ISBN 978-1-330-38434-3
PIBN 10047061

For support please visit www.forgottenbooks.com

1987

Census of Agriculture

AC87-A-16

Volume 1
GEOGRAPHIC AREA SERIES

Part 16

Kansas·
State and County Data

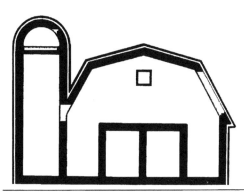

U.S. Department of Commerce
BUREAU OF THE CENSUS

ACKNOWLEDGMENTS

This report was prepared in the Agriculture Division. Many other divisions contributed to this preparation: Data Preparation performed the clerical processing; Administrative Services provided the forms design and other administrative services; Publications Services contributed in publication planning and design, editorial review, composition, and printing procurement; Computer Services provided the computer processing facilities; Field provided selected data collection activities; Economic Programming prepared the·computer programs; and Economic Surveys assisted in preparation of data collection and processing procedures and computer programs.

Members of the Census Advisory Committee on Agriculture Statistics and representatives of both public and private organizations made significant recommendations which helped establish data content.

Members of various agencies of the U.S. Department of Agriculture provided valuable advice in the planning, publicizing, and processing phases of the census, and in helping farmers and ranchers complete the report forms.

The press, farm magazines, radio and television stations, and farm organizations were most helpful in publicizing the census and encouraging cooperation of farm and ranch operators.

Special tribute is paid to the millions of farm and ranch operators who furnished the information requested. Only through their cooperation was it possible to collect and publish the data in this report.

If you have any questions concerning the statistics in this report, call:
(301) 763-8555 Division Chief
(301) 763-8567 Crops Branch
(301) 763-8569 Livestock Branch
(301) 763-8566 Farm Economics Branch
(301) 763-1113 General Information
(301) 763-8558 Statistical Methodology

VOLUME 1
GEOGRAPHIC AREA SERIES

1987
Census of Agriculture
AC87-A-16
Changed November 1989

CHANGE SHEET
Kansas

Following are changes to the 1987 Census of Agriculture volume 1 publications:

Table 17. **Selected Characteristics of Farms Operated by Females, Persons of Spanish Origin, and Specified Racial Groups: 1987 and 1982**

[For meaning of abbreviations and symbols, see introductory text]

Characteristics	Female operators	Operators of Spanish origin[1]	Farms operated by Black and other races			
			Black	American Indian	Asian	Other (see text)
1987 OPERATOR CHARACTERISTICS						
Operators by days of work off farm:						
Any.	1 348	71	83	85	6	12
100 to 199 days	270	11	8	9	–	2

[1] See chapter 1, table 16, for operators not of or not reporting Spanish origin.

Following are changes to appendix C:

Table G. **State Coverage Evaluation Estimates of Farms Not on the Mail List: 1987**

[During additional processing for coverage evaluation estimates, minor errors in estimates and relative standard errors were discovered for selected data items in some States. Corrected estimates will be published in Volume 2, Subject Series, Part 2, Coverage Evaluation]

U.S. Department of Commerce
BUREAU OF THE CENSUS

1987
Census of Agriculture

AC87-A-16

Volume 1
GEOGRAPHIC AREA SERIES

Part 16
Kansas
State and County Data

Issued June 1989

U.S. Department of Commerce
Robert A. Mosbacher, Secretary
BUREAU OF THE CENSUS

BUREAU OF THE CENSUS
C. L. Kincannon, Deputy Director

Charles A. Waite, Associate Director for
Economic Programs
Roger H. Bugenhagen, Assistant Director for
Economic and Agriculture Censuses

Thomas L. Mesenbourg, Chief,
Economic Census Staff

AGRICULTURE DIVISION
Charles P. Pautler, Jr., Chief

Library of Congress Cataloging-in-Publication Data

Census of agriculture (1987). Geographic area series.
  1987 census of agriculture. Geographic area series.

  Includes indexes.
  Supt. of Docs. no.: C 3.31/4:987/v.1
  1. Agriculture—Economic aspects—United States—
Statistics. 2. Agriculture—Economic aspects—United
States—States—Statistics. 3. Agriculture—Economic
aspects—United States—Territories and possessions
—Statistics. I. United States. Bureau of the Census.
II. Title.
HD1769.C46   1987   338.1'0973'021   88-600103

For sale by Superintendent of Documents, U.S. Government
Printing Office, Washington, DC 20402.

CONTENTS

FIGURES

TABLES

CHAPTER 1. State Data

*Not published for this State.

INTRODUCTION

HISTORY

The 1987 Census of Agriculture is the 23d taken by the U.S. Department of Commerce, Bureau of the Census. The first agriculture census was taken in 1840 as part of the sixth decennial census of population. From 1840 to 1950, an agriculture census was taken as part of the decennial census. A separate mid-decade census of agriculture was conducted in 1925, 1935, and 1945. From 1954 to 1974, a census of agriculture was taken for the years ending in 4 and 9. In 1976, Congress authorized the census of agriculture to be taken for 1978 and 1982 to adjust the data reference year so that it coincided with the economic censuses covering manufacturing, mining, construction, retail trade, wholesale trade, service industries, and selected transportation activities. This adjustment in timing established the agriculture census on a 5-year cycle collecting data for years ending in 2 and 7.

USES OF THE CENSUS

The census of agriculture is the leading source of statistics about the Nation's agricultural production and the only source of consistent, comparable data at the county, State, and national levels. Census statistics are used by Congress in developing and changing farm programs and for determining the effects of these programs. Many national and State programs are designed or allocated on the basis of census data, such as funds for extension services, research, and soil conservation projects. Private industry uses census statistics to provide a more effective production and distribution system for the agricultural community.

AUTHORITY AND AREA COVERED

The census of agriculture is required by law under Title 13, United States Code, sections 142(a) and 191, which directs that a census be taken in 1979, 1983, and in every fifth year after 1983 covering the prior year. The 1987 census includes each State, Puerto Rico, Guam, and the Virgin Island of the United States. A census of agriculture will be conducted in American Samoa and the Commonwealth of the Northern Mariana Islands in conjunction with the 1990 Census of Population and Housing.

FARM DEFINITION

Since 1850, when minimum criteria defining a farm for census purposes first were established, the farm definition has been changed nine times. The current definition, first used for the 1974 census, is any place from which $1,000 or more of agricultural products were produced and sold or normally would have been sold during the census year. The farm definition used for the outlying areas varies according to area. The report for each area includes a discussion of the farm definition.

COMPARABILITY OF DATA

Data on acreages and inventories for 1987 and 1982 are generally comparable. Dollar figures shown for expenses and agricultural product sales are expressed in current dollars and have not been adjusted for inflation or deflation. In general, data for censuses since 1974 are not fully comparable with data for 1969 and earlier censuses due to changes in the farm definition.

The 1978 U.S., region, and State data shown in the 1978 Census of Agriculture publications included data for farms on the mail list plus estimates from an area sample for farms not on the mail list. For comparability, the 1978 data in the 1987 publications include only farms on the mail list.

TABULAR PRESENTATION

State data—Tables 1 through 47 in chapter 1 show detailed State-level data usually accompanied by historical data for one or more past censuses. Tables 48 through 53 provide 1987 State data cross-tabulated by various farm classifications.

County data—Chapter 2 presents selected data items by county. Tables 1 through 16 include general data for all counties. The counties are listed in alphabetical order in the column headings. Tables 17 through 36 include only counties reporting the data item. Counties not having the item, or with a limited number of farms reporting the item, have data combined and presented as "all other counties."

ADVANCE REPORTS

Advance reports of 1987 census data have been published separately for each county with 10 farms or more, each State, and the United States. This series provided, at the earliest possible date, final data on major data items together with comparable final data from the 1982 census. Data items are standard across States except information on selected crops harvested, which vary by State according to their relative importance in the State.

ELECTRONIC DATA DISSEMINATION

The volume 1 data are available on computer tapes and compact disc. The advance report data are available on computer tapes, computer diskettes, and through electronic data services such as the AGRIDATA network, the CENDATA package on Dialog, CompuServe on-line services, and the Census Bureau's State Data Center Bulletin Board. Computer tapes, diskettes, and compact discs are sold by the Customer Services Branch, Data User Services Division, Bureau of the Census, Washington, D.C. 20233 (telephone (301) 763-4100).

SPECIAL TABULATIONS

Custom designed tabulations can be developed to individual user specifications on a programming cost reimbursable basis. Inquiries about special tabulations should be directed to the Chief, Agriculture Division, Bureau of the Census, Washington, D.C. 20233.

CENSUS DISCLOSURE RULES

In keeping with the provisions of Title 13, United States Code, no data are published that would disclose the operations of an individual farm. However, the number of farms in a given size category or other classification, such as size of farm, is not considered a release of confidential information and is provided even though other information is withheld.

INVENTORIES, PRODUCTION, AND SALES DATA

Inventories of livestock, poultry, and machinery and equipment are measured as of December 31 of the census year. Crop and livestock production, sales, and expense data are for the calendar year, except for a few crops (such as citrus) for which the production year overlaps the calendar year.

ABBREVIATIONS AND SYMBOLS

The following abbreviations and symbols are used throughout the tables:

–	Represents zero.
(D)	Withheld to avoid disclosing data for individual farms.
(IC)	Independent city.
(NA)	Not available.
(S)	Withheld because estimate did not meet publication standards on the basis of either the response rate (associated relative standard error) or a consistency review.
(X)	Not applicable.
(Z)	Less than half of the unit shown.
cwt	Hundredweight.
sq ft	Square feet.

Highlights of the State's Agriculture: 1987 and 1982

[Dollar figures are in current dollars with no adjustment for price changes. For meaning of abbreviations and symbols, see introductory text.]

Item	All farms		
	1987	1982	Percent change from 1982 to 1987
Farms...number..	68 579	73 315	-6.5
Land in farms..................................acres..	46 628 519	47 052 213	-.9
Average size of farm..........................acres..	680	642	5.9
Value of land and buildings[1]:			
Average per farm............................dollars..	278 047	384 197	-27.6
Average per acre............................dollars..	413	601	-31.3
Farms by size:			
1 to 9 acres	3 689	3 547	4 0
10 to 49 acres	6 222	6 837	-9.0
50 to 179 acres	15 510	16 720	-7.2
180 to 499 acres	16 705	18 693	-10.6
500 to 999 acres	12 093	13 600	-11.1
1,000 to 1,899 acres	9 304	9 428	-1.3
2,000 acres or more	5 056	4 490	12.6
Harvested cropland ....farms..	57 822	62 860	-8.0
acres..	17 729 394	20 186 974	-12.2
Irrigated land................................farms..	7 352	7 257	1.3
acres..	2 463 073	2 675 167	-7.9
Market value of agricultural products sold ....$1,000..	6 476 669	6 190 861	4.6
Average per farm...........................dollars..	94 441	84 442	11.8
Crops, including nursery and greenhouse crops .....$1,000..	1 693 609	2 143 047	-21.0
Grain.....................................$1,000..	1 550 403	2 009 729	-22.9
Cotton and cottonseed......................$1,000..	186	–	–
Tobacco...................................$1,000..	80	77	4.7
Hay, silage, and field seeds ....$1,000..	109 574	100 169	9.4
Vegetables, sweet corn, and melons ....$1,000..	4 151	3 206	29.5
Fruits, nuts, and berries ....$1,000..	1 693	1 398	21.1
Nursery and greenhouse crops ....$1,000..	26 805	21 515	24.6
Other crops ....$1,000..	716	6 954	-89.7
Livestock, poultry, and their products ....$1,000..	4 783 060	4 047 815	18.2
Poultry and poultry products ....$1,000..	25 284	25 755	-1.8
Dairy products ....$1,000..	140 232	162 232	-13.6
Cattle and calves ....$1,000..	4 305 335	3 516 670	22.4
Hogs and pigs ....$1,000..	284 375	316 882	-10.3
Sheep, lambs, and wool....................$1,000..	18 561	15 502	19.7
Other livestock and livestock products (see text)..$1,000..	9 273	10 773	-13.9
Farms by type of organization:			
Individual or family (sole proprietorship)	60 202	64 313	-6.4
Partnership	5 889	6 702	-12.1
Corporation	2 100	1 876	11.9
Other—cooperative, estate or trust, institutional, etc. ..	388	424	-8.5
Operators by principal occupation:			
Farming	42 807	47 293	-9.9
Other	25 972	26 022	-.2
Operators by days worked off farm:			
Any	34 654	35 521	-2.4
200 days or more	21 677	21 306	1.7
Average age of operator ....years..	52.0	50.9	2.2
Total farm production expenses[1] ....$1,000..	5 516 518	(NA)	(NA)
Selected farm production expenses[1]:			
Livestock and poultry purchased ....$1,000..	2 426 149	1 900 272	27.7
Feed for livestock and poultry ....$1,000..	887 270	920 415	-3.6
Commercial fertilizer[2] ....$1,000..	216 166	254 590	-15.1
Agricultural chemicals[2] ....$1,000..	125 003	94 957	31.6
Petroleum products ....$1,000..	243 568	358 860	-32.1
Hired farm labor ....$1,000..	226 075	153 404	47.4
Interest expense[2] ....$1,000..	314 163	467 054	-32.7
Livestock and poultry inventory:			
Cattle and calves............................farms..	40 785	47 008	-13.2
number..	5 539 992	5 800 138	-4.5
Milk cows..................................farms..	3 093	4 631	-33.2
number..	96 675	123 009	-21.4
Hogs and pigs ....farms..	6 768	9 241	-26.8
number..	1 515 878	1 708 770	-11.2
Chickens 3 months old or older ....farms..	4 206	6 044	-30.4
number..	2 094 610	2 093 245	.1
Selected crops harvested:			
Corn for grain or seed ....farms..	8 944	8 346	7.2
acres..	1 243 969	1 161 875	7.1
Corn for silage or green chop ....farms..	2 009	3 020	-33.5
acres..	109 230	154 307	-29.2
Sorghum for grain or seed ....farms..	32 492	26 908	20.8
acres..	3 399 564	3 187 148	6.7
Wheat for grain ....farms..	38 638	49 231	-21.5
acres..	8 679 588	11 664 006	-25.6
Oats for grain ....farms..	5 313	6 644	-20.0
acres..	126 091	166 982	-24.2
Soybeans for beans ....farms..	18 654	17 116	10.2
acres..	1 878 978	1 692 288	11.0
Hay—alfalfa, other tame, small grain, wild, grass silage, green chop, etc. (see text).........................farms..	33 964	37 341	-9.0
acres..	2 254 082	2 233 631	.9

[1]Data are based on a sample of farms.
[2]Data for 1987 include cost of custom applications.
[3]Data for 1982 do not include imputation for item nonresponse.

Figure 1. **State Map**

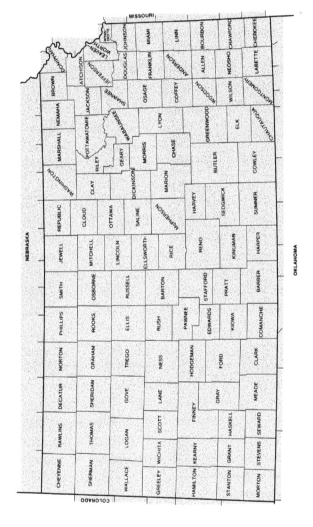

Figure 2. **Profile of State's Agriculture: 1987**

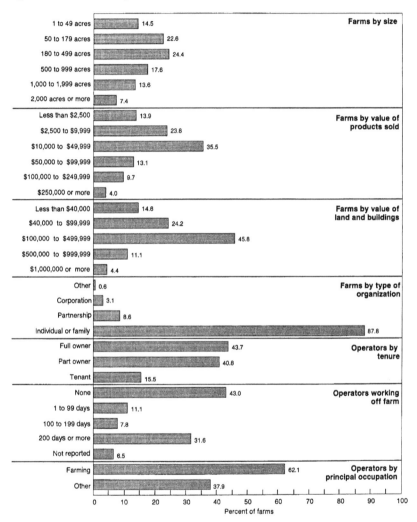

Figure 3. **Percent of Farms and of Value of Products Sold: 1987**

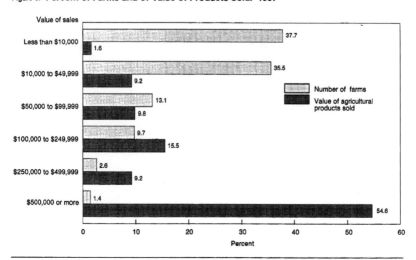

Figure 4. **Farms by Value of Agricultural Products Sold: 1959 to 1987**

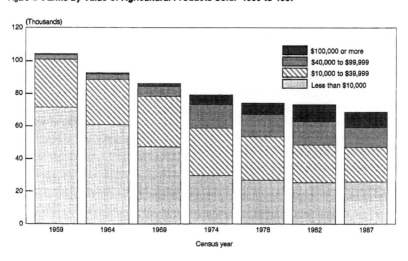

Figure 5. **Land Use: 1987**

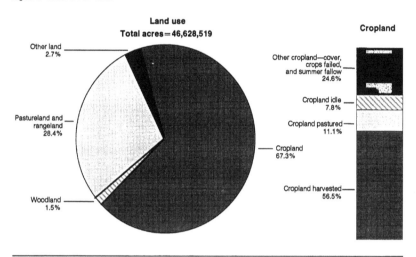

Land use
Total acres = 46,628,519

Other land 2.7%

Pastureland and rangeland 28.4%

Woodland 1.5%

Cropland

Other cropland—cover, crops failed, and summer fallow 24.6%

Cropland idle 7.8%

Cropland pastured 11.1%

Cropland 67.3%

Cropland harvested 56.5%

Figure 6. **Selected Crops Harvested: 1987**

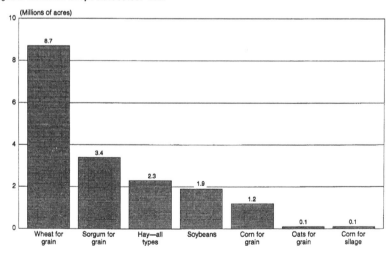

(Millions of acres)

Wheat for grain	Sorgum for grain	Hay—all types	Soybeans	Corn for grain	Oats for grain	Corn for silage
8.7	3.4	2.3	1.9	1.2	0.1	0.1

Figure 7. **Value of Livestock and Poultry Sold: 1987**

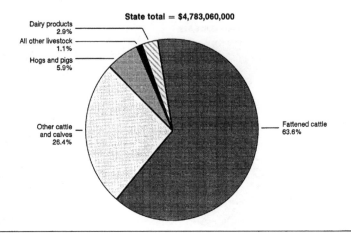

State total = $4,783,060,000

Dairy products
2.9%

All other livestock
1.1%

Hogs and pigs
5.9%

Other cattle
and calves
26.4%

Fattened cattle
63.6%

Figure 8. **Production Expenses: 1987**

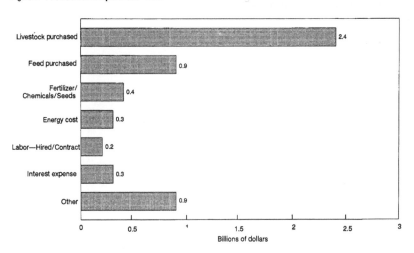

	Billions of dollars
Livestock purchased	2.4
Feed purchased	0.9
Fertilizer/Chemicals/Seeds	0.4
Energy cost	0.3
Labor—Hired/Contract	0.2
Interest expense	0.3
Other	0.9

Billions of dollars

Table 1. Historical Highlights: 1987 and Earlier Census Years

[For meaning of abbreviations and symbols, see introductory text]

All farms	1987	1982	1978	1974	1969	1964	1959	1954
Farms ..... number..	68 579	73 315	74 171	79 188	86 057	92 440	104 347	120 167
Land in farms ..... acres..	46 628 519	47 052 213	47 499 831	47 945 722	49 390 369	50 271 117	50 152 870	50 023 538
Average size of farm ..... acres..	680	642	640	605	574	544	481	416
Value of land and buildings[1]:								
Average per farm ..... dollars..	278 047	384 197	322 165	179 454	91 131	66 397	48 084	33 117
Average per acre ..... dollars..	413	601	498	296	159	122	100	80
Estimated market value of all machinery and equipment[1] ..... $1,000..	3 447 663	3 830 616	3 137 696	2 109 529	1 008 608	(NA)	(NA)	(NA)
Average per farm ..... dollars..	50 411	52 304	42 385	29 069	12 124	(NA)	(NA)	(NA)
Farms by size:								
1 to 9 acres	3 689	3 547	3 186	2 797	3 460	2 366	2 952	6 542
10 to 49 acres	6 222	6 837	5 379	5 127	5 231	6 465	7 610	8 810
50 to 179 acres	15 510	16 720	16 971	18 974	19 025	20 796	24 458	30 116
180 to 499 acres	16 705	16 693	20 044	23 231	27 334	31 514	39 547	47 097
500 to 999 acres	12 093	13 600	14 671	16 047	18 394	19 564	19 710	18 890
1,000 to 1,999 acres	9 304	9 428	9 501	9 193	9 272	8 519	10 070	8 712
2,000 acres or more	5 056	4 490	4 219	3 819	3 341	3 117		
Total cropland ..... farms..	61 615	66 461	68 430	74 306	80 455	86 535	97 420	110 350
acres..	31 385 090	30 598 850	29 843 255	29 984 268	31 767 739	29 421 414	29 623 874	29 577 170
Harvested cropland ..... farms..	57 822	62 860	64 862	70 573	76 110	84 171	94 918	107 602
acres..	17 729 394	20 186 974	18 987 644	19 870 535	17 649 231	18 160 353	20 528 357	21 440 232
Irrigated land ..... farms..	7 352	7 257	7 961	6 710	6 271	5 102	4 592	2 736
acres..	2 463 073	2 675 167	2 665 757	2 010 385	1 522 317	1 004 210	762 101	331 551
Market value of agricultural products sold[2] ..... $1,000..	6 476 669	6 190 861	4 995 543	3 682 044	1 818 018	1 174 563	1 110 817	802 340
Average per farm ..... dollars..	94 441	84 442	67 352	46 497	21 125	12 706	10 645	6 677
Crops, including nursery and greenhouse crops ..... $1,000..	1 693 609	2 143 047	1 440 843	1 794 548	579 188	448 267	485 902	428 282
Livestock, poultry, and their products ..... $1,000..	4 783 060	4 047 815	3 554 701	1 886 980	1 238 353	725 535	624 603	373 890
Farms by value of sales[2]:								
Less than $2,500	9 502	9 637	7 967	10 897	16 266	23 670	25 522	41 849
$2,500 to $4,999	6 619	6 565	7 897	7 698	12 260	15 622	19 469	26 325
$5,000 to $9,999	9 430	9 163	10 944	11 067	16 699	21 421	26 434	29 828
$10,000 to $24,999	14 070	15 130	17 284				32 673	18 849
$25,000 to $49,999	10 282	11 627	13 426	43 422	37 115	30 962		3 601
$50,000 to $99,999	8 897	10 459	9 587					
$100,000 to $499,999	8 422	9 584	6 324	5 659	1 534	748		
$500,000 or more	957	895	604	412	142			
Farms by type of organization:								
Individual or family (sole proprietorship)	60 202	64 313	65 380	(NA)	(NA)	(NA)	(NA)	(NA)
Partnership	5 889	6 702	7 092	(NA)	(NA)	(NA)	(NA)	(NA)
Corporation	2 100	1 876	1 478	(NA)	(NA)	(NA)	(NA)	(NA)
Other—cooperative, estate or trust, institutional, etc.	388	424	221	(NA)	(NA)	(NA)	(NA)	(NA)
Operators by days worked off farm[3]:								
None	29 462	30 524	34 255	31 086	(NA)	(NA)	(NA)	66 606
Any	34 654	35 521	36 256	29 601	43 708	40 865	45 169	52 066
200 days or more	21 677	21 306	20 390	16 970	21 147	18 086	17 881	17 988
Operators by principal occupation[3]:								
Farming	42 607	47 293	49 104	57 633	(NA)	(NA)	(NA)	(NA)
Other	25 972	26 022	25 067	20 722	(NA)	(NA)	(NA)	(NA)
Average age of operator[4] ..... years..	52.0	50.9	50.7	52.2	51.1	51.3	50.5	49.4
Total farm production expenses[1] ..... $1,000..	5 516 518	(NA)	(NA)	2 676 186	1 531 075	(NA)	(NA)	(NA)
Selected farm production expenses[1]:								
Livestock and poultry purchased ..... $1,000..	2 426 149	1 900 272	1 674 241	738 839	573 566	267 759	231 466	(NA)
Feed for livestock and poultry ..... $1,000..	887 270	920 415	803 712	602 285	234 254	158 573	102 041	96 792
Commercial fertilizer[7] ..... $1,000..	216 166	254 590	252 403	205 630	72 564	44 808	(NA)	24 044
Petroleum products ..... $1,000..	243 568	358 660	207 732	138 140	76 882	72 103	65 601	58 266
Hired farm labor ..... $1,000..	226 075	153 404	131 444	85 140	53 816	38 399	33 496	31 717
Interest expense[8] ..... $1,000..	314 163	467 054	(NA)	(NA)	(NA)	(NA)	(NA)	(NA)
Agricultural chemicals[7] ..... $1,000..	125 003	94 957	68 543	43 071	16 856	(NA)	(NA)	(NA)
Livestock and poultry:								
Cattle and calves inventory ..... farms..	40 785	47 008	48 215	54 045	60 299	71 558	81 372	102 678
number..	5 539 292	5 800 138	5 930 016	5 590 626	5 753 261	5 149 607	4 324 106	4 304 950
Beef cows ..... farms..	31 475	36 497	37 656	43 545	(NA)	54 633	(NA)	(NA)
number..	1 354 549	1 523 697	1 579 322	1 890 367	1 696 614	1 598 226	1 160 221	1 355 015
Milk cows ..... farms..	3 093	4 631	5 691	7 823	12 563	25 990	44 889	77 982
number..	96 675	123 009	120 775	149 477	172 099	240 522	316 470	452 924
Cattle and calves sold ..... farms..	41 498	47 032	49 162	54 803	61 404	70 334	78 843	69 804
number..	7 310 338	6 519 159	6 758 343	5 104 331	4 711 037	3 920 543	2 610 987	2 332 667
Hogs and pigs inventory ..... farms..	6 768	9 801	13 329	13 065	19 764	24 819	37 615	41 594
number..	1 516 678	1 708 770	2 014 541	1 520 269	1 638 904	1 264 348	1 341 300	902 220
Hogs and pigs sold ..... farms..	7 090	9 778	13 794	14 558	21 071	25 088	34 602	36 005
number..	2 759 676	3 036 205	3 344 600	2 829 467	2 934 653	2 257 937	1 709 695	1 051 367
Chickens 3 months old or older inventory[9] ..... farms..	4 206	6 044	7 137	9 615	16 211	35 657	62 823	89 258
number..	2 094 610	2 093 245	2 796 152	2 728 432	3 889 910	5 058 037	7 705 091	10 801 470
Broilers and other meat-type chickens sold ..... farms..	132	210	220	270	194	10	24	110
number..	176 061	94 543	259 001	438 326	132 876	82 950	560 189	841 460

See footnotes at end of table.

Table 1. Historical Highlights: 1987 and Earlier Census Years—Con.

[For meaning of abbreviations and symbols, see introductory text]

All farms	1987	1982	1978	1974	1969	1964	1959	1954
Selected crops harvested:								
Corn for grain or seed .... farms...	8 944	8 346	10 618	13 300	17 131	23 570	39 223	29 557
acres...	1 243 966	1 161 875	1 567 013	1 597 279	1 152 878	988 065	1 674 816	1 317 485
bushels...	144 133 581	130 662 235	154 173 376	126 247 120	90 136 720	44 103 321	69 902 423	31 223 389
Sorghum for grain or seed .... farms...	32 492	26 908	34 778	34 821	40 159	46 969	59 661	48 879
acres...	3 399 564	3 187 148	3 664 560	3 238 489	3 167 318	2 878 091	3 835 328	3 545 992
bushels...	228 045 100	192 400 229	176 218 600	132 210 153	178 300 694	92 530 503	123 201 103	49 824 979
Wheat for grain .... farms...	38 638	49 231	46 191	55 895	62 204	71 703	63 005	84 203
acres...	8 679 588	11 664 008	9 501 848	11 040 335	9 342 569	9 034 093	9 856 222	9 483 480
bushels...	292 899 442	372 590 045	268 457 130	299 416 699	268 780 083	196 896 894	199 604 763	163 108 142
Oats for grain .... farms...	5 313	6 544	4 666	(NA)	(NA)	16 744	31 580	47 417
acres...	128 091	166 962	94 399	(NA)	(NA)	295 602	667 153	1 021 584
bushels...	4 775 729	7 799 056	3 483 394	(NA)	(NA)	8 561 555	16 080 166	33 359 310
Soybeans for beans ...... farms...	16 864	17 116	16 254	14 236	15 066	16 909	11 947	10 440
acres...	1 878 976	1 692 288	1 480 800	931 135	765 450	518 919	416 193	279 509
bushels...	55 769 994	43 042 471	26 436 742	18 634 361	17 124 661	10 948 094	8 715 280	1 913 268
Hay—alfalfa, other tame, small grain, grass silage, green chop, etc. (see text) .... farms...	33 964	37 341	39 244	42 504	43 761	(NA)	(NA)	(NA)
acres...	2 254 062	2 233 631	2 241 268	2 066 168	1 902 475	2 402 209	1 857 502	2 500 840
tons, dry...	5 080 847	5 092 039	4 462 796	4 032 977	4 312 407	4 214 548	3 388 855	3 323 660

[1] Data are based on a sample of farms.
[2] Data for 1974 and prior years include the value of forest products sold.
[3] Data for 1982 and prior years exclude abnormal farms.
[4] Data for 1959 are for $10,000 or more.
[5] Data for 1954 are for $25,000 or more.
[6] Data for 1974 apply only to individual or family operations (sole proprietorship) and partnerships; see text.
[7] Data for 1987 include cost of custom applications; data for agricultural chemicals exclude the cost of lime for 1987 and 1982.
[8] Data for 1982 do not include imputation for item nonresponse.
[9] Data for 1964 and prior years are for chickens 4 months old or older.

Table 2. **Market Value of Agricultural Products Sold: 1987, 1982, and 1978**

[For meaning of abbreviations and symbols, see introductory text]

Item	1987	Percent of total in 1987	1982	1978
Total sales (see text) ... farms..	68 579	100.0	73 315	74 171
$1,000..	6 476 669	100.0	6 190 861	4 995 543
Average per farm ... dollars..	94 441	(X)	84 442	67 352
Value of sales[1]:				
Less than $1,000 (see text) ... farms..	4 536	6.6	4 357	2 269
$1,000..	1 380	(Z)	1 433	1 086
$1,000 to $2,499 ... farms..	4 964	7.2	5 280	5 678
$1,000..	8 455	.1	8 977	9 697
$2,500 to $4,999 ... farms..	6 919	10.1	6 565	7 897
$1,000..	25 267	.4	24 009	28 927
$5,000 to $9,999 ... farms..	9 430	13.6	9 183	10 944
$1,000..	68 474	1.1	66 849	79 307
$10,000 to $19,999 ... farms..	10 504	15.3	11 236	12 847
$1,000..	150 932	2.3	162 118	184 511
$20,000 to $24,999 ... farms..	3 566	5.2	3 894	4 437
$1,000..	79 440	1.2	86 796	99 007
$25,000 to $39,999 ... farms..	7 150	10.4	8 007	9 353
$1,000..	227 493	3.5	255 798	296 555
$40,000 to $49,999 ... farms..	3 132	4.6	3 820	4 073
$1,000..	139 656	2.2	170 777	181 539
$50,000 to $99,999 ... farms..	8 997	13.1	10 459	9 687
$1,000..	637 837	9.8	741 372	675 787
$100,000 to $249,999 ... farms..	6 656	9.7	7 644	5 114
$1,000..	1 006 123	15.5	1 150 070	761 924
$250,000 to $499,999 ... farms..	1 766	2.6	1 940	1 210
$1,000..	597 614	9.2	654 510	407 435
$500,000 to $999,999[2] ... farms..	568	.8	895	604
$1,000..	378 027	5.8	2 885 670	2 266 010
$1,000,000 or more ... farms..	589	.6	-	-
$1,000..	3 155 768	48.7	-	-
Sales by commodity or commodity group:				
Crops, including nursery and greenhouse crops ... farms..	51 773	75.5	56 791	59 075
$1,000..	1 693 609	26.1	2 143 047	1 440 843
Grains ... farms..	48 606	70.9	54 146	56 180
$1,000..	1 550 403	23.9	2 009 729	1 327 136
Corn for grain ... farms..	7 426	10.8	6 297	(NA)
$1,000..	255 791	3.9	263 913	(NA)
Wheat ... farms..	38 365	55.9	49 000	(NA)
$1,000..	694 147	10.7	1 162 533	(NA)
Soybeans ... farms..	18 724	27.3	16 993	(NA)
$1,000..	263 742	4.1	215 700	(NA)
Sorghum for grain ... farms..	28 719	41.9	21 864	(NA)
$1,000..	311 649	4.8	350 828	(NA)
Barley ... farms..	1 715	2.5	(NA)	(NA)
$1,000..	3 953	.1	(NA)	(NA)
Oats ... farms..	2 416	3.5	2 828	(NA)
$1,000..	3 328	.1	6 275	(NA)
Other grains[3] ... farms..	1 656	2.4	1 011	(NA)
$1,000..	17 793	.3	10 880	(NA)
Cotton and cottonseed ... farms..	10	(Z)	-	-
$1,000..	186	(Z)	-	-
Tobacco ... farms..	13	(Z)	13	5
$1,000..	80	(Z)	77	27
Hay, silage, and field seeds ... farms..	12 801	18.7	12 376	14 198
$1,000..	109 574	1.7	100 189	84 927
Vegetables, sweet corn, and melons ... farms..	418	.6	360	361
$1,000..	4 151	.1	3 206	2 687
Fruits, nuts, and berries ... farms..	278	.4	213	227
$1,000..	1 893	(Z)	1 398	1 119
Nursery and greenhouse crops ... farms..	272	.4	296	288
$1,000..	26 805	.4	21 515	15 848
Other crops ... farms..	80	.1	180	232
$1,000..	716	(Z)	6 954	9 099
Livestock, poultry, and their products ... farms..	45 882	66.9	51 701	54 221
$1,000..	4 783 060	73.9	4 047 815	3 554 701
Poultry and poultry products ... farms..	1 550	2.3	2 385	2 774
$1,000..	25 284	.4	25 755	26 195
Dairy products ... farms..	2 004	2.9	2 667	3 224
$1,000..	140 232	2.2	162 232	117 412
Cattle and calves ... farms..	41 498	60.5	47 032	49 162
$1,000..	4 305 335	66.5	3 516 570	3 093 572
Hogs and pigs ... farms..	7 090	10.3	9 778	13 794
$1,000..	284 375	4.4	316 882	297 439
Sheep, lambs, and wool ... farms..	2 456	3.6	2 535	1 977
$1,000..	16 561	.3	15 502	13 549
Other livestock and livestock products (see text) ... farms..	2 869	4.2	2 858	2 581
$1,000..	9 273	.1	10 773	6 534

[1]Data for 1982 and 1978 exclude abnormal farms.
[2]Data for 1982 and 1978 are for $500,000 or more.
[3]Data for 1982 include barley.

Table 3. **Farm Production Expenses: 1987, 1982, and 1978**

[Data are based on a sample of farms: see text. For meaning of abbreviations and symbols, see introductory text]

Item	1987		1982	1978
	Farms	Expenses ($1,000)		
Total farm production expenses .... farms..	66 580	(X)	(NA)	(NA)
$1,000..	(X)	5 516 518	(NA)	(NA)
Average per farm ....dollars..	(X)	80 439	(NA)	(NA)
Farms with expenses of—				
$1 to $4,999	16 362	42 964	(NA)	(NA)
$5,000 to $9,999	10 827	79 502	(NA)	(NA)
$10,000 to $24,999	16 576	269 924	(NA)	(NA)
$25,000 to $49,999	10 260	366 015	(NA)	(NA)
$50,000 to $99,999	7 770	547 453	(NA)	(NA)
$100,000 to $249,999	4 832	726 131	(NA)	(NA)
$250,000 to $499,999	1 203	408 533	(NA)	(NA)
$500,000 or more	750	3 077 996	(NA)	(NA)
Livestock and poultry purchased .... farms..	23 380	(X)	26 892	30 792
$1,000..	(X)	2 426 149	1 900 272	1 674 241
percent of total..	(X)	44.0	(NA)	(NA)
Farms with expenses of—				
$1 to $999	4 453	2 123	6 974	9 033
$1,000 to $4,999	7 470	17 931	8 019	8 652
$5,000 to $9,999	3 217	22 273	2 947	3 442
$10,000 to $24,999[1]	3 253	51 084		9 665
$25,000 to $49,999	1 944	68 023	5 973	
$50,000 to $99,999	1 363	96 370		
$100,000 to $249,999	1 023	155 899	2 979	
$250,000 or more	657	2 012 445		
Feed for livestock and poultry .... farms..	38 347	(X)	45 184	49 543
$1,000..	(X)	887 270	920 415	803 712
percent of total..	(X)	16.1	(NA)	(NA)
Farms with expenses of—				
$1 to $999	13 929	5 975	17 364	19 724
$1,000 to $4,999	14 399	32 080	16 005	17 677
$5,000 to $9,999	3 785	25 460	4 694	5 500
$10,000 to $24,999	3 566	54 593		6 642
$25,000 to $49,999[1]	1 346	46 027	6 257	
$50,000 to $79,999	522	31 773		
$80,000 to $99,999	160	13 930	864	
$100,000 or more	640	677 402		
Commercially mixed formula feeds .... farms..	14 988	(X)	16 595	18 854
$1,000..	(X)	163 561	194 615	172 220
percent of total..	(X)	3.0	(NA)	(NA)
Farms with expenses of—				
$1 to $999	6 568	2 416	6 013	7 829
$1,000 to $4,999	4 759	10 559	5 621	6 720
$5,000 to $9,999	1 468	9 961	1 836	1 926
$10,000 to $24,999[1]	1 386	21 021		2 577
$25,000 to $49,999	402	13 545	2 626	
$50,000 to $79,999	175	10 430		
$80,000 or more	230	95 728	497	
Seeds, bulbs, plants, and trees .... farms..	48 233	(X)	47 466	49 820
$1,000..	(X)	95 302	83 505	72 966
percent of total..	(X)	1.7	(NA)	(NA)
Farms with expenses of—				
$1 to $499	18 299	4 146	17 366	23 574
$500 to $999	9 948	6 795	10 221	9 093
$1,000 to $4,999	15 265	32 861	16 180	13 872
$5,000 to $9,999	2 990	19 938	2 511	2 355
$10,000 to $19,999	1 330	17 463	897	740
$20,000 to $24,999	153	3 281		186
$25,000 or more	248	10 816	291	
Commercial fertilizer[2] .... farms..	47 731	(X)	49 644	54 046
$1,000..	(X)	216 166	254 590	252 403
percent of total..	(X)	3.9	(NA)	(NA)
Farms with expenses of—				
$1 to $499	8 665	2 235	8 207	6 976
$500 to $999	6 780	4 807	7 339	6 679
$1,000 to $4,999	19 444	47 294	19 444	24 902
$5,000 to $9,999	6 995	47 660	7 466	9 019
$10,000 to $24,999[1]	4 745	68 611		6 470
$25,000 to $29,999	355	9 426	6 054	
$30,000 to $49,999	529	18 872		
$50,000 to $99,999	188	12 166	1 114	
$100,000 or more	30	4 896		
Agricultural chemicals[2] .... farms..	46 318	(X)	34 068	42 427
$1,000..	(X)	125 003	94 957	68 543
percent of total..	(X)	2.3	(NA)	(NA)
Farms with expenses of—				
$1 to $499	14 169	3 120	10 638	18 406
$500 to $999	7 776	5 392	5 719	7 883
$1,000 to $4,999	17 511	39 695	12 858	13 031
$5,000 to $9,999	4 127	27 761	2 809	2 118
$10,000 to $24,999	2 349	33 510		969
$25,000 to $49,999	322	10 459	2 044	
$50,000 or more	64	5 047		
Petroleum products .... farms..	65 460	(X)	73 030	73 806
$1,000..	(X)	243 568	358 860	207 732
percent of total..	(X)	4.4	(NA)	(NA)
Farms with expenses of—				
$1 to $999	24 444	10 592	24 222	29 926
$1,000 to $4,999	27 397	68 030	27 036	33 646
$5,000 to $9,999	8 430	56 287	12 347	6 921
$10,000 to $24,999[1]	4 222	60 852	8 717	3 311
$25,000 to $39,999	616	16 646		
$40,000 to $49,999	144	6 340	708	
$50,000 or more	207	20 821		

See footnotes at end of table.

Table 3. **Farm Production Expenses: 1987, 1982, and 1978**—Con.

[Data are based on a sample of farms; see text. For meaning of abbreviations and symbols, see introductory text]

Item	1987 Farms	1987 Expenses ($1,000)	1982	1978
Total farm production expenses—Con.				
Electricity ... farms..	48 797	(X)	51 533	52 213
$1,000..	(X)	54 103	53 184	39 160
percent of total..	(X)	1.0	(NA)	(NA)
Farms with expenses of—				
$1 to $499..	25 802	5 780	26 355	33 552
$500 to $999..	11 056	7 390	12 758	10 413
$1,000 to $1,999..	6 627	8 679	7 249	5 012
$2,000 to $4,999..	3 936	11 362	3 905	2 302
$5,000 to $9,999..	849	5 493		
$10,000 to $24,999..	387	5 537	1 266	934
$25,000 or more ..	136	9 860		
Hired farm labor... farms..	24 715	(X)	25 274	26 531
$1,000..	(X)	226 075	153 404	131 444
percent of total..	(X)	4.1	(NA)	(NA)
Farms with expenses of—				
$1 to $999..	12 145	4 140	11 088	14 521
$1,000 to $4,999..	6 384	14 679	8 366	8 578
$5,000 to $9,999..	1 961	13 588	2 323	2 578
$10,000 to $24,999[1]..	2 568	39 109		2 854
$25,000 to $49,999..	998	33 230	3 114	
$50,000 to $79,999..	328	20 006		-
$80,000 to $99,999..	65	5 742	381	-
$100,000 or more ..	266	95 482		
Contract labor... farms..	7 882	(X)	3 346	4 187
$1,000..	(X)	23 691	8 123	7 922
percent of total..	(X)	.4	(NA)	(NA)
Farms with expenses of—				
$1 to $999..	3 892	1 743	1 603	2 254
$1,000 to $4,999..	2 895	6 096	1 340	1 536
$5,000 to $9,999..	660	4 374	262	298
$10,000 to $24,999..	363	5 267		
$25,000 to $49,999..	43	1 395	120	99
$50,000 or more ..	29	4 816		
Repair and maintenance ... farms..	56 961	(X)	(NA)	(NA)
$1,000..	(X)	252 018	(NA)	(NA)
percent of total..	(X)	4.6	(NA)	(NA)
Farms with expenses of—				
$1 to $999..	18 441	7 979	(NA)	(NA)
$1,000 to $4,999..	23 943	56 348	(NA)	(NA)
$5,000 to $9,999..	8 249	55 417	(NA)	(NA)
$10,000 to $24,999..	5 228	74 085	(NA)	(NA)
$25,000 to $49,999..	644	27 023	(NA)	(NA)
$50,000 or more ..	256	31 167	(NA)	(NA)
Customwork, machine hire, and rental of machinery and equipment[3] ...	30 603	(X)	30 844	37 238
$1,000..	(X)	107 366	104 886	84 572
percent of total..	(X)	1.9	(NA)	(NA)
Farms with expenses of—				
$1 to $999..	13 298	5 555	13 362	19 534
$1,000 to $4,999..	11 636	26 527	11 949	13 445
$5,000 to $9,999..	2 911	19 921	3 195	2 879
$10,000 to $24,999..	2 071	30 563		
$25,000 to $49,999..	373	12 053	2 338	1 380
$50,000 or more ..	114	12 747		
Interest[4] ...	39 549	(X)	40 559	(NA)
$1,000..	(X)	314 183	467 054	(NA)
percent of total..	(X)	5.7	(NA)	(NA)
Farms with expenses of—				
$1 to $999..	9 664	4 091	7 578	(NA)
$1,000 to $4,999..	14 469	37 094	13 762	(NA)
$5,000 to $9,999..	6 545	44 993	6 715	(NA)
$10,000 to $24,999..	6 130	92 297		
$25,000 to $49,999..	1 978	65 520	12 504	(NA)
$50,000 to $99,999..	579	37 640		
$100,000 or more ..	183	32 528		
Interest paid on debt:				
Secured by real estate ..	26 406	188 166	(NA)	(NA)
Not secured by real estate ..	24 307	125 997	(NA)	(NA)
Cash rent... farms..	21 234	(X)	(NA)	(NA)
$1,000..	(X)	123 531	(NA)	(NA)
percent of total..	(X)	2.2	(NA)	(NA)
Farms with expenses of—				
$1 to $499..	3 028	755	(NA)	(NA)
$500 to $999..	2 592	1 829	(NA)	(NA)
$1,000 to $4,999..	9 009	22 280	(NA)	(NA)
$5,000 to $9,999..	3 298	23 007	(NA)	(NA)
$10,000 to $24,999..	2 511	37 645	(NA)	(NA)
$25,000 to $49,999..	587	19 627	(NA)	(NA)
$50,000 or more ..	209	18 188	(NA)	(NA)
Property taxes paid ... farms..	63 359	(X)	(NA)	(NA)
$1,000..	(X)	112 201	(NA)	(NA)
percent of total..	(X)	2.0	(NA)	(NA)
Farms with expenses of—				
$1 to $499..	18 289	4 513	(NA)	(NA)
$500 to $999..	13 120	9 243	(NA)	(NA)
$1,000 to $4,999..	27 653	59 987	(NA)	(NA)
$5,000 to $9,999..	3 248	21 167	(NA)	(NA)
$10,000 to $24,999..	956	12 949	(NA)	(NA)
$25,000 or more ..	93	4 342	(NA)	(NA)

See footnotes at end of table.

Table 3. **Farm Production Expenses: 1987, 1982, and 1978**—Con.

[Data are based on a sample of farms; see text. For meaning of abbreviations and symbols, see introductory text]

Item	1987		1982	1978
	Farms	Expenses ($1,000)		
Total farm production expenses—Con.				
All other farm production expenses ... farms..	64 491	(X)	(NA)	(NA)
$1,000..	(X)	309 614	(NA)	(NA)
percent of total..	(X)	5.6	(NA)	(NA)
Farms with expenses of—				
$1 to $999	26 760	11 114	(NA)	(NA)
$1,000 to $4,999	25 092	57 293	(NA)	(NA)
$5,000 to $9,949	6 895	46 221	(NA)	(NA)
$10,000 to $24,999	4 186	60 765	(NA)	(NA)
$25,000 to $49,999	1 005	33 054	(NA)	(NA)
$50,000 to $99,999	340	22 234	(NA)	(NA)
$100,000 or more	223	79 233	(NA)	(NA)

[1] Data for 1978 are for $10,000 or more.
[2] Data for 1987 include cost of custom applications; data for agricultural chemicals exclude the cost of lime for 1987 and 1982.
[3] Data for 1987 exclude cost of custom applications for commercial fertilizer and agricultural chemicals.
[4] Data for 1982 do not include imputation for item nonresponse.

Table 4. **Net Cash Return From Agricultural Sales: 1987**

[Data are based on a sample of farms; see text. For meaning of abbreviations and symbols, see introductory text]

Item	All farms	Farms with sales of $10,000 or more	Farms with sales of less than $10,000
Net cash return from agricultural sales for the farm unit (see text) ... farms..	66 580	42 865	25 715
$1,000..	822 225	956 268	-34 043
Average per farm ... dollars..	13 447	22 309	-1 324
Farms with net gains[1] ... number..	41 673	31 351	10 322
$1,000..	1 140 553	1 119 077	21 476
Average per farm ... dollars..	27 369	35 695	2 081
Gain of—			
Less than $1,000	4 994	1 425	3 569
$1,000 to $4,999	11 424	5 432	5 992
$5,000 to $9,999	6 954	6 193	761
$10,000 to $24,999	8 626	8 626	–
$25,000 to $49,999	5 063	5 063	–
$50,000 or more	4 412	4 412	–
Farms with net losses ... number..	26 907	11 514	15 393
$1,000..	218 328	162 809	55 519
Average per farm ... dollars..	8 114	14 140	3 607
Loss of—			
Less than $1,000	5 287	1 252	4 035
$1,000 to $4,999	11 215	3 465	7 750
$5,000 to $9,999	5 338	2 608	2 730
$10,000 to $24,999	3 632	2 839	793
$25,000 to $49,999	1 031	951	80
$50,000 or more	404	399	5

[1] Farms with total production expenses equal to market value of agricultural products sold are included as farms with gains of less than $1,000.

Table 5. Government Payments and Other Farm-Related Income: 1987 and 1982

[For meaning of abbreviations and symbols, see introductory text.]

Item	All farms		Farms with sales of $10,000 or more	
	Farms	Value ($1,000)	Farms	Value ($1,000)
Government payments .... 1987..	41 627	573 647	32 463	547 846
Average per farm[1] .... 1987..	(X)	13 781	(X)	16 676
Farms with receipts of—				
$1 to $999	4 031	2 037	1 356	725
$1,000 to $4,999	12 727	34 951	7 593	22 297
$5,000 to $9,999	8 218	58 774	7 145	51 601
$10,000 to $24,999	9 862	155 890	9 610	152 378
$25,000 to $49,999	4 638	160 460	4 614	159 707
$50,000 or more	2 151	161 536	2 145	161 137
Amount received in cash .... 1987..	35 909	247 737	29 146	238 588
Value of certificates received .... 1987..	38 992	325 910	30 797	309 258
Other farm-related income, gross before taxes and expenses[2] .... 1987..	18 682	69 944	13 245	57 798
Average per farm[1] .... 1987..	(X)	3 744	(X)	4 364
Farms with receipts of—				
$1 to $999	7 008	2 824	4 751	1 908
$1,000 to $4,999	7 881	18 123	5 322	12 449
$5,000 to $9,999	2 128	14 190	1 607	10 637
$10,000 to $24,999	1 275	19 069	1 193	17 835
$25,000 to $49,999	336	10 923	319	(D)
$50,000 or more	54	4 817	53	(D)
Customwork and other agricultural services[3] .... 1987..	7 463	32 115	6 068	29 029
.... 1982..	7 742	35 309	6 771	33 583
Average per farm[1] .... 1987..	(X)	4 303	(X)	4 784
.... 1982..	(X)	4 561	(X)	4 960
1987 farms with receipts of—				
$1 to $999	2 291	1 027	1 704	782
$1,000 to $4,999	3 233	7 463	2 634	6 106
$5,000 to $9,999	1 067	7 182	858	5 698
$10,000 to $24,999	678	10 001	678	10 001
$25,000 to $49,999	194	6 443	194	6 443
$50,000 or more	–	–	–	–
Rental of farmland .... 1987..	7 899	30 403	4 546	22 613
Average per farm[1] .... 1987..	(X)	3 849	(X)	4 974
Farms with receipts of—				
$1 to $999	2 394	1 241	1 095	604
$1,000 to $4,999	4 115	9 254	2 399	5 610
$5,000 to $9,999	754	5 009	510	3 417
$10,000 to $24,999	470	6 896	394	5 737
$25,000 or more	166	8 003	148	7 244
Sales of forest products and Christmas trees .... 1987..	439	1 087	229	741
Average per farm[1] .... 1987..	(X)	2 477	(X)	3 236
Farms with receipts of—				
$1 to $999	231	72	126	50
$1,000 to $4,999	133	280	45	77
$5,000 to $9,999	42	290	23	169
$10,000 to $24,999	32	(D)	32	(D)
$25,000 or more	1	(D)	1	(D)
Other farm-related income sources .... 1987..	6 669	6 340	5 565	5 415
Average per farm[1] .... 1987..	(X)	951	(X)	973
Farms with receipts of—				
$1 to $999	5 166	1 369	4 296	1 203
$1,000 to $4,999	1 235	2 454	1 041	1 982
$5,000 to $9,999	191	1 233	151	946
$10,000 to $24,999	68	982	68	982
$25,000 or more	9	302	9	302

[1]Data are in whole dollars.
[2]Data are based on a sample of farms.
[3]Data for 1987 are based on a sample of farms; data for 1982 are nonsample and exclude abnormals from farms with sales of $10,000 or more.

Table 6. Commodity Credit Corporation Loans: 1987 and 1982

[For meaning of abbreviations and symbols, see introductory text]

CCC loans	1987 Farms	1987 Value ($1,000)	1982 Farms	1982 Value ($1,000)
Total	15 832	336 298	14 306	364 770
Average per farm[1]	(X)	21 368	(X)	25 498
Farms with loans of—				
$1 to $999	741	410	1 288	652
$1,000 to $4,999	3 893	11 018	3 097	8 421
$5,000 to $9,999	3 011	21 646	2 341	16 946
$10,000 to $19,999	3 316	46 771	2 644	37 337
$20,000 to $24,999	1 007	22 206		
$25,000 to $49,999	2 150	74 766	4 936	301 415
$50,000 or more	1 714	161 480		
Corn	3 591	108 314	(NA)	(NA)
Average per farm[1]	(X)	30 163	(X)	(NA)
Farms with loans of—				
$1 to $999	120	68	(NA)	(NA)
$1,000 to $9,999	1 223	5 791	(NA)	(NA)
$10,000 to $24,999	965	15 569	(NA)	(NA)
$25,000 or more	1 283	86 886	(NA)	(NA)
Wheat	7 282	95 942	10 341	187 661
Average per farm[1]	(X)	13 175	(X)	18 147
Farms with loans of—				
$1 to $999	501	243	(NA)	(NA)
$1,000 to $9,999	3 518	16 268	(NA)	(NA)
$10,000 to $24,999	2 237	34 755	(NA)	(NA)
$25,000 or more	1 026	44 677	(NA)	(NA)
Soybeans	1 246	20 764	(NA)	(NA)
Average per farm[1]	(X)	16 638	(X)	(NA)
Farms with loans of—				
$1 to $999	92	42	(NA)	(NA)
$1,000 to $9,999	566	2 646	(NA)	(NA)
$10,000 to $24,999	355	5 706	(NA)	(NA)
$25,000 or more	235	12 372	(NA)	(NA)
Sorghum, barley, and oats	10 032	112 774	(NA)	(NA)
Average per farm[1]	(X)	11 241	(X)	(NA)
Farms with loans of—				
$1 to $999	776	433	(NA)	(NA)
$1,000 to $9,999	5 656	25 543	(NA)	(NA)
$10,000 to $24,999	2 501	38 322	(NA)	(NA)
$25,000 or more	1 099	48 477	(NA)	(NA)
Cotton	–	–	–	
Average per farm[1]	(X)	–	(X)	
Farms with loans of—				
$1 to $999	–	–	(NA)	(NA)
$1,000 to $9,999	–	–	(NA)	(NA)
$10,000 to $24,999	–	–	(NA)	(NA)
$25,000 or more	–	–	(NA)	(NA)
Peanuts, rye, rice, tobacco, and honey	22	503	(NA)	(NA)
Average per farm[1]	(X)	22 843	(X)	(X)
Farms with loans of—				
$1 to $999	3	2	(NA)	(NA)
$1,000 to $9,999	8	(D)	(NA)	(NA)
$10,000 to $24,999	1	(D)	(NA)	(NA)
$25,000 or more	10	449	(NA)	(NA)

[1]Data are in whole dollars.

All farms		1987	Percent of total in 1987	1982	1978
Farms	number..	68 579	100.0	73 315	74 171
Land in farms	acres..	46 628 519	100.0	47 052 213	47 499 831
Total cropland	farms..	61 615	89.8	66 481	68 430
	acres..	31 385 090	67.3	30 598 859	29 843 255
Harvested cropland	farms..	57 822	84.3	62 860	64 862
	acres..	17 729 394	38.0	20 186 974	18 987 844
Farms by acres harvested:					
1 to 49 acres		12 372	18.0	12 391	11 874
1 to 9 acres		2 149	3.1	2 142	1 716
10 to 19 acres		2 967	4.3	3 097	2 870
20 to 29 acres		2 694	3.9	2 630	2 634
30 to 49 acres		4 562	6.7	4 522	4 654
50 to 99 acres		8 853	12.9	8 832	9 792
100 to 199 acres		10 361	15.1	11 638	12 874
200 to 499 acres		14 761	21.5	17 228	19 162
500 to 999 acres		8 150	11.9	9 046	8 327
1,000 acres or more		3 325	4.8	3 725	2 833
1,000 to 1,999 acres		2 876	4.2	3 142	2 414
2,000 acres or more		449	.7	583	419
Cropland used only for pasture or grazing	farms..	22 575	32.9	23 055	24 226
	acres..	3 485 445	7.5	3 231 652	3 122 683
Other cropland	farms..	43 046	62.8	34 770	43 552
	acres..	10 170 251	21.8	7 180 233	7 732 928
Cropland in cover crops, legumes, and soil-improvement grasses, not harvested and not pastured	farms..	11 212	16.3	5 739	9 657
	acres..	1 103 315	2.4	290 742	463 615
Cropland on which all crops failed	farms..	3 341	4.9	5 059	5 325
	acres..	206 231	.4	365 959	368 550
Cropland in cultivated summer fallow	farms..	25 408	37.0	22 060	26 863
	acres..	6 409 506	13.7	5 475 611	5 654 847
Cropland idle	farms..	20 610	30.1	12 304	17 755
	acres..	2 451 199	5.3	1 027 921	1 245 916
Total woodland	farms..	12 587	18.4	13 184	12 764
	acres..	718 261	1.5	753 577	674 721
Woodland pastured	farms..	6 382	9.3	6 657	6 751
	acres..	366 136	.8	377 954	354 817
Woodland not pastured	farms..	7 991	11.7	8 039	7 683
	acres..	352 125	.8	375 623	319 904
Pastureland and rangeland other than cropland and woodland pastured	farms..	32 362	47.2	34 510	37 780
	acres..	13 254 094	28.4	14 085 336	15 523 943
Land in house lots, ponds, roads, wasteland, etc.	farms..	44 335	64.6	50 409	50 188
	acres..	1 271 074	2.7	1 614 441	1 457 912
Cropland under federal acreage reduction programs:					
Annual commodity acreage adjustment programs	farms..	34 658	(X)	14 825	35 233
	acres..	3 966 196	(X)	896 640	2 159 904
Conservation reserve program	farms..	5 630	(X)	(NA)	(NA)
	acres..	810 862	(X)	(NA)	(NA)

Table 8. **Land in Farms, Harvested Cropland, and Irrigated Land, by Size of Farm: 1987 and 1982**

[For meaning of abbreviations and symbols, see introductory text]

All farms	Farms		Land in farms (acres)		Harvested cropland (acres)		Irrigated land (acres)	
	1987	1982	1987	1982	1987	1982	1987	1982
Land in farms ------------------	68 579	73 315	46 626 519	47 052 213	17 729 394	20 186 974	2 463 073	2 675 167
Farms by size:								
1 to 9 acres ------------------	3 689	3 547	9 327	9 498	1 792	1 715	288	224
10 to 49 acres ----------------	6 222	6 837	172 040	191 041	82 424	77 944	2 463	2 266
50 to 69 acres ----------------	1 849	2 053	107 904	119 295	37 812	50 235	1 184	1 363
70 to 99 acres ----------------	4 690	5 014	379 846	405 812	145 968	177 381	4 173	4 584
100 to 139 acres --------------	3 117	3 333	363 799	389 029	140 440	177 309	5 120	6 608
140 to 179 acres --------------	5 854	6 320	927 599	1 001 210	371 929	462 336	21 194	27 692
180 to 219 acres --------------	2 307	2 457	455 738	484 816	182 448	223 641	5 670	6 394
220 to 259 acres --------------	2 845	3 209	677 474	765 139	269 308	370 138	9 306	12 393
260 to 499 acres --------------	11 553	13 027	4 296 061	4 830 682	1 811 003	2 401 338	128 620	177 788
500 to 999 acres --------------	12 093	13 600	8 673 395	9 740 321	3 806 268	4 863 099	378 941	412 456
1,000 to 1,999 acres ----------	9 304	9 428	12 925 252	12 918 501	5 444 815	5 981 289	797 399	835 059
2,000 acres or more -----------	5 056	4 490	17 640 082	16 196 969	5 455 187	5 400 569	1 106 715	1 188 340
5,000 acres or more ---------	632	601	5 199 243	5 089 262	964 274	1 060 244	252 272	275 746
Farms with harvested cropland-----	57 822	62 860	44 493 191	45 090 954	17 729 394	20 186 974	2 458 502	2 668 300
Farms by size:								
1 to 9 acres ------------------	559	561	2 697	2 668	1 792	1 715	273	224
10 to 49 acres ----------------	3 746	4 328	106 254	126 468	82 424	77 944	2 346	2 159
50 to 69 acres ----------------	1 246	1 473	73 233	85 600	37 812	50 235	1 104	1 330
70 to 99 acres ----------------	3 658	4 005	296 508	324 498	145 968	177 381	4 074	4 582
100 to 139 acres --------------	2 500	2 761	292 952	322 877	140 440	177 309	5 095	6 550
140 to 179 acres --------------	5 084	5 490	805 525	870 185	371 929	462 336	20 674	27 572
180 to 219 acres --------------	1 972	2 143	389 161	423 295	182 448	223 641	5 610	6 394
220 to 259 acres --------------	2 555	2 962	608 654	706 591	269 308	370 138	9 306	12 326
260 to 499 acres --------------	10 777	12 248	4 018 557	4 552 094	1 811 003	2 401 338	127 395	176 966
500 to 999 acres --------------	11 707	13 247	8 409 034	9 494 849	3 806 268	4 863 099	378 217	411 896
1,000 to 1,999 acres ----------	9 092	9 256	12 641 615	12 699 557	5 444 815	5 981 289	797 399	835 059
2,000 acres or more -----------	4 924	4 386	16 848 501	15 482 072	5 455 187	5 400 569	1 107 109	1 183 340
5,000 acres or more ---------	578	557	4 834 492	4 552 998	964 274	1 060 244	252 272	270 746
Farms with irrigated land -------	7 352	7 257	10 653 734	10 344 665	4 816 179	5 300 114	2 463 073	2 675 167
Farms by size:								
1 to 9 acres ------------------	126	95	553	411	324	240	288	224
10 to 49 acres ----------------	226	192	5 939	5 033	3 188	2 919	2 463	2 266
50 to 69 acres ----------------	56	48	3 307	2 664	1 740	1 659	1 184	1 363
70 to 99 acres ----------------	104	114	8 482	9 276	5 292	8 484	4 179	4 584
100 to 139 acres --------------	103	100	12 247	11 852	7 496	8 961	5 120	6 608
140 to 179 acres --------------	259	281	41 328	44 857	25 335	33 391	21 194	27 692
180 to 219 acres --------------	83	83	16 500	16 427	9 172	10 975	5 670	6 394
220 to 259 acres --------------	110	118	26 092	27 946	14 800	20 479	9 306	12 393
260 to 499 acres --------------	842	998	325 321	360 791	190 290	271 350	128 620	177 788
500 to 999 acres --------------	1 646	1 626	1 225 444	1 210 524	672 649	766 702	378 941	412 456
1,000 to 1,999 acres ----------	2 113	2 033	3 039 274	2 907 417	1 662 973	1 856 814	797 399	835 059
2,000 acres or more -----------	1 680	1 569	5 949 249	5 727 467	2 322 720	2 520 160	1 106 715	1 188 340
5,000 acres or more ---------	215	227	1 750 081	1 816 244	497 487	595 271	252 272	275 746

Table 9. **Irrigation: 1987, 1982, and 1978**

[For meaning of abbreviations and symbols, see introductory text]

Farms with irrigation	1987	1982	1978	Farms with irrigation	1987	1982	1978
Farms --------------------number..	7 352	7 257	7 961	Irrigated land—Con.			
Proportion of farms ----------percent..	10.7	9.9	10.7	Acres irrigated—Con.			
				200 to 499 acres ------------- farms..	1 953	2 047	2 072
				acres..	623 475	659 494	660 831
Irrigated land -----------------acres..	2 463 073	2 675 167	2 685 757	500 to 999 acres ------------- farms..	1 012	984	989
Average per farm ------------acres..	335	369	337	acres..	700 303	680 582	677 550
				1,000 acres or more ---------- farms..	504	615	575
Acres irrigated:				acres..	822 643	1 031 775	988 849
1 to 9 acres ----------------- farms..	416	315	370	Irrigated land use:			
acres..	1 324	1 020	1 291	Harvested cropland ------------- farms..	7 268	7 211	7 827
10 to 49 acres --------------- farms..	897	846	1 044	acres..	2 408 176	2 639 024	2 546 894
acres..	25 518	24 098	29 641	Pastureland and other land ----- farms..	365	279	(NA)
50 to 99 acres --------------- farms..	996	901	1 143	acres..	54 897	36 143	138 863
acres..	71 219	63 619	80 674	Land in irrigated farms --------acres..	10 653 734	10 344 665	10 793 174
100 to 199 acres ------------- farms..	1 574	1 549	1 768	Cropland -------------------acres..	6 163 623	7 740 490	7 563 814
acres..	218 591	214 579	246 921	Harvested cropland -----------acres..	4 816 179	5 300 114	4 986 423

Table 10. Selected Characteristics of Irrigated and Nonirrigated Farms: 1987 and 1982

[For meaning of abbreviations and symbols, see introductory text]

Characteristics	All farms		Irrigated farms				Nonirrigated farms	
			Any land irrigated		All harvested cropland irrigated			
	1987	1982	1987	1982	1987	1982	1987	1982
Farms ... number	68 579	73 315	7 352	7 257	1 722	1 527	61 227	66 058
Land in farms ... acres	46 628 519	47 052 213	10 653 734	10 344 665	1 632 530	1 311 863	35 974 765	36 707 548
Value of land and buildings[1]:								
Average per farm ... dollars	278 047	384 197	641 180	891 850	499 350	632 682	235 418	328 935
Average per acre ... dollars	413	601	445	614	549	710	404	597
Irrigated land ... acres	2 463 073	2 675 167	2 463 073	2 675 167	835 419	793 192	(X)	(X)
Land in farms according to use:								
Total cropland ... farms	61 615	66 481	7 339	7 246	1 722	1 527	54 276	59 235
acres	31 385 090	30 598 859	8 163 623	7 740 490	1 291 003	1 028 498	23 221 467	22 858 369
Harvested cropland ... farms	57 822	62 860	7 307	7 233	1 722	1 527	50 515	55 627
acres	17 729 394	20 186 974	4 816 179	5 300 114	809 530	778 096	12 913 215	14 886 860
Pastureland, excluding woodland pastured ... farms	47 598	51 075	4 411	4 438	587	568	43 187	46 637
acres	16 739 539	17 316 988	2 689 836	2 665 537	372 156	276 732	14 049 703	14 651 451
Land set aside in federal farm programs ... farms	36 246	(NA)	5 943	(NA)	1 161	(NA)	30 303	(NA)
acres	4 767 068	(NA)	1 443 724	(NA)	239 425	(NA)	3 323 334	(NA)
Owned and rented land in farms:								
Owned land in farms ... farms	57 923	(NA)	5 931	(NA)	1 274	(NA)	51 992	(NA)
acres	21 178 322	(NA)	4 245 087	(NA)	744 485	(NA)	16 933 235	(NA)
Rented or leased land in farms ... farms	38 623	41 349	5 698	6 516	1 030	(NA)	32 925	(NA)
acres	25 450 197	23 666 545	6 408 647	(NA)	868 045	(NA)	19 041 550	(NA)
Market value of agricultural products sold ... $1,000	6 476 669	6 190 861	1 941 973	1 842 586	598 880	443 247	4 534 696	4 348 275
Average per farm ... dollars	94 441	84 442	264 142	253 905	347 782	290 273	74 084	65 825
Crops, including nursery and greenhouse crops ... farms	51 773	58 791	7 165	7 096	1 648	1 445	44 608	49 695
$1,000	1 693 609	2 143 047	652 451	803 466	165 112	172 792	1 041 158	1 339 581
Livestock, poultry, and their products ... farms	45 882	51 701	4 060	4 404	640	613	41 822	47 297
$1,000	4 783 060	4 047 815	1 289 522	1 039 120	433 767	270 455	3 493 538	3 008 694
Total farm production expenses[1] ... $1,000	5 516 518	(NA)	1 666 516	(NA)	531 291	(NA)	3 850 001	(NA)
Average per farm ... dollars	80 439	(NA)	231 300	(NA)	304 639	(NA)	62 729	(NA)
Livestock and poultry purchased ... farms	23 380	26 892	2 649	(NA)	458	(NA)	20 731	(NA)
$1,000	2 426 149	1 900 272	745 987	(NA)	288 839	(NA)	1 680 161	(NA)
Feed for livestock and poultry ... farms	38 347	45 184	3 541	3 843	579	602	34 806	41 341
$1,000	887 270	920 415	229 504	212 495	77 580	61 300	657 766	707 921
Seeds, bulbs, plants, and trees ... farms	48 233	47 466	6 935	6 731	1 588	1 383	41 298	40 735
$1,000	95 302	83 505	38 064	31 129	10 032	7 528	57 237	52 376
Commercial fertilizer[2] ... farms	47 731	49 644	6 853	6 516	1 571	1 338	40 878	43 128
$1,000	216 166	254 590	74 402	86 261	16 379	17 643	141 765	168 309
Agricultural chemicals[2] ... farms	46 318	34 068	6 691	5 782	1 586	1 255	39 627	28 286
$1,000	125 003	94 957	42 377	38 401	9 622	8 947	82 626	56 557
Petroleum products ... farms	65 460	73 030	7 099	(NA)	1 648	(NA)	58 361	(NA)
$1,000	243 568	358 860	81 186	(NA)	21 143	(NA)	162 382	(NA)
Electricity ... farms	48 797	51 538	6 107	(NA)	1 326	(NA)	42 690	(NA)
$1,000	54 103	53 184	17 784	(NA)	4 566	(NA)	36 319	(NA)
Hired farm labor ... farms	24 715	25 274	4 383	4 206	861	661	20 332	21 068
$1,000	226 075	153 404	82 230	62 252	25 937	14 877	143 845	91 152
Contract labor ... farms	7 882	3 345	1 514	683	329	122	6 368	2 662
$1,000	23 691	8 123	6 754	2 775	1 623	495	16 937	5 349
Repairs and maintenance ... farms	56 961	(NA)	6 653	(NA)	1 477	(NA)	50 308	(NA)
$1,000	252 018	(NA)	72 979	(NA)	15 797	(NA)	179 039	(NA)
Customwork, machine hire, and rental of machinery and equipment[3] ... farms	30 603	30 844	4 441	(NA)	973	(NA)	26 162	(NA)
$1,000	107 366	104 886	38 089	(NA)	9 846	(NA)	69 277	(NA)
Interest[4] ... farms	39 549	40 559	5 453	5 731	1 197	1 145	34 096	34 828
$1,000	314 163	467 054	90 142	142 472	17 443	28 234	224 021	324 582
Cash rent paid for land and buildings ... farms	21 234	(NA)	3 028	(NA)	491	(NA)	18 206	(NA)
$1,000	123 531	(NA)	32 787	(NA)	5 628	(NA)	90 744	(NA)
Property taxes paid ... farms	63 359	(NA)	6 855	(NA)	1 543	(NA)	56 704	(NA)
$1,000	112 201	(NA)	22 974	(NA)	4 135	(NA)	89 227	(NA)
All other farm production expenses ... farms	64 491	(NA)	7 124	(NA)	1 709	(NA)	57 367	(NA)
$1,000	309 914	(NA)	91 257	(NA)	22 703	(NA)	218 656	(NA)
Commodity Credit Corporation loans ... farms	15 832	14 306	3 598	(NA)	652	(NA)	12 234	(NA)
$1,000	338 298	364 770	164 904	(NA)	34 063	(NA)	173 394	(NA)
Government payments received ... farms	41 627	(NA)	6 125	(NA)	1 218	(NA)	35 502	(NA)
$1,000	573 547	(NA)	208 472	(NA)	41 645	(NA)	365 175	(NA)
Other farm-related income[1] ... farms	18 682	(NA)	2 292	(NA)	363	(NA)	16 390	(NA)
$1,000	69 944	(NA)	14 929	(NA)	2 742	(NA)	55 016	(NA)
Estimated market value of all machinery and equipment[1] ... farms	68 391	73 238	7 205	7 174	1 744	1 549	61 186	66 064
$1,000	3 447 663	3 830 616	850 255	901 847	180 912	164 854	2 597 408	2 928 769
Average per farm ... dollars	50 411	52 304	118 009	125 710	103 734	106 426	42 451	44 332
Inventory of livestock:								
Cattle and calves ... farms	40 795	47 008	3 589	4 019	534	524	37 196	42 989
number	5 539 292	5 800 138	1 286 912	1 318 217	325 568	263 693	4 252 980	4 481 921
Milk cows ... farms	3 093	4 631	267	356	31	39	2 826	4 275
number	96 675	123 009	13 776	14 778	1 658	1 021	82 899	108 231
Hogs and pigs ... farms	6 788	9 241	616	695	72	85	6 172	8 546
number	1 516 878	1 708 770	198 119	186 929	16 632	13 112	1 318 759	1 521 841
Sheep and lambs ... farms	2 400	2 478	190	222	25	30	2 210	2 256
number	249 303	278 616	36 094	71 952	1 227	5 345	213 209	206 664

[1] Data are based on a sample of farms.
[2] Data for 1987 include cost of custom applications.
[3] Data for 1987 exclude cost of custom applications for commercial fertilizer and agricultural chemicals.
[4] Data for 1982 do not include imputation for item nonresponse.

Table 11. **Value of Land and Buildings: 1987, 1982, and 1978**

[Data are based on a sample of farms; see text. For meaning of abbreviations and symbols, see introductory text]

Value of land and buildings	1987		1982	1978
	Farms	Value ($1,000)		
Estimated market value of land and buildings......farms..	68 580	(X)	73 077	74 171
$1,000..	(X)	19 066 461	28 075 971	23 895 307
Average per farm.....................................dollars..	(X)	278 047	384 197	322 165
Average per acre.....................................dollars..	(X)	413	601	498
Farms by value group:				
$1 to $39,999..	10 024	186 463	7 733	8 678
$40,000 to $69,999..	9 571	507 673	7 558	9 199
$70,000 to $99,999..	7 001	581 565	6 560	7 031
$100,000 to $149,999..	8 596	1 037 123	8 049	8 367
$150,000 to $199,999..	6 313	1 080 117	6 275	6 546
$200,000 to $499,999..	16 476	5 164 005	19 892	20 346
$500,000 to $999,999..	7 579	5 187 765	10 810	9 820
$1,000,000 to $1,999,999....................................	2 396	3 132 664		
$2,000,000 to $4,999,999....................................	535	1 482 084	6 102	4 182
$5,000,000 or more..	89	708 802		

Table 12. **Value of Machinery and Equipment on Place: 1987 and 1982**

[Data are based on a sample of farms; see text. For meaning of abbreviations and symbols, see introductory text]

Value of machinery and equipment	1987		1982	
	Farms	Value ($1,000)	Farms	Value ($1,000)
Estimated market value of all machinery and equipment	68 391	9 447 663	79 238	3 630 616
Average per farm[1]	(X)	50 411	(X)	52 304
By value group:				
$1 to $4,999..	5 812	15 447	4 006	12 055
$5,000 to $9,999...	11 585	77 411	13 687	91 476
$10,000 to $19,999...	11 722	154 418	12 077	157 750
$20,000 to $29,999...	8 003	182 924	8 690	199 806
$30,000 to $49,999...	8 721	320 105	9 765	363 797
$50,000 to $69,999...	6 850	376 231	7 074	392 622
$70,000 to $99,999...	5 326	431 090	5 536	449 343
$100,000 to $199,999.......................................	7 277	938 932	8 617	1 109 011
$200,000 to $499,999.......................................	2 860	730 659	3 546	899 833
$500,000 to $999,999.......................................	195	115 954	220	154 922
$1,000,000 or more...	40	102 593		

[1]Data are in whole dollars.

Table 13. **Selected Machinery and Equipment on Place: 1987 and 1982**

[Data are based on a sample of farms; see text. For meaning of abbreviations and symbols, see introductory text]

Selected machinery and equipment	1987						1982		
	Total		Manufactured 1983 to 1987		Manufactured prior to 1983				Number manufactured 1978 to 1982
	Farms	Number	Farms	Number	Farms	Number	Farms	Number	
Motortrucks, including pickups............................	63 093	159 329	19 029	23 314	57 552	136 015	66 885	159 424	39 814
2 or 3	28 169	67 381	2 487	5 444	25 422	60 547	29 735	70 664	12 396
4 or more	13 617	70 641	300	1 628	10 735	54 063	12 500	63 910	3 646
Wheel tractors...	60 459	150 647	7 633	10 363	58 487	140 284	62 969	149 870	21 129
2 or 3	29 707	72 014	1 543	3 462	26 590	68 604	32 456	77 977	7 758
4 or more	12 243	50 124	207	998	10 742	52 325	10 940	52 320	1 637
Less than 40 horsepower (PTO).............................	25 210	38 591	1 685	2 079	24 148	36 612	(NA)	(NA)	(NA)
40 horsepower (PTO) or more...............................	50 577	112 056	6 449	8 284	48 649	103 772	(NA)	(NA)	(NA)
Grain and bean combines[1]................................	35 608	43 801	2 824	3 075	33 195	40 726	36 503	46 662	7 681
Cottonpickers and strippers...............................	1	(D)	–	–	1	(D)			
Mower conditioners..	18 793	20 167	2 309	2 402	16 612	17 765	17 416	18 932	4 637
Pickup balers...	26 083	31 892	3 708	3 952	23 408	27 940	27 088	31 998	7 271

[1]Data for 1982 include self-propelled only.

Table 14. Petroleum Products Expenses: 1987, 1982, and 1978

[Data are based on a sample of farms; see text. For meaning of abbreviations and symbols, see introductory text.]

Item	1987 Farms	1987 Expenses ($1,000)	1982	1978
Petroleum products .... farms..	65 460	(X)	73 030	73 806
$1,000..	(X)	243 568	358 860	207 732
Average per farm .... dollars..	(X)	3 721	4 914	2 815
Gasoline and gasohol .... farms..	57 245	(X)	68 308	70 292
$1,000..	(X)	80 737	127 211	86 050
Average per farm .... dollars..	(X)	1 410	1 862	1 224
Farms with expenses of—				
$1 to $499	20 147	4 622	20 073	24 666
$500 to $999	11 825	7 952	11 763	16 376
$1,000 to $1,999	12 264	16 257	13 856	16 470
$2,000 to $4,999	10 453	29 274	17 109	10 902
$5,000 to $9,999	1 998	12 615	4 292	1 501
$10,000 to $24,999	492	6 584	} 1 225	377
$25,000 or more	66	3 432		
Diesel fuel .... farms..	46 376	(X)	48 725	45 058
$1,000..	(X)	110 961	155 737	69 886
Average per farm .... dollars..	(X)	2 393	3 196	1 551
Farms with expenses of—				
$1 to $499	11 766	2 730	9 341	15 087
$500 to $999	8 258	5 590	7 345	9 840
$1,000 to $1,999	8 947	12 058	8 986	9 470
$2,000 to $4,999	11 254	33 865	13 336	8 254
$5,000 to $9,999	4 625	29 975	6 542	1 713
$10,000 to $24,999	1 325	17 775	} 3 175	694
$25,000 or more	201	8 984		
Natural gas .... farms..	4 956	(X)	5 660	5 962
$1,000..	(X)	26 371	31 617	21 570
Average per farm .... dollars..	(X)	5 321	5 586	3 618
Farms with expenses of—				
$1 to $99	218	12	271	427
$100 to $499	890	256	1 036	1 665
$500 to $999	660	443	773	603
$1,000 to $1,999	778	1 026	739	812
$2,000 to $4,999	998	3 063	1 135	1 198
$5,000 to $9,999	672	4 714	} 1 706	1 257
$10,000 or more	740	16 857		
LP gas, fuel oil, kerosene, motor oil, grease, etc. .... farms..	52 549	(X)	(NA)	(NA)
$1,000..	(X)	25 478	44 295	30 226
Average per farm .... dollars..	(X)	485	(NA)	(NA)
Farms with expenses of—				
$1 to $99	13 526	686	(NA)	(NA)
$100 to $499	23 892	5 533	(NA)	(NA)
$500 to $999	8 473	5 455	(NA)	(NA)
$1,000 to $1,999	4 464	5 607	(NA)	(NA)
$2,000 to $4,999	1 875	5 029	(NA)	(NA)
$5,000 to $9,999	236	1 454	(NA)	(NA)
$10,000 or more	83	1 715	(NA)	(NA)

Table 15. Agricultural Chemicals Used, Including Fertilizer and Lime: 1987, 1982, and 1978

[Data are based on a sample of farms; see text. For meaning of abbreviations and symbols, see introductory text.]

Chemicals used	1987	1982	1978	Chemicals used	1987	1982	1978
Any chemicals, fertilizer, or lime used .... farms..	54 462	53 833	59 096	Any chemicals, fertilizer, or lime used—Con.			
Commercial fertilizer¹ .... farms..	47 731	49 644	54 046	Sprays, dusts, granules, fumigants, etc., to control—			
acres on which used..	13 852 822	14 569 402	14 127 330	Insects on hay and other crops .... farms..	19 416	14 733	16 035
$1,000..	216 166	254 590	252 403	acres on which used..	3 015 580	2 861 551	2 980 702
Lime .... farms..	2 685	2 514	3 662	Nematodes in crops .... farms..	716	699	1 292
acres on which used..	154 622	148 897	215 038	acres on which used..	87 904	130 368	167 310
tons..	369 024	375 467	527 020	Diseases in crops and orchards .... farms..	1 055	925	1 429
Farms by tons used:				acres on which used..	125 065	131 390	221 675
1 to 49 tons	917	751	1 212	Weeds, grass, or brush in crops and pasture .... farms..	36 950	28 058	33 257
50 to 99 tons	676	538	857	acres on which used..	8 637 062	5 907 509	6 070 765
100 to 199 tons	582	676	774				
200 to 499 tons	385	419	635				
500 to 999 tons	101	105	141	Chemicals used for defoliation or for growth control of crops			
1,000 tons or more	24	25	43	or thinning of fruit .... farms..	614	737	606
Agricultural chemicals¹ .... farms..	46 318	34 068	42 427	acres on which used..	66 639	95 589	64 314
$1,000..	125 003	94 957	68 543				

¹Data for 1987 include cost of custom applications; data for agricultural chemicals exclude the cost of lime for 1987 and 1982.

Table 16. **Tenure and Characteristics of Operator and Type of Organization for All Farms and Farms Operated by Black and Other Races: 1987, 1982, and 1978**

[For meaning of abbreviations and symbols, see introductory text]

Characteristics	All farms			Farms operated by Black and other races[1]		
	1987	1982	1978	1987	1982	1978
Tenure of operator:						
All operators _____ farms__	68 579	73 315	74 171	275	269	325
acres__	46 626 519	47 052 213	47 499 831	73 470	94 052	143 839
Harvested cropland _____ farms__	57 822	82 860	64 862	176	192	259
acres__	17 729 394	20 186 974	18 987 844	26 005	36 025	60 306
Full owners _____ farms__	29 956	31 834	30 061	172	155	156
acres__	8 839 919	10 524 633	9 138 120	26 446	22 554	36 564
Harvested cropland _____ farms__	21 783	23 963	23 012	90	93	107
acres__	2 909 784	3 955 987	3 199 878	7 046	7 335	11 956
Part owners _____ farms__	27 967	29 862	31 647	66	69	109
acres__	30 896 557	30 378 105	31 792 701	32 317	51 422	84 815
Harvested cropland _____ farms__	26 819	26 775	30 751	56	84	101
acres__	11 996 753	13 330 829	12 955 820	12 553	19 408	35 087
Tenants _____ farms__	10 656	11 619	12 463	37	45	60
acres__	6 892 043	6 149 575	6 569 010	14 707	20 076	22 460
Harvested cropland _____ farms__	9 220	10 122	11 099	30	35	51
acres__	2 822 857	2 900 358	2 831 946	6 406	9 282	13 263
Percent of tenancy _____ percent__	15.5	15.8	16.8	13.5	16.7	18.5
Operators by place of residence:						
On farm operated _____	45 527	48 356	48 900	173	175	179
Not on farm operated _____	17 871	17 026	16 889	77	79	93
Not reported _____	5 181	7 933	8 382	25	15	53
Operators by principal occupation:						
Farming _____	42 607	47 293	49 104	112	120	173
Other _____	25 972	26 022	25 067	163	149	152
Operators by days of work off farm:						
None _____	29 462	30 524	34 255	73	87	125
Any _____	34 654	35 521	36 256	186	164	181
1 to 49 days _____	5 265	6 247	7 839	12	15	33
50 to 99 days _____	2 355	2 405	2 492	7	8	7
100 to 149 days _____	2 246	2 350	2 452	10	3	13
150 to 199 days _____	3 111	3 213	3 083	9	13	20
200 days or more _____	21 677	21 306	20 390	148	125	108
Not reported _____	4 463	7 270	5 000	16	18	19
Operators by years on present farm:						
2 years or less _____	3 511	3 376	(NA)	12	13	(NA)
3 or 4 years _____	3 873	5 484	(NA)	20	26	(NA)
5 to 9 years _____	8 552	10 297	(NA)	50	51	(NA)
10 years or more _____	40 624	39 238	(NA)	137	123	(NA)
Average years on present farm _____	21.3	20.2	(NA)	16.4	16.2	(NA)
Not reported _____	12 019	14 920	(NA)	56	56	(NA)
Operators by age group:						
Under 25 years _____	1 712	2 840	3 215	3	7	11
25 to 34 years _____	9 531	10 670	9 708	38	24	46
35 to 44 years _____	12 471	12 232	12 031	55	55	68
45 to 49 years _____	5 928	} 14 815	16 837	} 30 36	} 62	79
50 to 54 years _____	6 781					
55 to 59 years _____	7 581	} 17 746	18 401	} 23 30	} 67	78
60 to 64 years _____	8 407					
65 to 69 years _____	6 584	} 15 012	13 979	} 24 38	} 50	50
70 years and over _____	9 606					
Average age _____	52.0	50.9	50.7	52.2	51.4	49.3
Operators by sex:						
Male _____ farms__	65 619	70 674	71 566	258	248	304
acres__	45 466 481	46 024 059	46 420 296	70 156	87 764	134 162
Female _____ farms__	2 960	2 641	2 605	17	21	21
acres__	1 140 038	1 028 154	1 079 535	3 314	6 288	9 677
Operators of Spanish origin (see text) _____ farms__	108	118	118	20	15	15
Operators not of Spanish origin _____ farms__	55 373	50 860	83 834	5 088	4 114	7 817
Spanish origin not reported _____ farms__	47 928	(NA)	(NA)	147	(NA)	(NA)
	20 543	(NA)	(NA)	108	(NA)	(NA)
Type of organization:						
Individual or family (sole proprietorship) _____ farms__	60 202	64 313	65 380	242	232	273
acres__	36 420 471	36 885 296	37 997 141	57 566	74 479	115 594
Partnership _____ farms__	6 689	6 702	7 092	26	28	44
acres__	6 151 580	6 196 310	6 420 883	8 694	11 227	19 360
Corporation _____ farms__	2 100	1 876	1 478	2	5	6
acres__	3 606 121	3 452 797	2 793 293	(D)	5 015	(D)
Family held:						
More than 10 stockholders _____ farms__	23	30	22	-	-	-
acres__	40 087	37 014	36 662	-	-	-
10 or less stockholders _____ farms__	1 919	1 665	1 294	2	5	6
acres__	3 405 858	3 169 047	2 497 313	(D)	5 015	(D)
Other than family held:						
More than 10 stockholders _____ farms__	17	33	20	-	-	-
acres__	5 299	21 462	11 650	-	-	-
10 or less stockholders _____ farms__	141	148	142	-	-	-
acres__	154 077	225 274	237 668	-	-	-
Other—cooperative, estate or trust, institutional, etc. _____ farms__	388	424	221	3	4	2
acres__	450 347	517 810	298 534	(D)	3 331	(D)

[1]For classification of social and ethnic groups, see text.

Table 17. **Selected Characteristics of Farms Operated by Females, Persons of Spanish Origin, and Specified Racial Groups: 1987 and 1982**

[For meaning of abbreviations and symbols, see introductory text]

Characteristics	Female operators	Operators of Spanish origin[1]	Farms operated by Black and other races				
			Total	Black	American Indian	Asian	Other (see text)
FARMS AND LAND IN FARMS							
Farms............................. number, 1987..	2 960	108	275	129	121	9	16
1982..	2 641	113	269	137	101	19	12
Land in farms............................ acres, 1987..	1 140 038	55 373	73 470	36 759	26 897	5 616	4 198
1982..	1 028 154	50 850	94 052	42 710	34 163	13 869	3 310
Harvested cropland....................farms, 1987..	2 136	79	178	98	65	9	6
1982..	1 998	90	192	106	66	15	5
acres, 1987..	380 102	22 310	26 005	13 880	6 839	2 232	3 054
1982..	371 855	23 168	36 025	18 174	11 268	4 801	1 782
1987 FARMS BY SIZE							
1 to 9 acres	294	7	22	9	11	1	1
10 to 49 acres	439	17	72	31	34	2	5
50 to 139 acres..	551	29	69	28	36	1	6
140 to 219 acres.......................................	458	5	40	26	14	–	–
220 to 499 acres.......................................	599	14	36	18	18	–	–
500 acres or more	619	36	36	19	8	5	4
1987 OWNED AND RENTED LAND IN FARMS							
Owned land in farms ....farms..	2 652	86	238	111	108	7	12
acres..	760 311	20 363	41 274	20 595	18 361	1 786	533
Rented or leased land in farms ....farms..	883	60	103	54	38	4	7
acres..	379 727	35 010	32 196	16 164	8 536	3 831	3 665
TENURE OF OPERATOR							
Full owners...................................farms, 1987..	2 077	48	172	75	83	5	9
1982..	1 853	55	155	73	67	1	7
acres, 1987..	510 218	10 267	26 446	11 866	13 037	1 293	450
1982..	472 811	8 357	22 554	11 088	9 810	(D)	(D)
Part owners.................................farms, 1987..	575	40	66	36	25	2	3
1982..	543	33	69	42	22	4	1
acres, 1987..	511 034	34 621	32 317	16 986	11 350	(D)	(D)
1982..	446 877	36 416	51 422	25 431	21 893	(D)	(D)
Tenants ....farms, 1987..	308	20	37	18	13	2	4
1982..	245	25	45	22	12	7	4
acres, 1987..	118 786	10 485	14 707	8 107	2 510	(D)	(D)
1982..	108 466	6 077	20 076	8 191	2 460	8 795	2 640
1987 FARMS BY TYPE OF ORGANIZATION							
Individual or family (sole proprietorship)	2 529	89	242	116	106	8	12
Partnership	226	15	28	12	12	1	3
Family held corporation	60	3	2	1	1	–	–
Other than family held corporation	8	–	–	–	–	–	–
Other—cooperative, estate or trust, institutional, etc..........................	37	1	3	–	2	–	1
1987 MARKET VALUE OF AGRICULTURAL PRODUCTS SOLD							
Total sales .... farms..	2 960	108	275	129	121	9	16
$1,000..	88 462	5 935	4 293	1 813	1 808	355	317
Crops, including nursery and greenhouse crops .... farms..	1 800	63	147	80	52	9	6
$1,000..	35 146	2 011	2 086	983	575	3	(D)
Livestock, poultry, and their products .... farms..	1 790	75	196	83	99	3	10
$1,000..	53 316	3 924	2 207	830	1 233	(D)	(D)
Farms by value of sales:							
Less than $2,500	739	24	78	29	41	3	5
$2,500 to $9,999	1 070	32	103	50	46	2	5
$10,000 to $19,999............................	410	13	44	29	14	–	1
$20,000 to $24,999............................	141	6	11	7	3	–	1
$25,000 or more	600	33	39	14	17	4	4
1987 FARMS BY STANDARD INDUSTRIAL CLASSIFICATION							
Cash grains (011)	1 177	41	85	52	26	4	3
Field crops, except cash grains (013)	127	4	15	3	6	3	3
Cotton (0131)	–	–	–	–	–	–	–
Tobacco (0132)	–	–	–	–	–	–	–
Sugarcane and sugar beets; Irish potatoes; field crops, except cash grains, n.e.c. (0133, 0134, 0139)	127	4	15	3	6	3	3
Vegetables and melons (016)	18	1	1	1	–	–	–
Fruits and tree nuts (017)	9	1	–	–	–	–	–
Horticultural specialties (018)	29	–	2	–	2	–	–
General farms, primarily crop (019)..........	60	2	3	3	–	–	–
Livestock, except dairy, poultry, and animal specialties (021)	1 269	51	149	63	75	1	10
Beef cattle, except feedlots (0212)	1 051	43	99	33	56	1	9
Dairy farms (024)..................................	50	2	4	2	2	–	–
Poultry and eggs (025)..........................	16	–	3	2	1	–	–
Animal specialties (027).........................	143	6	10	2	8	–	–
General farms, primarily livestock and animal specialties (029)	42	–	3	1	2	–	–

See footnotes at end of table.

Table 17. **Selected Characteristics of Farms Operated by Females, Persons of Spanish Origin, and Specified Racial Groups: 1987 and 1982**—Con.

[For meaning of abbreviations and symbols, see introductory text]

Characteristics	Female operators	Operators of Spanish origin[1]	Farms operated by Black and other races				
			Total	Black	American Indian	Asian	Other (see text)
1987 OPERATOR CHARACTERISTICS							
Operators by place of residence:							
On farm operated	1 868	75	173	72	82	5	14
Not on farm operated	857	29	77	41	30	4	2
Not reported	235	4	25	16	9	-	-
Operators by principal occupation:							
Farming	1 508	58	112	56	46	3	7
Other	1 452	50	163	73	75	6	9
Operators by days of work off farm:							
None	1 404	33	73	38	31	3	1
Any	2 210	119	186	148	153	12	21
1 to 99 days	216	12	19	10	8	-	1
100 to 199 days	1 132	59	19	73	77	6	11
200 days or more	862	48	148	65	68	6	9
Not reported	208	4	16	8	5	-	3
Operators by years on present farm:							
2 years or less	201	10	12	2	8	-	2
3 or 4 years	222	14	20	9	8	1	4
5 to 9 years	394	12	50	16	26	3	3
10 years or more	1 479	56	137	69	56	5	7
Average years on present farm	20.7	15.7	16.4	16.7	14.6	14.6	14.6
Not reported	664	16	56	31	25	-	-
Operators by age group:							
Under 25 years	65	8	3	-	3	-	-
25 to 34 years	195	18	36	14	19	-	3
35 to 44 years	370	24	55	12	33	4	6
45 to 54 years	489	29	66	34	27	2	3
55 to 59 years	305	7	23	15	7	1	-
60 to 64 years	397	10	30	18	10	1	1
65 to 69 years	374	5	24	13	8	1	2
70 years and over	785	9	38	23	14	-	1
Average age	58.2	47.2	52.2	56.0	48.9	50.0	47.8
Operators by sex:							
Male	(X)	97	258	119	114	9	16
Female	2 960	11	17	10	7	-	-
Operators of Spanish origin[1]	11	108	20	2	2	-	16
1987 COMMODITY CREDIT CORPORATION LOANS AND GOVERNMENT PAYMENTS							
Amount received from Commodity Credit Corporation loans .... farms..	355	14	24	10	7	4	3
$1,000..	6 899	275	377	231	70	63	13
Government payments received .... farms..	1 417	50	79	40	29	5	5
$1,000..	12 056	674	774	333	303	60	77

[1]See chapter 1, table 16 for operators not of or not reporting Spanish origin.

Table 18. Selected Characteristics of Farms by Standard Industrial Classification: 1987

[For meaning of abbreviations and symbols, see introductory text]

SIC code	Farms	Land in farms (acres)	Harvested cropland (acres)	Value of selected capital assets[1], average per farm (dollars) Land and buildings	Machinery and equipment	Market value of agricultural products sold ($1,000) Total	Crops, including nursery and greenhouse crops	Livestock, poultry, and their products
Total	68 579	46 628 519	17 729 394	278 047	50 411	6 476 869	1 693 609	4 783 060
Crops (01)	35 836	25 991 871	12 434 005	317 949	57 720	1 570 462	1 337 434	233 028
Cash grains (011)	31 789	24 396 997	11 737 683	331 138	60 503	1 429 353	1 223 712	205 641
Wheat (0111)	14 290	11 021 008	4 900 659	312 339	55 376	446 463	402 730	43 732
Rice (0112)	–	–	–	–	–	–	–	–
Corn (0115)	1 685	(D)	(D)	524 758	108 216	180 195	172 025	8 170
Soybeans (0116)	4 704	1 939 894	1 134 305	219 485	43 282	(D)	(D)	12 140
Cash grains, n.e.c. (0119)	11 110	(D)	(D)	373 354	67 325	(D)	(D)	141 599
Field crops, except cash grains (013)	2 010	641 893	326 417	192 475	31 777	47 372	44 341	3 031
Cotton (0131)	1	(D)	(D)	(D)	(D)	(D)	(D)	(D)
Tobacco (0132)	3	(D)	(D)	(D)	(D)	(D)	(D)	–
Sugarcane and sugar beets (0133)	–	–	–	–	–	–	–	–
Irish potatoes (0134)	–	–	–	–	–	–	–	–
Field crops, except cash grains, n.e.c. (0139)	2 006	639 598	325 604	190 806	31 388	47 246	(D)	(D)
Vegetables and melons (016)	179	12 759	6 499	103 752	22 611	3 658	3 517	141
Fruits and tree nuts (017)	171	8 923	3 983	91 108	16 886	1 323	1 289	34
Berry crops (0171)	24	388	104	82 966	9 324	62	(D)	(D)
Grapes (0172)	4	212	43	–	–	10	10	–
Tree nuts (0173)	19	1 942	1 153	121 208	33 829	236	229	7
Citrus fruits (0174)	–	–	–	–	–	–	–	–
Deciduous tree fruits (0175)	57	2 590	1 194	90 133	22 900	914	890	25
Fruits and tree nuts, n.e.c. (0179)	67	3 791	1 489	77 705	8 086	101	(D)	(D)
Horticultural specialties (018)	224	19 302	6 069	246 343	49 950	26 681	26 645	36
Ornamental floriculture and nursery products (0181)...	221	19 264	6 057	249 882	50 815	26 452	26 416	36
Food crops grown under cover (0182) ...	3	38	12	85 000	10 500	229	229	–
General farms, primarily crop (019)	1 463	911 997	353 354	282 794	45 499	62 075	37 931	24 144
Livestock and animal specialties (02)	32 743	20 636 648	5 295 369	235 056	42 551	4 906 207	356 174	4 550 033
Livestock, except dairy, poultry, and animal specialties (021)	29 037	19 106 721	4 789 005	237 604	42 447	4 680 257	325 945	4 354 311
Beef cattle feedlots (0211)	2 069	2 164 512	694 460	446 512	117 139	3 061 190	56 114	3 005 076
Beef cattle, except feedlots (0212)	21 861	14 512 574	3 100 134	225 319	34 468	1 207 132	195 347	1 011 784
Hogs (0213)	2 857	957 581	424 004	153 193	45 143	263 782	30 691	233 092
Sheep and goats (0214)	691	85 228	25 881	86 965	15 066	13 712	1 443	12 269
General livestock, except dairy, poultry, and animal specialties (0219)	1 559	1 386 826	544 526	343 830	61 617	134 441	42 350	92 091
Dairy farms (024)	1 391	805 354	(D)	288 873	76 162	162 066	19 001	143 065
Poultry and eggs (025)	197	34 376	13 106	140 394	27 852	25 902	1 145	24 757
Broiler, fryer, and roaster chickens (0251)	7	304	(D)	78 000	6 000	131	–	131
Chicken eggs (0252)	133	29 678	11 906	199 766	36 488	20 598	1 066	19 533
Turkeys and turkey eggs (0253)	13	1 996	347	87 846	35 138	1 772	(D)	(D)
Poultry hatcheries (0254)	4	20	–	31 000	43 143	2 827	–	2 827
Poultry and eggs, n.e.c. (0259)	40	2 376	853	53 063	10 502	574	(D)	(D)
Animal specialties (027)	1 452	126 440	(D)	94 293	13 620	7 065	286	6 779
Fur-bearing animals and rabbits (0271)	25	3 361	(D)	155 000	5 114	68	(D)	(D)
Horses and other equines (0272)	1 336	110 157	9 527	95 628	13 884	3 946	271	3 675
Animal aquaculture (0273)	17	2 043	66	197 000	18 517	769	(D)	(D)
Animal specialties, n.e.c. (0279)	74	10 859	283	57 860	11 019	2 282	10	2 272
General farms, primarily livestock and animal specialties (029)	666	583 757	120 501	333 957	42 706	30 917	9 797	21 120

[1]Data are based on a sample of farms.

Table 19. Selected Characteristics of Abnormal Farms: 1987 and 1982

[For meaning of abbreviations and symbols, see introductory text]

Characteristics	1987	1982	Characteristics	1987	1982
Farms .... number..	38	35	Market value of agricultural products sold ..... $1,000..	~4 028	2 483
Land in farms .... acres..	164 950	166 900	Average per farm .... dollars..	111 881	70 942
Average size of farm .... acres..	4 582	4 769			
			Crops, including nursery and greenhouse crops .... $1,000..	1 018	431
Value of land and buildings[1] .... $1,000..	32 661	35 778	Livestock, poultry, and their products .... $1,000..	3 009	2 052
Average per farm .... dollars..	907 250	1 022 229			
Average per acre .... dollars..	198	214	Total farm production expenses[1] .... $1,000..	5 505	(NA)
			Average per farm .... dollars..	152 911	(NA)
Estimated market value of all machinery and equipment[1] .... $1,000..	5 916	2 131	Tenure of operator:		
			Full owners	20	20
			Part owners	6	6
Land in farms according to use:			Tenants	10	9
Total cropland .... farms..	26	25			
acres..	12 855	9 579	Abnormal farms by standard industrial classification:		
Harvested cropland .... farms..	25	23	Cash grains (011)	10	8
acres..	7 398	5 135	Field crops, except cash grains (013)	-	-
Cropland used only for pasture or grazing .. farms..	8	5	Cotton (0131)	-	-
acres..	3 345	1 574	Tobacco (0132)	-	-
Other cropland .... farms..	19	(NA)	Sugarcane and sugar beets; Irish potatoes; field crops, except cash grains, n.e.c. (0133, 0134, 0139)	-	-
acres..	2 112	2 870			
Total woodland .... farms..	6	6	Vegetables and melons (016)	2	1
acres..	217	313	Fruits and tree nuts (017)	2	1
Woodland pastured .... farms..	3	3	Horticultural specialties (018)	-	1
acres..	128	250	General farms, primarily crop (019)	1	3
Woodland not pastured .... farms..	4	4			
acres..	89	63	Livestock, except dairy, poultry, and animal specialties (021)	11	12
			Beef cattle, except feedlots (0212)	3	8
Pastureland and rangeland other than cropland and woodland pastured .... farms..	18	15	Dairy farms (024)	-	-
acres..	150 376	155 473	Poultry and eggs (025)	-	-
Land in house lots, ponds, roads, wasteland, etc... farms..	26	20	Animal specialties (027)	1	2
acres..	1 502	1 535	General farms, primarily livestock and animal specialties (029)	9	7
Irrigated land .... farms..	11	11			
acres..	642	259			

[1]Data are based on a sample of farms.

Table 20. **Livestock and Poultry—Inventory and Sales: 1987, 1982, and 1978**

[For meaning of abbreviations and symbols, see introductory text]

Item		Inventory			Sales		
		Farms	Number	Value[1] ($1,000)	Farms	Number	Value ($1,000)
Livestock and poultry	1987..	47 467	(X)	2 783 201	45 882	(X)	4 783 060
	1982..	53 281	(X)	2 179 679	51 701	(X)	4 047 815
	1978..	54 579	(X)	2 340 047	54 221	(X)	3 554 701
Poultry	1987..	4 691	(X)	3 388	1 550	(X)	25 284
	1982..	6 535	(X)	4 237	2 385	(X)	25 755
	1978..	7 789	(X)	4 417	2 774	(X)	26 195
Livestock	1987..	47 039	(X)	2 779 813	45 654	(X)	4 757 776
	1982..	52 761	(X)	2 175 442	51 376	(X)	4 022 060
	1978..	53 978	(X)	2 335 630	53 685	(X)	3 528 505
Any cattle, hogs, or sheep	1987..	43 600	(X)	2 752 014	44 522	(X)	4 608 271
	1982..	49 891	(X)	2 157 357	50 386	(X)	3 849 055
	1978..	51 846	(X)	2 327 893	53 123	(X)	3 404 560
Cattle and calves	1987..	40 785	5 539 292	2 625 128	41 498	7 310 338	4 305 395
	1982..	47 008	5 800 138	1 997 082	47 032	6 519 159	3 516 670
	1978..	48 215	5 930 018	2 151 677	49 162	6 758 343	3 093 572
Cows and heifers that had calved	1987..	33 157	1 451 324	895 918	(NA)	(NA)	(NA)
	1982..	38 796	1 646 706	647 216	(NA)	(NA)	(NA)
	1978..	40 277	1 700 097	751 573	(NA)	(NA)	(NA)
Beef cows	1987..	31 475	1 354 649	799 243	(NA)	(NA)	(NA)
	1982..	36 497	1 523 697	518 057	(NA)	(NA)	(NA)
	1978..	37 856	1 579 322	679 108	(NA)	(NA)	(NA)
Milk cows	1987..	3 093	96 675	96 675	(NA)	(NA)	(NA)
	1982..	4 631	123 009	129 159	(NA)	(NA)	(NA)
	1978..	5 691	120 775	72 465	(NA)	(NA)	(NA)
Hogs and pigs	1987..	8 768	1 516 878	108 941	7 090	2 759 876	284 375
	1982..	9 241	1 706 770	144 394	9 778	3 036 205	316 882
	1978..	13 329	2 014 541	161 163	13 794	3 344 500	297 439
Feeder pigs sold	1987..	(X)	(X)	(X)	1 869	514 394	23 029
	1982..	(X)	(X)	(X)	2 741	555 066	24 918
	1978..	(X)	(X)	(X)	4 233	733 119	30 765
Sheep and lambs[2]	1987..	2 400	249 303	19 944	2 396	257 152	18 561
	1982..	2 478	278 616	15 661	2 462	262 947	15 562
	1978..	1 930	224 662	15 052	1 931	208 642	13 549
Horses and ponies	1987..	12 879	55 598	27 799	2 260	8 467	5 496
	1982..	14 069	60 285	19 086	2 353	8 743	8 490
	1978..	14 015	51 579	7 737	2 210	7 125	4 959
Chickens 3 months old or older[3]	1987..	4 206	2 094 610	2 664	363	2 380 936	(NA)
	1982..	6 044	2 093 245	3 648	692	2 714 323	(NA)
	1978..	7 137	2 796 152	4 211	932	3 074 161	(NA)
Hens and pullets of laying age	1987..	4 150	1 797 313	2 337	336	1 384 767	(NA)
	1982..	5 986	1 794 673	3 230	674	1 312 177	(NA)
	1978..	7 078	2 305 443	3 573	909	1 892 993	(NA)
Broilers and other meat-type chickens	1987..	592	49 559	34	132	176 061	(NA)
	1982..	954	64 603	39	210	94 543	(NA)
	1978..	975	113 000	75	220	259 001	(NA)
Turkeys	1987..	331	112 661	691	88	230 719	(NA)
	1982..	368	38 556	550	57	65 161	(NA)
	1978..	211	13 065	131	42	49 805	(NA)

[1]Data are estimated; see text.
[2]Value of sales includes sheep, lambs, and wool sold.
[3]Sales for 1987 include pullets of less than 3 months old.

Table 21. **Poultry—Inventory and Sales: 1987 and 1982**

[For meaning of abbreviations and symbols, see introductory text]

Item	1987		1982		Item	1987		1982	
	Farms	Number	Farms	Number		Farms	Number	Farms	Number
INVENTORY					**SALES**				
Chickens 3 months old or older	4 206	2 094 610	6 044	2 093 245	Hens and pullets[1]	363	2 380 936	692	2 714 323
Farms with—					Farms with—				
1 to 3,199	4 147	159 829	5 961	266 291	1 to 3,199	296	21 969	600	71 360
3,200 to 9,999	12	65 397	30	205 132	3,200 to 9,999	21	144 434	42	285 665
10,000 or more	47	1 849 384	53	1 621 822	10,000 or more	46	2 214 533	50	2 357 298
Hens and pullets of laying age	4 150	1 797 313	5 986	1 794 673	Hens and pullets of laying age	336	1 384 767	674	1 312 177
Farms with—					Farms with —				
1 to 99	3 824	87 718	5 346	134 076	1 to 99	238	5 979	407	13 067
100 to 399	248	37 708	513	80 859	100 to 399	35	5 849	159	28 492
400 to 3,199	28	32 156	49	35 788	400 to 3,199	9	9 472	29	28 895
3,200 to 9,999	14	98 247	30	201 803	3,200 to 9,999	20	136 534	38	257 805
10,000 to 19,999	14	214 175	25	339 696	10,000 to 19,999	11	169 001	21	277 170
20,000 to 49,999	15	501 663	17	494 214	20,000 to 49,999	17	502 740	16	446 708
50,000 to 99,999	7	(D)	4	(D)	50,000 to 99,999	4	(D)	4	260 020
100,000 or more	2	(D)	2	(D)	100,000 or more	2	(D)		
Broilers and other meat-type chickens	592	49 559	954	64 603	Broilers and other meat-type chickens	132	176 061	210	94 543
Turkeys	331	112 661	368	38 556	Turkeys	88	230 719	57	65 161
For slaughter	181	(D)	201	2 773	For slaughter	75	(D)	43	(D)
Hens kept for breeding	194	(D)	237	35 783	Hens kept for breeding	20	(D)	20	(D)
Ducks, geese, and other poultry	1 084	(X)	1 183	(X)	Ducks, geese, and other poultry	167	(X)	207	(X)

[1]Sales for 1987 include pullets of less than 3 months old.

Table 22. **Broilers and Started Pullets—Sales: 1987 and 1982**

[For meaning of abbreviations and symbols, see introductory text]

Number sold	Broilers and other meat-type chickens				Pullets not of laying age		Pullets 3 months old or older not of laying age	
	1987		1982		1987		1982	
	Farms	Number	Farms	Number	Farms	Number	Farms	Number
Total	132	176 061	210	94 543	39	996 169	33	1 402 146
Farms with—								
1 to 1,999	123	16 160	208	(D)	26	3 669	19	886
2,000 to 15,999	7	(D)	1	(D)	2	(D)	7	66 260
16,000 to 29,999	-	-	-	-	1	(D)	2	(D)
30,000 to 59,999	-	-	-	-	4	153 000	1	(D)
60,000 to 99,999	2	(D)	1	(D)	4	302 900	3	253 000
100,000 to 199,999	-	-	-	-	1	(D)	-	-
200,000 to 499,999	-	-	-	-	1	(D)	-	-
200,000 to 299,999	-	-	(NA)	(NA)	(NA)	(NA)	(NA)	(NA)
300,000 to 499,999	-	-	(NA)	(NA)	(NA)	(NA)	(NA)	(NA)
500,000 or more	-	-	-	-	-	-	1	(D)

Table 23. **Poultry—Inventory and Sales by Size of Flock: 1987**

[For meaning of abbreviations and symbols, see introductory text]

Chickens 3 months old or older	Inventory									
	Chickens 3 months old or older						Pullet chicks and pullets under 3 months old		Broilers and other meat-type chickens	
	Total		Hens and pullets of laying age		Pullets 3 months old or older not of laying age					
	Farms	Number	Farms	Number	Farms	Number	Farms	Number	Farms	Number
Total inventory	4 206	2 094 610	4 150	1 797 313	415	297 297	80	126 155	471	35 665
Farms with—										
1 to 99	3 835	90 166	3 766	85 292	333	4 876	66	1 251	419	23 556
100 to 399	282	43 760	280	39 449	65	4 331	10	629	47	3 304
400 to 1,599	26	17 092	26	15 892	4	1 200	-	-	3	(D)
1,600 to 3,199	4	8 789	4	(D)	1	(D)	1	(D)	1	(D)
3,200 to 9,999	12	85 397	12	(D)	2	(D)	1	(D)	1	(D)
10,000 to 19,999	18	281 075	16	230 975	4	50 100	1	(D)	-	-
20,000 to 49,999	19	632 663	15	501 663	4	131 000	-	-	-	-
50,000 to 99,999	7	473 000	6	(D)	1	(D)	1	(D)	-	-
100,000 or more	3	462 646	3	(D)	1	(D)	-	-	-	-
No inventory	(X)	(X)	(X)	(X)	(X)	(X)	18	147 516	121	13 894

Chickens 3 months old or older	Sales									
	Hens and pullets						Broilers and other meat-type chickens		Poultry and poultry products	
	Total		Hens and pullets of laying age		Pullets not of laying age					
	Farms	Number	Farms	Number	Farms	Number	Farms	Number	Farms	Value ($1,000)
Total inventory	305	2 033 028	289	1 370 283	26	662 745	87	31 527	1 351	19 442
Farms with—										
1 to 99	183	30 503	176	29 852	12	651	78	20 328	1 000	341
100 to 399	53	5 337	51	4 943	5	394	6	458	262	418
400 to 1,599	9	(D)	9	(D)	-	-	1	(D)	26	154
1,600 to 3,199	1	(D)	1	(D)	-	-	1	(D)	4	101
3,200 to 9,999	12	77 344	12	(D)	1	(D)	1	(D)	12	767
10,000 to 19,999	18	248 892	16	(D)	3	(D)	-	-	18	2 551
20,000 to 49,999	19	594 339	15	388 339	4	206 000	-	-	19	5 466
50,000 to 99,999	7	758 592	6	(D)	1	(D)	-	-	7	5 428
100,000 or more	3	313 000	3	313 000	-	-	-	-	3	4 216
No inventory	56	347 908	47	14 484	13	333 424	45	144 534	199	5 842

Table 24. **Turkeys—Sales by Number Sold Per Farm: 1987**

[For meaning of abbreviations and symbols, see introductory text]

Turkeys	Total		Sales for slaughter		Sales of hens kept for breeding	
	Farms	Number	Farms	Number	Farms	Number
Total sold	88	230 719	75	(D)	20	(D)
Farms with—						
1 to 1,999	74	5 806	62	5 411	18	395
2,000 to 7,999	4	18 966	4	18 966	–	–
8,000 to 15,999	5	(D)	4	(D)	1	(D)
16,000 to 29,999	2	(D)	2	(D)	1	(D)
30,000 to 59,999	3	(D)	3	(D)	–	–
60,000 to 99,999	–	–	–	–	–	–
100,000 or more	–	–	–	–	–	–

Table 25. **Cattle and Calves—Inventory: 1987 and 1982**

[For meaning of abbreviations and symbols, see introductory text]

Item	1987		1982	
	Farms	Number	Farms	Number
Cattle and calves	40 785	5 539 292	47 008	5 800 138
Farms with—				
1 to 9	4 367	23 155	4 715	25 526
10 to 19	5 573	77 961	6 086	84 765
20 to 49	11 268	360 946	13 181	422 804
50 to 99	8 529	589 156	10 146	703 817
100 to 199	6 150	830 620	7 336	990 498
200 to 499	3 580	1 046 310	4 163	1 198 771
500 to 999	868	574 878	959	632 047
1,000 to 2,499	305	420 454	294	417 750
2,500 or more	145	1 615 812	128	1 324 160
Cows and heifers that had calved	33 157	1 451 324	38 796	1 646 706
Farms with—				
1 to 9	6 607	33 450	7 680	38 251
10 to 19	6 730	93 049	7 848	107 263
20 to 49	10 902	337 150	12 865	396 776
50 to 99	5 654	377 360	6 765	448 743
100 to 199	2 335	299 973	2 730	348 523
200 to 499	748	205 939	793	214 691
500 to 999	96	59 713	90	57 971
1,000 or more	25	44 690	25	34 488
Beef cows	31 475	1 354 649	36 497	1 523 697
Farms with—				
1 to 9	6 299	32 615	7 252	37 360
10 to 19	6 677	91 238	7 687	104 856
20 to 49	10 446	320 969	12 218	373 597
50 to 99	5 108	339 951	6 024	398 882
100 to 199	2 115	271 669	2 449	313 572
200 to 499	714	196 616	753	203 889
500 to 999	91	56 901	89	57 056
1,000 or more	25	44 690	25	34 485
Milk cows	3 093	96 675	4 631	123 009
Farms with—				
1 to 4	1 195	1 904	1 986	2 963
5 to 9	150	967	238	1 552
10 to 29	495	9 164	758	13 985
30 to 49	484	18 085	708	26 489
50 to 99	582	38 874	712	46 402
100 to 199	163	20 491	200	23 999
200 to 499	21	5 540	28	6 999
500 or more	3	1 650	1	(D)
Heifers and heifer calves	31 410	1 632 193	37 146	1 610 349
Steers, steer calves, bulls, and bull calves	35 035	2 455 775	41 395	2 543 083

Table 26. **Cattle and Calves—Sales: 1987 and 1982**

[For meaning of abbreviations and symbols, see introductory text]

Item	1987			1982		
	Farms	Number	Value ($1,000)	Farms	Number	Value ($1,000)
Cattle and calves sold	41 498	7 310 336	4 305 335	47 032	6 519 159	3 516 670
Farms with—						
1 to 9	8 828	44 436	17 718	10 478	52 388	17 814
10 to 19	8 136	112 031	44 311	9 476	130 691	43 698
20 to 49	11 824	367 698	149 258	13 419	415 246	143 324
50 to 99	6 066	415 257	180 892	6 882	466 452	173 860
100 to 199	3 224	433 691	201 072	3 497	466 209	190 124
200 to 499	2 125	631 044	314 096	2 141	633 107	280 733
500 to 999	726	477 009	256 039	650	423 807	208 213
1,000 to 2,499	335	472 893	265 032	310	446 560	230 937
2,500 or more	214	4 356 279	2 876 916	179	3 484 599	2 227 967
Cattle sold	34 216	6 842 010	4 159 374	37 556	5 935 940	3 361 124
Farms with—						
1 to 9	9 697	42 993	19 429	11 326	49 632	19 502
10 to 19	6 135	82 997	37 188	6 924	93 897	-36 706
20 to 49	8 254	255 949	116 834	8 961	275 564	109 717
50 to 99	4 434	303 172	144 001	4 711	320 453	134 533
100 to 199	2 586	348 357	171 569	2 723	364 248	160 624
200 to 499	1 902	564 770	293 501	1 832	543 249	254 275
500 to 999	675	445 084	244 862	609	398 365	201 523
1,000 or more	533	4 798 688	3 131 992	470	3 890 532	2 444 143
Cattle fattened on grain and concentrates sold	4 620	4 551 726	3 041 522	5 853	3 879 210	2 488 360
Farms with—						
1 to 9	1 554	5 583	3 073	1 969	7 008	3 460
10 to 19	539	7 276	3 669	801	10 832	5 297
20 to 49	799	24 533	14 207	1 056	32 764	17 138
50 to 99	528	36 731	21 637	623	42 576	23 906
100 to 199	395	53 944	33 126	497	66 285	38 141
200 to 499	372	109 970	70 439	429	130 832	76 425
500 to 999	185	123 179	81 202	211	140 484	85 612
1,000 to 2,499	102	156 677	98 931	119	181 189	111 991
2,500 or more	146	4 033 831	2 713 838	128	3 267 240	2 128 130
Calves sold	16 516	468 326	145 961	22 120	583 219	155 547
Farms with—						
1 to 9	7 205	31 769	9 522	8 078	36 650	8 966
10 to 19	4 501	59 850	18 383	5 436	72 816	18 415
20 to 49	4 744	139 558	43 043	5 859	173 224	44 446
50 to 99	1 368	89 246	29 286	1 872	122 026	32 666
100 to 199	488	63 624	20 767	618	79 436	21 947
200 to 499	175	50 782	16 539	213	58 570	15 924
500 or more	37	34 499	9 420	42	40 496	13 155

Table 27. **Cattle and Calves—Inventory and Sales by Size of Herd: 1987**

[For meaning of abbreviations and symbols, see introductory text]

Cattle and calves	Cattle and calves inventory								Cattle and calves sales		
	Total		Cows and heifers that had calved		Heifers and heifer calves		Steers, steer calves, bulls, and bull calves				
	Farms	Number	Farms	Number	Farms	Number	Farms	Number	Farms	Number	Value ($1,000)
Total inventory	40 785	5 539 292	33 157	1 451 324	31 410	1 632 193	35 035	2 455 775	39 343	7 112 790	4 205 819
Farms with—											
1 to 9	4 367	23 155	2 847	10 109	2 552	6 075	2 900	6 971	2 931	31 298	13 502
10 to 19	5 573	77 961	4 551	36 716	3 926	19 283	4 492	19 962	5 570	63 019	25 511
20 to 49	11 266	360 946	9 611	184 447	8 718	84 451	9 844	92 048	11 266	245 295	98 825
50 to 99	8 529	589 156	7 474	283 371	7 093	145 908	7 764	159 677	8 528	360 074	153 497
100 to 199	6 150	830 620	5 201	359 852	5 232	225 737	5 561	247 031	6 150	527 213	238 685
200 to 499	3 580	1 046 310	2 633	348 505	2 896	301 498	3 258	396 307	3 580	757 835	393 209
500 to 999	868	574 878	490	(D)	637	169 655	783	(D)	868	548 741	300 722
1,000 to 2,499	305	420 454	132	(D)	228	139 759	272	(D)	305	507 451	279 943
2,500 or more	145	1 615 812	18	27 130	126	541 827	141	1 046 855	145	4 041 864	2 702 124
No inventory	(X)	(X)	(X)	(X)	(X)	(X)	(X)	(X)	2 155	197 548	99 515

Table 28. **Cattle and Calves—Inventory and Sales by Size of Cow Herd: 1987**

[For meaning of abbreviations and symbols, see introductory text]

Cows and heifers that had calved	Cattle and calves inventory								Cattle and calves sales		
	Total		Cows and heifers that had calved		Heifers and heifer calves		Steers, steer calves, bulls, and bull calves				
	Farms	Number	Farms	Number	Farms	Number	Farms	Number	Farms	Number	Value ($1,000)
Total inventory	33 157	3 009 363	33 157	1 451 324	27 113	761 614	29 188	796 425	32 289	2 139 840	1 031 727
Farms with—											
1 to 4	2 779	43 137	2 779	7 144	2 037	16 576	2 114	19 417	2 008	43 855	21 061
5 to 9	3 828	62 365	3 828	26 306	2 962	16 894	3 212	19 165	3 734	46 876	19 703
10 to 19	6 790	202 722	6 790	93 049	5 415	50 715	5 973	58 958	6 789	134 245	57 414
20 to 29	5 040	254 949	5 040	117 804	4 145	67 744	4 529	69 401	5 040	175 831	83 076
30 to 49	5 862	444 754	5 862	219 346	4 886	109 788	5 309	115 620	5 860	268 596	117 430
50 to 99	5 654	762 816	5 654	377 360	4 898	194 765	5 155	190 693	5 654	431 446	193 357
100 to 199	2 335	641 092	2 335	299 973	2 041	163 183	2 146	177 936	2 335	464 433	236 747
200 to 499	748	407 637	748	205 939	631	96 072	653	105 626	748	277 891	140 088
500 to 999	96	103 817	96	59 713	78	21 424	77	22 660	96	92 895	48 624
1,000 or more	25	86 072	25	44 690	20	24 453	20	16 929	25	203 772	114 227
No inventory	7 628	2 529 929	(X)	(X)	4 297	870 579	5 847	1 859 350	9 209	5 170 498	3 273 607

Table 29. **Cattle and Calves—Inventory and Sales by Size of Beef Cow Herd: 1987**

[For meaning of abbreviations and symbols, see introductory text]

Beef cows	Cattle and calves inventory									
	Total		Cows and heifers that had calved				Heifers and heifer calves		Steers, steer calves, bulls, and bull calves	
			Total		Beef cows					
	Farms	Number	Farms	Number	Farms	Number	Farms	Number	Farms	Number
Total Inventory	31 475	2 849 099	31 475	1 378 560	31 475	1 354 649	25 669	703 538	27 997	787 001
Farms with—										
1 to 4	2 531	36 554	2 531	8 947	2 531	6 732	1 889	14 040	1 952	13 567
5 to 9	3 768	63 466	3 768	27 197	3 768	25 883	2 923	17 219	3 172	19 050
10 to 19	6 677	204 260	6 677	94 509	6 677	91 238	5 324	50 912	5 912	58 859
20 to 29	4 932	255 746	4 932	118 665	4 932	115 142	4 046	67 101	4 464	69 980
30 to 49	5 514	424 976	5 514	210 598	5 514	205 827	4 573	102 289	5 062	112 091
50 to 99	5 108	697 488	5 108	344 983	5 108	339 951	4 386	170 255	4 752	182 270
100 to 199	2 115	587 513	2 115	274 163	2 115	271 668	1 835	145 210	1 964	168 140
200 to 499	714	394 520	714	197 842	714	196 616	600	92 336	626	104 342
500 to 999	91	98 482	91	56 986	91	56 901	73	19 723	73	21 773
1,000 or more	25	86 072	25	44 690	25	44 690	20	24 453	20	16 929
No inventory	9 310	2 690 193	1 682	72 764	(X)	(X)	5 741	926 855	7 038	1 688 774

Beef cows	Cattle and calves sales											
	Total			Cattle						Calves		
				Total			Fattened on grain and concentrates					
	Farms	Number	Value ($1,000)	Farms	Number	Value ($1,000)	Farms	Number	Value ($1,000)	Farms	Number	Value ($1,000)
Total inventory	30 717	2 068 216	1 000 705	24 794	1 699 125	882 600	2 915	547 314	337 503	15 122	369 091	118 104
Farms with—												
1 to 4	1 859	30 246	13 199	1 492	23 756	11 393	217	1 700	988	892	6 490	1 806
5 to 9	3 685	46 857	19 811	2 768	32 956	15 684	268	3 603	2 219	2 005	13 901	4 127
10 to 19	6 676	134 945	57 721	5 128	94 652	45 564	511	12 440	7 587	3 651	40 293	12 126
20 to 29	4 932	176 477	83 600	3 856	132 106	69 891	399	41 683	29 566	2 883	44 371	13 709
30 to 49	5 512	260 270	114 291	4 513	192 769	93 427	476	32 137	19 919	2 686	67 501	20 864
50 to 99	5 108	405 867	183 357	4 404	317 596	154 213	580	41 935	26 027	2 161	88 271	29 144
100 to 199	2 115	444 823	228 229	1 865	381 065	206 935	289	144 162	93 627	816	63 758	21 294
200 to 499	714	275 198	138 489	660	239 609	126 463	142	65 812	41 210	220	35 589	12 036
500 to 999	91	89 761	47 781	83	82 694	45 268	24	29 801	18 199	24	7 067	2 513
1,000 or more	25	203 772	114 227	25	201 922	113 742	9	174 041	98 161	4	1 850	485
No inventory	10 761	5 242 122	3 304 630	9 422	5 142 885	3 276 774	1 705	4 004 412	2 704 019	3 396	99 237	27 856

Table 30. Cattle and Calves—Inventory and Sales by Size of Milk Cow Herd: 1987

[For meaning of abbreviations and symbols, see introductory text]

	Cattle and calves inventory									
Milk cows	Total		Cows and heifers that had calved				Heifers and heifer calves		Steers, steer calves, bulls, and bull calves	
			Total		Milk cows					
	Farms	Number	Farms	Number	Farms	Number	Farms	Number	Farms	Number
Total inventory	3 093	317 967	3 093	152 826	3 093	96 675	2 699	98 307	2 475	66 834
Farms with—										
1 to 4	1 195	81 822	1 195	34 175	1 195	1 904	977	21 802	1 023	25 845
5 to 9	150	5 590	150	2 882	150	967	117	1 281	114	1 427
10 to 19	254	11 027	254	5 673	254	3 551	217	2 991	194	2 363
20 to 29	241	16 387	241	8 626	241	5 613	211	4 609	183	3 150
30 to 49	484	(D)	484	(D)	484	18 065	449	(D)	377	10 928
50 to 99	582	(D)	582	(D)	582	38 874	555	(D)	442	14 089
100 to 199	163	45 963	163	23 063	163	20 491	152	15 891	124	7 009
200 to 499	21	11 828	21	6 240	21	5 540	18	(D)	16	(D)
500 or more	3	2 890	3	1 650	3	1 650	3	(D)	2	(D)
No inventory	37 692	5 221 325	30 064	1 298 498	(X)	(X)	28 711	1 533 866	32 580	2 388 941

	Cattle and calves sales								Dairy product sales	
Milk cows	Total			Cattle		Calves				
	Farms	Number	Value ($1,000)	Farms	Number	Farms	Number	Farms	Value ($1,000)	
Total inventory	2 955	145 647	63 547	2 475	105 775	1 760	39 872	1 929	137 626	
Farms with—										
1 to 4	1 065	51 242	24 891	884	41 162	549	10 080	134	244	
5 to 9	142	3 317	1 306	109	2 253	84	1 064	66	504	
10 to 19	254	4 845	1 809	195	2 828	161	2 017	235	3 645	
20 to 29	241	6 983	2 780	194	4 125	156	2 858	241	6 041	
30 to 49	484	(D)	(D)	420	(D)	298	5 628	484	(D)	
50 to 99	582	(D)	(D)	508	(D)	388	11 882	582	(D)	
100 to 199	163	17 099	7 190	146	11 927	107	5 172	163	32 244	
200 to 499	21	4 853	1 656	16	(D)	15	(D)	21	8 560	
500 or more	3	574	212	3	(D)	2	(D)	3	2 997	
No inventory	38 543	7 164 691	4 241 787	31 741	6 736 235	16 758	428 456	75	2 606	

Table 31. Cattle and Calves—Sales by Number Sold Per Farm: 1987

[For meaning of abbreviations and symbols, see introductory text]

	Cattle and calves			Cattle						Calves		
Cattle and calves				Total			Fattened on grain and concentrates					
	Farms	Number	Value ($1,000)	Farms	Number	Value ($1,000)	Farms	Number	Value ($1,000)	Farms	Number	Value ($1,000)
Total sold	41 496	7 310 338	4 305 335	34 216	6 842 010	4 159 374	4 620	4 551 726	3 041 522	18 516	468 328	145 961
Farms with—												
1 to 4	3 763	9 703	4 055	2 748	6 336	3 047	498	1 065	606	1 544	3 367	1 008
5 to 9	5 065	34 733	13 663	3 744	20 758	9 359	358	1 701	687	2 721	13 975	4 303
10 to 19	8 136	112 031	44 311	6 285	68 657	30 865	565	5 026	2 680	4 323	43 374	13 447
20 to 49	11 824	367 698	149 258	9 700	244 387	111 243	961	19 687	11 193	5 914	123 311	38 015
50 to 99	6 086	415 257	180 892	5 456	313 561	148 398	706	33 590	19 875	2 503	101 696	32 504
100 to 199	3 224	433 691	201 072	2 991	359 875	176 719	516	51 540	31 542	964	73 816	24 353
200 to 499	2 125	631 044	314 096	2 038	571 506	296 147	489	111 611	71 402	398	59 538	17 980
500 to 999	726	477 009	256 039	710	450 627	247 807	231	124 139	81 310	89	26 382	8 232
1,000 or more	549	4 829 172	3 141 948	544	4 806 303	3 135 801	278	4 203 467	2 822 027	42	22 869	6 147

Table 32. Hogs and Pigs—Inventory: 1987 and 1982

[For meaning of abbreviations and symbols, see introductory text]

	1987		1982	
Item	Farms	Number	Farms	Number
Total hogs and pigs	6 768	1 516 878	9 241	1 708 770
Farms with—				
1 to 24	1 916	19 902	2 812	27 953
25 to 49	828	29 265	1 144	40 471
50 to 99	1 087	74 758	1 582	109 247
100 to 199	1 092	147 160	1 551	209 570
200 to 499	1 226	386 822	1 415	420 095
500 to 999	372	249 374	490	310 600
1,000 to 1,999	161	206 547	176	228 480
2,000 to 4,999	73	216 247	56	155 838
5,000 or more	13	206 803	15	199 516
Hogs and pigs used or to be used for breeding	4 596	191 079	6 360	207 873
Farms with—				
1 to 24	2 741	28 676	4 248	42 132
25 to 49	898	30 806	1 069	36 367
50 to 99	572	37 411	643	41 961
100 to 199	267	33 239	264	32 496
200 or more	118	60 947	116	54 917
Other hogs and pigs	6 286	1 325 799	8 501	1 500 897

Table 33. **Hogs and Pigs—Sales: 1987 and 1982**

[For meaning of abbreviations and symbols, see introductory text]

Item	1987			1982		
	Farms	Number	Value ($1,000)	Farms	Number	Value ($1,000)
Total hogs and pigs sold	7 090	2 759 676	284 375	9 778	3 036 205	316 882
Farms with—						
1 to 24	1 265	13 716	1 448	1 915	20 722	2 289
25 to 49	844	29 704	2 990	1 228	43 785	4 509
50 to 99	1 060	74 489	7 298	1 615	113 426	11 613
100 to 199	1 143	157 706	15 740	1 651	227 088	22 896
200 to 499	1 466	448 491	45 309	1 871	561 843	56 017
500 to 999	729	492 919	49 388	900	618 559	63 453
1,000 to 1,999	371	482 477	47 993	397	524 306	54 155
2,000 to 4,999	158	441 596	46 474	160	442 564	47 017
5,000 or more	54	618 578	67 748	41	483 912	54 943
Feeder pigs sold	1 869	514 394	23 029	2 741	555 066	24 918
Farms with—						
1 to 9	107	594	26	183	994	43
10 to 49	538	14 276	585	521	21 930	896
50 to 99	360	24 420	1 008	526	36 793	1 578
100 to 199	301	40 515	1 715	488	67 191	2 872
200 to 499	303	93 862	4 174	466	140 947	6 151
500 to 999	163	110 519	4 934	175	118 197	5 440
1,000 or more	97	230 088	10 586	81	169 014	7 937
Other hogs and pigs sold	6 536	2 245 282	261 346	9 006	2 481 139	291 965
Farms with—						
1 to 24	1 613	16 173	2 003	(NA)	(NA)	(NA)
25 to 49	825	28 741	3 447	(NA)	(NA)	(NA)
50 to 99	892	62 225	7 226	(NA)	(NA)	(NA)
100 to 199	959	131 786	15 237	(NA)	(NA)	(NA)
200 to 499	1 207	368 381	42 282	(NA)	(NA)	(NA)
500 to 999	578	390 379	44 733	(NA)	(NA)	(NA)
1,000 to 1,999	282	367 475	41 806	(NA)	(NA)	(NA)
2,000 to 4,999	139	387 911	44 781	(NA)	(NA)	(NA)
5,000 or more	41	492 209	59 831	(NA)	(NA)	(NA)

Table 34. **Hogs and Pigs—Litters Farrowed: 1987 and 1982**

[For meaning of abbreviations and symbols, see introductory text]

Litters	1987		1982	
	Farms	Number of litters	Farms	Number of litters
Litters farrowed between Dec. 1 of preceding year and Nov. 30	4 819	295 974	6 713	322 989
Farms with—				
1 to 9	1 239	5 378	2 050	8 935
10 to 19	910	12 006	1 326	17 733
20 to 49	1 264	38 412	1 736	51 811
50 to 99	737	50 676	864	57 602
100 to 199	413	55 336	471	61 123
200 to 499	196	55 286	218	61 340
500 or more	60	78 880	48	64 445
Dec. 1 of preceding year and May 31	4 455	149 414	6 140	164 086
June 1 and Nov. 30	4 403	146 560	5 907	158 903

Table 35. **Hogs and Pigs—Inventory and Sales by Size of Herd: 1987**

[For meaning of abbreviations and symbols, see introductory text]

Hogs and pigs	Hogs and pigs inventory						Hogs and pigs sales					
	Total		Used or to be used for breeding		Other hogs and pigs		Total			Feeder pigs		
	Farms	Number	Farms	Number	Farms	Number	Farms	Number	Value ($1,000)	Farms	Number	Value ($1,000)
Total inventory	6 768	1 516 876	4 596	191 079	6 266	1 325 799	6 480	2 681 343	275 990	1 802	506 926	22 677
Farms with—												
1 to 9	942	4 347	414	1 802	704	2 745	654	24 473	2 336	188	6 366	248
10 to 24	974	15 555	598	5 161	805	10 394	974	56 372	4 803	301	21 969	875
25 to 99	1 915	104 023	1 264	18 975	1 849	85 048	1 915	227 971	20 891	558	72 637	3 123
100 to 199	1 092	147 160	816	21 423	1 086	125 737	1 092	266 364	25 257	306	72 798	3 176
200 to 499	1 226	366 822	955	44 476	1 224	322 344	1 226	643 553	63 832	303	141 449	6 459
500 to 999	372	249 374	309	30 394	372	218 980	372	424 524	44 436	95	62 190	2 800
1,000 or more	247	629 597	210	69 046	246	560 551	247	1 038 066	114 436	51	129 517	5 996
No inventory	(X)	(X)	(X)	(X)	(X)	(X)	610	78 333	8 385	67	7 468	352

Table 36. **Hogs and Pigs—Inventory and Sales by Number Sold Per Farm: 1987**

[For meaning of abbreviations and symbols, see introductory text]

Hogs and pigs	Hogs and pigs inventory						Hogs and pigs sales					
	Total		Used or to be used for breeding		Other hogs and pigs		Total			Feeder pigs		
	Farms	Number	Farms	Number	Farms	Number	Farms	Number	Value ($1,000)	Farms	Number	Value ($1,000)
Total sold	6 480	1 515 871	4 517	190 904	6 042	1 324 967	7 090	2 759 676	284 375	1 869	514 394	23 029
Farms with—												
1 to 9	437	4 385	182	714	390	3 671	587	2 671	302	48	257	12
10 to 49	1 308	36 223	746	5 439	1 183	30 784	1 522	40 749	4 135	327	7 692	309
50 to 99	969	56 246	689	8 739	859	49 507	1 080	74 489	7 286	324	17 363	679
100 to 199	1 077	101 313	809	14 745	992	86 568	1 143	157 706	15 740	336	33 063	1 378
200 to 499	1 395	260 158	1 078	34 110	1 343	226 046	1 466	448 491	45 309	425	87 977	3 852
500 to 999	719	251 027	556	31 290	708	219 737	729	492 919	49 388	225	102 454	4 610
1,000 or more	575	804 521	477	95 867	567	708 654	583	1 542 651	162 215	184	265 588	12 189
None sold	288	1 007	79	175	244	832	(X)	(X)	(X)	(X)	(X)	(X)

Table 37. **Hogs and Pigs—Inventory, Sales, and Litters by Total Litters Farrowed: 1987**

[For meaning of abbreviations and symbols, see introductory text]

Litters farrowed	Hogs and pigs inventory						Hogs and pigs sales					
	Total		Used or to be used for breeding		Other hogs and pigs		Total			Feeder pigs		
	Farms	Number	Farms	Number	Farms	Number	Farms	Number	Value ($1,000)	Farms	Number	Value ($1,000)
Total litters farrowed	4 718	1 256 229	4 595	(D)	4 237	(D)	4 734	2 216 928	223 480	1 864	513 088	22 952
Farms with—												
1	124	1 188	111	313	85	875	93	1 770	193	34	223	9
2 to 4	549	12 499	507	2 124	424	10 375	534	18 957	1 924	202	3 961	182
5 to 9	513	22 624	485	4 358	433	18 266	527	40 736	3 991	240	9 481	382
10 to 19	882	58 548	865	12 479	757	46 075	910	102 620	9 070	307	20 021	1 072
20 to 49	1 248	167 407	1 231	26 281	1 161	139 126	1 264	283 621	27 689	474	71 753	3 091
50 to 99	734	205 905	729	34 076	716	171 829	737	369 048	35 246	289	102 986	4 488
100 to 199	412	218 992	412	33 011	409	185 981	413	408 574	39 246	163	105 443	4 880
200 or more	256	569 066	255	76 440	252	492 626	256	991 602	105 320	95	192 620	8 868
No litters farrowed	2 050	260 649	1	(D)	2 049	(D)	2 358	542 750	60 895	6	1 306	77

Litters farrowed	Litters farrowed between Dec. 1, 1986, and Nov. 30, 1987					
	Total		Dec. 1, 1986, and May 31, 1987		June 1, 1987, and Nov. 30, 1987	
	Farms	Litters	Farms	Litters	Farms	Litters
Total litters farrowed	4 819	295 974	4 455	149 414	4 403	146 560
Farms with—						
1	130	130	88	88	42	42
2 to 4	582	1 693	476	868	468	825
5 to 9	527	3 555	433	1 716	461	1 839
10 to 19	910	12 006	826	6 000	836	6 006
20 to 49	1 264	38 412	1 236	19 576	1 206	18 836
50 to 99	737	50 676	730	25 458	723	25 218
100 to 199	413	55 336	411	27 893	411	27 443
200 or more	256	134 166	256	67 815	254	66 351

Table 38. **Sheep and Lambs—Inventory and Sales: 1987 and 1982**

[For meaning of abbreviations and symbols, see introductory text]

Item	1987		1982	
	Farms	Number	Farms	Number
Sheep and lambs inventory	2 400	249 303	2 478	278 616
Farms with—				
1 to 24	1 050	12 217	1 041	11 766
25 to 99	850	40 263	854	41 504
100 to 299	342	53 813	397	64 610
300 to 999	123	55 794	144	69 968
1,000 to 2,499	28	36 996	34	46 723
2,500 or more	7	47 220	8	44 145
Ewes 1 year old or older	2 195	129 607	2 247	150 502
Sheep and lambs shorn	2 183	218 980	2 220	231 018
Pounds of wool	(X)	1 510 863	(X)	1 607 200
Sheep and lambs sold	2 396	267 152	2 462	262 947
Value of sales from sheep, lambs, and wool ($1,000)	2 456	18 561	2 535	15 502

Table 39. **Sheep and Lambs—Inventory and Sales by Size of Flock: 1987**

[For meaning of abbreviations and symbols, see introductory text]

Sheep and lambs	Sheep and lambs inventory				Sheep and lambs shorn			Sales			
	Total		Ewes 1 year old or older					Sheep and lambs		Sheep, lambs, and wool	
	Farms	Number	Farms	Number	Farms	Number	Pounds of wool	Farms	Number	Farms	Value ($1,000)
Total inventory	2 400	249 303	2 195	129 607	2 107	210 346	1 449 657	2 213	253 446	2 273	17 531
Farms with—											
1 to 24	1 050	12 217	873	8 822	784	10 933	79 013	868	12 626	923	900
25 to 99	850	40 263	830	28 741	831	32 056	229 061	848	30 226	850	2 202
100 to 299...................	342	53 813	339	35 724	339	42 178	308 731	341	41 307	342	3 398
300 to 999...................	123	58 794	121	34 307	121	44 735	316 788	123	43 489	123	3 530
1,000 to 2,499	28	36 996	25	16 901	25	27 267	201 024	26	26 557	28	2 061
2,500 to 4,999	4	13 020	4	3 645	4	6 900	50 920	4	10 241	4	695
5,000 or more..............	3	34 200	3	1 467	3	48 277	264 120	3	89 000	3	4 744
No inventory	(X)	(X)	(X)	(X)	76	8 634	61 006	183	13 706	183	1 030

Table 40. **Sheep and Lambs—Inventory and Sales by Size of Ewe Flock: 1987**

[For meaning of abbreviations and symbols, see introductory text]

Ewes 1 year old or older	Sheep and lambs inventory				Sheep and lambs shorn			Sales			
	Total		Ewes 1 year old or older					Sheep and lambs		Sheep, lambs, and wool	
	Farms	Number	Farms	Number	Farms	Number	Pounds of wool	Farms	Number	Farms	Value ($1,000)
Total inventory	2 195	242 102	2 195	129 607	2 061	209 652	1 445 243	2 078	245 151	2 125	16 879
Farms with—											
1 to 24	1 098	19 115	1 096	12 787	962	15 379	111 657	984	15 519	1 026	1 094
25 to 99	765	53 374	765	36 194	765	40 908	291 333	763	38 241	765	2 931
100 to 199...................	200	41 786	200	25 946	200	34 026	248 167	196	34 723	200	2 869
200 to 499...................	102	73 984	102	30 902	102	71 746	444 377	102	91 635	102	5 827
500 to 999...................	28	43 573	28	18 958	28	42 356	306 076	27	57 264	28	3 682
1,000 to 2,499	4	10 270	4	4 820	4	5 237	43 633	4	7 769	4	456
2,500 to 4,999	–	–	–	–	–	–	–	–	–	–	–
5,000 or more..............	–	–	–	–	–	–	–	–	–	–	–
No inventory	205	7 201	(X)	(X)	122	9 328	65 420	318	22 001	331	1 682

Table 41. Other Livestock and Livestock Products—Inventory and Sales: 1987 and 1982

[For meaning of abbreviations and symbols, see introductory text]

Item	Inventory		Sales	
	1987	1982	1987	1982
Horses and ponies .... farms..	12 879	14 069	2 260	2 353
number..	55 598	60 285	8 467	8 743
$1,000..	(X)	(X)	5 496	8 490
Mules, burros, and donkeys .... farms..	533	193	62	26
number..	1 308	453	175	130
$1,000..	(X)	(X)	58	51
Colonies of bees .... farms..	544	683	25	22
number..	24 943	22 851	3 992	271
Honey sold .... farms..	(X)	(X)	199	147
pounds..	(X)	(X)	1 433 599	1 134 878
Bees and honey sold .... farms..	(X)	(X)	210	(NA)
$1,000..	(X)	(X)	1 827	705
Goats .... farms..	862	891	258	237
number..	8 831	4 841	2 679	1 840
Angora goats .... farms..	55	9	17	2
number..	3 978	(D)	960	(D)
Mohair sold .... farms..	(X)	(X)	43	2
pounds..	(X)	(X)	43 086	(D)
Angora goats and mohair sold .... farms..	(X)	(X)	48	(NA)
$1,000..	(X)	(X)	160	(D)
Milk goats .... farms..	438	733	106	193
number..	2 297	3 312	552	1 147
Goats milk sold .... farms..	(X)	(X)	79	41
gallons..	(X)	(X)	36 773	(D)
Milk goats and goats milk sold .... farms..	(X)	(X)	144	(NA)
$1,000..	(X)	(X)	104	(D)
Other goats... farms..	516	219	156	56
$1,000..	2 556	(D)	1 147	(D)
Mink and their pelts.. farms..	6	6	6	3
number..	394	895	462	1 134
$1,000..	(X)	(X)	14	25
Rabbits and their pelts .... farms..	288	196	104	85
number..	8 214	7 517	20 430	14 873
$1,000..	(X)	(X)	74	64
Fish and other aquaculture products sold .... farms..	(X)	(X)	51	44
$1,000..	(X)	(A)	1 008	905
Other livestock and livestock products .... farms..	87	(NA)	36	(NA)
$1,000..	(X)	(X)	706	(D)

Table 42. **Crops Harvested and Value of Production: 1987 and 1982**

[For meaning of abbreviations and symbols, see introductory text]

Crop	1987				1982			
	Farms	Acres	Quantity	Value of production[1] ($1,000)	Farms	Acres	Quantity	Value of production[1] ($1,000)
Harvested cropland	57 822	17 729 394	(X)	1 960 714	62 860	20 186 974	(X)	2 622 578
Corn for grain or seed (bushels)	8 944	1 243 969	144 133 581	259 440	8 346	1 161 875	130 662 235	287 457
Corn for silage or green chop or cut for dry fodder, hogged or grazed	2 009	109 230	(X)	25 041	3 020	154 307	(X)	46 300
Sorghum for grain or seed (bushels)	32 492	3 399 564	226 045 100	342 068	26 908	3 167 148	192 400 229	430 976
Sorghum for silage or green chop, cut for dry forage or hay, or hogged or grazed	3 988	170 629	(X)	26 726	6 632	286 687	(X)	51 921
Wheat for grain (bushels)	38 638	8 679 588	292 999 442	703 199	49 231	11 664 008	372 590 045	1 248 176
Barley for grain (bushels)	2 307	95 465	3 639 224	5 095	666	34 820	1 490 498	2 906
Oats for grain (bushels)	5 313	128 091	4 775 729	6 686	6 644	168 982	7 799 056	13 258
Rye for grain (bushels)	131	7 620	213 924	235	95	2 583	60 806	116
Rice (cwt)	–	–	–	–	–	–	–	–
Flaxseed (bushels)	1 196	113 449	134 339 654	9 404	380	42 328	48 509 547	4 851
Sunflower seed (pounds)	18 864	1 878 978	55 789 994	290 108	17 116	1 692 288	43 042 471	225 973
Soybeans for beans (bushels)	192	30 460	441 318	5 737	223	25 287	262 041	3 747
Dry edible beans, excluding dry limas (cwt)								
Peanuts for nuts (pounds)	–							
Cotton (bales)	10	542	595	208	–	–	–	–
Tobacco (pounds)	13	30	60 805	91	13	30	50 869	56
Irish potatoes (cwt)	97	643	138 764	666	210	827	144 655	579
Sweetpotatoes (bushels)	10	26	2 462	14	19	122	18 432	101
Pineapples harvested (tons)	–							
Sugar beets for sugar (tons)	–	–	–	–	76	12 110	210 570	6 422
Sugarcane for sugar (tons)	–							
Hay—alfalfa, other tame, small grain, wild, grass silage, green chop, etc. (see text) (tons, dry)	33 964	2 254 082	5 080 847	245 448	37 341	2 233 631	5 092 039	270 373
Vegetables harvested for sale (see text)	418	5 424	(X)	4 151	362	4 808	(X)	3 206
Land in orchards	503	5 999	(X)	1 579	603	6 408	(X)	1 347
Berries harvested for sale	131	275	(X)	215	107	205	(X)	174
Nursery and greenhouse crops, mushrooms, and sod grown for sale (see text)	272	4 274	(X)	26 805	298	4 316	(X)	21 515
Other crops	1 511	85 422	(X)	6 799	(NA)	(NA)	(X)	3 123

[1]Data are estimated; see text.

Table 43. **Specified Crops Harvested—Yield Per Acre Irrigated and Nonirrigated: 1987**

[For meaning of abbreviations and symbols, see introductory text]

Crop	Entire crop irrigated			Part of crop irrigated				None of crop irrigated		
	Farms	Acres	Average yield per acre	Farms	Acres irrigated	Acres not irrigated	Average yield per acre	Farms	Acres	Average yield per acre
Corn for grain or seed (bushels)	3 359	772 149	130.6	288	44 843	25 990	114.3	5 297	400 867	87.7
Corn for silage or green chop (tons, green)	626	51 943	18.4	33	1 271	1 315	15.3	1 350	54 701	12.3
Sorghum for grain or seed (bushels)	1 540	255 912	89.9	1 597	208 207	221 280	74.1	29 355	2 714 165	63.8
Wheat for grain (bushels)	1 296	323 908	41.0	1 750	311 616	594 530	36.6	35 892	7 449 534	33.1
Oats for grain (bushels)	44	2 132	48.8	4	146	172	39.1	5 268	125 641	37.1
Barley for grain (bushels)	122	5 263	42.6	44	2 076	2 053	39.0	2 141	86 053	37.8
Soybeans for beans (bushels)	1 416	135 290	39.7	523	39 763	47 285	36.4	16 925	1 656 640	28.5
Peanuts for nuts (pounds)	–	–	–	–	–	–	–	–	–	–
Dry edible beans, excluding dry limas (cwt)	163	27 352	15.2	4	830	231	11.7	25	2 047	6.5
Cotton (bales)	2	(D)	(D)	–	–	–	–	8	(D)	(D)
Tobacco (pounds)	3	6	2 386.8	–	–	–	–	10	23	1 896.2
Irish potatoes (cwt)	21	551	228.1	–	–	–	–	76	92	142.2
Sugar beets for sugar (tons)	–									
Sugarcane for sugar (tons)	–									
Alfalfa hay (tons, dry)	838	156 794	4.9	236	24 158	17 432	4.1	14 310	543 412	2.9
Small grain hay (tons, dry)	107	4 813	2.2	28	1 172	767	2.0	4 725	143 020	1.8
Tame hay other than alfalfa, small grain, and wild hay (see text) (tons, dry)	171	8 833	2.4	59	1 862	2 619	2.6	16 254	710 547	1.9
Wild hay (tons, dry)	12	892	1.1	3	429	69	1.3	11 419	553 959	1.3
Grass silage, haylage, and green chop hay (tons, green)	89	(D)	(D)	16	958	(D)	(D)	1 472	69 023	5.9
Alfalfa seed (pounds)	3	(D)	(D)	3	201	(D)	(D)	351	10 770	86.9
Vegetables harvested for sale (see text)	124	1 599	(X)	42	252	252	(X)	252	3 322	(X)
Land in orchards	79	595	(X)	11	162	189	(X)	413	5 053	(X)
Strawberries harvested for sale (pounds)	58	142	2 324.6	1	(C)	(C)	(D)	50	(D)	(D)

Table 44. **Specified Crops by Acres Harvested: 1987 and 1982**

[For meaning of abbreviations and symbols, see introductory text]

Crop	1987					1982				
				Irrigated land					Irrigated land	
	Farms	Acres	Quantity	Farms	Acres	Farms	Acres	Quantity	Farms	Acres
Corn for grain or seed (bushels)	8 944	1 243 969	144 133 581	3 647	816 992	8 346	1 161 875	130 662 235	3 007	755 272
1 to 14 acres	1 101	9 071	653 453	65	558	1 108	9 186	613 105	56	410
15 to 24 acres	883	16 866	1 301 785	97	1 862	876	16 547	1 236 049	103	1 935
25 to 49 acres	1 527	54 042	4 730 682	321	11 513	1 494	52 031	4 211 573	267	9 354
50 to 99 acres	1 752	119 832	11 626 333	685	47 271	1 632	112 394	10 138 396	512	34 856
100 to 249 acres	2 196	340 092	38 351 668	1 327	206 033	1 941	292 719	30 585 925	1 068	160 311
250 to 499 acres	1 044	351 431	42 481 959	778	254 271	860	298 551	35 704 864	637	210 744
500 to 999 acres	366	233 564	29 636 177	307	188 766	324	212 731	26 643 037	280	182 908
1,000 acres or more	75	119 069	15 151 524	67	106 728	91	167 716	21 529 286	84	154 754
1,000 to 1,999 acres	63	(X)	(X)	56	(X)	72	(X)	(X)	65	(X)
2,000 to 2,999 acres	8	(X)	(X)	7	(X)	}				
3,000 to 4,999 acres	3	(X)	(X)	3	(X)	} 19	(X)	(X)	19	(X)
5,000 acres or more	1	(X)	(X)	1	(X)					
Corn for silage or green chop (tons, green)	2 009	109 230	1 669 413	659	53 214	3 020	154 307	2 280 790	903	71 132
1 to 14 acres	401	3 635	44 799	77	709	619	5 729	67 338	106	983
15 to 24 acres	396	7 451	89 249	80	1 518	540	12 041	152 070	136	2 602
25 to 49 acres	542	18 397	249 054	182	5 156	819	27 896	364 827	218	7 276
50 to 99 acres	402	26 215	380 879	186	11 901	559	36 114	502 008	220	14 126
100 to 249 acres	207	29 175	456 683	123	17 673	313	43 042	668 804	171	24 360
250 to 499 acres	43	14 031	253 788	29	8 831	57	17 920	308 596	41	12 320
500 to 999 acres	15	(D)	(D)	12	7 426	9	5 605	104 667	7	4 805
1,000 acres or more	1	(D)	(D)	–		5	5 960	112 490	4	4 660
Sorghum for grain or seed (bushels)	32 492	3 399 554	228 045 100	3 137	464 119	26 906	3 187 148	192 400 029	3 474	643 658
1 to 14 acres	3 585	32 363	1 888 063	60	500	2 280	20 662	1 037 279	40	344
15 to 24 acres	3 695	70 905	4 195 725	103	1 895	2 696	51 507	2 599 701	86	1 594
25 to 49 acres	6 552	231 862	14 247 398	267	8 430	5 445	191 097	10 222 788	263	8 663
50 to 99 acres	7 587	526 959	32 818 225	596	34 361	6 498	444 333	25 171 295	595	35 841
100 to 249 acres	7 830	1 182 330	79 896 465	1 156	128 803	6 891	1 038 351	63 682 517	1 279	163 000
250 to 499 acres	2 503	820 525	57 969 199	644	147 987	2 226	742 681	48 005 214	791	201 304
500 to 999 acres	650	413 010	29 903 244	270	111 466	702	461 055	28 185 657	325	147 839
1,000 acres or more	90	121 610	7 036 681	41	30 677	170	237 462	13 495 778	95	84 633
1,000 to 1,999 acres	84	(X)	(X)	40	(X)	154	(X)	(X)	88	(X)
2,000 to 2,999 acres	6	(X)	(X)	1	(X)	}				
3,000 to 4,999 acres	–	(X)	(X)	–	(X)	} 16	(X)	(X)	7	(X)
5,000 acres or more	–	(X)	(X)	–	(X)					
Sorghum for silage or green chop (tons, green)	3 944	168 654	2 189 924	452	22 109	5 559	231 330	2 800 231	577	33 599
Wheat for grain (bushels)	38 635	8 679 588	292 999 442	3 046	635 524	49 231	11 664 008	372 590 045	3 111	715 445
1 to 14 acres	2 157	18 800	578 101	37	241	2 424	21 723	570 675	32	245
15 to 24 acres	2 073	39 732	1 195 143	61	1 162	2 797	53 244	1 408 743	38	705
25 to 49 acres	4 510	160 536	5 038 853	144	5 039	5 909	209 770	5 728 351	118	4 131
50 to 99 acres	9 841	485 313	15 643 634	256	19 994	8 463	597 226	17 491 741	232	14 516
100 to 249 acres	11 111	1 787 405	56 263 191	796	98 430	14 021	2 242 550	68 297 092	715	84 554
250 to 499 acres	7 248	2 510 796	84 953 793	853	175 677	9 291	3 219 487	102 776 097	856	169 555
500 to 999 acres	3 733	2 468 904	85 403 823	687	217 135	4 306	3 254 983	107 964 855	775	239 509
1,000 acres or more	865	1 204 902	40 922 904	212	121 846	1 421	2 065 020	68 342 491	345	202 227
1,000 to 1,999 acres	774	(X)	(X)	186	(X)	1 231	(X)	(X)	293	(X)
2,000 to 2,999 acres	74	(X)	(X)	20	(X)	}				
3,000 to 4,999 acres	13	(X)	(X)	4	(X)	} 190	(X)	(X)	52	(X)
5,000 acres or more	4	(X)	(X)	2	(X)					
Barley for grain (bushels)	2 307	95 465	3 639 224	166	7 359	666	34 820	1 490 498	84	9 599
Oats for grain (bushels)	5 313	128 091	4 775 729	48	2 276	6 644	168 962	7 799 056	108	7 176
1 to 14 acres	2 456	20 144	763 905	10	85	3 012	25 200	1 093 159	16	140
15 to 24 acres	1 272	23 522	888 685	6	69	1 588	29 336	1 329 707	19	522
25 to 49 acres	1 001	33 290	1 235 374	18	633	1 309	43 176	2 016 034	26	834
50 to 99 acres	439	27 348	1 050 921	10	611	540	34 461	1 708 842	19	1 141
100 to 249 acres	131	17 140	637 104	3	(D)	158	21 650	1 014 966	24	3 326
250 to 499 acres	8	2 722	85 040	–		29	9 968	484 180	3	(D)
500 to 999 acres	3	3 925	144 700	1	(D)	7	(D)	(D)	1	(D)
1,000 acres or more	–			–		2	(D)	(D)	–	
Soybeans for beans (bushels)	19 864	1 878 976	55 789 994	1 939	175 053	17 116	1 692 288	43 042 471	1 725	199 270
1 to 14 acres	2 438	21 642	593 770	124	1 142	1 965	17 778	400 789	69	614
15 to 24 acres	2 570	48 970	1 330 447	166	3 088	2 091	39 776	908 032	89	1 680
25 to 49 acres	4 247	146 749	4 075 843	378	12 064	3 685	136 044	3 227 194	294	10 102
50 to 99 acres	4 006	272 373	7 907 106	499	29 480	3 783	258 156	6 371 224	446	26 206
100 to 249 acres	3 775	568 578	17 195 456	573	71 342	3 831	568 451	14 686 851	585	76 180
250 to 499 acres	1 316	438 410	13 344 021	147	36 206	1 189	391 455	10 086 363	190	52 153
500 to 999 acres	436	275 119	8 029 916	45	17 911	321	200 232	5 125 984	42	19 555
1,000 acres or more	77	107 137	3 313 935	7	3 620	51	80 387	2 234 034	10	10 780
1,000 to 1,999 acres	68	(X)	(X)	6	(X)	42	(X)	(X)	9	(X)
2,000 to 2,999 acres	8	(X)	(X)	1	(X)	}				
3,000 to 4,999 acres	1	(X)	(X)	–	(X)	} 9	(X)	(X)	1	(X)
5,000 acres or more	–									
Dry edible beans, excluding dry limas (cwt)	192	30 460	441 316	167	28 162	223	25 287	262 041	186	23 111
Hay—alfalfa, other tame, small grain, wild, grass silage, green chop, etc. (see text)(tons, dry)	33 964	2 264 082	5 080 847	1 492	205 961	37 241	2 233 831	5 092 039	1 841	187 173
1 to 14 acres	5 966	51 229	100 781	104	819	7 307	60 754	126 580	171	1 477
15 to 24 acres	5 425	102 141	199 447	116	1 929	6 455	116 641	242 494	179	3 003
25 to 49 acres	8 452	294 489	598 169	271	8 296	9 855	342 061	733 745	365	10 612
50 to 99 acres	7 659	520 426	1 097 427	364	18 177	8 013	539 868	1 181 112	364	20 871
100 to 249 acres	5 297	756 972	1 658 679	390	43 486	5 017	710 082	1 607 244	524	58 098
250 to 499 acres	913	298 661	692 780	151	41 613	819	265 044	642 254	153	30 322
500 to 999 acres	202	(D)	(D)	73	39 400	149	97 645	253 797	41	21 700
1,000 acres or more	50	(D)	(D)	23	53 299	56	101 136	304 813	24	32 980
1,000 to 1,999 acres	32	(X)	(X)	12	(X)	44	(X)	(X)	17	(X)
2,000 to 2,999 acres	15	(X)	(X)	8	(X)	}				
3,000 to 4,999 acres	1	(X)	(X)	2	(X)	} 12	(X)	(X)	7	(X)
5,000 acres or more	2	(X)	(X)	1	(X)					
Alfalfa hay (tons, dry)	15 484	741 856	2 529 635	1 174	180 552	20 032	875 567	2 820 549	1 530	182 974
1 to 14 acres	4 391	37 534	98 886	120	994	5 806	49 445	134 881	164	1 402
15 to 24 acres	3 221	60 185	164 107	132	2 399	4 187	78 178	221 009	185	3 316
25 to 49 acres	3 917	133 043	390 107	219	6 848	5 150	173 873	610 078	300	9 882
50 to 99 acres	3 408	156 517	495 598	217	13 079	3 094	201 552	613 839	315	18 714
100 to 249 acres	1 225	167 733	583 190	267	36 625	1 470	201 187	676 418	381	46 819
250 to 499 acres	224	74 363	261 597	121	37 491	234	74 636	277 686	126	38 161
500 to 999 acres	67	44 035	203 458	58	33 671	64	41 598	162 840	35	21 393
1,000 acres or more	31	67 526	322 702	20	49 845	27	54 922	223 798	20	26 910
1,000 to 1,999 acres	17	(X)	(X)	10	(X)	21	(X)	(X)	14	(X)

36 **KANSAS**

1987 CENSUS OF AGRICULTURE—STATE DATA

Table 44. Specified Crops by Acres Harvested: 1987 and 1982—Con.

[For meaning of abbreviations and symbols, see introductory text]

Crop	1987					1982				
				Irrigated land					Irrigated land	
	Farms	Acres	Quantity	Farms	Acres	Farms	Acres	Quantity	Farms	Acres
Hay—alfalfa, other tame, small grain, wild, grass silage, green chop, etc. (see text)(tons, dry)—Con.										
Alfalfa hay (tons, dry)—Con.										
2,000 to 2,999 acres	12	(X)	(X)	8	(X)	} 6	(X)	(X)	6	(X)
3,000 to 4,999 acres	-	(X)	(X)	-	(X)					
5,000 acres or more	2	(X)	(X)	2	(X)					
Small grain hay (tons, dry)	4 860	154 772	278 785	135	5 965	3 233	95 569	177 085	133	6 667
Tame hay other than alfalfa, small grain, and wild hay (see text)(tons, dry)	18 484	723 851	1 409 236	230	10 695	18 439	664 805	1 243 821	227	8 842
1 to 14 acres	5 285	43 510	79 130	56	464	5 825	46 117	82 017	62	473
15 to 24 acres	3 912	72 753	135 143	32	537	3 875	71 586	128 266	43	703
25 to 49 acres	4 715	159 519	302 780	57	1 680	4 729	158 087	299 665	61	1 659
50 to 99 acres	2 978	192 627	382 207	55	2 791	2 682	171 891	324 521	34	1 859
100 to 249 acres	1 426	190 199	380 354	25	2 235	1 183	156 085	299 433	22	1 828
250 to 499 acres	143	45 638	88 578	3	(D)	118	38 316	73 834	3	(D)
500 to 999 acres	19	10 915	26 464	1	(D)	20	12 678	23 120	1	(D)
1,000 acres or more	6	8 700	14 580	1	(D)	7	9 845	12 965	1	(D)
Wild hay (tons, dry)	11 434	555 349	699 410	15	1 321	11 621	519 040	677 488	19	701
1 to 14 acres	3 119	25 648	36 432	2	(D)	3 416	27 036	39 175	3	15
15 to 24 acres	2 227	41 152	55 340	-	-	2 305	42 412	57 475	5	89
25 to 49 acres	2 676	91 418	121 103	6	205	2 742	94 024	125 644	7	(D)
50 to 99 acres	1 941	127 563	160 549	4	222	1 912	124 693	164 453	1	(D)
100 to 249 acres	1 238	172 889	211 893	1	(D)	1 054	145 079	164 948	3	420
250 to 499 acres	178	57 370	71 587	2	(D)	147	47 832	60 929	-	-
500 to 999 acres	47	(D)	(D)	-	-	33	20 997	25 794	-	-
1,000 acres or more	8	(D)	(D)	-	-	12	16 987	19 070	-	-
1,000 to 1,999 acres	7	(X)	(X)	-	(X)	9	(X)	(X)	-	(X)
2,000 to 2,999 acres	1	(X)	(X)	-	(X)	} 3	(X)	(X)	-	(X)
3,000 to 4,999 acres	-	(X)	(X)	-	(X)					
5,000 acres or more	-	(X)	(X)	-	(X)					
Grass silage, haylage, and green chop hay (tons, green)	1 577	78 244	491 391	105	8 008	1 507	78 650	519 336	117	7 989
Field seed and grass seed crops	1 188	56 460	(X)	12	2 222	1 049	36 382	(X)	12	1 227
Alfalfa seed (pounds)	357	11 060	963 164	6	(D)	774	24 065	2 376 363	10	913
Vegetables harvested for sale (see text)	418	5 424	(X)	166	1 851	362	4 808	(X)	123	1 201
0.1 to 0.9 acres	44	16	(X)	12	4	72	27	(X)	25	8
1.0 to 4.9 acres	200	453	(X)	79	158	141	360	(X)	37	81
5.0 to 14.9 acres	104	610	(X)	39	263	104	628	(X)	44	310
15.0 to 24.9 acres	26	486	(X)	8	94	19	344	(X)	7	111
25.0 to 49.9 acres	29	970	(X)	20	599	12	408	(X)	5	(D)
50.0 to 99.9 acres	10	691	(X)	6	(D)	5	300	(X)	2	(D)
100.0 to 249.9 acres	4	(D)	(X)	2	(D)	8	(D)	(X)	3	431
250.0 to 499.9 acres	-	-	(X)	-	-	-	-	(X)	-	-
500.0 to 749.9 acres	-	-	(X)	-	-	} -	-	(X)	-	-
750.0 to 999.9 acres	-	-	(X)	-	-					
1,000.0 acres or more	1	(D)	(X)	-	(X)					
1,000.0 to 1,999.9 acres	1	(X)	(X)	-	(X)	} 1	(X)	(X)	-	(X)
2,000.0 to 2,999.9 acres	-	(X)	(X)	-	(X)					
3,000.0 acres or more	-	(X)	(X)	-	(X)					
Land in orchards	503	5 999	(X)	90	757	603	6 408	(X)	83	589
0.1 to 0.9 acres	61	32	(X)	4	3	78	39	(X)	7	4
1.0 to 4.9 acres	248	536	(X)	52	116	299	622	(X)	28	62
5.0 to 14.9 acres	116	988	(X)	20	166	139	1 086	(X)	17	128
15.0 to 24.9 acres	31	549	(X)	4	46	36	689	(X)	2	(D)
25.0 to 49.9 acres	27	826	(X)	6	165	26	908	(X)	4	125
50.0 to 99.9 acres	12	717	(X)	3	(D)	14	913	(X)	4	159
100.0 to 499.9 acres	6	(D)	(X)	1	(D)	8	(D)	(X)	1	(D)
250.0 to 499.9 acres	1	(D)	(X)	-	-	-	-	(X)	-	-
500.0 to 749.9 acres	-	-	(X)	-	-	} 1	(D)	(X)	-	-
750.0 to 999.9 acres	1	(D)	(X)	-	-					
1,000.0 acres or more	-	-	(X)	-	(X)					
1,000.0 to 1,999.9 acres	-	(X)	(X)	-	(X)	} -	(X)	(X)	-	(X)
2,000.0 to 2,999.9 acres	-	(X)	(X)	-	(X)					
3,000.0 acres or more	-	(X)	(X)	-	(X)					

Table 45. Specified Fruits and Nuts by Acres: 1987 and 1982

[Not published for this State]

Table 46. **Nursery and Greenhouse Crops, Mushrooms, and Sod Grown for Sale by Value of Sales: 1987 and 1982**

[For meaning of abbreviations and symbols, see introductory text]

Crop	Under glass or other protection		In the open		Sales	
	Farms	Square feet	Farms	Acres	Farms	Value ($1,000)
Nursery and greenhouse crops, mushrooms, and sod grown for sale (see text) .... 1987...	170	3 488 306	137	4 195	272	26 805
1982...	187	2 984 220	153	4 248	298	21 515
1987 value of sales:						
$1 to $2,499 sales............	38	30 434	25	75	58	72
$2,500 to $9,999 sales............	22	57 447	39	138	60	308
$10,000 to $39,999 sales	56	350 932	38	368	83	1 536
$40,000 to $99,999 sales	23	363 260	10	191	26	1 663
$100,000 to $199,999 sales	14	399 583	11	776	19	2 706
$200,000 to $499,999 sales	11	836 836	5	660	12	3 928
$500,000 sales or more	7	1 450 814	9	2 046	14	16 592
Bedding plants .... 1987...	139	1 737 613	13	(D)	142	7 946
1982...	144	1 286 564	14	61	149	5 471
Foliage and potted flowering plants, total .... 1987...	64	1 527 831	11	28	71	9 202
1982...	65	1 228 329	12	27	74	7 086
Foliage plants .... 1987...	30	324 521	2	(D)	31	2 580
Potted flowering plants .... 1987...	52	1 203 310	9	(D)	58	6 622
Nursery crops .... 1987...	11	67 704	82	1 410	88	3 864
1982...	16	245 003	87	1 826	91	5 314

Table 47. Farms by Concentration of Market Value of Agricultural Products Sold: 1987

[For meaning of abbreviations and symbols, see introductory text]

Characteristics	All farms	Fewest number of farms accounting for—			
		10 percent of sales	25 percent of sales	50 percent of sales	75 percent of sales
Farms................................number..	68 579	8	30	483	6 905
percent..	100.0	(Z)	(Z)	.7	10.1
Land in farms...........................acres..	46 628 519	7 774	43 221	1 869 674	15 957 143
Average size of farm..............acres..	680	972	1 441	3 871	2 311
Value of land and buildings[1]................farms..	66 580	8	30	483	6 728
$1,000..	19 068 461	28 353	63 021	858 878	6 390 608
Average per farm ....dollars..	278 047	3 544 125	2 100 700	1 778 215	949 853
Average per acre ....dollars..	413	3 647	1 458	459	408
Estimated market value of all machinery and equipment...........$1,000..	3 447 663	13 359	67 055	194 098	1 098 189
percent..	100.0	.4	1.9	5.6	31.9
Land in farms according to use:					
Total cropland ....acres..	31 365 090	3 452	15 426	847 877	9 887 740
Harvested cropland.................acres..	17 729 394	2 700	6 964	541 749	6 181 215
Pastureland, excluding woodland pastured ....acres..	16 739 539	690	19 340	1 021 699	6 257 087
Market value of agricultural products sold...........$1,000..	6 476 669	685 846	1 623 170	3 238 910	4 857 653
Average per farm ....dollars..	94 441	85 730 752	54 105 668	6 705 818	703 496
Grains ....farms..	48 606	2	7	323	6 175
$1,000..	1 550 403	(D)	547	59 700	670 607
Cotton and cottonseed ....farms..	10	–	–	–	7
$1,000..	166	–	–	–	105
Tobacco ....farms..	13	–	–	–	1
$1,000..	80	–	–	–	(D)
Hay, silage, and field seeds ....farms..	12 801	2	3	131	1 897
$1,000..	109 574	(D)	668	18 949	60 924
Vegetables, sweet corn, and melon ......farms..	418	–	–	2	36
$1,000..	4 151	–	–	(D)	1 641
Fruits, nuts, and berries.............farms..	278	–	–	5	18
$1,000..	1 693	–	–	(D)	592
Nursery and greenhouse crops ....farms..	272	–	–	10	42
$1,000..	26 805	–	–	13 247	22 388
Other crops ....farms..	80	–	–	3	12
$1,000..	716	–	–	495	(D)
Poultry and poultry products.............farms..	1 550	–	–	9	135
$1,000..	25 284	–	–	9 649	22 584
Dairy products ....farms..	2 004	–	–	8	603
$1,000..	140 232	–	–	4 662	89 895
Cattle and calves ....farms..	41 498	8	30	432	5 479
$1,000..	4 305 335	685 174	1 621 949	3 064 739	3 784 508
Hogs and pigs ....farms..	7 090	–	–	62	1 282
$1,000..	284 375	–	–	61 694	190 849
Sheep, lambs, and wool ....farms..	2 456	–	–	7	185
$1,000..	18 561	–	–	4 711	9 537
Other livestock and livestock products (see text) ....farms..	2 869	1	3	29	232
$1,000..	9 273	(D)	6	1 014	3 232
Total farm production expenses[1]..........farms..	68 580	8	30	483	6 728
$1,000..	5 518 518	651 734	1 476 079	2 910 944	4 148 224
Selected farm production expenses[1]:					
Livestock and poultry purchased ....farms..	23 380	8	29	455	4 674
$1,000..	2 426 149	492 276	1 085 280	1 928 735	2 274 588
Feed for livestock and poultry ....farms..	38 347	8	30	461	5 375
$1,000..	887 270	129 364	330 410	642 526	785 333
Commercial fertilizer ....farms..	47 731	3	8	341	6 062
$1,000..	218 166	56	169	11 061	93 733
Agricultural chemicals ....farms..	46 318	3	13	344	5 926
$1,000..	125 003	67	129	6 846	52 951
Petroleum products................farms..	65 480	8	30	475	6 681
$1,000..	243 568	1 639	4 471	21 470	101 066
Electricity......................farms..	48 797	8	29	466	6 374
$1,000..	54 103	2 002	4 062	11 164	26 330
Hired farm labor ....farms..	24 715	8	30	470	5 481
$1,000..	226 075	12 951	26 405	97 262	184 013
Interest ....farms..	39 549	6	28	448	5 929
$1,000..	314 153	848	4 883	38 146	153 377
Payments from government programs ....farms..	41 627	2	5	291	5 629
$1,000..	573 647	(D)	260	18 311	215 404
Inventory of selected livestock:					
Cattle and calves ....farms..	40 785	8	30	417	5 243
number..	5 539 292	337 083	833 780	1 868 348	3 397 893
Milk cows ....farms..	3 093	–	–	12	645
number..	96 675	–	–	2 393	53 011
Hogs and pigs ....farms..	6 766	–	–	63	1 237
number..	1 516 878	–	–	301 957	942 329

[1]Data are based on a sample of farms.

Table 48. **Summary by Tenure of Operator: 1987**

[For meaning of abbreviations and symbols, see introductory text]

Item	All farms				Farms with sales of $10,000 or more			
	Total	Full owners	Part owners	Tenants	Total	Full owners	Part owners	Tenants
FARMS AND LAND IN FARMS								
Farms ....number...	68 579	29 956	27 967	10 656	42 728	11 862	23 793	7 073
...........................percent...	100.0	43.7	40.8	15.5	62.3	17.3	34.7	10.3
Land in farms ....acres...	46 626 519	8 839 919	30 896 557	6 892 043	42 829 070	6 717 881	29 906 320	6 204 869
Average size of farm ....acres...	680	295	1 105	647	1 002	566	1 257	877
MARKET VALUE OF AGRICUL-TURAL PRODUCTS SOLD								
Total sales (see text) ....farms...	68 579	29 956	27 967	10 656	42 728	11 862	23 793	7 073
...........................$1,000...	6 476 669	2 967 544	2 803 505	805 620	6 373 092	2 901 198	2 762 466	789 427
Average per farm ....dollars...	94 441	95 725	100 243	75 602	149 155	236 149	116 945	111 611
Farms by value of sales:								
Less than $1,000 (see text)	4 538	3 703	419	416	-	-	-	-
$1,000 to $2,499	4 964	3 776	549	639	-	-	-	-
$2,500 to $4,999	6 919	4 874	1 072	973	-	-	-	-
$5,000 to $9,999	9 430	5 741	2 134	1 555	-	-	-	-
$10,000 to $19,999	10 504	4 906	3 712	1 886	10 504	4 906	3 712	1 886
$20,000 to $24,999	3 566	1 294	1 679	593	3 566	1 294	1 679	593
$25,000 to $39,999	7 150	1 987	3 825	1 338	7 150	1 987	3 825	1 338
$40,000 to $49,999	3 132	732	1 840	560	3 132	732	1 840	560
$50,000 to $99,999	8 997	1 510	6 038	1 449	8 997	1 510	6 038	1 449
$100,000 to $249,999	6 656	898	4 843	915	6 656	898	4 843	915
$250,000 to $499,999	1 766	277	1 284	205	1 766	277	1 284	205
$500,000 to $999,999	568	107	382	79	568	107	382	79
$1,000,000 or more	389	151	190	48	389	151	190	48
Grains ....farms...	48 606	15 638	24 475	8 493	36 677	8 308	22 109	6 262
...........................$1,000...	1 550 403	238 496	1 047 988	263 918	1 504 937	213 139	1 037 927	253 872
Sales of $50,000 or more ......farms...	8 994	906	6 642	1 448	8 994	906	6 642	1 448
...........................$1,000...	976 864	105 190	712 792	158 882	976 864	105 190	712 792	158 882
Corn for grain ....farms...	7 426	1 849	4 241	1 336	6 776	1 395	4 132	1 249
...........................$1,000...	255 791	43 867	159 465	52 459	254 432	42 922	159 279	52 231
Wheat ....farms...	38 365	10 875	20 437	7 052	30 471	6 308	18 790	5 373
...........................$1,000...	694 147	106 212	469 948	117 989	669 098	93 192	464 059	111 847
Soybeans ....farms...	18 724	5 787	10 112	2 825	14 988	3 331	9 392	2 265
...........................$1,000...	263 742	42 257	184 927	36 558	263 888	35 854	182 977	35 028
Sorghum for grain ....farms...	28 719	7 076	16 352	5 291	23 980	4 406	15 317	4 257
...........................$1,000...	311 649	42 050	217 105	52 494	302 969	37 324	215 167	50 478
Barley ....farms...	1 715	268	1 076	371	1 598	201	1 062	335
...........................$1,000...	3 953	462	2 742	748	3 881	425	2 730	776
Oats ....farms...	2 416	597	1 410	409	2 033	366	1 319	348
...........................$1,000...	3 328	656	2 144	528	3 093	503	2 098	492
Other grains ....farms...	1 656	277	1 062	317	1 553	229	1 040	284
...........................$1,000...	17 793	2 992	11 659	3 142	17 606	2 919	11 617	3 070
Cotton and cottonseed ....farms...	10	-	8	2	10	-	8	2
...........................$1,000...	186	-	(D)	(D)	186	-	(D)	(D)
Sales of $50,000 or more ......farms...	2	-	1	1	2	-	1	1
...........................$1,000...	(D)	-	(D)	(D)	(D)	-	(D)	(D)
Tobacco ....farms...	13	5	6	2	10	3	6	1
...........................$1,000...	80	29	(D)	(D)	73	(D)	(D)	(D)
Sales of $50,000 or more ......farms...	-	-	-	-	-	-	-	-
...........................$1,000...	-	-	-	-	-	-	-	-
Hay, silage, and field seeds ....farms...	12 801	4 372	6 605	1 824	9 398	1 952	5 968	1 478
...........................$1,000...	109 574	25 567	64 710	19 298	104 350	21 948	63 696	18 705
Sales of $50,000 or more ......farms...	316	54	217	45	316	54	217	45
...........................$1,000...	47 030	11 108	26 519	9 403	47 030	11 108	26 519	9 403
Vegetables, sweet corn, and melons ....farms...	418	217	144	57	223	75	118	30
...........................$1,000...	4 151	1 248	2 344	559	3 664	903	2 290	471
Sales of $50,000 or more ......farms...	10	3	6	1	10	3	6	1
...........................$1,000...	1 767	(D)	1 442	(D)	1 767	(D)	1 442	(D)
Fruits, nuts, and berries ....farms...	276	175	76	25	125	53	58	14
...........................$1,000...	1 693	597	1 004	92	1 442	402	967	72
Sales of $50,000 or more ......farms...	6	1	5	-	6	1	5	-
...........................$1,000...	732	(D)	(D)	-	732	(D)	(D)	-
Nursery and greenhouse crops ....farms...	272	209	43	20	171	122	38	11
...........................$1,000...	26 805	19 589	5 901	1 315	26 474	19 287	5 893	1 294
Sales of $50,000 or more ......farms...	62	42	15	5	62	42	15	5
...........................$1,000...	24 509	17 755	5 578	1 176	24 509	17 755	5 578	1 176
Other crops ....farms...	80	30	38	12	57	12	35	10
...........................$1,000...	716	52	378	286	701	(D)	374	(D)
Sales of $50,000 or more ......farms...	3	-	2	1	3	-	2	1
...........................$1,000...	558	-	(D)	(D)	558	-	(D)	(D)
Poultry and poultry products ....farms...	1 550	776	595	179	861	264	475	122
...........................$1,000...	25 264	14 152	9 288	1 824	24 996	13 917	9 257	1 824
Sales of $50,000 or more ......farms...	75	35	34	6	75	35	34	6
...........................$1,000...	23 851	13 391	8 751	1 709	23 851	13 391	8 751	1 709
Dairy products ....farms...	2 004	584	1 206	214	1 801	509	1 185	207
...........................$1,000...	140 232	29 536	98 636	12 058	139 968	29 358	98 595	12 045
Sales of $50,000 or more ......farms...	979	184	707	88	979	184	707	88
...........................$1,000...	119 518	22 546	87 304	9 667	119 518	22 546	87 304	9 667
Cattle and calves ....farms...	41 498	16 587	19 555	5 356	29 267	7 905	17 297	4 065
...........................$1,000...	4 305 335	2 425 821	1 408 581	470 932	4 261 066	2 394 857	1 399 844	466 366
Sales of $50,000 or more ......farms...	5 932	1 147	4 015	770	5 932	1 147	4 015	770
...........................$1,000...	3 891 456	2 295 913	1 177 116	418 427	3 891 456	2 295 913	1 177 116	418 427

See footnotes at end of table.

Table 48. **Summary by Tenure of Operator: 1987**—Con.

[For meaning of abbreviations and symbols. see Introductory text]

Item	All farms				Farms with sales of $10,000 or more			
	Total	Full owners	Part owners	Tenants	Total	Full owners	Part owners	Tenants
MARKET VALUE OF AGRICULTURAL PRODUCTS SOLD—Con.								
Total sales (see text)—Con.								
Hogs and pigs .... farms..	7 090	2 510	3 599	981	5 791	1 561	3 391	839
$1,000..	284 375	101 832	152 310	30 233	281 082	99 294	151 905	29 863
Sales of $50,000 or more .... farms..	1 278	331	798	149	1 278	331	798	149
$1,000..	213 369	80 856	112 767	19 745	213 369	80 856	112 767	19 745
Sheep, lambs, and wool .... farms..	2 458	1 092	1 025	339	1 430	354	857	219
$1,000..	16 581	4 043	10 273	4 245	16 929	2 908	10 010	4 012
Sales of $50,000 or more .... farms..	44	11	25	8	44	11	25	8
$1,000..	9 169	1 278	5 133	2 758	9 169	1 278	5 133	2 758
Other livestock and livestock products (see text) .... farms..	2 869	1 498	1 022	349	1 273	374	715	184
$1,000..	9 273	6 581	1 933	759	7 212	5 119	1 552	541
Sales of $50,000 or more .... farms..	21	18	1	2	21	18	1	2
$1,000..	3 849	3 319	(D)	(D)	3 849	3 319	(D)	(D)
FARM PRODUCTION EXPENSES[1]								
Total farm production expenses............ farms..	68 580	29 814	27 791	10 975	42 865	11 945	23 673	7 247
$1,000..	5 516 518	2 569 223	2 281 264	666 030	5 376 664	2 480 680	2 251 399	646 585
Average per farm....................... dollars..	80 439	86 175	82 086	60 686	125 478	207 675	95 104	89 221
Livestock and poultry purchased .... farms..	23 380	8 376	11 637	3 367	18 117	4 732	10 672	2 713
$1,000..	2 426 149	1 517 189	640 215	268 745	2 415 351	1 510 168	637 990	267 193
Farms with expenses of—								
$1 to $4,999	11 923	5 264	5 079	1 580	7 095	1 847	4 225	1 023
$5,000 to $24,999	6 470	2 023	3 353	1 094	6 068	1 823	3 248	997
$25,000 to $99,999	3 307	708	2 125	474	3 274	681	2 119	474
$100,000 or more	1 680	381	1 080	219	1 680	381	1 080	219
Feed for livestock and poultry .... farms..	38 347	15 192	18 032	5 123	27 518	7 633	16 063	3 822
$1,000..	887 270	510 721	282 260	94 269	677 309	504 052	280 229	93 029
Farms with expenses of—								
$1 to $4,999	28 328	12 644	11 748	3 936	17 643	5 178	9 799	2 666
$5,000 to $24,999	7 351	1 863	4 522	966	7 207	1 770	4 502	935
$25,000 to $99,999	2 028	457	1 418	153	2 028	457	1 418	153
$100,000 or more	640	228	344	68	640	228	344	68
Commercially mixed formula feeds .... farms..	14 968	5 588	7 220	2 160	11 221	3 099	6 506	1 616
$1,000..	163 561	86 223	63 638	11 700	161 449	86 830	63 205	11 415
Farms with expenses of—								
$1 to $4,999	11 327	4 671	4 875	1 781	7 574	2 196	4 161	1 217
$5,000 to $24,999	2 854	684	1 829	341	2 840	670	1 829	341
$25,000 to $79,999	577	131	405	41	577	131	405	41
$80,000 or more	230	102	111	17	230	102	111	17
Seeds, bulbs, plants, and trees .... farms..	48 233	15 729	24 128	8 376	36 438	8 454	21 762	6 222
$1,000..	95 302	17 317	61 977	16 007	91 270	14 962	61 091	15 217
Farms with expenses of—								
$1 to $999	28 247	12 239	10 979	5 029	17 105	5 319	8 758	3 028
$1,000 to $4,999	15 265	2 901	9 812	2 552	14 624	2 558	9 667	2 399
$5,000 to $24,999	4 473	541	3 177	755	4 461	529	3 177	755
$25,000 or more	248	48	160	40	248	48	160	40
Commercial fertilizer .... farms..	47 731	16 513	23 433	7 785	35 204	8 399	20 970	5 835
$1,000..	216 166	36 924	145 725	33 617	207 371	31 845	143 661	31 864
Farms with expenses of—								
$1 to $4,999	34 889	14 889	14 130	5 870	22 422	6 777	11 705	3 940
$5,000 to $24,999	11 740	1 485	8 504	1 751	11 580	1 483	8 466	1 731
$25,000 to $49,999	884	103	652	129	884	103	652	129
$50,000 or more	218	36	147	35	218	36	147	35
Agricultural chemicals.................... farms..	46 318	16 134	22 560	7 624	34 474	8 373	20 302	5 799
$1,000..	125 003	21 855	82 620	20 528	118 865	18 179	81 202	19 485
Farms with expenses of—								
$1 to $4,999	39 456	15 257	17 677	6 522	27 693	7 541	15 447	4 705
$5,000 to $24,999	6 476	829	4 604	1 043	6 395	784	4 576	1 035
$25,000 to $49,999	322	38	237	47	322	38	237	47
$50,000 or more	64	10	42	12	64	10	42	12
Petroleum products .... farms..	65 480	27 413	27 371	10 676	42 296	11 638	23 512	7 146
$1,000..	243 568	53 767	149 653	40 148	227 993	44 522	146 155	37 316
Farms with expenses of—								
$1 to $4,999	51 841	25 641	17 587	8 613	28 696	9 672	13 739	5 085
$5,000 to $24,999	12 652	1 603	9 157	1 892	12 633	1 595	9 146	1 892
$25,000 to $49,999	760	104	521	135	760	104	521	135
$50,000 or more	207	65	106	36	207	65	106	36
Gasoline and gasohol .... farms..	57 245	23 636	24 672	8 937	37 599	10 187	21 307	6 105
$1,000..	80 737	20 638	47 727	12 372	72 306	15 289	45 964	11 052
Diesel fuel .... farms..	46 376	15 034	23 205	8 137	35 421	8 353	20 961	6 107
$1,000..	110 981	20 554	72 395	18 032	106 235	18 059	71 212	16 964
Natural gas .... farms..	4 956	1 227	2 795	944	4 549	942	2 719	888
$1,000..	26 371	6 346	14 062	5 961	26 231	6 259	14 046	5 926
LP gas, fuel oil, kerosene, motor oil, grease, etc. .... farms..	52 549	19 501	25 238	8 810	39 013	10 003	22 529	6 481
$1,000..	25 478	6 227	15 469	3 782	23 222	4 915	14 933	3 374

See footnotes at end of table.

Table 48. **Summary by Tenure of Operator: 1987**—Con.

[For meaning of abbreviations and symbols, see introductory text]

Item	All farms				Farms with sales of $10,000 or more			
	Total	Full owners	Part owners	Tenants	Total	Full owners	Part owners	Tenants
FARM PRODUCTION EXPENSES[1] —Con.								
Total farm production expenses—Con.								
Electricity ... farms	48 797	19 413	22 932	6 452	35 071	9 532	20 613	4 926
$1,000	54 103	18 095	29 445	6 563	50 132	15 274	28 720	6 137
Farms with expenses of—								
$1 to $999	36 860	16 690	15 143	5 027	23 645	7 190	12 904	3 551
$1,000 to $4,999	10 565	2 403	6 875	1 287	10 055	2 022	6 795	1 238
$5,000 to $24,999	1 236	251	862	123	1 235	251	862	122
$25,000 or more	136	69	52	15	136	69	52	15
Hired farm labor ... farms	24 715	7 208	14 018	3 489	20 551	4 467	13 133	2 951
$1,000	226 075	88 254	110 116	27 694	223 983	86 957	109 706	27 320
Farms with expenses of—								
$1 to $4,999	18 529	5 965	9 814	2 750	14 369	3 244	8 930	2 215
$5,000 to $24,999	4 529	856	3 172	501	4 509	837	3 172	500
$25,000 to $99,999	1 391	258	926	206	1 367	258	925	204
$100,000 or more	266	128	106	32	266	128	106	32
Contract labor ... farms	7 862	2 648	4 071	1 163	6 184	1 538	3 709	937
$1,000	23 691	7 809	12 485	3 397	22 375	6 886	12 229	3 260
Farms with expenses of—								
$1 to $999	3 892	1 565	1 727	600	2 578	697	1 467	414
$1,000 to $4,999	2 895	801	1 709	385	2 628	576	1 607	345
$5,000 to $24,999	1 023	256	599	168	1 006	239	599	168
$25,000 or more	72	26	36	10	72	26	36	10
Repair and maintenance ... farms	56 961	22 329	25 599	9 033	38 771	10 193	22 366	6 212
$1,000	252 018	58 523	157 643	35 852	235 054	47 960	154 164	32 931
Farms with expenses of—								
$1 to $4,999	42 384	20 194	15 055	7 135	24 456	8 191	11 882	4 383
$5,000 to $24,999	13 477	1 942	9 790	1 745	13 215	1 809	9 730	1 676
$25,000 to $49,999	844	118	606	120	844	118	606	120
$50,000 or more	256	75	148	33	256	75	148	33
Customwork, machine hire, and rental of machinery and equipment ... farms	30 603	10 536	15 282	4 785	23 220	5 712	13 844	3 664
$1,000	107 366	24 773	62 255	20 338	101 691	21 412	61 089	19 190
Farms with expenses of—								
$1 to $999	13 298	6 045	5 365	1 888	7 763	2 277	4 353	1 133
$1,000 to $4,999	11 836	3 455	6 469	1 912	10 016	2 420	6 043	1 553
$5,000 to $24,999	4 982	945	3 172	865	4 954	924	3 172	858
$25,000 or more	487	91	276	120	487	91	276	120
Interest expense ... farms	39 549	13 471	20 532	5 546	29 923	6 917	18 581	4 425
$1,000	314 163	75 961	215 926	22 277	295 316	62 348	211 786	21 182
Farms with expenses of—								
$1 to $4,999	24 133	10 068	9 642	4 423	15 347	4 140	7 898	3 309
$5,000 to $24,999	12 676	2 938	8 731	1 007	11 837	2 312	8 525	1 000
$25,000 to $99,999	2 557	400	2 050	107	2 556	400	2 049	107
$100,000 or more	183	65	109	9	183	65	109	9
Secured by real estate ... farms	26 408	10 596	15 812	-	19 713	5 313	14 400	-
$1,000	188 166	50 823	137 343	-	173 150	39 052	134 098	-
Farms with expenses of—								
$1 to $999	5 315	2 991	2 324	-	2 980	1 189	1 791	-
$1,000 to $4,999	10 417	4 954	5 463	-	6 755	2 008	4 747	-
$5,000 to $24,999	9 280	2 395	6 885	-	8 582	1 860	6 722	-
$25,000 or more	1 396	256	1 140	-	1 396	258	1 140	-
Not secured by real estate ... farms	24 307	6 083	12 676	5 548	19 818	3 684	11 709	4 425
$1,000	125 997	25 138	76 582	22 277	122 166	23 296	77 688	21 182
Farms with expenses of—								
$1 to $999	8 203	3 090	3 159	1 954	5 115	1 351	2 507	1 257
$1,000 to $4,999	9 540	2 073	4 998	2 469	8 163	1 428	4 685	2 052
$5,000 to $24,999	5 766	761	3 998	1 007	5 742	748	3 994	1 000
$25,000 or more	798	159	523	116	798	159	523	116
Cash rent ... farms	21 234	-	16 014	5 220	17 942	-	14 019	3 923
$1,000	123 531	-	91 969	31 562	119 525	-	89 826	29 698
Farms with expenses of—								
$1 to $4,999	14 629	-	10 973	3 656	11 424	-	9 019	2 405
$5,000 to $9,999	3 298	-	2 497	801	3 217	-	2 462	755
$10,000 to $24,999	2 511	-	1 964	547	2 505	-	1 958	547
$25,000 or more	796	-	580	216	796	-	580	216
Property taxes ... farms	63 359	29 591	27 770	5 998	40 045	11 894	23 668	4 483
$1,000	112 201	42 740	64 979	4 482	96 361	30 035	62 360	3 966
Farms with expenses of—								
$1 to $4,999	59 062	28 365	24 804	5 893	35 825	10 738	20 709	4 378
$5,000 to $9,999	3 248	835	2 331	82	3 186	780	2 324	82
$10,000 to $24,999	956	343	591	22	942	329	591	22
$25,000 or more	93	48	44	1	92	47	44	1
All other farm production expenses ... farms	64 491	26 951	27 328	10 212	42 856	11 939	23 670	7 247
$1,000	309 914	95 285	173 998	40 631	296 067	86 081	171 189	38 796
Farms with expenses of—								
$1 to $4,999	51 852	24 859	18 563	8 430	30 235	9 858	14 912	5 465
$5,000 to $24,999	11 071	1 778	7 696	1 597	11 053	1 767	7 689	1 597
$25,000 to $49,999	1 005	158	736	111	1 005	158	736	111
$50,000 or more	563	156	333	74	563	156	333	74

See footnotes at end of table.

Table 48. Summary by Tenure of Operator: 1987—Con.

[For meaning of abbreviations and symbols, see introductory text]

Item	All farms				Farms with sales of $10,000 or more			
	Total	Full owners	Part owners	Tenants	Total	Full owners	Part owners	Tenants
NET CASH RETURN FROM AGRICULTURAL SALES FOR THE FARM UNIT[1]								
All terms................number..	68 580	29 814	27 791	10 975	42 865	11 945	23 673	7 247
$1,000..	922 2±5	296 601	496 136	129 489	956 268	319 601	505 312	131 355
Average per farm.................dollars..	13 447	9 948	17 852	11 799	22 309	26 756	21 345	18 125
Farms with net gains[2]................number..	41 673	15 574	18 488	7 611	31 351	8 511	17 073	5 767
Average net gain ....dollars..	27 369	24 638	32 676	20 066	35 695	43 399	35 216	25 742
Gain of—								
Less than $1,000	4 994	3 040	1 158	796	1 425	507	692	226
$1,000 to $9,999	18 378	8 535	6 198	3 645	11 625	4 005	5 249	2 371
$10,000 to $49,999	13 889	3 135	8 227	2 527	13 889	3 135	8 227	2 527
$50,000 or more	4 412	864	2 905	643	4 412	864	2 905	643
Farms with net losses.................number..	26 907	14 240	9 303	3 364	11 514	3 434	6 600	1 480
Average net loss ....dollars..	8 114	8 118	11 607	8 907	14 140	14 493	14 536	11 555
Loss of—								
Less than $1,000	5 287	3 403	1 115	769	1 252	465	590	197
$1,000 to $9,999	16 553	9 412	5 104	2 037	6 073	2 094	3 176	803
$10,000 to $49,999	4 663	1 344	2 814	505	3 790	796	2 565	429
$50,000 or more	404	81	270	53	399	79	269	51
GOVERNMENT PAYMENTS AND OTHER FARM-RELATED INCOME								
Government payments ....farms..	41 627	12 822	21 645	7 160	32 463	7 049	19 871	5 543
$1,000..	573 647	92 243	388 142	93 262	547 846	77 579	381 583	88 684
Other farm-related income[1] ....farms..	18 682	6 911	8 861	2 910	13 245	2 933	8 043	2 269
$1,000..	69 944	22 959	35 936	11 049	57 798	13 889	34 557	9 352
Customwork and other agricultural services ....farms..	7 463	1 400	4 391	1 672	6 068	640	4 113	1 315
$1,000..	32 115	4 284	21 094	6 738	29 029	2 586	20 572	5 871
Gross cash rent or share payments ...... farms..	7 899	4 511	2 715	673	4 546	1 742	2 326	478
$1,000..	30 403	16 489	10 428	3 506	22 613	10 022	9 811	2 780
Forest products and Christmas trees .... farms..	439	296	118	25	229	110	100	19
$1,000..	1 087	778	276	33	741	476	256	9
Other farm-related income sources ....farms..	8 669	1 708	3 915	1 046	5 565	1 001	3 652	912
$1,000..	6 340	1 429	4 138	773	5 415	804	3 919	692
COMMODITY CREDIT CORPORATION LOANS								
Total ....farms..	15 832	3 056	9 898	2 878	14 398	2 252	9 587	2 557
$1,000..	338 298	39 165	239 448	59 685	334 877	37 410	238 607	58 860
Corn ....farms..	3 591	554	2 360	677	3 514	499	2 353	662
$1,000..	108 314	14 502	70 421	23 391	108 157	14 390	70 413	23 354
Wheat ....farms..	7 282	1 466	4 466	1 350	6 453	999	4 285	1 169
$1,000..	95 942	11 266	68 926	15 749	94 085	10 314	68 447	15 324
Soybeans ....farms..	1 248	244	817	187	1 166	198	800	168
$1,000..	20 764	2 194	(D)	(D)	20 615	(D)	(D)	(D)
Sorghum, barley, and oats ....farms..	10 032	1 599	6 634	1 799	9 313	1 229	6 458	1 626
$1,000..	112 774	10 711	83 691	18 172	111 537	10 107	83 584	17 845
Cotton ....farms..	–	–	–	–	–	–	–	–
$1,000..	–	–	–	–	–	–	–	–
Peanuts, rye, rice, tobacco, and honey .... farms..	22	17	2	3	15	13	1	1
$1,000..	503	491	(D)	(D)	483	(D)	(D)	(D)
LAND IN FARMS ACCORDING TO USE								
Total cropland ....farms..	61 615	24 560	27 324	9 731	40 638	10 373	23 515	6 750
acres..	31 385 092	5 518 065	20 948 350	4 918 685	29 090 488	4 278 536	20 303 353	4 508 597
Harvested cropland ....farms..	57 822	21 783	26 819	9 220	39 674	9 790	23 316	6 568
acres..	17 729 394	2 909 784	11 996 753	2 822 857	16 756 210	2 375 247	11 745 760	2 635 203
Farms by acres harvested:								
1 to 49 acres	12 372	8 983	2 130	1 259	2 072	1 236	596	240
50 to 99 acres	8 853	4 961	2 357	1 535	3 589	1 802	1 273	514
100 to 199 acres	10 361	3 972	4 347	2 042	8 083	2 997	3 580	1 506
200 to 499 acres	14 761	2 783	9 234	2 744	14 461	2 672	9 120	2 669
500 to 999 acres	8 150	814	6 138	1 198	8 145	814	6 134	1 197
1,000 to 1,999 acres	2 876	220	2 289	367	2 875	219	2 289	367
2,000 acres or more	449	50	324	75	449	50	324	75
Cropland:								
Pasture or grazing only..................farms..	22 575	9 171	10 629	2 775	15 052	3 940	9 071	2 041
acres..	3 485 445	903 025	2 156 744	425 676	2 955 754	586 169	2 010 516	359 049
In cover crops, legumes, and soil-improvement grasses, not harvested and not pastured ....farms..	11 212	3 777	5 907	1 528	8 413	1 936	5 315	1 162
acres..	1 103 315	248 025	705 586	149 704	955 326	162 683	661 810	130 833
On which all crops failed ....farms..	3 341	1 109	1 733	499	2 264	468	1 460	336
acres..	206 231	50 971	126 064	29 196	169 141	30 460	115 407	23 274
In cultivated summer fallow ....farms..	25 408	8 336	14 245	4 827	20 818	3 900	13 147	3 771
acres..	6 409 508	902 749	4 399 753	1 107 004	6 053 078	746 976	4 289 290	1 016 812
Idle ....farms..	20 610	6 570	10 625	3 415	15 618	3 506	9 524	2 588
acres..	2 451 199	503 501	1 563 450	384 248	2 200 979	376 983	1 480 570	343 426
Total woodland ....farms..	12 587	6 005	5 470	1 112	7 616	2 271	4 557	788
acres..	718 261	267 731	388 527	62 003	537 091	137 542	349 040	50 509
Woodland pastured ....farms..	6 382	3 211	2 667	504	3 702	1 186	2 176	340
acres..	366 136	139 276	197 309	29 551	268 846	69 453	176 271	23 122
Woodland not pastured ....farms..	7 991	3 648	3 706	737	5 137	1 438	3 150	549
acres..	352 125	128 455	191 218	32 452	268 245	68 089	172 769	27 387

See footnotes at end of table.

Table 48. **Summary by Tenure of Operator: 1987**—Con.

[For meaning of abbreviations and symbols, see introductory text]

Item	All farms				Farms with sales of $10,000 or more			
	Total	Full owners	Part owners	Tenants	Total	Full owners	Part owners	Tenants
LAND IN FARMS ACCORDING TO USE—Con.								
Pastureland and rangeland other than cropland and woodland pastured .... farms..	32 362	12 353	15 731	4 278	22 213	5 412	13 751	3 050
acres..	13 254 094	2 679 207	8 800 184	1 774 703	12 143 432	2 071 683	8 543 439	1 528 310
Land in house lots, ponds, roads, wasteland, etc. .... farms..	44 335	20 585	18 998	4 752	27 802	8 153	16 261	3 388
acres..	1 271 074	374 926	759 496	136 652	1 056 059	230 118	710 488	117 453
Cropland under federal acreage reduction programs:								
Annual commodity acreage adjustment programs .... farms..	34 858	8 698	19 853	6 307	29 094	5 591	18 399	5 104
acres..	3 956 196	527 440	2 729 295	699 461	3 612 266	460 241	2 689 090	662 935
Conservation reserve program .... farms..	5 630	1 723	3 283	624	4 403	873	3 039	491
acres..	810 862	181 483	536 642	92 737	696 782	115 851	500 158	80 773
Value of land and buildings[1] .... farms..	68 580	29 814	27 791	10 975	42 885	11 945	23 673	7 247
$1,000..	19 068 461	4 449 660	11 980 767	2 638 134	16 828 379	3 029 425	11 476 087	2 322 867
Average per farm........................dollars..	278 047	149 244	431 102	240 377	392 590	253 614	484 775	320 526
Average per acre........................dollars..	413	515	392	379	397	459	388	374
Farms by value group:								
$1 to $39,999	10 024	7 558	707	1 759	1 963	1 424	164	375
$40,000 to $69,999	9 571	6 280	1 634	1 657	2 771	1 428	638	705
$70,000 to $99,999	7 001	4 059	1 760	1 182	3 143	1 478	1 046	619
$100,000 to $149,999	8 596	3 913	3 134	1 549	5 158	1 833	2 173	1 152
$150,000 to $199,999	6 313	2 553	2 707	1 053	4 799	1 578	2 353	868
$200,000 to $499,999	16 476	3 982	10 066	2 428	14 771	2 925	9 602	2 244
$500,000 to $999,999	7 579	1 039	5 549	991	7 276	858	5 480	938
$1,000,000 to $1,999,999	2 396	301	1 836	259	2 367	296	1 820	251
$2,000,000 to $4,999,999	535	109	340	86	529	105	339	85
$5,000,000 or more	89	20	58	11	88	20	58	10
VALUE OF MACHINERY AND EQUIPMENT[1]								
Estimated market value of all machinery and equipment .... farms..	68 391	29 677	27 770	10 944	42 831	11 937	23 659	7 235
$1,000..	3 447 663	940 365	1 994 094	513 205	3 028 837	675 234	1 909 429	444 173
Farms by value group:								
$1 to $4,999	5 812	4 097	854	861	1 353	633	387	333
$5,000 to $9,999	11 585	7 904	1 901	1 780	2 418	1 143	756	519
$10,000 to $19,999	11 722	6 173	3 545	2 004	6 000	2 469	2 447	1 084
$20,000 to $49,999	16 724	6 273	7 484	2 967	12 246	3 541	6 466	2 239
$50,000 to $99,999	12 176	3 203	7 067	1 906	10 904	2 374	6 786	1 744
$100,000 to $199,999	7 277	1 368	4 907	1 002	6 899	1 171	4 822	906
$200,000 to $499,999	2 860	610	1 854	396	2 776	557	1 837	382
$500,000 or more	235	49	158	28	235	49	158	28
SELECTED MACHINERY AND EQUIPMENT[1]								
Motortrucks, including pickups .... farms..	63 093	26 126	26 763	10 204	41 188	11 196	23 079	6 913
number..	159 329	51 245	83 399	24 685	123 782	28 197	76 670	18 915
Wheel tractors .... farms..	60 459	25 430	25 883	9 146	39 758	10 902	22 469	6 387
number..	150 647	53 082	76 038	21 527	113 793	28 068	69 204	16 521
Less than 40 horsepower (PTO) .... farms..	25 210	12 585	9 535	3 090	14 125	4 341	7 803	1 981
number..	36 591	18 946	15 249	4 394	36 910	7 075	12 611	2 859
40 horsepower (PTO) or more .... farms..	50 577	18 401	23 875	6 301	36 910	9 446	21 348	6 116
number..	112 056	34 134	60 789	17 133	91 248	20 993	56 593	13 662
Grain and bean combines .... farms..	35 608	10 563	19 218	5 827	28 372	6 344	17 594	4 434
number..	43 801	12 321	24 339	7 141	35 670	7 666	22 507	5 497
Cottonpickers and strippers................... farms..	1	-	1	-	1	-	1	-
number..	(D)	-	(D)	-	(D)	-	(D)	-
Mower conditioners .... farms..	18 793	6 358	9 990	2 445	14 303	3 534	8 838	1 931
number..	20 167	6 641	10 738	2 588	15 417	3 818	9 525	2 074
Pickup balers .... farms..	26 083	9 111	13 661	3 311	19 563	4 855	12 085	2 623
number..	31 892	10 484	17 354	4 054	24 558	5 771	15 540	3 247
AGRICULTURAL CHEMICALS[1]								
Commercial fertilizer .... farms..	47 723	16 513	23 425	7 785	35 196	8 399	20 962	5 835
acres on which used..	13 852 822	2 145 196	9 455 144	2 252 482	13 190 009	1 802 211	9 287 740	2 100 058
Lime .... farms..	2 665	889	1 537	259	2 104	468	1 401	235
acres on which used..	154 522	37 424	97 239	19 959	137 056	24 849	93 093	19 114
tons..	369 024	87 968	229 175	51 881	327 379	56 652	220 883	49 844
Sprays, dusts, granules, fumigants, etc., to control—								
Insects on hay and other crops .... farms..	19 416	4 957	11 196	3 263	16 992	3 428	10 671	2 893
acres on which used..	3 015 580	483 798	1 997 987	533 795	2 849 695	446 188	1 881 798	521 709
Nematodes in crops .... farms..	716	244	325	147	561	153	293	115
acres on which used..	87 904	19 836	53 137	15 931	81 963	15 631	51 098	15 234
Diseases in crops and orchards .... farms..	1 055	482	428	145	724	207	397	120
acres on which used..	125 065	24 347	81 024	19 694	120 052	22 028	79 760	18 264
Weeds, grass, or brush in crops and pasture .... farms..	36 950	11 932	18 714	6 304	28 305	6 519	16 918	4 868
acres on which used..	8 637 062	1 362 439	5 854 090	1 420 533	8 177 411	1 117 024	5 727 259	1 333 128
Chemicals for defoliation or for growth control of crops or thinning of fruit .... farms..	614	199	323	93	443	103	284	56
acres on which used..	68 639	16 742	42 994	9 103	65 338	14 456	42 553	8 329

See footnotes at end of table.

Table 48. **Summary by Tenure of Operator: 1987**—Con.

[For meaning of abbreviations and symbols, see introductory text]

Item	All farms				Farms with sales of $10,000 or more			
	Total	Full owners	Part owners	Tenants	Total	Full owners	Part owners	Tenants
TENURE AND RACE OF OPERATOR								
All operators	68 579	29 956	27 967	10 656	42 728	11 862	23 793	7 073
Full owners	29 956	29 956	-	-	11 862	11 862	-	-
Part owners	27 967	-	27 967	-	23 793	-	23 793	-
Tenants	10 656	-	-	10 656	7 073	-	-	7 073
White	68 304	29 784	27 901	10 619	42 634	11 827	23 754	7 053
Full owners	29 784	29 784	-	-	11 827	11 827	-	-
Part owners	27 901	-	27 901	-	23 754	-	23 754	-
Tenants	10 619	-	-	10 619	7 053	-	-	7 053
Black and other races	275	172	66	37	94	35	39	20
Full owners	172	172	-	-	35	35	-	-
Part owners	66	-	66	-	39	-	39	-
Tenants	37	-	-	37	20	-	-	20
OWNED AND RENTED LAND								
Land owned .... farms..	58 533	29 956	27 967	610	36 040	11 862	23 793	385
acres..	24 331 897	10 933 599	13 159 770	238 528	20 743 827	7 943 690	12 633 753	166 384
Owned land in farms.............. farms..	57 923	29 956	27 967	-	35 655	11 862	23 793	-
acres..	21 178 322	8 839 919	12 338 403	-	18 610 740	6 717 881	11 892 859	-
Land rented or leased from others .... farms..	38 906	285	27 967	10 656	31 048	182	23 793	7 073
acres..	25 865 815	107 117	18 756 314	7 002 384	24 579 331	85 332	18 199 360	6 294 639
Rented or leased land in farms.. farms..	38 623	-	27 967	10 656	30 866	-	23 793	7 073
acres..	25 450 197	-	18 558 154	6 892 043	24 218 330	-	18 013 461	6 204 869
Land rented or leased to others............. farms..	11 944	7 420	3 647	877	6 575	2 952	3 053	570
acres..	3 569 193	2 200 797	1 019 527	348 869	2 494 088	1 311 141	926 793	256 154
OPERATOR CHARACTERISTICS								
Operators by place of residence:								
On farm operated	45 527	18 632	21 962	4 933	30 071	7 343	18 962	3 766
Not on farm operated	17 871	8 162	4 579	5 130	9 808	3 163	3 689	2 956
Not reported	5 181	3 162	1 426	593	2 849	1 356	1 142	351
Operators by principal occupation:								
Farming	42 607	14 609	21 582	6 416	33 778	8 317	20 153	5 308
Other	25 972	15 347	6 385	4 240	8 950	3 545	3 640	1 765
Operators by days of work off farm:								
None	29 462	11 483	14 438	3 541	22 373	5 935	13 525	2 913
Any	34 654	16 114	11 854	6 686	17 268	4 682	8 762	3 824
1 to 99 days	7 620	2 205	3 693	1 722	5 799	1 041	3 388	1 370
100 to 199 days	5 357	2 079	2 108	1 170	3 229	755	1 700	774
200 days or more	21 677	11 830	6 053	3 794	8 240	2 886	3 674	1 680
Not reported	4 463	2 359	1 675	429	3 087	1 245	1 506	336
Operators by years on present farm:								
2 years or less	3 511	1 710	587	1 214	1 600	535	351	714
3 or 4 years	3 873	1 739	831	1 303	1 800	469	533	798
5 to 9 years	8 552	3 531	2 709	2 312	4 651	1 050	2 053	1 548
10 years or more	40 624	16 425	20 048	4 151	27 950	7 235	17 680	3 035
Average years on present farm	21.3	21.3	24.3	13.2	23.5	25.5	25.4	13.9
Not reported	12 019	6 551	3 792	1 676	6 727	2 573	3 176	978
Operators by age group:								
Under 25 years	1 712	486	258	968	945	152	210	583
25 to 34 years	9 531	2 691	3 418	3 422	6 161	969	2 871	2 321
35 to 44 years	12 471	4 598	5 566	2 307	7 754	1 493	4 649	1 612
45 to 49 years	5 926	2 481	2 699	746	3 578	835	2 255	488
50 to 54 years	5 781	2 889	3 199	693	4 249	1 065	2 746	438
55 to 59 years	7 581	3 133	3 776	672	5 091	1 297	3 322	472
60 to 64 years	8 407	3 805	3 916	686	5 667	1 744	3 458	465
65 to 69 years	6 564	3 526	2 556	482	4 084	1 589	2 184	311
70 years and over	9 606	6 347	2 579	680	5 199	2 718	2 098	383
Average age	52.0	55.9	51.6	41.9	51.6	57.4	51.7	41.7
Operators by sex:								
Male	65 619	27 879	27 392	10 348	41 577	11 248	23 397	6 932
Female	2 960	2 077	575	308	1 151	614	396	141
Operators of Spanish origin (see text)	108	48	40	20	52	12	29	11
FARMS BY TYPE OF ORGANIZATION								
Individual or family (sole proprietorship) ..... farms..	60 202	26 808	24 616	8 778	36 327	10 050	20 696	5 581
acres..	36 420 471	6 971 881	24 831 477	4 617 113	33 110 291	5 079 486	23 919 350	4 111 455
Partnership .... farms..	5 689	2 131	2 336	1 422	4 309	1 009	2 118	1 092
acres..	6 151 580	961 050	3 713 203	1 477 327	5 881 210	816 410	3 652 363	1 412 437
Corporation:								
Family held .... farms..	1 942	677	897	368	1 758	536	885	337
acres..	3 445 745	664 141	2 166 058	616 546	3 397 256	633 554	2 153 884	609 818
More than 10 stockholders .... farms..	23	16	4	3	22	16	3	3
10 or less stockholders .... farms..	1 919	661	893	365	1 736	520	882	334
Other than family held .... farms..	158	88	45	25	122	64	37	21
acres..	159 376	52 074	76 196	31 106	152 533	47 225	74 764	30 544
More than 10 stockholders .... farms..	17	9	6	2	8	5	2	1
10 or less stockholders .... farms..	141	79	39	23	114	59	35	20
Other—cooperative, estate or trust, institutional, etc. .... farms..	388	252	73	63	212	113	57	42
acres..	450 347	190 773	109 623	149 951	287 780	141 206	105 959	40 615

See footnotes at end of table.

Table 48. **Summary by Tenure of Operator: 1987**—Con.

[For meaning of abbreviations and symbols, see introductory text]

Item	All farms				Farms with sales of $10,000 or more			
	Total	Full owners	Part owners	Tenants	Total	Full owners	Part owners	Tenants
FARMS BY SIZE								
1 to 9 acres	3 689	3 407	59	223	1 104	1 031	8	65
10 to 49 acres	6 222	4 902	581	739	578	429	65	84
50 to 69 acres	1 549	1 235	299	315	218	140	40	38
70 to 99 acres	4 690	3 528	522	645	687	494	84	109
100 to 139 acres	3 117	1 886	708	523	853	454	224	175
140 to 179 acres	5 854	3 798	956	1 100	2 044	1 208	377	459
180 to 219 acres	2 307	1 165	730	412	1 168	524	410	234
220 to 259 acres	2 845	1 425	874	546	1 603	693	580	330
260 to 499 acres	11 553	4 393	5 009	2 151	8 949	3 066	4 157	1 726
500 to 999 acres	12 093	2 560	7 449	2 084	11 352	2 239	7 154	1 959
1,000 to 1,999 acres	9 304	1 107	6 888	1 309	9 152	1 050	6 815	1 287
2,000 acres or more	5 056	550	3 892	614	5 020	534	3 879	607
FARMS BY STANDARD INDUSTRIAL CLASSIFICATION								
Cash grains (011)	31 789	10 576	14 855	6 358	22 225	4 770	13 081	4 374
Field crops, except cash grains (013)	2 010	1 318	467	225	569	184	276	109
Cotton (0131)	1	1	-	-	1	-	1	-
Tobacco (0132)	3	2	-	1	-	-	-	-
Sugarcane and sugar beets; Irish potatoes; field crops, except cash grains, n.e.c. (0133, 0134, 0139)	2 006	1 316	466	224	568	184	275	109
Vegetables and melons (016)	179	113	35	31	59	26	23	10
Fruits and tree nuts (017)	171	144	19	8	24	14	8	2
Horticultural specialties (018)	224	185	23	16	145	114	22	9
General farms, primarily crop (019)	1 463	749	557	157	718	141	474	103
Livestock, except dairy, poultry, and animal specialties (021)	29 037	14 817	10 729	3 491	17 179	6 049	8 854	2 276
Beef cattle, except feedlots (0212)	21 861	11 534	7 709	2 618	12 004	4 295	6 093	1 616
Dairy farms (024)	1 391	416	821	154	1 348	381	817	150
Poultry and eggs (025)	197	139	42	16	83	45	33	5
Animal specialties (027)	1 452	1 128	186	138	104	83	17	4
General farms, primarily livestock and animal specialties (029)	666	371	233	62	274	55	188	31
LIVESTOCK								
Cattle and calves inventory .... farms	40 785	16 382	19 186	5 217	28 111	7 430	16 818	3 863
number	5 539 292	2 107 043	2 794 463	637 786	5 266 525	1 926 032	2 731 099	609 394
Farms with—								
1 to 9	4 367	2 902	916	549	952	324	475	153
10 to 49	16 841	8 799	5 721	2 321	8 569	3 019	4 096	1 464
50 to 99	8 529	2 645	4 794	1 090	7 662	2 124	4 525	1 013
100 to 199	8 150	1 155	4 281	714	6 040	1 090	4 249	701
200 to 499	3 580	570	2 618	392	3 572	563	2 618	391
500 or more	1 318	311	956	151	1 316	310	855	151
Cows and heifers that had calved .... farms	33 157	13 142	15 959	4 056	22 650	5 829	13 878	2 943
number	1 451 324	386 245	908 135	156 944	1 314 791	295 587	875 914	143 290
Beef cows .... farms	31 475	12 540	15 065	3 860	21 232	5 415	13 022	2 795
number	1 354 649	363 623	842 812	148 214	1 219 690	274 047	810 886	134 697
Farms with—								
1 to 9	6 299	3 873	1 624	802	1 777	557	917	303
10 to 49	17 123	7 102	7 770	2 251	11 554	3 385	6 486	1 683
50 to 99	5 108	1 032	3 524	552	4 973	951	3 487	535
100 to 199	2 115	361	1 557	197	2 101	352	1 553	196
200 to 499	714	134	514	66	712	132	514	66
500 or more	116	38	66	12	115	38	65	12
Milk cows .... farms	3 093	1 075	1 676	342	2 514	681	1 549	284
number	96 675	22 622	65 323	8 730	95 161	21 540	65 028	8 593
Farms with—								
1 to 4	1 195	534	531	130	701	197	423	81
5 to 9	150	73	54	23	86	32	37	16
10 to 49	979	326	526	127	960	311	524	125
50 to 99	562	105	425	52	581	104	425	52
100 to 199	163	30	125	8	163	30	125	8
200 to 499	21	5	15	1	21	5	15	1
500 or more	3	2	-	1	3	2	-	1
Heifers and heifer calves .... farms	31 410	11 950	15 516	3 944	22 032	5 493	13 516	2 923
number	1 632 193	677 113	781 972	173 108	1 564 381	632 391	766 151	165 839
Steers, steer calves, bulls, and bull calves .... farms	35 035	13 516	17 082	4 437	24 681	6 303	15 043	3 335
number	2 455 775	1 043 585	1 104 356	307 734	2 387 353	998 054	1 089 034	300 265
Cattle and calves sold .... farms	41 498	16 587	19 555	5 356	29 267	7 905	17 297	4 065
number	7 310 338	3 835 818	2 660 549	814 171	7 185 342	3 746 155	2 635 769	801 420
$1,000	4 305 335	2 425 821	1 408 581	470 932	4 261 066	2 394 857	1 399 844	466 366
Calves .... farms	18 518	8 292	7 910	2 316	11 574	3 373	6 609	1 592
number	468 326	149 568	257 557	61 203	408 979	108 107	245 732	55 140
$1,000	145 961	45 622	81 998	18 340	129 095	33 815	78 666	16 613
Cattle .... farms	34 216	13 074	16 727	4 415	25 323	6 764	15 067	3 492
number	6 842 010	3 686 050	2 402 992	752 968	6 776 363	3 640 048	2 390 037	746 280
$1,000	4 159 374	2 380 199	1 326 583	452 592	4 131 971	2 361 041	1 321 178	449 752
Fattened on grain and concentrates ... farms	4 620	648	2 433	539	3 710	1 015	2 238	457
number	4 551 726	3 155 848	952 400	443 378	4 547 436	3 152 895	951 437	443 004
$1,000	3 041 522	2 126 081	612 557	302 885	3 039 410	2 124 613	612 103	302 694

See footnotes at end of table.

Table 48. **Summary by Tenure of Operator: 1987**—Con.

[For meaning of abbreviations and symbols, see introductory text]

Item	All farms				Farms with sales of $10,000 or more			
	Total	Full owners	Part owners	Tenants	Total	Full owners	Part owners	Tenants
LIVESTOCK—Con.								
Hogs and pigs inventory .... farms..	6 768	2 366	3 465	937	5 480	1 448	3 239	793
number..	1 516 878	538 270	823 118	155 490	1 486 304	516 288	818 003	152 013
Farms with—								
1 to 24	1 916	912	746	258	1 006	273	570	163
25 to 49	828	312	385	131	599	148	347	104
50 to 99	1 087	360	580	147	975	270	574	131
100 to 199	1 092	294	624	174	1 067	278	620	169
200 to 499	1 226	317	735	174	1 217	310	734	173
500 or more	619	171	395	53	616	169	394	53
Used or to be used for breeding .... farms..	4 596	1 555	2 373	668	3 847	1 013	2 269	565
number..	191 079	70 290	99 930	20 859	184 633	65 643	99 055	19 935
Other .... farms..	6 286	2 146	3 305	835	5 187	1 356	3 101	730
number..	1 325 799	467 980	723 188	134 631	1 301 671	450 646	718 948	132 078
Hogs and pigs sold .... farms..	7 090	2 510	3 599	981	5 791	1 561	3 391	839
number..	2 759 676	1 002 250	1 455 627	301 799	2 713 592	967 343	1 450 327	295 922
$1,000..	284 375	101 832	152 310	30 233	281 062	99 294	151 905	29 863
Feeder pigs .... farms..	1 869	784	808	297	1 392	414	744	234
number..	514 394	220 489	225 745	68 160	489 501	201 936	223 305	64 260
$1,000..	23 029	9 731	10 262	3 036	22 115	9 043	10 177	2 895
Litters of pigs farrowed between—								
Dec. 1 of preceding year and Nov. 30 .... farms..	4 819	1 647	2 475	697	4 009	1 057	2 368	584
number..	295 974	107 616	157 490	30 868	289 308	102 627	156 733	29 948
Dec. 1 and May 31 .... farms..	4 455	1 495	2 317	643	3 773	991	2 235	547
number..	149 414	54 149	79 702	15 563	146 163	51 710	79 350	15 103
June 1 and Nov. 30 .... farms..	4 403	1 454	2 308	641	3 731	964	2 220	547
number..	146 560	53 467	77 786	15 305	143 145	50 917	77 383	14 845
Sheep and lambs of all ages inventory...... farms..	2 400	1 065	1 003	332	1 987	340	833	214
number..	249 303	63 086	140 257	45 960	217 992	41 084	134 912	41 996
Ewes 1 year old or older .... farms..	2 195	969	914	312	1 276	317	757	202
number..	129 607	34 853	74 678	20 076	107 922	19 729	70 831	17 362
Sheep and lambs sold .... farms..	2 396	1 056	1 007	333	1 405	348	840	217
number..	267 152	54 663	146 970	65 519	243 837	38 493	143 296	62 048
Sheep and lambs shorn .... farms..	2 183	958	921	304	1 286	319	768	199
number..	218 980	49 928	128 414	40 638	193 541	32 343	123 952	37 246
pounds of wool..	1 510 663	367 484	860 515	282 664	1 329 437	239 951	831 675	257 811
Horses and ponies inventory.............. farms..	12 879	5 582	5 707	1 590	7 341	1 722	4 602	1 017
number..	55 598	25 765	23 606	6 227	29 705	7 819	18 146	3 740
Horses and ponies sold .... farms..	2 260	1 122	855	283	1 022	279	594	149
number..	8 467	4 339	3 046	1 082	4 984	2 059	2 265	660
Goats inventory .... farms..	862	451	311	100	348	83	219	44
number..	8 831	4 681	3 547	603	5 219	1 861	3 147	191
Goats sold .... farms..	258	160	77	21	88	32	49	7
number..	2 679	1 670	627	182	1 378	779	567	32
POULTRY								
Chickens 3 months old or older inventory .. farms..	4 206	2 047	1 709	450	2 236	611	1 340	285
number..	2 094 610	1 014 404	886 552	193 654	2 038 101	971 752	876 916	189 433
Farms with—								
1 to 399	4 117	2 011	1 661	445	2 151	579	1 292	280
400 to 3,199	30	14	15	1	26	10	15	1
3,200 to 9,999	12	4	8	-	12	4	8	-
10,000 to 19,999	18	7	9	2	18	7	9	2
20,000 to 49,999	19	5	13	1	19	5	13	1
50,000 to 99,999	7	4	3	-	7	4	3	-
100,000 or more	3	2	-	1	3	2	-	1
Hens and pullets of laying age .... farms..	4 150	2 015	1 692	443	2 214	602	1 330	282
number..	1 797 313	841 395	834 439	121 479	1 745 164	801 889	825 562	117 713
Pullets 3 months old or older not of laying age .... farms..	415	208	153	54	193	61	105	27
number..	297 297	173 009	52 113	72 175	292 937	169 863	51 354	71 720
Hens and pullets sold .... farms..	363	176	151	36	216	69	121	26
number..	2 380 936	1 445 336	841 594	94 006	2 372 808	1 441 050	838 009	93 749
Broilers and other meat-type chickens sold .... farms..	132	68	37	27	72	27	28	17
number..	176 061	132 364	10 867	32 830	166 699	127 129	10 318	29 252
Farms with—								
1 to 1,999	123	65	36	22	64	24	27	13
2,000 to 59,999	7	1	1	5	6	1	1	4
60,000 to 99,999	2	2	-	-	2	2	-	-
100,000 or more	-	-	-	-	-	-	-	-
Turkey hens kept for breeding .... farms..	194	113	67	14	89	36	48	5
number..	(D)	29 996	227	(D)	(D)	29 614	145	(D)
Turkeys sold .... farms..	88	39	30	19	56	22	19	15
number..	230 719	137 853	62 797	30 069	229 860	137 180	62 683	29 997

See footnotes at end of table.

Table 48. **Summary by Tenure of Operator: 1987**—Con.

[For meaning of abbreviations and symbols, see introductory text]

Item	All farms				Farms with sales of $10,000 or more			
	Total	Full owners	Part owners	Tenants	Total	Full owners	Part owners	Tenants
CROPS HARVESTED								
Corn for grain or seed .... farms..	8 944	2 360	5 113	1 471	8 028	1 736	4 923	1 369
acres..	1 243 969	213 147	801 983	228 839	1 228 426	202 588	799 265	226 573
bushels..	144 133 581	23 707 805	92 231 443	28 194 233	143 105 352	22 995 450	92 067 155	28 042 747
Irrigated .... farms..	3 647	641	2 228	778	3 594	608	2 221	765
acres..	816 992	132 468	506 972	177 552	815 633	131 610	506 849	177 174
Farms by acres harvested:								
1 to 24 acres	1 964	892	832	260	1 272	411	670	191
25 to 99 acres	3 279	900	1 853	526	3 080	758	1 827	495
100 to 249 acres	2 196	373	1 403	420	2 191	372	1 401	418
250 to 499 acres	1 044	132	733	179	1 044	132	733	179
500 acres or more	441	63	292	86	441	63	292	86
Corn for silage or green chop.............. farms..	2 009	411	1 360	238	1 946	373	1 343	230
acres..	109 230	19 958	75 097	14 175	107 988	19 112	74 902	13 974
tons, green..	1 669 413	301 196	1 136 170	232 047	1 657 553	294 263	1 133 639	229 651
Irrigated .... farms..	659	98	462	99	646	94	458	94
acres..	53 214	8 161	36 464	8 589	52 741	7 895	36 403	8 443
Farms by acres harvested:								
1 to 24 acres	799	193	511	95	752	165	495	92
25 to 99 acres	944	170	676	98	930	162	675	93
100 to 249 acres	207	36	136	35	205	34	136	35
250 to 499 acres	43	10	25	8	43	10	25	8
500 acres or more	16	2	12	2	16	2	12	2
Sorghum for grain or seed.............. farms..	32 492	8 298	18 504	5 690	27 102	5 234	17 268	4 600
acres..	3 399 564	477 229	2 364 333	558 002	3 262 294	406 891	2 329 345	526 158
bushels..	226 045 100	30 785 731	160 364 823	36 894 546	221 098 837	27 092 540	158 734 059	35 272 238
Irrigated .... farms..	3 137	472	2 022	643	3 021	405	2 001	615
acres..	484 119	54 188	311 435	96 496	460 555	52 242	310 636	97 677
Farms by acres harvested:								
1 to 24 acres	7 280	3 346	2 706	1 228	3 964	1 316	2 007	641
25 to 99 acres	14 139	3 787	7 710	2 642	12 150	2 784	7 207	2 159
100 to 249 acres	7 830	883	5 613	1 334	7 752	855	5 580	1 317
250 to 499 acres	2 503	212	1 906	385	2 496	209	1 905	382
500 acres or more	740	70	569	101	740	70	569	101
Wheat for grain .... farms..	36 638	11 053	20 500	7 085	30 569	6 356	18 826	5 387
acres..	8 679 588	1 323 364	5 875 126	1 481 078	8 225 848	1 101 348	5 754 223	1 370 277
bushels..	292 999 442	43 578 447	198 587 002	50 535 993	280 906 658	37 734 986	195 686 059	47 485 613
Irrigated .... farms..	3 046	558	1 767	721	2 919	469	1 765	695
acres..	635 524	88 566	391 963	154 995	690 691	04 750	391 527	154 314
Farms by acres harvested:								
1 to 24 acres	4 230	2 346	1 283	601	1 969	762	923	284
25 to 99 acres	11 451	4 836	4 333	2 282	6 891	2 200	3 448	1 243
100 to 249 acres	11 111	2 589	6 263	2 259	9 639	2 126	5 870	1 643
250 to 499 acres	7 246	864	5 124	1 260	7 187	850	5 092	1 245
500 acres or more	4 596	416	3 497	683	4 593	418	3 493	682
Barley for grain.............. farms..	2 307	375	1 495	437	2 138	280	1 464	394
acres..	95 465	11 704	66 385	17 376	93 426	10 654	65 945	16 827
bushels..	3 639 224	417 982	2 570 236	651 004	3 573 070	383 043	2 556 497	633 530
Irrigated .... farms..	166	27	95	44	161	22	95	44
acres..	7 359	1 041	4 859	1 459	7 319	1 001	4 859	1 459
Oats for grain .... farms..	5 313	1 432	3 172	709	4 491	923	2 956	612
acres..	128 001	26 969	83 918	17 214	117 316	20 637	81 006	15 673
bushels..	4 775 729	1 001 420	3 166 220	608 089	4 463 199	815 041	3 079 378	568 780
Irrigated .... farms..	48	12	27	9	48	12	27	9
acres..	2 278	983	983	312	2 278	983	983	312
Soybeans for beans .... farms..	18 864	5 874	10 147	2 843	15 037	3 347	9 414	2 276
acres..	1 878 978	307 530	1 312 620	258 828	1 779 543	246 659	1 291 195	241 789
bushels..	55 789 994	8 879 599	39 150 833	7 759 462	53 527 794	7 449 343	38 689 523	7 388 928
Irrigated .... farms..	1 939	284	1 279	376	1 886	248	1 269	369
acres..	175 053	20 711	121 581	32 761	173 634	19 947	121 269	32 598
Farms by acres harvested:								
1 to 24 acres	5 008	2 349	1 910	749	2 769	790	1 522	457
25 to 99 acres	8 253	2 750	4 236	1 265	6 713	1 803	3 907	1 003
100 to 249 acres	3 775	642	2 528	605	3 727	621	2 514	582
250 to 499 acres	1 315	102	1 040	173	1 315	102	1 040	173
500 acres or more	513	31	431	51	513	31	431	51
Dry edible beans, excluding dry limas ...... farms..	192	30	129	33	189	30	128	31
acres..	30 460	5 599	18 715	5 146	30 365	5 599	(D)	(D)
cwt..	441 316	103 292	264 587	73 639	440 367	103 292	(D)	(D)
Irrigated .... farms..	167	26	113	28	166	26	113	27
acres..	28 182	6 432	16 884	4 866	(D)	6 432	16 884	(D)
Irish potatoes .... farms..	97	39	47	11	75	23	43	9
acres..	643	52	313	278	623	(D)	312	(D)
cwt..	136 764	7 404	52 036	79 324	136 796	(D)	51 626	(D)
Irrigated .... farms..	21	6	9	3	15	6	6	3
acres..	(D)	(D)	273	260	(D)	16	(D)	2
Hay—alfalfa, other tame, small grain, wild, grass silage, green chop, etc. (see text) .. farms..	33 964	12 364	17 477	4 123	24 304	5 615	15 411	3 278
acres..	2 254 082	531 755	1 459 164	263 163	1 990 641	362 943	1 388 751	238 947
tons, dry..	5 080 647	1 124 326	3 311 724	644 797	4 689 290	870 301	3 210 222	608 767
Irrigated .... farms..	1 642	324	922	394	1 404	262	907	235
acres..	206 961	51 566	116 374	39 021	205 220	50 228	116 090	38 902
Farms by acres harvested:								
1 to 24 acres	11 391	6 049	3 932	1 410	5 491	1 711	2 879	901
25 to 99 acres	16 111	5 255	8 835	2 021	12 641	2 982	7 944	1 715
100 to 249 acres	5 297	889	3 819	589	5 015	810	3 700	559
250 to 499 acres	913	127	705	81	906	123	702	81
500 acres or more	252	44	186	22	251	43	186	22

See footnotes at end of table.

Table 48. **Summary by Tenure of Operator: 1987**—Con.

[For meaning of abbreviations and symbols, see introductory text]

Item	All farms				Farms with sales of $10,000 or more			
	Total	Full owners	Part owners	Tenants	Total	Full owners	Part owners	Tenants
CROPS HARVESTED—Con.								
Hay—alfalfa, other tame, small grain, wild, grass silage, green chop, etc. (see text) —Con.								
Alfalfa hay .... farms..	15 484	4 550	9 007	1 927	12 700	2 679	8 364	1 657
acres..	741 856	168 536	470 920	102 400	698 959	139 394	459 916	97 649
tons, dry..	2 529 635	559 028	1 603 367	367 240	2 433 646	495 667	1 580 644	357 135
Irrigated .... farms..	1 174	246	737	191	1 121	213	726	182
acres..	180 952	45 157	100 805	34 990	179 852	44 375	100 606	34 871
Vegetables harvested for sale (see text) ... farms..	418	217	144	57	223	75	118	30
acres..	5 424	1 515	3 297	613	4 738	1 026	3 205	506
Irrigated .... farms..	166	83	55	28	92	34	43	15
acres..	1 851	581	922	347	1 594	410	885	299
Farms by acres harvested:								
0.1 to 4.9 acres	244	140	75	29	104	36	56	12
5.0 to 24.9 acres	130	62	48	20	78	25	41	10
25.0 to 99.9 acres	39	14	17	8	38	13	17	8
100.0 to 249.9 acres	4	1	3	–	4	1	3	–
250.0 acres or more	1	–	1	–	1	–	1	–
Field seed and grass seed crops .... farms..	1 188	362	710	116	1 013	224	685	104
acres..	58 480	11 605	40 910	5 945	54 702	8 604	40 472	5 626
Irrigated .... farms..	12	5	6	1	10	3	6	1
acres..	2 222	(D)	1 672	(D)	(D)	(D)	1 672	(D)
Land in orchards .... farms..	503	343	127	33	182	76	86	20
acres..	5 999	3 374	2 360	265	3 940	1 869	1 946	125
Irrigated .... farms..	90	59	20	11	34	13	14	7
acres..	757	356	316	85	386	84	274	29
Farms by bearing and nonbearing acres:								
0.1 to 4.9 acres	309	221	69	19	97	44	40	13
5.0 to 24.9 acres	147	98	36	11	52	17	29	6
25.0 to 99.9 acres	39	21	15	3	26	12	13	1
100.0 to 249.9 acres	6	2	4	–	5	2	3	–
250.0 acres or more	2	1	1	–	2	1	1	–

¹Data are based on a sample of farms.
²Farms with total production expenses equal to market value of agricultural products sold are included as farms with gains of less than $1,000.

Table 49. **Summary by Type of Organization: 1987**

[For meaning of abbreviations and symbols, see introductory text]

Item	Total	Individual or family	Partnership	Corporation Family held Total	Corporation Family held 10 or less stock-holders	Corporation Other than family held Total	Corporation Other than family held 10 or less stock-holders	Other— cooperative, estate or trust, institutional, etc.
FARMS AND LAND IN FARMS								
Farms _____ number..	68 579	60 202	5 889	2 100	1 942	1 919	158	141	388
_____ percent..	100.0	87.8	8.6	3.1	2.8	2.8	.2	.2	.6
Land in farms _____ acres..	46 628 519	36 420 471	6 151 580	3 606 121	3 446 745	3 406 656	159 376	154 077	450 347
Average size of farm _____ acres..	680	605	1 045	1 717	1 775	1 775	1 009	1 093	1 161
MARKET VALUE OF AGRICUL- TURAL PRODUCTS SOLD								
Total sales (see text) _____ farms..	68 579	60 202	5 889	2 100	1 942	1 919	158	141	388
_____ $1,000..	6 476 669	2 860 402	743 863	2 814 605	1 968 512	1 722 933	846 093	783 752	37 799
Average per farm _____ dollars..	94 441	47 846	126 314	1 340 288	1 013 652	897 829	5 355 019	5 558 524	97 419
Farms by value of sales:								
Less than $1,000 (see text) _____	4 538	4 219	221	51	44	44	7	4	47
$1,000 to $2,499 _____	4 964	4 650	250	39	30	30	9	6	25
$2,500 to $4,999 _____	6 619	6 364	458	41	38	38	3	3	56
$5,000 to $9,999 _____	9 430	8 642	651	89	72	71	17	14	46
$10,000 to $19,999 _____	10 504	9 537	614	105	95	93	10	8	46
$20,000 to $24,999 _____	3 566	3 230	268	47	42	42	5	5	21
$25,000 to $39,999 _____	7 150	6 365	626	113	111	110	2	2	46
$40,000 to $49,999 _____	3 132	2 791	246	94	87	87	7	7	11
$50,000 to $99,999 _____	8 997	7 766	851	343	331	329	12	12	37
$100,000 to $249,999 _____	6 656	5 154	937	529	500	494	29	28	26
$250,000 to $499,999 _____	1 766	1 068	372	313	298	295	15	15	13
$500,000 to $999,999 _____	568	284	127	154	143	142	11	10	3
$1,000,000 or more _____	366	132	68	162	151	144	31	27	7
Grains _____ farms..	48 606	42 180	4 552	1 616	1 537	1 525	81	71	256
_____ $1,000..	1 550 403	1 174 422	221 603	146 370	141 984	141 230	4 386	4 266	8 008
Sales of $50,000 or more _____ farms..	8 994	6 775	1 246	929	898	892	31	30	44
_____ $1,000..	976 864	669 904	170 468	131 211	127 564	126 948	3 647	(D)	5 281
Corn for grain _____ farms..	7 426	5 901	908	564	536	532	28	28	53
_____ $1,000..	255 791	166 222	49 869	38 387	37 252	37 063	1 136	1 136	1 312
Wheat _____ farms..	38 365	33 047	3 678	1 440	1 379	1 368	61	55	200
_____ $1,000..	694 147	542 465	89 939	57 308	55 682	55 922	1 626	1 631	4 406
Soybeans _____ farms..	18 724	16 170	1 876	607	575	570	32	31	71
_____ $1,000..	263 742	203 979	36 140	22 773	21 857	21 699	916	(D)	850
Sorghum for grain _____ farms..	28 719	24 840	2 776	967	930	924	37	31	136
_____ $1,000..	311 649	244 044	41 575	24 862	24 212	24 165	650	633	1 168
Barley _____ farms..	1 715	1 389	190	120	119	119	1	1	16
_____ $1,000..	3 953	2 899	620	342	(D)	(D)	(D)	(D)	92
Oats _____ farms..	2 416	2 100	247	56	54	54	2	2	13
_____ $1,000..	3 328	2 742	396	172	(D)	(D)	(D)	(D)	19
Other grains _____ farms..	1 656	1 334	184	124	121	120	3	3	14
_____ $1,000..	17 793	12 070	3 063	2 527	2 473	(D)	54	54	132
Cotton and cottonseed _____ farms..	10	8	2	-	-	-	-	-	-
_____ $1,000..	166	(D)	(D)	-	-	-	-	-	-
Sales of $50,000 or more _____ farms..	2	1	1	-	-	-	-	-	-
_____ $1,000..	(D)	(D)	(D)	-	-	-	-	-	-
Tobacco _____ farms..	13	12	1	-	-	-	-	-	-
_____ $1,000..	80	(D)	(D)	-	-	-	-	-	-
Sales of $50,000 or more _____ farms..	-	-	-	-	-	-	-	-	-
_____ $1,000..	-	-	-	-	-	-	-	-	-
Hay, silage, and field seeds _____ farms..	12 801	11 099	1 151	491	484	461	27	27	60
_____ $1,000..	109 574	72 325	21 997	14 839	12 644	12 962	2 195	2 195	414
Sales of $50,000 or more _____ farms..	316	181	70	65	54	53	9	9	2
_____ $1,000..	47 030	22 651	14 421	(D)	7 800	(D)	(D)	(D)	(D)
Vegetables, sweet corn, and melons ____ farms..	418	358	37	17	17	17	-	-	6
_____ $1,000..	4 151	2 671	518	906	906	906	-	-	56
Sales of $50,000 or more _____ farms..	10	8	1	1	1	1	-	-	-
_____ $1,000..	1 767	(D)	(D)	(D)	(D)	(D)	-	-	-
Fruits, nuts, and berries _____ farms..	278	232	26	15	14	14	1	1	5
_____ $1,000..	1 693	1 053	132	483	(D)	(D)	(D)	(D)	26
Sales of $50,000 or more _____ farms..	6	3	-	3	2	2	1	1	-
_____ $1,000..	732	288	-	444	(D)	(D)	(D)	(D)	-
Nursery and greenhouse crops _____ farms..	272	196	19	54	50	49	4	4	3
_____ $1,000..	26 805	6 022	834	19 821	18 751	(D)	1 070	1 070	128
Sales of $50,000 or more _____ farms..	62	22	5	34	31	31	3	3	1
_____ $1,000..	24 509	4 224	(D)	19 532	(D)	(D)	(D)	(D)	(D)
Other crops _____ farms..	80	61	10	3	3	3	-	-	3
_____ $1,000..	716	457	254	2	2	2	-	-	3
Sales of $50,000 or more _____ farms..	3	2	1	-	-	-	-	-	-
_____ $1,000..	558	(D)	(D)	-	-	-	-	-	-
Poultry and poultry products _____ farms..	1 550	1 398	109	36	31	29	5	5	7
_____ $1,000..	25 284	13 332	1 588	10 327	9 019	(D)	1 308	1 308	38
Sales of $50,000 or more _____ farms..	75	54	6	16	13	11	2	2	-
_____ $1,000..	23 851	12 046	1 494	10 309	(D)	6 028	(D)	(D)	-
Dairy products _____ farms..	2 004	1 604	312	81	75	73	6	6	7
_____ $1,000..	140 232	92 321	32 709	14 239	13 582	(D)	658	658	963
Sales of $50,000 or more _____ farms..	488	339	93	72	57	65	5	5	5
_____ $1,000..	119 516	74 295	30 277	(D)	13 423	(D)	5	5	(D)
Cattle and calves _____ farms..	41 498	36 503	3 593	1 228	1 140	1 125	88	82	174
_____ $1,000..	4 305 335	1 318 694	415 503	2 544 686	1 712 719	1 471 950	831 967	769 760	26 452
Sales of $50,000 or more _____ farms..	5 932	4 309	882	702	645	635	57	51	39
_____ $1,000..	3 891 456	954 060	377 623	2 535 024	1 703 475	1 462 149	831 549	769 342	24 748

See footnotes at end of table.

Table 49. **Summary by Type of Organization: 1987**—Con.

[For meaning of abbreviations and symbols, see introductory text]

Item	Total	Individual or family	Partnership	Corporation Total	Family held Total	Family held 10 or less stockholders	Other than family held Total	Other than family held 10 or less stockholders	Other— cooperative, estate or trust, institutional, etc.
MARKET VALUE OF AGRICULTURAL PRODUCTS SOLD—Con.									
Total sales (see text)—Con.									
Hogs and pigs .... farms..	7 090	6 143	732	191	179	179	12	11	24
$1,000..	284 375	180 435	46 289	56 136	51 704	51 704	4 432	(D)	1 515
Sales of $50,000 or more .... farms..	1 278	946	196	128	119	119	9	9	8
$1,000..	213 369	118 203	38 691	55 065	(D)	(D)	(D)	(D)	1 410
Sheep, lambs, and wool .... farms..	2 456	2 217	185	44	43	43	1	-	10
$1,000..	18 561	11 619	1 304	5 478	(D)	(D)	(D)	-	159
Sales of $50,000 or more .... farms..	44	30	4	9	9	9	-	-	1
$1,000..	9 169	3 696	(D)	5 214	5 214	5 214	-	-	(D)
Other livestock and livestock products (see text) .... farms..	2 869	2 598	197	60	54	53	6	5	14
$1,000..	9 273	6 865	1 054	1 318	(D)	(D)	(D)	(D)	37
Sales of $50,000 or more .... farms..	21	15	3	3	3	3	-	-	-
$1,000..	3 649	1 760	743	1 146	1 146	1 146	-	-	-
FARM PRODUCTION EXPENSES[1]									
Total farm production expenses .... farms..	68 580	60 156	5 911	2 061	1 905	1 873	156	136	452
$1,000..	5 516 518	2 351 601	602 017	2 527 998	1 773 121	1 555 132	754 876	697 717	34 902
Average per farm .... dollars..	80 439	39 092	101 847	1 226 588	930 772	830 290	4 838 952	5 130 275	77 217
Livestock and poultry purchased .... farms..	23 380	20 146	2 246	874	815	805	59	53	114
$1,000..	2 426 149	565 833	229 291	1 616 836	1 106 851	947 192	509 985	471 119	14 188
Farms with expenses of—									
$1 to $4,999	11 923	10 844	902	105	104	103	1	1	72
$5,000 to $24,999	6 470	5 611	658	189	185	185	4	4	12
$25,000 to $99,999	3 307	2 676	422	192	184	184	8	8	17
$100,000 or more	1 680	1 015	264	388	342	333	46	40	13
Feed for livestock and poultry .... farms..	38 347	33 839	3 230	1 139	1 066	1 052	73	60	139
$1,000..	887 270	260 758	85 761	535 768	351 177	310 557	184 591	171 365	4 962
Farms with expenses of—									
$1 to $4,999	28 326	25 941	1 978	311	299	297	12	5	98
$5,000 to $24,999	7 351	6 151	805	374	363	360	11	10	21
$25,000 to $99,999	2 028	1 470	327	223	211	209	12	12	8
$100,000 or more	640	277	120	231	193	186	38	33	12
Commercially mixed formula feeds ...... farms..	14 988	13 003	1 345	576	534	523	42	30	64
$1,000..	163 561	66 897	19 300	76 247	56 499	53 301	19 746	17 147	1 117
Farms with expenses of—									
$1 to $4,999	11 327	10 228	871	189	180	179	9	2	39
$5,000 to $24,999	2 854	2 333	315	190	180	176	10	8	16
$25,000 to $79,999	577	352	117	103	102	101	1	1	5
$80,000 or more	230	90	42	94	72	67	22	19	4
Seeds, bulbs, plants, and trees .... farms..	46 233	41 794	4 506	1 631	1 551	1 528	80	72	302
$1,000..	95 302	70 579	13 179	11 073	10 649	10 571	424	(D)	470
Farms with expenses of—									
$1 to $999	28 247	25 307	2 311	402	367	364	35	28	227
$1,000 to $4,999	15 265	13 101	1 493	614	589	572	25	25	57
$5,000 to $24,999	4 473	3 261	641	554	537	534	17	16	17
$25,000 or more	248	125	61	61	58	58	3	3	1
Commercial fertilizer .... farms..	47 731	41 469	4 443	1 566	1 484	1 471	72	63	253
$1,000..	216 166	163 930	30 660	20 509	19 788	19 451	721	686	1 068
Farms with expenses of—									
$1 to $4,999	34 889	31 334	2 827	531	501	491	30	22	197
$5,000 to $24,999	11 740	9 508	1 354	825	789	779	36	35	53
$25,000 to $49,999	884	526	195	162	157	155	5	5	1
$50,000 or more	218	101	67	48	47	46	1	1	2
Agricultural chemicals .... farms..	46 318	40 123	4 314	1 586	1 511	1 492	75	60	295
$1,000..	125 003	93 887	17 843	12 667	12 176	12 053	491	465	606
Farms with expenses of—									
$1 to $4,999	39 456	35 004	3 350	845	800	786	45	31	257
$5,000 to $24,999	6 478	4 922	877	640	616	613	24	23	37
$25,000 to $49,999	322	173	66	82	76	74	6	6	1
$50,000 or more	64	24	21	19	19	19	-	-	-
Petroleum products .... farms..	65 460	57 351	5 728	1 978	1 831	1 800	147	134	403
$1,000..	243 586	178 353	33 195	30 511	25 896	24 394	4 615	4 270	1 509
Farms with expenses of—									
$1 to $4,999	51 841	46 929	3 842	731	676	665	55	47	339
$5,000 to $24,999	12 652	9 966	1 885	942	864	870	58	57	59
$25,000 to $49,999	760	397	142	217	203	202	14	12	4
$50,000 or more	207	59	59	88	68	63	20	18	1
Gasoline and gasohol .... farms..	57 245	50 054	5 052	1 714	1 579	1 555	135	122	359
$1,000..	80 737	62 380	9 629	8 156	6 981	6 221	1 175	1 123	572
Diesel fuel .... farms..	48 376	39 954	4 489	1 664	1 553	1 532	111	100	269
$1,000..	110 981	82 233	15 217	12 831	10 998	10 745	1 834	1 734	700
Natural gas .... farms..	4 956	3 929	520	461	426	413	35	34	46
$1,000..	26 371	14 465	5 240	6 551	5 563	5 192	988	(D)	115
LP gas, fuel oil, kerosene, motor oil, grease, etc. .... farms..	52 549	45 670	4 779	1 768	1 644	1 619	124	114	332
$1,000..	25 478	19 274	3 109	2 972	2 353	2 236	619	(D)	123

See footnotes at end of table.

Table 49. Summary by Type of Organization: 1987—Con.

[For meaning of abbreviations and symbols, see introductory text]

Item	Total	Individual or family	Partnership	Corporation — Total	Family held — Total	Family held — 10 or less stockholders	Other than family held — Total	Other than family held — 10 or less stockholders	Other—cooperative, estate or trust, institutional, etc.
FARM PRODUCTION EXPENSES[1] —Con.									
Total farm production expenses—Con.									
Electricity ...... farms..	46 797	42 488	4 301	1 743	1 634	1 610	109	100	265
$1,000..	54 103	34 492	6 963	12 353	9 533	8 750	2 820	2 599	296
Farms with expenses of—									
$1 to $999	36 660	33 169	2 838	648	626	621	22	18	205
$1,000 to $4,999	10 565	8 597	1 197	726	693	682	33	32	45
$5,000 to $24,999	1 236	693	245	285	256	254	29	28	13
$25,000 or more	136	29	21	84	59	53	25	22	2
Hired farm labor ...... farms..	24 715	20 882	2 242	1 442	1 347	1 325	95	85	149
$1,000..	226 075	97 270	29 079	95 970	76 959	71 363	19 011	17 492	3 756
Farms with expenses of—									
$1 to $4,999	18 529	16 715	1 389	348	338	336	10	7	77
$5,000 to $24,999	4 529	3 413	560	491	454	443	37	35	45
$25,000 to $99,999	1 391	689	226	456	442	440	14	13	20
$100,000 or more	266	65	47	147	113	106	34	30	7
Contract labor ...... farms..	7 662	6 705	729	428	402	396	26	25	20
$1,000..	23 691	15 452	2 747	5 407	4 713	3 623	694	(D)	84
Farms with expenses of—									
$1 to $999	3 892	3 563	251	74	74	73	–	–	4
$1,000 to $4,999	2 895	2 364	333	171	161	160	10	10	7
$5,000 to $24,999	1 023	723	131	160	149	148	11	10	9
$25,000 or more	72	35	14	23	18	15	5	5	–
Repair and maintenance ...... farms..	56 961	49 894	4 917	1 853	1 712	1 682	141	123	297
$1,000..	252 018	180 278	32 467	37 814	31 167	28 527	6 447	6 180	1 668
Farms with expenses of—									
$1 to $4,999	42 384	36 388	3 057	695	629	627	66	54	244
$5,000 to $24,999	13 477	10 968	1 627	837	797	777	40	36	45
$25,000 to $49,999	844	465	173	201	189	186	12	11	5
$50,000 or more	256	73	60	120	97	92	23	22	3
Customwork, machine hire, and rental of machinery and equipment ...... farms..	30 603	26 606	2 627	1 182	1 119	1 094	63	58	188
$1,000..	107 366	79 091	14 353	12 724	10 932	10 414	1 793	1 729	1 100
Farms with expenses of—									
$1 to $999	13 296	12 166	941	118	116	113	2	1	73
$1,000 to $4,999	11 636	10 205	1 096	471	440	438	31	29	64
$5,000 to $24,999	4 982	3 939	509	489	470	453	19	18	45
$25,000 or more	487	296	81	104	93	90	11	10	6
Interest expense ...... farms..	39 549	34 690	3 315	1 437	1 341	1 318	96	83	107
$1,000..	314 163	237 870	36 896	38 093	32 692	32 242	5 401	5 151	1 304
Farms with expenses of—									
$1 to $4,999	24 133	21 789	1 819	464	438	429	26	19	61
$5,000 to $24,999	12 676	10 965	1 103	556	521	511	35	33	32
$25,000 to $99,999	2 557	1 842	360	343	320	317	23	20	12
$100,000 or more	183	74	33	74	62	61	12	11	2
Secured by real estate ...... farms..	26 406	23 476	1 915	946	887	867	59	46	69
$1,000..	188 166	150 598	19 208	17 779	16 588	16 382	1 165	1 114	597
Farms with expenses of—									
$1 to $999	5 315	4 844	328	122	112	111	10	3	21
$1,000 to $4,999	10 417	9 507	675	213	195	187	18	17	22
$5,000 to $24,999	9 280	8 151	710	400	380	371	20	18	19
$25,000 or more	1 396	976	202	211	200	198	11	10	7
Not secured by real estate ...... farms..	24 307	21 066	2 231	945	879	875	66	61	65
$1,000..	125 997	87 282	17 688	20 320	16 104	15 860	4 216	4 038	707
Farms with expenses of—									
$1 to $999	8 203	7 535	501	163	154	153	9	9	4
$1,000 to $4,999	8 540	7 409	896	201	192	192	9	8	32
$5,000 to $24,999	6 766	5 675	677	389	361	360	28	26	25
$25,000 or more	798	447	155	192	172	170	20	18	4
Cash rent ...... farms..	21 234	18 250	2 118	788	755	752	33	27	78
$1,000..	123 531	90 324	19 813	13 113	11 864	11 852	1 249	1 230	281
Farms with expenses of—									
$1 to $4,999	14 629	13 006	1 273	283	268	266	15	10	67
$5,000 to $9,999	3 298	2 819	335	141	138	137	3	3	3
$10,000 to $24,999	2 511	1 988	308	210	204	204	6	5	5
$25,000 or more	796	437	202	154	145	145	9	9	3
Property taxes ...... farms..	63 359	55 915	5 110	1 959	1 809	1 778	150	130	375
$1,000..	112 201	69 324	11 671	10 306	9 109	8 806	1 197	1 126	901
Farms with expenses of—									
$1 to $4,999	59 062	52 674	4 492	1 364	1 254	1 233	110	93	332
$5,000 to $9,999	3 248	2 445	437	344	325	320	19	17	22
$10,000 to $24,999	956	557	161	219	204	201	15	14	19
$25,000 or more	93	38	20	32	26	24	6	6	2
All other farm production expenses ...... farms..	64 491	56 614	5 538	1 991	1 845	1 813	146	135	348
$1,000..	309 914	194 161	36 089	75 053	59 615	55 338	15 438	13 215	2 611
Farms with expenses of—									
$1 to $4,999	51 652	46 544	4 047	959	890	880	69	64	302
$5,000 to $24,999	11 071	9 165	1 209	663	630	617	33	32	34
$25,000 to $49,999	1 005	658	173	168	160	158	8	8	6
$50,000 or more	563	247	109	201	165	158	36	31	6

See footnotes at end of table.

Table 49. Summary by Type of Organization: 1987—Con.

[For meaning of abbreviations and symbols, see introductory text]

Item	Total	Individual or family	Partnership	Corporation — Total	Family held — Total	Family held — 10 or less stockholders	Other than family held — Total	Other than family held — 10 or less stockholders	Other—cooperative, estate or trust, institutional, etc.
NET CASH RETURN FROM AGRICULTURAL SALES FOR THE FARM UNIT[1]									
All farms ... number	68 580	60 156	5 911	2 061	1 905	1 873	156	136	452
... $1,000	922 225	513 815	129 004	276 656	184 819	156 219	91 837	86 658	2 750
Average per farm ... dollars	13 447	8 541	21 824	134 234	97 018	83 406	588 697	637 191	6 085
Farms with net gains[2] ... number	41 673	35 733	4 225	1 441	1 325	1 306	116	109	274
Average net gain ... dollars	27 369	19 242	34 395	209 847	158 537	138 529	795 932	798 849	19 267
Gain of—									
Less than $1,000	4 994	4 535	347	54	50	50	4	4	58
$1,000 to $9,999	18 378	16 406	1 551	274	254	252	20	18	147
$10,000 to $49,999	13 889	11 818	1 496	526	498	487	28	28	49
$50,000 or more	4 412	2 974	831	587	523	517	64	59	20
Farms with net losses ... number	26 907	24 423	1 686	620	580	567	40	27	178
Average net loss ... dollars	8 114	7 114	9 677	41 505	43 520	43 563	12 284	15 426	14 206
Loss of—									
Less than $1,000	5 287	4 848	312	70	54	54	16	15	57
$1,000 to $9,999	16 553	15 265	981	219	204	195	15	4	88
$10,000 to $49,999	4 663	4 024	336	282	276	273	6	5	21
$50,000 or more	404	286	57	49	46	45	3	3	12
GOVERNMENT PAYMENTS AND OTHER FARM-RELATED INCOME									
Government payments ... farms	41 627	35 984	3 990	1 438	1 374	1 362	64	62	215
... $1,000	573 647	440 294	81 097	49 240	47 634	47 287	1 606	(D)	3 016
Other farm-related income[1] ... farms	18 682	16 569	1 424	613	590	574	23	23	76
... $1,000	69 944	57 772	5 597	5 799	5 496	5 163	303	303	776
Customwork and other agricultural services ... farms	7 463	6 573	665	217	203	194	14	14	8
... $1,000	32 115	26 869	3 118	2 120	1 888	1 802	232	232	8
Gross cash rent or share payments ... farms	7 899	7 123	495	241	236	232	3	3	40
... $1,000	30 403	24 971	1 831	2 885	2 680	2 639	5	5	715
Forest products and Christmas trees ... farms	439	384	43	11	10	10	1	1	1
... $1,000	1 087	844	152	(D)	(D)	(D)	(D)	(D)	(D)
Other farm-related income sources ... farms	6 669	5 898	463	275	263	256	12	12	33
... $1,000	6 340	5 088	495	(D)	(D)	(D)	(D)	(D)	(D)
COMMODITY CREDIT CORPORATION LOANS									
Total ... farms	15 832	13 396	1 623	765	736	730	29	29	48
... $1,000	338 298	239 491	55 205	42 914	41 288	40 978	1 626	1 626	688
Corn ... farms	3 591	2 761	463	354	336	333	18	18	13
... $1,000	108 314	66 842	22 489	18 727	18 153	17 914	574	574	256
Wheat ... farms	7 262	6 176	737	346	332	330	14	14	23
... $1,000	96 942	73 316	12 922	9 513	9 146	(D)	366	366	190
Soybeans ... farms	1 246	1 033	145	70	63	61	7	7	–
... $1,000	20 764	14 348	3 365	3 052	2 891	(D)	160	160	–
Sorghum, barley, and oats ... farms	10 032	8 522	1 048	438	429	425	9	9	24
... $1,000	112 774	84 534	16 377	11 622	11 098	11 083	524	524	241
Cotton ... farms	–	–	–	–	–	–	–	–	–
... $1,000	–	–	–	–	–	–	–	–	–
Peanuts, rye, rice, tobacco, and honey ... farms	22	19	3	–	–	–	–	–	–
... $1,000	503	451	52	–	–	–	–	–	–
LAND IN FARMS ACCORDING TO USE									
Total cropland ... farms	61 615	54 066	5 329	1 899	1 780	1 763	119	106	321
... acres	31 385 092	24 690 748	4 004 360	2 319 538	2 240 738	2 216 410	78 800	76 243	170 444
Harvested cropland ... farms	57 822	50 626	5 077	1 819	1 710	1 694	109	96	300
... acres	17 729 394	13 891 648	2 364 889	1 381 699	1 330 347	1 320 807	51 352	49 511	91 158
Farms by acres harvested:									
1 to 49 acres	12 372	11 465	672	164	139	137	25	19	71
50 to 99 acres	8 653	8 046	675	86	73	71	13	11	46
100 to 199 acres	10 361	9 323	841	141	128	128	13	10	56
200 to 499 acres	14 761	12 974	1 334	379	357	353	22	21	74
500 to 999 acres	8 150	6 881	916	515	494	490	21	20	38
1,000 to 1,999 acres	2 676	1 930	499	435	425	421	10	10	12
2,000 acres or more	449	207	140	99	94	94	5	5	3
Cropland:									
Pasture or grazing only ... farms	22 575	19 987	1 891	596	559	555	37	37	101
... acres	3 485 445	2 971 712	351 647	144 756	138 972	138 668	5 788	5 788	17 328
In cover crops, legumes, and soil-improvement grasses, not harvested and not pastured ... farms	11 212	9 763	1 038	354	327	322	27	24	57
... acres	1 103 315	884 502	145 906	66 691	63 776	(D)	2 915	2 590	6 216
On which all crops failed ... farms	3 341	2 892	328	92	83	82	9	9	29
... acres	206 231	169 676	22 331	10 626	(D)	(D)	(D)	(D)	3 596
In cultivated summer fallow ... farms	25 408	21 629	2 427	1 013	961	949	52	47	139
... acres	6 409 506	5 018 398	812 997	537 761	523 416	519 126	14 345	13 962	40 350
Idle ... farms	20 610	17 818	2 028	663	621	618	42	40	101
... acres	2 451 199	1 954 810	306 590	178 003	(D)	(D)	165 163	(D)	11 796
Total woodland ... farms	12 587	11 236	1 015	280	260	257	20	19	56
... acres	718 261	598 731	82 994	34 133	32 258	32 174	1 875	(D)	2 403
Woodland pastured ... farms	6 382	5 744	462	122	116	116	6	6	34
... acres	366 136	303 003	42 622	18 943	18 348	(D)	595	595	1 568
Woodland not pastured ... farms	7 991	7 072	691	198	179	177	19	18	30
... acres	352 125	295 728	40 372	15 190	13 910	(D)	1 280	(D)	635

See footnotes at end of table.

Table 49. **Summary by Type of Organization: 1987**—Con.

[For meaning of abbreviations and symbols, see introductory text]

Item	Total	Individual or family	Partnership	Corporation Family held — Total	Family held — 10 or less stockholders	Other than family held — Total	Other than family held — 10 or less stockholders	Other—cooperative, estate or trust, institutional, etc.
LAND IN FARMS ACCORDING TO USE—Con.								
Pastureland and rangeland other than cropland and woodland pastured ... farms..	32 362	28 484	2 759	979	921	911	58	54	140
acres..	13 254 094	9 887 734	1 936 059	1 162 792	1 094 374	1 080 751	68 418	67 091	267 509
Land in house lots, ponds, roads, wasteland, etc. ... farms..	44 335	39 117	3 619	1 322	1 208	1 191	114	99	277
acres..	1 271 074	1 043 258	128 167	89 658	79 375	77 323	10 283	(D)	9 991
Cropland under federal acreage reduction programs:								
Annual commodity acreage adjustment programs ... farms..	34 658	29 824	3 363	1 312	1 258	1 247	54	52	159
acres..	3 956 196	3 070 787	539 806	324 373	314 882	313 402	9 491	(D)	21 230
Conservation reserve program ... farms..	5 630	4 796	566	238	230	226	6	6	30
acres..	810 862	635 476	111 651	58 610	56 608	56 319	2 202	2 202	4 925
Value of land and buildings[1] ... farms..	68 580	60 156	5 911	2 061	1 905	1 873	156	136	452
$1,000..	19 068 461	14 852 829	2 523 365	1 530 043	1 439 899	1 417 203	90 144	85 210	162 204
Average per farm ... dollars..	278 047	246 905	426 896	742 379	755 852	756 649	577 846	626 544	358 858
Average per acre ... dollars..	413	410	418	441	435	436	571	564	350
Farms by value group:								
$1 to $39,999	10 024	9 103	697	150	136	136	14	12	74
$40,000 to $69,999	9 571	8 870	582	89	78	77	11	10	30
$70,000 to $99,999	7 001	6 436	408	90	68	67	2	1	67
$100,000 to $149,999	6 596	7 722	712	117	96	95	21	11	45
$150,000 to $199,999	6 313	5 665	517	92	80	78	12	11	39
$200,000 to $499,999	16 476	14 391	1 485	483	449	440	34	32	117
$500,000 to $999,999	7 579	6 047	943	534	501	487	33	31	55
$1,000,000 to $1,999,999	2 396	1 593	403	386	364	361	22	21	14
$2,000,000 to $4,999,999	535	288	141	98	91	90	7	7	6
$5,000,000 or more	89	41	23	22	22	22	-	-	3
VALUE OF MACHINERY AND EQUIPMENT[1]								
Estimated market value of all machinery and equipment ... farms..	68 391	59 994	5 896	2 049	1 893	1 861	156	138	452
$1,000..	3 447 663	2 658 256	417 422	347 479	317 916	311 476	29 563	28 112	24 506
Farms by value group:								
$1 to $4,999	5 812	5 341	364	49	47	47	2	2	58
$5,000 to $9,999	11 585	10 684	698	117	109	109	8	8	66
$10,000 to $19,999	11 722	10 686	858	121	106	106	15	7	57
$20,000 to $49,999	16 724	15 012	1 268	349	331	328	18	16	95
$50,000 to $99,999	12 176	10 446	1 263	374	355	346	19	15	93
$100,000 to $199,999	7 277	5 783	964	490	447	435	43	39	40
$200,000 to $499,999	2 860	1 955	428	457	418	412	39	37	20
$500,000 or more	235	87	53	92	80	78	12	12	3
SELECTED MACHINERY AND EQUIPMENT[1]								
Motortrucks, including pickups ... farms..	63 093	55 318	5 438	1 938	1 798	1 767	140	127	399
number..	159 329	132 708	16 871	8 661	7 975	7 789	686	621	1 089
Wheel tractors ... farms..	60 459	52 902	5 257	1 896	1 759	1 727	137	117	404
number..	150 647	127 140	15 812	6 754	6 293	6 172	461	408	1 141
Less than 40 horsepower (PTO) ... farms..	25 210	22 159	2 168	661	623	616	58	46	202
number..	38 591	33 603	3 382	1 227	1 119	1 095	108	92	379
40 horsepower (PTO) or more ... farms..	50 577	43 902	4 630	1 731	1 615	1 583	116	104	314
number..	112 056	93 537	12 230	5 527	5 174	5 077	353	316	762
Grain and bean combines ... farms..	35 608	30 671	3 461	1 252	1 194	1 172	58	50	224
number..	43 801	37 254	4 462	1 770	1 673	1 650	97	82	315
Cottonpickers and strippers ... farms..	1	(D)	-	-	-	-	-	-	-
number..	(D)	(D)	-	-	-	-	-	-	-
Mower conditioners ... farms..	18 793	16 049	1 966	651	607	597	44	39	127
number..	20 167	17 096	2 156	767	700	687	67	59	148
Pickup balers ... farms..	26 083	22 773	2 505	690	639	632	51	49	115
number..	31 892	27 764	3 086	882	820	807	62	(D)	160
AGRICULTURAL CHEMICALS[1]								
Commercial fertilizer ... farms..	47 723	41 461	4 443	1 566	1 494	1 471	72	63	253
acres on which used..	13 652 822	10 813 890	1 877 796	1 089 163	1 052 058	1 036 404	37 105	35 394	72 003
Lime ... farms..	2 685	2 233	335	111	108	108	3	-	6
acres on which used..	154 622	118 313	22 925	12 707	12 607	12 607	100	-	677
tons..	369 024	283 473	51 193	32 810	32 509	32 509	301	-	1 548
Sprays, dusts, granules, fumigants, etc., to control—								
Insects on hay and other crops ... farms..	19 416	16 346	2 028	942	908	893	34	31	100
acres on which used..	3 015 580	2 180 865	480 445	337 895	324 083	321 073	13 812	12 790	16 375
Nematodes in crops ... farms..	716	614	56	43	43	43	-	-	3
acres on which used..	87 904	66 997	9 485	11 385	11 385	11 385	-	-	37
Diseases in crops and orchards ... farms..	1 055	928	70	52	49	49	3	1	5
acres on which used..	125 065	86 386	16 574	20 015	19 944	19 944	71	(D)	90
Weeds, grass, or brush in crops and pasture ... farms..	36 950	31 910	3 542	1 291	1 238	1 221	53	45	207
acres on which used..	8 637 062	6 695 245	1 216 811	682 425	655 471	650 765	26 954	25 444	40 581
Chemicals for defoliation or for growth control of crops or thinning of fruit ... farms..	614	490	69	52	44	44	8	1	3
acres on which used..	66 839	58 366	5 185	5 111	4 930	4 930	181	(D)	155

See footnotes at end of table.

Table 49. Summary by Type of Organization: 1987—Con.

[For meaning of abbreviations and symbols, see introductory text]

Item	Total	Individual or family	Partnership	Corporation Total	Family held — Total	Family held — 10 or less stockholders	Other than family held — Total	Other than family held — 10 or less stockholders	Other—cooperative, estate or trust, institutional, etc.
TENURE AND RACE OF OPERATOR									
All operators	68 579	60 202	5 889	2 100	1 942	1 919	158	141	368
Full owners	29 956	26 808	2 131	765	677	661	88	79	252
Part owners	27 967	24 616	2 336	942	897	893	45	39	73
Tenants	10 656	8 778	1 422	393	368	365	25	23	63
White	68 304	59 960	5 861	2 098	1 940	1 917	158	141	385
Full owners	29 784	26 653	2 117	764	676	660	88	79	250
Part owners	27 901	24 560	2 327	942	897	893	45	39	72
Tenants	10 619	8 747	1 417	392	367	364	25	23	63
Black and other races	275	242	28	2	2	2	–	–	3
Full owners	172	156	14	1	1	1	–	–	2
Part owners	66	56	9	–	–	–	–	–	1
Tenants	37	31	5	1	1	1	–	–	–
OWNED AND RENTED LAND									
Land owned ... farms	58 533	51 981	4 501	1 723	1 590	1 570	133	118	328
acres	24 331 897	19 378 461	2 701 613	1 942 610	1 843 898	1 806 619	98 712	94 207	309 213
Owned land in farms ... farms	57 823	51 424	4 467	1 707	1 574	1 554	133	118	325
acres	21 178 322	16 742 566	2 435 379	1 747 241	1 652 698	1 621 611	94 543	90 038	253 134
Land rented or leased from others ... farms	38 908	33 629	3 789	1 347	1 277	1 270	70	62	143
acres	25 865 815	20 028 228	3 752 871	1 885 654	1 820 281	1 811 381	65 373	(D)	199 062
Rented or leased land in farms ... farms	38 623	33 394	3 758	1 335	1 265	1 258	70	62	136
acres	25 450 197	19 677 903	3 716 201	1 858 880	1 794 047	1 785 147	64 833	64 039	197 213
Land rented or leased to others ... farms	11 944	10 606	887	346	322	314	24	23	105
acres	3 569 193	2 986 218	302 904	222 143	217 434	211 342	4 709	(D)	57 928
OPERATOR CHARACTERISTICS									
Operators by place of residence:									
On farm operated	45 527	40 865	3 318	1 207	1 169	1 158	38	38	137
Not on farm operated	17 871	14 846	2 133	688	577	567	111	94	204
Not reported	5 181	4 491	438	205	196	194	9	9	47
Operators by principal occupation:									
Farming	42 607	36 673	4 048	1 654	1 567	1 552	87	83	232
Other	25 972	23 529	1 841	446	375	367	71	58	156
Operators by days of work off farm:									
None	29 462	25 204	2 794	1 299	1 219	1 206	80	73	165
Any	34 654	31 125	2 677	671	596	587	75	66	181
1 to 99 days	7 620	6 655	707	213	198	196	15	14	45
100 to 199 days	5 357	4 787	427	113	96	95	17	16	30
200 days or more	21 677	19 683	1 543	345	302	296	43	36	106
Not reported	4 463	3 873	418	130	127	126	3	2	42
Operators by years on present farm:									
2 years or less	3 511	3 014	345	120	105	103	15	11	32
3 or 4 years	3 873	3 341	407	96	83	82	13	12	29
5 to 9 years	8 552	7 446	828	215	185	184	30	25	63
10 years or more	40 624	36 007	3 191	1 278	1 206	1 191	72	66	148
Average years on present farm	21.3	21.4	20.6	21.2	21.8	21.7	14.3	15.2	15.7
Not reported	12 019	10 394	1 118	391	363	359	28	27	116
Operators by age group:									
Under 25 years	1 712	1 511	178	17	17	17	–	–	6
25 to 34 years	9 531	8 356	939	200	179	179	21	18	36
35 to 44 years	12 471	10 894	1 064	430	398	393	32	29	83
45 to 49 years	5 926	5 269	409	207	190	189	17	15	41
50 to 54 years	6 781	5 970	517	258	231	229	27	22	36
55 to 59 years	7 581	6 546	684	297	277	274	20	19	52
60 to 64 years	8 407	7 380	703	279	262	258	17	15	45
65 to 69 years	6 564	5 777	577	172	163	162	9	8	38
70 years and over	9 606	8 497	818	240	225	216	15	15	51
Average age	52.0	52.0	51.3	52.4	52.6	52.5	50.6	50.9	52.7
Operators by sex:									
Male	65 619	57 573	5 663	2 032	1 882	1 859	150	133	351
Female	2 960	2 629	226	68	60	60	8	8	37
Operators of Spanish origin (see text)	108	89	15	3	3	3	–	–	1
FARMS BY TYPE OF ORGANIZATION									
Individual or family (sole proprietorship) ... farms	60 202	60 202	–	–	–	–	–	–	–
acres	36 420 471	36 420 471	–	–	–	–	–	–	–
Partnership ... farms	5 889	–	5 889	–	–	–	–	–	–
acres	6 151 580	–	6 151 580	–	–	–	–	–	–
Corporation:									
Family held ... farms	1 942	–	–	–	1 942	1 919	–	–	–
acres	3 446 745	–	–	–	3 446 745	3 406 658	–	–	–
More than 10 stockholders ... farms	23	–	–	–	23	–	–	–	–
10 or less stockholders ... farms	1 919	–	–	–	1 919	1 919	–	–	–
Other than family held ... farms	158	–	–	–	–	–	158	141	–
acres	159 376	–	–	–	–	–	159 376	154 077	–
More than 10 stockholders ... farms	17	–	–	–	–	–	17	–	–
10 or less stockholders ... farms	141	–	–	–	–	–	141	141	–
Other—cooperative, estate or trust, institutional, etc. ... farms	388	–	–	–	–	–	–	–	388
acres	450 347	–	–	–	–	–	–	–	450 347

See footnotes at end of table.

Table 49. **Summary by Type of Organization: 1987**—Con.

[For meaning of abbreviations and symbols, see introductory text]

Item	Total	Individual or family	Partnership	Corporation Total	Family held Total	Family held 10 or less stockholders	Other than family held Total	Other than family held 10 or less stockholders	Other—cooperative, estate or trust, institutional, etc.
FARMS BY SIZE									
1 to 9 acres	3 689	3 186	352	113	104	104	9	8	38
10 to 49 acres	6 222	5 803	285	88	74	73	15	11	46
50 to 69 acres	1 849	1 727	98	20	17	17	3	3	4
70 to 99 acres	4 690	4 367	263	40	34	33	6	4	20
100 to 139 acres	3 117	2 810	247	37	31	31	6	6	23
140 to 179 acres	5 854	5 349	407	59	50	48	9	8	39
180 to 219 acres	2 307	2 104	153	38	31	30	7	6	12
220 to 259 acres	2 845	2 572	220	35	32	32	3	1	18
260 to 499 acres	11 553	10 348	973	186	149	145	37	32	46
500 to 999 acres	12 093	10 696	1 027	314	289	286	25	25	56
1,000 to 1,999 acres	9 304	7 706	1 010	545	533	527	12	12	43
2,000 acres or more	5 056	3 536	854	624	598	593	26	25	42
FARMS BY STANDARD INDUSTRIAL CLASSIFICATION									
Cash grains (011)	31 769	27 794	2 841	976	921	914	55	46	178
Field crops, except cash grains (013)	2 010	1 809	140	55	47	46	8	6	6
Cotton (0131)	1	-	1	-	-	-	-	-	-
Tobacco (0132)	3	3	-	-	-	-	-	-	-
Sugarcane and sugar beets; Irish potatoes; field crops, except cash grains, n.e.c. (0133, 0134, 0139)	2 006	1 806	139	55	47	46	8	8	6
Vegetables and melons (016)	179	159	13	5	5	5	-	-	2
Fruits and tree nuts (017)	171	149	13	7	7	7	-	-	2
Horticultural specialties (018)	224	158	15	51	47	47	4	4	-
General farms, primarily crop (019)	1 463	1 309	113	30	29	29	1	-	11
Livestock, except dairy, poultry, and animal specialties (021)	29 037	25 645	2 379	853	772	761	81	75	160
Beef cattle, except feedlots (0212)	21 861	19 611	1 664	475	434	430	41	39	121
Dairy farms (024)	1 391	1 085	248	55	53	51	2	2	3
Poultry and eggs (025)	197	174	9	13	11	9	2	2	1
Animal specialties (027)	1 452	1 357	61	22	21	21	1	-	12
General farms, primarily livestock and animal specialties (029)	666	563	57	33	29	29	4	4	13
LIVESTOCK									
Cattle and calves inventory .... farms	40 785	35 931	3 499	1 183	1 098	1 063	85	79	172
number	5 539 292	3 193 177	632 453	1 674 304	1 168 450	1 070 096	505 854	480 826	39 358
Farms with—									
1 to 9	4 367	4 093	220	35	31	31	4	4	19
10 to 49	16 841	15 488	1 134	162	144	143	18	18	57
50 to 99	8 529	7 693	651	150	145	145	4	4	36
100 to 199	6 150	5 215	705	203	196	196	6	6	27
200 to 499	3 580	2 724	534	304	289	286	15	14	18
500 or more	1 318	719	255	329	290	282	39	34	15
Cows and heifers that had calved ...... farms	33 157	29 453	2 810	760	726	716	34	34	134
number	1 451 324	1 157 476	183 969	99 832	95 010	93 020	4 822	4 622	10 227
Beef cows .... farms	31 475	28 069	2 578	700	667	659	33	33	128
number	1 354 649	1 090 337	163 516	91 279	67 074	85 222	4 205	4 205	9 515
Farms with—									
1 to 9	6 299	5 833	386	60	55	54	5	5	20
10 to 49	17 123	15 822	1 219	220	208	206	12	12	62
50 to 99	5 108	4 408	523	153	148	148	5	5	24
100 to 199	2 115	1 679	279	145	141	139	4	4	12
200 to 499	714	469	145	92	87	87	5	5	8
500 or more	116	58	26	30	28	25	2	2	2
Milk cows .... farms	3 093	2 591	395	93	87	83	6	6	14
number	96 675	67 139	20 471	8 353	7 936	7 798	417	417	712
Farms with—									
1 to 4	1 195	1 093	62	13	12	10	1	1	7
5 to 9	180	128	20	2	2	2	-	-	-
10 to 49	979	853	111	13	13	13	-	-	2
50 to 99	582	425	126	29	25	23	4	4	2
100 to 199	163	82	49	30	29	29	1	1	2
200 to 499	21	8	8	6	6	6	-	-	1
500 or more	3	2	1	-	-	-	-	-	-
Heifers and heifer calves .... farms	31 410	27 539	2 747	906	837	824	69	64	118
number	1 632 193	874 756	173 781	569 341	386 946	363 158	179 396	183 139	14 315
Steers, steer calves, bulls, and bull calves .... farms	35 035	30 822	3 056	1 012	935	922	77	71	145
number	2 455 775	1 160 945	274 683	1 005 331	683 494	619 918	321 837	293 065	14 816
Cattle and calves sold .... farms	41 498	36 503	3 593	1 228	1 140	1 125	88	82	174
number	7 310 336	2 692 922	726 045	3 840 025	2 562 272	2 218 031	1 277 753	1 179 571	51 346
$1,000	4 305 335	1 316 894	415 503	2 544 686	1 712 719	1 471 350	831 967	769 760	26 452
Calves .... farms	18 518	16 629	1 478	338	318	315	20	20	75
number	468 325	391 758	47 427	24 351	24 351	24 283	1 656	1 656	3 136
$1,000	145 961	121 595	15 079	8 205	7 623	7 614	581	581	1 082
Cattle .... farms	34 216	29 910	3 054	1 105	1 028	1 013	77	71	147
number	6 842 010	2 301 164	678 618	3 814 018	2 537 921	2 193 748	1 276 097	1 177 915	48 210
$1,000	4 159 374	1 197 099	400 424	2 536 482	1 705 096	1 463 736	831 386	769 179	25 370
Fattened on grain and concentrates ... farms	4 620	3 704	524	364	328	317	39	34	28
number	4 551 726	679 417	333 303	3 530 967	2 296 169	1 952 763	1 234 798	1 143 118	8 039
$1,000	3 041 522	415 036	225 675	2 395 178	1 579 895	1 338 904	816 283	757 254	4 632

See footnotes at end of table.

Table 49. **Summary by Type of Organization: 1987**—Con.

[For meaning of abbreviations and symbols, see introductory text]

Item	Total	Individual or family	Partnership	Corporation Total	Family held Total	Family held 10 or less stockholders	Other than family held Total	Other than family held 10 or less stockholders	Other—cooperative, estate or trust, institutional, etc.
LIVESTOCK—Con.									
Hogs and pigs inventory......farms..	6 768	5 859	699	185	173	172	12	11	25
number..	1 516 878	974 119	245 784	288 503	268 883	(D)	19 620	(D)	8 472
Farms with—									
1 to 24	1 916	1 745	148	15	13	12	2	1	8
25 to 49	828	748	71	7	7	7	–	–	2
50 to 99	1 067	966	103	14	14	14	–	–	4
100 to 199	1 092	958	114	18	18	18	–	–	2
200 to 499	1 226	1 048	141	34	31	31	3	3	3
500 or more	619	394	122	97	90	90	7	7	6
Used or to be used for breeding ......farms..	4 596	3 984	475	125	118	117	7	7	12
number..	181 079	125 997	28 156	36 168	33 715	(D)	2 453	2 453	758
Other ......farms..	6 286	5 425	658	181	170	169	11	10	22
number..	1 325 799	848 122	217 628	252 335	235 168	(D)	17 167	(D)	7 714
Hogs and pigs sold ......farms..	7 090	6 143	732	191	179	179	12	11	24
number..	2 759 675	1 803 796	441 669	500 322	452 978	452 978	47 344	(D)	13 889
$1,000..	284 375	180 435	46 269	56 136	51 704	51 704	4 432	(D)	1 515
Feeder pigs ......farms..	1 869	1 673	156	36	32	32	4	4	4
number..	514 394	385 283	54 557	73 570	55 676	55 676	17 894	17 894	984
$1,000..	23 029	17 188	2 281	3 522	2 744	2 744	779	779	38
Litters of pigs farrowed between—									
Dec. 1 of preceding year and Nov. 30 ...farms..	4 819	4 188	494	125	118	117	7	7	12
number..	295 974	189 242	46 752	58 768	53 675	(D)	5 093	5 093	1 212
Dec. 1 and May 31 ......farms..	4 455	3 857	470	119	112	112	7	7	9
number..	149 414	96 377	23 489	28 940	26 378	26 378	2 562	2 562	608
June 1 and Nov. 30 ......farms..	4 403	3 804	464	124	117	116	7	7	11
number..	146 560	92 865	23 263	29 828	27 297	(D)	2 531	2 531	604
Sheep and lambs of all ages inventory......farms..	2 400	2 161	184	43	42	42	1	(D)	12
number..	249 303	181 436	28 016	38 174	(D)	(D)	(D)	–	1 677
Ewes 1 year old or older ......farms..	2 195	1 975	171	41	41	41	–	–	8
number..	129 607	105 744	15 923	(D)	(D)	(D)	–	–	(D)
Sheep and lambs sold ......farms..	2 396	2 167	178	44	43	43	1	(D)	9
number..	267 152	151 897	16 842	96 961	(D)	(D)	(D)	–	1 452
Sheep and lambs shorn ......farms..	2 183	1 964	170	41	41	41	–	–	8
number..	218 980	146 497	22 517	48 559	48 559	48 559	–	–	1 407
pounds of wool..	1 510 663	1 048 351	166 153	287 104	287 104	287 104	–	–	9 055
Horses and ponies inventory......farms..	12 879	11 488	956	370	343	338	27	22	65
number..	55 598	48 356	4 559	2 206	1 914	1 864	292	220	477
Horses and ponies sold ......farms..	2 260	2 035	164	50	45	44	5	4	11
number..	8 467	7 569	574	251	232	(D)	19	(D)	73
Goats inventory ......farms..	862	803	46	5	5	5	–	–	8
number..	8 931	7 714	793	206	206	206	–	–	118
Goats sold ......farms..	258	243	13	1	1	1	–	–	1
number..	2 679	2 448	(D)	(D)	(D)	(D)	–	–	(D)
POULTRY									
Chickens 3 months old or older inventory ...farms..	4 206	3 842	291	53	46	46	5	5	20
number..	2 094 610	1 183 405	159 709	744 255	659 066	(D)	85 190	85 190	7 241
Farms with—									
1 to 399	4 117	3 770	285	43	39	39	4	4	19
400 to 3,199	30	29	1	–	–	–	–	–	–
3,200 to 9,999	12	10	–	1	1	1	–	–	1
10,000 to 19,999	18	14	2	2	2	2	–	–	–
20,000 to 49,999	19	15	2	2	2	2	–	–	–
50,000 to 99,999	7	4	1	2	1	1	1	1	–
100,000 or more	3	–	–	3	3	3	–	–	–
Hens and pullets of laying age ......farms..	4 150	3 792	289	51	46	44	5	5	18
number..	1 797 313	1 061 243	130 948	599 243	514 053	(D)	85 190	85 190	5 879
Pullets 3 months old or older not of laying age ......farms..	415	369	35	6	6	6	–	–	5
number..	297 297	122 162	28 761	145 012	145 012	145 012	–	–	1 362
Hens and pullets sold ......farms..	363	326	19	16	14	12	2	2	2
number..	2 380 936	1 206 168	(D)	1 008 693	(D)	631 262	(D)	(D)	(D)
Broilers and other meat-type chickens sold ......farms..	132	125	4	2	2	2	–	–	1
number..	176 061	174 231	250	(D)	(D)	(D)	–	–	(D)
Farms with—									
1 to 1,999	123	118	4	2	2	2	–	–	1
2,000 to 59,999	7	7	–	–	–	–	–	–	–
60,000 to 99,999	2	2	–	–	–	–	–	–	–
100,000 or more	–	–	–	–	–	–	–	–	–
Turkey hens kept for breeding ......farms..	194	173	16	2	1	1	1	1	3
number..	(D)	14 001	60	(D)	(D)	(D)	(D)	(D)	14
Turkeys ......farms..	88	78	7	2	1	1	1	1	1
number..	230 719	173 224	39 061	(D)	(D)	(D)	(D)	(D)	(D)

See footnotes at end of table.

Table 49. **Summary by Type of Organization: 1987**—Con.

[For meaning of abbreviations and symbols, see introductory text]

Item	Total	Individual or family	Partnership	Corporation Family held Total	Family held 10 or less stockholders	Other than family held Total	Other than family held 10 or less stockholders	Other—cooperative, estate or trust, institutional, etc.
CROPS HARVESTED								
Corn for grain or seed .... farms..	8 944	7 158	1 109	619	590	584	29	29	58
acres..	1 243 969	840 452	221 594	175 050	169 126	168 151	5 922	5 922	6 873
bushels..	144 133 581	94 698 627	26 640 571	21 978 145	21 324 921	21 194 851	653 224	653 224	816 238
Irrigated .... farms..	3 647	2 592	509	417	399	394	18	18	29
acres..	816 992	527 160	158 443	126 571	122 163	121 486	4 408	4 408	4 818
Farms by acres harvested:								
1 to 24 acres	1 984	1 763	186	20	20	18	–	–	15
25 to 99 acres	3 279	2 734	389	130	124	123	6	6	26
100 to 249 acres	2 196	1 719	277	192	177	177	15	15	8
250 to 499 acres	1 044	704	148	186	179	176	7	7	6
500 acres or more	441	238	109	91	90	90	1	1	3
Corn for silage or green chop ...... farms..	2 009	1 440	364	191	180	178	11	10	14
acres..	109 230	66 130	22 940	18 089	17 688	(D)	1 401	(D)	1 071
tons, green..	1 669 413	965 027	362 066	325 170	301 507	(D)	23 669	(D)	17 150
Irrigated .... farms..	659	427	132	94	89	87	5	5	6
acres..	53 214	28 927	11 758	11 864	11 083	(D)	761	761	665
Farms by acres harvested:								
1 to 24 acres	769	561	102	32	31	29	1	1	4
25 to 99 acres	944	636	204	96	93	93	6	6	5
100 to 249 acres	207	114	45	44	42	42	2	2	4
250 to 499 acres	43	20	10	12	11	11	1	–	–
500 acres or more	16	9	3	4	3	3	1	1	1
Sorghum for grain or seed .... farms..	32 492	26 071	3 189	1 075	1 034	1 025	41	35	157
acres..	3 399 564	2 689 596	452 312	241 451	235 843	234 827	5 608	5 388	18 205
bushels..	226 045 100	177 665 777	30 995 167	16 229 705	17 801 324	17 726 917	428 381	413 507	954 431
Irrigated .... farms..	3 137	2 432	421	256	247	244	9	8	28
acres..	464 119	330 295	80 923	49 397	47 104	46 942	2 293	(D)	3 504
Farms by acres harvested:								
1 to 24 acres	7 280	6 503	542	93	84	84	9	8	42
25 to 99 acres	14 139	12 495	1 283	288	270	266	18	13	73
100 to 249 acres	7 830	6 651	633	325	316	311	9	9	21
250 to 499 acres	2 503	1 861	379	249	247	247	2	2	14
500 acres or more	740	461	152	120	117	117	3	3	7
Wheat for grain .... farms..	36 638	33 298	3 697	1 441	1 379	1 368	62	56	202
acres..	8 679 588	6 873 954	1 107 398	649 069	630 520	626 097	18 549	17 523	49 167
bushels..	292 999 442	230 050 456	37 537 779	23 726 795	23 075 547	22 917 602	648 746	609 197	1 674 424
Irrigated .... farms..	3 046	2 274	421	330	312	310	17	17	21
acres..	635 524	417 034	128 189	86 582	81 439	(D)	5 143	(D)	3 719
Farms by acres harvested:								
1 to 24 acres	4 230	3 798	47	39	39	8	7	25	
25 to 99 acres	11 451	10 247	955	192	178	174	8	12	57
100 to 249 acres	11 111	9 754	988	306	290	290	16	14	63
250 to 499 acres	7 248	6 139	703	380	367	362	13	13	26
500 acres or more	4 598	3 360	691	516	505	503	11	10	31
Barley for grain............ farms..	2 307	1 875	263	150	149	149	1	1	19
acres..	95 465	70 908	13 768	8 683	(D)	8 655	(D)	(D)	2 106
bushels..	3 639 224	2 656 210	555 662	347 233	(D)	345 733	(D)	(D)	80 119
Irrigated .... farms..	166	108	34	21	21	21	–	–	3
acres..	7 359	4 487	1 254	966	966	966	–	–	672
Oats for grain .... farms..	5 313	4 637	509	141	137	137	4	4	26
acres..	126 091	107 178	13 945	6 213	6 180	6 150	63	63	755
bushels..	4 775 729	3 944 013	540 010	267 654	265 194	265 194	2 460	2 460	24 052
Irrigated .... farms..	48	34	9	5	5	5	–	–	–
acres..	2 276	1 657	428	193	193	193	–	–	–
Soybeans for beans .... farms..	18 664	16 296	1 664	611	579	574	32	31	73
acres..	1 878 978	1 493 072	247 948	132 762	126 630	125 710	6 132	(D)	5 196
bushels..	55 789 994	43 447 268	7 611 338	4 560 266	4 359 213	4 323 463	201 073	(D)	171 102
Irrigated .... farms..	1 939	1 451	278	191	180	178	11	10	19
acres..	175 053	116 019	31 644	24 257	22 629	(D)	1 628	(D)	1 133
Farms by acres harvested:								
1 to 24 acres	5 008	4 496	417	72	69	69	3	3	23
25 to 99 acres	8 253	7 256	776	192	183	181	9	8	29
100 to 249 acres	3 775	3 176	413	164	152	150	12	12	20
250 to 499 acres	1 315	1 017	161	116	111	111	5	5	1
500 acres or more	513	349	97	67	64	63	3	3	–
Dry edible beans, excluding dry limas ...... farms..	192	139	25	27	26	26	1	1	1
acres..	30 460	19 804	6 406	(D)	(D)	4 170	(D)	(D)	(D)
cwt..	441 318	272 652	96 905	(D)	(D)	71 026	(D)	(D)	(D)
Irrigated .... farms..	167	117	22	27	26	26	1	1	1
acres..	28 182	17 961	5 971	(D)	(D)	4 170	(D)	(D)	(D)
Irish potatoes .... farms..	97	75	17	2	2	(D)	–	–	3
cwt..	643	343	297	(D)	(D)	(D)	–	–	(D)
Irrigated .... farms..	138 764	90 953	47 217	(D)	(D)	(D)	–	–	(D)
acres..	21	13	5	–	–	–	–	–	3
farms..	(D)		271	(D)	(D)	(D)			(D)
Hay—alfalfa, other tame, small grain, wild, grass silage, green chop, etc. (see text) .. farms..	33 954	29 993	2 903	934	886	875	48	45	134
tons, dry..	2 254 082	1 816 682	291 393	137 125	124 608	122 327	12 517	12 230	8 882
Irrigated .... farms..	5 080 947	3 882 191	758 522	422 226	378 394	369 404	43 842	43 437	17 908
acres..	1 492	1 086	219	174	162	157	12	11	13
	206 981	117 423	51 638	37 499	31 527	30 387	5 972	(D)	401
Farms by acres harvested:								
1 to 24 acres	11 391	10 520	691	129	123	120	6	6	51
25 to 99 acres	16 111	14 349	1 327	374	358	355	16	15	61
100 to 249 acres	5 297	4 311	670	300	287	264	13	11	16
250 to 499 acres	913	658	159	91	84	84	7	7	5
500 acres or more	252	155	56	40	34	32	7	6	1

See footnotes at end of table.

Table 49. Summary by Type of Organization: 1987—Con.

[For meaning of abbreviations and symbols, see introductory text]

Item	Total	Individual or family	Partnership	Corporation					Other—cooperative, estate or trust, institutional, etc.
				Total	Family held		Other than family held		
					Total	10 or less stock-holders	Total	10 or less stock-holders	
CROPS HARVESTED—Con.									
Hay—alfalfa, other tame, small grain, wild, grass silage, green chop, etc. (see text)—Con.									
Alfalfa hay .... farms..	15 484	13 326	1 549	543	515	508	28	28	64
acres..	741 856	552 876	116 180	69 603	60 727	59 457	9 076	9 076	2 997
tons, dry..	2 529 635	1 796 517	437 896	286 575	248 476	241 582	38 099	38 099	8 647
Irrigated .... farms..	1 174	849	169	145	135	130	10	10	11
acres..	180 952	100 567	46 267	33 804	28 112	26 982	5 692	5 692	314
Vegetables harvested for sale (see text) .... farms..	418	358	37	17	17	17	-	-	6
acres..	5 424	3 063	557	1 726	1 728	1 728	-	-	77
Irrigated .... farms..	166	138	13	10	10	10	-	-	5
acres..	1 851	1 315	242	251	251	251	-	-	44
Farms by acres harvested:									
0.1 to 4.9 acres	244	221	18	3	3	3	-	-	2
5.0 to 24.9 acres	130	109	12	6	6	6	-	-	3
25.0 to 99.9 acres	39	24	7	7	7	7	-	-	1
100.0 to 249.9 acres	4	4	-	-	-	-	-	-	-
250.0 acres or more	1	-	-	1	1	1	-	-	-
Field seed and grass seed crops .... farms..	1 188	1 022	117	39	37	37	2	2	10
acres..	58 460	48 158	7 176	2 951	(D)	2 671	(D)	(D)	175
Irrigated .... farms..	12	9	3	-	-	-	-	-	-
acres..	2 222	576	1 644	-	-	-	-	-	-
Land in orchards .... farms..	503	445	32	19	17	17	2	2	7
acres..	5 999	4 239	251	1 403	(D)	437	(D)	(D)	105
Irrigated .... farms..	90	73	10	6	6	6	-	-	1
acres..	757	498	(D)	210	210	210	-	-	(D)
Farms by bearing and nonbearing acres:									
0.1 to 4.9 acres	309	280	20	6	5	5	1	1	3
5.0 to 24.9 acres	147	126	11	7	7	7	-	-	3
25.0 to 99.9 acres	39	33	1	4	4	4	-	-	1
100.0 to 249.9 acres	6	5	-	1	1	1	-	-	-
250.0 acres or more	2	1	-	1	-	-	1	1	-

[1]Data are based on a sample of farms.
[2]Farms with total production expenses equal to market value of agricultural products sold are included as farms with gains of less than $1,000.

Table 50. **Summary by Age and Principal Occupation of Operator: 1987**

[For meaning of abbreviations and symbols, see introductory text]

Item	Total farming and other occupations	Farming						
					Age of operator (years)			
		Total	Under 25	25 to 34	35 to 44	45 to 54	55 to 64	65 and over
FARMS AND LAND IN FARMS								
Farms .... number..	68 579	42 607	1 013	5 436	6 422	6 505	10 552	12 676
percent..	100.0	62.1	1.5	7.9	9.4	9.5	15.4	18.5
Land in farms .... acres..	48 628 519	40 030 217	496 608	4 494 024	7 504 372	8 165 985	11 124 115	8 245 113
Average size of farm .... acres..	680	940	490	827	1 169	1 255	1 054	650
MARKET VALUE OF AGRICUL-TURAL PRODUCTS SOLD								
Total sales (see text) .... farms..	68 579	42 607	1 013	5 436	6 422	6 508	10 552	12 676
$1,000..	6 476 669	5 198 211	42 553	452 904	1 063 328	1 346 869	1 577 137	715 420
Average per farm .... dollars..	94 441	122 004	42 007	83 316	165 576	206 958	149 463	56 439
Farms by value of sales:								
Less than $1,000 (see text)	4 538	936	29	73	98	96	201	439
$1,000 to $2,499	4 964	1 240	38	105	160	130	236	571
$2,500 to $4,999	6 919	2 459	71	207	212	243	431	1 295
$5,000 to $9,999	9 430	4 194	142	369	390	400	624	2 129
$10,000 to $19,999	10 504	6 308	158	693	638	651	1 379	2 789
$20,000 to $24,999	3 566	2 504	71	308	249	305	613	958
$25,000 to $39,999	7 150	5 504	177	768	736	734	1 522	1 567
$40,000 to $49,999	3 132	2 651	78	429	409	420	733	582
$50,000 to $99,999	8 997	8 054	153	1 286	1 545	1 498	2 263	1 309
$100,000 to $249,999	6 656	6 236	83	929	1 449	1 394	1 671	712
$250,000 to $499,999	1 766	1 665	11	194	391	416	454	199
$500,000 to $999,999	568	527	2	51	128	138	135	73
$1,000,000 or more	389	327	-	24	77	83	90	53
Grains .... farms..	48 606	35 182	825	4 641	5 522	5 589	8 964	9 641
$1,000..	1 550 403	1 389 864	21 929	191 776	294 591	301 848	364 878	214 842
Sales of $50,000 or more .... farms..	8 994	8 491	111	1 197	1 977	1 965	2 233	1 008
$1,000..	976 864	931 478	10 276	124 674	223 636	230 153	238 788	103 951
Corn for grain .... farms..	7 426	6 225	176	1 028	1 248	1 171	1 560	1 044
$1,000..	255 791	239 631	4 721	39 953	57 680	57 701	54 956	24 421
Wheat .... farms..	38 365	29 147	601	3 887	4 658	4 747	7 473	7 781
$1,000..	615 979	615 979	8 045	76 003	116 810	128 861	169 891	114 348
Soybeans .... farms..	18 724	13 759	390	1 957	2 318	2 331	3 527	3 208
$1,000..	263 742	229 939	4 032	33 149	43 596	49 250	56 628	22 295
Sorghum for grain .... farms..	28 719	22 204	549	3 233	3 742	3 646	5 936	5 096
$1,000..	311 649	281 228	4 848	39 044	60 924	61 039	75 390	39 982
Barley .... farms..	1 715	1 466	13	208	255	284	360	328
$1,000..	3 955	3 558	12	423	612	812	1 027	672
Oats .... farms..	2 416	1 967	41	281	301	315	504	525
$1,000..	3 328	2 872	53	405	542	467	809	597
Other grains .... farms..	1 656	1 465	27	270	282	254	366	266
$1,000..	17 793	16 658	216	2 799	3 227	3 698	4 179	2 538
Cotton and cottonseed .... farms..	10	8	-	1	1	3	3	-
$1,000..	186	(D)	-	(D)	(D)	71	(D)	-
Sales of $50,000 or more .... farms..	2	2	-	-	-	1	1	-
$1,000..	(D)	(D)	-	-	-	(D)	(D)	-
Tobacco .... farms..	13	8	-	1	1	-	2	4
$1,000..	80	(D)	-	(D)	(D)	-	(D)	47
Sales of $50,000 or more .... farms..	-	-	-	-	-	-	-	-
$1,000..	-	-	-	-	-	-	-	-
Hay, silage, and field seeds .... farms..	12 901	8 856	173	1 205	1 522	1 443	2 224	2 289
$1,000..	109 574	94 437	1 100	11 581	22 582	19 485	26 287	13 401
Sales of $50,000 or more .... farms..	316	286	-	40	61	89	75	40
$1,000..	47 030	43 356	(D)	(D)	12 286	9 948	12 519	4 133
Vegetables, sweet corn, and melons .... farms..	418	237	3	25	53	41	44	71
$1,000..	4 151	3 385	48	238	1 207	559	660	674
Sales of $50,000 or more .... farms..	10	10	-	1	3	2	2	(D)
$1,000..	1 767	1 767	-	(D)	785	(D)	(D)	(D)
Fruits, nuts, and berries .... farms..	278	143	-	10	24	20	40	49
$1,000..	1 693	1 417	-	228	126	398	293	372
Sales of $50,000 or more .... farms..	6	6	-	-	2	-	1	2
$1,000..	732	732	-	-	(D)	-	(D)	(D)
Nursery and greenhouse crops .... farms..	272	126	1	13	28	25	34	25
$1,000..	26 805	23 002	(D)	3 233	3 450	5 967	1 118
Sales of $50,000 or more .... farms..	62	51	-	5	13	14	13	6
$1,000..	24 509	21 987	-	4 069	3 003	8 290	5 657	967
Other crops .... farms..	80	58	-	7	12	9	14	16
$1,000..	716	676	-	279	30	254	86	26
Sales of $50,000 or more .... farms..	1	3	-	1	-	-	-	-
$1,000..	558	558	-	(D)	-	(D)	(D)	-
Poultry and poultry products .... farms..	1 550	1 004	4	108	157	129	232	374
$1,000..	25 284	17 942	(D)	747	(D)	3 364	5 839	5 302
Sales of $50,000 or more .... farms..	75	63	-	4	8	14	28	9
$1,000..	23 851	16 873	-	604	2 587	3 262	5 433	4 987
Dairy products .... farms..	2 004	1 781	19	248	346	384	518	266
$1,000..	140 232	133 265	722	16 722	29 627	30 895	39 269	16 029
Sales of $50,000 or more .... farms..	979	936	4	126	215	215	266	108
$1,000..	119 518	114 684	417	14 156	26 445	26 786	33 663	13 216
Cattle and calves .... farms..	41 498	28 068	529	3 441	4 284	4 439	7 311	8 064
$1,000..	4 305 335	3 276 587	15 078	180 887	646 669	920 903	1 075 272	437 756
Sales of $50,000 or more .... farms..	5 932	5 293	78	659	1 065	1 144	1 483	864
$1,000..	3 891 456	2 957 355	9 917	141 449	595 839	868 989	986 406	354 755

See footnotes at end of table.

[For meaning of abbreviations and symbols, see introductory text]

Item		Other occupations						
			Age of operator (years)					
		Total	Under 25	25 to 34	35 to 44	45 to 54	55 to 64	65 and over
FARMS AND LAND IN FARMS								
Farms	number	25 972	899	4 095	6 049	6 199	5 436	3 494
	percent	37.0	1.0	6.0	8.8	9.0	7.9	5.1
Land in farms	acres	6 598 302	100 160	868 403	1 424 482	1 679 369	1 520 029	1 005 859
Average size of farm	acres	254	143	212	235	271	280	288
MARKET VALUE OF AGRICUL-TURAL PRODUCTS SOLD								
Total sales (see text)	farms	25 972	899	4 095	6 049	6 199	5 436	3 494
	$1,000	1 276 458	8 618	151 798	306 850	213 389	502 824	94 980
Average per farm	dollars	49 224	12 329	37 069	50 727	34 423	92 499	27 184
Farms by value of sales:								
Less than $1,000 (see text)		3 602	67	490	929	907	738	471
$1,000 to $2,499		3 724	122	593	898	841	693	577
$2,500 to $4,999		4 460	137	689	969	1 068	947	650
$5,000 to $9,999		5 236	161	844	1 121	1 195	1 160	755
$10,000 to $19,999		4 196	122	706	944	1 012	900	512
$20,000 to $24,999		1 062	18	180	251	272	227	114
$25,000 to $39,999		1 646	40	262	425	409	329	181
$40,000 to $49,999		481	7	81	121	123	98	51
$50,000 to $99,999		943	15	162	241	228	197	100
$100,000 to $249,999		418	7	62	101	104	89	55
$250,000 to $499,999		101	2	13	26	22	27	11
$500,000 to $999,999		41	1	3	7	9	11	10
$1,000,000 or more		62	–	10	16	9	20	7
Grains	farms	13 424	371	2 177	2 987	3 197	2 863	1 829
	$1,000	160 539	3 350	25 097	37 735	39 731	34 307	20 318
Sales of $50,000 or more	farms	503	4	72	119	131	109	68
	$1,000	45 366	320	6 693	10 328	11 196	9 955	6 894
Corn for grain	farms	1 201	37	217	256	302	253	136
	$1,000	16 160	389	3 308	3 116	3 990	3 625	1 732
Wheat	farms	9 218	264	1 514	2 005	2 142	1 995	1 298
	$1,000	78 169	1 537	10 850	18 413	19 188	17 419	10 761
Soybeans	farms	4 965	136	819	1 154	1 248	1 000	608
	$1,000	33 902	701	5 356	8 261	8 748	6 500	4 217
Sorghum for grain	farms	6 515	190	1 181	1 548	1 522	1 283	791
	$1,000	30 422	706	5 380	7 619	7 340	6 066	3 311
Barley	farms	247	7	34	46	59	64	37
	$1,000	395	8	37	82	100	115	53
Oats	farms	449	10	75	101	109	92	62
	$1,000	456	5	48	76	136	120	70
Other grains	farms	191	3	27	35	56	48	22
	$1,000	1 134	3	118	147	230	462	174
Cotton and cottonseed	farms	2	–	–	1	1	–	–
	$1,000	(D)	–	–	(D)	(D)	–	–
Sales of $50,000 or more	farms	–	–	–	–	–	–	–
	$1,000	–	–	–	–	–	–	–
Tobacco	farms	5	1	–	1	1	2	–
	$1,000	(D)	(D)	–	(D)	(D)	(D)	–
Sales of $50,000 or more	farms	–	–	–	–	–	–	–
	$1,000	–	–	–	–	–	–	–
Hay, silage, and field seeds	farms	3 945	52	634	1 006	943	846	464
	$1,000	15 137	265	1 897	3 038	3 611	3 902	2 423
Sales of $50,000 or more	farms	30	1	2	5	9	8	5
	$1,000	3 674	(D)	(D)	969	866	1 356	871
Vegetables, sweet corn, and melons	farms	181	–	21	47	46	48	19
	$1,000	766	–	128	200	184	187	68
Sales of $50,000 or more	farms	–	–	–	–	–	–	–
	$1,000	–	–	–	–	–	–	–
Fruits, nuts, and berries	farms	135	1	15	28	44	35	12
	$1,000	276	(D)	(D)	(D)	(D)	(D)	17
Sales of $50,000 or more	farms	–	–	–	–	–	–	–
	$1,000	–	–	–	–	–	–	–
Nursery and greenhouse crops	farms	146	–	15	37	36	37	21
	$1,000	3 803	–	1 608	570	717	522	387
Sales of $50,000 or more	farms	11	–	4	2	3	1	1
	$1,000	2 522	–	1 515	(D)	422	(D)	(D)
Other crops	farms	22	–	–	6	5	6	5
	$1,000	41	–	–	18	18	3	2
Sales of $50,000 or more	farms	–	–	–	–	–	–	–
	$1,000	–	–	–	–	–	–	–
Poultry and poultry products	farms	546	5	108	156	114	89	76
	$1,000	7 342	(D)	(D)	375	2 590	2 171	2 111
Sales of $50,000 or more	farms	12	–	–	2	1	7	2
	$1,000	6 978	–	–	(D)	(D)	2 142	(D)
Dairy products	farms	223	5	39	53	61	46	19
	$1,000	6 967	162	1 025	1 315	2 580	1 329	557
Sales of $50,000 or more	farms	43	1	3	9	17	9	4
	$1,000	4 835	(D)	(D)	905	1 862	1 000	416
Cattle and calves	farms	13 430	327	2 130	3 124	3 245	2 827	1 777
	$1,000	1 028 768	3 540	115 937	233 292	156 189	454 172	65 638
Sales of $50,000 or more	farms	639	15	104	149	139	160	72
	$1,000	934 101	1 757	101 397	211 918	133 100	433 594	52 335

See footnotes at end of table.

[For meaning of abbreviations and symbols, see introductory text]

Item	Total farming and other occupations	Farming						
		Total	Under 25	25 to 34	35 to 44	45 to 54	55 to 64	65 and over
					Age of operator (years)			
MARKET VALUE OF AGRICULTURAL PRODUCTS SOLD—Con.								
Total sales (see text)—Con.								
Hogs and pigs .... farms..	7 090	5 041	150	972	1 004	925	1 199	791
$1,000..	284 375	236 625	3 365	43 710	53 427	57 253	55 207	23 663
Sales of $50,000 or more .... farms..	1 276	1 152	10	248	285	249	273	87
$1,000..	213 369	180 267	1 135	32 776	42 600	46 901	41 155	15 700
Sheep, lambs, and wool .... farms..	2 456	1 364	33	193	318	239	309	272
$1,000..	18 561	15 606	192	1 945	7 429	2 167	2 489	1 362
Sales of $50,000 or more .... farms..	44	38	-	6	14	9	6	3
$1,000..	9 169	8 656	-	924	5 783	951	676	342
Other livestock and livestock products (see text) .... farms..	2 869	1 327	20	175	261	249	294	327
$1,000..	9 273	5 190	100	579	1 699	1 190	796	826
Sales of $50,000 or more .... farms..	21	18	-	2	4	6	2	2
$1,000..	3 649	2 313	-	(D)	1 149	637	(D)	(D)
FARM PRODUCTION EXPENSES[1]								
Total farm production expenses .... farms..	68 580	43 272	966	5 285	8 311	6 438	10 490	12 762
$1,000..	5 516 518	4 375 785	31 068	339 578	900 918	1 167 608	1 385 515	571 097
Average per farm .... dollars..	80 439	103 515	31 510	64 253	142 754	181 362	130 173	44 750
Livestock and poultry purchased .... farms..	23 380	16 068	366	2 344	2 875	2 734	4 170	3 557
$1,000..	2 426 149	1 832 592	7 334	90 997	394 900	544 960	618 326	176 075
Farms with expenses of—								
$1 to $4,999	11 923	6 792	205	904	1 021	953	1 781	1 928
$5,000 to $24,999	6 470	4 893	101	838	882	791	1 201	1 080
$25,000 to $99,999	3 307	2 880	66	442	615	626	793	338
$100,000 or more	1 680	1 503	16	160	357	364	395	211
Feed for livestock and poultry .... farms..	38 347	25 592	447	3 210	4 121	4 108	6 852	6 854
$1,000..	887 270	674 379	2 728	36 973	135 623	192 929	224 173	79 954
Farms with expenses of—								
$1 to $4,999	28 328	17 092	318	2 062	2 396	2 307	4 509	5 500
$5,000 to $24,999	7 351	6 074	116	856	1 193	1 204	1 692	1 013
$25,000 to $99,999	2 028	1 874	10	245	408	454	497	260
$100,000 or more	640	552	3	47	124	149	154	61
Commercially mixed formula feeds ..... farms..	14 988	10 306	195	1 376	1 893	1 777	2 726	2 339
$1,000..	163 561	134 641	564	11 376	27 431	34 851	45 620	14 798
Farms with expenses of—								
$1 to $4,999	11 327	7 077	157	956	1 205	1 036	1 834	1 889
$5,000 to $24,999	2 854	2 501	37	336	527	553	690	358
$25,000 to $79,999	577	537	-	73	116	137	147	64
$80,000 or more	230	191	1	11	45	51	55	28
Seeds, bulbs, plants, and trees .... farms..	48 233	34 474	761	4 542	5 392	5 634	8 876	9 269
$1,000..	95 302	84 740	1 285	11 125	17 578	19 584	22 292	12 877
Farms with expenses of—								
$1 to $999	28 247	17 185	490	2 026	2 010	2 047	4 255	6 357
$1,000 to $4,999	15 265	12 875	196	1 937	2 347	2 517	3 516	2 362
$5,000 to $24,999	4 473	4 175	75	557	974	1 003	1 042	524
$25,000 or more	248	239	-	22	61	67	63	26
Commercial fertilizer .... farms..	47 731	33 276	724	4 426	5 076	5 340	8 546	9 164
$1,000..	216 186	192 873	2 599	24 136	39 266	43 431	52 435	31 005
Farms with expenses of—								
$1 to $4,999	34 669	21 331	544	2 894	2 589	2 669	5 152	7 483
$5,000 to $24,999	11 740	10 892	172	1 435	2 224	2 357	3 131	1 563
$25,000 to $49,999	884	846	7	77	214	248	213	87
$50,000 or more	218	207	1	20	49	56	50	31
Agricultural chemicals .... farms..	46 318	32 566	761	4 306	5 098	5 269	8 368	8 764
$1,000..	125 003	110 913	1 571	14 550	22 711	23 539	30 007	18 535
Farms with expenses of—								
$1 to $4,999	99 456	26 161	671	3 473	3 687	3 835	6 641	7 854
$5,000 to $24,999	6 476	6 033	89	788	1 314	1 335	1 641	866
$25,000 to $49,999	322	309	1	36	83	86	68	35
$50,000 or more	64	63	-	9	14	13	18	9
Petroleum products .... farms..	65 460	41 320	918	5 204	6 220	6 270	10 329	12 379
$1,000..	243 568	207 976	2 868	25 713	40 161	44 892	57 945	36 396
Farms with expenses of—								
$1 to $4,999	51 841	28 687	732	3 582	3 602	3 369	6 725	10 677
$5,000 to $24,999	12 652	11 726	175	1 516	2 421	2 648	3 385	1 581
$25,000 to $49,999	760	722	11	88	158	204	159	102
$50,000 or more	207	185	-	18	39	49	60	19
Gasoline and gasohol .... farms..	57 245	36 804	743	4 514	5 569	5 673	9 322	10 983
$1,000..	80 737	66 266	806	7 647	12 068	13 330	18 734	13 681
Diesel fuel .... farms..	46 376	32 824	715	4 419	5 281	5 398	8 543	8 468
$1,000..	110 981	96 313	1 197	11 955	18 841	20 984	27 111	16 245
Natural gas .... farms..	4 956	4 194	90	566	798	820	1 091	719
$1,000..	26 371	24 146	586	3 613	5 149	6 180	6 036	2 580
LP gas, fuel oil, kerosene, motor oil, grease, etc.	52 549	36 741	703	4 669	5 561	5 835	9 400	10 573
$1,000..	25 478	21 251	277	2 498	4 103	4 418	6 065	3 890

See footnotes at end of table.

[For meaning of abbreviations and symbols, see introductory text]

Item		Other occupations						
			Age of operator (years)					
		Total	Under 25	25 to 34	35 to 44	45 to 54	55 to 64	65 and over
MARKET VALUE OF AGRICULTURAL PRODUCTS SOLD—Con.								
Total sales (see text)—Con.								
Hogs and pigs	farms..	2 049	99	454	639	408	318	131
	$1,000..	47 750	1 171	5 043	27 473	6 056	5 175	2 832
Sales of $50,000 or more	farms..	126	1	22	46	26	20	11
	$1,000..	33 102	(D)	(D)	22 890	3 234	3 005	2 086
Sheep, lambs, and wool	farms..	1 092	36	230	325	266	158	77
	$1,000..	2 956	67	623	971	651	464	180
Sales of $50,000 or more	farms..	6	–	1	4	–	1	–
	$1,000..	513	–	(D)	(D)	–	(D)	–
Other livestock and livestock products (see text)	farms..	1 542	29	226	497	410	249	129
	$1,000..	4 083	32	339	1 766	972	507	447
Sales of $50,000 or more	farms..	5	–	–	2	1	–	2
	$1,000..	1 336	–	–	(D)	(D)	–	(D)
FARM PRODUCTION EXPENSES[1]								
Total farm production expenses	farms..	26 306	655	4 111	6 103	6 030	5 602	3 807
	$1,000..	1 140 733	6 861	136 440	284 989	195 861	430 887	85 696
Average per farm	dollars..	43 361	10 474	33 189	46 697	32 481	76 917	22 510
Livestock and poultry purchased	farms..	7 312	186	1 479	2 043	1 413	1 471	720
	$1,000..	593 557	1 773	71 299	137 444	89 333	264 587	29 121
Farms with expenses of—								
$1 to $4,999		5 131	149	991	1 406	1 101	1 026	458
$5,000 to $24,999		1 577	14	380	605	193	295	190
$25,000 to $99,999		427	22	79	90	83	102	51
$100,000 or more		177	1	29	42	36	48	21
Feed for livestock and poultry	farms..	12 755	359	2 109	3 388	2 876	2 632	1 391
	$1,000..	212 891	955	21 496	60 320	33 048	83 675	13 397
Farms with expenses of—								
$1 to $4,999		11 236	306	1 899	2 987	2 517	2 333	1 194
$5,000 to $24,999		1 277	52	170	341	306	247	161
$25,000 to $99,999		154	1	28	35	39	22	29
$100,000 or more		88	–	12	25	14	30	7
Commercially mixed formula feeds	farms..	4 682	130	918	1 243	978	974	439
	$1,000..	26 919	46	3 395	9 343	7 639	6 133	2 163
Farms with expenses of—								
$1 to $4,999		4 250	130	812	1 123	879	884	422
$5,00u to $24,999		353	–	96	104	76	68	9
$25,000 to $79,999		40	–	4	5	16	10	5
$80,000 or more		39	–	6	11	7	12	3
Seeds, bulbs, plants, and trees	farms..	13 759	307	2 202	3 139	3 152	3 093	1 868
	$1,000..	10 561	203	1 596	2 309	2 499	2 424	1 530
Farms with expenses of—								
$1 to $999		11 062	223	1 793	2 544	2 525	2 468	1 509
$1,000 to $4,999		2 390	84	343	540	539	571	313
$5,000 to $24,999		298	–	65	53	88	49	43
$25,000 or more		9	–	1	2	–	5	1
Commercial fertilizer	farms..	14 455	315	2 235	3 399	3 302	3 183	2 021
	$1,000..	23 293	364	3 127	5 216	5 981	5 161	3 445
Farms with expenses of—								
$1 to $4,999		13 556	314	2 113	3 235	3 048	2 994	1 854
$5,000 to $24,999		848	–	121	155	238	177	157
$25,000 to $49,999		38	1	1	6	14	8	9
$50,000 or more		11	–	–	3	2	4	2
Agricultural chemicals	farms..	13 752	298	2 184	3 293	3 089	2 950	1 938
	$1,000..	14 090	245	1 812	3 404	3 176	3 327	2 127
Farms with expenses of—								
$1 to $4,999		13 295	298	2 114	3 201	2 984	2 847	1 851
$5,000 to $24,999		443	–	70	89	102	98	84
$25,000 to $49,999		13	–	–	3	3	5	2
$50,000 or more		1	–	–	–	–	–	1
Petroleum products	farms..	24 140	610	3 814	5 610	5 520	5 122	3 464
	$1,000..	35 592	795	4 985	9 119	7 665	8 304	4 723
Farms with expenses of—								
$1 to $4,999		23 154	579	3 681	5 429	5 265	4 881	3 319
$5,000 to $24,999		926	30	126	164	245	223	138
$25,000 to $49,999		38	–	3	13	8	9	5
$50,000 or more		22	1	4	4	2	9	2
Gasoline and gasohol	farms..	20 441	458	3 204	4 818	4 715	4 386	2 860
	$1,000..	14 471	307	2 081	3 792	3 245	3 025	2 020
Diesel fuel	farms..	13 552	368	2 333	3 176	3 083	2 773	1 819
	$1,000..	14 689	343	2 242	3 824	3 124	3 291	1 843
Natural gas	farms..	762	27	89	161	156	217	112
	$1,000..	2 225	70	114	460	341	977	263
LP gas, fuel oil, kerosene, motor oil, grease, etc.	farms..	15 808	363	2 427	3 820	3 602	3 469	2 127
	$1,000..	4 227	74	549	1 042	956	1 011	597

See footnotes at end of table.

Table 50. **Summary by Age and Principal Occupation of Operator: 1987**—Con.

[For meaning of abbreviations and symbols, see introductory text]

Item	Total farming and other occupations	Farming						
		Total	Under 25	25 to 34	35 to 44	45 to 54	55 to 64	65 and over
FARM PRODUCTION EXPENSES[1] —Con.								
Total farm production expenses—Con.								
Electricity .... farms..	48 797	33 323	505	3 782	5 158	5 407	8 926	9 546
$1,000..	54 103	44 261	349	4 320	8 586	10 698	12 822	7 486
Farms with expenses of—								
$1 to $999	36 660	22 839	412	2 580	3 032	3 046	5 921	7 848
$1,000 to $4,999	10 565	9 215	81	1 098	1 833	2 021	2 660	1 522
$5,000 to $24,999	1 236	1 163	12	94	272	305	313	167
$25,000 or more	136	106	–	10	21	35	31	9
Hired farm labor .... farms..	24 715	18 787	286	2 161	3 324	3 428	4 921	4 667
$1,000..	225 075	186 707	613	15 715	35 347	51 001	58 998	27 033
Farms with expenses of—								
$1 to $4,999	18 529	13 189	262	1 586	2 111	2 045	3 410	3 773
$5,000 to $24,999	4 529	4 089	21	433	899	1 001	1 079	656
$25,000 to $99,999	1 391	1 295	3	125	269	324	366	208
$100,000 or more	266	214	–	15	45	58	66	30
Contract labor......................... farms..	7 882	5 472	94	725	1 032	911	1 324	1 386
$1,000..	23 691	17 665	155	1 976	3 980	3 907	4 599	3 248
Farms with expenses of—								
$1 to $999	3 892	2 374	77	314	429	375	442	737
$1,000 to $4,999	2 895	2 203	4	300	408	365	637	466
$5,000 to $24,999	1 023	835	13	103	176	155	233	155
$25,000 or more	72	60	–	8	19	13	12	8
Repair and maintenance .... farms..	56 961	37 415	719	4 706	5 640	5 840	9 547	10 963
$1,000..	252 018	214 413	2 123	22 954	40 733	46 246	61 552	36 804
Farms with expenses of—								
$1 to $4,999	42 384	24 106	578	3 169	2 933	2 675	5 694	8 854
$5,000 to $24,999	13 477	12 277	136	1 454	2 489	2 677	3 557	1 964
$25,000 to $49,999	844	807	5	70	174	210	239	109
$50,000 or more	256	225	–	13	44	75	57	36
Customwork, machine hire, and rental of machinery and equipment .... farms..	30 603	21 280	355	2 567	3 169	3 390	5 657	6 142
$1,000..	107 366	89 109	2 015	11 746	15 214	17 845	23 246	19 043
Farms with expenses of—								
$1 to $999	13 298	7 629	117	836	1 017	1 083	1 935	2 641
$1,000 to $4,999	11 836	8 801	139	1 095	1 273	1 389	2 483	2 512
$5,000 to $24,999	4 982	4 319	81	583	780	817	1 126	919
$25,000 or more	487	431	18	53	86	91	113	70
Interest expense .... farms..	39 549	26 597	519	3 734	4 873	4 895	7 053	5 523
$1,000..	314 163	261 284	1 754	26 950	57 151	66 511	72 043	36 875
Farms with expenses of—								
$1 to $4,999	24 133	13 938	419	2 083	2 054	1 930	3 631	3 821
$5,000 to $24,999	12 676	10 121	93	1 471	2 213	2 245	2 685	1 414
$25,000 to $99,999	2 557	2 380	7	173	576	672	693	259
$100,000 or more	183	158	–	7	30	48	44	29
Secured by real estate................ farms..	26 408	17 499	180	1 925	3 334	3 459	5 039	3 562
$1,000..	188 166	153 825	773	14 290	31 734	39 052	44 867	23 109
Farms with expenses of—								
$1 to $999	5 315	2 966	52	220	363	380	874	1 077
$1,000 to $4,999	10 417	5 868	89	729	1 121	1 046	1 655	1 228
$5,000 to $24,999	9 280	7 366	37	893	1 572	1 653	2 121	1 090
$25,000 or more	1 396	1 299	2	83	278	380	389	167
Not secured by real estate .... farms..	24 307	17 228	432	2 847	3 375	3 272	4 176	3 126
$1,000..	125 997	107 459	981	12 660	25 417	27 459	27 175	13 766
Farms with expenses of—								
$1 to $999	8 203	4 636	213	667	543	516	1 168	1 429
$1,000 to $4,999	9 640	6 773	160	1 380	1 381	1 222	1 545	1 085
$5,000 to $24,999	5 766	5 183	58	746	1 268	1 314	1 264	533
$25,000 or more	798	736	1	54	183	220	199	79
Cash rent............................... farms..	21 234	16 026	439	2 459	3 047	3 024	4 148	2 911
$1,000..	123 531	108 772	2 877	17 705	24 467	24 239	25 352	14 132
Farms with expenses of—								
$1 to $4,999	14 629	10 111	213	1 495	1 705	1 701	2 790	2 207
$5,000 to $9,999	3 298	2 891	127	450	614	646	706	348
$10,000 to $24,999	2 511	2 270	82	368	562	493	490	275
$25,000 or more	796	754	17	146	166	184	160	81
Property taxes .... farms..	63 359	39 755	600	4 548	5 941	6 180	10 223	12 263
$1,000..	112 201	90 209	527	6 047	12 864	17 140	28 007	25 623
Farms with expenses of—								
$1 to $4,999	59 062	35 855	583	4 340	5 376	5 300	8 908	11 346
$5,000 to $9,999	3 248	2 967	14	170	437	667	976	703
$10,000 to $24,999	956	855	3	35	116	196	316	189
$25,000 or more	93	78	–	3	10	17	23	25
All other farm production expenses...... farms..	64 491	41 120	866	5 138	6 178	6 328	10 330	12 282
$1,000..	309 914	257 693	2 269	26 672	52 336	58 686	73 718	44 011
Farms with expenses of—								
$1 to $4,999	51 852	29 644	726	3 697	3 771	3 781	7 099	10 570
$5,000 to $24,999	11 071	10 015	135	1 278	2 062	2 171	2 836	1 533
$25,000 to $49,999	1 005	956	5	121	212	236	269	111
$50,000 or more	563	505	–	42	131	138	126	68

See footnotes at end of table.

[For meaning of abbreviations and symbols, see introductory text]

| Item | Other occupations | | | | | | |
| | Total | Age of operator (years) | | | | | |
		Under 25	25 to 34	35 to 44	45 to 54	55 to 64	65 and over
FARM PRODUCTION EXPENSES[1] —Con.							
Total farm production expenses—Con.							
Electricity .... farms..	15 474	279	2 088	3 589	3 712	3 598	2 206
$1,000..	9 842	115	985	2 729	2 239	2 759	1 016
Farms with expenses of—							
$1 to $999	14 021	249	1 914	3 307	3 342	3 205	2 004
$1,000 to $4,999	1 350	29	162	258	342	368	191
$5,000 to $24,999	73	1	9	16	21	13	11
$25,000 or more	30	-	3	6	7	12	2
Hired farm labor .... farms..	5 928	66	830	1 462	1 474	1 266	788
$1,000..	37 368	145	4 090	10 073	6 404	10 130	6 527
Farms with expenses of—							
$1 to $4,999	5 340	63	791	1 371	1 301	1 155	659
$5,000 to $24,999	440	1	23	84	132	101	99
$25,000 to $99,999	96	2	7	14	33	16	24
$100,000 or more	52	-	9	13	8	16	6
Contract labor .... farms..	2 410	9	378	633	519	571	300
$1,000..	5 826	2	586	1 757	901	1 857	721
Farms with expenses of—							
$1 to $999	1 516	8	246	469	294	339	162
$1,000 to $4,999	692	1	92	122	194	192	91
$5,000 to $24,999	188	-	40	36	30	16	46
$25,000 or more	12	-	-	6	1	4	1
Repair and maintenance .... farms..	19 546	365	3 055	4 750	4 449	4 279	2 628
$1,000..	37 605	540	4 738	10 317	7 915	9 401	4 694
Farms with expenses of—							
$1 to $4,999	18 278	375	2 923	4 452	4 131	3 982	2 415
$5,000 to $24,999	1 200	8	124	284	307	273	204
$25,000 to $49,999	37	2	1	6	8	12	8
$50,000 or more	31	-	7	8	3	12	1
Customwork, machine hire, and rental of machinery and equipment .... farms..	9 323	225	1 487	2 138	2 160	2 066	1 247
$1,000..	16 257	184	2 940	4 235	4 077	4 263	2 558
Farms with expenses of—							
$1 to $999	5 669	154	903	1 340	1 251	1 302	719
$1,000 to $4,999	2 935	70	467	679	699	605	415
$5,000 to $24,999	663	1	91	111	207	144	109
$25,000 or more	56	-	26	8	3	15	4
Interest expense .... farms..	12 952	332	2 293	3 442	3 080	2 605	1 200
$1,000..	52 872	690	7 223	15 525	13 104	12 032	4 306
Farms with expenses of—							
$1 to $4,999	10 195	302	1 866	2 664	2 330	2 016	1 017
$5,000 to $24,999	2 555	29	417	726	687	535	161
$25,000 to $99,999	177	-	8	46	60	45	18
$100,000 or more	25	1	2	6	3	9	4
Secured by real estate .... farms..	8 909	127	1 335	2 515	2 275	1 912	745
$1,000..	34 341	243	4 546	9 391	9 940	7 358	2 863
Farms with expenses of—							
$1 to $999	2 349	51	329	518	571	612	258
$1,000 to $4,999	4 549	65	710	1 456	1 127	626	365
$5,000 to $24,999	1 914	-	291	522	536	456	109
$25,000 or more	97	1	5	19	41	18	13
Not secured by real estate .... farms..	7 079	262	1 450	1 857	1 517	1 307	686
$1,000..	18 538	447	2 676	6 134	3 164	4 674	1 443
Farms with expenses of—							
$1 to $999	3 667	166	821	899	695	702	364
$1,000 to $4,999	2 767	73	536	800	674	454	330
$5,000 to $24,999	583	22	87	139	141	130	64
$25,000 or more	62	1	6	19	7	21	8
Cash rent .... farms..	5 208	166	1 075	1 601	1 020	974	372
$1,000..	14 759	239	3 089	4 032	3 105	2 940	1 354
Farms with expenses of—							
$1 to $4,999	4 518	166	909	1 423	854	845	321
$5,000 to $9,999	407	-	95	108	96	85	23
$10,000 to $24,999	241	-	61	61	59	37	23
$25,000 or more	42	-	10	9	11	7	5
Property taxes .... farms..	23 604	389	3 373	5 456	5 500	5 338	3 548
$1,000..	21 992	192	1 895	4 433	5 318	5 656	4 497
Farms with expenses of—							
$1 to $4,999	23 207	387	3 346	5 389	5 420	5 246	3 419
$5,000 to $24,999	281	1	16	52	58	61	93
$10,000 to $24,999	101	-	10	12	20	26	32
$25,000 or more	15	-	1	3	2	5	4
All other farm production expenses .... farms..	23 371	519	3 581	5 451	5 383	5 107	3 330
$1,000..	52 221	419	8 579	14 076	11 095	14 371	5 681
Farms with expenses of—							
$1 to $4,999	22 208	510	3 409	5 215	5 098	4 817	3 159
$5,000 to $24,999	1 056	9	156	214	252	266	159
$25,000 to $49,999	49	-	8	7	23	5	6
$50,000 or more	58	-	8	15	10	19	6

See footnotes at end of table.

Table 50. **Summary by Age and Principal Occupation of Operator: 1987** — Con.

[For meaning of abbreviations and symbols, see introductory text]

Item	Total farming and other occupations	Farming						
		Total	Under 25	25 to 34	35 to 44	45 to 54	55 to 64	65 and over
NET CASH RETURN FROM AGRICULTURAL SALES FOR THE FARM UNIT[1]								
All farms............number..	68 580	42 272	986	5 285	6 311	6 438	10 490	12 762
$1,000..	922 225	788 592	10 295	92 136	143 208	185 760	207 746	149 447
Average per farm....................dollars..	13 447	18 655	10 441	17 433	22 692	28 854	19 804	11 710
Farms with net gains[2]..............number..	41 673	29 161	732	3 830	4 366	4 527	7 239	8 447
Average net gain..................dollars..	27 369	32 230	16 331	28 161	39 654	47 264	34 855	21 189
Gain of—								
Less than $1,000	4 994	2 282	83	205	226	347	415	1 006
$1,000 to $9,999	18 378	10 973	366	1 290	1 243	1 304	2 491	4 279
$10,000 to $49,999	13 889	11 797	222	1 748	2 004	1 920	3 267	2 636
$50,000 or more	4 412	4 109	61	587	913	956	1 066	526
Farms with net losses ....number..	26 907	13 111	254	1 455	1 925	1 911	3 251	4 315
Average net loss ....dollars..	8 114	11 538	6 532	10 805	16 411	14 759	13 709	6 844
Loss of—								
Less than $1,000	5 287	1 935	22	214	207	242	441	809
$1,000 to $9,999	16 553	7 414	194	761	1 022	899	1 754	2 784
$10,000 to $49,999	4 663	3 404	34	453	607	675	948	687
$50,000 or more	404	358	4	27	89	95	108	95
GOVERNMENT PAYMENTS AND OTHER FARM-RELATED INCOME								
Government payments ....farms..	41 627	30 972	690	4 195	4 994	5 008	7 925	8 160
$1,000..	573 647	512 413	6 974	65 015	102 660	107 887	142 260	87 416
Other farm-related income[1]..............farms..	78 682	13 098	234	1 753	2 184	1 971	3 187	3 689
$1,000..	69 944	55 790	1 117	7 061	10 701	10 149	13 941	12 821
Customwork and other agricultural services ....farms..	7 463	5 839	203	1 197	1 390	1 019	1 379	651
$1,000..	32 115	27 203	671	5 603	6 756	5 921	5 536	2 516
Gross cash rent or share payments ...... farms..	7 899	4 836	49	288	493	622	1 128	2 256
$1,000..	30 403	22 332	169	1 144	2 608	3 007	6 619	8 766
Forest products and Christmas trees ..... farms..	439	230	16	10	28	35	58	83
$1,000..	1 087	683	8	12	213	65	135	251
Other farm-related income sources ...... farms..	6 668	5 310	98	601	865	824	1 457	1 465
$1,000..	6 340	5 572	49	302	1 125	1 156	1 652	1 288
COMMODITY CREDIT CORPORATION LOANS								
Total ....farms..	15 832	13 166	342	2 229	2 574	2 369	3 427	2 225
$1,000..	338 298	314 188	5 168	46 291	74 328	72 058	81 800	34 544
Corn ....farms..	3 591	3 225	90	592	744	640	791	368
$1,000..	108 314	102 526	1 879	17 355	26 053	24 517	24 103	8 619
Wheat ....farms..	7 282	5 969	128	992	1 167	1 082	1 479	1 121
$1,000..	95 942	87 099	1 222	11 453	18 548	19 986	23 974	11 916
Soybeans ....farms..	1 248	1 054	24	196	255	228	(D)	133
$1,000..	20 764	19 055	(D)	(D)	(D)	4 251	(D)	(D)
Sorghum, barley, and oats..............farms..	10 032	8 490	220	1 491	1 695	1 521	2 254	1 309
$1,000..	112 774	105 158	1 662	15 003	23 681	23 240	29 340	12 032
Cotton..................farms..	–	–	–	–	–	–	–	–
$1,000..	–	–	–	–	–	–	–	–
Peanuts, rye, rice, tobacco, and honey.... farms..	22	13	2	2	2	3	2	2
$1,000..	503	350	(D)	(D)	(D)	65	(D)	(D)
LAND IN FARMS ACCORDING TO USE								
Total cropland...................farms..	61 615	40 105	897	5 046	6 038	6 209	10 108	11 807
acres..	31 385 090	27 168 013	384 536	3 334 442	5 196 747	5 512 407	7 491 906	5 247 975
Harvested cropland..................farms..	57 822	38 785	870	4 915	5 890	6 039	9 847	11 224
acres..	17 729 394	15 569 768	221 690	1 968 275	3 093 112	3 226 981	4 285 845	2 773 865
Farms by acres harvested:								
1 to 49 acres	12 372	4 150	106	341	384	379	844	2 096
50 to 99 acres	8 653	4 510	151	441	428	502	829	2 159
100 to 199 acres	10 961	6 914	220	857	784	743	1 627	2 683
200 to 499 acres	14 761	12 356	279	1 870	1 908	1 908	3 550	2 841
500 to 999 acres	9 150	7 642	97	1 099	1 617	1 663	2 114	1 052
1,000 to 1,999 acres...................	2 875	2 776	16	278	670	728	748	336
2,000 acres or more	449	437	1	29	99	116	135	57
Cropland:								
Pasture or grazing only..............farms..	22 575	14 792	260	1 685	2 129	2 259	3 935	4 524
acres..	3 485 445	2 754 584	35 731	328 740	475 369	494 315	750 555	669 854
In cover crops, legumes, and soil-improvement grasses, not harvested and not pastured ....farms..	11 212	8 054	141	945	1 316	1 316	2 215	2 181
acres..	1 103 315	906 030	12 867	100 662	159 472	163 022	256 221	213 786
On which all crops failed ....farms..	3 941	2 324	43	258	385	359	648	631
acres..	206 231	170 445	4 597	13 937	30 284	31 162	54 162	36 203
In cultivated summer fallow..............farms..	25 408	19 915	408	2 610	3 093	3 273	5 310	5 223
acres..	6 409 506	5 710 493	78 986	660 613	1 039 151	1 175 861	1 595 107	1 160 775
Idle ....farms..	20 610	14 839	355	2 028	2 440	2 475	3 799	3 905
acres..	2 461 199	2 056 713	30 665	262 215	399 359	421 066	550 016	393 392
Total woodland...................farms..	12 587	7 712	114	691	1 029	1 246	2 103	2 529
acres..	718 261	510 580	5 675	43 160	77 816	101 955	145 159	137 015
Woodland pastured ....farms..	6 382	3 824	54	315	457	642	1 097	1 319
acres..	366 136	259 484	3 144	17 060	36 089	54 616	73 359	75 216
Woodland not pastured ....farms..	7 991	5 116	75	492	706	826	1 402	1 613
acres..	352 125	251 096	2 531	26 100	41 527	47 339	71 800	61 799

See footnotes at end of table.

Table 50. **Summary by Age and Principal Occupation of Operator: 1987**—Con.

[For meaning of abbreviations and symbols, see introductory text]

Item		Other occupations						
			Age of operator (years)					
		Total	Under 25	25 to 34	35 to 44	45 to 54	55 to 64	65 and over
NET CASH RETURN FROM AGRICULTURAL SALES FOR THE FARM UNIT[1]								
All farms	number	26 308	655	4 111	6 103	6 030	5 602	3 807
	$1,000	133 633	1 157	13 958	18 565	15 815	69 958	14 179
Average per farm	dollars	5 080	1 767	3 395	3 042	2 623	12 488	3 725
Farms with net gains[2]	number	12 512	346	2 004	2 663	2 853	2 681	1 965
Average net gain	dollars	16 039	7 115	11 569	14 923	10 505	31 166	11 081
Gain of—								
Less than $1,000		2 712	88	439	575	592	592	426
$1,000 to $9,999		7 405	217	1 157	1 527	1 729	1 588	1 187
$10,000 to $49,999		2 092	31	357	501	452	441	310
$50,000 or more		303	10	51	60	80	60	42
Farms with net losses	number	13 796	309	2 107	3 440	3 177	2 921	1 842
Average net loss	dollars	4 860	4 221	4 379	6 155	4 455	4 655	4 123
Loss of—								
Less than $1,000		3 352	93	546	622	790	752	549
$1,000 to $9,999		9 139	205	1 367	2 483	2 090	1 845	1 149
$10,000 to $49,999		1 259	11	182	326	290	322	128
$50,000 or more		46	–	12	9	7	2	16
GOVERNMENT PAYMENTS AND OTHER FARM-RELATED INCOME								
Government payments	farms	10 655	273	1 688	2 326	2 601	2 278	1 489
	$1,000	61 234	1 122	8 641	13 707	16 085	14 223	7 457
Other farm-related income[1]	farms	5 584	151	794	1 217	1 266	1 241	915
	$1,000	14 154	479	1 662	2 664	3 124	3 482	2 744
Customwork and other agricultural services	farms	1 624	117	286	463	354	268	136
	$1,000	4 911	395	903	1 251	1 045	867	451
Gross cash rent or share payments	farms	3 063	9	306	560	705	772	711
	$1,000	8 071	78	576	1 218	1 715	2 290	2 193
Forest products and Christmas trees	farms	209	9	15	22	57	77	29
	$1,000	404	5	46	21	180	131	23
Other farm-related income sources	farms	1 359	27	283	300	284	261	204
	$1,000	768	1	138	174	184	195	77
COMMODITY CREDIT CORPORATION LOANS								
Total	farms	2 666	94	523	661	618	483	287
	$1,000	24 110	564	4 397	5 258	6 165	4 624	3 103
Corn	farms	366	15	75	83	84	73	36
	$1,000	5 788	208	1 556	831	1 486	1 037	670
Wheat	farms	1 313	40	252	318	305	231	167
	$1,000	8 843	135	1 309	2 042	2 145	1 902	1 311
Soybeans	farms	194	5	27	49	53	38	22
	$1,000	1 710	8	(D)	345	478	(D)	377
Sorghum, barley, and oats	farms	1 542	50	329	405	358	268	132
	$1,000	7 617	212	1 323	2 034	1 974	1 329	745
Cotton	farms	–	–	–	–	–	–	–
	$1,000	–	–	–	–	–	–	–
Peanuts, rye, rice, tobacco, and honey	farms	9	–	1	3	3	2	–
	$1,000	152	–	(D)	8	83	(D)	–
LAND IN FARMS ACCORDING TO USE								
Total cropland	farms	21 510	487	3 218	4 949	5 223	4 899	2 934
	acres	4 217 077	76 849	572 103	952 193	1 062 580	941 025	612 327
Harvested cropland	farms	19 037	431	2 862	4 395	4 543	4 157	2 549
	acres	2 159 626	43 732	308 866	500 994	544 684	471 182	290 188
Farms by acres harvested:								
1 to 49 acres		8 222	159	1 146	1 988	1 974	1 827	1 128
50 to 99 acres		4 343	114	722	903	1 032	947	625
100 to 199 acres		3 447	106	580	763	848	718	432
200 to 499 acres		2 405	45	332	606	616	540	264
500 to 999 acres		508	5	71	110	150	95	77
1,000 to 1,999 acres		100	2	11	20	21	27	19
2,000 acres or more		12	–	–	3	2	3	4
Cropland:								
Pasture or grazing only	farms	7 783	138	1 062	1 829	1 963	1 754	1 037
	acres	730 681	9 335	91 933	164 719	188 669	166 980	109 245
In cover crops, legumes, and soil-improvement grasses, not harvested and not pastured	farms	3 158	60	419	729	854	712	384
	acres	197 285	1 929	20 947	43 697	58 480	48 450	23 782
On which all crops failed	farms	1 017	25	130	229	276	221	136
	acres	35 786	860	4 455	6 226	10 371	8 557	5 315
In cultivated summer fallow	farms	5 493	148	884	1 153	1 290	1 221	797
	acres	699 013	13 741	96 074	146 493	165 291	159 288	118 186
Idle	farms	5 771	133	925	1 280	1 390	1 249	794
	acres	394 486	7 252	49 828	90 062	95 165	86 568	65 611
Total woodland	farms	4 875	64	555	1 100	1 333	1 130	693
	acres	207 681	2 106	19 812	35 232	57 962	59 709	32 860
Woodland pastured	farms	2 558	33	254	584	717	594	376
	acres	106 652	944	9 823	17 543	28 373	31 527	18 442
Woodland not pastured	farms	2 675	37	349	636	765	692	394
	acres	101 029	1 162	9 989	17 689	29 589	28 182	14 418

See footnotes at end of table.

[For meaning of abbreviations and symbols, see introductory text]

Item	Total farming and other occupations	Farming						
					Age of operator (years)			
		Total	Under 25	25 to 34	35 to 44	45 to 54	55 to 64	65 and over
LAND IN FARMS ACCORDING TO USE—Con.								
Pastureland and rangeland other than cropland and woodland pastured ... farms..	32 362	21 789	324	2 329	3 266	3 542	5 881	6 447
acres..	13 254 094	11 350 846	94 837	1 032 321	2 057 893	2 351 750	3 202 110	2 611 935
Land in house lots, ponds, roads, wasteland, etc. ... farms..	44 335	28 094	493	2 888	3 962	4 442	7 452	8 847
acres..	1 271 074	1 000 778	11 560	84 101	172 116	199 873	284 940	248 188
Cropland under federal acreage reduction programs:								
Annual commodity acreage adjustment programs ... farms..	34 658	27 026	611	3 828	4 554	4 524	7 099	6 410
acres..	3 958 196	3 640 757	52 596	471 417	717 604	736 895	974 094	588 151
Conservation reserve program ... farms..	5 630	4 215	54	535	695	726	1 151	1 054
acres..	810 882	665 958	6 943	79 661	107 825	125 673	182 669	163 187
Value of land and buildings¹ ... farms..	68 580	42 272	966	5 285	6 311	6 438	10 490	12 762
$1,000..	19 068 461	15 700 807	181 783	1 769 428	2 932 918	3 290 269	4 284 426	3 241 983
Average per farm ... dollars..	278 047	371 423	184 364	334 802	464 731	511 070	408 430	254 034
Average per acre ... dollars..	413	397	402	406	402	406	387	391
Farms by value group:								
$1 to $39,999 ...	10 024	3 430	176	448	483	361	592	1 370
$40,000 to $59,999 ...	9 571	3 784	100	424	396	324	624	1 896
$70,000 to $99,999 ...	7 001	3 143	173	344	371	286	675	1 294
$100,000 to $149,999 ...	8 596	4 881	148	638	448	529	1 191	1 927
$150,000 to $199,999 ...	6 313	4 253	80	565	470	446	1 095	1 597
$200,000 to $499,999 ...	16 476	13 190	242	1 803	2 095	2 207	3 599	3 144
$500,000 to $999,999 ...	7 579	6 793	55	807	1 396	1 582	1 831	1 122
$1,000,000 to $1,999,999 ...	2 396	2 260	12	213	535	561	628	311
$2,000,000 to $4,999,999 ...	535	476	–	37	108	120	120	63
$5,000,000 or more ...	89	82	–	6	11	22	25	18
VALUE OF MACHINERY AND EQUIPMENT¹								
Estimated market value of all machinery and equipment ... farms..	68 391	42 250	981	5 285	6 904	6 436	10 489	12 753
$1,000..	3 447 669	2 810 791	42 184	307 827	511 112	574 497	786 644	588 526
Farms by value group:								
$1 to $4,999 ...	5 812	1 821	77	270	187	121	299	867
$5,000 to $9,999 ...	11 565	4 043	190	398	494	391	641	1 931
$10,000 to $19,999 ...	11 722	5 977	110	862	668	665	1 164	2 508
$20,000 to $49,999 ...	16 724	11 020	262	1 588	1 493	1 450	2 820	3 367
$50,000 to $99,999 ...	12 176	9 964	237	1 236	1 628	1 712	2 874	2 299
$100,000 to $199,999 ...	7 277	6 546	58	677	1 262	1 383	1 857	1 309
$200,000 to $499,999 ...	2 860	2 639	27	247	516	652	778	421
$500,000 or more ...	235	220	–	9	58	64	58	31
SELECTED MACHINERY AND EQUIPMENT¹								
Motortrucks, including pickups ... farms..	63 093	40 353	899	5 013	6 052	6 233	10 154	12 002
number..	159 329	117 452	2 013	12 285	18 762	21 474	32 972	29 946
Wheel tractors ... farms..	60 459	38 684	805	4 612	5 822	6 025	9 994	11 826
number..	150 847	109 467	1 754	11 146	16 396	16 986	30 750	30 445
Less than 40 horsepower (PTO) ... farms..	25 210	14 960	247	1 367	1 842	2 181	4 020	5 303
number..	36 591	23 969	360	1 905	2 670	3 316	6 985	8 731
40 horsepower (PTO) or more ... farms..	50 577	34 842	729	4 331	5 452	5 650	9 070	9 610
number..	112 056	85 498	1 394	9 241	13 716	15 668	23 765	21 714
Grain and bean combines ... farms..	35 608	27 116	508	3 066	4 277	4 666	7 434	7 175
number..	43 801	33 896	627	3 609	5 395	5 994	9 445	8 925
Cottonpickers and strippers ... farms..	1	1	–	–	1	–	–	–
number..	(D)	(D)	–	–	(D)	–	–	–
Mower conditioners ... farms..	18 793	13 455	166	1 318	2 039	2 336	3 725	3 869
number..	20 167	14 480	169	1 388	2 188	2 543	4 030	4 162
Pickup balers ... farms..	26 083	16 983	294	1 972	2 863	3 111	5 403	5 320
number..	31 692	23 691	325	2 439	3 718	4 045	6 601	6 365
AGRICULTURAL CHEMICALS¹								
Commercial fertilizer ... farms..	47 723	33 268	724	4 426	5 070	5 340	8 645	9 163
acres on which used..	13 882 822	12 256 603	174 753	1 569 161	2 429 817	2 658 847	3 345 357	2 078 868
Lime ... farms..	2 685	1 972	1	224	435	292	461	559
acres on which used..	154 822	129 546	(D)	(D)	37 330	22 152	30 930	27 090
tons..	369 024	316 377	(D)	(D)	88 476	56 591	78 651	64 789
Sprays, dusts, granules, fumigants, etc., to control—								
Insects on hay and other crops ... farms..	19 416	15 679	278	2 191	2 682	2 921	4 192	3 415
acres on which used..	3 015 560	2 758 634	36 776	351 212	557 354	633 323	762 244	417 725
Nematodes in crops ... farms..	716	586	35	80	65	110	164	162
acres on which used..	87 904	79 910	4 660	11 260	13 992	17 854	22 859	9 265
Diseases in crops and orchards ... farms..	1 055	755	20	124	107	125	188	191
acres on which used..	125 065	112 916	691	20 239	21 422	28 632	26 251	15 481
Weeds, grass, or brush in crops and pasture ... farms..	36 950	26 367	650	3 643	4 192	4 301	6 658	6 923
acres on which used..	8 837 062	7 558 078	129 879	1 019 349	1 510 991	1 521 576	2 055 300	1 320 983
Chemicals for defoliation or for growth control of crops or thinning of fruit ... farms..	614	412	6	64	74	78	78	112
acres on which used..	68 839	61 952	268	15 526	10 509	10 439	10 868	14 300

See footnotes at end of table.

[For meaning of abbreviations and symbols. see introductory text]

Item	Total	Under 25	25 to 34	35 to 44	45 to 54	55 to 64	65 and over
				Other occupations			
				Age of operator (years)			
LAND IN FARMS ACCORDING TO USE—Con.							
Pastureland and rangeland other than cropland and woodland pastured .... farms..	10 573	193	1 565	2 485	2 679	2 295	1 356
acres..	1 903 248	18 143	241 789	379 477	493 111	456 369	314 359
Land in house lots, ponds, roads, wasteland, etc. .... farms..	16 241	342	2 330	3 748	4 041	3 538	2 244
acres..	270 296	3 062	34 899	57 580	65 716	52 926	46 313
Cropland under federal acreage reduction programs:							
Annual commodity acreage adjustment programs .... farms..	7 632	213	1 303	1 720	1 847	1 609	940
acres..	415 439	9 433	80 023	96 667	108 485	90 847	50 204
Conservation reserve program .... farms..	1 415	14	180	325	377	320	199
acres..	144 904	711	17 299	29 921	45 243	34 247	17 483
Value of land and buildings¹ .... farms..	26 308	655	4 111	6 103	6 030	5 602	3 807
$1,000..	3 367 654	39 025	385 836	761 609	850 850	771 642	558 692
Average per farm ....dollars..	128 009	59 580	93 855	124 793	141 103	137 744	146 754
Average per acre ....dollars..	508	497	450	545	509	512	502
Farms by value group:							
$1 to $39,999	6 594	295	1 345	1 408	1 387	1 153	1 006
$40,000 to $69,999	5 807	116	1 034	1 469	1 172	1 144	872
$70,000 to $99,999	3 858	125	620	832	914	835	532
$100,000 to $149,999	3 715	62	461	869	921	1 012	390
$150,000 to $199,999	2 060	32	262	565	491	451	259
$200,000 to $499,999	3 286	24	295	740	672	790	565
$500,000 to $999,999	786	1	85	184	209	169	138
$1,000,000 to $1,999,999	136	–	7	26	41	31	31
$2,000,000 to $4,999,999	59	–	2	8	21	16	12
$5,000,000 or more	7	–	–	2	2	1	2
VALUE OF MACHINERY AND EQUIPMENT¹							
Estimated market value of all machinery and equipment .... farms..	26 141	651	4 094	6 054	5 993	5 594	3 755
$1,000..	636 672	12 457	83 496	145 242	134 632	174 285	86 860
Farms by value group:							
$1 to $4,999	3 991	125	784	982	780	622	518
$5,000 to $9,999	7 542	213	1 267	1 573	1 833	1 564	1 092
$10,000 to $19,999	5 745	181	852	1 318	1 299	1 253	842
$20,000 to $49,999	5 704	80	730	1 457	1 321	1 286	830
$50,000 to $99,999	2 192	36	354	490	560	429	323
$100,000 to $199,999	731	8	78	199	157	172	117
$200,000 to $499,999	221	8	26	52	41	62	32
$500,000 or more	15	–	3	3	2	6	1
SELECTED MACHINERY AND EQUIPMENT¹							
Motortrucks, including pickups .... farms..	22 740	581	3 592	5 307	5 213	4 833	3 214
number..	41 877	1 009	6 006	9 789	9 919	9 085	6 069
Wheel tractors .... farms..	21 575	405	2 996	4 929	5 140	4 674	3 229
number..	41 180	754	5 026	9 042	10 304	9 564	6 490
Less than 40 horsepower (PTO) .... farms..	10 250	203	1 177	2 194	2 464	2 640	1 572
number..	14 622	347	1 602	2 984	3 605	3 750	2 334
40 horsepower (PTO) or more .... farms..	15 735	255	2 233	3 773	3 864	3 334	2 276
number..	26 558	407	3 424	6 058	6 699	5 814	4 156
Grain and bean combines .... farms..	8 492	181	1 029	1 967	2 154	1 938	1 223
number..	9 903	212	1 152	2 253	2 582	2 297	1 407
Cottonpickers and strippers .... farms..	–	–	–	–	–	–	–
number..	–	–	–	–	–	–	–
Mower conditioners .... farms..	5 338	59	717	1 259	1 359	1 194	750
number..	5 687	66	773	1 296	1 457	1 299	797
Pickup balers .... farms..	7 100	86	870	1 753	1 790	1 668	933
number..	8 201	110	979	1 975	2 072	1 906	1 159
AGRICULTURAL CHEMICALS¹							
Commercial fertilizer .... farms..	14 455	315	2 235	3 399	3 302	3 183	2 021
acres on which used..	1 596 219	29 174	225 166	370 700	404 686	335 985	230 508
Lime .... farms..	713	5	102	176	186	172	72
acres on which used..	25 074	450	3 506	6 141	7 696	5 147	2 134
tons..	52 647	1 350	7 006	14 880	12 924	11 391	5 096
Sprays, dusts, granules, fumigants, etc., to control—							
Insects on hay and other crops .... farms..	3 737	76	546	904	866	799	546
acres on which used..	258 946	4 126	29 625	55 543	64 769	58 701	44 182
Nematodes in crops .... farms..	130	9	44	45	18	10	4
acres on which used..	7 994	63	2 572	1 104	1 388	1 245	1 622
Diseases in crops and orchards .... farms..	300	–	71	39	61	82	47
acres on which used..	12 149	–	3 892	2 331	2 361	2 129	1 436
Weeds, grass, or brush in crops and pasture .... farms..	10 583	243	1 730	2 533	2 448	2 248	1 381
acres on which used..	1 078 984	16 174	143 825	265 415	266 685	244 058	142 827
Chemicals for defoliation or for growth control of crops or thinning of fruit .... farms..	202	13	54	60	15	15	45
acres on which used..	6 887	350	1 563	1 878	664	140	2 262

See footnotes at end of table.

Table 50. Summary by Age and Principal Occupation of Operator: 1987—Con.

[For meaning of abbreviations and symbols, see introductory text]

Item	Total farming and other occupations	Farming						
		Total	Under 25	25 to 34	35 to 44	45 to 54	55 to 64	65 and over
TENURE AND RACE OF OPERATOR								
All operators	68 579	42 607	1 013	5 436	6 422	6 508	10 552	12 676
Full owners	29 956	14 609	227	837	1 341	1 624	3 344	7 136
Part owners	27 967	21 582	203	2 434	3 829	4 133	6 333	4 650
Tenants	10 656	6 416	583	2 065	1 252	751	875	890
White	68 304	42 495	1 010	5 428	6 404	6 489	10 527	12 637
Full owners	29 784	14 552	224	834	1 339	1 614	3 326	7 115
Part owners	27 901	21 544	203	2 433	3 818	4 127	6 326	4 637
Tenants	10 619	6 399	583	2 061	1 247	748	875	885
Black and other races	275	112	3	8	18	19	25	39
Full owners	172	57	3	3	2	10	18	21
Part owners	66	38	-	1	11	6	7	13
Tenants	37	17	-	4	5	3	-	5
OWNED AND RENTED LAND								
Land owned .... farms..	58 533	36 607	443	3 416	5 216	5 806	9 743	11 981
acres..	24 331 697	19 680 602	106 099	1 095 483	2 486 230	3 603 801	6 030 575	6 358 414
Owned land in farms .... farms..	57 923	36 191	430	3 371	5 170	5 757	9 677	11 786
acres..	21 178 322	17 476 469	90 490	1 012 062	2 243 015	3 366 001	5 484 394	5 280 507
Land rented or leased from others ... farms..	38 908	28 187	788	4 509	5 096	4 900	7 255	5 638
acres..	25 665 815	22 901 822	412 154	3 537 112	5 327 775	4 840 667	5 722 971	3 061 143
Rented or leased land in farms ... farms..	38 623	27 898	786	4 499	5 081	4 884	7 208	5 540
acres..	25 450 197	22 553 748	406 118	3 481 962	5 281 357	4 799 984	5 639 721	2 964 606
Land rented or leased to others ... farms..	11 944	7 314	74	407	713	802	1 742	3 576
acres..	3 569 193	2 552 207	21 645	138 571	309 633	276 483	629 431	1 174 444
OPERATOR CHARACTERISTICS								
Operators by place of residence:								
On farm operated	45 527	30 841	506	3 455	4 619	4 931	8 188	9 142
Not on farm operated	17 871	8 676	454	1 619	1 354	1 101	1 677	2 471
Not reported	5 181	3 090	53	362	449	476	687	1 063
Operators by principal occupation:								
Farming	42 607	42 607	1 013	5 436	6 422	6 508	10 552	12 676
Other	25 972	-	-	-	-	-	-	-
Operators by days of work off farm:								
None	29 462	26 647	414	2 433	3 396	3 819	7 111	9 474
Any	34 654	11 497	527	2 618	2 470	2 071	2 424	1 387
1 to 99 days	7 620	6 562	307	1 475	1 313	1 104	1 403	960
100 to 199 days	5 357	2 499	123	518	566	492	562	236
200 days or more	21 677	2 436	97	625	589	475	459	191
Not reported	4 463	4 463	72	385	556	618	1 017	1 815
Operators by years on present farm:								
2 years or less	3 511	1 474	294	520	259	136	148	117
3 or 4 years	3 873	1 586	290	583	312	150	151	100
5 to 9 years	8 552	3 933	209	1 766	920	401	335	282
10 years or more	40 624	28 303	-	1 738	3 908	4 690	8 244	9 723
Average years on present farm	21.3	25.3	3.4	8.1	13.5	21.9	30.8	37.9
Not reported	12 019	7 311	220	829	1 023	1 131	1 654	2 454
Operators by age group:								
Under 25 years	1 712	1 013	1 013	-	-	-	-	-
25 to 34 years	9 531	5 436	-	5 436	-	-	-	-
35 to 44 years	12 471	6 422	-	-	6 422	-	-	-
45 to 49 years	5 926	2 896	-	-	-	2 896	-	-
50 to 54 years	6 781	3 612	-	-	-	3 612	-	-
55 to 59 years	7 561	4 689	-	-	-	-	4 689	-
60 to 64 years	6 407	5 863	-	-	-	-	5 863	-
65 to 69 years	6 564	5 058	-	-	-	-	-	5 058
70 years and over	9 608	7 618	-	-	-	-	-	7 618
Average age	52.0	54.1	22.0	30.1	39.3	49.7	59.8	72.0
Operators by sex:								
Male	65 619	41 099	997	5 369	6 287	6 307	10 183	11 956
Female	2 960	1 508	16	67	135	201	369	720
Operators of Spanish origin (see text)	108	58	3	7	13	14	10	11
FARMS BY TYPE OF ORGANIZATION								
Individual or family (sole proprietorship) ... farms..	60 202	36 673	885	4 658	5 387	5 548	9 015	11 180
acres..	36 420 471	30 942 639	421 096	3 594 694	5 667 172	6 447 795	6 421 996	6 369 886
Partnership ... farms..	5 689	4 048	116	509	642	664	1 025	1 092
acres..	6 151 580	5 429 815	61 055	654 187	959 742	902 937	1 661 507	1 190 187
Corporation:								
Family held ... farms..	1 942	1 567	9	140	329	329	437	323
acres..	3 446 745	3 167 869	13 337	213 225	675 707	735 337	910 746	619 517
More than 10 stockholders ... farms..	23	15	-	-	3	2	4	6
10 or less stockholders ... farms..	1 919	1 552	9	140	326	327	433	317
Other than family held ... farms..	158	87	-	7	16	27	20	15
acres..	159 376	109 386	-	17 858	24 429	14 258	29 516	23 265
More than 10 stockholders ... farms..	17	4	-	-	-	3	1	-
10 or less stockholders ... farms..	141	83	-	7	16	24	19	15
Other—cooperative, estate or trust, institutional, etc. ... farms..	388	232	3	22	46	40	55	66
acres..	450 347	380 766	1 120	14 060	157 322	65 658	100 350	42 258

See footnotes at end of table.

Table 50. **Summary by Age and Principal Occupation of Operator: 1987**—Con.

[For meaning of abbreviations and symbols, see introductory text]

Item		Other occupations						
			Age of operator (years)					
	Total	Under 25	25 to 34	35 to 44	45 to 54	55 to 64	65 and over
TENURE AND RACE OF OPERATOR							
All operators	25 972	699	4 095	8 049	8 199	5 436	3 494
Full owners	15 347	259	1 754	3 257	3 746	3 594	2 737
Part owners	6 385	55	984	1 737	1 765	1 359	485
Tenants	4 240	385	1 357	1 055	668	483	272
White	25 809	699	4 067	8 012	8 152	5 408	3 471
Full owners	15 232	259	1 744	3 228	3 714	3 572	2 715
Part owners	6 357	55	979	1 733	1 751	1 355	484
Tenants	4 220	385	1 344	1 051	687	481	272
Black and other races	163	-	28	37	47	28	23
Full owners	115	-	10	29	32	22	22
Part owners	28	-	5	4	14	4	1
Tenants	20	-	13	4	1	2	-
OWNED AND RENTED LAND							
Land owned farms..	21 926	322	2 763	5 037	5 553	4 996	3 256
acres..	4 661 295	34 066	341 450	757 379	1 199 625	1 243 920	1 074 855
Owned land in farms farms..	21 732	314	2 738	4 994	5 511	4 953	3 222
acres..	3 701 853	23 722	275 681	632 870	991 415	1 002 783	775 362
Land rented or leased from others farms..	10 721	441	2 348	2 810	2 473	1 860	789
acres..	2 963 993	77 173	604 820	802 333	705 786	535 012	238 869
Rented or leased land in farms farms..	10 625	440	2 341	2 792	2 453	1 842	757
acres..	2 896 449	76 438	592 722	791 612	687 954	517 246	230 477
Land rented or leased to others farms..	4 630	41	381	812	1 174	1 146	1 076
acres..	1 016 986	11 079	77 867	135 230	226 042	258 903	307 865
OPERATOR CHARACTERISTICS							
Operators by place of residence:							
On farm operated	14 686	271	2 148	3 682	3 808	3 079	1 698
Not on farm operated	9 195	391	1 636	1 936	1 916	1 932	1 384
Not reported	2 091	37	311	431	475	425	412
Operators by principal occupation:							
Farming	-	-	-	-	-	-	-
Other	25 972	699	4 095	8 049	8 199	5 436	3 494
Operators by days of work off farm:							
None	2 815	39	117	172	213	500	1 774
Any	23 157	660	3 978	5 877	5 986	4 936	1 720
1 to 99 days	1 058	68	97	146	162	248	337
100 to 199 days	2 858	120	405	610	732	548	343
200 days or more	19 241	472	3 476	5 121	5 092	4 040	1 040
Not reported	-	-	-	-	-	-	-
Operators by years on present farm:							
2 years or less	2 037	214	702	535	324	192	70
3 or 4 years	2 287	159	749	690	395	210	84
5 to 9 years	4 619	109	1 347	1 521	940	515	187
10 years or more	12 321	-	659	2 415	3 548	3 546	2 153
Average years on present farm	14.7	3.2	6.1	9.5	14.7	20.8	29.1
Not reported	4 708	217	838	888	992	973	1 000
Operators by age group:							
Under 25 years	699	699	-	-	-	-	-
25 to 34 years	4 095	-	4 095	-	-	-	-
35 to 44 years	8 049	-	-	8 049	-	-	-
45 to 49 years	3 030	-	-	-	3 030	-	-
50 to 54 years	3 169	-	-	-	3 169	-	-
55 to 59 years	2 892	-	-	-	-	2 892	-
60 to 64 years	2 544	-	-	-	-	2 544	-
65 to 69 years	1 506	-	-	-	-	-	1 506
70 years and over	1 988	-	-	-	-	-	1 988
Average age	48.4	21.6	30.1	39.6	49.5	59.2	72.1
Operators by sex:							
Male	24 520	650	3 967	5 814	5 911	5 103	3 075
Female	1 452	49	128	235	288	333	419
Operators of Spanish origin (see text)	50	3	11	11	15	7	3
FARMS BY TYPE OF ORGANIZATION							
Individual or family (sole proprietorship) farms..	23 529	626	3 698	5 507	5 691	4 913	3 094
acres..	5 477 832	86 929	739 011	1 185 098	1 433 739	1 215 846	817 209
Partnership farms..	1 841	62	330	422	362	362	303
acres..	721 965	10 107	98 388	180 705	159 632	156 516	116 417
Corporation:							
Family held farms..	375	8	39	69	92	102	65
acres..	278 876	3 063	23 106	25 520	54 990	110 495	61 702
More than 10 stockholders farms..	8	-	2	2	1	3	2
10 or less stockholders farms..	367	8	39	67	91	99	63
Other than family held farms..	71	-	14	14	17	17	9
acres..	50 050	-	5 723	7 557	12 113	21 238	3 419
More than 10 stockholders farms..	13	-	3	3	4	2	1
10 or less stockholders farms..	58	-	11	11	13	15	8
Other—cooperative, estate or trust, institutional, etc. farms..	156	3	14	37	37	42	23
acres..	69 579	61	2 175	25 602	18 695	15 934	7 112

See footnotes at end of table.

Table 50. **Summary by Age and Principal Occupation of Operator: 1987**—Con.

[For meaning of abbreviations and symbols, see introductory text]

Item	Total farming and other occupations	Farming						
				Age of operator (years)				
		Total	Under 25	25 to 34	35 to 44	45 to 54	55 to 64	65 and over
FARMS BY SIZE								
1 to 9 acres	3 689	1 465	78	252	225	190	246	474
10 to 49 acres	6 222	1 348	57	144	164	136	256	571
50 to 69 acres	1 849	532	22	51	56	56	88	259
70 to 99 acres	4 690	1 584	54	182	150	142	309	747
100 to 139 acres	3 117	1 191	59	119	117	122	210	564
140 to 179 acres	5 854	2 785	93	303	267	233	499	1 390
180 to 219 acres	2 307	1 127	46	132	101	115	213	520
220 to 259 acres	2 945	1 614	58	155	167	169	379	686
260 to 499 acres	11 553	7 684	229	1 044	900	864	1 786	2 861
500 to 999 acres	12 093	9 942	178	1 514	1 553	1 554	2 758	2 385
1,000 to 1,999 acres	9 304	8 538	108	1 117	1 672	1 750	2 442	1 449
2,000 acres or more	5 056	4 797	31	423	1 030	1 177	1 366	770
FARMS BY STANDARD INDUSTRIAL CLASSIFICATION								
Cash grains (011)	31 789	21 948	583	2 945	3 420	3 380	5 401	6 219
Field crops, except cash grains (013)	2 010	776	14	90	114	90	185	283
Cotton (0131)	1	1	-	-	-	-	1	-
Tobacco (0132)	3	-	-	-	-	-	-	-
Sugarcane and sugar beets; Irish potatoes; field crops, except cash grains, n.e.c. (0133, 0134, 0139)	2 006	775	14	90	114	90	184	283
Vegetables and melons (016)	179	80	-	8	12	10	13	37
Fruits and tree nuts (017)	171	51	-	5	3	6	17	20
Horticultural specialties (018)	224	98	1	11	22	21	22	21
General farms, primarily crop (019)	1 463	767	13	93	130	133	199	199
Livestock, except dairy, poultry, and animal specialties (021)	29 037	16 840	375	2 018	2 336	2 435	4 164	5 512
Beef cattle, except feedlots (0212)	21 661	12 216	242	1 272	1 486	1 653	2 993	4 870
Dairy farms (024)	1 391	1 262	14	170	265	290	343	180
Poultry and eggs (025)	197	102	-	7	17	18	31	29
Animal specialties (027)	1 452	301	10	42	55	52	64	78
General farms, primarily livestock and animal specialties (029)	666	382	3	47	48	73	113	98
LIVESTOCK								
Cattle and calves inventory .... farms	40 765	27 374	507	3 361	4 207	4 348	7 133	7 818
number	5 539 292	4 511 209	41 893	418 664	863 368	1 064 996	1 342 429	779 829
Farms with—								
1 to 9	4 967	1 486	42	212	179	189	297	567
10 to 49	16 841	9 262	227	1 079	1 085	1 086	2 100	3 685
50 to 99	8 529	6 699	118	896	1 025	969	1 628	1 833
100 to 199	6 150	5 417	66	694	908	1 041	1 581	1 037
200 to 499	3 580	3 330	47	365	661	743	1 009	505
500 or more	1 318	1 180	7	115	259	290	318	191
Cows and heifers that had calved .... farms	33 157	22 420	374	2 587	3 315	3 547	5 966	6 631
number	1 451 324	1 197 522	12 293	118 592	205 094	235 278	348 544	277 721
Beef cows .... farms	31 476	21 071	355	2 389	3 030	3 262	5 606	6 429
number	1 354 649	1 107 509	11 662	107 477	186 025	213 978	322 543	265 804
Farms with—								
1 to 9	6 299	2 575	74	308	306	310	533	1 044
10 to 49	17 123	11 960	213	1 389	1 435	1 524	2 894	3 905
50 to 99	5 108	4 438	43	471	777	825	1 365	957
100 to 199	2 115	1 933	23	166	366	423	588	366
200 or more	714	667	2	49	132	160	198	126
500 or more	116	98	-	6	16	20	28	29
Milk cows .... farms	3 093	2 439	29	303	514	479	661	453
number	96 675	90 013	611	11 115	19 069	21 300	26 001	11 917
Farms with—								
1 to 4	1 195	744	10	63	175	107	181	208
5 to 9	150	84	2	16	18	13	20	15
10 to 49	979	677	14	137	161	175	257	133
50 to 99	582	557	3	72	120	142	147	73
100 to 199	163	155	-	13	36	37	48	22
200 to 499	21	19	-	1	5	4	7	2
500 or more	3	3	-	1	1	-	1	-
Heifers and heifer calves .... farms	31 410	21 357	383	2 546	3 295	3 457	5 665	6 011
number	1 632 193	1 330 473	13 074	113 732	276 035	340 508	366 911	220 213
Steers, steer calves, bulls and bull calves .... farms	35 035	23 910	430	2 893	3 678	3 606	6 299	6 804
number	2 455 775	1 983 214	16 526	188 360	382 259	489 200	626 974	261 895
Cattle and calves sold .... farms	41 498	28 068	529	3 441	4 284	4 439	7 311	8 064
number	7 310 338	5 589 363	31 538	355 729	1 095 516	1 510 321	1 784 393	831 866
$1,000	4 305 335	3 276 567	15 078	180 887	646 669	920 903	1 075 272	437 758
Calves .... farms	18 618	11 657	166	1 290	1 711	1 769	2 981	3 720
number	468 326	366 614	4 458	42 231	71 358	64 819	96 751	89 197
$1,000	146 961	116 848	1 514	13 375	22 365	20 714	30 274	27 707
Cattle .... farms	34 216	23 671	480	2 930	3 666	3 774	6 195	6 666
number	6 842 010	5 220 549	27 080	313 498	1 024 158	1 445 502	1 667 642	742 669
$1,000	4 159 374	3 160 719	13 564	167 512	624 404	900 189	1 044 998	410 051
Fattened on grain and concentrates ... farms	4 620	3 357	60	390	571	579	920	837
number	4 851 726	3 284 545	4 851	92 899	631 574	1 004 340	1 158 948	391 933
$1,000	3 041 522	2 210 486	2 946	59 759	427 829	680 363	796 993	242 596

See footnotes at end of table.

Table 50. **Summary by Age and Principal Occupation of Operator: 1987** —Con.

[For meaning of abbreviations and symbols, see introductory text]

Item		Other occupations					
			Age of operator (years)				
	Total	Under 25	25 to 34	35 to 44	45 to 54	55 to 64	65 and over
FARMS BY SIZE							
1 to 9 acres	2 221	151	491	543	412	316	311
10 to 49 acres	4 874	127	750	1 345	1 164	937	551
50 to 69 acres	1 317	31	207	309	299	282	189
70 to 99 acres	3 106	84	492	687	757	666	420
100 to 139 acres	1 926	53	333	413	441	432	254
140 to 179 acres	3 069	89	485	633	709	656	497
180 to 219 acres	1 180	22	190	254	307	255	152
220 to 259 acres	1 231	23	172	256	295	293	192
260 to 499 acres	3 869	92	584	887	965	854	487
500 to 999 acres	2 161	19	277	505	576	502	272
1,000 to 1,999 acres	766	6	94	169	214	171	112
2,000 acres or more	259	2	20	48	60	72	57
FARMS BY STANDARD INDUSTRIAL CLASSIFICATION							
Cash grains (011)	9 841	308	1 587	2 174	2 319	2 048	1 397
Field crops. except cash grains (013)	1 234	13	164	307	297	297	156
Cotton (0131)	-	-	-	-	-	-	-
Tobacco (0132)	3	1	-	1	1	-	-
Sugarcane and sugar beets; irish potatoes; field crops, except cash grains, n.e.c. (0133, 0134, 0139)	1 231	12	164	306	296	297	156
Vegetables and melons (016)	99	-	13	25	26	21	14
Fruits and tree nuts (017)	120	1	7	16	43	37	16
Horticultural specialties (018)	126	-	12	32	30	33	19
General farms, primarily crop (019)	696	11	89	173	173	150	100
Livestock, except dairy, poultry, and animal specialties (021)	12 197	344	1 997	2 869	2 837	2 533	1 617
Beef cattle, except feedlots (0212)	9 645	232	1 447	2 151	2 296	2 122	1 395
Dairy farms (024)	129	5	26	23	37	27	11
Poultry and eggs (025)	95	2	18	26	16	20	13
Animal specialties (027)	1 151	14	139	350	344	208	97
General farms, primarily livestock and animal specialties (029)	284	1	34	54	77	64	54
LIVESTOCK							
Cattle and calves inventory .... farms	13 411	324	2 132	3 179	3 228	2 821	1 727
number	1 028 083	9 080	127 238	246 442	215 270	325 203	104 850
Farms with—							
1 to 9	2 861	93	527	802	631	511	317
10 to 49	7 579	191	1 216	1 703	1 873	1 588	1 008
50 to 99	1 830	22	230	432	469	452	235
100 to 199	733	11	115	153	174	158	111
200 to 499	250	7	31	59	66	54	33
500 or more	138	-	13	30	26	47	23
Cows and heifers that had calved .... farms	10 737	262	1 612	2 477	2 644	2 317	1 425
number	253 802	4 005	33 481	49 688	60 800	66 109	39 719
Beef cows .... farms	10 404	256	1 538	2 393	2 566	2 257	1 394
number	247 140	3 871	32 577	46 345	58 609	64 608	39 130
Farms with—							
1 to 49	3 724	131	612	931	859	724	467
10 to 49	5 763	117	820	1 278	1 475	1 311	762
50 to 99	670	5	89	140	164	159	113
100 to 199	162	-	15	38	52	43	34
200 to 499	47	3	1	4	14	13	12
500 or more	18	-	1	2	2	7	6
Milk cows .... farms	654	12	119	164	155	132	72
number	6 662	134	904	1 343	2 191	1 501	589
Farms with—							
1 to 4	451	8	90	122	97	93	51
5 to 9	66	3	17	12	12	13	9
10 to 49	102	-	19	20	35	19	9
50 to 99	25	-	1	8	9	6	1
100 to 199	8	1	2	1	2	-	2
200 to 499	2	-	-	-	1	1	-
500 or more	-	-	-	-	-	-	-
Heifers and heifer calves .... farms	10 053	241	1 579	2 404	2 456	2 140	1 233
number	301 720	2 658	37 712	57 944	68 542	105 770	29 094
Steers, steer calves, bulls, and bull calves .... farms	11 125	251	1 731	2 632	2 742	2 361	1 408
number	472 561	2 417	56 045	138 810	85 928	153 324	36 037
Cattle and calves sold .... farms	13 430	327	2 130	3 124	3 245	2 827	1 777
number	1 720 975	7 869	191 788	383 257	284 434	726 070	127 557
$1,000	1 026 788	3 540	115 937	233 292	156 189	454 172	65 638
Calves .... farms	6 861	145	1 027	1 573	1 676	1 513	927
number	99 614	1 436	13 689	22 225	24 322	23 366	14 476
$1,000	30 112	410	4 152	6 611	7 467	6 964	4 509
Cattle .... farms	10 545	259	1 673	2 448	2 570	2 214	1 381
number	1 621 461	6 433	178 099	361 032	260 112	702 704	113 081
$1,000	998 655	3 131	111 785	226 681	148 722	447 208	61 130
Fattened on grain and concentrates ... farms	1 263	41	219	328	296	235	146
number	1 267 181	277	132 213	291 795	186 226	610 785	45 885
$1,000	831 037	157	89 982	193 159	114 546	400 702	32 490

See footnotes at end of table.

Table 50. Summary by Age and Principal Occupation of Operator: 1987—Con.

[For meaning of abbreviations and symbols, see introductory text]

Item	Total farming and other occupations	Farming						
					Age of operator (years)			
		Total	Under 25	25 to 34	35 to 44	45 to 54	55 to 64	65 and over
LIVESTOCK—Con.								
Hogs and pigs inventory .... farms..	6 768	4 837	141	940	972	891	1 142	751
number..	1 516 878	1 267 843	25 806	233 409	280 506	303 649	300 014	124 457
Farms with—								
1 to 24	1 916	992	21	149	173	163	240	246
25 to 49	828	515	12	102	86	89	106	120
50 to 99	1 087	811	28	165	145	131	212	130
100 to 199	1 092	878	40	174	199	171	185	109
200 to 499	1 226	1 059	35	241	227	201	253	102
500 or more	619	582	5	109	142	136	146	44
Used or to be used for breeding .... farms..	4 596	3 400	102	664	868	631	808	526
number..	191 079	155 477	3 093	29 736	34 645	34 698	37 447	15 858
Other .... farms..	6 286	4 579	136	890	924	846	1 081	702
number..	1 325 799	1 112 166	22 513	203 673	245 863	268 951	262 567	108 599
Hogs and pigs sold .... farms..	7 090	5 041	150	972	1 004	925	1 199	791
number..	2 759 676	2 299 615	40 120	437 126	535 168	544 819	617 956	224 427
$1,000..	284 375	236 626	3 365	43 710	53 427	57 263	55 207	23 663
Feeder pigs .... farms..	1 869	1 212	52	269	270	185	268	168
number..	514 394	406 862	17 768	109 895	109 605	72 835	59 605	37 174
$1,000..	23 029	19 303	736	5 090	4 962	3 202	2 548	1 745
Litters of pigs farrowed between—								
Dec. 1 of preceding year and Nov. 30 .... farms..	4 819	3 546	107	691	692	660	843	553
number..	295 974	244 967	4 755	44 782	56 640	57 192	57 615	24 003
Dec. 1 and May 31 .... farms..	4 455	3 333	99	643	649	626	801	515
number..	149 414	124 066	2 248	22 322	28 195	28 822	29 743	12 736
June 1 and Nov. 30 .... farms..	4 403	3 277	99	659	657	606	775	481
number..	146 560	120 921	2 507	22 460	28 445	26 370	27 872	11 267
Sheep and lambs of all ages inventory ...... farms..	2 400	1 326	31	183	312	241	296	265
number..	249 303	202 196	2 302	36 141	66 996	28 210	45 481	23 066
Ewes 1 year old or older .... farms..	2 195	1 226	26	176	275	219	279	249
number..	129 607	100 061	1 121	15 570	25 914	16 946	26 031	14 479
Sheep and lambs sold .... farms..	2 396	1 335	33	188	309	234	305	266
number..	267 152	225 204	2 613	25 184	121 480	26 698	31 368	17 661
Sheep and lambs shorn .... farms..	2 183	1 232	26	176	273	221	256	248
number..	218 980	193 848	1 631	30 154	79 097	26 154	32 181	19 929
pounds of wool..	1 610 863	1 251 287	10 973	210 499	453 700	196 655	237 191	142 269
Horses and ponies inventory .... farms..	12 879	6 919	96	856	1 366	1 225	1 634	1 742
number..	55 598	29 073	446	3 163	5 715	5 981	6 618	7 150
Horses and ponies sold .... farms..	2 260	1 035	13	141	198	199	222	262
number..	8 467	4 585	35	664	759	977	1 181	969
Goats inventory .... farms..	862	396	8	61	106	75	79	67
number..	8 831	6 223	252	1 064	2 070	928	1 074	635
Goats sold .... farms..	258	112	–	14	35	17	31	15
number..	2 679	1 198	–	71	410	125	334	258
POULTRY								
Chickens 3 months old or older inventory .. farms..	4 206	2 498	23	272	363	345	602	873
number..	2 094 610	1 681 643	573	62 216	224 897	298 926	535 941	559 090
Farms with—								
1 to 399	4 117	2 421	23	269	375	330	573	851
400 to 3,199	30	25	–	1	2	2	7	13
3,200 to 9,999	12	11	–	–	–	2	6	3
10,000 to 19,999	16	16	–	–	2	7	6	1
20,000 to 49,999	19	17	–	2	3	3	8	1
50,000 to 99,999	7	6	–	–	1	1	2	2
100,000 or more	3	2	–	–	–	–	–	2
Hens and pullets of laying age .... farms..	4 150	2 470	23	269	362	338	595	866
number..	1 797 313	1 464 771	556	37 573	223 815	283 326	462 966	456 533
Pullets 3 months old or older not of laying age .... farms..	415	297	3	30	35	34	58	79
number..	297 297	216 872	15	24 643	1 082	15 600	72 975	102 557
Hens and pullets sold .... farms..	363	228	–	23	34	39	54	78
number..	2 380 938	1 933 747	–	122 911	282 800	264 535	591 990	671 511
Broilers and other meat-type chickens sold .... farms..	132	70	2	17	19	11	13	8
number..	176 061	145 983	(D)	(D)	3 026	1 317	121 475	602
Farms with—								
1 to 1,999	123	65	2	14	19	11	11	8
2,000 to 59,999	7	3	–	3	–	–	–	–
60,000 to 99,999	2	2	–	–	–	–	2	–
100,000 or more	–	–	–	–	–	–	–	–
Turkey hens kept for breeding .... farms..	194	97	–	12	17	23	28	17
number..	(D)	(D)	–	(D)	38	12 448	116	62
Turkeys sold .... farms..	88	54	1	12	12	11	8	10
number..	230 719	164 281	(D)	(D)	33 896	30 912	92 977	1 562

See footnotes at end of table.

Table 50. **Summary by Age and Principal Occupation of Operator: 1987**—Con.

[For meaning of abbreviations and symbols, see introductory text]

Item	Total	Other occupations					
		Age of operator (years)					
	Total	Under 25	25 to 34	35 to 44	45 to 54	55 to 64	65 and over
LIVESTOCK—Con.							
Hogs and pigs inventory .... farms..	1 931	84	437	586	386	307	131
number..	249 235	6 614	26 613	144 232	33 609	23 992	12 175
Farms with—							
1 to 24	924	35	201	281	172	164	71
25 to 49	313	17	81	91	57	45	22
50 to 99	276	13	62	71	69	43	18
100 to 199	214	11	51	70	43	29	10
200 to 499	167	7	40	59	33	22	6
500 or more	37	1	2	14	12	4	4
Used or to be used for breeding .... farms..	1 196	47	295	357	244	185	68
number..	35 602	917	4 817	19 375	5 735	3 631	1 127
Other .... farms..	1 707	70	383	522	348	267	117
number..	213 633	5 697	23 796	124 857	27 874	20 361	11 048
Hogs and pigs sold .... farms..	2 049	99	454	639	408	318	131
number..	460 060	11 506	59 218	246 865	65 447	51 980	25 044
$1,000..	47 750	1 171	5 043	27 473	6 056	5 175	2 832
Feeder pigs .... farms..	657	35	185	197	124	88	28
number..	107 512	2 545	24 213	51 640	15 552	11 249	2 313
$1,000..	4 726	107	1 065	2 325	632	500	97
Litters of pigs farrowed between—							
Dec. 1 of preceding year and Nov. 30 ... farms..	1 273	53	310	383	257	194	76
number..	50 987	1 048	6 408	29 478	6 964	5 199	1 890
Dec. 1 and May 31 .... farms..	1 122	43	264	339	230	177	69
number..	25 348	520	3 031	14 710	3 501	2 831	955
June 1 and Nov. 30 .... farms..	1 126	47	289	331	231	166	62
number..	25 639	528	3 377	14 768	3 463	2 568	935
Sheep and lambs of all ages inventory..... farms..	1 072	35	229	316	265	150	77
number..	47 107	1 236	9 996	15 739	10 470	6 409	3 263
Ewes 1 year old or older .... farms..	969	33	202	283	240	137	74
number..	29 546	(D)	(D)	8 676	7 435	4 266	2 081
Sheep and lambs sold .... farms..	1 061	36	220	316	261	151	77
number..	41 948	933	8 544	14 705	8 442	6 800	2 524
Sheep and lambs shorn .... farms..	951	33	195	272	239	139	73
number..	36 134	1 097	7 263	10 879	6 874	5 396	2 605
pounds of wool..	259 376	7 288	52 698	75 168	61 979	43 230	19 013
Horses and ponies inventory................. farms..	5 960	92	891	1 762	1 600	1 114	501
number..	26 525	265	3 299	7 567	7 502	5 550	2 342
Horses and ponies sold .... farms..	1 225	22	178	398	325	200	102
number..	3 882	48	461	1 159	1 073	666	475
Goats inventory .... farms..	468	9	68	153	131	83	22
number..	2 608	67	321	793	926	374	127
Goats sold .... farms..	146	5	31	41	46	17	6
number..	1 481	24	271	418	634	89	45
POULTRY							
Chickens 3 months old or older inventory .. farms..	1 708	16	302	494	393	305	198
number..	412 967	3 499	7 602	27 098	9 435	185 964	179 369
Farms with—							
1 to 399	1 696	15	302	492	391	299	197
400 to 3,199	5	1	–	1	2	1	–
3,200 to 9,999	1	–	–	–	–	1	–
10,000 to 19,999	2	–	–	1	–	1	–
20,000 to 49,999	2	–	–	–	–	2	–
50,000 to 99,999	1	–	–	–	–	1	–
100,000 or more	1	–	–	–	–	–	1
Hens and pullets of laying age .... farms..	1 680	16	298	484	387	301	194
number..	332 542	(D)	(D)	25 918	8 623	110 297	178 986
Pullets 3 months old or older not of							
laying age .... farms..	178	2	29	52	46	29	20
number..	80 425	(D)	(D)	1 180	612	75 867	383
Hens and pullets sold .... farms..	135	–	22	42	27	24	20
number..	447 189	–	1 252	18 403	1 153	250 675	175 706
Broilers and other meat-type chickens							
sold.. farms..	62	1	17	20	11	10	3
number..	30 078	(D)	(D)	6 653	1 044	2 840	160
Farms with—							
1 to 1,999	58	–	16	18	11	10	3
2,000 to 59,999	4	1	1	2	–	–	–
60,000 to 99,999	–	–	–	–	–	–	–
100,000 or more	–	–	–	–	–	–	–
Turkey hens kept for breeding .... farms..	97	–	19	32	28	8	10
number..	17 558	–	132	151	1 025	16 219	31
Turkeys sold .... farms..	34	–	7	9	12	3	3
number..	46 438	–	2 476	19 360	159	18 431	6 012

See footnotes at end of table.

Table 50. **Summary by Age and Principal Occupation of Operator: 1987** —Con.

[For meaning of abbreviations and symbols, see introductory text]

Item	Total farming and other occupations	Farming						
		Total	Under 25	25 to 34	35 to 44	45 to 54	55 to 64	65 and over
CROPS HARVESTED								
Corn for grain or seed .... farms..	8 944	7 482	193	1 151	1 455	1 408	1 909	1 366
acres..	1 243 969	1 157 111	21 367	182 620	271 444	264 828	282 397	134 455
bushels..	144 133 587	135 061 428	2 651 266	22 194 570	32 158 677	31 273 370	32 263 232	14 520 314
Irrigated .... farms..	3 547	3 327	99	601	724	674	812	417
acres..	816 992	772 044	15 883	131 766	181 769	184 789	178 698	79 139
Farms by acres harvested:								
1 to 24 acres	1 984	1 324	47	162	163	188	320	444
25 to 99 acres	3 279	2 716	69	462	478	458	727	522
100 to 249 acres	2 196	2 025	58	296	445	432	536	258
250 to 499 acres	1 044	989	15	162	257	219	236	100
500 acres or more	441	428	4	69	112	111	90	42
Corn for silage or green chop .... farms..	2 009	1 861	22	225	358	378	556	322
acres..	109 230	102 857	946	11 860	20 849	21 976	29 959	17 267
tons, green..	1 669 413	1 571 827	14 657	193 567	308 817	342 494	454 522	257 770
Irrigated .... farms..	659	610	7	87	115	123	188	90
acres..	53 214	49 619	516	6 922	8 914	10 957	14 150	8 159
Farms by acres harvested:								
1 to 24 acres	799	723	8	90	134	138	212	141
25 to 99 acres	944	889	12	106	167	187	279	138
100 to 249 acres	207	193	2	21	46	39	48	37
250 to 499 acres	43	41	–	7	8	10	13	3
500 acres or more	16	15	–	1	3	4	4	3
Sorghum for grain or seed .... farms..	3 492	25 175	601	3 595	4 213	4 199	6 722	5 845
acres..	3 399 564	3 043 331	50 016	416 436	633 356	648 532	825 366	469 525
bushels..	228 045 100	206 296 146	3 479 540	26 776 228	43 434 430	45 081 580	55 533 317	29 991 041
Irrigated .... farms..	3 137	2 808	67	409	572	531	792	437
acres..	464 119	437 059	8 195	57 586	90 739	101 310	122 551	56 678
Farms by acres harvested:								
1 to 24 acres	7 260	4 205	137	478	459	460	1 024	1 649
25 to 99 acres	14 139	10 747	289	1 600	1 557	1 538	2 889	2 664
100 to 249 acres	7 830	7 114	139	1 145	1 442	1 418	1 983	989
250 to 499 acres	2 503	2 392	34	293	577	580	641	267
500 acres or more	740	717	2	81	168	205	185	76
Wheat for grain .... farms..	38 638	29 285	602	3 898	4 673	4 766	7 507	7 839
acres..	8 679 586	7 637 092	96 560	925 505	1 425 665	1 570 717	2 137 297	1 481 348
bushels..	292 999 442	260 051 333	3 410 662	32 057 835	49 887 257	53 673 065	72 061 548	49 140 966
Irrigated .... farms..	3 046	2 702	77	471	607	529	663	385
acres..	635 524	599 722	11 782	86 181	134 127	139 979	149 582	78 091
Farms by acres harvested:								
1 to 24 acres	4 230	2 297	78	245	257	280	532	905
25 to 99 acres	11 451	7 421	208	985	976	918	1 656	2 678
100 to 249 acres	11 111	8 688	200	1 339	1 293	1 252	2 237	2 367
250 to 499 acres	7 248	6 539	79	854	1 244	1 270	1 841	1 251
500 acres or more	4 598	4 340	37	475	903	1 046	1 241	638
Barley for grain....................... farms..	2 307	2 000	24	265	351	386	537	437
acres..	95 465	87 176	572	6 795	15 557	18 487	24 731	18 034
bushels..	3 639 224	3 326 879	15 959	390 778	594 472	712 133	943 304	669 233
Irrigated .... farms..	166	158	–	26	27	40	30	35
acres..	7 359	7 161	–	893	1 410	1 614	1 152	2 092
Oats for grain .... farms..	5 313	4 407	72	526	646	727	1 245	1 191
acres..	128 091	111 499	1 716	13 789	18 627	19 696	32 545	25 126
bushels..	4 775 729	4 232 631	71 738	513 402	710 883	762 072	1 263 356	911 180
Irrigated .... farms..	48	45	–	8	9	7	14	7
acres..	2 278	2 164	–	322	849	267	440	286
Soybeans for beans .... farms..	18 864	13 830	392	967	2 326	2 337	3 542	3 264
acres..	1 878 974	1 616 735	31 184	231 996	359 845	346 472	411 958	235 260
bushels..	55 789 994	48 621 277	866 121	7 096 936	11 045 153	10 362 334	12 376 849	6 873 884
Irrigated .... farms..	1 939	1 752	38	289	400	341	433	251
acres..	175 053	163 890	1 912	25 274	41 144	36 568	37 467	19 525
Farms by acres harvested:								
1 to 24 acres	5 508	2 996	113	392	379	391	691	1 030
25 to 99 acres	8 253	5 926	174	853	878	692	1 547	1 582
100 to 249 acres	3 775	3 196	82	471	640	629	876	498
250 to 499 acres	1 315	1 213	21	165	287	293	313	114
500 acres or more	513	499	2	66	144	132	115	40
Dry edible beans, excluding dry limas ...... farms..	192	182	2	35	36	35	51	23
acres..	30 460	28 662	(D)	(D)	5 403	7 560	7 168	3 513
cwt..	441 316	418 433	(D)	(D)	72 803	114 626	108 041	52 511
Irrigated .... farms..	167	160	2	33	33	28	49	15
acres..	28 182	26 505	(D)	(D)	4 921	6 837	6 968	2 956
Irish potatoes .... farms..	97	71	–	5	7	8	18	33
acres..	643	612	–	262	16	285	18	32
cwt..	136 764	136 307	–	79 125	2 616	46 620	2 551	5 393
Irrigated .... farms..	21	13	–	4	2	2	1	4
acres..	(D)	547	–	262	(D)	272	(D)	(D)
Hay—alfalfa, other tame, small grain, wild,								
grass silage, green chop, etc. (see text) . farms..	33 964	23 597	348	2 766	3 646	3 602	6 380	6 855
acres..	2 254 082	1 847 119	21 979	196 357	354 257	340 362	537 007	397 157
tons, dry..	5 080 647	4 326 895	46 866	477 115	918 104	836 812	1 241 421	806 577
Irrigated .... farms..	1 492	1 296	19	178	296	262	329	214
acres..	206 961	187 376	844	16 633	55 446	39 894	51 128	23 429
Farms by acres harvested:								
1 to 24 acres	11 391	6 083	136	693	785	759	1 446	2 264
25 to 99 acres	16 111	11 863	144	1 484	1 769	1 855	3 231	3 380
100 to 249 acres	5 297	4 502	56	499	963	979	1 385	819
250 to 499 acres	913	828	8	70	166	170	262	152
500 acres or more	252	221	2	21	63	39	56	40

See footnotes at end of table.

[For meaning of abbreviations and symbols, see introductory text]

Item	Total	Other occupations					
		Age of operator (years)					
		Under 25	25 to 34	35 to 44	45 to 54	55 to 64	65 and over
CROPS HARVESTED							
Corn for grain or seed ... farms..	1 462	42	261	318	362	305	174
acres..	86 858	2 057	15 879	17 438	22 011	18 868	10 605
bushels..	9 072 153	226 263	1 814 863	1 800 401	2 192 383	1 995 732	1 040 511
Irrigated ... farms..	320	12	69	67	73	71	28
acres..	44 948	1 358	10 016	8 496	10 704	9 567	4 807
Farms by acres harvested:							
1 to 24 acres	660	18	131	145	144	135	87
25 to 99 acres	563	18	88	124	163	113	57
100 to 249 acres	171	5	26	37	40	42	21
250 to 499 acres	55	1	12	11	11	12	8
500 acres or more	13	-	4	1	4	3	1
Corn for silage or green chop ... farms..	148	2	18	32	36	38	22
acres..	6 373	(D)	(D)	1 238	1 817	1 735	1 003
tons, green..	97 566	(D)	(D)	16 237	30 025	26 605	16 431
Irrigated ... farms..	49	-	9	12	12	8	8
acres..	3 595	-	391	431	1 140	928	705
Farms by acres harvested:							
1 to 24 acres	76	2	10	17	16	21	10
25 to 99 acres	55	-	7	11	16	13	8
100 to 249 acres	14	-	1	3	3	3	4
250 to 499 acres	2	-	-	1	1	-	-
500 acres or more	1	-	-	-	-	1	-
Sorghum for grain or seed ... farms..	7 317	203	1 287	1 728	1 741	1 481	877
acres..	356 233	8 670	58 315	84 972	86 983	74 126	41 167
bushels..	21 748 954	548 747	3 730 167	5 317 592	5 405 841	4 376 016	2 368 591
Irrigated ... farms..	329	10	56	77	85	72	29
acres..	27 060	564	3 200	6 226	6 530	7 074	3 466
Farms by acres harvested:							
1 to 24 acres	3 075	80	561	710	718	604	402
25 to 99 acres	3 392	106	598	814	803	690	381
100 to 249 acres	716	16	109	173	188	154	76
250 to 499 acres	111	1	15	25	27	29	14
500 acres or more	23	-	4	6	5	4	4
Wheat for grain ... farms..	9 353	270	1 537	2 035	2 171	2 025	1 315
acres..	1 042 496	21 261	143 772	245 255	254 420	229 241	148 527
bushels..	32 948 109	677 501	4 548 291	7 686 776	7 932 732	7 443 961	4 658 848
Irrigated ... farms..	314	14	45	65	67	72	31
acres..	35 802	868	4 624	7 746	8 575	9 010	4 979
Farms by acres harvested:							
1 to 24 acres	1 933	67	321	416	468	389	272
25 to 99 acres	4 030	139	730	829	856	891	585
100 to 249 acres	2 423	53	379	547	586	525	333
250 to 499 acres	709	8	80	162	195	163	81
500 acres or more	258	3	27	61	66	57	44
Barley for grain ... farms..	307	7	47	59	71	81	42
acres..	8 289	137	824	1 772	1 827	2 371	1 358
bushels..	313 345	6 124	29 352	68 789	69 964	101 225	37 891
Irrigated ... farms..	8	-	1	(D)	(D)	3	1
acres..	198	-	(D)	(D)	(D)	134	(D)
Oats for grain ... farms..	906	14	124	223	225	201	119
acres..	16 592	202	2 071	3 763	4 220	4 000	2 336
bushels..	543 098	5 706	59 085	116 728	144 709	144 151	72 719
Irrigated ... farms..	3	1	-	2	-	-	-
acres..	114	(D)	-	(D)	-	-	-
Soybeans for beans ... farms..	5 034	136	827	1 175	1 264	1 006	626
acres..	262 243	6 334	43 020	63 394	68 591	50 279	30 625
bushels..	7 168 717	151 195	1 161 050	1 739 645	1 882 683	1 362 916	871 228
Irrigated ... farms..	167	3	30	50	44	47	13
acres..	11 163	76	2 312	2 917	2 327	2 545	986
Farms by acres harvested:							
1 to 24 acres	2 012	58	338	456	487	386	287
25 to 99 acres	2 327	55	375	537	591	494	275
100 to 249 acres	579	23	95	155	149	109	48
250 to 499 acres	102	-	18	23	32	15	14
500 acres or more	14	-	1	4	5	2	2
Dry edible beans, excluding dry limas ... farms..	10	-	4	-	3	2	1
acres..	1 798	-	263	-	285	(D)	(D)
cwt..	22 865	-	2 757	-	3 279	(D)	(D)
Irrigated ... farms..	7	-	2	-	3	1	-
acres..	1 677	-	(D)	-	269	(D)	(D)
Irish potatoes ... farms..	26	-	-	6	4	7	9
acres..	31	-	-	12	4	4	11
cwt..	2 457	-	-	389	615	880	573
Irrigated ... farms..	8	-	-	1	-	5	2
acres..	(D)	-	-	(D)	-	3	(D)
Hay—alfalfa, other tame, small grain, wild, grass silage, green chop, etc. (see text) ... farms..	10 367	151	1 426	2 527	2 646	2 327	1 290
acres..	406 963	5 679	50 111	89 642	108 798	94 196	58 537
tons, dry..	753 952	11 737	89 151	161 001	199 444	178 536	114 083
Irrigated ... farms..	194	2	26	39	54	45	28
acres..	19 585	(D)	(D)	2 926	6 926	3 548	4 151
Farms by acres harvested:							
1 to 24 acres	5 308	78	779	1 319	1 328	1 128	676
25 to 99 acres	4 248	60	554	1 036	1 091	1 017	490
100 to 249 acres	695	12	84	150	194	158	97
250 to 499 acres	85	-	9	20	21	16	19
500 acres or more	31	1	-	2	12	8	8

See footnotes at end of table.

Table 50. **Summary by Age and Principal Occupation of Operator: 1987**—Con.

[For meaning of abbreviations and symbols, see introductory text]

Item	Total farming and other occupations	Farming						
		Total	Age of operator (years)					
			Under 25	25 to 34	35 to 44	45 to 54	55 to 64	65 and over
CROPS HARVESTED—Con.								
Hay—alfalfa, other tame, small grain, wild, grass silage, green chop, etc. (see text) —Con.								
Alfalfa hay .... farms..	15 484	12 058	149	1 416	1 996	2 094	3 407	2 996
acres..	741 856	544 256	5 437	74 099	134 098	122 541	186 828	121 253
tons, dry..	2 529 635	2 246 122	19 557	252 449	515 836	453 037	634 462	370 781
Irrigated .... farms..	1 174	1 025	13	132	227	213	272	168
acres..	180 952	163 566	627	13 654	47 277	35 451	46 707	19 870
Vegetables harvested for sale (see text) ... farms..	418	237	3	25	53	41	44	71
acres..	5 424	4 331	23	363	2 027	526	679	713
Irrigated .... farms..	166	95	3	11	20	16	22	23
acres..	1 851	1 425	23	119	338	313	416	215
Farms by acres harvested:								
0.1 to 4.9 acres	244	126	1	11	31	22	22	39
5.0 to 24.9 acres	130	77	2	9	12	14	14	26
25.0 to 99.9 acres	39	29	–	4	9	4	7	5
100.0 to 249.9 acres	4	4	–	1	–	1	1	1
250.0 acres or more	1	1	–	–	–	1	–	–
Field seed and grass seed crops .... farms..	1 188	927	14	113	189	148	252	211
acres..	58 460	47 221	673	5 689	12 943	7 600	11 868	9 448
Irrigated .... farms..	12	9	–	–	2	2	4	1
acres..	2 222	2 181	–	–	(D)	(D)	1 656	(D)
Land in orchards .... farms..	503	211	–	17	22	33	48	91
acres..	5 999	4 150	–	294	401	734	1 560	1 162
Irrigated .... farms..	90	42	–	5	4	11	6	16
acres..	757	431	–	68	23	201	33	106
Farms by bearing and nonbearing acres:								
0.1 to 4.9 acres	309	113	–	9	11	18	20	55
5.0 to 24.9 acres	147	63	–	3	8	7	16	27
25.0 to 99.9 acres	39	28	–	5	2	6	9	6
100.0 to 249.9 acres	6	5	–	–	1	–	–	2
250.0 acres or more	2	2	–	–	–	–	1	1

See footnotes at end of table.

Table 50. **Summary by Age and Principal Occupation of Operator: 1987**—Con.

[For meaning of abbreviations and symbols, see introductory text]

Item	Other occupations						
	Total	Age of operator (years)					
		Under 25	25 to 34	35 to 44	45 to 54	55 to 64	65 and over
CROPS HARVESTED—Con.							
Hay—alfalfa, other tame, small grain, wild, grass silage, green chop, etc. (see text) —Con.							
Alfalfa hay .... farms..	3 426	43	485	840	865	778	417
acres..	97 600	1 698	11 329	19 824	25 344	23 819	15 786
tons, dry..	283 513	5 563	31 074	56 546	70 589	69 681	50 040
Irrigated .... farms..	149	1	20	91	43	36	18
acres..	17 366	(D)	(D)	2 439	8 248	3 254	3 765
Vegetables harvested for sale (see text) ... farms..	181	–	21	47	46	48	19
acres..	1 093	–	167	253	357	240	76
Irrigated .... farms..	71	–	10	16	20	18	7
acres..	426	–	73	106	116	107	24
Farms by acres harvested:							
0.1 to 4.9 acres	118	–	14	31	25	34	14
5.0 to 24.9 acres	53	–	4	15	17	12	5
25.0 to 99.9 acres	10	–	3	1	4	2	–
100.0 to 249.9 acres	–	–	–	–	–	–	–
250.0 acres or more	–	–	–	–	–	–	–
Field seed and grass seed crops .... farms..	261	2	37	89	56	56	21
acres..	11 239	(D)	(D)	4 237	3 012	2 046	1 085
Irrigated .... farms..	3	–	1	–	–	–	2
acres..	41	–	(D)	–	–	–	(D)
Land in orchards .... farms..	292	2	27	65	90	74	34
acres..	1 849	(D)	(D)	434	595	522	105
Irrigated .... farms..	48	2	5	12	11	12	6
acres..	326	(D)	(D)	65	48	166	15
Farms by bearing and nonbearing acres:							
0.1 to 4.9 acres	196	2	16	55	53	44	26
5.0 to 24.9 acres	84	–	9	7	33	27	8
25.0 to 99.9 acres	11	–	2	2	4	3	–
100.0 to 249.9 acres	1	–	–	1	–	–	–
250.0 acres or more	–	–	–	–	–	–	–

[1] Data are based on a sample of farms.
[2] Farms with total production expenses equal to market value of agricultural products sold are included as farms with gains of less than $1,000.

Table 51. **Summary by Size of Farm: 1987**

[For meaning of abbreviations and symbols, see introductory text]

Item	Total	1 to 9 acres	10 to 49 acres	50 to 69 acres	70 to 99 acres	100 to 139 acres
FARMS AND LAND IN FARMS						
Farms _____ number__	68 579	3 689	6 222	1 849	4 690	3 117
percent__	100.0	5.4	9.1	2.7	6.8	4.5
Land in farms _____acres__	46 628 519	9 327	172 040	107 904	379 846	363 799
Average size of farm_____acres__	680	3	28	58	81	117
MARKET VALUE OF AGRICUL-TURAL PRODUCTS SOLD						
Total sales (see text) _____ farms__	68 579	3 689	6 222	1 849	4 690	3 117
$1,000__	8 476 669	184 405	67 069	34 533	193 464	132 746
Average per farm _____dollars__	94 441	49 986	10 994	18 677	41 250	42 586
Farms by value of sales:						
Less than $1,000 (see text)_____	4 538	662	1 890	336	515	276
$1,000 to $2,499 _____	4 964	732	1 771	400	883	315
$2,500 to $4,999 _____	6 519	636	1 270	551	1 446	721
$5,000 to $9,999 _____	9 430	559	719	544	1 157	952
$10,000 to $19,999 _____	10 504	434	269	142	465	569
$20,000 to $24,999 _____	3 566	112	54	15	61	90
$25,000 to $39,999 _____	7 150	160	87	24	59	109
$40,000 to $49,999 _____	3 132	76	25	6	22	21
$50,000 to $99,999 _____	8 997	132	56	16	46	36
$100,000 to $249,999_____	6 656	103	47	6	17	18
$250,000 to $499,999_____	1 766	39	17	4	5	5
$500,000 to $999,999_____	568	13	13	-	2	5
$1,000,000 or more_____	369	16	10	5	10	-
Grains _____ farms__	48 608	172	1 713	707	2 392	1 743
$1,000__	1 550 403	113	3 181	2 311	6 890	9 935
Sales of $50,000 or more _____ farms__	8 994	-	-	-	-	-
$1,000__	976 864	-	-	-	-	-
Corn for grain _____ farms__	7 426	8	141	71	191	186
$1,000__	255 791	6	249	185	668	965
Wheat_____ farms__	36 365	127	810	330	1 359	985
$1,000__	894 147	54	935	520	3 258	3 136
Soybeans_____ farms__	16 724	35	618	326	916	834
$1,000__	263 742	44	1 327	1 018	3 064	3 790
Sorghum for grain _____ farms__	28 719	23	472	264	933	801
$1,000__	311 649	10	656	448	1 854	1 967
Barley_____ farms__	1 715	-	5	6	6	15
$1,000__	3 953	-	1	1	4	6
Oats _____ farms__	2 415	-	28	21	72	80
$1,000__	3 328	-	10	11	32	41
Other grains _____ farms__	1 656	-	7	3	10	16
$1,000__	17 793	-	3	28	10	31
Cotton and cottonseed_____ farms__	10	-	-	-	-	-
$1,000__	186	-	-	-	-	-
Sales of $50,000 or more _____ farms__	2	-	-	-	-	-
$1,000__	(D)	-	-	-	-	-
Tobacco_____ farms__	13	2	-	2	-	-
$1,000__	80	(D)	-	(D)	-	-
Sales of $50,000 or more _____ farms__	-	-	-	-	-	-
$1,000__	-	-	-	-	-	-
Hay, silage, and field seeds _____ farms__	12 601	29	814	267	748	504
$1,000__	109 574	13	915	392	1 315	1 023
Sales of $50,000 or more _____ farms__	316	-	-	-	-	-
$1,000__	47 030	-	-	-	-	-
Vegetables, sweet corn, and melons ____ farms__	418	51	127	28	33	24
$1,000__	4 151	145	746	110	324	347
Sales of $50,000 or more _____ farms__	10	-	-	-	2	1
$1,000__	1 767	-	-	-	(D)	(D)
Fruits, nuts, and berries _____ farms__	278	24	100	18	23	21
$1,000__	1 693	44	281	202	119	144
Sales of $50,000 or more _____ farms__	6	-	-	2	-	1
$1,000__	732	-	-	(D)	-	(D)
Nursery and greenhouse crops_____ farms__	272	122	73	11	12	7
$1,000__	26 805	11 151	3 652	(D)	674	119
Sales of $50,000 or more _____ farms__	62	30	11	2	4	-
$1,000__	24 509	10 101	2 981	(D)	579	-
Other crops_____ farms__	80	6	21	-	3	3
$1,000__	716	(D)	25	-	10	14
Sales of $50,000 or more _____ farms__	3	-	-	-	-	-
$1,000__	558	-	-	-	-	-
Poultry and poultry products _____ farms__	1 550	148	256	62	107	68
$1,000__	25 294	4 123	4 771	513	378	398
Sales of $50,000 or more _____ farms__	75	7	13	1	3	2
$1,000__	23 851	3 915	4 635	(D)	284	(D)
Dairy products _____ farms__	2 004	77	73	22	50	40
$1,000__	140 232	1 475	1 429	616	1 812	1 277
Sales of $50,000 or more _____ farms__	979	4	9	3	10	7
$1,000__	119 516	815	865	395	986	625
Cattle and calves_____ farms__	41 498	2 194	2 653	978	2 429	1 682
$1,000__	4 305 335	146 031	43 461	19 873	172 926	114 104
Sales of $50,000 or more _____ farms__	5 932	166	27	9	27	19
$1,000__	3 891 456	130 391	33 724	15 472	160 921	103 647

See footnotes at end of table.

Table 51. **Summary by Size of Farm:** 1987—Con.

[For meaning of abbreviations and symbols, see introductory text]

Item	140 to 179 acres	180 to 219 acres	220 to 259 acres	260 to 499 acres	500 to 999 acres	1,000 to 1,999 acres	2,000 acres or more
FARMS AND LAND IN FARMS							
Farms number	5 854	2 307	2 845	11 553	12 093	9 304	5 056
percent	8.5	3.4	4.1	16.8	17.6	13.6	7.4
Land in farms acres	927 599	455 738	677 474	4 296 061	8 673 395	12 925 252	17 640 082
Average size of farm acres	158	198	238	372	717	1 389	3 489
MARKET VALUE OF AGRICUL-TURAL PRODUCTS SOLD							
Total sales (see text) farms	5 854	2 307	2 845	11 553	12 093	9 304	5 056
$1,000	250 504	112 472	121 661	938 026	1 328 933	1 496 960	1 593 896
Average per farm dollars	42 792	48 753	42 763	81 193	109 893	161 109	315 248
Farms by value of sales:							
Less than $1,000 (see text)	305	117	99	168	91	43	16
$1,000 to $2,499	432	94	89	167	52	7	2
$2,500 to $4,999	1 103	293	252	489	127	23	4
$5,000 to $9,999	1 970	635	802	1 740	471	79	14
$10,000 to $19,999	1 346	742	927	3 630	1 875	264	41
$20,000 to $24,999	194	120	208	1 291	1 120	263	38
$25,000 to $39,999	233	165	255	2 001	2 830	1 063	144
$40,000 to $49,999	69	33	46	579	1 288	841	125
$50,000 to $99,999	134	69	102	974	2 911	3 462	1 059
$100,000 to $249,999	47	25	50	365	1 262	2 567	2 129
$250,000 to $499,999	5	5	6	62	171	535	912
$500,000 to $999,999	3	3	3	18	39	99	375
$1,000,000 or more	13	6	4	29	36	58	197
Grains farms	4 094	1 543	2 069	9 554	11 063	8 843	4 723
$1,000	26 804	12 954	19 150	142 484	324 067	502 155	498 359
Sales of $50,000 or more farms	–	–	6	253	1 714	3 822	3 197
$1,000	–	–	490	16 834	131 265	370 361	457 914
Corn for grain farms	357	173	224	1 248	1 882	1 883	1 053
$1,000	2 894	1 134	1 661	17 985	50 001	86 280	93 763
Wheat farms	2 939	999	1 455	7 459	9 376	8 029	4 497
$1,000	11 672	4 615	7 521	58 770	134 569	220 288	248 709
Soybeans farms	1 404	729	918	3 674	4 568	3 279	1 223
$1,000	6 600	4 430	5 566	34 534	69 159	83 930	50 390
Sorghum for grain farms	1 857	791	1 124	5 590	7 293	6 307	3 264
$1,000	5 325	2 669	4 260	30 052	66 876	103 462	94 069
Barley farms	45	14	27	177	337	568	513
$1,000	37	20	30	168	439	1 120	2 128
Oats farms	160	64	89	481	641	571	209
$1,000	140	53	84	446	857	1 065	591
Other grains farms	56	16	13	143	345	570	473
$1,000	136	31	39	529	2 165	6 110	8 710
Cotton and cottonseed farms	–	–	–	–	2	6	2
$1,000	–	–	–	–	(D)	102	(D)
Sales of $50,000 or more farms	–	–	–	–	–	1	1
$1,000	–	–	–	–	–	(D)	(D)
Tobacco farms	1	–	–	–	7	1	–
$1,000	(D)	–	–	–	60	(D)	–
Sales of $50,000 or more farms	–	–	–	–	–	–	–
$1,000	–	–	–	–	–	–	–
Hay, silage, and field seeds farms	908	409	558	2 239	2 740	2 310	1 275
$1,000	2 906	1 417	1 728	9 585	17 943	26 967	45 471
Sales of $50,000 or more farms	1	2	1	9	36	97	166
$1,000	(D)	(D)	(D)	882	3 055	9 900	33 141
Vegetables, sweet corn, and melons farms	23	11	6	43	34	25	13
$1,000	134	129	105	751	236	958	166
Sales of $50,000 or more farms	1	–	–	3	–	2	1
$1,000	(D)	–	–	548	–	(D)	(D)
Fruits, nuts, and berries farms	20	7	7	24	13	13	10
$1,000	50	318	22	279	100	44	110
Sales of $50,000 or more farms	–	1	–	1	–	–	1
$1,000	–	(D)	–	(D)	–	–	(D)
Nursery and greenhouse crops farms	8	5	3	13	11	2	6
$1,000	23	(D)	(D)	1 514	(D)	(D)	2 167
Sales of $50,000 or more farms	–	3	2	4	9	–	2
$1,000	–	(D)	(D)	1 428	2 280	–	(D)
Other crops farms	5	6	1	11	8	11	5
$1,000	(D)	(D)	(D)	25	102	16	(D)
Sales of $50,000 or more farms	–	–	–	–	1	–	2
$1,000	–	–	–	–	(D)	–	(D)
Poultry and poultry products farms	111	53	68	252	237	130	59
$1,000	2 670	2 092	1 523	3 970	2 973	1 673	204
Sales of $50,000 or more farms	7	3	6	16	10	6	1
$1,000	2 571	2 040	1 431	3 548	2 816	1 581	(D)
Dairy products farms	127	70	105	432	602	329	77
$1,000	5 655	2 901	4 688	27 289	47 910	34 311	11 166
Sales of $50,000 or more farms	44	23	37	193	365	228	56
$1,000	4 309	2 069	3 376	21 660	42 325	31 853	10 520
Cattle and calves farms	2 912	1 337	1 701	7 008	8 060	6 999	3 854
$1,000	202 675	87 999	84 530	694 408	868 421	672 885	998 021
Sales of $50,000 or more farms	62	27	42	355	1 004	1 803	2 391
$1,000	182 538	77 492	70 303	621 659	764 269	770 974	960 064

See footnotes at end of table.

Table 51. **Summary by Size of Farm: 1987**—Con.

[For meaning of abbreviations and symbols. see introductory text]

Item	Total	1 to 9 acres	10 to 49 acres	50 to 69 acres	70 to 99 acres	100 to 139 acres
MARKET VALUE OF AGRICUL- TURAL PRODUCTS SOLD—Con.						
Total sales (see text)—Con.						
Hogs and pigs .... farms..	7 090	723	650	106	288	224
$1,000..	284 375	19 112	23 321	6 522	5 872	4 583
Sales of $50,000 or more .... farms..	1 278	89	71	14	23	24
$1,000..	213 369	13 495	19 307	6 002	3 422	2 596
Sheep, lambs, and wool.................. farms..	2 456	262	356	71	177	115
$1,000..	18 561	1 038	3 027	178	443	391
Sales of $50,000 or more .... farms..	44	2	4	-	-	1
$1,000..	9 169	(D)	2 291	-	-	(D)
Other livestock and livestock products (see text) .... farms..	2 869	312	625	138	225	153
$1,000..	9 273	1 147	2 280	249	1 001	412
Sales of $50,000 or more .... farms..	21	4	4	-	1	1
$1,000..	3 649	260	1 107	-	(D)	(D)
FARM PRODUCTION EXPENSES[1]						
Total farm production expenses .... farms..	68 580	3 644	6 274	1 918	4 772	2 966
$1,000..	5 516 516	165 747	81 460	32 346	184 778	123 390
Average per farm .... dollars..	80 439	45 485	12 984	16 864	38 721	41 573
Livestock and poultry purchased .... farms..	23 380	1 515	1 895	551	1 226	750
$1,000..	2 426 149	97 728	30 038	13 111	107 309	64 995
Farms with expenses of—						
$1 to $4,999	11 923	880	1 553	393	968	494
$5,000 to $24,999	6 470	426	285	138	234	216
$25,000 to $99,999	3 307	154	36	15	12	34
$100,000 or more	1 680	55	21	5	12	6
Feed for livestock and poultry .... farms..	36 347	2 342	3 335	1 049	2 121	1 385
$1,000..	887 270	33 700	16 253	6 831	44 432	26 657
Farms with expenses of—						
$1 to $4,999	26 328	1 851	3 143	955	1 989	1 241
$5,000 to $24,999	7 361	367	127	55	106	129
$25,000 to $99,999	2 028	77	31	32	14	7
$100,000 or more	640	27	34	7	12	8
Commercially mixed formula feeds ..... farms..	14 988	1 049	1 343	427	719	481
$1,000..	163 561	8 121	5 375	1 769	3 055	8 840
Farms with expenses of—						
$1 to $4,999	11 327	872	1 287	375	686	440
$5,000 to $24,999	2 854	143	37	46	19	33
$25,000 to $79,999	577	23	6	2	9	4
$80,000 or more	230	11	13	4	5	4
Seeds, bulbs, plants, and trees .... farms..	48 233	513	1 964	717	2 421	1 738
$1,000..	95 302	1 199	690	617	742	774
Farms with expenses of—						
$1 to $999	28 247	463	1 900	673	2 296	1 570
$1,000 to $4,999	15 265	28	51	43	123	156
$5,000 to $24,999	4 473	10	9	-	2	12
$25,000 or more	248	12	4	1	-	-
Commercial fertilizer .... farms..	47 791	261	2 530	834	2 722	1 940
$1,000..	216 166	110	857	465	1 554	1 646
Farms with expenses of—						
$1 to $4,999	34 889	259	2 529	833	2 714	1 934
$5,000 to $24,999	11 740	2	-	-	8	6
$25,000 to $49,999	884	-	-	1	-	-
$50,000 or more	218	-	-	-	-	-
Agricultural chemicals .... farms..	46 318	842	2 385	833	2 423	1 823
$1,000..	125 003	293	574	346	1 041	952
Farms with expenses of—						
$1 to $4,999	39 456	840	2 385	831	2 421	1 823
$5,000 to $24,999	6 476	1	-	1	2	-
$25,000 to $49,999	322	1	-	1	-	-
$50,000 or more	64	-	-	-	-	-
Petroleum products .... farms..	65 460	3 110	5 303	1 691	4 439	2 810
$1,000..	243 568	4 517	3 124	1 252	3 268	2 896
Farms with expenses of—						
$1 to $4,999	51 841	2 942	5 258	1 672	4 412	2 790
$5,000 to $24,999	12 652	157	38	18	22	15
$25,000 to $49,999	760	6	3	-	2	1
$50,000 or more	207	5	4	1	3	4
Gasoline and gasohol .... farms..	57 245	2 897	4 627	1 421	3 840	2 442
$1,000..	90 737	1 614	1 715	638	1 694	1 471
Diesel fuel .... farms..	46 376	1 306	1 690	643	2 041	1 621
$1,000..	110 981	1 298	722	242	1 033	1 004
Natural gas .... farms..	4 956	144	166	45	59	58
$1,000..	26 371	944	209	204	128	69
LP gas, fuel oil, kerosene, motor oil, grease, etc .... farms..	52 549	1 780	2 404	896	2 430	1 892
$1,000..	25 478	480	477	168	413	352

See footnotes at end of table.

Item	140 to 179 acres	180 to 219 acres	220 to 259 acres	260 to 499 acres	500 to 999 acres	1,000 to 1,999 acres	2,000 acres or more
MARKET VALUE OF AGRICULTURAL PRODUCTS SOLD—Con.							
Total sales (see text)—Con.							
Hogs and pigs .... farms..	401	194	270	1 220	1 518	1 078	418
$1,000..	6 600	2 984	6 067	54 612	61 460	55 971	35 271
Sales of $50,000 or more .... farms..	38	14	32	185	323	290	175
$1,000..	4 587	1 066	3 475	41 219	43 363	43 572	31 245
Sheep, lambs, and wool.................. farms..	188	78	93	351	393	261	111
$1,000..	621	306	2 798	2 021	2 681	3 104	1 953
Sales of $50,000 or more .... farms..	2	1	1	2	6	12	11
$1,000..	(D)	(D)	(D)	(D)	734	1 228	1 304
Other livestock and livestock products (see text) .... farms..	183	87	104	291	287	279	185
$1,000..	384	493	357	1 087	602	839	442
Sales of $50,000 or more .... farms..	–	1	1	6	1	2	–
$1,000..	–	(D)	(D)	580	(D)	(D)	–
FARM PRODUCTION EXPENSES[1]							
Total farm production expenses .... farms..	5 865	2 461	2 687	11 657	12 144	9 197	4 993
$1,000..	238 767	106 427	100 010	820 118	1 110 550	1 258 266	1 294 660
Average per farm........................dollars..	40 711	43 245	37 220	70 354	91 448	136 813	259 295
Livestock and poultry purchased .... farms..	1 364	675	659	3 503	4 376	4 103	2 761
$1,000..	126 738	57 350	50 144	413 439	481 425	499 691	484 179
Farms with expenses of—							
$1 to $4,999	937	469	398	1 966	2 046	1 270	529
$5,000 to $24,999	308	140	209	1 067	1 387	1 369	691
$25,000 to $99,999	95	56	37	377	734	1 025	732
$100,000 or more	24	10	15	73	211	439	809
Feed for livestock and poultry .... farms..	2 543	1 221	1 351	6 010	7 332	6 114	3 544
$1,000..	48 343	20 051	18 034	166 668	193 725	160 106	148 470
Farms with expenses of—							
$1 to $4,999	2 200	1 044	1 156	4 763	5 090	3 703	1 193
$5,000 to $24,999	268	140	152	968	1 751	1 800	1 468
$25,000 to $99,999	57	29	34	215	412	487	633
$100,000 or more	18	8	9	64	79	124	250
Commercially mixed formula feeds ..... farms..	847	436	466	2 383	2 865	2 417	1 555
$1,000..	10 048	2 890	3 814	33 208	26 336	29 062	31 042
Farms with expenses of—							
$1 to $4,999	696	362	395	1 915	2 040	1 534	725
$5,000 to $24,999	119	62	55	370	670	714	586
$25,000 to $79,999	19	6	10	54	127	139	178
$80,000 or more	13	6	6	44	28	30	66
Seeds, bulbs, plants, and trees .... farms..	3 903	1 682	1 929	9 306	10 845	8 550	4 665
$1,000..	2 043	1 266	1 190	8 981	19 955	28 081	29 763
Farms with expenses of—							
$1 to $999	3 407	1 363	1 589	6 532	5 067	2 615	782
$1,000 to $4,999	468	302	331	2 615	4 892	4 143	2 113
$5,000 to $24,999	26	16	9	158	693	1 755	1 561
$25,000 or more	–	1	–	1	3	37	189
Commercial fertilizer .... farms..	3 942	1 796	1 972	8 996	10 185	8 165	4 386
$1,000..	4 435	2 119	2 874	20 567	47 043	57 565	66 832
Farms with expenses of—							
$1 to $4,999	3 897	1 783	1 940	8 129	6 557	3 276	1 058
$5,000 to $24,999	45	33	32	865	3 569	4 569	2 610
$25,000 to $49,999	–	–	–	2	56	289	536
$50,000 or more	–	–	–	–	3	31	184
Agricultural chemicals .... farms..	3 554	1 564	1 763	8 641	10 094	8 040	4 386
$1,000..	2 469	1 254	1 701	12 425	27 596	37 663	38 787
Farms with expenses of—							
$1 to $4,999	3 547	1 561	1 748	8 288	8 457	5 426	2 129
$5,000 to $24,999	7	2	15	353	1 628	2 527	1 940
$25,000 to $49,999	–	1	–	–	8	83	228
$50,000 or more	–	–	–	–	1	4	59
Petroleum products .... farms..	5 610	2 417	2 597	11 373	12 052	9 111	4 947
$1,000..	7 946	3 106	3 541	27 948	49 847	68 620	67 804
Farms with expenses of—							
$1 to $4,999	5 530	2 380	2 565	10 558	9 091	3 759	864
$5,000 to $24,999	71	33	30	788	2 879	5 122	3 479
$25,000 to $49,999	3	3	2	13	71	200	456
$50,000 or more	6	1	–	14	11	30	128
Gasoline and gasohol .... farms..	4 662	2 146	2 181	9 774	10 650	8 220	4 565
$1,000..	3 991	1 433	1 852	10 648	16 201	16 917	18 917
Diesel fuel .... farms..	3 556	1 544	1 717	8 655	10 702	8 295	4 606
$1,000..	2 709	1 081	1 227	11 665	24 211	33 527	32 261
Natural gas .... farms..	150	35	59	714	1 094	1 341	1 091
$1,000..	227	149	53	2 261	3 830	7 807	10 492
LP gas, fuel oil, kerosene, motor oil, grease, etc. .... farms..	4 049	1 927	2 181	9 995	11 370	8 806	4 836
$1,000..	1 020	443	408	3 474	5 304	6 824	6 134

See footnotes at end of table.

Table 51. **Summary by Size of Farm: 1987**—Con.

[For meaning of abbreviations and symbols, see introductory text]

Item	Total	1 to 9 acres	10 to 49 acres	50 to 69 acres	70 to 99 acres	100 to 139 acres
FARM PRODUCTION EXPENSES[1] —Con.						
Total farm production expenses—Con.						
Electricity .... farms..	48 797	2 296	3 265	1 082	2 680	1 799
$1,000...	54 103	1 822	1 504	561	1 205	914
Farms with expenses of—						
$1 to $999	36 860	1 959	3 098	1 006	2 555	1 709
$1,000 to $4,999	10 565	307	135	69	112	81
$5,000 to $24,999	1 236	27	26	4	6	5
$25,000 or more	136	3	6	3	6	4
Hired farm labor .... farms..	24 715	615	770	364	740	732
$1,000...	226 075	7 360	5 078	1 905	4 124	5 865
Farms with expenses of—						
$1 to $4,999	18 529	505	681	356	710	698
$5,000 to $24,999	4 529	70	50	2	11	27
$25,000 to $99,999	1 391	25	29	1	10	2
$100,000 or more	266	15	10	5	9	5
Contract labor............................. farms..	7 862	214	437	99	295	257
$1,000...	23 691	481	969	59	535	228
Farms with expenses of—						
$1 to $999	3 892	126	345	84	220	199
$1,000 to $4,999	2 895	66	73	13	56	56
$5,000 to $24,999	1 023	19	17	2	18	2
$25,000 or more	72	3	2	-	2	-
Repair and maintenance .... farms..	56 961	2 386	3 987	1 415	3 380	2 308
$1,000...	252 016	3 554	4 032	1 381	4 440	3 393
Farms with expenses of—						
$1 to $999	42 384	2 260	3 895	1 388	3 330	2 241
$5,000 to $24,999	13 477	120	78	23	40	62
$25,000 to $49,999	844	5	9	-	3	1
$50,000 or more	256	3	5	4	7	4
Customwork, machine hire, and rental of machinery and equipment .... farms..	30 603	762	1 478	461	1 422	1 080
$1,000...	107 366	1 039	942	260	1 022	1 061
Farms with expenses of—						
$1 to $999	13 298	580	1 326	427	1 177	820
$1,000 to $4,999	11 896	156	133	63	235	239
$5,000 to $24,999	4 962	22	15	1	8	20
$25,000 or more	487	4	4	-	2	1
Interest expense .... farms..	39 549	1 515	2 209	708	1 891	1 358
$1,000...	314 163	3 984	4 558	1 813	4 453	4 276
Farms with expenses of—						
$1 to $4,999	24 133	1 359	2 079	614	1 698	1 089
$5,000 to $24,999	12 676	128	120	91	187	266
$25,000 to $99,999	2 557	25	7	3	4	2
$100,000 or more	183	3	3	-	2	1
Secured by real estate .... farms..	26 408	957	1 574	493	1 364	994
$1,000...	188 166	1 321	3 035	1 356	3 032	3 119
Farms with expenses of—						
$1 to $999	5 315	676	582	136	431	231
$1,000 to $4,999	10 417	241	914	297	803	555
$5,000 to $24,999	9 280	35	73	59	129	208
$25,000 or more	1 396	5	5	1	1	-
Not secured by real estate .... farms..	24 307	927	959	373	885	634
$1,000...	125 997	2 664	1 523	457	1 421	1 156
Farms with expenses of—						
$1 to $999	8 203	534	666	239	636	350
$1,000 to $4,999	9 540	289	258	123	222	259
$5,000 to $24,999	5 766	81	26	9	22	23
$25,000 or more	798	23	5	2	5	2
Cash rent............................. farms..	21 234	101	610	260	569	622
$1,000...	123 531	135	594	343	492	737
Farms with expenses of—						
$1 to $4,999	14 629	93	581	257	567	619
$5,000 to $9,999	3 298	6	27	1	1	2
$10,000 to $24,999	2 511	2	-	2	1	1
$25,000 or more	796	-	2	2	-	-
Property taxes .... farms..	63 359	3 365	5 746	1 670	4 410	2 527
$1,000...	112 201	1 659	2 943	996	2 840	2 146
Farms with expenses of—						
$1 to $4,999	59 062	3 331	5 731	1 660	4 393	2 514
$5,000 to $9,999	3 248	23	14	8	14	11
$10,000 to $24,999	956	9	1	2	1	2
$25,000 or more	93	2	-	-	-	-
All other farm production expenses....... farms..	64 491	3 242	5 021	1 638	4 070	2 708
$1,000...	309 914	8 155	7 302	2 407	7 322	4 850
Farms with expenses of—						
$1 to $4,999	51 852	3 039	4 899	1 615	4 019	2 655
$5,000 to $24,999	11 071	165	99	18	33	46
$25,000 to $49,999	1 005	23	7	-	8	2
$50,000 or more	563	15	16	4	10	5

See footnotes at end of table.

Table 51. Summary by Size of Farm: 1987—Con.

[For meaning of abbreviations and symbols, see introductory text]

Item	140 to 179 acres	180 to 219 acres	220 to 259 acres	260 to 499 acres	500 to 899 acres	1,000 to 1,999 acres	2,000 acres or more
FARM PRODUCTION EXPENSES¹ —Con.							
Total farm production expenses—Con.							
Electricity .... farms..	3 555	1 586	1 639	8 472	9 810	8 059	4 554
$1,000..	2 301	900	987	7 276	10 851	12 359	13 424
Farms with expenses of—							
$1 to $999..	3 137	1 454	1 475	7 145	7 055	4 666	1 600
$1,000 to $4,999..	398	124	155	1 250	2 550	3 030	2 354
$5,000 to $24,999..	11	4	7	59	186	345	555
$25,000 or more..	9	4	2	18	19	18	44
Hired farm labor .... farms..	1 346	751	755	3 849	5 376	5 513	3 904
$1,000..	7 000	3 101	2 508	23 281	31 584	50 979	83 289
Farms with expenses of—							
$1 to $4,999..	1 266	715	722	3 561	4 490	3 599	1 226
$5,000 to $24,999..	59	20	22	227	776	1 493	1 772
$25,000 to $99,999..	10	8	7	28	87	391	793
$100,000 or more..	11	8	4	33	23	30	113
Contract labor .... farms..	443	193	218	1 291	1 610	1 732	1 092
$1,000..	485	263	378		3 565	6 958	6 883
Farms with expenses of—							
$1 to $999..	317	132	157	686	778	609	239
$1,000 to $4,999..	119	52	46	503	658	788	465
$5,000 to $24,999..	5	9	14	94	169	320	354
$25,000 or more..	2	-	1	8	5	15	34
Repair and maintenance .... farms..	4 592	2 075	2 161	10 117	11 016	8 720	4 802
$1,000..	8 209	3 808	3 819	29 345	53 444	68 706	67 888
Farms with expenses of—							
$1 to $4,999..	4 454	1 957	2 041	8 906	7 245	3 537	1 130
$5,000 to $24,999..	127	112	116	1 182	3 687	4 909	3 021
$25,000 to $49,999..	1	3	3	11	63	233	512
$50,000 or more..	10	3	1	18	21	41	139
Customwork, machine hire, and rental of machinery and equipment .... farms..	2 252	1 015	1 104	5 512	6 542	5 562	3 383
$1,000..	3 475	1 447	1 522	12 001	20 647	28 754	35 197
Farms with expenses of—							
$1 to $999..	1 266	543	588	2 582	2 271	1 313	405
$1,000 to $4,999..	906	432	460	2 391	3 156	2 491	1 174
$5,000 to $24,999..	78	39	56	519	1 065	1 638	1 523
$25,000 or more..	4	1	-	20	50	120	281
Interest expense .... farms..	2 594	1 374	1 296	6 603	8 496	7 276	4 229
$1,000..	9 890	3 770	4 645	30 981	61 049	88 462	96 282
Farms with expenses of—							
$1 to $4,999..	2 168	1 166	985	4 706	4 663	2 627	987
$5,000 to $24,999..	410	205	306	1 821	3 450	3 749	1 943
$25,000 to $99,999..	7	2	5	62	380	875	1 185
$100,000 or more..	9	1	-	12	13	25	114
Secured by real estate .... farms..	1 594	861	804	3 994	5 719	4 954	3 005
$1,000..	5 654	2 530	3 182	18 348	38 953	53 112	54 513
Farms with expenses of—							
$1 to $999..	456	254	193	868	922	378	188
$1,000 to $4,999..	913	467	380	1 782	2 073	1 454	538
$5,000 to $24,999..	319	138	228	1 325	2 535	2 651	1 580
$25,000 or more..	6	2	3	19	183	471	700
Not secured by real estate .... farms..	1 494	828	773	4 213	5 441	4 871	2 909
$1,000..	4 226	1 241	1 462	12 632	22 096	35 349	41 769
Farms with expenses of—							
$1 to $999..	839	501	398	1 712	1 437	643	246
$1,000 to $4,999..	580	303	298	2 016	2 584	1 838	770
$5,000 to $24,999..	62	22	75	464	1 358	2 205	1 417
$25,000 or more..	13	2	2	21	62	185	476
Cash rent .... farms..	871	552	608	3 568	5 227	5 134	3 112
$1,000..	1 276	1 186	1 204	10 086	22 967	37 612	45 919
Farms with expenses of—							
$1 to $4,999..	829	500	568	3 034	3 746	2 756	1 079
$5,000 to $9,999..	35	48	31	373	936	1 217	621
$10,000 to $24,999..	7	2	9	146	495	938	910
$25,000 or more..	-	2	-	15	50	223	502
Property taxes .... farms..	5 250	2 221	2 383	10 612	11 546	8 719	4 810
$1,000..	4 676	2 255	2 610	15 194	24 362	26 785	25 714
Farms with expenses of—							
$1 to $4,999..	5 215	2 214	2 367	10 417	10 888	7 251	2 981
$5,000 to $9,999..	28	4	5	166	582	1 202	1 191
$10,000 to $24,999..	5	3	11	24	71	254	573
$25,000 or more..	2	-	-	5	5	12	65
All other farm production expenses ...... farms..	5 369	2 377	2 520	11 317	12 052	9 186	4 991
$1,000..	9 480	4 570	4 855	39 049	62 767	75 927	83 231
$1 to $4,999..	5 210	2 265	2 447	10 204	9 007	4 969	1 523
$5,000 to $24,999..	141	103	69	1 048	2 851	3 812	2 686
$25,000 to $49,999..	5	1	1	30	140	294	493
$50,000 or more..	13	8	3	35	54	111	289

See footnotes at end of table.

Table 51. **Summary by Size of Farm: 1987**—Con.

[For meaning of abbreviations and symbols, see introductory text]

Item	Total	1 to 9 acres	10 to 49 acres	50 to 69 acres	70 to 99 acres	100 to 139 acres
NET CASH RETURN FROM AGRICULTURAL SALES FOR THE FARM UNIT[1]						
All farms ... number	68 580	3 644	6 274	1 918	4 772	2 968
... $1,000	922 225	18 096	5 142	5 302	7 202	11 519
Average per farm ... dollars	13 447	4 967	820	2 765	1 509	3 881
Farms with net gains[2] ... number	41 673	1 971	2 471	895	2 297	1 494
Average net gain ... dollars	27 369	12 429	6 263	9 655	6 671	12 091
Gain of—						
Less than $1,000	4 994	481	951	330	636	324
$1,000 to $9,999	16 378	1 071	1 330	483	1 532	997
$10,000 to $49,999	13 669	306	131	59	106	128
$50,000 or more	4 412	113	59	23	24	45
Farms with net losses ... number	26 907	1 673	3 803	1 023	2 475	1 474
Average net loss ... dollars	8 114	3 825	2 717	3 264	3 281	4 440
Loss of—						
Less than $1,000	5 287	565	1 366	277	762	316
$1,000 to $9,999	16 553	993	2 335	705	1 587	1 056
$10,000 to $49,999	4 663	110	97	41	123	102
$50,000 or more	404	5	5	–	3	–
GOVERNMENT PAYMENTS AND OTHER FARM-RELATED INCOME						
Government payments ... farms	41 627	567	849	453	1 560	1 302
... $1,000	573 647	1 378	801	490	2 443	2 836
Other farm-related income[1] ... farms	18 682	763	1 228	506	1 008	767
... $1,000	69 944	2 611	2 594	1 211	2 323	1 696
Customwork and other agricultural services ... farms	7 483	201	318	110	327	256
... $1,000	32 115	729	954	272	645	344
Gross cash rent or share payments ... farms	7 899	543	717	344	561	434
... $1,000	30 403	1 767	1 263	769	1 500	1 133
Forest products and Christmas trees ... farms	439	16	50	10	42	35
... $1,000	1 087	64	100	27	49	131
Other farm-related income sources ... farms	6 669	59	250	90	215	171
... $1,000	6 340	61	278	143	130	88
COMMODITY CREDIT CORPORATION LOANS						
Total ... farms	15 832	22	113	58	287	252
... $1,000	338 296	437	169	111	620	890
Corn ... farms	3 591	–	18	9	38	46
... $1,000	106 314	–	24	24	123	332
Wheat ... farms	7 282	5	53	24	130	103
... $1,000	95 942	1	35	28	186	195
Soybeans ... farms	1 248	–	6	8	25	25
... $1,000	20 764	–	10	17	45	49
Sorghum, barley, and oats ... farms	10 032	1	42	32	148	130
... $1,000	112 734	(D)	(D)	41	(D)	(D)
Cotton ... farms	–	–	–	–	–	–
... $1,000	–	–	–	–	–	–
Peanuts, rye, rice, tobacco, and honey ... farms	22	17	1	–	1	1
... $1,000	503	(D)	(D)	–	(D)	(D)
LAND IN FARMS ACCORDING TO USE						
Total cropland ... farms	61 615	734	4 794	1 505	4 135	2 819
... acres	31 385 090	2 726	102 054	64 411	245 593	244 985
Harvested cropland ... farms	57 822	559	3 746	1 248	3 658	2 500
... acres	17 729 394	1 792	62 424	37 812	145 968	140 440
Farms by acres harvested:						
1 to 49 acres	12 372	559	3 746	997	2 426	1 108
50 to 99 acres	8 853	–	–	251	1 232	1 105
100 to 199 acres	10 361	–	–	–	–	287
200 to 499 acres	14 761	–	–	–	–	–
500 to 999 acres	8 160	–	–	–	–	–
1,000 to 1,999 acres	2 876	–	–	–	–	–
2,000 acres or more	449	–	–	–	–	–
Cropland:						
Pasture or grazing only ... farms	22 575	194	1 699	492	1 410	1 029
... acres	3 485 445	761	28 940	16 184	55 609	56 765
In cover crops, legumes, and soil-improvement grasses, not harvested and not pastured ... farms	11 212	26	273	136	368	363
... acres	1 103 315	67	2 929	2 599	9 843	8 598
On which all crops failed ... farms	3 341	7	122	66	171	116
... acres	206 231	21	1 261	1 103	3 427	2 329
In cultivated summer fallow ... farms	25 408	10	210	131	574	521
... acres	6 409 506	22	2 242	2 512	13 943	17 619
Idle ... farms	20 610	24	434	261	850	726
... acres	2 451 189	63	4 268	4 201	16 603	19 214
Total woodland ... farms	12 587	53	872	422	1 040	756
... acres	718 261	145	6 619	7 570	23 530	21 939
Woodland pastured ... farms	6 382	25	468	230	575	402
... acres	366 136	82	5 091	4 104	13 527	11 214
Woodland not pastured ... farms	7 991	30	443	225	552	428
... acres	352 125	63	3 528	3 466	10 003	10 725

See footnotes at end of table.

Table 51. **Summary by Size of Farm: 1987**—Con.

[For meaning of abbreviations and symbols, see introductory text]

Item	140 to 179 acres	180 to 219 acres	220 to 259 acres	260 to 499 acres	500 to 999 acres	1,000 to 1,999 acres	2,000 acres or more
NET CASH RETURN FROM AGRICULTURAL SALES FOR THE FARM UNIT[1]							
All farms............number..	5 865	2 461	2 687	11 657	12 144	9 197	4 993
$1,000..	19 312	7 341	17 183	111 238	209 310	220 722	269 856
Average per farm.................dollars..	3 293	2 983	6 395	9 543	17 236	23 999	58 053
Farms with net gains[2]............number..	3 357	1 318	1 591	7 526	8 389	6 576	3 790
Average net gain..................dollars..	9 831	10 365	13 803	18 964	30 347	40 600	65 926
Gain of—							
Less than $1,000	577	264	175	578	387	199	92
$1,000 to $9,999	2 274	820	992	4 199	2 858	1 411	411
$10,000 to $49,999	458	204	392	2 489	4 417	3 535	1 665
$50,000 or more	48	28	32	260	727	1 431	1 622
Farms with net losses............number..	2 508	1 145	1 096	4 131	3 755	2 621	1 203
Average net loss..................dollars..	5 459	5 501	4 359	7 622	12 057	17 650	29 761
Loss of—							
Less than $1,000	449	178	307	487	394	116	70
$1,000 to $9,999	1 916	875	701	2 793	2 084	1 151	357
$10,000 to $49,999	134	91	87	840	1 218	1 217	603
$50,000 or more	9	1	1	11	59	137	173
GOVERNMENT PAYMENTS AND OTHER FARM-RELATED INCOME							
Government payments.................farms..	3 211	1 218	1 707	8 337	10 044	8 096	4 283
$1,000..	9 630	4 117	6 700	52 867	123 976	186 329	182 280
Other farm-related income[1]...............farms..	1 249	675	665	3 069	3 985	3 210	1 557
$1,000..	4 226	1 642	1 584	6 724	15 343	16 060	11 930
Customwork and other agricultural services................farms..	315	171	232	1 160	1 859	1 683	831
$1,000..	884	397	616	3 717	7 473	9 599	6 483
Gross cash rent or share payments.....farms..	719	393	334	1 283	1 276	868	427
$1,000..	3 062	1 163	850	4 229	6 282	4 573	3 821
Forest products and Christmas trees....farms..	40	17	7	71	55	55	5
$1,000..	20	34	16	195	338	88	23
Other farm-related income sources........farms..	385	162	191	1 225	1 640	1 459	793
$1,000..	260	47	96	583	1 251	1 799	1 603
COMMODITY CREDIT CORPORATION LOANS							
Total.................farms..	759	313	495	2 724	4 351	4 215	2 243
$1,000..	3 197	1 503	2 564	23 902	70 275	118 464	116 167
Corn................farms..	112	47	76	495	1 011	1 115	824
$1,000..	1 029	311	552	6 850	23 513	37 110	38 445
Wheat.................farms..	353	129	215	1 132	1 876	2 022	1 840
$1,000..	691	384	667	5 997	17 163	32 839	37 543
Soybeans................farms..	34	27	53	209	360	351	148
$1,000..	152	180	262	1 551	4 557	7 691	6 251
Sorghum, barley, and oats.............farms..	427	173	278	1 691	2 835	2 820	1 455
$1,000..	1 125	(D)	1 063	9 504	25 051	(D)	33 927
Cotton.................farms..	-	-	-	-	-	-	-
$1,000..	-	(D)	-	-	-	-	-
Peanuts, rye, rice, tobacco, and honey....farms..	-	-	-	-	-	1	-
$1,000..	-	(D)	-	-	-	(D)	-
LAND IN FARMS ACCORDING TO USE							
Total cropland.........................farms..	5 477	2 122	2 705	11 217	11 957	9 184	4 966
acres..	663 220	305 240	481 098	3 210 534	6 719 349	9 554 822	9 791 276
Harvested cropland.....................farms..	5 084	1 972	2 565	10 727	11 707	9 092	4 924
acres..	371 929	182 448	269 306	1 811 003	3 806 268	5 444 815	5 455 187
Farms by acres harvested:							
1 to 49 acres	1 425	442	455	838	272	76	28
50 to 99 acres	2 366	666	758	1 688	602	133	52
100 to 199 acres	1 293	806	1 183	4 445	1 802	426	119
200 to 499 acres	-	58	159	3 806	7 271	2 885	582
500 to 999 acres	-	-	-	-	1 760	4 694	1 696
1,000 to 1,999 acres	-	-	-	-	-	878	1 998
2,000 acres or more	-	-	-	-	-	-	449
Cropland:							
Pasture or grazing only.................farms..	1 941	747	1 045	4 292	4 848	3 470	1 408
acres..	126 428	57 602	89 236	527 647	966 738	1 062 266	497 249
In cover crops, legumes, and soil-improvement grasses, not harvested and not pastured.................farms..	796	319	546	2 323	2 592	2 121	1 239
On which all crops failed................farms..	25 674	11 095	22 577	126 529	225 741	290 754	376 663
acres..	266	105	146	608	759	646	329
In cultivated summer fallow..............farms..	6 714	3 081	4 349	23 183	46 937	57 160	56 666
acres..	1 676	519	884	4 878	6 516	8 029	3 461
Idle.................farms..	77 679	26 761	54 453	464 544	1 134 866	2 012 622	2 602 243
acres..	1 852	667	936	4 228	5 003	3 776	2 053
	54 796	24 253	41 175	257 402	538 799	687 185	803 250
Total woodland.........................farms..	1 138	613	669	2 490	2 382	1 517	635
Woodland pastured.....................farms..	39 491	26 460	27 782	128 529	171 331	148 616	114 249
acres..	554	316	316	1 203	1 189	717	347
Woodland not pastured.................farms..	19 277	13 492	14 526	64 791	85 900	70 043	64 089
acres..	708	398	426	1 672	1 616	1 082	411
	20 214	12 968	13 256	63 738	85 431	78 573	50 160

See footnotes at end of table.

Item	Total	1 to 9 acres	10 to 49 acres	50 to 69 acres	70 to 99 acres	100 to 139 acres
LAND IN FARMS ACCORDING TO USE—Con.						
Pastureland and rangeland other than cropland and woodland pastured .... farms..	32 362	187	1 949	743	1 908	1 847
acres..	13 254 084	709	35 566	26 095	82 185	75 372
Land in house lots, ponds, roads, wasteland, etc. .... farms..	44 335	3 279	4 019	1 077	2 844	1 909
acres..	1 271 074	5 747	25 761	9 826	28 760	21 523
Cropland under federal acreage reduction programs:						
Annual commodity acreage adjustment programs .... farms..	34 658	22	351	229	994	803
acres..	3 956 195	28	2 212	2 164	13 617	14 650
Conservation reserve program .... farms..	5 630	2	39	32	123	127
acres..	810 862	(D)	(D)	848	3 474	4 151
Value of land and buildings[1] .... farms..	68 560	3 644	6 274	1 918	4 772	2 968
$1,000..	19 068 461	126 546	354 484	136 078	345 547	278 261
Average per farm ....dollars..	278 047	34 727	56 500	70 948	72 411	93 754
Average per acre ....dollars..	413	13 777	2 003	1 217	894	798
Farms by value group:						
$1 to $39,999	10 024	2 879	3 035	810	1 760	563
$40,000 to $69,999	9 571	369	1 522	567	1 541	1 029
$70,000 to $99,999	7 001	193	784	195	544	535
$100,000 to $149,999	8 596	65	545	177	468	404
$150,000 to $199,999	6 313	28	169	74	207	200
$200,000 to $499,999	16 478	41	208	77	209	172
$500,000 to $999,999	7 579	34	9	7	42	35
$1,000,000 to $1,999,999	2 396	14	1	5	1	10
$2,000,000 to $4,999,999	535	1	1	1	-	-
$5,000,000 or more	89	-	-	1	-	-
VALUE OF MACHINERY AND EQUIPMENT[1]						
Estimated market value of all machinery and equipment .... farms..	68 391	3 622	6 188	1 901	4 756	2 968
$1,000..	3 447 663	80 102	71 230	29 891	79 526	66 790
Farms by value group:						
$1 to $4,999	5 812	660	1 647	393	850	294
$5,000 to $9,999	11 585	1 407	2 740	677	1 547	844
$10,000 to $19,999	11 722	626	862	446	1 201	749
$20,000 to $49,999	16 724	505	611	269	594	755
$50,000 to $99,999	12 176	273	121	74	168	236
$100,000 to $199,999	7 277	88	65	32	84	65
$200,000 to $499,999	2 860	61	22	10	12	32
$500,000 or more	235	2	-	-	2	1
SELECTED MACHINERY AND EQUIPMENT[1]						
Motortrucks, including pickups .... farms..	63 093	3 052	5 132	1 629	4 017	2 686
number..	159 329	5 382	7 469	2 555	6 427	4 668
Wheel tractors .... farms..	60 459	2 593	4 801	1 481	3 914	2 665
number..	150 647	4 881	7 092	2 533	7 129	5 216
Less than 40 horsepower (PTO) .... farms..	25 210	1 403	3 058	843	2 001	1 300
number..	38 591	2 006	4 060	1 191	2 955	2 068
40 horsepower (PTO) or more .... farms..	50 577	1 598	2 348	916	2 715	2 001
number..	112 056	2 875	3 032	1 342	4 174	3 150
Grain and bean combines .... farms..	35 608	650	699	408	1 240	1 056
number..	43 801	756	742	450	1 418	1 196
Cottonpickers and strippers.............. farms..	1	-	-	-	-	-
number..	(D)	-	-	-	-	-
Mower conditioners .... farms..	18 793	304	813	335	828	708
number..	20 167	325	853	340	939	756
Pickup balers .... farms..	26 083	532	911	474	1 301	1 043
number..	31 892	561	989	503	1 480	1 179
AGRICULTURAL CHEMICALS[1]						
Commercial fertilizer .... farms..	47 723	281	2 530	834	2 722	1 940
acres on which used..	13 852 822	855	44 966	24 529	102 716	102 115
Lime .... farms..	2 685	15	119	24	131	97
acres on which used..	154 622	19	1 558	384	3 118	2 663
tons..	389 024	47	4 084	838	7 503	6 062
Sprays, dusts, granules, fumigants, etc., to control—						
Insects on hay and other crops .... farms..	19 416	146	527	134	491	548
acres on which used..	3 015 580	361	6 100	1 913	12 845	15 891
Nematodes in crops .... farms..	716	14	44	5	29	16
acres on which used..	87 904	26	464	15	633	760
Diseases in crops and orchards.......... farms..	1 055	67	175	32	43	43
acres on which used..	125 065	96	1 199	365	840	1 067
Weeds, grass, or brush in crops and pasture .... farms..	36 950	137	1 772	873	1 675	1 436
acres on which used..	8 637 062	422	30 721	18 537	66 313	68 602
Chemicals for defoliation or for growth control of crops or thinning of fruit ...... farms..	614	18	49	22	17	35
acres on which used..	68 839	23	441	200	231	1 180

See footnotes at end of table.

Table 51. **Summary by Size of Farm: 1987**—Con.

[For meaning of abbreviations and symbols, see introductory text]

Item	140 to 179 acres	180 to 219 acres	220 to 259 acres	260 to 499 acres	500 to 999 acres	1,000 to 1,999 acres	2,000 acres or more
LAND IN FARMS ACCORDING TO USE—Con.							
Pastureland and rangeland other than							
cropland and woodland pastured .... farms..	2 470	1 023	1 372	5 803	6 362	5 686	3 814
acres..	176 405	99 256	137 846	782 827	1 511 457	2 893 514	7 433 062
Land in house lots, ponds, roads,							
wasteland, etc. .... farms..	3 497	1 418	1 809	7 388	7 852	6 077	3 166
acres..	48 483	24 762	30 948	174 171	271 256	328 300	301 493
Cropland under federal acreage reduction programs:							
Annual commodity acreage adjustment							
programs .... farms..	2 369	904	1 307	6 912	9 027	7 679	4 061
acres..	57 777	25 044	42 455	345 574	843 201	1 310 131	1 299 345
Conservation reserve program .... farms..	290	106	173	810	1 297	1 366	1 145
acres..	13 935	5 869	11 559	66 828	130 802	221 989	351 176
Value of land and buildings[1] .... farms..	5 865	2 481	2 687	11 857	12 144	9 197	4 993
$1,000..	542 977	285 144	324 275	2 015 812	3 647 789	4 928 584	6 082 964
Average per farm .... dollars..	92 579	115 865	120 683	172 927	300 376	535 890	1 218 296
Average per acre .... dollars..	584	584	508	468	424	387	349
Farms by value group:							
$1 to $39,999	646	95	94	104	9	8	1
$40,000 to $69,999	2 172	684	576	1 004	76	12	-
$70,000 to $99,999	1 425	564	634	1 914	207	5	1
$100,000 to $149,999	847	622	787	3 331	1 273	75	2
$150,000 to $199,999	408	204	282	2 410	2 070	246	15
$200,000 to $499,999	324	261	295	2 546	7 218	4 579	544
$500,000 to $999,999	41	29	10	314	1 184	3 710	2 164
$1,000,000 to $1,999,999	2	2	9	13	97	506	1 730
$2,000,000 to $4,999,999	-	-	-	20	7	51	454
$5,000,000 or more	-	-	-	-	3	3	82
VALUE OF MACHINERY AND EQUIPMENT[1]							
Estimated market value of all machinery							
and equipment .... farms..	5 865	2 444	2 686	11 637	12 135	9 196	4 993
$1,000..	146 173	58 261	82 527	439 200	752 636	876 136	763 191
Farms by value group:							
$1 to $4,999	607	192	235	589	214	111	10
$5,000 to $9,999	1 323	529	474	1 371	469	162	42
$10,000 to $19,999	10 029	738	636	2 514	1 593	549	137
$20,000 to $49,999	1 551	684	830	4 098	4 144	1 789	549
$50,000 to $99,999	541	243	377	2 218	3 705	3 018	1 204
$100,000 to $199,999	158	33	96	667	1 636	2 631	1 730
$200,000 to $499,999	57	24	34	171	357	916	1 164
$500,000 or more	2	1	2	9	17	42	167
SELECTED MACHINERY AND EQUIPMENT[1]							
Motortrucks, including pickups .... farms..	5 298	2 197	2 449	10 898	11 797	9 006	4 934
number..	9 569	4 135	4 798	24 884	32 707	32 536	24 209
Wheel tractors .... farms..	5 016	2 130	2 409	10 531	11 348	8 718	4 855
number..	10 029	4 496	5 420	25 601	31 486	27 970	18 782
Less than 40 horsepower (PTO) .... farms..	2 211	925	1 100	1 977	3 922	2 869	1 571
number..	3 245	1 371	1 696	6 407	6 353	4 384	2 855
40 horsepower (PTO) or more .... farms..	4 067	1 756	2 018	9 469	10 663	8 325	4 701
number..	6 784	3 125	3 724	19 194	25 133	23 586	15 937
Grain and bean combines .... farms..	2 506	1 151	1 440	6 867	8 730	7 079	3 782
number..	2 750	1 255	1 692	8 087	10 709	9 196	5 539
Cottonpickers and strippers .... farms..	-	-	-	-	-	-	1
number..	-	-	-	-	-	-	(D)
Mower conditioners .... farms..	1 281	675	665	3 310	4 259	3 551	2 094
number..	1 301	725	683	3 515	4 515	3 814	2 401
Pickup balers .... farms..	1 905	1 048	1 091	4 675	6 015	4 542	2 546
number..	2 164	1 235	1 175	5 633	7 601	5 910	3 562
AGRICULTURAL CHEMICALS[1]							
Commercial fertilizer .... farms..	3 942	1 796	1 972	8 996	10 179	8 165	4 366
acres on which used..	279 750	141 956	190 184	1 346 416	2 962 218	4 358 642	4 276 473
Lime .... farms..	229	137	81	623	627	432	180
acres on which used..	9 249	5 806	3 309	27 316	33 389	45 467	22 344
tons..	19 522	14 893	9 370	60 191	76 385	117 297	52 832
Sprays, dusts, granules, fumigants, etc., to							
control—							
Insects on hay and other crops .... farms..	984	433	570	3 336	5 022	4 478	2 747
acres on which used..	40 399	16 961	30 814	229 662	582 910	933 746	1 141 936
Nematodes in crops .... farms..	77	7	27	155	134	119	89
acres on which used..	2 995	915	2 522	15 377	14 585	18 410	31 002
Diseases in crops and orchards .... farms..	59	23	20	151	150	167	125
acres on which used..	832	1 356	570	11 890	18 103	36 214	52 443
Weeds, grass, or brush in crops and							
pasture .... farms..	2 735	1 282	1 420	6 965	8 368	6 726	3 541
acres on which used..	173 678	96 559	121 308	893 125	2 015 596	2 667 392	2 484 809
Chemicals for defoliation or for growth							
control of crops or thinning of fruit .... farms..	32	10	8	101	163	93	66
acres on which used..	677	335	880	5 337	14 908	21 456	22 971

See footnotes at end of table.

Table 51. **Summary by Size of Farm: 1987**—Con.

[For meaning of abbreviations and symbols, see introductory text]

Item	Total	1 to 9 acres	10 to 49 acres	50 to 69 acres	70 to 99 acres	100 to 139 acres
TENURE AND RACE OF OPERATOR						
All operators	68 579	3 689	6 222	1 849	4 690	3 117
Full owners	29 956	3 407	4 902	1 235	3 528	1 886
Part owners	27 967	59	581	299	522	708
Tenants	10 656	223	739	315	640	523
White	68 304	3 667	6 150	1 841	4 647	3 099
Full owners	29 784	3 389	4 844	1 226	3 493	1 877
Part owners	27 901	59	574	299	517	702
Tenants	10 619	219	732	314	637	520
Black and other races	275	22	72	8	43	16
Full owners	172	18	58	7	35	9
Part owners	66	-	7	-	5	6
Tenants	37	4	7	1	3	3
OWNED AND RENTED LAND						
Land owned .... farms..	58 533	3 466	5 518	1 544	4 095	2 625
acres..	24 331 697	471 410	261 418	144 669	454 846	379 091
Owned land in farms .... farms..	57 923	3 466	5 483	1 534	4 050	2 594
acres..	21 178 322	8 161	140 354	78 671	301 578	254 739
Land rented or leased from others .... farms..	38 908	324	1 345	617	1 179	1 255
acres..	25 865 815	23 530	43 106	30 927	83 634	116 665
Rented or leased land in farms .... farms..	38 623	282	1 320	614	1 162	1 231
acres..	25 450 197	1 146	31 686	29 233	78 270	109 060
Land rented or leased to others............ farms..	11 944	1 253	1 159	538	859	799
acres..	3 569 193	485 613	152 484	67 712	158 634	131 857
OPERATOR CHARACTERISTICS						
Operators by place of residence:						
On farm operated	45 527	1 943	4 333	1 166	2 750	1 833
Not on farm operated	17 871	1 113	1 432	527	1 607	1 049
Not reported	5 181	633	457	156	333	235
Operators by principal occupation:						
Farming	42 607	1 465	1 348	532	1 584	1 191
Other	25 972	2 224	4 874	1 317	3 106	1 926
Operators by days of work off farm:						
None	29 462	1 132	1 273	471	1 203	881
Any	34 654	2 293	4 766	1 299	3 239	2 066
1 to 99 days	7 620	319	331	132	329	245
100 to 199 days	5 357	268	460	146	364	293
200 days or more	21 677	1 705	3 975	1 021	2 545	1 528
Not reported	4 463	264	183	79	249	170
Operators by years on present farm:						
2 years or less	3 511	376	553	127	387	231
3 or 4 years	3 873	367	627	157	396	265
5 to 9 years	8 552	519	1 251	337	737	464
10 years or more	40 624	1 177	2 706	893	2 362	1 600
Average years on present farm	21.3	13.9	13.0	16.0	16.5	17.7
Not reported	12 019	1 248	1 085	335	788	557
Operators by age group:						
Under 25 years	1 712	229	184	53	138	112
25 to 34 years	8 531	743	884	268	674	452
35 to 44 years	12 471	768	1 529	365	837	530
45 to 49 years	5 926	293	662	161	441	267
50 to 54 years	6 781	309	638	194	458	296
55 to 59 years	7 581	252	590	189	463	315
60 to 64 years	8 407	310	603	181	512	327
65 to 69 years	6 564	284	452	151	438	291
70 years and over	9 606	501	670	297	729	527
Average age	52.0	48.3	49.5	51.6	52.0	52.1
Operators by sex:						
Male	65 619	3 395	6 783	1 739	4 422	2 944
Female	2 960	294	439	110	268	173
Operators of Spanish origin (see text)	108	7	17	7	18	4
FARMS BY TYPE OF ORGANIZATION						
Individual or family (sole proprietorship) ..... farms..	60 202	3 186	5 803	1 727	4 367	2 810
acres..	36 420 471	8 379	160 737	100 726	353 634	328 149
Partnership .... farms..	5 889	352	265	98	263	247
acres..	6 151 580	641	7 876	5 775	21 453	28 584
Corporation:						
Family held .... farms..	1 942	104	74	17	34	31
acres..	3 446 745	245	1 751	990	2 691	3 652
More than 10 stockholders .... farms..	23	-	1	-	1	-
10 or less stockholders .... farms..	1 919	104	73	17	33	31
Other than family held .... farms..	158	9	15	3	6	6
acres..	159 766	15	409	175	469	728
More than 10 stockholders .... farms..	17	1	4	-	2	-
10 or less stockholders .... farms..	141	8	11	3	4	6
Other—cooperative, estate or trust, institutional, etc. .... farms..	388	38	45	4	20	23
acres..	450 347	47	1 267	238	1 601	2 686

See footnotes at end of table.

Item	140 to 179 acres	180 to 219 acres	220 to 259 acres	260 to 499 acres	500 to 999 acres	1,000 to 1,999 acres	2,000 acres or more
TENURE AND RACE OF OPERATOR							
All operators	5 854	2 307	2 845	11 553	12 093	9 304	5 056
Full owners	3 798	1 165	1 425	4 393	2 560	1 107	550
Part owners	956	730	874	5 009	7 449	6 888	3 892
Tenants	1 100	412	546	2 151	2 084	1 309	614
White	5 825	2 296	2 840	11 522	12 075	9 292	5 050
Full owners	3 784	1 158	1 425	4 379	2 555	1 104	548
Part owners	944	726	870	4 998	7 440	6 883	3 889
Tenants	1 097	412	545	2 145	2 080	1 305	613
Black and other races	29	11	5	31	18	12	6
Full owners	14	7	–	14	5	3	2
Part owners	12	4	4	11	9	5	3
Tenants	3	1	1	6	4	4	1
OWNED AND RENTED LAND							
Land owned farms..	4 854	1 918	2 339	9 553	10 092	8 053	4 474
acres..	896 597	421 472	538 797	2 974 735	4 548 126	5 625 726	7 594 988
Owned land in farms farms..	4 754	1 895	2 299	9 402	10 009	7 995	4 442
acres..	663 265	295 492	436 250	2 443 124	4 088 499	5 220 012	7 248 157
Land rented or leased from others farms..	2 089	1 152	1 434	7 202	9 569	8 217	4 525
acres..	301 998	166 616	246 839	1 902 166	4 646 310	7 799 651	10 500 371
Rented or leased land in farms farms..	2 056	1 142	1 420	7 160	9 533	8 197	4 506
acres..	264 334	160 246	241 224	1 852 937	4 584 896	7 705 240	10 391 925
Land rented or leased to others farms..	1 000	539	501	1 861	1 619	1 161	655
acres..	270 896	134 350	108 162	580 842	523 041	500 325	455 277
OPERATOR CHARACTERISTICS							
Operators by place of residence:							
On farm operated	3 261	1 441	1 824	7 417	8 739	7 068	3 752
Not on farm operated	2 141	707	804	3 366	2 645	1 602	878
Not reported	452	159	217	770	709	634	426
Operators by principal occupation:							
Farming	2 785	1 127	1 614	7 684	9 942	8 538	4 797
Other	3 069	1 180	1 231	3 869	2 151	766	259
Operators by days of work off farm:							
None	2 017	746	1 117	4 903	6 353	5 778	3 568
Any	3 466	1 414	1 536	5 825	4 869	2 843	1 039
1 to 99 days	534	232	257	1 394	1 814	1 477	556
100 to 199 days	500	225	262	1 113	1 044	529	153
200 days or more	2 432	957	1 017	3 318	2 011	837	330
Not reported	371	147	192	825	871	683	429
Operators by years on present farm:							
2 years or less	431	139	131	492	385	184	73
3 or 4 years	414	162	149	549	436	253	98
5 to 9 years	825	299	336	1 446	1 299	744	295
10 years or more	3 136	1 299	1 752	7 168	8 202	6 637	3 672
Average years on present farm	20.1	20.5	22.6	23.2	24.3	25.3	26.4
Not reported	1 048	408	477	1 898	1 771	1 486	918
Operators by age group:							
Under 25 years	182	66	81	321	197	114	33
25 to 34 years	788	322	327	1 628	1 791	1 211	443
35 to 44 years	900	355	423	1 787	2 058	1 841	1 078
45 to 49 years	416	205	211	847	987	891	545
50 to 54 years	526	217	253	982	1 143	1 073	692
55 to 59 years	540	236	299	1 132	1 528	1 296	739
60 to 64 years	615	232	373	1 508	1 732	1 315	699
65 to 69 years	710	240	353	1 297	1 171	769	408
70 years and over	1 177	432	525	2 051	1 486	792	419
Average age	53.9	53.1	54.5	53.4	52.0	51.2	51.9
Operators by sex:							
Male	5 510	2 193	2 722	11 077	11 769	9 090	4 975
Female	344	114	123	476	324	214	81
Operators of Spanish origin (see text)	3	2	2	12	18	12	6
FARMS BY TYPE OF ORGANIZATION							
Individual or family (sole proprietorship) farms..	5 349	2 104	2 572	10 346	10 696	7 706	3 536
acres..	847 670	415 352	612 458	3 842 581	7 664 367	10 647 224	11 439 194
Partnership farms..	407	153	220	973	1 027	1 010	654
acres..	64 417	30 471	52 273	364 791	734 139	1 420 590	3 420 470
Corporation:							
Family held farms..	50	31	32	149	289	533	598
acres..	7 891	6 238	7 751	57 715	214 617	779 581	2 363 623
More than 10 stockholders farms..	2	1	1	4	3	6	5
10 or less stockholders farms..	48	30	32	145	286	527	593
Other than family held farms..	9	7	3	37	25	12	26
acres..	1 444	1 333	743	13 399	19 216	18 030	103 415
More than 10 stockholders farms..	1	1	2	5	–	–	1
10 or less stockholders farms..	8	6	1	32	25	12	25
Other — cooperative, estate or trust, institutional, etc. farms..	39	12	18	48	56	43	42
acres..	6 177	2 344	4 249	17 575	41 056	59 727	313 380

See footnotes at end of table.

Table 51. **Summary by Size of Farm: 1987**—Con.

[For meaning of abbreviations and symbols, see Introductory text]

Item	Total	1 to 9 acres	10 to 49 acres	50 to 69 acres	70 to 99 acres	100 to 139 acres
FARMS BY SIZE						
1 to 9 acres	3 689	3 689	-	-	-	-
10 to 49 acres	6 222	-	6 222	-	-	-
50 to 69 acres	1 849	-	-	1 849	-	-
70 to 99 acres	4 690	-	-	-	4 690	-
100 to 139 acres	3 117	-	-	-	-	3 117
140 to 179 acres	5 654	-	-	-	-	-
180 to 219 acres	2 307	-	-	-	-	-
220 to 259 acres	2 845	-	-	-	-	-
260 to 499 acres	11 553	-	-	-	-	-
500 to 999 acres	12 093	-	-	-	-	-
1,000 to 1,999 acres	9 304	-	-	-	-	-
2,000 acres or more	5 056	-	-	-	-	-
FARMS BY STANDARD INDUSTRIAL CLASSIFICATION						
Cash grains (011)	31 789	139	1 351	549	1 747	1 270
Field crops, except cash grains (013)	2 010	11	475	125	293	138
Cotton (0131)	1	-	-	-	-	-
Tobacco (0132)	3	2	-	1	-	-
Sugarcane and sugar beets; Irish potatoes; field crops, except cash grains, n.e.c. (0133, 0134, 0139)	2 006	9	475	124	293	138
Vegetables and melons (016)	179	38	87	8	17	10
Fruits and tree nuts (017)	171	37	83	16	15	10
Horticultural specialties (018)	224	116	63	9	10	5
General farms, primarily crop (019)	1 463	38	279	89	125	61
Livestock, except dairy, poultry, and animal specialties (021)	29 037	2 882	3 155	944	2 289	1 454
Beef cattle, except feedlots (0212)	21 861	1 834	2 186	794	1 897	1 213
Dairy farms (024)	1 391	61	37	19	39	34
Poultry and eggs (025)	197	46	54	5	14	4
Animal specialties (027)	1 452	315	602	101	131	86
General farms, primarily livestock and animal specialties (029)	666	6	36	4	10	45
LIVESTOCK						
Cattle and calves inventory .... farms..	40 785	2 162	2 818	980	2 402	1 876
number..	5 539 292	155 982	60 726	26 638	141 347	97 618
Farms with—						
1 to 9	4 367	600	1 393	275	499	255
10 to 49	16 841	1 032	1 319	663	1 772	1 247
50 to 99	8 529	287	69	32	94	151
100 to 199	6 150	148	20	2	20	13
200 to 499	3 580	62	11	6	8	4
500 or more	1 318	33	6	2	9	6
Cows and heifers that had calved .... farms..	33 157	1 520	1 952	799	1 932	1 412
number..	1 451 324	34 721	16 490	7 834	22 374	19 973
Beef cows .... farms..	31 475	1 416	1 828	763	1 858	1 356
number..	1 354 649	33 044	14 865	7 276	21 162	18 883
Farms with—						
1 to 9	6 299	565	1 370	466	885	470
10 to 49	17 123	700	440	293	952	881
50 to 99	5 108	103	12	4	20	5
100 to 199	2 115	28	5	-	1	2
200 to 499	714	20	1	-	-	-
500 or more	116	-	-	-	-	-
Milk cows .... farms..	3 093	149	212	56	123	93
number..	96 675	1 677	1 625	558	1 212	1 090
Farms with—						
1 to 4	1 195	78	162	36	80	50
5 to 9	150	16	18	7	14	8
10 to 49	979	48	26	11	24	31
50 to 99	582	4	3	1	4	4
100 to 199	163	3	3	1	1	-
200 to 499	21	-	-	-	-	-
500 or more	3	-	-	-	-	-
Heifers and heifer calves .... farms..	31 410	1 425	1 946	740	1 812	1 273
number..	1 632 193	42 167	21 755	8 204	51 461	33 579
Steers, steer calves, bulls, and bull calves .... farms..	35 035	1 662	2 119	773	1 957	1 427
number..	2 455 775	79 094	22 481	10 600	67 512	44 066
Cattle and calves sold .... farms..	41 498	2 194	2 653	978	2 429	1 682
number..	7 310 338	244 742	77 878	33 786	281 216	178 108
$1,000..	4 305 335	146 031	43 461	19 873	172 926	114 104
Calves .... farms..	18 518	1 011	1 337	556	1 277	936
number..	468 328	16 344	9 965	5 011	12 238	10 756
$1,000..	145 961	5 188	2 788	1 491	3 663	3 067
Cattle .... farms..	34 216	1 685	2 050	730	1 866	1 312
number..	6 842 010	228 398	67 913	28 775	268 978	167 352
$1,000..	4 159 374	140 843	40 673	18 382	169 263	111 016
Fattened on grain and concentrates .... farms..	4 620	315	331	98	176	136
number..	4 551 726	177 793	23 344	21 639	240 114	160 595
$1,000..	3 041 522	116 440	17 124	15 283	154 719	103 597

See footnotes at end of table.

Table 51. Summary by Size of Farm: 1987—Con.

[For meaning of abbreviations and symbols, see introductory text]

Item	140 to 179 acres	180 to 219 acres	220 to 259 acres	260 to 499 acres	500 to 999 acres	1,000 to 1,999 acres	2,000 acres or more
FARMS BY SIZE							
1 to 9 acres	-	-	-	-	-	-	-
10 to 49 acres	-	-	-	-	-	-	-
50 to 69 acres	-	-	-	-	-	-	-
70 to 99 acres	-	-	-	-	-	-	-
100 to 139 acres	-	-	-	-	-	-	-
140 to 179 acres	5 854	-	-	-	-	-	-
180 to 219 acres	-	2 307	-	-	-	-	-
220 to 259 acres	-	-	2 845	-	-	-	-
260 to 499 acres	-	-	-	11 553	-	-	-
500 to 999 acres	-	-	-	-	12 093	-	-
1,000 to 1,999 acres	-	-	-	-	-	9 304	-
2,000 acres or more	-	-	-	-	-	-	5 056
FARMS BY STANDARD INDUSTRIAL CLASSIFICATION							
Cash grains (011)	2 958	1 000	1 354	6 215	7 025	5 580	2 603
Field crops, except cash grains (013)	227	99	98	237	175	85	47
Cotton (0131)	-	-	-	-	-	-	1
Tobacco (0132)	-	-	-	-	-	-	-
Sugarcane and sugar beets; Irish potatoes; field crops, except cash grains, n.e.c. (0133, 0134, 0139)	227	99	98	237	175	85	46
Vegetables and melons (016)	4	3	1	8	1	2	-
Fruits and tree nuts (017)	1	2	2	2	3	-	-
Horticultural specialties (018)	2	4	3	7	4	-	1
General farms, primarily crop (019)	111	40	53	199	213	170	105
Livestock, except dairy, poultry, and animal specialties (021)	2 261	1 027	1 190	4 366	4 081	3 160	2 228
Beef cattle, except feedlots (0212)	1 849	858	969	3 342	2 955	2 287	1 677
Dairy farms (024)	99	53	75	323	435	188	28
Poultry and eggs (025)	22	6	6	26	7	7	-
Animal specialties (027)	81	36	18	45	23	9	5
General farms, primarily livestock and animal specialties (029)	90	37	45	125	126	103	39
LIVESTOCK							
Cattle and calves inventory ...... farms	2 883	1 299	1 703	6 833	7 813	6 484	3 732
number	206 510	103 560	100 829	737 601	1 073 720	1 226 352	1 608 409
Farms with—							
1 to 9	366	106	167	381	202	90	33
10 to 49	2 050	871	1 033	3 520	2 250	934	150
50 to 99	369	262	405	2 125	2 861	1 552	322
100 to 199	74	44	77	626	1 927	2 349	850
200 to 499	10	9	16	132	470	1 345	1 507
500 or more	14	7	5	49	103	214	870
Cows and heifers that had calved ...... farms	2 401	1 127	1 462	5 788	6 581	5 308	2 875
number	41 946	23 454	35 475	161 175	285 291	360 683	441 908
Beef cows ...... farms	2 271	1 065	1 364	5 430	6 156	5 129	2 837
number	37 816	21 303	32 159	141 836	253 823	337 695	434 787
Farms with—							
1 to 9	659	235	262	715	436	185	51
10 to 49	1 555	795	1 034	4 216	3 928	1 937	392
50 to 99	53	31	59	440	1 549	2 123	709
100 to 199	2	3	8	55	217	782	1 012
200 to 499	2	-	-	3	21	87	580
500 or more	-	1	1	1	5	15	93
Milk cows ...... farms	216	104	154	603	782	457	144
number	4 130	2 151	3 316	19 339	31 468	22 988	7 121
Farms with—							
1 to 4	91	38	53	190	212	135	70
5 to 9	17	6	11	20	22	10	1
10 to 49	80	47	75	242	273	100	22
50 to 99	25	11	12	124	225	147	22
100 to 199	3	2	3	23	44	57	23
200 to 499	-	-	-	4	4	7	6
500 or more	-	-	-	-	2	1	-
Heifers and heifer calves ...... farms	2 161	1 012	1 304	5 342	6 253	5 149	2 993
number	56 838	34 068	29 742	231 770	315 387	351 313	455 919
Steers, steer calves, bulls, and bull calves ...... farms	2 405	1 133	1 453	5 970	6 937	5 823	3 376
number	107 726	46 048	35 612	344 656	473 042	514 356	710 582
Cattle and calves sold ...... farms	2 912	1 337	1 701	7 008	8 060	6 690	3 854
number	321 879	149 068	134 437	1 157 376	1 440 305	1 523 422	1 768 121
$1,000	202 675	87 999	84 530	694 408	868 421	872 885	998 021
Calves ...... farms	1 526	714	903	3 406	3 382	2 373	1 097
number	19 622	11 706	14 557	65 584	90 060	102 123	110 360
$1,000	5 891	3 120	4 387	19 598	27 198	32 879	36 670
Cattle ...... farms	2 312	1 068	1 349	5 651	6 805	5 881	3 487
number	302 257	137 360	119 880	1 091 792	1 350 245	1 421 299	1 657 761
$1,000	196 764	84 879	80 143	674 810	841 224	840 006	961 351
Fattened on grain and concentrates ... farms	218	99	129	683	883	876	676
number	264 955	115 795	93 439	902 402	993 929	852 973	714 748
$1,000	179 776	75 311	68 228	591 390	672 155	503 027	484 473

See footnotes at end of table.

Item	Total	1 to 9 acres	10 to 49 acres	50 to 69 acres	70 to 99 acres	100 to 139 acres
LIVESTOCK—Con.						
Hogs and pigs inventory .... farms..	6 768	656	825	94	298	217
number..	1 516 878	96 984	127 611	29 980	34 009	24 979
Farms with—						
1 to 24	1 916	239	330	54	138	85
25 to 49	828	104	76	12	48	32
50 to 99	1 087	105	62	10	33	40
100 to 199	1 092	83	52	4	31	24
200 to 499	1 226	86	61	6	41	22
500 or more	619	39	42	8	7	14
Used or to be used for breeding .... farms..	4 596	450	392	53	190	148
number..	191 079	14 641	17 230	2 492	4 841	3 951
Other .... farms..	6 286	585	556	84	266	191
number..	1 325 799	82 343	110 581	27 488	29 168	21 028
Hogs and pigs sold .... farms..	7 090	723	650	106	288	224
number..	2 759 676	214 095	253 372	57 374	57 573	44 923
$1,000..	284 375	19 112	23 321	6 522	5 672	4 583
Feeder pigs .... farms..	1 869	247	236	32	102	80
number..	514 394	73 173	73 536	5 637	13 781	11 503
$1,000..	23 029	3 182	3 308	273	588	534
Litters of pigs farrowed between—						
Dec. 1 of preceding year and Nov. 30 ... farms..	4 819	474	418	57	202	167
number..	295 974	23 005	29 774	3 978	6 690	5 243
Dec. 1 and May 31 .... farms..	4 455	423	376	49	178	138
number..	149 414	11 405	15 018	2 085	3 313	2 695
June 1 and Nov. 30 .... farms..	4 403	430	361	47	173	141
number..	146 560	11 600	14 756	1 893	3 377	2 548
Sheep and lambs of all ages inventory...... farms..	2 400	245	351	63	173	113
number..	249 303	16 780	23 352	2 755	9 505	5 599
Ewes 1 year old or older .... farms..	2 195	220	321	59	157	103
number..	129 607	6 095	8 922	1 764	5 791	3 696
Sheep and lambs sold .... farms..	2 396	255	349	69	168	113
number..	267 152	15 115	47 904	2 425	5 916	5 274
Sheep and lambs shorn .... farms..	2 183	219	307	62	157	99
number..	218 980	13 119	26 412	2 353	7 072	4 827
pounds of wool..	1 510 663	91 007	176 211	17 633	57 238	34 739
Horses and ponies inventory .... farms..	12 879	701	1 791	462	953	563
number..	55 598	2 966	8 124	2 157	4 342	2 526
Horses and ponies sold .... farms..	2 260	194	488	106	183	124
number..	6 467	578	1 380	349	568	397
Goats inventory .... farms..	862	90	184	34	80	50
number..	8 831	494	2 179	255	460	419
Goats sold.............................. farms..	256	41	67	10	28	14
number..	2 679	406	602	47	208	167
POULTRY						
Chickens 3 months old or older inventory ... farms..	4 206	299	640	155	347	206
number..	2 094 610	122 717	497 307	4 246	43 796	47 726
Farms with—						
1 to 399	4 117	293	631	155	343	204
400 to 3,199	30	2	2	–	1	–
3,200 to 9,999	12	1	–	–	1	–
10,000 to 19,999	16	3	2	–	2	1
20,000 to 49,999	19	1	2	–	–	–
50,000 to 99,999	7	1	1	–	–	1
100,000 or more	3	–	2	–	–	–
Hens and pullets of laying age .... farms..	4 150	296	629	154	339	202
number..	1 797 313	107 854	403 311	3 889	43 036	47 210
Pullets 3 months old or older not of laying age .... farms..	415	34	67	18	38	36
number..	297 297	14 863	93 996	357	760	516
Hens and pullets sold .... farms..	363	37	58	16	19	19
number..	2 380 936	108 613	494 524	932	31 697	38 455
Broilers and other meat-type chickens sold............................... farms..	132	20	32	3	5	5
number..	176 061	3 952	136 359	135	1 095	2 310
Farms with—						
1 to 1,999	123	19	29	3	8	4
2,000 to 59,999	7	1	1	–	–	1
60,000 to 99,999	2	–	2	–	–	–
100,000 or more	–	–	–	–	–	–
Turkey hens kept for breeding .... farms..	194	19	30	14	28	10
number..	(D)	(D)	12 506	16 327	101	29
Turkeys sold .... farms..	66	9	16	4	7	3
number..	230 719	4 008	28 888	18 419	6 026	19

See footnotes at end of table.

Table 51. **Summary by Size of Farm: 1987**—Con.

[For meaning of abbreviations and symbols, see introductory text]

Item	140 to 179 acres	180 to 219 acres	220 to 259 acres	260 to 499 acres	500 to 999 acres	1,000 to 1,999 acres	2,000 acres or more
LIVESTOCK—Con.							
Hogs and pigs inventory ----------------- farms..	378	187	258	1 182	1 442	1 033	398
number..	45 471	17 447	33 844	296 760	322 821	307 410	179 362
Farms with—							
1 to 24 -----------------------------------	145	54	83	298	283	148	59
25 to 49 ---------------------------------	47	41	32	154	148	108	24
50 to 99 ---------------------------------	57	35	52	216	240	191	44
100 to 199 -------------------------------	61	30	37	224	286	192	68
200 to 499 -------------------------------	55	24	42	210	336	245	98
500 or more -----------------------------	13	3	12	78	149	149	105
Used or to be used for breeding --------- farms..	259	123	173	830	1 005	709	264
number..	6 032	2 443	4 120	39 003	39 132	38 035	19 159
Other ----------------------------------- farms..	337	175	250	1 099	1 371	998	374
number..	39 439	15 004	29 724	257 757	283 689	269 375	160 203
Hogs and pigs sold --------------------- farms..	401	194	270	1 220	1 516	1 078	418
number..	90 792	32 116	62 078	513 206	580 230	528 647	325 270
$1,000..	8 600	2 984	6 067	54 612	61 480	55 971	35 271
Feeder pigs --------------------------- farms..	122	67	62	319	339	203	60
number..	26 075	9 049	11 817	103 664	81 809	73 400	30 970
$1,000..	1 098	367	487	4 782	3 745	3 296	1 367
Litters of pigs farrowed between—							
Dec. 1 of preceding year and Nov. 30 ... farms..	268	127	184	870	1 051	736	275
number..	8 799	3 510	6 877	58 206	59 276	57 129	33 488
Dec. 1 and May 31 -------------------- farms..	235	113	166	819	1 000	688	267
number..	4 447	1 693	3 489	29 086	30 218	29 191	16 774
June 1 and Nov. 30 ------------------ farms..	235	117	172	797	976	693	261
number..	4 352	1 817	3 388	29 120	29 058	27 937	16 714
Sheep and lambs of all ages inventory----- farms..	190	76	96	341	378	265	109
number..	11 827	5 244	20 112	26 629	43 681	51 940	29 879
Ewes 1 year old or older --------------- farms..	169	72	92	321	350	242	89
number..	7 728	2 869	4 192	18 820	25 114	29 048	15 548
Sheep and lambs sold -------------------- farms..	182	76	89	342	386	257	110
number..	8 397	3 916	53 427	25 620	34 155	38 813	26 188
Sheep and lambs shorn ------------------ farms..	168	69	86	322	357	242	93
number..	10 741	3 023	28 972	27 342	34 366	39 242	21 611
pounds of wool..	82 808	19 704	154 208	197 268	233 838	284 484	161 545
Horses and ponies inventory------------- farms..	837	395	448	1 633	1 864	1 744	1 468
number..	3 401	1 925	1 882	7 563	6 837	6 775	7 101
Horses and ponies sold ----------------- farms..	152	65	80	224	239	244	163
number..	499	339	479	1 407	745	1 062	654
Goats inventory ------------------------ farms..	64	20	27	119	97	63	34
number..	1 265	88	132	965	1 548	708	348
Goats sold ---------------------------- farms..	18	9	12	19	17	18	5
number..	129	83	122	205	111	582	17
POULTRY							
Chickens 3 months old or older inventory .. farms..	319	133	169	662	660	403	173
number..	221 253	204 568	121 703	300 950	318 396	198 675	13 273
Farms with—							
1 to 399 ----------------------------------	310	130	164	656	666	391	172
400 to 3,199 -----------------------------	3	-	-	15	2	8	-
3,200 to 9,999 ---------------------------	2	-	2	2	2	-	1
10,000 to 19,999 -------------------------	-	2	1	3	3	2	-
20,000 to 49,999 -------------------------	2	-	1	6	3	4	-
50,000 to 99,999 -------------------------	2	1	1	-	2	-	-
100,000 or more --------------------------	-	1	-	-	-	-	-
Hens and pullets of laying age ---------- farms..	313	131	166	675	670	402	173
number..	137 768	204 408	120 844	265 466	263 846	198 105	11 578
Pullets 3 months old or older not of							
laying age ---------------------------- farms..	36	9	17	65	51	26	17
number..	83 485	162	859	45 484	54 550	570	1 695
Hens and pullets sold------------------- farms..	31	7	21	50	55	25	13
number..	526 637	206 015	207 116	363 662	246 358	151 820	5 707
Broilers and other meat-type chickens							
sold ---------------------------------- farms..	10	6	1	15	18	7	7
number..	1 246	(D)	(D)	18 753	5 015	815	931
Farms with—							
1 to 1,999 --------------------------------	10	4	1	14	17	7	7
2,000 to 59,999 --------------------------	-	1	-	2	1	-	-
60,000 to 99,999 -------------------------	-	-	-	-	-	-	-
100,000 or more --------------------------	-	-	-	-	-	-	-
Turkey hens kept for breeding ----------- farms..	15	4	9	10	36	9	10
number..	74	10	44	56	119	13	27
Turkeys sold --------------------------- farms..	3	7	4	14	10	3	8
number..	953	562	110	141 788	6 197	38	23 711

See footnotes at end of table.

Table 51. **Summary by Size of Farm:** 1987—Con.

[For meaning of abbreviations and symbols, see introductory text]

Item	Total	1 to 9 acres	10 to 49 acres	50 to 69 acres	70 to 99 acres	100 to 139 acres
CROPS HARVESTED						
Corn for grain or seed .... farms..	6 944	14	183	86	253	246
acres..	1 243 969	44	1 967	1 533	5 188	6 615
bushels..	144 133 561	4 070	166 077	119 179	450 310	826 968
Irrigated .... farms..	3 647	–	10	7	26	34
acres..	816 992	–	97	211	891	1 913
Farms by acres harvested:						
1 to 24 acres	1 964	14	174	57	174	140
25 to 99 acres	3 279	–	9	29	79	103
100 to 249 acres	2 196	–	–	–	–	3
250 to 499 acres	1 044	–	–	–	–	–
500 acres or more	441	–	–	–	–	–
Corn for silage or green chop.............. farms..	2 009	–	15	2	18	16
acres..	109 230	–	(D)	(D)	284	349
tons, green..	1 669 413	–	(D)	(D)	2 497	4 646
Irrigated .... farms..	659	–	4	1	–	2
acres..	53 214	–	82	(D)	–	(D)
Farms by acres harvested:						
1 to 24 acres	799	–	13	1	16	9
25 to 99 acres	944	–	2	1	2	7
100 to 249 acres	207	–	–	–	–	–
250 to 499 acres	43	–	–	–	–	–
500 acres or more	16	–	–	–	–	–
Sorghum for grain or seed................ farms..	32 482	40	580	298	1 074	891
acres..	3 399 564	150	6 450	5 661	23 395	23 823
bushels..	228 045 100	7 392	506 002	359 323	1 412 859	1 479 683
Irrigated .... farms..	3 187	–	21	5	30	25
acres..	464 119	–	287	104	1 198	1 160
Farms by acres harvested:						
1 to 24 acres	7 280	40	490	208	722	506
25 to 99 acres	14 139	–	90	90	352	366
100 to 249 acres	7 830	–	–	–	–	17
250 to 499 acres	2 503	–	–	–	–	–
500 acres or more	740	–	–	–	–	–
Wheat for grain .... farms..	38 638	177	847	344	1 383	997
acres..	8 679 588	668	13 863	9 124	46 366	44 420
bushels..	292 999 442	20 747	403 386	270 669	1 393 677	1 386 910
Irrigated .... farms..	3 046	5	20	9	25	21
acres..	635 524	14	380	233	952	883
Farms by acres harvested:						
1 to 24 acres	4 230	177	651	168	511	282
25 to 99 acres	11 461	–	196	156	872	664
100 to 249 acres	11 111	–	–	–	–	51
250 to 499 acres	7 248	–	–	–	–	–
500 acres or more	4 598	–	–	–	–	–
Barley for grain................ farms..	2 307	–	12	8	19	23
acres..	95 465	–	133	91	163	192
bushels..	3 639 224	–	6 186	3 300	5 128	6 661
Irrigated .... farms..	166	–	–	–	1	1
acres..	7 359	–	–	–	(D)	(D)
Oats for grain .... farms..	5 313	2	60	51	144	141
acres..	126 091	(D)	(D)	506	1 422	1 696
bushels..	4 775 729	(D)	(D)	15 416	44 086	49 405
Irrigated .... farms..	48	–	–	–	–	–
acres..	2 278	–	–	–	–	–
Soybeans for beans .... farms..	18 864	46	639	332	931	840
acres..	1 878 978	207	10 125	7 927	25 052	26 155
bushels..	55 789 994	7 732	281 538	218 402	657 805	793 250
Irrigated .... farms..	1 639	1	13	9	22	29
acres..	175 063	(D)	(D)	110	627	773
Farms by acres harvested:						
1 to 24 acres	6 008	46	511	187	501	377
25 to 99 acres	6 253	–	128	145	430	435
100 to 249 acres	3 775	–	–	–	–	28
250 to 499 acres	1 315	–	–	–	–	–
500 acres or more	513	–	–	–	–	–
Dry edible beans, excluding dry limes .... farms..	192	–	–	1	–	1
acres..	30 460	–	–	(D)	–	(D)
cwt..	441 318	–	–	(D)	–	(D)
Irrigated .... farms..	167	–	–	1	–	–
acres..	26 182	–	–	(D)	–	–
Irish potatoes .... farms..	97	2	22	1	5	2
acres..	643	(D)	29	(D)	9	(D)
cwt..	136 764	(D)	3 755	(D)	1 810	(D)
Irrigated .... farms..	21	2	6	–	1	2
acres..	(D)	(D)	2	–	(D)	(D)
Hay—alfalfa, other tame, small grain, wild,						
grass silage, green chop, etc. (see text) ... farms..	33 964	119	2 038	697	2 017	1 375
acres..	2 254 082	413	27 533	13 853	45 067	37 461
tons, dry..	5 080 847	799	44 385	21 563	73 238	61 692
Irrigated .... farms..	1 492	6	37	7	7	10
acres..	206 961	26	498	149	332	233
Farms by acres harvested:						
1 to 24 acres	11 391	119	1 773	500	1 321	783
25 to 99 acres	16 111	–	265	197	696	559
100 to 249 acres	5 297	–	–	–	–	33
250 to 499 acres	913	–	–	–	–	–
500 acres or more	252	–	–	–	–	–

See footnotes at end of table.

Table 51. **Summary by Size of Farm: 1987**—Con.

[For meaning of abbreviations and symbols, see introductory text]

Item	140 to 179 acres	180 to 219 acres	220 to 259 acres	260 to 499 acres	500 to 999 acres	1,000 to 1,999 acres	2,000 acres or more
CROPS HARVESTED							
Corn for grain or seed .... farms..	457	226	302	1 560	2 243	2 137	1 237
acres..	15 881	8 093	11 728	101 173	259 384	404 925	426 436
bushels..	1 678 348	743 826	1 070 792	10 630 050	28 827 235	47 495 084	52 319 852
Irrigated .... farms..	110	35	48	400	894	1 189	894
acres..	7 289	2 023	3 964	46 627	145 090	270 541	338 946
Farms by acres harvested:							
1 to 24 acres	202	106	130	472	300	172	43
25 to 99 acres	220	107	151	743	966	628	244
100 to 249 acres	35	13	21	312	703	735	374
250 to 499 acres	-	-	-	33	256	450	305
500 acres or more	-	-	-	-	18	152	271
Corn for silage or green chop .... farms..	61	36	51	292	531	531	454
acres..	1 777	1 166	1 166	7 633	19 974	29 995	46 614
tons, green..	25 103	12 569	15 397	100 081	263 112	445 888	776 196
Irrigated .... farms..	14	2	6	43	141	186	260
acres..	591	(D)	181	1 849	6 782	13 783	29 809
Farms by acres harvested:							
1 to 24 acres	35	27	34	173	245	166	79
25 to 99 acres	24	6	16	113	249	284	240
100 to 249 acres	2	5	1	6	33	69	91
250 to 499 acres	-	-	-	-	2	10	31
500 acres or more	-	-	-	-	1	2	13
Sorghum for grain or seed .... farms..	2 108	907	1 290	6 377	8 226	6 990	3 711
acres..	64 374	31 968	50 793	349 897	756 167	1 084 234	1 000 632
bushels..	4 002 245	2 025 273	3 276 189	22 839 325	50 676 494	74 874 854	66 585 461
Irrigated .... farms..	72	19	35	311	693	1 066	860
acres..	3 212	628	1 631	21 401	67 507	164 917	202 074
Farms by acres harvested:							
1 to 24 acres	1 085	408	483	1 738	1 091	405	102
25 to 99 acres	970	469	745	3 699	4 162	2 443	753
100 to 249 acres	53	30	62	908	2 592	2 835	1 333
250 to 499 acres	-	-	-	32	357	1 103	1 011
500 acres or more	-	-	-	-	24	204	512
Wheat for grain .... farms..	2 952	1 012	1 465	7 507	9 406	8 039	4 499
acres..	161 265	64 155	105 222	794 357	1 770 944	2 723 291	2 945 902
bushels..	4 994 670	2 009 796	3 239 612	25 445 811	57 558 071	93 213 519	103 060 774
Irrigated .... farms..	98	18	23	343	644	959	881
acres..	4 888	822	1 289	30 070	65 906	203 022	307 065
Farms by acres harvested:							
1 to 24 acres	519	222	243	757	490	157	33
25 to 99 acres	2 138	569	845	2 997	2 037	739	218
100 to 249 acres	305	201	376	3 451	4 241	2 020	466
250 to 499 acres	-	-	1	302	2 402	3 439	1 104
500 acres or more	-	-	-	-	236	1 684	2 678
Barley for grain .... farms..	64	17	38	252	463	763	658
acres..	869	458	703	4 701	11 330	28 140	48 685
bushels..	34 908	20 676	27 258	173 373	405 024	1 128 345	1 828 345
Irrigated .... farms..	4	-	3	9	24	61	63
acres..	(D)	-	54	226	738	2 430	3 861
Oats for grain .... farms..	323	137	215	1 187	1 401	1 165	487
acres..	4 623	1 805	3 352	21 146	31 202	38 979	22 884
bushels..	153 407	62 206	114 198	740 741	1 155 571	1 461 939	963 658
Irrigated .... farms..	-	-	-	1	8	20	14
acres..	-	-	-	142	249	787	1 100
Soybeans for beans .... farms..	1 421	734	926	3 903	4 578	3 286	1 226
acres..	49 999	34 526	44 438	259 313	514 613	574 972	329 649
bushels..	1 399 269	953 121	1 202 136	7 414 184	14 861 542	17 606 995	10 394 020
Irrigated .... farms..	72	17	32	239	483	654	390
acres..	2 020	527	1 258	13 531	32 813	62 896	60 359
Farms by acres harvested:							
1 to 24 acres	633	258	298	980	748	383	84
25 to 99 acres	723	391	529	2 033	1 937	1 156	246
100 to 249 acres	65	85	96	821	1 342	954	384
250 to 499 acres	-	-	3	69	493	523	227
500 acres or more	-	-	-	-	58	270	185
Dry edible beans, excluding dry limas ...... farms..	4	-	2	10	37	76	61
acres..	95	-	(D)	585	3 754	11 896	14 061
cwt..	866	-	(D)	8 181	44 582	166 279	220 082
Irrigated .... farms..	1	-	2	7	31	70	55
acres..	(D)	-	(D)	423	3 316	10 973	13 386
Irish potatoes .... farms..	8	7	1	14	14	15	6
acres..	4	9	(D)	18	14	27	522
cwt..	399	1 791	(D)	2 057	2 958	4 209	120 115
Irrigated .... farms..	-	-	-	(D)	(D)	4	4
acres..	-	-	-	-	-	7	521
Hay—alfalfa, other tame, small grain, wild, grass silage, green chop, etc. (see text) .. farms..	2 517	1 161	1 561	6 271	7 297	5 810	3 101
acres..	77 068	43 731	59 616	301 047	496 458	575 482	573 353
tons, dry..	143 067	77 528	105 956	578 105	1 054 975	1 333 468	1 586 073
Irrigated .... farms..	39	19	26	154	296	407	484
acres..	2 135	1 051	1 416	10 692	26 450	48 665	115 114
Farms by acres harvested:							
1 to 24 acres	1 331	500	630	2 045	1 507	686	196
25 to 99 acres	1 092	594	848	3 554	4 238	3 007	1 061
100 to 249 acres	94	67	82	630	1 400	1 759	1 232
250 to 499 acres	-	-	1	42	124	297	449
500 acres or more	-	-	-	-	28	61	163

See footnotes at end of table.

Table 51. **Summary by Size of Farm: 1987**—Con.

[For meaning of abbreviations and symbols, see introductory text]

Item	Total	1 to 9 acres	10 to 49 acres	50 to 69 acres	70 to 99 acres	100 to 139 acres
CROPS HARVESTED—Con.						
Hay—alfalfa, other tame, small grain, wild, grass silage, green chop. etc. (see text) —Con.						
Alfalfa hay .... farms..	15 484	60	564	184	542	380
acres..	741 856	185	5 901	2 722	9 214	7 698
tons, dry..	2 529 635	383	14 988	6 074	22 841	18 565
Irrigated .... farms..	1 174	6	23	3	5	3
acres..	180 952	26	328	101	181	86
Vegetables harvested for sale (see text) ... farms..	418	51	127	28	33	24
acres..	5 424	156	918	166	385	407
Irrigated .... farms..	166	26	50	15	7	12
acres..	1 851	66	350	103	102	281
Farms by acres harvested:						
0.1 to 4.9 acres	244	40	67	21	16	10
5.0 to 24.9 acres	130	11	52	4	12	7
25.0 to 99.9 acres	39	-	8	3	5	7
100.0 to 249.9 acres	4	-	-	-	-	-
250.0 acres or more	1	-	-	-	-	-
Field seed and grass seed crops .... farms..	1 188	3	34	8	60	34
acres..	56 460	7	488	200	1 218	869
Irrigated .... farms..	12	-	1	-	-	-
acres..	2 222	-	(D)	-	-	-
Land in orchards .... farms..	503	42	148	42	40	36
acres..	5 999	144	767	367	494	371
Irrigated .... farms..	90	13	31	8	8	2
acres..	757	46	159	84	151	(D)
Farms by bearing and nonbearing acres:						
0.1 to 4.9 acres	309	33	96	27	22	21
5.0 to 24.9 acres	147	9	49	10	12	8
25.0 to 99.9 acres	39	-	3	5	6	7
100.0 to 249.9 acres	6	-	-	-	-	-
250.0 acres or more	2	-	-	-	-	-

See footnotes at end of table.

Table 51. **Summary by Size of Farm: 1987**—Con.

[For meaning of abbreviations and symbols, see introductory text]

Item	140 to 179 acres	180 to 219 acres	220 to 259 acres	260 to 499 acres	500 to 999 acres	1,000 to 1,999 acres	2,000 acres or more
CROPS HARVESTED—Con.							
Hay—alfalfa, other tame, small grain, wild, grass silage, green chop, etc. (see text) —Con.							
Alfalfa hay .... farms..	805	455	628	2 847	3 853	3 340	1 826
acres..	16 548	10 108	14 245	83 146	158 936	195 002	236 151
tons, dry..	45 502	27 748	37 679	233 818	498 922	666 327	956 790
Irrigated .... farms..	27	16	23	118	235	324	391
acres..	1 637	959	1 166	8 997	23 146	43 137	101 186
Vegetables harvested for sale (see text) ... farms..	23	11	8	43	34	25	13
acres..	122	263	122	646	217	1 827	196
Irrigated .... farms..	10	1	4	12	14	10	5
acres..	(D)	(D)	116	327	32	341	54
Farms by acres harvested:							
0.1 to 4.9 acres	15	4	2	26	20	15	8
5.0 to 24.9 acres	7	3	2	12	13	4	3
25.0 to 99.9 acres	1	4	2	3	1	4	1
100.0 to 249.9 acres	–	–	–	2	–	1	1
250.0 acres or more	–	–	–	–	–	1	–
Field seed and grass seed crops .... farms..	75	37	46	245	290	252	104
acres..	2 019	1 178	981	8 082	13 181	16 190	14 046
Irrigated .... farms..	1	–	1	1	2	4	2
acres..	(D)	–	(D)	(D)	(D)	236	(D)
Land in orchards .... farms..	43	11	15	52	46	17	11
acres..	239	517	145	1 040	464	209	1 242
Irrigated .... farms..	9	4	1	6	4	2	2
acres..	34	131	(D)	33	28	(D)	(D)
Farms by bearing and nonbearing acres:							
0.1 to 4.9 acres	29	5	8	27	31	6	4
5.0 to 24.9 acres	11	2	5	17	12	8	4
25.0 to 99.9 acres	3	2	2	5	2	3	1
100.0 to 249.9 acres	–	2	–	2	1	–	1
250.0 acres or more	–	–	–	1	–	–	1

[1]Data are based on a sample of farms.
[2]Farms with total production expenses equal to market value of agricultural products sold are included as farms with gains of less than $1,000.

Table 52. Summary by Value of Agricultural Products Sold: 1987

[For meaning of abbreviations and symbols, see introductory text]

| Item | All farms | $500,000 or more | | $250,000 to $499,999 | $100,000 to $249,999 | $50,000 to $99,999 | $40,000 to $49,999 |
		$1,000,000 or more	Total				
FARMS AND LAND IN FARMS							
Farms .... number..	68 579	389	957	1 766	6 656	8 997	3 132
percent..	100.0	.6	1.4	2.6	9.7	13.1	4.6
Land in farms .... acres..	46 628 519	1 560 676	3 504 324	4 541 221	11 683 980	10 326 376	2 676 482
Average size of farm.................. acres..	680	4 012	3 662	2 571	1 755	1 148	855
MARKET VALUE OF AGRICULTURAL PRODUCTS SOLD							
Total sales (see text) .... farms..	68 579	389	957	1 766	6 656	8 997	3 132
$1,000..	6 476 669	3 155 768	3 533 796	597 614	1 006 123	637 837	139 856
Average per farm.................. dollars..	94 441	8 112 515	9 692 576	338 400	151 160	70 894	44 654
Farms by value of sales:							
Less than $1,000 (see text)....................	4 538	-	-	-	-	-	-
$1,000 to $2,499	4 964	-	-	-	-	-	-
$2,500 to $4,999	6 919	-	-	-	-	-	-
$5,000 to $9,999	9 430	-	-	-	-	-	-
$10,000 to $19,999	10 504	-	-	-	-	-	-
$20,000 to $24,999	3 566	-	-	-	-	-	-
$25,000 to $39,999	7 150	-	-	-	-	-	-
$40,000 to $49,999	3 132	-	-	-	-	-	3 132
$50,000 to $99,999	8 997	-	-	-	-	8 997	-
$100,000 to $249,999	6 656	-	-	-	6 656	-	-
$250,000 to $499,999	1 766	-	-	1 766	-	-	-
$500,000 to $999,999	568	-	568	-	-	-	-
$1,000,000 or more	389	389	389	-	-	-	-
Grains.............................. farms..	48 606	245	730	1 602	6 127	8 289	2 825
$1,000..	1 550 403	47 312	121 504	203 631	492 104	356 675	80 382
Sales of $50,000 or more .... farms..	6 994	169	515	1 119	3 945	3 415	-
$1,000..	976 664	45 783	116 750	191 828	438 692	229 594	-
Corn for grain .... farms..	7 426	87	285	629	1 897	1 735	441
$1,000..	255 791	19 262	44 638	58 665	93 221	39 259	5 696
Wheat.............................. farms..	36 365	226	662	1 436	5 455	7 125	2 363
$1,000..	684 147	16 573	43 051	71 538	210 658	167 662	41 707
Soybeans........................... farms..	18 724	72	288	699	2 687	3 673	1 160
$1,000..	263 742	5 969	16 333	92 927	79 040	63 824	14 309
Sorghum for grain .... farms..	28 719	110	360	955	4 196	6 052	1 966
$1,000..	311 649	4 750	14 904	36 896	100 259	80 539	17 380
Barley............................. farms..	1 715	18	42	92	393	443	131
$1,000..	3 953	93	209	463	1 434	965	182
Oats .... farms..	2 418	8	22	56	371	537	159
$1,000..	3 328	36	79	192	785	651	237
Other grains .... farms..	1 656	18	49	110	454	458	120
$1,000..	17 793	1 234	2 290	2 920	6 706	3 554	673
Cotton and cottonseed.............. farms..	10	-	-	1	7	2	-
$1,000..	188	-	-	(D)	188	(D)	-
Sales of $50,000 or more .... farms..	2	-	-	-	2	-	-
$1,000..	(D)	-	-	-	(D)	-	-
Tobacco............................ farms..	13	-	-	-	2	-	3
$1,000..	80	-	-	-	(D)	-	(D)
Sales of $50,000 or more .... farms..	-	-	-	-	-	-	-
$1,000..	-	-	-	-	-	-	-
Hay, silage, and field seeds .... farms..	12 801	102	270	520	1 745	2 222	713
$1,000..	109 574	17 571	27 815	15 181	24 956	16 581	4 274
Sales of $50,000 or more .... farms..	316	40	88	82	112	34	-
$1,000..	47 030	16 520	25 047	9 961	10 061	1 961	-
Vegetables, sweet corn, and melons .... farms..	418	2	5	8	31	46	15
$1,000..	4 151	(D)	695	753	535	559	200
Sales of $50,000 or more .... farms..	10	-	1	3	2	4	-
$1,000..	1 767	-	(D)	683	(D)	(D)	-
Fruits, nuts, and berries .... farms..	278	2	3	5	15	19	6
$1,000..	1 693	(D)	22	346	249	337	59
Sales of $50,000 or more .... farms..	6	-	-	1	2	3	-
$1,000..	732	-	-	(D)	(D)	228	-
Nursery and greenhouse crops........... farms..	272	8	16	11	26	27	8
$1,000..	26 805	11 497	16 731	3 147	3 510	1 440	295
Sales of $50,000 or more .... farms..	82	7	15	8	23	16	-
$1,000..	24 509	(D)	(D)	(D)	3 495	(D)	-
Other crops........................ farms..	80	3	3	3	7	12	1
$1,000..	716	495	495	(D)	(D)	(D)	(D)
Sales of $50,000 or more .... farms..	3	2	2	-	1	-	-
$1,000..	558	(D)	(D)	-	(D)	-	-
Poultry and poultry products .... farms..	1 550	8	18	34	134	165	62
$1,000..	25 284	8 842	13 487	6 199	3 654	1 092	73
Sales of $50,000 or more .... farms..	75	6	14	23	26	12	-
$1,000..	23 851	(D)	(D)	6 162	3 451	789	-
Dairy products .... farms..	2 004	6	24	148	666	526	126
$1,000..	140 232	4 310	10 584	29 978	66 587	23 998	3 134
Sales of $50,000 or more .... farms..	979	6	23	139	568	229	-
$1,000..	119 516	4 310	(D)	(D)	54 457	(D)	-
Cattle and calves .... farms..	41 498	354	853	1 456	4 987	6 436	2 151
$1,000..	4 305 335	3 010 392	3 250 880	283 829	335 567	191 836	42 620
Sales of $50,000 or more .... farms..	5 932	347	822	1 202	2 643	1 265	-
$1,000..	3 891 456	3 010 196	3 250 206	277 865	282 664	80 721	-

See footnotes at end of table.

Table 52. **Summary by Value of Agricultural Products Sold: 1987**—Con.

[For meaning of abbreviations and symbols, see introductory text]

Item	$25,000 to $39,999	$20,000 to $24,999	$10,000 to $19,999	$5,000 to $9,999	$2,500 to $4,999	Less than $2,500
FARMS AND LAND IN FARMS						
Farms.......................number..	7 150	3 566	10 504	9 430	6 919	9 502
percent..	10.4	5.2	15.3	13.8	10.1	13.9
Land in farms.......................acres..	4 679 979	1 815 942	3 596 766	1 934 778	862 367	1 002 304
Average size of farm.......................acres..	655	509	343	205	125	105
MARKET VALUE OF AGRICULTURAL PRODUCTS SOLD						
Total sales (see text) ....farms..	7 150	3 566	10 504	9 430	6 919	9 502
$1,000..	227 493	79 440	150 932	68 474	25 267	9 835
Average per farm.......................dollars..	31 817	22 277	14 369	7 261	3 652	1 035
Farms by value of sales:						
Less than $1,000 (see text)..........................	-	-	-	-	-	4 538
$1,000 to $2,499	-	-	-	-	-	4 964
$2,500 to $4,999	-	-	-	-	6 919	-
$5,000 to $9,999	-	-	-	9 430	-	-
$10,000 to $19,999	-	-	10 504	-	-	-
$20,000 to $24,999	-	3 566	-	-	-	-
$25,000 to $39,999	7 150	-	-	-	-	-
$40,000 to $49,999	-	-	-	-	-	-
$50,000 to $99,999	-	-	-	-	-	-
$100,000 to $249,999	-	-	-	-	-	-
$250,000 to $499,999	-	-	-	-	-	-
$500,000 to $999,999	-	-	-	-	-	-
$1,000,000 or more..........................	-	-	-	-	-	-
Grains.......................farms..	6 242	2 942	7 920	5 898	3 370	2 661
$1,000..	128 169	44 043	78 430	31 927	10 237	3 302
Sales of $50,000 or more ....farms..	-	-	-	-	-	-
$1,000..	-	-	-	-	-	-
Corn for grain.......................farms..	795	323	671	361	157	132
$1,000..	7 654	2 012	3 157	967	276	116
Wheat.......................farms..	5 125	2 323	5 982	4 102	2 197	1 595
$1,000..	68 352	23 657	42 453	17 618	5 681	1 751
Soybeans.......................farms..	2 413	1 142	2 918	2 064	1 022	650
$1,000..	22 999	8 712	15 715	6 902	2 260	722
Sorghum for grain.......................farms..	4 092	1 878	4 481	2 691	1 274	774
$1,000..	27 676	9 172	16 143	6 082	1 920	677
Barley.......................farms..	222	83	192	74	33	10
$1,000..	327	83	216	47	20	5
Oats.......................farms..	378	133	377	223	101	59
$1,000..	452	138	359	148	62	26
Other grains ....farms..	179	66	118	77	18	8
$1,000..	809	266	386	164	18	5
Cotton and cottonseed.......................farms..	-	-	-	-	-	-
$1,000..	-	-	-	-	-	-
Sales of $50,000 or more ....farms..	-	-	-	-	-	-
$1,000..	-	-	-	-	-	-
Tobacco.......................farms..	4	-	1	-	2	1
$1,000..	(D)	-	(D)	-	(D)	(D)
Sales of $50,000 or more ....farms..	-	-	-	-	-	-
$1,000..	-	-	-	-	-	-
Hay, silage, and field seeds ....farms..	1 514	855	1 759	1 356	873	1 174
$1,000..	7 566	2 456	5 539	3 054	1 347	823
Sales of $50,000 or more ....farms..	-	-	-	-	-	-
$1,000..	-	-	-	-	-	-
Vegetables, sweet corn, and melons ....farms..	35	16	65	77	63	55
$1,000..	444	101	378	307	133	48
Sales of $50,000 or more ....farms..	-	-	-	-	-	-
$1,000..	-	-	-	-	-	-
Fruits, nuts, and berries ....farms..	18	14	45	46	35	71
$1,000..	119	95	215	127	68	56
Sales of $50,000 or more ....farms..	-	-	-	-	-	-
$1,000..	-	-	-	-	-	-
Nursery and greenhouse crops.......................farms..	21	13	49	36	35	30
$1,000..	531	271	589	202	85	44
Sales of $50,000 or more ....farms..	-	-	-	-	-	-
$1,000..	-	-	-	-	-	-
Other crops.......................farms..	12	6	13	8	7	8
$1,000..	(D)	7	(D)	7	(D)	(D)
Sales of $50,000 or more ....farms..	-	-	-	-	-	-
$1,000..	-	-	-	-	-	-
Poultry and poultry products ....farms..	159	91	218	194	177	298
$1,000..	216	95	183	130	65	71
Sales of $50,000 or more ....farms..	-	-	-	-	-	-
$1,000..	-	-	-	-	-	-
Dairy products ....farms..	195	75	139	45	26	30
$1,000..	3 715	859	1 041	167	34	13
Sales of $50,000 or more ....farms..	-	-	-	-	-	-
$1,000..	-	-	-	-	-	-
Cattle and calves.......................farms..	4 708	2 302	6 374	5 376	3 672	3 183
$1,000..	72 356	27 531	55 448	26 811	11 314	4 144
Sales of $50,000 or more ....farms..	-	-	-	-	-	-
$1,000..	-	-	-	-	-	-

See footnotes at end of table.

Table 52. **Summary by Value of Agricultural Products Sold: 1987**—Con.

[For meaning of abbreviations and symbols, see introductory text]

Item	All farms	$500,000 or more		$250,000 to $499,999	$100,000 to $249,999	$50,000 to $99,999	$40,000 to $49,999
		$1,000,000 or more	Total				
MARKET VALUE OF AGRICUL-TURAL PRODUCTS SOLD—Con.							
Total sales (see text)—Con.							
Hogs and pigs .... farms..	7 090	41	137	364	1 230	1 462	432
$1,000..	284 375	50 668	84 988	51 848	73 933	41 456	7 584
Sales of $50,000 or more .... farms..	1 278	38	122	267	605	284	-
$1,000..	213 369	50 628	84 556	49 911	61 224	17 677	-
Sheep, lambs, and wool .... farms..	2 456	5	17	45	196	313	102
$1,000..	16 561	4 541	4 898	1 938	3 708	2 553	683
Sales of $50,000 or more .... farms..	44	2	4	10	23	7	-
$1,000..	9 169	(D)	4 810	1 646	2 350	363	-
Other livestock and livestock products (see text) .... farms..	2 869	23	50	61	193	242	111
$1,000..	9 273	72	1 699	751	1 068	1 300	409
Sales of $50,000 or more .... farms..	21	-	2	3	5	11	-
$1,000..	3 849	-	(D)	(D)	(D)	788	-
FARM PRODUCTION EXPENSES[1]							
Total farm production expenses .... farms..	68 580	389	957	1 766	8 530	8 856	3 033
$1,000..	5 516 518	2 842 036	3 149 710	470 286	747 998	492 084	113 649
Average per farm .... dollars..	80 439	7 306 005	3 291 233	266 300	114 548	55 565	37 471
Livestock and poultry purchased .... farms..	23 380	369	878	1 354	3 788	4 063	1 122
$1,000..	2 426 149	1 898 725	2 027 911	143 686	135 347	61 489	10 520
Farms with expenses of—							
$1 to $4,999	11 923	1	8	71	790	1 481	543
$5,000 to $24,999	8 470	5	25	155	1 159	1 650	464
$25,000 to $99,999	3 307	14	67	481	1 594	923	115
$100,000 or more	1 680	349	778	647	245	9	-
Feed for livestock and poultry .... farms..	38 347	373	892	1 488	4 890	6 213	1 855
$1,000..	887 270	629 623	675 007	58 220	72 760	37 876	7 606
Farms with expenses of—							
$1 to $4,999	28 328	4	16	142	1 603	3 719	1 331
$5,000 to $24,999	7 351	11	114	585	2 367	2 290	506
$25,000 to $99,999	2 028	44	266	637	901	203	19
$100,000 or more	640	014	490	124	19	1	-
Commercially mixed formula feeds ..... farms..	14 986	213	481	791	2 397	2 450	687
$1,000..	163 561	83 426	95 531	19 961	25 859	11 122	2 037
Farms with expenses of—							
$1 to $4,999	11 327	7	26	167	1 048	1 671	560
$5,000 to $24,999	2 654	28	153	382	1 110	755	127
$25,000 to $79,999	577	56	139	191	224	23	-
$80,000 or more	230	122	163	51	15	1	-
Seeds, bulbs, plants, and trees .... farms..	48 233	262	762	1 617	6 082	8 164	2 710
$1,000..	95 302	5 054	11 035	12 572	27 904	19 256	4 921
Farms with expenses of—							
$1 to $999	28 247	25	65	139	1 133	2 695	1 191
$1,000 to $4,999	15 265	67	221	623	2 963	4 493	1 334
$5,000 to $24,999	4 473	123	373	777	1 939	965	177
$25,000 or more	248	47	103	78	47	11	8
Commercial fertilizer .... farms..	47 731	262	760	1 608	5 996	7 843	2 564
$1,000..	216 166	9 146	21 005	26 969	63 044	47 686	11 033
Farms with expenses of—							
$1 to $4,999	34 689	39	104	214	1 520	3 843	1 655
$5,000 to $24,999	11 740	118	370	1 045	4 058	3 954	907
$25,000 to $49,999	864	57	184	265	366	44	2
$50,000 or more	216	48	102	84	30	2	-
Agricultural chemicals .... farms..	46 316	264	755	1 549	5 859	7 679	2 531
$1,000..	125 003	5 672	12 506	15 624	36 085	26 784	5 920
Farms with expenses of—							
$1 to $4,999	39 456	87	232	559	3 226	5 879	2 249
$5,000 to $24,999	6 476	118	389	867	2 510	1 791	282
$25,000 to $49,999	322	32	92	102	119	9	-
$50,000 or more	64	27	42	21	1	-	-
Petroleum products .... farms..	65 460	384	945	1 746	6 495	8 765	2 995
$1,000..	243 568	19 545	31 260	27 038	63 225	46 981	12 101
Farms with expenses of—							
$1 to $4,999	51 841	19	79	198	1 579	4 729	2 199
$5,000 to $24,999	12 652	174	526	1 265	4 587	4 041	796
$25,000 to $49,999	760	96	197	231	317	15	-
$50,000 or more	207	95	143	52	12	-	-
Gasoline and gasohol .... farms..	57 245	364	901	1 609	5 975	7 936	2 686
$1,000..	80 737	5 225	8 488	7 295	17 862	15 917	4 219
Diesel fuel .... farms..	46 376	340	863	1 623	6 029	7 894	2 599
$1,000..	110 981	7 691	12 864	12 327	30 638	23 975	6 003
Natural gas .... farms..	4 956	133	304	453	1 247	1 176	310
$1,000..	26 371	4 697	6 995	4 826	8 596	4 052	664
LP gas, fuel oil, kerosene, motor oil, grease, etc. .... farms..	52 549	376	932	1 730	6 368	8 489	2 841
$1,000..	25 478	1 932	2 914	2 590	6 139	5 037	1 214

See footnotes at end of table.

Table 52. **Summary by Value of Agricultural Products Sold:** 1987—Con.

[For meaning of abbreviations and symbols, see introductory text]

Item	$25,000 to $39,999	$20,000 to $24,999	$10,000 to $19,999	$5,000 to $9,999	$2,500 to $4,999	Less than $2,500
MARKET VALUE OF AGRICULTURAL PRODUCTS SOLD—Con.						
Total sales (see text)—Con.						
Hogs and pigs _____ farms__	917	334	895	560	388	351
$1,000__	12 392	2 855	5 908	2 116	873	323
Sales of $50,000 or more _____ farms__	-	-	-	-	-	-
$1,000__	-	-	-	-	-	-
Sheep, lambs, and wool _____ farms__	238	142	377	323	284	419
$1,000__	1 257	688	1 204	757	482	393
Sales of $50,000 or more _____ farms__	-	-	-	-	-	-
$1,000__	-	-	-	-	-	-
Other livestock and livestock products (see text) _____ farms__	202	105	309	408	363	805
$1,000__	665	341	978	849	598	615
Sales of $50,000 or more _____ farms__	-	-	-	-	-	-
$1,000__	-	-	-	-	-	-
FARM PRODUCTION EXPENSES[1]						
Total farm production expenses _____ farms__	7 219	3 471	11 033	9 628	6 786	9 301
$1,000__	188 422	65 355	151 159	72 723	33 109	32 022
Average per farm _____ dollars__	26 101	18 829	13 701	7 553	4 879	3 443
Livestock and poultry purchased _____ farms__	2 587	1 095	3 230	2 060	1 474	1 729
$1,000__	17 897	5 583	12 919	5 729	2 673	2 396
Farms with expenses of—						
$1 to $4,999 _____	1 345	656	2 201	1 765	1 411	1 652
$5,000 to $24,999 _____	1 173	439	1 003	279	57	66
$25,000 to $99,999 _____	69	-	25	16	6	11
$100,000 or more _____	-	-	1	-	-	-
Feed for livestock and poultry _____ farms__	4 274	1 993	5 913	4 153	2 918	3 758
$1,000__	11 660	4 301	9 879	4 600	2 332	3 028
Farms with expenses of—						
$1 to $4,999 _____	3 523	1 767	5 542	4 084	2 912	3 689
$5,000 to $24,999 _____	750	226	369	69	6	69
$25,000 to $99,999 _____	1	-	2	-	-	-
$100,000 or more _____	-	-	-	-	-	-
Commercially mixed formula feeds ____ farms__	1 683	631	2 101	1 316	834	1 617
$1,000__	3 200	1 015	2 705	837	491	783
Farms with expenses of—						
$1 to $4,999 _____	1 515	569	2 018	1 316	834	1 603
$5,000 to $24,999 _____	166	62	83	-	-	14
$25,000 to $79,999 _____	-	-	-	-	-	-
$80,000 or more _____	1	-	-	-	-	-
Seeds, bulbs, plants, and trees _____ farms__	6 092	2 820	8 191	5 743	3 291	2 761
$1,000__	7 525	2 455	5 702	2 491	945	595
Farms with expenses of—						
$1 to $999 _____	3 325	1 987	6 570	5 257	3 180	2 705
$1,000 to $4,999 _____	2 646	797	1 547	486	111	44
$5,000 to $24,999 _____	120	36	74	-	-	12
$25,000 or more _____	1	-	-	-	-	-
Commercial fertilizer _____ farms__	5 884	2 614	7 935	5 863	3 408	3 256
$1,000__	17 691	5 855	12 088	5 424	1 909	1 463
Farms with expenses of—						
$1 to $4,999 _____	4 972	2 393	7 721	5 811	3 408	3 248
$5,000 to $24,999 _____	911	221	214	52	-	8
$25,000 to $49,999 _____	1	-	-	-	-	-
$50,000 or more _____	-	-	-	-	-	-
Agricultural chemicals _____ farms__	5 810	2 620	7 871	5 295	3 279	3 270
$1,000__	10 039	3 609	8 299	3 638	1 394	1 106
Farms with expenses of—						
$1 to $4,999 _____	5 470	2 570	7 505	5 238	3 272	3 253
$5,000 to $24,999 _____	340	50	166	57	7	17
$25,000 to $49,999 _____	-	-	-	-	-	-
$50,000 or more _____	-	-	-	-	-	-
Petroleum products _____ farms__	7 132	3 405	10 793	9 284	6 255	7 625
$1,000__	20 579	7 467	17 342	8 790	3 890	2 894
Farms with expenses of—						
$1 to $4,999 _____	6 173	3 207	10 532	9 272	6 255	7 618
$5,000 to $24,999 _____	959	198	261	12	-	7
$25,000 to $49,999 _____	-	-	-	-	-	-
$50,000 or more _____	-	-	-	-	-	-
Gasoline and gasohol _____ farms__	6 092	2 994	9 406	7 825	5 267	6 554
$1,000__	7 801	2 943	7 781	4 363	2 285	1 783
Diesel fuel _____ farms__	5 957	2 723	7 733	5 327	2 857	2 771
$1,000__	9 883	3 484	7 060	3 021	1 048	676
Natural gas _____ farms__	450	160	449	230	57	120
$1,000__	563	138	408	103	14	23
LP gas, fuel oil, kerosene, motor oil, grease, etc. _____ farms__	6 553	2 989	9 111	6 533	3 691	3 312
$1,000__	2 333	902	2 093	1 304	543	410

See footnotes at end of table.

Table 52. **Summary by Value of Agricultural Products Sold: 1987** —Con.

[For meaning of abbreviations and symbols, see introductory text]

Item	All farms	$500,000 or more		$250,000 to $499,999	$100,000 to $249,999	$50,000 to $99,999	$40,000 to $49,999
		$1,000,000 or more	Total				
FARM D N EXPENSES[1] **—CeRO UCTIO**							
Total farm production expenses—Con.							
Electricity .... farms..	48 797	376	918	1 713	6 031	7 771	2 509
$1,000..	54 103	10 479	13 612	6 511	11 889	8 141	2 047
Farms with expenses of—							
$1 to $999...........................	36 880	21	80	354	2 273	4 697	1 841
$1,000 to $4,999	10 585	111	422	958	3 306	2 985	657
$5,000 to $24,999	1 236	144	301	383	449	89	11
$25,000 or more	136	100	115	18	3	-	-
Hired farm labor .... farms..	24 715	380	934	1 555	4 555	4 705	1 335
$1,000..	226 075	91 385	116 708	36 958	40 873	17 117	2 953
Farms with expenses of—							
$1 to $4,999........................	18 529	8	20	107	2 282	3 672	1 168
$5,000 to $24,999	4 529	38	256	922	1 884	971	164
$25,000 to $99,999	1 391	151	419	503	366	61	3
$100,000 or more	266	185	239	23	3	1	-
Contract labor...................... farms..	7 882	119	282	432	1 398	1 311	402
$1,000..	23 691	4 329	6 586	3 438	5 016	3 275	763
Farms with expenses of—							
$1 to $999..........................	3 892	4	24	50	357	528	217
$1,000 to $4,999	2 895	36	78	185	716	577	137
$5,000 to $24,999	1 023	52	143	169	319	205	48
$25,000 or more	72	27	37	28	6	1	-
Repair and maintenance .... farms..	56 961	379	933	1 707	6 268	8 276	2 822
$1,000..	252 018	28 986	40 116	27 014	61 589	47 984	12 303
Farms with expenses of—							
$1 to $4,999........................	42 384	32	124	236	1 685	4 161	1 797
$5,000 to $24,999	13 477	108	408	1 155	4 270	4 060	1 023
$25,000 to $49,999	844	91	212	275	290	53	1
$50,000 or more	256	148	189	41	23	2	1
Customwork, machine hire, and rental of							
machinery and equipment .... farms..	30 603	261	660	1 213	3 876	5 053	1 675
$1,000..	107 366	10 560	15 847	11 238	26 002	21 297	5 342
Farms with expenses of—							
$1 to $999..........................	13 298	9	49	117	798	1 384	719
$1,000 to $4,999	11 836	54	175	489	1 842	2 379	800
$5,000 to $24,999	4 982	100	295	511	1 386	1 211	355
$25,000 or more	487	98	141	96	170	79	1
Interest expense .... farms..	39 549	364	892	1 601	5 537	6 923	2 129
$1,000..	314 163	34 736	55 246	41 082	82 013	58 440	13 790
Farms with expenses of—							
$1 to $4,999........................	24 133	25	72	249	1 457	2 931	1 125
$5,000 to $24,999	12 676	61	224	674	2 997	3 654	981
$25,000 to $99,999	2 557	157	448	649	1 079	338	23
$100,000 or more	183	121	150	29	4	-	-
Secured by real estate .... farms..	26 408	225	577	1 149	4 023	4 787	1 951
$1,000..	188 166	12 726	22 581	23 779	50 834	37 718	8 926
Farms with expenses of—							
$1 to $999..........................	5 315	4	16	68	213	459	178
$1,000 to $4,999	10 417	14	53	152	907	1 652	466
$5,000 to $24,999	9 280	69	207	589	2 337	2 510	697
$25,000 or more	1 396	138	301	340	566	168	10
Not secured by real estate .... farms..	24 307	276	685	1 185	3 648	4 528	1 350
$1,000..	125 997	22 010	32 685	17 303	31 179	20 722	4 865
Farms with expenses of—							
$1 to $999..........................	8 203	7	15	61	433	800	229
$1,000 to $4,999	9 540	20	69	201	1 246	2 018	777
$5,000 to $24,999	5 768	57	231	704	1 979	1 699	341
$25,000 or more	798	192	375	219	190	11	3
Cash rent........................... farms..	21 234	177	542	1 122	3 734	4 441	1 286
$1,000..	123 531	8 411	16 712	16 527	35 800	25 480	5 653
Farms with expenses of—							
$1 to $4,999........................	14 629	28	110	360	1 724	2 723	888
$5,000 to $9,999	3 298	24	94	244	811	931	243
$10,000 to $24,999	2 511	47	152	325	897	685	152
$25,000 or more	796	78	186	193	302	102	3
Property taxes .... farms..	63 359	370	909	1 717	6 260	8 364	2 865
$1,000..	112 201	5 048	8 718	8 769	22 550	21 596	6 289
Farms with expenses of—							
$1 to $4,999........................	59 062	129	389	1 029	4 852	7 391	2 633
$5,000 to $9,999	3 248	89	258	485	1 045	839	190
$10,000 to $24,999	956	111	209	192	338	126	41
$25,000 or more	93	41	53	11	15	8	1
All other farm production expenses....... farms..	64 491	388	958	1 766	6 528	8 854	3 033
$1,000..	309 914	80 337	97 438	32 643	64 202	46 684	12 406
Farms with expenses of—							
$1 to $4,999........................	51 852	13	82	306	2 362	5 963	2 098
$5,000 to $24,999	11 071	75	358	1 018	3 646	3 402	935
$25,000 to $49,999	1 005	68	176	312	428	88	-
$50,000 or more	563	232	340	130	92	1	-

See footnotes at end of table.

Table 52. **Summary by Value of Agricultural Products Sold: 1987**—Con.

[For meaning of abbreviations and symbols, see introductory text]

Item	$25,000 to $39,999	$20,000 to $24,999	$10,000 to $19,999	$5,000 to $9,999	$2,500 to $4,999	Less than $2,500
FARM PRODUCTION EXPENSES[1] —Con.						
Total farm production expenses—Con.						
Electricity _____ farms..	5 632	2 594	7 903	5 665	3 963	4 098
$1,000..	3 460	1 336	3 137	1 896	1 080	994
Farms with expenses of—						
$1 to $999 _____	4 648	2 288	7 464	5 351	3 882	3 982
$1,000 to $4,999 _____	982	306	438	314	81	115
$5,000 to $24,999 _____	2	–	–	–	–	1
$25,000 or more _____	–	–	–	–	–	–
Hired farm labor _____ farms..	2 874	1 266	3 327	2 023	1 201	940
$1,000..	4 780	1 505	3 291	1 003	502	587
Farms with expenses of—						
$1 to $4,999 _____	2 683	1 214	3 243	2 014	1 200	926
$5,000 to $24,999 _____	178	52	82	7	1	12
$25,000 to $99,999 _____	13	–	2	2	–	2
$100,000 or more _____	–	–	–	–	–	–
Contract labor _____ farms..	889	403	1 067	871	413	414
$1,000..	1 413	504	1 381	843	242	231
Farms with expenses of—						
$1 to $999 _____	487	246	669	599	346	369
$1,000 to $4,999 _____	337	140	358	256	67	44
$5,000 to $24,998 _____	65	17	40	16	–	1
$25,000 or more _____	–	–	–	–	–	–
Repair and maintenance _____ farms..	6 427	3 026	9 312	7 484	4 898	5 808
$1,000..	21 160	7 497	17 369	9 263	3 667	3 713
Farms with expenses of—						
$1 to $4,999 _____	5 077	2 637	8 739	7 292	4 653	5 783
$5,000 to $24,999 _____	1 337	389	573	192	45	25
$25,000 to $49,999 _____	13	–	–	–	–	–
$50,000 or more _____	–	–	–	–	–	–
Customwork, machine hire, and rental of machinery and equipment _____ farms..	3 954	1 735	4 954	3 255	2 015	2 113
$1,000..	10 102	3 499	8 365	3 269	1 517	889
Farms with expenses of—						
$1 to $999 _____	1 537	721	2 438	2 106	1 531	1 898
$1,000 to $4,999 _____	1 773	813	2 145	1 121	464	215
$5,000 to $24,999 _____	644	201	371	28	–	–
$25,000 or more _____	–	–	–	–	–	–
Interest expense _____ farms..	4 926	2 060	5 853	3 954	2 504	3 168
$1,000..	21 130	6 630	16 984	8 675	4 478	5 693
Farms with expenses of—						
$1 to $4,999 _____	3 235	1 572	4 706	3 536	2 326	2 924
$5,000 to $24,999 _____	1 676	482	1 147	417	178	244
$25,000 to $99,999 _____	15	6	–	1	–	–
$100,000 or more _____	–	–	–	–	–	–
Secured by real estate _____ farms..	2 997	1 198	3 631	2 510	1 663	2 522
$1,000..	13 204	4 206	11 921	6 512	3 637	4 867
Farms with expenses of—						
$1 to $999 _____	633	340	1 073	736	559	1 038
$1,000 to $4,999 _____	1 293	556	1 676	1 434	946	1 282
$5,000 to $24,999 _____	1 064	296	882	338	158	202
$25,000 or more _____	7	6	–	–	–	–
Not secured by real estate _____ farms..	3 213	1 326	3 678	2 164	1 160	1 165
$1,000..	7 927	2 422	5 063	2 163	841	826
Farms with expenses of—						
$1 to $999 _____	1 076	590	1 911	1 374	845	869
$1,000 to $4,999 _____	1 635	589	1 628	766	315	294
$5,000 to $24,999 _____	502	147	139	22	–	2
$25,000 or more _____	–	–	–	–	–	–
Cash rent_____ farms..	2 908	1 136	2 773	1 629	853	810
$1,000..	9 982	2 972	6 396	2 573	913	521
Farms with expenses of—						
$1 to $4,999 _____	2 203	956	2 460	1 562	837	806
$5,000 to $9,999 _____	499	150	245	61	16	4
$10,000 to $24,999 _____	199	29	66	6	–	–
$25,000 or more _____	7	1	2	–	–	–
Property taxes _____ farms..	6 724	3 216	9 970	8 621	6 190	8 503
$1,000..	11 149	4 943	12 346	7 327	3 801	4 712
Farms with expenses of—						
$1 to $4,999 _____	6 534	3 133	9 834	8 579	6 183	8 475
$5,000 to $9,999 _____	176	72	121	42	7	13
$10,000 to $24,999 _____	13	11	12	–	–	14
$25,000 or more _____	1	–	3	–	–	1
All other farm production expenses _____ farms..	7 219	3 471	11 029	8 650	5 769	7 316
$1,000..	19 854	7 199	15 640	7 202	3 447	3 198
Farms with expenses of—						
$1 to $4,999 _____	6 142	3 201	10 681	8 632	5 769	7 316
$5,000 to $24,999 _____	1 076	270	348	18	–	–
$25,000 to $49,999 _____	1	–	–	–	–	–
$50,000 or more _____	–	–	–	–	–	–

See footnotes at end of table.

Table 52. **Summary by Value of Agricultural Products Sold: 1987**—Con.

[For meaning of abbreviations and symbols, see introductory text]

Item	All farms	$500,000 or more — $1,000,000 or more	$500,000 or more — Total	$250,000 to $499,999	$100,000 to $249,999	$50,000 to $99,999	$40,000 to $49,999
NET CASH RETURN FROM AGRICULTURAL SALES FOR THE FARM UNIT[1]							
All farms........number..	68 580	389	957	1 766	6 530	8 856	3 033
$1,000..	922 225	313 733	384 065	127 326	229 830	132 452	22 267
Average per farm........dollars..	13 447	806 510	401 343	72 100	35 196	14 958	7 342
Farms with net gains[2]........number..	41 673	356	841	1 523	5 471	6 922	2 187
Average net gain........dollars..	27 369	939 505	489 685	90 843	47 160	23 794	15 008
Gain of—							
Less than $1,000..........	4 994	9	15	25	88	132	74
$1,000 to $9,999..........	18 378	17	34	84	504	1 261	674
$10,000 to $49,999..........	13 889	22	88	362	2 922	5 130	1 439
$50,000 or more..........	4 412	310	704	1 052	2 257	399	–
Farms with net losses........number..	26 907	31	116	243	1 059	1 934	846
Average net loss........dollars..	6 114	729 364	239 205	45 375	26 718	16 674	12 476
Loss of—							
Less than $1,000..........	5 287	–	2	6	40	113	85
$1,000 to $9,999..........	16 553	1	21	50	290	794	407
$10,000 to $49,999..........	4 663	4	38	128	609	929	331
$50,000 or more..........	404	26	55	59	120	98	23
GOVERNMENT PAYMENTS AND OTHER FARM-RELATED INCOME							
Government payments........farms..	41 627	218	665	1 467	5 619	7 581	2 505
$1,000..	573 847	14 238	37 195	64 360	168 113	137 708	32 366
Other farm-related income[1]........farms..	18 882	95	261	538	2 312	3 090	843
$1,000..	69 944	2 180	3 880	3 997	12 941	13 724	4 886
Customwork and other agricultural services........farms..	7 463	29	123	313	1 293	1 689	448
$1,000..	32 115	349	1 092	2 229	7 357	8 467	2 796
Gross cash rent or share payments........farms..	7 899	39	73	113	592	887	319
$1,000..	30 403	1 638	2 329	1 084	3 703	4 071	1 604
Forest products and Christmas trees........farms..	439	–	1	7	39	56	20
$1,000..	1 087	–	(D)	(D)	165	53	(D)
Other farm-related income sources........farms..	5 659	43	116	271	1 119	1 922	547
$1,000..	6 340	193	(D)	(D)	1 716	1 133	(D)
COMMODITY CREDIT CORPORATION LOANS							
Total........farms..	15 832	111	358	867	3 925	3 975	1 161
$1,000..	338 298	14 260	34 499	52 940	121 509	76 588	14 309
Corn........farms..	3 591	65	187	416	1 189	937	203
$1,000..	108 314	8 932	16 266	24 304	41 489	17 744	2 257
Wheat........farms..	7 282	47	155	381	1 544	1 710	620
$1,000..	95 942	2 474	6 406	10 964	33 697	23 924	5 239
Soybeans........farms..	1 248	5	37	112	319	319	70
$1,000..	20 764	555	2 567	4 191	7 149	4 398	697
Sorghum, barley, and oats........farms..	10 032	53	194	515	2 150	2 741	762
$1,000..	112 774	2 299	7 260	13 581	39 173	30 441	6 035
Cotton........farms..	–	–	–	–	–	–	–
$1,000..	–	–	–	–	–	–	–
Peanuts, rye, rice, tobacco, and honey........farms..	22	–	–	–	–	4	3
$1,000..	503	–	–	–	–	181	81
LAND IN FARMS ACCORDING TO USE							
Total cropland........farms..	61 615	306	837	1 898	6 471	8 764	2 997
acres..	31 385 090	654 368	1 720 822	2 793 823	8 031 275	7 360 850	1 936 234
Harvested cropland........farms..	57 822	283	805	1 674	6 403	8 647	2 957
acres..	17 729 394	424 448	1 107 857	1 795 327	4 853 026	4 212 806	1 058 306
Farms by acres harvested:							
1 to 49 acres..........	12 372	10	21	21	81	160	73
50 to 99 acres..........	8 853	7	14	26	104	297	129
100 to 199 acres..........	10 361	17	36	52	293	648	398
200 to 499 acres..........	14 781	38	101	233	1 508	3 736	1 751
500 to 999 acres..........	8 150	57	197	556	2 748	3 418	592
1,000 to 1,999 acres..........	2 876	89	269	614	1 572	579	22
2,000 acres or more..........	449	65	167	173	97	10	2
Cropland:							
Pasture or grazing only........farms..	22 575	108	279	587	2 266	3 301	1 164
acres..	3 485 445	44 087	90 903	166 689	593 073	771 133	231 269
In cover crops, legumes, and soil-improvement grasses, not harvested and not pastured........farms..	11 212	51	171	367	1 397	1 891	633
acres..	1 103 315	21 876	59 025	66 615	225 983	229 792	68 423
On which all crops failed........farms..	3 341	14	44	81	376	512	174
acres..	206 231	2 271	6 936	9 901	37 224	43 149	12 409
In cultivated summer fallow........farms..	25 408	143	416	908	3 796	5 020	1 646
acres..	6 409 506	111 966	314 474	543 466	1 743 180	1 585 795	422 203
Idle........farms..	20 610	112	341	751	2 686	3 487	1 212
acres..	2 451 199	49 720	141 627	221 825	578 789	518 175	143 624
Total woodland........farms..	12 587	39	122	268	1 059	1 577	568
acres..	718 261	6 962	21 305	35 472	95 611	191 480	37 163
Woodland pastured........farms..	6 382	18	65	151	453	811	262
acres..	366 136	4 410	11 961	22 297	39 635	67 900	18 227
Woodland not pastured........farms..	7 991	24	77	166	769	1 067	400
acres..	352 125	2 552	9 344	13 175	55 976	63 580	18 956

See footnotes at end of table.

Table 52. **Summary by Value of Agricultural Products Sold: 1987**—Con.

[For meaning of abbreviations and symbols, see introductory text]

Item	$25,000 to $39,999	$20,000 to $24,999	$10,000 to $19,999	$5,000 to $9,999	$2,500 to $4,999	Less than $2,500
NET CASH RETURN FROM AGRICULTURAL SALES FOR THE FARM UNIT[1]						
All farms................number..	7 219	3 471	11 033	9 628	6 766	9 301
$1,000..	40 491	11 976	7 837	-3 134	-6 465	-22 444
Average per farm...............dollars..	5 609	3 451	710	-326	-1 247	-2 413
Farms with net gains[2]..............number..	5 287	2 494	6 626	5 452	3 007	1 863
Average net gain..............dollars..	11 242	7 668	5 234	2 935	1 430	629
Gain of—						
Less than $1,000	245	196	650	694	1 206	1 469
$1,000 to $9,999	2 199	1 521	5 348	4 558	1 801	394
$10,000 to $49,999	2 843	777	628	-	-	-
$50,000 or more	-	-	-	-	-	-
Farms with net losses..............number..	1 932	977	4 407	4 176	3 779	7 438
Average net loss..............dollars..	9 806	7 315	6 092	4 583	3 378	3 175
Loss of—						
Less than $1,000	180	120	706	910	934	2 191
$1,000 to $9,999	1 066	590	2 855	2 884	2 703	4 893
$10,000 to $49,999	652	266	837	379	142	352
$50,000 or more	34	1	9	3	-	2
GOVERNMENT PAYMENTS AND OTHER FARM-RELATED INCOME						
Government payments .... farms..	5 489	2 540	6 597	4 627	2 545	1 992
$1,000..	53 770	19 226	35 106	16 113	5 621	4 068
Other farm-related income[1]..................... farms..	2 219	1 046	2 836	2 247	1 492	1 698
$1,000..	6 685	3 795	7 889	4 860	3 495	3 791
Customwork and other agricultural services .... farms..	974	414	814	609	419	357
$1,000..	3 270	1 174	2 544	1 137	1 040	908
Gross cash rent or share payments ...... farms..	786	402	1 372	1 316	959	1 078
$1,000..	2 945	2 183	4 595	3 173	2 298	2 319
Forest products and Christmas trees ..... farms..	23	19	64	70	52	88
$1,000..	98	194	159	166	39	142
Other farm-related income sources .... farms..	886	419	1 083	661	221	322
$1,000..	673	245	391	385	118	423
COMMODITY CREDIT CORPORATION LOANS						
Total .... farms..	2 107	846	1 757	890	359	187
$1,000..	20 270	5 932	8 731	2 599	660	161
Corn .... farms..	307	111	164	47	19	11
$1,000..	2 729	559	808	122	29	7
Wheat.................................... farms..	943	350	950	491	208	130
$1,000..	7 795	2 244	3 815	1 376	377	104
Soybeans................................ farms..	140	46	121	55	21	6
$1,000..	924	306	383	121	23	5
Sorghum, barley, and oats .... farms..	1 389	555	1 007	481	183	55
$1,000..	8 673	2 750	3 624	967	231	40
Cotton.................................... farms..	-	-	-	-	-	-
$1,000..	-	-	-	-	-	-
Peanuts, rye, rice, tobacco, and honey..... farms..	5	3	-	3	-	4
$1,000..	148	73	-	14	-	6
LAND IN FARMS ACCORDING TO USE						
Total cropland............................ farms..	6 849	3 347	9 675	8 241	5 637	7 099
acres..	3 389 542	1 293 223	2 564 719	1 303 966	542 991	447 625
Harvested cropland .... farms..	6 694	3 261	9 233	7 571	4 996	5 591
acres..	1 797 241	662 916	1 276 731	603 172	233 719	136 293
Farms by acres harvested:						
1 to 49 acres	298	230	1 168	2 314	3 028	4 958
50 to 99 acres	459	360	2 201	3 112	1 600	552
100 to 199 acres	1 604	1 114	3 938	1 673	327	78
200 to 499 acres	3 815	1 473	1 844	267	30	3
500 to 999 acres	500	83	61	5	-	-
1,000 to 1,999 acres	18	1	1	-	1	-
2,000 acres or more	-	-	-	-	-	-
Cropland:						
Pasture or grazing only .... farms..	2 575	1 288	3 592	2 996	1 999	2 528
acres..	469 954	198 847	433 886	267 329	126 888	135 474
In cover crops, legumes, and soil-improvement grasses, not harvested and not pastured .... farms..	1 434	685	1 645	1 281	737	781
acres..	116 106	55 188	134 194	70 430	30 372	47 187
On which all crops failed .... farms..	381	188	508	471	243	363
acres..	24 227	12 496	22 799	17 114	6 347	13 629
In cultivated summer fallow .... farms..	3 545	1 581	3 904	2 468	1 256	844
acres..	713 221	259 762	470 977	213 172	84 414	58 842
Idle .... farms..	2 635	1 201	3 305	2 349	1 396	1 247
acres..	268 793	104 014	224 132	132 769	61 251	56 200
Total woodland .... farms..	1 344	698	1 980	1 878	1 358	1 735
acres..	85 142	36 690	94 208	76 117	48 240	56 813
Woodland pastured .... farms..	869	329	962	1 006	755	919
acres..	43 055	18 126	47 645	42 700	25 818	28 772
Woodland not pastured .... farms..	895	464	1 299	1 107	753	994
acres..	42 087	18 564	46 563	33 417	22 422	28 041

See footnotes at end of table.

Table 52. **Summary by Value of Agricultural Products Sold: 1987**—Con.

[For meaning of abbreviations and symbols, see introductory text]

Item	All farms	$500,000 or more $1,000,000 or more	$500,000 or more Total	$250,000 to $499,999	$100,000 to $249,999	$50,000 to $99,999	$40,000 to $49,999
LAND IN FARMS ACCORDING TO USE—Con.							
Pastureland and rangeland other than cropland and woodland pastured .... farms..	32 362	210	582	1 079	3 865	5 018	1 645
acres..	13 254 094	857 974	1 684 323	1 622 277	3 310 160	2 572 352	643 984
Land in house lots, ponds, roads, wasteland, etc. .... farms..	44 335	295	653	1 173	4 401	5 949	2 023
acres..	1 271 074	41 372	77 674	89 649	246 934	261 694	61 081
Cropland under federal acreage reduction programs:							
Annual commodity acreage adjustment programs .... farms..	34 658	202	626	1 404	5 391	7 134	2 289
acres..	3 956 196	85 766	235 912	396 391	1 152 881	995 002	238 425
Conservation reserve program .... farms..	5 650	40	126	262	876	1 062	353
acres..	810 862	16 078	47 447	57 523	165 629	167 761	52 450
Value of land and buildings¹ .... farms..	68 580	389	957	1 766	6 530	8 856	3 033
$1,000..	19 068 461	728 073	1 580 029	1 849 173	4 430 903	3 770 672	1 006 480
Average per farm ....dollars..	278 047	1 871 653	1 630 124	1 047 097	678 546	425 776	331 843
Average per acre ....dollars..	413	467	445	407	387	376	378
Farms by value group:							
$1 to $39,999	10 024	10	21	41	111	193	80
$40,000 to $69,999	9 571	7	19	12	83	188	151
$70,000 to $99,999	7 001	4	7	10	87	233	125
$100,000 to $149,999	8 596	16	23	22	169	472	261
$150,000 to $199,999	6 313	15	24	28	224	684	346
$200,000 to $499,999	16 476	44	122	313	2 060	4 303	1 579
$500,000 to $999,999	7 579	83	253	627	2 614	2 406	439
$1,000,000 to $1,999,999	2 396	101	288	543	1 037	330	39
$2,000,000 to $4,999,999	535	77	159	150	132	46	11
$5,000,000 or more	89	32	50	20	13	1	2
VALUE OF MACHINERY AND EQUIPMENT¹							
Estimated market value of all machinery and equipment .... farms..	68 391	389	957	1 766	6 529	8 849	3 033
$1,000..	3 447 663	174 162	294 542	302 819	783 829	686 179	186 327
Farms by value group:							
$1 to $4,999	5 812	1	4	8	24	111	50
$5,000 to $9,999	11 585	4	5	8	69	176	134
$10,000 to $19,999	11 722	4	8	41	283	546	308
$20,000 to $49,999	16 724	21	62	164	891	2 173	933
$50,000 to $99,999	12 176	32	127	323	1 800	3 322	1 058
$100,000 to $199,999	7 277	106	292	606	2 356	2 073	434
$200,000 to $499,999	2 860	152	349	554	1 056	439	105
$500,000 or more	235	69	110	64	50	9	1
SELECTED MACHINERY AND EQUIPMENT¹							
Motortrucks, including pickups .... farms..	63 093	384	944	1 749	6 402	8 602	2 921
number..	159 329	2 843	6 113	8 703	24 698	28 154	8 320
Wheel tractors .... farms..	60 459	376	923	1 711	6 254	8 378	2 834
number..	150 647	1 835	4 429	7 175	21 465	25 628	7 942
Less than 40 horsepower (PTO) .... farms..	25 210	129	323	548	2 010	2 803	1 044
number..	38 591	266	735	1 060	3 174	4 284	1 668
40 horsepower (PTO) or more .... farms..	50 677	359	883	1 677	5 977	8 056	2 642
number..	112 056	1 549	3 694	6 115	18 291	21 344	6 274
Grain and bean combines .... farms..	35 606	191	591	1 342	4 982	6 603	2 105
number..	43 801	309	915	1 827	6 546	8 397	2 544
Cottonpickers and strippers .... farms..	1	-	-	1	-	-	-
number..	(D)	-	-	(D)	-	-	-
Mower conditioners .... farms..	18 793	123	373	732	2 551	3 349	1 021
number..	20 167	164	465	827	2 817	3 586	1 087
Pickup balers .... farms..	26 083	138	411	897	3 262	4 426	1 381
number..	31 892	209	603	1 212	4 357	5 727	1 681
AGRICULTURAL CHEMICALS¹							
Commercial fertilizer .... farms..	47 723	262	760	1 607	5 995	7 843	2 564
acres on which used..	13 852 822	385 378	972 919	1 520 101	3 858 015	3 249 093	796 908
Lime .... farms..	2 685	19	61	131	458	468	102
acres on which used..	154 622	4 528	11 066	17 662	36 814	23 275	6 541
tons..	369 024	11 825	29 108	40 909	92 854	56 112	14 352
Sprays, dusts, granules, fumigants, etc., to control—							
Insects on hay and other crops .... farms..	19 416	176	524	1 062	3 678	4 242	1 344
acres on which used..	3 015 580	149 212	358 816	462 312	941 298	614 272	161 115
Nematodes in crops .... farms..	716	13	24	40	159	150	20
acres on which used..	87 904	5 424	8 849	16 854	26 235	19 313	1 639
Diseases in crops and orchards .... farms..	1 055	14	34	46	177	146	43
acres on which used..	125 065	7 008	13 448	15 150	51 678	18 105	3 798
Weeds, grass, or brush in crops and pasture .... farms..	36 950	212	623	1 263	4 924	6 369	2 054
acres on which used..	8 637 062	209 156	567 404	868 628	2 401 923	2 031 740	468 902
Chemicals for defoliation or for growth control of crops or thinning of fruit .... farms..	614	5	14	25	97	102	29
acres on which used..	68 639	5 308	8 731	4 511	21 445	13 279	1 655

See footnotes at end of table.

Table 52. **Summary by Value of Agricultural Products Sold: 1987**—Con.

[For meaning of abbreviations and symbols, see introductory text]

Item	$25,000 to $39,999	$20,000 to $24,999	$10,000 to $19,999	$5,000 to $9,999	$2,500 to $4,999	Less than $2,500
LAND IN FARMS ACCORDING TO USE—Con.						
Pastureland and rangeland other than cropland and woodland pastured .... farms..	3 566	1 771	4 687	3 930	2 718	3 501
acres..	1 074 689	428 668	806 979	461 538	220 187	428 937
Land in house lots, ponds, roads, wasteland, etc. .... farms..	4 586	2 312	6 705	5 923	4 329	6 281
acres..	130 606	57 361	132 860	93 137	50 949	68 929
Cropland under federal acreage reduction programs:						
Annual commodity acreage adjustment programs .... farms..	4 888	2 165	5 197	3 221	1 512	831
acres..	407 157	140 955	245 543	101 255	31 566	11 009
Conservation reserve program .... farms..	676	297	751	570	274	363
acres..	81 426	39 294	85 052	52 471	18 579	43 030
Value of land and buildings[1] .... farms..	7 219	3 471	11 033	9 828	6 786	9 301
$1,000..	1 840 514	685 559	1 685 049	986 007	535 096	718 977
Average per farm .... dollars..	254 954	197 511	152 728	102 410	78 853	77 301
Average per acre .... dollars..	386	395	454	499	651	738
Farms by value group:						
$1 to $39,999	242	188	1 067	2 073	2 358	3 630
$40,000 to $69,999	333	242	1 752	2 505	1 925	2 370
$70,000 to $99,999	494	373	1 814	1 502	1 004	1 352
$100,000 to $149,999	1 027	775	2 409	1 793	782	863
$150,000 to $199,999	1 211	632	1 650	780	268	466
$200,000 to $499,999	3 289	1 133	1 972	828	375	502
$500,000 to $999,999	579	99	259	140	62	101
$1,000,000 to $1,999,999	35	23	72	6	10	13
$2,000,000 to $4,999,999	9	6	16	1	2	3
$5,000,000 or more	–	–	2	–	–	1
VALUE OF MACHINERY AND EQUIPMENT[1]						
Estimated market value of all machinery and equipment .... farms..	7 218	3 471	11 008	9 608	6 744	9 208
$1,000..	334 437	133 528	327 175	223 215	116 769	78 842
Farms by value group:						
$1 to $4,999	145	162	851	1 311	1 298	1 850
$5,000 to $9,999	353	189	1 484	1 849	1 666	5 652
$10,000 to $19,999	1 195	678	2 941	2 750	1 940	1 032
$20,000 to $49,999	2 884	1 486	3 653	2 493	1 425	560
$50,000 to $99,999	1 913	737	1 814	884	283	105
$100,000 to $199,999	584	192	362	257	118	3
$200,000 to $499,999	144	26	103	64	14	6
$500,000 or more	–	1	–	–	–	–
SELECTED MACHINERY AND EQUIPMENT[1]						
Motortrucks, including pickups .... farms..	6 979	3 304	10 267	8 595	5 832	7 478
number..	18 476	7 733	21 585	15 540	9 688	10 319
Wheel tractors .... farms..	6 648	3 238	9 772	8 117	5 408	7 176
number..	17 361	8 119	21 874	16 542	9 571	10 741
Less than 40 horsepower (PTO) ...... farms..	2 334	1 160	3 913	3 803	2 878	4 404
number..	3 623	1 928	6 073	5 711	4 159	6 176
40 horsepower (PTO) or more .... farms..	6 290	2 955	8 490	6 376	3 667	3 622
number..	13 738	6 191	15 801	10 831	5 412	4 565
Grain and bean combines .... farms..	4 856	2 193	5 700	4 097	2 223	916
number..	5 910	2 646	6 885	4 673	2 486	972
Cottonpickers and strippers .... farms..	–	–	–	–	–	–
number..	–	–	–	–	–	–
Mower conditioners .... farms..	2 384	1 077	2 816	2 140	1 340	1 010
number..	2 526	1 140	2 969	2 279	1 404	1 067
Pickup balers .... farms..	3 409	1 434	4 343	3 150	2 138	1 232
number..	4 201	1 674	5 103	3 585	2 447	1 302
AGRICULTURAL CHEMICALS[1]						
Commercial fertilizer .... farms..	5 884	2 614	7 929	5 863	3 408	3 256
acres on which used..	1 409 660	453 447	929 866	424 817	142 871	95 125
Lime .... farms..	332	155	397	250	196	135
acres on which used..	19 224	6 411	16 063	9 898	4 409	3 259
tons..	41 054	14 876	38 114	24 206	9 702	7 737
Sprays, dusts, granules, fumigants, etc., to control—						
Insects on hay and other crops .... farms..	2 662	1 148	2 332	1 241	661	522
acres on which used..	219 445	67 601	124 836	43 185	14 411	8 289
Nematodes in crops .... farms..	89	21	58	83	41	31
acres on which used..	5 190	1 285	2 598	4 490	1 146	305
Diseases in crops and orchards .... farms..	97	51	130	86	58	187
acres on which used..	10 725	2 798	4 350	2 618	909	1 466
Weeds, grass, or brush in crops and pasture................................. farms..	4 767	2 059	6 246	4 060	2 398	2 187
acres on which used..	868 835	292 918	677 161	285 550	101 665	72 436
Chemicals for defoliation or for growth control of crops or thinning of fruit .... farms..	55	28	93	62	39	70
acres on which used..	7 011	2 543	6 163	2 279	346	876

See footnotes at end of table.

Table 52. **Summary by Value of Agricultural Products Sold: 1987**—Con.

[For meaning of abbreviations and symbols, see introductory text]

Item	All farms	$500,000 or more $1,000,000 or more	$500,000 or more Total	$250,000 to $499,999	$100,000 to $249,999	$50,000 to $99,999	$40,000 to $49,999
TENURE AND RACE OF OPERATOR							
All operators	68 579	389	957	1 766	6 656	8 997	3 132
Full owners	29 956	151	258	277	898	1 510	732
Part owners	27 967	190	572	1 284	4 843	6 038	1 840
Tenants	10 656	48	127	205	915	1 449	560
White	68 304	389	957	1 765	6 649	8 985	3 126
Full owners	29 784	151	258	277	897	1 506	732
Part owners	27 901	190	572	1 283	4 839	6 033	1 836
Tenants	10 619	48	127	205	913	1 446	558
Black and other races	275	-	-	1	7	12	6
Full owners	172	-	-	-	1	4	-
Part owners	66	-	-	1	4	5	4
Tenants	37	-	-	-	2	3	2
OWNED AND RENTED LAND							
Land owned ___ farms	58 533	343	836	1 575	5 791	7 597	2 596
acres	24 331 897	779 007	1 639 184	1 992 156	4 845 202	4 628 951	1 313 681
Owned land in farms ___ farms	57 923	341	830	1 561	5 741	7 548	2 572
acres	21 178 322	719 592	1 538 683	1 921 718	4 518 532	4 227 381	1 166 200
Land rented or leased from others ___ farms	36 908	241	705	1 493	5 791	7 504	2 411
acres	25 865 815	846 277	2 012 613	2 644 348	7 247 398	6 174 002	1 539 653
Rented or leased land in farms ___ farms	38 623	238	699	1 489	5 758	7 487	2 400
acres	25 450 197	841 084	1 965 641	2 619 505	7 165 448	6 098 995	1 512 282
Land rented or leased to others ___ farms	11 944	62	125	189	819	1 166	440
acres	3 569 193	64 608	147 473	95 283	408 620	476 577	173 852
OPERATOR CHARACTERISTICS							
Operators by place of residence:							
On farm operated	45 527	200	605	1 343	5 155	6 867	2 260
Not on farm operated	17 871	153	267	271	1 037	1 628	642
Not reported	5 181	36	85	152	464	502	210
Operators by principal occupation:							
Farming	42 607	327	854	1 665	6 238	8 054	2 651
Other	25 972	62	103	101	418	943	481
Operators by days of work off farm:							
None	29 462	297	727	1 291	4 474	5 317	1 654
Any	34 654	67	163	331	1 673	3 051	1 239
1 to 99 days	7 620	17	56	166	940	1 486	483
100 to 199 days	5 357	9	29	57	232	569	271
200 days or more	21 677	41	78	108	501	996	485
Not reported	4 463	25	67	144	509	629	239
Operators by years on present farm:							
2 years or less	3 511	10	18	48	168	254	106
3 or 4 years	3 873	19	26	38	162	343	127
5 to 9 years	8 552	24	70	110	556	971	346
10 years or more	40 624	262	669	1 251	4 705	6 209	2 051
Average years on present farm	21.3	22.2	23.9	24.6	23.5	23.7	23.7
Not reported	12 019	74	174	319	1 065	1 220	502
Operators by age group:							
Under 25 years	1 712	-	3	13	90	168	85
25 to 34 years	9 531	34	88	207	991	1 448	510
35 to 44 years	12 471	93	228	417	1 550	1 786	530
45 to 49 years	5 926	43	113	194	678	811	243
50 to 54 years	6 781	49	128	244	620	915	300
55 to 59 years	7 581	62	142	254	917	1 184	411
60 to 64 years	8 407	48	114	227	843	1 276	420
65 to 69 years	6 564	22	64	124	393	720	279
70 years and over	9 606	38	79	86	374	689	354
Average age	52.0	51.6	51.2	49.8	49.1	50.0	51.0
Operators by sex:							
Male	65 619	381	937	1 745	6 560	8 827	3 057
Female	2 960	8	20	21	96	170	75
Operators of Spanish origin (see text)	108	1	1	2	10	7	6
FARMS BY TYPE OF ORGANIZATION							
Individual or family (sole proprietorship) ___ farms	60 202	132	418	1 068	5 164	7 766	2 781
acres	36 420 471	562 516	1 528 660	2 604 319	6 739 363	8 601 940	2 398 834
Partnership ___ farms	5 689	66	195	372	937	851	246
acres	6 151 580	511 203	993 345	1 038 386	1 803 552	1 017 905	185 468
Corporation:							
Family held ___ farms	1 942	151	294	298	500	331	87
acres	3 446 745	443 151	898 552	819 600	1 014 066	437 722	77 723
More than 10 stockholders ___ farms	23	7	8	3	6	2	-
10 or less stockholders ___ farms	1 919	144	286	295	494	329	87
Other than family held ___ farms	158	31	42	15	29	12	7
acres	159 376	14 345	31 958	27 644	59 051	16 550	3 998
More than 10 stockholders ___ farms	17	4	5	1	1	-	-
10 or less stockholders ___ farms	141	27	37	15	28	12	7
Other—cooperative, estate or trust, institutional, etc. ___ farms	388	7	10	13	26	37	11
acres	450 347	29 461	51 809	51 272	67 948	52 259	12 459

See footnotes at end of table.

Table 52. **Summary by Value of Agricultural Products Sold: 1987** —Con.

[For meaning of abbreviations and symbols, see introductory text]

Item	$25,000 to $39,999	$20,000 to $24,999	$10,000 to $19,999	$5,000 to $9,999	$2,500 to $4,999	Less than $2,500
TENURE AND RACE OF OPERATOR						
All operators	7 150	3 566	10 504	9 430	6 919	9 502
Full owners	1 987	1 294	4 906	5 741	4 874	7 479
Part owners	3 825	1 679	3 712	2 134	1 072	968
Tenants	1 338	593	1 886	1 555	973	1 055
White	7 137	3 555	10 460	9 370	6 876	9 424
Full owners	1 983	1 289	4 885	5 701	4 844	7 412
Part owners	3 820	1 675	3 696	2 120	1 065	962
Tenants	1 334	591	1 879	1 549	967	1 050
Black and other races	13	11	44	60	43	78
Full owners	4	5	21	40	30	67
Part owners	5	4	16	14	7	6
Tenants	4	2	7	6	6	5
OWNED AND RENTED LAND						
Land owned .... farms..	5 897	3 003	8 745	7 993	6 007	8 493
acres..	2 576 872	1 163 716	2 562 065	1 710 567	858 519	1 018 984
Owned land in farms .... farms..	5 812	2 973	8 618	7 875	5 946	8 447
acres..	2 204 277	951 111	2 082 840	1 262 938	605 527	699 117
Land rented or leased from others .... farms..	5 188	2 292	6 664	3 738	2 072	2 053
acres..	2 512 564	884 916	1 565 437	691 601	271 599	323 284
Rented or leased land in farms .... farms..	5 163	2 272	6 598	3 689	2 045	2 023
acres..	2 475 702	864 831	1 515 926	671 840	256 840	303 187
Land rented or leased to others .... farms..	1 147	640	2 049	2 032	1 476	1 861
acres..	411 457	232 090	548 736	467 390	267 751	339 964
OPERATOR CHARACTERISTICS						
Operators by place of residence:						
On farm operated	4 963	2 378	6 480	5 529	4 000	5 927
Not on farm operated	1 741	961	3 261	3 128	2 288	2 647
Not reported	446	227	763	773	631	928
Operators by principal occupation:						
Farming	5 504	2 504	6 308	4 194	2 459	2 176
Other	1 646	1 062	4 196	5 236	4 460	7 326
Operators by days of work off farm:						
None	3 308	1 579	4 023	3 071	1 927	2 091
Any	3 338	1 732	5 741	5 797	4 598	6 991
1 to 99 days	1 066	454	1 148	753	478	590
100 to 199 days	704	354	1 013	860	599	669
200 days or more	1 568	924	3 580	4 184	3 521	5 732
Not reported	504	255	740	562	394	420
Operators by years on present farm:						
2 years or less	321	144	541	584	536	791
3 or 4 years	353	161	590	658	599	816
5 to 9 years	836	452	1 300	1 321	1 012	1 668
10 years or more	4 567	2 226	6 272	5 093	3 307	4 274
Average years on present farm	23.5	23.7	22.7	20.2	17.6	14.9
Not reported	1 073	573	1 801	1 774	1 465	2 053
Operators by age group:						
Under 25 years	217	89	280	303	208	256
25 to 34 years	1 030	488	1 399	1 213	896	1 261
35 to 44 years	1 181	500	1 582	1 451	1 181	2 085
45 to 49 years	526	269	744	737	613	998
50 to 54 years	617	308	919	858	698	976
55 to 59 years	803	393	987	898	677	915
60 to 64 years	1 048	447	1 292	1 086	701	953
65 to 69 years	766	450	1 298	1 046	670	764
70 years and over	982	622	2 013	1 838	1 275	1 294
Average age	52.2	53.8	54.0	53.8	53.1	51.0
Operators by sex:						
Male	6 932	3 425	10 094	8 846	6 433	8 763
Female	218	141	410	584	486	739
Operators of Spanish origin (see text)	7	8	13	16	14	24
FARMS BY TYPE OF ORGANIZATION						
Individual or family (sole proprietorship) .... farms..	6 365	3 230	9 537	8 642	6 364	8 869
acres..	4 138 451	1 643 184	3 255 540	1 750 158	787 617	772 405
Partnership .... farms..	626	268	814	651	458	471
acres..	416 423	136 992	289 139	139 888	65 456	65 026
Corporation:						
Family held .... farms..	111	42	95	72	38	74
acres..	92 248	23 613	33 732	31 590	3 011	14 888
More than 10 stockholders .... farms..	1	–	2	1	–	–
10 or less stockholders .... farms..	110	42	93	71	38	74
Other than family held .... farms..	2	5	10	17	3	16
acres..	(D)	(D)	3 212	2 669	170	3 964
More than 10 stockholders .... farms..	–	–	2	3	–	6
10 or less stockholders .... farms..	2	5	8	14	3	10
Other—cooperative, estate or trust, institutional, etc. .... farms..	46	21	48	48	56	72
acres..	(D)	(D)	17 143	10 453	6 113	146 001

See footnotes at end of table.

Table 52. Summary by Value of Agricultural Products Sold: 1987—Con.

[For meaning of abbreviations and symbols, see introductory text]

Item	All farms	$500,000 or more — $1,000,000 or more	$500,000 or more — Total	$250,000 to $499,999	$100,000 to $249,999	$50,000 to $99,999	$40,000 to $49,999
FARMS BY SIZE							
1 to 9 acres	3 689	16	29	39	103	132	75
10 to 49 acres	6 222	10	23	17	47	56	25
50 to 69 acres	1 849	8	5	4	8	16	6
70 to 99 acres	4 690	10	12	5	17	46	22
100 to 139 acres	3 117	6	5	5	18	36	21
140 to 179 acres	5 854	13	16	5	47	134	69
180 to 219 acres	2 307	6	9	5	25	69	33
220 to 259 acres	2 845	4	7	6	50	102	48
260 to 499 acres	11 553	29	47	62	365	974	579
500 to 999 acres	12 093	36	75	171	1 282	2 911	1 266
1,000 to 1,999 acres	9 304	58	157	535	2 567	3 452	841
2,000 acres or more	5 056	197	572	912	2 129	1 059	126
FARMS BY STANDARD INDUSTRIAL CLASSIFICATION							
Cash grains (011)	31 789	14	79	492	3 145	5 112	1 854
Field crops, except cash grains (013)	2 010	4	12	16	62	86	32
Cotton (0131)	1	-	-	-	1	-	-
Tobacco (0132)	3	-	-	-	-	-	-
Sugarcane and sugar beets; Irish potatoes; field crops, except cash grains, n.e.c. (0133, 0134, 0139)	2 006	4	12	16	61	86	32
Vegetables and melons (016)	179	-	1	3	1	5	4
Fruits and tree nuts (017)	171	-	1	1	1	3	1
Horticultural specialties (018)	224	6	14	8	23	18	7
General farms, primarily crop (019)	1 463	4	13	26	117	159	52
Livestock, except dairy, poultry, and animal specialties (021)	29 037	351	805	1 072	2 682	3 130	1 075
Beef cattle, except feedlots (0212)	21 861	115	359	630	1 632	1 970	738
Dairy farms (024)	1 391	4	15	99	516	381	76
Poultry and eggs (025)	197	6	14	20	22	14	2
Animal specialties (027)	1 452	-	2	2	5	13	6
General farms, primarily livestock and animal specialties (029)	666	-	2	25	82	76	21
LIVESTOCK							
Cattle and calves inventory .... farms	40 785	344	617	1 388	4 769	6 184	2 056
number	5 539 292	1 812 875	2 154 661	564 606	959 898	709 995	172 942
Farms with—							
1 to 9	4 367	-	3	8	68	145	44
10 to 49	16 841	1	12	46	407	1 142	583
50 to 99	8 529	2	12	52	705	1 865	766
100 to 199	6 150	7	27	210	1 690	2 151	557
200 to 499	3 580	22	142	639	1 661	856	103
500 or more	1 318	312	621	423	238	25	3
Cows and heifers that had calved .... farms	33 157	87	287	776	3 551	5 145	1 752
number	1 451 324	45 135	92 757	130 362	344 852	315 323	83 023
Beef cows .... farms	31 478	80	264	667	3 057	4 755	1 870
number	1 354 649	42 654	87 222	113 447	302 169	296 103	79 818
Farms with—							
1 to 9	6 299	-	9	24	126	275	102
10 to 49	17 123	14	43	124	871	1 970	916
50 to 99	5 108	8	35	158	927	1 631	503
100 to 199	2 115	16	56	154	771	778	135
200 to 499	714	20	77	161	351	99	13
500 or more	116	23	44	46	21	2	1
Milk cows .... farms	3 093	9	28	162	719	643	178
number	96 675	2 261	5 535	16 915	42 683	19 220	3 205
Farms with—							
1 to 4	1 195	3	6	17	79	136	60
5 to 9	150	-	-	1	4	17	5
10 to 49	979	-	1	9	144	380	106
50 to 99	582	1	2	39	424	105	7
100 to 199	163	-	6	88	65	3	-
200 to 499	21	2	10	8	3	-	-
500 or more	3	3	3	-	-	-	-
Heifers and heifer calves .... farms	31 410	260	561	983	3 717	4 950	1 653
number	1 632 193	609 262	714 718	172 792	279 490	183 063	43 081
Steers, steer calves, bulls, and bull calves .... farms	35 035	311	724	1 202	4 111	5 519	1 829
number	2 455 775	1 159 478	1 347 386	261 452	335 656	211 609	46 838
Cattle and calves sold .... farms	41 498	354	653	1 456	4 987	6 436	2 151
number	7 310 336	4 565 793	4 993 601	542 337	711 938	440 449	101 236
$1,000	4 305 335	3 010 392	3 250 680	283 829	335 567	191 838	42 620
Calves .... farms	18 518	25	81	270	1 482	2 344	896
number	488 328	12 008	25 211	26 850	96 995	94 759	26 042
$1,000	146 961	2 845	7 528	9 403	30 035	30 371	9 934
Cattle .... farms	34 216	351	835	1 403	4 576	5 715	1 832
number	6 842 010	4 553 785	4 968 390	513 487	616 543	345 690	73 194
$1,000	4 159 374	3 007 547	3 243 352	274 425	305 532	161 467	33 227
Fattened on grain and concentrates ... farms	4 620	229	428	396	803	795	218
number	4 551 726	4 147 435	4 284 617	112 354	67 905	37 965	6 544
$1,000	3 041 522	2 790 479	2 878 966	73 134	53 031	21 180	3 691

See footnotes at end of table.

Table 52. Summary by Value of Agricultural Products Sold: 1987—Con.

[For meaning of abbreviations and symbols, see introductory text]

Item	$25,000 to $39,999	$20,000 to $24,999	$10,000 to $19,999	$5,000 to $9,999	$2,500 to $4,999	Less than $2,500
FARMS BY SIZE						
1 to 9 acres	180	112	434	553	638	1 394
10 to 49 acres	87	54	269	713	1 270	3 661
50 to 69 acres	24	15	142	344	551	736
70 to 99 acres	59	61	485	1 157	1 448	1 398
100 to 139 acres	109	90	569	952	721	591
140 to 179 acres	233	194	1 346	1 970	1 103	737
180 to 219 acres	165	120	742	635	293	211
220 to 259 acres	255	208	927	802	252	188
260 to 499 acres	2 001	1 291	3 630	1 740	489	375
500 to 999 acres	2 830	1 120	1 675	471	127	143
1,000 to 1,999 acres	1 063	263	264	79	23	50
2,000 acres or more	144	38	41	14	4	18
FARMS BY STANDARD INDUSTRIAL CLASSIFICATION						
Cash grains (011)	4 080	2 028	5 435	4 369	2 750	2 445
Field crops, except cash grains (013)	110	45	206	302	313	826
Cotton (0131)	-	-	-	-	-	-
Tobacco (0132)	-	-	-	-	2	1
Sugarcane and sugar beets; Irish potatoes; field crops, except cash grains, n.e.c. (0133, 0134, 0139)	110	45	206	302	311	825
Vegetables and melons (016)	15	4	26	47	36	37
Fruits and tree nuts (017)	1	4	13	18	21	108
Horticultural specialties (018)	18	13	44	28	25	26
General farms, primarily crop (019)	141	48	160	81	29	635
Livestock, except dairy, poultry, and animal specialties (021)	2 610	1 347	4 458	4 446	3 555	3 847
Beef cattle, except feedlots (0212)	1 886	1 075	3 714	3 842	3 001	3 014
Dairy farms (024)	126	51	82	24	8	11
Poultry and eggs (025)	5	1	5	8	18	66
Animal specialties (027)	11	12	53	91	141	1 116
General farms, primarily livestock and animal specialties (029)	33	18	22	16	13	363
LIVESTOCK						
Cattle and calves inventory ...... farms..	4 511	2 237	6 149	5 254	3 586	3 834
number..	313 372	123 567	267 284	157 569	69 388	45 810
Farms with—						
1 to 9	154	95	435	563	744	2 108
10 to 49	1 663	1 080	3 636	3 922	2 704	1 646
50 to 99	1 741	785	1 726	662	120	65
100 to 199	820	256	329	81	18	11
200 to 499	130	21	20	4	-	4
500 or more	3	-	3	2	-	-
Cows and heifers that had calved .... farms..	3 894	1 935	5 310	4 493	3 026	2 966
number..	153 387	61 753	133 334	79 798	35 196	21 536
Beef cows	3 753	1 862	5 174	4 407	2 960	2 656
number..	149 182	60 535	131 154	78 024	34 894	21 101
Farms with—						
1 to 9	289	215	737	1 002	1 331	2 189
10 to 49	2 341	1 303	3 986	3 296	1 622	649
50 to 99	959	331	429	95	26	14
100 to 199	156	90	21	10	1	3
200 to 499	7	3	1	1	-	1
500 or more	1	-	-	1	-	-
Milk cows............................ farms..	317	136	391	213	134	232
number..	4 205	1 218	2 180	775	302	437
Farms with—						
1 to 4	125	68	206	159	119	216
5 to 9	16	9	33	40	12	13
10 to 49	173	59	88	13	3	3
50 to 99	2	-	2	1	-	-
100 to 199	1	-	-	-	-	-
200 to 499	-	-	-	-	-	-
500 or more	-	-	-	-	-	-
Heifers and heifer calves .... farms..	3 589	1 758	4 821	3 980	2 677	2 721
number..	76 685	26 770	65 782	38 462	17 277	12 073
Steers, steer calves, bulls, and bull calves .... farms..	3 996	1 964	5 336	4 499	2 946	2 909
number..	83 300	33 044	68 168	39 308	16 915	12 199
Cattle and calves sold .... farms..	4 708	2 302	6 374	5 376	3 672	3 183
number..	177 302	89 363	149 115	79 744	32 429	12 823
$1,000..	72 356	27 531	55 446	28 811	11 314	4 144
Calves .... farms..	2 105	1 104	3 292	3 050	2 171	1 729
number..	54 298	23 053	59 371	36 115	16 399	6 835
$1,000..	17 430	7 229	17 706	10 591	4 596	1 676
Cattle .... farms..	3 950	1 908	5 094	4 074	2 707	2 112
number..	123 004	66 310	89 745	43 629	16 030	5 988
$1,000..	54 926	20 302	38 741	18 220	6 718	2 468
Fattened on grain and concentrates .... farms..	407	198	465	338	265	307
number..	9 487	3 419	6 155	2 511	1 122	657
$1,000..	5 088	1 753	2 567	1 206	572	334

See footnotes at end of table.

Table 52. **Summary by Value of Agricultural Products Sold: 1987**—Con.

[For meaning of abbreviations and symbols, see introductory text]

Item	All farms	$500,000 or more		$250,000 to $499,999	$100,000 to $249,999	$50,000 to $99,999	$40,000 to $49,999
		$1,000,000 or more	Total				
LIVESTOCK—Con.							
Hogs and pigs inventory ____ farms..	6 768	42	132	350	1 178	1 411	411
number..	1 516 878	249 159	409 860	263 942	383 169	234 565	49 964
Farms with—							
1 to 24	1 916	2	4	20	106	173	70
25 to 49	828	1	2	7	56	132	52
50 to 99	1 087	1	2	23	128	246	90
100 to 199	1 092	2	6	28	182	372	106
200 to 499	1 226	4	13	83	442	437	89
500 or more	619	32	105	189	264	51	4
Used or to be used for breeding ____ farms..	4 596	27	96	235	833	991	311
number..	191 079	26 298	44 164	30 600	46 171	31 716	7 812
Other ____ farms..	6 286	42	132	340	1 146	1 361	366
number..	1 325 799	222 861	365 696	233 342	336 998	202 849	42 152
Hogs and pigs sold ____ farms..	7 090	41	137	364	1 230	1 482	432
number..	2 759 676	419 750	730 792	508 541	705 934	433 727	89 632
$1,000..	264 375	50 688	84 986	51 848	73 933	41 456	7 684
Feeder pigs ____ farms..	1 869	5	18	53	231	359	112
number..	514 394	24 725	53 413	86 025	102 797	119 509	32 364
$1,000..	23 029	1 370	2 774	3 721	4 744	5 559	1 345
Litters of pigs farrowed between—							
Dec. 1 of preceding year and Nov. 30 ___ farms..	4 819	27	98	237	861	1 030	322
number..	295 974	45 547	77 253	49 956	72 630	48 109	11 195
Dec. 1 and May 31 ____ farms..	4 455	27	97	231	827	991	290
number..	149 414	22 202	36 993	25 403	36 479	24 491	5 710
June 1 and Nov. 30 ____ farms..	4 403	26	96	233	827	967	302
number..	146 560	23 345	38 260	24 555	36 151	23 618	5 485
Sheep and lambs of all ages inventory ____ farms..	2 400	5	15	45	183	297	101
number..	249 303	27 457	31 942	28 368	47 443	42 485	12 682
Ewes 1 year old or older ____ farms..	2 195	4	12	39	166	274	94
number..	129 607	(D)	2 997	8 692	26 705	25 000	7 284
Sheep and lambs sold ____ farms..	2 396	4	15	45	195	308	100
number..	267 152	85 305	89 305	26 888	42 431	32 505	9 052
Sheep and lambs shorn ____ farms..	2 183	5	14	41	175	280	91
number..	218 980	40 344	43 456	25 579	40 851	33 267	7 462
pounds of wool..	1 510 663	225 908	250 745	106 642	203 561	298 066	56 283
Horses and ponies inventory ____ farms..	12 879	139	317	452	1 309	1 570	463
number..	55 596	1 349	2 259	1 881	5 362	5 933	1 750
Horses and ponies sold ____ farms..	2 260	22	46	53	164	195	87
number..	8 467	100	231	178	892	1 312	277
Goats inventory ____ farms..	862	1	3	8	46	57	33
number..	8 831	(D)	152	28	355	892	848
Goats sold ____ farms..	256	-	-	1	11	9	7
number..	2 679	-	-	(D)	(D)	369	51
POULTRY							
Chickens 3 months old or older inventory ___ farms..	4 206	14	25	63	274	401	179
number..	2 094 610	529 537	1 075 740	468 019	320 969	104 779	9 760
Farms with—							
1 to 399	4 117	8	11	45	251	388	177
400 to 3,199	30	1	1	1	3	5	2
3,200 to 9,999	12	-	1	1	5	5	-
10,000 to 19,999	18	-	-	4	12	2	-
20,000 to 49,999	19	-	3	12	3	1	-
50,000 to 99,999	7	2	3	-	-	-	-
100,000 or more	3	3	3	-	-	-	-
Hens and pullets of laying age ____ farms..	4 150	13	24	62	271	396	179
number..	1 797 313	526 237	974 440	420 933	221 776	65 501	9 542
Pullets 3 months old or older not of laying age ____ farms..	415	3	3	4	22	31	9
number..	297 297	101 300	101 300	47 086	99 193	39 278	238
Hens and pullets sold ____ farms..	363	7	15	21	43	46	6
number..	2 380 936	783 283	1 175 495	415 841	629 490	143 801	153
Broilers and other meat-type chickens sold ____ farms..	132	-	-	-	16	17	6
number..	176 061	-	-	-	14 745	123 010	370
Farms with—							
1 to 1,999	123	-	-	-	14	15	5
2,000 to 59,999	7	-	-	-	2	-	-
60,000 to 99,999	2	-	-	-	-	2	-
100,000 or more	-	-	-	-	-	-	-
Turkey hens kept for breeding ____ farms..	194	-	-	3	13	12	9
number..	(D)	-	-	16 204	12 415	46	27
Turkeys sold ____ farms..	66	-	-	7	11	9	7
number..	230 719	-	-	155 826	55 755	11 996	69

See footnotes at end of table.

Table 52. **Summary by Value of Agricultural Products Sold: 1987**—Con.

[For meaning of abbreviations and symbols, see introductory text]

Item	$25,000 to $39,999	$20,000 to $24,999	$10,000 to $19,999	$5,000 to $9,999	$2,500 to $4,999	Less than $2,500
LIVESTOCK—Con.						
Hogs and pigs inventory ___ farms__	854	318	826	526	385	377
number__	81 513	20 914	42 377	18 300	7 899	4 375
Farms with—						
1 to 24	199	105	329	305	280	325
25 to 49	120	59	171	115	68	46
50 to 99	210	65	191	81	27	4
100 to 199	212	46	113	14	9	2
200 to 499	111	20	22	8	1	-
500 or more	2	1	-	3	-	-
Used or to be used for breeding ____ farms__	602	211	568	332	231	186
number__	12 944	3 745	7 461	3 575	1 751	1 120
Other ____ farms__	795	287	740	445	328	326
number__	68 569	17 169	34 896	14 725	6 148	3 255
Hogs and pigs sold ____ farms__	917	334	895	560	388	351
number__	141 052	33 499	70 415	28 552	11 908	5 324
$1,000__	12 392	2 855	5 908	2 116	873	323
Feeder pigs ____ farms__	244	96	279	226	132	117
number__	51 647	12 795	28 951	14 940	6 584	3 369
$1,000__	2 283	511	1 178	563	246	102
Litters of pigs farrowed between—						
Dec. 1 of preceding year and Nov. 30 ___ farms__	638	221	602	361	245	204
number__	17 171	3 886	9 106	3 771	1 871	1 024
Dec. 1 and May 31 ____ farms__	599	197	541	307	204	171
number__	8 638	1 923	4 526	1 814	913	524
June 1 and Nov. 30 ____ farms__	587	194	525	310	206	156
number__	8 533	1 963	4 580	1 957	958	500
Sheep and lambs of all ages inventory ____ farms__	237	146	363	330	269	414
number__	21 425	11 511	22 138	12 657	9 872	8 782
Ewes 1 year old or older ____ farms__	212	134	343	305	245	369
number__	14 273	7 635	15 136	8 815	6 951	5 919
Sheep and lambs sold ____ farms__	236	139	367	313	275	403
number__	17 590	9 322	16 644	10 488	6 752	6 075
Sheep and lambs shorn ____ farms__	218	127	340	293	246	358
number__	16 900	8 650	17 356	10 659	7 826	6 952
pounds of wool__	122 053	59 797	123 290	77 560	54 623	49 043
Horses and ponies inventory____ farms__	1 063	543	1 604	1 416	1 301	2 821
number__	4 236	2 156	6 128	5 971	5 123	14 799
Horses and ponies sold ____ farms__	154	83	240	320	286	632
number__	772	374	948	1 122	939	1 422
Goats inventory ____ farms__	62	41	96	148	133	235
number__	1 438	491	1 015	1 220	791	1 601
Goats sold____ farms__	15	11	34	48	48	74
number__	257	156	367	432	374	495
POULTRY						
Chickens 3 months old or older Inventory __ farms__	414	238	642	595	501	874
number__	21 883	10 521	26 410	20 111	16 480	19 918
Farms with—						
1 to 399	408	234	636	593	499	874
400 to 3,199	5	4	6	2	2	-
3,200 to 9,999	-	-	-	-	-	-
10,000 to 19,999	-	-	-	-	-	-
20,000 to 49,999	-	-	-	-	-	-
50,000 to 99,999	-	-	-	-	-	-
100,000 or more	-	-	-	-	-	-
Hens and pullets of laying age ____ farms__	413	238	633	587	498	851
number__	19 079	9 193	24 700	18 790	15 429	17 930
Pullets 3 months old or older not of laying age ____ farms__	31	23	70	50	52	120
number__	2 804	1 328	1 710	1 321	1 051	1 988
Hens and pullets sold ____ farms__	29	15	39	47	35	65
number__	3 775	1 371	2 882	4 248	2 188	1 692
Broilers and other meat-type chickens sold ____ farms__	12	11	11	17	9	34
number__	13 161	14 363	1 050	4 747	1 152	3 463
Farms with—						
1 to 1,999	10	9	11	16	9	34
2,000 to 59,999	2	2	-	1	-	-
60,000 to 99,999	-	-	-	-	-	-
100,000 or more	-	-	-	-	-	-
Turkey hens kept for breeding ____ farms__	12	12	28	24	30	51
number__	43	(D)	(D)	(D)	144	(D)
Turkeys sold ____ farms__	8	10	7	14	8	10
number__	2 139	186	3 889	447	254	158

See footnotes at end of table.

Table 52. **Summary by Value of Agricultural Products Sold: 1987**—Con.

[For meaning of abbreviations and symbols, see introductory text]

Item	All farms	$500,000 or more $1,000,000 or more	Total	$250,000 to $499,999	$100,000 to $249,999	$50,000 to $99,999	$40,000 to $49,999
CROPS HARVESTED							
Corn for grain or seed .... farms...	8 944	111	345	742	2 199	2 023	515
acres...	1 243 969	73 968	185 556	249 347	439 570	218 196	37 792
bushels...	144 133 581	9 384 549	23 741 290	31 425 972	52 283 118	23 470 784	3 672 357
Irrigated .... farms...	3 547	88	261	466	1 298	946	167
acres...	816 992	63 442	155 659	181 408	304 090	125 632	17 404
Farms by acres harvested:							
1 to 24 acres	1 984	2	11	27	126	211	81
25 to 99 acres	3 279	10	29	135	548	890	296
100 to 249 acres	2 198	24	82	186	615	781	131
250 to 499 acres	1 044	31	99	202	589	135	7
500 acres or more	441	44	124	190	121	6	-
Corn for silage or green chop .... farms...	2 009	77	196	303	646	418	88
acres...	109 230	15 013	25 836	23 279	34 432	13 850	2 983
tons, green...	1 669 413	251 504	432 010	363 990	526 983	189 050	36 446
Irrigated .... farms...	659	49	108	141	217	103	41
acres...	53 214	9 361	15 416	13 003	16 197	4 957	922
Farms by acres harvested:							
1 to 24 acres	799	3	19	54	207	227	53
25 to 99 acres	944	27	94	181	369	165	31
100 to 249 acres	207	29	57	54	53	25	-
250 to 499 acres	43	11	17	11	14	1	-
500 acres or more	16	7	9	3	3	-	1
Sorghum for grain or seed .... farms...	32 492	147	497	1 189	4 883	6 706	2 202
acres...	3 399 584	61 877	162 148	338 902	986 619	882 524	210 846
bushels...	228 045 100	4 033 124	12 566 551	26 260 526	70 859 197	56 324 990	13 241 792
Irrigated .... farms...	3 137	45	151	300	980	833	164
acres...	464 119	10 375	34 316	76 161	191 343	101 768	17 196
Farms by acres harvested:							
1 to 24 acres	7 260	4	19	28	240	523	*
25 to 99 acres	14 139	19	78	229	1 260	2 576	1 146
100 to 249 acres	7 830	50	159	386	1 973	2 806	736
250 to 499 acres	2 503	38	131	364	1 098	698	79
500 acres or more	740	36	110	182	312	105	14
Wheat for grain .... farms...	38 638	227	663	1 438	5 458	7 143	2 376
acres...	9 679 568	165 076	449 448	776 853	2 354 618	2 115 866	556 253
bushels...	292 999 442	6 431 870	16 687 056	28 511 365	85 392 251	71 432 801	18 358 021
Irrigated .... farms...	3 046	69	197	363	1 038	715	150
acres...	635 524	33 462	83 537	137 871	244 009	104 780	17 713
Farms by acres harvested:							
1 to 24 acres	4 230	3	7	32	154	310	151
25 to 99 acres	11 451	21	66	144	660	1 190	440
100 to 249 acres	11 111	37	113	280	1 196	1 994	817
250 to 499 acres	7 248	52	150	340	1 506	2 413	757
500 acres or more	4 598	114	327	642	1 942	1 236	211
Barley for grain .... farms...	2 307	25	68	143	537	584	172
acres...	95 485	3 002	6 182	11 208	30 567	24 041	2 034
bushels...	3 639 224	130 234	286 487	419 216	1 219 538	899 480	174 044
Irrigated .... farms...	166	7	18	20	62	39	5
acres...	7 359	1 081	1 554	986	2 926	1 024	150
Oats for grain .... farms...	5 313	11	48	160	796	1 156	358
acres...	126 091	617	2 886	8 368	26 889	31 187	8 496
bushels...	4 775 729	29 630	138 819	337 945	1 139 535	1 202 883	320 028
Irrigated .... farms...	48	1	2	6	18	11	2
acres...	2 278	(D)	(D)	241	1 241	413	(D)
Soybeans for beans .... farms...	15 864	72	289	699	2 702	3 689	1 161
acres...	1 876 978	25 472	84 624	193 969	508 853	474 767	115 183
bushels...	55 789 994	960 888	3 153 563	6 643 701	16 259 373	13 772 147	3 166 179
Irrigated .... farms...	1 939	34	112	229	660	544	102
acres...	175 063	5 528	19 818	35 620	70 272	34 476	4 222
Farms by acres harvested:							
1 to 24 acres	5 008	3	17	51	266	536	214
25 to 99 acres	8 253	21	77	173	931	1 467	511
100 to 249 acres	3 775	19	100	225	792	1 114	350
250 to 499 acres	1 315	17	57	134	471	476	77
500 acres or more	513	12	43	116	242	96	9
Dry edible beans, excluding dry limas ...... farms...	192	3	11	21	83	47	4
acres...	30 460	2 836	4 916	7 905	12 736	5 705	375
cwt...	441 318	47 445	87 608	84 424	166 868	65 271	4 582
Irrigated .... farms...	167	3	11	21	75	40	2
acres...	28 182	2 835	4 916	5 559	11 701	5 048	(D)
Irish potatoes .... farms...	97	3	4	5	7	8	1
acres...	843	(D)	521	15	15	21	(D)
cwt...	136 764	(D)	119 790	2 132	752	4 083	(D)
Irrigated .... farms...	21	3	4	3	1	-	(D)
acres...	(D)	(D)	521	10	(D)	-	(D)
Hay—alfalfa, other tame, small grain, wild, grass silage, green chop, etc. (see text) .. farms...	33 964	184	545	1 107	4 159	6 603	1 805
tons, dry...	2 254 082	80 470	169 772	183 125	475 533	468 776	125 408
acres...	5 080 847	330 050	621 925	526 643	1 186 390	1 045 616	255 972
Irrigated .... farms...	1 492	51	150	209	451	330	64
acres...	206 961	45 073	77 985	37 719	48 489	27 358	4 009
Farms by acres harvested:							
1 to 24 acres	11 391	14	29	77	450	961	397
25 to 99 acres	16 111	38	153	423	1 929	3 002	1 024
100 to 249 acres	5 297	69	203	390	1 364	1 395	336
250 to 499 acres	913	29	86	156	326	210	42
500 acres or more	252	34	74	61	64	35	6

See footnotes at end of table.

1987 CENSUS OF AGRICULTURE—STATE DATA

Table 52. **Summary by Value of Agricultural Products Sold: 1987**—Con.

[For meaning of abbreviations and symbols, see introductory text]

Item	$25,000 to $39,999	$20,000 to $24,999	$10,000 to $19,999	$5,000 to $9,999	$2,500 to $4,999	Less than $2,500
CROPS HARVESTED						
Corn for grain or seed ... farms	960	390	854	510	208	198
acres	54 096	15 927	27 942	10 301	3 176	2 066
bushels	4 949 929	1 385 722	2 176 180	715 947	202 892	109 390
Irrigated ... farms	245	84	127	40	8	5
acres	19 923	4 868	6 629	1 093	210	56
Farms by acres harvested:						
1 to 24 acres	239	158	419	355	174	163
25 to 99 acres	575	199	408	151	33	15
100 to 249 acres	136	33	25	4	1	-
250 to 499 acres	10	-	2	-	-	-
500 acres or more	-	-	-	-	-	-
Corn for silage or green chop ... farms	155	52	88	45	11	7
acres	4 442	1 208	1 958	971	215	56
tons, green	63 497	13 915	29 662	9 149	1 620	1 091
Irrigated ... farms	36	8	10	12	-	1
acres	1 532	416	298	(D)	-	(D)
Farms by acres harvested:						
1 to 24 acres	93	38	61	31	9	7
25 to 99 acres	53	12	25	13	1	-
100 to 249 acres	9	2	2	1	1	-
250 to 499 acres	-	-	-	-	-	-
500 acres or more	-	-	-	-	-	-
Sorghum for grain or seed ... farms	4 566	2 070	4 989	3 004	1 457	929
acres	340 236	122 714	220 505	89 587	32 092	15 591
bushels	20 554 944	6 886 791	12 403 046	4 736 615	1 563 377	646 271
Irrigated ... farms	316	95	162	79	18	19
acres	24 793	6 448	8 530	2 769	484	291
Farms by acres harvested:						
1 to 24 acres	735	481	1 711	1 577	993	746
25 to 99 acres	2 680	1 289	2 692	1 356	452	181
100 to 249 acres	1 056	275	361	64	12	2
250 to 499 acres	81	22	25	7	-	-
500 acres or more	14	3	-	-	-	-
Wheat for grain ... farms	5 141	2 332	6 018	4 146	2 227	1 696
acres	960 208	352 395	656 007	301 487	108 797	43 456
bushels	30 394 903	10 731 181	19 399 090	8 379 376	2 783 066	930 302
Irrigated ... farms	235	66	155	76	25	26
acres	25 482	6 047	11 152	3 355	1 026	550
Farms by acres harvested:						
1 to 24 acres	353	214	748	705	549	1 007
25 to 99 acres	1 287	658	2 436	2 410	1 501	659
100 to 249 acres	2 044	1 059	2 436	972	170	30
250 to 499 acres	1 274	375	372	54	7	-
500 acres or more	183	26	26	5	-	-
Barley for grain ... farms	290	106	238	101	48	20
acres	8 752	2 390	5 252	1 304	605	230
bushels	309 043	78 110	185 152	42 548	18 471	5 135
Irrigated ... farms	12	4	3	3	2	-
acres	269	355	55	(D)	(D)	-
Oats for grain ... farms	823	336	814	486	202	134
acres	17 942	6 519	15 030	5 901	2 422	1 452
bushels	632 226	213 728	478 055	201 794	72 540	36 196
Irrigated ... farms	5	1	3	-	-	-
acres	215	(D)	40	-	-	-
Soybeans for beans ... farms	2 420	1 144	2 933	2 086	1 046	695
acres	189 849	74 036	138 242	65 480	23 411	10 544
bushels	5 082 350	1 951 037	3 499 444	1 562 352	508 103	191 745
Irrigated ... farms	121	53	65	38	10	6
acres	5 196	2 580	1 950	907	268	44
Farms by acres harvested:						
1 to 24 acres	503	276	906	985	690	584
25 to 99 acres	1 229	617	1 713	1 080	349	111
100 to 249 acres	603	235	308	41	7	-
250 to 499 acres	80	14	6	-	-	-
500 acres or more	5	2	-	-	-	-
Dry edible beans, excluding dry limas ... farms	14	3	6	3	-	-
acres	753	147	174	95	-	-
cwt	7 558	836	3 162	961	-	-
Irrigated ... farms	11	2	4	1	-	-
acres	547	(D)	129	(D)	-	-
Irish potatoes ... farms	19	7	24	10	8	4
acres	(D)	7	10	8	12	1
cwt	(D)	1 255	2 193	1 010	830	125
Irrigated ... farms	3	-	3	2	3	1
acres	8	-	2	(D)	1	(D)
Hay—alfalfa, other tame, small grain, wild, grass silage, green chop, etc. (see text) ... farms	4 013	1 910	5 168	3 981	2 513	3 166
acres	240 909	97 818	229 300	134 278	65 667	63 496
tons, dry	480 458	178 285	392 601	214 341	96 334	78 882
Irrigated ... farms	114	31	55	44	18	26
acres	6 575	1 474	1 611	1 245	298	198
Farms by acres harvested:						
1 to 24 acres	1 043	600	1 934	2 023	1 548	2 329
25 to 99 acres	2 278	1 069	2 763	1 763	903	804
100 to 249 acres	640	229	438	190	60	32
250 to 499 acres	45	10	31	5	1	1
500 acres or more	7	2	2	-	1	1

See footnotes at end of table.

Table 52. **Summary by Value of Agricultural Products Sold: 1987**—Con.

[For meaning of abbreviations and symbols, see introductory text]

Item	All farms	$500,000 or more $1,000,000 or more	$500,000 or more Total	$250,000 to $499,999	$100,000 to $249,999	$50,000 to $99,999	$40,000 to $49,999
CROPS HARVESTED—Con.							
Hay—alfalfa, other tame, small grain, wild, grass silage, green chop, etc. (see text)—Con.							
Alfalfa hay .... farms..	15 484	109	341	671	2 475	3 201	1 012
acres..	741 856	54 352	101 923	81 559	178 062	155 142	37 816
tons, dry..	2 529 635	278 458	485 214	324 518	630 924	498 719	112 295
Irrigated .... farms..	1 174	40	120	166	349	275	51
acres..	180 952	42 205	69 917	33 269	41 035	24 647	3 079
Vegetables harvested for sale (see text) .... farms..	418	2	5	8	31	46	15
acres..	5 424	(D)	1 444	546	616	653	246
Irrigated .... farms..	166	2	4	5	13	23	6
acres..	1 851	(D)	50	508	204	299	120
Farms by acres harvested:							
0.1 to 4.9 acres	244	-	1	1	16	25	5
5.0 to 24.9 acres	130	2	2	2	6	12	5
25.0 to 99.9 acres	39	-	1	3	6	8	5
100.0 to 249.9 acres	4	-	-	2	1	1	-
250.0 acres or more	1	-	1	-	-	-	-
Field seed and grass seed crops .... farms..	1 188	6	20	59	200	281	88
acres..	58 460	685	3 291	6 713	13 452	15 049	3 489
Irrigated .... farms..	12	-	1	1	6	-	-
acres..	2 222	-	(D)	(D)	487	-	-
Land in orchards .... farms..	503	1	2	5	19	30	13
acres..	5 999	(D)	(D)	(D)	1 712	488	(D)
Irrigated .... farms..	90	-	1	3	2	7	2
acres..	757	-	(D)	162	(D)	71	(D)
Farms by bearing and nonbearing acres:							
0.1 to 4.9 acres	309	-	1	-	7	13	9
5.0 to 24.9 acres	147	1	1	2	7	12	2
25.0 to 99.9 acres	39	-	-	2	2	4	2
100.0 to 249.9 acres	6	-	-	1	1	1	-
250.0 acres or more	2	-	-	1	2	-	-

See footnotes at end of table.

Table 52. Summary by Value of Agricultural Products Sold: 1987—Con.

[For meaning of abbreviations and symbols, see introductory text]

Item	$25,000 to $39,999	$20,000 to $24,999	$10,000 to $19,999	$5,000 to $9,999	$2,500 to $4,999	Less than $2,500
CROPS HARVESTED—Con.						
Hay—alfalfa, other tame, small grain, wild, grass silage, green chop, etc. (see text) —Con.						
Alfalfa hay .... farms..	2 008	876	2 116	1 391	669	704
acres..	66 997	23 497	52 163	26 300	10 442	8 155
tons, dry..	192 022	61 117	128 837	59 649	21 906	14 432
Irrigated .... farms..	94	24	43	27	10	16
acres..	5 484	1 190	1 231	827	176	97
Vegetables harvested for sale (see text) ... farms..	35	18	65	77	63	55
acres..	600	134	496	360	201	127
Irrigated .... farms..	15	7	19	33	22	19
acres..	250	39	123	132	86	39
Farms by acres harvested:						
0.1 to 4.9 acres	13	11	32	43	45	52
5.0 to 24.9 acres	12	6	31	34	18	2
25.0 to 99.9 acres	10	1	2	-	-	1
100.0 to 249.9 acres	-	-	-	-	-	-
250.0 acres or more	-	-	-	-	-	-
Field seed and grass seed crops .... farms..	145	62	158	93	39	43
acres..	5 395	2 012	5 301	2 185	866	707
Irrigated .... farms..	1	-	1	-	1	1
acres..	(D)	-	(D)	-	(D)	(D)
Land in orchards .... farms..	27	23	63	67	55	199
acres..	278	348	655	760	255	1 045
Irrigated .... farms..	4	3	12	8	9	39
acres..	40	6	51	51	38	282
Farms by bearing and nonbearing acres:						
0.1 to 4.9 acres	15	11	41	36	41	135
5.0 to 24.9 acres	10	5	13	23	13	59
25.0 to 99.9 acres	2	7	7	7	1	5
100.0 to 249.9 acres	-	-	2	1	-	-
250.0 acres or more	-	-	-	-	-	-

[1]Data are based on a sample of farms.
[2]Farms with total production expenses equal to market value of agricultural products sold are included as farms with gains of less than $1,000.

Table 53. Summary by Standard Industrial Classification of Farm: 1987

[For meaning of abbreviations and symbols, see introductory text]

Item	Total	Cash grains (011)	Field crops, except cash grains (013) Total	Cotton (0131)	Tobacco (0132)	Sugarcane and sugar beets; Irish potatoes; field crops, except cash grains, n.e.c. (0133, 0134, 0139)	Vegetables and melons (016)	Fruits and tree nuts (017)
FARMS AND LAND IN FARMS								
Farms..............................number..	68 579	31 789	2 010	1	3	2 006	179	171
...............................percent..	100.0	46.4	2.9	(Z)	(Z)	2.9	.3	.2
Land in farms.....................acres..	46 628 519	24 398 997	641 893	(D)	(D)	639 598	12 759	8 923
Average size of farm............acres..	680	767	319	(D)	(D)	319	71	52
MARKET VALUE OF AGRICUL- TURAL PRODUCTS SOLD								
Total sales (see text) ....farms..	68 579	31 789	2 010	1	3	2 006	178	171
...................................$1,000..	6 476 669	1 429 353	47 372	(D)	(D)	47 248	3 658	1 323
Average per farm................dollars..	94 441	44 964	23 568	(D)	(D)	23 553	20 435	7 736
Farms by value of sales:								
Less than $1,000 (see text)...........	4 538	776	480	-	-	480	16	85
$1,000 to $2,499	4 964	1 669	346	-	1	345	21	23
$2,500 to $4,999	6 919	2 750	313	-	2	311	36	21
$5,000 to $9,999	9 430	4 368	302	-	-	302	47	18
$10,000 to $19,999	10 504	5 435	205	-	-	206	26	13
$20,000 to $24,999	3 566	2 028	45	-	-	45	4	4
$25,000 to $39,999	7 150	4 080	110	-	-	110	15	1
$40,000 to $49,999	3 132	1 854	32	-	-	32	4	1
$50,000 to $99,999	8 997	5 112	86	-	-	86	5	3
$100,000 to $249,999	6 656	3 145	62	1	-	61	1	1
$250,000 to $499,999	1 766	492	16	-	-	16	3	1
$500,000 to $999,999	566	65	8	-	-	8	1	-
$1,000,000 or more	389	14	4	-	-	4	-	-
Grains................................farms..	48 606	31 766	640	1	-	638	53	13
...................................$1,000..	1 550 403	1 188 845	8 321	(D)	(D)	(D)	281	30
Sales of $50,000 or more ....farms..	8 994	7 131	38	-	-	38	1	-
...................................$1,000..	976 864	794 579	3 727	-	-	3 727	(D)	-
Corn for grain ....farms..	7 426	5 449	69	-	-	69	6	3
...................................$1,000..	255 791	213 917	1 474	-	-	1 474	25	2
Wheat...............................farms..	38 365	25 477	441	1	-	440	28	3
...................................$1,000..	694 147	510 363	4 228	(D)	-	(D)	50	2
Soybeans...........................farms..	18 724	12 418	159	-	-	158	26	9
...................................$1,000..	263 742	205 158	780	(D)	-	(D)	190	20
Sorghum for grain ....farms..	28 719	19 989	294	1	-	292	6	4
...................................$1,000..	311 649	238 584	1 753	(D)	(D)	(D)	16	7
Barley..............................farms..	1 715	1 294	9	-	-	9	-	-
...................................$1,000..	3 953	3 161	19	-	-	19	-	-
Oats ....farms..	2 418	1 540	49	-	-	49	-	-
...................................$1,000..	3 328	2 333	55	-	-	55	-	-
Other grains ....farms..	1 656	1 333	6	-	-	6	3	-
...................................$1,000..	17 793	15 626	12	-	-	12	(Z)	-
Cotton and cottonseed ....farms..	10	7	1	1	-	-	-	-
...................................$1,000..	186	59	(D)	(D)	-	-	-	-
Sales of $50,000 or more ....farms..	2	-	-	-	-	-	-	-
...................................$1,000..	(D)	-	(D)	(D)	-	-	-	-
Tobacco.............................farms..	13	6	3	-	3	-	-	-
...................................$1,000..	80	43	(D)	-	8	-	-	-
Sales of $50,000 or more ....farms..	-	-	-	-	-	-	-	-
Hay, silage, and field seeds ....farms..	12 801	5 670	2 004	1	-	2 003	9	5
...................................$1,000..	109 574	33 941	35 920	(D)	-	(D)	11	9
Sales of $50,000 or more ....farms..	316	82	123	-	-	123	-	-
...................................$1,000..	47 030	8 279	24 054	-	-	24 054	-	-
Vegetables, sweet corn, and melons ....farms..	418	82	8	-	-	8	179	19
...................................$1,000..	4 151	336	16	-	-	16	3 001	91
Sales of $50,000 or more ....farms..	10	-	-	-	-	-	9	-
...................................$1,000..	1 767	-	-	-	-	-	(D)	-
Fruits, nuts, and berries ....farms..	278	45	6	-	-	6	38	115
...................................$1,000..	1 693	160	2	-	-	2	108	1 154
Sales of $50,000 or more ....farms..	6	-	-	-	-	-	-	5
...................................$1,000..	732	-	-	-	-	-	-	(D)
Nursery and greenhouse crops..........farms..	272	10	1	-	-	(D)	9	2
...................................$1,000..	26 805	69	(D)	-	-	(D)	69	(D)
Sales of $50,000 or more ....farms..	62	-	-	-	-	-	-	-
...................................$1,000..	24 509	-	-	-	-	-	-	-
Other crops.........................farms..	80	22	4	-	-	4	22	1
...................................$1,000..	716	260	8	-	-	8	47	(D)
Sales of $50,000 or more ....farms..	3	1	-	-	-	-	-	-
...................................$1,000..	558	(D)	-	-	-	-	-	-
Poultry and poultry products ....farms..	1 550	399	25	-	-	25	6	3
...................................$1,000..	25 284	355	(D)	-	-	10	1	(Z)
Sales of $50,000 or more ....farms..	75	1	-	-	-	-	-	-
...................................$1,000..	23 851	(D)	-	-	-	-	-	-
Dairy products ....farms..	2 004	105	2	-	-	2	-	-
...................................$1,000..	140 232	1 886	(D)	-	-	(D)	-	-
Sales of $50,000 or more ....farms..	979	7	-	-	-	-	-	-
...................................$1,000..	119 518	645	-	-	-	-	-	-
Cattle and calves ....farms..	41 498	12 066	261	1	-	260	17	6
...................................$1,000..	4 305 335	181 436	2 764	(D)	-	(D)	108	29
Sales of $50,000 or more ....farms..	5 932	606	10	-	-	10	-	-
...................................$1,000..	3 891 456	53 351	1 657	-	-	1 657	(D)	-

See footnotes at end of table.

[For meaning of abbreviations and symbols, see introductory text]

Item	Horticultural specialties (016)	General farms, primarily crop (019)	Livestock, except dairy, poultry, and animal specialties (021) Total	Beef cattle, except feedlots (0212)	Dairy farms (024)	Poultry and eggs (025)	Animal specialties (027)	General farms, primarily livestock and animal specialties (029)
FARMS AND LAND IN FARMS								
Farms ....number..	224	1 463	29 037	21 861	1 391	197	1 452	666
percent..	.3	2.1	42.3	31.9	2.0	.3	2.1	1.0
Land in farms ....acres..	19 302	911 997	19 106 721	14 512 574	805 354	34 376	126 440	563 757
Average size of farm ....acres..	86	623	658	664	579	174	87	846
MARKET VALUE OF AGRICULTURAL PRODUCTS SOLD								
Total sales (see text) ....farms..	224	1 463	29 037	21 861	1 391	197	1 452	666
$1,000..	26 681	62 075	4 680 257	1 207 132	162 066	25 902	7 065	30 917
Average per farm ....dollars..	119 112	42 430	161 183	55 218	116 511	131 482	4 866	46 422
Farms by value of sales:								
Less than $1,000 (see text)....................	1	627	1 291	1 032	5	63	847	347
$1,000 to $2,499	25	8	2 556	1 982	6	25	269	16
$2,500 to $4,999	25	29	3 565	3 001	8	18	141	13
$5,000 to $9,999	28	81	4 446	3 642	24	6	91	16
$10,000 to $19,999	44	160	4 458	3 714	82	5	53	22
$20,000 to $24,999	13	48	1 347	1 075	51	1	12	13
$25,000 to $39,999	16	141	2 610	1 886	126	5	11	33
$40,000 to $49,999	7	52	1 075	736	78	2	6	21
$50,000 to $99,999	18	159	3 130	1 970	381	14	13	76
$100,000 to $249,999	23	117	2 682	1 632	516	22	5	82
$250,000 to $499,999.............................	8	26	1 072	630	99	20	2	25
$500,000 to $999,999.............................	8	9	454	244	11	8	2	2
$1,000,000 or more..............................	6		351	115	4	8	–	–
Grains................................farms..	15	634	13 891	9 630	990	55	50	269
$1,000..	90	25 352	299 880	179 727	17 274	1 055	212	9 062
Sales of $50,000 or more ....farms..	–	129	1 566	910	66	6	1	56
$1,000..	–	15 242	152 480	84 833	5 152	(D)	(D)	5 079
Corn for grain ....farms..	2	140	1 559	884	133	4	2	59
$1,000..	(D)	4 160	33 862	17 849	1 460	46	(D)	1 113
Wheat ....farms..	10	643	10 759	7 414	709	40	31	224
$1,000..	41	12 592	155 677	103 176	7 451	428	139	3 175
Soybeans ....farms..	5	367	5 093	2 985	449	16	10	172
$1,000..	31	3 422	47 134	23 183	4 306	101	20	2 581
Sorghum for grain ....farms..	5	563	7 153	4 916	456	40	9	198
$1,000..	(D)	4 912	59 759	35 449	3 972	(D)	44	2 120
Barley ....farms..	–	26	358	262	19	–	–	5
$1,000..	–	53	687	476	27	–	–	8
Oats ....farms..	–	94	676	425	35	1	1	21
$1,000..	–	97	759	463	46	(D)	(D)	(D)
Other grains ....farms..	–	22	274	167	7	–	2	8
$1,000..	–	116	1 983	1 131	13	(D)	(D)	(D)
Cotton and cottonseed ....farms..	–	1	1	1	–	–	–	–
$1,000..	–	(D)	(D)	(D)	–	–	–	–
Sales of $50,000 or more ....farms..	–	1	–	–	–	–	–	–
$1,000..	–	(D)	–	–	–	–	–	–
Tobacco ....farms..	–	1	2	–	–	1	–	–
$1,000..	–	(D)	(D)	–	–	(D)	–	–
Sales of $50,000 or more ....farms..	–	–	–	–	–	–	–	–
$1,000..	–	–	–	–	–	–	–	–
Hay, silage, and field seeds ....farms..	13	818	3 909	2 689	209	17	57	90
$1,000..	21	11 850	25 300	15 299	1 648	72	72	730
Sales of $50,000 or more ....farms..	–	39	67	36	3	–	–	2
$1,000..	–	5 462	8 858	4 640	(D)	–	–	(D)
Vegetables, sweet corn, and melons ...farms..	10	25	45	45	5	2	1	4
$1,000..	87	216	367	178	12	(D)	(D)	4
Sales of $50,000 or more ....farms..	–	1	–	–	–	–	–	–
$1,000..	–	(D)	–	–	–	–	–	–
Fruits, nuts, and berries ....farms..	3	13	52	35	3	3	–	–
$1,000..	11	92	165	104	(D)	1	–	–
Sales of $50,000 or more ....farms..	–	–	1	1	–	–	–	–
$1,000..	–	–	(D)	(D)	–	–	–	–
Nursery and greenhouse crops..........farms..	224	6	14	153	1	2	–	3
$1,000..	26 434	(D)	(D)	(D)	(D)	(D)	–	1
Sales of $50,000 or more ....farms..	61	–	1	1	–	–	–	–
$1,000..	(D)	–	(D)	(D)	–	–	–	–
Other crops ....farms..	2	9	18	14	1	1	–	–
$1,000..	(D)	298	34	32	(D)	(D)	–	–
Sales of $50,000 or more ....farms..	–	1	–	–	1	–	–	–
$1,000..	–	(D)	–	–	(D)	–	–	–
Poultry and poultry products ....farms..	2	31	745	457	61	181	32	65
$1,000..	(D)	(D)	(D)	160	40	23 801	(D)	576
Sales of $50,000 or more ....farms..	–	–	1	–	–	66	–	5
$1,000..	–	–	(D)	–	–	23 314	–	(D)
Dairy products ....farms..	–	22	245	145	1 387	3	–	240
$1,000..	–	5 732	2 822	121 597	3	–	10 439
Sales of $50,000 or more ....farms..	–	3	35	18	859	–	–	75
$1,000..	–	324	3 727	1 794	107 858	–	–	6 964
Cattle and calves ....farms..	7	777	26 557	21 521	1 379	44	70	312
$1,000..	(D)	20 971	4 070 015	993 193	19 982	797	(D)	8 961
Sales of $50,000 or more ....farms..	–	100	5 110	3 697	51	3	1	50
$1,000..	–	11 771	3 814 836	784 186	4 106	(D)	(D)	5 041

See footnotes at end of table.

Table 53. Summary by Standard Industrial Classification of Farm: 1987—Con.

[For meaning of abbreviations and symbols, see introductory text]

Item	Total	Cash grains (011)	Field crops, except cash grains (013) Total	Cotton (0131)	Tobacco (0132)	Sugarcane and sugar beets; Irish potatoes; field crops, except cash grains, n.e.c. (0133, 0134, 0139)	Vegetables and melons (016)	Fruits and tree nuts (017)
MARKET VALUE OF AGRICULTURAL PRODUCTS SOLD—Con.								
Total sales (see text)—Con.								
Hogs and pigs .... farms..	7 090	1 415	26	-	-	26	6	1
$1,000..	284 375	17 931	84	-	-	84	15	(D)
Sales of $50,000 or more .... farms..	1 278	63	-	-	-	-	-	-
$1,000..	213 369	5 256	-	-	-	-	-	-
Sheep, lambs, and wool.............. farms..	2 456	686	34	-	-	34	6	3
$1,000..	18 561	3 229	73	-	-	73	16	(D)
Sales of $50,000 or more .... farms..	44	6	-	-	-	-	-	-
$1,000..	9 169	483	-	-	-	-	-	-
Other livestock and livestock products (see text) .... farms..	2 869	485	75	-	-	75	6	3
$1,000..	9 273	804	66	-	-	66	1	1
Sales of $50,000 or more .... farms..	21	-	-	-	-	-	-	-
$1,000..	3 649	-	-	-	-	-	-	-
FARM PRODUCTION EXPENSES[1]								
Total farm production expenses .... farms..	68 580	31 424	2 028	7	2	2 019	222	195
$1,000..	5 516 518	1 115 529	37 576	(D)	(D)	(D)	3 308	1 445
Average per farm.....................dollars..	80 439	35 499	18 528	(D)	(D)	(D)	14 902	7 412
Livestock and poultry purchased .... farms..	23 380	5 713	163	7	-	156	20	-
$1,000..	2 426 149	54 319	1 390	6	-	1 384	37	-
Farms with expenses of—								
$1 to $4,999	11 923	3 559	134	7	-	127	19	-
$5,000 to $24,999	6 470	1 589	18	-	-	18	1	-
$25,000 to $99,999	3 307	514	9	-	-	9	-	-
$100,000 or more	1 680	51	2	-	-	2	-	-
Feed for livestock and poultry .... farms..	38 347	10 237	411	-	1	410	50	44
$1,000..	887 270	24 678	477	-	(D)	(D)	34	32
Farms with expenses of—								
$1 to $4,999	28 328	9 024	391	-	1	390	49	44
$5,000 to $24,999	7 351	1 137	19	-	-	19	1	-
$25,000 to $99,999	2 028	74	1	-	-	1	-	-
$100,000 or more	640	2	-	-	-	-	-	-
Commercially mixed formula feeds .... farms..	14 988	3 323	144	-	-	144	24	20
$1,000..	163 581	6 053	126	-	-	126	14	6
Farms with expenses of—								
$1 to $4,999	11 327	3 027	139	-	-	139	24	20
$5,000 to $24,999	2 854	281	4	-	-	4	-	-
$25,000 to $79,999	577	14	1	-	-	1	-	-
$80,000 or more	230	1	-	-	-	-	-	-
Seeds, bulbs, plants, and trees .... farms..	46 233	26 480	899	7	1	891	175	53
$1,000..	95 302	62 021	1 408	(D)	(D)	1 394	225	14
Farms with expenses of—								
$1 to $999	26 247	15 703	666	-	1	665	123	53
$1,000 to $4,999	15 265	9 485	165	7	-	158	36	-
$5,000 to $24,999	4 473	3 123	64	-	-	64	16	-
$25,000 or more	248	169	4	-	-	4	1	-
Commercial fertilizer .... farms..	47 731	26 519	1 154	7	2	1 145	179	122
$1,000..	216 166	134 435	3 634	56	(D)	(D)	230	54
Farms with expenses of—								
$1 to $4,999	34 889	18 426	1 002	-	2	1 000	162	121
$5,000 to $24,999	11 740	7 389	133	7	-	128	17	1
$25,000 to $49,999	884	562	10	-	-	10	-	-
$50,000 or more	218	142	9	-	-	9	-	-
Agricultural chemicals..................... farms..	46 318	25 366	1 181	-	2	1 179	157	152
$1,000..	125 003	79 785	2 287	-	(D)	(D)	238	120
Farms with expenses of—								
$1 to $4,999	39 456	20 765	1 102	-	2	1 100	149	150
$5,000 to $24,999	6 476	4 341	67	-	-	67	8	1
$25,000 to $49,999	322	222	9	-	-	9	-	1
$50,000 or more	64	38	3	-	-	3	-	-
Petroleum products....................... farms..	65 460	30 855	1 806	7	2	1 797	217	170
$1,000..	243 568	132 588	4 676	(D)	(D)	4 612	333	94
Farms with expenses of—								
$1 to $4,999	51 841	22 877	1 649	-	2	1 647	207	169
$5,000 to $24,999	12 652	7 437	132	7	-	125	9	1
$25,000 to $49,999	760	458	12	-	-	12	-	-
$50,000 or more	207	85	13	-	-	13	1	-
Gasoline and gasohol .... farms..	57 245	26 130	1 582	7	2	1 573	200	157
$1,000..	80 737	36 853	1 316	(D)	(D)	1 312	212	51
Diesel fuel .... farms..	46 376	26 026	866	7	1	858	66	72
$1,000..	110 981	65 796	1 798	(D)	(D)	1 749	64	29
Natural gas .... farms..	4 956	3 052	160	-	-	160	32	-
$1,000..	26 371	16 936	1 183	-	-	1 183	34	-
LP gas, fuel oil, kerosene, motor oil, grease, etc. .... farms..	52 546	26 645	985	7	2	976	118	79
$1,000..	25 478	12 983	375	(D)	(D)	368	22	14

See footnotes at end of table.

Table 53. **Summary by Standard Industrial Classification of Farm: 1987**—Con.

[For meaning of abbreviations and symbols, see introductory text]

Item	Horticultural specialties (018)	General farms, primarily crop (019)	Livestock, except dairy, poultry, and animal specialties (021) Total	Beef cattle, except feedlots (0212)	Dairy farms (024)	Poultry and eggs (025)	Animal specialties (027)	General farms, primarily livestock and animal specialties (029)
MARKET VALUE OF AGRICULTURAL PRODUCTS SOLD—Con.								
Total sales (see text)—Con.								
Hogs and pigs .... farms..	1	123	5 305	1 080	124	10	13	66
$1,000..	(D)	2 183	261 867	13 262	(D)	71	61	942
Sales of $50,000 or more .... farms..	–	11	1 195	58	4	–	–	5
$1,000..	–	1 033	206 523	6 373	255	–	–	303
Sheep, lambs, and wool.............. farms..	1	39	1 595	516	35	10	25	20
$1,000..	(D)	386	14 518	1 099	174	75	30	59
Sales of $50,000 or more .... farms..	–	2	34	–	1	1	–	–
$1,000..	–	(D)	8 338	–	(D)	(D)	–	–
Other livestock and livestock products (see text) .... farms..	8	40	1 252	892	41	18	884	57
$1,000..	11	43	1 702	1 249	52	11	6 438	142
Sales of $50,000 or more .... farms..	–	–	1	1	–	–	20	–
$1,000..	–	–	(D)	(D)	–	–	(D)	–
FARM PRODUCTION EXPENSES[1]								
Total farm production expenses .... farms..	233	1 466	29 410	22 388	1 359	221	1 385	657
$1,000..	20 567	52 796	4 114 522	1 040 987	112 211	23 383	10 408	24 772
Average per farm..................... dollars..	88 270	36 014	139 902	46 495	82 569	105 805	7 625	37 705
Livestock and poultry purchased .... farms..	8	481	15 870	10 774	614	200	345	166
$1,000..	32	7 439	2 346 563	420 189	5 699	5 976	1 451	3 243
Farms with expenses of—								
$1 to $4,999	8	305	7 102	4 983	294	129	289	64
$5,000 to $24,999	–	106	4 378	3 117	268	26	42	42
$25,000 to $99,999	–	54	2 599	1 736	50	31	14	36
$100,000 or more	–	16	1 591	938	2	14	–	4
Feed for livestock and poultry .... farms..	13	838	23 990	17 474	1 349	186	924	305
$1,000..	10	2 700	808 259	116 500	34 260	11 500	1 653	3 667
Farms with expenses of—								
$1 to $4,999	13	706	16 781	13 651	242	108	855	115
$5,000 to $24,999	–	118	5 178	3 075	667	20	65	146
$25,000 to $99,999	–	14	1 473	593	403	17	4	42
$100,000 or more	–	–	558	155	37	41	–	2
Commercially mixed formula feeds .... farms..	5	361	8 941	5 825	1 340	177	408	245
$1,000..	1	629	125 495	25 827	17 583	11 325	409	1 922
Farms with expenses of—								
$1 to $4,999	5	329	6 643	4 906	505	108	390	137
$5,000 to $24,999	–	30	1 752	750	670	11	18	88
$25,000 to $79,999	–	2	379	138	147	14	–	20
$80,000 or more	–	–	167	31	18	44	–	–
Seeds, bulbs, plants, and trees .... farms..	181	840	15 899	11 388	1 168	89	107	342
$1,000..	2 192	1 913	24 372	14 549	2 236	66	34	801
Farms with expenses of—								
$1 to $999	82	493	10 357	7 976	446	71	96	157
$1,000 to $4,999	63	254	4 465	2 827	630	14	11	143
$5,000 to $24,999	15	86	1 035	563	92	4	–	38
$25,000 or more	21	7	42	22	–	–	–	4
Commercial fertilizer .... farms..	134	914	16 970	12 566	1 136	56	263	284
$1,000..	537	4 870	64 184	39 125	6 030	225	101	1 867
Farms with expenses of—								
$1 to $4,999	121	648	13 263	10 446	690	46	261	149
$5,000 to $24,999	10	234	3 389	1 967	433	7	2	125
$25,000 to $49,999	1	23	264	122	12	3	–	9
$50,000 or more	2	9	54	31	1	–	–	1
Agricultural chemicals .... farms..	196	874	16 436	12 080	1 102	111	356	385
$1,000..	457	2 376	35 730	21 642	2 654	132	209	1 015
Farms with expenses of—								
$1 to $4,999	178	756	14 605	11 034	970	104	348	329
$5,000 to $24,999	14	111	1 735	1 003	130	7	8	54
$25,000 to $49,999	2	4	80	37	2	–	–	2
$50,000 or more	2	3	18	6	–	–	–	–
Petroleum products .... farms..	225	1 269	27 833	21 113	1 339	192	1 013	541
$1,000..	1 807	4 570	90 485	54 122	6 385	382	616	1 853
Farms with expenses of—								
$1 to $4,999	159	999	23 306	18 239	857	176	1 006	436
$5,000 to $24,999	54	252	4 174	2 729	469	15	7	102
$25,000 to $49,999	6	14	255	120	13	1	–	3
$50,000 or more	6	4	98	25	–	–	–	–
Gasoline and gasohol................... farms..	213	1 129	25 030	18 979	1 283	185	877	479
$1,000..	488	1 600	36 773	23 979	2 337	185	375	543
Diesel fuel .... farms..	105	860	16 541	12 060	1 096	72	343	309
$1,000..	289	2 051	37 059	21 576	2 826	87	126	855
Natural gas .... farms..	63	73	1 346	845	144	21	34	31
$1,000..	906	445	6 604	2 637	193	16	18	34
LP gas, fuel oil, kerosene, motor oil, grease, etc. .... farms..	167	950	21 322	15 844	1 279	147	491	366
$1,000..	123	475	10 049	5 929	1 028	94	96	220

See footnotes at end of table.

Table 53. **Summary by Standard Industrial Classification of Farm: 1987**—Con.

[For meaning of abbreviations and symbols, see introductory text]

Item	Total	Cash grains (011)	Field crops, except cash grains (013)				Vegetables and melons (016)	Fruits and tree nuts (017)
			Total	Cotton (0131)	Tobacco (0132)	Sugarcane and sugar beets; Irish potatoes; field crops, except cash grains, n.e.c. (0133, 0134, 0139)		
FARM PRODUCTION EXPENSES[1] —Con.								
Total farm production expenses—Con.								
Electricity .... farms..	48 797	21 611	1 138	7	2	1 129	130	107
$1,000..	54 103	19 972	890	(D)	(D)	866	84	40
Farms with expenses of—								
$1 to $999............................	36 860	16 380	1 009	7	2	1 000	91	95
$1,000 to $4,999	10 565	4 714	89	-	-	89	37	11
$5,000 to $24,999	1 236	499	38	-	-	38	2	1
$25,000 or more	138	18	2	-	-	2	-	-
Hired farm labor .... farms..	24 715	12 123	460	-	2	458	60	49
$1,000..	226 075	58 727	3 374	-	(D)	(D)	328	374
Farms with expenses of—								
$1 to $4,999.........................	18 529	9 358	364	-	2	362	43	39
$5,000 to $24,999	4 529	2 264	63	-	-	63	14	7
$25,000 to $99,999	1 391	474	28	-	-	28	3	2
$100,000 or more	266	27	5	-	-	5	-	1
Contract labor.......................... farms..	7 882	3 553	208	-	-	209	44	17
$1,000..	23 691	8 556	519	-	-	519	461	21
Farms with expenses of—								
$1 to $999...........................	3 892	1 693	129	-	-	129	25	9
$1,000 to $4,999	2 895	1 366	62	-	-	62	9	8
$5,000 to $24,999	1 023	481	15	-	-	15	9	-
$25,000 or more	72	13	3	-	-	3	1	-
Repair and maintenance .... farms..	56 961	26 644	1 452	7	2	1 443	176	141
$1,000..	252 018	123 416	4 228	(D)	(D)	4 115	280	194
Farms with expenses of—								
$1 to $4,999.........................	42 384	18 491	1 276	-	2	1 274	168	135
$5,000 to $24,999	13 477	7 690	153	7	-	146	8	5
$25,000 to $49,999	844	402	12	-	-	12	-	1
$50,000 or more	256	61	11	-	-	11	-	-
Customwork, machine hire, and rental of machinery and equipment .... farms..	30 903	16 273	571	-	-	571	93	90
$1,000..	107 366	65 828	2 328	-	-	2 328	61	13
Farms with expenses of—								
$1 to $999...........................	13 298	5 957	359	-	-	359	61	33
$1,000 to $4,999	11 836	6 638	134	-	-	134	32	-
$5,000 to $24,999	4 982	3 379	63	-	-	63	-	-
$25,000 or more	487	299	15	-	-	15	-	-
Interest expense .... farms..	39 549	18 259	846	7	1	838	65	59
$1,000..	314 163	133 302	5 010	(D)	(D)	4 908	313	164
Farms with expenses of—								
$1 to $4,999.........................	24 133	10 642	607	-	1	606	55	49
$5,000 to $24,999	12 576	6 507	204	7	-	197	7	10
$25,000 to $99,999	2 557	1 087	32	-	-	32	3	-
$100,000 or more	183	23	3	-	-	3	-	-
Secured by real estate .... farms..	26 408	11 756	612	7	1	604	49	58
$1,000..	188 166	85 904	3 515	(D)	(D)	3 416	264	147
Farms with expenses of—								
$1 to $999...........................	5 915	1 913	200	-	1	199	13	10
$1,000 to $4,999	10 417	4 464	216	-	-	218	27	38
$5,000 to $24,999	9 280	4 753	172	7	-	165	7	10
$25,000 or more	1 396	606	22	-	-	22	2	-
Not secured by real estate .... farms..	24 307	11 613	418	7	-	411	25	7
$1,000..	125 997	47 398	1 495	4	-	1 492	49	16
Farms with expenses of—								
$1 to $999...........................	8 203	3 567	179	7	-	172	13	-
$1,000 to $4,999	9 540	4 968	177	-	-	177	9	6
$5,000 to $24,999	5 766	2 853	52	-	-	52	3	1
$25,000 or more	798	205	10	-	-	10	-	-
Cash rent.............................. farms..	21 234	10 218	359	7	-	352	37	18
$1,000..	123 531	57 016	1 855	14	-	1 641	141	8
Farms with expenses of—								
$1 to $4,999.........................	14 629	6 982	301	7	-	294	20	18
$5,000 to $9,999	3 298	1 616	30	-	-	30	16	-
$10,000 to $24,999	2 511	1 281	20	-	-	20	1	-
$25,000 or more	796	339	8	-	-	8	-	-
Property taxes .... farms..	63 359	28 081	1 943	7	2	1 934	206	192
$1,000..	112 201	53 416	2 163	(D)	(D)	2 145	153	153
Farms with expenses of—								
$1 to $4,999.........................	59 062	25 978	1 900	7	2	1 891	204	192
$5,000 to $9,999	3 246	1 671	19	-	-	19	2	-
$10,000 to $24,999	956	405	22	-	-	22	-	-
$25,000 or more	93	27	2	-	-	2	-	-
All other farm production expenses ...... farms..	64 491	29 614	1 679	7	2	1 670	199	161
$1,000..	309 914	107 490	3 540	(D)	(D)	3 535	403	175
Farms with expenses of—								
$1 to $4,999.........................	51 852	23 549	1 562	7	2	1 553	181	160
$5,000 to $24,999	11 071	5 590	99	-	-	99	16	-
$25,000 to $49,999	1 005	359	9	-	-	9	-	-
$50,000 or more	563	116	9	-	-	9	2	1

See footnotes at end of table.

Table 53. Summary by Standard Industrial Classification of Farm: 1987—Con.

[For meaning of abbreviations and symbols, see introductory text]

Item	Horticultural specialties (018)	General farms, primarily crop (019)	Livestock, except dairy, poultry, and animal specialties (021) Total	Beef cattle, except feedlots (0212)	Dairy farms (024)	Poultry and eggs (025)	Animal specialties (027)	General farms, primarily livestock and animal specialties (029)
FARM PRODUCTION EXPENSES[1] —Con.								
Total farm production expenses—Con.								
Electricity .... farms..	177	972	22 061	16 331	1 321	170	701	409
$1,000..	445	1 082	26 643	10 949	3 535	526	316	570
Farms with expenses of—								
$1 to $999	72	751	17 187	13 615	295	115	627	238
$1,000 to $4,999	81	205	4 295	2 522	878	36	68	151
$5,000 to $24,999	22	11	480	187	143	14	6	20
$25,000 or more	2	5	99	7	5	5	-	-
Hired farm labor .... farms..	138	413	10 234	7 302	754	83	229	171
$1,000..	8 045	3 077	140 690	43 848	7 650	1 736	460	1 814
Farms with expenses of—								
$1 to $4,999	54	273	7 617	5 760	412	41	206	120
$5,000 to $24,999	32	119	1 701	1 098	255	27	18	29
$25,000 to $99,999	33	17	721	379	80	10	3	20
$100,000 or more	20	4	195	45	7	5	-	2
Contract labor .... farms..	42	191	9 357	2 461	271	90	121	47
$1,000..	279	774	11 361	6 251	802	162	664	92
Farms with expenses of—								
$1 to $999	8	95	1 722	1 308	83	18	86	24
$1,000 to $4,999	17	53	1 176	858	149	6	31	18
$5,000 to $24,999	16	41	412	274	36	5	3	5
$25,000 or more	1	2	47	21	3	1	1	-
Repair and maintenance .... farms..	219	1 085	24 336	16 212	1 241	184	957	526
$1,000..	1 075	4 532	105 931	56 524	8 587	583	953	2 239
Farms with expenses of—								
$1 to $4,999	177	790	19 267	15 109	592	153	940	395
$5,000 to $24,999	33	268	4 552	2 873	613	25	15	115
$25,000 to $49,999	4	24	351	192	29	5	2	14
$50,000 or more	5	3	166	38	7	1	-	2
Customwork, machine hire, and rental of machinery and equipment .... farms..	47	583	11 613	8 635	794	56	288	252
$1,000..	178	2 263	33 905	21 202	2 087	44	130	510
Farms with expenses of—								
$1 to $999	33	309	5 812	4 414	284	44	268	138
$1,000 to $4,999	13	159	4 350	3 914	394	12	19	85
$5,000 to $24,999	-	102	1 297	921	112	-	-	28
$25,000 or more	1	13	154	86	4	-	-	1
Interest expense .... farms..	130	863	17 164	12 449	1 064	121	566	412
$1,000..	1 519	7 278	149 586	87 453	11 903	689	1 746	2 673
Farms with expenses of—								
$1 to $4,999	74	539	10 947	8 260	415	97	439	269
$5,000 to $24,999	43	244	4 869	3 419	524	21	125	122
$25,000 to $99,999	11	78	1 201	711	120	2	2	21
$100,000 or more	2	2	147	59	5	1	-	-
Secured by real estate .... farms..	113	633	11 556	8 236	756	104	445	326
$1,000..	1 086	4 892	80 966	50 123	7 733	427	1 427	1 805
Farms with expenses of—								
$1 to $999	19	97	2 747	2 140	68	40	131	77
$1,000 to $4,999	52	285	4 705	3 370	219	44	212	133
$5,000 to $24,999	31	207	3 474	2 381	405	17	100	104
$25,000 or more	11	44	630	347	64	3	2	12
Not secured by real estate .... farms..	82	479	10 465	7 573	723	53	241	201
$1,000..	433	2 386	68 600	37 330	4 170	262	319	868
Farms with expenses of—								
$1 to $999	33	141	3 911	2 871	130	22	124	83
$1,000 to $4,999	16	191	3 655	2 813	296	22	115	62
$5,000 to $24,999	31	136	2 353	1 593	280	7	1	49
$25,000 or more	2	11	546	296	14	2	1	7
Cash rent .... farms..	34	501	9 032	6 725	684	38	131	182
$1,000..	128	2 828	56 279	39 621	4 256	122	127	974
Farms with expenses of—								
$1 to $4,999	29	363	6 147	4 658	452	31	130	136
$5,000 to $9,999	2	53	1 435	1 046	125	4	1	16
$10,000 to $24,999	2	36	1 064	752	81	2	-	24
$25,000 or more	1	29	386	271	26	1	-	6
Property taxes .... farms..	218	1 391	27 895	21 280	1 322	206	1 261	644
$1,000..	444	2 330	48 023	32 825	3 253	224	810	1 233
Farms with expenses of—								
$1 to $4,999	197	1 307	26 067	20 152	1 170	198	1 252	597
$5,000 to $9,999	14	66	1 305	830	130	8	8	25
$10,000 to $24,999	5	15	465	274	22	-	1	21
$25,000 or more	2	3	58	24	-	-	-	1
All other farm production expenses .... farms..	227	1 279	27 942	21 235	1 339	221	1 228	602
$1,000..	3 420	4 743	172 533	76 189	12 875	994	1 138	2 602
Farms with expenses of—								
$1 to $4,999	164	1 055	22 714	18 005	606	198	1 203	460
$5,000 to $24,999	34	206	4 344	2 770	619	17	23	123
$25,000 to $49,999	20	8	510	308	84	1	-	14
$50,000 or more	9	10	374	152	30	5	2	5

See footnotes at end of table.

[For meaning of abbreviations and symbols, see introductory text]

Item	Total	Cash grains (011)	Field crops, except cash grains (013) Total	Cotton (0131)	Tobacco (0132)	Sugarcane and sugar beets; Irish potatoes; field crops, except cash grains, n.e.c. (0133, 0134, 0139)	Vegetables and melons (016)	Fruits and tree nuts (017)
NET CASH RETURN FROM AGRICULTURAL SALES FOR THE FARM UNIT [1]								
All farms........................number..	68 580	31 424	2 028	7	2	2 019	222	195
$1,000..	922 225	274 819	9 112	(D)	(D)	8 704	701	-382
Average per farm..................dollars..	13 447	8 746	4 493	(D)	(D)	4 311	3 157	-1 959
Farms with net gains[2]............number..	41 673	20 170	949	7	2	940	152	43
Average net gain..................dollars..	27 369	17 978	14 362	56 115	(D)	(D)	6 852	4 062
Gain of—								
Less than $1,000	4 994	2 167	222	–	2	220	33	10
$1,000 to $9,999	18 378	9 050	469	–	–	469	105	32
$10,000 to $49,999	13 889	7 299	192	–	–	192	10	–
$50,000 or more	4 412	1 654	46	7	–	39	4	1
Farms with net losses.............number..	26 907	11 254	1 079	–	–	1 079	70	152
Average net loss..................dollars..	8 114	7 801	4 187	–	–	4 187	4 867	3 662
Loss of—								
Less than $1,000	5 287	1 955	365	–	–	365	27	64
$1,000 to $9,999	16 553	6 861	608	–	–	608	33	84
$10,000 to $49,999	4 663	2 300	93	–	–	93	9	2
$50,000 or more	404	138	13	–	–	13	1	2
GOVERNMENT PAYMENTS AND OTHER FARM-RELATED INCOME								
Government payments ....farms..	41 627	25 317	629	1	–	628	32	17
$1,000..	573 647	396 772	5 278	(D)	–	(D)	76	51
Other farm-related income[1]........farms..	18 682	9 281	611	7	–	604	56	73
$1,000..	69 944	34 950	1 724	14	–	1 710	33	410
Customwork and other agricultural services ....farms..	7 463	3 905	180	7	–	173	16	1
$1,000..	32 115	17 434	860	14	–	846	3	(D)
Gross cash rent or share payments ....farms..	7 899	3 574	392	–	–	392	31	58
$1,000..	30 403	13 843	741	–	–	741	30	330
Forest products and Christmas trees ....farms..	439	123	20	–	–	20	–	22
$1,000..	1 087	261	20	–	–	20	–	(D)
Other farm-related income sources ....farms..	6 689	3 659	147	–	–	147	9	10
$1,000..	6 340	3 412	102	–	–	102	1	15
COMMODITY CREDIT CORPORATION LOANS								
Total ....farms..	15 832	10 834	113	–	–	113	4	–
$1,000..	339 298	252 480	1 469	–	–	1 469	20	–
Corn ....farms..	3 591	2 617	18	–	–	18	2	–
$1,000..	108 314	87 736	433	–	–	433	(D)	–
Wheat.......................farms..	7 282	4 874	66	–	–	66	–	–
$1,000..	95 942	67 339	578	–	–	578	(D)	–
Soybeans....................farms..	1 248	939	5	–	–	5	–	–
$1,000..	20 764	(D)	27	–	–	27	(D)	–
Sorghum, barley, and oats..........farms..	10 032	6 867	63	–	–	63	1	–
$1,000..	112 774	80 668	432	–	–	432	(D)	–
Cotton.......................farms..	–	–	–	–	–	–	–	–
$1,000..	–	–	–	–	–	–	–	–
Peanuts, rye, rice, tobacco, and honey....farms..	22	1	–	–	–	–	–	–
$1,000..	503	(D)	–	–	–	–	–	–
LAND IN FARMS ACCORDING TO USE								
Total cropland....................farms..	61 615	31 789	2 010	1	3	2 006	179	171
acres..	31 385 090	19 955 591	488 775	(D)	(D)	488 837	9 119	5 593
Harvested cropland ....farms..	57 822	31 789	2 010	1	3	2 006	179	171
acres..	17 729 394	11 737 683	326 417	(D)	(D)	325 604	6 499	3 983
Farms by acres harvested:								
1 to 49 acres	12 372	3 789	960	–	3	957	149	152
50 to 99 acres	8 853	4 616	400	–	–	400	16	14
100 to 199 acres	10 361	6 058	300	–	–	300	8	1
200 to 499 acres	14 761	9 342	202	–	–	202	5	4
500 to 999 acres	8 150	5 620	90	1	–	89	1	–
1,000 to 1,999 acres...........	2 876	2 049	41	–	–	41	–	–
2,000 acres or more	449	315	17	–	–	17	–	–
Cropland:								
Pasture or grazing only................farms..	22 575	8 758	479	–	–	479	27	14
acres..	3 485 445	1 373 280	39 474	–	–	39 474	975	454
In cover crops, legumes, and soil-improvement grasses, not harvested and not pastured ....farms..	11 212	6 296	263	1	–	262	25	14
acres..	1 103 315	645 753	24 898	(D)	–	(D)	496	380
On which all crops failed ....farms..	3 341	1 689	65	–	–	65	18	2
acres..	206 231	115 617	3 020	–	–	3 020	233	(D)
In cultivated summer fallow ....farms..	25 408	16 552	360	–	–	360	9	4
acres..	6 409 506	4 526 428	57 947	–	–	57 947	300	(D)
Idle ....farms..	20 610	12 388	423	1	–	422	37	35
acres..	2 451 199	1 556 830	38 019	(D)	–	(D)	616	594
Total woodland....................farms..	12 587	5 042	460	–	1	459	26	39
acres..	718 261	291 436	15 754	–	(D)	(D)	574	1 002
Woodland pastured ....farms..	6 362	2 911	201	–	1	200	8	14
acres..	366 136	118 157	6 808	–	(D)	(D)	198	282
Woodland not pastured ....farms..	7 991	3 760	297	–	–	297	20	30
acres..	352 125	173 279	8 946	–	–	8 946	376	720

See footnotes at end of table.

Table 53. Summary by Standard Industrial Classification of Farm: 1987—Con.

[For meaning of abbreviations and symbols, see introductory text]

Item	Horticultural specialties (018)	General farms, primarily crop (019)	Livestock, except dairy, poultry, and animal specialties (021) Total	Beef cattle, except feedlots (0212)	Dairy farms (024)	Poultry and eggs (025)	Animal specialties (027)	General farms, primarily livestock and animal specialties (029)
NET CASH RETURN FROM AGRICULTURAL SALES FOR THE FARM UNIT [1]								
All farms .... number..	233	1 466	29 410	22 388	1 359	221	1 365	657
$1,000..	8 215	8 617	568 101	179 640	48 266	2 167	−4 223	6 832
Average per farm .... dollars..	35 258	5 878	19 317	8 024	35 516	9 806	−3 094	10 400
Farms with net gains [2] .... number..	167	538	17 920	13 101	1 232	87	171	244
Average net gain .... dollars..	51 281	25 374	37 824	18 576	40 158	32 744	10 372	36 764
Gain of—								
Less than $1,000	7	16	2 416	1 975	27	3	71	22
$1,000 to $9,999	78	228	7 983	6 497	253	33	74	53
$10,000 to $49,999	31	230	5 377	3 589	591	31	19	109
$50,000 or more	51	64	2 144	1 129	361	20	7	60
Farms with net losses .... number..	66	928	11 490	9 167	127	134	1 194	413
Average net loss .... dollars..	5 283	5 425	9 548	7 111	9 517	5 087	5 022	5 177
Loss of—								
Less than $1,000	21	120	2 410	1 961	21	41	203	60
$1,000 to $9,999	26	692	6 944	5 570	60	80	852	313
$10,000 to $49,999	19	108	1 904	1 522	43	11	137	37
$50,000 or more	–	8	232	144	3	2	2	3
GOVERNMENT PAYMENTS AND OTHER FARM-RELATED INCOME								
Government payments .... farms..	10	782	13 436	9 552	870	58	105	371
$1,000..	31	11 154	145 933	83 399	6 373	491	241	5 247
Other farm-related income [1] .... farms..	44	1 136	7 373	5 625	422	53	315	149
$1,000..	182	1 136	28 438	21 136	1 152	116	871	934
Customwork and other agricultural services .... farms..	–	142	2 883	2 082	196	13	78	49
$1,000..	–	720	12 176	8 815	522	(D)	203	164
Gross cash rent or share payments .... farms..	19	98	3 373	2 804	76	27	172	79
$1,000..	23	282	13 630	10 515	297	68	441	718
Forest products and Christmas trees ..... farms..	23	6	213	177	26	1	5	–
$1,000..	(D)	36	528	429	13	(D)	2	–
Other farm-related income sources .... farms..	2	120	2 316	1 618	244	16	83	63
$1,000..	(D)	97	2 105	1 378	319	(D)	226	52
COMMODITY CREDIT CORPORATION LOANS								
Total .... farms..	1	288	4 126	2 433	309	13	20	124
$1,000..	(D)	6 306	71 767	36 314	3 480	(D)	(D)	2 057
Corn .... farms..	–	55	793	353	73	1	–	32
$1,000..	–	1 756	17 092	7 248	732	(D)	–	643
Wheat .... farms..	1	135	2 011	1 347	134	5	–	55
$1,000..	(D)	2 306	(D)	15 837	1 054	34	–	527
Soybeans .... farms..	–	20	265	123	19	–	–	9
$1,000..	–	242	3 402	(D)	222	–	–	132
Sorghum, barley, and oats .... farms..	–	187	2 624	1 424	191	11	–	88
$1,000..	–	2 003	27 169	12 051	1 473	(D)	–	854
Cotton .... farms..	–	–	–	–	–	–	–	–
$1,000..	–	–	–	–	–	–	–	–
Peanuts, rye, rice, tobacco, and honey.... farms..	–	–	1	1	–	–	20	–
$1,000..	–	–	(D)	(D)	–	–	(D)	–
LAND IN FARMS ACCORDING TO USE								
Total cropland .... farms..	224	1 463	23 068	17 351	1 309	135	749	518
acres..	12 410	617 385	9 386 031	6 521 143	583 989	26 843	51 230	247 124
Harvested cropland .... farms..	224	1 391	20 041	14 834	1 260	89	330	338
acres..	6 069	353 354	4 789 005	3 100 134	362 864	13 108	9 911	120 501
Farms by acres harvested:								
1 to 49 acres	201	579	6 064	4 947	96	40	286	56
50 to 99 acres	8	142	3 415	2 787	170	14	26	32
100 to 199 acres	5	189	3 409	2 522	303	20	14	54
200 to 499 acres	9	255	4 332	2 838	495	7	1	109
500 to 999 acres	–	160	2 038	1 272	171	7	3	60
1,000 to 1,999 acres	1	55	680	412	23	1	–	26
2,000 acres or more	–	11	103	56	2	–	–	1
Cropland:								
Pasture or grazing only .... farms..	15	551	11 168	8 579	761	58	475	269
acres..	796	83 774	1 790 736	1 397 278	109 795	5 699	25 408	55 054
In cover crops, legumes, and soil-improvement grasses, not harvested and not pastured .... farms..	19	256	3 920	2 887	220	26	56	117
acres..	568	26 671	364 275	279 015	15 667	1 257	4 409	18 841
On which all crops failed .... farms..	4	144	1 257	945	87	11	35	29
acres..	(D)	9 426	70 928	52 601	4 484	431	1 296	747
In cultivated summer fallow .... farms..	5	466	7 326	5 254	426	27	60	173
acres..	(D)	102 067	1 626 671	1 176 183	53 762	1 999	7 230	32 869
Idle .... farms..	35	405	6 501	4 521	483	44	82	177
acres..	4 777	42 093	744 416	515 932	37 417	4 349	2 976	19 112
Total woodland .... farms..	37	345	5 913	4 492	364	29	222	110
acres..	990	16 092	349 385	273 346	24 311	984	6 736	10 997
Woodland pastured .... farms..	7	168	3 656	2 882	216	13	193	65
acres..	195	7 377	207 670	168 619	14 291	463	3 605	6 890
Woodland not pastured .... farms..	32	233	3 201	2 321	218	20	113	67
acres..	795	8 715	141 715	104 727	10 020	521	2 931	4 107

See footnotes at end of table.

Table 53. **Summary by Standard Industrial Classification of Farm: 1987** —Con.

[For meaning of abbreviations and symbols, see introductory text]

Item	Total	Cash grains (011)	Field crops, except cash grains (013)				Vegetables and melons (016)	Fruits and tree nuts (017)
			Total	Cotton (0131)	Tobacco (0132)	Sugarcane and sugar beets; Irish potatoes; field crops, except cash grains, n.e.c. (0133, 0134, 0139)		
LAND IN FARMS ACCORDING TO USE—Con.								
Pastureland and rangeland other than cropland and woodland pastured .... farms..	32 362	13 074	680	1	1	678	27	28
acres..	13 254 094	3 519 986	113 031	(D)	(D)	(D)	2 166	788
Land in house lots, ponds, roads, wasteland, etc. .... farms..	44 335	19 254	1 309	1	2	1 306	120	124
acres..	1 271 074	629 984	23 333	(D)	(D)	23 318	900	1 540
Cropland under federal acreage reduction programs:								
Annual commodity acreage adjustment programs .... farms..	34 658	22 723	360	1	-	359	21	4
acres..	3 956 196	2 810 100	27 102	(D)	-	(D)	381	(D)
Conservation reserve program .... farms..	5 630	2 965	148	1	-	147	4	2
acres..	810 662	453 827	20 429	(D)	-	(D)	145	(D)
Value of land and buildings[1] .... farms..	68 580	31 424	2 028	7	2	2 019	222	195
$1,000..	19 068 481	10 405 684	390 339	(D)	(D)	(D)	23 033	17 766
Average per farm .... dollars..	278 047	331 138	192 475	(D)	(D)	(D)	103 752	91 108
Average per acre .... dollars..	413	437	604	(D)	(D)	(D)	1 453	2 312
Farms by value group:								
$1 to $39,999	10 024	2 156	372	-	1	371	78	57
$40,000 to $69,999	9 571	3 534	344	-	1	343	39	95
$70,000 to $99,999	7 001	2 910	301	-	-	301	37	30
$100,000 to $149,999	8 596	4 059	341	-	-	341	32	21
$150,000 to $199,999	6 313	3 175	226	-	-	226	8	16
$200,000 to $499,999	16 476	9 223	296	-	-	296	24	36
$500,000 to $999,999	7 579	4 679	107	7	-	100	3	-
$1,000,000 to $1,999,999	2 396	1 579	33	-	-	33	1	-
$2,000,000 to $4,999,999	535	282	5	-	-	5	-	-
$5,000,000 or more	89	27	3	-	-	3	-	-
VALUE OF MACHINERY AND EQUIPMENT[1]								
Estimated market value of all machinery and equipment .... farms..	68 391	31 333	1 998	7	2	1 989	222	195
$1,000..	3 447 863	1 895 756	83 491	(D)	(D)	62 430	5 020	3 293
Farms by value group:								
$1 to $4,999	5 812	1 290	325	-	1	324	58	47
$5,000 to $9,999	11 585	3 732	672	-	1	671	66	64
$10,000 to $19,999	11 722	4 644	308	-	-	306	11	31
$20,000 to $49,999	16 724	8 400	380	-	-	380	61	34
$50,000 to $99,999	12 176	7 018	141	-	-	141	16	17
$100,000 to $199,999	7 277	4 448	115	-	-	108	9	2
$200,000 to $499,999	2 860	1 700	50	-	-	50	1	-
$500,000 or more	235	101	7	-	-	7	-	-
SELECTED MACHINERY AND EQUIPMENT[1]								
Motortrucks, including pickups .... farms..	63 093	29 345	1 645	7	2	1 636	199	156
number..	159 329	81 885	3 242	(D)	(D)	3 190	365	212
Wheel tractors .... farms..	60 459	28 693	1 666	7	2	1 657	216	158
number..	160 647	74 408	3 389	(D)	(D)	3 357	459	267
Less than 40 horsepower (PTO) .... farms..	25 210	9 910	821	-	2	819	146	117
number..	36 591	14 981	1 120	-	(D)	(D)	247	171
40 horsepower (PTO) or more .... farms..	50 577	26 179	1 165	7	1	1 157	113	74
number..	112 056	59 427	2 269	(D)	(D)	(D)	212	96
Grain and bean combines .... farms..	35 608	21 277	537	7	1	529	30	10
number..	43 501	26 687	607	(D)	(D)	599	30	10
Cottonpickers and strippers .... farms..	1	1	-	-	-	-	-	-
number..	(D)	(D)	-	-	-	-	-	-
Mower conditioners .... farms..	18 793	7 151	628	7	-	621	61	43
number..	20 167	7 646	702	7	-	695	69	47
Pickup balers .... farms..	26 083	10 102	789	7	-	782	16	11
number..	31 892	12 157	990	14	-	976	16	11
AGRICULTURAL CHEMICALS[1]								
Commercial fertilizer .... farms..	47 723	26 519	1 154	7	2	1 145	179	122
acres on which used..	13 852 822	8 939 076	211 760	(D)	(D)	205 437	6 041	2 427
Lime .... farms..	2 685	1 172	75	7	-	68	21	-
acres on which used..	154 622	80 609	3 176	700	-	2 476	426	-
tons..	369 024	186 908	7 239	1 400	-	5 839	1 290	-
Sprays, dusts, granules, fumigants, etc., to control—								
Insects on hay and other crops .... farms..	19 416	10 691	514	-	2	512	113	62
acres on which used..	3 015 580	1 952 382	104 837	-	(D)	(D)	3 439	1 099
Nematodes in crops .... farms..	716	387	16	-	1	15	15	-
acres on which used..	87 304	52 629	2 186	-	(D)	(D)	38	-
Diseases in crops and orchards .... farms..	1 055	477	47	-	1	46	59	88
acres on which used..	125 065	88 160	719	-	(D)	(D)	1 391	1 287
Weeds, grass, or brush in crops and pasture .... farms..	38 950	20 830	762	7	1	754	83	95
acres on which used..	8 637 062	5 521 094	107 134	(D)	(D)	103 633	4 344	1 431
Chemicals for defoliation or for growth control of crops or thinning of fruit .... farms..	614	292	19	-	1	18	9	20
acres on which used..	68 839	35 337	125	-	(D)	(D)	360	480

See footnotes at end of table.

Table 53. **Summary by Standard Industrial Classification of Farm: 1987**—Con.

[For meaning of abbreviations and symbols, see introductory text]

Item	Horticultural specialties (018)	General farms, primarily crop (019)	Livestock, except dairy, poultry, and animal specialties (021) Total	Beef cattle, except feedlots (0212)	Dairy farms (024)	Poultry and eggs (025)	Animal specialties (027)	General farms, primarily livestock and animal specialties (029)
LAND IN FARMS ACCORDING TO USE—Con.								
Pastureland and rangeland other than cropland and woodland pastured .... farms..	26	714	15 904	12 555	739	63	642	463
acres..	4 496	253 771	8 838 835	7 341 082	167 602	4 337	58 201	290 881
Land in house lots, ponds, roads, wasteland, etc. .... farms..	127	1 025	19 732	14 411	1 069	159	1 015	401
acres..	1 406	24 749	532 470	377 003	29 452	2 212	10 273	14 755
Cropland under federal acreage reduction programs:								
Annual commodity acreage adjustment programs .... farms..	2	638	9 896	6 627	744	34	10	228
acres..	(D)	71 065	969 007	614 868	51 772	3 222	505	22 634
Conservation reserve program .... farms..	2	143	2 142	1 692	70	6	23	125
acres..	(D)	22 822	261 046	233 202	5 504	623	1 962	24 238
Value of land and buildings[1] .... farms..	233	1 468	29 410	22 388	1 359	221	1 365	657
$1,000..	57 398	414 578	6 987 939	5 044 439	392 579	31 027	128 710	219 410
Average per farm .... dollars..	246 343	282 794	237 604	225 319	288 873	140 394	94 293	333 957
Average per acre .... dollars..	2 730	455	364	343	491	1 185	1 074	374
Farms by value group:								
$1 to $39,999	85	219	6 417	4 811	91	80	455	14
$40,000 to $69,999	31	239	4 856	3 849	75	27	322	69
$70,000 to $99,999	31	196	3 090	2 435	113	31	202	60
$100,000 to $149,999	13	134	3 521	2 798	149	31	185	110
$150,000 to $199,999	6	108	2 367	1 912	216	13	92	84
$200,000 to $499,999	47	348	5 673	4 193	529	21	73	206
$500,000 to $999,999	10	171	2 347	1 531	143	15	16	88
$1,000,000 to $1,999,999	6	37	859	598	37	3	20	21
$2,000,000 to $4,999,999	2	10	228	152	4	–	–	4
$5,000,000 or more	2	4	52	39	–	–	–	1
VALUE OF MACHINERY AND EQUIPMENT[1]								
Estimated market value of all machinery and equipment .... farms..	233	1 458	29 350	22 333	1 359	221	1 365	657
$1,000..	11 638	88 338	1 245 820	769 772	103 504	6 155	18 591	28 058
Farms by value group:								
$1 to $4,999	31	96	3 502	2 812	80	35	269	79
$5,000 to $9,999	50	430	5 500	4 412	29	89	710	243
$10,000 to $19,999	34	294	5 594	4 414	124	35	205	42
$20,000 to $49,999	61	229	6 975	5 354	326	23	131	104
$50,000 to $99,999	27	196	4 206	2 956	419	16	25	95
$100,000 to $199,999	8	142	2 177	1 355	284	19	5	68
$200,000 to $499,999	20	68	882	497	89	4	20	26
$500,000 or more	2	3	114	33	8	–	–	–
SELECTED MACHINERY AND EQUIPMENT[1]								
Motortrucks, including pickups .... farms..	201	1 303	27 080	20 508	1 259	211	1 152	542
number..	616	3 168	63 015	45 403	3 469	408	1 626	1 319
Wheel tractors .... farms..	199	1 315	25 232	19 068	1 266	147	993	574
number..	499	3 177	60 869	43 778	4 299	349	1 465	1 466
Less than 40 horsepower (PTO) .... farms..	138	670	11 855	8 936	504	100	650	301
number..	273	979	18 455	13 820	837	150	910	468
40 horsepower (PTO) or more .... farms..	107	959	19 877	14 838	1 162	99	437	405
number..	226	2 198	42 414	29 958	3 462	199	555	998
Grain and bean combines .... farms..	44	598	11 836	8 307	890	49	59	278
number..	51	766	14 157	9 928	1 043	66	59	325
Cottonpickers and strippers .... farms..	–	–	–	–	–	–	–	–
number..	–	–	–	–	–	–	–	–
Mower conditioners .... farms..	35	449	9 299	7 218	795	23	129	190
number..	44	493	9 949	7 704	856	23	135	203
Pickup balers .... farms..	31	541	13 085	10 143	982	28	154	244
number..	32	797	16 084	12 407	1 296	30	155	324
AGRICULTURAL CHEMICALS[1]								
Commercial fertilizer .... farms..	134	914	16 962	12 558	1 136	56	263	284
acres on which used..	5 280	268 752	3 982 044	2 598 906	315 574	10 470	6 889	104 509
Lime .... farms..	26	58	1 079	724	164	1	19	70
acres on which used..	610	2 612	56 922	36 519	6 315	(D)	(D)	3 464
tons..	1 092	5 028	142 141	85 784	16 254	(D)	(D)	8 242
Sprays, dusts, granules, fumigants, etc.. to control—								
Insects on hay and other crops .... farms..	104	489	6 463	4 294	757	26	36	161
acres on which used..	2 478	80 070	771 279	436 025	75 079	2 017	422	22 478
Nematodes in crops .... farms..	6	11	261	145	12	–	–	8
acres on which used..	11	1 497	29 394	12 105	1 762	–	–	387
Diseases in crops and orchards .... farms..	52	23	267	163	8	8	14	12
acres on which used..	679	1 133	27 288	13 457	1 526	32	924	1 926
Weeds, grass, or brush in crops and pasture .... farms..	116	682	12 975	9 490	838	65	211	293
acres on which used..	5 608	162 554	2 589 730	1 701 437	152 119	8 355	9 327	75 386
Chemicals for defoliation or for growth control of crops or thinning of fruit .... farms..	26	7	218	150	22	1	–	–
acres on which used..	195	(D)	26 982	10 995	4 893	(D)	–	–

See footnotes at end of table.

[For meaning of abbreviations and symbols, see introductory text]

Item	Total	Cash grains (011)	Field crops, except cash grains (013)				Vegetables and melons (016)	Fruits and tree nuts (017)
			Total	Cotton (0131)	Tobacco (0132)	Sugarcane and sugar beets; Irish potatoes; field crops, except cash grains, n.e.c. (0133, 0134, 0139)		
TENURE AND RACE OF OPERATOR								
All operators	68 579	31 789	2 010	1	3	2 006	179	171
Full owners	29 956	10 576	1 318	-	2	1 316	113	144
Part owners	27 967	14 855	467	1	-	466	35	19
Tenants	10 656	6 358	225	-	1	224	31	8
White	68 304	31 704	1 995	1	3	1 991	178	171
Full owners	29 784	10 534	1 306	-	2	1 304	113	144
Part owners	27 901	14 828	467	1	-	466	35	19
Tenants	10 619	6 342	222	-	1	221	30	8
Black and other races	275	85	15	-	-	15	1	-
Full owners	172	42	12	-	-	12	-	-
Part owners	66	27	-	-	-	-	-	-
Tenants	37	16	3	-	-	3	1	-
OWNED AND RENTED LAND								
Land owned _____ farms	58 533	25 642	1 799	1	2	1 796	149	163
acres	24 331 897	11 493 940	455 638	(D)	(D)	(D)	9 400	12 745
Owned land in farms _____ farms	57 929	25 431	1 786	1	2	1 782	148	163
acres	21 178 322	10 125 830	357 073	(D)	(D)	(D)	7 483	7 830
Land rented or leased from others _____ farms	38 908	21 335	701	1	1	699	66	27
acres	25 865 815	14 448 943	295 049	(D)	(D)	(D)	5 320	1 303
Rented or leased land in farms _____ farms	36 623	21 213	692	1	1	690	66	27
acres	25 450 197	14 271 167	284 820	(D)	(D)	(D)	5 276	1 293
Land rented or leased to others _____ farms	11 944	5 076	407	-	-	407	27	40
acres	3 569 193	1 545 886	108 794	-	-	108 794	1 961	5 125
OPERATOR CHARACTERISTICS								
Operators by place of residence:								
On farm operated	45 527	19 323	1 250	1	3	1 246	136	113
Not on farm operated	17 871	10 196	604	-	-	604	35	47
Not reported	5 181	2 270	156	-	-	156	8	11
Operators by principal occupation:								
Farming	42 607	21 948	776	1	-	775	80	51
Other	25 972	9 841	1 234	-	3	1 231	99	120
Operators by days of work off farm:								
None	29 462	14 497	548	-	-	548	67	43
Any	34 654	15 098	1 343	1	3	1 339	107	125
1 to 99 days	7 620	4 178	198	1	-	197	17	15
100 to 199 days	5 357	2 715	162	-	-	162	19	21
200 days or more	21 677	8 207	983	-	3	980	71	89
Not reported	4 463	2 194	119	-	-	119	5	3
Operators by years on present farm:								
2 years or less	3 511	1 521	129	-	-	129	13	10
3 or 4 years	3 873	1 723	159	-	1	158	16	10
5 to 9 years	8 552	3 715	337	-	-	337	37	45
10 years or more	40 624	19 397	1 060	1	1	1 058	76	88
Average years on present farm	21.3	22.4	17.0	28.0	15.0	17.0	15.8	13.5
Not reported	12 019	5 433	325	-	1	324	37	18
Operators by age group:								
Under 25 years	1 712	891	27	-	-	26	-	1
25 to 34 years	9 531	4 542	254	-	1	254	21	12
35 to 44 years	12 471	5 594	421	-	1	420	37	19
45 to 49 years	5 926	2 693	168	-	-	168	22	26
50 to 54 years	6 781	3 006	219	-	1	218	14	21
55 to 59 years	7 581	3 496	244	1	-	243	12	27
60 to 64 years	8 407	3 951	238	-	-	238	22	27
65 to 69 years	6 564	3 117	173	-	-	173	17	13
70 years and over	9 606	4 499	266	-	-	266	34	23
Average age	52.0	52.0	52.0	56.0	39.7	52.1	54.1	54.7
Operators by sex:								
Male	65 619	30 612	1 883	1	3	1 879	161	162
Female	2 960	1 177	127	-	-	127	18	9
Operators of Spanish origin (see text)	108	41	4	-	-	4	1	1
FARMS BY TYPE OF ORGANIZATION								
Individual or family (sole proprietorship) _____ farms	60 202	27 794	1 809	-	3	1 806	159	149
acres	36 420 471	19 703 723	505 436	-	(D)	(D)	10 059	6 258
Partnership _____ farms	5 889	2 841	140	1	-	139	13	13
acres	6 151 580	2 971 874	84 522	(D)	-	(D)	1 386	1 856
Corporation:								
Family held _____ farms	1 942	921	47	-	-	47	5	7
acres	3 446 745	1 545 607	43 184	-	-	43 184	(D)	(D)
More than 10 stockholders _____ farms	23	7	1	-	-	1	-	-
10 or less stockholders _____ farms	1 919	914	46	-	-	46	5	7
Other than family held _____ farms	158	55	8	-	-	8	-	-
acres	159 376	52 733	8 180	-	-	8 180	-	-
More than 10 stockholders _____ farms	17	9	-	-	-	-	-	-
10 or less stockholders _____ farms	141	46	8	-	-	8	-	-
Other—cooperative, estate or trust, institutional, etc: _____ farms	388	178	6	-	-	6	2	2
acres	450 347	123 060	571	-	-	571	(D)	(D)

See footnotes at end of table.

Table 53. **Summary by Standard Industrial Classification of Farm: 1987**—Con.

[For meaning of abbreviations and symbols, see introductory text]

Item	Horticultural specialties (018)	General farms, primarily crop (019)	Livestock, except dairy, poultry, and animal specialties (021) Total	Beef cattle, except feedlots (0212)	Dairy farms (024)	Poultry and eggs (025)	Animal specialties (027)	General farms, primarily livestock and animal specialties (029)
TENURE AND RACE OF OPERATOR								
All operators	224	1 463	29 037	21 861	1 391	197	1 452	666
Full owners	185	749	14 817	11 534	416	139	1 126	371
Part owners	23	557	10 729	7 709	821	42	186	233
Tenants	16	157	3 491	2 618	154	16	138	62
White	222	1 460	28 888	21 762	1 387	194	1 442	663
Full owners	183	748	14 715	11 463	414	137	1 121	369
Part owners	23	555	10 697	7 690	819	41	185	232
Tenants	16	157	3 476	2 609	154	16	136	62
Black and other races	2	3	149	99	4	3	10	3
Full owners	2	1	102	71	2	2	7	2
Part owners	-	2	32	19	2	1	1	1
Tenants	-	-	15	9	-	-	2	-
OWNED AND RENTED LAND								
Land owned ... farms	208	1 309	25 714	19 381	1 240	181	1 316	610
acres	12 172	435 195	11 019 759	8 475 098	403 201	23 870	144 834	321 243
Owned land in farms ... farms	208	1 306	25 546	19 243	1 237	181	1 314	604
acres	10 445	402 054	9 493 475	7 196 696	385 722	19 284	92 874	276 352
Land rented or leased from others ... farms	39	718	14 355	10 436	977	61	331	298
acres	8 857	516 023	9 611 596	7 487 846	423 300	16 009	50 005	289 410
Rented or leased land in farms ... farms	39	714	14 220	10 327	975	58	324	295
acres	8 857	509 943	9 613 246	7 315 878	419 632	15 092	33 466	287 405
Land rented or leased to others ... farms	20	202	5 835	4 681	104	43	251	139
acres	1 727	39 221	1 724 634	1 450 370	21 147	5 303	68 499	46 896
OPERATOR CHARACTERISTICS								
Operators by place of residence:								
On farm operated	123	1 079	20 612	15 027	1 237	154	1 096	404
Not on farm operated	84	282	6 135	5 068	75	24	236	153
Not reported	17	102	2 290	1 766	79	19	120	109
Operators by principal occupation:								
Farming	98	767	16 840	12 216	1 262	102	301	382
Other	126	696	12 197	9 645	129	95	1 151	284
Operators by days of work off farm:								
None	102	544	12 011	8 752	1 015	78	261	296
Any	111	852	15 152	11 641	295	109	1 150	312
1 to 99 days	26	160	2 731	1 994	135	16	84	62
100 to 199 days	16	103	2 123	1 663	39	17	115	25
200 days or more	67	589	10 298	7 984	121	76	951	225
Not reported	11	67	1 874	1 466	81	12	41	56
Operators by years on present farm:								
2 years or less	9	78	1 528	1 096	45	11	145	22
3 or 4 years	20	79	1 624	1 204	43	14	155	30
5 to 9 years	34	196	3 684	2 698	136	29	275	64
10 years or more	133	883	16 934	12 837	972	103	628	350
Average years on present farm	16.6	20.2	20.9	21.3	23.0	19.9	12.3	22.3
Not reported	28	227	5 267	4 026	195	40	249	200
Operators by age group:								
Under 25 years	1	24	719	474	19	2	24	4
25 to 34 years	23	162	4 015	2 719	196	25	180	81
35 to 44 years	54	303	5 205	3 637	288	43	405	102
45 to 49 years	29	128	2 430	1 764	133	13	200	73
50 to 54 years	22	178	2 842	2 197	194	21	187	77
55 to 59 years	31	176	3 175	2 401	187	21	123	89
60 to 64 years	24	173	3 522	2 714	183	30	149	88
65 to 69 years	10	114	2 886	2 362	91	14	74	53
70 years and over	30	185	4 241	3 603	100	28	101	99
Average age	51.5	51.7	52.2	53.4	50.1	52.3	48.4	53.5
Operators by sex:								
Male	195	1 403	27 748	20 810	1 341	181	1 309	624
Female	29	60	1 289	1 051	50	16	143	42
Operators of Spanish origin (see text)	-	2	51	43	2	-	6	-
FARMS BY TYPE OF ORGANIZATION								
Individual or family (sole proprietorship) ... farms	158	1 309	25 645	19 611	1 085	174	1 357	563
acres	6 123	697 197	14 472 707	11 257 360	561 918	28 198	111 643	317 209
Partnership ... farms	15	113	2 379	1 654	248	9	81	57
acres	543	154 380	2 686 098	1 938 464	179 749	3 642	9 720	57 809
Corporation:								
Family held ... farms	47	29	772	434	53	11	21	29
acres	12 310	56 686	1 682 438	1 109 047	58 834	2 461	2 975	40 298
More than 10 stockholders ... farms	-	-	11	4	2	2	-	-
10 or less stockholders ... farms	47	29	761	430	51	9	21	29
Other than family held ... farms	4	1	81	41	2	2	1	4
acres	326	(D)	89 887	70 592	(D)	(D)	(D)	5 401
More than 10 stockholders ... farms	-	1	6	2	-	-	1	-
10 or less stockholders ... farms	4	-	75	39	2	2	-	4
Other—cooperative, estate or trust, institutional, etc. ... farms	-	11	160	121	3	1	12	13
acres	-	(D)	175 590	137 111	(D)	(D)	(D)	143 040

See footnotes at end of table.

Table 53. Summary by Standard Industrial Classification of Farm: 1987—Con.

[For meaning of abbreviations and symbols, see introductory text]

Item	Total	Cash grains (011)	Field crops, except cash grains (013)				Vegetables and melons (016)	Fruits and tree nuts (017)
			Total	Cotton (0131)	Tobacco (0132)	Sugarcane and sugar beets; Irish potatoes; field crops, except cash grains, n.e.c. (0133, 0134, 0139)		
FARMS BY SIZE								
1 to 9 acres	3 669	139	11	–	2	9	38	37
10 to 49 acres	6 222	1 351	475	–	–	475	87	83
50 to 69 acres	1 849	549	125	–	1	124	8	16
70 to 99 acres	4 690	1 747	293	–	–	293	17	15
100 to 139 acres	3 117	1 270	138	–	–	138	10	10
140 to 179 acres	5 854	2 956	227	–	–	227	4	1
180 to 219 acres	2 307	1 000	99	–	–	99	3	2
220 to 259 acres	2 845	1 354	98	–	–	98	1	2
260 to 499 acres	11 553	6 215	237	–	–	237	8	2
500 to 999 acres	12 093	7 025	175	–	–	175	1	3
1,000 to 1,999 acres	9 304	5 580	85	–	–	85	2	–
2,000 acres or more	5 056	2 603	47	1	–	46	–	–
FARMS BY STANDARD INDUSTRIAL CLASSIFICATION								
Cash grains (011)	31 789	31 789	–	–	–	–	–	–
Field crops, except cash grains (013)	2 010	–	2 010	1	3	2 008	–	–
Cotton (0131)	1	–	1	1	–	–	–	–
Tobacco (0132)	3	–	3	–	3	–	–	–
Sugarcane and sugar beets; Irish potatoes; field crops, except cash grains, n.e.c. (0133, 0134, 0139)	2 008	–	2 008	–	–	2 008	–	–
Vegetables and melons (016)	179	–	–	–	–	–	179	–
Fruits and tree nuts (017)	171	–	–	–	–	–	–	171
Horticultural specialties (018)	224	–	–	–	–	–	–	–
General farms, primarily crop (019)	1 463	–	–	–	–	–	–	–
Livestock, except dairy, poultry, and animal specialties (021)	29 037	–	–	–	–	–	–	–
Beef cattle, except feedlots (0212)	21 861	–	–	–	–	–	–	–
Dairy farms (024)	1 391	–	–	–	–	–	–	–
Poultry and eggs (025)	197	–	–	–	–	–	–	–
Animal specialties (027)	1 452	–	–	–	–	–	–	–
General farms, primarily livestock and animal specialties (029)	668	–	–	–	–	–	–	–
LIVESTOCK								
Cattle and calves inventory ...... farms	40 785	12 152	348	1	1	346	23	15
number	5 539 292	849 354	12 964	(D)	(D)	(D)	508	251
Farms with—								
1 to 9	4 367	1 159	157	–	1	156	12	8
10 to 49	16 841	5 345	132	1	–	131	6	7
50 to 99	8 529	2 939	31	–	–	31	2	–
100 to 199	6 150	1 982	18	–	–	18	–	–
200 to 499	3 580	700	6	–	–	6	1	–
500 or more	1 318	57	4	–	–	4	–	–
Cows and heifers that had calved ...... farms	33 157	10 466	259	1	1	257	17	13
number	1 451 324	386 622	4 694	(D)	(D)	(D)	233	97
Beef cows ...... farms	31 475	10 321	251	–	1	249	15	11
number	1 354 649	383 996	4 637	(D)	(D)	(D)	230	(D)
Farms with—								
1 to 9	6 299	1 788	125	–	1	124	11	7
10 to 49	17 123	5 943	106	1	–	105	3	4
50 to 99	5 108	1 873	16	–	–	16	1	–
100 to 199	2 115	608	2	–	–	2	–	–
200 to 499	714	103	1	–	–	1	–	–
500 or more	116	6	1	–	–	1	–	–
Milk cows ...... farms	3 093	385	16	–	–	16	3	2
number	96 675	2 626	57	–	–	57	3	(D)
Farms with—								
1 to 4	1 195	284	15	–	–	15	3	2
5 to 9	150	27	–	–	–	–	–	–
10 to 49	979	66	1	–	–	1	–	–
50 to 99	582	7	–	–	–	–	–	–
100 to 199	163	1	–	–	–	–	–	–
200 to 499	21	–	–	–	–	–	–	–
500 or more	3	–	–	–	–	–	–	–
Heifers and heifer calves ...... farms	31 410	9 510	237	1	1	235	18	10
number	1 632 193	211 607	4 222	(D)	(D)	(D)	153	66
Steers, steer calves, bulls, and bull calves ...... farms	35 035	10 617	252	1	1	250	16	11
number	2 455 775	250 925	4 048	(D)	(D)	(D)	122	86
Cattle and calves sold ...... farms	41 498	12 066	291	(D)	1	260	17	8
number	7 310 338	437 109	6 923	(D)	–	(D)	242	79
$1,000	4 905 335	181 436	2 764	(D)	–	(D)	106	29
Calves ...... farms	18 518	5 339	124	–	–	123	9	4
number	468 328	114 570	1 897	(D)	–	(D)	43	37
$1,000	145 961	36 227	571	(D)	–	(D)	12	12
Cattle ...... farms	34 216	9 473	179	–	–	178	11	7
number	6 842 010	322 539	5 026	(D)	–	(D)	199	42
$1,000	4 159 374	145 209	2 193	(D)	–	(D)	96	17
Fattened on grain and concentrates ...... farms	4 620	978	25	–	–	25	1	2
number	4 551 726	32 288	259	–	–	259	(D)	(D)
$1,000	3 041 522	18 537	128	–	–	128	(D)	(D)

See footnotes at end of table.

[For meaning of abbreviations and symbols, see introductory text]

Item	Horticultural specialties (018)	General farms, primarily crop (019)	Livestock, except dairy, poultry, and animal specialties (021) Total	Beef cattle, except feedlots (0212)	Dairy farms (024)	Poultry and eggs (025)	Animal specialties (027)	General farms, primarily livestock and animal specialties (029)
FARMS BY SIZE								
1 to 9 acres	116	38	2 882	1 534	61	46	315	6
10 to 49 acres	63	279	3 155	2 186	37	54	602	36
50 to 69 acres	9	69	944	794	19	5	101	4
70 to 99 acres	10	125	2 289	1 897	39	14	131	10
100 to 139 acres	5	61	1 454	1 213	34	4	86	45
140 to 179 acres	2	111	2 261	1 849	99	22	81	90
180 to 219 acres	4	40	1 027	858	53	6	96	37
220 to 259 acres	3	53	1 190	969	75	6	18	45
260 to 499 acres	7	199	4 366	3 342	323	26	45	125
500 to 999 acres	4	213	4 061	2 955	435	7	23	126
1,000 to 1,999 acres	-	170	3 160	2 287	188	7	9	103
2,000 acres or more	1	105	2 228	1 677	28	-	5	39
FARMS BY STANDARD INDUSTRIAL CLASSIFICATION								
Cash grains (011)	-	-	-	-	-	-	-	-
Field crops, except cash grains (013)	-	-	-	-	-	-	-	-
Cotton (0131)	-	-	-	-	-	-	-	-
Tobacco (0132)	-	-	-	-	-	-	-	-
Sugarcane and sugar beets; Irish potatoes; field crops, except cash grains, n.e.c. (0133, 0134, 0139)	-	-	-	-	-	-	-	-
Vegetables and melons (016)	-	-	-	-	-	-	-	-
Fruits and tree nuts (017)	-	-	-	-	-	-	-	-
Horticultural specialties (018)	224	-	-	-	-	-	-	-
General farms, primarily crop (019)	-	1 463	-	-	-	-	-	-
Livestock, except dairy, poultry, and animal specialties (021)	-	-	29 037	21 861	-	-	-	-
Beef cattle, except feedlots (0212)	-	-	21 861	21 861	-	-	-	-
Dairy farms (024)	-	-	-	-	1 391	-	-	-
Poultry and eggs (025)	-	-	-	-	-	197	-	-
Animal specialties (027)	-	-	-	-	-	-	1 452	-
General farms, primarily livestock and animal specialties (029)	-	-	-	-	-	-	-	666
LIVESTOCK								
Cattle and calves inventory ... farms..	12	830	25 425	20 447	1 387	65	162	336
number..	179	76 054	4 391 648	2 184 387	167 607	1 881	1 462	37 384
Farms with—								
1 to 9	9	150	2 643	1 994	20	32	124	53
10 to 49	2	270	10 668	9 134	273	23	32	81
50 to 99	-	181	4 875	3 923	417	6	5	73
100 to 199	1	136	3 479	2 712	463	2	1	68
200 to 499	-	75	2 543	1 920	199	2	-	54
500 or more	-	18	1 217	764	15	-	-	7
Cows and heifers that had calved ... farms..	6	691	19 891	16 380	1 382	48	86	298
number..	92	31 196	922 339	732 722	87 917	463	698	16 973
Beef cows ... farms..	5	671	19 609	16 206	285	44	76	187
number..	(D)	30 633	916 085	729 046	9 610	454	681	8 137
Farms with—								
1 to 9	4	150	4 091	3 376	62	25	57	39
10 to 49	-	316	10 462	8 781	158	18	16	97
50 to 99	1	132	3 001	2 354	53	1	2	28
100 to 199	-	57	1 421	1 151	8	-	1	18
200 to 499	-	14	587	465	4	-	-	5
500 or more	-	2	107	79	-	-	-	-
Milk cows ... farms..	1	49	1 005	706	1 377	8	13	234
number..	(D)	563	6 254	3 674	78 307	9	17	8 836
Farms with—								
1 to 4	1	31	792	568	15	8	13	31
5 to 9	-	1	81	59	33	-	-	8
10 to 49	-	13	104	67	666	-	-	129
50 to 99	-	3	22	8	496	-	-	52
100 to 199	-	1	5	4	143	-	-	13
200 to 499	-	-	1	-	19	-	-	1
500 or more	-	-	-	-	3	-	-	-
Heifers and heifer calves ... farms..	9	642	19 276	15 487	1 279	41	94	294
number..	83	20 540	1 326 273	609 714	57 929	397	308	10 446
Steers, steer calves, bulls, and bull calves ... farms..	10	721	21 947	17 540	1 017	54	105	285
number..	24	24 318	2 143 036	841 951	21 764	1 031	456	9 965
Cattle and calves sold ... farms..	7	777	26 557	21 521	1 379	44	70	312
number..	65	47 947	6 741 671	2 088 907	65 103	1 452	681	19 066
$1,000..	24	20 971	4 070 015	993 193	19 982	797	248	8 961
Calves ... farms..	4	315	11 555	10 204	949	20	46	153
number..	46	8 058	316 519	285 972	22 201	192	413	4 352
$1,000..	16	2 605	100 858	91 367	4 248	44	104	1 265
Cattle ... farms..	5	669	22 386	17 839	1 159	34	31	262
number..	19	39 889	6 425 152	1 802 935	32 902	1 260	268	14 714
$1,000..	8	18 366	3 969 157	901 826	15 734	753	144	7 696
Fattened on grain and concentrates ... farms..	-	95	3 332	577	122	7	8	50
number..	-	4 887	4 508 740	14 644	3 156	354	94	1 945
$1,000..	-	3 047	3 016 496	8 253	1 764	245	64	1 240

See footnotes at end of table.

Table 53. **Summary by Standard Industrial Classification of Farm: 1987**—Con.

[For meaning of abbreviations and symbols, see introductory text]

Item	Total	Cash grains (011)	Field crops, except cash grains (013)				Vegetables and melons (016)	Fruits and tree nuts (017)
			Total	Cotton (0131)	Tobacco (0132)	Sugarcane and sugar beets; Irish potatoes; field crops, except cash grains, n.e.c. (0133, 0134, 0139)		
LIVESTOCK—Con.								
Hogs and pigs inventory .... farms..	6 768	1 340	34	-	-	34	7	5
number..	1 516 878	119 948	600	-	-	600	258	(D)
Farms with—								
1 to 24	1 916	467	25	-	-	25	3	5
25 to 49	828	205	7	-	-	7	2	-
50 to 99	1 087	258	1	-	-	1	2	-
100 to 199	1 092	243	1	-	-	1	-	-
200 to 499	1 226	143	-	-	-	-	-	-
500 or more	619	24	-	-	-	-	-	-
Used or to be used for breeding .... farms..	4 596	818	11	-	-	11	2	1
number..	191 079	15 546	89	-	-	89	(D)	(D)
Other .... farms..	6 286	1 240	32	-	-	32	7	5
number..	1 325 799	104 402	511	-	-	511	(D)	16
Hogs and pigs sold .... farms..	7 090	1 415	26	-	-	26	6	1
number..	2 759 676	185 337	1 116	-	-	1 116	(D)	(D)
$1,000..	284 375	17 931	84	-	-	84	(D)	(D)
Feeder pigs .... farms..	1 869	297	7	-	-	7	2	1
number..	514 394	40 055	428	-	-	428	(D)	(D)
$1,000..	23 029	1 661	12	-	-	12	(D)	(D)
Litters of pigs farrowed between—								
Dec. 1 of preceding year and Nov. 30 ... farms..	4 819	878	12	-	-	12	3	1
number..	295 974	20 255	107	-	-	107	(D)	(D)
Dec. 1 and May 31 .... farms..	4 455	775	10	-	-	10	2	1
number..	149 414	10 023	47	-	-	47	(D)	(D)
June 1 and Nov. 30 .... farms..	4 403	794	11	-	-	11	3	1
number..	146 560	10 232	60	-	-	60	(D)	(D)
Sheep and lambs of all ages inventory..... farms..	2 400	684	37	-	-	37	7	3
number..	249 303	64 953	977	-	-	977	206	(D)
Ewes 1 year old or older .... farms..	2 195	625	29	-	-	29	7	3
number..	129 607	40 174	750	-	-	750	193	34
Sheep and lambs sold .... farms..	2 396	666	33	-	-	33	6	2
number..	267 152	45 469	1 271	-	-	1 271	176	(D)
Sheep and lambs shorn .... farms..	2 183	612	32	-	-	32	6	3
number..	218 980	45 609	1 152	-	-	1 152	193	(D)
pounds of wool..	1 510 663	341 520	8 109	-	-	8 109	1 064	(D)
Horses and ponies inventory............... farms..	12 879	3 247	397	-	(D)	396	11	22
number..	55 598	11 602	1 801	-	-	(D)	40	117
Horses and ponies sold .... farms..	2 260	386	49	-	-	49	-	-
number..	8 467	1 479	126	-	-	126	-	-
Goats inventory .... farms..	862	164	31	-	-	31	3	1
number..	8 831	1 117	423	-	-	423	(D)	(D)
Goats sold....................... farms..	258	29	6	-	-	6	-	-
number..	2 679	610	32	-	-	32	-	-
POULTRY								
Chickens 3 months old or older inventory ... farms..	4 206	1 176	105	-	-	105	16	9
number..	2 094 610	59 879	2 517	-	-	2 517	440	210
Farms with—								
1 to 399	4 117	1 168	105	-	-	105	16	9
400 to 3,199	30	7	-	-	-	-	-	-
3,200 to 9,999	12	-	-	-	-	-	-	-
10,000 to 19,999	18	1	-	-	-	-	-	-
20,000 to 49,999	19	-	-	-	-	-	-	-
50,000 to 99,999	7	-	-	-	-	-	-	-
100,000 or more	3	-	-	-	-	-	-	-
Hens and pullets of laying age .... farms..	4 150	1 168	101	-	-	101	14	9
number..	1 797 313	57 171	2 440	-	-	2 440	361	(D)
Pullets 3 months old or older not of laying age .... farms..	415	98	7	-	-	7	3	1
number..	297 297	2 706	77	-	-	77	79	(D)
Hens and pullets sold .... farms..	363	72	5	-	-	5	1	1
number..	2 380 936	19 510	422	-	-	422	(D)	(D)
Broilers and other meat-type chickens sold .... farms..	132	35	1	-	-	1	1	-
number..	176 061	6 908	(D)	-	-	(D)	(D)	-
Farms with—								
1 to 1,999	123	34	1	-	-	1	1	-
2,000 to 59,999	7	1	-	-	-	-	-	-
60,000 to 99,999	2	-	-	-	-	-	-	-
100,000 or more	-	-	-	-	-	-	-	-
Turkey hens kept for breeding .... farms..	194	37	8	-	-	8	-	1
number..	(D)	113	42	-	-	42	-	(D)
Turkeys sold....................... farms..	86	11	-	-	-	-	-	-
number..	230 719	4 699	-	-	-	-	-	-

See footnotes at end of table.

[For meaning of abbreviations and symbols, see introductory text]

Item	Horticultural specialties (018)	General farms, primarily crop (019)	Livestock, except dairy, poultry, and animal specialties (021) Total	Beef cattle, except feedlots (0212)	Dairy farms (024)	Poultry and eggs (025)	Animal specialties (027)	General farms, primarily livestock and animal specialties (029)
LIVESTOCK—Con.								
Hogs and pigs inventory ... farms..	1	124	5 049	1 066	120	12	16	60
number..	(D)	11 355	1 372 548	80 164	6 396	686	241	4 815
Farms with—								
1 to 24	1	49	1 266	553	58	7	14	21
25 to 49	-	17	572	157	16	-	2	7
50 to 99	-	19	765	144	25	2	2	13
100 to 199	-	22	801	119	12	2	-	11
200 to 499	-	16	1 052	69	7	1	-	7
500 or more	-	1	593	24	-	-	-	1
Used or to be used for breeding ... farms..	-	71	3 578	500	55	8	8	44
number..	-	1 673	171 873	9 745	829	116	70	865
Other ... farms..	1	117	4 695	962	111	10	14	54
number..	(D)	9 682	1 200 675	70 419	5 567	570	171	3 950
Hogs and pigs sold ... farms..	1	123	5 305	1 080	124	10	13	66
number..	(D)	22 343	2 525 408	131 458	13 227	673	640	10 746
$1,000..	(D)	2 163	261 867	13 262	1 220	71	61	942
Feeder pigs ... farms..	-	39	1 470	266	22	3	3	25
number..	-	6 052	460 408	25 938	3 158	67	93	4 091
$1,000..	-	273	20 775	1 103	134	2	3	166
Litters of pigs farrowed between—								
Dec. 1 of preceding year and Nov. 30 ... farms..	-	75	3 730	644	58	8	9	45
number..	-	2 114	270 885	13 539	1 131	74	79	1 308
Dec. 1 and May 31 ... farms..	-	65	3 500	585	49	3	7	43
number..	-	1 025	136 998	6 878	568	7	44	697
June 1 and Nov. 30 ... farms..	-	68	3 420	545	55	7	4	40
number..	-	1 089	133 887	6 661	563	67	35	611
Sheep and lambs of all ages inventory ... farms..	2	40	1 537	520	33	11	26	20
number..	(D)	7 732	168 226	20 313	3 667	1 183	1 395	905
Ewes 1 year old or older ... farms..	2	35	1 421	459	28	10	17	18
number..	(D)	2 820	80 979	13 584	2 005	(D)	836	(D)
Sheep and lambs sold ... farms..	-	38	1 567	499	34	10	20	20
number..	-	4 941	211 122	14 404	2 264	1 001	(D)	737
Sheep and lambs shorn ... farms..	1	32	1 425	438	31	10	15	16
number..	(D)	3 247	161 786	15 832	2 901	1 993	1 359	681
pounds of wool..	(D)	27 927	1 071 482	117 365	20 934	19 050	14 624	5 461
Horses and ponies inventory ... farms..	16	391	7 095	5 614	255	32	1 304	109
number..	51	1 676	25 939	20 868	848	139	12 604	781
Horses and ponies sold ... farms..	8	30	924	730	34	3	777	51
number..	11	70	2 612	2 077	72	4	3 833	260
Goats inventory ... farms..	5	28	543	291	8	12	56	11
number..	23	155	6 650	1 902	35	75	300	35
Goats sold ... farms..	1	4	191	79	-	6	14	7
number..	(D)	(D)	1 892	653	-	17	69	29
POULTRY								
Chickens 3 months old or older inventory ... farms..	5	99	2 303	1 534	133	151	121	88
number..	194	2 855	86 368	44 540	5 365	1 839 363	2 137	95 282
Farms with—								
1 to 399	5	99	2 293	1 531	133	90	121	78
400 to 3,199	-	-	8	3	-	10	-	5
3,200 to 9,999	-	-	2	-	-	8	-	2
10,000 to 19,999	-	-	-	-	-	15	-	2
20,000 to 49,999	-	-	-	-	-	18	-	1
50,000 to 99,999	-	-	-	-	-	7	-	-
100,000 or more	-	-	-	-	-	3	-	-
Hens and pullets of laying age ... farms..	5	99	2 278	1 514	132	141	116	87
number..	(D)	2 789	80 514	41 815	5 043	1 605 932	1 931	40 820
Pullets 3 months old or older not of laying age ... farms..	2	7	231	146	10	23	18	15
number..	(D)	66	5 854	2 725	322	233 431	206	54 462
Hens and pullets sold ... farms..	1	4	152	93	15	85	6	19
number..	(D)	81	23 052	4 501	1 175	2 259 215	126	77 227
Broilers and other meat-type chickens sold ... farms..	2	1	54	36	8	18	5	7
number..	(D)	(D)	8 796	6 927	9 924	136 018	454	13 269
Farms with—								
1 to 1,999	2	1	53	35	7	14	5	5
2,000 to 59,999	-	-	1	1	1	2	-	2
60,000 to 99,999	-	-	-	-	-	2	-	-
100,000 or more	-	-	-	-	-	-	-	-
Turkey hens kept for breeding ... farms..	1	5	107	69	7	17	4	7
number..	(D)	16	369	238	13	29 670	21	33
Turkeys sold ... farms..	1	4	41	24	2	19	1	9
number..	(D)	1 415	10 964	684	(D)	197 990	(D)	15 598

See footnotes at end of table.

Table 53. Summary by Standard Industrial Classification of Farm: 1987—Con.

[For meaning of abbreviations and symbols, see introductory text]

Item	Total	Field crops, except cash grains (013)					Vegetables and melons (016)	Fruits and tree nuts (017)
		Cash grains (011)	Total	Cotton (0131)	Tobacco (0132)	Sugarcane and sugar beets; Irish potatoes; field crops, except cash grains, n.e.c. (0133, 0134, 0139)		
CROPS HARVESTED								
Corn for grain or seed .... farms..	8 944	5 765	77	-	-	77	8	3
acres..	1 243 969	955 154	6 712	-	-	6 712	205	(D)
bushels..	144 133 581	113 615 525	800 365	-	-	800 365	21 295	(D)
Irrigated .... farms..	3 647	2 781	37	-	-	37	2	-
acres..	816 992	657 684	5 647	-	-	5 647	(D)	-
Farms by acres harvested:								
1 to 24 acres	1 984	906	31	-	-	31	5	3
25 to 99 acres	3 279	2 008	25	-	-	25	3	-
100 to 249 acres	2 196	1 668	13	-	-	13	-	-
250 to 499 acres	1 044	826	6	-	-	6	-	-
500 acres or more	441	357	2	-	-	2	-	-
Corn for silage or green chop .... farms..	2 009	482	71	-	-	71	1	-
acres..	109 230	25 854	8 526	-	-	8 526	(D)	-
tons, green..	1 669 413	430 584	154 101	-	-	154 101	(D)	-
Irrigated .... farms..	659	241	46	-	-	46	-	-
acres..	53 214	18 073	7 210	-	-	7 210	-	-
Farms by acres harvested:								
1 to 24 acres	799	220	11	-	-	11	1	-
25 to 99 acres	944	186	29	-	-	29	-	-
100 to 249 acres	207	62	22	-	-	22	-	-
250 to 499 acres	43	11	6	-	-	6	-	-
500 acres or more	16	3	3	-	-	3	-	-
Sorghum for grain or seed .... farms..	32 492	20 590	319	1	1	317	10	5
acres..	3 399 564	2 334 453	20 625	(D)	(D)	(D)	218	315
bushels..	225 045 100	157 614 613	1 268 010	(D)	(D)	(D)	10 861	6 040
Irrigated .... farms..	3 137	2 367	58	-	-	58	1	-
acres..	464 119	376 531	5 709	-	-	5 709	(D)	-
Farms by acres harvested:								
1 to 24 acres	7 280	4 127	124	-	-	124	8	3
25 to 99 acres	14 139	8 930	137	1	1	135	2	-
100 to 249 acres	7 830	5 181	41	-	-	41	-	2
250 to 499 acres	2 503	1 776	13	-	-	13	-	-
500 acres or more	740	576	4	-	-	4	-	-
Wheat for grain .... farms..	68 608	25 544	451	1	-	450	31	4
acres..	8 679 588	6 202 909	67 616	(D)	-	(D)	909	25
bushels..	292 999 442	213 169 754	1 955 071	(D)	-	(D)	25 240	691
Irrigated .... farms..	3 046	2 317	94	-	-	94	-	1
acres..	635 524	497 355	16 807	-	-	16 807	-	(D)
Farms by acres harvested:								
1 to 24 acres	4 230	2 193	93	-	-	93	16	4
25 to 99 acres	11 451	7 125	165	-	-	165	13	-
100 to 249 acres	11 111	7 625	109	-	-	109	2	-
250 to 499 acres	7 248	5 200	57	1	-	56	-	-
500 acres or more	4 598	3 401	27	-	-	27	-	-
Barley for grain .... farms..	2 307	1 494	13	-	-	13	-	-
acres..	95 485	66 107	338	-	-	338	-	-
bushels..	3 639 224	2 521 005	13 504	-	-	13 504	-	-
Irrigated .... farms..	166	124	5	-	-	5	-	-
acres..	7 359	4 855	136	-	-	136	-	-
Oats for grain .... farms..	5 313	2 603	72	-	-	72	2	-
acres..	128 091	66 671	1 968	-	-	1 968	(D)	-
bushels..	4 775 729	2 635 911	53 635	-	-	53 635	(D)	-
Irrigated .... farms..	48	29	3	-	-	3	-	-
acres..	2 276	1 773	(D)	-	-	(D)	-	-
Soybeans for beans .... farms..	18 664	12 489	160	1	-	159	27	9
acres..	1 878 978	1 435 816	7 025	(D)	-	(D)	1 306	310
bushels..	55 789 994	42 870 104	177 188	(D)	-	(D)	43 848	4 408
Irrigated .... farms..	1 939	1 509	19	-	-	19	6	-
acres..	175 053	141 689	1 503	-	-	1 503	(D)	-
Farms by acres harvested:								
1 to 24 acres	5 008	2 801	76	-	-	76	13	6
25 to 99 acres	8 253	5 397	66	1	-	67	9	1
100 to 249 acres	3 775	2 779	11	-	-	11	5	2
250 to 499 acres	1 315	1 068	2	-	-	2	-	-
500 acres or more	513	444	1	-	-	1	-	-
Dry edible beans, excluding dry limas .... farms..	192	167	1	-	-	1	-	-
cwt..	30 460	27 174	(D)	-	-	(D)	-	-
441 318	394 755	(D)	-	-	(D)	-	-
Irrigated .... farms..	167	147	-	-	-	-	-	-
acres..	26 182	25 396	-	-	-	-	-	-
Irish potatoes .... farms..	97	29	-	-	-	-	23	-
acres..	843	289	-	-	-	-	46	-
cwt..	138 764	48 059	-	-	-	-	7 129	-
Irrigated .... farms..	21	5	-	-	-	-	8	-
acres..	(D)	263	-	-	-	-	19	-
Hay—alfalfa, other tame, small grain, wild, grass silage, green chop, etc. (see text) .. farms..	33 964	12 985	1 920	1	-	1 919	26	31
tons, dry..	2 254 082	712 171	213 426	(D)	-	(D)	416	790
	5 080 847	1 576 831	669 170	(D)	-	(D)	749	1 025
Irrigated .... farms..	1 492	664	173	-	-	173	2	-
acres..	206 961	58 312	74 675	-	-	74 675	(D)	-
Farms by acres harvested:								
1 to 24 acres	11 391	4 769	547	-	-	547	20	24
25 to 99 acres	16 111	6 283	895	1	-	894	6	5
100 to 249 acres	5 297	1 661	325	-	-	325	-	2
250 to 499 acres	913	233	85	-	-	85	-	-
500 acres or more	252	39	68	-	-	68	-	-

See footnotes at end of table.

[For meaning of abbreviations and symbols, see introductory text]

Item	Horticultural specialties (018)	General farms, primarily crop (019)	Livestock, except dairy, poultry, and animal specialties (021) Total	Beef cattle, except feedlots (0212)	Dairy farms (024)	Poultry and eggs (025)	Animal specialties (027)	General farms, primarily livestock and animal specialties (029)
CROPS HARVESTED								
Corn for grain or seed .... farms..	2	163	2 477	1 258	338	8	4	99
acres..	(D)	20 693	231 728	104 169	20 845	606	37	7 927
bushels..	(D)	2 501 053	24 726 312	11 044 393	1 897 006	36 690	2 302	726 053
Irrigated .... farms..		55	705	376	43	2	–	21
acres..	(D)	14 506	133 092	69 167	3 302	(D)	–	2 326
Farms by acres harvested:								
1 to 24 acres	1	48	865	518	95	5	4	21
25 to 99 acres	1	69	930	453	168	1	–	54
100 to 249 acres	–	25	427	178	44	1	–	18
250 to 499 acres	–	12	183	75	11	1	–	5
500 acres or more	–	9	72	34	–	–	–	1
Corn for silage or green chop.............. farms..	–	54	891	527	451	–	2	57
acres..	–	3 088	51 083	27 722	18 011	–	(D)	2 505
tons, green..	–	49 562	769 243	406 985	230 581	–	(D)	33 262
Irrigated .... farms..	–	26	264	185	55	–	1	6
acres..	–	1 863	23 132	11 625	2 477	–	(D)	(D)
Farms by acres harvested:								
1 to 24 acres	–	17	341	205	188	–	1	20
25 to 99 acres	–	29	434	259	235	–	–	31
100 to 249 acres	–	6	85	47	25	–	1	6
250 to 499 acres	–	2	22	14	2	–	–	–
500 acres or more	–	–	9	2	1	–	–	–
Sorghum for grain or seed.................. farms..	5	604	9 808	6 238	836	45	20	250
acres..	73	51 636	890 545	467 900	69 975	4 435	773	26 516
bushels..	5 215	3 543 856	58 684 591	29 036 224	4 714 767	335 336	38 633	1 823 066
Irrigated .... farms..	–	88	604	389	38	1	–	13
acres..	–	7 046	68 178	44 184	3 451	(D)	–	(D)
Farms by acres harvested:								
1 to 24 acres	4	136	2 663	2 009	155	14	13	33
25 to 99 acres	1	289	4 202	2 761	428	19	5	126
100 to 249 acres	–	143	2 175	1 129	212	7	1	68
250 to 499 acres	–	31	623	279	36	4	1	19
500 acres or more	–	5	145	60	5	1	–	4
Wheat for grain .... farms..	10	701	10 877	7 501	716	41	37	226
acres..	638	153 516	2 103 730	1 463 730	102 458	5 624	1 904	40 259
bushels..	15 176	5 262 505	67 813 748	45 494 123	3 207 501	169 997	60 671	1 319 088
Irrigated .... farms..	–	55	552	376	16	2	3	567
acres..	(D)	16 231	102 605	69 373	1 807	(D)	144	
Farms by acres harvested:								
1 to 24 acres	7	112	1 646	1 159	93	8	23	37
25 to 99 acres	1	199	3 586	2 473	277	14	10	61
100 to 249 acres	1	183	2 875	1 919	224	14	2	76
250 to 499 acres	1	128	1 728	1 201	94	6	1	33
500 acres or more	–	79	1 042	749	28	1	1	19
Barley for grain........................... farms..	–	33	682	424	69	–	–	16
acres..	–	1 131	25 238	15 686	2 317	–	–	334
bushels..	–	51 110	935 193	564 593	105 625	–	–	12 787
Irrigated .... farms..	–	1	33	17	1	–	–	2
acres..	–	(D)	2 288	1 139	(D)	–	–	(D)
Oats for grain .... farms..	1	155	2 169	1 368	234	4	6	67
acres..	(D)	3 194	47 367	29 689	5 087	56	137	1 551
bushels..	(D)	111 079	1 736 856	1 013 175	168 408	2 665	5 390	60 825
Irrigated .... farms..	–	–	14	12	2	–	–	–
acres..	–	–	313	(D)	(D)	–	–	–
Soybeans for beans .... farms..	5	371	5 147	3 016	455	17	11	173
acres..	167	24 868	357 312	172 585	31 268	747	203	19 956
bushels..	8 200	738 329	10 396 281	4 734 684	946 338	20 280	4 260	582 789
Irrigated .... farms..	–	27	338	171	29	2	–	11
acres..	–	2 312	26 544	12 453	2 037	(D)	–	639
Farms by acres harvested:								
1 to 24 acres	1	117	1 806	1 210	125	7	9	45
25 to 99 acres	4	178	2 283	1 329	231	8	1	73
100 to 249 acres	–	63	801	383	80	2	1	31
250 to 499 acres	–	10	204	76	16	–	–	15
500 acres or more	–	3	53	18	3	–	–	9
Dry edible beans, excluding dry limas .... farms..	–	–	23	14	–	–	–	1
acres..	–	–	(D)	2 304	–	–	–	(D)
cwt..	–	–	(D)	29 705	–	–	–	(D)
Irrigated .... farms..	–	–	16	12	–	–	–	1
acres..	–	–	(D)	1 899	–	–	–	(D)
Irish potatoes .... farms..	2	8	33	22	–	1	1	–
acres..	(D)	29	26	22	–	(D)	(D)	–
cwt..	(D)	79 633	3 733	3 111	–	(D)	(D)	–
Irrigated .... farms..	1	2	4	1	–	–	–	–
acres..	(D)	(D)	1	(D)	–	–	(D)	–
Hay—alfalfa, other tame, small grain, wild, grass silage, green chop, etc. (see text) .. farms..	23	1 305	15 908	12 026	1 139	56	279	292
acres..	721	98 688	1 079 338	810 058	115 019	1 844	6 688	24 961
tons, dry..	867	283 909	2 184 875	1 591 246	291 477	3 941	9 205	56 798
Irrigated .... farms..	1	–	516	368	50	–	8	10
acres..	(D)	16 168	54 364	37 547	2 663	–	63	407
Farms by acres harvested:								
1 to 24 acres	19	508	5 058	3 815	132	33	208	73
25 to 99 acres	3	495	7 642	5 833	566	18	60	138
100 to 249 acres	–	233	2 628	1 952	371	5	10	62
250 to 499 acres	–	54	465	336	61	–	1	14
500 acres or more	–	15	115	86	9	–	1	5

See footnotes at end of table.

Table 53. **Summary by Standard Industrial Classification of Farm: 1987**—Con.

[For meaning of abbreviations and symbols, see introductory text]

Item	Total	Cash grains (011)	Field crops, except cash grains (013)				Vegetables and melons (016)	Fruits and tree nuts (017)
			Total	Cotton (0131)	Tobacco (0132)	Sugarcane and sugar beets; Irish potatoes; field crops, except cash grains, n.e.c. (0133, 0134, 0139)		
CROPS HARVESTED—Con.								
Hay—alfalfa, other tame, small grain, wild, grass silage, green chop, etc. (see text) —Con.								
Alfalfa hay .... farms..	15 484	5 951	823	-	-	823	10	7
acres..	741 856	232 015	128 327	-	-	128 327	82	47
tons, dry..	2 529 635	751 976	539 165	-	-	539 165	266	62
Irrigated .... farms..	1 174	524	164	-	-	164	1	-
acres..	180 952	49 713	74 065	-	-	74 065	(D)	-
Vegetables harvested for sale (see text) .... farms..	418	82	8	-	-	8	179	19
acres..	5 424	460	15	-	-	15	3 952	101
Irrigated .... farms..	166	24	3	-	-	3	79	6
acres..	1 851	194	(D)	-	-	(D)	1 194	50
Farms by acres harvested:								
0.1 to 4.9 acres	244	62	8	-	-	8	71	15
5.0 to 24.9 acres	130	16	-	-	-	-	81	2
25.0 to 99.9 acres	39	4	-	-	-	-	23	2
100.0 to 249.9 acres	4	-	-	-	-	-	3	-
250.0 acres or more	1	-	-	-	-	-	1	-
Field seed and grass seed crops .... farms..	1 188	394	96	1	-	95	-	-
acres..	58 460	14 429	8 629	(D)	-	(D)	-	-
Irrigated .... farms..	12	3	4	-	-	4	-	-
acres..	2 222	(D)	1 592	-	-	1 592	-	-
Land in orchards .... farms..	503	107	20	-	-	20	27	148
acres..	5 999	1 328	85	-	-	85	172	2 414
Irrigated .... farms..	90	15	2	-	-	2	11	40
acres..	757	74	(D)	-	-	(D)	75	535
Farms by bearing and nonbearing acres:								
0.1 to 4.9 acres	309	73	15	-	-	15	17	64
5.0 to 24.9 acres	147	22	5	-	-	5	9	62
25.0 to 99.9 acres	39	8	-	-	-	-	1	19
100.0 to 249.9 acres	6	4	-	-	-	-	-	2
250.0 acres or more	2	-	-	-	-	-	-	1

See footnotes at end of table.

[For meaning of abbreviations and symbols. see introductory text]

Item	Horticultural specialties (018)	General farms, primarily crop (019)	Livestock, except dairy, poultry, and animal specialties (021)		Dairy farms (024)	Poultry and eggs (025)	Animal specialties (027)	General farms, primarily livestock and animal specialties (029)
			Total	Beef cattle, except feedlots (0212)				
CROPS HARVESTED—Con.								
Hay—alfalfa, other tame, small grain, wild, grass silage, green chop, etc. (see text) —Con.								
Alfalfa hay .... farms...	9	658	6 906	4 828	841	22	78	181
acres...	176	48 317	276 707	190 930	46 044	615	1 426	8 100
tons, dry...	273	188 903	871 561	591 620	148 215	1 774	2 027	25 411
irrigated .... farms...	1	64	368	250	40	–	4	8
acres...	(D)	14 975	39 758	26 238	2 067	–	(D)	318
Vegetables harvested for sale (see text) .... farms...	10	25	83	45	5	2	1	4
acres...	125	330	405	174	20	(D)	(D)	8
irrigated .... farms...	9	8	31	11	1	1	–	4
acres...	40	101	256	99	(D)	(D)	–	7
Farms by acres harvested:								
0.1 to 4.9 acres	7	9	62	35	4	2	1	3
5.0 to 24.9 acres	1	12	16	8	1	–	–	1
25.0 to 99.9 acres	2	3	5	2	–	–	–	–
100.0 to 249.9 acres	–	1	–	–	–	–	–	–
250.0 acres or more	–	–	–	–	–	–	–	–
Field seed and grass seed crops .... farms...	–	101	540	349	41	4	2	10
acres...	–	5 033	28 003	18 650	1 902	(D)	(D)	284
irrigated .... farms...	–	1	4	3	–	–	–	–
acres...	–	(D)	479	(D)	–	–	–	–
Land in orchards .... farms...	6	11	160	118	5	6	12	2
acres...	39	124	1 776	1 635	(D)	18	26	(D)
irrigated .... farms...	3	1	11	7	–	3	3	–
acres...	29	(D)	19	12	–	8	8	(D)
Farms by bearing and nonbearing acres:								
0.1 to 4.9 acres	3	4	112	79	4	5	10	2
5.0 to 24.9 acres	1	5	39	31	1	1	2	–
25.0 to 99.9 acres	1	2	8	7	–	–	–	–
100.0 to 249.9 acres	–	–	1	–	–	–	–	–
250.0 acres or more	–	–	1	1	–	–	–	–

[1]Data are based on a sample of farms.
[2]Farms with total production expenses equal to market value of agricultural products sold are included as farms with gains of less than $1,000.

Item	Kansas	Allen	Anderson	Atchison	Barber	Barton	Bourbon
Farms .... number..	68 579	665	727	694	535	937	842
Land in farms .... acres..	46 628 519	276 555	352 141	233 619	700 147	556 433	318 958
Average size of farm .... acres..	680	416	484	337	1 309	594	379
Value of land and buildings[1]:							
Average per farm .... dollars..	278 047	177 737	172 158	176 069	371 298	260 449	145 606
Average per acre .... dollars..	413	445	352	564	298	451	393
Estimated market value of all machinery and equipment[1]:							
Average per farm .... dollars..	50 411	37 659	39 287	38 521	56 038	61 698	22 346
Farms by size:							
1 to 9 acres	3 689	28	47	48	49	80	34
10 to 49 acres	6 222	64	59	76	21	59	83
50 to 179 acres	15 510	177	177	222	60	160	312
180 to 499 acres	16 705	236	210	200	101	258	227
500 to 999 acres	12 093	85	135	104	80	215	118
1,000 acres or more	14 360	75	99	42	224	165	68
Total cropland .... farms..	61 615	595	640	630	449	845	733
acres..	31 385 090	189 229	230 898	178 038	255 328	487 019	167 985
Harvested cropland .... farms..	57 822	564	611	589	415	806	845
acres..	17 729 394	125 078	161 985	122 717	149 449	262 060	90 939
Irrigated land .... farms..	7 352	7	10	11	27	111	9
acres..	2 463 073	(D)	1 152	478	2 954	29 147	763
Market value of agricultural products sold .... $1,000..	6 476 669	23 025	34 226	26 262	45 715	125 117	23 062
Average per farm .... dollars..	94 441	34 624	47 078	37 842	85 448	133 529	27 389
Crops, including nursery and greenhouse crops .... $1,000..	1 693 609	11 747	16 771	14 121	9 652	24 053	6 058
Livestock, poultry, and their products .... $1,000..	4 783 060	11 278	17 455	12 142	36 063	101 064	17 004
Farms by value of sales:							
Less than $2,500	9 502	102	103	77	62	118	172
$2,500 to $4,999	6 919	95	85	78	34	86	130
$5,000 to $9,999	9 430	112	115	108	58	116	163
$10,000 to $24,999	14 070	131	158	158	91	247	195
$25,000 to $49,999	10 282	105	106	113	93	176	79
$50,000 to $99,999	8 997	64	98	95	84	104	56
$100,000 or more	9 379	58	82	65	113	88	47
Operators by principal occupation:							
Farming	42 607	407	430	426	367	608	426
Other	25 972	258	297	268	168	329	416
Operators by days worked off farm:							
Any	34 654	320	382	333	237	460	434
200 days or more	21 677	197	246	230	140	243	309
Average age of operator .... years..	52.0	54.7	51.2	50.2	52.0	52.1	54.2
Total farm production expenses[1] .... $1,000..	5 516 518	18 027	24 959	21 043	41 388	104 395	20 185
Average per farm .... dollars..	80 439	27 109	34 379	30 365	77 506	111 414	23 972
Livestock and poultry:							
Cattle and calves inventory .... farms..	40 785	492	522	456	386	540	635
number..	5 539 292	30 062	35 758	29 344	89 515	85 041	46 560
Beef cows .... farms..	31 475	423	432	368	269	468	515
number..	1 354 649	12 799	14 924	10 970	28 337	14 700	17 494
Milk cows .... farms..	3 093	54	53	49	13	36	59
number..	95 675	2 419	1 655	1 332	811	951	1 481
Cattle and calves sold .... farms..	41 498	488	526	463	393	538	645
number..	7 310 338	16 932	26 577	15 993	69 121	150 497	32 536
Hogs and pigs inventory .... farms..	6 768	59	60	134	29	67	71
number..	1 516 878	6 612	10 240	17 675	3 900	5 473	7 261
Hogs and pigs sold .... farms..	7 090	62	60	144	32	71	74
number..	2 759 876	12 015	16 843	28 541	5 509	14 919	11 596
Sheep and lambs inventory .... farms..	2 400	15	29	14	19	17	24
number..	249 303	421	1 171	1 716	5 455	1 515	721
Chickens 3 months old or older inventory .... farms..	4 206	54	68	38	30	76	46
number..	2 094 610	1 686	21 514	(D)	692	(D)	2 247
Broilers and other meat-type chickens sold .... farms..	132	2	2	2	–	4	–
number..	176 061	(D)	(D)	(D)	–	(D)	–
Selected crops harvested:							
Corn for grain or seed .... farms..	8 944	103	199	285	–	43	105
acres..	1 243 969	7 562	13 596	22 627	–	9 382	5 937
bushels..	144 133 581	600 173	1 111 323	1 910 556	–	1 188 646	482 711
Corn for silage or green chop .... farms..	2 009	17	32	33	2	14	27
acres..	109 230	900	1 484	918	(D)	964	1 039
tons, green..	1 669 413	12 264	18 280	12 621	(D)	17 398	11 295
Sorghum for grain or seed .... farms..	32 492	294	330	381	104	501	213
acres..	3 399 564	19 291	22 705	32 153	6 932	41 882	12 311
bushels..	228 045 100	1 392 031	1 701 589	2 555 518	348 987	2 893 658	707 820
Wheat for grain .... farms..	38 638	141	135	133	375	750	65
acres..	8 679 588	9 519	6 676	5 160	121 445	167 887	3 442
bushels..	292 999 442	273 355	197 151	137 915	3 341 963	5 428 175	85 687
Oats for grain .... farms..	5 313	77	84	107	14	52	63
acres..	126 091	1 965	2 144	2 589	779	880	1 434
bushels..	4 775 729	75 541	80 947	127 246	29 834	39 723	45 437
Soybeans for beans .... farms..	18 864	398	449	435	16	77	317
acres..	1 878 976	61 809	80 630	43 701	1 416	6 945	32 777
bushels..	55 789 994	1 787 211	2 616 386	1 474 034	45 929	266 240	817 832
Hay—alfalfa, other tame, small grain, wild, grass silage, green chop, etc. (see text) .... farms..	33 964	463	463	395	222	492	522
acres..	2 254 082	30 385	39 800	19 182	18 355	37 437	36 721
tons, dry..	5 080 947	48 927	62 070	36 644	51 611	106 817	61 439

See footnotes at end of table.

Table 1. **County Summary Highlights: 1987**—Con.

[For meaning of abbreviations and symbols, see introductory text]

Item	Brown	Butler	Chase	Chautauqua	Cherokee	Cheyenne	Clark
Farms .... number..	728	1 300	288	421	841	493	290
Land in farms .... acres..	339 863	699 487	328 905	320 956	280 704	619 870	587 574
Average size of farm .... acres..	467	538	1 142	762	334	1 257	2 026
Value of land and buildings[1]:							
Average per farm .... dollars..	308 734	261 728	320 139	187 026	173 944	396 783	520 769
Average per acre .... dollars..	654	497	288	239	541	311	242
Estimated market value of all machinery and equipment[1]:							
Average per farm .... dollars..	59 723	34 129	35 704	23 760	35 078	58 749	52 902
Farms by size:							
1 to 9 acres	48	62	10	23	32	17	16
10 to 49 acres	52	191	22	18	157	14	6
50 to 179 acres	189	375	47	103	281	49	26
180 to 499 acres	216	298	71	126	192	87	56
500 to 999 acres	129	169	64	63	108	104	53
1,000 acres or more	94	205	74	88	71	222	133
Total cropland .... farms..	657	1 075	247	307	725	454	256
acres..	272 083	341 336	84 665	73 008	210 941	403 719	198 178
Harvested cropland .... farms..	637	934	223	248	657	426	233
acres..	197 847	210 975	45 580	35 741	156 409	176 293	92 271
Irrigated land .... farms..	3	21	-	3	7	151	28
acres..	(D)	1 588	-	31	376	40 651	8 030
Market value of agricultural products sold .... $1,000..	62 567	99 269	34 012	15 707	22 029	51 543	54 942
Average per farm .... dollars..	85 944	76 376	118 098	37 309	26 194	104 549	189 466
Crops, including nursery and greenhouse crops .... $1,000..	26 709	14 466	3 690	4 895	14 551	18 765	6 107
Livestock, poultry, and their products .... $1,000..	35 859	84 823	30 322	10 812	7 478	32 778	48 835
Farms by value of sales:							
Less than $2,500	53	321	27	97	202	32	23
$2,500 to $4,999	46	167	21	53	133	30	10
$5,000 to $9,999	86	162	29	81	132	47	28
$10,000 to $24,999	174	232	59	75	153	101	53
$25,000 to $49,999	103	123	53	45	96	108	38
$50,000 to $99,999	124	128	43	37	79	92	46
$100,000 or more	142	167	57	30	46	83	92
Operators by principal occupation:							
Farming	543	657	189	222	438	373	203
Other	185	643	99	199	403	120	87
Operators by days worked off farm:							
Any	284	746	146	236	481	209	140
200 days or more	162	533	84	155	343	99	80
Average age of operator .... years..	51.2	53.9	52.7	53.5	51.9	53.2	52.6
Total farm production expenses[1] .... $1,000..	50 552	85 827	26 893	13 629	18 347	43 570	50 743
Average per farm .... dollars..	69 345	66 021	93 379	32 295	21 790	88 378	174 976
Livestock and poultry:							
Cattle and calves inventory .... farms..	442	788	197	328	551	254	197
number..	39 705	107 777	39 591	34 230	22 329	42 329	66 325
Beef cows .... farms..	336	561	147	288	484	210	97
number..	12 065	24 896	9 452	15 854	10 568	15 303	(D)
Milk cows .... farms..	55	52	15	18	13	8	2
number..	1 732	1 214	349	498	138	18	(D)
Cattle and calves sold .... farms..	447	631	219	324	528	259	214
number..	43 045	137 769	57 451	21 126	(D)	55 568	90 994
Hogs and pigs inventory .... farms..	135	130	36	40	51	35	5
number..	42 810	37 102	7 829	7 682	6 217	5 134	(D)
Hogs and pigs sold .... farms..	142	142	35	39	51	36	4
number..	77 802	60 660	15 609	11 334	10 054	8 566	(D)
Sheep and lambs inventory .... farms..	31	63	17	27	10	14	7
number..	1 997	2 336	1 993	1 094	153	877	132
Chickens 3 months old or older inventory .... farms..	35	110	13	42	39	24	9
number..	1 709	(D)	(D)	1 039	1 163	596	229
Broilers and other meat-type chickens sold .... farms..	-	2	2	-	1	1	-
number..	-	(D)	(D)	-	(D)	(D)	-
Selected crops harvested:							
Corn for grain or seed .... farms..	349	43	36	12	80	98	-
acres..	48 227	3 180	2 323	658	5 166	11 604	-
bushels..	4 726 726	250 012	163 141	42 190	502 149	2 367 733	-
Corn for silage or green chop .... farms..	59	36	23	5	9	23	1
acres..	1 940	1 952	2 262	123	97	1 239	(D)
tons, green..	27 753	21 842	32 958	1 410	1 563	21 762	(D)
Sorghum for grain or seed .... farms..	354	496	122	65	248	131	108
acres..	28 762	66 302	7 794	5 306	20 936	11 063	9 362
bushels..	2 296 531	4 789 767	521 325	285 900	1 445 829	707 778	521 390
Wheat for grain .... farms..	367	488	135	78	158	409	213
acres..	26 577	63 946	11 898	8 028	16 296	109 225	70 665
bushels..	1 030 105	1 865 760	330 110	179 242	372 571	4 063 922	2 097 680
Oats for grain .... farms..	114	49	31	14	50	25	7
acres..	2 277	951	827	793	1 186	1 107	260
bushels..	101 458	27 958	20 228	25 175	34 397	58 106	7 718
Soybeans for beans .... farms..	539	279	121	48	457	33	3
acres..	76 311	23 625	9 639	8 401	100 264	4 029	(D)
bushels..	2 532 198	714 386	339 233	225 752	2 089 323	167 976	(D)
Hay—alfalfa, other tame, small grain, wild, grass silage, green chop, etc. (see text) .... farms..	354	676	180	208	411	156	110
acres..	16 003	54 005	12 737	13 125	16 011	11 353	11 181
tons, dry..	36 477	86 301	26 011	21 664	27 319	31 386	31 085

See footnotes at end of table.

Table 1. County Summary Highlights: 1987—Con.

[For meaning of abbreviations and symbols, see introductory text]

Item	Clay	Cloud	Coffey	Comanche	Cowley	Crawford	Decatur
Farms ___ number__	672	659	606	277	907	809	486
Land in farms ___ acres__	392 321	397 383	330 435	481 136	619 647	283 589	543 466
Average size of farm ___ acres__	584	603	545	1 737	622	351	1 118
Value of land and buildings[1]:							
Average per farm ___ dollars__	242 641	262 663	195 295	417 993	230 291	154 295	350 809
Average per acre ___ dollars__	426	407	357	266	385	436	292
Estimated market value of all machinery and equipment[1]:							
Average per farm ___ dollars__	61 035	53 311	35 139	47 321	35 698	35 478	78 024
Farms by size:							
1 to 9 acres	44	41	25	26	52	40	22
10 to 49 acres	29	34	46	8	111	100	18
50 to 179 acres	125	153	160	29	269	255	47
180 to 499 acres	185	166	157	36	237	257	84
500 to 999 acres	158	121	125	54	176	96	98
1,000 acres or more	131	144	93	124	152	61	217
Total cropland ___ farms__	614	611	549	230	859	706	452
acres__	283 874	293 364	208 391	187 433	269 262	161 598	356 393
Harvested cropland ___ farms__	588	583	515	209	760	649	438
acres__	176 217	184 007	142 688	93 062	160 651	116 714	175 861
Irrigated land ___ farms__	49	76	8	28	19	11	92
acres__	10 626	10 139	466	4 424	1 410	1 447	10 433
Market value of agricultural products sold ___ $1,000__	39 675	30 672	32 459	29 146	55 906	21 741	72 560
Average per farm ___ dollars__	59 040	46 847	53 563	105 220	56 075	26 873	149 300
Crops, including nursery and greenhouse crops ___ $1,000__	16 083	17 193	14 123	5 626	11 396	10 254	17 476
Livestock, poultry, and their products ___ $1,000__	23 592	13 680	18 336	23 520	44 511	11 487	55 082
Farms by value of sales:							
Less than $2,500	80	62	76	29	186	142	27
$2,500 to $4,999	45	70	48	24	139	116	21
$5,000 to $9,999	79	91	78	20	173	175	47
$10,000 to $24,999	143	138	141	44	211	176	93
$25,000 to $49,999	121	113	93	41	115	102	86
$50,000 to $99,999	121	108	94	35	90	61	106
$100,000 or more	103	77	76	84	83	37	106
Operators by principal occupation:							
Farming	497	449	368	200	516	447	382
Other	175	210	238	77	491	362	104
Operators by days worked off farm:							
Any	285	301	318	117	603	403	215
200 days or more	135	166	199	60	428	281	85
Average age of operator ___ years__	51.8	50.6	51.4	54.3	52.9	52.9	51.3
Total farm production expenses[1] ___ $1,000__	29 763	23 426	25 314	21 845	51 239	16 809	61 688
Average per farm ___ dollars__	44 290	35 546	41 703	78 861	51 444	20 804	126 930
Livestock and poultry:							
Cattle and calves inventory ___ farms__	446	374	363	203	614	574	902
number__	39 466	31 448	31 584	50 945	61 082	31 162	57 326
Beef cows ___ farms__	367	325	266	131	505	513	254
number__	14 394	13 958	8 335	14 951	20 584	14 508	16 631
Milk cows ___ farms__	38	16	17	8	33	36	11
number__	775	293	217	277	711	766	216
Cattle and calves sold ___ farms__	455	381	371	218	629	576	315
number__	25 540	20 930	27 790	46 538	71 675	21 606	85 340
Hogs and pigs inventory ___ farms__	147	71	51	17	119	44	68
number__	42 511	16 703	5 827	2 035	24 267	2 859	12 546
Hogs and pigs sold ___ farms__	156	77	55	17	117	41	73
number__	75 529	33 133	11 755	3 406	48 321	5 365	29 981
Sheep and lambs inventory ___ farms__	21	25	21	5	41	18	78
number__	1 496	2 261	1 287	133	5 692	1 003	785
Chickens 3 months old or older inventory ___ farms__	35	28	45	9	68	36	37
number__	(D)	978	(D)	194	1 697	1 059	1 626
Broilers and other meat-type chickens sold ___ farms__	-	1	-	-	2	-	1
number__	-	(D)	(D)	-	(D)	-	(D)
Selected crops harvested:							
Corn for grain or seed ___ farms__	75	59	136	7	12	108	114
acres__	7 405	7 338	7 862	809	612	7 737	17 038
bushels__	886 470	880 934	620 771	127 385	46 912	675 502	1 741 211
Corn for silage or green chop ___ farms__	21	10	16	2	8	10	13
acres__	742	267	878	(D)	379	384	474
tons, green__	7 776	3 678	11 142	(D)	4 580	6 326	6 434
Sorghum for grain or seed ___ farms__	464	410	342	78	385	326	326
acres__	41 625	37 418	24 807	7 311	29 662	26 330	37 348
bushels__	2 964 750	3 004 763	1 692 593	333 660	1 795 900	1 787 148	2 567 910
Wheat for grain ___ farms__	519	501	182	162	549	69	396
acres__	79 221	109 897	11 740	71 867	95 945	3 989	93 716
bushels__	2 715 122	3 909 381	313 911	1 846 967	2 695 979	121 569	3 999 819
Oats for grain ___ farms__	135	62	36	2	33	98	42
acres__	2 298	1 769	629	(D)	667	3 003	1 448
bushels__	106 359	80 251	18 763	(D)	15 647	109 140	57 297
Soybeans for beans ___ farms__	349	231	434	9	123	475	12
acres__	23 165	12 176	70 481	774	5 627	59 552	954
bushels__	743 352	357 497	2 150 726	28 709	141 824	1 259 435	23 712
Hay—alfalfa, other tame, small grain, wild, grass silage, green chop, etc. (see text) ___ farms__	424	326	330	119	500	439	226
acres__	25 074	18 121	31 082	9 870	31 618	21 593	13 517
tons, dry__	50 497	39 301	41 420	27 747	61 034	36 858	42 546

See footnotes at end of table.

Table 1. **County Summary Highlights: 1987**—Con.

[For meaning of abbreviations and symbols. see introductory text]

Item	Dickinson	Doniphan	Douglas	Edwards	Elk	Ellis	Ellsworth
Farms .... number..	1 028	630	852	361	409	795	499
Land in farms .... acres..	513 946	216 179	223 426	387 309	340 899	568 934	423 655
Average size of farm............................... acres..	500	408	262	1 073	833	716	849
Value of land and buildings[1]:							
Average per farm.................................. dollars..	209 824	279 453	195 964	455 709	237 000	264 675	276 723
Average per acre .... dollars..	446	741	827	423	277	361	338
Estimated market value of all machinery and equipment[1]:							
Average per farm.................................. dollars..	48 768	49 135	29 037	86 059	23 672	42 063	49 300
Farms by size:							
1 to 9 acres	68	47	48	10	16	53	18
10 to 49 acres	60	54	157	10	17	43	18
50 to 179 acres	239	133	345	36	89	176	82
180 to 499 acres	303	136	183	93	115	205	123
500 to 999 acres	207	92	74	68	82	173	103
1,000 acres or more	151	58	45	144	90	145	155
Total cropland....................................... farms..	940	474	757	339	334	718	470
acres..	392 686	166 755	154 565	316 104	85 006	333 282	247 187
Harvested cropland .... farms..	908	454	691	328	293	691	450
acres..	245 504	127 668	108 664	185 513	40 040	147 980	128 533
Irrigated land .... farms..	34	2	14	155	1	13	8
acres..	2 792	(D)	1 472	83 316	(D)	983	896
Market value of agricultural products sold .... $1,000..	65 235	34 650	28 024	57 867	17 905	46 993	21 448
Average per farm.................................. dollars..	63 458	65 378	32 892	160 296	43 777	59 111	42 978
Crops, including nursery and greenhouse crops....................................... $1,000..	17 841	22 155	12 357	24 380	2 097	9 528	9 152
Livestock, poultry, and their products .... $1,000..	47 394	12 496	15 667	33 487	15 808	37 465	12 295
Farms by value of sales:							
Less than $2,500	108	48	242	22	59	113	34
$2,500 to $4,999	107	45	126	24	48	104	29
$5,000 to $9,999	153	68	151	32	76	138	81
$10,000 to $24,999	211	96	138	63	93	197	110
$25,000 to $49,999	178	87	68	63	48	122	116
$50,000 to $99,999	126	80	59	43	49	70	84
$100,000 or more	145	106	68	114	36	51	45
Operators by principal occupation:							
Farming	670	364	360	284	245	471	349
Other	358	166	492	77	164	324	150
Operators by days worked off farm:							
Any	497	215	533	134	210	452	226
200 days or more	297	134	406	69	155	269	130
Average age of operator .... years..	51.7	50.4	53.8	52.6	56.7	51.3	54.3
Total farm production expenses[1] .... $1,000..	54 860	24 829	23 004	48 942	14 243	41 538	19 037
Average per farm.................................. dollars..	53 365	46 848	27 000	135 574	34 798	52 118	38 147
Livestock and poultry:							
Cattle and calves inventory .... farms..	635	299	512	194	321	528	344
number..	73 786	20 301	27 845	51 127	37 023	55 888	36 888
Beef cows .... farms..	422	246	394	112	282	462	305
number..	14 853	7 716	8 587	4 670	16 665	21 957	17 434
Milk cows... farms..	50	15	43	9	10	31	12
number..	1 649	580	2 093	184	125	1 306	135
Cattle and calves sold .... farms..	658	303	517	201	339	537	346
number..	77 223	15 426	21 697	61 840	29 016	64 199	22 831
Hogs and pigs inventory .... farms..	137	113	51	12	40	40	45
number..	19 486	18 432	8 120	1 333	9 613	4 096	6 985
Hogs and pigs sold .... farms..	144	116	50	15	40	35	41
number..	36 641	33 659	12 945	2 185	18 624	9 577	14 020
Sheep and lambs inventory .... farms..	61	22	41	7	10	15	10
number..	3 800	1 054	1 296	(D)	468	1 797	1 120
Chickens 3 months old or older inventory .... farms..	54	41	60	10	29	82	61
number..	18 274	1 441	2 634	892	1 071	2 762	2 356
Broilers and other meat-type chickens sold .... farms..	2	–	2	–	–	1	2
number..	(D)	–	(D)	–	–	(D)	(D)
Selected crops harvested:							
Corn for grain or seed .... farms..	44	362	175	100	8	4	6
bushels..	1 915	56 130	15 643	38 522	307	207	231
	148 123	6 228 898	1 513 650	4 203 683	21 270	9 840	16 945
Corn for silage or green chop....................... farms..	85	25	40	13	3	2	9
acres..	3 208	806	1 720	708	31	(D)	189
tons, green..	35 499	15 706	21 964	12 130	248	(D)	2 785
Sorghum for grain or seed .... farms..	619	80	242	194	104	314	291
acres..	47 319	4 352	18 903	20 830	5 465	21 586	18 469
bushels..	2 702 408	378 074	1 374 834	1 290 586	290 331	1 182 640	1 227 419
Wheat for grain .... farms..	818	118	76	296	99	611	405
acres..	135 344	7 949	2 844	87 995	6 405	99 562	85 816
bushels..	4 377 284	328 510	92 999	2 921 112	148 994	3 181 838	2 976 878
Oats for grain .... farms..	201	34	82	9	24	25	51
acres..	4 012	425	1 611	355	507	650	1 046
bushels..	128 951	22 486	49 741	10 060	13 300	20 211	34 586
Soybeans for beans .... farms..	336	376	373	90	98	–	31
acres..	14 637	52 547	42 051	21 083	9 348	–	1 582
bushels..	413 709	1 931 717	1 399 719	806 148	269 817	–	45 930
Hay—alfalfa, other tame, small grain, wild, grass silage, green chop, etc. (see text) .... farms..	650	210	540	145	250	358	312
acres..	39 964	6 512	27 405	19 249	19 341	22 783	23 590
tons, dry..	90 833	16 496	50 418	76 879	27 687	51 546	48 505

See footnotes at end of table.

Table 1. **County Summary Highlights: 1987**—Con.

[For meaning of abbreviations and symbols, see introductory text]

Item		Finney	Ford	Franklin	Geary	Gove	Graham	Grant
Farms	number	534	812	979	296	534	452	303
Land in farms	acres	722 748	674 986	312 783	170 339	676 575	503 589	323 136
Average size of farm	acres	1 353	831	319	577	1 267	1 114	1 066
Value of land and buildings[1]:								
Average per farm	dollars	658 750	341 901	181 876	237 777	350 782	412 626	535 611
Average per acre	dollars	499	429	585	429	297	317	513
Estimated market value of all machinery and equipment[1]:								
Average per farm	dollars	105 935	106 473	29 307	46 123	59 818	57 672	121 294
Farms by size:								
1 to 9 acres		37	50	48	23	51	17	17
10 to 49 acres		25	55	163	32	17	19	8
50 to 179 acres		52	128	363	65	57	56	39
180 to 499 acres		90	167	233	72	79	90	57
500 to 999 acres		81	189	103	45	102	85	56
1,000 acres or more		249	223	71	58	228	183	126
Total cropland	farms	492	743	876	255	470	426	271
	acres	581 793	549 220	207 599	77 496	445 010	320 474	277 331
Harvested cropland	farms	463	703	799	239	454	403	258
	acres	323 807	284 042	135 087	48 216	194 728	146 177	156 356
Irrigated land	farms	283	213	16	22	87	53	190
	acres	184 177	77 629	1 503	1 516	15 941	8 519	99 429
Market value of agricultural products sold	$1,000	381 532	229 083	33 009	16 506	93 924	27 608	231 412
Average per farm	dollars	714 479	282 121	33 718	55 952	175 887	60 859	763 735
Crops, including nursery and greenhouse crops	$1,000	43 002	29 546	13 653	4 164	15 725	11 770	20 450
Livestock, poultry, and their products	$1,000	338 530	199 537	19 357	12 342	78 199	15 738	210 962
Farms by value of sales:								
Less than $2,500		42	84	247	42	35	41	21
$2,500 to $4,999		30	63	157	34	36	36	18
$5,000 to $9,999		41	86	165	41	53	43	24
$10,000 to $24,999		63	173	179	64	107	93	44
$25,000 to $49,999		73	119	93	42	94	105	50
$50,000 to $99,999		105	119	69	30	98	73	58
$100,000 or more		180	168	75	42	111	61	88
Operators by principal occupation:								
Farming		379	522	431	166	391	331	228
Other		155	290	548	129	143	121	75
Operators by days worked off farm:								
Any		217	404	606	156	224	205	106
200 days or more		126	240	470	114	114	108	49
Average age of operator	years	50.8	51.8	52.8	54.0	49.7	52.6	50.0
Total farm production expenses[1]	$1,000	342 909	213 012	26 450	12 135	83 875	25 413	226 675
Average per farm	dollars	640 951	262 330	26 990	40 998	101 079	56 225	748 101
Livestock and poultry:								
Cattle and calves inventory	farms	171	423	653	209	310	281	120
	number	193 533	137 745	35 740	22 321	81 975	36 291	149 230
Beef cows	farms	91	210	514	170	239	247	76
	number	6 224	14 024	12 776	8 819	16 992	16 306	3 872
Milk cows	farms	7	17	81	18	21	23	9
	number	15	609	3 364	798	546	737	78
Cattle and calves sold	farms	174	442	646	207	324	282	117
	number	484 784	333 262	24 035	14 246	124 523	27 797	307 689
Hogs and pigs inventory	farms	34	37	84	44	39	17	30
	number	6 046	4 936	17 076	19 056	6 628	2 223	3 797
Hogs and pigs sold	farms	33	38	90	44	33	23	27
	number	10 917	10 295	33 393	35 803	11 069	5 034	5 802
Sheep and lambs inventory	farms	19	22	34	7	12	7	10
	number	591	539	1 123	281	4 292	419	218
Chickens 3 months old or older inventory	farms	30	29	69	23	28	20	29
	number	607	825	3 367	2 316	634	661	650
Broilers and other meat-type chickens sold	farms	–	2	4	1	4	(D)	4
	number	–	(D)	160	(D)	350	(D)	760
Selected crops harvested:								
Corn for grain or seed	farms	142	81	182	22	37	25	110
	acres	50 415	19 058	11 765	952	5 013	3 302	26 236
	bushels	6 724 251	2 317 716	920 810	84 624	547 514	375 964	4 104 121
Corn for silage or green chop	farms	20	17	43	14	21	11	12
	acres	2 065	1 900	1 576	307	3 210	766	1 777
	tons, green	45 427	27 268	22 443	3 737	42 725	12 490	38 246
Sorghum for grain or seed	farms	266	428	322	168	308	267	174
	acres	55 532	52 001	21 469	10 601	40 514	30 316	42 463
	bushels	3 950 820	3 911 021	1 523 437	708 133	2 505 504	1 838 475	2 350 616
Wheat for grain	farms	431	644	87	170	435	379	232
	acres	174 488	181 190	4 832	16 731	117 701	91 909	72 047
	bushels	7 146 392	6 427 347	135 449	603 063	4 496 191	3 548 458	2 626 269
Oats for grain	farms	7	24	113	62	16	22	3
	acres	372	976	1 891	1 188	1 005	778	(D)
	bushels	13 838	24 292	67 971	40 289	32 069	31 190	4 200
Soybeans for beans	farms	87	85	498	113	3	3	43
	acres	8 644	6 586	62 225	5 462	(D)	205	3 793
	bushels	263 194	233 727	1 671 238	163 290	15 294	(D)	106 002
Hay—alfalfa, other tame, small grain, wild, grass silage, green chop, etc. (see text)	farms	169	273	813	189	162	165	64
	acres	30 042	19 770	33 840	13 587	14 985	11 912	7 349
	tons, dry	130 942	67 181	57 077	24 346	39 347	32 580	34 351

See footnotes at end of table.

Table 1. **County Summary Highlights: 1987** —Con.

[For meaning of abbreviations and symbols, see introductory text]

Item	Gray	Greeley	Greenwood	Hamilton	Harper	Harvey	Haskell
Farms _____ number__	547	294	587	279	648	874	315
Land in farms _____ acres__	532 284	475 278	549 507	538 449	484 471	309 123	369 850
Average size of farm _____ acres__	973	1 617	936	1 930	748	354	1 174
Value of land and buildings[1]:							
Average per farm _____ dollars__	479 429	668 113	314 348	568 527	314 046	253 936	757 035
Average per acre _____ dollars__	518	419	320	306	425	658	654
Estimated market value of all machinery and equipment[1]:							
Average per farm _____ dollars__	93 879	85 795	25 417	91 356	56 080	52 895	137 948
Farms by size:							
1 to 9 acres _____	37	14	36	8	36	79	16
10 to 49 acres _____	12	3	41	10	38	145	8
50 to 179 acres _____	77	36	131	22	97	215	32
180 to 499 acres _____	119	65	159	29	168	225	44
500 to 999 acres _____	119	47	93	52	138	146	76
1,000 acres or more _____	183	129	127	158	173	63	139
Total cropland _____ farms__	504	279	461	253	612	786	296
acres__	464 775	430 162	127 714	404 212	349 932	274 647	333 685
Harvested cropland _____ farms__	480	266	409	225	595	740	284
acres__	258 379	196 152	73 937	160 604	233 900	197 917	200 065
Irrigated land _____ farms__	304	58	8	58	10	118	223
acres__	154 369	25 410	819	18 805	584	20 939	154 476
Market value of agricultural products sold _____ $1,000__	236 428	81 569	35 382	80 154	55 261	52 369	248 969
Average per farm _____ dollars__	432 227	277 445	60 276	287 289	85 280	59 919	790 379
Crops, including nursery and greenhouse crops _____ $1,000__	38 117	16 515	4 076	12 813	16 224	19 340	30 327
Livestock, poultry, and their products _____ $1,000__	198 311	65 054	31 306	67 340	39 037	33 028	218 643
Farms by value of sales:							
Less than $2,500 _____	26	20	85	29	66	153	19
$2,500 to $4,999 _____	22	26	57	10	45	97	11
$5,000 to $9,999 _____	51	32	90	26	65	118	16
$10,000 to $24,999 _____	86	51	138	45	145	165	37
$25,000 to $49,999 _____	77	45	87	35	99	122	27
$50,000 to $99,999 _____	77	42	58	66	83	102	56
$100,000 or more _____	208	78	72	66	145	117	149
Operators by principal occupation:							
Farming _____	423	216	324	201	452	479	250
Other _____	124	78	263	78	196	395	65
Operators by days worked off farm:							
Any _____	245	126	312	119	298	520	109
200 days or more _____	118	56	213	62	172	330	53
Average age of operator _____ years__	47.6	53.1	55.5	49.2	53.4	51.3	48.5
Total farm production expenses[1] _____ $1,000__	218 171	75 624	29 538	50 215	47 187	41 276	221 461
Average per farm _____ dollars__	399 581	258 103	50 406	179 981	72 707	47 227	703 051
Livestock and poultry:							
Cattle and calves inventory _____ farms__	265	85	440	105	410	422	103
number__	148 250	52 354	63 675	58 221	70 210	33 335	134 383
Beef cows _____ farms__	90	43	352	75	245	264	40
number__	5 832	6 888	25 751	5 057	11 560	6 314	2 532
Milk cows _____ farms__	6	7	32	4	15	56	7
number__	19	13	967	4	479	1 365	7
Cattle and calves sold _____ farms__	274	89	457	116	422	408	112
number__	314 237	90 929	56 628	110 524	69 401	37 716	329 026
Hogs and pigs inventory _____ farms__	19	9	37	10	31	116	11
number__	4 607	1 030	5 848	1 007	4 205	30 478	4 882
Hogs and pigs sold _____ farms__	23	10	36	11	24	121	12
number__	9 771	1 571	7 687	2 529	5 678	51 767	16 039
Sheep and lambs inventory _____ farms__	16	5	24	5	28	68	9
number__	4 535	477	891	(D)	33 724	7 656	(D)
Chickens 3 months old or older inventory _____ farms__	23	9	36	10	23	57	11
number__	676	370	1 048	286	496	242 016	708
Broilers and other meat-type chickens sold _____ farms__	4	–	–	2	1	4	–
number__	610	–	–	(D)	(D)	668	–
Selected crops harvested:							
Corn for grain or seed _____ farms__	196	38	29	22	1	82	157
acres__	51 161	12 977	1 119	4 574	(D)	11 053	55 966
bushels__	6 327 646	1 678 904	90 970	624 772	(D)	1 370 794	7 401 004
Corn for silage or green chop _____ farms__	16	6	16	2	1	24	25
acres__	975	706	815	2	(D)	882	2 326
tons, green__	15 565	14 418	8 755	(D)	(D)	12 907	45 243
Sorghum for grain or seed _____ farms__	275	124	174	127	79	520	151
acres__	47 462	16 705	12 603	18 681	(D)	55 624	32 584
bushels__	4 043 766	745 922	723 755	724 726	(D)	4 377 977	2 843 263
Wheat for grain _____ farms__	453	252	160	207	579	602	259
acres__	133 809	145 703	9 895	125 546	212 192	103 013	99 081
bushels__	4 994 017	4 553 923	249 303	3 977 998	6 247 571	3 078 624	3 800 254
Oats for grain _____ farms__	4	4	36	4	20	33	3
acres__	105	306	891	132	1 045	854	37
bushels__	2 450	6 187	24 087	2 492	29 335	25 612	1 300
Soybeans for beans _____ farms__	68	9	197	2	3	217	53
acres__	5 462	499	17 664	(D)	(D)	12 996	3 719
bushels__	208 432	13 450	500 533	(D)	(D)	479 136	110 636
Hay—alfalfa, other tame, small grain, wild, grass silage, green chop, etc. (see text) _____ farms__	131	65	331	63	294	401	58
acres__	20 644	4 570	35 069	8 479	17 327	14 908	6 126
tons, dry__	103 541	11 021	51 958	26 944	41 069	36 505	23 904

See footnotes at end of table.

Item		Hodgeman	Jackson	Jefferson	Jewell	Johnson	Kearny	Kingman	Kiowa
Farms	number_	423	1 082	1 017	738	659	291	818	310
Land in farms	acres_	495 080	335 142	263 592	502 106	151 763	549 371	517 652	392 245
Average size of farm	acres_	1 170	310	259	682	230	1 888	633	1 265
Value of land and buildings[1]:									
Average per farm	dollars_	385 670	127 956	168 696	246 574	322 914	740 880	269 880	404 694
Average per acre	dollars_	312	427	619	389	1 334	378	434	340
Estimated market value of all machinery and equipment[1]:									
Average per farm	dollars_	61 233	24 046	29 394	50 311	40 152	130 792	49 007	77 994
Farms by size:									
1 to 9 acres		18	40	36	44	41	16	31	12
10 to 49 acres		20	138	179	42	195	8	62	8
50 to 179 acres		34	406	420	112	218	39	155	30
180 to 499 acres		82	293	239	207	124	34	235	56
500 to 999 acres		83	140	89	154	50	43	165	71
1,000 acres or more		186	65	54	177	31	151	170	133
Total cropland	farms_	390	957	900	669	568	257	759	294
	acres_	343 039	208 974	177 972	354 217	106 867	392 706	363 772	262 470
Harvested cropland	farms_	382	844	836	647	466	247	718	276
	acres_	159 903	114 691	112 895	208 645	69 445	202 166	219 446	129 425
Irrigated land	farms_	126	7	21	52	20	110	66	91
	acres_	22 795	2 276	1 763	7 087	259	83 178	14 798	37 144
Market value of agricultural products sold	$1,000_	89 476	27 790	25 301	44 073	22 878	118 990	35 879	24 592
Average per farm	dollars_	211 527	25 684	24 878	59 882	34 716	408 900	43 984	79 330
Crops, including nursery and greenhouse crops	$1,000_	13 153	7 857	11 966	18 626	10 623	26 689	15 862	13 133
Livestock, poultry, and their products	$1,000_	76 323	19 934	13 335	25 446	12 255	92 301	20 117	11 459
Farms by value of sales:									
Less than $2,500		28	203	236	45	199	22	81	30
$2,500 to $4,999		33	165	143	39	95	14	67	11
$5,000 to $9,999		28	196	216	109	104	27	133	35
$10,000 to $24,999		81	246	211	166	98	40	205	43
$25,000 to $49,999		77	138	89	124	70	42	139	60
$50,000 to $99,999		73	90	56	135	45	50	107	53
$100,000 or more		103	44	66	116	48	96	86	78
Operators by principal occupation:									
Farming		316	500	460	583	273	225	546	230
Other		107	582	557	153	386	66	272	80
Operators by days worked off farm:									
Any		174	667	623	293	424	114	457	135
200 days or more		97	485	479	143	326	62	240	79
Average age of operator	years_	49.7	51.7	52.2	51.2	53.4	50.4	51.3	53.1
Total farm production expenses[1]	$1,000_	83 847	24 765	22 508	32 443	17 165	103 314	31 421	20 820
Average per farm	dollars_	198 221	22 888	22 131	44 140	26 047	355 033	38 413	67 163
Livestock and poultry:									
Cattle and calves inventory	farms_	253	799	663	472	357	123	531	167
	number_	83 072	43 136	32 679	44 080	19 542	77 669	51 395	31 041
Beef cows	farms_	134	657	533	387	284	93	415	105
	number_	7 702	16 554	13 733	16 427	7 377	8 038	20 005	6 156
Milk cows	farms_	17	75	52	38	19	8	29	4
	number_	691	1 404	1 719	605	784	182	1 316	8
Cattle and calves sold	farms_	260	815	668	488	361	125	541	172
	number_	122 505	30 393	21 053	30 448	17 123	136 995	36 725	23 981
Hogs and pigs inventory	farms_	18	133	106	159	40	14	96	13
	number_	672	16 634	11 369	49 577	8 292	1 457	9 076	1 640
Hogs and pigs sold	farms_	17	137	111	164	46	14	101	15
	number_	1 934	33 122	19 935	85 126	16 839	2 261	18 366	3 041
Sheep and lambs inventory	farms_	8	37	29	39	16	8	32	2
	number_	1 577	3 141	689	6 180	1 890	1 976	1 838	(D)
Chickens 3 months old or older inventory	farms_	28	70	82	46	31	21	57	4
	number_	772	(D)	2 473	2 024	2 305	835	2 049	51
Broilers and other meat-type chickens sold	farms_	-	2	1	1	1	1	2	-
	number_	-	(D)	(D)	(D)	(D)	(D)	(D)	-
Selected crops harvested:									
Corn for grain or seed	farms_	35	205	282	87	104	39	26	52
	acres_	2 826	12 664	23 174	6 361	8 767	24 651	5 130	13 151
	bushels_	343 924	858 889	2 053 312	742 577	759 913	3 148 328	574 524	1 742 065
Corn for silage or green chop	farms_	44	24	29	8	14	17	12	3
	acres_	4 094	773	844	328	1 029	2 455	496	146
	tons, green_	77 011	10 139	10 436	5 865	10 582	40 610	6 746	2 685
Sorghum for grain or seed	farms_	282	365	279	523	103	145	231	160
	acres_	31 439	23 760	17 596	58 469	4 799	25 436	11 834	21 760
	bushels_	1 923 912	1 362 502	1 219 455	4 277 975	346 106	1 241 764	622 839	1 501 690
Wheat for grain	farms_	370	155	83	666	60	226	681	252
	acres_	105 731	9 222	3 836	109 628	2 575	4 521 318	176 798	74 813
	bushels_	3 654 253	240 021	126 760	4 379 120	74 630	4 521 318	4 985 931	2 338 400
Oats for grain	farms_	4	95	97	116	52	7	53	10
	acres_	131	2 156	1 945	2 973	928	516	1 540	717
	bushels_	3 670	89 656	68 835	132 963	33 361	12 519	51 915	18 010
Soybeans for beans	farms_	31	369	365	154	239	14	43	60
	acres_	1 918	25 243	36 268	6 942	33 097	1 596	3 644	6 698
	bushels_	59 874	666 413	1 155 963	254 175	1 030 735	32 278	146 047	270 966
Hay—alfalfa, other tame, small grain, wild, grass silage, green chop, etc. (see text)	farms_	170	708	638	629	336	100	426	102
	acres_	10 680	43 691	32 019	22 884	17 728	20 561	26 571	11 051
	tons, dry_	27 556	71 748	56 692	57 762	30 035	89 250	62 799	36 268

See footnotes at end of table.

Table 1. **County Summary Highlights: 1987**—Con.

[For meaning of abbreviations and symbols, see introductory text]

Item	Labette	Lane	Leavenworth	Lincoln	Linn	Logan	Lyon	McPherson
Farms .... number..	971	322	1 144	578	666	382	872	1 357
Land in farms .... acres..	350 010	467 005	211 370	454 341	273 211	610 480	469 908	533 432
Average size of farm .... acres..	360	1 450	185	786	397	1 598	539	393
Value of land and buildings[1]:								
Average per farm .... dollars..	153 151	592 398	170 089	253 820	157 301	382 249	177 835	222 022
Average per acre .... dollars..	430	371	939	326	407	243	320	562
Estimated market value of all machinery and equipment[1]:								
Average per farm .... dollars..	28 156	78 263	25 112	51 318	30 923	63 422	28 908	45 754
Farms by size:								
1 to 9 acres	36	13	65	30	22	16	37	86
10 to 49 acres	102	5	296	23	74	7	93	126
50 to 179 acres	367	41	455	89	222	38	249	356
180 to 499 acres	238	50	225	161	201	61	249	432
500 to 999 acres	143	48	74	112	109	72	128	234
1,000 acres or more	85	165	29	163	60	188	116	123
Total cropland .... farms..	857	299	1 011	535	611	349	761	1 244
acres..	230 002	342 035	145 457	271 940	156 403	349 206	248 896	432 078
Harvested cropland .... farms..	767	291	892	510	551	334	709	1 210
acres..	136 963	154 879	96 700	163 709	93 665	150 236	153 962	283 623
Irrigated land .... farms..	19	46	17	7	2	46	8	165
acres..	1 905	14 902	310	699	(D)	10 982	(D)	24 008
Market value of agricultural products sold .... $1,000..	48 962	88 214	26 702	36 636	21 703	22 420	56 178	77 962
Average per farm .... dollars..	50 424	273 955	23 341	66 844	31 545	58 692	66 718	57 451
Crops, including nursery and greenhouse crops.. $1,000..	11 323	14 159	12 736	11 365	8 012	11 406	11 978	26 571
Livestock, poultry, and their products .... $1,000..	37 638	74 054	13 966	27 271	13 691	11 014	46 201	51 390
Farms by value of sales:								
Less than $2,500	173	21	346	45	151	21	138	157
$2,500 to $4,999	139	26	216	47	79	34	123	128
$5,000 to $9,999	202	29	192	70	110	41	134	218
$10,000 to $24,999	231	59	192	149	167	76	211	350
$25,000 to $49,999	94	43	87	106	79	79	99	200
$50,000 to $99,999	77	59	55	87	45	61	82	153
$100,000 or more	55	85	56	73	57	70	86	151
Operators by principal occupation:								
Farming	465	242	458	437	341	266	460	776
Other	506	80	686	141	347	116	412	581
Operators by days worked off farm:								
Any	576	129	710	239	369	156	504	617
200 days or more	427	66	562	129	274	86	354	480
Average age of operator .... years..	52.2	52.5	52.7	52.7	55.1	50.3	52.1	51.5
Total farm production expenses[1] .... $1,000..	40 870	79 856	21 790	31 723	17 179	18 657	50 199	60 212
Average per farm .... dollars..	42 134	248 001	19 047	54 865	24 861	48 968	57 568	44 371
Livestock and poultry:								
Cattle and calves inventory .... farms..	704	129	781	357	483	180	535	670
number..	56 329	59 727	30 300	53 344	35 037	31 593	75 525	56 946
Beef cows .... farms..	595	79	651	321	403	153	398	449
number..	17 913	5 587	12 250	19 348	14 000	11 127	18 655	12 831
Milk cows .... farms..	31	7	86	26	29	18	36	80
number..	1 184	20	3 497	698	763	175	588	2 568
Cattle and calves sold .... farms..	708	142	745	371	472	191	554	677
number..	57 824	114 179	14 862	47 799	22 610	22 537	79 945	62 079
Hogs and pigs inventory .... farms..	61	14	145	52	45	20	106	129
number..	14 152	1 922	17 890	6 635	15 530	1 883	11 099	22 117
Hogs and pigs sold .... farms..	65	15	148	51	48	20	107	140
number..	29 029	2 180	32 772	14 086	26 842	4 601	18 004	40 812
Sheep and lambs inventory .... farms..	32	8	31	29	12	5	29	63
number..	1 066	261	1 075	5 137	224	(D)	857	8 899
Chickens 3 months old or older inventory ..... farms..	47	15	95	39	47	23	55	88
number..	999	550	2 618	1 151	1 506	747	(D)	364 291
Broilers and other meat-type chickens sold ..... farms..	–	–	3	1	–	1	–	5
number..	–	–	110	(D)	–	(D)	–	1 410
Selected crops harvested:								
Corn for grain or seed .... farms..	47	8	292	9	92	16	180	106
acres..	2 261	643	17 320	1 131	6 544	3 448	11 007	11 579
bushels..	175 848	66 966	1 525 704	37 506	485 739	368 647	805 657	1 498 266
Corn for silage or green chop .... farms..	16	17	49	12	4	5	55	38
acres..	591	3 690	1 866	255	132	900	3 783	1 320
tons, green..	8 954	66 540	24 990	2 315	1 666	18 450	49 028	17 320
Sorghum for grain or seed .... farms..	342	178	260	350	241	184	459	683
acres..	25 624	26 210	14 487	24 531	16 867	21 236	35 421	44 923
bushels..	1 819 205	1 400 041	1 030 845	1 624 789	1 144 733	1 019 214	2 360 796	3 602 374
Wheat for grain .... farms..	171	280	74	480	73	322	274	1 077
acres..	11 815	111 527	3 049	99 912	2 608	111 886	17 825	184 434
bushels..	252 913	4 240 788	86 650	3 442 697	70 854	3 567 380	498 181	6 198 954
Oats for grain .... farms..	179	13	90	77	61	21	47	53
acres..	5 485	645	1 647	1 845	1 225	1 329	1 332	675
bushels..	172 356	21 405	55 135	71 466	44 681	46 655	43 923	27 692
Soybeans for beans .... farms..	482	4	381	44	297	2	492	352
acres..	66 166	174	31 563	1 896	40 829	(D)	43 599	16 498
bushels..	1 536 005	5 240	974 966	48 261	1 208 979	(D)	1 340 498	554 623
Hay—alfalfa, other tame, small grain, wild, grass silage, green chop, etc. (see text) .... farms..	545	75	677	326	438	117	492	654
acres..	28 555	4 653	29 970	26 059	27 364	7 713	44 903	26 779
tons, dry..	47 709	8 716	55 874	67 549	46 141	15 478	59 188	66 796

See footnotes at end of table.

Item	Marion	Marshall	Meade	Miami	Mitchell	Montgomery	Morris	Morton
Farms..........number..	1 119	1 061	464	1 151	622	974	550	226
Land in farms..........acres..	577 700	553 436	582 454	272 290	473 829	327 193	396 556	457 440
Average size of farm..........acres..	516	522	1 255	237	762	336	721	2 024
Value of land and buildings[1]:								
Average per farm..........dollars..	214 644	237 714	483 019	193 407	345 722	154 431	241 545	563 862
Average per acre..........dollars..	436	451	412	854	445	470	336	280
Estimated market value of all machinery and equipment[1]:								
Average per farm..........dollars..	44 694	43 930	70 674	27 500	64 447	28 166	42 244	89 705
Farms by size:								
1 to 9 acres	67	82	18	44	34	25	28	6
10 to 49 acres	97	57	11	262	40	156	32	9
50 to 179 acres	243	181	42	446	93	397	105	34
180 to 499 acres	341	344	96	268	151	235	159	28
500 to 999 acres	232	264	113	78	132	86	105	24
1,000 acres or more	139	153	184	55	172	74	121	125
Total cropland..........farms..	1 041	972	434	984	587	809	505	202
..........acres..	391 244	409 347	394 670	177 466	382 878	185 730	195 470	291 295
Harvested cropland ....farms..	994	844	413	902	570	674	472	192
..........acres..	252 314	261 802	200 706	116 217	237 322	111 306	112 525	139 398
Irrigated land ....farms..	28	20	191	14	39	21	6	78
..........acres..	2 168	2 159	100 309	437	4 867	2 463	226	35 799
Market value of agricultural products sold ....$1,000..	56 631	53 792	85 291	24 920	59 911	22 988	39 229	20 191
Average per farm..........dollars..	52 396	50 700	119 161	21 651	96 319	23 601	71 326	89 342
Crops, including nursery and greenhouse								
crops..........$1,000..	17 354	24 033	22 752	13 227	21 589	9 396	6 591	9 780
Livestock, poultry, and their products ....$1,000..	41 278	29 760	32 539	11 694	38 321	13 592	32 639	10 411
Farms by value of sales:								
Less than $2,500	127	82	25	339	64	259	60	22
$2,500 to $4,999	104	73	25	217	37	165	46	11
$5,000 to $9,999	157	115	42	193	55	200	80	31
$10,000 to $24,999	262	248	96	195	158	186	133	36
$25,000 to $49,999	169	223	82	94	114	66	90	32
$50,000 to $99,999	162	190	75	56	93	56	74	42
$100,000 or more	138	130	119	56	111	42	67	52
Operators by principal occupation:								
Farming	727	767	344	433	442	417	376	166
Other	392	294	120	718	180	557	174	60
Operators by days worked off farm:								
Any	575	468	200	746	266	571	249	80
200 days or more	349	238	100	596	161	442	138	52
Average age of operator ....years..	51.7	49.8	52.5	51.8	50.4	54.3	54.3	49.8
Total farm production expenses[1] ....$1,000..	45 506	43 417	44 664	19 230	47 864	21 179	35 629	18 175
Average per farm..........dollars..	40 669	40 882	96 636	16 721	76 952	21 745	64 781	80 777
Livestock and poultry:								
Cattle and calves inventory ....farms..	660	668	213	771	312	695	391	103
..........number..	66 026	49 806	50 379	33 569	47 246	32 459	55 338	15 115
Beef cows ....farms..	432	542	122	660	254	592	311	84
..........number..	16 960	16 259	(D)	15 513	12 215	15 636	17 055	5 271
Milk cows ....farms..	103	77	6	58	15	25	52	6
..........number..	3 906	2 680	(D)	1 685	441	950	1 853	10
Cattle and calves sold ....farms..	690	676	226	783	320	701	402	111
..........number..	55 585	35 633	56 100	19 583	54 604	18 690	52 184	17 774
Hogs and pigs inventory ....farms..	158	267	13	62	64	60	81	7
..........number..	30 622	44 970	2 728	11 243	23 109	20 969	10 777	80
Hogs and pigs sold ....farms..	173	279	14	59	88	62	81	5
..........number..	57 777	85 900	5 672	16 471	42 278	43 551	21 411	(D)
Sheep and lambs inventory ....farms..	62	27	8	41	39	21	19	4
..........number..	4 454	1 529	514	904	5 400	491	599	(D)
Chickens 3 months old or older inventory ....farms..	73	55	16	86	32	56	40	10
..........number..	165 871	3 756	535	1 953	1 330	1 474	1 531	359
Broilers and other meat-type chickens sold ....farms..	2	-	2	-	1	4	-	-
..........number..	(D)	-	(D)	-	(D)	267	-	-
Selected crops harvested:								
Corn for grain or seed ....farms..	85	114	80	156	32	73	65	10
..........acres..	3 765	6 076	21 843	9 976	2 516	7 980	2 667	2 658
..........bushels..	319 364	516 618	2 651 087	857 078	265 085	717 163	205 977	361 115
Corn for silage or green chop ....farms..	71	20	12	26	8	7	31	4
..........acres..	2 128	514	909	1 063	207	351	896	881
..........tons, green..	23 383	8 264	14 726	12 678	3 384	3 731	13 074	(D)
Sorghum for grain or seed ....farms..	739	824	269	262	429	253	347	148
..........acres..	66 973	91 784	56 143	17 421	48 067	28 618	27 744	58 159
..........bushels..	4 561 421	6 350 013	4 632 870	1 208 594	3 569 899	1 921 024	1 494 922	2 548 003
Wheat for grain ....farms..	857	768	391	48	529	177	328	167
..........acres..	118 472	75 311	106 765	1 631	164 343	16 023	36 194	74 500
..........bushels..	3 717 501	2 580 342	3 452 545	44 393	6 254 876	365 771	1 020 099	2 058 391
Oats for grain ....farms..	148	145	2	89	79	64	83	4
..........acres..	2 925	2 320	(D)	1 520	1 503	1 552	1 759	268
..........bushels..	85 028	112 692	(D)	53 858	71 496	48 808	48 007	12 340
Soybeans for beans ....farms..	321	741	54	393	114	280	212	3
..........acres..	11 732	61 942	5 222	46 043	7 764	34 604	12 486	(D)
..........bushels..	301 506	1 639 693	202 530	1 462 632	194 245	913 282	329 534	(D)
Hay—alfalfa, other tame, small grain, wild, grass silage, green chop, etc. (see text) ....farms..	710	617	125	748	285	524	348	39
..........acres..	45 711	29 483	9 648	40 425	14 427	25 847	31 649	3 273
..........tons, dry..	91 483	56 624	25 891	70 017	36 215	40 851	60 014	6 196

See footnotes at end of table.

Table 1. **County Summary Highlights: 1987**—Con.

[For meaning of abbreviations and symbols, see introductory text]

Item	Nemaha	Neosho	Ness	Norton	Osage	Osborne	Ottawa	Pawnee
Farms ....number..	1 127	751	597	470	885	607	523	530
Land in farms ....acres..	436 761	305 492	673 189	507 626	357 199	545 417	385 542	486 999
Average size of farm ....acres..	388	407	1 128	1 080	404	899	737	919
Value of land and buildings[1]:								
Average per farm ....dollars..	167 203	158 283	284 851	341 366	154 963	279 455	266 295	397 967
Average per acre ....dollars..	442	380	257	322	399	309	392	423
Estimated market value of all machinery and equipment[1]:								
Average per farm ....dollars..	47 989	31 618	55 490	50 854	33 142	59 380	42 185	73 566
Farms by size:								
1 to 9 acres	56	25	20	21	33	27	26	28
10 to 49 acres	74	69	7	26	126	24	45	29
50 to 179 acres	258	257	70	47	267	73	84	76
180 to 499 acres	430	214	137	91	241	153	123	102
500 to 999 acres	245	116	115	108	136	130	114	134
1,000 acres or more	64	70	248	177	82	200	131	162
Total cropland .... farms..	1 042	669	560	439	782	565	483	496
acres..	331 086	197 149	464 503	323 300	214 840	347 966	244 551	404 356
Harvested cropland .... farms..	994	611	542	415	729	554	476	475
acres..	203 290	126 121	193 380	154 827	140 377	182 055	149 979	223 904
Irrigated land .... farms..	9	7	29	54	5	78	25	183
acres..	494	536	2 662	5 893	(D)	8 482	1 741	65 213
Market value of agricultural products sold .... $1,000..	61 420	26 111	28 019	33 417	30 765	33 264	37 539	91 433
Average per farm ....dollars..	54 499	34 768	46 932	71 101	34 762	54 800	71 777	172 515
Crops, including nursery and greenhouse crops .... $1,000..	16 044	11 218	13 666	13 685	13 063	14 996	11 403	25 274
Livestock, poultry, and their products .... $1,000..	45 376	14 893	14 353	19 732	17 702	18 268	26 137	66 159
Farms by value of sales:								
Less than $2,500	94	135	37	18	185	41	61	41
$2,500 to $4,999	71	118	53	34	111	49	44	33
$5,000 to $9,999	126	119	76	48	157	59	64	53
$10,000 to $24,999	253	157	129	119	182	132	124	107
$25,000 to $49,999	225	93	118	95	108	116	77	101
$50,000 to $99,999	199	69	102	82	79	125	87	96
$100,000 or more	159	60	82	74	63	85	66	99
Operators by principal occupation:								
Farming	802	431	426	350	407	447	339	398
Other	325	320	171	120	478	160	184	132
Operators by days worked off farm:								
Any	485	404	270	203	554	253	270	200
200 days or more	292	277	146	121	375	134	153	119
Average age of operator ....years..	48.7	52.6	52.3	51.9	51.7	51.7	52.8	53.5
Total farm production expenses[1] .... $1,000..	47 002	20 374	21 214	28 000	24 881	25 983	32 030	72 505
Average per farm ....dollars..	41 706	27 093	35 474	59 574	28 115	42 805	61 360	136 802
Livestock and poultry:								
Cattle and calves inventory .... farms..	748	528	382	310	517	372	301	232
number..	60 317	34 652	42 710	38 256	34 842	47 252	40 760	57 425
Beef cows .... farms..	481	452	269	265	405	324	231	164
number..	14 864	13 699	15 690	16 197	11 706	19 139	13 579	(D)
Milk cows .... farms..	145	42	14	14	26	20	23	3
number..	5 980	1 381	283	206	476	573	503	(D)
Cattle and calves sold .... farms..	741	532	387	316	532	379	307	240
number..	39 541	21 342	30 993	31 830	27 683	35 512	45 524	130 566
Hogs and pigs inventory .... farms..	308	51	18	60	82	53	34	38
number..	86 022	23 529	1 870	16 293	8 067	7 984	3 809	10 136
Hogs and pigs sold .... farms..	327	57	17	60	85	61	35	42
number..	151 416	33 580	2 322	34 919	16 834	13 912	6 862	17 760
Sheep and lambs inventory .... farms..	41	17	12	15	15	43	21	14
number..	1 997	644	1 352	1 354	284	3 491	2 337	2 177
Chickens 3 months old or older inventory .... farms..	49	47	32	34	55	41	40	16
number..	91 184	2 431	819	865	1 473	1 901	2 007	570
Broilers and other meat-type chickens sold .... farms..	1	–	2	–	2	2	–	–
number..	(D)	–	(D)	–	(D)	(D)	–	–
Selected crops harvested:								
Corn for grain or seed .... farms..	243	88	2	70	98	26	11	52
acres..	10 885	5 010	(D)	9 697	4 676	1 180	2 232	13 077
bushels..	711 109	443 841	(D)	881 532	360 132	121 174	301 182	1 819 964
Corn for silage or green chop .... farms..	104	11	1	4	15	6	6	8
acres..	3 625	798	(D)	224	842	68	136	411
tons, green..	41 155	14 617	(D)	4 100	11 877	730	1 530	8 496
Sorghum for grain or seed .... farms..	822	318	362	242	435	417	211	337
acres..	90 326	28 847	32 270	23 991	39 997	35 210	12 192	46 296
bushels..	6 296 279	2 130 009	1 744 228	1 713 245	2 864 632	2 602 595	869 169	3 497 382
Wheat for grain .... farms..	654	136	519	376	160	517	424	433
acres..	35 303	13 064	135 612	98 468	7 888	117 191	111 270	125 758
bushels..	1 080 637	335 523	4 654 378	3 942 665	205 292	4 308 743	3 482 863	4 295 992
Oats for grain .... farms..	120	147	12	62	63	61	40	12
acres..	2 034	4 216	297	2 896	1 040	1 344	625	324
bushels..	84 805	168 894	5 780	103 836	34 658	66 886	25 481	10 878
Soybeans for beans .... farms..	613	408	11	9	481	74	117	98
acres..	31 953	50 860	969	344	50 704	3 224	5 250	11 666
bushels..	839 157	1 290 328	9 850	4 846	1 508 243	84 719	155 104	461 282
Hay—alfalfa, other tame, small grain, wild, grass silage, green chop, etc. (see text) .... farms..	662	462	272	220	489	331	220	220
acres..	33 071	26 155	18 306	12 510	37 886	20 527	18 533	27 296
tons, dry..	70 183	45 326	43 749	34 952	52 307	50 319	43 177	96 658

See footnotes at end of table.

Table 1. **County Summary Highlights: 1987**—Con.

[For meaning of abbreviations and symbols, see introductory text]

Item	Phillips	Pottawatomie	Pratt	Rawlins	Reno	Republic	Rice	Riley
Farms_____number__	591	790	517	541	1 557	833	604	546
Land in farms_____acres__	542 578	443 660	466 245	641 810	717 764	440 215	429 065	247 609
Average size of farm_____acres__	918	562	902	1 186	461	528	710	453
Value of land and buildings[1]:								
Average per farm_____dollars__	274 172	204 275	418 988	325 342	263 020	262 151	315 447	183 629
Average per acre_____dollars__	321	374	466	272	565	482	448	448
Estimated market value of all machinery and equipment[1]:								
Average per farm_____dollars__	46 099	28 336	76 332	56 965	46 177	56 873	62 989	36 030
Farms by size:								
1 to 9 acres _____	23	50	15	27	99	42	30	26
10 to 49 acres _____	30	82	15	11	203	47	43	84
50 to 179 acres _____	99	189	79	48	356	196	117	126
180 to 499 acres _____	111	194	114	98	419	206	125	133
500 to 999 acres _____	126	151	124	119	261	205	131	114
1,000 acres or more _____	202	124	170	238	217	135	158	61
Total cropland_____farms__	555	667	487	506	1 424	765	556	489
_____acres__	333 728	188 003	392 119	414 811	582 519	342 576	347 501	132 841
Harvested cropland_____farms__	527	614	455	467	1 346	736	541	462
_____acres__	162 736	118 376	242 460	196 707	374 679	230 517	214 092	80 307
Irrigated land_____farms__	37	48	160	72	156	232	67	27
_____acres__	4 910	9 573	71 541	11 547	25 576	45 220	15 058	1 922
Market value of agricultural products sold _____$1,000__	34 621	39 295	97 669	31 808	82 925	97 295	69 583	25 444
Average per farm_____dollars__	58 581	49 741	188 914	58 795	53 259	116 801	115 204	46 601
Crops, including nursery and greenhouse crops_____$1,000__	13 746	9 232	27 034	17 077	33 141	29 926	20 715	7 197
Livestock, poultry, and their products _____$1,000__	20 875	30 064	70 635	14 731	49 784	67 369	48 869	18 248
Farms by value of sales:								
Less than $2,500 _____	52	156	38	37	242	62	70	84
$2,500 to $4,999 _____	50	77	32	37	160	67	55	69
$5,000 to $9,999 _____	61	101	56	44	249	77	52	68
$10,000 to $24,999 _____	109	155	104	96	333	168	116	114
$25,000 to $49,999 _____	139	125	93	126	233	165	99	81
$50,000 to $99,999 _____	98	92	84	120	174	168	101	68
$100,000 or more _____	82	84	110	81	166	126	99	62
Operators by principal occupation:								
Farming _____	449	440	368	428	927	609	401	325
Other _____	142	350	149	113	630	224	203	221
Operators by days worked off farm:								
Any _____	235	396	237	227	848	420	310	270
200 days or more _____	120	262	118	106	506	201	179	189
Average age of operator _____years__	52.1	52.6	52.5	51.3	51.5	49.6	51.9	52.9
Total farm production expenses[1] _____$1,000__	26 959	30 076	89 949	24 757	56 378	88 233	57 389	18 519
Average per farm_____dollars__	45 539	38 073	173 963	45 762	42 632	105 795	95 014	33 856
Livestock and poultry:								
Cattle and calves inventory _____farms__	421	544	276	321	795	498	320	352
_____number__	51 554	56 613	61 095	44 947	66 838	58 209	50 618	31 205
Beef cows_____farms__	367	456	178	262	535	433	235	277
_____number__	25 421	21 027	5 827	19 207	17 232	13 418	8 824	11 897
Milk cows_____farms__	28	63	10	15	145	22	23	31
_____number__	412	1 387	273	354	4 275	844	878	1 108
Cattle and calves sold _____farms__	426	560	276	325	783	513	323	363
_____number__	26 308	40 874	104 585	24 064	79 028	95 611	69 919	21 457
Hogs and pigs inventory_____farms__	101	166	29	68	140	110	30	99
_____number__	41 030	36 063	18 001	11 548	21 871	19 475	17 265	29 764
Hogs and pigs sold _____farms__	111	196	31	69	150	123	38	113
_____number__	67 272	64 890	25 403	25 292	41 754	33 206	26 149	50 123
Sheep and lambs inventory _____farms__	18	21	17	11	140	34	15	34
_____number__	1 025	460	1 221	2 438	13 858	3 951	1 217	2 893
Chickens 3 months old or older inventory _____farms__	46	61	21	43	129	47	25	36
_____number__	1 109	(D)	425	2 057	139 418	1 664	730	7 996
Broilers and other meat-type chickens sold _____farms__	2	1	-	-	11	-	-	2
_____number__	(D)	(D)	-	-	25 405	-	-	(D)
Selected crops harvested:								
Corn for grain or seed _____farms__	38	133	112	54	69	265	36	56
_____acres__	5 261	11 352	29 531	6 047	11 147	39 494	7 833	2 892
_____bushels__	604 232	1 167 310	2 996 866	639 516	1 243 297	5 110 811	1 015 410	263 926
Corn for silage or green chop_____farms__	7	33	7	16	36	13	12	47
_____acres__	279	1 917	810	498	814	260	1 069	1 349
_____tons, green__	6 355	23 665	12 610	6 665	10 796	3 977	21 416	19 932
Sorghum for grain or seed_____farms__	366	362	292	354	785	538	418	312
_____acres__	36 063	27 721	36 214	40 057	80 060	64 091	53 304	25 050
_____bushels__	2 659 290	1 707 764	2 301 925	2 357 618	5 271 312	5 252 038	4 174 853	1 717 217
Wheat for grain _____farms__	473	301	428	467	1 140	638	484	302
_____acres__	84 316	16 958	143 482	123 069	237 738	83 080	130 672	21 023
_____bushels__	3 467 434	524 558	4 258 898	4 776 125	6 848 396	3 356 029	4 465 243	723 631
Oats for grain _____farms__	77	95	12	59	55	111	22	68
_____acres__	1 834	1 421	464	2 150	1 157	2 162	889	1 027
_____bushels__	63 457	56 179	15 979	100 025	36 030	109 378	28 124	43 598
Soybeans for beans _____farms__	20	311	80	11	132	434	117	206
_____acres__	636	16 726	8 671	461	8 400	24 503	7 475	10 911
_____bushels__	26 816	584 291	334 145	8 451	297 067	852 680	253 945	341 081
Hay—alfalfa, other tame, small grain, wild, grass silage, green chop, etc. (see text) _____farms__	368	469	154	233	734	455	287	333
_____acres__	27 505	43 089	28 831	15 764	40 161	19 993	16 076	17 945
_____tons, dry__	74 247	71 446	127 661	46 473	106 117	52 593	45 925	34 821

See footnotes at end of table.

Table 1. **County Summary Highlights: 1987**—Con.

[For meaning of abbreviations and symbols, see introductory text]

Item	Rooks	Rush	Russell	Saline	Scott	Sedgwick	Seward	Shawnee
Farms .... number..	473	546	534	743	391	1 589	285	852
Land in farms .... acres..	547 539	422 826	461 014	403 798	470 774	523 580	331 397	221 098
Average size of farm .... acres..	1 158	774	863	543	1 204	330	1 163	260
Value of land and buildings[1]:								
Average per farm .... dollars..	328 368	236 672	241 090	248 793	443 652	289 538	562 074	189 910
Average per acre .... dollars..	310	322	280	471	373	861	461	804
Estimated market value of all machinery and equipment[1]:								
Average per farm .... dollars..	51 358	50 778	48 959	46 849	104 759	46 374	102 551	26 118
Farms by size:								
1 to 9 acres	16	25	28	39	31	135	10	60
10 to 49 acres	14	16	10	80	13	326	10	166
50 to 179 acres	53	94	95	211	53	412	38	325
180 to 499 acres	106	125	143	147	66	385	52	173
500 to 999 acres	98	132	103	142	63	216	53	85
1,000 acres or more	186	154	155	124	165	116	122	43
Total cropland .... farms..	443	508	490	683	342	1 434	247	718
acres..	322 396	347 130	287 618	288 689	375 948	445 408	247 336	149 707
Harvested cropland .... farms..	431	494	469	649	330	1 345	229	659
acres..	157 823	160 253	135 417	173 828	180 540	319 625	141 650	101 139
Irrigated land .... farms..	22	74	6	51	162	179	142	67
acres..	2 864	7 975	434	3 152	54 507	29 739	77 842	11 382
Market value of agricultural products sold ... $1,000..	24 933	20 057	20 315	30 700	280 233	59 327	130 390	21 859
Average per farm .... dollars..	52 713	36 734	38 043	41 318	716 708	37 336	457 508	25 656
Crops, including nursery and greenhouse crops .... $1,000..	12 907	12 740	9 476	12 261	18 858	30 494	15 373	12 792
Livestock, poultry, and their products ...... $1,000..	12 027	7 316	10 839	18 438	261 375	28 833	115 017	9 066
Farms by value of sales:								
Less than $2,500	36	41	45	145	22	372	35	229
$2,500 to $4,999	38	39	48	100	22	194	14	149
$5,000 to $9,999	63	97	100	99	31	234	26	135
$10,000 to $24,999	115	150	136	133	49	319	39	148
$25,000 to $49,999	81	87	76	103	75	183	38	80
$50,000 to $99,999	74	88	78	89	69	137	50	53
$100,000 or more	66	44	51	74	123	150	81	58
Operators by principal occupation:								
Farming	329	384	369	414	295	752	212	369
Other	144	162	165	329	96	837	73	483
Operators by days worked off farm:								
Any	230	262	256	410	153	973	121	510
200 days or more	127	126	130	271	85	685	65	392
Average age of operator .... years..	51.8	53.6	54.2	52.1	50.5	52.0	47.6	53.8
Total farm production expenses[1] .... $1,000..	17 662	14 904	14 939	25 085	249 582	47 864	123 869	16 655
Average per farm .... dollars..	37 341	27 296	28 029	33 716	638 316	30 122	434 628	19 571
Livestock and poultry:								
Cattle and calves inventory .... farms..	290	298	331	373	131	673	108	459
number..	35 599	23 531	34 604	36 119	169 825	41 135	86 120	19 849
Beef cows .... farms..	249	250	285	279	44	430	69	369
number..	16 746	10 168	16 436	13 844	(D)	10 344	3 348	7 764
Milk cows .... farms..	23	12	26	36	1	104	5	20
number..	798	276	822	1 413	(D)	6 989	6	370
Cattle and calves sold .... farms..	296	312	336	382	143	677	113	469
number..	23 034	15 492	21 249	25 262	393 502	25 327	145 857	14 737
Hogs and pigs inventory .... farms..	37	10	38	36	25	101	17	52
number..	2 903	581	4 125	21 121	29 994	15 370	(D)	4 620
Hogs and pigs sold .... farms..	37	10	37	39	24	107	17	54
number..	5 285	1 267	9 305	43 610	45 761	30 510	(D)	15 245
Sheep and lambs inventory .... farms..	16	9	12	20	3	86	5	5
number..	478	1 517	1 033	1 298	(D)	15 254	117	(D)
Chickens 3 months old or older inventory .... farms..	30	26	32	40	11	75	15	59
number..	965	5 743	903	3 506	248	115 757	275	1 181
Broilers and other meat-type chickens sold .... farms..	1	3	1	–	–	4	1	2
number..	(D)	265	(D)	–	–	375	(D)	(D)
Selected crops harvested:								
Corn for grain or seed .... farms..	11	15	8	27	53	79	51	176
acres..	1 303	1 005	102	1 324	8 948	13 005	11 367	20 588
bushels..	134 750	104 265	6 047	115 318	1 137 275	1 568 412	1 340 010	2 194 933
Corn for silage or green chop .... farms..	6	4	1	44	42	28	7	15
acres..	269	255	(D)	1 556	4 936	1 823	1 020	437
tons, green..	3 820	6 255	(D)	19 967	83 677	25 336	17 700	5 116
Sorghum for grain or seed .... farms..	284	337	253	303	203	709	165	260
acres..	30 101	30 125	21 517	16 514	35 551	83 831	49 622	20 453
bushels..	1 824 668	1 736 580	1 336 858	1 098 936	2 314 111	4 162 363	3 281 751	1 279 717
Wheat for grain .... farms..	408	461	414	541	315	1 041	208	148
acres..	100 707	113 315	92 100	126 775	115 140	189 806	66 948	7 719
bushels..	3 769 144	3 815 969	2 995 383	3 770 758	4 521 675	5 504 605	2 317 037	233 770
Oats for grain .... farms..	22	50	39	33	3	27	3	73
acres..	736	1 569	827	703	122	560	123	1 086
bushels..	23 120	46 850	30 517	25 825	6 500	15 865	3 777	30 440
Soybeans for beans .... farms..	9	36	17	183	14	240	15	323
acres..	880	3 179	659	7 565	1 046	21 042	824	30 060
bushels..	11 695	40 534	17 750	199 976	39 512	779 028	29 413	913 322
Hay—alfalfa, other tame, small grain, wild, grass silage, green chop, etc. (see text) .... farms..	208	213	265	362	86	669	59	443
acres..	16 051	12 056	20 371	22 883	6 975	35 692	9 678	23 711
tons, dry..	46 623	26 721	44 657	54 221	19 126	64 452	37 342	34 650

See footnotes at end of table.

Table 1. County Summary Highlights: 1987—Con.

[For meaning of abbreviations and symbols, see introductory text]

Item	Sheridan	Sherman	Smith	Stafford	Stanton	Stevens	Sumner	Thomas
Farms ... number	518	524	692	540	280	300	1 271	644
Land in farms ... acres	503 582	625 942	555 678	461 213	425 150	480 974	704 786	677 199
Average size of farm ... acres	972	1 195	803	854	1 518	1 537	555	1 052
Value of land and buildings[1]:								
Average per farm ... dollars	359 500	403 973	283 039	427 813	591 609	682 130	297 971	410 301
Average per acre ... dollars	370	360	347	492	409	438	535	396
Estimated market value of all machinery and equipment[1]:								
Average per farm ... dollars	70 197	74 064	59 417	80 891	111 903	145 329	56 488	79 020
Farms by size:								
1 to 9 acres	37	25	29	26	13	5	76	20
10 to 49 acres	9	8	36	22	11	8	106	18
50 to 179 acres	62	67	90	69	28	27	318	81
180 to 499 acres	102	92	158	128	31	33	286	130
500 to 999 acres	104	108	165	117	40	53	239	147
1,000 acres or more	204	224	214	178	157	174	244	248
Total cropland ... farms	470	487	648	506	265	281	1 178	606
... acres	374 043	497 494	381 501	376 008	379 898	392 622	599 210	565 763
Harvested cropland ... farms	461	470	630	488	241	260	1 137	592
... acres	183 013	251 534	213 337	230 807	184 701	238 566	415 440	296 047
Irrigated land ... farms	187	246	81	188	168	166	28	218
... acres	50 527	83 424	7 812	66 430	112 728	119 752	2 684	73 546
Market value of agricultural products sold ... $1,000	54 089	67 429	50 882	72 053	86 972	96 641	53 409	74 156
Average per farm ... dollars	104 419	128 681	73 486	133 432	310 613	322 138	42 021	115 150
Crops, including nursery and greenhouse crops ... $1,000	22 118	30 169	20 043	23 729	23 700	24 780	30 866	35 387
Livestock, poultry, and their products ... $1,000	31 971	37 260	30 809	48 324	63 271	71 861	22 543	38 770
Farms by value of sales:								
Less than $2,500	19	28	33	47	13	21	188	44
$2,500 to $4,999	33	27	35	49	17	22	112	31
$5,000 to $9,999	44	60	69	80	30	16	199	76
$10,000 to $24,999	102	92	132	74	30	37	263	121
$25,000 to $49,999	105	90	160	96	33	39	214	122
$50,000 to $99,999	113	98	152	96	53	67	155	118
$100,000 or more	102	129	111	126	104	98	140	132
Operators by principal occupation:								
Farming	394	384	536	396	238	222	741	450
Other	124	140	156	144	42	78	530	194
Operators by days worked off farm:								
Any	224	213	271	224	94	119	698	305
200 days or more	112	109	131	114	46	66	451	168
Average age of operator ... years	50.1	52.0	50.9	51.7	48.4	50.7	51.5	51.7
Total farm production expenses[1] ... $1,000	47 749	56 326	37 639	62 257	77 823	87 008	47 879	64 216
Average per farm ... dollars	92 179	107 492	54 391	115 505	276 951	290 028	37 749	99 563
Livestock and poultry:								
Cattle and calves inventory ... farms	291	187	451	255	101	113	598	217
... number	43 899	33 721	54 892	62 373	49 369	52 216	41 742	36 649
Beef cows ... farms	233	128	378	191	53	90	421	173
... number	(D)	8 262	20 908	(D)	1 504	5 332	12 163	9 257
Milk cows ... farms	14	11	42	4	3	-	36	12
... number	(D)	110	692	(D)	3	-	1 265	15
Cattle and calves sold ... farms	297	172	468	260	105	118	600	231
... number	48 624	54 185	43 689	86 803	99 059	(D)	33 680	55 597
Hogs and pigs inventory ... farms	59	24	103	28	12	9	97	24
... number	7 319	1 960	28 020	4 160	165	3 665	20 817	5 896
Hogs and pigs sold ... farms	56	27	113	33	11	9	102	26
... number	12 218	12 480	64 014	8 369	291	5 352	48 307	12 561
Sheep and lambs inventory ... farms	9	11	41	16	9	7	65	18
... number	1 294	1 382	2 755	1 112	147	699	9 493	1 758
Chickens 3 months old or older inventory ... farms	28	31	60	25	9	11	54	32
... number	819	903	2 209	677	362	283	2 068	757
Broilers and other meat-type chickens sold ... farms	-	1	6	-	-	-	4	2
... number	-	(D)	740	-	-	-	269	(D)
Selected crops harvested:								
Corn for grain or seed ... farms	130	188	50	108	96	65	17	184
... bushels	4 061 477	5 066 990	353 379	3 786 704	4 387 760	3 303 471	69 170	7 122 349
Corn for silage or green chop ... farms	20	33	2	18	13	2	15	27
... acres	1 138	1 741	(D)	1 262	1 854	(D)	559	2 719
... tons, green	19 932	34 885	(D)	21 218	37 442	(D)	6 140	47 201
Sorghum for grain or seed ... farms	304	115	507	328	146	225	412	396
... acres	35 704	10 329	61 168	47 264	31 419	114 832	31 913	36 425
... bushels	2 549 482	620 775	5 249 221	3 023 173	1 937 190	5 595 676	1 505 504	2 357 796
Wheat for grain ... farms	421	445	579	438	233	224	1 040	551
... acres	94 689	155 862	107 735	124 760	113 050	89 747	356 942	181 694
... bushels	3 742 447	5 887 056	4 438 271	3 532 057	4 136 357	3 172 411	10 409 785	6 513 764
Oats for grain ... farms	26	20	110	16	-	2	11	36
... acres	1 038	959	2 874	792	-	(D)	538	2 369
... bushels	33 054	49 845	123 453	21 879	-	(D)	13 000	113 468
Soybeans for beans ... farms	55	46	175	88	19	16	489	70
... acres	3 899	5 071	10 697	8 721	2 360	890	14 494	5 742
... bushels	169 748	211 544	307 315	324 309	75 869	26 397	305 850	183 371
Hay—alfalfa, other tame, small grain, wild, grass silage, green chop, etc. (see text) ... farms	180	113	401	215	40	47	489	122
... acres	10 891	9 169	22 323	20 695	3 734	7 048	22 688	6 733
... tons, dry	31 918	23 389	63 066	63 614	11 464	33 777	49 487	16 031

See footnotes at end of table.

Table 1. **County Summary Highlights: 1987** — Con.

[For meaning of abbreviations and symbols, see introductory text]

Item	Trego	Wabaunsee	Wallace	Washington	Wichita	Wilson	Woodson	Wyandotte
Farms .... number..	482	633	330	939	355	610	369	199
Land in farms .... acres..	480 159	460 304	529 749	518 501	440 467	299 462	253 967	23 936
Average size of farm .... acres..	996	727	1 605	552	1 241	491	688	120
Value of land and buildings[1]:								
Average per farm .... dollars..	249 226	286 829	558 106	216 607	488 611	178 589	226 190	159 588
Average per acre .... dollars..	256	385	351	406	373	365	309	1 609
Estimated market value of all machinery and equipment[1]:								
Average per term .... dollars..	58 721	29 901	68 372	53 671	87 013	39 118	34 552	25 453
Farms by size:								
1 to 9 acres	31	32	30	85	24	23	16	25
10 to 49 acres	7	65	4	44	9	50	26	93
50 to 179 acres	40	142	23	164	43	152	64	56
180 to 499 acres	104	173	55	281	59	178	126	15
500 to 999 acres	129	118	57	210	66	121	58	5
1,000 acres or more	171	103	161	155	154	86	78	5
Total cropland .... farms..	442	533	294	825	313	548	330	154
acres..	324 214	149 203	299 727	378 755	368 240	183 539	123 270	17 145
Harvested cropland .... farms..	426	488	283	794	307	505	303	125
acres..	139 788	90 028	146 695	239 242	182 673	114 733	85 309	12 112
Irrigated land .... farms..	30	32	116	82	172	18	3	7
acres..	3 076	6 749	45 733	8 293	73 438	1 555	(D)	14
Market value of agricultural products sold .... $1,000..	35 552	34 210	28 601	62 837	223 235	20 203	21 103	5 015
Average per farm .... dollars..	73 760	54 045	86 671	66 920	628 830	33 120	57 189	25 202
Crops, including nursery and greenhouse crops .... $1,000..	10 704	6 269	15 063	19 751	19 539	11 204	7 063	3 760
Livestock, poultry, and their products .... $1,000..	24 848	27 941	13 538	43 087	203 695	8 999	14 039	1 255
Farms by value of sales:								
Less than $2,500	25	106	15	51	23	106	46	87
$2,500 to $4,999	29	82	23	65	18	70	32	37
$5,000 to $9,999	47	88	35	117	32	91	68	34
$10,000 to $24,999	139	145	64	192	48	131	81	24
$25,000 to $49,999	129	77	56	186	54	86	54	5
$50,000 to $99,999	73	57	59	168	77	82	44	3
$100,000 or more	40	68	78	160	103	44	44	9
Operators by principal occupation:								
Farming	351	372	245	741	262	383	226	61
Other	131	261	85	198	93	227	143	138
Operators by days worked off farm:								
Any	230	330	163	365	147	329	183	131
200 days or more	95	223	86	164	78	192	112	108
Average age of operator .... years..	51.2	53.4	50.8	50.7	48.3	53.4	52.3	55.8
Total farm production expenses[1] .... $1,000..	30 660	29 463	23 242	50 203	190 626	16 037	15 204	3 898
Average per farm .... dollars..	63 611	46 619	70 429	53 521	538 492	26 334	41 316	19 587
Livestock and poultry:								
Cattle and calves inventory .... farms..	340	412	161	668	138	426	256	94
number..	38 838	51 872	22 920	87 997	90 559	28 333	22 297	1 867
Beef cows .... farms..	277	316	127	518	91	352	221	77
number..	15 468	18 420	10 441	20 017	5 934	12 076	(D)	3
Milk cows .... farms..	36	37	16	47	–	20	6	3
number..	884	958	104	2 230	–	659	(D)	(D)
Cattle and calves sold .... farms..	343	430	173	676	140	420	269	85
number..	43 119	42 728	22 603	41 984	294 835	15 095	26 356	(D)
Hogs and pigs inventory .... farms..	37	70	28	246	16	44	27	13
number..	2 771	19 702	2 526	92 927	1 600	12 236	2 585	1 052
Hogs and pigs sold .... farms..	36	75	34	254	17	44	31	14
number..	4 602	37 851	5 414	165 832	3 124	22 186	4 908	2 096
Sheep and lambs inventory .... farms..	14	21	18	43	15	17	22	4
number..	972	3 746	2 953	3 056	890	905	1 506	16
Chickens 3 months old or older inventory .... farms..	41	37	24	56	16	34	26	16
number..	1 102	(D)	704	4 251	407	847	535	305
Broilers and other meat-type chickens sold .... farms..	1	1	–	1	–	–	–	–
number..	(D)	(D)	–	(D)	–	–	–	–
Selected crops harvested:								
Corn for grain or seed .... farms..	10	75	96	129	94	38	28	21
acres..	520	6 814	22 478	8 272	16 401	2 231	1 515	2 104
bushels..	66 335	701 730	3 210 151	785 743	2 291 817	176 995	94 015	229 190
Corn for silage or green chop .... farms..	4	33	9	91	25	9	2	2
acres..	67	1 098	592	1 110	2 281	426	(D)	(D)
tons, green..	837	14 641	9 235	12 470	47 468	5 880	(D)	(D)
Sorghum for grain or seed .... farms..	273	292	61	689	187	289	191	6
acres..	26 500	19 382	9 731	98 823	24 374	26 603	17 603	(D)
bushels..	1 507 727	1 274 145	463 198	7 110 326	1 693 699	1 798 323	1 250 906	(D)
Wheat for grain .... farms..	413	222	267	852	300	210	114	9
acres..	91 726	11 153	93 419	74 196	118 864	16 950	7 822	482
bushels..	3 380 637	330 170	3 009 097	2 638 117	4 477 060	394 873	171 930	14 158
Oats for grain .... farms..	28	66	12	155	11	31	38	4
acres..	675	1 122	762	2 775	757	818	740	51
bushels..	24 243	42 886	25 960	143 002	32 630	29 093	27 145	1 730
Soybeans for beans .... farms..	–	227	13	475	23	329	210	35
acres..	–	14 271	845	30 869	1 295	52 601	30 000	5 417
bushels..	–	434 517	26 139	902 105	37 428	1 505 453	905 137	204 728
Hay—alfalfa, other tame, small grain, wild, grass silage, green chop, etc. (see text) .... farms..	225	360	105	581	87	353	240	66
acres..	13 979	36 781	10 267	29 903	6 973	20 675	31 246	2 063
tons, dry..	32 250	62 976	22 017	64 738	20 717	34 169	38 745	3 215

[1]Data are based on a sample of farms.

Table 2. Market Value of Agricultural Products Sold and Farms by Standard Industrial Classification: 1987 and 1982

[For meaning of abbreviations and symbols, see introductory text]

Item	Kansas	Allen	Anderson	Atchison	Barber	Barton	Bourbon
MARKET VALUE OF AGRICULTURAL PRODUCTS SOLD							
Total sales (see text) .... farms, 1987..	68 579	665	727	694	535	937	842
1982..	73 315	735	768	768	517	962	882
$1,000, 1987..	6 476 669	23 025	34 226	26 262	45 715	125 117	23 062
1982..	6 190 861	23 723	29 700	26 894	52 423	117 840	26 531
Average per farm........dollars, 1987..	94 441	34 624	47 078	37 842	85 448	133 529	27 389
1982..	84 442	32 276	37 264	35 016	101 398	122 495	30 080
1987 value of sales:							
Less than $1,000 .... farms..	4 538	40	40	18	34	61	72
$1,000..	1 980	11	14	6	5	21	24
$1,000 to $2,499 .... farms..	4 964	62	63	59	28	57	100
$1,000..	8 455	107	107	99	50	94	168
$2,500 to $4,999 .... farms..	5 919	95	95	78	34	86	130
$1,000..	25 287	342	234	292	122	306	478
$5,000 to $9,999 .... farms..	9 430	112	115	108	58	116	163
$1,000..	68 474	789	804	761	422	864	1 187
$10,000 to $19,999 .... farms..	10 504	103	118	124	72	188	153
$1,000..	150 932	1 477	1 665	1 824	1 073	2 678	2 214
$20,000 to $24,999 .... farms..	3 566	28	40	34	19	59	42
$1,000..	79 440	639	881	769	435	1 319	930
$25,000 to $39,999 .... farms..	7 150	74	75	67	74	136	65
$1,000..	227 493	2 337	2 432	2 169	2 391	4 310	2 068
$40,000 to $49,999 .... farms..	3 132	31	31	46	19	42	14
$1,000..	139 856	1 387	1 379	2 069	855	1 890	634
$50,000 to $99,999 .... farms..	8 997	64	98	95	84	104	56
$1,000..	637 837	4 435	7 091	6 853	6 024	7 252	3 871
$100,000 to $249,999 .... farms..	6 656	42	62	55	89	70	34
$1,000..	1 008 123	6 206	9 287	7 843	11 384	10 580	4 973
$250,000 to $499,999 .... farms..	1 766	12	17	9	33	11	9
$1,000..	597 614	(D)	5 659	(D)	11 437	3 706	2 835
$500,000 or more .... farms..	957	2	3	1	11	7	4
$1,000..	3 533 796	(D)	4 673	(D)	11 517	92 095	3 679
1982 value of sales[1]:							
Less than $1,000 .... farms..	4 357	42	56	43	19	47	93
$1,000..	1 433	17	23	14	5	9	33
$1,000 to $2,499 .... farms..	5 280	80	63	59	12	49	120
$1,000..	8 977	136	113	99	21	88	205
$2,500 to $4,999 .... farms..	5 566	87	75	95	22	60	110
$1,000..	24 008	323	348	346	77	229	400
$5,000 to $9,999 .... farms..	9 183	122	123	121	47	102	147
$1,000..	66 849	889	898	894	351	744	1 066
$10,000 to $19,999 .... farms..	11 236	139	133	123	73	181	145
$1,000..	162 118	2 028	1 982	1 757	1 097	2 622	2 110
$20,000 to $24,999 .... farms..	3 894	34	43	38	32	65	38
$1,000..	86 796	756	957	854	714	1 473	857
$25,000 to $39,999 .... farms..	8 007	77	81	92	44	153	65
$1,000..	255 798	2 410	2 550	2 998	1 421	4 859	2 062
$40,000 to $49,999 .... farms..	3 820	30	41	38	39	59	25
$1,000..	170 777	1 339	1 832	1 726	1 735	2 635	1 111
$50,000 to $99,999 .... farms..	10 459	73	103	96	97	157	73
$1,000..	741 372	5 143	7 302	6 774	6 954	11 030	5 268
$100,000 to $249,999 .... farms..	7 644	43	43	55	90	62	53
$1,000..	1 150 070	6 771	6 545	7 725	14 325	9 074	7 407
$250,000 to $499,999 .... farms..	1 940	5	15	7	26	15	9
$1,000..	654 510	1 691	4 427	(D)	8 794	4 909	2 976
$500,000 or more .... farms..	895	3	4	1	16	12	4
$1,000..	2 865 670	2 218	2 721	(D)	16 929	80 168	3 035
Sales by commodity or commodity group:							
Crops, including nursery and greenhouse crops........ farms, 1987..	51 773	444	518	527	388	786	462
1982..	56 791	530	581	560	425	827	529
$1,000, 1987..	1 693 808	11 747	16 771	14 121	9 552	24 063	6 058
1982..	2 143 047	11 755	15 341	12 644	20 351	34 036	8 621
Grains........ farms, 1987..	48 608	418	487	496	379	766	381
1982..	54 146	507	548	538	417	799	480
$1,000, 1987..	1 550 403	11 156	16 129	13 636	9 180	20 778	5 569
1982..	2 009 726	11 322	14 453	12 238	19 897	30 182	8 026
Corn for grain .... farms, 1987..	7 426	72	146	229	-	41	67
1982..	6 297	55	170	172	6	31	61
$1,000, 1987..	255 791	963	1 562	2 689	-	2 168	635
1982..	263 913	551	1 832	2 047	274	2 093	655
Wheat........ farms, 1987..	38 365	135	128	131	373	750	62
1982..	49 000	393	381	388	411	779	313
$1,000, 1987..	694 147	620	438	322	8 485	12 929	221
1982..	1 162 533	3 002	2 080	1 580	18 848	21 224	1 842
Soybeans........ farms, 1987..	18 724	392	448	435	16	77	316
1982..	16 993	423	476	438	8	38	391
$1,000, 1987..	263 742	7 676	11 896	6 960	292	1 366	3 861
1982..	215 700	6 094	8 462	5 463	311	1 243	4 310
Sorghum for grain .... farms, 1987..	28 719	249	293	355	79	468	171
1982..		193	237	304	48	427	170
$1,000, 1987..	311 649	1 645	2 230	3 579	387	4 262	828
1982..	350 628	1 591	2 008	3 051	424	5 526	1 163
Barley .... farms, 1987..	1 715	-	-	-	2	10	1
1982..	(NA)	(NA)	(NA)	(NA)	(NA)	(NA)	(NA)
$1,000, 1987..	3 963	-	-	-	(D)	(D)	(D)
1982..	(NA)	(NA)	(NA)	(NA)	(NA)	(NA)	(NA)
Oats .... farms, 1987..	2 416	29	32	45	6	30	19
1982..	2 828	32	47	40	13	11	30
$1,000, 1987..	3 328	(D)	(D)	(D)	(D)	30	(D)
1982..	6 275	78	(D)	54	26	16	(D)
Other grains[2] .... farms, 1987..	1 656	1	2	1	-	4	-
1982..	1 011	3	2	6	8	7	1
$1,000, 1987..	17 793	(D)	(D)	(D)	-	(D)	-
1982..	10 660	7	52	52	14	79	(D)

See footnotes at end of table.

Table 2. **Market Value of Agricultural Products Sold and Farms by Standard Industrial Classification: 1987 and 1982** —Con.

[For meaning of abbreviations and symbols, see introductory text]

Item	Brown	Butler	Chase	Chautauqua	Cherokee	Cheyenne	Clark
MARKET VALUE OF AGRICULTURAL PRODUCTS SOLD							
Total sales (see text) .... farms, 1987..	728	1 300	288	421	841	493	290
1982..	826	1 376	295	431	939	546	308
$1,000, 1987..	62 567	99 269	34 012	15 707	22 029	51 543	54 942
1982..	60 674	101 956	28 668	15 749	24 553	51 572	50 550
Average per farm ....dollars, 1987..	85 944	76 376	118 098	37 309	26 194	104 549	189 456
1982..	73 455	74 096	97 183	36 542	26 148	95 004	164 123
1987 value of sales:							
Less than $1,000 .... farms..	27	181	15	52	83	17	14
$1,000..	10	56	5	16	24	5	2
$1,000 to $2,499 .... farms..	26	140	12	45	119	15	9
$1,000..	44	226	21	76	201	26	17
$2,500 to $4,999 .... farms..	46	167	21	53	133	30	10
$1,000..	162	595	80	189	479	123	31
$5,000 to $9,999 .... farms..	86	162	29	81	132	47	28
$1,000..	598	1 148	207	606	940	346	199
$10,000 to $19,999 .... farms..	117	188	43	60	116	73	41
$1,000..	1 767	2 670	598	865	1 642	1 017	580
$20,000 to $24,999 .... farms..	57	44	15	15	37	28	12
$1,000..	1 276	975	337	325	819	635	267
$25,000 to $39,999 .... farms..	66	92	35	34	76	73	23
$1,000..	2 099	2 897	1 136	1 097	2 348	2 323	780
$40,000 to $49,999 .... farms..	37	31	18	14	20	35	15
$1,000..	1 621	1 395	792	635	904	1 572	649
$50,000 to $99,999 .... farms..	124	128	43	57	79	92	46
$1,000..	9 096	9 204	3 047	2 633	5 513	6 756	3 228
$100,000 to $249,999 .... farms..	97	106	37	19	34	62	45
$1,000..	15 311	16 418	5 650	2 937	4 902	9 148	6 581
$250,000 to $499,999 .... farms..	31	35	7	6	10	14	30
$1,000..	10 608	12 457	2 418	(D)	(D)	5 023	10 840
$500,000 or more .... farms..	14	26	13	2	2	7	17
$1,000..	19 954	51 248	19 722	(D)	(D)	24 569	31 768
1982 value of sales[1]:							
Less than $1,000 .... farms..	25	197	19	32	105	9	9
$1,000..	(D)	83	(D)	7	(D)	4	(D)
$1,000 to $2,499 .... farms..	38	150	12	51	141	7	11
$1,000..	70	258	20	86	(D)	12	(D)
$2,500 to $4,999 .... farms..	66	156	17	55	126	32	18
$1,000..	245	562	59	200	446	116	71
$5,000 to $9,999 .... farms..	79	216	38	70	123	42	23
$1,000..	583	1 533	289	485	887	294	162
$10,000 to $19,999 .... farms..	113	184	58	66	139	83	43
$1,000..	1 643	2 602	817	941	1 976	1 197	625
$20,000 to $24,999 .... farms..	52	51	6	17	32	31	16
$1,000..	1 137	1 137	137	381	719	698	360
$25,000 to $39,999 .... farms..	102	105	35	51	84	91	34
$1,000..	3 170	3 332	1 165	1 619	2 658	2 912	1 109
$40,000 to $49,999 .... farms..	51	49	16	17	25	39	16
$1,000..	2 272	2 172	717	753	1 126	1 752	727
$50,000 to $99,999 .... farms..	132	119	42	55	104	115	64
$1,000..	9 681	8 327	2 891	2 385	7 426	8 146	3 775
$100,000 to $249,999 .... farms..	114	93	32	30	54	74	46
$1,000..	17 754	14 848	4 917	4 568	7 144	11 100	7 668
$250,000 to $499,999 .... farms..	41	34	4	5	4	19	21
$1,000..	14 630	11 495	1 573	(D)	(D)	6 604	7 206
$500,000 or more .... farms..	11	22	15	2	1	4	16
$1,000..	9 225	55 637	15 916	(D)	(D)	19 035	26 826
Sales by commodity or commodity group:							
Crops, including nursery and greenhouse crops......................... farms, 1987..	609	745	183	137	529	419	222
1982..	681	839	206	185	633	481	245
$1,000, 1987..	26 709	14 466	3 690	4 895	14 551	18 785	6 107
1982..	28 394	15 903	3 453	4 805	18 656	24 061	9 002
Grains.................................. farms, 1987..	587	611	169	106	488	414	213
1982..	673	722	200	160	595	470	241
$1,000, 1987..	26 141	12 909	3 251	2 011	13 200	18 023	5 648
1982..	27 954	14 178	3 091	2 707	17 846	22 836	8 973
Corn for grain .... farms, 1987..	313	25	30	8	66	88	-
1982..	333	10	24	6	40	7	-
$1,000, 1987..	7 935	186	230	(D)	700	4 166	-
1982..	8 961	74	133	50	402	3 883	(D)
Wheat............................. farms, 1987..	565	483	133	76	157	409	212
1982..	565	650	178	143	519	459	237
$1,000, 1987..	2 570	4 297	758	476	800	9 785	4 849
1982..	4 896	8 699	1 512	2 014	7 233	16 274	8 090
Soybeans.......................... farms, 1987..	537	276	121	47	457	93	3
1982..	566	178	111	29	551	26	3
$1,000, 1987..	12 413	3 394	1 616	1 131	9 731	833	(D)
1982..	10 729	1 091	818	324	9 005	479	(D)
Sorghum for grain .... farms, 1987..	317	413	93	43	226	117	97
1982..	252	316	87	25	106	76	66
$1,000, 1987..	3 165	5 008	535	337	1 943	922	710
1982..	3 174	4 217	592	299	1 063	1 620	515
Barley .... farms, 1987..	-	-	1	-	-	44	2
1982..	(NA)	(NA)	(NA)	(NA)	(NA)	(NA)	(NA)
$1,000, 1987..	-	-	-	-	-	99	(D)
1982..	(NA)	(NA)	(NA)	(NA)	(NA)	(NA)	(NA)
Oats .... farms, 1987..	47	13	9	3	25	18	5
1982..	88	36	26	10	39	7	1
$1,000, 1987..	(D)	(D)	(D)	(D)	(D)	58	8
1982..	177	77	(D)	20	(D)	49	(D)
Other grains[2]...................... farms, 1987..	2	2	1	-	1	134	4
1982..	6	7	2	3	3	35	5
$1,000, 1987..	(D)	(D)	(D)	-	(D)	2 161	31
1982..	7	20	(D)	1	(D)	530	29

See footnotes at end of table.

[For meaning of abbreviations and symbols, see introductory text]

Item	Clay	Cloud	Coffey	Comanche	Cowley	Crawford	Decatur
MARKET VALUE OF AGRICULTURAL PRODUCTS SOLD							
Total sales (see text) ... farms, 1987	672	659	606	277	997	809	466
1982	719	726	671	259	1 101	915	516
$1,000, 1987	39 675	30 872	32 459	29 146	55 906	21 741	72 560
1982	36 579	34 568	29 630	23 921	79 555	27 795	71 557
Average per farm ... dollars, 1987	59 040	46 847	53 563	105 220	56 075	26 873	149 300
1982	53 856	47 816	44 158	92 359	72 257	30 377	138 677
1987 value of sales:							
Less than $1,000 ... farms	27	19	33	17	97	60	12
$1,000	9	5	9	5	23	17	5
$1,000 to $2,499 ... farms	33	43	43	12	89	82	15
$1,000	60	67	74	19	151	142	27
$2,500 to $4,999 ... farms	45	70	48	24	139	116	21
$1,000	158	254	176	88	503	432	83
$5,000 to $9,999 ... farms	79	91	78	20	173	175	47
$1,000	572	662	590	137	1 244	1 248	356
$10,000 to $19,999 ... farms	108	104	97	27	155	133	63
$1,000	1 554	1 543	1 351	440	2 182	1 867	981
$20,000 to $24,999 ... farms	35	34	44	17	56	43	30
$1,000	782	747	983	372	1 248	963	681
$25,000 to $39,999 ... farms	81	74	69	28	74	71	64
$1,000	2 802	2 361	2 180	880	2 260	2 272	2 083
$40,000 to $49,999 ... farms	40	39	24	13	41	31	22
$1,000	1 764	1 768	1 077	579	1 829	1 376	987
$50,000 to $99,999 ... farms	121	108	94	35	90	61	106
$1,000	8 509	7 864	6 862	2 540	6 103	4 088	7 771
$100,000 to $249,999 ... farms	79	61	50	50	49	30	79
$1,000	11 804	8 653	7 718	7 510	7 909	4 585	11 870
$250,000 to $499,999 ... farms	17	12	20	23	17	4	19
$1,000	5 751	4 059	6 238	7 660	5 807	1 345	6 522
$500,000 or more ... farms	7	4	6	11	17	3	8
$1,000	6 121	2 690	5 223	8 917	26 646	3 406	41 195
1982 value of sales:							
Less than $1,000 ... farms	16	23	29	8	78	83	13
$1,000	5	9	7	(D)	27	33	4
$1,000 to $2,499 ... farms	45	53	49	3	95	113	10
$1,000	90	87	80	(D)	182	188	19
$2,500 to $4,999 ... farms	42	66	61	10	111	109	17
$1,000	162	245	214	31	397	403	63
$5,000 to $9,999 ... farms	83	75	116	28	151	171	43
$1,000	599	527	835	198	1 067	1 271	331
$10,000 to $19,999 ... farms	119	126	120	25	179	138	72
$1,000	1 780	1 774	1 745	369	2 639	2 008	1 054
$20,000 to $24,999 ... farms	59	46	45	13	78	45	35
$1,000	1 317	1 001	1 004	286	1 736	999	788
$25,000 to $39,999 ... farms	98	87	71	24	119	79	59
$1,000	3 128	2 760	2 313	806	3 790	2 545	1 863
$40,000 to $49,999 ... farms	40	47	22	21	63	39	47
$1,000	1 812	2 087	977	938	2 768	1 769	2 108
$50,000 to $99,999 ... farms	122	108	78	47	115	81	115
$1,000	8 635	7 672	5 353	3 491	8 267	5 489	8 267
$100,000 to $249,999 ... farms	75	77	59	58	79	47	80
$1,000	11 213	10 978	8 643	8 531	11 796	7 044	12 076
$250,000 to $499,999 ... farms	17	15	16	16	19	8	14
$1,000	6 112	5 089	5 037	5 706	6 140	(D)	4 259
$500,000 or more ... farms	3	3	5	5	5	14	2
$1,000	3 725	2 342	3 422	3 559	40 806	(D)	40 727
Sales by commodity or commodity group:							
Crops, including nursery and greenhouse crops ... farms, 1987	566	559	465	196	646	529	430
1982	620	620	530	207	782	624	449
$1,000, 1987	16 083	17 193	14 123	5 626	11 396	10 254	17 478
1982	17 728	19 363	13 410	11 213	19 218	13 915	18 964
Grains ... farms, 1987	559	535	456	184	584	499	418
1982	513	595	508	203	742	603	439
$1,000, 1987	15 410	16 404	13 360	5 288	9 598	9 925	16 870
1982	17 046	18 382	12 549	10 690	17 471	13 513	18 294
Corn for grain ... farms, 1987	60	54	103	7	8	91	88
1982	65	47	94	1	2	74	51
$1,000, 1987	1 427	1 215	895	253	85	1 078	2 464
1982	(D)	1 450	697	(D)	(D)	662	1 066
Wheat ... farms, 1987	519	498	176	182	545	64	393
1982	595	577	399	202	730	408	426
$1,000, 1987	6 464	9 072	671	4 453	6 554	332	9 451
1982	9 666	12 633	2 701	9 715	14 941	2 628	14 098
Soybeans ... farms, 1987	346	225	432	9	121	468	12
1982	272	158	445	4	49	542	4
$1,000, 1987	3 646	1 711	9 803	182	647	5 988	123
1982	2 410	1 235	7 121	(D)	259	7 173	12
Sorghum for grain ... farms, 1987	399	386	303	54	312	305	296
1982	265	231	215	45	240	259	189
$1,000, 1987	3 701	4 319	1 966	(D)	2 253	2 421	3 685
1982	3 338	2 851	2 017	450	2 097	2 808	3 082
Barley ... farms, 1987	1	1	2	1	10	-	39
1982	(NA)	(NA)	(NA)	(NA)	(NA)	(NA)	(NA)
$1,000, 1987	(D)	(D)	(D)	(D)	33	-	33
1982	(NA)	(NA)	(NA)	(NA)	(NA)	(NA)	(NA)
Oats ... farms, 1987	64	46	16	1	12	50	23
1982	41	50	15	1	32	92	14
$1,000, 1987	67	73	12	-	(D)	(D)	33
1982	55	156	14	(D)	(D)	224	22
Other grains² ... farms, 1987	5	5	2	1	2	1	104
1982	8	11	-	(D)	18	3	7
$1,000, 1987	(D)	(D)	(D)	(D)	(D)	(D)	1 080
1982	(D)	58	-	(D)	86	21	15

See footnotes at end of table.

Table 2. **Market Value of Agricultural Products Sold and Farms by Standard Industrial Classification: 1987 and 1982**—Con.

[For meaning of abbreviations and symbols, see introductory text]

Item	Dickinson	Doniphan	Douglas	Edwards	Elk	Ellis	Ellsworth
MARKET VALUE OF AGRICULTURAL PRODUCTS SOLD							
Total sales (see text) .... farms, 1987..	1 028	530	852	361	409	795	499
1982..	1 149	620	896	402	467	790	527
$1,000, 1987..	65 235	34 650	28 024	57 867	17 905	46 993	21 446
1982..	64 669	37 807	28 242	67 304	15 641	38 387	22 324
Average per farm.........dollars, 1987..	63 458	65 378	32 892	160 296	43 777	59 111	42 978
1982..	56 283	60 978	31 520	167 423	33 492	48 591	42 360
1987 value of sales:							
Less than $1,000 .... farms..	52	15	122	12	31	44	13
$1,000..	22	4	38	2	6	16	4
$1,000 to $2,499 .... farms..	56	33	120	10	28	69	21
$1,000..	93	58	206	17	48	116	34
$2,500 to $4,999 .... farms..	107	45	126	24	48	104	29
$1,000..	379	173	461	90	193	378	109
$5,000 to $9,999 .... farms..	153	68	151	32	76	138	81
$1,000..	1 157	491	1 052	242	581	1 009	600
$10,000 to $19,999 .... farms..	187	74	104	32	61	159	76
$1,000..	2 468	1 052	1 444	474	871	2 271	1 082
$20,000 to $24,999 .... farms..	44	22	34	31	32	38	34
$1,000..	982	489	758	673	700	831	777
$25,000 to $39,999 .... farms..	124	56	57	48	37	95	82
$1,000..	3 769	1 722	1 715	1 514	1 193	2 939	2 658
$40,000 to $49,999 .... farms..	54	31	11	15	11	27	34
$1,000..	2 385	1 411	(D)	670	485	(D)	1 544
$50,000 to $99,999 .... farms..	126	80	59	43	49	70	84
$1,000..	9 045	5 585	(D)	3 028	3 435	(D)	6 017
$100,000 to $249,999 .... farms..	102	74	52	66	24	38	39
$1,000..	16 386	11 849	(D)	10 464	3 480	(D)	5 572
$250,000 to $499,999 .... farms..	26	28	10	26	7	8	6
$1,000..	9 239	9 372	(D)	8 381	2 516	(D)	(D)
$500,000 or more .... farms..	17	4	6	22	5	5	1
$1,000..	19 309	2 645	6 951	32 292	4 399	25 138	(D)
1982 value of sales[1]:							
Less than $1,000 .... farms..	42	15	112	3	33	31	12
$1,000..	9	3	(D)	1	8	8	2
$1,000 to $2,499 .... farms..	67	41	133	15	42	48	25
$1,000..	110	67	212	25	68	(D)	44
$2,500 to $4,999 .... farms..	92	61	136	23	54	72	37
$1,000..	329	233	499	87	195	266	132
$5,000 to $9,999 .... farms..	160	56	156	24	88	127	63
$1,000..	1 184	410	1 138	173	654	961	450
$10,000 to $19,999 .... farms..	183	79	129	59	69	181	98
$1,000..	2 677	1 090	1 824	842	1 018	2 565	1 382
$20,000 to $24,999 .... farms..	65	28	38	23	36	54	29
$1,000..	1 468	638	832	510	798	1 195	641
$25,000 to $39,999 .... farms..	161	72	55	51	40	93	87
$1,000..	5 132	2 254	1 761	1 648	1 288	2 941	2 815
$40,000 to $49,999 .... farms..	53	37	13	25	26	47	38
$1,000..	2 368	1 660	579	1 103	1 133	2 100	1 727
$50,000 to $99,999 .... farms..	166	118	67	68	46	85	89
$1,000..	11 483	8 619	4 851	4 907	3 034	5 930	6 364
$100,000 to $249,999 .... farms..	121	88	37	66	26	41	64
$1,000..	18 030	13 969	5 573	10 224	3 992	5 855	6 738
$250,000 to $499,999 .... farms..	27	22	11	29	6	8	4
$1,000..	9 740	7 146	3 592	9 494	(D)	(D)	(D)
$500,000 or more .... farms..	12	3	3	16	1	(D)	1
$1,000..	11 939	1 721	7 342	36 290	(D)	(D)	(D)
Sales by commodity or commodity group:							
Crops, including nursery and greenhouse crops .... farms, 1987..	856	427	526	317	193	635	427
1982..	974	510	549	366	233	634	454
$1,000, 1987..	17 841	22 155	12 357	24 380	2 097	9 528	9 152
1982..	25 605	25 629	10 331	28 932	3 369	13 277	13 521
Grains .... farms, 1987..	827	416	417	312	158	621	415
1982..	946	495	471	358	207	622	448
$1,000, 1987..	15 843	21 502	11 229	20 946	1 874	9 037	8 817
1982..	23 699	24 823	9 451	24 922	3 021	12 817	13 289
Corn for grain .... farms, 1987..	28	351	142	98	4	2	4
1982..	49	351	155	46	6	6	1
$1,000, 1987..	(D)	10 816	2 465	8 178	(D)	(D)	28
1982..	905	12 015	2 498	5 277	(D)	247	(D)
Wheat .... farms, 1987..	809	117	74	296	93	610	403
1982..	927	326	357	337	177	611	438
$1,000, 1987..	10 378	838	221	6 840	355	7 460	6 799
1982..	16 922	2 577	1 673	10 808	1 939	11 107	11 485
Soybeans .... farms, 1987..	332	375	368	90	97	-	31
1982..	259	421	325	84	80	3	14
$1,000, 1987..	2 011	9 295	6 560	4 011	1 262	-	225
1982..	1 354	9 288	3 784	4 689	598	82	116
Sorghum for grain .... farms, 1987..	496	72	213	173	68	262	260
1982..	538	91	165	178	47	144	170
$1,000, 1987..	3 108	537	1 897	1 781	247	1 530	1 719
1982..	3 004	832	1 436	3 966	439	1 374	1 648
Barley .... farms, 1987..	25	-	1	(NA)	-	6	4
1982..	(NA)	(NA)	(NA)	(NA)	(NA)	(NA)	(NA)
$1,000, 1987..	23	(NA)	(D)	85	(NA)	6	(D)
1982..	(NA)	(NA)	(NA)	(NA)	(NA)	(NA)	(NA)
Oats .... farms, 1987..	94	15	51	3	3	7	20
1982..	133	17	52	3	15	2	12
$1,000, 1987..	91	(D)	49	11	(D)	(D)	25
1982..	267	(D)	57	(D)	34	(D)	(D)
Other grains[2] .... farms, 1987..	3	2	6	7	1	9	7
1982..	16	5	3	49	13	1	(D)
$1,000, 1987..	(D)	(D)	(D)	41	(D)	22	(D)
1982..	47	(D)	4	(D)	(D)	(D)	-

See footnotes at end of table.

[For meaning of abbreviations and symbols, see introductory text]

Item	Finney	Ford	Franklin	Geary	Gove	Graham	Grant
MARKET VALUE OF AGRICULTURAL PRODUCTS SOLD							
Total sales (see text) .... farms, 1987	534	812	979	295	534	452	303
1982	558	835	1 087	299	548	495	276
$1,000, 1987	381 532	229 083	33 009	16 506	93 924	27 506	231 412
1982	224 756	202 101	32 978	13 920	79 092	30 577	140 283
Average per farm .... dollars, 1987	714 479	282 121	33 718	55 952	175 887	60 859	763 735
1982	402 788	241 747	30 338	46 556	144 329	61 771	508 272
1987 value of sales:							
Less than $1,000 .... farms	29	34	108	16	13	22	9
$1,000	12	12	27	5	6	7	1
$1,000 to $2,499 .... farms	13	50	139	26	22	19	12
$1,000	18	86	227	48	36	38	23
$2,500 to $4,999 .... farms	30	63	157	34	36	36	18
$1,000	108	220	573	119	145	131	66
$5,000 to $9,999 .... farms	41	86	165	41	53	43	24
$1,000	276	607	1 206	302	379	320	176
$10,000 to $19,999 .... farms	49	128	125	47	82	69	28
$1,000	681	1 949	1 774	699	1 195	991	414
$20,000 to $24,999 .... farms	14	45	48	17	25	24	16
$1,000	303	1 012	1 055	377	565	521	349
$25,000 to $39,999 .... farms	43	80	65	31	57	79	31
$1,000	1 397	2 544	2 070	963	1 811	2 487	1 076
$40,000 to $49,999 .... farms	30	39	28	11	37	26	19
$1,000	1 318	1 760	1 266	484	1 603	1 161	846
$50,000 to $99,999 .... farms	105	119	69	30	98	73	58
$1,000	7 412	8 600	5 111	1 985	6 901	5 026	4 211
$100,000 to $249,999 .... farms	110	107	52	32	74	55	58
$1,000	16 949	16 630	7 558	4 885	11 280	8 404	9 102
$250,000 to $499,999 .... farms	32	37	18	6	18	5	19
$1,000	10 622	12 375	5 474	2 173	5 849	(D)	6 694
$500,000 or more .... farms	38	24	7	4	19	1	11
$1,000	342 437	183 287	6 668	4 464	64 153	(D)	208 453
1982 value of sales[1]:							
Less than $1,000 .... farms	11	38	143	21	14	11	7
$1,000	7	12	(D)	9	1	2	(Z)
$1,000 to $2,499 .... farms	15	38	154	18	19	15	5
$1,000	21	67	250	30	34	29	9
$2,500 to $4,999 .... farms	16	50	164	36	25	28	16
$1,000	55	186	580	134	98	94	60
$5,000 to $9,999 .... farms	41	81	158	41	58	77	11
$1,000	305	595	1 147	275	412	580	91
$10,000 to $19,999 .... farms	52	135	161	58	84	90	18
$1,000	812	1 964	2 345	810	1 247	1 256	242
$20,000 to $24,999 .... farms	25	45	47	12	36	35	6
$1,000	571	1 008	1 048	272	807	783	137
$25,000 to $39,999 .... farms	43	99	65	29	79	41	24
$1,000	1 319	3 184	2 021	937	2 519	1 286	781
$40,000 to $49,999 .... farms	32	43	36	13	27	39	18
$1,000	1 405	1 931	1 600	580	1 230	1 773	734
$50,000 to $99,999 .... farms	102	152	79	33	82	95	50
$1,000	7 560	10 571	5 493	2 475	5 724	6 969	3 735
$100,000 to $249,999 .... farms	119	99	80	33	90	65	82
$1,000	21 558	15 020	8 737	5 070	13 513	8 031	13 980
$250,000 to $499,999 .... farms	45	34	11	3	15	6	31
$1,000	15 342	12 427	3 826	(D)	4 654	(D)	11 152
$500,000 or more .... farms	37	22	8	2	19	1	11
$1,000	175 800	155 136	5 855	(D)	48 655	(D)	109 982
Sales by commodity or commodity group:							
Crops, including nursery and greenhouse crops .... farms, 1987	457	680	613	209	444	393	252
1982	489	708	705	229	470	444	233
$1,000, 1987	43 002	29 548	13 653	4 164	15 725	11 770	20 450
1982	60 472	34 875	11 904	4 882	17 385	14 646	30 367
Grains .... farms, 1987	444	660	540	194	441	389	243
1982	477	687	634	207	457	440	226
$1,000, 1987	36 662	27 314	12 659	3 208	14 924	11 446	18 569
1982	53 510	32 946	10 815	4 169	16 484	14 310	29 214
Corn for grain .... farms, 1987	138	79	130	14	32	23	99
1982	127	55	146	20	23	22	75
$1,000, 1987	12 866	4 964	1 240	95	801	545	7 344
1982	19 423	4 249	1 600	134	1 040	741	8 206
Wheat .... farms, 1987	430	644	82	167	434	379	232
1982	463	666	369	189	416	425	209
$1,000, 1987	15 244	14 940	313	1 519	10 380	8 013	8 513
1982	24 448	21 295	1 350	2 398	10 428	11 240	10 967
Soybeans .... farms, 1987	84	64	497	112	3	3	43
1982	45	61	515	66	10	2	28
$1,000, 1987	1 222	1 078	9 101	723	77	(D)	545
1982	(D)	1 427	8 485	473	73	(D)	608
Sorghum for grain .... farms, 1987	257	408	272	142	260	256	168
1982	253	255	178	110	256	165	174
$1,000, 1987	6 197	5 918	1 955	856	3 291	2 537	2 736
1982	8 600	5 736	1 200	1 121	4 731	2 171	8 998
Barley .... farms, 1987	46	76	2	(NA)	74	23	22
1982	(NA)	(NA)	(NA)	(NA)	(NA)	(NA)	(NA)
$1,000, 1987	(D)	103	(D)	(D)	214	37	51
1982	(NA)	(NA)	(NA)	(NA)	(NA)	(NA)	(NA)
Oats .... farms, 1987	4	11	51	31	10	10	3
1982	3	8	93	21	8	8	2
$1,000, 1987	(D)	(D)	49	(D)	14	(D)	5
1982	(D)	35	170	29	12	(D)	(D)
Other grains[2] .... farms, 1987	21	28	1	-	24	34	19
1982	21	24	9	5	18	11	20
$1,000, 1987	202	(D)	(D)	-	148	257	373
1982	245	205	30	15	180	99	(D)

See footnotes at end of table.

Table 2. Market Value of Agricultural Products Sold and Farms by Standard Industrial Classification: 1987 and 1982—Con.

[For meaning of abbreviations and symbols, see introductory text]

Item	Gray	Greeley	Greenwood	Hamilton	Harper	Harvey	Haskell
MARKET VALUE OF AGRICULTURAL PRODUCTS SOLD							
Total sales (see text) .... farms, 1987..	547	294	587	279	648	874	315
1982..	552	277	651	270	660	923	324
$1,000, 1987..	236 428	61 559	35 382	80 154	55 261	52 969	248 969
1982..	161 354	112 143	31 518	57 631	59 288	57 099	344 157
Average per farm.............dollars, 1987..	432 227	277 445	60 276	287 289	85 280	59 919	790 379
1982..	292 307	404 847	48 415	213 077	89 830	61 863	1 062 212
1987 value of sales:							
Less than $1,000 .... farms..	7	5	45	13	35	62	5
$1,000..	2	2	15	2	13	20	2
$1,000 to $2,499 .... farms..	19	15	40	16	31	91	14
$1,000..	33	25	67	29	53	156	26
$2,500 to $4,999 .... farms..	22	26	57	10	45	97	11
$1,000..	87	97	208	43	166	365	41
$5,000 to $9,999 .... farms..	51	32	90	26	65	118	16
$1,000..	366	251	654	191	463	894	119
$10,000 to $19,999 .... farms..	59	33	107	32	103	125	26
$1,000..	852	472	1 493	448	1 488	1 800	386
$20,000 to $24,999 .... farms..	27	18	31	13	42	40	9
$1,000..	608	397	685	295	936	894	198
$25,000 to $39,999 .... farms..	45	30	84	28	59	87	18
$1,000..	1 469	926	2 020	971	2 176	2 784	589
$40,000 to $49,999 .... farms..	32	15	23	7	30	35	9
$1,000..	1 420	653	1 025	311	1 341	1 522	409
$50,000 to $99,999 .... farms..	77	42	58	68	83	102	56
$1,000..	5 479	3 266	4 155	4 740	5 763	7 554	3 702
$100,000 to $249,999 .... farms..	131	45	42	49	88	77	83
$1,000..	20 363	6 651	6 515	7 452	12 851	11 869	12 759
$250,000 to $499,999 .... farms..	42	16	17	10	44	27	46
$1,000..	14 183	5 612	5 583	3 293	14 501	8 882	15 079
$500,000 or more .... farms..	35	17	13	7	13	13	20
$1,000..	191 567	63 195	12 981	62 379	15 509	15 629	215 660
1982 value of sales[1]:							
Less than $1,000 .... farms..	8	3	40	9	14	45	5
$1,000..	1	(D)	15	2	3	(D)	2
$1,000 to $2,499 .... farms..	10	7	68	9	20	75	4
$1,000..	15	10	117	16	35	124	7
$2,500 to $4,999 .... farms..	25	15	70	16	34	75	6
$1,000..	88	49	264	64	123	269	24
$5,000 to $9,999 .... farms..	36	43	93	13	49	115	10
$1,000..	269	341	706	101	375	874	70
$10,000 to $19,999 .... farms..	37	29	105	34	95	159	27
$1,000..	543	416	1 459	473	1 392	2 290	468
$20,000 to $24,999 .... farms..	21	19	39	10	27	45	5
$1,000..	460	424	848	233	599	1 008	(D)
$25,000 to $39,999 .... farms..	61	25	70	24	73	109	8
$1,000..	1 978	771	2 248	784	2 393	3 542	(D)
$40,000 to $49,999 .... farms..	31	18	25	7	48	35	15
$1,000..	1 354	780	1 123	304	2 159	1 566	674
$50,000 to $99,999 .... farms..	84	44	72	69	143	130	58
$1,000..	6 178	3 054	4 974	4 783	10 188	9 307	4 151
$100,000 to $249,999 .... farms..	138	48	47	53	111	101	104
$1,000..	22 118	7 439	7 207	8 012	17 189	14 616	17 723
$250,000 to $499,999 .... farms..	72	10	12	18	34	16	52
$1,000..	24 404	3 846	4 602	5 571	11 034	5 135	17 922
$500,000 or more .... farms..	29	15	10	10	8	17	30
$1,000..	103 946	94 989	7 956	37 189	13 798	18 328	302 731
Sales by commodity or commodity group:							
Crops, including nursery and greenhouse crops............ farms, 1987..	478	265	309	218	584	593	282
1982..	501	259	370	232	604	785	289
$1,000, 1987..	38 117	16 515	4 076	12 813	16 224	19 340	30 327
1982..	55 098	17 847	4 125	16 418	31 205	24 635	48 748
Grains............ farms, 1987..	472	264	262	214	576	648	277
1982..	496	259	343	230	597	736	289
$1,000, 1987..	32 479	15 894	3 499	11 699	15 700	16 164	29 200
1982..	52 462	17 257	3 682	15 360	30 713	23 755	46 934
Corn for grain............ farms, 1987..	191	37	18	21	-	79	155
1982..	192	16	4	9	1	45	153
$1,000, 1987..	12 831	(D)	86	1 264	-	2 499	15 157
1982..	19 423	1 835	20	758	(D)	1 644	20 541
Wheat............ farms, 1987..	453	251	157	207	576	597	259
1982..	466	252	292	219	595	697	267
$1,000, 1987..	12 055	11 186	505	9 215	15 420	7 361	6 796
1982..	21 084	12 917	1 930	13 145	30 289	13 566	15 983
Soybeans............ farms, 1987..	66	9	196	2	3	214	52
1982..	84	1	173	2	2	195	71
$1,000, 1987..	1 019	47	2 220	(D)	(D)	2 425	(D)
1982..	1 907	(D)	1 261	(D)	(D)	2 176	1 324
Sorghum for grain............ farms, 1987..	265	116	126	125	54	489	147
1982..	217	48	87	77	30	424	160
$1,000, 1987..	6 469	1 015	671	1 096	192	5 621	4 457
1982..	9 831	2 391	440	1 379	348	6 112	6 879
Barley............ farms, 1987..	6	71	(NA)	20	4	12	7
1982..	(NA)	(NA)	(NA)	(NA)	(NA)	(NA)	(NA)
$1,000, 1987..	6	389	(NA)	66	17	(NA)	(D)
1982..	(NA)	(NA)	(NA)	(NA)	(NA)	(NA)	(NA)
Oats............ farms, 1987..	4	4	14	2	10	14	-
1982..	1	1	18	-	11	38	1
$1,000, 1987..	3	(D)	18	(D)	32	15	-
1982..	36	(D)	30	-	34	81	(D)
Other grains[2]............ farms, 1987..	13	45	-	6	3	11	9
1982..	13	16	-	8	8	13	17
$1,000, 1987..	98	299	-	52	(D)	26	207
1982..	168	(D)	-	(D)	19	76	(D)

See footnotes at end of table.

Table 2. **Market Value of Agricultural Products Sold and Farms by Standard Industrial Classification: 1987 and 1982**—Con.

[For meaning of abbreviations and symbols, see introductory text]

Item	Hodgeman	Jackson	Jefferson	Jewell	Johnson	Kearny	Kingman	Kiowa
MARKET VALUE OF AGRICULTURAL PRODUCTS SOLD								
Total sales (see text) ....farms, 1987..	423	1 082	1 017	736	659	291	818	310
1982..	468	1 156	1 047	808	766	297	960	354
$1,000, 1987..	89 476	27 790	25 901	44 073	22 878	118 690	35 979	24 592
1982..	74 532	26 814	27 124	50 003	24 809	148 708	41 928	28 428
Average per farm............dollars, 1987..	211 527	25 684	24 878	59 882	34 716	408 900	43 984	79 330
1982..	159 941	23 198	25 906	61 885	32 387	500 704	48 754	74 656
1987 value of sales:								
Less than $1,000 ....farms..	12	107	116	15	102	14	27	14
$1,000..	4	36	40	3	26	2	10	4
$1,000 to $2,499 ....farms..	16	96	118	30	97	6	54	16
$1,000..	28	160	200	49	163	16	92	26
$2,500 to $4,999 ....farms..	33	165	143	39	95	14	67	11
$1,000..	125	597	520	137	332	54	236	43
$5,000 to $9,999 ....farms..	28	198	216	109	104	27	133	36
$1,000..	199	1 433	1 512	805	767	199	987	254
$10,000 to $19,999 ....farms..	63	193	163	113	74	23	156	30
$1,000..	934	2 690	2 244	1 628	1 019	332	2 254	428
$20,000 to $24,999 ....farms..	18	53	48	55	24	17	47	13
$1,000..	396	1 177	1 067	1 202	536	398	1 052	295
$25,000 to $39,999 ....farms..	59	103	74	81	48	25	108	40
$1,000..	1 836	3 268	2 296	2 634	1 544	782	3 486	1 351
$40,000 to $49,999 ....farms..	18	35	15	43	22	17	31	20
$1,000..	809	1 560	688	1 875	942	745	1 373	896
$50,000 to $99,999 ....farms..	73	90	66	135	45	50	107	53
$1,000..	5 088	6 239	4 641	9 661	3 077	3 494	7 604	3 834
$100,000 to $249,999 ....farms..	70	36	61	91	37	69	64	61
$1,000..	10 842	5 087	7 597	13 972	6 027	10 368	9 715	9 960
$250,000 to $499,999 ....farms..	21	5	13	17	15	15	15	10
$1,000..	6 920	2 007	(D)	5 319	1 595	2 966	4 622	3 425
$500,000 or more ....farms..	12	3	2	8	6	16	7	7
$1,000..	62 297	3 537	(D)	6 788	6 850	99 614	4 247	4 376
1982 value of sales[1]:								
Less than $1,000 ....farms..	7	108	125	26	103	12	35	5
$1,000..	1	44	(D)	12	(D)	3	9	3
$1,000 to $2,499 ....farms..	17	122	127	37	122	14	35	10
$1,000..	26	214	(D)	64	209	21	62	19
$2,500 to $4,999 ....farms..	16	193	164	28	119	13	82	27
$1,000..	64	701	599	105	409	48	223	100
$5,000 to $9,999 ....farms..	47	193	182	87	118	23	92	21
$1,000..	362	1 389	1 294	662	829	164	670	156
$10,000 to $19,999 ....farms..	62	190	160	128	109	27	159	52
$1,000..	831	2 724	2 245	1 852	1 559	374	2 346	771
$20,000 to $24,999 ....farms..	22	51	42	65	17	13	54	16
$1,000..	478	1 138	943	1 455	372	293	1 202	405
$25,000 to $39,999 ....farms..	55	99	81	117	55	31	102	46
$1,000..	1 755	3 100	2 590	3 664	1 740	972	3 288	1 439
$40,000 to $49,999 ....farms..	27	52	26	44	17	22	65	26
$1,000..	1 187	2 343	1 164	1 996	785	982	2 880	1 160
$50,000 to $99,999 ....farms..	99	104	72	198	52	46	138	66
$1,000..	6 851	7 220	5 174	9 971	3 662	3 332	9 993	4 906
$100,000 to $249,999 ....farms..	70	37	52	110	41	57	102	62
$1,000..	10 613	5 758	7 486	16 176	5 668	8 857	15 385	9 664
$250,000 to $499,999 ....farms..	23	7	13	23	7	22	12	16
$1,000..	8 334	2 186	7 463	7 463	2 588	7 698	3 927	5 139
$500,000 or more ....farms..	17	1	2	7	5	17	4	4
$1,000..	44 029	–	(D)	6 542	6 982	125 966	2 244	2 665
Sales by commodity or commodity group:								
Crops, including nursery and greenhouse crops ....farms, 1987..	377	602	575	604	369	242	684	266
1982..	412	685	606	673	432	238	738	301
$1,000, 1987..	13 153	7 857	11 966	18 626	10 623	26 689	15 862	13 133
1982..	16 406	8 153	11 261	23 507	12 229	33 012	24 597	15 747
Grains ....farms, 1987..	376	481	458	596	272	230	664	261
1982..	409	591	526	665	327	234	720	295
$1,000, 1987..	12 022	6 902	11 090	18 132	6 859	20 993	15 145	12 154
1982..	15 700	7 447	10 571	23 003	8 337	29 105	23 993	14 619
Corn for grain ....farms, 1987..	30	142	203	55	56	39	29	49
1982..	11	116	186	46	76	23	7	20
$1,000, 1987..	618	1 277	3 296	1 073	1 213	7 485	1 064	3 200
1982..	344	1 236	3 131	982	1 076	12 163	294	1 161
Wheat ....farms, 1987..	370	152	82	565	49	225	655	252
1982..	402	448	358	640	228	230	712	284
$1,000, 1987..	8 974	544	293	10 315	167	10 500	12 555	5 279
1982..	13 115	1 811	1 615	16 733	1 806	14 235	22 201	8 258
Soybeans ....farms, 1987..	31	368	363	163	237	14	43	60
1982..	12	375	371	177	255	9	17	49
$1,000, 1987..	301	3 245	5 717	1 222	5 008	163	706	1 326
1982..	131	2 811	4 399	526	4 656	(D)	404	2 031
Sorghum for grain ....farms, 1987..	253	309	245	467	93	135	167	164
1982..	148	219	177	334	72	106	122	154
$1,000, 1987..	2 602	1 753	1 713	5 342	442	2 130	747	2 301
1982..	2 080	1 541	1 294	4 645	569	2 527	916	3 064
Barley ....farms, 1987..	57	1	–	10	–	50	9	5
1982..	(NA)	(NA)	(NA)	(NA)	(NA)	(NA)	(NA)	(NA)
$1,000, 1987..	98	(D)	–	61	–	268	26	5
1982..	(NA)	(NA)	(NA)	(NA)	(NA)	(NA)	(NA)	(NA)
Oats ....farms, 1987..	3	41	41	49	22	6	22	6
1982..	1	49	46	40	21	–	30	3
$1,000, 1987..	3	48	50	77	(D)	(D)	36	22
1982..	(D)	39	82	83	(D)	–	104	(D)
Other grains[2] ....farms, 1987..	9	3	1	19	2	1	6	7
1982..	2	5	9	12	2	3	14	1
$1,000, 1987..	26	(D)	23	41	(D)	(D)	11	22
1982..	(D)	5	50	33	(D)	(D)	64	(D)

See footnotes at end of table.

Table 2. **Market Value of Agricultural Products Sold and Farms by Standard Industrial Classification: 1987 and 1982** —Con.

[For meaning of abbreviations and symbols, see introductory text]

Item	Labette	Lane	Leavenworth	Lincoln	Linn	Logan	Lyon	McPherson
MARKET VALUE OF AGRICULTURAL PRODUCTS SOLD								
Total sales (see text) ... farms, 1987..	971	322	1 144	578	688	382	872	1 357
1982..	1 064	335	1 237	615	772	379	945	1 476
$1,000, 1987..	48 962	86 214	26 702	38 636	21 703	22 420	58 178	77 962
1982..	55 415	79 731	23 607	30 323	21 781	26 542	50 509	71 087
Average per farm ... dollars, 1987..	50 424	273 965	23 341	66 844	31 545	58 692	66 718	57 451
1982..	52 082	238 002	19 084	49 306	28 213	70 032	53 449	48 162
1987 value of sales:								
Less than $1,000 ... farms..	91	12	176	16	84	12	58	57
$1,000..	31	5	59	5	18	2	14	17
$1,000 to $2,499 ... farms..	82	9	170	30	67	9	80	100
$1,000..	144	17	285	53	107	15	141	174
$2,500 to $4,999 ... farms..	139	26	216	47	79	34	123	128
$1,000..	511	103	758	167	299	134	453	477
$5,000 to $9,999 ... farms..	202	29	192	70	110	41	134	218
$1,000..	1 489	209	1 366	513	766	310	967	1 637
$10,000 to $19,999 ... farms..	184	43	154	123	125	54	170	269
$1,000..	2 616	637	2 122	1 781	1 741	784	2 435	3 842
$20,000 to $24,999 ... farms..	47	16	38	26	42	22	41	81
$1,000..	1 036	366	818	580	945	475	910	1 796
$25,000 to $39,999 ... farms..	57	20	83	76	57	53	62	144
$1,000..	1 757	651	2 010	2 421	1 734	1 666	1 944	4 478
$40,000 to $49,999 ... farms..	37	23	24	30	22	26	36	56
$1,000..	1 700	1 023	1 062	1 352	974	1 164	1 627	2 496
$50,000 to $99,999 ... farms..	77	59	55	87	45	61	82	153
$1,000..	5 250	4 212	3 829	6 100	2 836	4 303	5 590	10 911
$100,000 to $249,999 ... farms..	42	58	48	55	42	52	52	114
$1,000..	6 685	8 427	6 804	7 732	6 343	7 399	7 396	16 581
$250,000 to $499,999 ... farms..	7	19	8	14	13	17	20	27
$1,000..	2 197	6 726	2 261	4 756	(D)	(D)	7 172	8 674
$500,000 or more ... farms..	6	8	4	4	2	1	14	10
$1,000..	25 564	65 837	5 324	13 175	(D)	(D)	29 529	26 878
1982 value of sales[1]:								
Less than $1,000 ... farms..	76	9	210	14	100	15	76	45
$1,000..	132	2	78	4	30	(D)	21	18
$1,000 to $2,499 ... farms..	132	11	197	23	78	10	75	80
$1,000..	231	17	326	37	137	(D)	123	132
$2,500 to $4,999 ... farms..	144	21	197	37	137	32	119	115
$1,000..	549	68	706	135	434	117	442	419
$5,000 to $9,999 ... farms..	187	18	219	50	122	39	163	179
$1,000..	1 335	142	1 555	375	882	290	1 149	1 307
$10,000 to $19,999 ... farms..	180	38	155	127	117	54	180	299
$1,000..	2 576	505	2 204	1 853	1 682	776	2 509	4 429
$20,000 to $24,999 ... farms..	81	19	47	43	26	13	34	85
$1,000..	1 349	435	1 048	950	589	289	739	1 862
$25,000 to $39,999 ... farms..	78	49	64	57	72	56	75	183
$1,000..	2 419	1 631	1 994	2 140	2 333	1 761	2 368	5 859
$40,000 to $49,999 ... farms..	42	18	23	61	26	24	50	81
$1,000..	1 854	791	1 023	2 755	1 194	1 095	2 224	3 593
$50,000 to $99,999 ... farms..	99	58	74	125	53	67	100	243
$1,000..	6 687	4 260	5 224	8 907	3 661	4 716	6 765	17 115
$100,000 to $249,999 ... farms..	53	67	40	56	48	51	49	142
$1,000..	8 039	10 532	5 746	8 409	7 512	7 495	7 137	20 451
$250,000 to $499,999 ... farms..	5	19	6	11	6	12	11	20
$1,000..	1 616	6 365	(D)	(D)	(D)	4 023	3 730	6 904
$500,000 or more ... farms..	5	10	2	2	1	7	14	4
$1,000..	28 323	54 982	(D)	(D)	(D)	5 958	23 311	8 979
Sales by commodity or commodity group:								
Crops, including nursery and greenhouse crops ... farms, 1987..	621	287	621	496	393	326	610	1 165
1982..	707	296	707	535	476	317	719	1 277
$1,000, 1987..	11 323	14 159	12 736	11 985	6 012	11 406	11 978	26 571
1982..	13 952	16 204	9 487	16 012	9 500	15 913	10 157	35 149
Grains ... farms, 1987..	548	285	493	489	320	323	551	1 119
1982..	593	293	595	521	440	317	676	1 249
$1,000, 1987..	10 607	12 389	8 213	10 548	7 530	11 157	10 976	25 269
1982..	13 570	15 021	8 608	14 982	9 165	15 659	9 222	33 956
Corn for grain ... farms, 1987..	31	7	222	7	56	15	137	94
1982..	39	10	158	7	59	18	90	71
$1,000, 1987..	249	80	2 116	43	612	836	1 119	2 633
1982..	(D)	335	1 510	(D)	463	1 089	606	1 744
Wheat ... farms, 1987..	166	280	73	478	67	320	268	1 072
1982..	593	290	380	517	296	291	547	1 212
$1,000, 1987..	596	9 970	191	8 294	169	8 539	1 123	14 874
1982..	7 144	12 417	1 341	13 168	1 608	12 102	2 749	23 895
Soybeans ... farms, 1987..	479	4	378	44	295	2	489	349
1982..	461	11	388	42	356	3	485	293
$1,000, 1987..	7 137	25	4 547	224	5 447	(D)	5 889	2 708
1982..	4 599	(D)	4 013	271	5 390	(D)	3 700	2 839
Sorghum for grain ... farms, 1987..	300	162	215	309	191	156	390	620
1982..	150	83	226	178	167	114	269	464
$1,000, 1987..	2 451	2 065	1 308	1 897	1 294	1 522	2 781	5 009
1982..	1 184	1 837	1 701	1 451	1 748	2 372	2 121	5 419
Barley ... farms, 1987..	1	77	3	4	-	39	2	7
1982..	(NA)	(NA)	(NA)	(NA)	(NA)	(NA)	(NA)	(NA)
$1,000, 1987..	(D)	204	2	18	-	67	(D)	6
1982..	(NA)	(NA)	(NA)	(NA)	(NA)	(NA)	(NA)	(NA)
Oats ... farms, 1987..	95	6	40	50	14	10	18	21
1982..	132	2	21	24	31	3	25	39
$1,000, 1987..	132	9	32	59	(D)	(D)	11	16
1982..	324	(D)	16	(D)	39	(D)	22	35
Other grains[2] ... farms, 1987..	4	6	7	5	1	13	2	2
1982..	1	16	5	-	-	4	3	7
$1,000, 1987..	(D)	37	17	14	(D)	108	(D)	19
1982..	(D)	220	27	-	-	10	23	24

See footnotes at end of table.

[For meaning of abbreviations and symbols, see introductory text]

Item	Marion	Marshall	Meade	Miami	Mitchell	Montgomery	Morris	Morton
MARKET VALUE OF AGRICULTURAL PRODUCTS SOLD								
Total sales (see text) .... farms, 1987..	1 119	1 061	464	1 151	622	974	550	226
1982..	1 184	1 149	489	1 223	642	1 021	571	235
$1,000, 1987..	58 631	53 792	55 291	24 920	59 911	22 968	39 229	20 191
1982..	59 682	56 641	70 792	24 991	51 567	26 797	42 438	21 190
Average per farm .... dollars, 1987..	52 396	50 700	119 161	21 651	96 319	23 601	71 326	89 342
1982..	50 391	49 295	144 768	20 434	80 323	26 246	74 322	90 170
1987 value of sales:								
Less than $1,000 .... farms..	61	23	12	179	22	130	31	16
$1,000..	19	7	4	57	4	37	4	(D)
$1,000 to $2,499 .... farms..	66	59	13	160	32	129	29	6
$1,000..	112	101	23	271	55	224	49	(D)
$2,500 to $4,999 .... farms..	104	73	25	217	37	165	46	11
$1,000..	362	260	95	754	136	590	171	44
$5,000 to $9,999 .... farms..	157	115	42	193	55	200	80	31
$1,000..	1 153	862	297	1 400	404	1 490	590	229
$10,000 to $19,999 .... farms..	185	188	71	158	115	148	98	26
$1,000..	2 714	2 670	1 036	2 237	1 658	2 100	1 373	(D)
$20,000 to $24,999 .... farms..	77	60	25	38	43	38	37	10
$1,000..	1 715	1 340	553	840	984	845	823	(D)
$25,000 to $39,999 .... farms..	126	171	57	67	72	45	66	22
$1,000..	3 978	5 464	1 787	2 063	2 347	1 468	2 074	(D)
$40,000 to $49,999 .... farms..	41	52	25	27	42	21	24	10
$1,000..	1 823	2 315	1 112	1 216	1 906	929	1 088	(D)
$50,000 to $99,999 .... farms..	162	180	75	55	93	56	74	42
$1,000..	11 588	13 736	5 494	3 825	6 529	3 991	5 060	(D)
$100,000 to $249,999 .... farms..	93	114	78	44	82	28	48	43
$1,000..	14 083	16 429	11 939	6 704	12 607	4 532	6 928	6 439
$250,000 to $499,999 .... farms..	30	14	33	7	19	10	10	7
$1,000..	9 869	(D)	11 542	2 556	6 350	3 625	3 402	(D)
$500,000 or more .... farms..	15	2	10	4	10	4	9	2
$1,000..	11 196	(D)	21 406	2 897	26 830	3 217	17 667	(D)
1982 value of sales[1]:								
Less than $1,000 .... farms..	56	38	14	194	17	128	28	6
$1,000..	22	14	(D)	(D)	(D)	44	11	(D)
$1,000 to $2,499 .... farms..	75	53	11	181	30	157	22	11
$1,000..	138	95	22	(D)	50	262	41	(D)
$2,500 to $4,999 .... farms..	74	65	29	200	30	164	55	15
$1,000..	271	238	114	728	110	595	204	53
$5,000 to $9,999 .... farms..	143	130	45	220	72	178	64	22
$1,000..	1 058	848	300	1 566	548	1 331	479	162
$10,000 to $19,999 .... farms..	207	176	62	167	98	180	89	28
$1,000..	3 030	2 617	915	2 371	1 366	2 247	1 272	402
$20,000 to $24,999 .... farms..	75	74	28	49	34	31	37	15
$1,000..	1 668	1 673	639	1 098	736	691	841	322
$25,000 to $39,999 .... farms..	159	179	47	60	78	65	91	22
$1,000..	4 948	5 750	1 526	1 890	2 495	2 042	2 934	720
$40,000 to $49,999 .... farms..	56	82	26	33	41	20	33	14
$1,000..	2 479	3 666	1 161	1 449	1 831	912	1 439	600
$50,000 to $99,999 .... farms..	172	225	103	64	120	59	83	38
$1,000..	12 237	16 334	7 411	4 606	8 481	4 356	5 647	2 795
$100,000 to $249,999 .... farms..	131	110	83	45	93	46	50	47
$1,000..	19 483	15 275	13 117	6 659	13 604	7 128	7 577	7 097
$250,000 to $499,999 .... farms..	28	15	26	6	17	13	14	14
$1,000..	9 373	(D)	8 740	(D)	5 681	(D)	4 971	(D)
$500,000 or more .... farms..	8	2	14	2	10	2	6	2
$1,000..	4 957	(D)	36 814	(D)	16 817	(D)	17 128	(D)
Sales by commodity or commodity group:								
Crops, including nursery and greenhouse crops .... farms, 1987..	931	908	405	611	549	466	405	191
1982..	1 030	987	428	653	563	538	442	204
$1,000, 1987..	17 354	24 033	22 752	13 227	21 589	9 396	6 591	9 780
1982..	21 218	28 785	28 328	11 409	24 352	11 474	8 338	14 134
Grains .... farms, 1987..	887	884	398	449	536	376	386	191
1982..	992	971	422	539	550	463	427	203
$1,000, 1987..	16 065	23 036	22 033	10 194	20 977	8 476	5 770	9 619
1982..	20 272	28 127	27 747	10 054	23 585	10 503	5 981	13 861
Corn for grain .... farms, 1987..	58	60	73	117	28	60	41	8
1982..	63	92	45	88	18	52	39	8
$1,000, 1987..	397	722	5 050	1 270	412	1 131	228	659
1982..	366	862	4 081	1 485	404	808	298	763
Wheat .... farms, 1987..	651	760	391	43	526	171	317	167
1982..	968	900	410	333	548	423	398	174
$1,000, 1987..	8 722	5 875	8 204	98	14 970	890	2 349	4 796
1982..	13 317	9 537	12 043	1 474	19 446	5 719	3 338	6 745
Soybeans .... farms, 1987..	319	737	53	391	114	278	212	3
1982..	215	561	32	425	31	217	180	2
$1,000, 1987..	1 419	7 912	1 032	7 172	917	3 979	1 495	(D)
1982..	1 092	6 904	573	5 573	499	2 103	955	(D)
Sorghum for grain .... farms, 1987..	652	746	253	232	388	228	269	146
1982..	546	626	180	203	214	190	185	139
$1,000, 1987..	6 428	6 440	7 669	1 802	4 583	2 435	1 680	4 052
1982..	5 283	6 591	10 050	1 446	3 249	1 712	1 331	6 285
Barley .... farms, 1987..	22	-	24	-	4	2	2	10
1982..	14	(NA)	6	(NA)	(NA)	4	(NA)	(NA)
$1,000, 1987..	(D)	-	36	-	(D)	(D)	(D)	32
1982..	(NA)	(NA)	(NA)	(NA)	(NA)	(NA)	(NA)	(NA)
Oats .... farms, 1987..	82	-	2	52	38	24	17	3
1982..	119	109	2	52	24	61	38	-
$1,000, 1987..	47	82	-	(D)	50	38	12	(D)
1982..	136	223	(D)	(D)	79	110	44	-
Other grains[2] .... farms, 1987..	4	3	10	7	1	2	5	7
1982..	14	6	7	2	3	3	2	7
$1,000, 1987..	(D)	5	53	(D)	(D)	(D)	(D)	21
1982..	76	10	(D)	(D)	8	50	15	(D)

See footnotes at end of table.

Table 2. **Market Value of Agricultural Products Sold and Farms by Standard Industrial Classification: 1987 and 1982**—Con.

[For meaning of abbreviations and symbols, see introductory text]

Item	Nemaha	Neosho	Ness	Norton	Osage	Osborne	Ottawa	Pawnee
MARKET VALUE OF AGRICULTURAL PRODUCTS SOLD								
Total sales (see text) ....farms, 1987..	1 127	751	597	470	885	607	523	530
1982..	1 158	802	644	517	969	637	569	568
$1,000, 1987..	61 420	26 111	28 019	33 417	30 765	33 264	37 539	91 433
1982..	63 626	28 901	35 426	34 676	30 833	34 165	39 314	65 935
Average per farm ....dollars, 1987..	54 499	34 768	46 932	71 101	34 762	54 800	71 777	172 515
1982..	54 944	35 288	55 010	67 072	30 974	53 634	68 748	118 083
1987 value of sales:								
Less than $1,000 ....farms..	47	61	14	9	88	24	32	22
$1,000..	11	24	7	5	29	8	14	6
$1,000 to $2,499 ....farms..	47	74	23	9	97	17	29	19
$1,000..	87	125	40	13	161	30	45	33
$2,500 to $4,999 ....farms..	71	118	53	34	111	49	44	33
$1,000..	256	436	218	118	402	181	163	117
$5,000 to $9,999 ....farms..	126	119	76	48	157	59	64	53
$1,000..	943	862	561	352	1 186	437	457	397
$10,000 to $19,999 ....farms..	179	120	85	81	132	64	81	84
$1,000..	2 587	1 695	1 280	1 171	1 963	1 218	1 166	1 199
$20,000 to $24,999 ....farms..	74	37	44	38	50	48	43	23
$1,000..	1 648	811	960	835	1 103	1 091	962	512
$25,000 to $39,999 ....farms..	143	71	86	70	76	75	49	75
$1,000..	4 507	2 234	2 784	2 246	2 337	2 449	1 589	2 415
$40,000 to $49,999 ....farms..	82	22	32	25	32	41	28	26
$1,000..	3 648	978	1 406	1 106	1 435	1 816	1 252	1 155
$50,000 to $99,999 ....farms..	199	69	102	82	79	125	87	98
$1,000..	14 228	4 865	7 267	5 720	5 534	8 830	6 125	7 157
$100,000 to $249,999 ....farms..	126	46	72	58	41	76	48	58
$1,000..	18 989	6 634	10 215	8 985	6 332	11 404	7 140	8 565
$250,000 to $499,999 ....farms..	23	12	10	10	14	7	10	25
$1,000..	7 787	(D)	3 263	3 187	5 244	(D)	3 434	8 408
$500,000 or more ....farms..	8	2	—	8	8	2	8	16
$1,000..	6 732	(D)	—	9 681	5 018	(D)	15 192	61 470
1982 value of sales[1]:								
Less than $1,000 ....farms..	37	75	9	14	65	13	32	14
$1,000..	9	23	(D)	3	35	3	8	3
$1,000 to $2,499 ....farms..	51	87	22	15	106	33	26	16
$1,000..	86	151	(D)	24	172	51	48	26
$2,500 to $4,999 ....farms..	79	112	35	27	130	43	37	34
$1,000..	297	407	126	102	485	152	128	134
$5,000 to $9,999 ....farms..	126	130	75	40	190	66	54	43
$1,000..	939	904	547	291	1 359	471	417	315
$10,000 to $19,999 ....farms..	193	127	102	84	157	100	102	78
$1,000..	2 746	1 806	1 436	1 238	2 263	1 396	1 510	1 164
$20,000 to $24,999 ....farms..	66	37	35	20	43	39	36	35
$1,000..	1 482	826	782	449	970	858	804	773
$25,000 to $39,999 ....farms..	166	82	100	59	97	86	74	87
$1,000..	5 323	2 009	3 255	1 943	3 080	2 755	2 405	2 869
$40,000 to $49,999 ....farms..	75	33	40	52	39	66	38	37
$1,000..	3 378	1 464	1 776	2 302	1 741	2 955	1 666	1 661
$50,000 to $99,999 ....farms..	191	75	115	109	78	106	103	113
$1,000..	13 843	5 526	7 977	7 598	5 208	7 544	7 337	7 919
$100,000 to $249,999 ....farms..	144	45	91	91	44	68	65	75
$1,000..	20 835	6 424	12 995	11 591	6 435	9 610	9 478	11 671
$250,000 to $499,999 ....farms..	23	16	18	14	17	15	13	27
$1,000..	7 117	5 185	(D)	(D)	5 858	(D)	4 113	9 531
$500,000 or more ....farms..	7	2	1	(D)	3	(D)	9	9
$1,000..	7 513	3 554	(D)	(D)	3 027	(D)	11 381	29 868
Sales by commodity or commodity group:								
Crops, including nursery and greenhouse crops.....................................farms, 1987..	906	494	532	390	602	540	446	463
1982..	909	566	565	436	724	548	492	511
$1,000, 1987..	16 044	11 218	13 666	13 685	13 063	14 996	11 403	25 274
1982..	18 516	12 096	20 847	16 355	12 024	16 635	17 062	30 387
Grains..............................farms, 1987..	874	450	528	387	541	529	434	444
1982..	885	543	562	425	684	536	477	496
$1,000, 1987..	15 068	10 303	13 183	13 259	12 238	14 401	10 712	20 938
1982..	17 621	11 384	20 539	17 922	11 314	15 874	16 186	25 995
Corn for grain ....farms, 1987..	144	85	2	61	73	20	9	48
1982..	135	35	4	32	78	14	10	20
$1,000, 1987..	929	554	(D)	1 447	568	174	527	2 920
1982..	1 008	245	(D)	366	117	295	1 641	
Wheat.............................farms, 1987..	647	130	517	376	155	517	420	428
1982..	747	470	557	421	517	527	476	480
$1,000, 1987..	2 497	870	10 525	9 122	485	10 098	8 294	10 203
1982..	4 752	4 981	18 910	14 810	2 280	13 221	14 694	15 356
Soybeans.........................farms, 1987..	601	406	11	7	481	74	116	96
1982..	476	397	3	3	541	39	51	91
$1,000, 1987..	3 911	6 078	47	(D)	7 406	418	759	2 150
1982..	3 569	4 219	(D)	(D)	5 181	298	370	2 337
Sorghum for grain ....farms, 1987..	696	278	312	210	401	373	168	317
1982..	543	155	147	158	349	231	108	277
$1,000, 1987..	7 681	2 703	2 377	2 141	3 750	3 482	1 088	5 498
1982..	8 216	1 638	1 475	2 130	3 427	2 221	812	6 560
Barley.............................farms, 1987..	—	—	81	44	1	8	1	16
1982..	(NA)	(NA)	119	91	(NA)	(D)	(D)	(NA)
$1,000, 1987..	(NA)	(NA)	(NA)	(NA)	(NA)	(NA)	(NA)	(NA)
1982..	(NA)	(NA)	(NA)	(NA)	(NA)	(NA)	(NA)	(NA)
Oats ....farms, 1987..	38	73	6	36	20	30	25	7
1982..	49	82	3	21	26	7	5	6
$1,000, 1987..	43	(D)	(D)	(D)	(D)	54	(D)	(D)
1982..	66	(D)	(D)	54	50	(D)	(D)	(D)
Other grains[2]...................farms, 1987..	3	1	26	47	1	19	6	27
1982..	5	7	11	4	15	2	3	7
$1,000, 1987..	(D)	(D)	65	356	(D)	(D)	21	(D)
1982..	9	(D)	33	(D)	31	(D)	(D)	(D)

See footnotes at end of table.

Table 2. **Market Value of Agricultural Products Sold and Farms by Standard Industrial Classification: 1987 and 1982** —Con.

[For meaning of abbreviations and symbols, see introductory text]

Item	Phillips	Pottawatomie	Pratt	Rawlins	Reno	Republic	Rice	Riley
MARKET VALUE OF AGRICULTURAL PRODUCTS SOLD								
Total sales (see text) ....farms, 1987..	591	790	517	541	1 557	833	604	546
1982..	647	869	547	621	1 638	923	643	583
$1,000, 1987..	34 621	39 295	97 669	31 808	82 925	97 295	69 583	25 444
1982..	35 044	40 141	78 601	34 194	97 690	78 396	61 337	25 963
Average per farm...............dollars, 1987..	58 581	49 741	188 914	58 795	53 259	116 801	115 204	46 601
1982..	54 164	46 192	144 061	55 063	59 640	84 938	95 392	44 534
1987 value of sales:								
Less than $1,000 ....farms..	24	94	21	14	123	26	31	43
$1,000..	6	31	6	4	36	7	11	14
$1,000 to $2,499 ....farms..	28	62	17	23	119	36	39	41
$1,000..	50	98	28	43	203	65	64	74
$2,500 to $4,999 ....farms..	50	77	32	37	160	67	55	69
$1,000..	181	282	121	142	588	250	202	250
$5,000 to $9,999 ....farms..	61	101	56	44	249	77	62	68
$1,000..	447	725	416	314	1 809	539	447	499
$10,000 to $19,999 ....farms..	60	109	77	58	248	117	87	92
$1,000..	1 161	1 544	1 141	825	3 548	1 698	1 282	1 330
$20,000 to $24,999 ....farms..	29	46	27	38	85	51	31	22
$1,000..	658	1 009	595	855	1 883	1 159	682	498
$25,000 to $39,999 ....farms..	94	86	61	79	166	108	63	57
$1,000..	3 026	2 735	2 009	2 453	5 382	3 382	2 021	1 794
$40,000 to $49,999 ....farms..	45	39	32	47	67	57	36	24
$1,000..	2 010	1 736	1 414	2 098	3 008	2 602	1 649	1 061
$50,000 to $99,999 ....farms..	96	92	84	120	174	168	101	68
$1,000..	6 737	6 341	6 058	8 656	11 933	12 245	7 169	4 747
$100,000 to $249,999 ....farms..	61	50	72	66	129	108	71	46
$1,000..	9 294	7 443	10 730	9 636	19 044	15 851	11 126	7 075
$250,000 to $499,999 ....farms..	13	23	28	13	28	15	17	9
$1,000..	4 263	7 676	9 800	(D)	9 312	5 109	6 243	2 847
$500,000 or more ....farms..	8	11	10	2	9	3	11	7
$1,000..	6 768	9 676	65 352	(D)	26 176	54 387	38 688	5 255
1982 value of sales[1]:								
Less than $1,000 ....farms..	19	65	9	6	93	34	23	35
$1,000..	7	27	1	2	(D)	(D)	8	(D)
$1,000 to $2,499 ....farms..	21	60	24	7	132	35	28	52
$1,000..	36	98	40	12	211	64	53	(D)
$2,500 to $4,999 ....farms..	33	102	33	28	160	63	36	66
$1,000..	122	389	123	105	584	222	129	229
$5,000 to $9,999 ....farms..	88	117	44	68	161	111	74	85
$1,000..	652	861	326	480	1 145	816	547	605
$10,000 to $19,999 ....farms..	112	133	59	107	277	133	81	94
$1,000..	1 644	1 916	840	1 601	4 006	1 961	1 179	1 340
$20,000 to $24,999 ....farms..	56	51	35	33	84	54	39	31
$1,000..	1 253	1 123	772	743	1 884	1 212	875	694
$25,000 to $39,999 ....farms..	84	104	65	81	173	101	62	56
$1,000..	2 714	3 328	2 067	2 539	5 529	3 206	1 937	1 825
$40,000 to $49,999 ....farms..	33	33	25	48	103	73	41	34
$1,000..	1 498	1 437	1 107	2 166	4 616	3 235	1 831	1 549
$50,000 to $99,999 ....farms..	120	120	127	153	263	179	135	63
$1,000..	8 441	8 432	8 949	10 684	17 644	12 365	9 571	4 677
$100,000 to $249,999 ....farms..	61	60	90	78	166	118	86	51
$1,000..	9 103	8 712	13 526	11 335	24 619	17 060	12 688	7 324
$250,000 to $499,999 ....farms..	13	13	25	11	28	17	22	10
$1,000..	4 341	4 390	8 073	(D)	9 446	5 923	7 779	3 004
$500,000 or more ....farms..	7	11	11	1	7	4	16	5
$1,000..	5 234	9 427	42 978	(D)	27 943	32 320	24 540	4 619
Sales by commodity or commodity group:								
Crops, including nursery and greenhouse crops.....................farms, 1987..	497	497	445	487	1 242	711	521	400
1982..	564	610	495	563	1 322	790	563	411
$1,000, 1987..	13 746	9 232	27 034	17 077	33 141	29 926	20 715	7 197
1982..	16 276	9 793	30 805	20 894	47 067	30 766	28 563	7 969
Grains.....................farms, 1987..	483	440	438	478	1 183	693	503	361
1982..	548	574	466	555	1 267	780	548	386
$1,000, 1987..	12 630	7 755	20 905	16 249	28 409	28 766	19 703	5 567
1982..	15 433	8 611	28 754	19 998	43 473	30 003	25 446	6 435
Corn for grain ....farms, 1987..	33	85	105	46	57	241	34	32
1982..	28	96	58	27	33	218	26	35
$1,000, 1987..	991	1 745	5 395	1 061	2 162	8 993	1 594	380
1982..	859	1 616	(D)	1 159	1 143	7 864	1 325	524
Wheat.....................farms, 1987..	472	295	426	467	1 130	634	483	298
1982..	530	457	464	541	1 226	723	529	357
$1,000, 1987..	8 095	1 167	10 287	11 105	16 963	7 731	10 618	1 776
1982..	11 532	2 991	16 163	15 996	30 618	10 873	16 734	2 957
Soybeans.....................farms, 1987..	19	305	80	11	132	430	117	205
1982..	4	277	69	2	110	392	79	161
$1,000, 1987..	118	2 696	1 677	(D)	1 490	4 045	1 252	1 660
1982..	(D)	2 024	2 543	(D)	1 929	3 841	1 309	1 222
Sorghum for grain ....farms, 1987..	295	263	273	315	719	516	402	253
1982..	249	264	258	187	660	437	363	175
$1,000, 1987..	3 172	1 895	3 522	3 268	7 733	7 772	6 167	1 708
1982..	2 739	1 930	5 109	2 692	10 002	7 217	5 975	1 695
Barley.....................farms, 1987..	20	-	5	42	11	-	4	3
1982..	(NA)			(NA)	(NA)		(NA)	4
$1,000, 1987..	19	-		17		-	3
1982..	(NA)	(NA)	(NA)	(NA)	(NA)	(NA)	(NA)	(NA)
Oats ....farms, 1987..	47	23	3	29	18	64	15	26
1982..	28	36	10	6	59	97	9	30
$1,000, 1987..	42	33	(D)	82	21	77	46	40
1982..	35	(D)	(D)	(D)	266	155	71	(D)
Other grains[2].....................farms, 1987..	37	-	1	79	11	30	5	-
1982..	3	3	13	9	24	10	4	2
$1,000, 1987..	393	-	(D)	601	22	149	22	-
1982..	(D)	(D)	59	93	96	53	32	(D)

See footnotes at end of table.

Table 2. **Market Value of Agricultural Products Sold and Farms by Standard Industrial Classification: 1987 and 1982**—Con.

[For meaning of abbreviations and symbols, see introductory text]

Item	Rooks	Rush	Russell	Saline	Scott	Sedgwick	Seward	Shawnee
MARKET VALUE OF AGRICULTURAL PRODUCTS SOLD								
Total sales (see text) .... farms, 1987..	473	546	534	743	391	1 589	265	852
1982..	528	584	590	763	416	1 665	277	937
$1,000, 1987..	24 933	20 057	20 315	30 700	280 233	59 327	130 390	21 859
1982..	30 450	27 397	26 145	44 062	225 853	75 828	126 173	23 019
Average per farm.......... dollars, 1987..	52 713	36 734	38 043	41 318	716 708	37 336	457 508	25 656
1982..	57 670	46 912	44 314	57 748	542 915	45 422	455 498	24 567
1987 value of sales:								
Less than $1,000 .... farms..	20	14	16	75	12	184	19	108
$1,000..	4	2	5	24	2	52	4	30
$1,000 to $2,499 .... farms..	16	27	29	70	10	188	16	121
$1,000..	27	50	54	120	17	323	26	208
$2,500 to $4,999 .... farms..	38	39	48	100	22	194	14	149
$1,000..	136	146	174	354	87	716	55	535
$5,000 to $9,999 .... farms..	63	97	100	99	31	234	28	135
$1,000..	476	744	716	693	219	1 695	206	949
$10,000 to $19,999 .... farms..	60	112	99	101	40	242	28	126
$1,000..	1 122	1 612	1 391	1 458	629	3 447	418	1 818
$20,000 to $24,999 .... farms..	35	36	37	32	9	77	11	22
$1,000..	805	845	841	709	209	1 702	265	476
$25,000 to $39,999 .... farms..	59	60	51	72	51	123	23	65
$1,000..	1 936	1 960	1 625	2 289	1 658	3 775	781	2 076
$40,000 to $49,999 .... farms..	22	27	25	31	24	60	15	15
$1,000..	966	1 205	1 129	1 377	1 074	2 645	662	667
$50,000 to $99,999 .... farms..	74	88	76	89	69	137	50	53
$1,000..	5 285	5 897	5 209	6 247	4 880	9 389	3 646	3 760
$100,000 to $249,999 .... farms..	48	38	42	61	61	111	55	47
$1,000..	6 871	5 977	5 762	8 752	9 734	17 563	8 743	6 601
$250,000 to $499,999 .... farms..	17	5	7	7	24	29	13	8
$1,000..	(D)	1 619	(D)	2 428	7 438	9 371	4 790	3 021
$500,000 or more .... farms..	1	–	2	6	41	10	13	3
$1,000..	(D)	–	(D)	6 244	254 286	8 652	110 793	1 714
1982 value of sales[1]:								
Less than $1,000 .... farms..	8	14	24	35	9	152	13	154
$1,000..	2	4	(D)	1	4	(D)	(D)	(D)
$1,000 to $2,499 .... farms..	17	14	26	53	15	176	12	170
$1,000..	29	27	43	87	30	290	20	(D)
$2,500 to $4,999 .... farms..	29	32	43	57	25	173	14	160
$1,000..	103	119	157	208	92	625	55	590
$5,000 to $9,999 .... farms..	72	68	73	130	32	231	22	141
$1,000..	537	506	523	973	235	1 667	162	979
$10,000 to $19,999 .... farms..	98	121	112	134	44	242	28	114
$1,000..	1 388	1 801	1 636	1 861	625	3 477	392	1 640
$20,000 to $24,999 .... farms..	38	43	40	39	13	75	11	24
$1,000..	834	942	871	867	287	1 661	237	535
$25,000 to $39,999 .... farms..	61	100	89	85	41	170	33	54
$1,000..	1 928	3 097	2 817	2 782	1 361	5 417	1 064	1 747
$40,000 to $49,999 .... farms..	34	36	29	42	20	72	14	15
$1,000..	1 516	1 589	1 292	1 869	871	3 190	(D)	662
$50,000 to $99,999 .... farms..	92	93	86	86	67	186	38	47
$1,000..	6 516	6 506	5 934	6 036	4 747	13 272	(D)	3 244
$100,000 to $249,999 .... farms..	58	52	54	84	78	126	53	39
$1,000..	8 510	7 602	7 916	12 140	12 172	19 724	8 604	5 739
$250,000 to $499,999 .... farms..	17	8	10	12	33	49	25	16
$1,000..	5 314	2 886	3 124	3 962	11 346	17 338	8 472	(D)
$500,000 or more .... farms..	4	3	3	6	34	8	13	2
$1,000..	3 773	2 320	1 825	13 221	194 082	8 901	103 612	(D)
Sales by commodity or commodity group:								
Crops, including nursery and greenhouse crops................. farms, 1987..	418	477	433	600	328	1 231	222	515
1982..	469	514	481	646	349	1 289	222	538
$1,000, 1987..	12 907	12 740	9 478	12 261	18 858	30 494	15 373	12 792
1982..	16 385	17 031	16 449	18 899	26 553	41 690	19 525	13 232
Grains......... farms, 1987..	412	471	425	563	321	1 102	219	406
1982..	461	509	470	611	344	1 155	219	430
$1,000, 1987..	12 195	12 011	8 886	11 156	16 835	25 222	13 566	10 297
1982..	15 659	16 571	14 914	17 750	23 143	37 055	18 475	9 668
Corn for grain .... farms, 1987..	8	14	1	19	49	71	49	156
1982..	8	14	3	23	44	55	29	129
$1,000, 1987..	169	182	(D)	100	2 058	2 713	2 566	3 565
1982..	101	154	(D)	177	1 532	2 057	2 464	4 064
Wheat......... farms, 1987..	406	458	414	536	315	1 030	208	143
1982..	455	494	466	605	334	1 105	195	337
$1,000, 1987..	9 246	8 992	6 993	8 823	10 622	12 963	5 643	580
1982..	13 832	13 902	13 120	15 020	14 115	26 301	8 041	1 794
Soybeans......... farms, 1987..	8	36	17	182	14	239	16	322
1982..	5	23	3	111	24	159	21	264
$1,000, 1987..	59	199	85	868	212	3 825	136	4 370
1982..	(D)	(D)	(D)	510	814	2 149	437	2 154
Sorghum for grain .... farms, 1987..	253	326	220	258	189	649	181	232
1987..	142	207	142	137	159	447	152	164
$1,000, 1987..	2 513	2 508	1 757	1 328	3 491	5 673	5 250	1 761
1982..	1 606	2 264	1 612	967	4 642	6 330	7 446	1 586
Barley......... farms, 1987..	20	43	8	6	80	9	13	1
1982..	(NA)	(NA)	(NA)	(NA)	(NA)	(NA)	(NA)	(NA)
$1,000, 1987..	(D)	37	(D)	(D)	247	(D)	31	(D)
1982..	(NA)	(NA)	(NA)	(NA)	(NA)	(NA)	(NA)	(NA)
Oats .... farms, 1987..	13	31	20	12	2	14	3	29
1982..	10	25	9	26	2	37	1	31
$1,000, 1987..	(D)	44	20	23	(D)	14	6	(D)
1982..	85	113	28	(D)	(D)	133	(D)	22
Other grains[2]......... farms, 1987..	36	17	5	2	22	5	10	1
1982..	2	9	2	1	9	17	2	7
$1,000, 1987..	164	49	16	(D)	(D)	9	54	(D)
1982..	(D)	(D)	–	(D)	(D)	86	(D)	47

See footnotes at end of table.

[For meaning of abbreviations and symbols, see introductory text]

Item	Sheridan	Sherman	Smith	Stafford	Stanton	Stevens	Sumner	Thomas
MARKET VALUE OF AGRICUL-TURAL PRODUCTS SOLD								
Total sales (see text) ......farms, 1987..	518	524	692	540	280	300	1 271	644
1982..	571	550	761	557	231	325	1 386	628
$1,000, 1987..	54 089	67 429	50 852	72 053	96 972	96 641	53 409	74 156
1982..	58 695	69 425	54 463	63 961	79 356	70 171	71 802	77 919
Average per farm......dollars, 1987..	104 419	128 681	73 486	133 432	310 613	322 138	42 021	115 150
1982..	103 144	126 227	71 594	114 832	343 532	215 911	51 805	124 075
1987 value of sales:								
Less than $1,000 ......farms..	4	11	8	24	12	10	99	20
$1,000..	1	3	4	6	(D)	(D)	32	10
$1,000 to $2,499 ......farms..	15	17	25	23	1	11	89	24
$1,000..	29	29	42	38	(D)	(D)	145	38
$2,500 to $4,999 ......farms..	33	27	35	49	17	22	112	31
$1,000..	114	100	131	180	59	82	418	107
$5,000 to $9,999 ......farms..	44	60	69	50	30	16	199	76
$1,000..	320	440	497	371	225	125	1 406	568
$10,000 to $19,999 ......farms..	78	64	91	58	23	26	205	92
$1,000..	1 150	932	1 310	872	333	378	2 945	1 328
$20,000 to $24,999 ......farms..	24	28	41	16	7	11	58	25
$1,000..	518	632	901	352	156	247	1 302	555
$25,000 to $39,999 ......farms..	64	56	107	67	19	22	155	75
$1,000..	2 088	1 791	3 532	2 118	603	698	4 963	2 466
$40,000 to $49,999 ......farms..	41	34	52	29	14	17	59	47
$1,000..	1 854	1 544	2 372	1 321	631	773	(D)	2 080
$50,000 to $99,999 ......farms..	113	98	152	96	53	67	155	119
$1,000..	8 344	6 924	10 643	6 857	3 786	4 785	(D)	8 518
$100,000 to $249,999 ......farms..	76	82	78	65	69	63	115	93
$1,000..	11 371	14 426	11 204	13 245	11 074	10 016	(D)	14 301
$250,000 to $499,999 ......farms..	18	23	28	26	20	30	20	24
$1,000..	6 004	7 655	8 068	8 931	6 766	10 807	(D)	8 444
$500,000 or more ......farms..	9	14	12	17	15	5	5	15
$1,000..	22 267	32 954	11 949	37 763	63 331	68 712	5 021	35 642
1982 value of sales[1]:								
Less than $1,000 ......farms..	14	14	10	10	2	8	69	13
$1,000..	4	3	5	(D)	(D)	2	23	(D)
$1,000 to $2,499 ......farms..	9	15	31	13	4	9	77	17
$1,000..	16	27	54	24	(D)	15	133	30
$2,500 to $4,999 ......farms..	13	17	29	20	3	11	87	30
$1,000..	47	66	115	75	11	46	313	113
$5,000 to $9,999 ......farms..	40	45	69	33	19	20	136	48
$1,000..	285	357	508	259	132	136	1 001	366
$10,000 to $19,999 ......farms..	74	73	114	76	5	26	213	90
$1,000..	1 022	1 058	1 639	1 146	73	362	3 033	1 296
$20,000 to $24,999 ......farms..	36	32	37	49	7	10	70	41
$1,000..	800	711	813	1 103	157	225	1 548	908
$25,000 to $39,999 ......farms..	99	82	121	61	14	21	180	63
$1,000..	3 236	2 007	3 910	1 947	427	678	5 802	2 662
$40,000 to $49,999 ......farms..	36	27	47	35	7	17	85	49
$1,000..	1 610	1 219	2 111	1 574	300	774	3 827	2 200
$50,000 to $99,999 ......farms..	106	109	177	115	50	70	280	95
$1,000..	7 627	7 776	12 679	8 425	3 483	5 059	18 536	6 620
$100,000 to $249,999 ......farms..	104	95	99	100	71	68	182	109
$1,000..	15 568	14 930	14 821	14 969	11 277	13 223	27 276	16 572
$250,000 to $499,999 ......farms..	30	38	17	35	31	34	22	37
$1,000..	10 211	12 639	6 151	11 673	9 907	11 190	7 084	12 813
$500,000 or more ......farms..	10	23	10	9	18	11	5	15
$1,000..	18 468	28 832	11 677	22 733	53 582	38 462	3 224	34 176
Sales by commodity or commodity group:								
Crops, including nursery and greenhouse crops......farms, 1987..	454	467	610	481	239	258	1 098	584
1982..	506	505	651	518	207	290	1 226	567
$1,000, 1987..	22 118	30 169	20 043	23 729	23 700	24 780	30 566	35 387
1982..	26 588	43 276	22 394	33 354	30 446	(D)	52 859	42 787
Grains......farms, 1987..	443	484	594	462	239	265	1 064	580
1982..	495	498	630	513	207	288	1 188	564
$1,000, 1987..	21 262	29 406	19 235	21 760	22 937	23 350	29 775	34 682
1982..	27 456	37 743	21 623	31 151	29 794	33 137	51 482	42 202
Corn for grain ......farms, 1987..	123	179	44	100	93	61	14	181
1982..	122	163	21	48	67	44	3	136
$1,000, 1987..	7 903	9 002	540	6 908	6 023	6 523	108	13 022
1982..	9 746	(D)	319	4 515	8 976	4 507	(D)	12 566
Wheat ......farms, 1987..	420	445	579	437	233	224	1 037	560
1982..	457	478	612	482	205	237	1 184	536
$1,000, 1987..	8 396	14 137	9 957	8 623	9 600	7 281	26 157	16 207
1982..	13 243	22 332	14 961	15 737	19 525	10 776	49 729	25 044
Soybeans......farms, 1987..	54	48	175	88	19	16	192	69
1982..	39	41	34	89	31	11	39	39
$1,000, 1987..	837	1 100	1 492	1 657	365	126	1 502	853
1982..	906	677	173	3 260	1 095	89	185	836
Sorghum for grain ......farms, 1987..	275	103	464	314	138	223	353	306
1982..	193	74	391	318	123	260	186	163
$1,000, 1987..	3 480	882	7 009	4 519	3 098	9 083	1 871	3 370
1982..	3 415	925	6 096	7 515	5 819	17 682	1 371	3 465
Barley ......farms, 1987..	52	53	25	13	31	23	20	49
1982..	(NA)	(NA)	(NA)	(NA)	(NA)	(NA)	5	16
$1,000, 1987..	78	156	25	16	100	(D)	53	123
1982..	(NA)	(NA)	(NA)	(NA)	(NA)	(NA)	(NA)	(NA)
Oats ......farms, 1987..	15	13	8	15	1	1	23	23
1982..	11	20	33	15	1	7	15	18
$1,000, 1987..	29	46	95	11	(D)	(D)	16	106
1982..	36	(D)	46	62	(D)	-	(D)	(D)
Other grains[2]......farms, 1987..	66	198	28	17	23	15	14	86
1982..	16	120	7	18	19	5	18	16
$1,000, 1987..	540	4 085	117	32	730	274	68	972
1982..	109	2 216	28	63	(D)	72	107	(D)

See footnotes at end of table.

Table 2. **Market Value of Agricultural Products Sold and Farms by Standard Industrial Classification: 1987 and 1982**—Con.

[For meaning of abbreviations and symbols, see introductory text]

Item	Trego	Wabaunsee	Wallace	Washington	Wichita	Wilson	Woodson	Wyandotte
MARKET VALUE OF AGRICULTURAL PRODUCTS SOLD								
Total sales (see text) .... farms, 1987..	482	633	330	939	355	610	369	199
1982..	497	678	338	1 032	341	680	402	216
$1,000, 1987..	35 552	34 210	26 601	62 837	223 235	20 203	21 103	5 015
1982..	56 265	40 468	33 065	68 203	159 238	24 276	22 746	6 887
Average per farm .... dollars, 1987..	73 760	54 045	86 671	66 920	628 830	33 120	57 189	25 202
1982..	113 210	59 687	97 827	66 088	466 974	35 700	56 581	31 884
1987 value of sales:								
Less than $1,000 .... farms..	15	62	5	23	8	46	25	45
$1,000..	7	15	2	7	1	16	7	12
$1,000 to $2,499 .... farms..	10	44	10	28	15	60	21	42
$1,000..	17	76	18	49	27	106	37	71
$2,500 to $4,999 .... farms..	29	82	23	65	18	70	32	37
$1,000..	102	295	89	232	70	255	115	131
$5,000 to $9,999 .... farms..	47	88	35	117	32	91	68	34
$1,000..	336	617	241	851	225	643	500	246
$10,000 to $19,999 .... farms..	111	102	40	162	34	98	59	22
$1,000..	1 620	1 502	616	2 269	483	1 409	818	(D)
$20,000 to $24,999 .... farms..	26	43	24	30	14	33	22	2
$1,000..	640	959	543	671	316	744	491	(D)
$25,000 to $39,999 .... farms..	81	50	41	135	38	64	35	3
$1,000..	2 549	1 568	1 366	4 346	1 223	2 049	1 036	(D)
$40,000 to $49,999 .... farms..	48	27	15	51	16	22	19	2
$1,000..	2 142	1 227	646	2 265	721	984	843	(D)
$50,000 to $99,999 .... farms..	73	67	59	168	77	82	44	3
$1,000..	5 360	4 696	4 223	11 724	5 589	5 923	3 209	(D)
$100,000 to $249,999 .... farms..	33	45	59	115	71	38	34	3
$1,000..	4 570	6 803	9 098	16 938	10 531	5 744	5 029	454
$250,000 to $499,999 .... farms..	5	12	11	26	16	5	7	3
$1,000..	(D)	4 023	4 007	8 836	5 296	(D)	2 074	1 013
$500,000 or more .... farms..	2	11	8	19	16	1	3	3
$1,000..	(D)	12 430	7 752	14 630	198 752	(D)	6 942	2 312
1982 value of sales[1]:								
Less than $1,000 .... farms..	22	47	14	40	5	37	22	50
$1,000..	(D)	15	3	10	1	12	10	12
$1,000 to $2,499 .... farms..	18	60	13	25	7	70	38	54
$1,000..	33	105	22	45	13	123	66	87
$2,500 to $4,999 .... farms..	29	69	21	65	9	85	41	43
$1,000..	103	258	78	254	32	306	149	163
$5,000 to $9,999 .... farms..	52	96	30	117	29	78	74	23
$1,000..	396	709	223	838	207	588	540	166
$10,000 to $19,999 .... farms..	67	113	28	150	34	93	62	14
$1,000..	1 021	1 618	426	2 241	510	1 330	919	198
$20,000 to $24,999 .... farms..	46	44	20	61	14	44	28	4
$1,000..	1 040	986	458	1 384	315	985	623	(D)
$25,000 to $39,999 .... farms..	88	74	33	139	38	75	32	5
$1,000..	2 772	2 353	1 035	4 483	1 193	2 420	981	(D)
$40,000 to $49,999 .... farms..	28	29	26	74	15	36	17	4
$1,000..	1 250	1 291	1 163	3 343	675	1 634	752	(D)
$50,000 to $99,999 .... farms..	95	82	65	177	67	103	48	7
$1,000..	6 580	5 607	4 588	13 052	4 684	6 886	3 441	(D)
$100,000 to $249,999 .... farms..	40	46	64	121	78	50	31	9
$1,000..	6 067	6 777	10 285	17 668	12 356	7 522	4 471	1 366
$250,000 to $499,999 .... farms..	8	9	16	39	33	9	5	1
$1,000..	2 744	2 912	5 872	13 142	10 712	2 470	1 707	(D)
$500,000 or more .... farms..	3	9	8	14	12	-	4	2
$1,000..	34 254	17 835	8 913	11 765	128 559	-	9 089	(D)
Sales by commodity or commodity group:								
Crops, including nursery and greenhouse crops................. farms, 1987..	419	389	274	741	304	403	252	84
1982..	424	451	275	872	291	496	276	102
$1,000, 1987..	10 704	6 269	15 063	19 751	19 539	11 204	7 063	3 760
1982..	12 434	6 540	21 492	26 627	26 034	13 421	6 338	(D)
Grains .... farms, 1987..	415	343	272	734	302	371	224	45
1982..	423	411	270	858	290	478	260	54
$1,000, 1987..	10 238	5 402	14 603	19 241	18 215	10 742	6 315	1 477
1982..	11 947	5 667	20 509	25 958	24 456	12 856	5 798	1 409
Corn for grain .... farms, 1987..	9	54	95	96	90	30	16	17
1982..	7	59	76	95	73	27	12	14
$1,000, 1987..	102	1 104	5 724	981	(D)	245	91	359
1982..	324	735	5 667	1 163	4 537	258	96	312
Wheat .... farms, 1987..	413	217	258	648	299	206	112	9
1982..	411	348	255	783	288	437	205	36
$1,000, 1987..	7 859	764	7 082	5 795	10 681	957	374	36
1982..	10 053	1 805	10 102	10 939	13 626	5 455	1 780	365
Soybeans .... farms, 1987..	-	225	13	469	23	327	208	35
1982..	2	189	3	398	33	355	208	37
$1,000, 1987..	-	1 938	117	4 080	172	6 959	4 180	991
1982..	4	1 094	(D)	4 777	(O)	4 826	2 549	640
Sorghum for grain .... farms, 1987..	245	225	78	600	175	264	171	6
1982..	230	227	73	557	146	214	109	11
$1,000, 1987..	2 125	1 554	721	8 229	2 805	2 566	1 661	(D)
1982..	1 552	1 964	3 530	8 814	4 852	2 288	1 357	99
Barley .... farms, 1987..	38	-	35	1	74	1	-	-
1982..	48	-	52	(D)	233	(D)	-	-
$1,000, 1987..	(NA)	(NA)	(NA)	(NA)	(NA)	(NA)	(NA)	(NA)
1982..	(NA)	(NA)	(NA)	(NA)	(NA)	(NA)	(NA)	(NA)
Oats .... farms, 1987..	13	29	8	69	8	12	10	3
1982..	2	30	1	86	3	23	20	3
$1,000, 1987..	19	(D)	13	(D)	(D)	(D)	(D)	1
1982..	(D)	30	(D)	145	(D)	29	17	(D)
Other grains[2] .... farms, 1987..	20	2	52	12	63	-	1	1
1982..	4	11	54	19	49	-	2	2
$1,000, 1987..	84	(D)	894	79	933	-	(D)	(D)
1982..	8	18	1 174	121	1 082	-	-	(D)

See footnotes at end of table.

[For meaning of abbreviations and symbols, see introductory text]

Item	Kansas	Allen	Anderson	Atchison	Barber	Barton	Bourbon
MARKET VALUE OF AGRICULTURAL PRODUCTS SOLD—Con.							
Total sales (see text)-Con.							
Sales by commodity or commodity group-Con.							
Crops, including nursery and greenhouse crops-Con.							
Cotton and cottonseed .... farms, 1987..	10	--	--	--	--	--	--
1982..	-	--	--	--	--	--	--
$1,000, 1987..	186	--	--	--	--	--	--
1982..	-	--	--	--	--	--	--
Tobacco .... farms, 1987..	13	--	--	5	--	--	--
1982..	13	--	--	6	--	--	--
$1,000, 1987..	80	--	--	(D)	--	--	--
1982..	77	-	--	19	--	--	--
Hay, silage, and field seeds .... farms, 1987..	12 801	119	150	119	54	214	169
1982..	12 376	100	137	104	58	259	119
1987..	109 574	577	634	324	(D)	3 259	468
1982..	100 189	400	(D)	297	442	3 510	662
Vegetables, sweet corn, and melons .... farms, 1987..	418	5	4	2	2	1	--
1982..	360	4	--	4	2	4	--
$1,000, 1987..	4 151	6	2	(D)	(D)	(D)	--
1982..	3 206	12	--	3	(D)	(D)	--
Fruits, nuts, and berries .... farms, 1987..	278	5	3	3	--	--	4
1982..	213	3	--	2	1	--	3
$1,000, 1987..	1 693	(D)	(D)	(D)	(D)	--	(D)
1982..	1 398	(D)	1	(D)	--	--	(D)
Nursery and greenhouse crops.......... farms, 1987..	272	2	1	2	--	5	1
1982..	298	1	1	4	--	6	--
$1,000, 1987..	26 805	(D)	(D)	(D)	(D)	(D)	(D)
1982..	21 515	(D)	(D)	(D)	(D)	--	(D)
Other crops .... farms, 1987..	80	--	--	1	--	--	--
1982..	190	1	--	1	--	1	--
$1,000, 1987..	716	--	--	(D)	--	--	--
1982..	6 954	(D)	--	(D)	--	(D)	--
Livestock, poultry, and their products ...... farms, 1987..	45 882	511	563	504	419	594	681
1982..	51 701	608	637	602	404	600	730
$1,000, 1987..	4 765 000	11 276	17 455	12 142	36 063	101 064	17 004
1982..	4 047 815	11 967	14 358	14 250	32 072	83 804	17 910
Poultry and poultry products .... farms, 1987..	1 550	23	38	16	3	29	19
1982..	2 985	23	41	19	4	42	29
$1,000, 1987..	25 284	6	(D)	(D)	(D)	(D)	14
1982..	25 755	11	(D)	(D)	(Z)	(D)	16
Dairy products .... farms, 1987..	2 004	40	37	28	10	23	46
1982..	2 597	53	57	47	10	25	60
$1,000, 1987..	140 232	2 950	2 131	1 712	1 278	1 164	1 899
1982..	162 232	3 655	2 357	1 940	1 166	822	2 744
Cattle and calves.......... farms, 1987..	41 498	488	525	463	393	535	645
1982..	47 032	566	593	530	383	547	668
$1,000, 1987..	4 305 335	7 038	13 085	7 102	33 934	97 664	13 876
1982..	3 516 670	6 417	9 078	8 148	30 107	80 795	13 257
Hogs and pigs .... farms, 1987..	7 090	62	60	144	32	71	74
1982..	9 778	85	90	209	24	86	115
$1,000, 1987..	284 375	1 234	1 705	3 119	539	1 276	1 128
1982..	316 882	1 760	2 816	3 903	586	1 294	1 765
Sheep, lambs, and wool.......... farms, 1987..	2 456	28	28	14	20	16	25
1982..	2 535	30	34	18	14	23	26
$1,000, 1987..	16 561	27	68	96	160	(D)	41
1982..	15 502	61	55	108	141	113	36
Other livestock and livestock products (see text) .... farms, 1987..	2 669	26	23	17	27	31	44
1982..	2 858	42	22	22	34	29	37
$1,000, 1987..	9 273	24	(D)	(D)	(D)	180	47
1982..	10 773	63	(D)	(D)	72	(D)	90
1987 FARMS BY STANDARD INDUSTRIAL CLASSIFICATION							
Cash grains (011)	31 789	279	324	345	154	579	188
Field crops, except cash grains (013)	2 010	10	25	6	5	44	38
Cotton (0131)	1	--	--	--	--	--	--
Tobacco (0132)	3	--	--	1	--	--	--
Sugarcane and sugar beets; Irish potatoes; field crops, except cash grains, n.e.c. (0133, 0134, 0139)	2 006	10	25	5	5	44	38
Vegetables and melons (016)	179	--	--	--	2	--	--
Fruits and tree nuts (017)	171	1	1	2	--	--	2
Horticultural specialties (018)	224	2	1	2	--	3	1
General farms, primarily crop (019)	1 463	14	21	12	10	24	14
Livestock, except dairy, poultry, and animal specialties (021)	29 037	314	308	298	331	240	543
Beef cattle, except feedlots (0212)	21 861	259	257	185	299	185	468
Dairy farms (024)	1 391	28	25	17	8	12	35
Poultry and eggs (025)	197	2	5	2	3	1	1
Animal specialties (027)	1 452	9	7	3	18	26	12
General farms, primarily livestock and animal specialties (029)	666	6	12	7	4	8	8

See footnotes at end of table.

Table 2. **Market Value of Agricultural Products Sold and Farms by Standard Industrial Classification: 1987 and 1982**—Con.

[For meaning of abbreviations and symbols, see introductory text]

Item		Brown	Butler	Chase	Chautauqua	Cherokee	Cheyenne	Clark
MARKET VALUE OF AGRICULTURAL PRODUCTS SOLD—Con.								
Total sales (see text)-Con.								
Sales by commodity or commodity group-Con.								
Crops, including nursery and greenhouse crops-Con.								
Cotton and cottonseed	farms, 1987	-	1	-	-	-	-	-
	1982	-	-	-	-	-	-	-
	$1,000, 1987	-	(D)	-	-	-	-	-
	1982	-	-	-	-	-	-	-
Tobacco	farms, 1987	-	-	-	-	-	-	-
	1982	-	-	-	-	-	-	-
	$1,000, 1987	-	-	-	-	-	-	-
	1982	-	-	-	-	-	-	-
Hay, silage, and field seeds	farms, 1987	150	303	68	55	107	68	49
	1982	129	304	71	46	103	49	38
	$1,000, 1987	499	1 371	(D)	228	281	(D)	(D)
	1982	406	1 580	(D)	109	151	600	(D)
Vegetables, sweet corn, and melons	farms, 1987	2	7	-	2	1	1	1
	1982	1	3	-	1	2	-	1
	$1,000, 1987	(D)	(D)	-	(D)	(D)	(D)	(D)
	1982	(D)	(D)	-	(D)	(D)	-	(D)
Fruits, nuts, and berries	farms, 1987	1	8	1	3	14	-	-
	1982	2	2	-	1	11	-	-
	$1,000, 1987	(D)	35	(D)	11	(D)	-	-
	1982	(D)	9	-	(D)	21	-	-
Nursery and greenhouse crops	farms, 1987	3	9	1	1	1	1	-
	1982	1	9	1	1	2	3	-
	$1,000, 1987	(D)	120	(D)	(D)	(D)	(D)	-
	1982	(D)	132	(D)	(D)	(D)	44	-
Other crops	farms, 1987	-	2	-	1	-	-	1
	1982	-	2	-	1	-	5	2
	$1,000, 1987	-	-	-	(D)	-	-	(D)
	1982	-	(D)	-	(D)	-	582	(D)
Livestock, poultry, and their products	farms, 1987	514	956	233	354	557	280	217
	1982	621	1 012	243	388	651	341	222
	$1,000, 1987	35 659	64 623	30 322	10 612	7 479	32 776	48 835
	1982	32 280	86 053	25 215	10 944	5 898	27 811	41 548
Poultry and poultry products	farms, 1987	15	38	7	7	13	6	-
	1982	24	84	7	9	17	14	4
	$1,000, 1987	11	(D)	(D)	2	772	(D)	-
	1982	17	333	(D)	4	14	1	(Z)
Dairy products	farms, 1987	40	30	8	8	4	1	-
	1982	57	50	10	8	14	6	1
	$1,000, 1987	2 645	1 773	417	660	147	(D)	-
	1982	3 919	2 738	269	462	342	294	(D)
Cattle and calves	farms, 1987	447	831	219	324	528	259	214
	1982	565	893	231	368	615	317	215
	$1,000, 1987	25 265	75 618	27 990	9 132	5 447	31 950	48 797
	1982	20 640	75 860	23 156	9 343	4 597	25 654	41 313
Hogs and pigs	farms, 1987	142	142	35	39	51	36	4
	1982	185	179	40	49	79	54	14
	$1,000, 1987	7 768	6 455	1 665	963	1 075	749	(D)
	1982	7 603	6 493	1 572	1 055	900	1 822	156
Sheep, lambs, and wool	farms, 1987	32	62	15	28	8	14	6
	1982	34	51	9	16	9	10	6
	$1,000, 1987	127	(D)	91	39	5	63	(D)
	1982	87	97	13	41	7	26	7
Other livestock and livestock products (see text)	farms, 1987	19	90	29	25	26	8	11
	1982	14	87	26	21	26	11	21
	$1,000, 1987	43	506	(D)	15	32	4	10
	1982	14	532	(D)	39	38	14	(D)
1987 FARMS BY STANDARD INDUSTRIAL CLASSIFICATION								
Cash grains (011)		414	291	74	41	403	301	83
Field crops, except cash grains (013)		6	85	6	15	18	4	6
Cotton (0131)		-	-	-	-	-	-	-
Tobacco (0132)		-	-	-	-	-	-	-
Sugarcane and sugar beets; Irish potatoes; field crops, except cash grains, n.e.c. (0133, 0134, 0139)		6	85	6	15	18	4	6
Vegetables and melons (016)		1	5	-	-	-	-	1
Fruits and tree nuts (017)		1	2	1	1	8	-	-
Horticultural specialties (018)		3	6	-	1	1	-	-
General farms, primarily crop (019)		9	44	7	7	20	3	4
Livestock, except dairy, poultry, and animal specialties (021)		257	761	186	332	365	175	190
Beef cattle, except feedlots (0212)		116	566	157	262	321	134	169
Dairy farms (024)		23	15	4	5	2	-	-
Poultry and eggs (025)		1	6	1	-	5	1	-
Animal specialties (027)		3	68	3	11	16	4	3
General farms, primarily livestock and animal specialties (029)		11	17	6	8	3	5	3

See footnotes at end of table.

Table 2. **Market Value of Agricultural Products Sold and Farms by Standard Industrial Classification: 1987 and 1982**—Con.

[For meaning of abbreviations and symbols, see introductory text]

Item	Clay	Cloud	Coffey	Comanche	Cowley	Crawford	Decatur
MARKET VALUE OF AGRICULTURAL PRODUCTS SOLD—Con.							
Total sales (see text)-Con.							
Sales by commodity or commodity group-Con.							
Crops, including nursery and greenhouse crops-Con.							
Cotton and cottonseed .... farms, 1987..	–	–	–	–	3	–	–
1982..	–	–	–	–	–	–	–
$1,000, 1987..	–	–	–	–	(D)	–	–
1982..	–	–	–	–	–	–	–
Tobacco........................... farms, 1987..	–	–	–	–	–	–	–
1982..	–	–	–	–	–	–	–
$1,000, 1987..	–	–	–	–	–	–	–
1982..	–	–	–	–	–	–	–
Hay, silage, and field seeds .... farms, 1987..	143	116	97	50	174	116	86
1982..	127	144	104	47	230	116	86
$1,000, 1987..	655	606	530	341	1 292	283	(D)
1982..	670	778	474	(D)	1 560	321	670
Vegetables, sweet corn, and melons .... farms, 1987..	2	5	2	2	13	3	1
1982..	–	5	–	1	10	2	–
$1,000, 1987..	(D)	(D)	(D)	(D)	92	(D)	(D)
1982..	–	(D)	–	(D)	31	(D)	–
Fruits, nuts, and berries .... farms, 1987..	–	4	–	1	8	–	–
1982..	1	2	1	–	6	–	–
$1,000, 1987..	(D)	(D)	(D)	(D)	21	–	–
1982..	(D)	(D)	–	–	15	–	–
Nursery and greenhouse crops............ farms, 1987..	1	2	3	1	8	2	–
1982..	1	2	5	–	3	–	–
$1,000, 1987..	(D)	(D)	(D)	(D)	306	(D)	–
1982..	(D)	(D)	(D)	–	(D)	(D)	–
Other crops............................. farms, 1987..	–	–	–	–	4	–	1
1982..	1	1	–	–	3	–	–
$1,000, 1987..	–	–	–	–	(D)	–	(D)
1982..	(D)	(D)	–	–	(D)	–	–
Livestock, poultry, and their products ...... farms, 1987..	507	419	405	230	708	601	337
1982..	566	487	496	216	904	710	390
$1,000, 1987..	23 582	13 680	18 336	23 520	44 511	11 487	55 082
1982..	20 850	15 207	16 220	12 708	60 336	13 879	52 593
Poultry and poultry products .... farms, 1987..	12	11	18	2	21	12	14
1982..	35	14	24	4	29	18	11
$1,000, 1987..	(D)	5	(D)	(D)	8	5	9
1982..	(D)	12	(D)	(2)	11	10	13
Dairy products .... farms, 1987..	21	7	7	5	13	23	6
1982..	29	23	21	5	20	28	10
$1,000, 1987..	863	379	228	523	1 007	725	244
1982..	1 164	1 090	528	315	1 195	1 247	1 122
Cattle and calves...................... farms, 1987..	455	381	371	218	628	576	315
1982..	526	437	455	210	714	676	374
$1,000, 1987..	12 786	10 027	15 600	22 648	38 289	10 047	52 156
1982..	11 228	10 839	12 698	12 025	52 189	10 361	46 419
Hogs and pigs .... farms, 1987..	156	77	55	17	117	41	73
1982..	156	94	84	28	139	108	75
$1,000, 1987..	8 014	3 112	1 003	328	4 805	484	2 627
1982..	6 334	3 140	2 040	317	6 480	2 083	2 924
Sheep, lambs, and wool................ farms, 1987..	24	27	24	5	46	17	13
1982..	25	17	13	10	60	22	12
$1,000, 1987..	114	86	62	(D)	306	68	40
1982..	62	70	20	11	177	84	20
Other livestock and livestock products (see text) .... farms, 1987..	16	20	21	12	54	35	6
1982..	14	29	15	16	52	29	9
$1,000, 1987..	(D)	71	(D)	12	97	178	4
1982..	(D)	55	(D)	40	283	95	96
1987 FARMS BY STANDARD INDUSTRIAL CLASSIFICATION							
Cash grains (011)	337	384	300	66	353	354	267
Field crops, except cash grains (013)	7	13	12	4	30	14	10
Cotton (0131)	–	–	–	–	1	–	–
Tobacco (0132)	–	–	–	–	–	–	–
Sugarcane and sugar beets; Irish potatoes; field crops, except cash grains, n.e.c. (0133, 0134, 0139)	7	13	12	4	29	14	10
Vegetables and melons (016)	2	2	–	1	6	1	–
Fruits and tree nuts (017)	–	1	2	–	2	3	–
Horticultural specialties (018)	–	1	3	1	7	2	–
General farms, primarily crop (019)	13	11	9	4	33	24	5
Livestock, except dairy, poultry, and animal specialties (021)	284	236	262	184	519	373	198
Beef cattle, except feedlots (0212)	128	169	194	164	405	334	123
Dairy farms (024)	14	4	–	5	10	13	2
Poultry and eggs (025)	3	1	2	1	4	1	–
Animal specialties (027)	5	5	7	6	24	14	1
General farms, primarily livestock and animal specialties (029)	7	1	9	5	9	10	3

See footnotes at end of table.

Table 2. **Market Value of Agricultural Products Sold and Farms by Standard Industrial Classification: 1987 and 1982**—Con.

[For meaning of abbreviations and symbols, see introductory text]

Item	Dickinson	Doniphan	Douglas	Edwards	Elk	Ellis	Ellsworth
MARKET VALUE OF AGRICULTURAL PRODUCTS SOLD—Con.							
Total sales (see text)-Con.							
Sales by commodity or commodity group-Con.							
Crops, including nursery and greenhouse crops-Con.							
Cotton and cottonseed ... farms, 1987..	-	-	-	-	-	-	-
1982..	-	-	-	-	-	-	-
$1,000, 1987..	-	-	-	-	-	-	-
1982..	-	-	-	-	-	-	-
Tobacco ... farms, 1987..	-	2	-	-	-	-	-
1982..	-	5	-	-	-	-	-
$1,000, 1987..	-	(D)	-	-	-	-	-
1982..	-	(D)	-	-	-	-	-
Hay, silage, and field seeds ... farms, 1987..	258	53	219	79	67	97	80
1982..	283	71	169	95	75	57	60
$1,000, 1987..	1 940	207	677	(D)	219	413	329
1982..	1 662	206	579	4 010	331	(D)	231
Vegetables, sweet corn, and melons ... farms, 1987..	4	5	13	1	1	3	1
1982..	7	7	11	-	2	1	2
$1,000, 1987..	3	(D)	97	(D)	(D)	(D)	(D)
1982..	18	69	37	-	-	(D)	(D)
Fruits, nuts, and berries ... farms, 1987..	3	11	6	-	1	-	2
1982..	-	12	4	-	4	-	-
$1,000, 1987..	13	400	(D)	-	(D)	-	(D)
1982..	-	501	(D)	-	(D)	-	-
Nursery and greenhouse crops ... farms, 1987..	2	-	11	1	-	-	-
1982..	2	-	10	-	1	1	-
$1,000, 1987..	(D)	-	115	(D)	-	-	-
1982..	(D)	-	79	-	(D)	(D)	-
Other crops ... farms, 1987..	1	-	2	-	1	1	1
1982..	2	2	5	-	-	-	1
$1,000, 1987..	(D)	-	(D)	-	(D)	(D)	(D)
1982..	(D)	(D)	(D)	-	-	-	(D)
Livestock, poultry, and their products ... farms, 1987..	747	352	590	211	352	582	370
1982..	824	412	665	231	407	595	393
$1,000, 1987..	47 394	12 496	15 667	33 487	15 808	37 465	12 295
1982..	39 063	12 177	17 912	38 372	12 272	25 109	8 802
Poultry and poultry products ... farms, 1987..	27	17	35	4	8	22	31
1982..	34	17	45	9	11	34	27
$1,000, 1987..	(D)	6	159	(D)	5	8	9
1982..	279	9	22	7	(D)	13	11
Dairy products ... farms, 1987..	34	7	38	5	3	24	5
1982..	58	11	52	9	3	30	8
$1,000, 1987..	2 528	818	2 807	261	135	1 827	(D)
1982..	2 826	955	3 517	574	(D)	1 757	634
Cattle and calves ... farms, 1987..	658	303	517	201	339	537	346
1982..	740	344	600	219	392	571	378
$1,000, 1987..	40 616	7 942	10 957	32 958	13 713	34 845	10 611
1982..	31 409	7 015	10 914	37 528	9 187	22 453	6 575
Hogs and pigs ... farms, 1987..	144	116	50	15	40	35	41
1982..	196	198	86	18	72	46	50
$1,000, 1987..	3 765	3 638	1 426	200	1 891	652	1 390
1982..	4 308	4 116	3 034	145	2 776	729	1 540
Sheep, lambs, and wool ... farms, 1987..	61	22	40	7	10	14	9
1982..	46	31	26	10	15	11	4
$1,000, 1987..	211	59	46	(D)	31	103	65
1982..	188	55	82	87	70	56	8
Other livestock and livestock products (see text) ... farms, 1987..	33	14	55	10	26	23	25
1982..	33	8	55	11	22	25	19
$1,000, 1987..	(D)	33	270	8	32	33	(D)
1982..	52	28	341	30	(D)	101	34
1987 FARMS BY STANDARD INDUSTRIAL CLASSIFICATION							
Cash grains (011)	440	335	266	211	47	387	258
Field crops, except cash grains (013)	28	2	56	14	17	17	2
Cotton (0131)	-	-	-	-	-	-	-
Tobacco (0132)	-	-	-	-	-	-	-
Sugarcane and sugar beets; Irish potatoes; field crops, except cash grains, n.e.c. (0133, 0134, 0139)	28	2	56	14	17	17	2
Vegetables and melons (016)	1	3	3	-	1	-	1
Fruits and tree nuts (017)	2	3	4	-	2	1	2
Horticultural specialties (018)	2	-	8	1	-	-	3
General farms, primarily crop (019)	32	7	26	11	7	12	3
Livestock, except dairy, poultry, and animal specialties (021)	482	169	393	112	317	344	225
Beef cattle, except feedlots (0212)	328	80	303	96	287	306	192
Dairy farms (024)	25	4	26	3	2	19	2
Poultry and eggs (025)	2	1	2	-	1	1	-
Animal specialties (027)	6	4	49	4	11	9	4
General farms, primarily livestock and animal specialties (029)	8	2	12	5	4	5	2

See footnotes at end of table.

[For meaning of abbreviations and symbols, see introductory text]

Item		Finney	Ford	Franklin	Geary	Gove	Graham	Grant
MARKET VALUE OF AGRICULTURAL PRODUCTS SOLD—Con.								
Total sales (see text)-Con.								
Sales by commodity or commodity group-Con.								
Crops, including nursery and greenhouse crops-Con.								
Cotton and cottonseed	farms, 1987..	-	-	-	-	-	-	-
	1982..	-	-	-	-	-	-	-
	$1,000, 1987..	-	-	-	-	-	-	-
	1982..	-	-	-	-	-	-	-
Tobacco	farms, 1987..	-	-	-	-	-	-	-
	1982..	-	-	-	-	-	-	-
	$1,000, 1987..	-	-	-	-	-	-	-
	1982..	-	-	-	-	-	-	-
Hay, silage, and field seeds	farms, 1987..	134	107	204	56	84	53	49
	1982..	157	90	208	53	84	46	42
	$1,000, 1987..	6 003	2 112	595	259	(D)	(D)	1 869
	1982..	6 820	1 845	482	226	(D)	(D)	1 027
Vegetables, sweet corn, and melons	farms, 1987..	1	3	5	2	-	-	5
	1982..	2	1	6	5	-	2	2
	$1,000, 1987..	(D)	(D)	12	(D)	-	2	(D)
	1982..	(D)	(D)	7	6	-	(D)	(D)
Fruits, nuts, and berries	farms, 1987..	-	1	5	1	-	-	-
	1982..	-	1	1	1	-	-	-
	$1,000, 1987..	-	-	(D)	(D)	-	-	-
	1982..	-	(D)	(D)	(D)	-	-	-
Nursery and greenhouse crops	farms, 1987..	2	3	4	3	1	1	1
	1982..	2	4	7	5	1	-	1
	$1,000, 1987..	(D)	(D)	(D)	(D)	(D)	(D)	(D)
	1982..	(D)	(D)	(D)	(D)	(D)	-	(D)
Other crops	farms, 1987..	2	-	1	-	-	-	1
	1982..	-	-	-	-	-	-	1
	$1,000, 1987..	(D)	-	(D)	-	-	-	(D)
	1982..	-	-	-	-	-	-	(D)
Livestock, poultry, and their products	farms, 1987..	211	474	705	231	348	292	148
	1982..	240	473	807	239	363	335	154
	$1,000, 1987..	800 530	199 537	19 357	12 342	78 199	15 738	210 962
	1982..	164 284	167 226	21 073	9 039	61 707	15 930	109 917
Poultry and poultry products	farms, 1987..	11	14	39	13	12	3	12
	1982..	5	14	54	16	8	10	13
	$1,000, 1987..	(Z)	(D)	18	16	3	(D)	2
	1982..	2	2	18	11	(Z)	3	5
Dairy products	farms, 1987..	1	5	50	16	9	14	5
	1982..	2	13	67	16	12	15	4
	$1,000, 1987..	(D)	914	5 129	1 161	939	1 115	35
	1982..	(D)	1 248	5 129	1 416	996	913	(D)
Cattle and calves	farms, 1987..	174	442	646	207	324	282	117
	1982..	208	451	729	210	360	326	116
	$1,000, 1987..	337 030	197 377	11 277	7 212	75 809	13 951	210 294
	1982..	163 139	164 596	11 359	3 650	58 934	13 906	(D)
Hogs and pigs	farms, 1987..	33	38	90	44	44	23	27
	1982..	32	46	145	66	46	42	31
	$1,000, 1987..	1 296	1 109	2 792	3 900	1 116	623	583
	1982..	988	1 303	4 312	3 895	1 565	1 074	732
Sheep, lambs, and wool	farms, 1987..	23	22	35	7	13	7	6
	1982..	17	17	36	7	18	13	14
	$1,000, 1987..	157	(D)	82	34	305	(D)	22
	1982..	22	18	150	12	203	25	25
Other livestock and livestock products (see text)	farms, 1987..	17	29	44	16	14	18	18
	1982..	22	18	55	21	11	7	12
	$1,000, 1987..	(D)	65	61	20	25	24	25
	1982..	(D)	59	104	54	10	9	(D)
1987 FARMS BY STANDARD INDUSTRIAL CLASSIFICATION								
Cash grains (011)		351	463	344	86	285	279	213
Field crops, except cash grains (013)		21	13	43	7	1	5	11
Cotton (0131)		-	-	-	-	-	-	-
Tobacco (0132)		-	-	-	-	-	-	-
Sugarcane and sugar beets; Irish potatoes; field crops, except cash grains, n.e.c. (0133, 0134, 0139)		21	13	43	7	1	5	11
Vegetables and melons (016)		1	2	-	-	-	-	1
Fruits and tree nuts (017)		-	-	2	1	-	-	-
Horticultural specialties (018)		1	3	4	3	-	1	-
General farms, primarily crop (019)		9	7	40	8	8	5	1
Livestock, except dairy, poultry, and animal specialties (021)		132	295	463	169	232	134	63
Beef cattle, except feedlots (0212)		76	231	372	116	165	118	44
Dairy farms (024)		-	5	44	10	5	13	3
Poultry and eggs (025)		-	5	5	1	-	2	1
Animal specialties (027)		17	16	26	6	3	9	7
General farms, primarily livestock and animal specialties (029)		2	6	8	4	2	4	3

See footnotes at end of table.

1987 CENSUS OF AGRICULTURE—COUNTY DATA

[For meaning of abbreviations and symbols, see introductory text]

Item	Gray	Greeley	Greenwood	Hamilton	Harper	Harvey	Haskell
MARKET VALUE OF AGRICULTURAL PRODUCTS SOLD—Con.							
Total sales (see text)-Con.							
Sales by commodity or commodity group-Con.							
Crops, including nursery and greenhouse crops-Con.							
Cotton and cottonseed .... farms, 1987..	–	– –	–	–	–	1	–
1982..	–	–	–	–	–	–	–
$1,000, 1987..	–	–	–	–	–	(D)	–
1982..	–	–	–	–	–	–	–
Tobacco................................ farms, 1987..	–	–	–	–	–	–	–
1982..	–	–	–	–	–	–	–
$1,000, 1987..	–	–	–	–	–	–	–
1982..	–	–	–	–	–	–	–
Hay, silage, and field seeds .... farms, 1987..	61	45	126	41	93	184	43
1982..	76	18	105	33	95	233	50
$1,000, 1987..	(D)	(D)	(D)	1 114	524	762	1 108
1982..	2 536	(D)	(D)	1 057	418	781	1 813
Vegetables, sweet corn, and melons ..... farms, 1987..	1	–	–	–	–	17	2
1982..	–	–	–	–	–	9	–
$1,000, 1987..	(D)	–	–	–	–	116	(D)
1982..	–	–	–	–	(D)	68	–
Fruits, nuts, and berries .... farms, 1987..	–	–	–	–	–	8	1
1982..	–	–	–	–	–	6	–
$1,000, 1987..	–	–	–	–	–	37	(D)
1982..	–	–	–	–	–	19	–
Nursery and greenhouse crops........... farms, 1987..	–	1	1	–	–	3	–
1982..	–	1	–	–	1	3	–
$1,000, 1987..	–	(D)	(D)	–	–	(D)	–
1982..	–	(D)	–	–	(D)	(D)	–
Other crops.............................. farms, 1987..	–	–	–	–	–	4	–
1982..	–	–	2	–	1	3	–
$1,000, 1987..	–	–	–	–	–	(D)	–
1982..	–	–	(D)	–	(D)	(D)	–
Livestock, poultry, and their products ...... farms, 1987..	303	102	485	127	446	543	131
1982..	297	107	557	137	482	607	137
$1,000, 1987..	198 311	65 054	31 306	67 340	39 037	33 028	218 643
1982..	106 256	94 296	27 393	41 113	28 083	32 465	295 409
Poultry and poultry products .... farms, 1987..	6	2	14	6	8	36	4
1982..	23	2	20	9	11	42	3
$1,000, 1987..	2	(D)	4	(Z)	1	2 813	3
1982..	3	(D)	9	1	(D)	2 716	(D)
Dairy products .... farms, 1987..	2	–	17	–	9	41	–
1982..	4	–	17	1	13	55	1
$1,000, 1987..	(D)	–	1 729	–	619	2 649	–
1982..	(D)	–	1 844	(D)	784	2 977	(D)
Cattle and calves........................ farms, 1987..	274	89	457	116	422	406	112
1982..	250	93	533	122	466	449	119
$1,000, 1987..	197 008	64 851	28 689	66 995	32 500	21 393	216 725
1982..	104 871	94 026	23 922	40 743	26 413	20 336	293 626
Hogs and pigs .... farms, 1987..	23	10	36	11	29	121	12
1982..	45	17	60	16	49	139	19
$1,000, 1987..	1 086	181	794	306	829	5 375	1 635
1982..	1 230	241	1 428	314	772	5 749	1 566
Sheep, lambs, and wool................. farms, 1987..	18	5	24	5	31	70	9
1982..	9	8	31	5	21	95	8
$1,000, 1987..	187	18	51	19	5 247	538	(D)
1982..	84	8	50	6	79	496	49
Other livestock and livestock products (see text) .... farms, 1987..	15	3	34	13	16	44	10
1982..	20	3	44	18	17	47	12
$1,000, 1987..	(D)	(D)	39	20	42	260	(D)
1982..	(D)	(D)	140	(D)	(D)	190	24
1987 FARMS BY STANDARD INDUSTRIAL CLASSIFICATION							
Cash grains (011)	349	226	98	173	339	443	237
Field crops, except cash grains (013)	11	5	29	5	8	24	7
Cotton (0131)	–	–	–	–	–	–	–
Tobacco (0132)	–	–	–	–	–	–	–
Sugarcane and sugar beets; Irish potatoes; field crops, except cash grains, n.e.c. (0133, 0134, 0139)	11	5	29	5	8	24	7
Vegetables and melons (016)	–	–	–	–	–	4	1
Fruits and tree nuts (017)	–	–	–	–	–	8	–
Horticultural specialties (018)	–	–	1	–	–	3	–
General farms, primarily crop (019)	–	1	10	4	7	18	1
Livestock, except dairy, poultry, and animal specialties (021)	171	61	418	86	279	303	66
Beef cattle, except feedlots (0212)	132	31	374	69	246	148	44
Dairy farms (024)	–	–	8	–	4	22	–
Poultry and eggs (025)	1	–	–	–	–	13	–
Animal specialties (027)	6	–	14	4	10	31	3
General farms, primarily livestock and animal specialties (029)	1	1	9	7	1	5	–

See footnotes at end of table.

Table 2. **Market Value of Agricultural Products Sold and Farms by Standard Industrial Classification: 1987 and 1982**—Con.

[For meaning of abbreviations and symbols, see introductory text]

Item	Hodgeman	Jackson	Jefferson	Jewell	Johnson	Kearny	Kingman	Kiowa
MARKET VALUE OF AGRICUL-TURAL PRODUCTS SOLD—Con.								
Total sales (see text)-Con.								
Sales by commodity or commodity group-Con.								
Crops, including nursery and greenhouse crops-Con.								
Cotton and cottonseed ....farms, 1987..	-	-	-	-	-	-	-	-
1982..	-	-	-	-	-	-	-	-
$1,000, 1987..	-	-	-	-	-	-	-	-
1982..	-	-	-	-	-	-	-	-
Tobacco.........farms, 1987..	-	-	-	-	-	-	-	-
1982..	-	-	-	-	-	-	-	-
$1,000, 1987..	-	-	-	-	-	-	-	-
1982..	-	-	-	-	-	-	-	-
Hay, silage, and field seeds .... farms, 1987..	74	263	215	131	135	80	131	33
1982..	61	218	170	123	136	65	128	39
$1,000, 1987..	1 123	951	622	496	452	5 695	673	(D)
1982..	(D)	702	486	(D)	542	3 838	569	(D)
Vegetables, sweet corn, and melons ..... farms, 1987..	2	3	12	-	16	-	5	-
1982..	1	2	8	-	22	-	4	-
$1,000, 1987..	(D)	(D)	124	-	120	-	(D)	-
1982..	(D)	(D)	17	-	206	-	11	-
Fruits, nuts, and berries ....farms, 1987..	-	1	9	-	5	-	5	-
1982..	-	1	4	-	5	-	3	-
$1,000, 1987..	-	(D)	(D)	-	(D)	-	22	-
1982..	-	(D)	(D)	-	(D)	-	(D)	-
Nursery and greenhouse crops..........farms, 1987..	-	2	3	-	22	-	3	2
1982..	-		2	-	40	2	4	2
$1,000, 1987..	-	(D)	(D)	-	3 159	-	(D)	(D)
1982..	-	-	(D)	-	2 646	(D)	(D)	(D)
Other crops.........farms, 1987..	2	1	2	1	4	2	1	-
1982..	-		-		6	-	-	-
$1,000, 1987..	(D)		(D)		(D)	(D)	(D)	-
1982..	-	(D)	-	(D)	(D)	(D)	(D)	-
Livestock, poultry, and their products .... farms, 1987..	270	874	748	551	430	139	586	182
1982..	323	970	800	624	521	157	526	240
$1,000, 1987..	70 323	19 934	13 335	25 446	12 255	92 301	20 117	11 459
1982..	58 127	18 661	15 863	26 496	12 579	115 697	17 331	10 681
Poultry and poultry products ....farms, 1987..	8	27	20	17	15	6	19	2
1982..	11	51	46	31	19	11	29	5
$1,000, 1987..	2	(D)	16	13	17	6	8	(D)
1982..	5	(D)	30	17	(D)	3	19	(D)
Dairy products ....farms, 1987..	10	41	33	19	12	4	18	1
1982..	12	66	58	24	12	3	35	4
$1,000, 1987..	1 045	2 049	2 655	972	1 359	270	2 136	(D)
1982..	1 010	2 574	2 902	1 238	1 006	(D)	2 774	197
Cattle and calves.........farms, 1987..	260	815	666	488	361	125	541	172
1982..	316	910	721	554	447	139	597	228
$1,000, 1987..	74 986	13 915	8 549	14 681	8 567	91 659	15 738	11 097
1982..	56 623	11 609	9 177	15 844	9 088	(D)	12 645	9 330
Hogs and pigs ....farms, 1987..	17	137	111	164	48	14	101	15
1982..	25	220	179	230	54	26	101	28
$1,000, 1987..	184	3 438	1 955	9 145	1 209	240	1 783	347
1982..	427	3 871	3 654	9 018	1 629	594	1 545	(D)
Sheep, lambs, and wool.........farms, 1987..	9	38	34	42	18	8	34	2
1982..	13	29	28	41	23	5	34	2
$1,000, 1987..	84	204	54	605	45	62	177	(D)
1982..	32	135	27	336	39	(D)	66	(D)
Other livestock and livestock products (see text) ....farms, 1987..	15	56	49	13	71	19	41	11
1982..	11	49	45	17	74	18	35	20
$1,000, 1987..	22	(D)	106	30	1 057	64	275	9
1982..	30	(D)	74	43	(D)	(D)	281	(D)
1987 FARMS BY STANDARD INDUSTRIAL CLASSIFICATION								
Cash grains (011)	231	224	282	347	186	183	394	172
Field crops, except cash grains (013)	5	66	57	8	44	23	15	6
Cotton (0131)	-	-	-	-	-	-	-	-
Tobacco (0132)	-	-	-	-	-	-	-	-
Sugarcane and sugar beets; Irish potatoes; field crops, except cash grains, n.e.c. (0133, 0134, 0139)	5	66	57	8	44	23	15	6
Vegetables and melons (016)	-	-	4	-	7	-	1	-
Fruits and tree nuts (017)	-	-	5	-	6	-	1	-
Horticultural specialties (018)	-	-	3	-	22	-	2	2
General farms, primarily crop (019)	3	37	34	11	25	5	11	6
Livestock, except dairy, poultry, and animal specialties (021)	172	676	567	348	284	71	357	119
Beef cattle, except feedlots (0212)	146	537	445	185	222	49	272	108
Dairy farms (024)	6	37	30	13	10	1	15	-
Poultry and eggs (025)	-	2	3	1	1	1	1	1
Animal specialties (027)	2	28	27	2	68	4	14	2
General farms, primarily livestock and animal specialties (029)	4	12	5	6	4	3	7	2

See footnotes at end of table.

Table 2. **Market Value of Agricultural Products Sold and Farms by Standard Industrial Classification: 1987 and 1982**—Con.

[For meaning of abbreviations and symbols, see introductory text]

Item	Labette	Lane	Leavenworth	Lincoln	Linn	Logan	Lyon	McPherson
MARKET VALUE OF AGRICULTURAL PRODUCTS SOLD—Con.								
Total sales (see text)-Con.								
Sales by commodity or commodity group-Con.								
Crops, including nursery and greenhouse crops-Con.								
Cotton and cottonseed .... farms, 1987..	–	–	–	–	–	–	–	2
1982..	–	–	–	–	–	–	–	–
$1,000, 1987..	–	–	–	–	–	–	–	–
1982..	–	–	–	–	–	–	–	(D)
Tobacco................ farms, 1987..	–	–	6	–	–	–	–	–
1982..	–	–	2	–	–	–	–	–
$1,000, 1987..	–	–	34	–	–	–	–	–
1982..	–	–	(D)	–	–	–	–	–
Hay, silage, and field seeds .... farms, 1987..	186	54	210	126	154	50	203	307
1982..	133	38	214	160	107	29	198	336
$1,000, 1987..	553	1 770	541	817	399	249	992	1 216
1982..	334	(D)	585	(D)	266	254	921	1 158
Vegetables, sweet corn, and melons ..... farms, 1987..	4	–	20	–	5	–	3	10
1982..	10	–	12	–	6	–	–	2
$1,000, 1987..	(D)	–	201	–	(D)	–	(D)	12
1982..	14	–	69	–	10	–	–	(D)
Fruits, nuts, and berries .... farms, 1987..	8	3	5	–	16	–	1	3
1982..	14	–	5	–	9	–	–	–
$1,000, 1987..	41	–	12	–	37	–	(D)	(D)
1982..	(D)	–	18	–	37	–	–	–
Nursery and greenhouse crops........... farms, 1987..	4	–	13	–	1	–	1	7
1982..	1	1	10	–	2	–	4	3
$1,000, 1987..	47	–	(D)	–	(D)	–	(D)	59
1982..	(D)	(D)	(D)	–	(D)	–	(D)	(D)
Other crops................... farms, 1987..	2	–	2	–	–	–	2	1
1982..	1	2	2	1	1	–	1	1
$1,000, 1987..	(D)	–	(D)	–	–	–	(D)	(D)
1982..	(D)	(D)	(D)	(D)	(D)	–	(D)	(D)
Livestock, poultry, and their products .... farms, 1987..	747	155	836	402	510	201	618	809
1982..	877	192	928	448	599	230	704	935
$1,000, 1987..	37 638	74 054	13 966	27 271	13 691	11 014	46 201	51 390
1982..	41 463	63 527	14 120	14 311	12 261	10 829	40 352	35 938
Poultry and poultry products .... farms, 1987..	16	5	36	9	12	5	22	44
1982..	24	8	55	18	21	7	24	77
$1,000, 1987..	4	2	29	4	15	2	936	6 509
1982..	50	9	46	7	11	1	1 103	4 161
Dairy products .... farms, 1987..	23	–	70	17	15	3	15	58
1982..	46	–	88	24	27	3	26	91
$1,000, 1987..	1 841	–	4 936	1 304	1 197	(D)	786	4 259
1982..	2 985	–	5 359	1 086	1 949	(D)	801	4 926
Cattle and calves.................. farms, 1987..	708	142	745	371	472	191	554	677
1982..	818	179	839	427	566	218	622	775
$1,000, 1987..	32 556	73 772	5 555	24 105	9 510	10 341	42 482	35 541
1982..	32 221	62 368	6 141	11 094	7 324	9 930	34 875	20 425
Hogs and pigs .... farms, 1987..	65	15	146	51	48	20	107	140
1982..	116	23	173	72	89	22	188	195
$1,000, 1987..	3 309	215	3 297	1 331	2 914	480	1 862	4 133
1982..	6 016	1 055	2 431	1 819	2 926	604	3 404	5 345
Sheep, lambs, and wool................ farms, 1987..	32	8	31	30	11	6	27	60
1982..	39	13	32	38	18	14	26	69
$1,000, 1987..	44	19	48	411	12	10	48	548
1982..	58	26	23	271	26	41	34	668
Other livestock and livestock products (see text) .... farms, 1987..	44	12	54	13	32	9	53	58
1982..	54	15	60	16	22	16	39	66
$1,000, 1987..	84	46	97	115	43	(D)	66	399
1982..	134	47	120	33	44	(D)	136	414
1987 FARMS BY STANDARD INDUSTRIAL CLASSIFICATION								
Cash grains (011)	325	208	291	277	165	238	325	774
Field crops, except cash grains (013)	30	8	67	13	32	2	46	35
Cotton (0131)	–	–	–	–	–	–	–	–
Tobacco (0132)	–	–	2	–	–	–	–	–
Sugarcane and sugar beets; Irish potatoes; field crops, except cash grains, n.e.c. (0133, 0134, 0139)	30	8	65	13	32	2	46	35
Vegetables and melons (016)	2	–	11	–	1	–	–	2
Fruits and tree nuts (017)	1	–	8	–	7	–	1	3
Horticultural specialties (018)	4	–	12	–	1	–	1	6
General farms, primarily crop (019)	22	6	45	23	21	7	21	26
Livestock, except dairy, poultry, and animal specialties (021)	538	97	604	239	397	126	437	418
Beef cattle, except feedlots (0212)	476	73	469	180	337	106	317	285
Dairy farms (024)	17	–	55	12	9	2	10	38
Poultry and eggs (025)	3	–	7	–	2	–	4	13
Animal specialties (027)	14	2	34	8	24	3	15	26
General farms, primarily livestock and animal specialties (029)	9	1	10	6	9	4	12	12

See footnotes at end of table.

Table 2. **Market Value of Agricultural Products Sold and Farms by Standard Industrial Classification: 1987 and 1982**—Con.

[For meaning of abbreviations and symbols, see introductory text]

Item	Marion	Marshall	Meade	Miami	Mitchell	Montgomery	Morris	Morton
MARKET VALUE OF AGRICULTURAL PRODUCTS SOLD—Con.								
Total sales (see text)-Con.								
Sales by commodity or commodity group-Con.								
Crops, including nursery and greenhouse crops-Con.								
Cotton and cottonseed .... farms, 1987..	-	-	-	-	-	-	-	-
1982..	-	-	-	-	-	-	-	-
$1,000, 1987..	-	-	-	-	-	-	-	-
1982..	-	-	-	-	-	-	-	-
Tobacco................................ farms, 1987..	-	-	-	-	-	-	-	-
1982..	-	-	-	-	-	-	-	-
$1,000, 1987..	-	-	-	-	-	-	-	-
1982..	-	-	-	-	-	-	-	-
Hay, silage, and field seeds .... farms, 1987..	291	175	60	268	97	164	113	12
1982..	307	157	56	199	104	145	105	10
$1,000, 1987..	1 168	920	(D)	849	537	451	(D)	161
1982..	861	(D)	(D)	700	608	410	334	272
Vegetables, sweet corn, and melons ...... farms, 1987..	3	2	-	5	4	7	-	-
1982..	10	-	-	3	4	8	-	-
$1,000, 1987..	(D)	(D)	-	12	(D)	53	-	-
1982..	13	-	-	(D)	7	(D)	-	-
Fruits, nuts, and berries .... farms, 1987..	4	2	1	6	2	8	1	-
1982..	3	1	2	9	1	8	4	-
$1,000, 1987..	4	(D)	(D)	(D)	(D)	(D)	(D)	-
1982..	(D)	(D)	(D)	(D)	(D)	11	(D)	-
Nursery and greenhouse crops.... farms, 1987..	4	2	1	16	5	5	1	-
1982..	2	-	-	15	3	7	-	-
$1,000, 1987..	(D)	(D)	(D)	2 056	67	395	(D)	-
1982..	(D)	-	-	626	(D)	500	(D)	-
Other crops.......................... farms, 1987..	-	2	-	-	1	1	-	-
1982..	-	1	-	-	-	1	-	-
$1,000, 1987..	-	(D)	-	-	(D)	(D)	-	-
1982..	-	-	-	-	-	(D)	-	-
Livestock, poultry, and their products .... farms, 1987..	789	774	241	848	364	754	429	121
1982..	891	864	264	931	410	828	479	133
$1,000, 1987..	41 278	29 760	32 699	11 694	36 021	19 602	82 809	10 411
1982..	36 444	27 656	42 464	13 562	27 215	15 323	36 100	7 056
Poultry and poultry products .... farms, 1987..	35	20	6	96	7	17	14	9
1982..	61	42	11	43	9	26	14	8
$1,000, 1987..	1 593	152	(D)	14	3	3	7	(D)
1982..	1 739	141	1	(D)	6	9	6	2
Dairy products .... farms, 1987..	88	59	3	33	9	18	40	-
1982..	114	67	4	43	15	35	44	-
$1,000, 1987..	6 298	3 738	(D)	1 685	616	1 484	2 296	-
1982..	6 910	3 591	591	2 850	(D)	1 784	2 138	-
Cattle and calves.................... farms, 1987..	690	676	226	783	320	701	402	111
1982..	791	771	244	860	366	769	453	124
$1,000, 1987..	27 560	17 343	31 493	7 845	33 262	7 234	29 189	10 335
1982..	24 135	14 239	23 880	8 173	21 366	7 455	30 734	5 927
Hogs and pigs .... farms, 1987..	173	279	14	57	88	62	81	5
1982..	222	291	31	111	113	119	128	9
$1,000, 1987..	5 544	8 392	647	1 790	4 073	4 662	2 063	(D)
1982..	5 426	9 641	(D)	2 158	4 843	5 536	3 145	112
Sheep, lambs, and wool.............. farms, 1987..	63	29	7	39	40	21	18	4
1982..	54	29	11	38	42	29	17	5
$1,000, 1987..	237	93	48	53	260	35	33	(D)
1982..	170	59	(D)	42	347	26	27	5
Other livestock and livestock products (see text) .... farms, 1987..	42	17	18	76	19	61	24	15
1982..	36	26	16	62	14	56	24	8
$1,000, 1987..	48	43	29	167	87	173	50	16
1982..	64	154	52	(D)	(D)	512	49	10
1987 FARMS BY STANDARD INDUSTRIAL CLASSIFICATION								
Cash grains (011)	603	552	304	274	401	211	169	158
Field crops, except cash grains (013)	26	7	9	88	4	50	7	2
Cotton (0131)	-	-	-	-	-	-	-	-
Tobacco (0132)	-	-	-	-	-	-	-	-
Sugarcane and sugar beets; irish potatoes; field crops, except cash grains, n.e.c. (0133, 0134, 0139)	26	7	9	88	4	50	7	2
Vegetables and melons (016)	1	2	-	3	1	3	-	-
Fruits and tree nuts (017)	4	2	1	2	-	1	-	-
Horticultural specialties (018)	3	2	-	14	5	4	1	-
General farms, primarily crop (019)	36	14	1	42	4	31	14	-
Livestock, except dairy, poultry, and animal specialties (021)	443	417	139	627	186	605	309	59
Beef cattle, except feedlots (0212)	275	298	127	554	106	535	227	52
Dairy farms (024)	66	34	2	23	8	17	26	-
Poultry and eggs (025)	9	4	-	4	-	3	1	-
Animal specialties (027)	15	7	5	58	7	44	10	4
General farms, primarily livestock and animal specialties (029)	11	20	3	16	2	5	11	3

See footnotes at end of table.

[For meaning of abbreviations and symbols, see introductory text]

Item		Nemaha	Neosho	Ness	Norton	Osage	Osborne	Ottawa	Pawnee
MARKET VALUE OF AGRICULTURAL PRODUCTS SOLD—Con.									
Total sales (see text)-Con.									
Sales by commodity or commodity group-Con.									
Crops, including nursery and greenhouse crops-Con.									
Cotton and cottonseed	farms, 1987..	-	-	-	-	-	-	-	-
	1982..	-	-	-	-	-	-	-	-
	$1,000, 1987..	-	-	-	-	-	-	-	-
	1982..	-	-	-	-	-	-	-	-
Tobacco	farms, 1987..	-	-	-	-	-	-	-	-
	1982..	-	-	-	-	-	-	-	-
	$1,000, 1987..	-	-	-	-	-	-	-	-
	1982..	-	-	-	-	-	-	-	-
Hay, silage, and field seeds	farms, 1987..	231	152	96	71	176	126	116	142
	1982..	162	103	68	74	169	87	133	184
	$1,000, 1987..	(D)	551	(D)	(D)	752	531	663	4 251
	1982..	883	383	(D)	(D)	668	698	860	(D)
Vegetables, sweet corn, and melons	farms, 1987..	-	13	1	1	1	3	-	4
	1982..	1	5	-	-	2	3	2	1
	$1,000, 1987..	-	(D)	(D)	-	(D)	(D)	(D)	(D)
	1982..	(D)	7	-	(D)	(D)	(D)	(D)	(D)
Fruits, nuts, and berries	farms, 1987..	-	10	1	-	2	1	1	1
	1982..	1	4	-	-	-	2	-	-
	$1,000, 1987..	(D)	102	(D)	-	(D)	(D)	(D)	(D)
	1982..	(D)	(D)	-	-	-	(D)	-	-
Nursery and greenhouse crops	farms, 1987..	1	2	-	1	5	-	2	1
	1982..	-	1	-	-	2	-	2	1
	$1,000, 1987..	(D)	(D)	-	(D)	41	-	(D)	(D)
	1982..	-	(D)	-	-	(D)	-	(D)	(D)
Other crops	farms, 1987..	1	-	-	-	-	1	-	-
	1982..	3	-	1	-	2	1	5	-
	$1,000, 1987..	(D)	-	-	-	-	(D)	-	-
	1982..	(D)	-	(D)	-	(D)	(D)	6	-
Livestock, poultry, and their products	farms, 1987..	851	557	399	339	590	407	343	272
	1982..	977	621	468	387	714	458	368	305
	$1,000, 1987..	45 376	14 893	14 353	19 732	17 702	18 266	26 137	66 159
	1982..	45 108	16 205	14 579	16 321	18 609	17 530	22 253	35 546
Poultry and poultry products	farms, 1987..	22	12	11	5	16	17	15	6
	1982..	39	16	10	16	28	12	24	10
	$1,000, 1987..	521	12	2	2	9	10	62	3
	1982..	812	27	2	6	29	5	54	6
Dairy products	farms, 1987..	128	29	6	11	14	16	10	2
	1982..	153	51	10	24	18	19	13	6
	$1,000, 1987..	8 978	1 744	360	336	491	885	676	(D)
	1982..	8 868	3 316	406	(D)	664	(D)	865	253
Cattle and calves	farms, 1987..	741	532	387	316	532	379	307	240
	1982..	895	591	458	368	637	441	352	260
	$1,000, 1987..	19 934	9 119	13 708	16 382	14 511	15 768	24 599	64 244
	1982..	22 040	8 016	13 794	12 800	14 967	15 191	19 442	32 996
Hogs and pigs	farms, 1987..	327	57	17	60	85	61	35	42
	1982..	363	109	25	56	136	76	51	55
	$1,000, 1987..	15 731	3 959	193	2 869	1 620	1 264	672	1 738
	1982..	13 278	4 774	275	2 263	2 436	1 421	1 751	2 170
Sheep, lambs, and wool	farms, 1987..	41	18	15	15	12	45	23	14
	1982..	36	18	17	25	20	36	18	18
	$1,000, 1987..	163	29	76	112	(D)	252	114	81
	1982..	89	29	67	103	35	154	81	83
Other livestock and livestock products (see text)	farms, 1987..	11	36	14	18	46	27	27	13
	1982..	17	23	16	16	43	18	20	24
	$1,000, 1987..	51	30	14	31	(D)	66	14	(D)
	1982..	20	41	35	(D)	278	(D)	60	39
1987 FARMS BY STANDARD INDUSTRIAL CLASSIFICATION									
Cash grains (011)		396	294	312	266	345	322	255	341
Field crops, except cash grains (013)		21	20	5	3	40	8	9	31
Cotton (0131)		-	-	-	-	-	-	-	-
Tobacco (0132)		-	-	-	-	-	-	-	-
Sugarcane and sugar beets; Irish potatoes; field crops, except cash grains, n.e.c. (0133, 0134, 0139)		21	20	5	3	40	8	9	31
Vegetables and melons (016)		-	4	-	-	4	1	-	-
Fruits and tree nuts (017)		-	3	-	-	3	-	-	-
Horticultural specialties (018)		1	2	-	-	4	-	2	1
General farms, primarily crop (019)		15	13	6	4	21	11	12	19
Livestock, except dairy, poultry, and animal specialties (021)		562	367	263	183	414	244	223	129
Beef cattle, except feedlots (0212)		253	317	239	129	334	182	182	89
Dairy farms (024)		95	21	5	5	8	9	8	1
Poultry and eggs (025)		4	1	-	-	8	4	1	-
Animal specialties (027)		7	14	1	7	31	5	9	5
General farms, primarily livestock and animal specialties (029)		26	12	3	2	11	7	4	3

See footnotes at end of table.

Table 2. **Market Value of Agricultural Products Sold and Farms by Standard Industrial Classification: 1987 and 1982**—Con.

[For meaning of abbreviations and symbols, see introductory text]

Item	Phillips	Pottawatomie	Pratt	Rawlins	Reno	Republic	Rice	Riley
MARKET VALUE OF AGRICULTURAL PRODUCTS SOLD—Con.								
Total sales (see text)-Con.								
Sales by commodity or commodity group-Con.								
Crops, including nursery and greenhouse crops-Con.								
Cotton and cottonseed .... farms, 1987..	–	–	–	–	–	–	2	–
1982..	–	–	–	–	–	–	–	–
$1,000, 1987..	–	–	–	–	–	–	(D)	–
1982..	–	–	–	–	–	–	–	–
Tobacco .... farms, 1987..	–	–	–	–	–	–	–	–
1982..	–	–	–	–	–	–	–	–
$1,000, 1987..	–	–	–	–	–	–	–	–
1982..	–	–	–	–	–	–	–	–
Hay, silage, and field seeds .... farms, 1987..	118	136	49	83	340	150	130	126
1982..	139	133	58	111	363	154	142	99
$1,000, 1987..	895	659	827	827	2 009	966	894	450
1982..	834	533	2 026	(D)	1 936	726	1 105	443
Vegetables, sweet corn, and melons ...... farms, 1987..	4	7	4	–	26	5	3	15
1982..	3	11	4	1	26	3	4	8
$1,000, 1987..	(D)	28	–	–	168	(D)	(D)	339
1982..	(D)	25	6	(D)	79	2	(D)	(D)
Fruits, nuts, and berries .... farms, 1987..	–	4	1	–	6	3	1	8
1982..	–	3	1	–	12	1	(D)	3
$1,000, 1987..	–	(D)	(D)	–	(D)	(D)	(D)	15
1982..	–	(D)	(D)	–	38	–	(D)	7
Nursery and greenhouse crops............ farms, 1987..	1	3	1	–	9	–	2	5
1982..	–	7	1	–	11	1	(D)	5
$1,000, 1987..	(D)	(D)	(D)	–	2 515	1	(D)	(D)
1982..	–	596	–	–	1 537	(D)	(D)	676
Other crops.......................... farms, 1987..	1	–	1	–	4	2	1	3
1982..	2	2	1	–	5	–	–	5
$1,000, 1987..	(D)	–	(D)	–	(D)	(D)	(D)	(D)
1982..	(D)	(D)	–	–	4	(D)	–	7
Livestock, poultry, and their products .... farms, 1987..	459	620	296	352	958	563	350	405
1982..	527	693	303	432	1 096	706	409	454
$1,000, 1987..	20 875	30 064	70 635	14 731	49 784	67 369	48 869	18 248
1982..	16 767	30 388	47 988	13 300	56 622	47 832	34 774	17 994
Poultry and poultry products .... farms, 1987..	12	26	6	12	83	20	7	14
1982..	19	34	20	17	118	28	15	26
$1,000, 1987..	2	(D)	(D)	10	1 777	6	2	(D)
1982..	10	(D)	(D)	(D)	1 920	24	8	87
Dairy products .... farms, 1987..	11	40	8	11	105	12	19	22
1982..	15	65	9	26	125	19	29	32
$1,000, 1987..	435	1 345	529	590	6 315	1 176	1 171	1 822
1982..	293	2 024	587	2 022	5 719	903	1 478	1 967
Cattle and calves...................... farms, 1987..	426	550	278	325	783	513	323	363
1982..	491	619	281	413	897	642	376	393
$1,000, 1987..	12 418	20 667	66 769	11 962	36 531	62 420	44 587	11 059
1982..	13 327	19 247	43 747	9 306	37 608	41 242	29 526	11 127
Hogs and pigs .... farms, 1987..	111	196	31	69	150	123	38	113
1982..	128	256	31	79	215	179	62	182
$1,000, 1987..	7 926	6 645	2 880	2 055	4 167	3 490	3 030	5 231
1982..	6 029	6 667	3 161	1 779	4 401	5 216	3 675	4 894
Sheep, lambs, and wool................ farms, 1987..	20	20	16	18	143	37	16	24
1982..	26	19	12	22	150	35	14	23
$1,000, 1987..	65	(D)	55	(D)	662	261	54	242
1982..	30	67	21	133	639	192	37	105
Other livestock and livestock products (see text) .... farms, 1987..	30	38	20	19	92	15	25	25
1982..	35	34	18	19	99	18	20	25
$1,000, 1987..	28	56	(D)	(D)	331	14	25	(D)
1982..	78	(D)	(D)	(D)	335	56	49	92
1987 FARMS BY STANDARD INDUSTRIAL CLASSIFICATION								
Cash grains (011)	234	165	345	324	828	546	386	166
Field crops, except cash grains (013)	7	25	9	10	39	11	20	14
Cotton (0131)	–	–	–	–	–	–	–	–
Tobacco (0132)	–	–	–	–	–	–	–	–
Sugarcane and sugar beets; Irish potatoes; field crops, except cash grains, n.e.c. (0133, 0134, 0139)	7	25	9	10	39	11	20	14
Vegetables and melons (016)	–	3	–	–	11	–	1	10
Fruits and tree nuts (017)	–	7	–	–	5	2	1	1
Horticultural specialties (018)	1	3	1	–	6	–	1	4
General farms, primarily crop (019)	16	9	1	15	42	16	12	15
Livestock, except dairy, poultry, and animal specialties (021)	313	507	147	177	467	240	152	306
Beef cattle, except feedlots (0212)	214	352	115	116	314	146	110	183
Dairy farms (024)	4	24	2	6	83	9	10	15
Poultry and eggs (025)	–	2	1	2	17	–	–	–
Animal specialties (027)	9	32	6	–	52	4	16	9
General farms, primarily livestock and animal specialties (029)	7	13	5	7	15	5	5	8

See footnotes at end of table.

Table 2. **Market Value of Agricultural Products Sold and Farms by Standard Industrial Classification: 1987 and 1982** — Con.

[For meaning of abbreviations and symbols, see introductory text]

Item	Rooks	Rush	Russell	Saline	Scott	Sedgwick	Seward	Shawnee
MARKET VALUE OF AGRICULTURAL PRODUCTS SOLD — Con.								
Total sales (see text)-Con.								
Sales by commodity or commodity group-Con.								
Crops, including nursery and greenhouse crops-Con.								
Cotton and cottonseed .... farms, 1987..	-	-	-	-	-	-	-	-
1982..	-	-	-	-	-	-	-	-
$1,000, 1987..	-	-	-	-	-	-	-	-
1982..	-	-	-	-	-	-	-	-
Tobacco .... farms, 1987..	-	-	-	-	-	-	-	-
1982..	-	-	-	-	-	-	-	-
$1,000, 1987..	-	-	-	-	-	-	-	-
1982..	-	-	-	-	-	-	-	-
Hay, silage, and field seeds .... farms, 1987..	67	78	81	154	102	336	26	181
1982..	80	58	95	174	73	368	32	169
$1,000, 1987..	690	724	564	936	(D)	2 052	(D)	449
1982..	(D)	(D)	476	866	3 410	1 870	(D)	633
Vegetables, sweet corn, and melons ..... farms, 1987..	1	-	1	9	2	33	-	11
1982..	-	-	-	4	-	33	-	12
$1,000, 1987..	(D)	-	(D)	33	(D)	222	-	(D)
1982..	-	-	-	(D)	-	132	-	663
Fruits, nuts, and berries .... farms, 1987..	-	2	-	2	-	22	-	5
1982..	-	1	-	5	-	13	-	3
$1,000, 1987..	-	(D)	-	(D)	-	60	-	(D)
1982..	-	(D)	-	17	-	(D)	-	(D)
Nursery and greenhouse crops............ farms, 1987..	2	1	2	5	-	26	-	11
1982..	2	-	3	5	-	34	1	20
$1,000, 1987..	(D)	(D)	(D)	135	-	2 931	-	1 476
1982..	(D)	-	(D)	259	-	2 578	(D)	2 134
Other crops .... farms, 1987..	-	-	1	2	-	4	1	6
1982..	-	-	1	3	-	1	-	8
$1,000, 1987..	-	-	(D)	(D)	-	9	(D)	25
1982..	-	-	(D)	(D)	-	(D)	-	(D)
Livestock, poultry, and their products .... farms, 1987..	314	324	430	430	172	847	130	533
1982..	355	392	420	465	214	933	135	630
$1,000, 1987..	12 027	7 316	10 839	18 438	261 375	28 833	115 017	9 066
1982..	14 065	10 366	10 696	25 163	199 300	33 936	106 648	9 787
Poultry and poultry products .... farms, 1987..	11	12	8	16	5	29	2	13
1982..	16	17	16	36	9	66	7	36
$1,000, 1987..	2	(D)	1	43	1	1 280	(D)	21
1982..	2	(D)	5	32	7	2 599	2	120
Dairy products .... farms, 1987..	15	8	22	24	1	93	-	10
1982..	25	7	26	40	2	100	-	23
$1,000, 1987..	1 068	403	909	2 816	(D)	12 020	-	520
1982..	1 530	216	986	2 349	(D)	10 873	-	907
Cattle and calves........................ farms, 1987..	298	312	336	362	143	677	113	469
1982..	335	374	401	421	176	736	117	551
$1,000, 1987..	10 504	6 655	9 182	11 774	255 682	11 037	95 689	6 994
1982..	11 159	9 706	8 719	17 823	194 293	12 129	104 598	6 843
Hogs and pigs .... farms, 1987..	37	10	37	39	24	107	17	54
1982..	41	20	39	56	31	162	21	102
$1,000, 1987..	397	106	687	3 977	5 501	2 993	(D)	1 381
1982..	1 293	171	919	4 821	4 863	4 174	2 012	1 716
Sheep, lambs, and wool................. farms, 1987..	16	9	12	20	5	88	4	8
1982..	6	15	10	23	16	87	6	10
$1,000, 1987..	25	86	40	77	(D)	965	6	4
1982..	20	141	36	86	52	2 894	5	20
Other livestock and livestock products (see text) .... farms, 1987..	22	6	11	36	10	107	14	56
1982..	22	9	20	27	14	90	11	56
$1,000, 1987..	32	(D)	19	51	134	538	20	146
1982..	60	(D)	30	52	(D)	1 269	32	181
1987 FARMS BY STANDARD INDUSTRIAL CLASSIFICATION								
Cash grains (011)	272	354	270	391	224	807	169	279
Field crops, except cash grains (013)	4	10	11	24	21	76	10	62
Cotton (0131)	-	-	-	-	-	-	-	-
Tobacco (0132)	-	-	-	-	-	-	-	-
Sugarcane and sugar beets; Irish potatoes; field crops, except cash grains, n.e.c. (0133, 0134, 0139)	4	10	11	24	21	76	10	62
Vegetables and melons (016)	1	-	-	4	1	25	-	9
Fruits and tree nuts (017)	-	2	-	1	-	22	-	1
Horticultural specialties (018)	2	-	1	4	-	23	-	10
General farms, primarily crop (019)	17	11	11	21	3	52	2	28
Livestock, except dairy, poultry, and animal specialties (021)	156	156	213	251	134	389	89	392
Beef cattle, except feedlots (0212)	136	146	179	217	67	266	70	336
Dairy farms (024)	10	7	12	17	-	80	-	7
Poultry and eggs (025)	-	1	-	2	-	10	-	3
Animal specialties (027)	5	1	8	23	6	92	10	54
General farms, primarily livestock and animal specialties (029)	6	4	8	5	2	13	5	7

See footnotes at end of table.

Table 2. **Market Value of Agricultural Products Sold and Farms by Standard Industrial Classification: 1987 and 1982**—Con.

[For meaning of abbreviations and symbols, see introductory text]

Item	Sheridan	Sherman	Smith	Stafford	Stanton	Stevens	Sumner	Thomas
MARKET VALUE OF AGRICULTURAL PRODUCTS SOLD—Con.								
Total sales (see text)-Con.								
Sales by commodity or commodity group-Con.								
Crops, including nursery and greenhouse crops-Con.								
Cotton and cottonseed ... farms, 1987	-	-	-	1	-	-	-	-
1982	-	-	-	(D)	-	-	-	-
$1,000, 1987	-	-	-	-	-	-	-	-
1982	-	-	-	-	-	-	-	-
Tobacco ... farms, 1987	-	-	-	-	-	-	-	-
1982	-	-	-	-	-	-	-	-
$1,000, 1987	-	-	-	-	-	-	-	-
1982	-	-	-	-	-	-	-	-
Hay, silage, and field seeds ... farms, 1987	98	66	138	132	26	27	210	69
1982	70	80	144	141	20	37	225	48
$1,000, 1987	(D)	761	806	1 784	1 430	1 632	967	(D)
1982	907	(D)	772	2 059	653	1 041	578	
Vegetables, sweet corn, and melons ... farms, 1987	1	3	-	2	4	-	5	1
1982	-	-	-	-	9	-	9	
$1,000, 1987	(D)	-	(D)	(D)	(D)	-	39	(D)
1982	-	(D)	-	-	57	-	38	
Fruits, nuts, and berries ... farms, 1987	-	-	2	2	1	1	11	3
1982	-	-	-	1	-	-	8	
$1,000, 1987	-	-	(D)	(D)	(D)	(D)	45	(D)
1982	-	-	-	-	-	-	29	
Nursery and greenhouse crops ... farms, 1987	1	-	1	3	-	-	4	1
1982	2	-	-	1	-	-	2	2
$1,000, 1987	(D)	-	(D)	(D)	-	-	13	(D)
1982	(D)	-	-	(D)	-	-	(D)	(D)
Other crops ... farms, 1987	-	-	1	2	-	-	4	-
1982	2	58	-	1	-	-	4	1
$1,000, 1987	-	-	(D)	(D)	-	-	(D)	-
1982	(D)	4 616	-	(D)	-	-	(D)	(D)
Livestock, poultry, and their products ... farms, 1987	313	200	517	286	115	130	695	264
1982	374	251	528	308	97	140	819	269
$1,000, 1987	31 971	37 260	30 809	48 324	63 271	71 861	22 543	38 770
1982	30 327	26 147	32 068	30 608	48 910	(D)	19 140	38 132
Poultry and poultry products ... farms, 1987	5	7	21	9	3	2	18	10
1982	9	13	26	12	4	6	31	9
$1,000, 1987	(D)	1	7	(D)	(D)	(D)	10	2
1982	6	5	11	4	(D)	4	(D)	5
Dairy products ... farms, 1987	4	4	18	3	1	-	23	3
1982	15	13	25	3	1	1	21	3
$1,000, 1987	(D)	104	1 041	48	(D)	-	2 063	-
1982	1 084	315	910	(D)	-	-	1 921	
Cattle and calves ... farms, 1987	297	172	466	260	105	116	600	231
1982	354	213	569	286	84	128	740	249
$1,000, 1987	29 622	36 193	23 072	47 341	63 188	71 166	15 385	37 357
1982	26 879	24 339	23 301	29 472	48 813	(D)	13 026	32 857
Hogs and pigs ... farms, 1987	56	27	113	33	11	9	102	26
1982	91	55	162	27	14	13	119	43
$1,000, 1987	1 136	741	6 545	777	28	592	4 410	1 229
1982	2 134	1 349	(D)	690	89	502	3 639	2 120
Sheep, lambs, and wool ... farms, 1987	10	14	42	15	12	5	67	20
1982	16	16	51	14	4	4	65	20
$1,000, 1987	68	123	136	127	8	(D)	604	119
1982	215	81	(D)	56	1	(D)	403	243
Other livestock and livestock products (see text) ... farms, 1987	9	22	12	18	9	12	49	26
1982	5	15	20	22	7	8	40	25
$1,000, 1987	9	99	7	(D)	44	16	70	62
1982	10	57	28	(D)	(D)	11	(D)	(D)
1987 FARMS BY STANDARD INDUSTRIAL CLASSIFICATION								
Cash grains (011)	342	401	352	340	204	233	846	525
Field crops, except cash grains (013)	13	6	12	18	2	5	25	4
Cotton (0131)	-	-	-	-	-	-	-	-
Tobacco (0132)	-	-	-	-	-	-	-	-
Sugarcane and sugar beets; Irish potatoes; field crops, except cash grains, n.e.c. (0133, 0134, 0139)	13	6	12	18	2	5	25	4
Vegetables and melons (016)	-	-	-	2	-	-	4	-
Fruits and tree nuts (017)	-	-	-	1	-	-	10	-
Horticultural specialties (018)	-	-	-	3	-	-	2	-
General farms, primarily crop (019)	12	6	13	8	3	2	17	4
Livestock, except dairy, poultry, and animal specialties (021)	145	97	300	154	62	49	314	105
Beef cattle, except feedlots (0212)	96	52	188	113	41	35	215	65
Dairy farms (024)	4	2	10	-	-	-	14	-
Poultry and eggs (025)	-	1	-	2	-	-	2	1
Animal specialties (027)	1	8	2	6	7	6	29	3
General farms, primarily livestock and animal specialties (029)	1	5	3	7	2	5	6	2

See footnotes at end of table.

[For meaning of abbreviations and symbols, see introductory text]

Item	Trego	Wabaunsee	Wallace	Washington	Wichita	Wilson	Woodson	Wyandotte
MARKET VALUE OF AGRICULTURAL PRODUCTS SOLD—Con.								
Total sales (see text)-Con.								
Sales by commodity or commodity group-Con.								
Crops, including nursery and greenhouse crops-Con.								
Cotton and cottonseed .... farms, 1987..	-	-	-	-	-	-	-	-
1982..	-	-	-	-	-	-	-	-
$1,000, 1987..	-	-	-	-	-	-	-	-
1982..	-	-	-	-	-	-	-	-
Tobacco............................... farms, 1987..	-	-	-	-	-	-	-	-
1982..	-	-	-	-	-	-	-	-
$1,000, 1987..	-	-	-	-	-	-	-	-
1982..	-	-	-	-	-	-	-	-
Hay, silage, and field seeds .... farms, 1987..	69	141	46	152	66	100	101	21
1982..	48	149	31	179	48	105	73	41
$1,000, 1987..	(D)	814	460	490	(D)	359	709	62
1982..	467	839	(D)	(D)	1 576	497	538	98
Vegetables, sweet corn, and melons ..... farms, 1987..	-	3	-	2	1	7	4	20
1982..	-	4	-	1	-	4	1	16
$1,000, 1987..	-	39	-	(D)	(D)	96	(D)	911
1982..	-	(D)	-	(D)	-	(D)	(D)	864
Fruits, nuts, and berries .... farms, 1987..	2	1	-	-	-	5	4	12
1982..	-	1	-	-	-	4	3	9
$1,000, 1987..	(D)	(O)	-	-	-	8	(D)	58
1982..	-	(O)	-	-	-	5	(D)	10
Nursery and greenhouse crops............ farms, 1987..	-	1	-	1	1	-	-	6
1982..	-	-	-	1	-	1	1	8
$1,000, 1987..	-	(D)	-	(D)	(D)	-	-	(D)
1982..	-	-	-	(D)	-	(D)	(D)	(D)
Other crops .... farms, 1987..	-	5	-	-	1	-	-	2
1982..	-	1	6	-	-	2	-	7
$1,000, 1987..	-	(D)	-	-	(D)	-	-	(D)
1982..	-	(D)	(D)	-	-	(D)	-	16
Livestock, poultry, and their products .... farms, 1987..	355	474	192	758	164	456	283	114
1982..	372	560	205	838	197	530	344	119
$1,000, 1987..	24 848	27 941	13 538	43 087	203 695	8 999	14 039	1 255
1982..	43 832	33 928	11 573	41 576	133 204	10 855	16 408	(O)
Poultry and poultry products .... farms, 1987..	6	11	3	30	4	9	5	5
1982..	21	28	12	43	5	12	11	15
$1,000, 1987..	1	(D)	(D)	20	(Z)	5	2	(D)
1982..	4	(D)	1	35	(D)	7	2	(D)
Dairy products .... farms, 1987..	22	18	3	41	-	13	2	2
1982..	29	30	2	68	-	19	13	5
$1,000, 1987..	1 123	1 152	(D)	3 295	-	684	(D)	(D)
1982..	1 154	1 330	(D)	4 006	207	867	488	277
Cattle and calves........................... farms, 1987..	343	430	173	676	140	420	269	85
1982..	349	500	184	752	165	483	327	95
$1,000, 1987..	23 211	21 315	12 535	21 919	202 946	6 206	13 310	855
1982..	41 549	27 782	10 185	22 033	131 207	6 527	14 764	746
Hogs and pigs .... farms, 1987..	36	75	34	254	17	44	31	14
1982..	53	126	32	295	43	80	65	14
$1,000, 1987..	451	3 910	554	17 487	351	2 049	457	189
1982..	1 024	3 255	787	15 169	(D)	3 384	1 037	(D)
Sheep, lambs, and wool.................... farms, 1987..	15	21	19	44	14	16	22	4
1982..	13	15	13	53	13	22	26	2
$1,000, 1987..	50	267	344	155	(D)	33	106	5
1982..	74	111	410	165	(D)	39	68	(D)
Other livestock and livestock products (see text) .... farms, 1987..	12	24	11	33	15	26	20	19
1982..	21	20	20	37	8	32	27	19
$1,000, 1987..	13	(D)	23	210	(D)	23	(O)	68
1982..	26	(D)	(D)	167	(D)	32	48	38
1987 FARMS BY STANDARD INDUSTRIAL CLASSIFICATION								
Cash grains (011) -----------------------------------	266	159	197	381	250	257	132	30
Field crops, except cash grains (013) -----------------	4	33	2	3	8	15	23	13
Cotton (0131) --	-	-	-	-	-	-	-	-
Tobacco (0132) --------------------------------------	-	-	-	-	-	-	-	-
Sugarcane and sugar beets; Irish potatoes; field crops, except cash grains, n.e.c. (0133, 0134, 0139) -------------------------	4	33	2	3	8	15	23	13
Vegetables and melons (016) -----------------------	-	2	-	-	-	2	2	16
Fruits and tree nuts (017) --------------------------	-	-	-	-	-	2	4	10
Horticultural specialties (018) ---------------------	-	1	-	1	1	-	-	5
General farms, primarily crop (019) ----------------	10	10	4	9	4	10	7	7
Livestock, except dairy, poultry, and animal specialties (021) -----------------------------------	180	384	125	487	89	296	189	94
Beef cattle, except feedlots (0212) ----------------	151	307	98	261	57	265	161	70
Dairy farms (024) -----------------------------------	12	15	-	32	-	10	1	1
Poultry and eggs (025) ------------------------------	-	1	-	1	-	2	-	-
Animal specialties (027) ----------------------------	2	15	2	17	2	12	4	22
General farms, primarily livestock and animal specialties (029) ------------------------------------	8	13	-	8	1	4	7	1

¹Data for 1982 exclude abnormal farms.
²Data for 1982 include market value of barley sold.

Table 3. Farm Production Expenses: 1987 and 1982

[Data are based on a sample of farms. For meaning of abbreviations and symbols, see introductory text]

Item	Kansas	Allen	Anderson	Atchison	Barber	Barton	Bourbon
Total farm production expenses ..... farms, 1987..	68 580	666	726	693	534	937	842
$1,000, 1987..	5 816 518	18 027	24 959	21 043	41 388	104 395	20 185
Average per farm ..... dollars, 1987..	80 439	27 109	34 379	30 365	77 506	111 414	23 972
Livestock and poultry purchased ..... farms, 1987..	23 380	213	281	272	278	267	233
1982..	26 692	197	250	306	257	250	282
$1,000, 1987..	2 426 143	2 297	4 534	3 029	15 301	44 482	5 036
1982..	1 900 272	1 417	3 472	3 421	13 774	47 600	5 159
Feed for livestock and poultry ..... farms, 1987..	38 347	421	450	443	352	469	550
1982..	45 184	484	562	486	376	494	626
$1,000, 1987..	887 270	2 272	2 003	2 176	5 019	29 112	2 653
1982..	920 415	2 604	2 797	3 335	4 334	23 811	3 535
Commercially mixed formula feeds ..... farms, 1987..	14 988	134	169	177	190	184	188
1982..	16 595	164	213	263	116	123	284
$1,000, 1987..	163 561	570	887	989	875	3 152	676
1982..	194 615	1 097	1 093	1 067	1 684	1 954	1 860
Seeds, bulbs, plants, and trees ..... farms, 1987..	48 233	461	513	495	346	690	427
1982..	47 466	417	556	544	285	695	476
$1,000, 1987..	95 302	748	1 094	1 117	606	953	557
1982..	83 505	663	793	895	552	826	617
Commercial fertilizer[1] ..... farms, 1987..	47 731	479	508	504	352	681	496
1982..	49 844	461	544	594	351	641	516
$1,000, 1987..	216 166	1 349	1 650	1 960	2 022	2 477	1 070
1982..	254 590	1 574	1 743	2 133	2 454	2 947	1 454
Agricultural chemicals[1] ..... farms, 1987..	46 318	384	510	556	272	779	415
1982..	34 068	291	361	502	134	315	307
$1,000, 1987..	125 003	882	1 298	1 401	753	1 691	518
1982..	94 957	646	1 009	1 403	270	897	498
Petroleum products ..... farms, 1987..	65 460	615	855	637	489	916	798
1982..	73 030	735	791	768	517	956	882
$1,000, 1987..	243 586	1 337	1 774	1 714	2 276	3 095	1 340
1982..	358 860	2 119	2 471	2 427	3 590	4 832	1 950
Gasoline and gasohol ..... farms, 1987..	57 245	559	602	563	441	791	715
1982..	68 308	709	750	708	474	884	804
$1,000, 1987..	80 737	557	812	629	887	1 029	668
1982..	127 211	1 083	1 102	1 126	1 382	1 728	886
Diesel fuel ..... farms, 1987..	46 376	418	461	464	358	770	352
1982..	48 725	417	503	481	407	751	473
$1,000, 1987..	110 981	635	809	851	1 140	1 611	514
1982..	155 737	829	1 088	1 074	1 823	2 128	753
Natural gas ..... farms, 1987..	4 956	10	22	13	11	86	9
1982..	5 660	32	14	13	19	93	12
$1,000, 1987..	26 371	7	10	10	35	121	6
1982..	31 617	15	6	10	30	310	5
LP gas, fuel oil, kerosene, motor oil, grease, etc. ..... farms, 1987..	52 549	473	514	517	447	808	576
1982..	(NA)	(NA)	(NA)	(NA)	(NA)	(NA)	(NA)
$1,000, 1987..	25 476	138	144	224	214	333	132
1982..	44 295	193	275	217	374	666	206
Electricity ..... farms, 1987..	48 797	432	543	540	393	692	553
1982..	51 533	498	553	516	361	661	644
$1,000, 1987..	54 103	365	364	423	371	820	287
1982..	53 184	335	384	292	(D)	964	324
Hired farm labor ..... farms, 1987..	24 715	231	219	288	243	328	177
1982..	25 274	203	181	254	227	349	209
$1,000, 1987..	226 076	984	947	603	1 895	2 496	537
1982..	153 404	797	496	701	2 010	2 237	494
Contract labor ..... farms, 1987..	7 882	61	58	32	122	98	98
1982..	3 345	39	7	12	47	39	40
$1,000, 1987..	23 691	118	443	59	385	330	163
1982..	8 123	49	19	26	131	73	27
Repair and maintenance ..... farms, 1987..	56 961	530	623	574	487	790	673
$1,000, 1987..	252 016	1 788	1 991	1 966	2 305	4 364	1 471
Customwork, machine hire, and rental of machinery and equipment[2] ..... farms, 1987..	30 603	257	247	295	253	393	188
1982..	30 844	262	277	249	254	398	259
$1,000, 1987..	107 366	332	586	553	1 243	834	307
1982..	104 886	380	338	445	2 175	988	358
Interest paid[3] ..... farms, 1987..	39 549	374	383	346	314	457	487
1982..	40 559	346	408	357	320	459	434
$1,000, 1987..	314 163	2 204	2 998	2 642	3 504	2 982	2 906
1982..	467 054	2 672	3 487	2 601	6 578	4 665	4 273
Interest paid on debt: Secured by real estate ..... farms, 1987..	26 408	255	273	235	193	295	381
$1,000, 1987..	186 166	1 429	2 182	1 774	1 709	1 837	1 863
Not secured by real estate ..... farms, 1987..	24 307	193	198	236	180	292	226
$1,000, 1987..	125 997	775	816	868	1 795	1 144	1 043
Cash rent ..... farms, 1987..	21 234	190	258	166	218	261	227
$1,000, 1987..	123 531	636	1 469	697	2 134	967	650
Property taxes paid ..... farms, 1987..	63 359	533	703	658	482	859	811
$1,000, 1987..	112 201	850	1 011	868	1 166	1 590	1 012
All other farm production expenses ..... farms, 1987..	64 491	633	887	672	488	892	726
$1,000, 1987..	309 914	1 884	2 807	1 835	2 429	8 211	1 679

See footnotes at end of table.

Table 3. Farm Production Expenses: 1987 and 1982—Con.

[Data are based on a sample of farms. For meaning of abbreviations and symbols, see introductory text]

Item		Brown	Butler	Chase	Chautauqua	Cherokee	Cheyenne	Clark
Total farm production expenses	farms, 1987..	729	1 300	288	422	842	493	290
	$1,000, 1987..	50 552	85 827	26 893	13 629	18 347	43 570	50 743
Average per farm	dollars, 1987..	69 345	66 021	93 379	32 295	21 790	88 378	174 978
Livestock and poultry purchased	farms, 1987..	281	496	113	179	176	169	201
	1982..	310	586	156	152	277	199	158
	$1,000, 1987..	12 706	40 379	14 097	2 365	1 614	17 617	29 671
	1982..	11 003	39 029	10 799	2 441	1 166	14 561	19 354
Feed for livestock and poultry	farms, 1987..	490	863	177	321	456	275	225
	1982..	540	903	224	369	590	277	206
	$1,000, 1987..	7 953	13 764	3 986	2 314	1 414	4 671	5 465
	1982..	5 787	19 128	2 906	2 537	1 503	6 494	6 681
Commercially mixed formula feeds	farms, 1987..	209	393	80	82	118	115	58
	1982..	250	425	73	114	154	138	72
	$1,000, 1987..	2 430	3 575	2 148	643	795	554	1 283
	1982..	2 107	3 194	1 033	955	604	948	3 371
Seeds, bulbs, plants, and trees	farms, 1987..	603	589	167	163	433	380	214
	1982..	650	660	184	156	440	363	183
	$1,000, 1987..	1 925	877	158	356	1 174	1 177	305
	1982..	1 858	769	200	329	1 134	822	287
Commercial fertilizer[1]	farms, 1987..	568	702	157	164	536	332	193
	1982..	674	683	183	198	582	380	200
	$1,000, 1987..	3 353	2 813	356	390	2 203	2 012	773
	1982..	3 822	2 673	434	712	2 577	2 177	825
Agricultural chemicals[1]	farms, 1987..	593	657	163	182	464	301	183
	1982..	605	442	157	104	374	197	112
	$1,000, 1987..	2 588	1 318	399	248	1 105	1 064	562
	1982..	2 650	751	191	228	1 185	768	245
Petroleum products	farms, 1987..	692	1 205	288	390	804	476	282
	1982..	826	1 372	295	431	940	546	302
	$1,000, 1987..	2 320	2 685	797	898	1 628	2 629	1 630
	1982..	3 986	3 804	1 120	1 253	2 633	3 982	1 666
Gasoline and gasohol	farms, 1987..	579	1 093	281	334	706	412	242
	1982..	758	1 316	289	413	851	461	261
	$1,000, 1987..	835	1 172	413	332	820	737	642
	1982..	1 390	1 687	657	701	1 037	1 154	740
Diesel fuel	farms, 1987..	495	715	159	236	505	328	217
	1982..	638	657	160	137	613	461	213
	$1,000, 1987..	1 176	1 057	304	231	818	1 017	692
	1982..	2 047	1 414	309	288	1 351	1 740	818
Natural gas	farms, 1987..	28	10	–	2	8	101	18
	1982..	31	31	–	8	5	91	8
	$1,000, 1987..	34	147	–	(D)	32	596	36
	1982..	24	112	7	(D)	4	614	32
LP gas, fuel oil, kerosene, motor oil, grease, etc.	farms, 1987..	587	821	226	268	533	447	261
	1982..	(NA)	(NA)	(NA)	(NA)	(NA)	(NA)	(NA)
	$1,000, 1987..	275	309	79	(D)	158	260	260
	1982..	525	591	147	(D)	240	474	278
Electricity	farms, 1987..	576	853	228	212	461	357	209
	1982..	652	866	249	262	629	332	201
	$1,000, 1987..	610	677	175	180	229	642	249
	1982..	635	696	176	143	259	752	202
Hired farm labor	farms, 1987..	355	450	86	132	164	198	115
	1982..	328	384	125	139	246	194	124
	$1,000, 1987..	4 637	3 525	1 091	1 448	1 197	1 835	1 933
	1982..	2 052	2 428	574	956	709	1 413	1 100
Contract labor	farms, 1987..	58	196	25	67	93	81	81
	1982..	15	64	8	8	15	34	27
	$1,000, 1987..	321	450	82	80	116	209	356
	1982..	30	99	26	34	6	97	88
Repair and maintenance	farms, 1987..	635	1 107	249	343	634	445	260
	$1,000, 1987..	2 779	3 003	1 200	774	1 745	2 208	1 531
Customwork, machine hire, and rental of machinery and equipment[2]	farms, 1987..	448	404	110	127	269	309	142
	1982..	378	473	116	126	270	318	157
	$1,000, 1987..	1 040	576	316	255	510	1 451	736
	1982..	880	865	285	249	343	1 809	1 103
Interest paid[3]	farms, 1987..	391	712	150	245	462	342	182
	1982..	490	664	182	239	364	369	191
	$1,000, 1987..	4 281	4 968	1 227	1 321	2 231	3 068	2 614
	1982..	6 323	6 237	2 215	2 522	3 173	5 157	2 795
Interest paid on debt:								
Secured by real estate	farms, 1987..	294	525	100	170	363	208	115
	$1,000, 1987..	2 572	2 602	661	825	1 584	1 855	1 301
Not secured by real estate	farms, 1987..	230	383	81	112	201	238	134
	$1,000, 1987..	1 709	2 386	566	496	647	1 213	1 313
Cash rent	farms, 1987..	171	394	82	119	205	139	178
	$1,000, 1987..	1 048	2 494	763	532	643	871	1 773
Property taxes paid	farms, 1987..	682	1 243	261	414	811	460	262
	$1,000, 1987..	1 669	1 923	560	542	1 112	997	577
All other farm production expenses	farms, 1987..	694	1 186	282	375	797	468	288
	$1,000, 1987..	3 322	6 373	1 686	1 926	1 427	2 820	2 549

See footnotes at end of table.

Table 3. Farm Production Expenses: 1987 and 1982—Con.

[Data are based on a sample of farms. For meaning of abbreviations and symbols, see introductory text]

Item	Clay	Cloud	Coffey	Comanche	Cowley	Crawford	Decatur
Total farm production expenses .... farms, 1987..	672	659	607	277	996	808	486
$1,000, 1987..	29 763	23 426	25 314	21 845	51 239	16 809	61 688
Average per farm ....dollars, 1987..	44 290	35 546	41 703	78 861	51 444	20 804	126 930
Livestock and poultry purchased .... farms, 1987..	309	237	274	144	375	205	181
1982..	290	216	229	126	424	270	222
$1,000, 1987..	5 989	3 370	8 061	8 606	19 467	2 758	29 157
1982..	5 403	3 956	4 955	5 077	26 145	3 719	13 962
Feed for livestock and poultry .... farms, 1987..	451	322	401	211	599	436	293
1982..	405	263	401	193	777	645	352
$1,000, 1987..	5 361	2 073	3 482	2 475	6 455	1 853	10 984
1982..	5 425	1 967	3 026	1 901	19 547	3 035	10 766
Commercially mixed formula feeds .... farms, 1987..	134	147	175	80	227	139	78
1982..	154	132	100	74	263	209	120
$1,000, 1987..	1 929	294	1 371	494	2 218	466	817
1982..	2 839	529	968	552	3 240	1 163	1 488
Seeds, bulbs, plants, and trees .... farms, 1987..	556	507	494	152	595	477	393
1982..	494	481	459	174	566	558	421
$1,000, 1987..	791	639	968	291	532	731	934
1982..	604	711	602	290	628	1 007	601
Commercial fertilizer[1] .... farms, 1987..	577	530	402	146	690	533	366
1982..	587	491	470	169	746	590	347
$1,000, 1987..	2 436	2 477	1 118	727	1 999	1 770	1 990
1982..	2 671	2 283	1 354	1 091	2 920	2 334	1 994
Agricultural chemicals[1] .... farms, 1987..	550	518	480	149	531	385	350
1982..	443	347	355	83	390	323	250
$1,000, 1987..	1 276	1 198	1 064	392	729	796	1 161
1982..	866	747	792	111	704	782	670
Petroleum products .... farms, 1987..	665	635	583	256	984	788	463
1982..	713	726	671	250	1 098	909	516
$1,000, 1987..	2 159	2 127	1 623	1 156	2 227	1 411	2 353
1982..	2 935	3 385	2 223	1 674	3 517	2 839	2 952
Gasoline and gasohol........................ farms, 1987..	604	517	557	237	819	666	387
1982..	643	682	649	241	998	825	483
$1,000, 1987..	787	654	756	485	902	575	725
1982..	1 062	1 224	948	698	1 478	1 016	1 006
Diesel fuel .... farms, 1987..	500	482	390	209	668	459	386
1982..	489	519	417	233	679	505	396
$1,000, 1987..	1 117	1 236	589	527	1 057	664	1 317
1982..	1 372	1 675	1 035	774	1 518	1 343	1 365
Natural gas .... farms, 1987..	22	33	14	8	50	18	45
1982..	34	17	9	3	30	12	32
$1,000, 1987..	26	26	146	18	15	21	70
1982..	18	9	2	11	14	7	86
LP gas, fuel oil, kerosene, motor oil, grease, etc. .... farms, 1987..	579	482	486	226	712	489	368
1982..	(NA)	(NA)	(NA)	(NA)	(NA)	(NA)	(NA)
$1,000, 1987..	228	211	132	127	253	151	240
1982..	482	477	238	191	507	271	494
Electricity .... farms, 1987..	530	485	445	232	542	418	437
1982..	514	463	470	196	719	642	461
$1,000, 1987..	503	(D)	311	193	411	291	(D)
1982..	372	372	(D)	165	511	361	611
Hired farm labor .... farms, 1987..	232	345	158	101	321	176	242
1982..	173	246	182	87	353	187	174
$1,000, 1987..	1 338	964	1 022	1 147	2 710	561	1 596
1982..	779	672	972	538	1 830	488	1 253
Contract labor .... farms, 1987..	38	67	39	43	139	74	63
1982..	50	54	29	1	73	21	19
$1,000, 1987..	122	(D)	80	42	335	83	(D)
1982..	63	69	55	(D)	93	24	122
Repair and maintenance .... farms, 1987..	568	507	497	246	808	615	412
$1,000, 1987..	2 282	2 153	1 608	1 017	2 913	1 454	2 245
Customwork, machine hire, and rental of machinery and equipment[2] .... farms, 1987..	346	321	230	141	319	252	299
1982..	366	295	198	172	459	311	241
$1,000, 1987..	337	550	372	556	495	511	981
1982..	425	451	325	1 026	899	355	900
Interest paid[3] .... farms, 1987..	417	447	365	196	600	357	293
1982..	401	384	334	180	564	353	356
$1,000, 1987..	2 594	3 009	2 128	1 816	4 270	1 597	3 542
1982..	4 061	4 281	2 335	2 363	4 844	3 441	4 767
Interest paid on debt: Secured by real estate .... farms, 1987..	272	250	293	131	459	279	184
$1,000, 1987..	1 585	1 860	1 195	1 101	2 382	1 109	2 468
Not secured by real estate .... farms, 1987..	302	314	235	126	330	176	175
$1,000, 1987..	1 009	1 128	933	717	1 888	488	1 074
Cash rent................................... farms, 1987..	229	192	241	102	300	190	197
$1,000, 1987..	880	1 070	983	1 129	1 514	638	1 178
Property taxes paid .... farms, 1987..	612	584	571	246	957	794	444
$1,000, 1987..	1 183	1 124	602	585	1 554	854	1 015
All other farm production expenses........... farms, 1987..	645	638	592	277	876	758	477
$1,000, 1987..	2 513	2 084	1 911	1 710	3 626	1 514	3 843

See footnotes at end of table.

Table 3. **Farm Production Expenses: 1987 and 1982**—Con.

[Data are based on a sample of farms. For meaning of abbreviations and symbols, see introductory text]

Item	Dickinson	Doniphan	Douglas	Edwards	Elk	Ellis	Ellsworth
Total farm production expenses .... farms, 1987..	1 028	530	852	361	410	797	499
$1,000, 1987..	54 860	24 629	23 004	48 942	14 243	41 538	18 037
Average per farm ....dollars, 1987..	53 365	46 848	27 000	135 574	34 738	52 118	36 147
Livestock and poultry purchased .... farms, 1987..	364	192	286	139	147	211	228
1982..	511	218	424	147	172	239	157
$1,000, 1987..	23 474	3 883	6 970	17 504	3 547	15 491	3 053
1982..	16 662	2 851	5 841	22 173	2 693	9 609	2 181
Feed for livestock and poultry .... farms, 1987..	541	269	491	190	300	440	308
1982..	637	353	609	199	397	476	275
$1,000, 1987..	6 311	1 896	2 222	5 476	2 677	7 498	1 312
1982..	7 231	2 837	4 057	7 899	3 335	8 157	1 525
Commercially mixed formula feeds .... farms, 1987..	197	124	191	93	132	203	143
1982..	258	107	244	33	147	207	90
$1,000, 1987..	1 378	584	744	581	1 119	1 573	574
1982..	2 526	647	1 727	857	1 005	1 685	364
Seeds, bulbs, plants, and trees .... farms, 1987..	707	419	470	303	205	596	399
1982..	775	538	473	316	249	471	304
$1,000, 1987..	891	1 496	926	1 574	230	442	354
1982..	847	1 411	821	1 081	261	378	317
Commercial fertilizer[1] .... farms, 1987..	847	387	630	285	205	450	379
1982..	819	443	633	330	213	381	372
$1,000, 1987..	3 047	2 214	1 750	3 452	378	651	1 226
1982..	3 847	3 056	2 221	3 111	513	791	1 178
Agricultural chemicals[1] .... farms, 1987..	816	428	532	277	186	563	381
1982..	559	475	444	205	92	266	179
$1,000, 1987..	1 302	2 224	1 001	1 750	192	957	758
1982..	758	1 813	882	1 185	119	396	463
Petroleum products .... farms, 1987..	970	506	818	361	398	759	482
1982..	1 148	619	895	402	459	785	527
$1,000, 1987..	2 768	1 710	1 287	2 758	775	2 102	1 545
1982..	4 419	2 903	2 053	3 778	1 105	3 176	2 020
Gasoline and gasohol .... farms, 1987..	847	454	733	328	397	717	461
1982..	1 032	575	835	369	418	707	496
$1,000, 1987..	1 017	645	603	696	477	856	603
1982..	1 766	1 120	890	1 079	674	1 500	749
Diesel fuel .... farms, 1987..	700	320	390	342	174	591	418
1982..	853	406	478	329	172	613	409
$1,000, 1987..	1 414	868	516	1 190	223	977	780
1982..	2 180	1 296	846	1 620	278	1 240	972
Natural gas .... farms, 1987..	23	4	7	88	10	65	12
1982..	27	11	11	115	21	69	47
$1,000, 1987..	16	(D)	5	590	1	72	11
1982..	14	21	15	689	5	28	29
LP gas, fuel oil, kerosene, motor oil, grease, etc. .... farms, 1987..	807	389	543	332	261	635	406
1982..	(NA)	(NA)	(NA)	(NA)	(NA)	(NA)	(NA)
$1,000, 1987..	322	(D)	163	282	74	197	161
1982..	457	475	301	396	151	407	270
Electricity .... farms, 1987..	798	389	507	301	275	615	426
1982..	803	434	592	328	303	459	368
$1,000, 1987..	550	273	377	566	149	550	266
1982..	479	330	427	615	131	448	168
Hired farm labor .... farms, 1987..	394	197	234	210	148	238	150
1982..	344	231	245	196	178	296	221
$1,000, 1987..	1 579	1 445	790	2 712	643	2 265	690
1982..	1 003	922	1 041	1 692	604	1 842	462
Contract labor .... farms, 1987..	71	54	43	93	86	91	65
1982..	8	26	26	36	23	31	16
$1,000, 1987..	140	215	89	336	160	117	54
1982..	9	133	27	93	88	56	76
Repair and maintenance .... farms, 1987..	867	414	661	323	352	717	412
$1,000, 1987..	3 099	2 245	1 549	2 234	835	2 542	2 186
Customwork, machine hire, and rental of machinery and equipment[2] .... farms, 1987..	422	308	257	231	124	337	287
1982..	426	329	310	274	143	407	172
$1,000, 1987..	634	941	299	1 548	266	488	719
1982..	687	949	343	1 600	274	651	334
Interest paid[2] .... farms, 1987..	626	285	397	258	266	393	298
1982..	657	351	475	294	280	287	272
$1,000, 1987..	4 444	2 755	2 346	3 841	1 289	2 611	1 652
1982..	6 112	3 388	4 030	6 775	2 604	3 268	1 983
Interest paid on debt: Secured by real estate .... farms, 1987..	415	192	291	187	202	249	172
$1,000, 1987..	2 158	1 801	1 494	2 470	831	1 689	1 041
Not secured by real estate .... farms, 1987..	391	184	231	177	90	198	178
$1,000, 1987..	2 286	954	852	1 370	458	922	612
Cash rent................................. farms, 1987..	366	145	138	143	117	335	198
$1,000, 1987..	2 053	1 172	651	1 747	992	1 611	1 224
Property taxes paid .... farms, 1987..	961	473	809	335	376	729	432
$1,000, 1987..	1 348	883	1 094	811	807	1 192	745
All other farm production expenses........... farms, 1987..	964	518	741	355	393	724	456
$1,000, 1987..	3 406	1 497	1 654	2 634	1 303	2 721	2 249

See footnotes at end of table.

Table 3. **Farm Production Expenses: 1987 and 1982**—Con.

[Data are based on a sample of farms. For meaning of abbreviations and symbols, see introductory text]

Item	Finney	Ford	Franklin	Geary	Gove	Graham	Grant
Total farm production expenses ... farms, 1987	535	812	980	296	533	452	303
$1,000, 1987	342 909	213 012	26 450	12 135	53 675	25 413	226 675
Average per farm ... dollars, 1987	640 951	262 330	26 990	40 998	101 079	56 225	748 101
Livestock and poultry purchased ... farms, 1987	133	281	306	103	178	115	84
1982	193	357	401	151	239	157	78
$1,000, 1987	213 537	131 226	4 332	2 743	23 984	5 301	159 445
1982	100 676	95 496	4 006	1 390	27 551	6 269	74 092
Feed for livestock and poultry ... farms, 1987	189	393	638	183	272	232	122
1982	210	498	765	192	327	233	102
$1,000, 1987	72 832	36 862	3 678	2 276	7 516	3 104	41 367
1982	34 085	39 959	4 325	1 540	6 223	3 543	(D)
Commercially mixed formula feeds ... farms, 1987	77	146	232	81	122	65	59
1982	61	120	374	89	117	51	48
$1,000, 1987	8 210	1 645	1 216	486	1 319	778	(D)
1982	5 997	4 945	2 125	1 009	3 369	392	(D)
Seeds, bulbs, plants, and trees ... farms, 1987	439	610	576	200	381	402	240
1982	405	506	556	189	354	412	231
$1,000, 1987	1 943	1 569	1 062	184	892	725	1 043
1982	1 817	1 046	761	180	864	487	1 024
Commercial fertilizer[1] ... farms, 1987	375	547	555	198	347	379	215
1982	331	432	533	238	307	389	215
$1,000, 1987	4 328	3 659	1 610	648	1 874	1 336	1 960
1982	5 171	2 652	1 594	677	1 962	1 271	3 632
Agricultural chemicals[1] ... farms, 1987	401	570	553	245	353	361	238
1982	324	307	533	179	176	157	216
$1,000, 1987	2 715	2 501	1 247	295	1 060	1 142	1 276
1982	2 845	1 035	764	221	626	340	1 962
Petroleum products ... farms, 1987	512	770	927	267	491	441	296
1982	554	835	1 087	298	538	495	276
$1,000, 1987	6 740	4 565	1 643	603	2 567	1 974	2 927
1982	8 523	6 001	2 326	982	4 193	2 558	4 682
Gasoline and gasohol ... farms, 1987	445	638	825	256	415	384	263
1982	500	745	1 021	298	531	449	244
$1,000, 1987	1 643	1 256	757	341	746	706	630
1982	2 110	1 819	1 040	491	1 510	1 028	1 076
Diesel fuel ... farms, 1987	409	653	537	193	384	395	251
1982	487	604	589	121	388	392	243
$1,000, 1987	3 108	1 807	676	342	1 214	1 008	1 005
1982	3 607	2 451	957	310	1 798	1 168	1 714
Natural gas ... farms, 1987	178	153	14	5	65	52	132
1982	229	150	72	16	29	14	175
$1,000, 1987	1 431	1 079	9	10	298	52	1 053
1982	2 050	1 123	20	29	(D)	11	1 960
LP gas, fuel oil, kerosene, motor oil, grease, etc. ... farms, 1987	443	635	569	219	415	420	264
1982	(NA)	(NA)	(NA)	(NA)	(NA)	(NA)	(NA)
$1,000, 1987	558	422	200	111	309	207	240
1982	755	607	310	153	(D)	351	532
Electricity ... farms, 1987	370	598	608	201	438	384	224
1982	417	532	610	217	420	338	206
$1,000, 1987	1 530	989	464	207	(D)	452	946
1982	1 457	862	662	138	723	366	761
Hired farm labor ... farms, 1987	321	285	268	94	232	257	176
1982	311	298	227	74	114	180	173
$1,000, 1987	13 120	4 873	1 922	838	2 181	1 250	5 011
1982	6 802	2 357	1 197	442	1 848	698	3 334
Contract labor ... farms, 1987	98	141	70	16	80	59	68
1982	58	36	35	5	32	18	22
$1,000, 1987	444	439	133	31	(D)	153	170
1982	257	152	25	5	82	71	51
Repair and maintenance ... farms, 1987	488	662	791	257	453	403	264
$1,000, 1987	6 203	4 539	2 238	1 016	2 382	2 094	3 708
Customwork, machine hire, and rental of machinery and equipment[2] ... farms, 1987	314	406	405	73	262	247	171
1982	265	390	365	97	201	223	141
$1,000, 1987	3 638	2 546	692	236	1 647	927	1 527
1982	3 172	1 836	339	148	742	945	1 434
Interest paid[3] ... farms, 1987	394	488	480	205	339	293	197
1982	339	453	534	156	342	284	198
$1,000, 1987	5 921	6 062	2 668	1 345	3 635	2 801	2 348
1982	9 787	6 575	3 774	1 253	6 350	3 405	3 641
Interest paid on debt:							
Secured by real estate ... farms, 1987	240	297	340	153	213	202	120
$1,000, 1987	2 533	2 772	1 739	713	2 448	(D)	1 437
Not secured by real estate ... farms, 1987	265	312	311	135	214	166	136
$1,000, 1987	3 389	3 290	929	632	1 187	(D)	911
Cash rent ... farms, 1987	141	187	229	89	143	278	71
$1,000, 1987	1 294	1 890	1 105	344	810	1 121	759
Property taxes paid ... farms, 1987	452	732	946	258	497	417	287
$1,000, 1987	1 438	1 851	1 194	438	1 094	907	615
All other farm production expenses ... farms, 1987	519	777	900	280	522	442	290
$1,000, 1987	7 224	7 453	2 462	731	3 553	2 128	3 573

See footnotes at end of table.

Table 3. **Farm Production Expenses: 1987 and 1982**—Con.

[Data are based on a sample of farms. For meaning of abbreviations and symbols, see introductory text]

Item	Gray	Greeley	Greenwood	Hamilton	Harper	Harvey	Haskell
Total farm production expenses .... farms, 1987..	546	293	586	279	649	874	315
$1,000, 1987..	218 171	75 624	29 538	50 215	47 187	41 276	221 461
Average per farm .... dollars, 1987..	399 581	258 103	50 406	179 981	72 707	47 227	703 051
Livestock and poultry purchased .... farms, 1987..	220	76	230	83	276	306	93
1982..	206	84	229	98	235	299	90
$1,000, 1987..	135 695	40 783	10 765	19 036	18 668	11 656	137 078
1982..	57 839	60 970	7 480	15 473	12 776	11 150	171 623
Feed for livestock and poultry .... farms, 1987..	267	96	404	112	359	455	97
1982..	269	92	482	130	428	573	104
$1,000, 1987..	35 515	13 109	4 472	(D)	4 961	6 964	43 750
1982..	32 668	22 528	5 580	(D)	4 747	8 477	58 051
Commercially mixed formula feeds .... farms, 1987..	91	52	199	37	181	198	37
1982..	81	24	232	49	127	296	23
$1,000, 1987..	4 201	1 831	1 512	396	379	2 761	9 694
1982..	1 932	(D)	2 789	(D)	602	3 603	5 243
Seeds, bulbs, plants, and trees .... farms, 1987..	449	251	322	191	420	691	234
1982..	405	158	307	172	385	703	288
$1,000, 1987..	2 152	949	319	759	785	1 042	1 559
1982..	2 361	573	307	400	535	733	1 964
Commercial fertilizer[1] .... farms, 1987..	429	149	288	144	523	631	212
1982..	376	50	336	90	564	699	278
$1,000, 1987..	4 376	1 431	829	846	2 794	2 792	3 028
1982..	5 345	1 304	892	676	3 643	3 068	5 052
Agricultural chemicals[1] .... farms, 1987..	397	198	268	174	345	607	253
1982..	328	68	171	131	217	620	255
$1,000, 1987..	2 835	945	386	541	816	1 294	2 271
1982..	2 701	566	246	364	398	1 108	3 201
Petroleum products .... farms, 1987..	544	291	569	258	647	830	314
1982..	552	277	651	269	660	922	324
$1,000, 1987..	6 144	2 249	1 258	1 712	2 852	2 379	4 305
1982..	8 732	3 163	1 842	2 556	4 222	3 018	7 665
Gasoline and gasohol .... farms, 1987..	459	228	509	216	582	699	278
1982..	466	267	610	263	597	836	301
$1,000, 1987..	1 212	519	753	440	1 061	673	838
1982..	1 719	762	1 021	600	1 576	1 118	1 524
Diesel fuel .... farms, 1987..	481	232	293	214	545	616	264
1982..	469	236	284	219	510	606	291
$1,000, 1987..	2 518	1 133	332	898	1 459	1 333	1 452
1982..	3 510	1 810	546	1 448	2 126	1 384	2 282
Natural gas .... farms, 1987..	198	50	4	23	23	37	141
1982..	268	29	20	39	16	50	232
$1,000, 1987..	1 833	340	6	242	24	75	1 614
1982..	2 717	433	7	250	44	80	3 026
LP gas, fuel oil, kerosene, motor oil, grease, etc. .... farms, 1987..	442	246	463	230	579	641	267
1982..	(NA)	(NA)	(NA)	(NA)	(NA)	(NA)	(NA)
$1,000, 1987..	580	258	167	135	308	298	402
1982..	786	358	268	258	473	436	932
Electricity .... farms, 1987..	414	183	397	221	466	694	224
1982..	386	194	454	187	498	659	259
$1,000, 1987..	1 356	518	267	562	343	640	920
1982..	(D)	(D)	290	(D)	371	544	(D)
Hired farm labor .... farms, 1987..	258	131	157	121	265	320	210
1982..	244	110	186	131	285	302	192
$1,000, 1987..	6 260	2 878	1 336	2 047	1 486	1 316	9 134
1982..	3 055	1 726	1 171	1 395	1 141	967	4 843
Contract labor .... farms, 1987..	114	33	125	37	45	80	69
1982..	62	15	50	13	40	29	42
$1,000, 1987..	(D)	330	297	(D)	314	161	(D)
1982..	224	125	98	42	172	86	138
Repair and maintenance .... farms, 1987..	466	236	514	231	560	725	275
$1,000, 1987..	4 497	2 121	1 589	1 825	2 859	2 605	4 561
Customwork, machine hire, and rental of machinery and equipment[2] .... farms, 1987..	336	189	168	163	312	426	172
1982..	291	176	192	146	353	444	222
$1,000, 1987..	3 081	1 790	444	1 324	1 526	1 051	1 297
1982..	2 220	1 613	396	886	2 505	650	2 472
Interest paid[3] .... farms, 1987..	366	190	294	192	422	519	209
1982..	339	161	294	178	469	551	238
$1,000, 1987..	6 007	2 950	2 394	1 831	4 467	3 888	4 070
1982..	6 951	4 609	3 528	3 460	6 258	5 079	8 558
Interest paid on debt: Secured by real estate .... farms, 1987..	221	105	199	100	295	350	130
$1,000, 1987..	3 110	1 745	1 510	1 025	2 335	2 426	1 736
Not secured by real estate .... farms, 1987..	266	137	171	131	270	322	137
$1,000, 1987..	2 897	1 205	883	606	2 152	1 462	2 335
Cash rent .... farms, 1987..	121	55	236	59	243	368	60
$1,000, 1987..	(D)	676	1 793	651	1 014	1 788	(D)
Property taxes paid .... farms, 1987..		237	538	244	577	765	290
$1,000, 1987..	1 547	675	1 018	591	1 193	1 091	902
All other farm production expenses .... farms, 1987..	535	293	559	278	643	845	314
$1,000, 1987..	7 028	4 220	2 368	1 970	3 088	2 627	7 394

See footnotes at end of table.

Table 3. **Farm Production Expenses: 1987 and 1982**—Con.

[Data are based on a sample of farms. For meaning of abbreviations and symbols, see introductory text]

Item		Hodgeman	Jackson	Jefferson	Jewell	Johnson	Kearny	Kingman	Kiowa
Total farm production expenses	farms, 1987__	423	1 082	1 017	735	659	291	818	310
	$1,000, 1987__	83 847	24 765	22 508	32 443	17 165	103 314	31 421	20 820
Average per farm	dollars, 1987__	198 221	22 888	22 131	44 140	26 047	355 033	38 413	67 163
Livestock and poultry purchased	farms, 1987__	211	474	343	260	135	93	347	97
	1982__	198	594	430	337	242	97	359	153
	$1,000, 1987__	47 975	5 302	3 243	6 554	3 477	56 507	7 009	4 063
	1982__	28 512	3 904	3 870	7 766	3 269	78 684	5 882	4 797
Feed for livestock and poultry	farms, 1987__	272	804	683	460	308	133	497	196
	1982__	310	947	764	563	460	145	548	239
	$1,000, 1987__	12 606	4 307	2 862	4 667	1 716	18 267	2 733	916
	1982__	11 845	3 621	3 617	5 675	2 404	23 970	3 452	2 012
Commercially mixed formula feeds	farms, 1987__	76	290	197	204	124	36	243	31
	1982__	53	331	347	215	210	44	146	84
	$1,000, 1987__	1 171	1 087	959	1 330	591	2 065	905	138
	1982__	1 657	1 948	1 375	1 362	1 029	2 916	983	520
Seeds, bulbs, plants, and trees	farms, 1987__	370	563	543	607	381	225	554	272
	1982__	330	630	454	644	315	163	547	295
	$1,000, 1987__	653	887	914	682	737	1 264	796	916
	1982__	559	676	769	941	738	1 192	977	725
Commercial fertilizer[1]	farms, 1987__	277	758	743	548	448	186	618	250
	1982__	202	804	673	612	455	86	672	253
	$1,000, 1987__	1 095	2 098	2 222	2 458	1 106	2 523	3 416	2 276
	1982__	1 092	2 601	2 196	3 369	1 115	2 201	3 838	2 072
Agricultural chemicals[1]	farms, 1987__	332	736	672	562	389	204	487	206
	1982__	216	571	458	454	316	102	278	142
	$1,000, 1987__	1 113	1 321	1 228	1 348	881	1 585	957	904
	1982__	497	1 018	986	914	1 012	1 150	281	629
Petroleum products	farms, 1987__	410	990	933	715	616	278	810	309
	1982__	459	1 148	1 047	800	766	297	860	346
	$1,000, 1987__	2 921	1 888	1 423	2 343	1 066	3 782	2 678	1 724
	1982__	2 820	2 625	2 248	4 275	1 776	4 073	4 297	2 501
Gasoline and gasohol	farms, 1987__	325	909	826	637	567	230	644	235
	1982__	440	1 067	974	778	707	272	800	314
	$1,000, 1987__	1 349	821	728	933	426	844	834	446
	1982__	1 064	1 286	1 125	1 489	839	1 053	1 627	706
Diesel fuel	farms, 1987__	371	510	465	524	443	296	604	252
	1982__	344	491	453	643	341	256	630	264
	$1,000, 1987__	1 069	593	498	1 106	447	1 230	1 424	851
	1982__	1 199	975	730	2 157	658	1 613	2 093	1 125
Natural gas	farms, 1987__	63	11	11	39	37	76	42	64
	1982__	27	12	17	15	38	100	58	62
	$1,000, 1987__	196	8	6	33	28	1 453	61	268
	1982__	146	6	35	27	38	(D)	62	317
LP gas, fuel oil, kerosene, motor oil, grease, etc.	farms, 1987__	379	718	697	657	441	256	724	280
	1982__	(NA)	(NA)	(NA)	(NA)	(NA)	(NA)	(NA)	(NA)
	$1,000, 1987__	305	173	191	271	165	255	359	159
	1982__	411	357	358	601	240	(D)	525	363
Electricity	farms, 1987__	299	779	705	614	414	200	595	196
	1982__	342	820	749	622	470	208	665	251
	$1,000, 1987__	534	398	358	646	343	678	502	206
	1982__	(D)	464	378	572	324	(D)	608	267
Hired farm labor	farms, 1987__	167	286	283	333	145	156	346	172
	1982__	198	325	314	294	239	162	277	125
	$1,000, 1987__	3 750	621	895	1 521	1 823	4 520	1 180	1 020
	1982__	1 438	615	786	1 183	1 618	3 647	831	927
Contract labor	farms, 1987__	49	92	73	67	84	60	120	62
	1982__	19	81	48	32	39	22	29	26
	$1,000, 1987__	163	117	109	154	(D)	532	156	166
	1982__	19	25	60	42	64	172	93	71
Repair and maintenance	farms, 1987__	068	845	797	667	416	265	711	256
	$1,000, 1987__	3 740	1 769	1 605	2 512	1 327	3 093	2 882	1 578
Customwork, machine hire, and rental of machinery and equipment[2]	farms, 1987__	213	375	379	410	172	170	410	209
	1982__	212	458	301	451	166	153	417	213
	$1,000, 1987__	1 059	455	495	892	(D)	3 239	1 129	1 224
	1982__	1 022	446	372	1 405	277	1 908	1 297	1 197
Interest paid[3]	farms, 1987__	312	610	446	481	210	179	469	200
	1982__	263	598	477	485	254	154	562	210
	$1,000, 1987__	3 159	2 287	2 578	3 144	1 324	2 814	2 706	1 966
	1982__	4 021	3 564	3 396	6 152	1 788	4 159	5 172	3 188
Interest paid on debt:									
Secured by real estate	farms, 1987__	223	481	337	258	135	84	285	114
	$1,000, 1987__	1 823	1 404	1 921	2 043	798	1 114	1 683	1 151
Not secured by real estate	farms, 1987__	181	309	215	329	112	129	299	170
	$1,000, 1987__	1 337	883	757	1 101	527	1 700	1 025	815
Cash rent	farms, 1987__	175	262	273	285	172	111	319	123
	$1,000, 1987__	974	528	893	1 658	569	1 069	1 581	1 551
Property taxes paid	farms, 1987__	397	1 074	979	674	637	253	721	283
	$1,000, 1987__	1 125	1 078	1 105	1 319	969	592	1 183	529
All other farm production expenses	farms, 1987__	400	1 014	933	699	573	280	746	304
	$1,000, 1987__	2 981	1 910	2 278	2 325	1 403	2 853	2 510	1 760

See footnotes at end of table.

Table 3. **Farm Production Expenses: 1987 and 1982**—Con.

[Data are based on a sample of farms. For meaning of abbreviations and symbols, see introductory text]

Item	Labette	Lane	Leavenworth	Lincoln	Linn	Logan	Lyon	McPherson
Total farm production expenses........farms, 1987..	970	322	1 144	578	691	381	872	1 357
$1,000, 1987..	40 870	79 856	21 790	31 723	17 179	18 657	50 199	60 212
Average per farm........................dollars, 1987..	42 134	248 001	19 047	54 885	24 861	48 968	57 568	44 371
Livestock and poultry purchased ....farms, 1987..	286	78	410	207	213	90	299	430
1982..	319	111	395	234	264	131	336	480
$1,000, 1987..	19 254	39 368	1 636	10 948	2 995	4 159	19 791	20 430
1982..	21 519	37 773	1 552	4 454	2 549	4 446	20 154	11 545
Feed for livestock and poultry ....farms, 1987..	578	149	703	295	448	157	528	676
1982..	793	201	795	408	577	221	670	761
$1,000, 1987..	5 563	19 206	2 779	3 211	2 334	1 210	8 000	6 893
1982..	8 775	16 365	2 990	3 152	2 563	1 376	6 890	7 266
Commercially mixed formula feeds ....farms, 1987..	135	57	283	121	-178	61	163	243
1982..	236	78	304	154	206	91	289	344
$1,000, 1987..	1 371	(D)	1 216	566	700	335	1 544	3 623
1982..	1 682	2 076	1 692	1 354	1 118	405	2 782	3 982
Seeds, bulbs, plants, and trees ....farms, 1987..	579	262	635	469	385	295	604	997
1982..	505	240	618	402	397	260	659	1 047
$1,000, 1987..	849	554	1 346	578	592	478	861	1 272
1982..	930	442	730	397	531	528	882	1 131
Commercial fertilizer[1] ....farms, 1987..	589	165	728	469	434	148	553	1 035
1982..	710	179	766	507	429	148	684	1 156
$1,000, 1987..	1 694	968	1 599	1 704	1 309	895	1 527	3 900
1982..	2 694	1 031	1 736	1 889	1 352	839	1 959	4 726
Agricultural chemicals[1] ....farms, 1987..	460	249	676	464	433	186	537	958
1982..	325	146	542	323	288	140	372	792
$1,000, 1987..	800	1 044	1 124	989	821	571	981	1 574
1982..	624	574	707	595	692	477	848	1 425
Petroleum products ....farms, 1987..	921	316	1 075	560	652	370	793	1 322
1982..	1 064	335	1 237	615	766	373	945	1 473
$1,000, 1987..	1 661	2 283	1 715	2 072	1 263	1 659	1 954	2 498
1982..	2 671	2 907	2 076	2 814	2 115	2 701	2 793	4 935
Gasoline and gasohol..........................farms, 1987..	836	266	989	514	576	280	724	1 169
1982..	981	329	1 208	562	743	367	926	1 367
$1,000, 1987..	760	748	716	719	573	572	865	1 193
1982..	1 125	919	1 057	1 172	1 114	988	1 268	1 872
Diesel fuel ....farms, 1987..	522	270	568	450	410	268	591	1 078
1982..	603	279	483	471	465	267	528	1 039
$1,000, 1987..	713	1 088	584	1 161	499	797	861	1 809
1982..	1 169	1 300	630	1 296	783	1 243	1 165	2 250
Natural gas ....farms, 1987..	41	43	55	30	4	36	6	96
1982..	38	60	43	1	5	34	7	91
$1,000, 1987..	13	216	191	19	(D)	105	11	103
1982..	12	316	124	(D)	5	134	1	78
LP gas, fuel oil, kerosene, motor oil, grease, etc. ....farms, 1987..	676	278	729	468	541	272	603	1 089
1982..	(NA)	(NA)	(NA)	(NA)	(NA)	(NA)	(NA)	(NA)
$1,000, 1987..	175	231	225	173	(D)	185	227	392
1982..	365	372	265	(D)	213	336	359	736
Electricity ....farms, 1987..	568	256	747	424	486	284	573	1 040
1982..	751	225	792	401	532	276	645	1 072
$1,000, 1987..	301	(D)	473	353	312	342	391	993
1982..	375	424	426	279	349	329	419	664
Hired farm labor ....farms, 1987..	257	163	223	219	195	164	299	456
1982..	211	167	294	171	194	168	225	639
$1,000, 1987..	1 983	4 200	1 829	1 368	865	(D)	2 470	1 627
1982..	689	1 473	870	546	488	968	1 047	1 599
Contract labor................................farms, 1987..	63	63	136	66	74	34	66	94
1982..	30	5	78	41	20	25	21	52
$1,000, 1987..	78	(D)	144	72	121	(D)	215	256
1982..	54	(D)	51	29	17	43	29	96
Repair and maintenance ....farms, 1987..	805	260	822	487	620	333	679	1 142
$1,000, 1987..	2 119	2 071	2 135	1 974	1 328	1 805	2 500	3 748
Customwork, machine hire, and rental of machinery and equipment[2] ....farms, 1987..	330	200	355	277	202	186	339	572
1982..	213	192	415	314	261	135	402	809
$1,000, 1987..	442	1 781	416	659	333	922	785	1 222
1982..	275	1 614	364	567	281	865	487	1 563
Interest paid[3] ....farms, 1987..	495	214	581	348	411	226	515	806
1982..	486	229	483	369	455	279	526	973
$1,000, 1987..	2 159	2 784	2 321	2 849	1 892	2 696	3 809	4 889
1982..	3 613	3 290	2 523	4 144	3 043	4 766	5 115	6 922
Interest paid on debt: Secured by real estate ....farms, 1987..	341	135	407	237	306	141	392	515
$1,000, 1987..	1 480	1 683	1 888	1 623	1 319	1 760	2 437	3 120
Not secured by real estate ....farms, 1987..	300	135	276	205	193	155	282	541
$1,000, 1987..	679	1 101	633	1 226	573	936	1 372	1 768
Cash rent....................................farms, 1987..	207	134	224	198	185	99	285	436
$1,000, 1987..	717	938	1 153	1 089	858	549	1 501	1 731
Property taxes paid ....farms, 1987..	890	313	1 082	259	559	329	839	1 233
$1,000, 1987..	1 178	916	1 151	1 071	605	777	1 162	1 777
All other farm production expenses.........$1,000, 1987..	877	322	1 013	532	631	350	817	1 305
$1,000, 1987..	2 071	3 193	2 169	2 763	1 551	1 480	4 223	4 203

See footnotes at end of table.

Table 3. Farm Production Expenses: 1987 and 1982—Con.

[Data are based on a sample of farms. For meaning of abbreviations and symbols, see introductory text]

Item		Marion	Marshall	Meade	Miami	Mitchell	Montgomery	Morris	Morton
Total farm production expenses	farms, 1987	1 119	1 062	465	1 150	622	974	550	225
	$1,000, 1987	45 508	43 417	44 564	19 230	47 864	21 179	35 529	18 175
Average per farm	dollars, 1987	40 669	40 882	95 836	16 721	76 952	21 746	64 781	80 777
Livestock and poultry purchased	farms, 1987	430	391	137	330	164	222	214	71
	1982	563	400	118	504	228	416	257	60
	$1,000, 1987	12 416	7 638	(D)	1 256	16 792	2 490	12 705	4 127
	1982	11 689	7 304	11 216	3 376	11 658	3 587	13 392	2 364
Feed for livestock and poultry	farms, 1987	641	592	172	666	272	710	324	98
	1982	800	670	216	632	365	757	426	136
	$1,000, 1987	6 385	5 259	5 399	1 760	7 078	3 425	6 703	2 462
	1982	6 498	6 173	10 453	2 797	7 879	3 597	6 870	1 971
Commercially mixed formula feeds	farms, 1987	250	233	58	318	108	267	172	36
	1982	300	263	67	208	153	315	199	26
	$1,000, 1987	2 543	1 155	922	696	2 451	1 541	1 108	126
	1982	3 394	1 742	1 340	1 067	2 816	1 303	1 127	19
Seeds, bulbs, plants, and trees	farms, 1987	922	896	373	539	537	459	419	161
	1982	925	931	368	513	398	359	434	195
	$1,000, 1987	809	1 500	1 248	1 289	863	619	505	692
	1982	933	1 123	1 021	731	709	666	472	441
Commercial fertilizer[1]	farms, 1987	916	877	341	667	488	481	370	128
	1982	977	900	290	752	453	586	462	108
	$1,000, 1987	3 559	3 847	2 707	1 892	3 042	1 396	1 486	945
	1982	3 856	3 887	2 457	1 880	3 401	2 715	1 664	1 082
Agricultural chemicals[1]	farms, 1987	789	876	353	682	523	364	404	143
	1982	745	841	262	540	324	290	336	115
	$1,000, 1987	1 424	2 159	1 683	1 622	1 694	743	663	736
	1982	1 044	2 083	1 054	1 042	915	679	424	842
Petroleum products	farms, 1987	1 088	1 047	446	1 102	619	678	534	222
	1982	1 170	1 144	468	1 210	642	1 021	571	235
	$1,000, 1987	2 697	3 171	3 526	1 603	2 723	1 666	1 934	1 459
	1982	4 151	4 902	5 872	2 267	3 965	2 384	2 186	2 535
Gasoline and gasohol	farms, 1987	959	933	347	1 023	561	795	520	216
	1982	1 095	1 106	453	1 162	626	971	549	222
	$1,000, 1987	987	1 135	733	775	877	759	910	491
	1982	1 747	1 842	1 179	1 198	1 454	1 070	1 044	579
Diesel fuel	farms, 1987	773	814	376	508	508	449	334	157
	1982	870	829	392	509	511	429	393	205
	$1,000, 1987	1 284	1 629	1 160	632	1 438	717	726	581
	1982	1 757	2 420	1 823	759	2 026	950	888	1 081
Natural gas	farms, 1987	35	7	158	12	22	24	15	44
	1982	54	26	135	21	7	48	16	70
	$1,000, 1987	30	(D)	1 374	(D)	33	15	53	220
	1982	24	24	1 618	18	13	93	11	(D)
LP gas, fuel oil, kerosene, motor oil, grease, etc.	farms, 1987	853	914	407	768	524	637	463	177
	1982	(NA)	(NA)	(NA)	(NA)	(NA)	(NA)	(NA)	(NA)
	$1,000, 1987	295	(D)	258	(D)	375	176	244	167
	1982	623	517	1 254	282	472	271	242	(D)
Electricity	farms, 1987	916	779	343	769	467	601	441	151
	1982	948	819	335	674	435	723	470	165
	$1,000, 1987	693	690	506	368	509	448	397	216
	1982	659	591	623	316	434	343	288	216
Hired farm labor	farms, 1987	434	368	234	332	278	226	223	124
	1982	399	427	201	387	280	247	154	90
	$1,000, 1987	1 947	1 806	1 991	1 109	1 965	1 083	2 040	1 500
	1982	1 085	832	3 769	998	1 519	1 092	664	723
Contract labor	farms, 1987	127	86	68	125	69	141	49	43
	1982	50	26	33	52	21	48	58	16
	$1,000, 1987	176	176	(D)	235	171	182	116	146
	1982	70	54	96	94	59	211	96	63
Repair and maintenance	farms, 1987	993	894	425	1 016	515	796	492	197
	$1,000, 1987	3 119	3 459	2 499	1 824	2 513	1 909	2 157	1 651
Customwork, machine hire, and rental of machinery and equipment[2]	farms, 1987	553	590	269	330	344	244	171	73
	1982	382	634	224	352	223	205	160	84
	$1,000, 1987	897	1 198	1 701	459	1 050	448	366	791
	1982	512	1 167	1 327	386	696	285	203	588
Interest paid[3]	farms, 1987	734	708	253	480	404	472	318	145
	1982	815	709	312	544	386	378	395	124
	$1,000, 1987	3 924	5 049	2 237	2 337	3 923	2 557	2 303	1 253
	1982	6 389	6 620	5 807	3 855	6 845	3 023	3 454	2 123
Interest paid on debt:									
Secured by real estate	farms, 1987	473	516	138	326	291	301	209	79
	$1,000, 1987	2 325	3 134	1 242	1 536	2 453	1 601	1 017	550
Not secured by real estate	farms, 1987	467	437	181	288	271	267	198	97
	$1,000, 1987	1 599	1 915	994	801	1 471	956	1 286	703
Cash rent	farms, 1987	511	288	132	276	200	243	230	41
	$1,000, 1987	2 526	1 328	1 994	1 285	791	1 304	226	703
Property taxes paid	farms, 1987	1 045	995	408	1 092	550	931	521	192
	$1,000, 1987	1 507	1 859	736	1 143	1 420	1 160	873	315
All other farm production expenses	farms, 1987	1 049	1 049	433	1 039	604	906	535	207
	$1,000, 1987	3 528	4 265	2 923	1 498	2 846	2 261	2 045	1 451

See footnotes at end of table.

Table 3. **Farm Production Expenses: 1987 and 1982**—Con.

[Data are based on a sample of farms. For meaning of abbreviations and symbols, see introductory text.]

Item	Nemaha	Neosho	Ness	Norton	Osage	Osborne	Ottawa	Pawnee
Total farm production expenses ... farms, 1987	1 127	752	598	470	885	607	522	530
$1,000, 1987	47 002	20 374	21 214	26 000	24 881	25 983	32 030	72 505
Average per farm ... dollars, 1987	41 706	27 093	35 474	59 574	28 115	42 806	61 360	136 802
Livestock and poultry purchased ... farms, 1987	573	268	232	192	281	253	152	210
1982	504	253	224	221	406	281	227	164
$1,000, 1987	9 371	2 856	4 848	8 114	5 798	3 796	13 539	30 325
1982	11 445	2 812	5 380	5 974	6 289	6 967	10 243	15 221
Feed for livestock and poultry ... farms, 1987	613	501	356	341	523	365	288	234
1982	768	549	374	299	660	391	367	268
$1,000, 1987	9 707	2 634	1 398	3 437	2 397	2 432	3 853	13 616
1982	8 195	4 495	1 472	3 283	2 907	3 168	4 097	8 863
Commercially mixed formula feeds ... farms, 1987	399	205	119	103	163	183	120	75
1982	368	148	139	120	228	100	143	118
$1,000, 1987	3 356	552	253	784	542	908	640	573
1982	3 282	1 464	291	1 319	609	639	780	2 430
Seeds, bulbs, plants, and trees ... farms, 1987	911	493	464	366	571	534	356	434
1982	891	437	498	377	598	431	372	425
$1,000, 1987	1 263	623	487	593	933	748	415	1 145
1982	1 200	765	508	446	741	436	458	843
Commercial fertilizer¹ ... farms, 1987	929	522	415	302	582	505	410	437
1982	899	528	392	348	638	432	440	376
$1,000, 1987	3 523	1 861	929	1 963	1 721	2 016	1 796	2 208
1982	3 643	2 142	1 077	2 133	2 381	2 010	2 291	2 264
Agricultural chemicals¹ ... farms, 1987	922	411	439	348	649	499	355	447
1982	755	299	243	214	506	272	296	320
$1,000, 1987	1 825	725	889	840	1 629	1 328	751	1 361
1982	1 748	577	461	728	1 019	423	695	951
Petroleum products ... farms, 1987	1 104	732	581	450	860	594	479	511
1982	1 141	764	637	517	969	629	587	568
$1,000, 1987	3 065	1 716	2 034	1 855	1 583	2 323	1 824	2 700
1982	4 974	2 291	3 546	2 906	2 410	2 965	2 638	4 115
Gasoline and gasohol ... farms, 1987	971	614	483	369	788	561	420	466
1982	1 078	750	604	504	839	579	571	544
$1,000, 1987	1 283	702	744	690	677	799	675	782
1982	1 911	1 068	1 547	1 161	1 059	1 186	990	1 257
Diesel fuel ... farms, 1987	800	437	452	344	527	481	383	427
1982	763	423	475	379	541	474	430	441
$1,000, 1987	1 381	789	1 021	922	722	1 246	952	1 411
1982	1 628	923	1 484	1 353	1 077	1 346	1 344	2 030
Natural gas ... farms, 1987	22	46	7	35	24	18	6	82
1982	33	16	20	32	3	23	7	98
$1,000, 1987	24	62	6	53	12	11	8	154
1982	7	58	8	22	(D)	6	9	192
LP gas, fuel oil, kerosene, motor oil, grease, etc. ... farms, 1987	969	543	545	370	625	518	416	431
1982	(NA)	(NA)	(NA)	(NA)	(NA)	(NA)	(NA)	(NA)
$1,000, 1987	377	163	263	190	172	267	188	353
1982	628	243	508	380	(D)	425	295	636
Electricity ... farms, 1987	892	539	435	391	608	451	407	392
1982	937	594	453	386	622	477	415	466
$1,000, 1987	851	356	269	485	325	353	299	708
1982	935	357	331	488	280	310	285	873
Hired farm labor ... farms, 1987	373	262	245	206	206	249	252	210
1982	438	210	304	164	230	248	339	266
$1,000, 1987	1 606	1 129	713	1 096	823	1 151	1 334	2 646
1982	1 341	814	843	957	516	971	1 221	1 902
Contract labor ... farms, 1987	98	68	61	63	66	46	67	65
1982	14	21	42	1	15	19	68	42
$1,000, 1987	217	144	76	156	611	70	109	179
1982	29	24	38	(D)	32	87	26	143
Repair and maintenance ... farms, 1987	981	629	491	386	735	544	421	441
$1,000, 1987	3 522	1 667	1 783	1 869	1 811	2 042	1 968	3 292
Customwork, machine hire, and rental of machinery and equipment² ... farms, 1987	554	276	355	270	377	396	231	266
1982	527	288	370	222	350	313	334	265
$1,000, 1987	848	388	1 212	626	447	1 243	406	2 233
1982	769	369	1 303	829	524	1 167	640	1 058
Interest paid³ ... farms, 1987	675	417	390	324	547	378	343	346
1982	669	338	374	347	452	406	430	296
$1,000, 1987	4 174	1 966	2 344	2 946	2 573	3 048	2 173	4 167
1982	6 903	3 248	3 967	4 461	3 370	4 060	3 278	5 790
Interest paid on debt:								
Secured by real estate ... farms, 1987	445	306	238	215	393	260	197	234
$1,000, 1987	2 663	1 350	1 369	1 477	1 703	2 117	1 349	2 305
Not secured by real estate ... farms, 1987	458	229	254	210	271	197	246	247
$1,000, 1987	1 511	616	975	1 469	870	930	824	1 862
Cash rent ... farms, 1987	276	194	236	211	217	236	143	189
$1,000, 1987	1 462	610	1 238	1 252	845	999	895	1 952
Property taxes paid ... farms, 1987	1 058	691	636	428	850	563	469	500
$1,000, 1987	1 570	1 145	1 134	1 002	1 115	1 146	848	1 424
All other farm production expenses ... farms, 1987	1 083	691	570	455	828	600	471	508
$1,000, 1987	3 990	2 156	1 861	2 165	2 259	3 288	1 740	4 547

See footnotes at end of table.

Table 3. **Farm Production Expenses: 1987 and 1982**—Con.

[Data are based on a sample of farms. For meaning of abbreviations and symbols, see introductory text]

Item	Phillips	Pottawatomie	Pratt	Rawlins	Reno	Republic	Rice	Riley
Total farm production expenses .... farms, 1987..	592	790	517	541	1 557	834	604	547
$1,000, 1987..	26 959	30 078	89 949	24 757	66 378	88 233	57 389	18 519
Average per farm .... dollars, 1987..	45 539	38 073	173 983	45 762	42 632	105 795	95 014	33 856
Livestock and poultry purchased .... farms, 1987..	250	292	175	187	554	239	149	206
1982..	258	269	180	238	590	361	222	275
$1,000, 1987..	4 033	7 190	44 958	3 548	17 686	40 424	25 674	4 343
1982..	3 852	7 673	26 597	2 863	23 786	25 853	17 632	4 645
Feed for livestock and poultry .... farms, 1987..	304	481	238	296	853	468	240	362
1982..	479	581	259	376	918	519	349	399
$1,000, 1987..	5 823	5 548	13 915	2 226	9 630	16 153	7 690	2 801
1982..	5 847	6 803	9 735	2 830	11 365	12 945	7 703	3 561
Commercially mixed formula feeds .... farms, 1987..	107	211	92	103	373	201	78	125
1982..	142	251	137	116	370	163	151	162
$1,000, 1987..	738	1 657	2 367	638	5 916	1 226	1 703	1 026
1982..	1 575	3 691	1 857	872	8 263	2 614	3 566	1 137
Seeds, bulbs, plants, and trees .... farms, 1987..	422	501	414	455	1 137	709	489	406
1982..	489	600	409	400	1 166	710	501	384
$1,000, 1987..	650	695	1 740	726	1 570	1 636	842	422
1982..	579	657	910	553	1 790	1 460	809	494
Commercial fertilizer[1] .... farms, 1987..	433	500	439	384	1 043	724	446	373
1982..	512	561	432	445	1 180	673	521	397
$1,000, 1987..	1 519	1 612	4 447	1 626	4 932	4 160	2 505	1 106
1982..	1 876	1 848	4 226	1 436	6 739	4 816	3 817	1 234
Agricultural chemicals[1] .... farms, 1987..	408	532	378	369	939	718	489	396
1982..	272	444	224	184	598	598	371	365
$1,000, 1987..	1 036	1 013	1 977	934	1 793	2 048	1 427	655
1982..	449	738	1 007	342	1 242	1 683	1 550	691
Petroleum products .... farms, 1987..	565	727	502	523	1 491	800	579	525
1982..	647	869	547	621	1 838	905	642	583
$1,000, 1987..	2 044	1 723	3 349	2 330	4 373	3 284	2 451	1 062
1982..	3 106	2 725	4 018	3 582	6 832	4 465	4 169	1 763
Gasoline and gasohol .... farms, 1987..	503	664	425	410	1 333	676	518	482
1982..	620	841	466	583	1 473	878	590	575
$1,000, 1987..	821	852	760	816	1 458	1 139	718	501
1982..	1 297	1 400	1 218	1 402	2 386	1 773	1 303	864
Diesel fuel .... farms, 1987..	447	364	407	416	1 101	611	475	272
1982..	467	476	441	429	1 225	677	524	345
$1,000, 1987..	937	670	1 769	1 016	2 274	1 678	1 357	434
1982..	1 377	901	1 833	1 565	3 440	2 038	2 280	638
Natural gas .... farms, 1987..	15	4	87	34	88	25	34	17
1982..	44	39	60	50	43	93	76	23
$1,000, 1987..	55	(D)	514	143	110	78	65	11
1982..	87	26	448	151	210	40	144	33
LP gas, fuel oil, kerosene, motor oil, grease, etc. .... farms, 1987..	451	598	438	451	1 186	693	499	430
1982..	(NA)	(NA)	(NA)	(NA)	(NA)	(NA)	(NA)	(NA)
$1,000, 1987..	231	(D)	287	355	530	389	.310	116
1982..	365	398	518	464	795	613	441	228
Electricity .... farms, 1987..	423	577	391	418	1 069	664	468	328
1982..	444	656	421	423	1 092	728	535	399
$1,000, 1987..	481	456	520	447	1 010	713	681	249
1982..	388	545	(D)	479	837	765	501	316
Hired farm labor .... farms, 1987..	231	226	228	225	637	369	302	203
1982..	195	296	306	277	591	285	286	201
$1,000, 1987..	1 313	1 623	2 891	1 007	4 077	2 379	2 694	1 301
1982..	1 201	1 429	1 702	1 166	3 261	1 324	2 128	1 253
Contract labor .... farms, 1987..	58	55	66	92	182	63	61	31
1982..	25	28	18	26	53	17	66	13
$1,000, 1987..	103	74	481	381	294	179	105	39
1982..	36	60	68	52	58	31	112	17
Repair and maintenance .... farms, 1987..	484	609	430	459	1 295	688	457	476
$1,000, 1987..	1 884	2 227	3 447	2 366	4 956	3 270	3 237	1 933
Customwork, machine hire, and rental of machinery and equipment[2] .... farms, 1987..	330	241	281	267	606	504	338	230
1982..	316	262	302	323	680	476	309	218
$1,000, 1987..	810	316	1 762	1 512	1 304	1 522	1 475	305
1982..	827	505	1 351	1 540	1 724	1 127	1 191	238
Interest paid[3] .... farms, 1987..	319	430	328	318	856	508	353	245
1982..	364	482	344	394	791	576	364	305
$1,000, 1987..	3 162	2 701	3 827	3 194	5 514	4 668	3 249	1 368
1982..	4 171	3 620	4 865	4 682	5 774	5 586	4 279	3 048
Interest paid on debt: Secured by real estate .... farms, 1987..	206	321	163	253	508	328	238	160
$1,000, 1987..	1 916	1 819	1 945	2 145	3 151	3 336	1 649	857
Not secured by real estate .... farms, 1987..	190	231	236	188	601	318	254	170
$1,000, 1987..	1 246	882	1 882	1 049	2 363	1 432	1 599	511
Cash rent .... farms, 1987..	215	174	198	177	528	357	221	125
$1,000, 1987..	1 893	1 237	1 370	907	1 980	2 392	900	549
Property taxes paid .... farms, 1987..	554	730	437	518	1 397	743	547	524
$1,000, 1987..	1 092	945	1 144	1 281	1 939	1 781	1 098	746
All other farm production expenses .... farms, 1987..	540	707	503	526	1 404	799	549	509
$1,000, 1987..	3 116	2 718	4 021	2 268	5 320	3 628	3 262	1 539

See footnotes at end of table.

Table 3. **Farm Production Expenses: 1987 and 1982**—Con.

[Data are based on a sample of farms. For meaning of abbreviations and symbols, see introductory text]

Item	Rooks	Rush	Russell	Saline	Scott	Sedgwick	Seward	Shawnee
Total farm production expenses ....farms, 1987..	473	546	533	744	391	1 589	285	851
$1,000, 1987..	17 662	14 904	14 939	25 085	249 582	47 864	123 869	16 855
Average per farm ....dollars, 1987..	37 341	27 295	28 029	33 716	638 316	30 122	434 628	19 571
Livestock and poultry purchased ....farms, 1987..	121	140	148	202	128	424	83	244
1982..	161	216	167	311	138	496	85	314
$1,000, 1987..	2 692	1 757	2 330	4 599	162 111	6 495	73 731	2 487
1982..	2 429	3 493	3 276	8 000	120 717	10 202	61 637	2 856
Feed for livestock and poultry ....farms, 1987..	242	293	242	371	187	646	103	446
1982..	315	380	300	436	196	905	104	560
$1,000, 1987..	1 291	738	962	2 986	51 564	5 948	22 117	1 241
1982..	2 192	1 777	1 808	6 198	53 966	9 810	(D)	2 040
Commercially mixed formula feeds ....farms, 1987..	74	77	100	130	80	321	42	183
1982..	121	128	91	146	118	284	23	185
$1,000, 1987..	343	138	330	736	13 096	2 589	(D)	488
1982..	583	461	464	1 561	3 611	5 172	1 123	793
Seeds, bulbs, plants, and trees ....farms, 1987..	334	396	457	527	311	1 103	214	440
1982..	379	353	421	448	303	935	182	467
$1,000, 1987..	488	351	441	542	778	1 555	842	1 101
1982..	468	414	514	601	609	1 271	592	739
Commercial fertilizer[1] ....farms, 1987..	326	359	343	559	231	1 129	204	518
1982..	385	386	449	572	222	1 178	198	554
$1,000, 1987..	1 194	1 079	960	1 705	1 515	4 291	1 879	1 180
1982..	1 187	1 107	1 562	2 540	1 866	4 901	2 517	1 658
Agricultural chemicals[1] ....farms, 1987..	341	429	370	472	267	1 041	217	517
1982..	215	273	199	300	229	675	121	432
$1,000, 1987..	933	985	790	828	1 009	2 010	1 157	1 063
1982..	378	350	209	424	864	1 486	828	1 058
Petroleum products ....farms, 1987..	460	545	512	673	375	1 505	260	798
1982..	528	584	573	763	416	1 650	277	937
$1,000, 1987..	1 597	1 664	1 441	1 858	3 468	3 973	2 713	1 197
1982..	2 754	2 483	2 727	2 873	4 901	8 259	3 031	1 859
Gasoline and gasohol ....farms, 1987..	409	455	371	620	313	1 227	192	672
1982..	495	559	545	743	404	1 510	242	906
$1,000, 1987..	624	634	491	678	998	1 271	467	504
1982..	1 120	922	1 096	1 097	1 335	2 304	633	825
Diesel fuel ....farms, 1987..	335	433	451	497	332	1 048	223	436
1982..	438	419	429	512	319	1 136	183	417
$1,000, 1987..	770	824	771	959	1 168	2 016	1 031	521
1982..	1 360	1 132	1 305	1 475	1 771	3 008	1 083	823
Natural gas ....farms, 1987..	26	47	13	30	125	100	115	13
1982..	41	60	20	27	170	74	120	14
$1,000, 1987..	33	21	10	60	864	157	1 002	31
1982..	24	35	22	43	1 249	161	892	22
LP gas, fuel oil, kerosene, motor oil, grease, etc. ....farms, 1987..	403	474	427	522	337	1 145	217	475
1982..	(NA)	(NA)	(NA)	(NA)	(NA)	(NA)	(NA)	(NA)
$1,000, 1987..	171	205	168	152	326	529	213	141
1982..	250	394	304	258	546	786	423	190
Electricity ....farms, 1987..	296	369	305	490	233	1 120	214	572
1982..	371	458	371	508	321	1 065	177	579
$1,000, 1987..	291	199	177	434	1 167	1 198	1 507	290
1982..	356	363	223	361	1 092	949	(D)	341
Hired farm labor ....farms, 1987..	153	241	136	242	180	468	136	176
1982..	197	267	194	269	178	634	136	200
$1,000, 1987..	990	767	676	1 626	8 789	3 391	6 085	810
1982..	757	927	915	1 459	4 426	2 901	1 846	1 250
Contract labor ....farms, 1987..	41	46	118	45	59	235	43	79
1982..	18	26	36	97	97	86	24	33
$1,000, 1987..	63	100	207	106	624	477	199	127
1982..	66	39	57	48	234	163	110	100
Repair and maintenance ....farms, 1987..	396	487	391	617	319	1 297	214	611
1982..	1 559	1 736	1 107	2 175	2 899	4 014	2 724	1 599
Customwork, machine hire, and rental of machinery and equipment[2] ....farms, 1987..	258	262	202	307	226	569	145	254
1982..	274	308	302	255	233	631	138	240
$1,000, 1987..	1 169	569	552	452	2 164	930	1 612	215
1982..	1 051	777	1 099	560	2 148	1 236	1 256	268
Interest paid[2] ....farms, 1987..	248	267	295	366	249	804	204	433
1982..	283	348	307	433	277	801	172	383
$1,000, 1987..	2 023	1 843	1 515	2 257	4 363	4 495	2 056	1 960
1982..	3 749	4 092	2 492	5 500	7 467	7 877	3 096	2 740
Interest paid on debt: Secured by real estate ....farms, 1987..	155	179	137	209	129	600	105	337
$1,000, 1987..	1 496	1 542	690	1 232	1 901	3 585	1 103	1 342
Not secured by real estate ....farms, 1987..	180	140	206	253	175	441	154	212
$1,000, 1987..	527	301	825	1 025	2 462	1 430	955	638
Cash rent ....farms, 1987..	226	158	172	218	99	367	103	217
$1,000, 1987..	1 051	614	1 429	1 403	1 249	1 861	1 140	681
Property taxes paid ....farms, 1987..	428	490	466	658	344	1 461	227	815
$1,000, 1987..	713	930	797	830	841	2 317	725	1 136
All other farm production expenses ....$1,000, 1987..	440	534	523	680	372	1 445	253	821
$1,000, 1987..	1 608	1 552	1 554	3 185	7 000	4 410	5 381	1 546

See footnotes at end of table.

Table 3. **Farm Production Expenses: 1987 and 1982**—Con.

[Data are based on a sample of farms. For meaning of abbreviations and symbols, see introductory text]

Item		Sheridan	Sherman	Smith	Stafford	Stanton	Stevens	Sumner	Thomas
Total farm production expenses	farms, 1987..	518	524	692	539	261	300	1 271	645
	$1,000, 1987..	47 749	56 328	37 639	62 257	77 823	87 008	47 979	64 218
Average per farm	dollars, 1987..	92 179	107 492	54 391	115 505	276 951	290 028	37 749	99 563
Livestock and poultry purchased	farms, 1987..	229	117	261	180	78	47	364	163
	1982..	210	156	356	188	73	94	401	197
	$1,000, 1987..	15 292	21 049	8 963	26 390	36 650	48 263	7 786	22 468
	1982..	12 902	15 140	11 935	15 067	27 280	(D)	8 023	16 895
Feed for livestock and poultry	farms, 1987..	306	204	418	260	94	88	632	218
	1982..	356	217	562	209	123	148	720	283
	$1,000, 1987..	7 351	5 638	4 166	10 273	12 389	(D)	4 582	6 546
	1982..	5 640	4 561	8 760	8 219	12 290	6 796	4 316	5 773
Commercially mixed formula feeds	farms, 1987..	148	76	113	97	30	14	244	93
	1982..	122	64	178	61	20	26	193	80
	$1,000, 1987..	1 023	492	649	996	265	145	1 233	1 278
	1982..	1 431	831	1 410	759	2 393	392	1 709	977
Seeds, bulbs, plants, and trees	farms, 1987..	434	427	570	482	230	256	865	566
	1982..	448	441	625	489	199	306	774	507
	$1,000, 1987..	1 091	1 756	848	1 400	1 286	1 385	1 350	1 942
	1982..	1 119	1 708	661	1 009	1 259	1 028	1 104	1 457
Commercial fertilizer[1]	farms, 1987..	372	350	570	453	206	244	1 018	476
	1982..	401	322	606	478	190	274	1 069	394
	$1,000, 1987..	2 081	2 728	2 537	4 002	2 553	3 060	4 759	2 913
	1982..	2 690	3 748	3 033	4 176	3 518	3 580	6 959	3 295
Agricultural chemicals[1]	farms, 1987..	404	380	623	379	218	230	671	465
	1982..	251	240	530	288	175	267	542	260
	$1,000, 1987..	1 485	1 716	1 804	1 554	1 614	1 779	1 364	2 092
	1982..	1 253	1 343	1 180	967	1 926	2 214	762	1 695
Petroleum products	farms, 1987..	500	498	671	526	271	294	1 262	587
	1982..	570	543	755	547	231	325	1 386	528
	$1,000, 1987..	3 214	4 092	2 610	2 928	3 627	3 632	4 601	3 979
	1982..	5 455	6 473	3 449	4 474	6 030	4 319	7 397	5 304
Gasoline and gasohol	farms, 1987..	430	416	576	431	208	246	1 089	440
	1982..	478	525	729	517	217	300	1 282	566
	$1,000, 1987..	935	783	893	872	740	749	1 298	762
	1982..	1 592	1 671	1 434	1 413	1 229	1 085	2 417	1 441
Diesel fuel	farms, 1987..	415	377	546	443	221	267	982	523
	1982..	505	441	593	493	217	272	696	498
	$1,000, 1987..	1 630	1 685	1 353	1 478	1 360	1 463	2 714	2 024
	1982..	2 350	2 376	1 613	2 167	2 143	1 873	4 081	2 383
Natural gas	farms, 1987..	81	175	15	78	139	129	36	162
	1982..	109	239	23	111	175	155	31	139
	$1,000, 1987..	449	1 345	12	268	1 261	1 163	71	865
	1982..	669	(D)	8	268	1 973	935	16	956
LP gas, fuel oil, kerosene, motor oil, grease, etc.	farms, 1987..	399	428	584	478	208	254	1 082	495
	1982..	(NA)	(NA)	(NA)	(NA)	(NA)	(NA)	(NA)	(NA)
	$1,000, 1987..	300	276	252	312	276	266	516	326
	1982..	843	(D)	393	625	684	426	883	523
Electricity	farms, 1987..	439	398	517	404	221	221	915	399
	1982..	438	375	594	411	203	225	1 012	381
	$1,000, 1987..	680	670	493	728	675	645	647	807
	1982..	(D)	789	462	445	847	446	696	1 293
Hired farm labor	farms, 1987..	229	214	301	258	146	161	491	186
	1982..	231	252	305	240	145	171	576	186
	$1,000, 1987..	1 887	2 384	2 075	2 084	5 152	3 349	1 956	3 475
	1982..	1 481	2 888	1 316	1 622	2 802	2 013	2 268	2 428
Contract labor	farms, 1987..	55	85	92	105	54	48	173	79
	1982..	31	55	36	28	31	55	41	17
	$1,000, 1987..	258	372	282	249	240	(D)	483	287
	1982..	112	198	45	484	124	153	187	81
Repair and maintenance	farms, 1987..	430	440	622	484	217	257	1 097	487
	$1,000, 1987..	2 746	2 887	2 873	3 010	3 201	3 175	4 169	3 645
Customwork, machine hire, and rental of machinery and equipment[2]	farms, 1987..	336	376	493	262	170	139	584	418
	1982..	337	334	393	386	139	128	639	365
	$1,000, 1987..	1 625	3 109	1 114	967	1 589	900	1 994	3 812
	1982..	1 496	3 951	999	1 887	2 384	1 155	2 326	3 319
Interest paid[3]	farms, 1987..	339	347	437	331	215	200	815	352
	1982..	363	336	478	357	186	236	632	419
	$1,000, 1987..	4 593	3 683	3 542	3 486	2 806	3 076	6 360	4 813
	1982..	6 857	6 178	6 008	4 242	3 885	3 977	9 128	6 620
Interest paid on debt:									
Secured by real estate	farms, 1987..	257	213	232	189	93	93	610	247
	$1,000, 1987..	3 210	2 261	1 918	1 928	1 023	1 424	4 614	3 333
Not secured by real estate	farms, 1987..	212	236	329	223	173	152	414	251
	$1,000, 1987..	1 184	1 422	1 624	1 540	1 783	1 654	1 766	1 480
Cash rent	farms, 1987..	172	139	297	190	63	78	423	135
	$1,000, 1987..	1 001	1 254	1 510	1 075	820	1 062	2 015	1 456
Property taxes paid	farms, 1987..	488	469	604	491	240	290	1 185	574
	$1,000, 1987..	1 189	1 184	1 316	1 008	578	591	2 256	1 862
All other farm production expenses	$1,000, 1987..	495	524	680	515	269	268	1 230	603
	$1,000, 1987..	3 255	3 802	3 605	2 902	4 644	3 058	3 638	4 121

See footnotes at end of table.

Table 3. Farm Production Expenses: 1987 and 1982—Con.

[Data are based on a sample of farms. For meaning of abbreviations and symbols, see introductory text]

Item	Trego	Wabaunsee	Wallace	Washington	Wichita	Wilson	Woodson	Wyandotte
Total farm production expenses ... farms, 1987..	482	632	330	938	354	609	368	199
$1,000, 1987..	30 660	29 463	23 242	50 203	190 626	16 037	15 204	3 898
Average per farm ... dollars, 1987..	63 611	46 619	70 429	53 521	538 492	26 334	41 316	19 587
Livestock and poultry purchased ... farms, 1987..	186	274	96	388	110	161	110	48
1982..	203	261	79	459	82	235	159	48
$1,000, 1987..	11 277	9 524	4 936	10 676	126 432	1 583	5 255	(D)
1982..	20 017	11 848	4 115	11 602	82 008	1 660	5 537	(D)
Feed for livestock and poultry ... farms, 1987..	326	383	126	611	150	325	179	90
1982..	273	474	148	714	130	436	272	123
$1,000, 1987..	5 299	4 817	1 528	8 838	34 713	1 374	791	264
1982..	12 879	5 317	1 830	9 735	39 486	2 431	2 690	500
Commercially mixed formula feeds ... farms, 1987..	131	138	57	263	73	148	71	39
1982..	93	203	45	252	90	154	129	51
$1,000, 1987..	482	1 234	446	3 750	1 094	395	261	123
1982..	598	2 378	264	3 054	3 247	1 004	475	165
Seeds, bulbs, plants, and trees ... farms, 1987..	384	376	262	716	303	413	216	58
1982..	370	464	207	853	277	448	226	51
$1,000, 1987..	444	430	935	1 294	951	621	309	326
1982..	426	593	882	1 063	886	694	371	440
Commercial fertilizer[1] ... farms, 1987..	327	449	195	694	193	451	245	71
1982..	326	434	132	821	228	504	278	101
$1,000, 1987..	964	1 069	1 507	3 541	1 426	1 832	814	225
1982..	1 114	1 549	1 878	4 450	2 455	1 846	1 056	193
Agricultural chemicals[1] ... farms, 1987..	357	449	207	751	245	410	241	104
1982..	156	296	114	671	269	357	205	107
$1,000, 1987..	663	687	667	2 149	1 007	861	470	148
1982..	269	541	523	1 789	1 497	704	504	146
Petroleum products ... farms, 1987..	481	555	317	893	351	560	318	187
1982..	497	678	338	1 031	340	672	402	216
$1,000, 1987..	1 641	1 290	2 810	2 948	3 614	1 422	778	373
1982..	2 453	2 217	3 797	5 015	4 685	2 118	1 156	875
Gasoline and gasohol ... farms, 1987..	418	487	253	769	295	482	304	175
1982..	400	671	325	978	311	627	376	199
$1,000, 1987..	589	606	556	995	651	572	369	187
1982..	933	1 057	1 003	2 005	880	892	670	171
Diesel fuel ... farms, 1987..	379	263	257	659	276	354	196	62
1982..	394	351	233	768	272	418	238	81
$1,000, 1987..	836	487	954	1 545	1 264	695	334	90
1982..	1 144	687	1 664	2 340	1 658	933	443	111
Natural gas ... farms, 1987..	42	40	92	40	133	12	7	7
1982..	16	9	92	56	187	8	10	24
$1,000, 1987..	27	67	762	56	1 455	6	(D)	(D)
1982..	17	19	808	33	1 624	3	4	(D)
LP gas, fuel oil, kerosene, motor oil, grease, etc. ... farms, 1987..	396	437	264	739	287	428	256	96
1982..	(NA)	(NA)	(NA)	(NA)	(NA)	(NA)	(NA)	(NA)
$1,000, 1987..	189	129	236	349	243	149	(D)	(D)
1982..	359	254	323	638	524	290	139	(D)
Electricity ... farms, 1987..	369	464	252	698	212	382	244	111
1982..	369	479	217	854	252	480	285	137
$1,000, 1987..	297	418	395	919	1 190	241	(D)	(D)
1982..	359	363	(D)	857	1 192	282	195	108
Hired farm labor ... farms, 1987..	164	192	121	309	136	128	111	55
1982..	174	248	102	326	167	197	148	43
$1,000, 1987..	799	1 656	1 147	2 407	4 739	419	(D)	765
1982..	633	839	993	1 538	3 362	(D)	605	(D)
Contract labor ... farms, 1987..	27	40	49	72	54	106	32	23
1982..	8	17	24	47	20	32	8	24
$1,000, 1987..	49	124	220	256	(D)	119	(D)	(D)
1982..	9	20	92	83	46	52	14	295
Repair and maintenance ... farms, 1987..	434	512	267	782	289	485	313	117
$1,000, 1987..	1 569	1 632	1 644	3 523	2 908	1 445	972	211
Customwork, machine hire, and rental of machinery and equipment[3] ... farms, 1987..	307	226	199	397	210	220	151	34
1982..	256	254	138	471	153	235	95	45
$1,000, 1987..	842	393	1 439	909	1 995	292	(D)	(D)
1982..	624	268	1 658	755	1 906	344	310	47
Interest paid[3] ... farms, 1987..	283	278	223	617	248	334	200	53
1982..	289	444	206	674	201	323	217	61
$1,000, 1987..	1 963	2 192	2 504	4 955	2 594	2 031	1 660	300
1982..	3 020	3 670	3 495	9 093	4 429	2 480	2 523	436
Interest paid on debt: Secured by real estate ... farms, 1987..	184	228	145	443	133	238	128	39
$1,000, 1987..	1 171	1 258	1 593	2 908	1 566	1 315	856	(D)
Not secured by real estate ... farms, 1987..	195	191	157	404	167	186	121	30
$1,000, 1987..	792	934	911	2 047	1 027	716	369	(D)
Cash rent ... farms, 1987..	196	194	117	325	76	204	174	19
$1,000, 1987..	1 010	1 519	1 008	2 008	(D)	1 242	1 053	85
Property taxes paid ... farms, 1987..	467	584	298	846	300	585	355	184
$1,000, 1987..	630	949	843	1 808	886	838	579	194
All other farm production expenses ... farms, 1987..	467	583	317	903	335	568	341	171
$1,000, 1987..	3 212	2 762	1 759	3 969	4 202	1 420	1 226	369

[1] Data for 1987 include cost of custom applications.
[2] Data for 1987 exclude cost of custom applications for commercial fertilizer and agricultural chemicals.
[3] Data for 1982 do not include imputation for item nonresponse.

Table 4. **Net Cash Return From Agricultural Sales, Government Payments, Other Farm-Related Income, and Commodity Credit Corporation Loans: 1987 and 1982**

[For meaning of abbreviations and symbols, see introductory text]

Item	Kansas	Allen	Anderson	Atchison	Barber	Barton	Bourbon
NET CASH RETURN							
Net cash return from agricultural sales for the farm unit (see text)[1] .... farms, 1987...	68 580	665	726	693	534	937	842
$1,000, 1987...	922 225	5 973	8 664	4 776	1 814	20 029	3 390
Average per farm.......................dollars, 1987...	13 447	8 983	11 934	6 892	3 397	21 375	4 026
Farms with net gains[2].................number, 1987...	41 673	423	443	431	287	670	446
$1,000, 1987...	1 140 553	7 211	10 693	6 185	5 958	23 282	5 236
Average per farm.......................dollars, 1987...	27 363	17 046	24 138	14 350	20 759	34 749	11 687
Farms with net losses...................number, 1987...	26 907	242	283	262	247	267	394
$1,000, 1987...	218 328	1 237	2 029	1 408	4 144	3 253	1 846
Average per farm.......................dollars, 1987...	8 114	5 112	7 170	5 376	16 778	12 185	4 680
GOVERNMENT PAYMENTS							
Total received................................ farms, 1987...	41 627	357	379	392	353	667	305
$1,000, 1987...	573 647	1 866	2 410	2 802	4 656	7 790	2 050
Average per farm.......................dollars, 1987...	13 781	5 227	6 360	7 149	13 189	11 679	6 721
Amount received in cash .... farms, 1987...	35 909	306	332	352	256	573	246
$1,000, 1987...	247 737	828	1 110	1 375	1 671	3 162	1 010
Value of commodity certificates received ..... farms, 1987...	38 992	329	350	367	336	623	278
$1,000, 1987...	325 910	1 038	1 300	1 428	2 985	4 629	1 040
OTHER FARM-RELATED INCOME							
Gross before taxes and expenses[1] .... farms, 1987...	18 682	172	160	109	159	252	180
$1,000, 1987...	69 944	714	659	643	914	392	598
Average per farm.......................dollars, 1987...	3 744	4 154	4 119	5 903	5 747	1 555	3 320
Customwork and other agricultural services[3] .... farms, 1987...	7 463	65	56	70	76	106	65
1982...	7 742	65	74	66	69	93	77
$1,000, 1987...	32 115	463	349	521	521	242	386
1982...	36 809	196	209	162	384	246	148
Rental of farmland.......................farms, 1987...	7 899	76	88	38	75	102	97
$1,000, 1987...	30 403	216	201	(D)	369	70	202
Sales of forest products and Christmas trees .... farms, 1987...	439	7	19	–	–	–	–
$1,000, 1987...	1 087	6	(D)	–	–	–	–
Other farm-related income sources .... farms, 1987...	6 669	32	15	4	36	93	9
$1,000, 1987...	6 340	30	(D)	(D)	24	80	10
COMMODITY CREDIT CORPORATION LOANS							
Total .... farms, 1987...	15 832	107	158	181	91	235	72
1982...	14 306	65	123	95	126	319	62
$1,000, 1987...	338 298	2 152	2 623	2 747	1 067	3 516	694
1982...	364 770	1 841	3 153	1 656	4 925	6 912	943
Corn .... farms, 1987...	3 591	23	77	85	–	20	30
$1,000, 1987...	106 314	448	900	948	–	809	275
Wheat.................................... farms, 1987...	7 262	8	8	8	82	135	2
$1,000, 1987...	95 942	(D)	13	4	948	1 255	(D)
Soybeans.................................... farms, 1987...	1 248	35	52	39	–	5	13
$1,000, 1987...	20 784	(D)	1 075	729	–	71	(D)
Sorghum, barley, and oats.................... farms, 1987...	10 032	82	101	126	18	152	45
$1,000, 1987...	112 774	545	634	1 056	119	1 482	277
Cotton.................................... farms, 1987...	–	–	–	–	–	–	–
$1,000, 1987...	–	–	–	–	–	–	–
Peanuts, rye, rice, tobacco, and honey........ farms, 1987...	22	–	–	–	–	–	–
$1,000, 1987...	503	–	–	–	–	–	–

See footnotes at end of table.

Table 4. **Net Cash Return From Agricultural Sales, Government Payments, Other Farm-Related Income, and Commodity Credit Corporation Loans: 1987 and 1982**—Con.

[For meaning of abbreviations and symbols, see introductory text]

Item	Brown	Butler	Chase	Chautauqua	Cherokee	Cheyenne	Clark
NET CASH RETURN							
Net cash return from agricultural sales for the farm unit (see text)[1] _____ farms, 1987_	729	1 300	268	422	842	493	290
$1,000, 1987_	12 397	13 039	6 530	1 927	3 209	7 638	9 755
Average per farm _____ dollars, 1987_	17 006	10 030	22 873	4 566	3 811	15 493	33 639
Farms with net gains[2] _____ number, 1987_	483	762	187	204	451	297	190
$1,000, 1987_	14 586	16 158	7 269	3 133	5 653	9 320	11 209
Average per farm _____ dollars, 1987_	30 198	21 205	38 871	15 359	12 534	31 379	58 992
Farms with net losses _____ number, 1987_	246	538	101	218	391	196	100
$1,000, 1987_	2 188	3 119	739	1 206	2 444	1 681	1 453
Average per farm _____ dollars, 1987_	8 896	5 797	7 317	5 534	6 250	8 578	14 531
GOVERNMENT PAYMENTS							
Total received _____ farms, 1987_	505	467	135	91	344	370	205
$1,000, 1987_	6 404	4 333	730	721	1 926	6 922	3 414
Average per farm _____ dollars, 1987_	12 682	9 277	5 409	7 923	5 600	18 706	16 653
Amount received in cash _____ farms, 1987_	462	382	117	68	253	324	162
$1,000, 1987_	3 083	1 969	325	284	758	2 887	1 204
Value of commodity certificates received _____ farms, 1987_	484	422	119	79	321	345	194
$1,000, 1987_	3 321	2 363	406	437	1 169	4 035	2 210
OTHER FARM-RELATED INCOME							
Gross before taxes and expenses[1] _____ farms, 1987_	276	405	64	94	159	151	96
$1,000, 1987_	920	1 223	439	256	719	1 195	850
Average per farm _____ dollars, 1987_	3 334	3 020	6 857	2 747	4 521	7 913	8 859
Customwork and other agricultural services[3] _____ farms, 1987_	131	146	22	22	62	79	57
1982_	132	117	39	31	44	85	35
$1,000, 1987_	402	328	38	86	269	579	472
1982_	458	367	168	91	135	492	231
Rental of farmland _____ farms, 1987_	95	231	30	70	96	75	16
$1,000, 1987_	425	804	393	145	440	602	225
Sales of forest products and Christmas trees _____ farms, 1987_	11	18	–	1	–	–	13
$1,000, 1987_	3	54	–	(D)	–	–	113
Other farm-related income sources _____ farms, 1987_	109	80	19	14	45	41	30
$1,000, 1987_	90	38	9	(D)	10	15	40
COMMODITY CREDIT CORPORATION LOANS							
Total _____ farms, 1987_	305	164	45	19	97	153	36
1982_	203	134	35	9	93	132	88
$1,000, 1987_	7 557	2 841	298	314	1 558	4 110	493
1982_	5 935	1 897	244	326	1 334	3 908	1 643
Corn _____ farms, 1987_	184	7	11	1	23	50	–
$1,000, 1987_	4 134	(D)	41	(D)	245	1 610	–
Wheat _____ farms, 1987_	36	57	14	8	13	123	23
$1,000, 1987_	158	462	55	(D)	52	1 932	306
Soybeans _____ farms, 1987_	71	11	8	6	32	10	–
$1,000, 1987_	1 754	(D)	82	111	787	219	–
Sorghum, barley, and oats _____ farms, 1987_	178	140	32	14	62	39	20
$1,000, 1987_	1 510	2 136	140	126	475	349	187
Cotton _____ farms, 1987_	–	–	–	–	–	–	–
$1,000, 1987_	–	–	–	–	–	–	–
Peanuts, rye, rice, tobacco, and honey _____ farms, 1987_	–	–	–	–	–	–	–
$1,000, 1987_	–	–	–	–	–	–	–

See footnotes at end of table.

[For meaning of abbreviations and symbols, see introductory text]

Item	Clay	Cloud	Coffey	Comanche	Cowley	Crawford	Decatur
NET CASH RETURN							
Net cash return from agricultural sales for the farm unit (see text)[1] .... farms, 1987..	672	659	607	277	996	808	486
$1,000, 1987..	7 584	7 750	7 985	5 613	4 691	4 301	11 829
Average per farm .... dollars, 1987..	11 285	11 760	13 154	20 265	4 710	5 323	24 339
Farms with net gains[2] .... number, 1987..	439	443	482	175	523	530	391
$1,000, 1987..	9 143	9 216	6 540	6 446	9 045	5 356	12 711
Average per farm .... dollars, 1987..	20 826	20 803	17 719	36 637	17 294	10 107	32 508
Farms with net losses .... number, 1987..	233	216	125	102	473	278	95
$1,000, 1987..	1 559	1 466	558	833	4 354	1 055	882
Average per farm .... dollars, 1987..	6 691	6 785	4 445	8 167	9 205	3 796	9 284
GOVERNMENT PAYMENTS							
Total received .... farms, 1987..	509	491	332	190	529	343	365
$1,000, 1987..	5 099	6 374	2 579	3 663	4 439	2 107	5 486
Average per farm .... dollars, 1987..	10 018	12 983	7 768	19 276	8 391	6 142	15 031
Amount received in cash .... farms, 1987..	457	444	290	151	425	276	323
$1,000, 1987..	2 175	2 906	1 038	1 492	1 690	956	2 524
Value of commodity certificates received ...... farms, 1987..	485	487	318	173	493	311	345
$1,000, 1987..	2 924	3 468	1 541	2 171	2 749	1 150	2 962
OTHER FARM-RELATED INCOME							
Gross before taxes and expenses[1] .... farms, 1987..	152	226	146	101	212	293	118
$1,000, 1987..	221	856	432	561	502	691	529
Average per farm .... dollars, 1987..	1 457	3 786	2 957	5 557	2 369	2 360	4 483
Customwork and other agricultural services[3] .... farms, 1987..	40	98	64	49	104	56	43
1982..	80	93	74	28	98	57	71
$1,000, 1987..	60	451	189	269	224	202	334
1982..	322	291	425	279	319	159	215
Rental of farmland .... farms, 1987..	67	79	100	51	80	119	68
$1,000, 1987..	146	314	236	266	217	270	141
Sales of forest products and Christmas trees .... farms, 1987..	–	10	9	9	–	32	–
$1,000, 1987..	–	4	(Z)	5	–	146	–
Other farm-related income sources .... farms, 1987..	59	129	21	37	70	138	52
$1,000, 1987..	15	87	6	22	61	73	53
COMMODITY CREDIT CORPORATION LOANS							
Total .... farms, 1987..	227	205	164	47	134	107	190
1982..	180	163	87	56	103	96	149
$1,000, 1987..	3 619	4 478	2 324	892	1 483	1 551	4 412
1982..	2 531	2 984	1 227	2 034	1 698	1 833	3 176
Corn .... farms, 1987..	34	31	53	5	–	35	50
$1,000, 1987..	701	902	414	75	–	397	1 269
Wheat .... farms, 1987..	137	114	23	42	88	12	114
$1,000, 1987..	1 195	1 763	102	796	820	(D)	1 855
Soybeans .... farms, 1987..	30	17	43	–	4	34	2
$1,000, 1987..	344	(D)	899	–	15	402	(D)
Sorghum, barley, and oats .... farms, 1987..	145	141	129	5	83	67	132
$1,000, 1987..	1 379	1 612	909	22	649	633	(D)
Cotton .... farms, 1987..	–	–	–	–	–	–	–
$1,000, 1987..	–	–	–	–	–	2	–
Peanuts, rye, rice, tobacco, and honey .... farms, 1987..	–	1	–	–	–	2	–
$1,000, 1987..	–	(D)	–	–	–	(D)	–

See footnotes at end of table.

Table 4. **Net Cash Return From Agricultural Sales, Government Payments, Other Farm-Related Income, and Commodity Credit Corporation Loans: 1987 and 1982**—Con.

[For meaning of abbreviations and symbols, see introductory text]

Item	Dickinson	Doniphan	Douglas	Edwards	Elk	Ellis	Ellsworth
NET CASH RETURN							
Net cash return from agricultural sales for the farm unit (see text)[1] ...... farms, 1987..	1 028	530	852	361	410	797	499
$1,000, 1987..	11 767	7 722	4 047	10 155	3 254	5 470	3 490
Average per farm...........................dollars, 1987..	11 447	14 570	4 749	28 130	7 938	6 863	6 994
Farms with net gains[2].......................number, 1987..	589	366	434	247	259	429	310
$1,000, 1987..	14 445	8 588	5 855	11 655	4 345	7 794	5 011
Average per farm...........................dollars, 1987..	24 525	23 463	13 490	47 185	16 775	18 166	16 165
Farms with net losses.......................number, 1987..	439	164	418	114	151	368	189
$1,000, 1987..	2 678	866	1 808	1 500	1 090	2 324	1 521
Average per farm...........................dollars, 1987..	6 100	5 277	4 326	13 156	7 220	6 316	8 048
GOVERNMENT PAYMENTS							
Total received............................. farms, 1987..	734	341	288	279	142	516	363
$1,000, 1987..	6 560	4 137	2 173	6 326	687	3 851	4 088
Average per farm...........................dollars, 1987..	8 937	12 131	7 546	22 673	4 839	7 463	10 673
Amount received in cash .... farms, 1987..	638	310	252	242	107	417	336
$1,000, 1987..	2 845	2 063	1 089	2 751	219	1 621	1 525
Value of commodity certificates received ..... farms, 1987..	695	321	255	266	131	479	362
$1,000, 1987..	3 715	2 073	1 064	3 574	468	2 230	2 562
OTHER FARM-RELATED INCOME							
Gross before taxes and expenses[1] .... farms, 1987..	292	131	237	118	107	238	178
$1,000, 1987..	802	532	841	510	192	1 032	364
Average per farm...........................dollars, 1987..	2 745	4 059	3 548	4 325	1 790	4 335	2 046
Customwork and other agricultural services[3] .... farms, 1987..	77	76	85	34	32	91	67
1982..	119	86	58	57	52	54	45
$1,000, 1987..	277	279	445	205	81	471	175
1982..	268	713	105	622	202	245	142
Rental of farmland......................... farms, 1987..	116	51	135	38	47	120	67
$1,000, 1987..	377	213	371	222	84	473	127
Sales of forest products and Christmas trees .... farms, 1987..	8	15	4	–	13	–	–
$1,000, 1987..	(Z)	34	(Z)	–	9	–	–
Other farm-related income sources .... farms, 1987..	131	16	52	78	32	132	102
$1,000, 1987..	148	6	25	84	17	88	63
COMMODITY CREDIT CORPORATION LOANS							
Total .... farms, 1987..	253	173	131	115	14	148	141
1982..	215	105	46	141	19	148	138
$1,000, 1987..	2 512	5 078	2 113	4 795	111	1 457	1 630
1982..	2 433	4 143	529	6 717	122	1 399	1 972
Corn .... farms, 1987..	9	161	69	49	1	–	2
$1,000, 1987..	(D)	4 050	1 064	3 298	(D)	–	(D)
Wheat.................................... farms, 1987..	147	8	8	58	5	128	96
$1,000, 1987..	1 167	43	45	798	7	1 083	1 000
Soybeans................................. farms, 1987..	20	34	20	7	2	–	3
$1,000, 1987..	(D)	889	184	(D)	(D)	–	(D)
Sorghum, barley, and oats.................... farms, 1987..	179	18	87	46	7	57	82
$1,000, 1987..	1 086	95	820	(D)	59	374	593
Cotton.................................... farms, 1987..	–	–	–	–	–	–	–
$1,000, 1987..	–	–	–	–	–	–	–
Peanuts, rye, rice, tobacco, and honey........ farms, 1987..	–	–	–	–	–	–	–
$1,000, 1987..	–	–	–	–	–	–	–

See footnotes at end of table.

Table 4. **Net Cash Return From Agricultural Sales, Government Payments, Other Farm-Related Income, and Commodity Credit Corporation Loans: 1987 and 1982**—Con.

[For meaning of abbreviations and symbols, see introductory text]

Item	Finney	Ford	Franklin	Geary	Gove	Graham	Grant
NET CASH RETURN							
Net cash return from agricultural sales for the farm unit (see text)¹ ... farms, 1987	535	812	980	296	593	452	303
$1,000, 1987	38 186	13 833	7 411	3 492	36 307	3 582	4 500
Average per farm ... dollars, 1987	71 375	17 036	7 562	11 797	71 870	7 924	14 851
Farms with net gains² ... number, 1987	379	472	511	153	348	264	210
$1,000, 1987	40 283	22 720	9 632	4 201	40 287	5 182	11 761
Average per farm ... dollars, 1987	106 287	48 135	18 850	27 456	115 768	19 630	56 007
Farms with net losses ... number, 1987	156	340	469	143	165	188	93
$1,000, 1987	2 097	8 887	2 222	709	1 981	1 601	7 262
Average per farm ... dollars, 1987	13 443	26 136	4 737	4 960	10 706	8 514	78 082
GOVERNMENT PAYMENTS							
Total received ... farms, 1987	383	580	343	166	374	330	219
$1,000, 1987	14 448	11 141	2 378	1 309	6 494	4 428	7 165
Average per farm ... dollars, 1987	37 724	19 895	6 934	7 886	17 363	13 417	32 717
Amount received in cash ... farms, 1987	349	494	297	150	337	263	201
$1,000, 1987	6 634	4 779	1 332	637	2 697	1 776	3 242
Value of commodity certificates received ... farms, 1987	364	530	320	153	362	315	212
$1,000, 1987	7 815	6 362	1 047	673	3 798	2 652	3 923
OTHER FARM-RELATED INCOME							
Gross before taxes and expenses¹ ... farms, 1987	130	234	249	55	161	158	79
$1,000, 1987	1 318	927	575	266	852	290	837
Average per farm ... dollars, 1987	10 136	3 960	2 309	4 831	5 290	1 834	10 596
Customwork and other agricultural services³ ... farms, 1987	44	94	41	20	67	51	21
1982	60	90	69	29	75	53	38
$1,000, 1987	340	634	72	221	433	157	152
1982	692	536	164	75	409	253	272
Rental of farmland ... farms, 1987	57	67	148	24	55	74	29
$1,000, 1987	896	202	299	15	359	105	607
Sales of forest products and Christmas trees ... farms, 1987	-	-	25	8	-	-	-
$1,000, 1987	-	-	26	20	-	-	-
Other farm-related income sources ... farms, 1987	50	123	57	15	92	77	44
$1,000, 1987	82	91	179	10	60	26	77
COMMODITY CREDIT CORPORATION LOANS							
Total ... farms, 1987	162	195	144	59	173	125	111
1982	189	232	83	56	184	130	99
$1,000, 1987	8 439	6 463	2 239	587	3 399	1 944	3 988
1982	9 084	7 105	1 460	794	2 167	2 465	5 110
Corn ... farms, 1987	72	36	57	3	25	12	64
$1,000, 1987	(D)	2 258	649	(D)	587	122	(D)
Wheat ... farms, 1987	81	119	5	17	110	78	55
$1,000, 1987	2 003	2 038	10	137	1 490	1 053	677
Soybeans ... farms, 1987	6	8	31	4	-	-	3
$1,000, 1987	(D)	104	746	(D)	-	-	(D)
Sorghum, barley, and oats ... farms, 1987	91	106	114	54	119	76	51
$1,000, 1987	2 089	2 064	834	372	1 323	768	876
Cotton ... farms, 1987	-	-	-	-	-	-	-
$1,000, 1987	-	-	-	-	-	-	-
Peanuts, rye, rice, tobacco, and honey ... farms, 1987	-	-	-	-	-	-	-
$1,000, 1987	-	-	-	-	-	-	-

See footnotes at end of table.

[For meaning of abbreviations and symbols, see introductory text]

Item	Gray	Greeley	Greenwood	Hamilton	Harper	Harvey	Haskell
NET CASH RETURN							
Net cash return from agricultural sales for the farm unit (see text)[1] .... farms, 1987..	546	293	586	279	649	874	315
$1,000, 1987..	16 758	5 141	7 073	29 400	7 392	10 036	25 625
Average per farm .... dollars, 1987..	30 693	17 547	12 070	105 377	11 390	11 483	81 349
Farms with net gains[2] .... number, 1987..	387	196	361	166	355	563	230
$1,000, 1987..	18 799	10 027	6 324	30 474	10 037	12 551	27 375
Average per farm .... dollars, 1987..	48 577	51 160	23 058	183 580	28 275	22 293	119 020
Farms with net losses .... number, 1987..	159	97	225	113	294	311	85
$1,000, 1987..	2 041	4 886	1 251	1 074	2 645	2 515	1 750
Average per farm .... dollars, 1987..	12 837	50 374	5 561	9 506	8 998	8 086	20 584
GOVERNMENT PAYMENTS							
Total received .... farms, 1987..	425	223	207	208	530	561	239
$1,000, 1987..	13 798	5 089	1 041	6 360	8 555	6 309	10 017
Average per farm .... dollars, 1987..	32 467	22 819	5 030	30 577	16 141	11 246	41 911
Amount received in cash .... farms, 1987..	397	194	185	164	429	514	221
$1,000, 1987..	6 258	2 132	456	1 997	3 135	2 973	4 700
Value of commodity certificates received ..... farms, 1987..	406	212	185	194	494	528	228
$1,000, 1987..	7 540	2 957	585	4 363	5 419	3 336	5 316
OTHER FARM-RELATED INCOME							
Gross before taxes and expenses[1] .... farms, 1987..	136	87	144	94	189	318	76
$1,000, 1987..	1 083	830	830	573	636	844	358
Average per farm .... dollars, 1987..	7 962	9 535	5 765	6 094	3 368	2 655	4 714
Customwork and other agricultural services[3] .... farms, 1987..	90	34	31	43	37	116	24
1982..	95	31	51	53	86	150	43
$1,000, 1987..	460	201	117	403	234	324	131
1982..	594	319	140	289	394	656	200
Rental of farmland .... farms, 1987..	34	38	103	22	66	101	23
$1,000, 1987..	515	597	628	86	236	309	173
Sales of forest products and Christmas trees .... farms, 1987..	–	1	–	–	–	1	–
$1,000, 1987..	–	(D)	–	–	–	(D)	–
Other farm-related income sources .... farms, 1987..	46	44	33	56	126	175	43
$1,000, 1987..	108	(D)	86	85	167	(D)	54
COMMODITY CREDIT CORPORATION LOANS							
Total .... farms, 1987..	202	85	34	58	122	256	109
1982..	191	96	15	104	162	256	124
$1,000, 1987..	10 318	3 067	290	1 570	1 903	5 437	6 281
1982..	9 282	4 428	(D)	4 160	6 935	4 773	8 282
Corn .... farms, 1987..	112	18	7	14	–	47	60
$1,000, 1987..	5 565	(D)	59	528	–	1 599	3 583
Wheat............................ farms, 1987..	82	83	10	33	116	117	51
$1,000, 1987..	(D)	1 665	48	724	1 856	1 031	1 128
Soybeans........................ farms, 1987..	1	–	6	–	–	11	7
$1,000, 1987..	(D)	–	42	–	–	(D)	66
Sorghum, barley, and oats .... farms, 1987..	103	21	28	32	7	203	52
$1,000, 1987..	2 674	(D)	130	217	47	2 536	1 504
Cotton............................ farms, 1987..	–	–	–	–	–	–	–
$1,000, 1987..	–	–	–	–	–	–	–
Peanuts, rye, rice, tobacco, and honey .... farms, 1987..	–	–	–	–	–	2	–
$1,000, 1987..	–	–	–	–	–	(D)	–

See footnotes at end of table.

Table 4. **Net Cash Return From Agricultural Sales, Government Payments, Other Farm-Related Income, and Commodity Credit Corporation Loans: 1987 and 1982**—Con.

[For meaning of abbreviations and symbols, see introductory text]

Item	Hodgeman	Jackson	Jefferson	Jewell	Johnson	Kearny	Kingman	Kiowa
NET CASH RETURN								
Net cash return from agricultural sales for the								
farm unit (see text)[1] ....farms, 1987..	423	1 062	1 017	735	659	291	818	310
$1,000, 1987..	5 042	4 239	3 041	10 138	4 926	17 084	4 280	2 122
Average per farm......................dollars, 1987..	11 920	3 918	2 991	13 794	7 475	58 709	5 233	6 845
Farms with net gains[2] ....number, 1987..	218	550	475	546	351	196	445	161
$1,000, 1987..	7 743	7 169	5 724	11 650	6 368	18 304	7 193	4 090
Average per farm......................dollars, 1987..	35 518	13 034	12 050	21 259	18 143	92 445	16 164	25 402
Farms with net losses......................number, 1987..	205	532	542	187	308	93	373	149
$1,000, 1987..	2 701	2 930	2 682	1 511	1 442	1 220	2 913	1 968
Average per farm......................dollars, 1987..	13 175	5 508	4 949	8 083	4 682	13 117	7 808	13 206
GOVERNMENT PAYMENTS								
Total received......................farms, 1987..	340	419	357	531	174	215	588	247
$1,000, 1987..	5 763	2 287	2 495	7 883	994	8 821	7 271	5 041
Average per farm......................dollars, 1987..	16 951	5 459	6 988	14 845	5 715	41 028	12 366	20 408
Amount received in cash ....farms, 1987..	298	354	297	487	149	194	472	205
$1,000, 1987..	2 508	1 034	1 211	3 598	486	3 415	2 798	1 890
Value of commodity certificates received ......farms, 1987..	319	379	320	504	154	203	547	237
$1,000, 1987..	3 256	1 254	1 284	4 284	508	5 406	4 473	3 150
OTHER FARM-RELATED INCOME								
Gross before taxes and expenses[1] ....farms, 1987..	135	235	182	178	100	100	204	131
$1,000, 1987..	608	764	720	459	135	1 091	562	1 160
Average per farm......................dollars, 1987..	4 505	3 252	3 955	2 577	1 348	10 909	2 755	8 859
Customwork and other agricultural								
services[3] ....farms, 1987..	56	112	50	111	47	53	127	61
1982..	71	87	80	107	43	43	98	43
$1,000, 1987..	465	390	189	317	44	681	352	722
1982..	416	133	172	531	60	745	397	312
Rental of farmland......................farms, 1987..	25	98	94	75	39	41	79	42
$1,000, 1987..	87	223	388	120	75	384	166	375
Sales of forest products and Christmas								
trees ....farms, 1987..	-	24	27	-	2	-	-	-
$1,000, 1987..	-	10	112	-	(D)	-	-	-
Other farm-related income sources ....farms, 1987..	88	38	22	39	16	31	45	71
$1,000, 1987..	56	142	32	21	(D)	26	44	64
COMMODITY CREDIT CORPORATION LOANS								
Total......................farms, 1987..	130	147	123	217	47	70	169	87
1982..	133	109	77	133	12	102	135	133
$1,000, 1987..	2 779	1 377	1 830	3 882	963	5 262	2 511	3 266
1982..	3 274	1 022	1 469	2 279	772	7 291	2 427	4 251
Corn ....farms, 1987..	12	51	65	24	33	16	14	34
$1,000, 1987..	(D)	418	906	(D)	451	3 496	569	1 539
Wheat......................farms, 1987..	209	8	3	2	46	1 343	1 604	639
$1,000, 1987..	1 636	41	10	1 667	(D)	1 343	1 604	639
Soybeans......................farms, 1987..	2	27	27	5	11	1	8	4
$1,000, 1987..	(D)	296	376	(D)	369	(D)	(D)	(D)
Sorghum, barley, and oats......................farms, 1987..	78	119	70	162	21	31	27	51
$1,000, 1987..	779	622	536	1 772	126	(D)	(D)	1 008
Cotton......................farms, 1987..	-	-	-	-	-	-	-	-
$1,000, 1987..	-	-	-	-	-	-	-	-
Peanuts, rye, rice, tobacco, and honey......................farms, 1987..	-	-	-	1	1	-	-	1
$1,000, 1987..	-	-	-	(D)	(D)	-	-	(D)

See footnotes at end of table.

Table 4. **Net Cash Return From Agricultural Sales, Government Payments, Other Farm-Related Income, and Commodity Credit Corporation Loans: 1987 and 1982** —Con.

[For meaning of abbreviations and symbols, see introductory text]

Item	Labette	Lane	Leavenworth	Lincoln	Linn	Logan	Lyon	McPherson
NET CASH RETURN								
Net cash return from agricultural sales for the farm unit (see text)[1] .... farms, 1987..	970	322	1 144	578	691	381	872	1 357
$1,000, 1987..	7 548	8 870	5 488	5 901	3 982	3 382	6 115	18 690
Average per farm................ dollars, 1987..	7 781	27 545	4 797	10 209	5 782	8 876	7 013	13 773
Farms with net gains[2] .... number, 1987..	551	219	495	389	386	265	490	935
$1,000, 1987..	10 266	10 308	7 893	7 097	5 397	5 828	8 673	21 353
Average per farm................ dollars, 1987..	18 632	47 069	15 946	18 245	13 981	21 994	17 701	22 838
Farms with net losses............ number, 1987..	419	103	649	189	305	116	382	422
$1,000, 1987..	2 718	1 438	2 406	1 197	1 415	2 447	2 558	2 664
Average per farm................ dollars, 1987..	6 488	13 965	3 707	6 332	4 640	21 093	6 696	6 312
GOVERNMENT PAYMENTS								
Total received.................... farms, 1987..	442	228	271	455	301	279	466	1 000
$1,000, 1987..	2 425	5 151	1 427	4 806	2 071	5 623	3 041	10 424
Average per farm................ dollars, 1987..	5 486	22 591	5 266	10 562	6 882	20 154	6 527	10 424
Amount received in cash .... farms, 1987..	380	192	226	382	245	237	403	882
$1,000, 1987..	1 030	2 184	647	1 865	937	2 271	1 362	4 580
Value of commodity certificates received ...... farms, 1987..	397	208	242	427	271	263	430	942
$1,000, 1987..	1 395	2 967	780	2 941	1 134	3 352	1 659	5 844
OTHER FARM-RELATED INCOME								
Gross before taxes and expenses[1] .... farms, 1987..	260	93	219	182	114	128	237	364
$1,000, 1987..	536	540	474	442	554	481	894	1 012
Average per farm................ dollars, 1987..	1 916	5 806	2 167	2 430	4 863	3 759	3 774	2 779
Customwork and other agricultural services[3] .... farms, 1987..	78	30	86	54	43	65	104	149
1982..	70	35	82	85	56	57	105	211
$1,000, 1987..	234	255	76	185	(D)	375	321	451
1982..	223	250	308	191	127	449	333	672
Rental of farmland................ farms, 1987..	108	26	120	80	55	44	149	116
$1,000, 1987..	169	119	360	190	378	80	571	461
Sales of forest products and Christmas trees .... farms, 1987..	22	-	9	-	11	-	13	7
$1,000, 1987..	81	-	(D)	-	13	-	7	8
Other farm-related income sources .... farms, 1987..	122	55	22	129	15	34	2	183
$1,000, 1987..	52	167	(D)	67	(D)	26	(D)	91
COMMODITY CREDIT CORPORATION LOANS								
Total .... farms, 1987..	96	98	92	147	94	104	185	331
1982..	86	97	40	144	76	115	125	355
$1,000, 1987..	1 254	2 085	960	2 121	1 393	2 211	2 264	4 452
1982..	1 118	3 496	613	2 261	1 115	2 741	1 531	4 960
Corn .... farms, 1987..	4	5	54	1	27	9	56	56
$1,000, 1987..	24	71	498	(D)	301	434	437	1 375
Wheat........................... farms, 1987..	12	70	1	115	7	84	26	188
$1,000, 1987..	28	1 299	(D)	1 389	15	1 359	(D)	1 546
Soybeans........................ farms, 1987..	27	-	7	-	18	-	16	10
$1,000, 1987..	519	-	(D)	-	316	-	194	72
Sorghum, barley, and oats........ farms, 1987..	80	49	62	80	76	44	162	178
$1,000, 1987..	683	715	387	(D)	760	417	1 456	1 457
Cotton.......................... farms, 1987..	-	-	-	-	-	-	-	-
$1,000, 1987..	-	-	-	-	-	-	-	-
Peanuts, rye, rice, tobacco, and honey........ farms, 1987..	-	-	-	1	-	-	1	-
$1,000, 1987..	-	-	-	(D)	-	-	(D)	-

See footnotes at end of table.

Table 4. **Net Cash Return From Agricultural Sales, Government Payments, Other Farm-Related Income, and Commodity Credit Corporation Loans: 1987 and 1982** —Con.

[For meaning of abbreviations and symbols, see introductory text]

Item	Marion	Marshall	Meade	Miami	Mitchell	Montgomery	Morris	Morton
NET CASH RETURN								
Net cash return from agricultural sales for the farm unit (see text)[1] ....farms, 1987..	1 119	1 062	465	1 150	522	974	550	225
$1,000, 1987..	13 356	9 670	10 098	5 291	11 115	2 897	3 791	1 470
Average per farm.............dollars, 1987..	11 936	9 105	21 715	4 601	17 870	2 974	6 893	6 534
Farms with net gains[2].............number, 1987..	716	652	297	610	422	416	311	92
$1,000, 1987..	15 326	12 272	11 949	7 401	12 730	5 559	5 675	3 255
Average per farm.............dollars, 1987..	21 345	18 823	40 233	12 133	30 167	13 364	18 246	35 380
Farms with net losses.............number, 1987..	401	410	168	540	200	558	239	133
$1,000, 1987..	1 970	2 603	1 852	2 110	1 615	2 663	1 884	1 785
Average per farm.............dollars, 1987..	4 912	6 348	11 021	3 908	8 077	4 772	7 881	13 419
GOVERNMENT PAYMENTS								
Total received.............farms, 1987..	775	789	357	330	465	354	347	173
$1,000, 1987..	6 654	8 414	8 749	1 706	7 687	2 702	2 789	5 460
Average per farm.............dollars, 1987..	8 586	10 664	24 508	5 169	16 531	7 632	8 037	31 562
Amount received in cash.............farms, 1987..	673	735	314	257	408	297	296	155
$1,000, 1987..	2 827	4 018	3 900	741	3 283	1 260	1 265	2 149
Value of commodity certificates received.....farms, 1987..	733	736	336	298	435	331	316	165
$1,000, 1987..	3 828	4 396	4 849	965	4 404	1 442	1 523	3 311
OTHER FARM-RELATED INCOME								
Gross before taxes and expenses[1].............farms, 1987..	430	330	139	298	244	183	132	56
$1,000, 1987..	811	1 322	1 056	681	647	375	492	238
Average per farm.............dollars, 1987..	1 885	4 005	7 601	2 884	2 651	2 051	3 725	4 253
Customwork and other agricultural services[3].............farms, 1987..	115	203	57	62	62	73	50	22
1982..	126	126	64	78	72	65	46	7
$1,000, 1987..	296	632	310	181	307	149	104	64
1982..	326	471	301	137	291	177	161	47
Rental of farmland.............farms, 1987..	180	87	72	150	70	111	63	15
$1,000, 1987..	350	365	735	407	(D)	212	379	60
Sales of forest products and Christmas trees.............farms, 1987..	7	5	-	14	1	15	5	-
$1,000, 1987..	(D)	(Z)	-	36	(D)	(D)	3	-
Other farm-related income sources.............farms, 1987..	279	128	34	28	156	10	14	42
$1,000, 1987..	(D)	124	11	57	216	(D)	6	114
COMMODITY CREDIT CORPORATION LOANS								
Total.............farms, 1987..	283	378	156	117	226	92	100	71
1982..	268	317	156	92	169	43	110	71
$1,000, 1987..	3 305	5 264	5 494	2 534	5 176	2 093	1 075	2 161
1982..	3 644	5 140	7 652	2 134	3 883	698	946	2 939
Corn.............farms, 1987..	20	37	42	51	12	26	18	2
$1,000, 1987..	226	339	1 802	(D)	229	612	117	(D)
Wheat.............farms, 1987..	117	86	88	2	159	16	27	29
$1,000, 1987..	919	550	1 197	(D)	2 990	99	216	(D)
Soybeans.............farms, 1987..	11	61	5	30	8	16	6	-
$1,000, 1987..	62	650	49	1 097	159	366	65	-
Sorghum, barley, and oats.............farms, 1987..	231	338	108	82	154	69	85	52
$1,000, 1987..	2 099	3 725	2 446	721	1 799	1 015	677	1 381
Cotton.............farms, 1987..	-	-	-	-	-	-	-	-
$1,000, 1987..	-	-	-	-	-	-	-	-
Peanuts, rye, rice, tobacco, and honey.........farms, 1987..	-	-	-	-	-	-	-	-
$1,000, 1987..	-	-	-	-	-	-	-	-

See footnotes at end of table.

Table 4. Net Cash Return From Agricultural Sales, Government Payments, Other Farm-Related Income, and Commodity Credit Corporation Loans: 1987 and 1982—Con.

[For meaning of abbreviations and symbols, see introductory text]

Item	Nemaha	Neosho	Ness	Norton	Osage	Osborne	Ottawa	Pawnee
NET CASH RETURN								
Net cash return from agricultural sales for the farm unit (see text)[1] ... farms, 1987	1 127	752	598	470	685	607	522	530
$1,000, 1987	13 336	5 675	5 180	5 103	6 278	7 656	4 815	18 174
Average per farm ... dollars, 1987	11 833	7 547	8 662	10 857	7 094	12 612	9 223	34 290
Farms with net gains[2] ... number, 1987	729	414	412	353	535	451	328	350
$1,000, 1987	16 291	7 184	6 315	6 281	7 616	9 187	6 292	19 967
Average per farm ... dollars, 1987	22 347	17 353	15 328	17 792	14 236	20 370	19 182	57 106
Farms with net losses ... number, 1987	398	338	186	117	350	156	194	180
$1,000, 1987	2 954	1 509	1 135	1 178	1 338	1 531	1 477	1 813
Average per farm ... dollars, 1987	7 423	4 464	6 105	10 067	3 824	9 814	7 614	10 074
GOVERNMENT PAYMENTS								
Total received ... farms, 1987	766	333	487	339	483	484	381	396
$1,000, 1987	6 607	2 036	5 962	5 578	3 200	6 207	4 541	7 207
Average per farm ... dollars, 1987	8 604	6 113	12 243	16 453	6 626	12 824	11 918	18 201
Amount received in cash ... farms, 1987	676	260	410	296	391	419	319	347
$1,000, 1987	3 133	674	2 279	2 398	1 488	2 642	1 694	3 199
Value of commodity certificates received ... farms, 1987	723	311	457	320	432	452	367	373
$1,000, 1987	3 475	1 162	3 683	3 180	1 713	3 565	2 847	4 009
OTHER FARM-RELATED INCOME								
Gross before taxes and expenses[1] ... farms, 1987	398	166	217	173	194	241	140	150
$1,000, 1987	934	590	802	1 155	590	886	295	924
Average per farm ... dollars, 1987	2 346	3 553	3 697	6 674	3 043	3 675	2 109	6 162
Customwork and other agricultural services[3] ... farms, 1987	180	70	102	86	83	110	60	90
farms, 1982	130	48	110	63	63	78	83	57
$1,000, 1987	659	207	437	339	251	569	82	640
$1,000, 1982	292	100	491	314	177	216	256	531
Rental of farmland ... farms, 1987	78	97	68	78	103	97	60	37
$1,000, 1987	174	344	292	800	300	241	192	247
Sales of forest products and Christmas trees ... farms, 1987	-	-	-	-	6	-	7	-
$1,000, 1987	-	-	-	-	25	-	3	-
Other farm-related income sources ... farms, 1987	216	40	131	43	14	69	29	46
$1,000, 1987	100	39	73	15	14	75	18	37
COMMODITY CREDIT CORPORATION LOANS								
Total ... farms, 1987	425	74	162	169	195	194	91	165
farms, 1982	249	52	178	148	84	172	125	170
$1,000, 1987	5 413	961	2 249	4 356	2 394	3 290	1 318	4 679
$1,000, 1982	3 697	760	3 531	4 045	1 450	3 069	2 064	5 489
Corn ... farms, 1987	79	19	-	40	35	9	5	20
$1,000, 1987	399	194	-	(D)	(D)	87	(D)	(D)
Wheat ... farms, 1987	92	8	123	125	11	125	70	106
$1,000, 1987	(D)	31	1 603	2 413	(D)	1 814	683	1 625
Soybeans ... farms, 1987	43	14	1	-	27	5	9	13
$1,000, 1987	405	257	(D)	-	496	24	111	(D)
Sorghum, barley, and oats ... farms, 1987	388	60	93	87	167	140	38	119
$1,000, 1987	4 376	479	(D)	(D)	1 582	1 384	(D)	1 808
Cotton ... farms, 1987	-	-	-	-	-	-	-	-
$1,000, 1987	-	-	-	-	-	-	-	-
Peanuts, rye, rice, tobacco, and honey ... farms, 1987	1	-	-	-	-	-	-	1
$1,000, 1987	(D)	-	-	-	-	-	-	(D)

See footnotes at end of table.

Table 4. **Net Cash Return From Agricultural Sales, Government Payments, Other Farm-Related Income, and Commodity Credit Corporation Loans: 1987 and 1982**—Con.

[For meaning of abbreviations and symbols, see introductory text]

Item		Phillips	Pottawatomie	Pratt	Rawlins	Reno	Republic	Rice	Riley
NET CASH RETURN									
Net cash return from agricultural sales for the farm unit (see text)[1]	farms, 1987	592	790	517	541	1 557	834	604	547
	$1,000, 1987	8 255	7 850	7 956	6 691	14 851	8 922	11 447	5 370
Average per farm	dollars, 1987	13 945	9 937	15 388	12 368	9 536	10 697	18 953	9 817
Farms with net gains[2]	number, 1987	397	448	302	368	953	552	399	350
	$1,000, 1987	9 334	9 366	10 681	8 357	19 156	10 719	12 979	6 161
Average per farm	dollars, 1987	23 511	20 906	35 369	22 708	20 101	19 418	32 528	17 604
Farms with net losses	number, 1987	195	342	215	173	604	282	205	197
	$1,000, 1987	1 079	1 516	2 726	1 666	4 305	1 797	1 531	791
Average per farm	dollars, 1987	5 532	4 432	12 676	9 626	7 127	6 372	7 470	4 017
GOVERNMENT PAYMENTS									
Total received	farms, 1987	419	394	386	424	973	636	436	300
	$1,000, 1987	5 370	2 833	7 932	7 209	12 542	10 276	6 607	1 778
Average per farm	dollars, 1987	12 816	7 191	20 549	17 002	12 890	16 161	15 154	5 925
Amount received in cash	farms, 1987	369	337	336	364	857	607	376	273
	$1,000, 1987	2 350	1 339	3 464	3 146	5 483	4 968	2 841	771
Value of commodity certificates received	farms, 1987	386	365	367	408	902	598	421	283
	$1,000, 1987	3 020	1 494	4 468	4 063	7 059	5 310	3 766	1 008
OTHER FARM-RELATED INCOME									
Gross before taxes and expenses[1]	farms, 1987	110	167	184	128	457	265	173	117
	$1,000, 1987	296	464	979	461	1 046	1 266	711	164
Average per farm	dollars, 1987	2 694	2 779	5 320	3 602	2 294	4 778	4 110	1 401
Customwork and other agricultural services[3]	farms, 1987	46	54	67	79	171	146	42	38
	1982	77	90	57	100	172	129	86	60
	$1,000, 1987	80	145	548	251	542	746	198	100
	1982	281	478	505	625	667	514	732	74
Rental of farmland	farms, 1987	74	89	54	30	170	109	83	46
	$1,000, 1987	216	306	297	(D)	372	381	291	56
Sales of forest products and Christmas trees	farms, 1987	-	5	-	-	1	-	-	-
	$1,000, 1987	-	2	-	-	(D)	-	-	-
Other farm-related income sources	farms, 1987	4	42	68	43	188	50	80	49
	$1,000, 1987	(Z)	11	144	(D)	(D)	139	222	9
COMMODITY CREDIT CORPORATION LOANS									
Total	farms, 1987	186	136	146	220	319	357	193	116
	1982	184	114	174	150	435	266	213	100
	$1,000, 1987	3 315	2 363	3 942	3 898	5 580	11 018	4 554	1 311
	1982	3 727	1 154	6 274	2 931	8 722	7 327	5 326	722
Corn	farms, 1987	21	47	44	24	29	154	24	15
	$1,000, 1987	(D)	1 115	1 469	(D)	(D)	5 027	(D)	170
Wheat	farms, 1987	127	28	84	147	180	120	104	31
	$1,000, 1987	1 558	(D)	1 248	2 110	1 845	1 609	1 248	144
Soybeans	farms, 1987	1	6	9	1	10	44	6	11
	$1,000, 1987	(D)	(D)	(D)	(D)	(D)	501	(D)	73
Sorghum, barley, and oats	farms, 1987	113	103	78	150	198	250	155	94
	$1,000, 1987	1 234	922	(D)	1 276	2 497	3 880	2 292	924
Cotton	farms, 1987	-	-	-	-	-	-	-	-
	$1,000, 1987	-	-	-	-	-	-	-	-
Peanuts, rye, rice, tobacco, and honey	farms, 1987	-	-	-	-	-	-	-	-
	$1,000, 1987	-	-	-	-	-	-	-	-

See footnotes at end of table.

[For meaning of abbreviations and symbols, see introductory text]

Item	Rooks	Rush	Russell	Saline	Scott	Sedgwick	Seward	Shawnee
NET CASH RETURN								
Net cash return from agricultural sales for the farm unit (see text)[1] ....farms, 1987..	473	546	533	744	391	1 589	285	851
$1,000, 1987..	5 657	4 385	2 974	5 796	29 979	11 648	8 373	2 566
Average per farm.........................dollars, 1987..	11 961	8 031	5 579	7 793	76 672	7 331	29 379	3 015
Farms with net gains[2] ....number, 1987..	330	375	355	471	252	801	183	410
$1,000, 1987..	6 453	5 677	4 022	7 377	32 307	15 849	13 574	5 101
Average per farm.........................dollars, 1987..	19 555	15 138	11 330	15 662	128 204	19 787	74 176	12 442
Farms with net losses.....................number, 1987..	143	171	178	273	139	788	102	441
$1,000, 1987..	796	1 292	1 048	1 579	2 329	4 201	5 201	2 536
Average per farm.........................dollars, 1987..	5 563	7 554	5 890	5 783	16 753	5 331	50 992	5 750
GOVERNMENT PAYMENTS								
Total received...............................farms, 1987..	376	436	360	517	284	821	194	308
$1,000, 1987..	5 285	5 321	4 517	5 597	7 580	8 287	5 396	2 350
Average per farm.........................dollars, 1987..	14 056	12 205	11 888	10 826	26 689	10 093	27 812	7 631
Amount received in cash ....farms, 1987..	308	372	305	417	262	705	169	242
$1,000, 1987..	2 118	2 241	1 812	1 996	3 420	3 452	2 262	1 080
Value of commodity certificates received ....farms, 1987..	353	406	358	486	271	763	182	281
$1,000, 1987..	3 167	3 080	2 706	3 601	4 160	4 835	3 133	1 271
OTHER FARM-RELATED INCOME								
Gross before taxes and expenses[1] ....farms, 1987..	157	113	145	179	103	287	47	206
$1,000, 1987..	318	301	353	318	843	571	700	436
Average per farm.........................dollars, 1987..	2 026	2 667	2 438	1 775	8 182	1 991	14 898	2 097
Customwork and other agricultural services[3] ....farms, 1987..	45	41	38	82	65	85	30	62
1982..	55	58	51	83	48	141	27	66
$1,000, 1987..	145	137	153	160	611	219	492	128
1982..	149	354	480	211	442	477	337	228
Rental of farmland......................farms, 1987..	59	52	80	87	13	89	8	131
$1,000, 1987..	156	146	127	153	203	208	172	269
Sales of forest products and Christmas trees.......................................farms, 1987..	-	-	-	-	-	24	-	-
$1,000, 1987..	-	-	-	-	-	62	-	-
Other farm-related income sources ....farms, 1987..	78	45	44	25	45	122	27	39
$1,000, 1987..	18	19	73	4	29	83	37	40
COMMODITY CREDIT CORPORATION LOANS								
Total ....farms, 1987..	138	146	125	89	116	255	68	104
1982..	126	156	129	133	130	270	78	63
$1,000, 1987..	2 086	2 082	1 526	967	4 563	3 966	2 467	2 315
1982..	2 150	2 962	2 394	2 073	4 962	4 703	4 489	1 340
Corn ....farms, 1987..	5	4	-	-	36	34	16	55
$1,000, 1987..	(D)	60	-	-	(D)	1 039	663	1 520
Wheat.......................................farms, 1987..	102	107	96	60	73	164	36	7
$1,000, 1987..	1 412	1 399	1 009	696	1 755	1 398	(D)	(D)
Soybeans....................................farms, 1987..	1	-	1	4	1	13	1	15
$1,000, 1987..	(D)	-	(D)	20	(D)	(D)	(D)	198
Sorghum, barley, and oats......................farms, 1987..	77	85	64	43	73	126	40	63
$1,000, 1987..	635	622	(D)	251	1 655	1 310	1 213	565
Cotton.......................................farms, 1987..	-	-	-	-	-	-	-	-
$1,000, 1987..	-	-	-	-	-	-	-	-
Peanuts, rye, rice, tobacco, and honey.........farms, 1987..	-	-	-	-	-	1	-	2
$1,000, 1987..	-	-	-	-	-	(D)	-	(D)

See footnotes at end of table.

Table 4. **Net Cash Return From Agricultural Sales, Government Payments, Other Farm-Related Income, and Commodity Credit Corporation Loans: 1987 and 1982**—Con.

[For meaning of abbreviations and symbols, see introductory text]

Item	Sheridan	Sherman	Smith	Stafford	Stanton	Stevens	Sumner	Thomas
NET CASH RETURN								
Net cash return from agricultural sales for the farm unit (see text)[1] .... farms, 1987..	518	524	692	539	261	300	1 271	645
$1,000, 1987..	6 698	8 550	13 048	10 052	8 253	9 762	6 344	10 096
Average per farm .... dollars, 1987..	12 930	16 317	18 855	18 649	29 369	32 541	4 992	15 653
Farms with net gains[2] .... number, 1987..	376	369	541	328	146	169	638	428
$1,000, 1987..	8 934	11 020	14 243	12 134	9 689	11 519	11 300	13 367
Average per farm .... dollars, 1987..	23 761	29 865	26 327	36 994	66 360	68 159	17 712	31 232
Farms with net losses...................... number, 1987..	142	155	151	211	135	131	633	217
$1,000, 1987..	2 237	2 470	1 195	2 082	1 436	1 757	4 956	3 271
Average per farm .... dollars, 1987..	15 752	15 936	7 916	9 867	10 636	13 409	7 829	15 074
GOVERNMENT PAYMENTS								
Total received .... farms, 1987..	380	428	530	396	214	229	947	494
$1,000, 1987..	8 093	10 418	7 709	8 165	9 168	8 916	13 478	13 870
Average per farm .... dollars, 1987..	21 298	24 340	14 545	20 619	42 794	38 935	14 233	28 078
Amount received in cash .... farms, 1987..	354	379	487	366	183	203	738	454
$1,000, 1987..	3 811	4 378	3 333	3 738	3 971	3 941	5 072	6 255
Value of commodity certificates received .... farms, 1987..	367	408	512	375	210	218	890	479
$1,000, 1987..	4 283	6 040	4 376	4 427	5 187	4 975	8 406	7 615
OTHER FARM-RELATED INCOME								
Gross before taxes and expenses[1] .... farms, 1987..	147	164	236	188	64	67	392	231
$1,000, 1987..	838	929	791	856	659	358	1 288	1 432
Average per farm .... dollars, 1987..	5 702	5 663	3 350	4 556	10 302	5 344	3 286	6 199
Customwork and other agricultural services[3] .... farms, 1987..	62	103	93	81	33	24	170	100
1982..	87	76	124	83	34	28	155	83
$1,000, 1987..	(D)	467	351	317	272	178	622	578
1982..	739	628	615	583	422	169	767	1 095
Rental of farmland...................... farms, 1987..	62	53	68	96	13	31	125	96
$1,000, 1987..	409	384	318	454	326	(D)	430	760
Sales of forest products and Christmas trees .... farms, 1987..	-	-	6	1	-	-	6	-
$1,000, 1987..	-	-	7	(D)	-	-	1	-
Other farm-related income sources .... farms, 1987..	39	62	113	98	30	18	184	86
$1,000, 1987..	(D)	77	114	(D)	60	(D)	236	94
COMMODITY CREDIT CORPORATION LOANS								
Total .... farms, 1987..	229	188	291	172	96	93	260	212
1982..	189	171	232	195	84	105	303	153
$1,000, 1987..	7 458	7 526	5 602	4 884	5 620	6 023	3 756	9 143
1982..	7 257	9 747	4 859	6 587	5 143	6 609	6 574	8 835
Corn .... farms, 1987..	79	107	24	56	51	25	4	109
$1,000, 1987..	4 104	5 139	(D)	2 677	3 272	2 517	31	6 144
Wheat........................... farms, 1987..	136	89	168	58	52	26	232	76
$1,000, 1987..	1 814	1 904	2 037	706	1 156	(D)	3 484	(D)
Soybeans........................... farms, 1987..	9	1	8	10	4	1	7	6
$1,000, 1987..	134	(D)	(D)	81	(D)	(D)	22	(D)
Sorghum, barley, and oats...................... farms, 1987..	137	49	243	116	55	76	53	111
$1,000, 1987..	1 406	(D)	3 181	1 440	(D)	2 802	239	1 242
Cotton........................... farms, 1987..	-	-	-	-	-	-	-	-
$1,000, 1987..	-	-	-	-	-	-	-	-
Peanuts, rye, rice, tobacco, and honey........ farms, 1987..	-	-	-	-	-	-	-	-
$1,000, 1987..	-	-	-	-	-	-	-	-

See footnotes at end of table.

Table 4. **Net Cash Return From Agricultural Sales, Government Payments, Other Farm-Related Income, and Commodity Credit Corporation Loans: 1987 and 1982** —Con.

[For meaning of abbreviations and symbols, see introductory text]

Item	Trego	Wabaunsee	Wallace	Washington	Wichita	Wilson	Woodson	Wyandotte
NET CASH RETURN								
Net cash return from agricultural sales for the farm unit (see text)[1] ....farms, 1987..	482	632	330	938	354	609	368	199
$1,000, 1987..	5 257	3 744	5 125	11 117	32 095	3 353	4 682	842
Average per farm............dollars, 1987..	10 906	5 923	15 531	11 852	90 663	5 505	13 267	4 231
Farms with net gains[2] ....number, 1987..	342	352	212	621	238	379	233	101
$1,000, 1987..	6 049	5 533	6 296	13 346	33 527	5 292	5 935	1 182
Average per farm............dollars, 1987..	17 688	15 718	29 700	21 490	140 872	13 964	25 472	11 699
Farms with net losses............number, 1987..	140	280	118	317	116	230	135	98
$1,000, 1987..	793	1 789	1 171	2 229	1 433	1 940	1 053	340
Average per farm............dollars, 1987..	5 663	6 390	9 927	7 031	12 351	8 433	7 797	3 465
GOVERNMENT PAYMENTS								
Total received..............farms, 1987..	377	273	242	665	276	328	195	15
$1,000, 1987..	4 236	1 743	5 782	8 415	7 654	2 226	1 663	89
Average per farm............dollars, 1987..	11 237	6 385	23 893	12 654	27 732	6 788	8 530	5 914
Amount received in cash ....farms, 1987..	324	236	214	618	254	271	169	12
$1,000, 1987..	1 712	796	2 464	4 077	3 366	976	766	47
Value of commodity certificates received ......farms, 1987..	357	248	232	632	263	304	181	10
$1,000, 1987..	2 524	947	3 318	4 338	4 287	1 251	897	42
OTHER FARM-RELATED INCOME								
Gross before taxes and expenses[1] ....farms, 1987..	158	165	116	275	90	149	98	55
$1,000, 1987..	392	407	545	691	666	421	263	120
Average per farm............dollars, 1987..	2 480	2 466	4 697	2 512	7 403	2 824	2 688	2 173
Customwork and other agricultural services[3] ....farms, 1987..	53	55	53	117	49	47	38	17
1982..	53	51	55	107	52	65	40	6
$1,000, 1987..	234	198	232	242	352	111	100	33
1982..	182	230	291	220	322	210	123	22
Rental of farmland..............farms, 1987..	65	93	32	107	29	108	44	36
$1,000, 1987..	127	164	237	320	281	306	126	63
Sales of forest products and Christmas trees ....farms, 1987..	1	1	-	9	-	1	7	-
$1,000, 1987..	(D)	(D)	-	81	-	(D)	19	-
Other farm-related income sources ....farms, 1987..	63	32	52	114	36	3	43	6
$1,000, 1987..	(D)	(D)	76	46	34	(D)	38	24
COMMODITY CREDIT CORPORATION LOANS								
Total ....farms, 1987..	153	89	100	331	124	116	84	-
1982..	131	78	100	259	129	86	48	2
$1,000, 1987..	1 895	1 260	3 691	5 880	4 091	1 505	1 173	-
1982..	2 136	673	6 341	5 614	5 733	1 231	723	(D)
Corn ....farms, 1987..	4	25	57	49	55	12	11	-
$1,000, 1987..	(D)	524	2 438	507	(D)	106	72	-
Wheat..............farms, 1987..	120	20	56	80	61	24	7	-
$1,000, 1987..	1 217	51	966	606	1 099	100	(D)	-
Soybeans..............farms, 1987..	-	16	1	32	6	27	15	-
$1,000, 1987..	-	192	(D)	(D)	(D)	340	(D)	-
Sorghum, barley, and oats............farms, 1987..	80	65	27	297	80	100	74	-
$1,000, 1987..	(D)	493	(D)	4 021	1 064	959	812	-
Cotton..............farms, 1987..	-	-	-	-	-	-	-	-
$1,000, 1987..	-	-	-	-	-	-	-	-
Peanuts, rye, rice, tobacco, and honey..........farms, 1987..	-	-	-	7	-	-	-	-
$1,000, 1987..	-	-	-	(D)	-	-	-	-

[1]Data are based on a sample of farms.
[2]Farms with total production expenses equal to market value of agricultural products sold are included as farms with gains.
[3]Data for 1987 are based on a sample of farms; data for 1982 are nonsample.

Table 5. **Farms, Land in Farms, and Land Use: 1987 and 1982**

[For meaning of abbreviations and symbols, see introductory text.]

All Farms	Kansas	Allen	Anderson	Atchison	Barber	Barton	Bourbon
FARMS AND LAND IN FARMS							
Farms........................number, 1987..	68 579	665	727	694	535	937	842
1982..	73 315	735	797	768	517	962	882
Land in farms................acres, 1987..	46 628 519	276 555	352 141	233 619	700 147	556 433	318 958
1982..	47 052 213	283 878	361 247	234 730	698 700	559 531	337 259
Average size of farm........acres, 1987..	680	416	484	337	1 309	594	379
1982..	642	386	453	306	1 351	562	382
Value of land and buildings[1]:							
Average per farm........dollars, 1987..	278 047	177 737	172 158	176 069	371 298	260 449	145 606
1982..	384 197	231 902	248 012	236 656	710 521	419 004	201 959
Average per acre........dollars, 1987..	413	445	352	554	298	451	393
1982..	601	613	593	768	522	729	541
Approximate land area..........acres, 1987..	52 337 984	323 321	373 452	275 712	727 276	573 081	408 441
Proportion in farms...........percent, 1987..	89.1	85.5	94.3	84.7	96.3	97.1	78.1
1987 size of farm:							
1 to 9 acres...............farms..	3 689	28	47	48	49	80	34
acres..	9 327	61	112	120	118	201	75
10 to 49 acres............farms..	6 222	64	59	78	21	59	83
acres..	172 040	1 955	1 776	2 293	426	1 514	2 437
50 to 69 acres............farms..	1 849	20	29	30	8	15	33
acres..	107 904	1 205	1 692	1 764	455	876	1 953
70 to 99 acres............farms..	4 690	71	58	54	17	51	122
acres..	379 545	5 604	4 717	4 462	1 363	4 192	10 086
100 to 139 acres..........farms..	3 117	35	32	54	14	19	69
acres..	363 799	4 035	3 649	6 341	1 531	2 152	8 077
140 to 179 acres..........farms..	5 554	51	58	84	21	75	88
acres..	927 599	8 116	9 152	13 211	3 320	11 617	14 163
180 to 219 acres..........farms..	2 907	37	32	27	19	20	53
acres..	455 738	7 422	6 266	5 374	3 702	4 004	10 581
220 to 259 acres..........farms..	2 845	47	41	36	13	45	34
acres..	677 474	11 227	9 907	8 532	3 116	10 754	8 121
260 to 499 acres..........farms..	11 553	152	137	137	69	193	140
acres..	4 298 061	55 918	50 985	51 023	25 531	73 448	50 298
500 to 999 acres..........farms..	12 093	135	104	80	80	215	118
acres..	8 673 395	60 397	94 094	72 063	55 423	155 173	84 478
1,000 to 1,999 acres......farms..	9 304	62	76	35	127	116	47
acres..	12 925 552	83 115	105 055	48 793	175 301	156 529	62 660
2,000 acres or more.......farms..	5 056	13	23	7	97	49	21
acres..	17 640 082	37 510	64 816	19 643	429 861	135 775	66 029
1982 size of farm:							
1 to 9 acres...............farms..	3 547	25	44	65	27	51	20
acres..	9 498	55	84	165	55	149	51
10 to 49 acres............farms..	6 837	84	66	86	20	65	100
acres..	191 041	2 626	2 078	2 445	449	1 753	2 912
50 to 69 acres............farms..	2 053	25	38	25	4	14	32
acres..	119 295	1 455	2 263	1 425	230	780	1 867
70 to 99 acres............farms..	5 014	66	74	69	18	44	92
acres..	405 812	5 293	5 985	5 635	1 438	3 629	7 670
100 to 139 acres..........farms..	3 333	51	45	69	18	29	74
acres..	389 029	5 922	5 321	8 137	2 093	3 396	8 555
140 to 179 acres..........farms..	6 320	67	54	87	33	91	92
acres..	1 001 210	10 670	8 445	13 626	5 333	14 399	14 541
180 to 219 acres..........farms..	2 457	29	40	41	11	27	56
acres..	484 816	5 746	8 040	8 007	2 152	5 380	11 511
220 to 259 acres..........farms..	3 209	55	49	40	21	53	40
acres..	765 139	13 197	11 744	9 682	4 941	12 726	9 521
260 to 499 acres..........farms..	13 027	148	156	131	71	205	172
acres..	4 830 582	54 470	57 017	49 251	26 284	78 939	60 370
500 to 999 acres..........farms..	13 800	124	137	114	91	213	123
acres..	9 740 321	86 212	96 076	78 510	65 913	150 245	84 865
1,000 to 1,999 acres......farms..	9 428	50	69	37	103	134	63
acres..	12 918 501	67 934	92 753	47 499	141 296	178 576	83 374
2,000 acres or more.......farms..	4 490	11	25	4	100	36	16
acres..	16 196 969	30 296	71 441	10 348	448 516	109 559	52 022
LAND IN FARMS ACCORDING TO USE							
Total cropland..............farms, 1987..	61 615	595	640	630	449	645	733
1982..	66 481	664	723	683	465	909	772
acres, 1987..	31 385 090	189 229	230 886	178 038	255 328	467 019	167 986
1982..	30 598 859	189 302	219 621	174 199	249 225	471 425	183 316
Harvested cropland ....farms, 1987..	57 822	564	611	589	415	606	645
1982..	62 860	614	667	637	445	871	705
acres, 1987..	17 729 394	125 078	161 985	122 717	149 449	262 060	90 939
1982..	20 186 974	137 642	167 000	129 487	190 605	314 881	121 086
Cropland used only for pasture or grazing ....farms, 1987..	22 575	277	216	216	279	365	354
1982..	23 055	319	287	342	188	339	353
acres, 1987..	3 485 445	38 884	32 956	29 757	(D)	52 077	49 123
1982..	3 231 652	38 806	41 508	34 029	32 823	36 279	50 164
Other cropland ....farms, 1987..	43 046	310	371	361	263	725	294
1982..	34 770	240	230	263	159	696	174
acres, 1987..	10 170 251	25 267	35 945	25 564	(D)	172 882	27 923
1982..	7 180 233	12 854	11 113	10 683	25 797	120 265	12 246
Cropland in cover crops, legumes, and soil-improvement grasses, not harvested and not pastured ....farms, 1987..	11 212	85	146	136	82	130	136
1982..	5 739	84	55	90	27	101	70
acres, 1987..	1 103 315	3 754	11 293	5 440	11 386	12 141	11 907
1982..	290 742	3 223	2 106	2 601	1 520	5 701	3 876

See footnotes at end of table.

Table 5. **Farms, Land in Farms, and Land Use: 1987 and 1982**—Con.

[For meaning of abbreviations and symbols, see introductory text]

All Farms	Brown	Butler	Chase	Chautauqua	Cherokee	Cheyenne	Clark
FARMS AND LAND IN FARMS							
Farms .... number, 1987..	728	1 300	268	421	841	493	290
1982..	826	1 376	295	431	939	546	308
Land in farms .... acres, 1987..	339 853	699 487	328 905	320 956	280 704	619 870	587 574
1982..	346 340	691 281	414 905	333 958	296 716	602 726	588 288
Average size of farm .... acres, 1987..	467	538	1 142	762	334	1 257	2 026
1982..	419	502	1 406	775	316	1 104	1 910
Value of land and buildings¹:							
Average per farm .... dollars, 1987..	308 734	261 726	320 139	187 026	173 944	396 783	520 769
1982..	450 533	309 690	542 193	349 061	226 822	474 695	699 301
Average per acre .... dollars, 1987..	854	497	268	239	541	311	242
1982..	1 065	629	404	458	666	442	360
Approximate land area .... acres, 1987..	365 785	923 673	497 254	412 019	377 843	653 356	624 032
Proportion in farms .... percent, 1987..	92.9	75.7	66.1	77.9	74.3	94.8	94.2
1987 size of farm:							
1 to 9 acres .... farms..	48	62	10	23	32	17	16
acres..	95	159	14	63	102	(D)	36
10 to 49 acres .... farms..	52	191	22	18	157	14	6
acres..	1 416	5 523	664	639	4 567	(D)	110
50 to 69 acres .... farms..	9	55	7	7	52	2	2
acres..	521	3 249	443	419	3 027	(D)	(D)
70 to 99 acres .... farms..	55	136	11	32	93	15	8
acres..	4 478	10 652	906	2 558	7 536	(D)	(D)
100 to 139 acres .... farms..	40	69	18	27	61	11	-
acres..	4 643	8 071	2 196	3 147	7 103	1 165	-
140 to 179 acres .... farms..	85	115	11	37	75	21	16
acres..	13 455	18 218	1 742	5 907	11 754	3 389	2 558
180 to 219 acres .... farms..	23	45	10	20	41	5	7
acres..	4 640	8 904	1 974	3 940	8 107	1 025	(D)
220 to 259 acres .... farms..	42	71	10	29	39	9	1
acres..	9 960	16 823	2 353	6 874	9 252	2 085	(D)
260 to 499 acres .... farms..	151	162	51	77	112	73	48
acres..	54 477	58 907	18 985	27 930	39 968	28 312	18 521
500 to 999 acres .... farms..	129	169	64	63	108	104	53
acres..	92 278	121 751	44 492	44 254	78 497	78 336	39 174
1,000 to 1,999 acres .... farms..	76	140	43	50	57	136	56
acres..	105 452	189 641	62 378	67 175	71 933	195 157	80 379
2,000 acres or more .... farms..	18	66	31	38	14	88	77
acres..	48 438	250 666	192 760	158 050	38 856	308 684	444 387
1982 size of farm:							
1 to 9 acres .... farms..	46	59	5	17	40	33	15
acres..	103	175	8	44	145	80	37
10 to 49 acres .... farms..	78	215	18	25	195	11	11
acres..	2 115	6 265	469	744	5 442	249	363
50 to 69 acres .... farms..	25	48	7	8	41	5	-
acres..	1 471	2 763	423	461	2 392	256	-
70 to 99 acres .... farms..	64	147	9	20	83	10	6
acres..	5 161	11 774	722	1 602	6 716	811	470
100 to 139 acres .... farms..	24	75	20	24	60	7	6
acres..	2 887	8 727	2 340	2 804	9 371	765	762
140 to 179 acres .... farms..	79	129	25	48	83	25	19
acres..	12 540	20 462	3 888	7 617	12 993	4 035	3 047
180 to 219 acres .... farms..	37	69	5	22	48	5	6
acres..	7 261	13 454	949	4 378	9 169	1 034	(D)
220 to 259 acres .... farms..	46	74	10	29	45	11	2
acres..	10 929	17 649	2 429	7 020	10 469	2 644	(D)
260 to 499 acres .... farms..	184	193	54	73	120	105	47
acres..	66 676	67 916	19 532	26 379	43 424	39 837	17 520
500 to 999 acres .... farms..	159	187	56	78	143	113	56
acres..	110 954	134 252	41 624	51 765	100 993	84 377	39 956
1,000 to 1,999 acres .... farms..	75	121	43	47	53	142	60
acres..	102 398	166 081	58 763	62 708	68 346	201 680	86 135
2,000 acres or more .... farms..	9	59	43	42	10	79	60
acres..	21 845	241 723	283 738	168 436	27 258	266 958	438 349
LAND IN FARMS ACCORDING TO USE							
Total cropland .... farms, 1987..	657	1 075	247	307	725	454	256
1982..	767	1 159	253	335	813	509	267
acres, 1987..	272 083	341 336	84 665	73 008	210 941	403 719	198 178
1982..	277 857	316 481	73 363	68 352	218 697	393 440	189 767
Harvested cropland .... farms, 1987..	637	934	223	248	657	426	233
1982..	732	1 053	238	294	729	491	254
acres, 1987..	197 847	210 975	45 580	35 741	156 409	176 293	92 271
1982..	226 953	225 388	49 790	40 581	166 648	197 174	113 399
Cropland used only for pasture or grazing .... farms, 1987..	265	449	101	126	251	122	115
1982..	351	467	88	162	311	132	61
acres, 1987..	25 179	67 067	23 523	20 444	20 566	32 327	23 227
1982..	35 119	58 961	13 883	24 614	21 914	28 629	(D)
Other cropland .... farms, 1987..	493	565	133	130	330	416	204
1982..	280	398	97	80	199	422	184
acres, 1987..	49 057	63 294	15 562	16 823	33 946	195 099	82 680
1982..	15 785	32 132	9 690	3 157	10 135	167 637	(D)
Cropland in cover crops, legumes, and soil-improvement grasses, not harvested and not pastured .... farms, 1987..	217	142	47	32	89	125	56
1982..	105	80	21	23	52	24	12
acres, 1987..	13 504	12 457	3 064	2 679	6 433	17 600	11 752
1982..	4 462	5 348	3 280	714	1 284	2 718	(D)

See footnotes at end of table.

Table 5. Farms, Land in Farms, and Land Use: 1987 and 1982—Con.

[For meaning of abbreviations and symbols, see introductory text]

All Farms	Clay	Cloud	Coffey	Comanche	Cowley	Crawford	Decatur
FARMS AND LAND IN FARMS							
Farms...number, 1987	672	659	606	277	997	809	486
1982	719	728	671	259	1 101	915	516
Land in farms...acres, 1987	392 321	397 383	330 435	481 136	619 647	283 589	543 466
1982	365 074	403 290	335 242	482 734	699 678	325 062	535 067
Average size of farm...acres, 1987	584	603	545	1 737	622	351	1 118
1982	508	555	500	1 787	635	355	1 037
Value of land and buildings[1]:							
Average per farm...dollars, 1987	242 841	262 653	195 295	417 993	230 291	154 295	350 809
1982	268 586	339 944	255 518	640 950	347 020	258 532	525 467
Average per acre...dollars, 1987	426	407	357	266	385	436	292
1982	568	635	848	362	551	748	500
Approximate land area...acres, 1987	404 185	459 315	393 580	504 832	721 753	380 697	571 993
Proportion in farms...percent, 1987	97.1	86.5	84.0	95.3	85.9	74.5	95.0
1987 size of farm:							
1 to 9 acres...farms	44	41	25	26	52	40	22
acres	116	114	72	(D)	147	121	30
10 to 49 acres...farms	29	34	46	4	111	100	18
acres	733	858	1 366	(D)	3 081	3 001	468
50 to 69 acres...farms	6	20	18	2	33	31	5
acres	345	1 198	1 076	(D)	1 885	1 762	294
70 to 99 acres...farms	37	37	51	4	85	91	12
acres	3 006	2 939	4 137	(D)	6 796	7 288	972
100 to 139 acres...farms	22	31	33	7	46	59	5
acres	2 528	3 605	3 811	818	5 478	7 015	530
140 to 179 acres...farms	60	65	58	16	105	74	26
acres	9 581	10 354	9 164	2 515	16 715	11 686	4 009
180 to 219 acres...farms	16	16	28	9	24	41	14
acres	3 219	3 188	5 548	1 806	4 718	7 901	2 812
220 to 259 acres...farms	42	34	31	5	43	66	10
acres	10 014	8 151	7 497	1 169	10 202	15 655	2 381
260 to 499 acres...farms	127	116	98	22	170	150	60
acres	47 350	43 533	36 264	8 346	64 304	54 651	23 511
500 to 999 acres...farms	158	121	125	54	176	96	98
acres	112 800	87 494	86 759	39 445	125 687	66 029	71 188
1,000 to 1,999 acres...farms	108	112	63	43	93	45	142
acres	144 610	151 010	84 758	57 986	125 575	60 564	207 083
2,000 acres or more...farms	23	32	30	61	59	16	75
acres	58 039	84 939	87 983	368 375	255 059	47 896	230 188
1982 size of farm:							
1 to 9 acres...farms	38	49	30	12	54	44	30
acres	104	147	107	28	152	144	76
10 to 49 acres...farms	39	59	60	7	148	151	10
acres	977	1 510	1 688	(D)	4 113	4 261	(D)
50 to 69 acres...farms	13	15	21	2	34	32	2
acres	755	848	1 194	(D)	1 955	1 831	(D)
70 to 99 acres...farms	32	43	60	3	72	76	11
acres	2 545	3 497	4 918	240	5 805	6 153	906
100 to 139 acres...farms	26	25	42	6	51	62	6
acres	2 859	2 840	4 749	941	6 076	7 309	683
140 to 179 acres...farms	69	61	52	14	97	92	27
acres	10 875	9 730	8 278	2 229	15 287	14 440	4 341
180 to 219 acres...farms	25	22	39	8	36	57	13
acres	4 669	4 348	7 633	1 590	7 077	11 302	2 580
220 to 259 acres...farms	52	41	37	4	58	58	10
acres	12 448	9 761	8 776	970	13 779	13 825	2 384
260 to 499 acres...farms	154	126	120	26	186	129	69
acres	57 316	46 196	43 109	9 097	69 163	46 822	24 552
500 to 999 acres...farms	163	154	123	56	184	149	127
acres	114 975	111 917	85 727	41 679	128 051	106 055	91 853
1,000 to 1,999 acres...farms	93	109	56	52	115	48	141
acres	120 461	148 033	77 326	73 278	155 933	62 433	197 438
2,000 acres or more...farms	15	22	31	67	66	17	70
acres	36 890	64 463	91 735	332 326	292 297	50 507	209 747
LAND IN FARMS ACCORDING TO USE							
Total cropland...farms, 1987	614	611	549	230	659	706	452
1982	668	663	610	230	666	782	472
acres, 1987	283 874	293 364	208 591	187 433	269 262	181 598	358 393
1982	253 377	279 045	198 328	178 526	269 653	202 892	338 557
Harvested cropland...farms, 1987	586	583	515	209	760	649	438
1982	647	642	572	215	885	725	459
acres, 1987	176 217	184 007	142 668	93 062	160 551	116 714	175 861
1982	189 827	214 074	157 589	118 915	212 326	155 932	172 883
Cropland used only for pasture or grazing...farms, 1987	249	203	209	93	328	321	157
1982	230	247	215	80	347	300	121
acres, 1987	44 220	37 971	36 977	(D)	50 343	32 769	39 965
1982	38 057	30 222	28 949	(D)	36 999	30 473	25 934
Other cropland...farms, 1987	510	507	333	192	520	316	393
1982	384	335	208	141	289	225	409
acres, 1987	63 437	71 386	28 746	(D)	58 368	32 115	140 567
1982	25 493	34 749	11 790	(D)	18 328	16 487	139 940
Cropland in cover crops, legumes, and soil-improvement grasses, not harvested and not pastured...farms, 1987	122	140	108	75	140	91	72
1982	76	76	51	18	94	55	34
acres, 1987	5 292	6 730	5 582	18 064	9 153	7 192	5 146
1982	2 246	6 140	3 337	(D)	4 487	2 413	5 950

See footnotes at end of table.

Table 5. **Farms, Land in Farms, and Land Use: 1987 and 1982**—Con.

[For meaning of abbreviations and symbols, see introductory text]

	All Farms						
	Dickinson	Doniphan	Douglas	Edwards	Elk	Ellis	Ellsworth
FARMS AND LAND IN FARMS							
Farms .... number, 1987..	1 028	530	852	361	409	795	499
1982..	1 149	620	896	402	467	790	527
Land in farms .... acres, 1987..	513 946	216 179	223 426	387 309	340 899	568 934	423 655
1982..	527 451	224 519	222 859	382 477	364 902	509 050	387 572
Average size of farm .... acres, 1987..	500	408	262	1 073	833	716	849
1982..	459	362	249	951	781	644	735
Value of land and buildings[1]:							
Average per farm .... dollars, 1987..	209 824	279 453	195 964	455 709	237 000	264 675	276 723
1982..	278 205	351 167	248 925	594 746	312 418	375 509	341 365
Average per acre .... dollars, 1987..	446	741	827	423	277	381	338
1982..	645	1 007	944	609	429	610	492
Approximate land area ...... acres, 1987..	545 356	248 083	294 886	396 531	416 019	576 288	458 867
Proportion in farms .... percent, 1987..	94.2	87.1	75.8	97.7	81.9	98.7	92.3
1987 size of farm:							
1 to 9 acres .... farms..	68	47	48	10	16	53	18
acres..	152	113	160	(D)	45	67	40
10 to 49 acres .... farms..	80	64	157	10	17	43	18
acres..	1 833	1 656	4 334	(D)	526	1 199	475
50 to 69 acres .... farms..	27	16	65	1	8	11	4
acres..	1 587	1 109	3 843	(D)	473	591	249
70 to 99 acres .... farms..	68	44	100	9	30	49	16
acres..	5 546	3 558	8 046	(D)	2 383	3 984	1 350
100 to 139 acres .... farms..	37	32	69	7	15	36	29
acres..	4 272	3 806	8 037	765	1 767	4 208	3 326
140 to 179 acres .... farms..	107	39	111	19	36	80	33
acres..	16 907	6 171	17 464	3 043	5 725	12 668	5 209
180 to 219 acres .... farms..	38	22	50	6	15	17	17
acres..	7 522	4 375	9 876	1 187	2 883	3 386	3 326
220 to 259 acres .... farms..	46	17	26	18	19	22	13
acres..	10 977	4 147	6 190	4 267	4 592	5 273	3 090
260 to 499 acres .... farms..	219	97	107	69	81	166	93
acres..	81 445	36 727	36 639	26 495	29 037	63 230	34 396
500 to 999 acres .... farms..	207	92	74	68	82	173	103
acres..	147 565	64 642	52 666	50 093	56 267	122 806	77 058
1,000 to 1,999 acres .... farms..	124	51	37	84	48	97	115
acres..	162 707	66 050	52 409	121 378	66 956	139 866	153 776
2,000 acres or more .... farms..	27	7	8	60	42	48	40
acres..	73 433	21 625	21 562	179 039	168 245	211 636	141 360
1982 size of farm:							
1 to 9 acres .... farms..	69	39	42	14	18	38	18
acres..	182	95	166	37	50	65	24
10 to 49 acres .... farms..	79	84	183	8	30	37	16
acres..	2 290	2 358	5 399	243	999	622	482
50 to 69 acres .... farms..	31	21	66	4	5	13	10
acres..	1 788	1 255	3 928	220	285	749	581
70 to 99 acres .... farms..	94	58	109	5	25	44	25
acres..	7 577	4 752	8 812	407	2 019	3 533	2 077
100 to 139 acres .... farms..	43	40	50	6	14	45	22
acres..	5 150	4 495	6 810	718	1 627	5 174	2 615
140 to 179 acres .... farms..	121	46	107	34	55	87	29
acres..	19 158	7 262	16 803	5 373	8 832	13 840	4 668
180 to 219 acres .... farms..	34	17	42	10	24	24	22
acres..	6 695	3 479	8 289	1 955	4 389	4 638	4 364
220 to 259 acres .... farms..	48	27	40	6	22	25	23
acres..	11 435	6 371	9 572	1 450	5 228	5 677	5 400
260 to 499 acres .... farms..	261	143	128	91	95	161	98
acres..	96 525	54 200	45 657	34 869	30 801	59 275	36 146
500 to 999 acres .... farms..	248	95	79	91	95	191	134
acres..	179 172	64 397	53 754	65 996	67 481	135 034	98 242
1,000 to 1,999 acres .... farms..	100	43	35	86	64	79	97
acres..	130 170	54 365	46 975	121 680	90 496	103 777	127 753
2,000 acres or more .... farms..	21	7	5	47	35	46	31
acres..	65 309	21 440	16 694	149 329	152 596	175 889	105 220
LAND IN FARMS ACCORDING TO USE							
Total cropland .... farms, 1987..	940	474	757	339	334	718	470
1982..	1 053	575	807	376	376	733	496
acres, 1987..	392 686	168 755	154 565	316 104	85 006	333 262	247 187
1982..	391 965	173 411	151 361	313 480	93 123	291 381	234 994
Harvested cropland .... farms, 1987..	908	454	691	328	293	691	450
1982..	1 012	543	740	373	348	640	471
acres, 1987..	245 504	127 666	108 664	186 513	40 040	147 980	128 533
1982..	297 527	150 592	112 308	206 856	54 719	162 248	146 178
Cropland used only for pasture or grazing .... farms, 1987..	394	170	342	110	163	272	184
1982..	418	213	339	82	175	209	160
acres, 1987..	57 415	13 278	25 677	19 829	31 102	54 475	40 990
1982..	62 366	16 766	28 469	14 195	31 584	(D)	28 777
Other cropland .... farms, 1987..	721	328	296	296	139	600	406
1982..	501	174	240	310	75	579	394
acres, 1987..	89 767	27 791	20 224	109 762	13 864	130 827	77 644
1982..	32 072	6 051	10 586	92 429	6 820	(D)	60 039
Cropland in cover crops, legumes, and soil-improvement grasses, not harvested and not pastured ..... farms, 1987..	179	151	128	49	66	94	108
1982..	121	73	47	20	22	48	64
acres, 1987..	16 132	6 975	5 379	9 903	3 971	10 464	6 265
1982..	4 428	1 727	1 443	2 808	2 987	2 642	2 053

See footnotes at end of table.

Table 5. Farms, Land in Farms, and Land Use: 1987 and 1982—Con.

[For meaning of abbreviations and symbols, see introductory text]

All Farms	Finney	Ford	Franklin	Geary	Gove	Graham	Grant
FARMS AND LAND IN FARMS							
Farms .... number, 1987..	534	812	979	295	534	452	309
1982..	558	838	1 087	299	548	495	276
Land in farms .... acres, 1987..	722 746	674 986	312 783	170 339	676 575	503 589	323 138
1982..	721 624	691 933	304 871	156 662	674 683	523 102	332 993
Average size of farm ...... acres, 1987..	1 353	831	319	577	1 267	1 114	1 066
1982..	1 293	826	280	524	1 231	1 057	1 206
Value of land and buildings[1]:							
Average per farm .... dollars, 1987..	656 750	341 901	181 876	237 777	350 782	412 628	535 811
1982..	893 068	431 192	202 411	255 435	621 394	412 152	901 322
Average per acre .... dollars, 1987..	499	429	585	429	397	317	513
1982..	680	526	727	518	462	397	777
Approximate land area .... acres, 1987..	833 356	703 187	369 427	241 203	685 968	575 014	368 108
Proportion in farms .... percent, 1987..	86.7	96.0	84.7	70.8	96.6	87.5	87.8
1987 size of farm:							
1 to 9 acres .... farms..	37	50	46	23	51	17	17
acres..	124	130	131	87	84	(D)	36
10 to 49 acres .... farms..	25	55	163	32	17	19	8
acres..	624	1 253	4 853	921	395	(D)	168
50 to 69 acres .... farms..	3	16	67	14	6	2	6
acres..	156	902	4 003	809	347	(D)	341
70 to 99 acres .... farms..	12	34	129	16	8	7	8
acres..	975	2 837	10 496	1 224	648	(D)	504
100 to 139 acres .... farms..	5	19	73	22	6	11	3
acres..	555	2 212	8 436	2 625	789	1 294	367
140 to 179 acres .... farms..	32	59	94	14	37	38	24
acres..	5 047	9 441	14 722	2 180	5 684	6 072	3 842
180 to 219 acres .... farms..	8	13	48	12	5	14	3
acres..	1 568	2 556	9 571	2 374	985	2 729	(D)
220 to 259 acres .... farms..	12	15	42	14	5	7	2
acres..	2 854	3 566	10 135	3 402	1 200	1 684	(D)
260 to 499 acres .... farms..	70	139	143	46	69	69	52
acres..	26 785	53 756	50 489	16 918	26 330	26 513	20 105
500 to 999 acres .... farms..	81	189	103	45	102	86	56
acres..	60 596	136 568	72 381	33 648	75 424	61 589	40 188
1,000 to 1,999 acres .... farms..	127	136	56	43	123	105	81
acres..	176 349	190 233	76 218	58 155	175 796	152 791	118 821
2,000 acres or more .... farms..	122	87	15	15	105	78	45
acres..	447 113	271 530	51 348	47 996	388 693	249 637	137 696
1982 size of farm:							
1 to 9 acres .... farms..	36	57	50	24	19	9	14
acres..	117	142	136	100	25	21	29
10 to 49 acres .... farms..	22	44	197	39	8	11	13
acres..	456	1 201	5 698	1 178	221	304	374
50 to 69 acres .... farms..	6	11	81	9	10	4	3
acres..	344	650	4 798	498	629	236	152
70 to 99 acres .... farms..	10	24	151	15	12	12	4
acres..	813	1 889	12 260	1 236	936	954	319
100 to 139 acres .... farms..	4	31	85	12	4	10	1
acres..	496	3 668	9 951	1 455	460	1 195	(D)
140 to 179 acres .... farms..	40	70	97	17	37	51	24
acres..	6 404	11 017	15 392	2 662	(D)	8 166	3 705
180 to 219 acres .... farms..	7	10	47	12	2	17	6
acres..	1 295	1 976	9 290	2 401	(D)	3 333	1 180
220 to 259 acres .... farms..	8	19	47	16	19	8	2
acres..	1 918	4 532	11 212	3 754	4 600	1 924	(D)
260 to 499 acres .... farms..	63	152	147	47	88	76	55
acres..	24 752	57 722	52 412	17 534	33 554	29 010	9 400
500 to 999 acres .... farms..	117	165	122	54	126	104	57
acres..	85 356	133 426	86 909	37 847	95 905	72 528	42 651
1,000 to 1,999 acres .... farms..	141	156	50	40	125	119	74
acres..	203 241	223 173	65 907	51 567	184 169	174 799	103 744
2,000 acres or more .... farms..	104	77	13	14	99	74	53
acres..	396 432	252 535	30 906	96 430	347 953	230 632	170 839
LAND IN FARMS ACCORDING TO USE							
Total cropland .... farms, 1987..	492	743	876	255	470	426	271
1982..	512	757	970	260	515	496	243
acres, 1987..	581 793	549 220	207 599	77 496	445 010	320 474	277 331
1982..	590 997	522 401	187 710	72 325	410 238	322 236	293 383
Harvested cropland .... farms, 1987..	463	703	799	239	454	403	258
1982..	494	730	895	250	485	464	236
acres, 1987..	323 607	284 042	135 097	46 216	194 728	148 177	156 356
1982..	384 552	301 832	142 823	50 305	195 149	161 560	199 136
Cropland used only for pasture or grazing ..... farms, 1987..	91	235	381	98	129	125	66
1982..	102	180	435	93	121	134	42
acres, 1987..	17 424	34 658	39 119	15 501	(D)	27 846	(D)
1982..	(D)	28 761	37 530	11 928	23 171	37 523	(D)
Other cropland .... farms, 1987..	422	618	397	161	438	383	225
1982..	404	588	312	113	462	398	169
acres, 1987..	240 762	230 520	33 363	13 779	(D)	144 451	(D)
1982..	(D)	191 808	17 257	10 092	191 918	123 153	(D)
Cropland in cover crops, legumes, and soil-improvement grasses, not harvested and not pastured .... farms, 1987..	71	96	153	33	77	117	47
1982..	18	31	69	14	14	45	17
acres, 1987..	19 452	13 398	6 432	2 904	6 288	19 693	(D)
1982..	(D)	2 623	1 807	2 820	1 043	2 359	(D)

See footnotes at end of table.

Table 5. **Farms, Land in Farms, and Land Use: 1987 and 1982**—Con.

[For meaning of abbreviations and symbols, see introductory text]

All Farms	Gray	Greeley	Greenwood	Hamilton	Harper	Harvey	Haskell
FARMS AND LAND IN FARMS							
Farms .... number, 1987	547	294	587	279	648	874	315
1982	552	277	651	270	660	923	324
Land in farms .... acres, 1987	532 284	475 278	549 507	538 449	484 471	309 123	369 850
1982	536 969	445 982	601 823	544 916	490 455	320 935	361 301
Average size of farm .... acres, 1987	973	1 617	936	1 930	748	354	1 174
1982	973	1 610	924	2 016	743	348	1 115
Value of land and buildings[1]:							
Average per farm .... dollars, 1987	479 429	668 113	314 348	568 527	314 048	253 936	757 035
1982	671 147	787 477	389 008	791 667	582 923	313 845	979 960
Average per acre .... dollars, 1987	518	419	320	306	425	658	654
1982	682	482	423	394	789	1 005	872
Approximate land area .... acres, 1987	555 276	498 156	726 214	638 425	513 318	345 862	369 696
Proportion in farms .... percent, 1987	95.9	95.4	75.7	84.3	94.4	89.4	100.0
1987 size of farm:							
1 to 9 acres .... farms	37	14	36	8	36	79	16
acres	79	25	53	22	78	199	20
10 to 49 acres .... farms	12	3	41	10	38	146	8
acres	284	84	1 165	323	1 022	3 705	139
50 to 69 acres .... farms	4	–	12	–	3	18	3
acres	226	–	709	–	181	1 116	167
70 to 99 acres .... farms	12	11	37	4	23	77	(D)
acres	1 021	906	3 046	(D)	1 848	6 227	(D)
100 to 139 acres .... farms	11	7	23	1	16	37	2
acres	1 304	748	2 656	(D)	1 887	4 388	(D)
140 to 179 acres .... farms	50	18	59	17	55	83	24
acres	7 975	2 851	9 392	2 723	6 722	13 167	3 766
180 to 219 acres .... farms	5	5	26	3	24	23	2
acres	1 053	(D)	5 215	(D)	4 723	4 544	(D)
220 to 259 acres .... farms	9	2	27	1	26	34	2
acres	2 168	(D)	6 471	(D)	6 176	8 034	(D)
260 to 499 acres .... farms	105	58	106	25	116	168	40
acres	41 235	22 210	38 657	10 284	44 653	62 725	15 208
500 to 999 acres .... farms	119	52	93	52	138	146	76
acres	87 538	33 962	65 179	39 428	100 082	104 539	55 923
1,000 to 1,999 acres .... farms	113	44	67	50	122	49	68
acres	158 424	63 438	95 335	74 606	172 557	62 965	129 660
2,000 acres or more .... farms	70	85	60	108	51	14	51
acres	230 957	349 578	321 629	409 750	142 340	37 494	163 612
1982 size of farm:							
1 to 9 acres .... farms	23	8	10	9	25	49	21
acres	57	(D)	24	19	39	156	22
10 to 49 acres .... farms	15	3	51	7	28	113	1
acres	339	95	1 483	245	757	3 133	(D)
50 to 69 acres .... farms	4	–	9	1	5	31	–
acres	219	–	504	(D)	275	1 817	–
70 to 99 acres .... farms	13	5	42	7	37	89	3
acres	1 109	395	3 319	580	2 983	7 121	240
100 to 139 acres .... farms	3	2	31	4	18	40	5
acres	350	(D)	3 689	490	2 082	4 624	590
140 to 179 acres .... farms	50	27	65	17	69	104	17
acres	(D)	4 306	10 433	2 694	10 922	16 549	2 706
180 to 219 acres .... farms	2	2	22	2	12	37	5
acres	11	(D)	4 379	(D)	2 395	7 263	870
220 to 259 acres .... farms	11	5	31	1	28	61	2
acres	2 650	1 200	7 382	(D)	6 670	14 534	(D)
260 to 499 acres .... farms	122	50	111	27	104	190	60
acres	47 697	17 980	43 956	9 686	39 601	68 929	22 265
500 to 999 acres .... farms	139	36	111	27	163	146	76
acres	101 013	26 517	80 266	20 693	117 477	99 614	57 689
1,000 to 1,999 acres .... farms	105	64	91	63	122	53	89
acres	145 893	89 648	123 237	93 386	185 636	69 802	128 641
2,000 acres or more .... farms	65	75	69	106	49	10	45
acres	229 274	305 203	323 151	416 456	141 618	27 387	(D)
LAND IN FARMS ACCORDING TO USE							
Total cropland .... farms, 1987	504	279	461	253	612	786	296
1982	516	267	559	249	630	853	292
acres, 1987	464 775	430 182	127 714	404 212	349 932	274 647	333 685
1982	462 344	401 691	135 634	424 189	343 378	273 373	329 514
Harvested cropland .... farms, 1987	480	266	409	225	595	740	284
1982	502	259	499	237	617	826	290
acres, 1987	258 379	196 152	73 937	160 504	233 900	197 917	200 065
1982	325 993	193 327	81 686	204 376	288 418	232 904	249 122
Cropland used only for pasture or grazing .... farms, 1987	142	53	186	61	215	262	72
1982	122	40	242	65	233	250	52
acres, 1987	(D)	12 671	36 489	15 022	42 398	15 930	(D)
1982	(D)	(D)	42 804	(D)	37 326	19 816	7 523
Other cropland .... farms, 1987	452	256	193	223	417	584	256
1982	406	240	173	207	180	410	225
acres, 1987	(D)	221 339	17 288	226 686	73 634	60 800	(D)
1982	(D)	(D)	11 144	(D)	17 634	20 653	72 869
Cropland in cover crops, legumes, and soil-improvement grasses, not harvested and not pastured .... farms, 1987	61	46	85	97	107	94	26
1982	29	18	43	11	42	66	4
acres, 1987	11 961	15 163	7 164	55 246	13 837	5 200	4 067
1982	4 669	(D)	2 784	(D)	2 154	1 956	(D)

See footnotes at end of table.

Table 5. **Farms, Land in Farms, and Land Use: 1987 and 1982**—Con.

[For meaning of abbreviations and symbols, see introductory text]

All Farms	Hodgeman	Jackson	Jefferson	Jewell	Johnson	Kearny	Kingman	Kiowa
FARMS AND LAND IN FARMS								
Farms_____ number, 1987__	423	1 082	1 017	738	659	291	816	310
1982__	466	1 156	1 047	808	766	297	860	354
Land in farms_____ acres, 1987__	495 080	335 142	263 592	502 106	151 763	549 371	517 662	392 245
1982__	482 739	376 330	271 691	510 447	169 986	532 077	492 197	422 852
Average size of farm_____ acres, 1987__	1 170	310	259	682	230	1 888	633	1 265
1982__	1 036	326	259	632	222	1 792	572	1 194
Value of land and buildings[1]:								
Average per farm_____ dollars, 1987__	385 670	127 956	168 696	246 574	322 914	740 880	269 880	404 694
1982__	514 236	199 151	223 582	357 588	400 038	806 626	390 653	485 102
Average per acre_____ dollars, 1987__	312	427	619	389	1 334	378	434	340
1982__	474	599	853	534	1 761	419	690	441
Approximate land area_____ acres, 1987__	550 656	420 825	342 630	582 182	305 849	555 315	553 875	462 572
Proportion in farms_____ percent, 1987__	89.9	79.6	76.9	86.2	49.6	98.9	93.5	84.8
1987 size of farm:								
1 to 9 acres_____ farms__	18	40	36	44	41	16	31	12
acres__	(D)	93	123	103	135	35	71	(D)
10 to 49 acres_____ farms__	20	138	179	42	195	8	62	6
acres__	(D)	4 147	5 009	1 136	5 151	209	1 787	(D)
50 to 69 acres_____ farms__	2	33	62	7	54	3	8	2
acres__	(D)	1 909	3 625	393	3 190	170	451	(D)
70 to 99 acres_____ farms__	7	158	136	21	72	8	51	7
acres__	(D)	12 810	11 125	1 655	5 825	665	4 219	(D)
100 to 139 acres_____ farms__	6	78	106	26	45	4	22	4
acres__	978	9 214	12 234	3 126	5 042	497	2 640	460
140 to 179 acres_____ farms__	17	137	116	58	47	24	74	17
acres__	2 710	21 707	18 506	9 260	7 399	3 766	11 787	2 718
180 to 219 acres_____ farms__	5	55	52	26	28	5	32	5
acres__	996	10 837	10 435	5 210	5 542	970	6 319	973
220 to 259 acres_____ farms__	8	64	48	37	19	4	41	9
acres__	1 926	15 268	11 442	8 623	4 529	985	9 825	2 115
260 to 499 acres_____ farms__	69	174	139	144	77	25	162	44
acres__	26 560	63 114	48 987	52 892	27 744	9 025	59 772	16 506
500 to 999 acres_____ farms__	83	140	89	154	50	43	165	71
acres__	61 217	99 226	58 823	110 024	33 634	30 996	119 627	52 715
1,000 to 1,999 acres_____ farms__	104	55	44	131	27	61	130	71
acres__	147 717	72 575	59 579	180 960	37 602	89 846	180 170	96 304
2,000 acres or more_____ farms__	82	10	10	46	4	90	62	62
acres__	251 671	24 240	23 703	128 720	15 970	412 205	120 984	219 616
1982 size of farm:								
1 to 9 acres_____ farms__	16	46	43	38	51	20	32	11
acres__	22	149	178	56	179	34	59	11
10 to 49 acres_____ farms__	17	152	196	34	207	15	59	15
acres__	(D)	4 473	5 624	822	5 855	336	1 615	363
50 to 69 acres_____ farms__	4	42	55	20	53	4	16	4
acres__	(D)	2 399	3 194	1 152	3 104	249	938	224
70 to 99 acres_____ farms__	3	169	138	37	85	4	44	13
acres__	220	13 689	11 099	2 987	6 978	324	3 607	1 059
100 to 139 acres_____ farms__	11	66	97	22	68	5	39	5
acres__	1 349	7 900	11 462	2 514	7 859	841	4 466	560
140 to 179 acres_____ farms__	35	134	105	67	57	27	73	16
acres__	5 590	21 294	16 518	10 706	8 952	4 250	11 638	(D)
180 to 219 acres_____ farms__	5	58	56	32	39	4	30	2
acres__	963	11 350	11 019	6 521	7 586	(D)	6 023	(D)
220 to 259 acres_____ farms__	12	71	46	42	34	2	49	12
acres__	2 773	17 068	10 877	10 031	8 158	(D)	11 716	2 827
260 to 499 acres_____ farms__	72	161	153	176	82	34	191	54
acres__	27 751	57 435	53 265	62 121	30 500	13 131	72 771	20 167
500 to 999 acres_____ farms__	111	174	106	178	54	44	175	86
acres__	84 778	118 060	72 698	126 204	42 254	33 565	127 031	62 974
1,000 to 1,999 acres_____ farms__	114	68	45	130	21	52	116	87
acres__	157 011	89 889	59 126	178 269	28 080	74 258	153 332	116 518
2,000 acres or more_____ farms__	89	11	7	43	5	84	36	50
acres__	201 689	32 604	16 642	109 062	20 701	403 848	98 986	215 214
LAND IN FARMS ACCORDING TO USE								
Total cropland_____ farms, 1987__	390	957	900	669	568	257	759	294
1982__	433	1 027	936	741	659	259	798	328
acres, 1987__	343 039	208 974	177 972	354 217	106 667	392 706	363 772	262 470
1982__	322 953	224 824	181 978	346 850	119 893	384 272	346 061	245 857
Harvested cropland_____ farms, 1987__	362	844	836	647	486	247	718	276
1982__	417	951	855	719	555	242	772	317
acres, 1987__	159 903	114 691	112 895	208 845	69 445	202 166	219 446	128 425
1982__	164 424	139 408	128 243	249 175	89 696	216 509	265 252	144 836
Cropland used only for pasture or grazing_____ farms, 1987__	124	458	435	271	281	64	306	109
1982__	94	473	429	246	306	76	265	83
acres, 1987__	(D)	56 955	42 296	44 175	21 139	15 802	56 372	(D)
1982__	22 522	62 841	38 801	45 670	24 105	(D)	56 857	11 686
Other cropland_____ farms, 1987__	364	440	348	544	164	227	587	260
1982__	364	365	288	420	135	203	302	273
acres, 1987__	(D)	37 328	22 781	101 397	16 283	174 838	87 954	(D)
1982__	136 007	22 575	15 034	52 005	6 090	(D)	23 952	89 336
Cropland in cover crops, legumes, and soil-improvement grasses, not harvested and not pastured__ farms, 1987__	64	170	165	160	64	64	198	108
1982__	12	102	82	102	31	16	73	16
acres, 1987__	7 345	11 895	9 250	11 721	3 410	18 935	18 625	22 266
1982__	1 017	2 382	2 025	8 325	975	(D)	2 226	1 534

See footnotes at end of table.

Table 5. **Farms, Land in Farms, and Land Use: 1987 and 1982**—Con.

[For meaning of abbreviations and symbols, see introductory text]

All Farms	Labette	Lane	Leavenworth	Lincoln	Linn	Logan	Lyon	McPherson
FARMS AND LAND IN FARMS								
Farms .... number, 1987..	971	322	1 144	578	688	382	872	1 357
1982..	1 064	335	1 237	615	772	379	945	1 476
Land in farms .... acres, 1987..	350 010	467 005	211 370	454 341	273 211	610 480	469 906	533 432
1982..	354 722	462 978	227 331	440 520	280 637	583 314	500 674	557 167
Average size of farm .... acres, 1987..	360	1 450	185	786	397	1 598	539	393
1982..	333	1 382	184	716	364	1 539	530	377
Value of land and buildings[1]:								
Average per farm .... dollars, 1987..	153 151	592 398	170 089	253 820	157 301	382 249	177 635	222 022
1982..	185 431	658 278	195 120	346 918	221 940	676 507	277 011	286 058
Average per acre .... dollars, 1987..	430	371	939	326	407	243	320	562
1982..	613	489	1 063	467	561	438	554	834
Approximate land area .... acres, 1987..	417 792	459 142	296 076	460 588	384 505	686 860	540 422	576 166
Proportion in farms .... percent, 1987..	83.8	101.7	71.4	98.6	71.1	88.9	87.0	92.6
1987 size of farm:								
1 to 9 acres .... farms..	36	13	65	30	22	16	37	86
acres..	99	52	252	49	48	22	114	240
10 to 49 acres .... farms..	102	6	296	23	74	7	93	126
acres..	2 861	148	8 260	664	2 445	205	2 697	3 622
50 to 69 acres .... farms..	58	6	84	8	29	–	20	33
acres..	3 346	270	4 969	471	1 702	–	1 174	1 897
70 to 99 acres .... farms..	130	8	185	21	60	6	81	94
acres..	10 636	662	14 926	1 689	4 902	478	6 566	7 513
100 to 139 acres .... farms..	67	9	84	24	62	11	68	72
acres..	7 814	1 030	9 691	2 788	7 270	(D)	7 874	8 611
140 to 179 acres .... farms..	112	19	102	36	71	21	80	157
acres..	17 652	3 036	16 099	5 779	11 300	(D)	12 790	24 861
180 to 219 acres .... farms..	39	4	57	25	42	1	52	61
acres..	7 705	818	11 256	4 849	8 285	(D)	10 205	12 052
220 to 259 acres .... farms..	65	10	48	23	29	6	49	66
acres..	15 517	2 319	11 417	5 523	6 944	(D)	11 571	20 464
260 to 499 acres .... farms..	134	36	120	113	130	54	148	285
acres..	47 767	14 020	41 532	42 728	49 613	19 804	55 519	103 138
500 to 999 acres .... farms..	143	48	74	112	109	72	128	234
acres..	99 546	36 240	49 286	79 286	75 810	54 438	87 485	159 496
1,000 to 1,999 acres .... farms..	70	80	24	106	45	93	78	99
acres..	94 465	118 395	32 066	152 696	63 832	130 990	101 398	126 244
2,000 acres or more .... farms..	15	85	5	55	15	95	40	24
acres..	42 600	290 021	11 614	161 819	40 862	396 337	172 645	65 274
1982 size of farm:								
1 to 9 acres .... farms..	43	15	62	30	24	17	37	68
acres..	149	33	257	43	83	21	118	188
10 to 49 acres .... farms..	126	10	327	17	99	7	89	148
acres..	3 570	(D)	9 164	553	3 128	165	2 476	4 150
50 to 69 acres .... farms..	51	6	99	14	27	5	33	50
acres..	3 179	(D)	5 793	840	1 557	300	2 010	2 974
70 to 99 acres .... farms..	134	14	177	28	66	9	102	95
acres..	10 843	1 117	14 361	2 319	5 425	700	8 341	7 628
100 to 139 acres .... farms..	74	3	106	20	69	5	78	55
acres..	8 518	347	12 437	2 396	7 940	590	8 902	7 771
140 to 179 acres .... farms..	124	20	118	47	89	14	67	166
acres..	19 336	3 184	18 691	7 540	14 042	2 172	10 516	26 306
180 to 219 acres .... farms..	43	1	57	18	37	3	49	70
acres..	8 495	(D)	11 122	3 544	7 202	598	9 677	13 936
220 to 259 acres .... farms..	46	4	55	18	36	7	43	91
acres..	10 950	927	13 063	4 252	8 598	1 640	10 253	21 621
260 to 499 acres .... farms..	197	45	136	122	147	58	174	358
acres..	70 855	17 080	47 887	45 816	54 672	21 287	63 741	132 307
500 to 999 acres .... farms..	156	63	75	150	160	80	144	257
acres..	111 480	46 980	50 507	108 367	75 271	57 617	102 489	175 185
1,000 to 1,999 acres .... farms..	50	76	19	109	56	92	97	89
acres..	66 636	113 728	26 827	148 682	75 177	135 507	131 328	114 474
2,000 acres or more .... farms..	16	83	6	42	12	82	32	18
acres..	40 711	279 129	17 212	116 155	27 542	362 716	150 925	50 647
LAND IN FARMS ACCORDING TO USE								
Total cropland .... farms, 1987..	857	299	1 011	535	611	349	781	1 244
1982..	926	309	1 081	571	692	347	868	1 362
acres, 1987..	230 002	342 035	145 457	271 940	156 409	349 206	248 896	432 076
1982..	227 401	318 080	150 415	273 185	168 922	337 068	234 231	425 619
Harvested cropland .... farms, 1987..	767	291	892	512	551	334	709	1 210
1982..	840	300	956	552	642	329	796	1 331
acres, 1987..	136 963	154 979	96 700	153 709	93 665	150 236	153 982	283 623
1982..	170 902	159 352	108 423	174 863	120 739	166 407	165 108	346 140
Cropland used only for pasture or grazing ..... farms, 1987..	367	73	514	177	290	67	292	362
1982..	408	77	495	202	323	59	324	418
acres, 1987..	40 832	71	30 528	41 327	34 413	(D)	49 437	42 306
1982..	45 199	18 393	29 761	49 138	40 654	14 942	41 912	39 928
Other cropland .... farms, 1987..	452	280	326	448	305	322	485	983
1982..	248	259	265	385	206	306	449	657
acres, 1987..	52 207	(D)	18 229	76 904	28 325	(D)	45 477	106 149
1982..	11 300	140 335	12 231	49 164	7 529	155 719	27 211	40 551
Cropland in cover crops, legumes, and soil-improvement grasses, not harvested and not pastured ..... farms, 1987..	136	66	151	97	131	54	210	202
1982..	70	3	85	63	77	13	145	133
acres, 1987..	7 132	13 562	7 449	6 760	8 806	9 834	13 967	10 867
1982..	1 802	(D)	1 810	5 268	2 536	542	5 601	4 793

See footnotes at end of table.

Table 5. **Farms, Land in Farms, and Land Use: 1987 and 1982**—Con.

[For meaning of abbreviations and symbols, see introductory text]

All Farms	Marion	Marshall	Meade	Miami	Mitchell	Montgomery	Morris	Morton
FARMS AND LAND IN FARMS								
Farms _____ number, 1987__	1 119	1 061	464	1 151	622	974	550	226
1982__	1 184	1 149	469	1 223	642	1 021	571	235
Land in farms _____ acres, 1987__	577 700	553 438	582 454	272 290	473 829	327 193	395 558	457 440
1982__	571 707	528 749	593 525	308 741	447 894	325 007	402 948	430 039
Average size of farm _____ acres, 1987__	516	522	1 255	237	762	336	721	2 024
1982__	483	460	1 214	252	698	318	706	1 830
Value of land and buildings[1]:								
Average per farm _____ dollars, 1987__	214 644	237 714	483 019	193 407	345 722	154 431	241 545	563 882
1982__	302 336	333 963	671 229	228 935	440 106	257 849	342 936	554 589
Average per acre _____ dollars, 1987__	436	451	412	854	445	470	336	280
1982__	628	683	509	916	650	741	467	312
Approximate land area _____ acres, 1987__	604 243	581 657	626 310	377 472	459 116	413 292	443 347	467 923
Proportion in farms _____ percent, 1987__	95.6	96.5	93.0	72.1	103.2	79.2	89.4	97.8
1987 size of farm:								
1 to 9 acres _____ farms__	67	62	18	44	34	25	28	6
acres__	170	99	28	123	86	88	74	7
10 to 49 acres _____ farms__	97	57	11	262	40	155	32	9
acres__	2 776	1 568	317	8 107	1 044	4 606	799	290
50 to 69 acres _____ farms__	21	16	5	65	10	56	17	3
acres__	1 231	908	274	3 779	580	3 272	996	163
70 to 99 acres _____ farms__	69	42	8	148	23	118	23	10
acres__	5 562	3 327	696	11 906	1 842	9 586	1 859	(D)
100 to 139 acres _____ farms__	49	39	6	116	25	116	22	2
acres__	5 700	4 495	733	13 366	2 995	13 581	2 457	(D)
140 to 179 acres _____ farms__	104	84	23	117	35	107	43	19
acres__	16 414	13 303	3 590	18 397	5 541	16 804	6 834	2 968
180 to 219 acres _____ farms__	42	42	3	63	20	46	19	2
acres__	8 372	8 190	549	12 602	3 876	9 029	3 745	(D)
220 to 259 acres _____ farms__	60	51	8	45	23	58	27	2
acres__	14 348	12 202	1 882	10 623	5 496	13 883	6 415	(D)
260 to 499 acres _____ farms__	239	251	85	160	106	131	113	24
acres__	88 118	94 164	33 794	56 065	40 623	47 518	42 774	9 337
500 to 999 acres _____ farms__	232	264	113	76	132	88	105	24
acres__	163 591	187 531	82 205	52 966	92 754	63 677	76 260	18 443
1,000 to 1,999 acres _____ farms__	110	131	103	47	121	46	76	62
acres__	138 868	176 624	146 212	61 993	169 017	67 164	108 299	91 064
2,000 acres or more _____ farms__	29	22	81	9	51	25	45	63
acres__	132 530	51 225	312 234	22 359	149 973	77 983	148 044	333 275
1982 size of farm:								
1 to 9 acres _____ farms__	55	64	24	33	34	40	23	10
acres__	158	111	24	137	66	142	73	17
10 to 49 acres _____ farms__	98	51	8	260	47	190	35	8
acres__	2 726	1 497	260	7 367	1 279	5 411	836	(D)
50 to 69 acres _____ farms__	21	28	3	72	9	56	9	1
acres__	1 206	1 618	182	4 095	550	3 229	494	(D)
70 to 99 acres _____ farms__	81	63	11	172	34	118	25	6
acres__	6 510	4 292	869	13 966	2 707	9 602	2 025	476
100 to 139 acres _____ farms__	40	49	11	98	16	91	16	5
acres__	4 656	5 678	1 290	13 286	1 900	10 800	2 040	530
140 to 179 acres _____ farms__	115	98	33	133	51	104	47	16
acres__	18 176	15 610	(D)	21 091	8 143	16 550	7 508	2 539
180 to 219 acres _____ farms__	41	50	1	62	14	54	23	1
acres__	7 917	9 869	(D)	12 265	2 785	10 693	4 468	(D)
220 to 259 acres _____ farms__	61	63	7	55	28	46	36	4
acres__	14 517	14 924	1 671	13 215	6 638	11 421	8 670	1 020
260 to 499 acres _____ farms__	298	266	115	163	113	146	114	23
acres__	110 132	109 257	36 834	57 854	42 178	52 390	41 173	7 712
500 to 999 acres _____ farms__	259	282	115	74	138	100	118	34
acres__	183 510	196 966	84 154	74 362	102 563	69 043	83 840	26 138
1,000 to 1,999 acres _____ farms__	90	117	108	47	117	54	92	67
acres__	115 929	151 957	151 039	59 861	158 023	75 773	121 248	90 452
2,000 acres or more _____ farms__	25	8	69	9	41	20	31	60
acres__	106 270	16 970	311 689	31 241	121 062	59 953	130 573	300 679
LAND IN FARMS ACCORDING TO USE								
Total cropland _____ farms, 1987__	1 041	972	434	984	587	809	505	202
1982__	1 103	1 069	452	1 088	599	825	523	216
acres, 1987__	391 244	409 347	394 670	177 466	382 878	165 730	195 470	291 295
1982__	384 780	377 572	339 183	198 649	338 381	178 223	189 170	281 969
Harvested cropland _____ farms, 1987__	994	944	413	902	570	674	472	192
1982__	1 072	1 045	436	972	583	696	494	210
acres, 1987__	252 314	261 802	200 706	116 217	237 322	111 306	112 525	139 398
1982__	292 672	279 758	215 390	129 869	248 161	129 397	117 842	170 522
Cropland used only for pasture or grazing _____ farms, 1987__	468	315	102	443	180	363	193	55
1982__	438	420	111	497	153	361	191	52
acres, 1987__	57 983	54 189	(D)	40 395	34 828	34 599	39 168	(D)
1982__	57 535	65 057	(D)	41 839	25 899	28 620	40 924	8 337
Other cropland _____ farms, 1987__	789	769	397	344	503	362	359	167
1982__	540	574	333	356	412	217	275	169
acres, 1987__	80 947	93 356	(D)	20 854	110 728	39 825	43 777	(D)
1982__	34 573	32 757	(D)	26 941	66 321	18 206	30 404	103 110
Cropland in cover crops, legumes, and soil-improvement grasses, not harvested and not pastured _____ farms, 1987__	194	187	48	146	110	98	113	82
1982__	96	140	32	63	76	65	54	26
acres, 1987__	10 016	9 844	7 702	5 909	7 071	4 977	5 514	30 757
1982__	3 115	4 939	3 348	3 197	2 787	2 466	3 875	3 677

See footnotes at end of table.

Table 5. Farms, Land in Farms, and Land Use: 1987 and 1982 —Con.

[For meaning of abbreviations and symbols, see introductory text]

		Nemaha	Neosho	Ness	Norton	Osage	Osborne	Ottawa	Pawnee
FARMS AND LAND IN FARMS									
Farms	number, 1987..	1 127	751	597	470	885	607	523	530
	1982..	1 158	802	644	517	989	637	569	568
Land in farms	acres, 1987..	436 761	305 492	673 189	507 626	357 199	545 417	385 542	466 898
	1982..	414 310	318 217	679 108	513 265	379 966	511 544	393 433	468 840
Average size of farm	acres, 1987..	388	407	1 128	1 080	404	899	737	919
	1982..	358	397	1 055	993	384	803	668	825
Value of land and buildings[1]:									
Average per farm	dollars, 1987..	167 203	158 283	284 851	341 366	154 963	279 455	266 295	397 987
	1982..	253 946	273 016	446 660	446 155	232 608	373 041	420 523	581 879
Average per acre	dollars, 1987..	442	380	257	322	399	309	392	423
	1982..	731	702	419	467	610	480	608	681
Approximate land area	acres, 1987..	459 897	368 716	687 660	558 585	444 716	564 339	461 273	483 097
Proportion in farms	percent, 1987..	95.0	82.9	97.9	90.9	80.3	96.6	83.6	100.8
1987 size of farm:									
1 to 9 acres	farms..	56	25	20	21	33	27	26	28
	acres..	108	105	26	31	90	38	71	77
10 to 49 acres	farms..	74	69	7	26	126	24	45	29
	acres..	2 095	1 980	195	655	3 657	649	1 217	686
50 to 69 acres	farms..	15	39	11	7	32	8	9	6
	acres..	905	2 257	638	423	1 879	454	513	342
70 to 99 acres	farms..	63	83	7	10	82	20	21	13
	acres..	5 140	6 769	546	810	6 631	1 664	1 746	1 062
100 to 139 acres	farms..	45	48	11	6	70	14	21	9
	acres..	5 189	5 601	1 242	701	8 308	1 554	2 442	1 059
140 to 179 acres	farms..	135	87	41	24	83	31	33	47
	acres..	21 524	13 807	6 469	3 787	13 025	4 888	5 287	7 460
180 to 219 acres	farms..	52	33	9	8	34	20	16	7
	acres..	10 101	6 580	1 789	1 599	6 802	3 942	3 160	1 380
220 to 259 acres	farms..	71	45	32	15	60	20	20	14
	acres..	17 004	10 663	7 683	3 526	14 263	4 775	4 782	3 294
260 to 499 acres	farms..	307	136	96	68	147	113	87	81
	acres..	115 518	48 660	35 976	25 425	52 762	41 402	33 075	31 287
500 to 999 acres	farms..	116	115	115	108	136	130	114	134
	acres..	168 551	81 761	82 685	77 201	93 967	96 996	82 957	97 401
1,000 to 1,999 acres	farms..	57	52	137	104	60	135	94	97
	acres..	71 200	69 102	197 838	143 776	79 822	189 509	130 907	141 223
2,000 acres or more	farms..	7	18	111	73	22	65	37	65
	acres..	19 426	58 207	338 102	249 692	75 993	199 546	119 385	201 728
1982 size of farm:									
1 to 9 acres	farms..	73	32	29	28	43	31	22	26
	acres..	157	82	29	64	151	49	66	75
10 to 49 acres	farms..	73	86	11	19	134	37	41	18
	acres..	2 119	2 535	368	537	4 058	1 077	1 248	405
50 to 69 acres	farms..	24	26	7	7	40	12	14	10
	acres..	1 421	1 444	391	428	2 266	719	796	571
70 to 99 acres	farms..	64	88	21	9	106	21	29	15
	acres..	5 169	7 044	1 695	744	8 576	1 680	2 349	1 211
100 to 139 acres	farms..	53	57	14	10	81	12	21	17
	acres..	6 225	6 637	1 584	1 177	9 529	1 389	2 471	1 992
140 to 179 acres	farms..	130	92	32	26	84	49	45	37
	acres..	20 644	14 594	5 073	4 058	13 369	7 787	7 180	5 824
180 to 219 acres	farms..	43	36	13	12	47	19	19	9
	acres..	8 469	7 170	2 566	2 369	9 193	3 760	3 803	1 805
220 to 259 acres	farms..	88	43	24	13	53	30	39	18
	acres..	21 078	10 305	5 771	3 102	12 621	7 062	9 354	4 292
260 to 499 acres	farms..	324	141	109	81	158	95	108	117
	acres..	120 983	50 062	40 181	31 622	56 802	36 798	40 215	45 162
500 to 999 acres	farms..	232	128	146	127	159	152	108	138
	acres..	154 676	90 805	108 061	98 421	110 225	110 430	77 806	100 191
1,000 to 1,999 acres	farms..	49	54	145	125	66	121	111	117
	acres..	61 284	70 100	214 005	168 551	88 805	170 702	149 127	165 488
2,000 acres or more	farms..	5	19	93	60	18	58	32	46
	acres..	12 083	57 439	299 404	202 192	64 371	170 071	99 038	141 904
LAND IN FARMS ACCORDING TO USE									
Total cropland	farms, 1987..	1 042	669	560	439	782	565	483	496
	1982..	1 063	702	596	477	885	588	538	533
	acres, 1987..	331 086	197 149	464 503	323 300	214 840	347 866	244 551	404 356
	1982..	294 676	195 640	448 818	308 192	213 598	316 788	238 542	386 156
Harvested cropland	farms, 1987..	994	611	542	415	729	554	475	475
	1982..	1 024	662	577	458	825	572	514	519
	acres, 1987..	203 290	126 121	193 380	154 827	140 377	182 056	149 979	223 904
	1982..	215 292	142 932	216 742	170 487	158 533	179 133	185 635	256 255
Cropland used only for pasture or grazing	farms, 1987..	424	303	175	175	256	170	151	144
	1982..	455	267	145	121	316	155	173	154
	acres, 1987..	54 123	38 569	45 203	42 022	39 982	50 805	28 828	19 202
	1982..	54 568	35 727	(D)	23 995	37 864	42 501	27 415	(D)
Other cropland	farms, 1987..	776	323	527	371	469	512	377	435
	1982..	630	260	553	392	315	472	261	406
	acres, 1987..	73 673	32 469	225 920	126 451	34 481	115 005	65 744	161 250
	1982..	24 816	16 981	(D)	113 710	17 201	95 154	23 492	(D)
Cropland in cover crops, legumes, and soil-improvement grasses, not harvested and not pastured	farms, 1987..	278	141	88	118	178	93	71	68
	1982..	154	85	26	41	79	68	73	20
	acres, 1987..	19 576	9 295	10 178	12 525	10 119	7 309	5 389	8 222
	1982..	5 096	3 201	(D)	3 161	3 290	3 850	4 594	(D)

See footnotes at end of table.

Table 5. **Farms, Land in Farms, and Land Use: 1987 and 1982**—Con.

[For meaning of abbreviations and symbols, see introductory text]

All Farms	Phillips	Pottawatomie	Pratt	Rawlins	Reno	Republic	Rice	Riley
FARMS AND LAND IN FARMS								
Farms .... number, 1987..	591	790	517	641	1 557	833	604	546
1982..	647	889	547	621	1 638	923	643	583
Land in farms .... acres, 1987..	542 578	443 660	466 245	641 810	717 764	440 218	429 065	247 609
1982..	544 332	464 739	438 501	686 471	701 435	441 118	429 881	252 903
Average size of farm.......... acres, 1987..	918	562	902	1 166	461	528	710	453
1982..	841	535	802	1 105	426	478	669	434
Value of land and buildings[1]:								
Average per farm.......... dollars, 1987..	274 172	204 275	416 988	326 342	263 020	282 151	315 447	183 629
1982..	426 362	296 386	425 567	486 419	374 657	387 225	446 946	292 513
Average per acre.......... dollars, 1987..	321	374	466	272	565	482	446	446
1982..	502	573	582	488	868	778	663	622
Approximate land area .... acres, 1987..	567 494	529 734	470 508	684 390	805 600	459 891	465 958	379 584
Proportion in farms .... percent, 1987..	95.6	83.8	99.1	93.8	89.1	95.7	92.1	65.2
1987 size of farm:								
1 to 9 acres .... farms..	23	50	15	27	99	42	30	28
acres..	50	149	44	37	340	86	76	84
10 to 49 acres .... farms..	30	82	15	44	203	47	43	64
acres..	746	2 219	384	223	5 113	1 201	1 100	2 222
50 to 69 acres .... farms..	12	23	5	4	41	23	12	24
acres..	684	1 317	282	246	2 383	1 322	667	1 389
70 to 99 acres .... farms..	33	61	22	8	111	55	33	37
acres..	2 680	4 837	1 795	645	8 989	4 471	2 669	2 965
100 to 139 acres .... farms..	20	32	10	7	67	43	24	27
acres..	2 317	3 734	1 087	797	7 873	5 065	2 838	3 125
140 to 179 acres .... farms..	34	73	42	29	139	75	48	38
acres..	5 368	11 714	6 743	4 655	22 023	12 012	7 663	6 003
180 to 219 acres .... farms..	16	31	12	10	65	34	16	20
acres..	3 140	6 172	2 377	1 957	12 706	6 599	3 148	3 909
220 to 259 acres .... farms..	25	31	20	7	95	27	17	25
acres..	5 907	7 495	4 788	1 655	22 657	6 434	4 080	5 897
260 to 499 acres .... farms..	70	132	82	81	259	147	92	88
acres..	25 710	48 134	30 433	31 916	93 761	54 854	35 995	32 606
500 to 999 acres .... farms..	126	151	124	119	261	205	131	114
acres..	93 294	106 605	91 673	91 638	186 445	143 917	95 087	80 283
1,000 to 1,999 acres .... farms..	134	79	115	134	178	116	117	44
acres..	169 947	105 555	162 495	191 400	242 937	159 040	163 603	57 663
2,000 acres or more .... farms..	98	45	55	104	39	19	41	17
acres..	212 735	145 729	164 144	317 341	112 517	45 214	112 159	50 983
1982 size of farm:								
1 to 9 acres .... farms..	28	48	19	22	123	43	33	45
acres..	106	153	35	39	435	111	97	96
10 to 49 acres .... farms..	30	82	25	9	200	51	43	84
acres..	809	2 275	749	225	5 187	1 432	1 256	2 218
50 to 69 acres .... farms..	6	28	3	10	51	25	11	26
acres..	328	1 635	170	647	2 972	1 459	591	1 527
70 to 99 acres .... farms..	23	60	26	10	128	49	34	38
acres..	1 863	4 680	2 156	801	10 275	4 024	2 720	3 080
100 to 139 acres .... farms..	20	39	12	9	69	45	21	40
acres..	2 381	4 497	1 357	1 108	8 226	5 175	2 356	4 715
140 to 179 acres .... farms..	32	59	44	33	132	82	47	44
acres..	5 002	9 364	6 990	5 236	20 850	13 032	7 367	6 965
180 to 219 acres .... farms..	14	22	13	4	72	45	11	11
acres..	2 681	4 349	2 521	815	13 964	8 797	2 233	2 194
220 to 259 acres .... farms..	34	51	14	13	94	56	39	24
acres..	8 143	12 289	3 397	3 136	22 271	13 290	9 290	5 695
260 to 499 acres .... farms..	114	160	78	85	305	216	93	96
acres..	43 119	59 104	28 932	32 995	113 572	78 909	34 663	35 936
500 to 999 acres .... farms..	150	178	145	162	256	199	154	117
acres..	105 905	123 709	105 184	121 701	184 335	142 039	113 611	83 244
1,000 to 1,999 acres .... farms..	141	85	131	182	174	92	122	42
acres..	195 672	106 724	177 222	262 577	226 188	124 443	164 390	55 542
2,000 acres or more .... farms..	55	37	37	82	34	20	35	16
acres..	178 423	134 160	109 788	257 191	91 160	48 407	91 087	51 691
LAND IN FARMS ACCORDING TO USE								
Total cropland.......... farms, 1987..	555	667	467	506	1 424	765	556	489
1982..	614	782	519	591	1 500	855	603	496
acres, 1987..	333 728	168 003	392 119	414 811	582 519	342 576	347 501	132 841
1982..	322 954	197 546	349 620	443 868	570 003	328 149	351 843	122 077
Harvested cropland .... farms, 1987..	527	614	465	497	1 346	736	541	462
1982..	506	732	511	579	1 438	831	586	466
acres, 1987..	162 736	118 376	242 480	196 707	374 679	230 817	214 092	80 307
1982..	173 288	134 722	249 755	217 218	446 426	259 275	248 311	84 221
Cropland used only for pasture or grazing .... farms, 1987..	238	227	146	138	587	263	200	178
1982..	237	248	143	163	574	278	199	170
acres, 1987..	61 292	39 545	25 293	38 660	56 910	40 283	28 756	27 945
1982..	62 075	41 908	18 404	(D)	54 334	32 262	26 917	25 388
Other cropland .... farms, 1987..	473	412	397	469	1 010	605	487	316
1982..	452	348	383	523	746	480	437	241
acres, 1987..	109 700	30 082	124 366	179 444	150 930	71 776	104 653	24 589
1982..	87 591	20 916	81 461	(D)	69 241	36 592	76 615	12 471
Cropland in cover crops, legumes, and soil-improvement grasses, not harvested and not pastured .... farms, 1987..	112	141	96	105	235	151	76	97
1982..	59	99	31	22	125	128	59	62
acres, 1987..	7 320	7 016	13 902	6 857	19 856	7 185	5 111	4 020
1982..	2 305	2 875	1 454	(D)	4 299	3 270	3 354	1 450

See footnotes at end of table.

Table 5. **Farms, Land in Farms, and Land Use: 1987 and 1982** —Con.

[For meaning of abbreviations and symbols, see introductory text]

		Rooks	Rush	Russell	Saline	Scott	Sedgwick	Seward	Shawnee
FARMS AND LAND IN FARMS									
Farms	number, 1987..	473	546	534	743	391	1 589	285	852
	1982..	528	584	590	763	418	1 665	277	937
Land in farms	acres, 1987..	547 539	422 826	461 014	403 798	470 774	523 580	331 397	221 098
	1982..	532 189	424 118	471 459	396 776	509 606	522 674	325 328	229 847
Average size of farm	acres, 1987..	1 158	774	863	543	1 204	330	1 163	260
	1982..	1 008	726	799	520	1 225	314	1 174	245
Value of land and buildings[1]:									
Average per farm	dollars, 1987..	328 368	236 672	241 090	248 793	443 652	289 538	562 074	189 910
	1982..	491 828	394 551	395 142	337 491	656 084	390 814	703 148	224 575
Average per acre	dollars, 1987..	310	322	280	471	373	861	461	804
	1982..	480	558	518	683	524	1 244	615	957
Approximate land area	acres, 1987..	568 627	458 513	556 377	461 587	459 225	644 633	409 657	351 212
Proportion in farms	percent, 1987..	96.3	92.0	82.9	87.5	102.5	81.2	80.9	63.0
1987 size of farm:									
1 to 9 acres	farms..	16	25	28	39	31	135	10	60
	acres..	21	40	43	130	72	495	11	238
10 to 49 acres	farms..	14	16	16	10	13	325	10	166
	acres..	442	490	490	301	2 005	8 194	281	4 656
50 to 69 acres	farms..	7	9	12	12	4	50	6	59
	acres..	430	499	708	1 427	254	2 907	337	3 445
70 to 99 acres	farms..	9	20	17	84	13	144	10	110
	acres..	732	1 628	1 376	6 632	1 030	11 669	791	8 942
100 to 139 acres	farms..	10	19	14	29	4	84	4	74
	acres..	1 073	2 156	1 682	3 483	485	9 808	532	8 676
140 to 179 acres	farms..	27	46	52	73	32	134	18	82
	acres..	4 358	7 285	8 284	11 484	5 153	20 989	2 886	12 888
180 to 219 acres	farms..	6	15	5	16	6	44	3	27
	acres..	1 192	2 945	1 000	3 139	(D)	8 657	617	5 296
220 to 259 acres	farms..	14	20	28	21	7	73	7	34
	acres..	3 290	4 754	6 643	5 032	(D)	17 345	1 657	8 052
260 to 499 acres	farms..	86	90	110	110	56	268	42	112
	acres..	31 022	35 190	41 278	41 865	21 908	99 078	15 753	40 206
500 to 999 acres	farms..	98	132	103	142	63	216	53	85
	acres..	71 091	95 863	74 581	104 684	46 501	151 884	38 854	58 577
1,000 to 1,999 acres	farms..	101	117	86	95	76	92	72	34
	acres..	141 262	162 607	118 730	129 120	111 653	122 479	102 861	46 596
2,000 acres or more	farms..	85	37	69	29	89	24	50	9
	acres..	292 626	109 569	206 408	94 797	281 319	70 065	166 817	23 526
1982 size of farm:									
1 to 9 acres	farms..	17	19	28	28	40	135	13	68
	acres..	34	38	67	86	100	462	28	230
10 to 49 acres	farms..	20	19	17	72	16	346	13	220
	acres..	599	606	487	1 750	397	9 251	295	5 869
50 to 69 acres	farms..	6	8	13	31	4	62	5	59
	acres..	334	469	775	1 810	206	3 500	297	3 408
70 to 99 acres	farms..	16	19	25	66	9	144	10	139
	acres..	1 343	1 467	2 068	5 301	715	11 630	800	11 388
100 to 139 acres	farms..	12	13	25	37	3	92	7	64
	acres..	1 408	1 585	2 870	4 509	371	10 811	852	7 423
140 to 179 acres	farms..	36	42	50	81	27	153	19	76
	acres..	5 714	6 700	7 944	12 814	4 317	23 994	3 040	11 916
180 to 219 acres	farms..	10	17	14	27	5	44	4	30
	acres..	1 931	3 370	2 689	5 401	940	8 750	820	5 951
220 to 259 acres	farms..	20	19	23	36	10	73	5	34
	acres..	4 716	4 509	5 473	8 605	2 350	17 384	1 204	8 011
260 to 499 acres	farms..	98	134	108	139	51	274	44	127
	acres..	35 073	50 744	41 032	50 143	18 741	100 343	16 352	46 022
500 to 999 acres	farms..	116	148	135	136	86	217	43	74
	acres..	87 283	105 523	101 516	100 061	62 739	150 907	32 350	51 897
1,000 to 1,999 acres	farms..	107	115	99	75	85	110	62	39
	acres..	152 458	158 072	133 866	97 572	125 998	141 935	87 938	56 171
2,000 acres or more	farms..	70	31	53	33	80	15	52	7
	acres..	241 296	91 055	172 673	108 724	292 732	43 707	181 352	21 761
LAND IN FARMS ACCORDING TO USE									
Total cropland	farms, 1987..	443	508	490	683	342	1 434	247	718
	1982..	504	547	542	720	366	1 497	245	810
	acres, 1987..	322 039	347 130	287 618	288 689	375 948	445 408	247 336	149 707
	1982..	308 565	332 152	284 829	287 446	380 960	437 228	236 709	148 655
Harvested cropland	farms, 1987..	431	494	469	649	330	1 345	229	559
	1982..	483	525	517	643	356	1 423	228	726
	acres, 1987..	157 823	160 253	135 417	173 828	180 540	319 625	141 650	101 139
	1982..	168 987	172 379	163 585	205 872	209 383	363 417	159 542	103 231
Cropland used only for pasture or grazing	farms, 1987..	113	196	195	223	61	427	61	262
	1982..	106	164	184	215	65	431	46	322
	acres, 1987..	25 365	(D)	37 464	37 603	(D)	31 920	(D)	28 646
	1982..	21 453	35 201	40 563	32 730	(D)	32 867	(D)	27 790
Other cropland	farms, 1987..	408	449	424	529	310	862	207	305
	1982..	405	458	405	285	309	526	166	306
	acres, 1987..	139 206	(D)	114 737	77 258	77 268	93 863	(D)	19 922
	1982..	118 125	124 572	80 681	28 844	(D)	40 944	(D)	17 634
Cropland in cover crops, legumes, and soil-improvement grasses, not harvested and not pastured	farms, 1987..	109	95	103	120	34	160	56	111
	1982..	45	44	47	83	8	92	11	55
	acres, 1987..	12 073	5 324	11 439	7 063	6 387	12 067	16 392	5 206
	1982..	2 123	5 147	2 656	2 021	(D)	3 713	(D)	1 761

See footnotes at end of table.

Table 5. **Farms, Land in Farms, and Land Use: 1987 and 1982**—Con.

[For meaning of abbreviations and symbols, see introductory text]

All Farms	Sheridan	Sherman	Smith	Stafford	Stanton	Stevens	Sumner	Thomas
FARMS AND LAND IN FARMS								
Farms .... number, 1987...	518	524	692	540	280	300	1 271	644
1982...	571	550	761	557	231	325	1 388	628
Land in farms .... acres, 1987...	503 582	625 942	555 676	461 213	425 150	460 974	704 788	677 199
1982...	513 458	672 254	546 068	458 403	445 129	456 595	734 576	658 558
Average size of farm................. acres, 1987...	972	1 195	803	854	1 518	1 537	555	1 052
1982...	899	1 222	718	823	1 927	1 405	530	1 049
Value of land and buildings[1]:								
Average per farm.................... dollars, 1987...	359 500	403 973	283 039	427 813	591 609	682 130	297 971	410 301
1982...	545 692	733 007	360 915	570 196	1 050 108	792 348	484 478	662 624
Average per acre................... dollars, 1987...	370	360	347	492	409	438	535	396
1982...	579	574	497	666	500	576	881	635
Approximate land area .... acres, 1987...	573 529	676 403	573 996	504 038	435 616	465 593	757 414	687 756
Proportion in farms .... percent, 1987...	87.8	92.5	96.8	91.5	97.6	99.0	93.1	98.5
1987 size of farm:								
1 to 9 acres .... farms...	37	25	29	26	13	5	76	20
acres...	43	32	86	86	42	9	258	37
10 to 49 acres .... farms...	9	6	36	22	11	6	106	16
acres...	221	204	936	439	275	204	2 791	427
50 to 69 acres .... farms...	5	8	4	3	1	3	27	9
acres...	275	478	233	173	(D)	170	1 591	484
70 to 99 acres .... farms...	4	11	28	28	3	5	94	7
acres...	325	861	2 254	2 255	(D)	400	7 701	575
100 to 139 acres .... farms...	8	6	13	5	3	6	57	14
acres...	910	712	1 514	560	375	730	6 730	1 855
140 to 179 acres .... farms...	45	42	45	33	21	13	140	51
acres...	7 158	6 719	7 169	5 251	3 296	(D)	22 244	8 072
180 to 219 acres .... farms...	9	5	16	10	1	1	30	8
acres...	1 790	932	3 162	1 931	(D)	(D)	5 813	1 547
220 to 259 acres .... farms...	5	10	35	15	1	3	47	10
acres...	1 202	2 352	8 422	3 507	(D)	(D)	11 228	2 353
260 to 499 acres .... farms...	88	77	107	103	29	29	209	112
acres...	34 528	28 370	40 991	38 186	(D)	11 475	79 923	41 503
500 to 999 acres .... farms...	104	108	185	117	40	53	239	147
acres...	77 999	76 786	120 861	85 342	29 332	39 966	175 399	108 510
1,000 to 1,999 acres .... farms...	142	128	161	126	78	86	194	158
acres...	199 404	180 227	220 421	174 835	115 043	122 042	262 404	222 964
2,000 acres or more .... farms...	62	96	53	52	79	69	50	90
acres...	179 727	326 269	149 629	146 668	265 587	282 977	128 606	289 072
1982 size of farm:								
1 to 9 acres .... farms...	24	14	44	13	11	2	66	18
acres...	33	45	82	53	11	(D)	223	30
10 to 49 acres .... farms...	13	11	38	18	4	4	112	24
acres...	365	249	865	467	68	(D)	2 934	563
50 to 69 acres .... farms...	7	7	5	6	–	4	42	4
acres...	416	400	290	346	–	240	2 466	228
70 to 99 acres .... farms...	7	10	29	22	4	11	91	13
acres...	577	777	2 346	1 803	320	865	7 395	1 036
100 to 139 acres .... farms...	11	4	15	9	–	3	58	12
acres...	1 254	470	1 627	1 067	–	340	6 941	1 311
140 to 179 acres .... farms...	36	50	51	40	12	16	118	59
acres...	5 677	8 025	8 127	6 386	1 904	2 552	18 680	9 404
180 to 219 acres .... farms...	11	9	16	13	–	–	35	6
acres...	2 129	1 724	3 180	2 540	–	–	6 956	1 219
220 to 259 acres .... farms...	6	14	25	12	–	4	47	7
acres...	1 454	3 296	5 941	2 865	–	945	11 256	1 642
260 to 499 acres .... farms...	116	87	138	123	20	40	259	118
acres...	45 952	32 906	52 146	48 902	7 198	15 202	97 307	45 555
500 to 999 acres .... farms...	147	119	199	134	31	69	329	146
acres...	110 205	87 842	144 898	95 935	21 752	53 907	234 440	112 060
1,000 to 1,999 acres .... farms...	136	135	150	126	66	102	199	141
acres...	188 179	188 927	210 268	175 289	100 391	146 514	263 631	199 017
2,000 acres or more .... farms...	57	90	41	41	83	70	30	80
acres...	157 215	347 591	116 298	123 350	313 485	235 928	82 349	286 493
LAND IN FARMS ACCORDING TO USE								
Total cropland...................... farms, 1987...	470	487	648	506	265	281	1 178	606
1982...	537	529	695	532	214	301	1 310	591
acres, 1987...	374 043	497 494	381 501	376 006	379 898	392 622	599 210	585 763
1982...	377 596	543 516	346 819	364 371	365 711	383 076	601 684	558 816
Harvested cropland.................. farms, 1987...	461	470	630	488	241	260	1 137	592
1982...	521	522	675	526	209	292	1 271	575
acres, 1987...	183 013	251 334	211 937	230 607	184 701	238 568	415 440	296 047
1982...	200 537	296 853	216 933	266 542	220 929	298 655	510 906	307 900
Cropland used only for pasture or grazing...... farms, 1987...	139	100	233	180	59	90	362	117
1982...	170	115	210	152	34	44	397	104
acres, 1987...	37 737	(D)	56 657	30 261	6 472	15 833	41 600	23 296
1982...	48 429	29 071	44 469	20 013	6 989	7 200	45 031	20 355
Other cropland..................... farms, 1987...	424	455	568	418	234	253	909	559
1982...	443	452	545	391	186	230	412	492
acres, 1987...	153 293	(D)	113 507	114 938	188 725	138 221	142 170	266 420
1982...	128 632	217 592	85 417	77 816	137 793	77 221	36 747	230 561
Cropland in cover crops, legumes, and soil-improvement grasses, not harvested and not pastured .... farms, 1987...	77	60	131	81	74	138	148	54
1982...	27	15	74	33	10	53	100	17
acres, 1987...	6 432	11 669	8 254	10 519	36 292	38 707	11 261	8 552
1982...	2 392	932	4 432	2 387	322	10 687	3 934	862

See footnotes at end of table.

Table 5. **Farms, Land in Farms, and Land Use: 1987 and 1982**—Con.

[For meaning of abbreviations and symbols, see introductory text]

	Trego	Wabaunsee	Wallace	Washington	Wichita	Wilson	Woodson	Wyandotte
FARMS AND LAND IN FARMS								
Farms _____ number, 1987..	482	633	330	939	355	610	369	199
1982..	497	678	338	1 032	341	680	402	216
Land in farms _____ acres, 1987..	480 159	460 304	529 749	518 501	440 467	299 462	253 967	23 936
1982..	499 771	442 489	505 916	530 203	427 542	332 902	276 081	25 337
Average size of farm _____ acres, 1987..	996	727	1 605	552	1 241	491	688	120
1982..	1 006	653	1 497	514	1 254	490	687	117
Value of land and buildings[1]:								
Average per farm _____ dollars, 1987..	249 226	286 829	558 106	216 607	488 511	178 589	226 190	159 568
1982..	416 014	268 808	633 692	322 151	663 249	286 695	338 378	189 250
Average per acre _____ dollars, 1987..	256	385	351	406	373	365	309	1 609
1982..	408	473	462	635	527	587	517	1 652
Approximate land area _____ acres, 1987..	569 817	510 163	584 697	575 027	459 865	367 955	318 745	95 411
Proportion in farms _____ percent, 1987..	84.3	90.2	90.6	90.2	95.8	81.4	79.7	25.1
1987 size of farm:								
1 to 9 acres _____ farms..	31	32	30	85	24	23	16	25
acres..	48	95	49	150	43	52	(D)	103
10 to 49 acres _____ farms..	7	65	4	44	9	50	26	93
acres..	208	1 938	146	1 107	199	1 347	(D)	2 246
50 to 69 acres _____ farms..	5	8	2	17	–	24	1	16
acres..	300	476	(D)	975	–	1 363	(D)	936
70 to 99 acres _____ farms..	4	55	6	48	6	53	33	19
acres..	315	4 417	469	3 871	493	4 287	(D)	1 517
100 to 139 acres _____ farms..	6	35	1	28	6	33	10	16
acres..	709	4 201	(D)	3 346	698	3 895	1 188	1 872
140 to 179 acres _____ farms..	25	44	14	71	31	42	20	5
acres..	3 987	6 895	2 207	11 084	4 996	6 570	3 163	812
180 to 219 acres _____ farms..	12	36	7	36	6	22	29	5
acres..	2 348	7 105	(D)	7 107	1 195	4 349	5 763	(D)
220 to 259 acres _____ farms..	8	31	2	44	7	48	25	2
acres..	1 920	7 269	(D)	10 338	1 718	11 397	5 960	(D)
260 to 499 acres _____ farms..	84	108	46	201	46	108	72	8
acres..	31 678	40 191	17 264	74 101	17 851	39 760	27 294	(D)
500 to 999 acres _____ farms..	129	118	57	210	66	121	58	5
acres..	95 364	81 632	43 045	150 792	(D)	85 949	40 503	(D)
1,000 to 1,999 acres _____ farms..	112	68	87	122	80	73	57	3
acres..	155 852	94 936	129 931	168 362	(D)	96 903	79 257	(D)
2,000 acres or more _____ farms..	59	35	74	33	74	13	22	2
acres..	187 430	211 149	334 532	87 288	(D)	43 590	87 301	(D)
1982 size of farm:								
1 to 9 acres _____ farms..	21	40	27	60	20	22	17	22
acres..	29	54	31	138	54	41	30	86
10 to 49 acres _____ farms..	9	56	7	54	1	46	33	97
acres..	200	1 638	(D)	1 374	(D)	1 260	912	2 438
50 to 69 acres _____ farms..	5	18	2	19	2	16	9	26
acres..	296	1 034	(D)	1 096	(D)	917	545	1 556
70 to 99 acres _____ farms..	17	55	7	55	3	62	30	28
acres..	1 384	4 338	560	4 418	233	5 062	2 420	2 238
100 to 139 acres _____ farms..	3	42	4	26	1	41	19	7
acres..	393	4 873	424	3 093	(D)	4 865	2 262	806
140 to 179 acres _____ farms..	34	38	21	95	38	60	29	7
acres..	5 443	6 037	3 271	14 988	6 116	9 531	4 591	1 053
180 to 219 acres _____ farms..	3	33	3	34	7	29	16	2
acres..	598	6 653	566	6 714	1 402	5 614	3 170	(D)
220 to 259 acres _____ farms..	10	34	6	55	5	47	26	4
acres..	2 374	8 014	1 419	13 257	1 200	11 393	6 207	942
260 to 499 acres _____ farms..	85	119	56	256	53	118	80	11
acres..	33 422	44 736	21 283	92 481	19 794	44 826	29 284	4 014
500 to 999 acres _____ farms..	124	142	57	245	55	142	73	7
acres..	91 303	100 923	43 713	172 047	44 760	100 740	54 559	5 122
1,000 to 1,999 acres _____ farms..	134	73	69	105	77	83	49	4
acres..	187 714	97 201	97 587	139 364	107 899	104 125	67 110	4 591
2,000 acres or more _____ farms..	52	28	79	28	79	15	21	1
acres..	176 619	167 078	336 716	81 233	245 850	44 528	104 991	(D)
LAND IN FARMS ACCORDING TO USE								
Total cropland_____ farms, 1987..	442	533	294	825	313	548	330	154
1982..	473	589	297	940	312	612	356	175
acres, 1987..	324 214	149 203	299 727	378 755	368 240	183 539	123 270	17 145
1982..	311 134	152 327	305 180	347 854	357 686	188 830	125 159	17 897
Harvested cropland _____ farms, 1987..	426	488	283	794	307	505	303	125
1982..	443	551	281	907	294	574	318	148
acres, 1987..	139 788	90 028	146 695	239 242	182 673	114 733	85 309	12 112
1982..	142 586	103 331	162 334	272 022	195 631	143 416	87 002	14 095
Cropland used only for pasture or grazing _____ farms, 1987..	155	211	54	315	57	57	111	62
1982..	126	205	60	338	67	245	195	63
acres, 1987..	416	37 726	(D)	55 176	9 491	31 046	17 498	3 542
1982..	32 091	28 632	11 282	50 536	(D)	30 023	31 106	3 311
Other cropland _____ farms, 1987..	405	283	267	627	283	313	210	35
1982..	416	216	249	451	266	218	143	27
acres, 1987..	(D)	21 449	(D)	84 337	176 076	37 760	20 463	1 491
1982..	136 457	20 364	131 564	25 296	(D)	15 391	7 051	491
Cropland in cover crops, legumes, and soil-improvement grasses, not harvested and not pastured _____ farms, 1987..	83	104	44	134	23	87	48	18
1982..	23	67	21	101	12	52	27	10
acres, 1987..	9 832	6 030	6 329	12 534	5 166	6 548	2 397	(D)
1982..	2 768	1 685	2 065	2 926	(D)	2 134	588	192

See footnotes at end of table.

Table 5. **Farms, Land in Farms, and Land Use: 1987 and 1982**—Con.

[For meaning of abbreviations and symbols, see introductory text]

All Farms		Kansas	Allen	Anderson	Atchison	Barber	~ Barton	Bourbon
LAND IN FARMS ACCORDING TO USE—Con.								
Total cropland-Con.								
Other cropland-Con.								
Cropland on which all crops failed	farms, 1987..	3 341	24	35	21	19	38	38
	1982..	5 059	56	48	81	30	37	40
	acres, 1987..	206 231	1 338	2 357	704	(D)	2 502	1 473
	1982..	385 959	2 688	2 256	2 796	2 676	1 782	1 562
Cropland in cultivated summer fallow	farms, 1987..	25 408	83	52	38	148	605	43
	1982..	22 060	56	48	34	102	583	28
	acres, 1987..	6 409 506	7 787	3 550	2 966	20 222	130 689	2 396
	1982..	5 475 611	2 862	2 167	1 049	10 669	89 235	2 319
Cropland idle	farms, 1987..	20 610	208	235	253	104	261	167
	1982..	12 304	116	138	114	58	245	92
	acres, 1987..	2 451 199	12 368	16 745	15 454	23 302	27 550	12 147
	1982..	1 027 921	4 061	4 584	4 237	10 932	23 547	4 489
Total woodland	farms, 1987..	12 587	158	221	276	49	76	256
	1982..	13 184	157	245	245	41	72	314
	acres, 1987..	718 261	7 220	17 959	16 423	5 407	2 403	19 780
	1982..	753 577	6 672	15 678	12 820	3 397	2 473	27 511
Woodland pastured	farms, 1987..	6 382	79	131	157	31	33	181
	1982..	6 857	80	150	155	24	35	209
	acres, 1987..	366 136	3 127	10 824	8 523	(D)	1 008	14 675
	1982..	377 954	2 943	7 760	7 016	2 478	1 508	19 037
Woodland not pastured	farms, 1987..	7 991	99	136	167	23	51	122
	1982..	8 039	88	154	123	22	40	138
	acres, 1987..	352 125	4 093	7 135	7 900	(D)	1 395	5 085
	1982..	375 623	3 729	7 898	5 804	919	965	8 474
Other land	farms, 1987..	53 891	564	599	527	442	706	688
	1982..	58 997	647	684	628	425	738	728
	acres, 1987..	14 525 188	80 106	103 296	39 158	439 412	67 011	131 213
	1982..	15 699 777	87 904	125 948	47 711	446 078	85 633	129 232
Pastureland and rangeland other than cropland and woodland pastured	farms, 1987..	32 362	376	374	256	332	334	451
	1982..	34 510	413	402	272	320	350	461
	acres, 1987..	13 254 094	69 944	90 081	26 270	428 182	55 294	119 492
	1982..	14 085 336	75 437	107 337	30 804	435 205	64 963	110 893
Land in house lots, ponds, roads, wasteland, etc.	farms, 1987..	44 335	466	497	459	283	604	560
	1982..	50 409	555	599	566	295	953	621
	acres, 1987..	1 271 074	10 162	13 215	10 879	11 230	11 717	11 721
	1982..	1 614 441	12 467	18 611	16 907	10 873	20 670	15 339
Pastureland, all types	farms, 1987..	48 663	551	532	495	427	616	722
	1982..	52 291	623	616	581	423	643	752
	acres, 1987..	17 105 675	111 955	133 861	86 558	481 965	108 379	183 290
	1982..	17 694 942	117 186	156 625	71 849	470 506	102 750	160 114
Cropland diverted under annual commodity acreage adjustment programs	farms, 1987..	34 658	268	303	324	276	565	195
	1982..	14 825	84	129	126	129	330	50
	acres, 1987..	3 956 196	10 837	13 500	16 261	37 561	66 940	7 091
	1982..	896 640	2 054	2 866	3 344	12 541	22 238	1 206
Cropland placed under the conservation reserve program	farms, 1987..	5 630	8	33	24	69	69	70
	acres, 1987..	810 862	324	2 531	854	12 335	8 987	5 970

See footnotes at end of table.

Table 5. Farms, Land in Farms, and Land Use: 1987 and 1982—Con.

[For meaning of abbreviations and symbols, see introductory text]

All Farms	Brown	Butler	Chase	Chautauqua	Cherokee	Cheyenne	Clark
LAND IN FARMS ACCORDING TO USE—Con.							
Total cropland-Con.							
Other cropland-Con.							
Cropland on which all crops failed .... farms, 1987..	21	76	11	27	39	41	11
1982..	57	99	21	17	46	31	19
acres, 1987..	394	2 766	712	1 586	3 838	1 443	725
1982..	1 990	6 782	1 857	550	1 640	2 903	1 963
Cropland in cultivated summer fallow ...... farms, 1987..	80	229	42	23	44	387	148
1982..	37	162	32	14	39	400	164
acres, 1987..	7 105	23 675	2 866	3 870	4 545	153 225	46 896
1982..	1 407	10 764	1 915	946	2 147	151 666	53 170
Cropland idle.............................. farms, 1987..	350	288	69	91	241	133	76
1982..	151	182	56	24	114	82	35
acres, 1987..	28 054	24 396	8 920	8 466	19 130	22 831	23 307
1982..	7 926	9 238	2 836	947	5 064	10 350	3 858
Total woodland.............................. farms, 1987..	213	282	75	135	238	39	14
1982..	207	289	76	167	260	33	12
acres, 1987..	12 415	12 625	5 050	23 899	11 866	4 029	2 273
1982..	13 150	11 865	4 162	25 929	15 958	4 806	2 282
Woodland pastured .... farms, 1987..	110	126	34	101	128	30	8
1982..	125	132	23	137	154	9	4
acres, 1987..	5 516	5 350	2 996	18 582	5 851	2 595	(D)
1982..	6 507	4 669	1 829	20 712	7 173	1 864	(D)
Woodland not pastured .... farms, 1987..	144	187	50	52	140	35	12
1982..	117	192	60	43	173	30	9
acres, 1987..	6 899	7 275	2 054	5 317	6 115	1 434	(D)
1982..	6 643	7 196	2 353	5 217	8 785	2 942	(D)
Other land .... farms, 1987..	608	1 095	240	365	660	378	233
1982..	703	1 158	265	381	771	406	259
acres, 1987..	55 356	345 526	239 190	224 049	57 797	212 122	387 123
1982..	55 333	362 935	337 360	239 677	62 063	204 480	396 239
Pastureland and rangeland other than cropland and woodland pastured .... farms, 1987..	292	701	181	296	364	271	192
1982..	292	663	190	295	409	268	204
acres, 1987..	35 228	320 248	224 157	215 400	41 684	200 299	(D)
1982..	32 234	333 106	328 064	230 146	43 347	192 516	(D)
Land in house lots, ponds, roads, wasteland, etc. .... farms, 1987..	565	894	184	260	552	289	140
1982..	665	967	209	294	672	345	166
acres, 1987..	20 127	25 278	15 033	8 649	16 113	11 623	(D)
1982..	23 099	29 829	9 296	9 531	18 716	11 964	(D)
Pastureland, all types .... farms, 1987..	506	1 011	242	376	587	334	225
1982..	586	1 023	242	372	683	357	237
acres, 1987..	65 923	392 665	250 676	254 426	68 121	235 221	405 127
1982..	73 860	396 736	343 776	275 472	72 434	223 009	404 436
Cropland diverted under annual commodity acreage adjustment programs................... farms, 1987..	438	375	107	56	234	301	151
1982..	150	153	55	12	79	97	76
acres, 1987..	33 946	34 240	6 293	3 683	12 755	41 606	23 272
1982..	4 140	5 349	1 717	504	2 294	5 800	6 708
Cropland placed under the conservation reserve program........................... farms, 1987..	44	27	8	25	14	100	78
acres, 1987..	4 733	1 655	398	2 617	1 024	14 957	24 883

See footnotes at end of table.

Table 5. **Farms, Land in Farms, and Land Use: 1987 and 1982**—Con.

[For meaning of abbreviations and symbols, see introductory text]

All Farms	Clay	Cloud	Coffey	Comanche	Cowley	Crawford	Decatur
LAND IN FARMS ACCORDING TO USE—Con.							
Total cropland-Con.							
Other cropland-Con.							
Cropland on which all crops failed...... farms, 1987..	29	35	31	13	64	48	21
1982..	52	60	37	25	62	50	15
acres, 1987..	896	1 035	622	(D)	2 450	2 021	1 362
1982..	2 850	4 011	1 873	4 826	2 788	2 445	1 506
Cropland in cultivated summer fallow .... farms, 1987..	372	327	87	143	205	36	364
1982..	262	212	48	120	74	51	390
acres, 1987..	39 033	42 025	6 904	36 931	19 940	4 607	116 126
1982..	13 495	16 514	1 973	32 918	3 301	5 869	124 546
Cropland idle................................ farms, 1987..	232	212	221	73	289	229	101
1982..	141	130	120	33	139	144	62
acres, 1987..	18 416	21 596	15 639	12 177	26 825	18 295	17 933
1982..	6 902	8 064	4 607	5 820	7 754	5 760	7 936
Total woodland................................ farms, 1987..	124	136	171	29	212	221	41
1982..	120	141	171	21	208	184	35
acres, 1987..	5 262	8 295	10 072	2 992	10 575	15 901	2 826
1982..	5 806	8 666	7 370	2 898	12 152	16 209	4 270
Woodland pastured .... farms, 1987..	31	31	78	16	95	122	24
1982..	34	40	73	10	89	115	20
acres, 1987..	850	1 347	4 323	(D)	4 866	8 106	2 081
1982..	1 185	1 489	2 095	(D)	5 903	8 548	1 068
Woodland not pastured .... farms, 1987..	106	119	125	15	140	139	22
1982..	96	121	118	13	142	91	20
acres, 1987..	4 412	6 948	5 749	(D)	5 709	7 795	745
1982..	4 621	7 197	5 275	(D)	6 249	7 661	3 202
Other land .... farms, 1987..	569	529	502	233	829	627	403
1982..	807	573	557	219	940	751	458
acres, 1987..	103 185	95 724	111 972	290 711	339 810	86 090	184 247
1982..	105 891	115 559	129 544	281 310	417 873	105 981	192 240
Pastureland and rangeland other than cropland and woodland pastured .... farms, 1987..	352	323	309	183	549	391	293
1982..	383	313	324	180	632	449	331
acres, 1987..	89 440	84 316	98 098	279 907	321 330	71 616	165 299
1982..	91 062	98 283	116 560	(D)	391 851	86 546	175 950
Land in house lots, ponds, roads, wasteland, etc. .... farms, 1987..	500	453	418	159	679	528	322
1982..	546	502	476	145	794	611	371
acres, 1987..	13 745	11 508	13 879	10 804	18 480	14 474	18 946
1982..	14 829	17 276	12 984	(D)	26 022	19 436	16 290
Pastureland, all types .... farms, 1987..	526	465	460	227	769	634	374
1982..	550	507	491	218	865	689	411
acres, 1987..	134 510	123 534	139 393	305 329	376 539	112 491	207 345
1982..	130 304	129 994	147 604	288 667	436 753	125 566	202 952
Cropland diverted under annual commodity acreage adjustment programs................... farms, 1987..	446	434	289	148	416	234	317
1982..	216	162	107	56	100	94	97
acres, 1987..	38 883	49 505	16 560	25 671	37 356	11 469	39 259
1982..	8 890	8 293	2 902	5 337	4 080	2 729	5 048
Cropland placed under the conservation reserve program............................... farms, 1987..	61	41	44	89	26	71	52
acres, 1987..	4 970	2 292	2 763	23 525	1 271	6 663	2 737

See footnotes at end of table.

Table 5. **Farms, Land in Farms, and Land Use: 1987 and 1982**—Con.

[For meaning of abbreviations and symbols, see introductory text]

All Farms		Dickinson	Doniphan	Douglas	Edwards	Elk	Ellis	Ellsworth
LAND IN FARMS ACCORDING TO USE—Con.								
Total cropland-Con.								
Other cropland-Con.								
Cropland on which all crops failed	farms, 1987..	43	15	20	15	19	53	33
	1982..	66	43	82	27	20	14	12
	acres, 1987..	1 500	592	464	915	1 169	4 711	1 628
	1982..	2 587	944	4 219	1 887	556	(D)	568
Cropland in cultivated summer fallow	farms, 1987..	414	39	47	227	26	495	341
	1982..	275	21	46	279	23	469	326
	acres, 1987..	41 008	3 379	2 859	66 884	1 294	82 771	57 480
	1982..	14 208	762	1 288	77 793	1 033	68 061	47 517
Cropland idle	farms, 1987..	396	210	188	152	76	286	127
	1982..	226	77	128	80	32	236	110
	acres, 1987..	31 127	16 845	11 522	30 060	7 430	32 881	12 271
	1982..	10 849	2 618	3 636	9 941	2 242	21 412	9 901
Total woodland	farms, 1987..	185	220	320	41	116	27	59
	1982..	185	240	336	33	115	27	41
	acres, 1987..	6 375	17 794	15 916	2 296	10 858	2 469	2 965
	1982..	6 058	20 940	17 007	2 976	11 639	1 714	2 081
Woodland pastured	farms, 1987..	58	109	196	20	69	13	24
	1982..	72	124	191	16	62	6	13
	acres, 1987..	1 957	7 628	9 722	1 251	7 306	899	535
	1982..	2 091	11 389	10 245	1 029	7 205	(D)	862
Woodland not pastured	farms, 1987..	136	148	165	28	63	15	52
	1982..	141	153	183	26	62	21	33
	acres, 1987..	4 418	10 166	6 194	1 045	3 552	1 570	2 430
	1982..	3 967	9 551	6 762	1 947	4 434	(D)	1 219
Other land	farms, 1987..	851	417	701	249	359	581	393
	1982..	938	477	741	310	405	517	410
	acres, 1987..	114 885	29 630	52 945	66 909	245 035	233 183	173 523
	1982..	129 428	30 168	54 491	66 021	260 140	215 955	150 497
Pastureland and rangeland other than cropland and woodland pastured	farms, 1987..	506	152	349	160	283	369	249
	1982..	506	149	382	178	334	429	263
	acres, 1987..	97 462	16 806	39 492	63 129	238 964	223 440	164 098
	1982..	97 147	14 635	41 820	57 603	250 058	(D)	136 691
Land in house lots, ponds, roads, wasteland, etc.	farms, 1987..	730	379	630	203	250	412	335
	1982..	835	451	665	256	298	503	348
	acres, 1987..	17 423	12 824	13 453	5 780	6 071	9 743	9 427
	1982..	32 281	15 533	12 671	8 418	10 082	(D)	11 806
Pastureland, all types	farms, 1987..	778	302	637	226	366	578	373
	1982..	809	357	669	237	416	565	387
	acres, 1987..	156 634	37 712	74 891	84 209	275 372	278 814	205 621
	1982..	161 604	42 792	80 534	72 827	288 847	238 683	168 330
Cropland diverted under annual commodity acreage adjustment programs	farms, 1987..	631	297	213	251	83	377	331
	1982..	246	76	47	123	32	159	164
	acres, 1987..	54 421	19 176	10 501	41 421	3 608	26 666	33 155
	1982..	8 911	1 778	1 107	10 172	688	7 855	9 396
Cropland placed under the conservation reserve program	farms, 1987..	60	26	34	57	46	63	96
	acres, 1987..	3 129	2 200	2 156	12 542	3 673	7 284	7 054

See footnotes at end of table.

Table 5. **Farms, Land in Farms, and Land Use: 1987 and 1982**—Con.

[For meaning of abbreviations and symbols, see introductory text]

All Farms		Finney	Ford	Franklin	Geary	Gove	Graham	Grant
LAND IN FARMS ACCORDING TO USE—Con.								
Total cropland-Con.								
Other cropland-Con.								
Cropland on which all crops failed	farms, 1987__	32	40	101	9	30	26	24
	1982__	18	34	128	20	160	29	13
	acres, 1987__	3 068	4 868	9 128	751	(D)	2 206	(D)
	1982__	2 303	3 265	4 741	1 169	33 997	2 358	3 135
Cropland in cultivated summer fallow	farms, 1987__	368	516	42	75	411	339	187
	1982__	358	519	53	43	402	359	170
	acres, 1987__	173 981	168 726	2 242	4 365	154 844	99 894	75 728
	1982__	162 661	166 346	2 764	3 054	138 811	106 911	72 249
Cropland idle	farms, 1987__	143	216	235	99	164	173	100
	1982__	92	137	159	58	96	105	59
	acres, 1987__	44 261	43 528	15 561	5 739	43 994	22 658	23 385
	1982__	16 113	19 574	7 945	3 049	18 067	11 527	7 875
Total woodland	farms, 1987__	16	36	385	89	11	33	8
	1982__	5	17	392	94	14	39	5
	acres, 1987__	1 178	1 006	19 524	5 220	1 934	2 066	(D)
	1982__	1 355	2 813	16 247	5 266	820	3 460	(D)
Woodland pastured	farms, 1987__	7	13	228	59	2	18	1
	1982__	1	8	243	50	10	22	2
	acres, 1987__	542	653	10 493	3 307	(D)	1 054	(D)
	1982__	(D)	837	10 477	2 223	326	1 043	(D)
Woodland not pastured	farms, 1987__	9	23	220	47	9	19	7
	1982__	4	15	206	67	5	22	3
	acres, 1987__	636	353	9 031	1 913	(D)	1 012	(D)
	1982__	(D)	1 976	7 770	3 043	494	2 417	(D)
Other land	farms, 1987__	341	559	814	258	407	358	219
	1982__	359	588	902	256	447	400	198
	acres, 1987__	139 775	124 760	85 660	87 623	229 631	181 049	(D)
	1982__	129 272	166 719	88 914	79 071	263 625	197 406	(D)
Pastureland and rangeland other than cropland and woodland pastured	farms, 1987__	169	345	456	172	261	267	107
	1982__	156	397	465	173	343	288	98
	acres, 1987__	129 510	114 372	68 986	81 083	(D)	170 129	36 690
	1982__	(D)	149 961	73 473	68 481	247 268	183 114	32 363
Land in house lots, ponds, roads, wasteland, etc.	farms, 1987__	278	402	716	216	309	265	173
	1982__	307	456	828	216	333	324	164
	acres, 1987__	10 265	10 387	16 672	5 730	(D)	10 920	(D)
	1982__	(D)	16 758	15 441	10 590	16 357	14 292	(D)
Pastureland, all types	farms, 1987__	236	520	765	238	346	345	145
	1982__	236	540	849	234	416	392	130
	acres, 1987__	147 476	149 684	118 600	100 701	257 849	199 029	49 127
	1982__	137 059	179 559	121 580	82 632	270 765	221 680	42 063
Cropland diverted under annual commodity acreage adjustment programs	farms, 1987__	341	478	263	141	331	249	206
	1982__	179	256	112	61	165	124	103
	acres, 1987__	83 838	71 496	10 572	8 730	44 822	30 991	44 108
	1982__	17 131	21 966	2 291	1 902	11 481	8 362	15 185
Cropland placed under the conservation reserve program	farms, 1987__	58	62	17	10	55	97	23
	acres, 1987__	20 946	10 670	591	879	6 420	12 258	4 478

See footnotes at end of table.

Table 5. **Farms, Land in Farms, and Land Use: 1987 and 1982**—Con.

[For meaning of abbreviations and symbols, see introductory text]

All Farms	Gray	Greeley	Greenwood	Hamilton	Harper	Harvey	Haskell
LAND IN FARMS ACCORDING TO USE—Con.							
Total cropland-Con.							
Other cropland-Con.							
Cropland on which all crops failed .... farms, 1987..	24	9	25	13	31	32	10
1982..	9	24	58	16	24	44	24
acres, 1987..	(D)	761	1 236	1 460	1 525	1 563	(D)
1982..	(D)	9 451	3 145	2 913	2 446	1 654	(D)
Cropland in cultivated summer fallow .... farms, 1987..	379	210	44	168	190	340	199
1982..	346	224	50	193	70	227	178
acres, 1987..	135 507	178 272	1 914	134 040	26 487	33 430	81 118
1982..	104 758	171 347	2 693	161 068	5 453	10 751	56 576
Cropland idle.............................. farms, 1987..	205	96	104	97	197	273	112
1982..	104	75	63	55	79	155	62
acres, 1987..	38 721	27 143	6 974	37 940	31 765	20 607	31 159
1982..	11 255	9 831	2 522	14 742	7 581	6 292	12 301
Total woodland...................... farms, 1987..	6	3	167	11	55	76	4
1982..	9	7	170	6	52	106	3
acres, 1987..	(D)	(D)	13 453	1 038	1 726	1 436	126
1982..	410	577	12 157	860	1 440	3 319	1 203
Woodland pastured .... farms, 1987..	2	–	98	4	19	21	2
1982..	5	1	101	2	16	30	3
acres, 1987..	(D)		8 551	376	742	617	(D)
1982..	(D)	(D)	6 545	(D)	717	512	1 203
Woodland not pastured .... farms, 1987..	4	3	102	7	36	60	2
1982..	6	6	89	4	37	80	–
acres, 1987..	(D)	(D)	4 902	660	984	819	(D)
1982..	(D)	(D)	5 612	(D)	723	2 807	–
Other land .... farms, 1987..	362	172	513	189	507	683	168
1982..	366	181	542	179	514	719	207
acres, 1987..	(D)	(D)	408 340	133 199	132 613	33 040	36 039
1982..	74 215	43 714	454 032	119 847	145 637	44 243	30 584
Pastureland and rangeland other than cropland and woodland pastured .... farms, 1987..	181	81	389	126	358	302	42
1982..	208	97	418	117	354	295	52
acres, 1987..	58 487	41 294	393 639	126 545	120 346	24 141	(D)
1982..	(D)	(D)	438 156	(D)	132 265	30 802	21 404
Land in house lots, ponds, roads, wasteland, etc. .... farms, 1987..	313	137	364	115	403	619	158
1982..	314	157	411	129	433	672	190
acres, 1987..	(D)	(D)	14 701	4 654	12 465	8 899	(D)
1982..	(D)	(D)	15 876	(D)	13 372	13 441	9 180
Pastureland, all types .... farms, 1987..	257	116	500	164	480	491	94
1982..	294	128	566	155	509	497	100
acres, 1987..	77 677	53 965	438 679	143 945	163 468	40 688	45 816
1982..	77 408	51 222	487 505	134 756	170 308	51 130	30 130
Cropland diverted under annual commodity acreage adjustment programs.................. farms, 1987..	387	188	137	167	473	515	227
1982..	190	116	36	125	142	223	107
acres, 1987..	76 359	52 905	5 955	42 605	71 926	45 780	54 828
1982..	16 358	17 875	712	19 123	11 885	7 725	10 975
Cropland placed under the conservation reserve program....................... farms, 1987..	31	30	24	106	42	17	18
acres, 1987..	5 962	15 491	2 116	67 832	5 285	1 223	6 321

See footnotes at end of table.

Table 5. **Farms, Land in Farms, and Land Use: 1987 and 1982**—Con.

[For meaning of abbreviations and symbols, see introductory text]

All Farms	Hodgeman	Jackson	Jefferson	Jewell	Johnson	Kearny	Kingman	Kiowa
LAND IN FARMS ACCORDING TO USE—Con.								
Total cropland-Con.								
Other cropland-Con.								
Cropland on which all crops failed .... farms, 1987..	16	65	25	21	21	15	20	13
1982..	32	148	94	41	34	15	41	33
acres, 1987..	(D)	4 171	525	1 174	337	1 289	769	(D)
1982..	3 039	9 193	5 042	2 022	1 230	1 323	2 085	4 708
Cropland in cultivated summer fallow .... farms, 1987..	324	69	32	428	23	178	313	209
1982..	329	44	37	304	10	183	150	230
acres, 1987..	114 702	2 877	1 398	67 320	537	123 787	39 573	64 497
1982..	116 484	2 671	1 390	32 738	423	140 538	12 245	70 419
Cropland idle .... farms, 1987..	141	281	209	191	123	88	287	102
1982..	86	212	142	113	77	44	127	91
acres, 1987..	21 605	18 365	11 608	21 182	11 999	30 927	28 987	25 300
1982..	15 467	8 329	6 577	6 920	3 462	11 644	7 394	12 675
Total woodland .... farms, 1987..	9	331	416	131	147	5	99	12
1982..	10	344	400	124	185	6	86	19
acres, 1987..	1 215	15 608	18 575	6 187	7 816	106	4 885	613
1982..	1 962	18 841	21 195	6 415	9 436	(D)	2 987	1 357
Woodland pastured .... farms, 1987..	2	193	252	51	83	2	45	3
1982..	5	192	255	41	114	2	33	6
acres, 1987..	(D)	8 008	9 336	1 796	4 644	(D)	1 944	(D)
1982..	400	10 797	12 288	1 800	5 564	(D)	995	1 177
Woodland not pastured .... farms, 1987..	7	185	229	96	79	3	68	9
1982..	9	201	208	94	96	3	66	13
acres, 1987..	(D)	7 600	9 239	4 391	3 172	(D)	2 941	(D)
1982..	1 562	8 044	8 937	4 615	3 872	(D)	1 872	180
Other land .... farms, 1987..	316	921	812	592	483	211	658	223
1982..	355	983	868	677	573	209	695	277
acres, 1987..	150 826	110 560	67 045	141 702	37 080	156 559	148 995	129 162
1982..	157 624	132 665	66 618	157 162	40 657	(D)	143 269	175 638
Pastureland and rangeland other than								
cropland and woodland pastured .... farms, 1987..	207	531	413	995	208	131	430	151
1982..	268	579	427	443	268	97	444	196
acres, 1987..	(Y)	89 846	52 211	124 000	26 631	149 047	134 240	(D)
1982..	149 988	107 199	52 653	137 568	32 505	134 571	129 254	169 344
Land in house lots, ponds, roads,								
wasteland, etc. .... farms, 1987..	228	780	714	488	415	147	525	173
1982..	245	668	768	576	482	173	583	206
acres, 1987..	(D)	20 714	14 834	17 364	8 449	7 512	14 755	(D)
1982..	7 836	25 466	15 965	19 617	8 152	(D)	14 015	6 294
Pastureland, all types .... farms, 1987..	280	897	788	566	476	164	652	217
1982..	324	963	822	613	549	144	674	250
acres, 1987..	181 431	154 809	103 843	170 909	54 414	(D)	192 556	144 915
1982..	172 910	160 837	103 512	184 735	62 174	148 137	187 106	162 206
Cropland diverted under annual commodity								
acreage adjustment programs.................. farms, 1987..	289	304	263	479	122	189	498	194
1982..	144	126	69	167	20	89	138	134
acres, 1987..	42 222	14 049	12 252	55 162	5 226	52 360	53 678	31 077
1982..	11 089	2 868	1 538	7 807	(D)	10 321	7 140	12 817
Cropland placed under the conservation								
reserve program......................... farms, 1987..	83	75	72	54	6	58	139	98
acres, 1987..	7 860	7 017	5 141	3 419	417	18 125	14 851	21 791

See footnotes at end of table.

Table 5. Farms, Land in Farms, and Land Use: 1987 and 1982—Con.

[For meaning of abbreviations and symbols, see introductory text]

All Farms		Labette	Lane	Leavenworth	Lincoln	Linn	Logan	Lyon	McPherson
LAND IN FARMS ACCORDING TO USE—Con.									
Total cropland-Con.									
Other cropland-Con.									
Cropland on which all crops failed	farms, 1987	105	23	50	10	22	30	48	34
	1982	54	17	76	39	43	69	133	80
	acres, 1987	8 200	(D)	1 815	581	607	(D)	1 209	611
	1982	1 934	(D)	3 845	3 189	1 253	14 885	7 168	2 346
Cropland in cultivated summer fallow	farms, 1987	106	242	23	390	39	293	94	689
	1982	47	237	27	315	23	293	101	409
	acres, 1987	10 729	135 868	742	54 896	2 805	137 771	5 647	65 487
	1982	2 481	124 680	796	35 725	1 315	124 006	4 530	23 991
Cropland idle	farms, 1987	298	97	179	159	189	98	312	376
	1982	129	53	136	95	99	74	212	245
	acres, 1987	26 147	19 006	8 423	14 667	16 107	28 600	24 654	29 164
	1982	5 083	13 241	5 780	5 002	2 425	16 286	9 912	9 419
Total woodland	farms, 1987	233	6	490	60	287	3	263	138
	1982	246	9	572	62	315	9	290	152
	acres, 1987	12 400	517	21 499	3 932	26 810	(D)	10 291	3 738
	1982	13 122	2 127	28 976	2 661	26 622	1 540	11 047	3 780
Woodland pastured	farms, 1987	139	1	313	18	191	2	86	34
	1982		-	398	19	210	3	107	37
	acres, 1987	6 136	(D)	12 633	2 121	17 450	(D)	2 948	1 079
	1982	6 743	-	17 763	971	18 232	304	3 328	1 524
Woodland not pastured	farms, 1987	121	6	252	43	144	3	205	114
	1982	123	9	266	48	160	9	212	118
	acres, 1987	6 264	(D)	8 866	1 611	9 360	(D)	7 343	2 659
	1982	6 379	2 127	11 213	1 690	8 390	1 236	7 719	2 256
Other land	farms, 1987	802	234	888	444	589	267	732	1 102
	1982	871	253	983	504	641	285	806	1 203
	acres, 1987	107 608	124 453	44 414	178 469	89 998	(D)	210 721	97 616
	1982	114 199	142 771	47 940	164 674	85 093	244 706	255 396	127 758
Pastureland and rangeland other than cropland and woodland pastured	farms, 1987	554	176	411	303	350	186	423	498
	1982	557	162	467	279	377	220	473	521
	acres, 1987	93 741	(D)	32 807	165 858	75 271	251 801	193 924	79 961
	1982	93 955	129 641	35 627	147 575	69 653	234 497	229 738	101 894
Land in house lots, ponds, roads, wasteland, etc.	farms, 1987	672	160	788	374	495	173	611	987
	1982	770	200	896	426	540	186	729	1 085
	acres, 1987	13 867	(D)	11 607	12 611	14 727	(D)	16 797	17 655
	1982	20 244	13 130	12 113	17 099	15 440	10 209	25 658	25 864
Pastureland, all types	farms, 1987	789	210	898	431	571	226	631	769
	1982	866	224	973	446	628	245	689	875
	acres, 1987	140 709	134 203	75 968	209 306	127 134	272 613	246 309	123 346
	1982	145 897	148 034	83 351	197 684	128 539	249 743	274 978	143 346
Cropland diverted under annual commodity acreage adjustment programs	farms, 1987	307	193	216	378	206	229	365	908
	1982	112	91	66	183	85	116	216	350
	acres, 1987	15 511	36 757	8 361	40 814	9 401	39 234	19 212	75 264
	1982	2 503	11 008	1 205	10 337	1 741	11 362	5 609	12 312
Cropland placed under the conservation reserve program	farms, 1987	25	49	24	62	82	52	89	59
	acres, 1987	1 211	7 614	1 903	3 642	8 147	10 283	6 929	4 290

See footnotes at end of table.

Table 5. **Farms, Land in Farms, and Land Use: 1987 and 1982**—Con.

[For meaning of abbreviations and symbols, see introductory text]

All Farms	Marion	Marshall	Meade	Miami	Mitchell	Montgomery	Morris	Morton
LAND IN FARMS ACCORDING TO USE—Con.								
Total cropland—Con.								
Other cropland—Con.								
Cropland on which all crops failed ‗‗‗‗‗ farms, 1987‗‗	51	48	24	31	17	76	34	10
1982‗‗	50	100	22	142	54	49	64	16
acres, 1987‗‗	1 197	2 361	(D)	929	912	4 073	1 676	(D)
1982‗‗	2 294	5 677	(D)	9 664	4 517	3 450	4 019	4 821
Cropland in cultivated summer fallow ‗‗‗‗‗‗‗ farms, 1987‗‗	412	287	313	49	422	80	214	120
1982‗‗	354	200	272	46	355	54	158	143
acres, 1987‗‗	36 424	31 300	126 552	2 076	84 372	6 866	24 295	82 352
1982‗‗	20 922	9 703	86 996	1 675	53 372	3 780	15 543	89 137
Cropland idle ‗‗‗‗‗‗‗‗‗‗‗‗‗‗‗‗‗‗ farms, 1987‗‗	392	535	177	200	183	230	172	56
1982‗‗	176	315	90	215	69	105	104	59
acres, 1987‗‗	31 310	49 651	40 448	11 940	18 373	23 907	12 292	26 290
1982‗‗	8 242	12 538	14 590	12 205	5 645	8 510	6 967	5 475
Total woodland ‗‗‗‗‗‗‗‗‗‗‗‗‗‗ farms, 1987‗‗	144	266	14	409	75	277	119	4
1982‗‗	140	303	17	464	74	293	123	11
acres, 1987‗‗	4 743	14 470	1 362	26 285	3 666	15 560	4 849	469
1982‗‗	5 210	15 315	1 655	23 871	3 711	17 691	5 404	1 167
Woodland pastured ‗‗‗‗‗‗‗‗‗ farms, 1987‗‗	58	111	2	274	27	195	51	2
1982‗‗	65	147	4	295	20	218	49	10
acres, 1987‗‗	1 427	5 754	(D)	17 520	917	10 714	1 529	(D)
1982‗‗	1 702	6 421	(D)	12 647	820	12 677	1 596	(D)
Woodland not pastured ‗‗‗‗‗‗‗‗‗‗‗ farms, 1987‗‗	111	201	12	220	59	114	96	4
1982‗‗	91	190	13	232	58	105	92	1
acres, 1987‗‗	3 316	8 716	(D)	8 765	2 749	4 846	3 320	(D)
1982‗‗	3 508	8 894	(D)	11 224	2 891	5 014	3 808	(D)
Other land ‗‗‗‗‗‗‗‗‗‗‗‗‗‗‗‗‗‗ farms, 1987‗‗	893	896	314	976	461	809	457	133
1982‗‗	972	997	384	1 019	503	869	490	137
acres, 1987‗‗	181 713	129 619	186 422	68 539	87 285	125 903	196 237	165 576
1982‗‗	181 717	135 662	252 687	86 221	105 802	131 093	208 374	146 903
Pastureland and rangeland other than cropland and woodland pastured ‗‗‗‗‗‗‗‗‗‗‗ farms, 1987‗‗	482	506	199	582	270	573	326	86
1982‗‗	477	531	219	557	293	595	339	67
acres, 1987‗‗	166 594	102 848	(D)	58 071	78 893	112 069	186 520	(D)
1982‗‗	155 634	99 681	(D)	68 121	86 152	113 623	195 654	142 455
Land in house lots, ponds, roads, wasteland, etc. ‗‗‗‗‗‗‗‗‗ farms, 1987‗‗	788	791	223	832	376	627	371	97
1982‗‗	886	906	307	887	431	717	416	113
acres, 1987‗‗	15 119	26 771	(D)	15 868	11 392	13 814	9 717	(D)
1982‗‗	26 083	36 181	(D)	18 100	19 650	17 470	12 720	4 448
Pastureland, all types ‗‗‗‗‗‗‗‗‗ farms, 1987‗‗	835	753	252	957	406	831	446	127
1982‗‗	827	862	300	1 005	409	860	466	113
acres, 1987‗‗	226 004	162 791	198 889	110 586	111 638	157 402	227 217	170 222
1982‗‗	214 871	171 159	256 388	122 607	112 871	154 920	238 174	(D)
Cropland diverted under annual commodity acreage adjustment programs ‗‗‗‗‗‗‗‗‗‗‗‗ farms, 1987‗‗	693	702	311	206	413	220	283	149
1982‗‗	306	333	153	93	175	75	135	61
acres, 1987‗‗	58 188	56 072	53 365	8 881	64 568	18 204	22 861	35 914
1982‗‗	9 893	10 207	13 597	2 031	12 868	2 196	4 912	12 363
Cropland placed under the conservation reserve program ‗‗‗‗‗‗‗‗‗‗‗‗‗‗ farms, 1987‗‗	49	53	53	78	37	21	28	80
acres, 1987‗‗	2 488	4 359	12 129	3 682	2 711	1 170	1 074	45 261

See footnotes at end of table.

Table 5. Farms, Land in Farms, and Land Use: 1987 and 1982—Con.

[For meaning of abbreviations and symbols, see introductory text]

	Nemaha	Neosho	Ness	Norton	Osage	Osborne	Ottawa	Pawnee
LAND IN FARMS ACCORDING TO USE—Con.								
Total cropland-Con.								
Other cropland-Con.								
Cropland on which all crops failed...farms, 1987..	48	41	26	27	29	28	22	24
1982..	127	86	23	14	111	56	55	13
acres, 1987..	1 935	1 803	1 302	1 141	1 048	1 945	988	3 063
1982..	6 946	4 094	2 226	973	8 813	5 162	3 873	1 702
Cropland in cultivated summer fallow.......farms, 1987..	133	45	477	341	69	447	281	355
1982..	81	43	506	359	47	418	159	353
acres, 1987..	9 409	6 959	169 622	96 598	4 118	91 039	42 237	114 325
1982..	3 223	2 509	165 688	101 457	1 883	76 223	10 835	96 363
Cropland idle.......farms, 1987..	570	196	243	124	321	151	137	199
1982..	280	130	142	75	162	131	83	85
acres, 1987..	42 753	14 412	44 818	16 187	19 196	14 712	17 130	35 640
1982..	9 551	7 177	32 782	8 119	5 215	9 919	4 390	13 412
Total woodland.......farms, 1987..	255	238	23	50	306	73	76	36
1982..	274	240	15	43	312	83	79	40
acres, 1987..	14 341	13 002	1 154	3 079	18 765	3 928	3 219	4 503
1982..	14 290	13 319	727	1 919	16 017	6 655	4 786	3 949
Woodland pastured.......farms, 1987..	126	140	6	25	147	18	12	20
1982..	129	134	1	24	160	37	11	25
acres, 1987..	6 793	7 774	961	1 130	8 923	917	425	3 295
1982..	7 675	6 229	(D)	1 064	6 742	1 817	186	(D)
Woodland not pastured.......farms, 1987..	164	140	17	37	207	62	69	25
1982..	174	139	14	27	197	67	70	19
acres, 1987..	7 548	5 228	193	1 949	9 842	3 011	2 794	1 208
1982..	6 615	7 090	(D)	865	9 275	4 838	4 600	(D)
Other land.......farms, 1987..	904	633	452	403	755	476	417	392
1982..	966	693	530	457	840	521	483	424
acres, 1987..	91 334	95 341	207 532	181 247	123 594	193 623	137 772	78 140
1982..	105 344	109 258	229 583	203 154	150 351	188 101	152 105	78 535
Pastureland and rangeland other than cropland and woodland pastured.......farms, 1987..	492	435	344	272	474	321	232	218
1982..	485	419	394	361	509	319	286	220
acres, 1987..	69 167	81 575	196 575	163 117	108 870	181 015	126 260	69 377
1982..	77 245	93 112	(D)	181 962	130 811	170 183	135 086	(D)
Land in house lots, ponds, roads, wasteland, etc.......farms, 1987..	792	525	312	328	639	373	351	306
1982..	858	602	376	394	732	443	397	361
acres, 1987..	22 167	13 766	8 957	18 130	14 724	12 606	11 512	8 763
1982..	26 099	16 146	(D)	21 192	19 540	17 918	17 019	(D)
Pastureland, all types.......farms, 1987..	848	634	443	378	657	425	348	329
1982..	674	630	498	436	740	432	413	355
acres, 1987..	130 083	127 908	244 739	206 269	157 775	232 737	155 513	91 874
1982..	139 488	135 068	248 626	207 011	175 417	214 501	162 687	83 050
Cropland diverted under annual commodity acreage adjustment programs.......farms, 1987..	682	229	409	269	357	420	335	331
1982..	227	78	171	124	124	193	126	169
acres, 1987..	41 687	12 189	49 406	33 642	16 265	47 406	40 989	53 776
1982..	5 458	1 782	12 406	6 971	2 002	11 763	6 156	15 951
Cropland placed under the conservation reserve program.......farms, 1987..	93	73	77	97	108	64	37	63
acres, 1987..	7 851	5 458	9 967	10 924	7 459	5 771	3 741	8 667

See footnotes at end of table.

Table 5. **Farms, Land in Farms, and Land Use: 1987 and 1982**—Con.

[For meaning of abbreviations and symbols, see introductory text]

All Farms	Phillips	Pottawatomie	Pratt	Rawlins	Reno	Republic	~.	Rice	Riley
LAND IN FARMS ACCORDING TO USE—Con.									
Total cropland-Con.									
Other cropland-Con.									
Cropland on which all crops failed .... farms, 1987..	41	36	29	20	109	17		18	20
1982..	7	120	24	58	80	53		41	54
acres, 1987..	1 268	782	2 445	1 622	3 546	227		976	473
1982..	623	6 155	2 435	8 494	4 143	3 449		2 197	2 860
Cropland in cultivated summer fallow .... farms, 1987..	421	97	318	440	847	394		383	111
1982..	420	72	309	488	486	340		377	91
acres, 1987..	78 205	5 245	83 977	154 894	67 705	43 395		82 249	7 076
1982..	76 353	3 628	61 535	160 007	44 761	22 048		60 044	3 399
Cropland idle .... farms, 1987..	167	273	144	134	405	248		149	193
1982..	74	169	122	83	293	168		118	115
acres, 1987..	22 907	17 039	24 042	16 071	39 823	20 969		16 317	13 018
1982..	6 310	8 258	16 037	13 009	16 038	7 825		11 020	4 762
Total woodland .... farms, 1987..	58	286	36	17	198	127		57	164
1982..	87	288	39	26	187	160		62	159
acres, 1987..	4 101	16 705	1 052	788	6 446	5 067		3 019	4 772
1982..	4 896	14 913	1 760	1 610	5 698	5 900		2 013	7 330
Woodland pastured .... farms, 1987..	26	160	13	9	68	54		13	76
1982..	32	156	16	7	79	73		19	85
acres, 1987..	1 213	9 072	322	509	2 342	1 947		1 107	1 977
1982..	2 272	8 050	366	(D)	2 624	2 445		1 219	4 308
Woodland not pastured .... farms, 1987..	39	177	25	9	146	88		49	108
1982..	66	186	31	22	121	113		48	94
acres, 1987..	2 888	6 733	730	279	4 104	3 120		1 912	2 795
1982..	2 626	6 863	1 374	(D)	3 074	3 455		794	3 021
Other land .... farms, 1987..	481	682	373	452	1 171	663		484	458
1982..	547	758	417	500	1 288	767		518	509
acres, 1987..	204 749	238 952	73 074	226 211	128 799	92 572		78 545	109 996
1982..	216 480	252 280	87 121	240 993	125 734	107 069		76 025	123 496
Pastureland and rangeland other than cropland and woodland pastured .... farms, 1987..	323	457	231	319	595	404		253	278
1982..	375	468	292	373	636	465		240	304
acres, 1987..	188 362	219 731	63 486	₤11 668	111 174	76 849		67 653	101 011
1982..	197 108	232 560	77 740	(D)	102 935	84 831		60 401	110 678
Land in house lots, ponds, roads, wasteland, etc. .... farms, 1987..	402	571	292	322	1 017	555		399	398
1982..	484	680	359	394	1 159	657		466	436
acres, 1987..	16 467	19 221	9 589	14 329	17 625	13 723		10 992	8 985
1982..	19 372	19 720	9 381	(D)	22 799	22 238		15 624	12 818
Pastureland, all types .... farms, 1987..	472	624	334	401	1 028	587		386	415
1982..	530	650	378	479	1 074	688		409	422
acres, 1987..	250 767	269 248	89 100	251 051	170 426	121 079		97 416	130 933
1982..	261 455	282 518	96 530	267 792	159 893	119 558		88 537	140 372
Cropland diverted under annual commodity acreage adjustment programs .... farms, 1987..	340	302	337	357	845	567		375	250
1982..	162	116	190	115	431	296		222	116
acres, 1987..	34 196	15 638	59 882	45 770	100 172	56 098		58 208	14 327
1982..	7 723	2 327	19 661	8 342	26 075	10 829		18 172	3 199
Cropland placed under the conservation reserve program .... farms, 1987..	71	66	78	97	128	21		34	25
acres, 1987..	5 909	3 656	11 793	6 951	14 270	1 760		2 854	1 055

See footnotes at end of table.

Table 5. **Farms, Land in Farms, and Land Use: 1987 and 1982**—Con.

[For meaning of abbreviations and symbols, see introductory text]

All Farms	Rooks	Rush	Russell	Saline	Scott	Sedgwick	Seward	Shawnee
LAND IN FARMS ACCORDING TO USE—Con.								
Total cropland—Con.								
Other cropland—Con.								
Cropland on which all crops failed .... farms, 1987..	42	40	9	37	24	61	13	40
1982..	12	24	24	41	26	92	13	117
acres, 1987..	3 765	(D)	500	1 376	(D)	2 270	(D)	1 253
1982..	788	2 250	980	2 147	2 881	5 372	2 166	7 191
Cropland in cultivated summer fallow .... farms, 1987..	371	375	341	331	276	392	139	20
1982..	379	361	350	153	280	211	127	35
acres, 1987..	98 486	105 953	75 856	46 100	150 731	41 339	47 589	1 181
1982..	103 765	85 784	63 401	17 518	139 377	12 679	53 914	1 694
Cropland idle .... farms, 1987..	188	214	206	232	107	441	101	202
1982..	98	188	127	93	69	248	59	158
acres, 1987..	24 884	33 391	26 940	22 719	20 165	38 187	27 810	12 282
1982..	11 448	31 391	13 644	7 158	14 792	19 180	13 103	8 988
Total woodland .... farms, 1987..	48	24	26	105	8	150	6	253
1982..	41	22	29	121	6	163	5	276
acres, 1987..	3 916	794	866	3 714	300	9 265	1 465	10 974
1982..	2 866	996	2 426	3 887	(D)	6 409	(D)	13 137
Woodland pastured .... farms, 1987..	12	2	16	35	6	62	2	135
1982..	20	5	13	37	2	70	3	162
acres, 1987..	1 854	(D)	423	1 008	(D)	4 033	(D)	5 636
1982..	819	458	1 475	1 332	(D)	3 191	(D)	6 228
Woodland not pastured .... farms, 1987..	39	22	16	79	2	99	4	150
1982..	31	18	20	95	5	105	2	166
acres, 1987..	2 062	(D)	463	2 706	(D)	5 232	(D)	5 338
1982..	2 047	538	951	2 555	(D)	3 218	(D)	6 909
Other land .... farms, 1987..	390	380	434	557	259	1 137	199	703
1982..	421	434	468	594	299	1 266	184	757
acres, 1987..	221 227	74 902	172 510	111 395	94 526	68 907	82 596	60 417
1982..	220 758	90 970	184 204	125 443	(D)	79 037	(D)	68 055
Pastureland and rangeland other than cropland and woodland pastured .... farms, 1987..	288	235	287	280	122	467	110	355
1982..	318	290	294	303	147	502	103	369
acres, 1987..	204 812	(D)	156 901	101 685	(D)	53 586	(D)	47 558
1982..	203 250	82 107	165 957	109 064	117 471	56 210	80 607	53 822
Land in house lots, ponds, roads, wasteland, etc. .... farms, 1987..	298	292	336	466	214	1 005	143	608
1982..	353	344	362	515	259	1 136	145	670
acres, 1987..	16 415	(D)	15 609	9 710	(D)	15 321	(D)	12 859
1982..	17 508	8 863	18 247	16 379	(D)	22 827	(D)	14 233
Pastureland, all types .... farms, 1987..	374	392	423	458	167	851	147	576
1982..	390	430	441	474	187	891	146	641
acres, 1982..	232 031	105 535	194 788	140 296	101 841	89 539	92 035	81 840
1982..	225 522	117 766	207 995	143 126	131 562	92 268	69 913	87 840
Cropland diverted under annual commodity acreage adjustment programs.................. farms, 1987..	297	378	291	424	254	725	168	238
1982..	131	165	161	135	129	296	92	84
acres, 1987..	38 382	43 673	35 121	48 063	48 492	67 157	33 525	13 802
1982..	10 080	14 886	11 624	6 763	12 158	11 544	13 091	2 293
Cropland placed under the conservation reserve program.......................... farms, 1987..	106	56	106	73	31	24	42	40
acres, 1987..	12 998	3 761	12 743	5 611	7 720	1 708	14 694	2 140

See footnotes at end of table.

Table 5. **Farms, Land in Farms, and Land Use: 1987 and 1982**—Con.

[For meaning of abbreviations and symbols, see introductory text]

All Farms	Sheridan	Sherman	Smith	Stafford	Stanton	Stevens	Sumner	Thomas
LAND IN FARMS ACCORDING TO USE—Con.								
Total cropland—Con.								
Other cropland—Con.								
Cropland on which all crops failed _____ farms, 1987__	48	36	28	27	31	25	66	43
1982__	9	41	23	20	23	10	66	58
acres, 1987__	5 183	(D)	1 553	2 338	6 861	2 175	3 451	3 794
1982__	710	8 841	1 537	1 636	4 788	1 083	4 071	10 915
Cropland in cultivated summer fallow _____ farms, 1987__	386	397	499	314	190	186	514	510
1982__	416	411	495	335	172	165	173	458
acres, 1987__	119 970	174 702	85 130	69 511	115 629	71 912	79 108	215 936
1982__	115 575	192 824	72 461	58 132	121 769	47 582	18 586	202 856
Cropland idle _____ farms, 1987__	142	172	164	163	93	84	415	187
1982__	63	103	111	194	36	81	163	102
acres, 1987__	21 708	34 270	16 570	32 570	29 943	25 427	48 350	38 138
1982__	9 955	14 995	6 967	15 661	10 914	17 869	12 176	18 108
Total woodland _____ farms, 1987__	20	13	96	105	1	–	172	12
1982__	19	14	84	74	2	1	183	14
acres, 1987__	1 490	(D)	6 208	3 800	(D)	–	8 992	379
1982__	1 689	686	4 089	3 463	(D)	(D)	6 627	1 052
Woodland pastured _____ farms, 1987__	9	7	40	30	–	–	60	3
1982__	8	5	29	24	2	1	56	6
acres, 1987__	371	(D)	3 141	1 038	–	–	3 277	30
1982__	1 251	97	1 624	1 052	(D)	(D)	2 632	508
Woodland not pastured _____ farms, 1987__	13	6	65	82	1	–	123	11
1982__	12	12	63	60	–	–	117	9
acres, 1987__	1 119	(D)	3 067	2 762	(D)	–	5 715	349
1982__	438	589	2 465	2 411	–	–	3 995	544
Other land _____ farms, 1987__	364	340	576	385	173	202	956	399
1982__	442	357	652	404	131	223	1 067	418
acres, 1987__	128 049	(D)	167 969	81 407	(D)	68 352	96 586	91 057
1982__	134 171	128 052	195 160	90 569	(D)	(D)	126 267	98 690
Pastureland and rangeland other than cropland and woodland pastured _____ farms, 1987__	240	179	364	226	74	117	541	231
1982__	278	192	434	218	59	149	599	236
acres, 1987__	119 296	115 736	146 041	78 463	35 028	63 541	77 833	81 327
1982__	121 432	116 075	176 110	80 549	67 720	67 436	96 251	87 075
Land in house lots, ponds, roads, wasteland, etc. _____ farms, 1987__	293	276	491	308	142	146	779	316
1982__	361	313	560	347	107	162	921	346
acres, 1987__	8 754	(D)	19 128	5 944	(D)	4 811	18 953	9 730
1982__	12 739	11 977	19 050	10 020	(D)	(D)	30 016	11 615
Pastureland, all types _____ farms, 1987__	338	250	533	351	113	165	828	320
1982__	406	275	582	325	87	176	912	314
acres, 1987__	157 403	137 875	208 639	106 762	41 500	79 374	122 510	104 653
1982__	171 112	145 243	222 203	101 614	(D)	(D)	143 914	107 938
Cropland diverted under annual commodity acreage adjustment programs _____ farms, 1987__	341	355	469	365	189	208	836	454
1982__	147	153	232	194	96	139	286	140
acres, 1987__	43 334	62 378	51 994	59 986	54 025	63 033	127 127	77 716
1982__	8 191	14 104	11 856	18 210	16 968	21 153	19 329	15 829
Cropland placed under the conservation reserve program _____ farms, 1987__	55	36	66	43	71	74	23	26
acres, 1987__	4 040	6 795	5 355	6 359	37 474	21 410	1 584	5 991

See footnotes at end of table.

Table 5. **Farms, Land in Farms, and Land Use: 1987 and 1982**—Con.

[For meaning of abbreviations and symbols, see introductory text]

All Farms		Trego	Wabaunsee	Wallace	Washington	Wichita	Wilson	Woodson	Wyandotte
LAND IN FARMS ACCORDING TO USE—Con.									
Total cropland—Con.									
Other cropland—Con.									
Cropland on which all crops failed	farms, 1987..	10	16	23	34	22	41	25	5
	1982..	55	88	15	60	27	48	42	7
	acres, 1987..	(D)	419	(D)	2 114	1 620	2 543	1 270	(D)
	1982..	7 384	7 018	2 022	2 494	3 652	2 516	1 956	101
Cropland in cultivated summer fallow	farms, 1987..	365	51	242	315	244	70	61	–
	1982..	376	45	221	220	241	48	37	–
	acres, 1987..	109 784	2 420	111 520	31 187	138 140	7 495	4 295	–
	1982..	109 027	3 723	117 089	11 260	130 925	3 649	1 647	–
Cropland idle	farms, 1987..	167	172	86	383	101	211	150	18
	1982..	109	128	51	209	58	121	80	11
	acres, 1987..	23 345	12 580	18 458	38 502	31 150	21 174	12 501	706
	1982..	17 278	7 938	10 388	8 616	13 463	6 992	2 860	198
Total woodland	farms, 1987..	15	165	8	209	1	169	127	59
	1982..	18	190	11	252	4	200	128	59
	acres, 1987..	924	12 137	723	10 721	(D)	10 858	8 396	2 027
	1982..	886	9 525	1 820	12 755	(D)	14 233	7 502	1 877
Woodland pastured	farms, 1987..	10	99	4	89	1	83	76	32
	1982..	8	83	6	110	1	113	69	27
	acres, 1987..	(D)	5 747	(D)	4 577	(D)	4 506	5 363	1 476
	1982..	770	3 535	654	5 616	(D)	8 822	3 490	429
Woodland not pastured	farms, 1987..	10	120	4	148	–	102	78	31
	1982..	10	143	11	174	4	113	85	38
	acres, 1987..	(D)	6 390	11	6 144	–	6 352	3 033	551
	1982..	116	5 990	1 166	7 139	(D)	5 411	4 012	1 448
Other land	farms, 1987..	384	559	242	777	233	508	308	159
	1982..	398	600	247	887	251	585	325	162
	acres, 1987..	155 021	298 964	229 298	129 025	(D)	105 065	122 301	4 764
	1982..	187 751	280 637	196 916	169 594	(D)	129 839	143 420	5 563
Pastureland and rangeland other than cropland and woodland pastured	farms, 1987..	271	366	156	497	131	354	228	61
	1982..	300	382	153	543	132	373	218	56
	acres, 1987..	145 465	262 681	219 923	107 471	64 484	93 029	115 209	3 180
	1982..	177 222	258 286	190 291	140 430	56 121	110 443	135 015	4 419
Land in house lots, ponds, roads, wasteland, etc	farms, 1987..	283	451	174	671	179	423	249	136
	1982..	326	509	200	799	214	466	264	150
	acres, 1987..	9 556	16 283	9 376	21 554	(D)	12 036	7 092	1 584
	1982..	10 529	22 371	6 625	29 164	(D)	19 396	8 405	1 144
Pastureland, all types	farms, 1987..	372	507	192	590	164	489	294	128
	1982..	392	528	191	810	172	524	344	124
	acres, 1987..	186 779	326 154	234 294	167 224	(D)	128 581	136 070	6 196
	1982..	210 083	290 433	202 227	196 582	69 733	149 288	169 611	6 159
Cropland diverted under annual commodity acreage adjustment programs	farms, 1987..	304	222	211	581	247	243	167	8
	1982..	146	90	65	264	121	97	94	2
	acres, 1987..	32 698	10 612	38 980	54 592	47 846	15 091	9 256	421
	1982..	8 956	1 842	9 244	8 588	10 869	3 200	2 251	(D)
Cropland placed under the conservation reserve program	farms, 1987..	82	43	21	69	28	38	14	–
	acres, 1987..	7 485	2 274	4 252	7 175	7 258	3 041	1 153	–

[1]Data are based on a sample of farms, see text.

[For meaning of abbreviations and symbols, see introductory text]

Farms with harvested cropland	Kansas	Allen	Anderson	Atchison	Barber	Barton	Bourbon
Farms .... number, 1987	57 822	564	611	589	415	808	645
1982	62 860	614	667	637	445	871	705
acres harvested, 1987	17 729 394	125 078	161 985	122 717	149 449	262 060	90 939
1982	20 186 974	137 642	167 000	129 487	190 605	314 881	121 086
HARVESTED CROPLAND BY SIZE OF FARM							
1987 size of farm:							
1 to 9 acres .... farms	559	3	4	5	6	7	4
acres harvested	1 792	8	4	22	26	12	13
10 to 49 acres .... farms	3 746	41	33	50	8	38	37
acres harvested	62 424	758	654	974	106	619	611
50 to 69 acres .... farms	1 248	14	19	23	4	12	19
acres harvested	37 812	487	559	687	145	480	426
70 to 99 acres .... farms	3 658	65	51	46	15	42	84
acres harvested	145 968	2 146	2 051	1 872	581	1 976	2 800
100 to 139 acres .... farms	2 500	25	23	44	9	16	56
acres harvested	140 440	1 220	1 539	2 299	596	1 136	2 450
140 to 179 acres .... farms	5 084	43	51	77	14	71	76
acres harvested	371 929	2 324	3 562	5 223	1 326	5 660	3 739
180 to 219 acres .... farms	1 972	35	31	26	15	17	39
acres harvested	182 448	3 382	3 256	2 684	1 244	1 669	2 396
220 to 259 acres .... farms	2 555	38	37	36	9	41	32
acres harvested	269 308	3 691	4 127	4 754	1 509	4 787	2 771
260 to 499 acres .... farms	10 777	147	130	137	56	188	124
acres harvested	1 811 003	22 549	21 913	26 786	9 175	34 514	14 884
500 to 999 acres .... farms	11 707	81	133	103	89	210	108
acres harvested	3 906 288	26 589	42 414	39 201	20 009	72 844	25 567
1,000 to 1,999 acres .... farms	9 092	51	76	95	119	115	46
acres harvested	5 444 915	44 348	54 778	26 956	52 219	75 414	20 851
2,000 acres or more .... farms	4 924	11	23	7	91	49	20
acres harvested	5 455 187	15 576	27 118	11 259	62 511	62 969	14 399
1982 size of farm:							
1 to 9 acres .... farms	581	1	5	9	4	10	2
acres harvested	1 715	(D)	25	23	24	17	(D)
10 to 49 acres .... farms	4 328	55	39	51	10	50	56
acres harvested	77 944	(D)	789	932	173	1 006	(D)
50 to 69 acres .... farms	1 473	16	22	20	3	13	21
acres harvested	50 235	578	800	506	110	437	659
70 to 99 acres .... farms	4 005	52	59	59	15	38	66
acres harvested	177 361	1 609	2 549	2 463	827	2 045	2 282
100 to 139 acres .... farms	2 761	37	37	62	16	27	54
acres harvested	177 309	1 774	2 726	9 093	1 152	2 483	2 646
140 to 179 acres .... farms	5 490	80	46	90	31	81	71
acres harvested	462 336	3 638	3 086	6 005	3 415	7 488	3 940
180 to 219 acres .... farms	2 149	26	35	92	10	25	53
acres harvested	223 641	2 186	3 458	3 901	1 515	3 372	3 634
220 to 259 acres .... farms	2 962	51	46	39	18	52	35
acres harvested	370 138	6 066	5 577	4 680	3 216	6 794	2 951
260 to 499 acres .... farms	12 248	137	148	130	61	194	152
acres harvested	2 401 338	24 342	28 654	26 602	11 632	41 799	20 553
500 to 999 acres .... farms	13 247	121	136	114	85	213	117
acres harvested	4 863 099	43 560	45 796	47 123	32 366	87 382	32 062
1,000 to 1,999 acres .... farms	9 256	49	69	37	95	132	62
acres harvested	5 981 289	38 182	46 122	28 488	45 805	98 644	40 874
2,000 acres or more .... farms	4 386	9	25	4	97	36	16
acres harvested	5 400 569	14 704	27 418	4 871	90 350	63 384	(D)
HARVESTED CROPLAND BY ACRES HARVESTED							
1987 acres harvested:							
1 to 9 acres .... farms	2 149	20	19	22	11	19	36
acres	10 659	126	83	115	58	84	216
10 to 19 acres .... farms	2 967	45	32	37	12	19	62
acres	40 217	566	441	476	155	234	816
20 to 29 acres .... farms	2 694	39	30	39	13	15	56
acres	62 776	892	680	959	297	352	1 340
30 to 49 acres .... farms	4 562	64	54	67	10	49	98
acres	173 886	2 400	2 098	2 655	388	1 932	3 707
50 to 99 acres .... farms	8 853	98	100	114	51	106	141
acres	634 398	6 986	7 228	8 272	3 652	7 780	10 035
100 to 199 acres .... farms	10 361	121	123	106	81	169	115
acres	1 472 924	16 764	16 956	15 099	11 097	24 722	15 896
200 to 499 acres .... farms	14 761	98	152	147	121	262	100
acres	4 750 260	30 510	47 690	46 490	38 358	81 005	31 064
500 to 999 acres .... farms	8 150	61	77	44	89	121	27
acres	5 613 200	42 130	53 511	30 900	59 044	81 572	18 988
1,000 acres or more .... farms	3 325	18	24	13	27	46	7
acres	4 971 084	24 702	33 304	17 751	36 400	64 379	8 873
1982 acres harvested:							
1 to 9 acres .... farms	2 142	22	19	25	8	30	33
acres	10 420	124	101	126	55	121	202
10 to 19 acres .... farms	3 097	54	37	44	8	16	62
acres	41 940	753	507	589	109	200	867
20 to 29 acres .... farms	2 630	29	26	41	12	15	67
acres	61 042	697	590	935	288	340	1 522
30 to 49 acres .... farms	4 522	71	62	62	15	49	78
acres	171 444	2 625	2 382	2 327	568	1 862	2 993
50 to 99 acres .... farms	8 832	99	108	117	43	100	159
acres	631 696	6 778	7 465	8 873	3 215	7 370	11 076
100 to 199 acres .... farms	11 838	117	141	126	84	174	132
acres	1 660 500	16 672	20 089	18 055	12 141	24 591	18 793
200 to 499 acres .... farms	17 228	156	181	157	141	282	119
acres	5 577 202	49 748	56 123	50 271	44 205	92 501	37 310
500 to 999 acres .... farms	9 046	45	71	56	91	181	38
acres	6 212 991	30 881	47 076	38 696	62 646	109 900	26 657
1,000 acres or more .... farms	3 725	21	24	10	43	44	17
acres	5 819 739	29 364	32 667	12 113	67 976	77 996	21 666

Table 6. Harvested Cropland by Size of Farm and Acres Harvested: 1987 and 1982 — Con.

[For meaning of abbreviations and symbols, see introductory text]

Farms with harvested cropland	Brown	Butler	Chase	Chautauqua	Cherokee	Cheyenne	Clark
Farms .... number, 1987	637	934	223	248	857	426	233
1982	732	1 063	238	294	729	491	254
acres harvested, 1987	197 847	210 975	45 580	35 741	158 409	176 293	92 371
1982	226 953	225 388	49 790	40 581	186 648	197 174	113 399

HARVESTED CROPLAND BY SIZE OF FARM

1987 size of farm:

	Brown	Butler	Chase	Chautauqua	Cherokee	Cheyenne	Clark
1 to 9 acres ..... farms	5	11	1	1	2	-	4
acres harvested	14	36	(D)	(D)	(D)	-	9
10 to 49 acres ..... farms	33	95	14	8	70	5	3
acres harvested	621	1 727	(D)	(D)	37	(D)	60
50 to 69 acres ..... farms	7	36	4	1	37	2	2
acres harvested	309	1 268	193	(D)	1 173	(D)	(D)
70 to 99 acres ..... farms	44	78	6	10	68	10	5
acres harvested	2 027	2 663	221	329	2 829	524	179
100 to 139 acres ..... farms	34	46	13	13	63	4	-
acres harvested	2 192	2 106	730	473	3 125	147	-
140 to 179 acres ..... farms	61	83	6	23	66	19	9
acres harvested	7 174	6 212	706	1 089	5 031	1 487	638
180 to 219 acres ..... farms	23	31	7	13	36	5	3
acres harvested	2 812	3 064	572	599	3 171	529	208
220 to 259 acres ..... farms	39	56	10	18	39	9	1
acres harvested	5 237	5 179	886	627	4 777	674	(D)
260 to 499 acres ..... farms	150	150	43	44	107	60	40
acres harvested	30 669	20 484	5 298	3 549	20 842	8 795	6 598
500 to 999 acres ..... farms	127	159	55	44	108	95	46
acres harvested	55 828	54 791	12 299	4 402	46 035	23 453	11 375
1,000 to 1,999 acres ..... farms	78	131	38	39	57	132	53
acres harvested	63 991	70 140	15 235	(D)	45 397	63 591	20 399
2,000 acres or more ..... farms	18	58	24	34	14	85	67
acres harvested	26 953	43 305	(D)	15 470	22 842	76 921	52 707

1982 size of farm:

	Brown	Butler	Chase	Chautauqua	Cherokee	Cheyenne	Clark
1 to 9 acres ..... farms	5	14	1	1	5	2	1
acres harvested	11	29	(D)	(D)	12	(D)	(D)
10 to 49 acres ..... farms	49	127	11	10	98	7	4
acres harvested	749	2 304	(D)	(D)	1 820	(D)	69
50 to 69 acres ..... farms	18	34	4	4	20	5	-
acres harvested	873	1 227	101	117	754	160	-
70 to 99 acres ..... farms	60	102	3	10	62	8	4
acres harvested	3 213	3 808	78	325	2 587	454	320
100 to 139 acres ..... farms	21	54	15	12	70	4	3
acres harvested	1 622	3 479	911	266	4 820	268	96
140 to 179 acres ..... farms	73	94	19	25	73	24	16
acres harvested	8 673	8 972	1 382	1 033	6 654	1 990	1 302
180 to 219 acres ..... farms	37	58	5	13	39	5	4
acres harvested	5 048	5 426	707	877	4 334	461	529
220 to 259 acres ..... farms	46	63	10	20	43	10	2
acres harvested	7 070	8 947	921	1 504	5 895	1 084	(D)
260 to 499 acres ..... farms	181	167	49	53	118	97	40
acres harvested	44 970	29 154	7 098	3 693	25 727	16 893	8 883
500 to 999 acres ..... farms	159	170	50	67	141	111	50
acres harvested	75 044	60 941	11 708	8 484	70 733	31 025	14 780
1,000 to 1,999 acres ..... farms	74	116	37	41	52	140	54
acres harvested	66 232	67 609	14 538	11 114	49 263	74 226	27 451
2,000 acres or more ..... farms	9	54	34	36	10	78	76
acres harvested	13 748	38 492	12 167	13 015	14 049	70 475	61 744

HARVESTED CROPLAND BY ACRES HARVESTED

1987 acres harvested:

	Brown	Butler	Chase	Chautauqua	Cherokee	Cheyenne	Clark
1 to 9 acres ..... farms	13	50	4	10	36	1	6
acres	64	241	18	62	207	(D)	19
10 to 19 acres ..... farms	12	61	9	34	54	4	7
acres	137	1 086	122	393	719	(D)	106
20 to 29 acres ..... farms	22	73	11	23	47	11	4
acres	484	1 653	254	542	1 083	283	103
30 to 49 acres ..... farms	37	112	14	44	78	14	5
acres	1 415	4 324	484	1 592	2 957	517	198
50 to 99 acres ..... farms	118	141	54	46	118	48	25
acres	8 463	9 627	3 688	3 175	8 132	3 543	1 626
100 to 199 acres ..... farms	136	161	54	50	100	78	41
acres	19 481	22 676	7 711	6 626	14 343	11 313	5 921
200 to 499 acres ..... farms	175	208	55	25	204	144	90
acres	58 634	62 322	17 202	7 664	37 705	47 705	28 288
500 to 999 acres ..... farms	90	100	20	12	82	94	39
acres	64 036	70 592	(D)	7 762	56 758	65 456	26 706
1,000 or more acres ..... farms	34	28	2	4	23	31	16
acres	47 133	38 254	(D)	7 925	34 505	47 407	29 304

1982 acres harvested:

	Brown	Butler	Chase	Chautauqua	Cherokee	Cheyenne	Clark
1 to 9 acres ..... farms	27	48	8	17	31	3	3
acres	134	226	43	88	185	10	19
10 to 19 acres ..... farms	22	90	11	23	83	9	6
acres	263	1 224	144	293	869	149	(D)
20 to 29 acres ..... farms	23	81	6	29	51	8	2
acres	526	1 895	146	650	1 159	179	(D)
30 to 49 acres ..... farms	40	128	20	46	61	16	5
acres	1 572	4 710	781	1 638	2 383	636	186
50 to 99 acres ..... farms	92	181	44	70	107	54	29
acres	6 311	12 245	3 167	4 638	7 504	4 002	2 275
100 to 199 acres ..... farms	183	162	55	45	146	85	33
acres	22 453	25 305	7 346	6 232	20 171	12 448	4 809
200 to 499 acres ..... farms	205	202	68	48	137	180	90
acres	77 003	63 768	21 670	12 777	45 895	60 019	28 944
500 to 999 acres ..... farms	101	107	25	10	108	101	54
acres	68 013	71 094	(D)	6 896	74 412	69 527	44 295
1,000 or more acres ..... farms	40	34	1	6	25	35	21
acres	50 676	44 921	(D)	7 369	34 090	50 204	32 739

Table 6. **Harvested Cropland by Size of Farm and Acres Harvested: 1987 and 1982**—Con.

[For meaning of abbreviations and symbols, see introductory text]

Farms with harvested cropland	Clay	Cloud	Coffey	Comanche	Cowley	Crawford	Decatur
Farms number, 1987	586	583	515	209	760	649	438
1982	647	642	572	215	885	725	459
acres harvested, 1987	176 317	184 007	142 668	93 062	160 551	116 714	175 861
1982	189 827	214 074	157 589	118 915	212 326	155 932	172 683

HARVESTED CROPLAND BY SIZE OF FARM

1987 size of farm:	Clay	Cloud	Coffey	Comanche	Cowley	Crawford	Decatur
1 to 9 acres farms	6	6	3	1	8	10	2
acres harvested	29	33	8	(D)	24	53	(D)
10 to 49 acres farms	23	20	27	3	57	59	10
acres harvested	325	295	465	57	938	898	(D)
50 to 69 acres farms	4	13	13	-	20	15	3
acres harvested	143	513	336	-	480	362	114
70 to 99 acres farms	27	34	37	2	58	68	11
acres harvested	1 061	1 299	1 685	(D)	2 273	2 792	463
100 to 139 acres farms	17	28	24	5	38	49	4
acres harvested	898	1 885	1 506	293	1 982	2 292	200
140 to 179 acres farms	52	59	55	11	80	63	23
acres harvested	4 320	4 090	4 179	936	5 679	4 244	1 977
180 to 219 acres farms	12	13	26	2	19	38	9
acres harvested	1 025	1 148	2 797	(D)	1 636	3 522	946
220 to 259 acres farms	39	31	29	-	37	61	9
acres harvested	3 768	3 218	3 649	-	2 501	4 961	775
260 to 499 acres farms	121	112	89	19	143	134	58
acres harvested	21 069	20 057	14 998	2 943	20 263	22 520	7 874
500 to 999 acres farms	157	121	120	47	163	96	93
acres harvested	53 270	43 405	41 934	12 311	48 839	31 918	24 424
1,000 to 1,999 acres farms	105	112	62	41	86	42	141
acres harvested	65 513	71 878	36 869	13 717	44 802	27 483	68 781
2,000 acres or more farms	23	32	30	78	51	14	75
acres harvested	24 608	36 266	34 242	52 601	31 132	15 569	70 651
1982 size of farm:							
1 to 9 acres farms	8	12	5	2	4	7	(1)
acres harvested	17	40	11	(D)	12	24	(D)
10 to 49 acres farms	24	42	38	-	90	84	5
acres harvested	421	917	670	-	1 631	1 574	(D)
50 to 69 acres farms	10	11	12	2	28	18	1
acres harvested	403	576	522	(D)	966	591	(D)
70 to 99 acres farms	26	38	45	3	56	64	10
acres harvested	1 235	2 066	2 177	195	2 730	2 425	627
100 to 139 acres farms	22	22	36	5	41	50	4
acres harvested	1 673	1 804	2 447	405	2 811	2 996	86
140 to 179 acres farms	63	56	46	11	83	74	24
acres harvested	5 414	5 098	3 852	982	6 339	5 991	2 020
180 to 219 acres farms	23	21	37	2	26	43	5
acres harvested	2 741	2 632	3 751	(D)	2 737	4 190	363
220 to 259 acres farms	52	39	32	2	53	57	7
acres harvested	6 478	5 541	3 504	(D)	6 804	6 717	641
260 to 499 acres farms	149	120	112	23	163	121	66
acres harvested	29 540	25 827	20 587	3 843	32 693	21 696	9 153
500 to 999 acres farms	162	151	122	48	170	144	125
acres harvested	64 142	64 243	44 710	17 135	58 823	56 075	29 672
1,000 to 1,999 acres farms	93	108	56	52	113	47	141
acres harvested	58 769	73 437	35 649	28 032	63 679	33 417	63 799
2,000 acres or more farms	15	22	31	65	58	16	70
acres harvested	19 095	31 893	39 709	67 778	33 301	20 236	65 966

HARVESTED CROPLAND BY ACRES HARVESTED

1987 acres harvested:	Clay	Cloud	Coffey	Comanche	Cowley	Crawford	Decatur
1 to 9 acres farms	19	17	12	3	39	32	5
acres	122	95	55	17	191	188	30
10 to 19 acres farms	14	18	31	6	54	58	5
acres	189	228	407	87	773	780	70
20 to 29 acres farms	18	27	18	4	57	46	11
acres	429	662	415	97	1 339	1 062	270
30 to 49 acres farms	28	44	45	7	89	92	23
acres	1 066	1 656	1 666	264	3 504	3 412	890
50 to 99 acres farms	87	92	95	21	168	123	49
acres	6 392	6 751	6 995	1 522	9 081	8 867	3 708
100 to 199 acres farms	111	89	86	29	134	128	64
acres	15 632	12 842	12 413	4 177	19 425	18 329	9 015
200 to 499 acres farms	186	161	149	66	173	113	143
acres	59 195	51 662	49 256	21 673	55 653	36 425	46 632
500 to 999 acres farms	105	105	59	54	74	43	105
acres	69 705	71 580	41 210	36 134	50 683	28 610	71 657
1,000 acres or more farms	18	30	20	19	17	14	33
acres	23 487	38 531	30 231	29 081	20 902	19 041	43 589
1982 acres harvested:							
1 to 9 acres farms	18	20	20	2	96	31	6
acres	58	63	106	(D)	208	164	26
10 to 19 acres farms	10	22	15	3	64	58	6
acres	147	281	208	31	881	797	72
20 to 29 acres farms	19	16	30	1	40	47	5
acres	443	390	674	(D)	940	1 107	124
30 to 49 acres farms	23	37	44	4	83	74	13
acres	1 259	1 434	1 592	162	3 137	2 771	494
50 to 99 acres farms	54	82	106	16	138	138	54
acres	6 166	5 700	7 669	1 166	9 577	9 720	4 163
100 to 199 acres farms	144	121	118	35	168	135	88
acres	20 063	17 014	16 601	4 854	23 999	18 530	12 679
200 to 499 acres farms	215	189	146	55	228	157	175
acres	68 551	61 855	47 039	18 200	71 853	50 788	58 866
500 to 999 acres farms	109	129	66	69	108	69	86
acres	72 573	88 551	45 368	47 395	72 120	47 021	59 234
1,000 acres or more farms	15	26	23	65	30	18	27
acres	20 547	36 766	38 332	47 076	29 621	25 034	37 023

1987 CENSUS OF AGRICULTURE—COUNTY DATA

[For meaning of abbreviations and symbols, see Introductory text]

Farms with harvested cropland	Dickinson	Doniphan	Douglas	Edwards	Elk	Ellis	Ellsworth
Farms number, 1987	908	454	691	328	293	691	450
1982	1 012	543	740	373	346	695	471
acres harvested, 1987	245 504	127 686	106 664	186 513	40 040	147 980	128 533
1982	297 527	150 592	112 306	206 856	54 719	162 348	146 178
HARVESTED CROPLAND BY SIZE OF FARM							
1987 size of farm:							
1 to 9 acres farms	9	6	11	-	1	4	4
acres harvested	27	22	37	-	(D)	8	12
10 to 49 acres farms	48	45	94	7	6	31	12
acres harvested	876	788	1 373	(D)	100	501	187
50 to 69 acres farms	17	13	56	1	2	8	3
acres harvested	405	515	1 404	(D)	(D)	229	125
70 to 99 acres farms	54	42	83	7	18	40	14
acres harvested	2 110	1 833	3 067	333	516	1 546	615
100 to 139 acres farms	30	30	59	5	6	26	24
acres harvested	2 155	2 025	2 628	250	254	1 296	1 446
140 to 179 acres farms	103	36	94	18	21	75	32
acres harvested	7 802	3 254	6 049	1 590	1 223	4 469	2 145
180 to 219 acres farms	36	19	47	6	10	16	14
acres harvested	3 453	1 922	4 585	380	535	1 264	1 323
220 to 259 acres farms	41	17	25	12	12	21	9
acres harvested	5 042	2 360	2 132	1 693	728	1 662	892
260 to 499 acres farms	213	96	105	65	70	154	87
acres harvested	36 587	20 922	16 918	11 660	8 557	18 889	12 180
500 to 999 acres farms	208	90	72	66	72	172	101
acres harvested	76 341	38 435	29 412	23 904	9 183	37 420	29 292
1,000 to 1,999 acres farms	124	51	37	82	42	98	112
acres harvested	77 765	44 601	27 818	55 959	10 747	41 174	51 161
2,000 acres or more farms	27	7	8	59	33	46	39
acres harvested	32 941	11 011	13 241	90 685	11 152	39 502	29 155
1982 size of farm							
1 to 9 acres farms	10	6	19	1	1	1	2
acres harvested	43	26	57	(D)	(D)	(D)	(D)
10 to 49 acres farms	56	61	117	4	12	23	9
acres harvested	1 181	1 096	1 660	(D)	(D)	(D)	(D)
50 to 69 acres farms	28	18	48	4	4	9	7
acres harvested	984	783	1 369	190	155	407	272
70 to 99 acres farms	86	52	83	4	18	37	20
acres harvested	4 726	2 540	3 153	205	468	1 605	1 142
100 to 139 acres farms	36	37	52	5	12	41	21
acres harvested	3 372	2 450	2 671	148	746	2 416	1 256
140 to 179 acres farms	107	45	89	34	35	78	25
acres harvested	10 519	4 270	6 465	3 406	1 730	5 684	1 969
180 to 219 acres farms	30	14	39	9	13	23	16
acres harvested	3 660	1 738	3 768	823	788	1 899	1 987
220 to 259 acres farms	46	25	39	4	16	20	18
acres harvested	7 005	3 872	3 600	418	1 073	845	2 016
260 to 499 acres farms	247	141	124	85	64	150	71
acres harvested	56 829	36 882	20 447	17 928	5 331	20 917	15 958
500 to 999 acres farms	245	94	79	91	86	169	109
acres harvested	105 026	46 333	30 686	35 503	13 451	49 601	46 941
1,000 to 1,999 acres farms	100	43	35	88	53	78	95
acres harvested	72 359	40 011	24 332	66 014	16 399	35 930	49 656
2,000 acres or more farms	21	7	8	46	32	46	31
acres harvested	31 821	10 591	13 898	82 100	14 221	41 277	24 601
HARVESTED CROPLAND BY ACRES HARVESTED							
1987 acres harvested:							
1 to 9 acres farms	28	20	58	3	4	23	12
acres	131	104	279	16	24	108	49
10 to 19 acres farms	30	33	60	4	27	33	12
acres	447	425	1 118	44	369	450	180
20 to 29 acres farms	35	16	67	5	19	31	8
acres	827	402	1 635	112	428	741	200
30 to 49 acres farms	72	37	110	11	46	46	26
acres	2 772	1 374	4 193	400	1 721	1 839	994
50 to 99 acres farms	146	65	136	36	79	157	76
acres	10 655	4 448	9 242	2 668	5 476	11 234	5 499
100 to 199 acres farms	170	81	89	46	57	174	91
acres	24 185	11 304	12 404	6 461	8 173	25 205	12 853
200 to 499 acres farms	275	123	97	97	46	163	144
acres	89 452	39 762	31 725	32 154	13 805	50 969	48 375
500 to 999 acres farms	123	58	40	62	13	45	71
acres	81 617	40 997	28 415	43 793	(D)	31 694	46 252
1,000 acres or more farms	28	21	12	64	2	19	11
acres	35 218	26 870	19 753	100 865	(D)	25 740	14 131
1982 acres harvested							
1 to 9 acres farms	30	26	73	2	6	16	6
acres	134	135	340	(D)	32	71	29
10 to 19 acres farms	28	32	86	2	16	20	4
acres	413	417	1 157	(D)	203	274	59
20 to 29 acres farms	31	18	52	9	37	22	10
acres	724	426	1 205	224	839	524	223
30 to 49 acres farms	50	39	112	13	81	54	23
acres	1 927	1 489	4 134	519	2 289	2 086	848
50 to 99 acres farms	160	84	155	31	76	136	75
acres	11 787	5 743	10 712	2 157	5 471	9 722	5 315
100 to 199 acres farms	210	98	177	67	90	158	91
acres	31 288	14 316	16 145	9 977	8 021	23 433	12 890
200 to 499 acres farms	323	152	91	112	66	204	172
acres	105 522	49 613	30 116	38 064	19 857	62 861	57 616
500 to 999 acres farms	151	73	40	77	17	57	80
acres	102 638	50 818	25 964	54 161	11 016	36 021	55 431
1,000 acres or more farms	29	21	14	60	6	18	10
acres	43 094	27 633	22 531	101 725	6 991	27 254	13 767

Table 6. Harvested Cropland by Size of Farm and Acres Harvested: 1987 and 1982—Con.

[For meaning of abbreviations and symbols, see introductory text]

Farms with harvested cropland	Finney	Ford	Franklin	Geary	Gove	Graham	Grant
Farms .... number, 1987	463	703	799	239	454	403	258
1982	494	730	895	250	485	464	236
acres harvested, 1987	323 607	284 042	135 097	48 216	194 728	148 177	156 356
1982	384 552	301 832	142 823	50 305	195 149	161 580	199 136
HARVESTED CROPLAND BY SIZE OF FARM							
1987 size of farm:							
1 to 9 acres .... farms	8	8	8	5	3	2	1
acres harvested	30	35	20	11	11	(D)	(D)
10 to 49 acres .... farms	11	34	101	17	7	11	1
acres harvested	(D)	607	1 662	329	130	176	(D)
50 to 69 acres .... farms	1	2	58	9	2	1	4
acres harvested	(D)	262	1 536	190	(D)	(D)	234
70 to 99 acres .... farms	11	23	103	11	5	6	3
acres harvested	591	1 084	3 600	330	243	287	123
100 to 139 acres .... farms	5	6	63	16	6	9	1
acres harvested	251	915	3 085	1 030	244	426	(D)
140 to 179 acres .... farms	26	52	60	12	35	31	20
acres harvested	2 066	3 907	5 043	573	2 671	1 566	1 706
180 to 219 acres .... farms	6	9	41	9	2	7	2
acres harvested	667	797	3 722	601	(D)	484	(D)
220 to 259 acres .... farms	9	14	39	11	5	4	2
acres harvested	1 047	1 664	3 448	1 121	347	378	45
260 to 499 acres .... farms	63	132	136	44	89	66	45
acres harvested	12 371	21 331	21 845	6 357	9 932	8 675	8 511
500 to 999 acres .... farms	78	187	99	46	97	83	54
acres harvested	33 109	57 648	32 753	9 711	26 048	19 474	19 544
1,000 to 1,999 acres .... farms	124	134	56	43	120	105	61
acres harvested	91 525	80 153	35 264	17 969	69 903	46 595	61 973
2,000 acres or more .... farms	121	86	15	15	104	78	44
acres harvested	181 621	115 419	23 019	9 974	94 952	70 084	63 702
1982 size of farm:							
1 to 9 acres .... farms	7	10	11	7	-	4	2
acres harvested	30	28	29	18	-	6	(D)
10 to 49 acres .... farms	15	26	125	24	4	6	2
acres harvested	(D)	573	2 161	503	51	77	142
50 to 69 acres .... farms	2	8	59	7	4	4	2
acres harvested	(D)	289	1 509	290	236	125	(D)
70 to 99 acres .... farms	9	18	122	9	7	12	4
acres harvested	508	724	4 252	384	302	426	166
100 to 139 acres .... farms	3	24	78	3	6	7	-
acres harvested	373	1 665	4 230	413	180	369	-
140 to 179 acres .... farms	33	65	90	16	30	46	19
acres harvested	3 073	4 915	5 693	1 098	(D)	3 159	1 990
180 to 219 acres .... farms	5	10	44	12	1	17	2
acres harvested	532	1 151	4 107	761	(D)	1 416	(D)
220 to 259 acres .... farms	8	17	41	14	14	4	-
acres harvested	1 447	1 974	3 714	1 357	2 006	531	-
260 to 499 acres .... farms	57	143	141	44	80	71	21
acres harvested	16 334	26 430	23 715	5 659	12 694	10 776	6 249
500 to 999 acres .... farms	111	179	121	54	115	98	65
acres harvested	49 816	60 603	45 899	13 527	30 209	19 406	28 973
1,000 to 1,999 acres .... farms	141	155	50	40	120	118	74
acres harvested	118 219	101 623	33 398	18 998	56 317	53 761	61 531
2,000 acres or more .... farms	103	75	13	13	99	74	53
acres harvested	194 063	101 867	14 110	7 297	90 496	71 508	99 589
HARVESTED CROPLAND BY ACRES HARVESTED							
1987 acres harvested:							
1 to 9 acres .... farms	10	21	54	13	5	6	3
acres	42	118	295	53	22	32	8
10 to 19 acres .... farms	6	22	82	14	6	8	3
acres	77	284	1 065	210	(D)	134	(D)
20 to 29 acres .... farms	4	18	82	15	2	12	(D)
acres	102	438	1 873	347	(D)	274	(D)
30 to 49 acres .... farms	15	32	129	26	18	21	3
acres	594	1 190	4 709	1 010	750	783	143
50 to 99 acres .... farms	43	80	150	32	55	53	21
acres	3 010	5 769	10 469	2 209	4 091	3 875	1 502
100 to 199 acres .... farms	42	114	100	54	87	70	34
acres	6 332	16 185	14 087	7 621	9 904	10 228	5 083
200 to 499 acres .... farms	104	236	134	59	168	128	71
acres	34 100	76 517	40 823	17 806	55 368	41 376	22 903
500 to 999 acres .... farms	124	116	49	22	90	76	75
acres	87 848	79 995	32 468	13 318	62 554	53 193	55 557
1,000 acres or more .... farms	115	64	19	4	43	29	47
acres	191 702	101 546	29 308	5 645	61 905	38 282	71 109
1982 acres harvested:							
1 to 9 acres .... farms	9	11	59	15	2	4	2
acres	41	29	278	54	(D)	14	(D)
10 to 19 acres .... farms	6	26	112	19	11	6	3
acres	83	350	1 474	244	(D)	165	(D)
20 to 29 acres .... farms	10	17	84	15	6	14	(D)
acres	235	419	2 002	371	149	349	(D)
30 to 49 acres .... farms	6	38	135	33	19	27	5
acres	226	1 425	5 078	1 297	671	1 037	173
50 to 99 acres .... farms	32	73	165	32	60	54	9
acres	2 393	5 347	11 568	2 232	4 332	3 889	617
100 to 199 acres .... farms	43	124	116	53	86	105	19
acres	6 329	16 397	16 262	7 552	12 519	15 248	2 771
200 to 499 acres .... farms	114	237	139	57	162	140	47
acres	39 469	76 485	48 784	17 199	51 859	44 920	17 356
500 to 999 acres .... farms	145	139	57	27	99	79	65
acres	100 195	96 554	37 350	18 004	67 174	57 853	60 474
1,000 acres or more .... farms	129	65	15	3	40	26	66
acres	235 679	102 817	20 027	3 352	56 477	36 093	117 701

Table 6. **Harvested Cropland by Size of Farm and Acres Harvested: 1987 and 1982**—Con.

[For meaning of abbreviations and symbols, see introductory text]

Farms with harvested cropland	Gray	Greeley	Greenwood	Hamilton	Harper	Harvey	Haskell
Farms .... number, 1987	480	266	409	225	595	740	284
1982	502	259	499	237	617	826	290
acres harvested, 1987	258 379	196 152	73 937	160 604	233 900	197 917	200 065
1982	325 993	193 327	81 686	204 376	288 418	232 904	349 122
HARVESTED CROPLAND BY SIZE OF FARM							
1987 size of farm:							
1 to 9 acres ... farms	2	1	1	-	13	8	-
acres harvested	(D)	(D)	(D)	-	38	24	-
10 to 49 acres ... farms	4	1	19	5	29	106	8
acres harvested	66	(D)	(D)	104	(D)	1 682	83
50 to 69 acres ... farms	2	-	7	-	2	13	3
acres harvested	(D)	-	242	-	(D)	461	157
70 to 99 acres ... farms	4	10	25	3	20		1
acres harvested	161	572	776	78	952	3 137	(D)
100 to 139 acres ... farms	11	6	19	-	10	35	-
acres harvested	836	273	1 415	-	611	2 549	-
140 to 179 acres ... farms	46	16	30	14	53	61	21
acres harvested	3 623	1 130	1 698	1 167	4 877	7 540	1 982
180 to 219 acres ... farms	5	5	19	-	24	23	2
acres harvested	358	404	1 384	-	2 590	2 891	(D)
220 to 259 acres ... farms	9	(D)	19	-	26	34	2
acres harvested	1 022	(D)	1 197	-	3 682	5 144	(D)
260 to 499 acres ... farms	99	54	82	22	113	166	37
acres harvested	19 796	9 950	8 269	4 054	23 778	36 944	7 841
500 to 999 acres ... farms	118	44	76	38	134	145	75
acres harvested	44 936	15 039	13 591	13 107	48 787	66 110	34 120
1,000 to 1,999 acres ... farms	111	44	57	42	120	49	86
acres harvested	83 973	25 793	18 335	22 237	89 008	43 366	77 837
2,000 acres or more ... farms	69	84	55	101	51	14	49
acres harvested	103 493	142 824	26 685	119 757	58 984	26 069	77 611
1982 size of farm:							
1 to 9 acres ... farms	-	-	1	-	4	6	1
acres harvested	-	-	(D)	-	9	27	(D)
10 to 49 acres ... farms	4	-	3	3	23	91	1
acres harvested	(D)	-	89	32	538	1 661	(D)
50 to 69 acres ... farms	1	-	-	1	3	21	-
acres harvested	(D)	-	42	(D)	138	640	-
70 to 99 acres ... farms	13	3	28	6	34	82	2
acres harvested	692	135	1 025	394	2 066	4 851	(D)
100 to 139 acres ... farms	3	-	24	1	16	35	3
acres harvested	360	-	1 494	161	1 211	3 004	300
140 to 179 acres ... farms	44	26	40	12	66	97	12
acres harvested	4 452	(D)	2 229	1 105	6 941	10 705	1 525
180 to 219 acres ... farms	1	2	17	2	11	36	3
acres harvested	(D)	(D)	1 776	(D)	1 327	4 945	477
220 to 259 acres ... farms	11	5	24	1	24	61	2
acres harvested	1 841	540	1 700	(D)	3 488	10 940	(D)
260 to 499 acres ... farms	117	47	98	19	102	188	56
acres harvested	32 869	7 728	10 935	3 405	26 807	50 485	17 147
500 to 999 acres ... farms	139	34	86	26	163	146	75
acres harvested	65 884	11 942	14 108	7 017	77 615	76 690	39 264
1,000 to 1,999 acres ... farms	105	64	83	59	122	53	89
acres harvested	94 049	36 943	19 930	38 431	101 681	50 273	91 523
2,000 acres or more ... farms	64	75	65	105	49	10	45
acres harvested	125 812	133 982	27 807	153 225	66 620	18 683	98 374
HARVESTED CROPLAND BY ACRES HARVESTED							
1987 acres harvested:							
1 to 9 acres ... farms	2	2	13	2	21	44	-
acres	(D)	(D)	70	(D)	83	188	-
10 to 19 acres ... farms	6	2	27	5	18	40	7
acres	(D)	(D)	354	(D)	263	555	(D)
20 to 29 acres ... farms	6	3	18	4	14	41	1
acres	160	66	426	92	334	958	(D)
30 to 49 acres ... farms	12	6	49	9	21	48	5
acres	459	224	1 886	322	810	1 914	192
50 to 99 acres ... farms	42	34	100	16	82	112	18
acres	3 039	2 579	7 050	1 075	4 817	8 090	1 378
100 to 199 acres ... farms	75	37	92	19	109	131	25
acres	10 157	5 763	12 314	2 891	15 377	18 667	3 631
200 to 499 acres ... farms	161	73	73	47	172	213	72
acres	54 773	24 333	23 517	16 355	56 749	69 693	25 554
500 to 999 acres ... farms	108	42	29	59	126	82	85
acres	78 090	30 022	17 996	41 598	86 190	54 587	63 397
1,000 acres or more ... farms	68	66	8	64	52	28	71
acres	111 596	133 125	10 324	96 080	69 477	43 255	105 800
1982 acres harvested:							
1 to 9 acres ... farms	-	-	12	-	6	37	1
acres	-	-	85	-	24	205	(D)
10 to 19 acres ... farms	3	1	28	3	15	36	-
acres	53	(D)	405	(D)	233	466	-
20 to 29 acres ... farms	3	1	33	2	15	32	-
acres	76	(D)	746	(D)	372	748	-
30 to 49 acres ... farms	7	7	78	19	54		-
acres	292	(D)	3 056	214	771	2 065	-
50 to 99 acres ... farms	34	31	97	20	59	116	6
acres	2 463	2 293	7 066	1 479	4 425	8 539	(D)
100 to 199 acres ... farms	53	43	124	25	98	157	26
acres	7 939	6 037	17 814	3 377	13 669	23 608	3 864
200 to 499 acres ... farms	180	59	96	36	178	241	84
acres	59 470	19 659	29 825	11 592	60 813	76 889	28 679
500 to 999 acres ... farms	126	51	24	66	157	107	94
acres	88 425	34 720	15 219	47 820	109 538	70 416	66 199
1,000 acres or more ... farms	96	66	6	80	70	36	79
acres	167 266	130 308	7 690	139 809	98 473	49 948	147 956

Table 6. **Harvested Cropland by Size of Farm and Acres Harvested: 1987 and 1982**—Con.

[For meaning of abbreviations and symbols, see introductory text]

Farms with harvested cropland	Hodgeman	Jackson	Jefferson	Jewell	Johnson	Kearny	Kingman	Kiowa
Farms................... number, 1987..	382	844	836	647	466	247	718	276
1982..	417	951	855	719	565	242	772	317
acres harvested, 1987..	159 903	114 691	112 865	208 645	69 445	202 164	219 446	128 425
1982..	164 424	139 408	128 243	249 175	89 698	216 509	265 252	144 836
HARVESTED CROPLAND BY SIZE OF FARM								
1987 size of farm:								
1 to 9 acres .... farms..	–	3	7	2	14	–	9	3
acres harvested..	–	4	28	(D)	40	–	27	6
10 to 49 acres .... farms..	14	71	109	24	120	5	35	2
acres harvested..	276	1 257	1 696	(D)	1 792	108	652	(D)
50 to 69 acres .... farms..	–	16	49	3	35	1	6	2
acres harvested..	–	481	1 266	88	1 020	(D)	137	(D)
70 to 99 acres .... farms..	6	114	113	17	56	2	43	7
acres harvested..	228	3 826	3 793	660	2 453	(D)	1 957	213
100 to 139 acres .... farms..	7	62	97	25	52	3	19	2
acres harvested..	486	3 156	4 269	1 464	1 810	162	1 051	(D)
140 to 179 acres .... farms..	12	115	97	56	39	19	87	16
acres harvested..	1 090	6 429	6 229	4 249	2 564	1 374	5 974	1 489
180 to 219 acres .... farms..	5	45	45	24	25	5	27	4
acres harvested..	534	3 045	3 658	2 273	2 607	566	2 312	534
220 to 259 acres .... farms..	7	55	43	35	15	4	34	9
acres harvested..	734	4 567	4 022	2 933	2 185	359	3 554	948
260 to 499 acres .... farms..	66	160	134	138	75	21	147	34
acres harvested..	9 782	21 641	20 311	21 885	12 654	3 677	25 382	5 143
500 to 999 acres .... farms..	81	137	89	146	48	42	161	69
acres harvested..	20 111	37 916	26 713	44 107	18 383	14 207	53 208	22 445
1,000 to 1,999 acres .... farms..	102	63	44	131	23	89	130	67
acres harvested..	50 142	23 913	33 021	80 317	18 842	36 762	78 050	38 569
2,000 acres or more .... farms..	82	10	9	46	4	86	40	61
acres harvested..	76 510	8 560	7 889	50 302	4 875	144 746	47 232	58 895
1982 size of farm:								
1 to 9 acres .... farms..	1	7	11	1	14	2	4	4
acres harvested..	(D)	24	55	(D)	34	(D)	11	4
10 to 49 acres .... farms..	6	95	114	20	119	6	35	4
acres harvested..	(D)	1 583	1 911	(D)	1 925	126	631	103
50 to 69 acres .... farms..	1	33	42	16	39	1	8	2
acres harvested..	(D)	1 050	1 059	645	1 244	(D)	277	(D)
70 to 99 acres .... farms..	3	127	112	29	67	4	40	9
acres harvested..	80	4 217	3 868	1 386	2 546	121	1 945	266
100 to 139 acres .... farms..	10	55	86	18	60	6	30	4
acres harvested..	663	3 066	3 970	1 051	3 049	407	2 723	225
140 to 179 acres .... farms..	23	108	92	62	47	21	70	15
acres harvested..	2 418	6 008	5 583	5 971	3 617	2 152	6 545	1 628
180 to 219 acres .... farms..	5	54	51	31	56	2	24	2
acres harvested..	663	4 246	4 259	2 965	3 042	(D)	2 439	(D)
220 to 259 acres .... farms..	10	70	42	37	29	2	46	11
acres harvested..	1 102	6 664	4 812	4 819	3 985	(D)	7 075	1 306
260 to 499 acres .... farms..	65	149	150	157	73	29	186	51
acres harvested..	10 095	19 980	23 408	29 970	15 677	6 477	45 406	10 394
500 to 999 acres .... farms..	109	172	104	176	60	40	171	80
acres harvested..	30 894	46 421	36 785	65 485	25 799	16 446	71 900	26 216
1,000 to 1,999 acres .... farms..	112	67	44	129	17	50	116	85
acres harvested..	54 403	35 226	34 399	84 259	15 350	34 787	81 929	55 697
2,000 acres or more .... farms..	69	11	7	43	4	60	36	50
acres harvested..	63 820	10 321	8 135	52 282	13 490	155 304	44 471	48 642
HARVESTED CROPLAND BY ACRES HARVESTED								
1987 acres harvested:								
1 to 9 acres .... farms..	3	34	50	17	60	1	23	6
acres..	11	198	300	99	298	(D)	87	17
10 to 19 acres .... farms..	4	70	102	17	63	4	28	3
acres..	76	980	1 361	232	881	61	394	42
20 to 29 acres .... farms..	9	78	96	19	51	2	24	3
acres..	224	1 768	2 313	443	1 193	(D)	567	76
30 to 49 acres .... farms..	7	127	137	37	64	9	42	10
acres..	260	4 776	5 187	1 403	2 324	341	1 587	332
50 to 99 acres .... farms..	45	209	177	100	81	19	96	25
acres..	3 379	14 459	12 146	7 473	5 448	1 371	6 996	1 816
100 to 199 acres .... farms..	72	160	125	129	70	31	157	55
acres..	10 302	20 578	17 050	18 883	9 716	4 737	22 483	7 762
200 to 499 acres .... farms..	123	139	93	183	62	58	202	70
acres..	40 936	44 109	27 929	58 064	20 372	19 236	64 321	23 913
500 to 999 acres .... farms..	87	31	43	116	27	56	116	77
acres..	60 172	20 229	30 191	79 969	18 751	42 810	78 218	53 913
1,000 acres or more .... farms..	32	6	13	30	8	69	30	27
acres..	44 521	7 574	16 416	42 039	10 461	133 552	44 793	40 454
1982 acres harvested:								
1 to 9 acres .... farms..	2	57	65	11	60	4	16	7
acres..	(D)	293	345	51	290	13	54	17
10 to 19 acres .... farms..	6	88	89	23	62	4	32	7
acres..	(D)	1 239	1 222	302	858	(D)	403	(D)
20 to 29 acres .... farms..	5	83	96	15	55	2	38	7
acres..	102	1 901	2 209	363	1 251	(D)	955	(D)
30 to 49 acres .... farms..	11	136	128	36	83	7	37	7
acres..	430	5 054	4 860	1 397	3 024	261	1 451	256
50 to 99 acres .... farms..	42	182	173	91	103	16	86	16
acres..	2 934	12 576	12 146	6 609	6 977	1 196	6 380	1 021
100 to 199 acres .... farms..	80	188	116	147	76	29	149	66
acres..	11 917	26 169	16 934	20 996	10 961	4 255	21 277	9 656
200 to 499 acres .... farms..	154	165	126	226	76	59	261	98
acres..	50 324	51 696	37 471	74 413	24 325	20 477	86 476	31 770
500 to 999 acres .... farms..	87	41	46	124	29	53	129	87
acres..	58 643	26 272	32 087	85 813	19 134	39 764	96 694	59 273
1,000 acres or more .... farms..	30	11	16	48	9	61	37	28
acres..	39 975	14 068	20 969	59 229	22 878	150 436	52 162	42 735

Table 6. **Harvested Cropland by Size of Farm and Acres Harvested: 1987 and 1982**—Con.

[For meaning of abbreviations and symbols, see introductory text]

Farms with harvested cropland	Labette	Lane	Leavenworth	Lincoln	Linn	Logan	Lyon	McPherson
Farms .... number, 1987	767	291	692	510	551	334	709	1 210
1982	840	300	956	552	642	329	796	1 331
acres harvested, 1987	136 963	154 979	96 700	153 709	93 665	150 236	153 982	363 623
1982	170 902	159 352	108 423	174 863	120 739	166 407	165 108	345 140

HARVESTED CROPLAND BY SIZE OF FARM

1987 size of farm:

	Labette	Lane	Leavenworth	Lincoln	Linn	Logan	Lyon	McPherson
1 to 9 acres .... farms	6	2	21	3	1	-	4	13
acres harvested	18	(D)	81	9	(D)	-	24	31
10 to 49 acres ...... farms	46	1	171	13	38	4	61	95
acres harvested	785	(D)	2 360	221	(D)	135	1 137	1 691
50 to 69 acres ...... farms	30	2	58	6	17	-	15	23
acres harvested	889	127	1 353	184	477	-	533	787
70 to 99 acres ...... farms	105	8	159	14	44	4	63	81
acres harvested	3 644	357	5 413	605	1 318	124	2 635	3 940
100 to 139 acres .... farms	51	7	70	19	54	6	52	69
acres harvested	2 651	480	3 277	1 309	2 056	337	3 066	4 786
140 to 179 acres .... farms	88	17	98	33	56	18	67	151
acres harvested	4 483	1 081	6 770	2 531	3 369	1 030	4 310	14 058
180 to 219 acres .... farms	34	3	53	22	33	-	42	60
acres harvested	2 166	268	4 747	1 923	2 432	-	3 195	6 431
220 to 259 acres .... farms	61	9	44	20	27	6	41	82
acres harvested	5 627	661	4 109	2 268	1 849	507	4 681	11 300
260 to 499 acres .... farms	126	32	117	107	122	63	135	280
acres harvested	16 344	4 716	18 428	16 965	15 452	8 277	20 185	56 892
500 to 999 acres .... farms	137	47	74	110	102	65	120	233
acres harvested	41 651	13 447	27 604	26 252	26 054	17 614	33 339	90 307
1,000 to 1,999 acres .. farms	69	78	22	108	43	88	72	99
acres harvested	41 699	39 972	15 607	55 262	27 526	41 938	41 826	66 990
2,000 acres or more .. farms	14	85	5	55	14	90	37	24
acres harvested	17 124	93 849	6 951	44 160	12 373	80 164	39 251	24 412

1982 size of farm:

	Labette	Lane	Leavenworth	Lincoln	Linn	Logan	Lyon	McPherson
1 to 9 acres .... farms	5	-	11	2	3	1	11	8
acres harvested	16	-	39	(D)	9	(D)	26	26
10 to 49 acres ...... farms	74	8	198	14	65	8	51	110
acres harvested	1 361	137	3 123	(D)	1 392	(D)	1 103	2 115
50 to 69 acres ...... farms	29	1	78	12	19	1	23	38
acres harvested	732	(D)	1 814	453	415	(D)	1 230	1 841
70 to 99 acres ...... farms	94	12	143	22	54	7	77	69
acres harvested	3 205	585	4 808	1 462	1 986	280	3 295	5 481
100 to 139 acres .... farms	56	1	87	15	55	4	63	63
acres harvested	3 213	(D)	3 879	1 465	2 462	272	4 038	5 606
140 to 179 acres .... farms	95	19	102	40	70	11	60	152
acres harvested	6 169	1 356	7 889	3 651	3 665	748	4 803	16 733
180 to 219 acres .... farms	40	1	53	17	33	2	42	68
acres harvested	3 882	(D)	4 739	1 652	2 232	(D)	3 462	9 627
220 to 259 acres .... farms	42	4	51	18	35	7	36	91
acres harvested	5 093	538	6 275	1 888	3 338	547	3 666	15 819
260 to 499 acres .... farms	184	41	134	116	116	51	160	355
acres harvested	32 437	6 556	25 512	21 304	21 237	6 799	23 080	95 623
500 to 999 acres .... farms	155	57	75	146	106	75	142	253
acres harvested	59 504	16 646	28 058	48 981	33 161	16 029	41 714	116 976
1,000 to 1,999 acres .. farms	80	75	19	108	61	88	95	86
acres harvested	36 116	43 262	16 976	54 534	35 660	45 323	47 127	60 549
2,000 acres or more .. farms	16	81	5	42	12	60	30	18
acres harvested	19 174	90 141	5 311	39 000	14 960	94 175	31 562	14 944

HARVESTED CROPLAND BY ACRES HARVESTED

1987 acres harvested:

	Labette	Lane	Leavenworth	Lincoln	Linn	Logan	Lyon	McPherson
1 to 9 acres .... farms	32	2	105	12	27	-	25	36
acres	170	(D)	553	61	154	-	156	159
10 to 19 acres ...... farms	71	3	132	10	54	-	26	50
acres	950	(D)	1 851	146	733	54	35	640
20 to 29 acres ...... farms	66	3	86	8	38	5	58	49
acres	1 477	71	2 000	202	868	102	1 340	1 165
30 to 49 acres ...... farms	117	10	133	33	80	14	87	81
acres	4 402	387	4 921	1 264	3 014	549	3 315	3 140
50 to 99 acres ...... farms	151	40	196	15	32	149	140	207
acres	10 224	2 861	13 550	4 488	6 232	2 224	10 803	15 271
100 to 199 acres .... farms	131	38	112	117	87	55	139	286
acres	18 462	5 227	15 218	16 047	11 774	7 958	19 824	40 790
200 to 499 acres .... farms	126	78	88	175	98	113	135	354
acres	39 295	25 892	25 304	56 422	29 374	37 025	41 324	111 041
500 to 999 acres .... farms	56	65	29	77	38	73	55	125
acres	37 933	44 757	19 165	52 111	25 349	50 231	36 926	81 500
1,000 acres or more .. farms	17	52	11	18	10	38	26	23
acres	24 050	75 736	14 138	22 968	14 167	52 093	40 033	29 917

1982 acres harvested:

	Labette	Lane	Leavenworth	Lincoln	Linn	Logan	Lyon	McPherson
1 to 9 acres .... farms	36	-	87	8	26	1	27	58
acres	176	-	457	40	127	(D)	114	200
10 to 19 acres ...... farms	74	7	151	14	67	3	47	48
acres	1 012	78	1 956	(9)	907	(D)	668	650
20 to 29 acres ...... farms	66	7	111	2	49	4	40	35
acres	1 501	164	2 545	(D)	1 098	91	930	853
30 to 49 acres ...... farms	102	14	146	15	97	17	87	58
acres	3 800	546	5 415	592	3 556	682	3 280	2 248
50 to 99 acres ...... farms	148	25	174	67	94	34	180	192
acres	10 851	1 899	12 169	4 910	6 253	2 401	12 955	13 736
100 to 199 acres .... farms	150	36	98	133	123	59	165	295
acres	21 384	5 109	19 311	18 790	17 044	8 045	23 028	42 457
200 to 499 acres .... farms	174	96	112	127	127	95	165	482
acres	57 988	31 490	34 522	65 437	39 342	31 465	51 057	154 988
500 to 999 acres .... farms	72	69	28	99	41	74	69	159
acres	49 884	50 728	19 353	65 700	27 221	53 261	46 430	105 251
1,000 acres or more .. farms	18	46	9	13	16	42	16	20
acres	24 308	69 336	12 675	(D)	25 191	70 430	26 646	24 779

[For meaning of abbreviations and symbols, see introductory text]

Farms with harvested cropland	Marion	Marshall	Meade	Miami	Mitchell	Montgomery	Morris	Morton
Farms number, 1987	994	944	413	902	570	674	472	192
1982	1 072	1 045	436	972	583	696	494	210
acres harvested, 1987	253 314	261 602	200 706	116 217	237 322	111 306	112 825	139 398
1982	292 872	279 758	215 390	129 869	246 161	129 397	117 842	170 522
HARVESTED CROPLAND BY SIZE OF FARM								
1987 size of farm:								
1 to 9 acres farms	15	6	–	5	9	6	8	–
acres harvested	45	13	–	7	29	24	24	–
10 to 49 acres farms	68	45	9	160	32	60	18	2
acres harvested	1 172	961	207	2 363	474	1 006	292	(D)
50 to 69 acres farms	15	11	3	41	9	26	10	3
acres harvested	474	310	133	1 063	369	843	281	155
70 to 99 acres farms	61	35	6	117	17	72	19	7
acres harvested	2 816	1 430	245	3 964	732	2 095	908	393
100 to 139 acres farms	40	28	4	105	21	74	19	–
acres harvested	2 487	1 917	324	4 555	1 523	3 282	1 076	13
140 to 179 acres farms	97	74	22	100	32	85	96	13
acres harvested	7 564	5 900	(D)	6 029	2 135	3 419	2 093	1 368
180 to 219 acres farms	40	39	2	51	20	41	15	1
acres harvested	4 597	4 168	(D)	4 426	2 638	2 407	1 206	(D)
220 to 259 acres farms	59	48	6	41	23	45	24	1
acres harvested	7 933	5 783	418	3 489	2 765	3 881	2 202	(D)
260 to 499 acres farms	232	244	77	152	104	109	104	23
acres harvested	48 140	45 708	14 464	20 496	19 847	12 213	12 783	4 174
500 to 999 acres farms	229	261	111	75	131	86	102	22
acres harvested	86 148	90 409	36 685	23 248	45 901	22 463	23 999	9 688
1,000 to 1,999 acres farms	110	131	97	47	121	45	74	58
acres harvested	62 903	82 595	66 179	34 346	84 783	27 518	32 241	38 502
2,000 acres or more farms	28	22	76	8	51	25	43	62
acres harvested	26 033	22 586	60 469	12 201	76 225	32 355	35 420	84 727
1982 size of farm:								
1 to 9 acres farms	14	6	–	3	5	9	7	–
acres harvested	50	30	–	7	7	19	35	–
10 to 49 acres farms	65	35	7	151	39	73	21	5
acres harvested	1 270	839	(D)	2 209	739	1 127	398	(D)
50 to 69 acres farms	20	26	1	51	5	28	7	1
acres harvested	778	1 042	(D)	1 004	222	994	274	(D)
70 to 99 acres farms	74	47	9	131	28	71	18	6
acres harvested	3 739	2 080	401	3 945	1 665	2 326	925	269
100 to 139 acres farms	38	41	10	97	15	68	15	3
acres harvested	2 762	2 716	813	4 619	1 345	3 649	1 023	304
140 to 179 acres farms	102	91	28	118	50	79	42	11
acres harvested	9 697	8 550	2 494	7 289	4 814	4 941	2 865	1 138
180 to 219 acres farms	39	47	1	54	14	37	20	1
acres harvested	5 143	5 696	(D)	3 984	1 784	2 710	1 737	(D)
220 to 259 acres farms	60	82	6	53	27	43	33	6
acres harvested	9 481	7 474	636	4 621	3 642	3 772	3 600	538
260 to 499 acres farms	291	283	94	151	109	121	98	22
acres harvested	69 584	62 224	19 692	22 256	23 213	17 607	13 710	4 050
500 to 999 acres farms	257	282	112	109	133	95	113	34
acres harvested	109 253	108 315	39 676	31 039	56 426	29 237	33 399	16 143
1,000 to 1,999 acres farms	89	117	105	46	117	54	92	67
acres harvested	57 381	73 913	73 765	26 582	85 549	36 817	36 652	54 562
2,000 acres or more farms	25	8	82	6	41	20	28	57
acres harvested	23 554	7 079	77 377	20 314	63 753	26 298	21 001	93 269
HARVESTED CROPLAND BY ACRES HARVESTED								
1987 acres harvested:								
1 to 9 acres farms	39	18	2	71	19	44	20	–
acres	196	83	(D)	361	74	232	105	–
10 to 19 acres farms	34	35	6	131	24	83	19	2
acres	453	468	(D)	1 827	348	1 116	229	(D)
20 to 29 acres farms	40	20	6	105	8	90	20	3
acres	944	458	150	2 379	176	2 044	488	84
30 to 49 acres farms	72	46	13	145	24	110	41	1
acres	2 822	1 857	488	5 486	890	4 131	1 625	(D)
50 to 99 acres farms	127	135	38	180	66	112	97	16
acres	9 096	10 210	2 855	12 484	4 927	7 595	6 930	1 413
100 to 199 acres farms	197	208	59	126	99	107	91	23
acres	28 279	29 720	8 350	17 560	14 432	15 359	12 797	3 163
200 to 499 acres farms	354	327	154	96	168	71	110	37
acres	111 406	104 293	49 930	31 091	55 017	21 799	33 239	12 239
500 to 999 acres farms	114	138	76	32	105	42	59	62
acres	77 090	89 936	53 061	22 308	74 174	30 290	38 041	45 549
1,000 acres or more farms	17	19	59	14	57	15	15	46
acres	22 058	24 777	85 766	22 701	87 284	28 800	19 073	76 875
1982 acres harvested:								
1 to 9 acres farms	35	19	2	82	12	51	16	1
acres	178	91	(D)	430	49	272	78	(D)
10 to 19 acres farms	30	38	5	132	19	74	15	2
acres	418	510	(D)	1 715	260	1 013	196	(D)
20 to 29 acres farms	32	32	4	112	19	61	12	5
acres	765	734	98	2 586	453	1 378	264	131
30 to 49 acres farms	71	41	15	159	20	88	40	2
acres	2 719	1 569	579	5 974	729	3 293	1 517	(D)
50 to 99 acres farms	125	131	40	170	59	148	94	12
acres	9 137	9 810	2 943	11 953	4 323	10 248	6 786	852
100 to 199 acres farms	226	238	75	151	107	142	102	23
acres	33 466	33 373	10 486	20 845	14 852	15 734	14 122	3 293
200 to 499 acres farms	386	396	151	118	175	90	153	34
acres	124 951	129 648	50 696	36 387	58 022	28 433	46 403	10 706
500 to 999 acres farms	148	138	90	36	122	50	54	69
acres	98 696	89 785	62 477	24 173	86 243	33 480	35 246	46 163
1,000 acres or more farms	17	12	54	12	50	22	8	68
acres	22 345	14 236	88 022	25 804	81 230	35 546	11 290	109 276

(For meaning of abbreviations and symbols, see introductory text)

Farms with harvested cropland	Nemaha	Neosho	Ness	Norton	Osage	Osborne	Ottawa	Pawnee
Farms number, 1987..	994	811	542	415	729	554	476	475
1982..	1 024	662	577	458	825	572	514	519
acres harvested, 1987..	203 290	126 121	193 380	154 827	140 377	182 056	149 979	223 904
1982..	215 292	142 932	216 742	170 497	158 533	179 133	185 635	256 255
HARVESTED CROPLAND BY SIZE OF FARM								
1987 size of farm:								
1 to 9 acres farms..	6	7	-	-	6	2	5	5
acres harvested..	13	36	-	-	19	(D)	11	9
10 to 49 acres farms..	51	33	3	13	73	14	39	18
acres harvested..	943	570	41	(D)	1 329	(D)	604	250
50 to 69 acres farms..	13	26	7	2	21	8	7	4
acres harvested..	460	739	293	(D)	653	213	231	114
70 to 99 acres farms..	47	55	6	7	65	19	19	12
acres harvested..	2 132	1 667	172	254	2 019	891	742	557
100 to 139 acres farms..	41	41	8	4	56	11	16	8
acres harvested..	2 479	2 019	479	262	2 471	560	1 008	540
140 to 179 acres farms..	117	74	37	20	70	29	30	41
acres harvested..	10 464	4 275	2 159	1 215	4 904	2 011	2 277	3 217
180 to 219 acres farms..	48	26	6	7	34	20	16	7
acres harvested..	5 009	2 257	533	788	2 926	2 076	1 213	597
220 to 259 acres farms..	69	42	27	14	54	20	17	13
acres harvested..	7 651	3 670	2 092	887	4 850	2 281	2 184	1 670
260 to 499 acres farms..	300	126	93	65	136	107	84	77
acres harvested..	53 248	16 918	12 833	8 407	19 236	16 499	14 874	15 210
500 to 999 acres farms..	238	111	109	107	133	125	114	130
acres harvested..	78 655	36 642	25 381	23 908	42 323	35 951	38 771	44 502
1,000 to 1,999 acres farms..	57	52	135	103	59	135	93	96
acres harvested..	31 881	31 838	59 147	46 119	33 979	66 878	50 472	63 484
2,000 acres or more farms..	7	18	111	73	22	64	36	64
acres harvested..	10 376	23 490	90 450	72 783	25 666	54 392	37 592	93 754
1982 size of farm:								
1 to 9 acres farms..	11	1	-	2	5	4	6	5
acres harvested..	45	(D)	-	(D)	12	4	22	10
10 to 49 acres farms..	48	51	8	12	91	28	29	7
acres harvested..	796	(D)	215	(D)	1 816	570	510	118
50 to 69 acres farms..	22	16	3	8	29	7	11	6
acres harvested..	845	598	67	226	1 012	228	393	277
70 to 99 acres farms..	56	66	10	7	86	19	25	13
acres harvested..	2 809	1 935	369	384	3 478	1 055	1 242	698
100 to 139 acres farms..	45	47	10	9	68	12	18	13
acres harvested..	2 959	2 899	578	463	3 808	824	1 302	1 016
140 to 179 acres farms..	126	76	25	22	73	40	33	36
acres harvested..	11 547	4 647	1 833	1 613	5 412	3 618	3 144	3 636
180 to 219 acres farms..	36	31	12	10	41	14	16	9
acres harvested..	3 669	2 849	947	970	3 563	2 036	1 777	1 256
220 to 259 acres farms..	79	39	22	11	47	28	35	17
acres harvested..	10 273	3 510	2 026	935	5 030	2 805	5 585	2 469
260 to 499 acres farms..	317	136	106	70	146	93	94	115
acres harvested..	54 375	23 018	13 914	11 212	22 435	15 902	22 036	26 949
500 to 999 acres farms..	232	126	145	125	157	149	106	135
acres harvested..	82 878	44 139	41 266	33 750	49 845	48 952	39 240	55 506
1,000 to 1,999 acres farms..	49	54	144	125	64	121	110	117
acres harvested..	28 174	35 355	73 001	58 967	40 196	61 030	75 078	68 312
2,000 acres or more farms..	5	19	92	59	18	57	31	46
acres harvested..	7 122	23 231	82 495	61 525	22 126	44 109	35 306	76 008
HARVESTED CROPLAND BY ACRES HARVESTED								
1987 acres harvested:								
1 to 9 acres farms..	20	24	3	8	36	5	20	9
acres..	86	141	19	36	187	29	91	24
10 to 19 acres farms..	29	60	8	17	53	9	26	12
acres..	380	813	111	237	705	142	292	154
20 to 29 acres farms..	27	45	5	9	71	10	18	13
acres..	617	1 032	123	212	1 651	226	438	294
30 to 49 acres farms..	79	81	20	22	85	37	25	15
acres..	3 001	3 030	761	838	3 193	1 368	985	615
50 to 99 acres farms..	160	107	68	37	147	69	60	48
acres..	11 912	7 747	6 071	2 733	10 531	5 350	4 234	3 665
100 to 199 acres farms..	295	103	104	76	131	112	84	84
acres..	41 540	14 301	14 990	10 823	17 802	15 756	12 203	11 825
200 to 499 acres farms..	321	125	170	147	129	204	148	134
acres..	98 675	39 689	54 479	46 037	41 097	67 645	47 919	43 805
500 to 999 acres farms..	54	49	113	64	57	81	76	107
acres..	34 268	34 139	75 222	45 387	37 154	55 237	52 812	74 437
1,000 or more acres farms..	9	17	31	35	18	27	20	53
acres..	12 809	25 235	41 604	48 524	28 057	36 303	31 005	89 085
1982 acres harvested:								
1 to 9 acres farms..	30	24	1	6	30	8	16	5
acres..	163	129	(D)	26	164	17	80	10
10 to 19 acres farms..	32	83	2	7	70	21	19	7
acres..	446	834	(D)	121	978	271	250	99
20 to 29 acres farms..	29	45	6	10	59	15	23	6
acres..	641	1 062	142	232	1 376	357	527	130
30 to 49 acres farms..	71	68	19	16	93	28	16	12
acres..	2 659	2 631	746	697	3 568	1 084	610	478
50 to 99 acres farms..	160	108	87	44	175	66	50	45
acres..	11 726	7 549	6 324	3 194	12 350	4 932	3 658	3 206
100 to 199 acres farms..	295	125	96	86	158	129	78	78
acres..	42 846	17 249	13 800	12 811	22 486	18 952	13 722	11 416
200 to 499 acres farms..	333	150	204	177	162	193	174	194
acres..	104 114	45 439	68 206	57 727	52 307	61 500	57 325	63 801
500 to 999 acres farms..	66	60	119	78	59	86	89	112
acres..	41 609	40 356	80 320	51 513	39 066	57 424	63 182	79 433
1,000 or more acres farms..	8	19	35	31	19	26	21	60
acres..	11 089	26 693	47 055	44 166	26 236	34 596	38 281	97 682

Table 6. **Harvested Cropland by Size of Farm and Acres Harvested: 1987 and 1982**—Con.

[For meaning of abbreviations and symbols, see introductory text]

Farms with harvested cropland		Phillips	Pottawatomie	Pratt	Rawlins	Reno	Republic	Rice	Riley
Farms	number, 1987..	527	614	465	497	1 346	736	541	462
	1982..	696	732	511	579	1 438	831	586	466
acres harvested,	1987..	162 736	118 376	242 460	196 707	374 679	230 517	214 092	80 307
	1982..	173 288	134 722	249 755	217 218	446 426	259 275	248 311	84 221

HARVESTED CROPLAND BY SIZE OF FARM

1987 size of farm:		Phillips	Pottawatomie	Pratt	Rawlins	Reno	Republic	Rice	Riley
1 to 9 acres	farms..	3	4	4	2	23	4	8	7
	acres harvested..	10	11	14	(D)	84	11	40	27
10 to 49 acres	farms..	22	48	7	10	129	28	26	63
	acres harvested..	306	548	98	(D)	1 846	443	443	1 073
50 to 69 acres	farms..	8	19	3	4	31	16	10	17
	acres harvested..	114	584	78	123	964	640	317	473
70 to 99 acres	farms..	27	40	19	4	102	45	28	29
	acres harvested..	1 183	1 496	783	126	5 018	2 301	1 328	1 457
100 to 139 acres	farms..	19	23	5	6	62	39	19	20
	acres harvested..	1 220	1 120	414	340	3 688	2 767	1 245	1 224
140 to 179 acres	farms..	26	51	35	27	132	70	45	34
	acres harvested..	1 856	3 374	3 092	1 586	11 511	6 311	3 804	2 641
180 to 219 acres	farms..	14	22	11	9	57	31	13	19
	acres harvested..	829	1 952	1 230	692	6 137	3 000	1 493	1 355
220 to 259 acres	farms..	23	26	17	7	69	27	15	21
	acres harvested..	2 045	1 955	2 157	444	12 562	3 498	1 523	1 631
260 to 499 acres	farms..	66	119	74	77	247	137	90	85
	acres harvested..	8 922	15 441	12 694	11 157	51 614	26 794	18 089	13 781
500 to 999 acres	farms..	120	144	123	116	259	204	190	108
	acres harvested..	26 347	31 430	48 996	31 161	97 734	77 586	50 143	26 651
1,000 to 1,999 acres	farms..	132	73	112	133	177	116	117	43
	acres harvested..	57 498	26 526	85 316	61 240	135 723	82 787	80 350	18 370
2,000 acres or more	farms..	67	45	55	102	38	19	40	16
	acres harvested..	62 405	33 929	87 587	89 647	47 598	24 359	55 317	11 624
1982 size of farm:									
1 to 9 acres	farms..	7	9	2	2	28	6	3	5
	acres harvested..	32	27	(D)	(D)	103	17	13	18
10 to 49 acres	farms..	21	57	20	6	147	35	34	62
	acres harvested..	386	953	472	(D)	2 409	708	672	1 135
50 to 69 acres	farms..	8	23		4	40	15	9	17
	acres harvested..	196	927	(D)	123	1 435	595	392	720
70 to 99 acres	farms..	20	61	21	8	114	46	31	90
	acres harvested..	883	3 003	693	362	6 188	2 667	1 864	1 198
100 to 139 acres	farms..	20	34	13	6	66	37	18	12
	acres harvested..	1 104	1 818	1 123	527	5 448	2 613	1 167	2 084
140 to 179 acres	farms..	29	49	43	31	124	75	44	36
	acres harvested..	2 007	3 323	3 978	2 129	13 730	6 644	4 201	2 730
180 to 219 acres	farms..	13	21	12	4	66	43	11	9
	acres harvested..	916	2 053	1 761	341	9 026	4 624	1 714	1 014
220 to 259 acres	farms..	34	47	12	11	92	55	37	23
	acres harvested..	3 045	4 616	2 911	1 379	15 033	7 979	5 270	2 026
260 to 499 acres	farms..	106	141	77	84	299	211	90	88
	acres harvested..	15 047	19 187	16 777	12 583	77 462	44 356	20 794	13 359
500 to 999 acres	farms..		171	145	157	255	196	153	110
	acres harvested..	30 581	37 933	63 672	40 580	119 884	86 198	69 965	31 531
1,000 to 1,999 acres	farms..	140	83	129	182	173	92	122	39
	acres harvested..	63 469	31 779	102 620	87 426	145 245	75 098	94 741	18 704
2,000 acres or more	farms..	55	36	37	81	34	20	34	16
	acres harvested..	55 622	29 003	56 110	71 498	50 445	27 776	47 518	11 702

HARVESTED CROPLAND BY ACRES HARVESTED

1987 acres harvested:		Phillips	Pottawatomie	Pratt	Rawlins	Reno	Republic	Rice	Riley
1 to 9 acres	farms..	15	21	7	8	85	12	15	34
	acres..	63	83	33	37	398	62	80	168
10 to 19 acres	farms..	18	45	11	5	66	18	18	36
	acres..	264	574	159	112	865	264	254	479
20 to 29 acres	farms..	15	50	12	6	57	24	18	31
	acres..	336	1 151	283	146	1 346	562	420	736
30 to 49 acres	farms..	36	56	11	23	78	41	31	36
	acres..	1 453	2 099	450	877	3 021	1 632	1 227	1 399
50 to 99 acres	farms..	82	112	44	51	212	66	67	88
	acres..	5 714	8 151	3 176	3 660	15 640	7 272	4 818	6 205
100 to 199 acres	farms..	93	155	88	88	262	164	71	89
	acres..	13 514	22 314	9 806	12 658	37 577	23 640	10 076	12 677
200 to 499 acres	farms..	164	127	127	170	334	222	159	116
	acres..	52 479	40 161	40 391	57 027	106 317	72 798	50 486	34 552
500 to 999 acres	farms..	78	35	122	108	193	122	110	28
	acres..	51 076	23 365	85 209	74 805	133 009	82 135	74 459	18 316
1,000 acres or more	farms..	26	13	63	37	59	34	52	4
	acres..	37 837	20 458	102 953	47 163	76 506	42 152	71 972	5 723
1982 acres harvested:									
1 to 9 acres	farms..	13	34	5	5	82	16	12	24
	acres..	65	173	13	24	377	91	60	116
10 to 19 acres	farms..	22	44	11	3	65	16	15	42
	acres..	320	599	165	37	860	222	213	588
20 to 29 acres	farms..	20	48	12	6	62	22	12	26
	acres..	483	1 129	283	144	1 461	511	274	605
30 to 49 acres	farms..	31	51	19	28	82	47	31	37
	acres..	1 252	1 909	691	1 084	3 141	1 781	1 231	1 396
50 to 99 acres	farms..	99	171	37	49	162	114	89	92
	acres..	7 569	11 941	2 714	4 959	11 801	8 483	4 093	6 451
100 to 199 acres	farms..	139	168	81	97	283	209	89	86
	acres..	19 943	23 753	11 669	14 259	40 209	24 605	12 824	13 277
200 to 499 acres	farms..	172	161	141	225	408	278	175	114
	acres..	55 999	48 735	47 825	73 633	131 252	89 328	60 049	33 809
500 to 999 acres	farms..	22	43	150	117	208	116	144	28
	acres..	53 099	27 411	104 429	84 935	143 308	78 005	98 830	16 983
1,000 acres or more	farms..	22	12	55	29	86	43		9
	acres..	34 558	19 072	81 966	38 143	114 029	56 249	70 737	10 996

Table 6. **Harvested Cropland by Size of Farm and Acres Harvested: 1987 and 1982**—Con.

[For meaning of abbreviations and symbols, see introductory text]

Farms with harvested cropland	Rooks	Rush	Russell	Saline	Scott	Sedgwick	Seward	Shawnee
Farms number, 1987	431	494	469	649	330	1 345	229	659
1982	483	525	517	694	356	1 423	228	726
acres harvested, 1987	157 823	160 253	135 417	173 828	180 540	319 625	141 650	101 139
1982	166 987	172 379	163 565	205 872	209 383	363 417	159 642	103 231
HARVESTED CROPLAND BY SIZE OF FARM								
1987 size of farm:								
1 to 9 acres farms	3	1	1	15	-	45	-	17
acres harvested	3	(D)	(D)	45	-	143	-	46
10 to 49 acres farms	10	13	8	60	5	225	3	107
acres harvested	178	(D)	(D)	1 045	(D)	3 675	61	1 971
50 to 69 acres farms	4	4	6	18	2	41	2	45
acres harvested	122	113	81	507	(D)	1 455	(D)	1 480
70 to 99 acres farms	8	20	15	69	9	123	5	88
acres harvested	358	757	638	2 780	503	6 578	320	2 976
100 to 139 acres farms	7	9	8	27	3	81	2	59
acres harvested	253	593	371	2 177	146	6 312	(D)	3 301
140 to 179 acres farms	23	41	47	63	29	124	12	66
acres harvested	983	2 990	3 084	4 896	2 395	12 163	1 029	3 258
180 to 219 acres farms	5	13	4	15	6	42	(D)	24
acres harvested	275	1 393	345	1 446	1 051	4 956	(D)	2 654
220 to 259 acres farms	13	19	28	20	3	70	5	31
acres harvested	856	2 379	2 314	1 694	425	10 283	624	3 251
260 to 499 acres farms	80	90	99	101	51	262	34	99
acres harvested	9 411	12 995	12 305	18 958	10 109	60 495	6 850	16 985
500 to 999 acres farms	93	132	101	139	80	216	51	80
acres harvested	21 484	34 486	23 226	51 980	19 020	96 552	19 534	30 742
1,000 to 1,999 acres farms	100	115	85	93	75	92	67	34
acres harvested	41 435	65 949	35 985	59 921	47 872	81 600	52 569	23 944
2,000 acres or more farms	85	37	67	29	67	24	46	9
acres harvested	82 465	38 339	56 997	28 396	98 678	35 411	60 011	10 331
1982 size of farm:								
1 to 9 acres farms	3	-	5	6	3	44	1	17
acres harvested	3	-	21	24	5	130	(D)	32
10 to 49 acres farms	15	13	7	62	9	254	7	152
acres harvested	(D)	348	148	1 116	236	4 865	107	2 404
50 to 69 acres farms	2	3	10	25	3	52	3	42
acres harvested	(D)	94	449	965	80	1 936	160	1 328
70 to 99 acres farms	15	13	19	62	8	121	7	110
acres harvested	898	386	853	3 602	524	7 019	504	4 213
100 to 139 acres farms	11	12	12	29	3	84	5	55
acres harvested	677	946	1 300	2 700	110	6 781	455	2 639
140 to 179 acres farms	31	39	48	76	24	141	14	61
acres harvested	2 315	2 808	3 453	7 795	1 966	16 367	1 819	3 212
180 to 219 acres farms	10	15	12	27	4	42	2	23
acres harvested	697	1 758	1 290	3 723	272	6 099	(D)	1 402
220 to 259 acres farms	19	17	21	34	7	72	3	29
acres harvested	1 832	1 919	2 437	4 506	90	12 364	405	2 323
260 to 499 acres farms	92	123	98	129	48	271	59	119
acres harvested	12 916	21 372	14 666	27 576	8 504	72 131	9 325	22 328
500 to 999 acres farms	111	147	128	135	86	217	41	72
acres harvested	29 963	44 939	40 109	60 316	33 066	110 780	19 886	24 982
1,000 to 1,999 acres farms	104	113	98	75	82	110	57	39
acres harvested	50 000	64 071	47 265	57 164	57 879	97 564	51 841	31 010
2,000 acres or more farms	70	30	53	33	79	15	49	7
acres harvested	69 332	33 748	51 594	36 369	106 242	27 359	75 089	7 158
HARVESTED CROPLAND BY ACRES HARVESTED								
1987 acres harvested:								
1 to 9 acres farms	7	5	13	46	2	129	1	52
acres	22	27	82	214	(D)	564	(D)	245
10 to 19 acres farms	9	17	11	35	4	87	3	92
acres	126	227	151	484	(D)	1 214	(D)	1 254
20 to 29 acres farms	16	12	5	32	5	73	4	65
acres	386	304	112	776	115	1 691	101	1 464
30 to 49 acres farms	26	23	31	50	14	105	7	98
acres	974	865	1 209	1 935	569	4 025	256	3 629
50 to 99 acres farms	55	61	96	103	26	208	18	110
acres	3 823	4 466	6 662	6 936	1 987	15 364	1 501	7 313
100 to 199 acres farms	84	105	104	104	50	227	23	102
acres	12 558	15 304	14 645	14 418	7 691	32 282	3 205	14 402
200 to 499 acres farms	127	156	128	163	91	330	75	76
acres	41 552	47 342	41 355	54 625	30 252	103 651	25 566	23 328
500 to 999 acres farms	77	100	61	92	90	137	58	52
acres	53 841	68 155	41 110	62 463	64 727	91 501	43 883	34 514
1,000 acres or more farms	30	16	20	20	48	49	40	12
acres	44 501	23 558	30 091	31 975	75 176	69 283	67 110	15 350
1982 acres harvested:								
1 to 9 acres farms	8	1	14	32	5	106	1	61
acres	26	(D)	81	147	21	473	(D)	396
10 to 19 acres farms	11	12	8	31	4	102	8	97
acres	152	(D)	109	407	55	1 395	(D)	1 345
20 to 29 acres farms	9	7	13	29	3	78	3	71
acres	188	159	299	690	63	1 790	66	1 667
30 to 49 acres farms	18	21	26	33	10	111	6	123
acres	690	639	1 052	1 262	379	4 166	216	4 628
50 to 99 acres farms	69	45	68	112	41	197	16	131
acres	5 097	3 082	5 062	6 030	2 973	14 084	1 137	9 174
100 to 199 acres farms	98	118	125	140	40	265	25	83
acres	13 779	16 377	17 705	19 230	5 907	37 735	3 562	11 567
200 to 499 acres farms	162	214	165	178	97	328	60	84
acres	52 710	66 407	54 335	56 077	32 105	104 448	20 470	28 234
500 to 999 acres farms	77	92	72	106	93	188	46	41
acres	51 636	62 697	47 386	73 707	65 732	128 933	31 344	27 624
1,000 acres or more farms	31	15	26	33	63	48	15	15
acres	44 709	22 654	37 566	46 922	102 148	70 393	102 639	18 396

Table 6. **Harvested Cropland by Size of Farm and Acres Harvested: 1987 and 1982**—Con.

[For meaning of abbreviations and symbols, see introductory text]

Farms with harvested cropland	Sheridan	Sherman	Smith	Stafford	Stanton	Stevens	Sumner	Thomas
Farms......................... number, 1987..	461	470	630	488	241	260	1 137	592
1982..	521	512	675	526	209	292	1 271	575
acres harvested, 1987..	183 013	251 334	211 337	230 607	194 701	238 568	415 440	296 047
1982..	200 637	296 853	216 933	266 542	220 929	298 656	519 906	307 900

HARVESTED CROPLAND BY SIZE OF FARM

	Sheridan	Sherman	Smith	Stafford	Stanton	Stevens	Sumner	Thomas
1987 size of farm:								
1 to 9 acres .... farms..	1	-	3	7	-	-	24	1
acres harvested..	(D)	-	14	22	-	-	93	(D)
10 to 49 acres .... farms..	6	5	27	9	1	4	74	10
acres harvested..	(D)	107	430	(D)	(D)	85	1 027	(D)
50 to 69 acres .... farms..	3	3	4	1	-	-	21	5
acres harvested..	78	102	133	(D)	-	-	636	165
70 to 99 acres .... farms..	4	6	23	27	-	-	81	5
acres harvested..	180	357	910	1 356	-	-	3 780	209
100 to 139 acres .... farms..	6	5	9	5	2	1	48	10
acres harvested..	374	239	586	401	(D)	(D)	3 136	507
140 to 179 acres .... farms..	40	40	38	31	16	12	132	47
acres harvested..	3 115	3 629	2 752	2 020	1 350	1 115	11 908	3 429
180 to 219 acres .... farms..	7	4	13	10	-	1	25	6
acres harvested..	572	486	1 161	1 197	-	(D)	2 943	524
220 to 259 acres .... farms..	4	8	31	14	1	-	46	9
acres harvested..	461	860	3 707	1 872	(D)	(D)	5 766	717
260 to 499 acres .... farms..	83	70	104	96	25	22	207	105
acres harvested..	12 315	11 506	15 642	20 257	5 016	4 963	45 576	18 961
500 to 999 acres .... farms..	104	107	165	114	39	48	237	147
acres harvested..	30 445	35 127	49 325	46 308	15 023	19 297	106 157	50 187
1,000 to 1,999 acres .... farms..	141	127	160	122	78	83	193	157
acres harvested..	77 604	82 134	82 779	85 953	54 945	65 634	160 917	98 624
2,000 acres or more .... farms..	62	95	53	52	79	68	49	90
acres harvested..	57 758	116 787	53 698	71 238	108 194	146 906	73 411	122 585
1982 size of farm:								
1 to 9 acres .... farms..	2	3	2	4	-	-	23	-
acres harvested..	(D)	7	(D)	21	-	-	89	-
10 to 49 acres .... farms..	3	7	24	12	1	2	81	18
acres harvested..	(D)	125	(D)	304	(D)	(D)	1 551	316
50 to 69 acres .... farms..	4	4	4	4	-	-	33	3
acres harvested..	317	177	173	208	-	-	1 247	138
70 to 99 acres .... farms..	5	10	22	17	4	6	85	11
acres harvested..	135	577	859	898	(D)	345	4 891	625
100 to 139 acres .... farms..	7	3	14	8	-	4	52	5
acres harvested..	718	180	888	830	-	(T)	4 815	169
140 to 179 acres .... farms..	34	45	46	38	10	8	114	53
acres harvested..	3 352	4 029	3 956	4 706	1 163	654	12 712	5 909
180 to 219 acres .... farms..	9	5	16	12	-	-	32	4
acres harvested..	742	472	1 641	1 992	-	-	4 322	245
220 to 259 acres .... farms..	6	14	22	11	-	4	44	5
acres harvested..	632	1 780	2 685	1 854	-	874	7 605	579
260 to 499 acres .... farms..	112	84	131	120	17	35	252	114
acres harvested..	18 605	17 834	22 182	29 621	3 892	8 366	69 287	21 700
500 to 999 acres .... farms..	143	116	195	133	28	64	327	146
acres harvested..	44 907	43 083	63 142	60 257	13 084	36 045	169 648	52 364
1,000 to 1,999 acres .... farms..	133	132	158	126	66	101	199	136
acres harvested..	74 698	85 911	77 584	106 129	55 602	101 765	190 826	94 542
2,000 acres or more .... farms..	55	89	41	41	83	70	29	60
acres harvested..	56 067	142 678	44 008	60 024	146 848	147 988	53 133	131 293

HARVESTED CROPLAND BY ACRES HARVESTED

	Sheridan	Sherman	Smith	Stafford	Stanton	Stevens	Sumner	Thomas
1987 acres harvested:								
1 to 9 acres .... farms..	1	-	15	9	-	1	57	5
acres..	(D)	-	72	34	-	(D)	298	29
10 to 19 acres .... farms..	11	4	10	12	-	1	46	6
acres..	(D)	60	132	160	-	(D)	574	91
20 to 29 acres .... farms..	5	5	16	7	2	1	36	10
acres..	111	125	341	172	(D)	(D)	794	237
30 to 49 acres .... farms..	21	13	30	18	7	5	49	13
acres..	827	482	1 205	710	(D)	180	1 919	481
50 to 99 acres .... farms..	48	50	79	52	13	9	199	56
acres..	3 655	3 742	5 828	3 776	956	620	12 201	4 037
100 to 199 acres .... farms..	82	75	118	60	23	19	189	98
acres..	12 061	10 976	16 956	8 555	3 296	2 477	26 957	14 237
200 to 499 acres .... farms..	145	141	221	141	48	48	279	187
acres..	47 453	46 839	72 980	47 654	15 391	18 549	92 224	62 742
500 to 999 acres .... farms..	119	107	112	139	79	78	222	148
acres..	82 231	77 610	74 911	96 879	55 708	58 740	155 881	102 146
1,000 acres or more .... farms..	29	75	29	50	69	91	92	67
acres..	36 494	109 500	38 912	72 957	109 061	157 957	124 592	112 048
1982 acres harvested:								
1 to 9 acres .... farms..	2	4	8	8	-	1	42	7
acres..	(D)	14	43	(D)	-	(D)	185	25
10 to 19 acres .... farms..	3	4	20	2	-	2	56	11
acres..	(D)	49	279	(D)	-	(D)	732	168
20 to 29 acres .... farms..	6	9	12	7	-	-	31	8
acres..	157	205	270	159	-	-	741	165
30 to 49 acres .... farms..	20	5	37	17	2	3	41	14
acres..	774	189	1 470	628	(D)	106	1 590	558
50 to 99 acres .... farms..	49	58	77	26	11	11	128	49
acres..	3 474	4 379	5 632	1 888	(D)	839	9 171	3 629
100 to 199 acres .... farms..	108	87	130	72	16	17	198	99
acres..	15 691	9 587	19 033	10 404	2 649	2 640	27 352	14 461
200 to 499 acres .... farms..	194	169	265	195	25	43	372	190
acres..	62 464	55 114	89 876	54 113	8 772	14 210	122 495	64 972
500 to 999 acres .... farms..	99	103	109	131	59	99	297	123
acres..	67 326	72 101	74 400	93 772	42 843	72 612	204 707	88 325
1,000 acres or more .... farms..	38	93	17	68	96	116	112	76
acres..	50 562	155 215	25 930	95 499	165 792	208 220	152 913	135 597

Table 6. **Harvested Cropland by Size of Farm and Acres Harvested: 1987 and 1982**—Con.

[For meaning of abbreviations and symbols. see introductory text]

Farms with harvested cropland	Trego	Wabaunsee	Wallace	Washington	Wichita	Wilson	Woodson	Wyandotte
Farms........................... number, 1987..	426	488	283	794	307	505	303	125
1982..	443	551	281	907	294	574	318	148
acres harvested, 1987..	139 788	90 028	146 695	239 242	182 673	114 733	85 309	12 112
1982..	142 586	103 331	162 334	272 022	195 631	143 416	87 002	14 095

HARVESTED CROPLAND BY SIZE OF FARM

1987 size of farm:

1 to 9 acres .... farms..	1	7	–	6	2	3	4	9
acres harvested..	(D)	19	–	16	(D)	5	13	21
10 to 49 acres .... farms..	4	34	2	31	2	26	17	56
acres harvested..	(D)	617	(D)	517	(D)	347	259	793
50 to 69 acres .... farms..	3	7	2	11	–	19	–	10
acres harvested..	63	293	(D)	422	–	420	–	321
70 to 99 acres .... farms..	1	42	5	37	4	43	25	14
acres harvested..	(D)	1 448	180	1 780	160	1 444	935	601
100 to 139 acres .... farms..	5	21	1	19	4	21	10	13
acres harvested..	163	1 056	(D)	1 207	349	978	644	764
140 to 179 acres .... farms..	22	32	12	67	29	35	16	2
acres harvested..	1 261	2 160	676	5 624	2 114	2 317	874	(D)
180 to 219 acres .... farms..	10	24	7	29	4	19	20	4
acres harvested..	967	1 739	801	2 678	493	1 089	1 304	397
220 to 259 acres .... farms..	5	26	2	41	6	46	17	1
acres harvested..	436	2 707	(D)	4 558	551	3 692	1 594	(D)
260 to 499 acres .... farms..	80	90	39	192	40	84	62	7
acres harvested..	10 161	11 613	5 694	33 309	7 312	14 291	10 145	1 048
500 to 999 acres .... farms..	126	114	56	206	85	114	55	5
acres harvested..	29 792	23 442	18 113	86 466	23 917	35 586	17 481	1 526
1,000 to 1,999 acres .... farms..	110	58	83	122	79	72	55	2
acres harvested..	45 404	21 262	44 906	80 666	54 032	41 661	30 659	(D)
2,000 acres or more .... farms..	59	34	74	33	72	13	22	2
acres harvested..	51 412	23 672	75 959	41 977	93 723	12 913	21 301	(D)

1982 size of farm:

1 to 9 acres .... farms..	3	3	–	9	–	3	2	10
acres harvested..	9	13	–	24	–	10	18	49
10 to 49 acres .... farms..	8	39	5	40	–	26	18	60
acres harvested..	124	761	(D)	745	–	358	(D)	886
50 to 69 acres .... farms..	5	11	2	15	2	15	7	18
acres harvested..	238	304	(D)	593	(D)	446	313	436
70 to 99 acres .... farms..	10	38	5	38	2	45	16	21
acres harvested..	318	1 355	172	1 834	119	1 886	412	862
100 to 139 acres .... farms..	2	33	–	20	–	30	14	23
acres harvested..	(D)	1 860	–	1 021	–	1 700	643	297
140 to 179 acres .... farms..	27	33	16	89	32	47	22	6
acres harvested..	1 798	2 361	1 203	8 810	3 254	3 195	1 427	586
180 to 219 acres .... farms..	2	25	3	30	6	22	8	2
acres harvested..	(D)	2 147	350	4 050	821	2 027	696	(D)
220 to 259 acres .... farms..	8	33	4	50	4	44	22	4
acres harvested..	657	3 468	555	6 644	735	5 075	1 922	501
260 to 499 acres .... farms..	80	106	50	241	43	109	69	10
acres harvested..	11 067	13 680	9 594	45 414	9 283	18 957	9 465	2 013
500 to 999 acres .... farms..	117	132	56	244	55	140	72	7
acres harvested..	26 768	30 770	20 321	89 891	23 641	50 392	24 427	3 321
1,000 to 1,999 acres .... farms..	131	71	64	103	73	76	48	1
acres harvested..	56 847	26 659	37 396	74 982	50 271	47 276	25 709	4 136
2,000 acres or more .... farms..	52	27	76	26	77	15	20	1
acres harvested..	44 445	19 953	91 888	38 414	107 450	12 092	21 647	(D)

HARVESTED CROPLAND BY ACRES HARVESTED

1987 acres harvested:

1 to 9 acres .... farms..	3	24	2	19	2	26	14	28
acres..	8	118	(D)	96	(D)	139	62	102
10 to 19 acres .... farms..	7	32	6	19	2	42	16	31
acres..	75	440	(D)	264	(D)	560	218	448
20 to 29 acres .... farms..	7	37	6	23	2	30	16	11
acres..	169	860	141	565	(D)	712	414	261
30 to 49 acres .... farms..	14	49	10	34	11	54	32	17
acres..	591	1 789	374	1 286	446	2 106	1 216	623
50 to 99 acres .... farms..	48	93	26	119	29	91	50	23
acres..	3 488	6 642	1 894	8 567	2 176	6 324	3 789	1 613
100 to 199 acres .... farms..	96	102	39	183	45	84	48	4
acres..	13 882	14 388	5 678	26 539	6 729	11 790	6 882	494
200 to 499 acres .... farms..	170	116	83	255	75	97	63	6
acres..	54 860	34 901	25 820	80 142	26 746	31 390	21 413	(D)
500 to 999 acres .... farms..	67	27	85	105	89	68	50	1
acres..	44 648	18 325	(D)	70 436	64 539	45 228	33 562	(D)
1,000 acres or more .... farms..	14	8	31	37	52	13	12	3
acres..	22 067	12 585	52 465	51 245	81 955	16 484	17 753	5 469

1982 acres harvested:

1 to 9 acres .... farms..	5	26	1	23	–	23	13	32
acres..	11	156	(D)	111	–	96	51	156
10 to 19 acres .... farms..	8	31	2	25	3	31	16	31
acres..	105	413	(D)	351	(D)	407	215	408
20 to 29 acres .... farms..	12	32	5	14	1	21	16	18
acres..	292	756	109	329	(D)	488	386	424
30 to 49 acres .... farms..	15	60	12	48	4	47	32	23
acres..	558	2 269	460	1 952	159	1 792	1 179	792
50 to 99 acres .... farms..	50	108	17	115	20	108	49	15
acres..	3 551	7 754	1 251	8 835	1 476	7 392	3 452	925
100 to 199 acres .... farms..	98	116	37	229	42	94	64	11
acres..	14 770	16 733	5 525	33 682	6 202	13 714	9 218	1 517
200 to 499 acres .... farms..	182	138	100	298	78	159	65	9
acres..	59 451	42 300	32 974	92 407	26 559	51 479	25 292	3 779
500 to 999 acres .... farms..	55	34	63	123	85	77	38	6
acres..	36 827	21 987	46 381	84 863	59 755	50 909	(D)	(D)
1,000 acres or more .... farms..	27	6	44	32	61	14	14	1
acres..	27 021	10 943	75 597	49 492	101 423	17 139	20 828	(D)

Table 7. **Irrigation: 1987 and 1982**

[For meaning of abbreviations and symbols, see introductory text]

Farms with Irrigation		Kansas	Allen	Anderson	Atchison	Barber	Barton	Bourbon
Farms	number, 1987__	7 352	7	10	11	27	111	9
	1982__	7 257	7	11	-	25	131	10
Land in irrigated farms	acres, 1987__	10 653 734	1 896	13 357	6 032	83 570	129 372	8 294
	1982__	10 344 665	1 949	15 106	-	52 894	152 513	8 235
Harvested cropland	farms, 1987__	7 307	7	9	11	27	111	8
	1982__	7 233	6	10	-	25	131	10
	acres, 1987__	4 816 179	1 407	6 356	3 452	14 233	73 242	3 224
	1982__	5 300 114	1 342	7 921	-	14 966	105 529	4 040
Other cropland, excluding cropland pastured	farms, 1987__	6 400	3	7	6	17	97	6
	1982__	5 365	1	7	-	12	96	3
	acres, 1987__	2 907 589	243	1 612	708	3 842	36 632	1 402
	1982__	2 096 276	(D)	984	-	2 053	26 361	555
Pastureland, excluding woodland pastured	farms, 1987__	4 411	2	8	8	20	77	7
	1982__	4 438	5	8	-	22	71	9
	acres, 1987__	2 689 836	(D)	3 936	1 552	(D)	14 917	2 861
	1982__	2 665 537	470	4 561	-	35 242	13 767	2 817
Irrigated land	acres, 1987__	2 463 073	(D)	1 152	478	2 954	29 147	763
	1982__	2 675 167	277	1 383	-	3 516	39 669	856
Harvested cropland	farms, 1987__	7 268	7	9	11	27	111	8
	1982__	7 211	6	10	-	25	131	9
	acres, 1987__	2 408 176	(D)	(D)	478	2 954	26 168	(D)
	1982__	2 639 024	(D)	(D)	-	(D)	39 499	(D)
Pastureland and other land	farms, 1987__	365	-	2	-	-	5	1
	1982__	279	1	1	-	1	8	1
	acres, 1987__	54 897	-	(D)	-	-	979	(D)
	1982__	36 143	(D)	(D)	-	(D)	170	(D)
1987 irrigated acres by size of farm:								
1 to 9 acres	farms__	128	1	-	2	2	1	1
	acres irrigated__	288	(D)	-	(D)	(D)	(D)	(D)
10 to 49 acres	farms__	226	2	-	1	-	6	4
	acres irrigated__	2 463	(D)	-	(D)	-	88	(D)
50 to 69 acres	farms__	58	1	1	-	-	1	-
	acres irrigated__	1 184	(D)	(D)	-	-	(D)	-
70 to 99 acres	farms__	104	-	1	-	-	-	-
	acres irrigated__	4 173	-	(D)	-	-	-	-
100 to 139 acres	farms__	103	-	1	-	-	1	-
	acres irrigated__	5 120	-	(D)	-	-	(D)	-
140 to 179 acres	farms__	259	-	-	-	-	4	-
	acres irrigated__	21 194	-	-	-	-	357	-
180 to 219 acres	farms__	83	-	-	1	-	2	1
	acres irrigated__	5 670	-	-	(D)	-	(D)	(D)
220 to 259 acres	farms__	110	2	-	-	3	2	-
	acres irrigated__	9 306	(D)	-	(D)	316	(D)	-
260 to 499 acres	farms__	842	-	-	3	3	17	-
	acres irrigated__	128 620	-	-	86	(D)	2 376	-
500 to 999 acres	farms__	1 646	-	1	2	1	32	1
	acres irrigated__	378 941	-	(D)	(D)	(D)	6 495	(D)
1,000 to 1,999 acres	farms__	2 113	-	2	1	8	31	4
	acres irrigated__	797 399	(D)	(D)	(D)	1 575	9 831	522
2,000 acres or more	farms__	1 680	-	4	1	8	18	1
	acres irrigated__	1 108 715	-	797	(D)	702	9 627	(D)
1982 irrigated acres by size of farm:								
1 to 9 acres	farms__	95	1	-	-	-	1	1
	acres irrigated__	224	(D)	-	-	-	(D)	(D)
10 to 49 acres	farms__	192	1	-	-	-	5	-
	acres irrigated__	2 266	(D)	-	-	-	(D)	-
50 to 69 acres	farms__	48	-	1	-	-	-	-
	acres irrigated__	1 363	-	(D)	-	-	-	-
70 to 99 acres	farms__	114	1	-	-	-	4	-
	acres irrigated__	4 584	(D)	-	-	-	235	-
100 to 139 acres	farms__	100	1	-	-	-	3	-
	acres irrigated__	6 608	(D)	-	-	-	180	(D)
140 to 179 acres	farms__	281	-	-	-	2	6	1
	acres irrigated__	27 692	(D)	-	-	(D)	868	(D)
180 to 219 acres	farms__	83	-	-	-	-	3	-
	acres irrigated__	6 094	-	-	-	-	414	-
220 to 259 acres	farms__	118	-	-	-	1	4	-
	acres irrigated__	12 393	-	-	-	(D)	275	-
260 to 499 acres	farms__	698	-	-	-	1	21	1
	acres irrigated__	177 788	-	-	-	(D)	2 929	(D)
500 to 999 acres	farms__	1 626	2	3	-	3	34	1
	acres irrigated__	412 456	(D)	(D)	-	206	5 376	(D)
1,000 to 1,999 acres	farms__	2 033	-	4	-	8	30	6
	acres irrigated__	835 059	-	276	-	1 597	11 421	605
2,000 acres or more	farms__	1 569	-	3	-	10	20	-
	acres irrigated__	1 186 340	-	692	-	1 220	17 899	-

Farms with irrigation	Brown	Butler	Chase	Chautauqua	Cherokee	Cheyenne	Clark
Farms _____number, 1987__	3	21	-	3	7	151	28
1982__	-	17	2	2	9	161	27
Land in irrigated farms _____acres, 1987__	38	10 741	-	328	2 418	305 849	116 263
1982__	-	5 728	(D)	(D)	3 890	274 743	114 275
Harvested cropland _____ farms, 1987__	3	19	-	3	7	149	28
1982__	-	17	2	2	9	161	27
acres, 1987__	33	6 003	-	231	1 466	97 749	20 539
1982__	-	3 992	(D)	(D)	2 362	98 082	24 500
Other cropland, excluding cropland pastured _____ farms, 1987__	1	10	-	2	1	140	24
1982__	-	9	1	-	2	131	18
acres, 1987__	(D)	2 025	-	(D)	(D)	91 026	17 159
1982__	-	70	(D)	-	(D)	68 062	9 000
Pastureland, excluding woodland pastured ___ farms, 1987__	-	10	2	-	5	107	21
1982__	-	10	-	1	8	110	20
acres, 1987__	-	1 471	-	-	665	108 466	(D)
1982__	-	724	(D)	(D)	864	101 288	78 796
Irrigated land_____acres, 1987__	(D)	1 588	-	31	376	40 651	6 030
1982__	-	614	(D)	(D)	394	44 496	5 605
Harvested cropland _____ farms, 1987__	3	19	-	3	7	149	28
1982__	-	17	2	2	9	159	27
acres, 1987__	(D)	(D)	-	31	376	40 555	(D)
1982__	-	614	(D)	(D)	394	44 281	5 605
Pastureland and other land _____ farms, 1987__	-	3	-	-	-	5	3
1982__	-	-	-	-	-	4	-
acres, 1987__	-	(D)	-	-	-	96	(D)
1982__	-	-	-	-	-	215	-
1987 irrigated acres by size of farm:							
1 to 9 acres _____ farms__	2	4	-	1	1	-	1
acres irrigated__	(D)	6	-	(D)	(D)	-	(D)
10 to 49 acres _____ farms__	1	2	-	-	2	5	-
acres irrigated__	(D)	(D)	-	-	(D)	124	-
50 to 69 acres _____ farms__	-	-	-	-	-	-	-
acres irrigated__	-	-	-	-	-	-	-
70 to 99 acres _____ farms__	-	1	-	-	-	1	-
acres irrigated__	-	(D)	-	-	-	(D)	-
100 to 139 acres _____ farms__	-	2	-	-	1	2	-
acres irrigated__	-	(D)	-	-	(D)	(D)	-
140 to 179 acres _____ farms__	-	2	-	2	-	3	-
acres irrigated__	-	(D)	-	(D)	-	125	-
180 to 219 acres _____ farms__	-	1	-	-	-	-	-
acres irrigated__	-	(D)	-	-	-	-	-
220 to 259 acres _____ farms__	-	-	-	-	-	-	-
acres irrigated__	-	-	-	-	-	-	-
260 to 499 acres _____ farms__	-	2	-	-	1	8	6
acres irrigated__	-	(D)	-	-	(D)	905	474
500 to 999 acres _____ farms__	-	2	-	-	1	25	3
acres irrigated__	-	(D)	-	-	(D)	3 523	(D)
1,000 to 1,999 acres_____ farms__	-	4	-	-	1	51	4
acres irrigated__	-	490	-	-	(D)	13 265	1 656
2,000 acres or more _____ farms__	-	1	-	-	-	56	14
acres irrigated__	-	(D)	-	-	-	22 568	3 481
1982 irrigated acres by size of farm:							
1 to 9 acres _____ farms__	-	3	-	1	-	-	1
acres irrigated__	-	7	-	(D)	-	-	(D)
10 to 49 acres _____ farms__	-	8	-	1	1	1	-
acres irrigated__	-	20	-	(D)	(D)	(D)	-
50 to 69 acres _____ farms__	-	1	-	-	-	2	-
acres irrigated__	-	(D)	-	-	-	(D)	-
70 to 99 acres _____ farms__	-	1	-	-	2	1	-
acres irrigated__	-	(D)	-	-	(D)	(D)	-
100 to 139 acres _____ farms__	-	-	1	-	-	1	-
acres irrigated__	-	-	(D)	-	-	(D)	-
140 to 179 acres _____ farms__	-	-	-	-	-	4	-
acres irrigated__	-	-	-	-	-	550	-
180 to 219 acres _____ farms__	-	-	-	-	-	2	-
acres irrigated__	-	-	-	-	-	(D)	-
220 to 259 acres _____ farms__	-	-	-	-	1	2	-
acres irrigated__	-	-	-	-	(D)	(D)	-
260 to 499 acres _____ farms__	-	1	-	-	2	17	1
acres irrigated__	-	(D)	-	-	(D)	3 323	(D)
500 to 999 acres _____ farms__	-	2	-	-	2	29	2
acres irrigated__	-	(D)	-	-	(D)	4 311	(D)
1,000 to 1,999 acres_____ farms__	-	3	1	-	1	54	5
acres irrigated__	-	390	(D)	-	(D)	14 007	965
2,000 acres or more _____ farms__	-	-	-	-	-	48	18
acres irrigated__	-	-	-	-	-	21 331	4 365

Table 7. **Irrigation: 1987 and 1982**—Con.

[For meaning of abbreviations and symbols, see introductory text]

Farms with irrigation	Clay	Cloud	Coffey	Comanche	Cowley	Crawford	Decatur
Farms _____ number, 1987__	49	76	8	26	19	11	92
1982__	60	70	10	27	13	16	94
Land in irrigated farms _____ acres, 1987__	53 203	85 035	4 229	83 559	12 021	13 006	169 095
1982__	55 834	73 327	5 279	81 056	9 356	16 567	156 482
Harvested cropland _____ farms, 1987__	49	76	8	26	19	11	91
1982__	60	70	10	27	13	16	93
acres, 1987__	27 499	40 911	2 896	19 206	7 049	7 183	51 035
1982__	32 604	42 406	2 831	22 006	5 299	10 544	46 522
Other cropland, excluding cropland pastured_____ farms, 1987__	45	69	5	24	11	9	81
1982__	36	35	5	16	4	7	82
acres, 1987__	7 054	13 443	539	12 125	1 375	1 299	36 385
1982__	2 060	3 921	318	11 534	447	407	39 072
Pastureland, excluding woodland pastured ____ farms, 1987__	35	61	6	24	11	8	64
1982__	46	59	6	26	7	12	86
acres, 1987__	15 906	26 120	550	(D)	2 712	2 766	75 939
1982__	18 597	22 470	1 534	46 546	2 542	3 675	67 461
Irrigated land_____ acres, 1987__	10 626	10 139	466	4 424	1 410	1 447	10 433
1982__	11 090	9 146	288	5 203	1 249	2 047	9 548
Harvested cropland _____ farms, 1987__	49	76	8	26	18	11	91
1982__	60	70	10	26	13	16	93
acres, 1987__	10 626	10 139	466	(D)	(D)	1 447	(D)
1982__	11 090	9 146	288	(D)	(D)	2 047	(D)
Pastureland and other land _____ farms, 1987__	-	-	-	1	1	-	1
1982__	-	-	-	1	2	-	1
acres, 1987__	-	-	-	(D)	(D)	-	(D)
1982__	-	-	-	(D)	(D)	-	(D)
1987 irrigated acres by size of farm:							
1 to 9 acres _____ farms__	-	1	1	-	1	1	-
acres irrigated__	-	(D)	(D)	-	(D)	(D)	-
10 to 49 acres _____ farms__	1	2	-	1	6	-	1
acres irrigated__	(D)	(D)	-	(D)	58	-	(D)
50 to 69 acres _____ farms__	-	1	1	-	-	-	1
acres irrigated__	-	(D)	(D)	-	-	-	(D)
70 to 99 acres _____ farms__	-	1	-	-	-	1	2
acres irrigated__	-	(D)	-	-	-	(D)	(D)
100 to 139 acres _____ farms__	-	2	-	-	-	-	-
acres irrigated__	-	(D)	-	-	-	-	-
140 to 179 acres _____ farms__	1	-	-	3	-	-	3
acres irrigated__	(D)	-	-	(D)	-	-	108
180 to 219 acres _____ farms__	1	1	-	-	-	-	1
acres irrigated__	(D)	(D)	-	-	-	-	(D)
220 to 259 acres _____ farms__	(D)	-	2	-	-	-	-
acres irrigated__	(D)	-	(D)	-	-	-	-
260 to 499 acres _____ farms__	6	6	-	1	2	1	5
acres irrigated__	731	510	-	(D)	(D)	(D)	310
500 to 999 acres _____ farms__	18	23	3	4	5	2	8
acres irrigated__	3 429	3 328	226	567	628	(D)	406
1,000 to 1,999 acres_____ farms__	16	29	1	4	4	1	37
acres irrigated__	4 190	3 878	(D)	663	483	801	4 177
2,000 acres or more _____ farms__	5	10	-	15	1	2	34
acres irrigated__	2 168	2 069	-	2 915	(D)	(D)	5 260
1982 irrigated acres by size of farm:							
1 to 9 acres _____ farms__	-	3	2	-	1	1	-
acres irrigated__	-	3	(D)	-	(D)	(D)	-
10 to 49 acres _____ farms__	2	-	-	-	1	-	2
acres irrigated__	(D)	-	-	-	(D)	-	(D)
50 to 69 acres _____ farms__	-	-	2	-	-	-	-
acres irrigated__	-	-	(D)	-	-	-	-
70 to 99 acres _____ farms__	2	1	-	-	1	-	4
acres irrigated__	(D)	(D)	-	-	(D)	-	(D)
100 to 139 acres _____ farms__	2	1	-	-	-	-	-
acres irrigated__	(D)	(D)	-	-	-	-	-
140 to 179 acres _____ farms__	2	1	-	1	-	-	-
acres irrigated__	(D)	(D)	-	(D)	-	-	-
180 to 219 acres _____ farms__	1	1	(D)	(D)	-	-	-
acres irrigated__	(D)	(D)	(D)	(D)	-	-	-
220 to 259 acres _____ farms__	-	-	-	-	1	-	-
acres irrigated__	-	-	-	-	(D)	-	-
260 to 499 acres _____ farms__	11	7	1	2	3	2	6
acres irrigated__	1 328	443	(D)	(D)	280	(D)	338
500 to 999 acres _____ farms__	20	22	3	4	2	8	19
acres irrigated__	4 021	2 160	139	1 002	(D)	745	1 175
1,000 to 1,999 acres_____ farms__	14	28	-	7	3	3	31
acres irrigated__	2 883	5 193	-	916	610	783	2 321
2,000 acres or more _____ farms__	6	6	1	12	1	2	32
acres irrigated__	2 419	1 090	(D)	2 959	(D)	(D)	5 502

Table 7. **Irrigation: 1987 and 1982**—Con.

[For meaning of abbreviations and symbols, see introductory text]

Farms with irrigation	Dickinson	Doniphan	Douglas	Edwards	Elk	Ellis	Ellsworth
Farms ... number, 1987	34	2	14	155	1	13	6
1982	23	3	15	161	1	32	8
Land in irrigated farms ... acres, 1987	30 595	(D)	10 562	231 462	(D)	17 159	6 867
1982	16 706	3 957	7 000	215 557	(D)	38 146	10 164
Harvested cropland ... farms, 1987	34	2	13	154	1	13	6
1982	23	3	15	161	1	32	8
acres, 1987	18 066	(D)	7 146	130 338	(D)	5 440	3 266
1982	12 178	1 308	5 129	130 284	(D)	11 107	4 697
Other cropland, excluding cropland pastured ... farms, 1987	30	1	6	140	1	11	5
1982	10	3	4	137	1	22	7
acres, 1987	5 474	(D)	908	58 975	(D)	3 766	1 378
1982	366	121	123	47 697	(D)	6 140	504
Pastureland, excluding woodland pastured ... farms, 1987	27	1	10	97	1	12	4
1982	17	1	9	92	1	21	7
acres, 1987	5 822	(D)	1 603	38 633	(D)	7 631	2 000
1982	3 178	(D)	995	34 632	(D)	17 654	4 631
Irrigated land ... acres, 1987	2 792	(D)	1 472	83 316	(D)	983	896
1982	1 637	(D)	1 196	74 298	(D)	3 008	861
Harvested cropland ... farms, 1987	33	2	13	154	1	13	6
1982	23	3	14	161	1	30	8
acres, 1987	(D)	(D)	(D)	82 708	(D)	(D)	896
1982	(D)	(D)	(D)	(D)	(D)	2 562	861
Pastureland and other land ... farms, 1987	1	-	1	8	-	1	-
1982	1	-	1	1	-	4	-
acres, 1987	(D)	-	(D)	608	-	(D)	-
1982	(D)	-	(D)	(D)	-	426	-
1987 irrigated acres by size of farm:							
1 to 9 acres ... farms	-	-	3	-	-	-	-
acres irrigated	-	-	10	-	-	-	-
10 to 49 acres ... farms	1	-	1	2	-	-	-
acres irrigated	(D)	-	(D)	(D)	-	-	-
50 to 69 acres ... farms	-	-	1	-	-	-	-
acres irrigated	-	-	(D)	-	-	-	-
70 to 99 acres ... farms	-	-	-	-	-	-	1
acres irrigated	-	-	-	-	-	-	(D)
100 to 139 acres ... farms	-	1	-	-	-	-	-
acres irrigated	-	(D)	-	-	-	-	-
140 to 179 acres ... farms	2	-	1	4	1	1	-
acres irrigated	(D)	-	(D)	410	(D)	(D)	-
180 to 219 acres ... farms	-	1	-	1	-	2	-
acres irrigated	-	(D)	-	(D)	-	(D)	-
220 to 259 acres ... farms	-	-	2	1	-	-	-
acres irrigated	(D)	-	(D)	550	-	-	-
260 to 499 acres ... farms	3	-	1	17	-	1	-
acres irrigated	164	-	(D)	3 144	-	(D)	-
500 to 999 acres ... farms	15	-	-	33	-	5	1
acres irrigated	1 177	-	-	8 784	-	223	(D)
1,000 to 1,999 acres ... farms	11	-	3	51	-	1	1
acres irrigated	1 238	-	125	22 596	-	(D)	(D)
2,000 acres or more ... farms	1	-	2	43	-	3	-
acres irrigated	(D)	-	(D)	47 745	-	412	-
1982 irrigated acres by size of farm:							
1 to 9 acres ... farms	-	-	4	-	-	-	-
acres irrigated	-	-	11	-	-	-	-
10 to 49 acres ... farms	2	-	-	3	-	3	-
acres irrigated	(D)	-	-	88	-	11	-
50 to 69 acres ... farms	-	-	-	-	-	-	-
acres irrigated	-	-	(D)	-	-	-	-
70 to 99 acres ... farms	1	1	2	-	-	-	-
acres irrigated	(D)	(D)	(D)	-	-	-	-
100 to 139 acres ... farms	-	-	1	-	-	2	-
acres irrigated	-	-	(D)	-	-	(D)	-
140 to 179 acres ... farms	1	-	2	7	1	6	-
acres irrigated	(D)	-	(D)	(D)	(D)	366	-
180 to 219 acres ... farms	-	-	1	1	-	-	-
acres irrigated	-	-	(D)	(D)	-	-	-
220 to 259 acres ... farms	-	-	-	-	-	-	-
260 to 499 acres ... farms	6	-	2	23	-	6	-
acres irrigated	316	-	(D)	4 667	-	227	-
500 to 999 acres ... farms	7	1	-	45	-	7	2
acres irrigated	768	(D)	-	11 598	-	1 182	(D)
1,000 to 1,999 acres ... farms	4	-	-	52	-	2	6
acres irrigated	325	-	(D)	25 783	-	(D)	(D)
2,000 acres or more ... farms	2	1	1	30	-	6	-
acres irrigated	(D)	(D)	(D)	31 297	-	912	-

Table 7. **Irrigation: 1987 and 1982**—Con.

[For meaning of abbreviations and symbols, see introductory text]

Farms with irrigation	Finney	Ford	Franklin	Geary	Gove	Graham	Grant
Farms _____ number, 1987__	283	213	16	22	87	53	190
1982__	301	216	16	17	85	70	173
Land in irrigated farms _____ acres, 1987__	431 681	302 969	26 295	21 221	170 648	99 697	254 735
1982__	464 899	298 721	12 444	15 988	215 854	132 485	263 046
Harvested cropland _____ farms, 1987__	279	210	16	22	87	53	189
1982__	299	214	16	17	85	70	171
acres, 1987__	237 909	144 284	9 773	8 566	59 930	31 764	131 061
1982__	288 422	153 146	5 716	8 492	67 381	45 442	154 212
Other cropland, excluding cropland pastured_____ farms, 1987__	245	178	10	17	82	45	172
1982__	226	169	8	8	81	58	148
acres, 1987__	139 029	98 725	1 570	2 376	46 473	26 701	85 400
1982__	100 730	66 283	343	1 083	48 222	28 139	64 599
Pastureland, excluding woodland pastured ____ farms, 1987__	111	161	11	18	65	43	86
1982__	119	163	14	14	73	61	76
acres, 1987__	48 371	66 186	12 945	8 006	(D)	40 071	31 477
1982__	63 491	71 876	5 667	5 411	95 942	55 305	29 123
Irrigated land_____ acres, 1987__	184 177	77 629	1 503	1 618	15 941	8 519	99 429
1982__	207 293	81 415	1 036	1 985	19 893	13 410	121 012
Harvested cropland _____ farms, 1987__	279	208	16	22	87	53	189
1982__	297	213	16	17	85	70	171
acres, 1987__	175 045	75 306	1 503	1 618	(D)	(D)	97 129
1982__	197 003	79 926	1 036	(D)	(D)	13 074	119 848
Pastureland and other land _____ farms, 1987__	29	15	-	-	3	1	16
1982__	29	13	-	1	2	7	16
acres, 1987__	9 132	2 323	-	-	(D)	(D)	2 300
1982__	10 290	1 489	-	(D)	(D)	336	1 364
1987 irrigated acres by size of farm:							
1 to 9 acres _____ farms__	3	4	2	1	-	1	2
acres irrigated__	11	11	(D)	(D)	-	(D)	(D)
10 to 49 acres _____ farms__	7	7	1	-	1	-	-
acres irrigated__	(D)	64	-	-	(D)	-	(D)
50 to 69 acres _____ farms__	1	-	1	1	2	-	1
acres irrigated__	(D)	-	(D)	(D)	(D)	-	(D)
70 to 99 acres _____ farms__	7	5	-	-	-	1	2
acres irrigated__	394	232	-	-	-	(D)	(D)
100 to 139 acres _____ farms__	1	2	-	-	-	-	1
acres irrigated__	(D)	(D)	(D)	-	-	-	(D)
140 to 179 acres _____ farms__	5	7	1	1	1	3	7
acres irrigated__	626	648	(D)	(D)	(D)	(D)	643
180 to 219 acres _____ farms__	4	1	-	1	-	-	2
acres irrigated__	381	(D)	-	(D)	-	-	(D)
220 to 259 acres _____ farms__	3	4	-	-	-	-	-
acres irrigated__	520	628	-	-	-	-	-
260 to 499 acres _____ farms__	35	17	2	2	4	4	31
acres irrigated__	7 325	2 322	(D)	(D)	1 065	266	6 294
500 to 999 acres _____ farms__	54	54	2	6	14	10	44
acres irrigated__	24 437	11 457	(D)	585	1 532	737	13 437
1,000 to 1,999 acres_____ farms__	90	56	1	8	35	13	62
acres irrigated__	59 943	22 959	270	642	4 867	1 639	38 240
2,000 acres or more _____ farms__	73	54	3	2	30	21	37
acres irrigated__	90 236	39 191	824	(D)	8 226	5 561	40 196
1982 irrigated acres by size of farm:							
1 to 9 acres _____ farms__	2	1	-	1	-	2	2
acres irrigated__	(D)	(D)	-	-	-	(D)	(D)
10 to 49 acres _____ farms__	12	5	2	-	-	-	2
acres irrigated__	211	72	(D)	-	-	-	(D)
50 to 69 acres _____ farms__	3	-	1	-	-	-	2
acres irrigated__	96	-	(D)	-	-	-	(D)
70 to 99 acres _____ farms__	4	3	-	1	-	1	1
acres irrigated__	194	108	-	(D)	-	(D)	(D)
100 to 139 acres _____ farms__	1	8	1	-	-	-	-
acres irrigated__	(D)	629	(D)	-	-	-	-
140 to 179 acres _____ farms__	8	9	1	2	1	5	9
acres irrigated__	894	857	(D)	(D)	(D)	571	1 150
180 to 219 acres _____ farms__	1	2	1	-	-	1	2
acres irrigated__	(D)	(D)	(D)	-	-	(D)	(D)
220 to 259 acres _____ farms__	5	1	1	-	-	-	-
acres irrigated__	1 053	(D)	(D)	-	-	-	-
260 to 499 acres _____ farms__	37	27	1	3	6	4	12
acres irrigated__	10 808	4 385	(D)	270	(D)	996	3 478
500 to 999 acres _____ farms__	69	41	3	2	14	9	44
acres irrigated__	32 405	11 366	360	(D)	1 943	1 042	19 680
1,000 to 1,999 acres_____ farms__	91	76	3	6	27	17	54
acres irrigated__	67 811	29 446	242	1 386	3 501	2 928	34 170
2,000 acres or more _____ farms__	68	43	2	2	37	31	45
acres irrigated__	93 763	34 325	(D)	(D)	12 860	7 709	61 945

Farms with irrigation		Gray	Greeley	Greenwood	Hamilton	Harper	Harvey	Haskell
Farms number, 1987..		304	58	8	58	10	118	223
1982..		328	40	6	51	18	123	238
Land in irrigated farms acres, 1987..		399 810	145 328	27 082	137 670	11 966	73 763	307 420
1982..		417 576	118 572	17 139	153 711	12 920	72 599	308 275
Harvested cropland farms, 1987..		303	58	8	58	10	118	222
1982..		327	40	6	51	18	123	238
acres, 1987..		207 280	64 112	2 781	38 501	5 291	50 070	174 880
1982..		269 693	59 208	2 454	59 374	7 373	56 487	222 318
Other cropland, excluding cropland pastured farms, 1987..		283	55	4	49	8	99	202
1982..		255	36	–	45	9	66	183
acres, 1987..		130 366	62 611	1 052	47 576	1 158	13 751	85 241
1982..		79 802	46 402	–	42 482	610	4 071	54 439
Pastureland, excluding woodland pastured farms, 1987..		158	26	6	34	9	68	72
1982..		169	21	6	38	15	63	74
acres, 1987..		56 548	17 305	22 822	49 793	5 356	8 235	42 348
1982..		59 048	10 547	14 084	50 694	4 560	9 143	23 346
Irrigated land acres, 1987..		154 369	25 410	819	18 805	584	20 939	154 476
1982..		191 175	28 730	244	23 419	1 440	20 725	180 843
Harvested cropland farms, 1987..		303	57	8	58	10	118	222
1982..		327	39	6	51	18	122	238
acres, 1987..		149 840	(D)	819	18 554	584	20 827	150 442
1982..		189 847	(D)	244	23 252	(D)	(D)	177 420
Pastureland and other land farms, 1987..		25	3	–	6	–	3	13
1982..		14	1	–	5	2	3	20
acres, 1987..		4 529	(D)	–	251	–	112	4 034
1982..		1 328	(D)	–	167	(D)	(D)	3 223
1987 irrigated acres by size of farm:								
1 to 9 acres farms..		–	1	1	–	–	2	–
acres irrigated..		–	(D)	(D)	–	–	(D)	–
10 to 49 acres farms..		1	–	–	1	–	14	3
acres irrigated..		(D)	–	–	(D)	–	150	48
50 to 69 acres farms..		–	–	–	–	–	–	–
acres irrigated..		–	–	–	–	–	–	–
70 to 99 acres farms..		1	–	–	2	–	3	–
acres irrigated..		(D)	–	–	(D)	–	134	–
100 to 139 acres farms..		8	–	–	–	–	2	–
acres irrigated..		(D)	–	–	–	–	(D)	–
140 to 179 acres farms..		11	2	–	3	2	3	14
acres irrigated..		1 209	(D)	–	214	(D)	(D)	1 403
180 to 219 acres farms..		3	1	–	–	–	2	–
acres irrigated..		82	(D)	–	–	–	(D)	–
220 to 259 acres farms..		4	–	–	–	–	3	–
acres irrigated..		522	(D)	–	–	(D)	256	–
260 to 499 acres farms..		54	7	1	2	–	26	25
acres irrigated..		11 508	1 432	(D)	(D)	–	3 363	5 308
500 to 999 acres farms..		80	12	2	12	2	46	63
acres irrigated..		29 145	4 216	(D)	2 894	(D)	7 772	26 881
1,000 to 1,999 acres farms..		85	6	2	14	4	15	61
acres irrigated..		51 645	2 524	(D)	5 449	226	7 174	61 197
2,000 acres or more farms..		57	28	2	24	1	3	37
acres irrigated..		59 777	16 894	(D)	9 883	(D)	1 492	59 639
1982 irrigated acres by size of farm:								
1 to 9 acres farms..		–	–	–	–	–	–	–
acres irrigated..		–	–	–	–	–	–	–
10 to 49 acres farms..		1	–	–	1	1	7	–
acres irrigated..		(D)	–	–	(D)	(D)	51	–
50 to 69 acres farms..		–	–	–	1	–	–	–
acres irrigated..		–	–	–	(D)	–	–	–
70 to 99 acres farms..		4	–	–	–	1	7	2
acres irrigated..		(D)	–	–	–	(D)	(D)	(D)
100 to 139 acres farms..		3	–	–	1	–	1	3
acres irrigated..		360	–	–	(D)	–	(D)	178
140 to 179 acres farms..		16	2	–	5	–	6	8
acres irrigated..		2 161	(D)	–	509	–	351	1 178
180 to 219 acres farms..		–	2	–	–	–	1	1
acres irrigated..		–	(D)	–	–	–	(D)	(D)
220 to 259 acres farms..		5	–	–	–	1	13	2
acres irrigated..		898	–	–	–	(D)	790	(D)
260 to 499 acres farms..		70	3	1	6	2	35	46
acres irrigated..		21 021	550	(D)	1 421	(D)	4 625	14 267
500 to 999 acres farms..		69	6	–	5	9	39	60
acres irrigated..		36 933	2 762	–	1 042	711	7 333	29 018
1,000 to 1,999 acres farms..		81	5	1	15	4	9	76
acres irrigated..		57 784	2 976	(D)	4 449	599	2 814	69 299
2,000 acres or more farms..		57	22	4	27	–	5	40
acres irrigated..		69 673	22 231	(D)	15 891	–	4 150	66 024

Table 7. **Irrigation: 1987 and 1982**—Con.

[For meaning of abbreviations and symbols, see introductory text]

Farms with irrigation	Hodgeman	Jackson	Jefferson	Jewell	Johnson	Kearny	Kingman	Kiowa
Farms _____ number, 1987__	126	7	21	52	20	110	66	91
1982__	126	8	7	52	23	114	67	96
Land in irrigated farms _____ acres, 1987__	230 646	10 907	6 016	43 740	3 244	275 919	96 059	154 387
1982__	194 301	4 799	5 526	40 775	4 129	266 034	75 024	149 503
Harvested cropland _____ farms, 1987__	126	7	20	52	19	109	66	91
1982__	128	6	7	52	22	113	66	96
acres, 1987__	76 912	3 739	4 337	18 342	1 402	106 093	44 260	68 492
1982__	70 487	2 669	4 780	19 768	2 958	125 297	41 011	75 149
Other cropland, excluding cropland pastured_____ farms, 1987__	119	3	6	42	7	95	57	83
1982__	111	5	2	30	4	91	34	81
acres, 1987__	61 764	1 208	873	5 945	707	67 898	13 479	41 457
1982__	45 531	100	(D)	3 793	443	63 978	2 565	30 605
Pastureland, excluding woodland pastured ____ farms, 1987__	101	6	9	42	11	64	55	63
1982__	101	5	4	41	7	64	58	69
acres, 1987__	(D)	5 026	225	17 184	561	99 129	34 624	(D)
1982__	76 120	1 944	170	15 257	644	68 893	29 569	40 400
Irrigated land _____ acres, 1987__	22 795	2 276	1 763	7 087	259	83 178	14 798	37 144
1982__	22 198	2 445	1 178	7 074	1 609	87 875	9 708	39 705
Harvested cropland _____ farms, 1987__	125	7	20	52	17	109	65	91
1982__	128	6	7	52	20	113	65	96
acres, 1987__	21 712	2 276	(D)	7 074	165	78 112	14 763	36 599
1982__	(D)	2 445	1 176	7 074	(D)	86 819	(D)	(D)
Pastureland and other land _____ farms, 1987__	8	-	1	1	5	12	4	4
1982__	2	-	-	-	3	13	2	2
acres, 1987__	1 083	-	(D)	(D)	94	5 066	35	545
1982__	(D)	-	-	-	(D)	1 056	(D)	(D)
1987 irrigated acres by size of farm:								
1 to 9 acres _____ farms__	-	-	2	-	2	-	1	2
acres irrigated__	-	-	(D)	-	(D)	-	(D)	(D)
10 to 49 acres _____ farms__	2	1	8	-	10	4	2	-
acres irrigated__	(D)	(D)	56	-	31	58	(D)	-
50 to 69 acres _____ farms__	-	-	-	-	1	-	1	-
acres irrigated__	-	-	-	-	(D)	-	(D)	-
70 to 99 acres _____ farms__	-	-	2	-	-	-	-	-
acres irrigated__	-	-	(D)	-	-	-	-	-
100 to 139 acres _____ farms__	-	-	-	2	-	3	-	-
acres irrigated__	-	-	(D)	(D)	-	162	(D)	-
140 to 179 acres _____ farms__	1	-	2	5	-	7	1	2
acres irrigated__	(D)	-	(D)	196	-	626	(D)	(D)
180 to 219 acres _____ farms__	1	-	-	2	3	2	1	1
acres irrigated__	(D)	-	-	(D)	111	(D)	(D)	(D)
220 to 259 acres _____ farms__	-	-	-	2	-	2	-	-
acres irrigated__	-	-	-	(D)	(D)	(D)	(D)	-
260 to 499 acres _____ farms__	14	2	3	9	1	10	4	9
acres irrigated__	1 400	(D)	132	904	(D)	2 063	121	1 608
500 to 999 acres _____ farms__	19	-	1	16	1	23	18	22
acres irrigated__	2 294	-	(D)	1 362	(D)	6 179	2 026	5 545
1,000 to 1,999 acres _____ farms__	37	-	1	13	1	23	24	22
acres irrigated__	5 096	(D)	(D)	3 850	(D)	14 166	4 721	7 803
2,000 acres or more _____ farms__	52	3	1	3	-	36	12	33
acres irrigated__	13 645	1 853	(D)	415	-	59 591	7 755	21 806
1982 irrigated acres by size of farm:								
1 to 9 acres _____ farms__	1	-	-	-	4	-	1	-
acres irrigated__	(D)	-	-	-	7	-	(D)	-
10 to 49 acres _____ farms__	3	1	1	-	9	1	5	-
acres irrigated__	60	(D)	(D)	-	41	(D)	29	-
50 to 69 acres _____ farms__	-	-	-	-	1	-	1	-
acres irrigated__	-	-	-	-	(D)	(D)	(D)	-
70 to 99 acres _____ farms__	-	1	-	2	2	1	-	-
acres irrigated__	-	(D)	-	(D)	(D)	(D)	-	-
100 to 139 acres _____ farms__	1	-	-	1	1	4	-	-
acres irrigated__	(D)	-	-	(D)	(D)	387	-	-
140 to 179 acres _____ farms__	2	-	-	6	-	9	3	2
acres irrigated__	(D)	-	-	543	-	957	50	(D)
180 to 219 acres _____ farms__	1	-	2	2	1	2	2	1
acres irrigated__	(D)	-	(D)	(D)	(D)	(D)	(D)	(D)
220 to 259 acres _____ farms__	4	-	-	2	1	2	-	-
acres irrigated__	398	-	-	(D)	(D)	(D)	-	-
260 to 499 acres _____ farms__	17	3	1	9	2	11	12	8
acres irrigated__	1 537	323	(D)	955	(D)	2 935	925	1 784
500 to 999 acres _____ farms__	30	1	1	17	1	21	13	21
acres irrigated__	4 291	-	(D)	1 886	(D)	7 273	2 838	5 123
1,000 to 1,999 acres _____ farms__	32	-	1	10	1	23	20	39
acres irrigated__	5 519	-	(D)	3 160	(D)	12 308	2 935	15 932
2,000 acres or more _____ farms__	37	1	1	3	-	39	10	25
acres irrigated__	10 058	(D)	(D)	325	-	63 247	2 600	16 470

Table 7. Irrigation: 1987 and 1982—Con.

[For meaning of abbreviations and symbols, see introductory text]

Farms with irrigation	Labette	Lane	Leavenworth	Lincoln	Linn	Logan	Lyon	McPherson
Farms ... number, 1987	19	46	17	7	2	46	8	165
1982	17	57	9	11	2	59	5	161
Land in irrigated farms ... acres, 1987	13 326	125 001	3 663	18 805	(D)	139 175	5 169	125 590
1982	10 262	125 829	4 948	13 608	(D)	154 553	3 733	106 763
Harvested cropland ... farms, 1987	18	46	17	7	2	46	8	163
1982	17	57	8	11	2	58	5	161
acres, 1987	6 304	42 261	1 471	6 833	(D)	37 784	2 088	70 704
1982	7 180	49 107	1 819	6 863	(D)	45 103	1 498	72 492
Other cropland, excluding cropland pastured ... farms, 1987	11	46	5	6	1	43	5	145
1982	6	49	4	6	1	50	3	100
acres, 1987	1 496	35 498	104	3 216	(D)	34 159	528	22 501
1982	58	33 502	1 297	1 447	(D)	36 431	117	5 930
Pastureland, excluding woodland pastured ... farms, 1987	13	34	7	7	2	29	8	88
1982	8	44	8	5	2	47	8	88
acres, 1987	4 661	(D)	1 158	7 916	(D)	64 619	2 245	27 927
1982	1 214	40 696	1 052	4 798	(D)	70 728	1 506	23 477
Irrigated land ... acres, 1987	1 905	14 902	310	699	(D)	10 982	(D)	24 008
1982	1 374	17 895	164	703	(D)	12 397	402	23 873
Harvested cropland ... farms, 1987	18	46	16	7	2	46	6	162
1982	17	57	8	11	2	58	5	161
acres, 1987	(D)	14 902	(D)	699	(D)	(D)	(D)	23 993
1982	1 374	17 895	(D)	703	(D)	(D)	402	(D)
Pastureland and other land ... farms, 1987	1	-	1	-	-	1	2	4
1982	-	-	2	-	-	2	-	1
acres, 1987	(D)	-	(D)	-	-	(D)	(D)	15
1982	-	-	(D)	-	-	(D)	-	(D)
1987 irrigated acres by size of farm:								
1 to 9 acres ... farms	3	-	3	-	-	-	-	5
acres irrigated	3	-	4	-	-	-	-	9
10 to 49 acres ... farms	2	-	1	-	-	-	-	6
acres irrigated	(D)	-	(D)	-	1	-	-	38
50 to 69 acres ... farms	-	-	3	-	1	-	-	3
acres irrigated	-	-	31	-	(D)	-	-	43
70 to 99 acres ... farms	-	-	4	-	1	-	2	3
acres irrigated	-	-	46	-	(D)	-	(D)	96
100 to 139 acres ... farms	2	-	-	-	-	1	-	9
acres irrigated	(D)	-	-	-	-	(D)	-	513
140 to 179 acres ... farms	1	3	-	-	-	-	2	6
acres irrigated	(D)	215	-	-	-	-	(D)	586
180 to 219 acres ... farms	-	-	-	-	-	-	-	5
acres irrigated	-	-	-	-	-	-	-	246
220 to 259 acres ... farms	-	-	1	-	-	-	1	7
acres irrigated	(D)	(D)	-	-	-	-	(D)	584
260 to 499 acres ... farms	-	2	2	-	-	2	-	35
acres irrigated	-	(D)	(D)	-	-	(D)	-	4 503
500 to 999 acres ... farms	4	3	4	-	-	6	-	47
acres irrigated	521	885	51	-	-	1 042	-	6 100
1,000 to 1,999 acres ... farms	5	13	-	5	-	13	2	28
acres irrigated	1 179	2 842	-	(D)	-	3 246	(D)	6 173
2,000 acres or more ... farms	1	24	-	2	-	24	1	11
acres irrigated	(D)	10 402	-	(D)	-	6 358	(D)	5 117
1982 irrigated acres by size of farm:								
1 to 9 acres ... farms	-	-	1	-	-	1	-	1
acres irrigated	-	-	(D)	-	-	(D)	-	(D)
10 to 49 acres ... farms	4	-	1	-	-	1	-	4
acres irrigated	17	-	(D)	-	-	(D)	-	116
50 to 69 acres ... farms	-	-	2	-	1	-	-	2
acres irrigated	-	-	(D)	-	(D)	-	-	(C)
70 to 99 acres ... farms	2	-	-	-	-	-	-	2
acres irrigated	(D)	-	-	-	-	-	-	(D)
100 to 139 acres ... farms	-	-	1	-	-	2	-	4
acres irrigated	-	-	(D)	-	-	(D)	-	172
140 to 179 acres ... farms	1	2	-	1	-	-	-	6
acres irrigated	-	(D)	-	(D)	-	-	-	324
180 to 219 acres ... farms	-	-	-	2	-	-	-	6
acres irrigated	-	-	-	(D)	-	-	-	441
220 to 259 acres ... farms	-	-	-	1	-	-	-	11
acres irrigated	-	-	-	-	-	-	-	1 180
260 to 499 acres ... farms	2	2	2	1	-	3	2	43
acres irrigated	(D)	(D)	(D)	-	-	277	(D)	5 597
500 to 999 acres ... farms	7	11	1	2	-	4	(D)	52
acres irrigated	893	2 486	(D)	(D)	-	1 350	(D)	7 391
1,000 to 1,999 acres ... farms	1	18	-	3	-	19	2	26
acres irrigated	(D)	5 467	(D)	228	-	2 288	(D)	6 634
2,000 acres or more ... farms	(D)	24	-	-	-	29	-	43
acres irrigated	(D)	9 478	(D)	156	-	8 348	-	1 861

Table 7. **Irrigation: 1987 and 1982**—Con.

[For meaning of abbreviations and symbols, see introductory text]

Farms with irrigation	Marion	Marshall	Meade	Miami	Mitchell	Montgomery	Morris	Morton
Farms _____ number, 1987__	28	20	191	14	39	21	5	78
1982__	25	14	188	6	36	20	5	80
Land in irrigated farms _____ acres, 1987__	26 892	12 266	271 941	6 199	48 761	17 106	7 113	192 712
1982__	20 877	16 179	299 950	8 752	42 380	19 297	2 430	152 890
Harvested cropland _____ farms, 1987__	28	20	191	14	38	21	5	78
1982__	25	14	188	6	36	19	5	60
acres, 1987__	14 657	6 842	135 655	4 012	28 221	11 440	888	77 073
1982__	11 353	8 944	142 700	7 600	27 713	10 426	1 351	80 556
Other cropland, excluding cropland pastured _____ farms, 1987__	24	13	184	6	34	11	5	71
1982__	12	10	145	2	28	7	2	85
acres, 1987__	3 479	1 970	76 272	927	10 735	2 613	2 728	81 098
1982__	1 324	1 635	50 315	(D)	5 353	3 699	(D)	52 666
Pastureland, excluding woodland pastured _____ farms, 1987__	24	14	87	8	27	15	4	39
1982__	20	11	105	6	27	12	5	32
acres, 1987__	7 869	2 420	(D)	609	8 341	1 714	2 966	(D)
1982__	6 622	3 951	98 661	923	7 185	2 957	963	18 532
Irrigated land _____ acres, 1987__	2 188	2 159	100 309	437	4 867	2 463	226	35 799
1982__	2 077	985	102 158	449	3 860	1 974	311	34 333
Harvested cropland _____ farms, 1987__	28	20	190	14	38	21	4	78
1982__	25	12	187	6	36	19	5	60
acres, 1987__	2 188	2 159	99 161	437	(D)	(D)	(D)	(D)
1982__	(D)	(D)	101 522	449	3 860	(D)	311	(D)
Pastureland and other land _____ farms, 1987__	-	-	9	-	1	1	1	1
1982__	1	2	12	-	1	1	-	1
acres, 1987__	(D)	(D)	1 148	-	(D)	(D)	(D)	(D)
1982__	(D)	(D)	636	-	-	(D)	-	(D)
1987 irrigated acres by size of farm:								
1 to 9 acres _____ farms __	1	2	-	2	4	3	1	-
acres irrigated __	(D)	(D)	-	(D)	4	7	(D)	-
10 to 49 acres _____ farms __	2	2	1	-	3	-	-	-
acres irrigated __	(D)	(D)	(D)	-	36	-	-	3
50 to 69 acres _____ farms __	-	-	-	-	-	-	-	3
acres irrigated __	-	-	-	-	-	-	-	155
70 to 99 acres _____ farms __	-	2	2	-	-	3	-	1
acres irrigated __	-	(D)	(D)	-	-	151	-	(D)
100 to 139 acres _____ farms __	2	-	2	2	-	4	-	-
acres irrigated __	(D)	-	(D)	(D)	-	94	-	-
140 to 179 acres _____ farms __	1	-	2	-	-	1	-	6
acres irrigated __	(D)	-	265	-	-	(D)	-	812
180 to 219 acres _____ farms __	-	-	-	-	-	-	-	1
acres irrigated __	-	-	-	-	-	-	-	(D)
220 to 259 acres _____ farms __	-	2	1	-	-	-	-	-
acres irrigated __	-	(D)	27	-	-	(D)	-	-
260 to 499 acres _____ farms __	1	1	2	1	5	-	1	2
acres irrigated __	(D)	(D)	5 986	(D)	65	-	(D)	(D)
500 to 999 acres _____ farms __	13	5	49	1	7	1	1	5
acres irrigated __	(D)	392	16 950	(D)	1 854	(D)	(D)	1 374
1,000 to 1,999 acres _____ farms __	5	6	62	-	12	4	-	22
acres irrigated __	743	1 505	35 656	-	1 762	1 099	-	11 195
2,000 acres or more _____ farms __	3	-	44	1	6	4	2	38
acres irrigated __	551	-	41 073	(D)	1 146	1 014	(D)	21 963
1982 irrigated acres by size of farm:								
1 to 9 acres _____ farms __	3	-	-	-	-	1	-	-
acres irrigated __	10	-	-	-	-	(D)	-	-
10 to 49 acres _____ farms __	1	-	2	-	2	2	-	1
acres irrigated __	(D)	-	(D)	-	(D)	(D)	-	(D)
50 to 69 acres _____ farms __	-	-	-	-	-	-	-	-
acres irrigated __	-	-	-	-	-	-	-	-
70 to 99 acres _____ farms __	1	-	3	1	1	4	1	-
acres irrigated __	(D)	-	50	(D)	(D)	119	(D)	-
100 to 139 acres _____ farms __	-	-	-	-	-	-	-	-
acres irrigated __	-	-	-	-	-	-	-	-
140 to 179 acres _____ farms __	2	-	5	-	-	2	-	-
acres irrigated __	(D)	-	738	-	-	(D)	-	-
180 to 219 acres _____ farms __	-	-	-	1	-	-	-	-
acres irrigated __	-	-	-	(D)	-	-	-	-
220 to 259 acres _____ farms __	-	-	1	1	-	-	2	-
acres irrigated __	-	-	(D)	(D)	-	-	(D)	-
260 to 499 acres _____ farms __	3	1	34	2	2	1	-	-
acres irrigated __	104	(D)	8 206	(D)	(D)	(D)	-	-
500 to 999 acres _____ farms __	8	5	50	-	3	1	1	8
acres irrigated __	943	(D)	15 815	-	1 713	220	(D)	(D)
1,000 to 1,999 acres _____ farms __	4	7	54	-	13	3	1	21
acres irrigated __	280	510	37 069	-	745	530	(D)	11 004
2,000 acres or more _____ farms __	3	1	39	1	4	4	-	32
acres irrigated __	650	(D)	40 003	(D)	1 240	995	-	21 041

Table 7. **Irrigation: 1987 and 1982**—Con.

[For meaning of abbreviations and symbols, see introductory text]

Farms with irrigation	Nemaha	Neosho	Ness	Norton	Osage	Osborne	Ottawa	Pawnee
Farms ... number, 1987..	9	7	29	54	5	78	25	183
1982..	8	8	34	64	12	48	25	174
Land in irrigated farms ... acres, 1987..	3 486	4 355	52 219	112 260	2 176	99 124	44 590	265 127
1982..	(D)	605	61 782	94 188	9 544	63 393	49 324	234 431
Harvested cropland ... farms, 1987..	9	7	29	54	5	76	25	180
1982..	1	8	34	64	12	48	25	173
acres, 1987..	2 155	2 199	14 938	37 496	1 043	42 385	18 643	137 931
1982..	(D)	274	19 349	33 248	4 302	26 003	25 690	141 526
Other cropland, excluding cropland pastured ... farms, 1987..	7	3	27	49	4	73	21	160
1982..	1	2	33	59	4	36	15	133
acres, 1987..	353	512	16 933	26 939	200	22 395	7 124	78 780
1982..	(D)	(D)	17 442	20 455	149	9 832	2 705	46 485
Pastureland, excluding woodland pastured ... farms, 1987..	7	5	26	48	3	52	15	113
1982..	1	4	29	58	9	38	19	111
acres, 1987..	885	901	19 388	44 145	825	30 304	17 119	42 146
1982..	(D)	278	24 506	35 722	4 134	22 104	19 551	40 758
Irrigated land ... acres, 1987..	494	536	2 662	5 893	(D)	8 462	1 741	65 213
1982..	(D)	39	3 865	6 255	1 340	3 393	3 094	65 207
Harvested cropland ... farms, 1987..	7	6	29	54	5	76	24	180
1982..	1	6	34	64	11	48	25	173
acres, 1987..	(D)	(D)	2 662	(D)	(D)	(D)	(D)	64 081
1982..	(D)	(D)	3 865	(D)	(D)	(D)	(D)	64 841
Pastureland and other land ... farms, 1987..	2	1	-	1	-	2	1	10
1982..	2	-	1	1	-	1	1	7
acres, 1987..	(D)	(D)	-	(D)	-	(D)	(D)	1 132
1982..	-	(D)	-	(D)	(D)	(D)	(D)	566
1987 irrigated acres by size of farm:								
1 to 9 acres ... farms..	1	-	-	-	-	-	2	-
acres irrigated..	(D)	-	-	-	-	-	(D)	-
10 to 49 acres ... farms..	2	-	1	-	2	2	-	2
acres irrigated..	(D)	-	(D)	-	(D)	(D)	-	(D)
50 to 69 acres ... farms..	-	-	-	-	1	-	1	-
acres irrigated..	-	(D)	-	-	(D)	-	(D)	-
70 to 99 acres ... farms..	-	-	2	-	-	3	-	6
acres irrigated..	-	(D)	(D)	-	-	43	-	364
100 to 139 acres ... farms..	-	1	-	-	-	1	1	-
acres irrigated..	-	-	-	-	-	(D)	(D)	-
140 to 179 acres ... farms..	-	-	-	-	-	1	-	12
acres irrigated..	-	-	-	-	-	(D)	-	1 124
180 to 219 acres ... farms..	-	-	2	1	-	2	-	1
acres irrigated..	-	-	(D)	(D)	-	(D)	-	(D)
220 to 259 acres ... farms..	-	-	-	3	-	1	-	4
acres irrigated..	-	-	(D)	(D)	-	(D)	-	428
260 to 499 acres ... farms..	3	1	3	6	-	9	2	19
acres irrigated..	26	(D)	112	574	-	388	(D)	3 976
500 to 999 acres ... farms..	2	1	1	5	-	20	6	41
acres irrigated..	(D)	(D)	(D)	574	-	1 302	459	9 351
1,000 to 1,999 acres ... farms..	(D)	2	9	12	2	25	7	51
acres irrigated..	(D)	(D)	(D)	1 059	(D)	2 273	586	15 420
2,000 acres or more ... farms..	-	-	11	25	-	14	6	47
acres irrigated..	-	-	1 792	3 560	-	4 220	553	34 416
1982 irrigated acres by size of farm:								
1 to 9 acres ... farms..	-	-	-	-	-	-	2	-
acres irrigated..	-	-	-	-	-	-	(D)	-
10 to 49 acres ... farms..	-	3	-	3	2	1	-	2
acres irrigated..	-	31	-	53	(D)	(D)	-	(D)
50 to 69 acres ... farms..	-	-	-	-	-	2	-	1
acres irrigated..	-	-	-	-	-	(D)	-	(D)
70 to 99 acres ... farms..	-	1	-	1	-	2	-	1
acres irrigated..	-	(D)	-	(D)	-	(D)	-	(D)
100 to 139 acres ... farms..	-	-	-	-	-	-	-	3
acres irrigated..	-	-	-	(D)	-	-	-	265
140 to 179 acres ... farms..	-	1	-	1	1	1	1	6
acres irrigated..	-	(D)	-	(D)	(D)	(D)	(D)	547
180 to 219 acres ... farms..	-	-	3	1	-	-	-	2
acres irrigated..	-	-	72	(D)	-	-	-	(D)
220 to 259 acres ... farms..	-	1	-	-	-	-	-	6
acres irrigated..	-	(D)	-	-	-	-	-	544
260 to 499 acres ... farms..	1	-	6	14	4	-	1	30
acres irrigated..	(D)	-	463	657	57	-	(D)	5 630
500 to 999 acres ... farms..	-	-	4	9	1	14	2	30
acres irrigated..	-	-	175	652	(D)	1 305	(D)	7 372
1,000 to 1,999 acres ... farms..	-	-	9	19	3	21	9	59
acres irrigated..	-	-	796	1 686	745	1 318	878	21 871
2,000 acres or more ... farms..	-	-	12	15	1	7	10	34
acres irrigated..	-	-	2 357	3 107	(D)	491	1 498	26 549

Farms with irrigation	Phillips	Pottawatomie	Pratt	Rawlins	Reno	Republic	Rice	Riley
Farms .... number, 1987..	37	48	160	72	156	232	67	27
1982..	42	47	153	95	135	208	64	23
Land in irrigated farms .... acres, 1987..	49 727	67 602	233 366	135 528	131 395	158 803	91 942	24 171
1982..	51 586	45 874	196 233	179 536	111 585	138 084	81 121	27 814
Harvested cropland .... farms, 1987..	37	48	160	72	156	232	67	25
1982..	42	47	153	95	135	208	64	23
acres, 1987..	16 775	27 156	134 803	45 685	76 360	90 917	53 504	8 372
1982..	18 748	23 079	122 956	57 547	77 670	90 439	55 258	9 709
Other cropland, excluding cropland pastured .... farms, 1987..	30	40	141	69	122	210	58	20
1982..	32	21	113	82	80	123	50	13
acres, 1987..	7 726	6 165	61 181	39 498	24 183	27 606	17 516	2 685
1982..	6 922	1 226	30 352	42 695	10 875	10 252	10 404	593
Pastureland, excluding woodland pastured .... farms, 1987..	27	31	89	64	113	165	43	15
1982..	37	23	104	80	82	147	44	10
acres, 1987..	18 092	31 335	32 462	47 942	27 301	34 457	18 816	12 113
1982..	23 335	19 097	41 400	76 922	19 803	25 889	13 076	15 711
Irrigated land .... acres, 1987..	4 910	9 573	71 541	11 547	25 576	45 220	15 058	1 922
1982..	4 506	7 796	53 114	17 719	23 563	42 871	16 232	2 131
Harvested cropland .... farms, 1987..	37	48	160	72	154	232	67	25
1982..	42	47	152	95	135	208	64	23
acres, 1987..	4 910	(D)	69 512	(D)	(D)	44 869	15 058	1 851
1982..	(D)	7 796	52 922	(D)	23 434	(D)	16 232	(D)
Pastureland and other land .... farms, 1987..	-	1	7	2	5	6	-	4
1982..	2			2	4	1		
acres, 1987..	(D)	(D)	2 029	(D)	(D)	351	-	71
1982..			192	(D)	129	(D)		(D)
1987 irrigated acres by size of farm:								
1 to 9 acres .... farms..	-	2	1	-	4	1	1	1
acres irrigated..	-	(D)	(D)	-	11	(D)	(D)	(D)
10 to 49 acres .... farms..	4	2	-	-	14	3	1	3
acres irrigated..	32	(D)	-	-	(D)	(D)	46	18
50 to 69 acres .... farms..	-	2	-	-	1	5	3	2
acres irrigated..	-	(D)	-	-	(D)	220	93	(D)
70 to 99 acres .... farms..	-	2	2	-	4	3	1	2
acres irrigated..	-	(D)	(D)	-	80	96	(D)	(D)
100 to 139 acres .... farms..	-	-	1	-	6	6	1	2
acres irrigated..	-	-	(D)	-	143	772	(D)	(D)
140 to 179 acres .... farms..	1	1	6	1	1	21	1	-
acres irrigated..	(D)	(D)	607	(D)	(D)	1 639	(D)	-
180 to 219 acres .... farms..	-	1	-	2	3	9	1	-
acres irrigated..	-	(D)	-	(D)	163	586	(D)	-
220 to 259 acres .... farms..	1	-	2	-	5	10		2
acres irrigated..	(D)	-	(D)	-	438	1 073	(D)	(D)
260 to 499 acres .... farms..	3	4	19	6	31	35	4	3
acres irrigated..	(D)	903	2 245	472	3 297	5 792	563	512
500 to 999 acres .... farms..	11	11	36	12	33	92	10	7
acres irrigated..	977	1 021	7 611	1 274	4 989	18 391	912	510
1,000 to 1,999 acres .... farms..	11	9	63	23	44	35	25	2
acres irrigated..	1 500	1 517	23 337	3 008	13 795	12 898	5 715	(D)
2,000 acres or more .... farms..	6	14	31	28	10	8	16	3
acres irrigated..	1 495	5 784	37 431	6 438	2 479	3 669	7 376	417
1982 irrigated acres by size of farm:								
1 to 9 acres .... farms..	-	2	-	-	3	-	-	1
acres irrigated..	-	(D)	-	(D)	10	-	-	(D)
10 to 49 acres .... farms..	-	3	3	-	13	2	1	3
acres irrigated..	-	4	34	-	103	(D)	(D)	24
50 to 69 acres .... farms..	-	1	-	-	-		3	
acres irrigated..	-	(D)	-	-	-	(D)	134	
70 to 99 acres .... farms..	2	3	4	-	3	3	1	-
acres irrigated..	(D)	102	118	-	71	214	(D)	-
100 to 139 acres .... farms..	1	1	1	1	2	11		3
acres irrigated..	(D)	(D)	(D)	(D)	(D)	625		195
140 to 179 acres .... farms..	-	2	8	1	4	10	2	1
acres irrigated..	-	(D)	750	(D)	195	903	(D)	(D)
180 to 219 acres .... farms..	-	1	2	-	2	11	-	-
acres irrigated..	-	(D)	(D)	-	(D)	640	-	-
220 to 259 acres .... farms..	-	-	3	2	7	13	2	-
acres irrigated..	-	-	432	(D)	362	13	(D)	-
260 to 499 acres .... farms..	8	7	13	10	24	55	6	4
acres irrigated..	424	544	1 932	1 257	3 798	7 321	373	603
500 to 999 acres .... farms..	12	14	33	20	30	61	11	6
acres irrigated..	1 041	1 199	7 205	2 308	6 224	12 057	2 562	870
1,000 to 1,999 acres .... farms..	15	10	64	28	37	35	28	1
acres irrigated..	1 797	2 018	20 586	4 995	8 296	14 333	6 123	(D)
2,000 acres or more .... farms..	7	6	24	32	10	8	11	4
acres irrigated..	1 178	3 485	21 602	8 709	4 249	5 094	6 476	596

Table 7. Irrigation: 1987 and 1982—Con.

[For meaning of abbreviations and symbols, see introductory text]

Farms with irrigation	Rooks	Rush	Russell	Saline	Scott	Sedgwick	Seward	Shawnee
Farms ... number, 1987	22	74	6	51	162	179	142	67
1982	27	86	5	34	186	187	127	60
Land in irrigated farms ... acres, 1987	53 128	94 607	3 871	38 294	271 227	96 423	210 987	38 132
1982	40 535	91 670	6 797	23 533	308 505	95 339	211 886	32 804
Harvested cropland ... farms, 1987	22	74	6	51	162	178	139	67
1982	27	86	5	34	185	183	127	59
acres, 1987	13 582	40 136	1 403	19 543	113 258	69 560	106 590	27 144
1982	13 575	39 132	3 193	13 307	139 056	75 156	118 562	24 489
Other cropland, excluding cropland pastured ... farms, 1987	20	66	3	41	156	109	124	46
1982	20	72		14	155	76	96	29
acres, 1987	10 156	26 906	728	8 296	100 012	16 955	56 816	5 191
1982	6 076	24 334	749	2 050	85 415	4 752	49 550	1 227
Pastureland, excluding woodland pastured ... farms, 1987	18	61	5	26	85	59	68	15
1982	20	73	3	23	100	67	56	18
acres, 1987	28 210	(D)	1 477	9 223	54 276	5 151	(D)	3 925
1982	19 638	25 359	(D)	7 140	77 929	9 948	40 113	5 344
Irrigated land ... acres, 1987	2 864	7 975	434	3 152	54 507	29 739	77 842	11 382
1982	2 988	9 284	(D)	1 886	67 592	29 761	77 455	9 995
Harvested cropland ... farms, 1987	22	74	6	50	162	176	139	66
1982	27	86	5	33	185	182	127	59
acres, 1987	(D)	7 780	434	(D)	54 147	29 446	75 210	(D)
1982	(D)	(D)	(D)	(D)	57 377	28 560	76 212	(D)
Pastureland and other land ... farms, 1987	1	8	–	2	5	10	16	3
1982	1	4	–	2	6	13	8	1
acres, 1987	(D)	195	–	(D)	360	293	2 632	(D)
1982	(D)	(D)	–	(D)	216	1 201	1 243	(D)
1987 irrigated acres by size of farm:								
1 to 9 acres ... farms	1	–	–	3	–	21	–	7
acres irrigated	(D)	–	–	4	–	64	–	14
10 to 49 acres ... farms	–	5	–	5	1	27	1	5
acres irrigated	–	110	–	33	(D)	240	(D)	153
50 to 69 acres ... farms	–	1	–	–	1	5	–	2
acres irrigated	–	(D)	–	–	(D)	145	–	(D)
70 to 99 acres ... farms	–	–	–	3	–	11	2	–
acres irrigated	–	–	–	120	–	562	(D)	–
100 to 139 acres ... farms	–	–	–	1	–	3	–	3
acres irrigated	–	–	–	87	–	124	–	104
140 to 179 acres ... farms	–	3	–	2	12	6	3	5
acres irrigated	–	242	–	(D)	921	(D)	305	452
180 to 219 acres ... farms	1	2	–	–	–	1	1	3
acres irrigated	(D)	(D)	–	–	–	(D)	(D)	159
220 to 259 acres ... farms	–	1	–	1	(D)	6	3	1
acres irrigated	–	(D)	–	(D)	(D)	772	386	(D)
260 to 499 acres ... farms	3	10	4	5	19	27	17	7
acres irrigated	(D)	893	(D)	233	2 750	3 901	3 983	1 245
500 to 999 acres ... farms	3	13	1	14	36	35	35	22
acres irrigated	143	1 109	(D)	815	6 938	7 107	13 966	5 611
1,000 to 1,999 acres ... farms	5	25	1	10	41	31	47	12
acres irrigated	1 102	3 643	(D)	1 121	14 686	11 534	32 380	3 604
2,000 acres or more ... farms	9	14	–	5	51	4	33	–
acres irrigated	1 146	1 794	–	710	28 994	4 775	26 621	–
1982 irrigated acres by size of farm:								
1 to 9 acres ... farms	–	–	(D)	5	–	21	–	7
acres irrigated	–	–	(D)	15	–	82	–	5
10 to 49 acres ... farms	1	3	–	6	4	26	2	8
acres irrigated	(D)	(D)	–	41	101	276	(D)	30
50 to 69 acres ... farms	–	1	–	–	3	4	1	–
acres irrigated	–	(D)	–	–	80	112	(D)	–
70 to 99 acres ... farms	–	–	–	–	4	8	4	1
acres irrigated	–	–	–	–	276	246	312	(D)
100 to 139 acres ... farms	1	–	–	–	2	9	2	5
acres irrigated	(D)	9	–	2	(D)	598	(D)	(D)
140 to 179 acres ... farms	–	–	–	–	2	6	3	1
acres irrigated	–	374	–	(D)	(D)	(D)	390	(D)
180 to 219 acres ... farms	–	3	–	–	–	2	–	3
acres irrigated	–	188	–	–	–	(D)	–	115
220 to 259 acres ... farms	1	1	1	–	1	7	–	–
acres irrigated	(D)	(D)	(D)	–	(D)	687	–	–
260 to 499 acres ... farms	4	16	–	6	21	29	18	11
acres irrigated	439	817	–	(D)	2 907	3 626	4 246	1 753
500 to 999 acres ... farms	4	24	–	6	51	36	21	15
acres irrigated	740	2 560	–	444	13 825	8 758	7 774	3 104
1,000 to 1,999 acres ... farms	9	16	–	4	47	33	38	12
acres irrigated	856	2 319	–	358	16 229	12 108	28 044	4 422
2,000 acres or more ... farms	7	13	2	5	51	4	38	–
acres irrigated	781	2 876	(D)	591	34 007	2 529	36 333	–

Table 7. **Irrigation: 1987 and 1982**—Con.

[For meaning of abbreviations and symbols, see Introductory text]

Farms with irrigation	Sheridan	Sherman	Smith	Stafford	Stanton	Stevens	Sumner	Thomas
Farms .... number, 1987..	187	246	81	188	168	166	28	216
1982..	206	261	49	170	147	161	21	196
Land in irrigated farms .... acres, 1987..	248 894	416 301	86 878	245 885	323 718	333 288	11 700	322 003
1982..	258 093	434 909	52 957	216 137	349 236	291 868	9 810	314 501
Harvested cropland .... farms, 1987..	187	243	81	188	168	164	28	216
1982..	206	261	49	170	147	161	21	196
acres, 1987..	101 029	176 400	33 863	131 538	155 965	184 086	6 313	155 647
1982..	116 254	208 159	22 001	134 002	185 051	196 335	7 216	169 803
Other cropland, excluding cropland pastured .... farms, 1987..	176	233	75	166	160	153	19	210
1982..	174	223	39	129	129	131	8	165
acres, 1987..	69 041	139 711	16 848	58 012	123 532	95 061	1 731	122 612
1982..	51 528	116 132	7 229	30 687	100 411	45 495	894	100 726
Pastureland, excluding woodland pastured ..... farms, 1987..	133	131	63	126	50	87	15	107
1987..	157	143	38	114	52	81	8	113
acres, 1987..	74 389	92 089	32 361	51 553	26 782	51 316	1 145	38 995
1982..	82 750	102 703	20 709	46 687	55 141	44 167	1 128	39 147
Irrigated land.............................. acres, 1987..	50 527	83 424	7 812	86 430	112 726	119 752	2 694	73 546
1982..	65 572	104 010	6 918	80 979	123 784	116 892	1 754	84 216
Harvested cropland .... farms, 1987..	187	241	81	186	158	161	28	214
1982..	206	261	49	170	147	161	21	196
acres, 1987..	49 232	82 671	(D)	65 784	110 331	116 787	(D)	72 347
1982..	65 255	(D)	5 918	60 765	120 784	115 696	1 754	(D)
Pastureland and other land .... farms, 1987..	5	11	1	11	9	13	2	9
1982..	3	3	-	5	10	7	-	2
acres, 1987..	1 295	753	(D)	646	2 397	2 965	(D)	1 199
1982..	317	(D)	-	214	3 000	1 196	-	(D)
1987 irrigated acres by size of farm:								
1 to 9 acres .... farms..	-	-	-	3	-	-	3	1
acres irrigated..	-	-	-	6	-	-	4	(D)
10 to 49 acres .... farms..	1	1	3	3	1	-	5	1
acres irrigated..	(D)	(D)	30	14	(D)	(D)	13	(D)
50 to 69 acres .... farms..	-	1	1	-	-	-	2	1
acres irrigated..	-	(D)	(D)	-	-	-	(D)	(D)
70 to 99 acres .... farms..	-	5	1	3	-	-	1	-
acres irrigated..	-	191	(D)	142	-	-	(D)	-
100 to 139 acres .... farms..	3	1	2	2	-	-	-	2
acres irrigated..	(D)	(D)	(D)	(D)	-	-	-	(D)
140 to 179 acres .... farms..	11	15	3	2	7	3	1	4
acres irrigated..	962	1 283	146	(D)	628	(D)	(D)	341
180 to 219 acres .... farms..	3	2	-	1	-	1	-	3
acres irrigated..	158	(D)	-	(D)	-	(D)	-	47
220 to 259 acres .... farms..	1	2	2	2	-	-	-	1
acres irrigated..	(D)	(D)	(D)	-	-	-	(D)	(D)
260 to 499 acres .... farms..	26	19	11	24	11	11	7	24
acres irrigated..	3 692	3 235	618	4 356	2 684	2 540	920	4 145
500 to 999 acres .... farms..	35	46	19	44	27	26	2	53
acres irrigated..	7 583	11 125	1 675	11 365	(D)	11 026	(D)	15 069
1,000 to 1,999 acres..................... farms..	69	85	28	69	57	53	-	60
acres irrigated..	24 597	33 075	2 717	23 576	33 958	29 453	1 377	26 952
2,000 acres or more .... farms..	36	71	11	37	65	71	-	48
acres irrigated..	13 305	33 970	2 336	26 576	66 937	76 298	-	26 740
1982 irrigated acres by size of farm:								
1 to 9 acres .... farms..	-	2	1	-	-	-	6	-
acres irrigated..	-	(D)	(D)	-	-	-	21	-
10 to 49 acres .... farms..	1	1	-	-	1	1	2	2
acres irrigated..	(D)	(D)	-	-	(D)	(D)	(D)	(D)
50 to 69 acres .... farms..	2	2	-	-	-	-	1	-
acres irrigated..	(D)	(D)	-	-	-	-	(D)	-
70 to 99 acres .... farms..	-	2	-	-	2	1	-	3
acres irrigated..	-	(D)	-	-	(D)	(D)	-	120
100 to 139 acres .... farms..	4	-	2	3	-	1	-	-
acres irrigated..	464	-	(D)	224	-	(D)	-	-
140 to 179 acres .... farms..	15	11	-	6	3	-	1	7
acres irrigated..	1 671	1 241	-	540	480	-	(D)	836
180 to 219 acres .... farms..	-	1	-	-	-	-	1	2
acres irrigated..	-	(D)	-	-	-	-	(D)	(D)
220 to 259 acres .... farms..	-	3	2	1	-	-	1	-
acres irrigated..	-	210	(D)	(D)	-	-	(D)	-
260 to 499 acres .... farms..	24	36	8	28	10	11	3	25
acres irrigated..	4 471	8 162	823	(D)	2 761	2 360	298	4 291
500 to 999 acres .... farms..	58	58	15	38	18	38	2	43
acres irrigated..	13 349	13 823	1 212	8 852	8 611	14 574	(D)	13 504
1,000 to 1,999 acres..................... farms..	66	80	13	66	44	58	5	64
acres irrigated..	26 725	33 456	1 795	26 650	32 529	37 134	783	27 886
2,000 acres or more .... farms..	36	87	8	38	69	60	-	50
acres irrigated..	18 757	46 830	1 851	17 985	79 243	62 648	-	37 382

Table 7. **Irrigation: 1987 and 1982**—Con.

[For meaning of abbreviations and symbols, see introductory text]

Farms with irrigation	Trego	Wabaunsee	Wallace	Washington	Wichita	Wilson	Woodson	Wyandotte
Farms number, 1987..	30	32	116	62	172	18	3	7
1982..	33	20	118	41	178	12	2	2
Land in irrigated farms acres, 1987..	62 871	106 569	242 966	68 847	252 140	12 960	1 175	244
1982..	79 085	79 684	227 007	49 860	271 264	9 570	(D)	(D)
Harvested cropland farms, 1987..	30	32	116	62	169	18	3	7
1982..	33	19	118	41	178	12	2	2
acres, 1987..	14 933	20 439	85 171	36 359	116 978	7 408	170	153
1982..	18 554	13 125	102 398	31 332	139 211	5 473	(D)	(D)
Other cropland, excluding cropland pastured farms, 1987..	25	22	113	54	163	7	-	-
1982..	30	7	100	22	159	7	1	1
acres, 1987..	12 995	2 873	72 020	9 420	101 346	1 133	-	-
1982..	15 404	776	53 450	1 989	88 676	1 027	(D)	(D)
Pastureland, excluding woodland pastured farms, 1987..	28	23	66	50	61	14	2	3
1982..	31	13	69	31	92	8	1	-
acres, 1987..	(D)	79 545	(D)	18 102	30 115	3 614	(D)	62
1982..	44 398	776	87 788	11 581	36 232	2 161	-	-
Irrigated land acres, 1987..	3 076	6 749	45 733	8 293	73 438	1 555	(D)	14
1982..	4 543	4 108	63 954	6 552	95 823	895	(D)	(D)
Harvested cropland farms, 1987..	29	32	115	61	169	18	3	7
1982..	33	19	118	41	178	12	2	2
acres, 1987..	(D)	(D)	45 435	(D)	72 811	(D)	(D)	14
1982..	(D)	(D)	63 954	(D)	95 738	895	(D)	(D)
Pastureland and other land farms, 1987..	1	1	3	1	8	1	-	-
1982..	2	1	-	1	3	-	-	-
acres, 1987..	(D)	(D)	298	(D)	627	(D)	-	-
1982..	(D)	(D)	-	(D)	85	-	-	-
1987 irrigated acres by size of farm:								
1 to 9 acres farms..	-	1	-	-	1	-	1	2
acres irrigated..	-	(D)	-	-	(D)	-	(D)	(D)
10 to 49 acres farms..	-	1	-	-	2	1	-	3
acres irrigated..	-	31	-	-	(D)	(D)	-	8
50 to 69 acres farms..	-	-	-	-	-	2	-	1
acres irrigated..	-	-	-	-	-	(D)	-	(D)
70 to 99 acres farms..	-	1	-	-	-	1	-	1
acres irrigated..	-	(D)	-	2	2	(D)	-	(D)
100 to 139 acres farms..	-	1	-	(D)	(D)	2	-	-
acres irrigated..	(D)	(D)	-	(D)	(D)	(D)	-	-
140 to 179 acres farms..	-	-	2	2	6	-	1	-
acres irrigated..	-	-	(D)	(D)	687	-	(D)	-
180 to 219 acres farms..	-	1	2	-	1	-	-	-
acres irrigated..	-	(D)	(D)	1	(D)	-	-	-
220 to 259 acres farms..	-	-	-	(D)	-	3	-	-
acres irrigated..	-	-	-	-	-	227	-	-
260 to 499 acres farms..	4	1	7	6	22	1	-	-
acres irrigated..	(D)	(D)	1 194	356	3 912	(D)	-	-
500 to 999 acres farms..	8	6	30	23	45	3	-	-
acres irrigated..	587	1 005	9 034	2 709	12 946	261	-	-
1,000 to 1,999 acres farms..	7	7	37	20	47	4	1	-
acres irrigated..	667	1 101	15 084	2 971	22 277	740	(D)	-
2,000 acres or more farms..	10	11	38	8	44	1	-	-
acres irrigated..	1 761	4 405	20 166	2 091	33 269	(D)	-	-
1982 irrigated acres by size of farm:								
1 to 9 acres farms..	-	1	-	-	-	1	-	-
acres irrigated..	-	(D)	-	-	-	(D)	-	-
10 to 49 acres farms..	-	2	-	-	-	1	-	1
acres irrigated..	-	(D)	-	-	-	(D)	-	(D)
50 to 69 acres farms..	-	-	2	-	1	-	-	1
acres irrigated..	-	-	(D)	-	(D)	-	-	(D)
70 to 99 acres farms..	1	1	-	-	-	-	-	-
acres irrigated..	(D)	(D)	-	-	-	-	-	-
100 to 139 acres farms..	-	1	-	-	-	-	1	-
acres irrigated..	-	(D)	-	-	-	-	(D)	-
140 to 179 acres farms..	1	1	2	1	19	-	1	-
acres irrigated..	(D)	(D)	(D)	(D)	2 277	-	(D)	-
180 to 219 acres farms..	-	2	1	-	5	-	-	-
acres irrigated..	-	(D)	(D)	-	595	-	-	-
220 to 259 acres farms..	-	-	2	-	2	-	-	-
acres irrigated..	-	-	(D)	-	(D)	-	-	-
260 to 499 acres farms..	3	-	15	6	21	1	-	-
acres irrigated..	(D)	-	3 527	(D)	4 873	(D)	-	-
500 to 999 acres farms..	4	3	26	13	28	5	-	-
acres irrigated..	322	492	7 395	1 402	10 886	539	-	-
1,000 to 1,999 acres farms..	14	4	30	17	45	4	-	-
acres irrigated..	1 803	473	15 529	3 065	24 195	327	-	-
2,000 acres or more farms..	10	5	40	4	57	-	-	-
acres irrigated..	2 217	2 795	36 699	1 690	52 633	-	-	-

Table 8. Machinery and Equipment on Place: 1987 and 1982

[Data are based on a sample of terms. For meaning of abbreviations and symbols, see introductory text]

All Farms	Kansas	Allen	Anderson	Atchison	Barber	Barton	Bourbon
VALUE OF MACHINERY AND EQUIPMENT							
Estimated market value of all machinery and							
equipment .... farms, 1987..	88 391	657	726	693	525	937	842
1982..	73 238	735	797	768	517	952	882
$1,000, 1987..	3 447 663	24 742	28 522	26 695	29 420	57 811	18 815
1982..	3 830 616	30 134	29 860	35 521	30 373	57 297	24 388
Average per farm.......................dollars, 1987..	50 411	37 659	39 287	38 521	56 038	61 698	22 346
1982..	52 304	40 999	37 090	46 251	58 749	59 581	27 651
Farms by value group:							
$1 to $9,999 ....1987..	17 397	231	192	170	124	203	345
1982..	17 693	207	226	179	104	130	372
$10,000 to $19,999 ....1987..	11 722	125	152	168	53	105	210
1982..	12 077	152	200	157	108	194	129
$20,000 to $29,999 ....1987..	8 003	88	94	85	96	88	131
1982..	8 890	83	75	52	44	105	149
$30,000 to $49,999 ....1987..	8 721	74	136	35	44	133	54
1982..	9 785	120	85	123	56	116	66
$50,000 to $69,999 ....1987..	8 850	47	38	102	70	99	52
1982..	7 074	52	92	88	41	147	72
$70,000 to $99,999 ....1987..	5 326	35	40	68	42	117	15
1982..	5 536	43	53	48	56	105	27
$100,000 to $199,999 ....1987..	7 277	64	45	57	64	117	32
1982..	8 617	57	40	90	75	104	57
$200,000 or more ....1987..	3 095	13	29	8	32	75	3
1982..	3 766	21	26	31	33	61	8
$200,000 to $499,999 ....1987..	2 860	12	28	7	30	71	2
$500,000 or more ....1987..	235	1	1	1	2	4	1
SELECTED MACHINERY AND EQUIPMENT							
Motortrucks, including pickups .... farms, 1987..	83 093	568	663	608	477	912	754
1982..	86 865	662	636	694	471	904	773
number, 1987..	159 329	1 149	1 461	1 473	1 354	2 447	1 298
1982..	169 424	1 300	1 357	1 483	1 252	2 481	1 227
Wheel tractors .... farms, 1987..	60 459	522	629	608	449	840	703
1982..	62 969	664	680	657	433	887	769
number, 1987..	150 284	1 285	1 649	1 779	1 071	2 370	1 385
1982..	149 870	1 450	1 661	1 839	1 005	2 457	1 398
Less than 40 horsepower (PTO) .... farms, 1987..	25 210	232	306	325	150	310	294
number, 1987..	38 591	390	494	492	195	416	453
40 horsepower (PTO) or more .... farms, 1987..	50 577	410	600	406	062	754	520
number, 1987..	112 056	895	1 055	1 281	876	1 954	932
Grain and bean combines¹ .... farms, 1987..	35 608	289	399	393	221	556	321
1982..	38 503	361	425	342	207	677	244
number, 1987..	43 801	329	448	444	319	870	361
1982..	46 662	379	439	367	271	919	260
Cottonpickers and strippers..................... farms, 1987..	1	-	-	-	-	-	-
1982..	-	-	-	-	-	-	-
number, 1987..	(D)	-	-	-	-	-	-
1982..	-	-	-	-	-	-	-
Mower conditioners .... farms, 1987..	18 793	213	361	178	144	278	308
1982..	17 416	238	247	137	132	291	224
number, 1987..	20 167	213	371	189	167	298	319
1982..	18 932	239	247	156	149	327	226
Pickup balers .... farms, 1987..	26 083	317	382	355	177	418	366
1982..	27 088	373	330	349	164	430	456
number, 1987..	31 892	417	490	429	258	481	409
1982..	31 998	471	435	411	225	529	527
1987 INVENTORY							
Manufactured 1983 to 1987:							
Motortrucks, including pickups .... farms..	19 029	193	177	177	218	279	261
number..	23 314	212	248	187	272	364	294
Wheel tractors .... farms..	7 633	79	88	52	49	88	37
number..	10 363	104	115	70	61	139	54
Less than 40 horsepower (PTO) .... farms..	1 685	5	23	15	6	10	22
number..	2 079	5	23	15	7	17	29
40 horsepower (PTO) or more .... farms..	6 449	74	76	46	44	87	22
number..	8 284	99	92	55	54	122	25
Grain and bean combines .... farms..	2 824	40	38	5	5	20	24
number..	3 075	43	39	5	6	22	24
Cottonpickers and strippers..................... farms..	-	-	-	-	-	-	-
number..	-	-	-	-	-	-	-
Mower conditioners .... farms..	2 309	47	28	14	11	22	50
number..	2 402	47	28	14	11	23	50
Pickup balers .... farms..	3 708	61	60	34	45	86	37
number..	3 952	61	60	34	46	93	37
Manufactured prior to 1983:							
Motortrucks, including pickups .... farms..	57 562	447	507	551	393	828	632
number..	136 015	937	1 243	1 286	1 082	2 083	1 004
Wheel tractors .... farms..	58 487	511	612	584	443	825	703
number..	140 284	1 181	1 434	1 709	1 010	2 231	1 331
Less than 40 horsepower (PTO) .... farms..	24 146	232	294	311	148	307	294
number..	36 512	385	471	477	188	399	424
40 horsepower (PTO) or more .... farms..	48 649	393	476	478	355	739	518
number..	103 772	796	963	1 226	822	1 832	907
Grain and bean combines .... farms..	33 195	250	361	388	216	640	297
number..	40 726	286	409	439	313	848	337
Cottonpickers and strippers..................... farms..	1	-	-	-	-	-	-
number..	(D)	-	-	-	-	-	-
Mower conditioners .... farms..	16 612	166	335	164	134	256	266
number..	17 765	166	343	175	156	275	268
Pickup balers .... farms..	23 408	273	334	323	145	337	335
number..	27 940	356	430	395	212	388	372

See footnotes at end of table.

Table 8. **Machinery and Equipment on Place: 1987 and 1982** – Con.

[Data are based on a sample of farms. For meaning of abbreviations and symbols, see introductory text]

All Farms	Brown	Butler	Chase	Chautauqua	Cherokee	Cheyenne	Clark
VALUE OF MACHINERY AND EQUIPMENT							
Estimated market value of all machinery and							
equipment .... farms, 1987..	729	1 300	288	414	842	493	290
1982..	826	1 376	295	431	940	546	308
$1,000, 1987..	43 538	44 368	10 283	9 837	29 536	28 963	15 342
1982..	59 347	41 478	11 855	11 062	37 654	35 729	14 676
Average per farm........................dollars, 1987..	59 723	34 129	35 704	23 760	35 078	58 749	52 902
1982..	71 848	30 144	39 509	25 667	40 057	65 437	47 648
Farms by value group:							
$1 to $9,999 ....1987..	102	424	76	137	285	105	57
1982..	122	472	56	206	347	101	92
$10,000 to $19,999 ....1987..	117	223	41	113	185	35	60
1982..	105	302	54	68	216	25	15
$20,000 to $29,999 ....1987..	42	203	46	81	66	53	27
1982..	109	231	54	33	71	97	38
$30,000 to $49,999 ....1987..	147	173	50	22	67	95	41
1982..	94	142	54	66	76	95	58
$50,000 to $69,999 ....1987..	137	90	30	46	123	74	35
1982..	89	57	25	29	67	52	45
$70,000 to $99,999 ....1987..	43	63	26	2	42	35	23
1982..	93	62	24	5	35	36	24
$100,000 to $199,999 ....1987..	85	106	14	8	81	61	36
1982..	115	94	26	20	80	89	28
$200,000 or more ....1987..	56	18	6	6	11	35	11
1982..	99	16	2	4	48	51	10
$200,000 to $499,999........................1987..	54	16	5	6	11	34	10
$500,000 or more ....1987..	2	-	-	-	-	1	1
SELECTED MACHINERY AND EQUIPMENT							
Motortrucks, including pickups .... farms, 1987..	659	1 235	276	368	766	470	273
1982..	726	1 279	269	411	916	504	276
number, 1987..	1 629	2 362	677	941	1 793	1 192	789
1982..	1 778	2 594	740	900	1 938	1 341	748
Wheel tractors .... farms, 1987..	694	1 142	263	349	722	443	263
1982..	731	1 136	246	323	793	436	219
number, 1987..	2 218	2 374	579	726	1 545	1 186	594
1982..	2 070	2 430	562	643	1 499	1 086	568
Less than 40 horsepower (PTO) .... farms, 1987..	334	562	116	143	291	199	78
number, 1987..	616	777	175	235	412	263	89
40 horsepower (PTO) or more .... farms, 1987..	605	845	210	275	552	405	240
number, 1987..	1 602	1 597	404	491	1 133	923	505
Grain and bean combines[1] .... farms, 1987..	477	469	148	137	358	267	84
1982..	496	517	148	148	384	297	119
number, 1987..	537	534	174	155	436	335	113
1982..	599	568	172	182	448	355	148
Cottonpickers and strippers.................... farms, 1987..	-	-	-	-	-	-	-
1982..	-	-	-	-	-	-	-
number, 1987..	-	-	-	-	-	-	-
1982..	-	-	-	-	-	-	-
Mower conditioners............................ farms, 1987..	195	412	111	86	156	109	76
1982..	278	404	117	107	129	97	33
number, 1987..	225	428	118	99	167	116	77
1982..	301	437	128	107	139	98	34
Pickup balers .... farms, 1987..	324	540	141	148	230	149	107
1982..	388	566	185	177	165	111	57
number, 1987..	409	702	175	161	239	177	131
1982..	456	665	223	213	188	139	61
1987 INVENTORY							
Manufactured 1983 to 1987:							
Motortrucks, including pickups .... farms..	190	305	83	143	202	132	108
number..	212	353	88	155	210	167	150
Wheel tractors .... farms..	73	117	17	17	145	56	41
number..	108	134	18	19	171	59	51
Less than 40 horsepower (PTO) .... farms..	6	25	-	12	83	24	4
number..	6	26	(D)	14	92	24	4
40 horsepower (PTO) or more .... farms..	71	100	16	5	63	32	38
number..	102	108	(D)	5	79	35	47
Grain and bean combines .... farms..	52	34	5	14	14	12	5
number..	54	34	6	14	24	17	6
Cottonpickers and strippers..................... farms..	-	-	-	-	-	-	-
number..	-	-	-	-	-	-	-
Mower conditioners............................ farms..	26	59	6	3	11	10	18
number..	26	59	6	3	12	10	18
Pickup balers .... farms..	52	114	7	22	6	34	49
number..	52	137	8	22	9	34	54
Manufactured prior to 1983:							
Motortrucks, including pickups .... farms..	614	1 131	258	321	707	405	252
number..	1 417	2 009	589	786	1 583	1 025	639
Wheel tractors .... farms..	686	1 118	262	344	699	427	266
number..	2 110	2 240	561	707	1 374	1 127	543
Less than 40 horsepower (PTO) .... farms..	328	545	117	131	281	175	76
number..	610	751	(D)	221	320	239	85
40 horsepower (PTO) or more .... farms..	594	820	205	272	538	402	234
number..	1 500	1 489	(D)	486	1 054	888	458
Grain and bean combines .... farms..	431	436	140	123	345	256	83
number..	483	500	166	141	412	318	107
Cottonpickers and strippers..................... farms..	-	-	-	-	-	-	-
number..	-	-	-	-	-	-	-
Mower conditioners............................ farms..	169	354	105	83	145	99	58
number..	199	369	112	96	155	106	59
Pickup balers .... farms..	277	474	136	127	225	131	69
number..	357	585	167	139	230	143	77

See footnotes at end of table.

Table 8. **Machinery and Equipment on Place: 1987 and 1982**—Con.

[Data are based on a sample of farms. For meaning of abbreviations and symbols, see introductory text]

All Farms	Clay	Cloud	Coffey	Comanche	Cowley	Crawford	Decatur
VALUE OF MACHINERY AND EQUIPMENT							
Estimated market value of all machinery and equipment .... farms, 1987..	672	653	607	277	996	800	466
1982..	720	726	671	259	1 102	915	516
$1,000, 1987..	41 015	34 812	21 329	13 108	35 655	28 383	37 919
1982..	39 396	40 877	26 221	15 658	45 904	33 371	39 765
Average per farm................dollars, 1987..	61 035	53 311	35 139	47 321	35 698	35 479	78 024
1982..	54 719	56 305	42 059	60 457	41 655	36 471	77 065
Farms by value group:							
$1 to $9,999 ...1987..	133	122	166	57	310	203	56
1982..	114	163	187	38	330	298	54
$10,000 to $19,999 ...1987..	82	54	137	52	204	201	53
1982..	88	125	119	38	253	232	52
$20,000 to $29,999 ...1987..	56	125	63	29	131	59	53
1982..	150	101	54	47	57	69	68
$30,000 to $49,999 ...1987..	91	113	77	53	137	154	53
1982..	122	62	136	44	145	107	33
$50,000 to $69,999 ...1987..	72	76	64	32	76	66	57
1982..	77	70	66	22	99	59	52
$70,000 to $99,999 ...1987..	90	49	28	13	41	46	67
1982..	59	85	32	11	61	56	73
$100,000 to $199,999...1987..	113	87	40	33	84	63	97
1982..	93	55	64	39	133	76	114
$200,000 or more ...1987..	35	27	12	8	13	6	30
1982..	37	65	13	20	24	18	50
$200,000 to $499,999...1987..	34	25	12	7	12	8	26
$500,000 or more ...1987..	1	2	-	1	1	-	4
SELECTED MACHINERY AND EQUIPMENT							
Motortrucks, including pickups ... farms, 1987..	663	602	580	247	970	707	460
1982..	661	631	601	244	1 028	852	495
number, 1987..	1 589	1 623	1 324	650	2 183	1 552	1 407
1982..	1 456	1 576	1 369	671	2 509	1 533	1 563
Wheel tractors ... farms, 1987..	625	587	483	240	898	678	412
1982..	663	642	612	206	943	806	442
number, 1987..	1 827	1 546	1 287	514	1 898	1 638	1 168
1982..	1 940	1 868	1 420	444	1 936	1 549	1 308
Less than 40 horsepower (PTO) ... farms, 1987..	245	177	184	89	421	289	150
number, 1987..	366	296	346	105	585	454	262
40 horsepower (PTO) or more ... farms, 1987..	460	550	413	200	663	515	370
number, 1987..	1 461	1 250	941	409	1 313	1 184	905
Grain and bean combines[1] ... farms, 1987..	512	378	302	92	465	393	272
1982..	504	432	371	107	549	420	293
number, 1987..	510	539	339	104	576	467	360
1982..	551	585	384	131	639	431	378
Cottonpickers and strippers... farms, 1987..	-	-	-	-	-	-	-
1982..	-	-	-	-	-	-	-
number, 1987..	-	-	-	-	-	-	-
1982..	-	-	-	-	-	-	-
Mower conditioners ... farms, 1987..	258	172	95	80	303	232	143
1982..	226	155	159	35	248	275	78
number, 1987..	272	183	98	82	316	255	146
1982..	244	169	166	106	267	278	79
Pickup balers ... farms, 1987..	331	247	240	128	340	379	195
1982..	369	243	276	101	461	393	112
number, 1987..	389	340	269	147	405	478	221
1982..	500	269	366	112	535	423	125
1987 INVENTORY							
Manufactured 1983 to 1987:							
Motortrucks, including pickups ... farms..	206	221	150	98	248	165	164
number..	216	254	167	119	305	171	189
Wheel tractors ... farms..	95	45	24	15	54	103	76
number..	112	54	30	22	85	110	99
Less than 40 horsepower (PTO) ... farms..	3	4	2	2	27	54	10
number..	3	7	(D)	(D)	37	55	10
40 horsepower (PTO) or more ... farms..	93	43	23	14	41	50	68
number..	109	47	(D)	(D)	48	55	89
Grain and bean combines ... farms..	56	33	14	7	5	4	59
number..	62	37	14	8	6	4	62
Cottonpickers and strippers... farms..	-	-	-	-	-	-	-
number..	-	-	-	-	-	-	-
Mower conditioners ... farms..	37	20	7	2	55	34	13
number..	39	20	7	(D)	56	34	13
Pickup balers ... farms..	26	54	20	15	26	28	65
number..	26	60	20	15	26	28	67
Manufactured prior to 1983:							
Motortrucks, including pickups ... farms..	620	552	536	216	902	684	441
number..	1 473	1 369	1 157	531	1 878	1 381	1 308
Wheel tractors ... farms..	617	566	474	237	877	670	410
number..	1 715	1 492	1 257	492	1 613	1 528	1 059
Less than 40 horsepower (PTO) ... farms..	244	174	183	69	395	283	149
number..	363	289	(D)	(D)	548	399	243
40 horsepower (PTO) or more ... farms..	534	532	404	197	651	506	356
number..	1 352	1 203	(D)	(D)	1 265	1 129	816
Grain and bean combines ... farms..	458	345	289	87	462	390	228
number..	548	502	325	96	570	483	298
Cottonpickers and strippers... farms..	-	-	-	-	-	-	-
number..	-	-	-	-	-	-	-
Mower conditioners ... farms..	222	153	88	79	249	198	130
number..	233	163	91	(D)	260	221	133
Pickup balers ... farms..	307	225	226	117	320	354	142
number..	361	280	259	132	379	450	154

See footnotes at end of table.

Table 8. Machinery and Equipment on Place: 1987 and 1982—Con.

[Data are based on a sample of farms. For meaning of abbreviations and symbols, see introductory text]

All Farms	Dickinson	Doniphan	Douglas	Edwards	Elk	Ellis	Ellsworth
VALUE OF MACHINERY AND EQUIPMENT							
Estimated market value of all machinery and equipment .... farms, 1987..	1 019	519	852	361	410	790	499
1982..	1 149	619	896	402	467	785	527
$1,000, 1987..	49 694	25 501	24 740	31 067	9 706	33 230	24 601
1982..	59 684	33 462	32 251	29 619	10 869	41 927	26 097
Average per farm ....dollars, 1987..	48 766	49 135	29 037	86 059	23 672	42 053	49 300
1982..	51 944	54 058	35 994	73 679	23 275	53 411	49 520
Farms by value group:							
$1 to $9,999 .... 1987..	275	181	328	43	138	196	82
1982..	257	127	329	54	158	116	107
$10,000 to $19,999 .... 1987..	104	74	237	57	109	205	102
1982..	162	71	190	53	169	126	55
$20,000 to $29,999 .... 1987..	142	28	90	25	62	52	85
1982..	72	62	65	38	44	139	52
$30,000 to $49,999 .... 1987..	131	43	44	44	48	68	51
1982..	187	111	151	64	33	143	91
$50,000 to $69,999 .... 1987..	105	69	64	18	23	105	59
1982..	111	113	51	19	19	79	87
$70,000 to $99,999 .... 1987..	104	35	42	68	15	92	30
1982..	192	48	21	43	33	58	55
$100,000 to $199,999 .... 1987..	137	70	27	57	12	53	77
1982..	131	46	60	86	10	69	71
$200,000 or more .... 1987..	21	19	20	49	3	19	13
1982..	37	41	29	35	1	35	8
$200,000 to $499,999 .... 1987..	13	16	18	44	3	18	13
$500,000 or more .... 1987..	8	3	2	5	-	1	-
SELECTED MACHINERY AND EQUIPMENT							
Motortrucks, including pickups .... farms, 1987..	928	518	748	359	389	719	474
1982..	1 081	565	772	380	405	708	470
number, 1987..	2 113	1 172	1 269	1 384	808	1 727	1 292
1982..	2 355	1 346	1 398	1 122	850	1 797	1 070
Wheel tractors .... farms, 1987..	948	455	764	339	348	704	451
1982..	992	564	729	338	355	720	415
number, 1987..	2 468	1 266	1 665	1 021	801	1 561	1 215
1982..	2 657	1 398	1 523	889	801	1 754	1 037
Less than 40 horsepower (PTO) .... farms, 1987..	392	212	374	118	175	297	234
number, 1987..	600	336	543	160	266	402	355
40 horsepower (PTO) or more .... farms, 1987..	823	354	590	329	282	600	413
number, 1987..	1 868	930	1 122	861	535	1 159	860
Grain and bean combines[1] .... farms, 1987..	680	233	240	270	208	413	377
1982..	771	287	283	255	154	475	354
number, 1987..	799	252	269	379	236	542	573
1982..	998	318	296	328	175	638	495
Cottonpickers and strippers..................... farms, 1987..	-	-	-	-	-	-	-
1982..	-	-	-	-	-	-	-
number, 1987..	-	-	-	-	-	-	-
1982..	-	-	-	-	-	-	-
Mower conditioners .... farms, 1987..	424	112	372	84	173	191	210
1982..	340	80	351	87	120	301	157
number, 1987..	438	129	385	111	175	198	213
1982..	376	95	354	82	129	330	345
Pickup balers .... farms, 1987..	525	111	354	133	193	325	220
1982..	555	157	403	90	210	356	225
number, 1987..	643	136	426	162	221	390	277
1982..	653	189	484	96	238	394	287
1987 INVENTORY							
Manufactured 1983 to 1987:							
Motortrucks, including pickups .... farms..	271	176	210	121	97	174	91
number..	287	198	220	160	111	247	119
Wheel tractors .... farms..	121	32	102	48	17	131	55
number..	139	37	168	72	23	166	69
Less than 40 horsepower (PTO) .... farms..	9	7	65	11	13	47	12
number..	14	8	66	13	13	48	12
40 horsepower (PTO) or more .... farms..	113	26	70	48	10	93	55
number..	125	29	102	59	10	118	57
Grain and bean combines .... farms..	63	31	22	39	7	21	16
number..	64	34	24	41	7	27	16
Cottonpickers and strippers..................... farms..	-	-	-	-	-	-	-
number..	-	-	-	-	-	-	-
Mower conditioners .... farms..	26	12	55	9	21	41	33
number..	26	19	51	17	21	43	33
Pickup balers .... farms..	99	7	48	34	12	63	42
number..	116	8	48	37	14	63	44
Manufactured prior to 1983:							
Motortrucks, including pickups .... farms..	825	449	627	340	358	650	471
number..	1 826	974	1 049	1 224	697	1 480	1 173
Wheel tractors .... farms..	939	452	690	336	341	653	433
number..	2 329	1 229	1 497	949	778	1 395	1 146
Less than 40 horsepower (PTO) .... farms..	385	209	311	116	162	262	222
number..	586	328	477	147	253	354	343
40 horsepower (PTO) or more .... farms..	815	350	534	324	282	569	393
number..	1 743	901	1 020	802	525	1 041	803
Grain and bean combines .... farms..	623	206	220	242	199	395	361
number..	735	218	245	338	229	515	557
Cottonpickers and strippers..................... farms..	-	-	-	-	-	-	-
number..	-	-	-	-	-	-	-
Mower conditioners .... farms..	398	101	318	75	152	152	177
number..	412	110	324	94	154	155	180
Pickup balers .... farms..	451	105	330	114	164	272	192
number..	527	130	378	125	207	327	233

See footnotes at end of table.

Table 8. **Machinery and Equipment on Place: 1987 and 1982**—Con.

[Data are based on a sample of farms. For meaning of abbreviations and symbols, see introductory text]

All Farms	Finney	Ford	Franklin	Geary	Gove	Graham	Grant
VALUE OF MACHINERY AND EQUIPMENT							
Estimated market value of all machinery and							
equipment .... farms, 1987..	535	800	980	296	533	452	303
1982..	557	836	1 087	299	543	495	276
$1,000, 1987..	56 675	85 178	28 721	13 652	31 883	26 068	36 752
1982..	61 167	51 954	33 206	12 846	40 863	29 035	34 139
Average per farm.....................dollars, 1987..	105 935	106 473	29 307	46 123	59 818	57 672	121 294
1982..	109 816	52 146	30 548	42 963	75 254	58 657	123 891
Farms by value group:							
$1 to $9,999 ....1987..	55	216	356	102	94	58	40
1982..	43	207	452	68	48	53	37
$10,000 to $19,999 ....1987..	86	128	277	48	53	54	14
1982..	40	79	197	96	32	63	10
$20,000 to $29,999 ....1987..	69	64	114	21	68	35	19
1982..	89	51	82	16	90	92	12
$30,000 to $49,999 ....1987..	54	81	86	37	70	85	62
1982..	42	132	177	41	94	94	10
$50,000 to $69,999 ....1987..	31	71	25	25	119	95	22
1982..	57	118	86	3	38	47	34
$70,000 to $99,999 ....1987..	36	52	51	20	40	40	26
1982..	41	75	41	35	89	44	26
$100,000 to $199,999.........................1987..	129	144	49	22	59	72	75
1982..	158	117	57	30	94	81	67
$200,000 or more ....1987..	73	44	22	21	30	13	45
1982..	89	57	15	10	58	21	60
$200,000 to $499,999.........................1987..	58	40	20	21	25	12	40
$500,000 or more ....1987..	15	4	2	-	5	1	5
SELECTED MACHINERY AND EQUIPMENT							
Motortrucks, including pickups .... farms, 1987..	487	749	832	293	458	409	287
1982..	532	770	925	277	519	470	266
number, 1987..	2 001	2 209	1 676	774	1 395	1 312	960
1982..	2 042	1 996	1 584	580	1 425	1 243	1 131
Wheel tractors .... farms, 1987	506	695	968	256	446	416	280
1982..	500	695	902	259	446	426	272
number, 1987..	1 465	1 462	2 009	706	1 043	1 068	701
1982..	1 366	1 519	1 885	709	1 151	1 079	701
Less than 40 horsepower (PTO) .... farms, 1987..	128	222	436	84	168	126	50
number, 1987..	186	264	716	157	208	205	70
40 horsepower (PTO) or more .... farms, 1987..	400	603	849	226	426	383	263
number, 1987..	1 279	1 198	1 294	549	834	861	631
Grain and bean combines[1] .... farms, 1987..	302	453	359	157	279	308	176
1982..	402	412	388	144	329	319	168
number, 1987..	375	567	440	168	330	383	224
1982..	520	490	433	160	462	386	211
Cottonpickers and strippers.................. farms, 1987..	-	-	1	-	-	-	-
1982..	-	-	-	-	-	-	-
number, 1987..	-	-	(D)	-	-	-	-
1982..	-	-	-	-	-	-	-
Mower conditioners......................... farms, 1987	95	103	385	136	57	128	53
1982..	114	100	360	131	162	139	23
number, 1987..	105	121	408	139	60	131	63
1982..	135	107	407	138	163	142	28
Pickup balers .... farms, 1987..	66	148	528	173	135	191	59
1982..	76	147	499	156	209	169	57
number, 1987..	82	197	644	217	143	242	60
1982..	92	161	566	175	235	190	59
1987 INVENTORY							
Manufactured 1983 to 1987:							
Motortrucks, including pickups .... farms..	237	240	208	49	134	102	136
number..	394	303	231	84	192	130	211
Wheel tractors .... farms..	120	97	49	32	90	40	72
number..	166	125	63	35	128	58	90
Less than 40 horsepower (PTO) .... farms..	13	8	18	7	15	11	6
number..	19	9	18	7	16	11	9
40 horsepower (PTO) or more .... farms..	112	91	41	25	82	40	66
number..	146	116	45	28	112	47	81
Grain and bean combines .... farms..	29	31	11	3	38	13	42
number..	35	35	11	4	40	13	43
Cottonpickers and strippers...................... farms..	-	-	-	-	-	-	-
number..	-	-	-	-	-	-	-
Mower conditioners.............................. farms..	9	7	40	17	5	13	26
number..	9	7	41	17	5	13	26
Pickup balers .... farms..	11	26	63	12	42	22	25
number..	13	26	63	14	42	22	25
Manufactured prior to 1983:							
Motortrucks, including pickups .... farms..	457	699	767	275	440	407	270
number..	1 607	1 906	1 445	690	1 204	1 182	749
Wheel tractors .... farms..	470	683	840	254	369	410	260
number..	1 300	1 337	1 946	671	915	1 008	611
Less than 40 horsepower (PTO) .... farms..	119	218	419	84	156	126	48
number..	167	255	697	150	193	194	61
40 horsepower (PTO) or more .... farms..	445	588	828	224	367	366	243
number..	1 133	1 082	1 249	521	722	814	550
Grain and bean combines .... farms..	276	427	350	154	242	298	139
number..	340	532	429	164	290	370	181
Cottonpickers and strippers...................... farms..	-	-	(D)	-	-	-	-
number..	-	-	1	-	-	-	-
Mower conditioners.............................. farms..	86	96	345	120	53	116	35
number..	96	114	367	122	55	118	37
Pickup balers .... farms..	63	131	487	169	95	175	34
number..	69	171	581	203	101	220	35

See footnotes at end of table.

1987 CENSUS OF AGRICULTURE—COUNTY DATA

Table 8. **Machinery and Equipment on Place: 1987 and 1982**—Con.

[Data are based on a sample of terms. For meaning of abbreviations and symbols, see introductory text]

All Farms	Gray	Greeley	Greenwood	Hamilton	Harper	Harvey	Haskell
VALUE OF MACHINERY AND EQUIPMENT							
Estimated market value of all machinery and							
equipment .... farms, 1987..	546	292	586	279	649	869	315
1982..	552	277	651	270	660	923	324
$1,000, 1987..	51 256	25 052	14 895	25 488	36 396	45 966	43 454
1982..	56 512	28 243	17 617	26 164	39 856	38 554	47 213
Average per farm.....................dollars, 1987..	93 879	85 796	25 417	91 356	56 080	52 895	137 948
1982..	102 377	101 961	27 061	96 905	60 388	41 771	145 719
Farms by value group:							
$1 to $9,999 .... 1987..	116	57	177	38	127	252	44
1982..	84	10	204	4	115	226	26
$10,000 to $19,999 .... 1987..	36	52	189	50	105	91	14
1982..	77	50	140	45	90	143	6
$20,000 to $29,999 .... 1987..	78	33	85	28	53	127	35
1982..	15	24	120	16	60	186	34
$30,000 to $49,999 .... 1987..	65	32	57	3	134	79	15
1982..	82	9	68	29	125	142	26
$50,000 to $69,999 .... 1987..	25	19	25	32	32	90	10
1982..	36	51	79	49	67	67	12
$70,000 to $99,999 .... 1987..	41	7	19	41	77	66	25
1982..	53	34	16	27	44	54	47
$100,000 to $199,999 .... 1987..	118	48	30	50	81	125	103
1982..	112	66	19	61	122	77	99
$200,000 or more .... 1987..	67	44	4	37	40	39	69
1982..	93	31	5	39	37	28	74
$200,000 to $499,999 .... 1987..	58	37	4	32	40	37	59
$500,000 or more .... 1987..	9	7	–	5	–	2	10
SELECTED MACHINERY AND EQUIPMENT							
Motortrucks, including pickups .... farms, 1987..	488	256	553	265	615	798	287
1982..	529	240	594	244	623	865	308
number, 1987..	1 725	1 011	1 165	996	1 787	1 751	1 214
1982..	1 758	904	1 277	943	1 810	1 842	1 093
Wheel tractors .... farms, 1987..	507	256	465	257	557	750	295
1982..	472	205	529	226	575	809	294
number, 1987..	1 174	653	1 004	616	1 401	1 846	775
1982..	1 090	488	1 218	595	1 395	1 971	705
Less than 40 horsepower (PTO) .... farms, 1987..	138	73	173	63	213	335	104
number, 1987..	216	124	250	80	281	468	165
40 horsepower (PTO) or more .... farms, 1987..	467	233	403	239	477	615	261
number, 1987..	958	529	754	536	1 120	1 378	610
Grain and bean combines¹ .... farms, 1987..	273	123	193	131	413	485	193
1982..	348	149	227	177	386	537	170
number, 1987..	327	154	214	197	567	573	214
1982..	389	232	228	264	529	624	181
Cottonpickers and strippers...................... farms, 1987..	–	–	–	–	–	–	–
1982..	–	–	–	–	–	–	–
number, 1987..	–	–	–	–	–	–	–
1982..	–	–	–	–	–	–	–
Mower conditioners .... farms, 1987..	43	29	210	48	177	145	58
1982..	70	9	177	33	174	101	45
number, 1987..	61	31	244	51	185	162	74
1982..	86	9	191	33	204	120	50
Pickup balers .... farms, 1987..	51	35	228	40	231	335	33
1982..	47	21	311	64	220	308	36
number, 1987..	66	37	313	43	287	386	44
1982..	72	23	410	73	284	315	47
1987 INVENTORY							
Manufactured 1983 to 1987:							
Motortrucks, including pickups .... farms..	233	116	144	116	214	162	135
number..	326	186	187	156	235	177	251
Wheel tractors .... farms..	110	45	31	49	67	98	77
number..	140	86	50	58	110	125	107
Less than 40 horsepower (PTO) .... number..	19	14	14	1	13	30	7
number..	26	21	16	(D)	29	30	8
40 horsepower (PTO) or more .... farms..	96	37	30	48	58	79	72
number..	114	65	34	(D)	81	95	99
Grain and bean combines .... farms..	48	13	2	13	24	19	42
number..	56	18	(D)	15	24	21	45
Cottonpickers and strippers...................... farms..	–	–	–	–	–	–	–
number..	–	–	–	–	–	–	–
Mower conditioners .... farms..	14	14	8	7	10	13	13
number..	19	14	8	7	10	13	25
Pickup balers .... farms..	13	6	48	16	46	49	16
number..	17	6	49	16	47	49	16
Manufactured prior to 1983:							
Motortrucks, including pickups .... farms..	464	242	481	247	554	738	247
number..	1 399	825	978	840	1 552	1 574	963
Wheel tractors .... farms..	460	243	450	238	530	736	283
number..	1 034	567	954	558	1 291	1 721	668
Less than 40 horsepower (PTO) .... farms..	125	68	159	62	202	305	100
number..	190	103	234	(D)	252	436	157
40 horsepower (PTO) or more .... farms..	414	220	387	220	455	593	240
number..	844	464	720	(D)	1 039	1 283	511
Grain and bean combines .... farms..	229	114	191	122	393	472	153
number..	269	136	(D)	162	543	552	169
Cottonpickers and strippers...................... farms..	–	–	–	–	–	–	–
number..	–	–	–	–	–	–	–
Mower conditioners .... farms..	35	16	202	41	169	132	45
number..	42	17	235	44	175	149	49
Pickup balers .... farms..	39	30	213	27	186	295	18
number..	49	31	264	27	240	337	28

See footnotes at end of table.

Table 8. **Machinery and Equipment on Place: 1987 and 1982**—Con.

[Data are based on a sample of farms. For meaning of abbreviations and symbols, see introductory text]

All Farms	Hodgeman	Jackson	Jefferson	Jewell	Johnson	Kearny	Kingman	Kiowa
VALUE OF MACHINERY AND EQUIPMENT								
Estimated market value of all machinery and								
equipment ....farms, 1987..	423	1 082	1 007	795	648	291	818	310
1982..	468	1 156	1 047	808	766	297	860	346
$1,000, 1987..	25 901	26 018	29 599	36 979	26 019	38 060	40 088	24 178
1982..	30 634	33 599	32 625	48 846	24 420	34 959	44 699	22 744
Average per farm.......................dollars, 1987..	61 233	24 046	29 394	50 311	40 152	130 792	49 007	77 994
1982..	65 524	29 065	31 161	60 452	31 880	117 706	51 976	65 734
Farms by value group:								
$1 to $9,999 ....1987..	59	419	458	146	193	30	161	29
1982..	100	458	348	137	314	57	156	62
$10,000 to $19,999 ....1987..	51	228	154	80	135	19	131	29
1982..	69	213	282	107	155	41	103	55
$20,000 to $29,999 ....1987..	44	136	113	103	99	14	110	47
1982..	60	147	142	163	91	6	121	37
$30,000 to $49,999 ....1987..	74	119	77	145	69	47	147	66
1982..	57	99	84	90	94	19	205	44
$50,000 to $69,999 ....1987..	55	118	98	102	65	20	65	35
1982..	11	137	60	73	30	35	86	27
$70,000 to $99,999 ....1987..	42	27	59	45	27	34	92	43
1982..	59	21	42	25	20	43	57	47
$100,000 to $199,999 ....1987..	80	22	30	84	37	78	79	29
1982..	77	64	59	149	30	55	90	42
$200,000 or more ....1987..	18	13	20	19	33	49	33	32
1982..	43	17	20	64	32	39	42	32
$200,000 to $499,999 ....1987..	18	13	18	29	32	41	31	30
$500,000 or more ....1987..	–	–	2	1	1	8	2	2
SELECTED MACHINERY AND EQUIPMENT								
Motortrucks, including pickups ....farms, 1987..	412	963	888	697	572	273	732	304
1982..	412	1 063	922	739	606	291	775	337
number, 1987..	1 654	1 804	1 695	1 751	1 123	1 235	1 939	804
1982..	1 327	1 889	1 684	1 863	1 115	1 271	1 929	924
Wheel tractors ....farms, 1987..	363	937	901	656	540	266	761	303
1982..	385	1 018	869	717	716	253	742	271
number, 1987..	998	1 651	2 069	1 822	1 346	696	1 866	676
1982..	851	2 130	1 817	1 883	1 320	770	1 776	687
Less than 40 horsepower (PTO) ....farms, 1987..	100	469	503	209	332	103	339	69
number, 1987..	120	730	776	353	583	187	445	76
40 horsepower (PTO) or more ....farms, 1987..	991	654	640	614	382	238	651	275
number, 1987..	878	1 121	1 293	1 469	763	708	1 421	603
Grain and bean combines[1] ....farms, 1987..	325	384	336	414	216	134	493	173
1982..	314	399	295	552	198	132	434	178
number, 1987..	444	472	399	494	220	182	650	191
1982..	433	468	310	661	202	165	576	200
Cottonpickers and strippers.....................farms, 1987..	–	–	–	–	–	–	–	–
1982..	–	–	–	–	–	–	–	–
number, 1987..	–	–	–	–	–	–	–	–
1982..	–	–	–	–	–	–	–	–
Mower conditioners ....farms, 1987..	114	310	311	148	212	28	230	45
1982..	53	354	322	190	264	36	194	73
number, 1987..	119	311	319	158	242	37	250	46
1982..	55	375	350	182	285	59	194	61
Pickup balers ....farms, 1987..	180	438	470	269	248	31	354	63
1982..	92	601	431	336	290	53	273	90
number, 1987..	244	534	578	334	291	44	455	71
1982..	98	710	518	398	349	65	342	120
1987 INVENTORY								
Manufactured 1983 to 1987:								
Motortrucks, including pickups ....farms..	170	273	168	129	266	158	185	89
number..	216	287	190	151	276	261	224	110
Wheel tractors ....farms..	54	90	23	93	82	51	46	21
number..	58	103	26	107	132	102	62	32
Less than 40 horsepower (PTO) ....farms..	–	44	1	8	52	10	20	1
number..	–	53	(D)	8	74	36	22	(D)
40 horsepower (PTO) or more ....farms..	54	48	23	86	49	49	30	20
number..	58	50	(D)	99	66	64	40	(D)
Grain and bean combines ....farms..	4	16	15	19	17	31	40	23
number..	4	16	15	19	17	36	43	24
Cottonpickers and strippers.........................farms..	–	–	–	–	–	–	–	–
number..	–	–	–	–	–	–	–	–
Mower conditioners ....farms..	13	43	42	7	18	6	27	5
number..	13	43	48	7	18	10	27	6
Pickup balers ....farms..	43	31	28	35	14	7	40	27
number..	45	31	29	35	14	8	40	28
Manufactured prior to 1983:								
Motortrucks, including pickups ....farms..	381	819	786	664	421	240	690	274
number..	1 338	1 517	1 505	1 600	847	974	1 715	694
Wheel tractors ....farms..	353	875	899	645	509	264	771	297
number..	940	1 748	2 043	1 715	1 214	793	1 804	646
Less than 40 horsepower (PTO) ....farms..	100	491	502	202	307	95	326	68
number..	120	677	(D)	345	509	149	423	(D)
40 horsepower (PTO) or more ....farms..	321	626	637	609	345	231	646	266
number..	820	1 071	(D)	1 370	705	644	1 381	(D)
Grain and bean combines ....farms..	322	370	325	404	199	111	469	151
number..	440	456	384	475	203	144	607	167
Cottonpickers and strippers.........................farms..	–	–	–	–	–	–	–	–
number..	–	–	–	–	–	–	–	–
Mower conditioners ....farms..	101	267	269	141	195	23	205	41
number..	106	268	271	149	224	27	223	43
Pickup balers ....farms..	160	409	447	243	237	26	336	39
number..	199	503	549	299	277	36	415	43

See footnotes at end of table.

Table 8. **Machinery and Equipment on Place: 1987 and 1982** – Con.

[Data are based on a sample of terms. For meaning of abbreviations and symbols, see introductory text]

	All Farms							
	Labette	Lane	Leavenworth	Lincoln	Linn	Logan	Lyon	McPherson

VALUE OF MACHINERY AND EQUIPMENT

Estimated market value of all machinery and

equipment .... farms, 1987..	970	322	1 137	577	691	381	872	1 356
1982..	1 064	335	1 236	615	772	378	945	1 476
$1,000, 1987..	27 312	26 201	28 553	29 610	21 368	24 164	25 208	62 042
1982..	31 519	22 714	35 030	30 668	22 902	25 700	31 039	63 804
Average per farm .... dollars, 1987..	28 156	78 263	25 112	51 318	30 923	63 422	28 908	45 754
1982..	29 624	67 803	28 341	49 867	29 666	67 988	32 846	43 227
Farms by value group:								
$1 to $9,999 .... 1987..	333	67	517	122	221	134	263	273
1982..	365	64	497	68	285	70	294	321
$10,000 to $19,999 .... 1987..	273	34	258	61	142	10	219	199
1982..	273	50	275	143	140	30	176	220
$20,000 to $29,999 .... 1987..	60	14	96	69	107	32	121	170
1982..	94	25	171	63	78	20	168	205
$30,000 to $49,999 .... 1987..	92	57	112	50	90	32	78	335
1982..	114	40	84	164	135	34	118	262
$50,000 to $69,999 .... 1987..	93	27	14	115	53	46	74	144
1982..	106	47	89	68	56	54	78	214
$70,000 to $99,999 .... 1987..	55	39	60	73	22	37	37	67
1982..	22	38	28	31	25	80	27	106
$100,000 to $199,999 .... 1987..	32	49	63	41	47	50	49	115
1982..	51	47	75	56	38	63	61	118
$200,000 or more .... 1987..	12	35	15	26	9	40	11	53
1982..	20	24	17	22	13	27	23	30
$200,000 to $499,999.............................. 1987..	11	31	15	25	9	40	10	51
$500,000 or more .... 1987..	1	4	-	1	-	-	1	2

SELECTED MACHINERY AND EQUIPMENT

Motortrucks, including pickups .... farms, 1987..	835	318	969	555	635	335	796	1 210
1982..	1 002	305	1 072	602	643	333	835	1 359
number, 1987..	1 824	1 124	1 826	1 464	1 235	1 003	1 726	2 979
1982..	1 920	978	1 934	1 456	1 227	1 127	1 760	2 889
Wheel tractors .... farms, 1987..	800	282	969	521	642	310	754	1 242
1982..	911	296	1 106	505	678	302	747	1 309
number, 1987..	1 643	746	2 006	1 448	1 487	815	1 935	3 086
1982..	1 788	713	2 265	1 350	1 465	708	1 870	2 816
Less than 40 horsepower (PTO) .... farms, 1987..	346	81	530	199	381	111	422	476
1987..	492	107	796	300	614	157	693	660
40 horsepower (PTO) or more .... farms, 1987..	582	266	665	494	501	291	599	1 086
number, 1987..	1 151	639	1 210	1 148	873	658	1 242	2 406
Grain and bean combines[†] .... farms, 1987..	321	139	294	423	274	196	391	939
1982..	496	188	424	402	280	241	449	1 028
number, 1987..	420	180	313	513	287	282	429	1 168
1982..	562	243	442	516	309	362	473	1 207
Cottonpickers and strippers .... farms, 1987..	-	-	-	-	-	-	-	-
1982..	-	-	-	-	-	-	-	-
number, 1987..	-	-	-	-	-	-	-	-
1982..	-	-	-	-	-	-	-	-
Mower conditioners .... farms, 1987..	236	65	402	201	266	102	229	293
1982..	173	52	320	205	293	47	191	269
number, 1987..	256	70	453	202	289	104	230	298
1982..	180	57	331	207	293	49	193	280
Pickup balers .... farms, 1987..	380	69	477	560	316	150	418	476
1987..	307	71	560	248	356	145	428	456
number, 1987..	479	78	549	359	368	205	516	586
1982..	381	77	659	287	450	190	505	474

1987 INVENTORY

Manufactured 1983 to 1987:

Motortrucks, including pickups .... farms..	207	141	257	134	144	123	255	306
number..	246	172	276	139	157	161	281	353
Wheel tractors .... farms..	112	89	69	64	60	56	39	74
number..	144	128	75	107	66	62	82	86
Less than 40 horsepower (PTO) .... farms..	59	5	47	11	10	6	15	13
number..	76	8	49	11	10	6	17	14
40 horsepower (PTO) or more .... farms..	62	84	22	57	50	52	38	61
number..	68	120	26	96	56	56	65	72
Grain and bean combines .... farms..	25	22	4	8	24	20	24	47
number..	26	29	4	8	24	23	25	53
Cottonpickers and strippers .... farms..	-	-	-	-	-	-	-	-
number..	-	-	-	-	-	-	-	-
Mower conditioners .... farms..	47	10	52	24	30	11	35	22
number..	47	11	52	24	31	11	35	22
Pickup balers .... farms..	54	23	53	39	48	24	67	54
number..	55	24	53	39	48	26	79	58
Manufactured prior to 1983:								
Motortrucks, including pickups .... farms..	769	298	826	527	591	321	728	1 184
number..	1 578	952	1 550	1 325	1 078	842	1 445	2 624
Wheel tractors .... farms..	768	268	965	498	602	304	742	1 226
number..	1 499	618	1 931	1 341	1 421	753	1 853	3 000
Less than 40 horsepower (PTO) .... farms..	307	77	490	188	372	109	410	472
number..	416	99	747	289	604	151	676	566
40 horsepower (PTO) or more .... farms..	572	242	688	470	470	286	586	1 076
number..	1 083	519	1 184	1 052	817	602	1 177	2 334
Grain and bean combines .... farms..	299	121	290	415	251	185	370	893
number..	394	151	309	505	263	259	404	1 115
Cottonpickers and strippers .... farms..	-	-	-	-	-	-	-	-
number..	-	-	-	-	-	-	-	-
Mower conditioners .... farms..	191	55	350	177	238	91	195	271
number..	209	59	401	178	258	93	195	276
Pickup balers .... farms..	345	51	446	280	275	129	368	436
number..	424	54	496	320	320	179	439	526

See footnotes at end of table.

Table 8. **Machinery and Equipment on Place: 1987 and 1982**—Con.

[Data are based on a sample of terms. For meaning of abbreviations and symbols, see introductory text]

All Farms	Marion	Marshall	Meade	Miami	Mitchell	Montgomery	Morris	Morton
VALUE OF MACHINERY AND EQUIPMENT								
Estimated market value of all machinery and equipment .... farms, 1987..	1 119	1 062	465	1 135	622	974	550	225
1982..	1 184	1 144	488	1 223	642	1 021	571	235
$1,000, 1987..	50 013	46 654	32 663	31 213	40 086	27 434	23 234	20 164
1982..	54 676	61 567	36 486	35 198	48 868	36 302	26 293	19 135
Average per farm........................ dollars, 1987..	44 694	43 930	70 674	27 800	64 447	28 166	42 244	89 705
1982..	46 350	53 817	74 766	28 780	76 119	35 555	46 047	81 424
Farms by value group:								
$1 to $9,999 .... 1987..	296	187	51	459	136	406	135	33
1982..	204	168	101	571	96	490	119	23
$10,000 to $19,999 .... 1987..	149	191	84	261	89	160	75	26
1982..	180	180	36	222	90	210	114	27
$20,000 to $29,999 .... 1987..	126	164	50	99	39	100	102	19
1982..	196	200	29	116	81	115	43	41
$30,000 to $49,999 .... 1987..	133	135	68	141	55	180	47	36
1982..	246	166	71	117	63	47	134	16
$50,000 to $69,999 .... 1987..	153	168	39	81	114	58	60	10
1982..	119	118	54	60	69	42	53	16
$70,000 to $99,999 .... 1987..	95	105	67	59	75	18	51	28
1982..	115	129	72	63	69	42	28	18
$100,000 to $199,999 .... 1987..	146	96	71	53	69	24	74	28
1982..	117	109	89	55	98	28	56	66
$200,000 or more .... 1987..	21	18	35	18	45	27	6	43
1982..	27	74	36	19	74	47	24	26
$200,000 to $499,999 .... 1987..	19	18	31	18	39	26	6	42
$500,000 or more .... 1987..	2	-	4	-	6	1	-	1
SELECTED MACHINERY AND EQUIPMENT								
Motortrucks, including pickups .... farms, 1987..	1 067	964	422	1 063	615	898	525	221
1982..	1 114	1 048	466	1 035	610	961	542	218
number, 1987..	2 438	2 157	1 292	1 903	1 732	1 679	1 268	833
1982..	2 639	2 025	1 396	1 769	1 727	1 885	1 164	800
Wheel tractors .... farms, 1987	1 022	964	430	990	550	868	518	183
1982..	1 064	1 022	421	1 048	591	841	508	215
number, 1987..	2 635	2 639	942	1 933	1 261	1 590	1 454	522
1982..	2 996	2 643	1 049	1 865	1 447	1 586	1 296	500
Less than 40 horsepower (PTO) .... farms, 1987..	439	353	147	540	192	383	189	47
number, 1987..	614	576	200	732	313	491	345	72
40 horsepower (PTO) or more .... farms, 1987..	878	866	392	689	469	588	457	172
number, 1987..	2 021	2 061	742	1 201	968	1 099	1 109	450
Grain and bean combines[1] .... farms, 1987..	672	740	302	293	371	319	318	113
1982..	643	766	322	332	400	316	339	127
number, 1987..	860	798	416	316	576	362	394	169
1982..	1 003	830	364	370	636	403	384	164
Cottonpickers and strippers...................... farms, 1987..	-	-	-	-	-	-	-	-
1982..	-	-	-	-	-	-	-	-
number, 1987..	-	-	-	-	-	-	-	-
1982..	-	-	-	-	-	-	-	-
Mower conditioners .... farms, 1987..	335	261	90	364	108	304	209	25
1982..	324	267	49	372	129	272	235	37
number, 1987..	336	264	115	381	122	326	223	40
1982..	342	279	55	404	133	280	251	41
Pickup balers .... farms, 1987..	515	429	75	428	164	387	284	45
1982..	596	545	89	395	186	401	342	48
number, 1987..	591	544	91	542	204	488	368	50
1982..	734	647	93	482	240	463	383	49
1987 INVENTORY								
Manufactured 1983 to 1987:								
Motortrucks, including pickups .... farms..	228	156	168	367	217	239	104	90
number..	278	165	239	432	250	253	134	132
Wheel tractors .... farms..	174	131	80	68	101	89	25	42
number..	239	152	103	75	146	93	26	60
Less than 40 horsepower (PTO) .... farms..	46	10	7	11	21	15	1	3
number..	46	17	8	14	23	15	(D)	4
40 horsepower (PTO) or more .... farms..	144	121	76	59	96	81	24	41
number..	193	135	94	61	125	78	(D)	56
Grain and bean combines .... farms..	62	55	42	24	63	23	4	25
number..	64	55	42	27	72	23	4	26
Cottonpickers and strippers...................... farms..	-	-	-	-	-	-	-	-
number..	-	-	-	-	-	-	-	-
Mower conditioners .... farms..	48	30	5	61	17	35	21	1
number..	48	30	8	70	18	35	21	(D)
Pickup balers .... farms..	63	52	7	55	15	69	33	6
number..	63	52	8	78	17	69	34	6
Manufactured prior to 1983:								
Motortrucks, including pickups .... farms..	1 017	934	358	867	569	828	489	200
number..	2 180	1 992	1 053	1 471	1 482	1 426	1 134	701
Wheel tractors .... farms..	980	923	401	957	518	844	517	176
number..	2 396	2 487	839	1 858	1 133	1 497	1 428	462
Less than 40 horsepower (PTO) .... farms..	397	346	141	530	190	371	188	46
number..	568	561	191	718	290	476	(D)	68
40 horsepower (PTO) or more .... farms..	818	852	363	657	456	570	456	164
number..	1 828	1 926	648	1 140	843	1 021	(D)	394
Grain and bean combines .... farms..	635	690	262	270	316	300	315	102
number..	796	743	374	289	504	339	390	141
Cottonpickers and strippers...................... farms..	-	-	-	-	-	-	-	-
number..	-	-	-	-	-	-	-	-
Mower conditioners .... farms..	287	231	85	303	92	269	188	25
number..	288	234	109	311	104	291	202	(D)
Pickup balers .... farms..	458	408	69	393	154	340	268	41
number..	522	492	83	464	187	399	324	44

See footnotes at end of table.

Table 8. **Machinery and Equipment on Place: 1987 and 1982**—Con.

[Data are based on a sample of farms. For meaning of abbreviations and symbols, see introductory text]

All Farms	Nemaha	Neosho	Ness	Norton	Osage	Osborne	Ottawa	Pawnee
VALUE OF MACHINERY AND EQUIPMENT								
Estimated market value of all machinery and								
equipment .... farms, 1987..	1 127	752	598	470	884	607	515	530
1982..	1 157	802	644	517	989	637	588	568
$1,000, 1987..	54 084	23 777	33 183	23 902	29 297	36 044	21 725	38 991
1982..	54 769	29 572	40 353	33 657	37 723	33 767	34 239	49 402
Average per farm..................... dollars, 1987..	47 969	31 618	55 490	50 854	33 142	59 380	42 185	73 568
1982..	47 337	36 873	62 659	65 101	38 143	53 009	58 229	86 975
Farms by value group:								
$1 to $9,999 .... 1987..	163	266	114	95	320	46	114	77
1982..	238	293	45	44	317	66	73	101
$10,000 to $19,999 .... 1987..	261	126	90	59	138	120	87	59
1982..	199	164	80	76	223	183	79	85
$20,000 to $29,999 .... 1987..	193	60	47	84	81	47	75	49
1982..	175	76	148	75	57	77	66	18
$30,000 to $49,999 .... 1987..	126	88	85	57	159	121	76	66
1982..	129	83	81	79	158	108	116	114
$50,000 to $69,999 .... 1987..	118	97	88	88	82	61	60	57
1982..	123	63	127	54	91	54	86	46
$70,000 to $99,999 .... 1987..	112	47	73	50	42	110	33	77
1982..	111	43	44	62	37	44	47	27
$100,000 to $199,999 .... 1987..	98	38	52	72	44	79	61	116
1982..	148	52	91	110	69	95	106	91
$200,000 or more .... 1987..	56	8	19	9	18	23	9	29
1982..	34	19	30	17	37	30	15	88
$200,000 to $499,999 .... 1987..	56	8	19	8	17	23	7	23
$500,000 or more .... 1987..	–	–	–	1	1	–	2	6
SELECTED MACHINERY AND EQUIPMENT								
Motortrucks, including pickups .... farms, 1987..	1 035	711	573	454	775	598	506	515
1982..	1 020	731	546	470	952	598	576	531
number, 1987..	1 968	1 477	1 675	1 315	1 662	1 622	1 400	1 680
1982..	1 722	1 490	1 776	1 283	1 952	1 490	1 387	1 572
Wheel tractors .... farms, 1987	1 003	607	510	443	764	594	458	483
1982..	1 044	655	570	466	803	524	536	504
number, 1987..	2 778	1 290	1 297	1 172	1 805	1 406	1 048	1 520
1982..	2 543	1 426	1 397	1 190	1 840	1 277	1 237	1 356
Less than 40 horsepower (PTO) .... farms, 1987..	443	287	155	178	400	185	132	223
number, 1987..	682	395	234	270	701	287	205	370
40 horsepower (PTO) or more .... farms, 1987..	865	439	485	408	542	538	425	441
number, 1987..	2 096	895	1 063	902	1 104	1 119	841	1 150
Grain and bean combines[1] .... farms, 1987..	628	344	395	277	409	435	348	348
1982..	676	389	367	360	490	428	408	340
number, 1987..	672	384	508	353	445	548	547	517
1982..	737	454	500	479	526	536	581	462
Cottonpickers and strippers............... farms, 1987..	–	–	–	–	–	–	–	–
1982..	–	–	–	–	–	–	–	–
number, 1987..	–	–	–	–	–	–	–	–
1982..	–	–	–	–	–	–	–	–
Mower conditioners .... farms, 1987..	334	236	148	146	239	248	137	107
1982..	209	186	182	139	216	152	170	153
number, 1987..	356	242	156	163	250	260	143	131
1982..	211	203	183	155	223	165	176	169
Pickup balers .... farms, 1987..	539	348	239	162	303	244	216	156
1982..	466	308	262	240	360	269	233	159
number, 1987..	653	414	279	198	376	288	234	216
1982..	516	364	325	283	409	336	268	257
1987 INVENTORY								
Manufactured 1983 to 1987:								
Motortrucks, including pickups .... farms..	365	191	200	171	247	192	119	162
number..	444	210	218	209	287	262	134	233
Wheel tractors .... farms..	113	26	76	57	92	104	41	61
number..	129	30	94	66	114	161	44	78
Less than 40 horsepower (PTO) .... farms..	21	2	8	2	35	14	1	2
number..	21	(D)	16	(D)	35	14	(D)	12
40 horsepower (PTO) or more .... farms..	92	26	66	55	59	93	40	61
number..	108	(D)	78	(D)	79	147	(D)	(D)
Grain and bean combines .... farms..	44	3	32	11	39	24	12	25
number..	44	3	34	14	40	29	12	32
Cottonpickers and strippers................ farms..	–	–	–	–	–	–	–	–
number..	–	–	–	–	–	–	–	–
Mower conditioners .... farms..	46	25	40	40	68	26	12	14
number..	46	25	40	40	68	26	12	17
Pickup balers .... farms..	70	37	32	22	62	43	21	16
number..	80	37	33	22	62	43	21	24
Manufactured 1983 to 1983:								
Motortrucks, including pickups .... farms..	885	637	504	426	682	567	480	456
number..	1 524	1 267	1 457	1 106	1 375	1 360	1 266	1 447
Wheel tractors .... farms..	967	603	475	420	730	557	441	478
number..	2 649	1 260	1 203	1 106	1 691	1 245	1 002	1 442
Less than 40 horsepower (PTO) .... farms..	428	285	147	176	375	182	131	221
number..	661	(D)	218	(D)	666	273	(D)	(D)
40 horsepower (PTO) or more .... farms..	856	433	448	373	512	492	411	435
number..	1 988	(D)	985	(D)	1 025	972	(D)	(D)
Grain and bean combines .... farms..	586	341	367	268	371	415	339	326
number..	628	381	474	339	405	519	535	485
Cottonpickers and strippers................ farms..	–	–	–	–	–	–	–	–
number..	–	–	–	–	–	–	–	–
Mower conditioners .... farms..	267	213	111	123	180	220	125	100
number..	308	217	116	123	182	232	131	114
Pickup balers .... farms..	489	324	209	143	257	214	197	147
number..	573	377	246	176	316	243	213	192

See footnotes at end of table.

Table 8. **Machinery and Equipment on Place: 1987 and 1982**—Con.

[Data are based on a sample of farms. For meaning of abbreviations and symbols, see introductory text]

All Farms	Phillips	Pottawatomie	Pratt	Rawlins	Reno	Republic	Rice	Riley
VALUE OF MACHINERY AND EQUIPMENT								
Estimated market value of all machinery and								
equipment .... farms, 1987..	592	765	517	534	1 557	834	604	547
1982..	647	862	547	621	1 638	911	642	583
$1,000, 1987..	27 290	22 246	39 464	30 420	71 897	47 432	38 046	20 803
1982..	30 490	30 818	38 466	41 428	78 593	50 534	48 151	23 493
Average per farm .... dollars, 1987..	46 099	28 336	76 332	56 965	46 177	56 873	62 989	38 030
1982..	47 125	35 752	70 321	66 712	47 981	55 471	75 002	40 297
Farms by value group:								
$1 to $9,999 .... 1987..	110	319	65	70	425	123	72	175
1982..	121	235	101	49	377	160	92	136
$10,000 to $19,999 .... 1987..	84	127	97	102	238	108	97	154
1982..	64	218	47	78	264	126	33	101
$20,000 to $29,999 .... 1987..	87	123	63	56	188	122	138	69
1982..	144	92	47	86	207	120	101	103
$30,000 to $49,999 .... 1987..	94	92	50	64	235	145	86	27
1982..	64	78	116	77	193	126	64	72
$50,000 to $69,999 .... 1987..	77	45	54	92	120	104	35	48
1982..	124	96	62	112	219	98	89	77
$70,000 to $99,999 .... 1987..	71	35	60	43	151	73	35	19
1982..	41	52	35	48	94	90	96	38
$100,000 to $199,999 .... 1987..	55	32	76	91	138	129	98	35
1982..	74	76	93	133	211	133	103	45
$200,000 or more .... 1987..	14	12	52	16	62	30	43	20
1982..	15	16	46	36	53	38	62	11
$200,000 to $499,999 .... 1987..	12	12	46	16	57	26	40	19
$500,000 or more .... 1987..	2	–	6	–	5	2	3	1
SELECTED MACHINERY AND EQUIPMENT								
Motortrucks, including pickups .... farms, 1987..	570	713	490	522	1 296	767	582	474
1982..	561	805	531	584	1 447	815	593	544
number, 1987..	1 544	1 514	1 595	1 466	3 437	1 932	1 552	1 060
1982..	1 356	1 596	1 395	1 564	3 333	1 932	1 651	1 126
Wheel tractors .... farms, 1987..	534	645	448	471	1 372	746	568	480
1982..	589	724	507	492	1 474	819	594	507
number, 1987..	1 860	1 727	1 189	1 449	3 548	2 213	1 536	1 421
1982..	1 478	1 831	1 198	1 391	3 408	2 185	1 560	1 508
Less than 40 horsepower (PTO) .... farms, 1987..	286	321	109	209	568	321	216	284
number, 1987..	593	617	171	336	815	580	351	452
40 horsepower (PTO) or more .... farms, 1987	476	469	407	410	1 170	679	300	388
number, 1987..	1 267	1 110	1 018	1 113	2 733	1 633	1 185	969
Grain and bean combines[1] .... farms, 1987..	338	356	318	325	910	564	388	265
1982..	364	363	383	376	873	570	427	294
number, 1987..	436	375	457	441	1 135	677	491	347
1982..	456	400	454	489	1 126	674	552	346
Cottonpickers and strippers............... farms, 1987..	–	–	–	–	–	–	–	–
1982..	–	–	–	–	–	–	–	–
number, 1987..	–	–	–	–	–	–	–	–
1982..	–	–	–	–	–	–	–	–
Mower conditioners .... farms, 1987..	215	194	113	162	447	224	175	209
1982..	216	285	86	166	367	191	188	196
number, 1987..	224	209	143	176	526	234	185	214
1982..	223	291	87	217	382	194	197	205
Pickup balers .... farms, 1987..	266	371	134	234	611	418	256	274
1982..	333	491	148	214	522	334	266	283
number, 1987..	333	459	171	296	771	489	317	351
1982..	366	635	152	247	593	377	327	336
1987 INVENTORY								
Manufactured 1983 to 1987:								
Motortrucks, including pickups .... farms..	174	127	178	135	427	210	177	117
number..	188	161	225	166	502	235	221	133
Wheel tractors .... farms..	72	53	70	77	119	87	91	42
number..	95	97	102	93	154	97	140	56
Less than 40 horsepower (PTO) .... farms..	27	28	12	3	23	9	20	15
number..	23	41	12	6	23	9	44	18
40 horsepower (PTO) or more .... farms..	64	33	58	75	97	78	77	28
number..	72	56	90	87	141	88	96	38
Grain and bean combines .... farms..	12	52	31	23	54	41	51	11
number..	12	54	33	23	71	41	54	12
Cottonpickers and strippers.................. farms..	–	–	–	–	–	–	–	–
number..	–	–	–	–	–	–	–	–
Mower conditioners .... farms..	10	46	20	5	41	13	20	18
number..	10	46	20	5	41	13	20	18
Pickup balers .... farms..	29	54	16	24	46	26	54	29
number..	30	54	23	24	58	26	67	30
Manufactured prior to 1983:								
Motortrucks, including pickups .... farms..	560	655	463	510	1 208	747	548	429
number..	1 356	1 353	1 371	1 298	2 935	1 697	1 331	927
Wheel tractors .... farms..	517	626	431	457	1 346	734	543	478
number..	1 765	1 630	1 087	1 356	3 384	2 116	1 396	1 365
Less than 40 horsepower (PTO) .... farms..	264	300	97	209	565	313	203	278
number..	570	576	159	330	792	571	307	434
40 horsepower (PTO) or more .... farms..	446	456	396	405	1 142	660	482	386
number..	1 195	1 054	928	1 026	2 592	1 545	1 089	931
Grain and bean combines .... farms..	327	304	289	318	879	537	340	275
number..	424	321	424	418	1 064	636	437	335
Cottonpickers and strippers.................. farms..	–	–	–	–	–	–	–	–
number..	–	–	–	–	–	–	–	–
Mower conditioners .... farms..	206	161	101	157	407	211	155	193
number..	214	163	123	171	485	221	165	196
Pickup balers .... farms..	264	339	119	211	584	394	217	258
number..	303	405	148	272	713	463	250	321

See footnotes at end of table.

Table 8. Machinery and Equipment on Place: 1987 and 1982—Con.

[Data are based on a sample of farms. For meaning of abbreviations and symbols, see introductory text]

All Farms	Rooks	Rush	Russell	Saline	Scott	Sedgwick	Seward	Shawnee
VALUE OF MACHINERY AND EQUIPMENT								
Estimated market value of all machinery and equipment ... farms, 1987	473	546	533	744	391	1 577	285	851
1982	528	564	573	763	416	1 665	277	937
$1,000, 1987	24 292	27 725	26 095	34 856	40 961	73 132	29 227	22 227
1982	28 776	43 806	30 158	39 055	36 017	79 203	19 320	26 910
Average per farm ... dollars, 1987	51 358	50 778	48 959	46 849	104 759	46 374	102 551	26 118
1982	54 501	75 010	52 633	51 186	86 580	47 570	69 748	28 719
Farms by value group:								
$1 to $9,999 ... 1987	146	109	82	242	53	520	66	357
1982	136	57	63	219	67	511	57	515
$10,000 to $19,999 ... 1987	71	48	100	94	35	246	32	181
1982	50	24	118	155	39	207	51	94
$20,000 to $29,999 ... 1987	33	83	82	109	47	107	12	123
1982	16	71	132	59	38	193	44	138
$30,000 to $49,999 ... 1987	50	103	75	100	36	149	28	70
1982	144	123	50	64	50	219	20	51
$50,000 to $69,999 ... 1987	73	70	79	36	57	249	17	44
1982	50	91	75	56	33	117	25	14
$70,000 to $99,999 ... 1987	30	43	68	38	26	93	11	38
1982	29	87	33	78	55	171	18	51
$100,000 to $199,999 ... 1987	39	80	49	93	71	135	80	25
1982	70	68	85	84	81	170	31	52
$200,000 or more ... 1987	31	10	18	32	66	78	39	13
1982	33	63	17	46	53	77	31	22
$200,000 to $499,999 ... 1987	31	10	18	32	55	73	36	13
$500,000 or more ... 1987	-	-	-	-	11	5	3	-
SELECTED MACHINERY AND EQUIPMENT								
Motortrucks, including pickups ... farms, 1987	417	508	500	669	384	1 439	250	737
1982	495	558	545	674	394	1 463	270	832
number, 1987	1 236	1 276	1 194	1 656	1 349	3 420	876	1 461
1982	1 342	1 742	1 225	1 542	1 351	3 148	721	1 531
Wheel tractors ... farms, 1987	379	455	495	653	350	1 371	247	796
1982	429	529	488	636	342	1 449	241	758
number, 1987	846	1 079	1 105	1 594	949	3 268	678	1 633
1982	1 061	1 395	1 140	1 533	849	3 088	473	1 522
Less than 40 horsepower (PTO) ... farms, 1987	121	177	178	250	105	600	101	440
number, 1987	144	281	258	361	205	866	163	626
40 horsepower (PTO) or more ... farms, 1987	344	361	451	571	323	1 132	211	562
number, 1987	702	798	847	1 233	744	2 402	515	1 007
Grain and bean combines[1] ... farms, 1987	248	333	263	393	197	820	159	297
1982	317	405	250	434	220	855	105	248
number, 1987	289	457	343	522	229	964	188	320
1982	354	564	365	555	261	1 013	133	263
Cottonpickers and strippers ... farms, 1987	-	-	-	-	-	-	-	-
1982	-	-	-	-	-	-	-	-
number, 1987	-	-	-	-	-	-	-	-
1982	-	-	-	-	-	-	-	-
Mower conditioners ... farms, 1987	107	141	137	215	51	397	56	292
1982	191	104	76	159	42	338	25	159
number, 1987	110	150	139	220	54	425	65	306
1982	200	113	94	167	59	447	32	165
Pickup balers ... farms, 1987	166	187	248	342	44	546	40	314
1982	228	256	183	313	29	521	8	292
number, 1987	200	233	276	409	62	677	65	379
1982	258	269	225	336	31	584	11	349
1987 INVENTORY								
Manufactured 1983 to 1987:								
Motortrucks, including pickups ... farms	121	155	91	205	188	475	103	142
number	154	198	107	225	265	806	166	157
Wheel tractors ... farms	51	64	82	97	72	200	76	68
number	69	142	90	139	95	325	121	81
Less than 40 horsepower (PTO) ... farms	12	14	2	10	2	51	32	31
number	12	54	(D)	10	(D)	78	38	31
40 horsepower (PTO) or more ... farms	43	50	82	96	72	175	58	37
number	57	88	(D)	129	(D)	247	83	50
Grain and bean combines ... farms	7	36	19	31	51	50	24	18
number	7	36	20	37	55	62	24	18
Cottonpickers and strippers ... farms	-	-	-	-	-	-	-	-
number	-	-	-	-	-	-	-	-
Mower conditioners ... farms	16	14	56	21	3	32	5	48
number	16	14	56	21	3	34	8	48
Pickup balers ... farms	37	17	65	35	4	102	11	38
number	39	17	73	37	4	106	19	38
Manufactured prior to 1983:								
Motortrucks, including pickups ... farms	400	481	456	626	333	1 279	239	686
number	1 082	1 078	1 087	1 431	1 084	2 814	710	1 304
Wheel tractors ... farms	362	443	438	634	337	1 334	229	777
number	777	937	1 015	1 455	854	2 943	557	1 552
Less than 40 horsepower (PTO) ... farms	110	164	176	248	105	561	88	427
number	132	227	(D)	351	(D)	788	125	595
40 horsepower (PTO) or more ... farms	327	344	392	543	306	1 072	184	555
number	645	710	(D)	1 104	(D)	2 155	432	957
Grain and bean combines ... farms	242	309	247	369	150	773	148	280
number	282	421	323	465	174	922	164	302
Cottonpickers and strippers ... farms	-	-	-	-	-	-	-	-
number	-	-	-	-	-	-	-	-
Mower conditioners ... farms	91	127	81	196	48	365	51	244
number	94	136	83	199	51	391	57	258
Pickup balers ... farms	132	171	189	318	42	479	29	291
number	161	216	203	372	58	571	46	341

See footnotes at end of table.

Table 8. Machinery and Equipment on Place: 1987 and 1982—Con.

[Data are based on a sample of farms. For meaning of abbreviations and symbols, see introductory text]

All Farms	Sheridan	Sherman	Smith	Stafford	Stanton	Stevens	Sumner	Thomas
VALUE OF MACHINERY AND EQUIPMENT								
Estimated market value of all machinery and equipment ... farms, 1987	518	524	692	529	281	300	1 266	632
1982	570	549	761	547	231	325	1 366	628
$1,000, 1987	36 362	38 810	41 116	43 600	31 445	43 599	71 514	49 941
1982	45 265	53 844	44 191	43 288	30 254	38 671	86 380	48 144
Average per farm ... dollars, 1987	70 187	74 064	59 417	80 891	111 903	145 329	56 488	79 020
1982	79 412	98 076	58 070	79 137	130 971	118 989	62 323	76 663
Farms by value group:								
$1 to $9,999 ... 1987	71	87	99	46	12	25	263	79
1982	45	55	116	42	27	34	243	118
$10,000 to $19,999 ... 1987	74	99	110	66	58	27	251	73
1982	92	41	112	55	3	18	210	89
$20,000 to $29,999 ... 1987	42	46	71	74	17	46	78	84
1982	52	64	106	93	9	25	93	57
$30,000 to $49,999 ... 1987	66	42	111	65	17	30	184	83
1982	87	61	131	76	8	31	244	85
$50,000 to $69,999 ... 1987	62	44	75	69	27	12	114	80
1982	27	62	72	70	11	33	135	48
$70,000 to $99,999 ... 1987	68	65	67	52	25	17	141	89
1982	86	34	77	61	60	23	122	56
$100,000 to $199,999 ... 1987	104	91	130	129	71	46	158	86
1982	124	130	119	92	41	113	254	119
$200,000 or more ... 1987	31	48	29	48	54	97	77	78
1982	47	82	28	69	52	48	85	56
$200,000 to $499,999 ... 1987	31	43	27	44	51	87	77	74
$500,000 or more ... 1987	-	5	2	4	3	10	-	4
SELECTED MACHINERY AND EQUIPMENT								
Motortrucks, including pickups ... farms, 1987	466	501	685	518	276	293	1 201	622
1982	561	501	677	535	222	315	1 291	575
number, 1987	1 497	1 426	2 010	1 009	1 263	3 239	1 846	1 846
1982	1 656	1 541	1 795	1 601	867	1 088	3 445	1 688
Wheel tractors ... farms, 1987	459	447	652	475	276	259	1 091	566
1982	469	494	641	480	210	291	1 206	449
number, 1987	1 238	1 177	2 012	1 339	734	792	2 778	1 454
1982	1 226	1 358	1 773	1 360	626	720	2 880	1 122
Less than 40 horsepower (PTO) ... farms, 1987	125	182	308	131	86	47	318	181
number, 1987	203	242	505	162	122	91	463	281
40 horsepower (PTO) or more ... farms, 1987	425	384	588	446	248	242	983	549
number, 1987	1 035	935	1 507	1 157	612	701	2 302	1 173
Grain and bean combines[1] ... farms, 1987	311	224	437	371	123	194	755	341
1982	379	293	501	401	141	209	905	307
number, 1987	380	273	551	408	136	227	1 051	405
1982	430	411	571	514	168	256	1 284	354
Cottonpickers and strippers ... farms, 1987	-	-	-	-	-	-	-	-
1982	-	-	-	-	-	-	-	-
number, 1987	-	-	-	-	-	-	-	-
1982	-	-	-	-	-	-	-	-
Mower conditioners ... farms, 1987	105	96	211	115	28	44	245	113
1982	96	86	126	115	21	64	262	63
number, 1987	112	116	256	116	42	52	280	130
1982	100	104	130	124	25	63	308	66
Pickup balers ... farms, 1987	164	92	278	178	26	29	350	104
1982	167	103	336	212	46	45	348	71
number, 1987	187	98	342	236	41	36	435	124
1982	190	120	353	235	49	48	397	82
1987 INVENTORY								
Manufactured 1983 to 1987:								
Motortrucks, including pickups ... farms	132	190	185	185	113	162	423	221
number	157	230	240	248	192	254	512	310
Wheel tractors ... farms	80	109	106	57	86	122	154	103
number	71	162	127	79	131	213	189	135
Less than 40 horsepower (PTO) ... farms	5	19	13	11	16	17	36	7
number	5	26	19	11	18	21	34	7
40 horsepower (PTO) or more ... farms	59	94	99	49	73	108	131	97
number	66	136	108	68	113	192	155	128
Grain and bean combines ... farms	40	34	42	28	19	50	36	53
number	52	37	43	29	19	55	37	60
Cottonpickers and strippers ... farms	-	-	-	-	-	-	-	-
number	-	-	-	-	-	-	-	-
Mower conditioners ... farms	15	17	22	8	1	5	19	12
number	15	17	22	6	(D)	10	20	13
Pickup balers ... farms	17	33	34	48	14	16	23	14
number	17	34	34	24	14	14	25	14
Manufactured prior to 1983:								
Motortrucks, including pickups ... farms	450	450	542	475	248	281	1 048	583
number	1 340	1 196	1 770	1 353	817	1 009	2 727	1 536
Wheel tractors ... farms	447	431	638	462	255	232	1 042	571
number	1 167	1 015	1 885	1 260	603	579	2 589	1 319
Less than 40 horsepower (PTO) ... farms	124	164	295	127	83	44	299	176
number	198	216	486	171	104	70	442	274
40 horsepower (PTO) or more ... farms	413	372	565	433	227	214	935	531
number	969	799	1 399	1 089	499	509	2 147	1 045
Grain and bean combines ... farms	274	192	398	346	106	149	736	297
number	336	236	508	399	117	172	1 014	345
Cottonpickers and strippers ... farms	-	-	-	-	-	-	-	-
number	-	-	-	-	-	-	-	-
Mower conditioners ... farms	94	79	189	109	27	39	228	103
number	97	99	234	110	(D)	42	260	117
Pickup balers ... farms	149	61	260	154	25	16	330	82
number	170	84	308	187	27	17	410	110

See footnotes at end of table.

Table 8. **Machinery and Equipment on Place: 1987 and 1982**—Con.

[Data are based on a sample of farms. For meaning of abbreviations and symbols, see introductory text]

All Farms	Trego	Wabaunsee	Wallace	Washington	Wichita	Wilson	Woodson	Wyandotte
VALUE OF MACHINERY AND EQUIPMENT								
Estimated market value of all machinery and equipment ... farms, 1987..	482	622	330	938	354	609	368	199
1982..	497	678	338	1 032	340	680	402	216
$1,000, 1987..	28 303	18 599	22 563	50 343	30 803	23 823	12 715	5 065
1982..	29 987	25 531	24 874	56 186	30 078	27 030	15 262	5 035
Average per farm ... dollars, 1987..	58 721	29 901	68 372	53 671	87 013	39 118	34 552	25 453
1982..	60 337	37 656	73 591	54 444	88 465	39 750	38 016	23 308
Farms by value group:								
$1 to $9,999 ... 1987..	59	196	33	178	55	183	121	126
1982..	73	132	62	176	29	222	166	137
$10,000 to $19,999 ... 1987..	136	125	57	130	43	95	51	38
1982..	85	222	86	128	61	128	80	30
$20,000 to $29,999 ... 1987..	30	102	89	138	24	62	47	6
1982..	48	66	23	167	19	92	21	17
$30,000 to $49,999 ... 1987..	82	92	24	144	21	80	61	12
1982..	82	77	36	194	37	54	25	21
$50,000 to $69,999 ... 1987..	37	50	35	105	37	58	38	4
1982..	61	85	28	99	31	57	24	-
$70,000 to $99,999 ... 1987..	67	32	18	90	57	47	22	-
1982..	49	13	31	103	27	36	33	1
$100,000 to $199,999 ... 1987..	32	16	46	117	86	56	23	9
1982..	69	75	33	115	101	78	44	4
$200,000 or more ... 1987..	39	9	28	36	31	8	5	4
1982..	30	8	39	50	35	13	6	6
$200,000 to $499,999 ... 1987..	38	9	26	32	28	8	5	1
$500,000 or more ... 1987..	1	-	2	4	3	-	-	3
SELECTED MACHINERY AND EQUIPMENT								
Motortrucks, including pickups ... farms, 1987..	442	581	317	842	339	588	325	143
1982..	442	634	273	922	301	638	359	188
number, 1987..	1 247	1 190	871	1 907	1 207	1 374	761	274
1982..	1 275	1 247	719	1 967	1 062	1 362	725	319
Wheel tractors ... farms, 1987..	425	523	265	827	302	557	340	162
1982..	429	571	271	897	245	570	328	190
number, 1987..	914	1 241	694	2 491	759	1 375	818	294
1982..	990	1 222	606	2 319	708	1 227	758	336
Less than 40 horsepower (PTO) ... farms, 1987..	181	297	107	343	60	300	180	121
number, 1987..	198	482	127	797	114	501	245	145
40 horsepower (PTO) or more ... farms, 1987..	408	384	256	720	286	384	265	73
number, 1987..	716	759	567	1 694	645	874	573	149
Grain and bean combines[1] ... farms, 1987..	328	276	153	568	177	336	148	11
1982..	339	296	142	659	146	398	180	12
number, 1987..	380	308	174	678	213	366	177	13
1982..	432	297	185	725	180	490	191	12
Cottonpickers and strippers ... farms, 1987..	-	-	-	-	-	-	-	-
1982..	-	-	-	-	-	-	-	-
number, 1987..	-	-	-	-	-	-	-	-
1982..	-	-	-	-	-	-	-	-
Mower conditioners ... farms, 1987..	164	167	52	306	46	179	121	37
1982..	129	179	56	268	26	183	113	58
number, 1987..	184	171	56	329	55	201	136	37
1982..	131	183	58	286	27	185	123	73
Pickup balers ... farms, 1987..	212	237	67	491	57	306	167	23
1982..	180	361	72	547	25	284	178	34
number, 1987..	244	331	81	575	64	362	260	24
1982..	237	456	80	660	32	306	215	36
1987 INVENTORY								
Manufactured 1983 to 1987:								
Motortrucks, including pickups ... farms..	120	139	113	260	174	133	112	47
number..	126	177	146	312	240	137	114	86
Wheel tractors ... farms..	30	52	50	141	95	41	37	16
number..	34	125	91	193	145	47	68	34
Less than 40 horsepower (PTO) ... farms..	3	30	8	11	16	7	6	16
number..	5	65	9	12	19	7	11	22
40 horsepower (PTO) or more ... farms..	27	30	45	138	95	35	37	7
number..	29	60	82	181	126	40	57	12
Grain and bean combines ... farms..	17	25	27	51	28	39	9	2
number..	17	28	27	52	32	55	12	(D)
Cottonpickers and strippers ... farms..	-	-	-	-	-	-	-	-
number..	-	-	-	-	-	-	-	-
Mower conditioners ... farms..	7	25	6	30	7	2	5	12
number..	7	26	6	30	12	(D)	8	12
Pickup balers ... farms..	20	30	18	49	17	25	22	8
number..	20	40	18	51	24	25	22	8
Manufactured prior to 1983:								
Motortrucks, including pickups ... farms..	421	517	301	758	319	578	295	125
number..	1 121	1 013	725	1 595	961	1 237	647	188
Wheel tractors ... farms..	418	494	273	801	286	549	326	150
number..	880	1 116	603	2 298	614	1 328	750	260
Less than 40 horsepower (PTO) ... farms..	158	277	104	333	58	294	174	105
number..	193	417	118	785	95	494	234	123
40 horsepower (PTO) or more ... farms..	399	335	245	682	254	382	250	72
number..	687	699	485	1 513	519	834	516	137
Grain and bean combines ... farms..	312	253	127	517	155	297	139	9
number..	363	280	147	624	181	311	165	(D)
Cottonpickers and strippers ... farms..	-	-	-	-	-	-	-	-
number..	-	-	-	-	-	-	-	-
Mower conditioners ... farms..	157	142	46	280	39	177	118	25
number..	177	145	50	299	43	(D)	131	25
Pickup balers ... farms..	196	219	56	462	40	291	181	15
number..	224	291	63	524	40	337	238	16

[1]Data for 1982 include self-propelled only.

[Data are based on a sample of farms. For meaning of abbreviations and symbols, see introductory text]

Chemicals used	Kansas	Allen	Anderson	Atchison	Barber	Barton	Bourbon
Commercial fertilizer ------- farms, 1987..	47 723	479	506	504	352	661	496
1982..	49 648	461	544	594	361	641	516
acres on which used, 1987..	13 852 822	74 870	83 380	99 117	123 668	203 441	64 933
1982..	14 569 402	84 052	83 568	102 512	156 246	234 087	77 744
Cropland fertilized, except pastureland ------- farms, 1987..	45 112	409	485	452	335	650	391
1982..	47 596	430	514	554	355	641	466
acres on which used, 1987..	13 282 488	64 545	73 227	60 741	122 863	202 724	42 566
1982..	14 023 310	75 414	75 482	78 782	155 677	233 987	57 245
Pastureland and rangeland fertilized ------- farms, 1987..	6 907	132	93	269	20	18	199
1982..	6 837	109	143	267	15	6	171
acres on which used, 1987..	570 334	10 325	10 153	18 376	825	717	22 367
1982..	548 092	8 836	8 086	23 730	568	120	20 499
Lime ------- farms, 1987..	2 885	29	55	70	1	1	62
1982..	2 514	63	55	26	-	-	107
acres on which used, 1987..	154 622	3 003	2 252	2 741	(D)	(D)	2 163
1982..	148 897	3 090	3 484	765	-	-	9 279
tons, 1987..	369 024	11 249	6 519	7 820	(D)	(D)	5 628
1982..	375 457	9 066	9 641	2 595	-	-	24 559
Sprays, dusts, granules, fumigants, etc., to control—							
insects on hay and other crops ------- farms, 1987..	19 416	95	199	148	65	359	97
1982..	14 733	124	125	130	55	90	135
acres on which used, 1987..	3 015 580	15 379	11 632	20 752	8 717	45 409	9 427
1982..	2 861 551	11 948	14 012	21 169	9 134	19 940	12 895
Nematodes in crops ------- farms, 1987..	716	-	7	12	7	-	-
1982..	699	5	12	9	-	17	12
acres on which used, 1987..	87 904	-	70	321	1 225	-	-
1982..	130 368	400	741	725	-	1 175	202
Diseases in crops and orchards ------- farms, 1987..	1 055	7	2	11	1	9	23
1982..	925	11	18	21	1	7	12
acres on which used, 1987..	125 065	(D)	(D)	161	(D)	(D)	244
1982..	131 390	440	1 663	1 480	(D)	(D)	72
Weeds, grass, or brush in crops and pasture ------- farms, 1987..	36 950	290	420	451	204	576	333
1982..	26 058	221	352	480	101	244	229
acres on which used, 1987..	8 637 062	55 166	68 228	76 469	64 409	125 711	31 968
1982..	5 907 509	39 109	77 270	95 409	26 436	40 876	34 171
Chemicals used for defoliation or for growth control of crops or thinning of fruit ------- farms, 1987..	614	-	-	-	9	-	-
1982..	737	-	4	12	7	-	1
acres on which used, 1987..	68 839	-	-	-	898	-	-
1982..	95 569	-	232	160	1 014	-	(D)

Chemicals used	Brown	Butler	Chase	Chautauqua	Cherokee	Cheyenne	Clark
Commercial fertilizer ------- farms, 1987..	568	702	157	164	536	332	193
1982..	674	663	183	198	562	380	200
acres on which used, 1987..	154 859	164 835	23 968	24 380	103 946	156 484	76 314
1982..	177 819	166 151	30 964	38 355	127 504	134 432	74 199
Cropland fertilized, except pastureland ------- farms, 1987..	528	634	120	157	494	332	191
1982..	653	665	171	159	509	380	200
acres on which used, 1987..	130 539	154 846	21 011	21 111	95 947	(D)	73 524
1982..	154 779	158 990	28 777	32 377	116 694	134 432	74 199
Pastureland and rangeland fertilized ------- farms, 1987..	261	128	42	33	120	2	3
1982..	251	101	25	76	128	-	-
acres on which used, 1987..	24 320	9 990	2 957	3 269	7 999	(D)	2 790
1982..	23 040	7 161	2 187	5 978	10 810	-	-
Lime ------- farms, 1987..	65	108	4	3	104	-	-
1982..	63	64	25	3	126	-	-
acres on which used, 1987..	6 467	8 162	242	174	6 105	-	-
1982..	4 221	7 781	1 803	1 100	9 948	-	-
tons, 1987..	17 623	20 430	780	(D)	17 301	-	-
1982..	8 998	18 263	3 995	1 625	31 869	-	-
Sprays, dusts, granules, fumigants, etc., to control—							
insects on hay and other crops ------- farms, 1987..	228	293	79	61	50	157	87
1982..	315	248	68	56	69	131	38
acres on which used, 1987..	35 029	36 531	5 978	2 582	7 664	29 769	10 032
1982..	57 528	38 091	5 517	2 994	7 527	23 606	5 592
Nematodes in crops ------- farms, 1987..	12	13	7	-	-	5	-
1982..	35	9	-	-	-	3	-
acres on which used, 1987..	2 242	3 491	79	-	-	1 965	-
1982..	4 636	2 282	-	-	-	650	-
Diseases in crops and orchards ------- farms, 1987..	19	10	-	6	3	9	-
1982..	10	32	-	-	13	18	-
acres on which used, 1987..	990	1 058	-	68	(D)	1 701	-
1982..	1 573	4 631	-	-	113	3 040	-
Weeds, grass, or brush in crops and pasture ------- farms, 1987..	499	493	143	122	383	255	152
1982..	523	329	117	81	336	153	80
acres on which used, 1987..	141 630	105 350	19 589	19 061	89 548	65 899	49 355
1982..	137 995	59 173	14 347	21 498	80 547	35 653	23 250
Chemicals used for defoliation or for growth control of crops or thinning of fruit ------- farms, 1987..	2	9	6	-	2	1	-
1982..	7	2	6	3	1	16	9
acres on which used, 1987..	(D)	(D)	120	-	(D)	(D)	-
1982..	715	-	413	(D)	-	650	585

Table 9. Agricultural Chemicals Used, Including Fertilizer and Lime: 1987 and 1982—Con.

[Data are based on a sample of farms. For meaning of abbreviations and symbols, see introductory text]

Chemicals used		Clay	Cloud	Coffey	Comanche	Cowley	Crawford	Decatur
Commercial fertilizer ... farms,	1987	577	530	402	146	690	533	386
	1982	567	491	470	169	746	590	347
acres on which used,	1987	154 558	169 878	58 121	61 242	136 925	83 574	161 619
	1982	141 755	159 341	75 040	94 150	188 563	96 648	138 486
Cropland fertilized, except pastureland ... farms,	1987	571	529	371	146	632	461	386
	1982	556	491	452	169	720	518	347
acres on which used,	1987	150 228	166 195	53 681	(D)	129 466	84 861	(D)
	1982	140 880	158 985	70 568	(D)	182 202	79 419	136 486
Pastureland and rangeland fertilized ... farms,	1987	40	31	56	1	99	201	1
	1982	24	17	70	1	66	175	-
acres on which used,	1987	4 330	3 681	4 440	(D)	7 459	18 713	(D)
	1982	875	356	4 472	(D)	6 361	17 429	-
Lime ... farms,	1987	24	10	30	1	23	85	-
	1982	13	-	77	-	24	153	-
acres on which used,	1987	1 172	188	1 461	(D)	2 070	3 049	-
	1982	519	-	3 467	-	1 810	5 297	-
tons,	1987	2 152	393	4 191	(D)	3 110	6 049	-
	1982	1 300	-	9 996	-	3 360	13 382	-
Sprays, dusts, granules, fumigants, etc., to control—								
insects on hay and other crops ... farms,	1987	310	278	120	50	194	79	217
	1982	162	114	90	29	166	101	146
acres on which used,	1987	35 671	26 375	13 875	9 495	14 927	12 740	34 066
	1982	19 666	16 126	12 758	4 516	20 542	9 277	22 981
Nematodes in crops ... farms,	1987	24	5	-	-	1	2	3
	1982	21	3	18	-	-	-	4
acres on which used,	1987	1 228	698	-	-	(D)	(D)	463
	1982	1 242	645	1 099	-	-	-	727
Diseases in crops and orchards ... farms,	1987	25	10	26	3	14	7	3
	1982	10	10	10	-	11	-	-
acres on which used,	1987	1 101	2 933	1 245	(D)	556	(D)	900
	1982	20	2 587	1 817	-	3 522	77	-
Weeds, grass, or brush in crops and pasture ... farms,	1987	456	425	354	132	377	301	251
	1982	415	297	323	57	315	268	163
acres on which used,	1987	101 183	120 933	72 310	25 602	60 263	65 830	61 002
	1982	72 991	74 082	81 461	5 887	62 274	47 952	33 036
Chemicals used for defoliation or for growth control of crops or thinning of fruit ... farms,	1987	-	7	16	-	9	8	9
	1982	3	19	15	-	14	11	1
acres on which used,	1987	-	550	93	-	390	510	(D)
	1982	(D)	532	555	-	970	262	(D)

Chemicals used		Dickinson	Doniphan	Douglas	Edwards	Elk	Ellis	Ellsworth
Commercial fertilizer ... farms,	1987	847	387	630	285	205	449	379
	1982	819	443	633	330	213	381	372
acres on which used,	1987	213 697	91 057	76 433	162 189	22 365	86 598	98 479
	1982	222 257	104 592	93 646	166 003	33 221	89 002	99 087
Cropland fertilized, except pastureland ... farms,	1987	828	318	535	285	172	449	379
	1982	811	422	544	330	195	381	365
acres on which used,	1987	207 685	79 495	63 717	(D)	18 993	86 598	98 354
	1982	218 113	88 269	76 648	(D)	27 773	89 002	98 342
Pastureland and rangeland fertilized ... farms,	1987	106	172	235	2	54	-	4
	1982	47	167	257	2	40	-	22
acres on which used,	1987	6 012	11 562	12 716	(D)	3 362	-	125
	1982	4 144	16 323	16 998	(D)	5 448	-	745
Lime ... farms,	1987	23	71	84	2	9	-	3
	1982	17	30	64	1	18	-	15
acres on which used,	1987	681	6 311	5 474	(D)	312	-	60
	1982	1 093	1 712	2 628	(D)	1 162	-	663
tons,	1987	2 060	13 262	11 991	(D)	1 041	-	127
	1982	1 849	4 476	6 886	(D)	2 733	-	1 683
Sprays, dusts, granules, fumigants, etc., to control—								
insects on hay and other crops ... farms,	1987	446	287	140	171	57	129	91
	1982	176	338	146	94	45	49	66
acres on which used,	1987	35 707	40 756	14 862	56 538	2 595	16 431	7 504
	1982	24 973	43 917	22 631	29 797	4 038	5 170	8 542
Nematodes in crops ... farms,	1987	27	15	16	2	-	-	9
	1982	7	6	15	5	-	-	-
acres on which used,	1987	1 063	858	288	(D)	-	-	226
	1982	253	610	2 712	2 466	-	-	-
Diseases in crops and orchards ... farms,	1987	6	7	6	10	6	29	24
	1982	11	10	5	-	1	-	-
acres on which used,	1987	1 630	829	296	1 642	(D)	1 860	3 048
	1982	4 720	1 851	598	(D)	(D)	-	-
Weeds, grass, or brush in crops and pasture ... farms,	1987	601	333	434	192	126	442	334
	1982	516	321	372	191	63	254	163
acres on which used,	1987	106 615	86 998	71 554	89 158	14 343	65 663	79 984
	1982	82 483	72 067	66 686	57 454	11 521	34 017	22 242
Chemicals used for defoliation or for growth control of crops or thinning of fruit ... farms,	1987	18	3	8	1	2	2	3
	1982	-	7	2	1	1	1	6
acres on which used,	1987	247	(D)	40	(D)	(D)	(D)	292
	1982	-	2 254	(D)	(D)	(D)	(D)	570

[Data are based on a sample of farms. For meaning of abbreviations and symbols, see introductory text]

Chemicals used	Finney	Ford	Franklin	Geary	Gove	Graham	Grant
Commercial fertilizer .... farms, 1987	375	547	555	198	347	379	215
1982	331	432	633	238	307	389	215
acres on which used, 1987	232 315	234 719	72 243	38 560	152 660	137 111	110 924
1982	248 075	189 130	78 658	38 282	140 953	121 426	157 003
Cropland fertilized, except pastureland .... farms, 1987	374	547	477	187	345	379	215
1982	325	430	601	237	307	379	215
acres on which used, 1987	231 217	234 199	56 748	33 766	(D)	136 901	(D)
1982	241 385	187 265	64 884	37 852	(D)	120 482	155 946
Pastureland and rangeland fertilized .... farms, 1987	4	10	189	33	2	9	1
1982	14	4	210	16	10	11	19
acres on which used, 1987	1 098	520	15 495	4 794	(D)	210	(D)
1982	6 690	1 865	13 774	440	(D)	944	1 057
Lime .... farms, 1987	-	-	55	16	-	-	.
1982	-	-	74	8	-	-	-
acres on which used, 1987	-	-	2 451	368	-	-	-
1982	-	-	4 090	2 245	-	-	-
tons, 1987	-	-	6 720	1 248	-	-	-
1982	-	-	11 864	(D)	-	-	-
Sprays, dusts, granules, fumigants, etc., to control—							
insects on hay and other crops .... farms, 1987	251	177	81	183	161	150	171
1982	237	112	110	67	60	39	179
acres on which used, 1987	97 945	55 268	8 064	9 961	22 650	21 262	64 642
1982	117 450	37 324	10 376	5 151	15 700	6 333	100 828
Nematodes in crops .... farms, 1987	15	10	3	8	13	8	4
1982	5	2	-	2	6	1	2
acres on which used, 1987	4 310	2 095	923	550	2 009	953	2 199
1982	(D)	(D)	-	(D)	6 534	(D)	(D)
Diseases in crops and orchards......... farms, 1987	16	1	3	-	17	12	12
1982	16	12	30	12	5	1	20
acres on which used, 1987	5 032	(D)	104	-	5 996	2 320	1 452
1982	7 189	1 317	1 450	(D)	1 941	(D)	7 980
Weeds, grass, or brush in crops and pasture......... farms, 1987	300	489	487	172	281	282	193
1982	244	267	156	156	129	129	164
acres on which used, 1987	131 052	164 224	88 091	25 422	65 619	70 362	75 640
1982	87 308	57 637	72 065	17 487	32 259	21 782	70 448
Chemicals used for defoliation or for growth control of crops or thinning of fruit .... farms, 1987	2	1	2	9	2	-	-
1982	3	9	11	-	2	1	-
acres on which used, 1987	(D)	(D)	(D)	(D)	(D)	-	-
1982	(D)	1 586	1 015	-	(D)	(D)	-

Chemicals used	Gray	Greeley	Greenwood	Hamilton	Harper	Harvey	Haskell
Commercial fertilizer .... farms, 1987	429	149	288	144	523	631	212
1982	376	50	336	90	564	703	278
acres on which used, 1987	219 685	108 750	42 402	83 233	215 953	193 540	153 876
1982	247 420	51 548	49 432	50 156	246 244	182 703	179 137
Cropland fertilized, except pastureland .... farms, 1987	429	143	239	144	517	631	211
1982	375	50	317	90	555	693	278
acres on which used, 1987	218 777	108 678	33 115	(D)	214 685	191 539	(D)
1982	246 642	51 548	46 422	(D)	240 569	182 287	178 700
Pastureland and rangeland fertilized .... farms, 1987	7	6	69	1	20	33	7
1982	11	-	49	1	57	22	6
acres on which used, 1987	908	72	9 287	(D)	1 267	2 001	(D)
1982	778	-	3 010	(D)	5 675	416	437
Lime .... farms, 1987	-	-	29	1	9	69	-
1982	-	-	514	-	15	37	-
acres on which used, 1987	-	-	1 871	(D)	637	3 916	-
1982	-	-	262	-	421	3 654	-
tons, 1987	-	-	4 241	(D)	1 022	9 372	-
1982	-	-	705	-	514	8 519	-
Sprays, dusts, granules, fumigants, etc., to control—							
insects on hay and other crops .... farms, 1987	281	111	94	65	111	297	221
1982	261	29	105	58	105	336	234
acres on which used, 1987	95 853	55 962	7 214	25 760	15 995	40 758	95 776
1982	110 682	18 159	7 065	14 837	20 755	57 964	119 626
Nematodes in crops .... farms, 1987	15	8	10	-	2	9	4
1982	20	2	9	1	4	7	26
acres on which used, 1987	4 956	1 331	847	-	(D)	397	2 203
1982	4 120	(D)	801	(D)	(D)	(D)	16 296
Diseases in crops and orchards......... farms, 1987	12	-	1	-	3	41	9
1982	15	-	2	-	-	31	7
acres on which used, 1987	7 459	-	(D)	-	(D)	2 040	3 331
1982	5 813	-	(D)	-	-	2 169	3 485
Weeds, grass, or brush in crops and pasture......... farms, 1987	336	133	191	143	230	487	194
1982	245	57	127	96	162	424	166
acres on which used, 1987	130 939	54 092	30 078	33 542	62 967	108 154	76 736
1982	94 599	44 760	20 897	33 425	26 599	67 552	76 476
Chemicals used for defoliation or for growth control of crops or thinning of fruit .... farms, 1987	17	7	1	-	12	1	20
1982	8	-	-	7	4	30	5
acres on which used, 1987	1 147	784	(D)	-	895	(D)	7 326
1982	3 449	-	-	1 120	(D)	819	7 478

Table 9. **Agricultural Chemicals Used, Including Fertilizer and Lime: 1987 and 1982**—Con.

[Data are based on a sample of farms. For meaning of abbreviations and symbols, see introductory text]

Chemicals used	Hodgeman	Jackson	Jefferson	Jewell	Johnson	Kearny	Kingman	Kiowa
Commercial fertilizer ... farms, 1987	277	758	743	548	448	186	618	250
1982	202	804	673	612	455	66	672	253
acres on which used, 1987	122 628	108 598	103 677	165 650	50 724	157 715	201 868	106 650
1982	84 366	131 609	100 443	199 195	59 349	89 690	233 788	107 748
Cropland fertilized, except pastureland ... farms, 1987	277	595	576	539	362	186	600	250
1982	201	644	505	603	353	86	670	253
acres on which used, 1987	(D)	79 256	71 751	163 398	42 347	(D)	198 788	106 650
1982	(D)	89 485	75 023	194 202	44 226	(D)	(D)	107 178
Pastureland and rangeland fertilized ... farms, 1987	2	349	328	52	168	2	46	-
1982	1	399	312	42	221	2	11	11
acres on which used, 1987	(D)	29 342	31 926	2 154	8 377	(D)	3 080	-
1982	(D)	42 124	25 420	4 993	15 123	(D)	(D)	570
Lime ... farms, 1987	-	58	55	9	44	-	52	-
1982	-	74	60	1	52	-	37	-
acres on which used, 1987	-	4 056	4 142	245	2 872	-	5 331	-
1982	-	2 403	2 214	(D)	2 327	-	2 080	-
tons, 1987	-	11 162	10 364	490	5 126	-	11 841	-
1982	-	6 931	4 009	(D)	5 485	-	3 157	-
Sprays, dusts, granules, fumigants, etc., to control—								
Insects on hay and other crops ... farms, 1987	115	164	162	315	97	108	201	90
1982	54	149	163	151	104	70	117	50
acres on which used, 1987	17 379	18 368	16 003	30 180	6 780	66 262	23 666	21 487
1982	14 523	12 316	19 816	24 798	19 394	43 748	8 918	13 482
Nematodes in crops ... farms, 1987	9	9	7	4	1	2	2	-
1982	1	-	1	27	17	1	-	-
acres on which used, 1987	691	63	562	290	(D)	(D)	(D)	-
1982	(D)	-	(D)	546	9 890	(D)	-	-
Diseases in crops and orchards ... farms, 1987	25	8	24	-	5	9	11	-
1982	1	6	9	16	10	-	5	17
acres on which used, 1987	2 376	238	216	-	(D)	2 270	1 942	-
1982	(D)	266	307	2 310	2 216	-	5	649
Weeds, grass, or brush in crops and pasture ... farms, 1987	277	640	580	479	301	145	327	180
1982	192	512	394	396	273	58	212	119
acres on which used, 1987	95 449	100 641	77 286	119 567	50 591	75 558	80 970	64 701
1982	37 376	78 658	67 307	68 428	49 891	25 072	25 563	38 707
Chemicals used for defoliation or for growth control of crops or thinning of fruit ... farms, 1987	-	19	4	2	9	12	1	-
1982	7	-	24	8	9	3	-	1
acres on which used, 1987	-	535	94	(D)	906	6 831	(D)	-
1982	300	-	907	924	268	(D)	-	(D)

Chemicals used	Labette	Lane	Leavenworth	Lincoln	Linn	Logan	Lyon	McPherson
Commercial fertilizer ... farms, 1987	589	165	728	469	434	148	553	1 035
1982	710	179	766	507	429	148	664	1 156
acres on which used, 1987	110 311	90 092	75 671	136 869	57 162	60 896	88 496	248 211
1982	150 294	78 283	86 289	132 031	68 227	64 931	94 564	274 154
Cropland fertilized, except pastureland ... farms, 1987	500	165	584	469	384	148	528	1 027
1982	642	179	676	507	399	379	627	1 147
acres on which used, 1987	79 997	(D)	57 044	136 579	47 334	60 896	80 796	244 820
1982	121 561	(D)	69 675	131 696	54 096	64 661	89 007	273 383
Pastureland and rangeland fertilized ... farms, 1987	242	1	310	15	137	-	105	36
1982	256	1	289	16	161	6	105	16
acres on which used, 1987	30 314	(D)	16 627	290	9 828	-	7 700	3 291
1982	26 733	(D)	16 614	335	14 131	270	5 557	771
Lime ... farms, 1987	56	-	76	1	46	-	43	53
1982	83	-	55	1	65	-	34	15
acres on which used, 1987	2 355	-	1 968	(D)	2 720	-	2 867	2 460
1982	3 511	-	1 849	(D)	2 391	-	1 383	1 814
tons, 1987	4 564	-	5 433	(D)	7 568	-	10 214	3 586
1982	8 353	-	6 580	(D)	6 506	-	3 478	2 930
Sprays, dusts, granules, fumigants, etc., to control—								
Insects on hay and other crops ... farms, 1987	83	61	190	290	60	49	183	427
1982	102	57	188	159	58	44	168	415
acres on which used, 1987	8 620	11 046	12 099	27 867	7 144	15 469	14 376	53 654
1982	9 346	14 732	18 214	16 124	8 950	13 523	23 064	59 356
Nematodes in crops ... farms, 1987	7	4	21	-	1	1	8	6
1982	-	8	8	13	-	-	11	8
acres on which used, 1987	770	959	869	1 090	(D)	(D)	233	911
1982	-	-	1 035	-	-	(D)	1 496	(D)
Diseases in crops and orchards ... farms, 1987	38	-	27	5	-	7	11	15
1982	14	-	29	8	1	1	2	1
acres on which used, 1987	293	-	979	200	-	1 707	288	(D)
1982	21	-	(D)	640	(D)	(D)	(D)	(D)
Weeds, grass, or brush in crops and pasture ... farms, 1987	361	226	567	390	369	162	454	759
1982	257	111	402	255	262	118	311	669
acres on which used, 1987	66 449	73 945	67 300	98 094	59 557	35 964	76 032	137 032
1982	47 221	36 573	42 065	41 034	57 412	43 876	52 467	78 265
Chemicals used for defoliation or for growth control of crops or thinning of fruit ... farms, 1987	16	12	15	13	-	-	-	22
1982	25	11	2	-	1	-	-	6
acres on which used, 1987	360	3 607	264	930	-	-	-	1 283
1982	4 333	799	579	-	(D)	-	8	3 005

[Data are based on a sample of farms. For meaning of abbreviations and symbols, see introductory text]

Chemicals used	Marion	Marshall	Meade	Miami	Mitchell	Montgomery	Morris	Morton
Commercial fertilizer .... farms, 1987..	916	677	341	667	488	481	370	126
1982..	977	900	290	752	453	586	462	108
acres on which used, 1987..	222 038	212 302	162 322	95 012	215 762	92 223	84 307	82 817
1982..	240 369	202 719	150 686	94 554	227 345	131 839	90 709	86 240
Cropland fertilized, except pastureland .... farms, 1987..	886	856	341	531	488	385	350	125
1982..	976	890	290	653	452	480	443	105
acres on which used, 1987..	212 625	196 237	162 185	69 364	214 387	74 690	80 096	(D)
1982..	237 126	196 072	150 315	71 575	226 222	119 916	88 122	85 535
Pastureland and rangeland fertilized .... farms, 1987..	142	141	4	292	19	170	59	1
1982..	62	73	11	270	18	189	63	16
acres on which used, 1987..	9 413	14 065	137	25 646	1 375	17 533	4 211	(D)
1982..	3 243	4 647	371	22 979	1 129	11 923	2 587	705
Lime .... farms, 1987..	23	112	-	87	-	82	27	-
1982..	91	39	-	73	-	84	27	-
acres on which used, 1987..	1 201	3 765	-	3 442	-	4 579	981	-
1982..	3 065	2 327	-	3 935	-	4 155	1 163	-
tons, 1987..	3 812	13 241	-	7 960	-	12 323	2 054	-
1982..	8 625	5 400	-	9 512	-	10 680	3 920	-
Sprays, dusts, granules, fumigants, etc., to control—								
Insects on hay and other crops .... farms, 1987..	453	440	198	53	277	138	184	69
1982..	426	262	149	116	129	159	114	99
acres on which used, 1987..	40 186	43 531	71 426	8 488	44 629	17 872	18 835	37 959
1982..	42 867	35 161	46 230	11 795	17 498	16 775	9 678	51 565
Nematodes in crops .... farms, 1987..	30	31	4	10	11	2	-	-
1982..	30	29	7	7	3	1	8	-
acres on which used, 1987..	5 034	2 969	1 925	1 850	478	(D)	-	-
1982..	3 804	2 063	(D)	1 160	370	(D)	250	-
Diseases in crops and orchards .... farms, 1987..	10	18	4	12	7	10	2	7
1982..	21	23	17	19	2	9	1	-
acres on which used, 1987..	904	1 853	2 971	96	(D)	1 252	(D)	700
1982..	2 969	1 364	4 920	82	(D)	(D)	(D)	-
Weeds, grass, or brush in crops and pasture .... farms, 1987..	628	739	266	615	428	322	316	93
1982..	624	703	212	492	294	204	276	85
acres on which used, 1987..	110 041	145 985	93 716	86 854	149 398	63 950	56 851	50 289
1982..	77 364	165 144	58 394	68 227	91 666	53 370	30 754	51 108
Chemicals used for defoliation or for growth control of crops or thinning of fruit .... farms, 1987..	2	11	7	9	7	-	7	5
1982..	20	35	7	17	8	1	8	2
acres on which used, 1987..	(D)	3 520	330	275	(D)	-	700	1 441
1982..	387	5 234	1 080	2 129	587	(D)	600	(D)

Chemicals used	Nemaha	Neosho	Ness	Norton	Osage	Osborne	Ottawa	Pawnee
Commercial fertilizer .... farms, 1987..	929	522	415	302	582	505	410	437
1982..	899	526	392	348	638	432	440	376
acres on which used, 1987..	182 318	104 534	123 520	120 711	79 826	157 060	127 811	161 401
1982..	181 867	96 698	131 295	134 186	103 322	140 689	173 347	162 660
Cropland fertilized, except pastureland .... farms, 1987..	853	463	401	302	551	505	402	436
1982..	856	468	384	346	583	432	440	370
acres on which used, 1987..	155 509	86 034	121 560	(D)	73 623	154 824	127 144	(D)
1982..	157 410	75 415	131 135	134 102	93 407	140 034	172 593	(D)
Pastureland and rangeland fertilized .... farms, 1987..	305	170	22	2	76	34	20	2
1982..	345	173	8	4	149	19	24	9
acres on which used, 1987..	25 809	18 500	1 960	(D)	6 203	2 236	667	(D)
1982..	24 457	21 283	160	84	9 915	855	754	(D)
Lime .... farms, 1987..	78	51	-	-	50	9	12	1
1982..	70	57	-	-	62	-	2	-
acres on which used, 1987..	3 140	1 830	-	-	3 508	540	300	(D)
1982..	6 732	3 167	-	-	3 399	-	(D)	-
tons, 1987..	8 151	5 482	-	-	8 085	882	701	(D)
1982..	20 852	8 168	-	-	10 012	-	(D)	-
Sprays, dusts, granules, fumigants, etc., to control—								
Insects on hay and other crops .... farms, 1987..	375	146	90	192	126	203	190	250
1982..	250	153	76	110	164	98	76	134
acres on which used, 1987..	33 244	11 051	6 996	24 543	20 054	21 195	12 350	43 127
1982..	33 192	18 569	4 248	21 978	18 845	11 687	4 873	25 560
Nematodes in crops .... farms, 1987..	33	2	-	-	4	-	7	1
1982..	15	4	-	2	7	1	2	2
acres on which used, 1987..	1 378	(D)	-	764	1 050	-	252	(D)
1982..	1 197	901	-	(D)	828	(D)	(D)	(D)
Diseases in crops and orchards .... farms, 1987..	19	12	3	3	10	3	7	2
1982..	26	13	2	2	13	-	20	1
acres on which used, 1987..	1 176	1 116	1 400	(D)	905	(D)	14	(D)
1982..	894	276	(D)	(D)	1 044	-	20	(D)
Weeds, grass, or brush in crops and pasture .... farms, 1987..	791	346	336	257	613	453	270	335
1982..	644	224	213	138	467	237	269	264
acres on which used, 1987..	126 112	69 671	111 936	49 584	109 421	125 515	76 024	99 587
1982..	99 469	38 917	30 917	30 326	80 903	40 117	76 752	51 207
Chemicals used for defoliation or for growth control of crops or thinning of fruit .... farms, 1987..	9	8	20	7	-	-	-	21
1982..	40	-	1	8	1	1	-	3
acres on which used, 1987..	122	76	1 184	1 815	-	-	-	810
1982..	3 948	-	-	(D)	469	(D)	(D)	665

Table 9. Agricultural Chemicals Used, Including Fertilizer and Lime: 1987 and 1982 — Con.

[Data are based on a sample of farms. For meaning of abbreviations and symbols, see introductory text]

Chemicals used	Phillips	Pottawatomie	Pratt	Rawlins	Reno	Republic	Rice	Riley
Commercial fertilizer .... farms, 1987..	433	500	439	384	1 043	724	446	373
1982..	512	561	432	445	1 160	673	521	397
acres on which used, 1987..	124 678	79 544	236 480	152 023	317 177	222 900	194 800	58 383
1982..	127 270	81 475	214 999	145 807	373 052	222 335	226 498	60 942
Cropland fertilized, except pastureland .... farms, 1987..	432	465	439	384	1 028	710	438	360
1982..	512	548	432	445	1 163	671	521	389
acres on which used, 1987..	123 868	74 897	235 511	(D)	315 879	220 852	194 415	57 015
1982..	126 210	74 603	213 087	145 767	368 862	218 189	226 126	60 266
Pastureland and rangeland fertilized .... farms, 1987..	10	92	11	1	33	50	12	51
1982..	6	81	13	4	55	78	18	24
acres on which used, 1987..	810	4 647	969	(D)	1 298	2 048	385	1 368
1982..	1 060	6 672	1 912	40	4 170	4 146	372	676
Lime .... farms, 1987..	-	31	10	-	143	15	44	13
1982..	8	52	-	-	57	15	20	11
acres on which used, 1987..	-	1 585	470	-	13 819	1 204	3 240	1 140
1982..	3 456	2 169	-	-	2 544	1 086	3 071	203
tons, 1987..	-	3 600	636	-	20 696	2 193	6 876	3 650
1982..	6 916	4 949	-	-	5 184	2 157	6 059	368
Sprays, dusts, granules, fumigants, etc., to control—								
Insects on hay and other crops .... farms, 1987..	202	256	158	225	475	400	217	166
1982..	64	188	64	104	347	249	215	91
acres on which used, 1987..	25 520	19 088	52 751	31 475	45 882	52 395	25 997	12 014
1982..	9 189	20 097	15 091	15 244	58 596	39 176	36 422	7 239
Nematodes in crops .... farms, 1987..	21	7	-	11	8	16	10	21
1982..	13	6	-	2	4	18	3	5
acres on which used, 1987..	4 562	539	-	1 327	433	1 397	1 085	441
1982..	2 059	1 694	-	(D)	394	1 596	395	300
Diseases in crops and orchards................ farms, 1987..	-	3	14	52	29	4	8	11
1982..	1	16	1	-	2	4	39	6
acres on which used, 1987..	-	(D)	2 090	3 419	3 786	1 407	1 993	(D)
1982..	(D)	1 485	(D)	-	(D)	1 382	1 755	1 347
Weeds, grass, or brush in crops and pasture... farms, 1987..	269	418	305	263	692	640	385	333
1982..	229	382	209	111	453	562	329	348
acres on which used, 1987..	73 481	84 933	105 304	63 807	113 606	171 232	116 754	56 402
1982..	31 858	59 166	88 776	20 166	75 177	139 888	80 559	56 037
Chemicals used for defoliation or for growth control of crops or thinning of fruit .... farms, 1987..	8	1	6	-	29	26	2	25
1982..	23	13	2	-	8	7	25	-
acres on which used, 1987..	984	(D)	6	-	1 268	1 368	(D)	266
1982..	3 231	1 489	(D)	-	1 687	1 311	1 423	-

Chemicals used	Rooks	Rush	Russell	Saline	Scott	Sedgwick	Seward	Shawnee
Commercial fertilizer .... farms, 1987..	325	359	343	559	231	1 129	204	518
1982..	385	386	449	572	222	1 176	198	554
acres on which used, 1987..	111 258	110 707	88 867	147 424	92 775	279 362	130 122	62 640
1982..	130 891	118 336	132 735	169 040	78 267	303 141	126 898	81 649
Cropland fertilized, except pastureland .... farms, 1987..	325	359	342	549	231	1 121	204	423
1982..	385	361	440	550	222	1 148	194	519
acres on which used, 1987..	111 258	109 597	(D)	147 076	92 775	279 061	(D)	52 452
1982..	(D)	117 596	130 630	168 516	(D)	300 680	128 836	76 672
Pastureland and rangeland fertilized .... farms, 1987..	1	9	5	17	-	11	2	170
1982..	1	5	30	42	1	76	4	85
acres on which used, 1987..	-	1 110	(D)	348	-	301	(D)	10 188
1982..	(D)	740	2 105	524	(D)	2 461	50	4 977
Lime .... farms, 1987..	-	-	2	4	-	125	-	25
1982..	-	-	1	25	-	86	-	23
acres on which used, 1987..	-	-	(D)	339	-	6 805	-	1 230
1982..	-	-	(D)	2 996	-	5 516	-	1 591
tons, 1987..	-	-	(D)	534	-	16 503	-	3 302
1982..	-	-	(D)	5 234	-	11 518	-	4 695
Sprays, dusts, granules, fumigants, etc., to control—								
Insects on hay and other crops .... farms, 1987..	136	102	95	266	100	461	148	179
1982..	131	45	36	90	163	455	84	168
acres on which used, 1987..	17 314	11 739	8 838	17 381	19 973	46 576	61 104	18 791
1982..	12 009	6 489	6 876	8 009	44 542	66 567	35 840	32 327
Nematodes in crops .... farms, 1987..	-	5	-	7	2	11	10	23
1982..	-	-	-	-	12	5	2	15
acres on which used, 1987..	-	105	-	345	(D)	352	2 245	619
1982..	-	-	(D)	504	2 441	(D)	663	663
Diseases in crops and orchards................ farms, 1987..	1	1	1	6	4	36	-	39
1982..	-	1	1	6	2	17	1	17
acres on which used, 1987..	(D)	(D)	(D)	(D)	495	990	-	1 210
1982..	(D)	(D)	(D)	(D)	(D)	840	(D)	337
Weeds, grass, or brush in crops and pasture... farms, 1987..	253	367	308	350	217	705	134	415
1982..	150	236	194	262	198	413	89	342
acres on which used, 1987..	74 975	86 021	71 159	77 155	69 577	144 346	64 088	67 275
1982..	20 057	24 766	25 376	46 766	53 961	85 468	47 517	59 431
Chemicals used for defoliation or for growth control of crops or thinning of fruit .... farms, 1987..	-	13	8	1	2	12	1	7
1982..	-	3	3	(D)	-	6	17	16
acres on which used, 1987..	-	3 120	320	(D)	-	(D)	(D)	203
1982..	-	-	150	(D)	-	4 461	2 172	261

Table 9. Agricultural Chemicals Used, Including Fertilizer and Lime: 1987 and 1982—Con.

[Data are based on a sample of farms. For meaning of abbreviations and symbols, see introductory text]

Chemicals used	Sheridan	Sherman	Smith	Stafford	Stanton	Stevens	Sumner	Thomas
Commercial fertilizer ... farms, 1987	372	350	570	453	206	244	1 018	476
1982	401	322	606	478	190	274	1 069	394
acres on which used, 1987	151 300	161 301	193 538	220 441	135 461	215 214	367 892	234 598
1982	149 189	153 728	205 310	221 721	149 075	231 274	470 954	171 329
Cropland fertilized, except pastureland ... farms, 1987	372	350	570	452	206	244	1 003	476
1982	401	322	599	478	190	273	1 066	394
acres on which used, 1987	(D)	161 301	193 359	219 213	135 261	215 214	365 013	234 598
1982	147 799	(D)	204 737	(D)	149 075	231 008	469 889	(D)
Pastureland and rangeland fertilized ... farms, 1987	2	-	4	12	10	-	34	-
1982	13	1	22	4	-	4	29	1
acres on which used, 1987	(D)	-	179	1 226	200	-	2 679	-
1982	1 390	(D)	573	(D)	-	266	1 065	(D)
Lime ... farms, 1987	-	-	-	19	-	-	51	-
1982	-	7	-	2	-	-	35	-
acres on which used, 1987	-	7	-	829	-	-	3 477	-
1982	-	280	-	(D)	-	-	2 132	-
tons, 1987	-	-	-	1 229	-	-	7 820	-
1982	-	700	-	(D)	-	-	6 320	-
Sprays, dusts, granules, fumigants, etc., to control—								
Insects on hay and other crops ... farms, 1987	304	247	338	222	155	106	242	254
1982	176	166	217	136	150	227	230	149
acres on which used, 1987	59 193	63 188	35 064	45 484	62 079	65 814	25 559	66 703
1982	44 268	54 247	30 943	34 962	82 153	140 068	28 807	48 790
Nematodes in crops ... farms, 1987	8	6	2	9	4	5	6	8
1982	14	17	20	2	4	5	7	14
acres on which used, 1987	1 424	1 871	(D)	771	1 341	2 290	1 199	1 453
1982	1 934	3 542	354	(D)	990	6 206	1 710	8 004
Diseases in crops and orchards ... farms, 1987	1	48	10	11	3	4	4	15
1982	3	46	2	6	1	-	13	15
acres on which used, 1987	(D)	7 235	5 712	1 792	516	970	2 170	2 076
1982	1 965	4 422	(D)	2 817	(D)	-	(D)	10 236
Weeds, grass, or brush in crops and pasture ... farms, 1987	228	297	562	304	157	205	578	329
1982	155	179	397	227	142	194	413	215
acres on which used, 1987	57 391	84 189	144 211	91 988	79 054	123 284	142 125	89 473
1982	43 627	61 791	72 107	50 958	89 696	130 333	100 662	72 006
Chemicals used for defoliation or for growth control of crops or thinning of fruit ... farms, 1987	7	3	20	1	-	9	4	2
1982	4	25	13	18	-	18	10	-
acres on which used, 1987	1 865	778	3 680	(D)	-	1 084	1 289	-
1982	1 145	2 945	1 906	967	-	2 116	80	(D)

Chemicals used	Trego	Wabaunsee	Wallace	Washington	Wichita	Wilson	Woodson	Wyandotte
Commercial fertilizer ... farms, 1987	327	449	195	694	193	451	239	71
1982	326	434	132	621	228	504	278	101
acres on which used, 1987	102 305	67 421	94 049	195 355	92 941	96 499	51 798	7 798
1982	105 057	64 620	86 667	223 105	110 848	98 328	53 763	7 812
Cropland fertilized, except pastureland ... farms, 1987	327	371	195	686	192	414	226	65
1982	326	412	132	611	226	483	235	88
acres on which used, 1987	(D)	58 139	(D)	191 067	(D)	90 815	40 878	6 151
1982	(D)	59 743	86 667	219 948	90 384	44 785	6 821	
Pastureland and rangeland fertilized ... farms, 1987	1	151	1	61	2	99	69	30
1982	1	61	-	74	2	88	101	21
acres on which used, 1987	(D)	9 282	(D)	4 288	(D)	5 664	11 120	1 647
1982	(D)	4 677	-	3 157		7 944	8 978	991
Lime ... farms, 1987	-	23	-	31	-	50	27	-
1982	-	23	-	30	-	25	25	-
acres on which used, 1987	-	726	-	1 590	-	3 005	497	-
1982	-	494	-	1 549	-	1 330	1 194	-
tons, 1987	-	1 852	-	2 644	-	6 740	1 359	-
1982	-	1 855	-	3 946	-	2 987	3 170	-
Sprays, dusts, granules, fumigants, etc., to control—								
Insects on hay and other crops ... farms, 1987	70	180	127	307	148	217	66	27
1982	14	137	71	270	209	171	72	42
acres on which used, 1987	5 829	16 924	35 772	38 656	34 787	19 450	7 880	972
1982	2 302	15 145	27 747	39 479	59 999	19 672	7 581	2 021
Nematodes in crops ... farms, 1987	5	1	1	12	7	1	6	2
1982	2	5	3	10	11	8	8	-
acres on which used, 1987	330	(D)	(D)	1 120	486	(D)	(D)	-
1982	(D)	100	200	699	938	250	570	(D)
Diseases in crops and orchards ... farms, 1987	2	1	5	1	4	4	9	13
1982	-	13	6	4	11	10	20	
acres on which used, 1987	(D)	13	1 009	(D)	1 843	1 294	93	73
1982	-	564	1 030	350	2 356	(D)	4 605	175
Weeds, grass, or brush in crops and pasture ... farms, 1987	334	327	149	651	184	272	205	73
1982	146	259	85	614	206	294	185	63
acres on which used, 1987	58 783	48 416	48 733	158 049	49 075	68 361	47 649	8 937
1982	20 209	34 063	39 443	135 533	101 663	57 933	36 914	5 855
Chemicals used for defoliation or for growth control of crops or thinning of fruit ... farms, 1987	2	-	-	2	4	-	1	1
1982	-	-	1	10	10	-	1	2
acres on which used, 1987	(D)	-	-	(D)	626	-	(D)	(D)
1982	-	-	(D)	2 733	1 663	-	(D)	(D)

[For meaning of abbreviations and symbols, see introductory text]

Characteristics	Kansas	Allen	Anderson	Atchison	Barber	Barton	Bourbon
FARMS							
Land in farms ... farms, 1987	68 579	665	727	694	535	937	842
1982	73 315	735	797	766	517	962	882
acres, 1987	46 628 519	276 555	352 141	233 619	700 147	556 433	318 958
1982	47 052 213	283 878	361 247	234 730	698 700	559 531	337 259
Harvested cropland ... farms, 1987	57 822	564	611	589	415	806	645
1982	62 860	614	667	637	445	871	705
acres, 1987	17 729 394	125 078	161 985	122 717	149 449	262 060	90 939
1982	20 186 974	137 642	167 000	129 487	190 605	314 881	121 086
TENURE OF OPERATOR							
Full owners ... farms, 1987	29 956	344	341	402	196	345	517
1982	31 834	372	403	421	163	332	497
acres, 1987	8 839 919	70 849	74 751	75 839	118 576	91 436	107 849
1982	10 524 533	72 623	98 700	69 237	127 076	101 409	104 870
Harvested cropland ... farms, 1987	21 783	268	252	308	123	240	348
1982	23 963	276	264	306	124	267	369
acres, 1987	2 909 784	25 981	31 702	33 526	21 911	39 826	25 393
1982	3 955 987	25 509	36 714	31 741	30 051	51 328	29 873
Part owners ... farms, 1987	27 987	272	291	291	199	396	272
1982	29 862	292	303	247	218	434	318
acres, 1987	30 896 557	187 919	247 115	132 666	433 718	367 004	176 732
1982	30 376 105	168 709	238 427	139 391	434 403	370 981	209 941
Owned land in farms ... acres, 1987	12 338 403	78 326	105 504	54 800	164 452	146 484	82 729
1982	12 888 497	89 965	111 227	63 679	209 267	151 063	104 660
Rented land in farms ... acres, 1987	18 558 154	109 593	141 611	77 866	269 266	220 520	94 003
1982	17 491 608	98 744	127 200	75 712	225 136	219 918	105 281
Harvested cropland ... farms, 1987	26 819	255	279	206	188	382	254
1982	26 775	282	298	241	208	430	289
acres, 1987	11 996 753	68 830	114 064	74 445	96 804	175 514	57 937
1982	13 330 629	100 351	115 892	61 708	125 248	215 916	80 908
Tenants ... farms, 1987	10 656	49	95	83	140	196	53
1982	11 619	71	91	100	136	196	66
acres, 1987	6 692 043	17 787	30 275	25 094	147 851	97 993	34 377
1982	6 149 575	22 546	24 120	26 102	137 221	87 141	22 448
Harvested cropland ... farms, 1987	9 220	41	80	75	104	184	43
1982	10 122	56	85	90	113	174	47
acres, 1987	2 822 857	10 267	16 229	14 746	30 734	46 720	7 609
1982	2 900 358	11 782	14 394	16 038	35 306	47 637	10 305
OPERATOR CHARACTERISTICS							
Operators by place of residence:							
On farm operated ... 1987	45 527	493	514	501	269	589	586
1982	46 356	533	586	537	252	608	635
Not on farm operated ... 1987	17 871	133	150	141	214	275	177
1982	17 026	124	124	149	208	260	155
Not reported ... 1987	5 181	39	63	52	52	73	79
1982	7 933	78	87	82	57	94	92
Operators by principal occupation:							
Farming ... 1987	42 607	407	430	426	367	608	426
1982	47 293	433	506	494	399	658	518
Other ... 1987	25 972	258	297	268	168	329	416
1982	26 022	302	291	274	118	304	364
Operators by days of work off farm:							
None ... 1987	29 462	290	288	309	247	400	345
1982	30 524	293	331	328	225	397	361
Any ... 1987	34 654	320	382	333	237	469	438
1982	35 521	358	389	365	228	461	436
1 to 49 days ... 1987	5 265	48	47	36	49	87	31
1982	6 247	60	59	57	46	74	66
50 to 99 days ... 1987	2 355	18	28	17	22	40	13
1982	2 405	18	31	19	19	46	33
100 to 149 days ... 1987	2 246	20	25	12	12	43	27
1982	2 350	16	29	22	24	35	27
150 to 199 days ... 1987	3 111	37	36	38	14	55	56
1982	3 213	32	34	38	11	46	48
200 days or more ... 1987	21 677	197	246	230	140	243	309
1982	21 306	232	236	229	128	260	262
Not reported ... 1987	4 463	55	57	52	51	68	61
1982	7 270	84	77	75	64	104	85
Operators by years on present farm:							
2 years or less ... 1987	3 511	20	34	35	42	47	42
1982	3 376	27	36	29	36	41	40
3 or 4 years ... 1987	3 873	34	32	39	28	70	51
1982	5 484	41	57	56	36	75	51
5 to 9 years ... 1987	8 552	66	95	75	58	99	120
1982	10 297	90	92	103	65	144	129
10 years or more ... 1987	40 624	427	421	420	295	533	459
1982	39 238	430	427	407	279	511	497
Average years on present farm ... 1987	21.3	22.6	21.0	20.9	21.7	22.4	20.1
1982	20.2	20.5	19.5	20.2	20.3	21.6	19.7
Not reported ... 1987	12 019	118	145	126	112	188	170
1982	14 920	147	185	173	102	191	165

[For meaning of abbreviations and symbols, see introductory text]

Characteristics		Brown	Butler	Chase	Chautauqua	Cherokee	Cheyenne	Clark
FARMS								
Land in farms	farms, 1987..	728	1 300	288	421	841	493	290
	1982..	826	1 376	295	431	939	546	308
	acres, 1987..	339 853	699 487	328 905	320 956	280 704	619 870	587 574
	1982..	346 340	691 281	414 905	333 958	296 718	602 726	588 288
Harvested cropland	farms, 1987..	637	934	223	248	657	426	233
	1982..	732	1 053	238	294	729	491	254
	acres, 1987..	197 847	210 975	45 580	35 741	156 409	176 293	92 271
	1982..	226 953	225 388	49 790	40 581	186 648	197 174	113 399
TENURE OF OPERATOR								
Full owners	farms, 1987..	357	691	122	246	452	167	90
	1982..	388	743	128	240	489	216	98
	acres, 1987..	85 408	162 345	61 677	111 628	63 442	132 208	74 705
	1982..	102 338	184 803	105 780	114 319	72 622	183 983	125 911
Harvested cropland	farms, 1987..	279	412	86	123	296	120	65
	1982..	311	502	95	140	320	183	70
	acres, 1987..	47 243	35 417	9 152	9 294	23 880	35 484	13 252
	1982..	56 859	43 763	12 211	11 072	35 322	57 061	26 051
Part owners	farms, 1987..	248	466	104	126	312	238	127
	1982..	282	481	122	149	357	238	137
	acres, 1987..	204 901	465 330	171 722	182 645	194 381	415 021	385 998
	1982..	192 534	455 904	226 260	193 606	203 697	372 363	329 561
Owned land in farms	acres, 1987..	79 487	179 134	70 867	74 447	76 523	210 102	149 415
	1982..	81 832	191 779	71 215	84 738	83 382	198 480	114 573
Rented land in farms	acres, 1987..	125 414	286 196	100 855	108 198	117 858	204 919	236 583
	1982..	110 702	264 125	155 045	108 870	120 515	173 883	214 988
Harvested cropland	farms, 1987..	243	418	87	99	292	232	114
	1982..	274	442	109	120	335	235	129
	acres, 1987..	119 469	153 057	24 886	21 579	117 272	116 173	63 559
	1982..	130 862	161 132	26 645	24 547	138 334	123 692	68 164
Tenants	farms, 1987..	123	143	62	49	77	88	73
	1982..	156	152	45	42	93	92	73
	acres, 1987..	49 544	71 812	95 506	26 683	22 861	72 641	126 871
	1982..	51 468	70 574	82 885	26 031	20 199	46 400	132 816
Harvested cropland	farms, 1987..	115	106	50	26	69	74	54
	1982..	147	109	34	34	74	73	55
	acres, 1987..	31 135	22 501	11 542	4 868	15 257	24 636	15 460
	1982..	37 232	20 493	10 934	4 962	12 992	16 421	19 184
OPERATOR CHARACTERISTICS								
Operators by place of residence:								
On farm operated	1987..	510	971	190	278	630	300	143
	1982..	575	964	199	288	702	305	154
Not on farm operated	1987..	168	254	78	114	145	149	128
	1982..	171	257	62	88	135	175	118
Not reported	1987..	50	75	20	29	66	44	19
	1982..	80	135	34	55	102	66	36
Operators by principal occupation:								
Farming	1987..	543	657	189	222	438	373	203
	1982..	637	656	214	248	487	420	236
Other	1987..	185	643	99	199	403	120	87
	1982..	189	720	81	183	452	126	72
Operators by days of work off farm:								
None	1987..	399	506	126	162	303	246	133
	1982..	449	482	125	158	375	270	155
Any	1987..	284	746	146	236	481	209	140
	1982..	289	827	137	231	482	213	119
1 to 49 days	1987..	55	77	24	24	46	55	26
	1982..	88	119	41	27	52	65	32
50 to 99 days	1987..	30	42	11	13	30	20	16
	1982..	21	47	11	13	35	25	8
100 to 149 days	1987..	20	42	11	11	29	13	4
	1982..	13	46	12	16	31	13	10
150 to 199 days	1987..	17	52	16	26	33	22	14
	1982..	20	50	13	26	34	16	7
200 days or more	1987..	162	533	84	155	343	99	80
	1982..	147	565	60	149	330	94	62
Not reported	1987..	45	48	16	23	57	38	17
	1982..	88	87	33	42	82	63	34
Operators by years on present farm:								
2 years or less	1987..	31	72	16	30	40	21	15
	1982..	36	69	14	19	48	26	11
3 or 4 years	1987..	42	80	16	20	43	26	22
	1982..	62	106	23	40	60	45	30
5 to 9 years	1987..	83	206	44	56	111	44	48
	1982..	101	262	46	65	128	64	37
10 years or more	1987..	469	760	171	253	477	306	161
	1982..	465	684	158	216	485	285	166
Average years on present farm	1987..	22.7	19.0	21.3	19.4	20.3	24.1	20.1
	1982..	21.6	17.7	22.0	16.3	19.1	22.3	20.5
Not reported	1987..	103	182	41	62	170	96	44
	1982..	162	255	54	91	218	126	64

Table 10. **Tenure and Characteristics of Operator and Type of Organization: 1987 and 1982**—Con.

[For meaning of abbreviations and symbols. see introductory text]

Characteristics		Clay	Cloud	Coffey	Comanche	Cowley	Crawford	Decatur
FARMS								
Land in farms	farms, 1987	672	659	606	277	997	809	486
	1982	719	726	671	259	1 101	915	516
	acres, 1987	392 321	397 363	330 435	481 136	619 647	283 589	543 466
	1982	365 074	403 290	335 242	462 734	599 678	325 082	535 067
Harvested cropland	farms, 1987	586	583	515	209	760	649	438
	1982	647	642	572	215	885	725	459
	acres, 1987	176 217	184 007	142 868	93 062	160 551	116 714	175 861
	1982	189 827	214 074	157 589	118 915	212 326	155 932	172 683
TENURE OF OPERATOR								
Full owners	farms, 1987	249	266	246	105	454	471	147
	1982	290	286	301	88	485	499	156
	acres, 1987	67 427	71 755	48 273	119 089	128 515	90 611	84 614
	1982	76 954	90 176	60 091	138 351	164 116	90 559	106 425
Harvested cropland	farms, 1987	179	208	186	62	267	338	119
	1982	226	221	219	69	341	338	118
	acres, 1987	25 140	31 236	18 352	19 363	24 639	26 077	29 669
	1982	36 230	42 535	22 651	24 929	38 305	32 966	33 071
Part owners	farms, 1987	306	280	272	117	402	270	236
	1982	299	283	263	107	437	338	265
	acres, 1987	266 333	269 104	251 336	302 048	406 175	171 366	371 094
	1982	242 691	254 032	245 004	243 040	462 231	217 840	375 228
Owned land in farms	acres, 1987	106 215	94 513	92 345	115 039	174 519	71 770	167 031
	1982	107 701	106 138	95 153	98 188	196 919	101 586	161 131
Rented land in farms	acres, 1987	160 118	174 591	158 991	187 009	231 656	99 596	204 063
	1982	134 990	147 894	149 851	144 852	265 312	116 254	214 497
Harvested cropland	farms, 1987	299	271	263	109	368	261	231
	1982	295	278	278	102	396	325	261
	acres, 1987	122 748	123 340	108 872	61 621	116 521	78 079	118 368
	1982	124 726	136 199	120 667	71 226	144 587	114 113	120 955
Tenants	farms, 1987	117	113	88	55	141	68	103
	1982	130	157	87	64	179	78	95
	acres, 1987	58 561	56 524	30 826	59 999	84 957	21 612	87 758
	1982	45 429	59 082	30 147	81 343	73 331	16 683	53 414
Harvested cropland	farms, 1987	108	104	66	38	105	52	88
	1982	124	143	75	54	148	52	80
	acres, 1987	28 329	29 431	15 444	12 078	19 391	12 558	27 624
	1982	28 869	35 340	14 251	22 760	29 434	8 853	18 656
OPERATOR CHARACTERISTICS								
Operators by place of residence:								
On farm operated	1987	456	417	425	146	703	566	290
	1982	495	429	482	143	793	637	316
Not on farm operated	1987	156	197	136	101	227	158	158
	1982	121	221	111	86	201	165	151
Not reported	1987	60	45	45	30	67	85	38
	1982	103	76	78	30	107	113	49
Operators by principal occupation:								
Farming	1987	497	449	368	200	516	447	382
	1982	540	502	428	194	605	500	406
Other	1987	175	210	238	77	481	362	104
	1982	179	224	243	65	496	415	110
Operators by days of work off farm:								
None	1987	333	309	253	132	352	347	239
	1982	345	339	290	115	361	368	248
Any	1987	265	301	318	117	603	403	215
	1982	283	323	316	107	654	478	215
1 to 49 days	1987	68	67	42	35	55	34	68
	1982	62	62	58	20	90	52	75
50 to 99 days	1987	28	19	34	9	33	35	21
	1982	29	20	18	8	41	22	20
100 to 149 days	1987	26	27	16	5	36	13	20
	1982	15	24	24	10	47	30	17
150 to 199 days	1987	28	22	27	8	51	40	21
	1982	26	29	33	12	71	51	30
200 days or more	1987	135	166	199	60	428	281	85
	1982	151	188	183	59	405	323	73
Not reported	1987	54	49	35	28	42	59	32
	1982	91	64	65	37	86	69	53
Operators by years on present farm:								
2 years or less	1987	34	33	35	14	62	27	34
	1982	27	47	38	15	42	23	26
3 or 4 years	1987	38	38	29	15	62	26	26
	1982	50	73	52	22	77	67	42
5 to 9 years	1987	75	74	92	32	124	97	63
	1982	69	93	84	40	174	142	57
10 years or more	1987	398	395	362	164	588	488	272
	1982	393	376	365	122	586	478	272
Average years on present farm	1987	23.3	22.4	21.0	23.6	20.6	21.5	22.4
	1982	22.8	19.8	19.3	19.2	19.2	19.1	21.9
Not reported	1987	129	119	88	52	161	169	89
	1982	180	137	132	60	222	205	114

Table 10. **Tenure and Characteristics of Operator and Type of Organization: 1987 and 1982**—Con.

[For meaning of abbreviations and symbols, see introductory text]

Characteristics		Dickinson	Doniphan	Douglas	Edwards	Elk	Ellis	Ellsworth
FARMS								
Land in farms	farms, 1987__	1 028	530	852	361	409	795	499
	1982__	1 149	520	896	402	467	790	527
	acres, 1987__	513 946	216 179	223 426	387 309	340 899	568 934	423 855
	1982__	527 451	224 519	222 859	382 477	364 902	509 050	387 572
Harvested cropland	farms, 1987__	908	454	691	328	293	691	450
	1982__	1 012	543	740	373	346	695	471
	acres, 1987__	245 504	127 586	106 664	166 513	40 040	147 980	128 533
	1982__	297 527	150 592	112 306	206 856	54 719	162 248	146 178
TENURE OF OPERATOR								
Full owners	farms, 1987__	442	250	526	100	205	302	146
	1982__	492	282	553	116	234	318	151
	acres, 1987__	96 734	44 806	69 430	57 267	106 386	113 114	48 064
	1982__	116 845	59 313	75 687	80 764	120 450	122 073	62 263
Harvested cropland	farms, 1987__	340	180	392	79	127	231	113
	1982__	390	215	425	97	150	254	115
	acres, 1987__	41 102	22 060	23 406	23 825	10 985	26 009	16 127
	1982__	60 664	35 720	25 835	36 961	15 406	37 631	23 533
Part owners	farms, 1987__	446	182	249	192	152	345	251
	1982__	484	204	263	186	178	314	252
	acres, 1987__	352 360	137 637	135 305	280 266	197 880	392 995	310 595
	1982__	354 276	125 907	126 725	240 602	214 581	319 998	258 420
Owned land in farms	acres, 1987__	129 104	53 199	53 409	108 347	84 715	184 403	125 465
	1982__	142 439	53 065	56 890	101 895	98 873	152 537	111 303
Rented land in farms	acres, 1987__	223 256	84 438	81 926	171 919	113 165	208 592	185 230
	1982__	211 837	72 842	69 835	138 907	115 708	167 461	147 117
Harvested cropland	farms, 1987__	435	179	232	187	131	337	247
	1982__	470	200	247	163	161	306	246
	acres, 1987__	171 331	83 943	73 806	137 734	22 437	104 413	92 354
	1982__	201 063	86 188	74 954	134 521	33 920	100 589	93 990
Tenants	farms, 1987__	140	98	77	69	52	148	102
	1982__	173	134	80	100	55	158	124
	acres, 1987__	64 852	33 736	18 661	49 776	36 633	62 825	64 896
	1982__	58 330	39 299	20 447	60 911	29 871	66 979	66 889
Harvested cropland	farms, 1987__	133	95	67	62	35	123	90
	1982__	152	128	68	93	35	135	110
	acres, 1987__	33 071	21 683	11 452	24 954	6 618	17 558	20 052
	1982__	35 800	28 684	11 517	33 374	5 393	23 828	28 655
OPERATOR CHARACTERISTICS								
Operators by place of residence:								
On farm operated	1987__	737	367	647	200	256	421	316
	1982__	824	402	693	215	289	447	332
Not on farm operated	1987__	215	122	148	127	110	294	146
	1982__	201	147	134	141	137	214	138
Not reported	1987__	76	41	57	34	43	80	37
	1982__	124	71	69	46	41	129	57
Operators by principal occupation:								
Farming	1987__	670	364	360	284	245	471	349
	1982__	804	433	426	323	280	475	406
Other	1987__	358	166	492	77	164	324	150
	1982__	345	187	470	79	187	315	121
Operators by days of work off farm:								
None	1987__	475	275	266	190	162	280	243
	1982__	529	299	309	201	169	279	246
Any	1987__	497	215	533	134	210	452	226
	1982__	498	262	522	152	257	439	214
1 to 49 days	1987__	66	44	38	36	21	77	37
	1982__	103	56	45	42	31	41	57
50 to 99 days	1987__	54	16	23	13	13	26	21
	1982__	38	21	20	14	14	24	20
100 to 149 days	1987__	38	6	30	7	10	22	12
	1982__	31	12	24	17	21	36	8
150 to 199 days	1987__	42	15	36	9	11	51	26
	1982__	54	31	37	13	48	42	13
200 days or more	1987__	297	134	406	69	155	260	130
	1982__	272	142	396	66	143	296	118
Not reported	1987__	56	40	53	37	37	63	30
	1982__	122	59	65	49	41	72	67
Operators by years on present farm:								
2 years or less	1987__	38	35	44	19	18	40	11
	1982__	45	44	50	24	26	28	25
3 or 4 years	1987__	57	20	48	19	19	48	31
	1982__	75	49	72	32	37	68	30
5 to 9 years	1987__	124	52	91	44	47	97	56
	1982__	128	75	133	62	65	113	78
10 years or more	1987__	643	326	528	208	250	416	310
	1982__	657	326	499	245	245	386	270
Average years on present farm	1987__	23.2	21.9	20.8	22.8	22.0	20.1	23.5
	1982__	23.2	18.6	19.6	21.2	20.0	20.3	22.5
Not reported	1987__	166	97	141	71	75	192	91
	1982__	244	126	142	87	94	195	124

290 KANSAS

Table 10. Tenure and Characteristics of Operator and Type of Organization: 1987 and 1982—Con.

[For meaning of abbreviations and symbols, see introductory text]

Characteristics	Finney	Ford	Franklin	Geary	Gove	Graham	Grant
FARMS							
Land in farms ... farms, 1987..	534	812	979	295	534	452	303
1982..	558	836	1 067	299	548	495	278
acres, 1987..	722 746	674 966	312 783	170 339	676 575	503 589	323 138
1982..	721 624	691 933	304 871	156 662	674 683	523 102	332 993
Harvested cropland ... farms, 1987..	463	703	798	239	454	403	258
1982..	494	730	895	250	485	464	236
acres, 1987..	323 607	284 042	135 097	48 216	194 728	148 177	156 356
1982..	384 552	301 832	142 823	50 305	195 149	161 560	199 136
TENURE OF OPERATOR							
Full owners ... farms, 1987..	164	304	583	136	194	134	84
1982..	171	321	651	130	188	152	70
acres, 1987..	142 765	133 600	86 592	44 476	128 049	61 947	35 735
1982..	128 435	173 194	94 346	27 114	147 083	88 661	48 606
Harvested cropland ... farms, 1987..	110	221	435	96	136	97	46
1982..	134	245	480	95	153	132	44
acres, 1987..	41 966	54 398	26 897	9 098	32 581	18 064	14 753
1982..	63 578	79 147	32 509	7 275	45 274	27 876	26 801
Part owners ... farms, 1987..	230	338	313	108	245	216	127
1982..	238	332	360	114	246	271	125
acres, 1987..	411 755	412 607	193 791	99 330	479 565	378 990	198 269
1982..	445 599	412 246	191 800	104 973	457 494	402 800	212 782
Owned land in farms ... acres, 1987..	142 468	174 868	73 636	46 467	208 297	152 131	49 674
1982..	168 573	170 817	90 848	47 479	212 921	174 362	61 448
Rented land in farms ... acres, 1987..	269 287	237 739	120 153	52 863	271 268	226 859	148 595
1982..	277 026	241 429	100 952	57 494	244 563	228 438	151 334
Harvested cropland ... farms, 1987..	226	329	292	101	238	211	123
1982..	230	322	347	112	241	264	123
acres, 1987..	195 852	173 726	90 833	29 824	141 711	109 306	95 726
1982..	234 283	170 996	99 263	33 323	127 443	121 070	123 910
Tenants ... farms, 1987..	140	170	83	51	95	102	92
1982..	149	183	76	55	112	72	81
acres, 1987..	168 226	128 779	30 400	26 533	68 961	62 652	89 134
1982..	147 590	106 493	18 725	24 575	70 116	31 641	71 605
Harvested cropland ... farms, 1987..	127	153	72	42	80	95	89
1982..	130	163	68	43	91	68	69
acres, 1987..	85 989	55 918	15 367	9 294	20 436	20 807	45 877
1982..	86 691	51 689	11 051	9 707	22 432	12 614	46 425
OPERATOR CHARACTERISTICS							
Operators by place of residence:							
On farm operated ... 1987..	296	448	729	223	311	240	178
1982..	292	424	820	213	291	255	172
Not on farm operated ... 1987..	193	301	186	51	174	171	98
1982..	180	303	174	57	165	192	73
Not reported ... 1987..	45	63	64	21	49	41	27
1982..	86	109	93	29	92	48	31
Operators by principal occupation:							
Farming ... 1987..	379	522	431	166	391	331	228
1982..	423	526	503	191	413	337	223
Other ... 1987..	155	290	548	129	143	121	75
1982..	135	310	584	108	135	158	53
Operators by days of work off farm:							
None ... 1987..	281	345	326	122	270	215	171
1982..	297	322	361	131	238	187	165
Any ... 1987..	217	404	606	156	224	205	106
1982..	195	422	669	139	232	243	82
1 to 49 days ... 1987..	39	66	45	18	42	40	26
1982..	39	87	90	24	46	60	23
50 to 99 days ... 1987..	20	22	21	10	15	24	8
1982..	14	21	39	6	19	22	5
100 to 149 days ... 1987..	10	38	24	9	19	16	6
1982..	9	28	36	13	20	7	5
150 to 199 days ... 1987..	22	38	46	8	34	19	17
1982..	18	28	44	9	29	26	4
200 days or more ... 1987..	126	240	470	114	114	106	49
1982..	115	258	460	87	118	128	45
Not reported ... 1987..	36	63	47	17	40	32	26
1982..	66	92	57	29	78	65	29
Operators by years on present farm:							
2 years or less ... 1987..	26	57	59	12	39	13	24
1982..	31	49	49	15	25	21	10
3 or 4 years ... 1987..	29	58	48	20	32	37	21
1982..	31	76	111	18	46	22	28
5 to 9 years ... 1987..	67	98	113	38	65	54	40
1982..	93	97	191	40	81	75	42
10 years or more ... 1987..	326	439	631	169	301	242	159
1982..	289	417	557	158	250	259	156
Average years on present farm ... 1987..	20.9	20.5	19.9	22.4	21.8	21.6	18.3
1982..	19.9	19.5	16.9	21.1	19.8	21.3	18.1
Not reported ... 1987..	86	160	130	56	97	106	59
1982..	114	197	179	68	146	118	40

Table 10. **Tenure and Characteristics of Operator and Type of Organization: 1987 and 1982**—Con.

[For meaning of abbreviations and symbols, see introductory text]

Characteristics		Gray	Greeley	Greenwood	Hamilton	Harper	Harvey	Haskell
FARMS								
Land in farms	farms, 1987..	547	294	587	279	648	874	315
	1982..	552	277	651	270	660	923	324
	acres, 1987..	532 284	475 278	549 507	538 449	484 471	309 123	369 850
	1982..	536 969	445 982	601 823	544 916	490 455	320 935	361 301
Harvested cropland	farms, 1987..	480	266	409	225	595	740	284
	1982..	502	259	499	237	617	826	290
	acres, 1987..	258 379	196 152	73 937	160 504	233 900	197 917	200 065
	1982..	325 993	193 327	81 666	204 376	288 418	232 904	249 122
TENURE OF OPERATOR								
Full owners	farms, 1987..	176	100	279	75	224	354	96
	1982..	150	88	298	78	205	351	103
	acres, 1987..	86 787	51 314	122 017	71 158	70 517	39 500	68 378
	1982..	87 460	66 673	113 241	64 044	67 818	56 289	72 941
Harvested cropland	farms, 1987..	120	79	163	50	188	244	68
	1982..	108	80	202	52	169	279	75
	acres, 1987..	43 326	21 635	14 836	16 415	31 257	20 811	36 919
	1982..	52 057	31 952	18 458	21 335	38 858	35 872	47 393
Part owners	farms, 1987..	232	124	233	144	291	393	133
	1982..	253	125	270	140	305	434	130
	acres, 1987..	327 954	335 619	375 036	392 496	323 249	229 378	210 260
	1982..	367 582	295 313	441 537	420 320	341 463	225 783	203 920
Owned land in farms	acres, 1987..	134 584	120 732	173 614	148 496	114 890	81 115	67 572
	1982..	154 534	111 480	162 140	170 885	136 811	83 169	76 763
Rented land in farms	acres, 1987..	193 390	214 887	201 422	244 000	208 559	148 263	142 708
	1982..	213 048	183 833	279 397	249 435	204 652	142 614	127 157
Harvested cropland	farms, 1987..	229	122	197	127	269	386	131
	1982..	251	125	240	137	304	424	129
	acres, 1987..	157 011	133 462	48 678	116 996	159 462	151 808	111 319
	1982..	219 299	123 741	55 344	158 317	200 656	167 456	143 859
Tenants	farms, 1987..	139	70	75	60	133	127	86
	1982..	149	64	83	52	150	138	91
	acres, 1987..	117 543	86 045	52 454	74 795	90 703	40 245	91 192
	1982..	81 927	83 996	47 045	60 552	81 174	38 863	84 440
Harvested cropland	farms, 1987..	131	65	49	48	118	110	85
	1982..	143	54	57	48	144	123	86
	acres, 1987..	58 042	41 055	10 421	27 093	43 181	25 298	51 827
	1982..	54 637	37 634	7 884	24 724	48 904	29 576	57 870
OPERATOR CHARACTERISTICS								
Operators by place of residence:								
On farm operated	1987..	298	150	396	146	381	662	170
	1982..	295	135	429	130	395	687	156
Not on farm operated	1987..	185	125	162	103	229	172	109
	1982..	209	105	171	103	190	154	109
Not reported	1987..	64	19	29	26	38	40	36
	1982..	48	37	51	37	75	82	59
Operators by principal occupation:								
Farming	1987..	423	216	324	201	452	479	250
	1982..	429	211	399	207	503	530	270
Other	1987..	124	78	263	78	196	395	65
	1982..	123	66	252	63	157	393	54
Operators by days of work off farm:								
None	1987..	265	151	230	144	306	322	173
	1982..	273	146	248	143	316	313	174
Any	1987..	245	126	312	119	298	520	109
	1982..	234	100	351	103	268	551	90
1 to 49 days	1987..	62	36	41	26	46	86	34
	1982..	68	25	46	20	59	84	24
50 to 99 days	1987..	26	8	13	12	23	24	11
	1982..	20	5	19	6	26	37	6
100 to 149 days	1987..	19	13	16	10	23	38	2
	1982..	15	16	27	8	27	39	2
150 to 199 days	1987..	18	13	29	7	34	45	9
	1982..	20	13	25	10	16	41	8
200 days or more	1987..	118	56	213	62	172	330	53
	1982..	111	41	224	59	138	350	50
Not reported	1987..	37	17	45	16	44	32	33
	1982..	45	31	52	24	76	59	60
Operators by years on present farm:								
2 years or less	1987..	33	25	24	20	36	49	19
	1982..	39	5	32	18	15	40	25
3 or 4 years	1987..	29	22	32	21	34	61	14
	1982..	50	16	43	15	45	70	19
5 to 9 years	1987..	32	32	81	38	72	109	40
	1982..	85	38	92	18	79	140	40
10 years or more	1987..	304	166	371	145	394	544	177
	1982..	279	147	364	155	403	540	153
Average years on present farm	1987..	19.3	20.4	21.5	19.9	22.3	20.7	20.5
	1982..	17.9	22.2	20.4	21.7	22.5	19.9	18.1
Not reported	1987..	98	49	79	55	112	111	65
	1982..	99	71	120	64	118	133	87

Table 10. **Tenure and Characteristics of Operator and Type of Organization: 1987 and 1982**—Con.

[For meaning of abbreviations and symbols, see introductory text]

Characteristics		Hodgeman	Jackson	Jefferson	Jewell	Johnson	Kearny	Kingman	Kiowa
FARMS									
Land in farms	farms, 1987..	423	1 082	1 017	736	659	291	818	310
	1982..	466	1 156	1 047	808	766	297	860	354
	acres, 1987..	495 080	335 142	263 592	502 106	151 763	549 371	517 652	392 245
	1982..	482 739	376 330	271 691	510 447	169 986	532 077	492 197	422 852
Harvested cropland	farms, 1987..	382	844	836	647	496	247	718	276
	1982..	417	951	855	719	555	242	772	317
	acres, 1987..	159 903	114 691	112 895	208 845	69 445	202 166	219 446	128 425
	1982..	164 424	139 408	128 243	249 175	89 698	218 509	265 252	144 636
TENURE OF OPERATOR									
Full owners	farms, 1987..	129	641	629	267	384	89	275	90
	1982..	126	684	660	322	462	96	300	101
	acres, 1987..	55 411	112 742	83 533	104 204	36 316	78 723	64 985	48 952
	1982..	77 873	127 314	97 127	129 228	47 771	108 243	82 392	58 969
Harvested cropland	farms, 1987..	98	449	482	203	257	60	216	69
	1982..	106	511	499	258	298	66	237	81
	acres, 1987..	19 348	33 429	27 165	37 701	12 265	34 642	25 035	12 734
	1982..	23 651	41 242	37 607	57 019	19 099	31 539	41 462	17 796
Part owners	farms, 1987..	223	361	315	328	208	133	372	157
	1982..	240	390	298	333	215	132	396	163
	acres, 1987..	369 249	197 032	162 774	330 982	94 478	354 594	360 570	261 480
	1982..	340 609	225 931	148 606	314 910	90 695	306 975	346 166	282 756
Owned land in farms	acres, 1987..	161 292	85 965	75 362	142 246	30 415	119 934	130 471	98 637
	1982..	150 274	100 923	70 863	152 137	27 536	119 320	136 532	101 223
Rented land in farms	acres, 1987..	207 957	111 067	87 412	188 736	64 063	234 660	230 099	162 843
	1982..	190 535	125 008	77 743	162 773	63 159	187 555	209 634	181 533
Harvested cropland	farms, 1987..	221	335	294	323	181	126	359	152
	1982..	232	370	279	325	193	120	388	161
	acres, 1987..	120 103	72 485	76 929	139 739	47 531	117 624	154 112	89 650
	1982..	114 842	89 247	75 839	155 634	57 047	127 200	187 652	101 196
Tenants	farms, 1987..	71	80	73	141	67	69	171	63
	1982..	98	82	89	153	89	69	164	90
	acres, 1987..	67 420	25 368	17 285	66 920	20 969	116 054	92 097	83 813
	1982..	64 057	23 085	25 958	66 309	31 520	116 959	63 639	81 127
Harvested cropland	farms, 1987..	63	50	60	121	48	61	143	55
	1982..	79	70	77	136	64	53	147	75
	acres, 1987..	20 451	8 797	8 801	31 205	9 649	49 900	40 299	26 041
	1982..	25 931	8 919	14 797	36 522	13 552	57 770	36 138	25 844
OPERATOR CHARACTERISTICS									
Operators by place of residence:									
On farm operated	1987..	245	850	786	471	483	154	567	187
	1982..	264	891	798	515	551	146	577	190
Not on farm operated	1987..	152	161	184	208	131	114	206	95
	1982..	154	159	161	207	157	103	175	118
Not reported	1987..	26	71	47	57	45	23	45	28
	1982..	48	106	88	86	58	48	108	46
Operators by principal occupation:									
Farming	1987..	316	500	460	583	273	225	546	230
	1982..	361	580	506	626	304	230	582	276
Other	1987..	107	582	557	153	386	66	272	80
	1982..	105	596	541	182	462	67	278	78
Operators by days of work off farm:									
None	1987..	212	361	334	378	211	161	329	151
	1982..	207	386	352	411	246	154	331	169
Any	1987..	174	667	623	293	424	114	457	135
	1982..	197	698	603	305	466	105	421	137
1 to 49 days	1987..	48	56	41	62	29	17	95	25
	1982..	45	57	45	76	39	27	73	34
50 to 99 days	1987..	11	34	30	32	20	12	28	9
	1982..	19	43	36	28	11	11	42	17
100 to 149 days	1987..	11	39	30	24	19	10	45	13
	1982..	11	34	27	18	21	9	33	3
150 to 199 days	1987..	7	53	43	18	32	13	49	9
	1982..	19	66	43	34	31	9	49	10
200 days or more	1987..	97	485	479	143	326	62	240	79
	1982..	103	494	452	149	366	49	224	73
Not reported	1987..	37	54	60	65	24	16	32	24
	1982..	62	74	92	92	52	36	108	48
Operators by years on present farm:									
2 years or less	1987..	22	60	68	43	26	12	53	21
	1982..	20	57	35	47	31	14	38	28
3 or 4 years	1987..	22	71	55	32	33	14	52	19
	1982..	38	101	88	62	60	19	53	28
5 to 9 years	1987..	52	125	137	93	100	46	94	29
	1982..	66	199	180	95	141	40	115	40
10 years or more	1987..	250	678	611	445	382	169	481	186
	1982..	233	594	559	439	375	164	466	185
Average years on present farm	1987..	22.2	19.9	19.1	21.8	18.8	21.2	21.7	23.0
	1982..	21.8	17.9	17.8	21.4	17.1	19.9	20.8	21.2
Not reported	1987..	77	148	146	123	118	50	138	55
	1982..	109	205	185	175	159	60	188	73

[For meaning of abbreviations and symbols, see introductory text]

Characteristics	Labette	Lane	Leavenworth	Lincoln	Linn	Logan	Lyon	McPherson
FARMS								
Land in farms .... farms, 1987	971	322	1 144	578	668	382	872	1 357
1982	1 064	335	1 237	615	772	379	945	1 478
acres, 1987	350 010	467 005	211 370	454 341	273 211	610 480	469 908	533 432
1982	354 722	482 978	227 331	440 520	280 637	583 314	500 674	557 157
Harvested cropland .... farms, 1987	767	291	892	510	551	334	709	1 210
1982	840	300	956	552	642	329	798	1 391
acres, 1987	136 963	154 979	96 700	153 709	93 665	150 236	153 982	283 623
1982	170 902	159 352	108 423	174 963	120 739	166 407	165 108	345 140
TENURE OF OPERATOR								
Full owners .... farms, 1987	551	94	808	192	394	124	415	490
1982	581	109	863	194	451	134	451	479
acres, 1987	99 136	60 360	86 357	69 254	85 544	141 972	82 326	73 175
1982	109 460	71 819	90 370	67 367	89 595	150 517	104 432	79 312
Harvested cropland .... farms, 1987	379	73	588	142	295	100	298	370
1982	397	86	613	146	349	107	343	383
acres, 1987	25 392	17 995	29 629	23 543	21 217	30 815	23 796	37 383
1982	38 912	25 026	31 418	26 483	29 203	37 853	30 324	48 736
Part owners .... farms, 1987	332	169	269	278	234	186	370	702
1982	359	175	261	297	259	180	400	769
acres, 1987	224 953	335 581	110 931	329 746	171 750	389 193	326 261	409 527
1982	216 820	338 938	116 644	308 481	171 407	379 300	360 953	418 740
Owned land in farms .... acres, 1987	103 023	126 723	41 697	121 051	74 570	201 340	124 850	152 350
1982	103 229	145 260	46 349	127 713	84 014	212 751	154 686	168 979
Rented land in farms .... acres, 1987	121 940	208 858	69 234	208 695	97 180	187 853	203 431	257 177
1982	113 591	193 678	70 495	190 766	87 393	166 549	206 267	249 761
Harvested cropland .... farms, 1987	315	163	249	274	220	179	342	689
1982	344	171	261	294	244	173	378	750
acres, 1987	98 932	110 498	59 289	107 907	65 174	97 737	114 763	215 484
1982	116 013	118 025	63 155	118 458	82 193	111 071	118 281	256 649
Tenants .... farms, 1987	88	59	67	108	60	72	87	165
1982	124	51	93	124	62	65	94	226
acres, 1987	26 911	71 064	14 072	55 341	15 917	79 315	59 301	50 730
1982	28 442	52 221	20 117	64 672	19 635	53 497	35 289	59 105
Harvested cropland .... farms, 1987	73	55	55	94	36	55	69	151
1982	99	43	82	112	49	49	75	198
acres, 1987	12 639	26 486	7 783	22 259	7 274	21 664	15 423	30 756
1982	15 977	16 301	13 650	29 922	9 343	17 483	16 503	39 755
OPERATOR CHARACTERISTICS								
Operators by place of residence:								
On farm operated 1987	704	163	907	375	493	175	648	949
1982	796	165	1 004	398	545	181	724	1 035
Not on farm operated 1987	200	127	155	125	172	149	163	306
1982	193	118	145	155	137	148	148	281
Not reported 1987	67	32	82	54	70	35	61	102
1982	75	52	88	62	90	49	73	160
Operators by principal occupation:								
Farming 1987	465	242	458	437	341	266	460	776
1982	564	275	490	466	396	263	537	868
Other 1987	506	80	686	141	347	116	412	581
1982	500	60	747	149	376	96	408	608
Operators by days of work off farm:								
None 1987	354	166	403	303	261	194	317	456
1982	388	178	383	292	253	159	339	467
Any 1987	576	129	710	239	369	156	504	817
1982	612	109	778	252	444	164	544	881
1 to 49 days 1987	56	27	56	64	34	30	59	112
1982	50	24	60	74	53	40	71	161
50 to 99 days 1987	29	12	14	7	13	11	20	65
1982	32	14	24	17	27	5	37	65
100 to 149 days 1987	18	14	24	16	15	10	25	67
1982	37	12	39	20	21	13	28	72
150 to 199 days 1987	46	9	54	23	33	19	48	93
1982	60	13	63	40	40	15	53	90
200 days or more 1987	427	66	562	129	274	86	354	480
1982	433	46	590	122	303	91	355	484
Not reported 1987	41	27	31	36	58	32	51	84
1982	64	48	78	71	75	56	62	128
Operators by years on present farm:								
2 years or less 1987	55	12	40	21	40	24	49	57
1982	49	12	55	21	31	16	40	66
3 or 4 years 1987	60	10	87	26	31	25	48	77
1982	93	24	111	29	63	23	75	101
5 to 9 years 1987	124	33	150	67	93	47	119	208
1982	180	41	218	91	113	62	139	208
10 years or more 1987	577	196	670	365	399	210	505	814
1982	567	170	623	344	380	190	526	837
Average years on present farm 1987	19.6	22.4	18.9	20.3	20.3	20.5	21.6	21.9
1982	17.9	20.6	16.6	22.8	19.0	20.1	21.0	21.3
Not reported 1987	155	71	197	97	125	76	151	216
1982	175	88	230	130	165	88	165	264

Table 10. **Tenure and Characteristics of Operator and Type of Organization: 1987 and 1982**—Con.

[For meaning of abbreviations and symbols, see introductory text]

Characteristics	Marion	Marshall	Meade	Miami	Mitchell	Montgomery	Morris	Morton
FARMS								
Land in farms .... farms, 1987..	1 119	1 061	464	1 151	622	974	550	226
1982..	1 184	1 149	489	1 223	642	1 021	571	235
acres, 1987..	577 700	553 436	582 454	272 290	473 829	327 193	396 556	457 440
1982..	571 707	528 749	593 525	308 741	447 894	325 007	402 948	430 039
Harvested cropland .... farms, 1987..	994	944	413	902	570	674	472	192
1982..	1 072	1 045	436	972	583	696	494	210
acres, 1987..	252 314	261 802	200 706	116 217	237 322	111 308	112 525	139 398
1982..	292 672	279 758	215 390	129 869	246 181	129 397	117 842	170 522
TENURE OF OPERATOR								
Full owners .... farms, 1987..	392	443	136	730	230	620	223	56
1982..	386	515	169	741	232	643	220	49
acres, 1987..	77 343	122 700	96 187	89 446	81 924	112 035	85 506	24 153
1982..	137 045	156 858	167 247	99 909	94 453	100 237	110 500	50 613
Harvested cropland .... farms, 1987..	295	346	102	520	194	380	170	36
1982..	302	423	128	541	191	366	170	39
acres, 1987..	30 990	49 239	30 157	24 750	37 332	21 230	20 417	11 880
1982..	50 313	77 332	44 943	29 740	50 090	25 974	21 788	28 575
Part owners .... farms, 1987..	557	444	208	330	263	277	253	118
1982..	596	430	217	366	293	309	257	114
acres, 1987..	429 467	358 447	364 582	155 851	323 827	188 119	279 524	268 108
1982..	369 893	297 232	350 997	176 778	309 722	199 711	257 561	218 757
Owned land in farms .... acres, 1987..	177 258	146 320	165 393	59 819	134 582	80 173	109 835	98 089
1982..	157 519	140 886	165 137	88 376	149 555	90 127	106 355	68 722
Rented land in farms .... acres, 1987..	252 209	212 127	219 189	97 032	189 245	107 946	169 689	170 019
1982..	212 374	156 346	185 860	108 402	160 167	109 584	151 206	150 035
Harvested cropland .... farms, 1987..	539	438	205	307	259	240	244	112
1982..	585	427	211	351	287	277	245	111
acres, 1987..	183 571	172 835	120 717	77 124	164 490	79 322	82 163	104 118
1982..	203 429	158 379	131 927	82 719	170 010	93 402	83 385	113 000
Tenants .... farms, 1987..	170	174	120	91	129	77	74	52
1982..	202	203	103	96	117	69	94	72
acres, 1987..	70 890	72 289	101 685	26 993	68 078	27 039	31 526	165 179
1982..	64 769	74 659	75 281	32 054	43 719	25 059	34 887	160 669
Harvested cropland .... farms, 1987..	160	160	106	75	117	54	58	44
1982..	185	195	97	80	105	53	79	60
acres, 1987..	37 753	39 726	49 832	14 343	35 500	10 754	9 945	23 400
1982..	38 930	44 047	38 520	17 410	26 061	10 021	12 669	28 947
OPERATOR CHARACTERISTICS								
Operators by place of residence:								
On farm operated .... 1987..	815	724	242	862	374	719	396	119
1982..	842	768	243	903	377	780	418	128
Not on farm operated .... 1987..	223	261	175	198	192	180	121	76
1982..	207	250	176	214	186	166	99	72
Not reported .... 1987..	81	76	47	91	56	75	33	31
1982..	135	131	70	106	79	73	54	35
Operators by principal occupation:								
Farming .... 1987..	727	767	344	433	442	417	376	166
1982..	805	870	362	482	482	437	416	191
Other .... 1987..	392	294	120	718	180	557	174	60
1982..	379	279	127	741	160	584	155	44
Operators by days of work off farm:								
None .... 1987..	465	517	225	353	295	355	259	124
1982..	465	577	224	362	302	336	269	120
Any .... 1987..	575	468	200	748	286	571	243	80
1982..	595	433	203	798	270	628	248	75
1 to 49 days .... 1987..	86	107	52	41	51	31	46	13
1982..	119	127	58	55	75	54	61	15
50 to 99 days .... 1987..	50	42	22	29	24	21	22	6
1982..	54	41	12	40	17	31	22	5
100 to 149 days .... 1987..	46	28	13	28	25	30	11	4
1982..	47	23	10	31	20	28	20	11
150 to 199 days .... 1987..	44	53	13	53	25	47	26	5
1982..	52	40	20	64	21	38	25	6
200 days or more .... 1987..	349	238	100	596	161	442	138	52
1982..	313	202	103	608	137	477	120	38
Not reported .... 1987..	79	76	39	52	41	48	48	22
1982..	124	139	62	63	70	57	54	40
Operators by years on present farm:								
2 years or less .... 1987..	36	44	25	63	26	47	22	2
1982..	42	37	29	34	31	48	26	22
3 or 4 years .... 1987..	53	51	29	78	58	54	27	18
1982..	82	91	36	96	32	98	27	12
5 to 9 years .... 1987..	133	131	55	162	67	118	65	26
1982..	142	146	48	227	83	155	65	21
10 years or more .... 1987..	701	647	242	642	357	611	353	122
1982..	663	613	267	658	349	550	332	125
Average years on present farm .... 1987..	22.8	21.4	21.9	18.3	22.9	20.0	23.8	22.0
1982..	21.7	20.2	22.1	17.3	23.4	18.4	22.6	21.2
Not reported .... 1987..	196	188	113	206	114	144	83	58
1982..	255	262	109	208	147	170	121	55

1987 CENSUS OF AGRICULTURE—COUNTY DATA

[For meaning of abbreviations and symbols, see introductory text]

Characteristics		Namaha	Neosho	Ness	Norton	Osage	Osborne	Ottawa	Pawnee
FARMS									
Land in farms	farms, 1987	1 127	751	597	470	885	607	523	530
	1982	1 158	802	644	517	969	637	589	568
	acres, 1987	436 761	305 492	673 189	507 626	357 199	545 417	385 542	466 999
	1982	414 310	318 217	679 106	513 265	379 966	511 544	393 433	468 640
Harvested cropland	farms, 1987	994	611	542	415	729	554	476	476
	1982	1 024	662	577	458	825	572	514	519
	acres, 1987	203 290	126 121	193 980	154 827	140 377	162 056	149 979	223 904
	1982	215 292	142 932	216 742	170 487	158 533	179 133	165 635	256 255
TENURE OF OPERATOR									
Full owners	farms, 1987	553	439	167	170	464	212	189	170
	1982	623	460	188	188	494	236	219	175
	acres, 1987	145 804	108 686	80 265	83 557	89 091	107 503	53 297	58 800
	1982	161 730	102 943	104 236	103 400	93 158	121 057	69 411	77 715
Harvested cropland	farms, 1987	449	325	127	126	332	178	153	126
	1982	513	338	140	140	377	191	173	143
	acres, 1987	61 251	36 050	20 502	20 435	25 477	34 933	18 523	23 669
	1982	81 396	35 906	30 232	32 748	32 527	41 655	31 978	43 281
Part owners	farms, 1987	390	248	311	246	343	280	243	246
	1982	360	272	309	267	406	283	260	299
	acres, 1987	233 497	179 351	512 660	389 477	250 217	373 868	271 542	337 582
	1982	201 661	189 007	476 892	365 845	263 524	332 865	252 297	335 415
Owned land in farms	acres, 1987	110 837	84 399	203 286	160 535	116 796	145 377	91 048	129 995
	1982	104 757	97 211	190 463	177 182	129 803	141 033	87 628	133 558
Rented land in farms	acres, 1987	122 660	94 952	309 604	228 942	133 421	228 491	180 594	207 587
	1982	96 904	92 696	285 429	178 663	133 721	191 832	164 669	201 857
Harvested cropland	farms, 1987	380	239	307	242	327	276	237	241
	1982	351	262	305	261	363	277	251	294
	acres, 1987	112 309	62 044	147 626	120 745	105 936	125 167	99 805	156 852
	1982	104 439	91 708	151 575	117 622	116 061	115 426	114 569	179 175
Tenants	farms, 1987	184	64	119	54	78	115	91	114
	1982	175	70	147	62	89	118	110	96
	acres, 1987	57 460	17 366	80 264	34 893	17 901	64 016	80 803	90 611
	1982	50 919	25 367	98 978	54 020	23 283	57 592	71 725	55 510
Harvested cropland	farms, 1987	165	47	108	47	70	96	86	108
	1982	160	62	132	57	65	104	90	82
	acres, 1987	29 730	6 027	25 252	13 647	6 962	21 936	31 651	43 383
	1982	29 457	15 318	34 935	20 119	9 945	22 053	38 768	33 799
OPERATOR CHARACTERISTICS									
Operators by place of residence:									
On farm operated	1987	801	535	318	287	643	355	342	305
	1982	824	569	365	337	741	352	337	350
Not on farm operated	1987	240	158	237	145	194	207	143	194
	1982	198	143	222	119	189	216	180	146
Not reported	1987	86	60	42	38	48	45	38	31
	1982	136	90	57	61	59	69	72	72
Operators by principal occupation:									
Farming	1987	802	431	426	350	407	447	339	398
	1982	882	459	502	410	471	481	408	444
Other	1987	325	320	171	120	478	160	184	132
	1982	276	343	142	107	518	156	181	124
Operators by days of work off farm:									
None	1987	556	294	296	229	293	313	222	289
	1982	591	299	298	250	325	303	244	283
Any	1987	485	404	270	203	554	253	270	200
	1982	429	418	273	190	614	260	287	212
1 to 49 days	1987	68	37	54	32	56	61	53	40
	1982	120	57	77	55	70	64	64	53
50 to 99 days	1987	44	27	22	15	90	19	19	13
	1982	26	22	19	26	23	22	31	15
100 to 149 days	1987	38	26	18	12	36	16	22	7
	1982	30	19	24	20	27	16	23	18
150 to 199 days	1987	43	37	30	23	57	23	23	21
	1982	30	42	20	7	52	29	33	12
200 days or more	1987	292	277	146	121	375	134	153	119
	1982	223	276	133	82	448	124	136	114
Not reported	1987	84	53	31	38	38	41	31	41
	1982	138	85	73	77	50	74	58	73
Operators by years on present farm:									
2 years or less	1987	60	41	13	21	50	30	18	33
3 or 4 years	1987	55	37	32	24	44	44	23	33
	1982	75	45	35	21	42	30	23	24
5 to 9 years	1987	89	49	36	31	93	45	47	21
	1982	150	81	77	57	124	75	49	64
10 years or more	1987	133	115	88	60	169	71	92	60
	1982	652	469	382	282	529	363	335	312
		610	451	357	269	522	354	314	326
Average years on present farm	1987	20.7	21.1	24.5	23.4	20.7	23.8	23.3	23.0
	1982	19.5	19.5	22.7	23.0	19.0	22.1	19.8	23.8
Not reported	1987	190	115	90	89	140	109	97	97
	1982	271	150	129	113	161	123	114	126

[For meaning of abbreviations and symbols, see introductory text]

Characteristics	Phillips	Pottawatomie	Pratt	Rawlins	Reno	Republic	Rice	Riley
FARMS								
Land in farms ... farms, 1987	591	790	517	541	1 557	833	604	546
1982	647	869	547	621	1 636	923	643	583
acres, 1987	542 578	443 660	466 245	641 810	717 764	440 215	429 065	247 609
1982	544 332	464 739	438 501	686 471	701 435	441 118	429 881	252 903
Harvested cropland ... farms, 1987	527	614	465	497	1 346	736	541	462
1982	596	732	511	579	1 438	831	566	466
acres, 1987	162 736	118 376	242 460	196 707	374 679	230 517	214 092	50 307
1982	173 288	134 722	249 755	217 218	446 426	259 275	248 311	84 221
TENURE OF OPERATOR								
Full owners ... farms, 1987	217	420	168	183	616	313	193	261
1982	229	471	156	208	649	352	205	264
acres, 1987	88 490	123 672	75 970	110 082	113 159	76 394	41 037	68 317
1982	132 169	168 929	57 891	157 010	126 923	113 579	55 691	73 414
Harvested cropland ... farms, 1987	173	262	139	151	461	241	138	218
1982	193	366	135	184	501	280	158	196
acres, 1987	29 098	29 711	39 797	33 082	56 384	37 007	15 161	17 275
1982	41 151	37 541	33 837	45 846	76 869	58 360	30 372	20 193
Part owners ... farms, 1987	282	269	228	260	662	379	311	189
1982	310	303	266	295	716	410	332	214
acres, 1987	389 781	273 333	284 657	429 195	476 811	313 031	314 677	150 457
1982	352 747	264 385	306 791	431 660	482 717	262 453	304 578	153 312
Owned land in farms ... acres, 1987	156 284	136 125	94 986	189 539	162 634	125 906	95 090	70 431
1982	156 349	131 599	105 007	205 441	170 693	127 134	90 648	75 535
Rented land in farms ... acres, 1987	233 477	137 208	189 669	239 646	314 177	187 125	219 787	80 026
1982	196 398	132 786	201 784	226 184	312 124	155 319	213 930	77 777
Harvested cropland ... farms, 1987	275	251	219	256	647	370	306	190
1982	304	285	264	292	697	402	323	201
acres, 1987	112 715	71 016	145 251	132 451	249 795	163 912	163 264	53 922
1982	113 073	84 270	174 135	136 653	308 370	171 412	179 862	52 893
Tenants ... farms, 1987	92	101	121	98	279	141	100	66
1982	108	95	123	118	273	161	106	85
acres, 1987	64 327	46 655	105 618	102 543	127 794	50 790	73 151	28 835
1982	59 416	81 425	73 819	97 636	91 795	45 086	69 612	26 177
Harvested cropland ... farms, 1987	79	79	107	90	238	125	97	54
1982	99	79	112	103	240	149	105	69
acres, 1987	20 923	17 649	57 412	31 174	68 500	29 598	35 647	9 110
1982	19 064	12 911	41 783	34 719	61 189	29 503	38 077	11 135
OPERATOR CHARACTERISTICS								
Operators by place of residence:								
On farm operated 1987	420	555	326	341	1 107	518	408	402
1982	429	629	321	402	1 162	577	432	411
Not on farm operated 1987	119	173	155	160	332	252	150	112
1982	148	164	163	155	322	238	132	110
Not reported 1987	52	62	36	40	118	63	46	32
1982	70	76	63	64	154	108	79	62
Operators by principal occupation:								
Farming 1987	449	440	368	428	927	609	401	325
1982	500	557	398	519	1 041	671	459	356
Other 1987	142	350	149	113	630	224	203	221
1982	147	312	149	102	597	252	184	227
Operators by days of work off farm:								
None 1987	310	346	250	277	613	366	254	239
1982	320	380	252	340	636	403	288	231
Any 1987	235	396	237	227	848	420	310	270
1982	255	406	240	196	848	393	288	289
1 to 49 days 1987	69	45	50	74	134	114	56	30
1982	76	79	48	58	180	104	50	55
50 to 99 days 1987	17	18	17	23	67	43	25	10
1982	14	28	19	24	63	29	35	18
100 to 149 days 1987	15	17	26	12	55	29	26	23
1982	18	19	24	15	53	25	26	11
150 to 199 days 1987	14	34	26	12	86	33	24	19
1982	12	35	22	21	73	33	32	24
200 days or more 1987	120	282	118	106	506	201	179	189
1982	135	245	127	78	499	202	145	181
Not reported 1987	46	48	30	37	96	45	40	37
1982	72	83	55	85	154	127	67	63
Operators by years on present farm:								
2 years or less 1987	21	38	19	23	60	37	35	27
1982	36	44	19	24	67	48	23	29
3 or 4 years 1987	26	48	26	12	95	42	31	29
1982	42	60	45	41	126	85	30	47
5 to 9 years 1987	64	104	59	61	198	106	66	69
1982	66	114	75	74	259	106	93	82
10 years or more 1987	342	444	335	358	939	507	363	331
1982	375	504	283	360	881	491	370	317
Average years on present farm 1987	23.4	21.8	23.4	23.3	21.7	21.9	22.1	21.2
1982	22.2	21.2	21.8	23.0	20.7	20.7	22.8	16.9
Not reported 1987	138	156	78	87	265	141	109	100
1982	128	147	125	122	303	193	127	115

Table 10. **Tenure and Characteristics of Operator and Type of Organization: 1987 and 1982**—Con.

[For meaning of abbreviations and symbols, see introductory text]

Characteristics	Rooks	Rush	Russell	Saline	Scott	Sedgwick	Seward	Shawnee
FARMS								
Land in farms .... farms, 1987..	473	546	534	743	391	1 589	285	852
1982..	528	584	590	763	416	1 665	277	937
acres, 1987..	547 539	422 826	461 014	403 798	470 774	523 580	331 397	221 098
1982..	532 189	424 118	471 459	396 776	509 608	522 674	325 328	229 847
Harvested cropland .... farms, 1987..	431	494	469	649	330	1 345	229	659
1982..	483	525	517	694	356	1 423	228	726
acres, 1987..	157 823	160 253	135 417	173 828	180 540	319 625	141 650	101 139
1982..	168 987	172 379	163 585	205 672	209 383	363 417	159 542	103 231
TENURE OF OPERATOR								
Full owners .... farms, 1987..	128	180	178	296	130	788	91	507
1982..	156	151	197	282	154	802	93	572
acres, 1987..	67 040	70 812	75 374	67 404	64 316	113 230	73 157	55 238
1982..	92 676	53 138	86 408	53 365	103 592	120 857	57 026	70 281
Harvested cropland .... farms, 1987..	100	150	137	229	85	590	53	356
1982..	132	116	151	235	109	614	60	411
acres, 1987..	17 227	25 380	17 601	20 656	23 317	58 768	25 317	16 533
1982..	32 641	20 946	30 159	23 915	44 479	73 036	26 016	22 084
Part owners .... farms, 1987..	244	259	227	309	155	560	109	267
1982..	267	315	243	341	160	592	108	277
acres, 1987..	397 893	290 806	295 929	276 736	303 244	328 091	184 151	139 179
1982..	371 484	304 767	302 261	297 783	326 662	326 020	201 294	136 476
Owned land in farms .... acres, 1987..	159 689	109 786	112 492	94 834	110 150	112 665	68 113	47 636
1982..	163 960	140 806	117 679	114 334	126 518	114 242	78 103	46 101
Rented land in farms .... acres, 1987..	238 204	181 020	183 437	183 902	193 094	215 426	116 038	91 543
1982..	207 524	163 961	184 582	183 449	200 346	210 778	123 191	90 377
Harvested cropland .... farms, 1987..	239	253	223	298	150	636	106	239
1982..	256	304	241	331	157	569	104	243
acres, 1987..	116 017	109 902	89 870	126 454	113 376	208 167	82 016	67 897
1982..	112 325	122 431	104 121	155 732	126 689	234 093	101 623	66 655
Tenants .... farms, 1987..	101	107	129	138	106	241	85	78
1982..	102	118	150	140	102	271	76	88
acres, 1987..	82 606	61 208	86 711	57 658	103 914	82 269	74 080	26 681
1982..	68 029	66 213	82 790	45 628	79 152	76 797	67 008	23 088
Harvested cropland .... farms, 1987..	92	91	109	122	95	219	70	64
1982..	95	105	125	128	90	240	64	72
acres, 1987..	24 579	24 971	27 946	26 718	43 847	52 690	34 317	16 709
1982..	24 021	29 002	29 305	26 225	38 215	56 288	31 901	14 492
OPERATOR CHARACTERISTICS								
Operators by place of residence:								
On farm operated .... 1987..	272	292	280	487	173	1 121	151	642
1982..	288	324	281	466	186	1 150	138	692
Not on farm operated .... 1987..	173	214	200	216	176	350	104	162
1982..	164	194	218	205	165	327	96	144
Not reported .... 1987..	28	40	54	40	42	118	30	48
1982..	76	66	91	72	65	188	43	101
Operators by principal occupation:								
Farming .... 1987..	329	384	369	414	295	752	212	369
1982..	348	422	389	467	327	814	205	364
Other .... 1987..	144	162	165	329	96	837	73	483
1982..	180	162	201	296	89	851	72	573
Operators by days of work off farm:								
None .... 1987..	214	250	241	286	208	531	137	293
1982..	198	250	261	292	198	509	121	276
Any .... 1987..	230	262	256	410	153	973	121	510
1982..	259	280	272	417	158	1 009	113	601
1 to 49 days .... 1987..	38	57	44	48	33	101	24	36
1982..	39	62	48	70	51	109	25	49
50 to 99 days .... 1987..	25	17	18	22	12	67	11	21
1982..	19	19	13	28	8	55	9	16
100 to 149 days .... 1987..	18	33	24	30	9	40	11	21
1982..	23	16	15	43	7	49	9	33
150 to 199 days .... 1987..	22	29	40	41	14	80	10	40
1982..	26	32	29	44	18	96	7	41
200 days or more .... 1987..	127	126	130	271	85	685	65	392
1982..	152	131	167	232	75	700	63	462
Not reported .... 1987..	29	34	37	47	30	85	27	49
1982..	71	74	57	54	62	147	43	56
Operators by years on present farm:								
2 years or less .... 1987..	19	25	24	41	33	82	22	48
1982..	15	29	24	39	17	99	22	46
3 or 4 years .... 1987..	31	16	24	49	21	99	19	56
1982..	38	43	42	66	30	147	31	68
5 to 9 years .... 1987..	54	82	56	56	46	230	49	131
1982..	66	70	59	124	46	260	37	174
10 years or more .... 1987..	293	301	343	435	213	811	131	482
1982..	271	307	315	401	210	820	118	467
Average years on present farm .... 1987..	23.3	24.1	23.7	20.9	20.2	19.5	16.8	19.3
1982..	22.6	23.0	21.9	19.6	20.3	18.1	16.3	17.6
Not reported .... 1987..	76	122	87	112	78	256	64	135
1982..	138	135	145	133	113	339	99	182

Table 10. **Tenure and Characteristics of Operator and Type of Organization: 1987 and 1982**—Con.

[For meaning of abbreviations and symbols, see introductory text]

Characteristics	Sheridan	Sherman	Smith	Stafford	Stanton	Stevens	Sumner	Thomas
FARMS								
Land in farms ... farms, 1987	518	524	692	540	260	300	1 271	644
1982	571	550	761	557	291	325	1 366	626
acres, 1987	503 582	625 942	555 678	461 213	425 150	460 974	704 788	677 199
1982	513 458	672 254	546 068	458 403	445 129	456 595	734 578	658 558
Harvested cropland ... farms, 1987	461	470	630	488	241	260	1 137	592
1982	521	512	675	526	209	292	1 271	576
acres, 1987	183 013	251 334	211 337	230 807	184 701	238 568	415 440	296 047
1982	200 537	296 853	216 933	266 542	220 929	298 855	519 906	307 900
TENURE OF OPERATOR								
Full owners ... farms, 1987	187	183	240	165	64	66	485	251
1982	221	208	275	172	56	67	464	279
acres, 1987	102 455	127 232	94 996	66 848	42 208	43 013	95 877	180 261
1982	144 550	153 061	106 122	97 524	72 708	59 007	111 785	208 287
Harvested cropland ... farms, 1987	145	143	193	127	41	43	391	217
1982	191	184	208	146	42	47	383	245
acres, 1987	36 545	47 302	36 045	31 917	12 740	24 629	50 593	74 397
1982	52 556	70 449	39 677	51 847	34 109	33 011	71 902	90 166
Part owners ... farms, 1987	241	243	334	258	118	162	564	268
1982	253	231	348	254	108	172	655	249
acres, 1987	341 971	393 550	393 246	317 372	248 592	319 962	491 884	397 208
1982	307 624	415 574	375 554	266 553	287 751	316 260	517 813	371 366
Owned land in farms ... acres, 1987	149 778	162 345	189 120	101 919	92 097	95 930	168 256	182 873
1982	140 825	173 734	190 202	92 718	115 482	106 222	186 432	178 330
Rented land in farms ... acres, 1987	191 593	231 205	204 126	215 453	156 495	224 032	323 626	214 535
1982	166 799	241 840	185 352	195 835	172 269	210 038	331 381	193 056
Harvested cropland ... farms, 1987	238	234	330	254	114	154	546	264
1982	248	225	346	252	106	171	636	243
acres, 1987	120 039	162 911	148 977	157 833	109 450	163 226	295 900	175 843
1982	122 174	182 253	148 135	167 439	136 461	209 871	370 232	179 204
Tenants ... farms, 1987	90	98	118	116	98	72	222	125
1982	97	111	138	131	67	66	267	100
acres, 1987	59 756	105 160	67 434	76 993	134 350	97 999	117 027	99 730
1982	61 284	93 619	84 392	72 326	84 670	81 328	104 980	78 885
Harvested cropland ... farms, 1987	78	93	107	107	86	63	200	111
1982	82	103	121	128	59	74	252	87
acres, 1987	26 429	41 121	26 315	41 257	62 511	50 713	68 947	45 807
1982	25 807	44 151	29 121	47 256	48 359	55 773	77 772	38 530
OPERATOR CHARACTERISTICS								
Operators by place of residence:								
On farm operated ... 1987	287	299	458	336	148	161	871	325
1982	316	317	503	321	118	166	957	318
Not on farm operated ... 1987	171	191	186	169	111	113	327	269
1982	180	174	190	158	80	116	319	238
Not reported ... 1987	80	34	48	35	21	26	73	50
1982	75	59	68	76	33	43	116	74
Operators by principal occupation:								
Farming ... 1987	394	384	536	396	238	222	741	450
1982	466	426	607	437	193	268	927	448
Other ... 1987	124	140	156	144	42	78	530	194
1982	105	124	154	120	38	57	459	180
Operators by days of work off farm:								
None ... 1987	243	270	376	257	164	161	498	298
1982	279	292	383	287	132	179	542	298
Any ... 1987	224	213	271	224	94	119	698	305
1982	212	198	303	199	73	108	711	254
1 to 49 days ... 1987	52	50	60	58	21	22	84	75
1982	74	42	99	46	20	27	106	59
50 to 99 days ... 1987	27	19	26	16	11	11	37	20
1982	19	19	30	18	4	5	42	19
100 to 149 days ... 1987	25	20	27	19	10	9	58	23
1982	19	11	15	29	5	4	83	20
150 to 199 days ... 1987	8	15	25	17	6	11	68	19
1982	11	13	30	21	6	11	81	26
200 days or more ... 1987	112	109	131	114	46	66	451	168
1982	89	113	129	85	38	61	399	130
Not reported ... 1987	51	41	45	59	22	20	75	41
1982	80	60	75	71	26	38	133	76
Operators by years on present farm:								
2 years or less ... 1987	30	41	24	30	28	13	54	63
1982	22	32	25	31	7	16	57	39
3 or 4 years ... 1987	26	23	35	29	19	17	86	51
1982	42	37	57	44	21	11	122	50
5 to 9 years ... 1987	68	72	78	79	40	29	153	76
1982	73	64	104	61	43	47	193	82
10 years or more ... 1987	282	292	444	307	144	166	771	351
1982	291	298	446	296	117	177	777	315
Average years on present farm ... 1987	21.3	21.2	23.4	22.1	18.2	22.2	20.8	20.6
1982	21.1	21.0	21.7	22.2	19.1	21.6	20.5	21.5
Not reported ... 1987	112	96	111	95	49	55	207	103
1982	143	99	129	125	43	74	237	142

Table 10. **Tenure and Characteristics of Operator and Type of Organization: 1987 and 1982**—Con.

[For meaning of abbreviations and symbols, see introductory text]

Characteristics	Trego	Wabaunsee	Wallace	Washington	Wichita	Wilson	Woodson	Wyandotte
FARMS								
Land in farms ... farms, 1987	482	633	330	939	355	610	369	199
1982	467	678	336	1 032	341	680	402	216
acres, 1987	480 159	460 304	529 749	518 501	440 467	299 462	253 967	23 936
1982	499 771	442 489	505 916	530 203	427 642	332 902	276 081	25 337
Harvested cropland ... farms, 1987	426	488	283	794	307	505	303	125
1982	443	551	281	907	294	574	318	148
acres, 1987	139 788	90 028	146 695	239 242	162 673	114 733	85 309	12 112
1982	142 586	103 331	162 334	272 022	195 631	143 416	87 002	14 095
TENURE OF OPERATOR								
Full owners ... farms, 1987	149	340	119	406	121	333	163	147
1982	149	352	139	467	111	323	186	150
acres, 1987	67 630	103 610	100 206	104 073	71 549	86 246	41 571	6 314
1982	82 112	110 321	156 980	148 665	93 152	87 993	68 144	7 256
Harvested cropland ... farms, 1987	108	232	79	283	87	242	114	85
1982	112	250	102	363	82	232	120	93
acres, 1987	19 719	20 002	32 226	42 908	28 699	20 925	12 915	1 955
1982	24 936	24 101	42 288	70 304	41 222	29 060	16 239	2 248
Part owners ... farms, 1987	235	220	144	399	156	225	165	33
1982	250	238	129	411	156	280	170	47
acres, 1987	343 236	290 625	337 932	345 667	260 380	193 633	194 359	11 690
1982	340 007	278 557	292 452	325 467	279 685	219 065	186 892	14 234
Owned land in farms ... acres, 1987	137 530	120 029	174 402	147 720	85 773	86 811	71 264	3 054
1982	154 928	116 245	156 918	157 845	102 448	99 553	73 138	5 421
Rented land in farms ... acres, 1987	205 706	170 596	163 530	197 947	194 607	106 822	123 105	8 636
1982	185 079	162 312	135 574	167 622	177 237	119 512	113 754	8 803
Harvested cropland ... farms, 1987	230	203	141	389	153	217	155	24
1982	241	228	123	402	155	271	160	40
acres, 1987	97 542	59 764	87 476	162 689	116 107	84 272	63 851	7 595
1982	92 899	62 977	91 380	167 888	132 615	100 945	61 396	8 696
Tenants ... farms, 1987	98	73	67	134	78	52	41	19
1982	98	88	70	154	74	77	46	19
acres, 1987	69 291	66 068	81 611	88 761	88 538	19 583	18 027	3 932
1982	77 652	53 611	56 464	56 071	54 705	25 844	21 045	3 857
Harvested cropland ... farms, 1987	88	53	63	122	67	46	34	16
1982	90	73	56	142	57	71	38	15
acres, 1987	22 527	10 262	26 993	33 645	37 867	9 536	8 533	2 562
1982	24 751	16 253	28 666	33 830	21 794	13 411	9 367	3 149
OPERATOR CHARACTERISTICS								
Operators by place of residence:								
On farm operated ... 1987	306	444	184	639	194	440	248	147
1982	319	500	166	683	170	499	275	155
Not on farm operated ... 1987	143	131	129	231	131	125	89	35
1982	130	109	108	211	122	112	78	40
Not reported ... 1987	33	58	17	69	30	45	32	17
1982	48	69	82	138	49	69	49	21
Operators by principal occupation:								
Farming ... 1987	351	372	245	741	262	383	226	61
1982	360	424	270	768	265	426	260	72
Other ... 1987	131	261	85	198	93	227	143	138
1982	137	254	68	244	76	254	142	144
Operators by days of work off farm:								
None ... 1987	230	262	155	481	184	240	161	56
1982	221	276	181	523	163	291	173	63
Any ... 1987	230	330	163	365	147	329	163	131
1982	223	335	141	379	135	330	200	137
1 to 49 days ... 1987	50	33	43	98	34	54	30	9
1982	43	50	41	95	28	47	42	17
50 to 99 days ... 1987	27	20	10	32	15	25	7	2
1982	18	23	9	33	12	23	15	7
100 to 149 days ... 1987	13	23	9	36	9	26	12	6
1982	20	20	16	30	9	27	18	12
150 to 199 days ... 1987	45	31	15	35	11	32	22	6
1982	26	36	13	30	17	33	12	7
200 days or more ... 1987	95	223	86	164	78	192	112	108
1982	114	206	62	191	69	200	111	94
Not reported ... 1987	22	41	12	93	24	41	25	12
1982	53	67	36	130	43	59	29	16
Operators by years on present farm:								
2 years or less ... 1987	25	46	21	54	24	16	20	8
1982	19	34	31	31	22	34	11	9
3 or 4 years ... 1987	25	30	14	41	28	28	16	20
1982	49	40	29	72	23	32	24	15
5 to 9 years ... 1987	62	97	45	125	42	105	48	38
1982	68	97	52	125	46	105	48	45
10 years or more ... 1987	289	353	202	562	191	397	222	96
1982	268	377	159	577	175	383	246	99
Average years on present farm ... 1987	21.5	21.7	20.6	22.8	19.6	22.6	21.5	16.9
1982	21.4	20.9	18.0	21.6	20.1	19.2	20.6	17.7
Not reported ... 1987	79	133	56	186	66	108	69	51
1982	99	130	74	236	79	126	73	55

Table 10. **Tenure and Characteristics of Operator and Type of Organization: 1987 and 1982** —Con.

[For meaning of abbreviations and symbols, see introductory text]

Characteristics	Kansas	Allen	Anderson	Atchison	Barber	Barton	Bourbon
OPERATOR CHARACTERISTICS— Con.							
Operators by age group:							
Under 25 years_____1987__	1 712	15	23	25	11	19	16
1982__	2 840	31	35	37	20	44	20
25 to 34 years _____1987__	9 531	71	111	105	82	145	84
1982__	10 670	100	118	116	96	119	108
35 to 44 years _____1987__	12 471	110	110	138	106	137	175
1982__	12 232	93	139	137	78	135	172
45 to 54 years _____1987__	12 707	99	169	135	77	175	142
1982__	14 815	138	153	183	94	206	164
55 to 64 years _____1987__	15 988	175	154	160	133	249	185
1982__	17 746	200	205	179	115	257	206
55 to 59 years _____1987__	7 581	79	69	78	76	125	82
60 to 64 years _____1987__	8 407	96	85	82	57	124	103
65 years and over _____1987__	16 170	195	160	131	126	212	238
1982__	15 012	175	147	116	111	201	212
65 to 69 years _____1987__	6 564	77	72	56	47	88	71
70 years and over _____1987__	9 606	118	88	75	79	124	167
Average age _____1987__	52.0	54.7	51.2	50.2	52.0	52.1	54.2
1982__	50.9	52.4	50.3	49.0	50.2	51.8	52.5
Operators by sex:							
Male _____ farms, 1987__	65 619	626	689	671	498	894	780
1982__	70 674	707	766	744	493	920	832
acres, 1987__	45 488 481	269 406	339 105	229 164	682 927	541 585	307 694
1982__	46 024 059	276 637	355 371	229 079	680 950	548 141	315 911
Female _____ farms, 1987__	2 960	37	38	23	37	43	62
1982__	2 641	28	31	24	24	42	50
acres, 1987__	1 140 038	7 149	13 036	4 455	17 220	14 848	11 064
1982__	1 028 154	7 241	5 876	5 651	17 750	11 390	21 348
TYPE OF ORGANIZATION							
Individual or family (sole proprietorship) _____ farms, 1987__	60 202	607	684	596	450	800	771
1982__	64 313	673	726	689	439	838	805
acres, 1987__	36 420 471	230 905	300 407	182 001	563 593	457 764	266 371
1982__	36 885 296	237 206	305 539	187 093	539 717	441 975	278 562
Partnership _____ farms, 1987__	5 889	52	54	78	66	106	53
1982__	6 702	51	66	87	63	105	69
acres, 1987__	6 151 580	37 137	41 657	35 153	108 881	71 319	38 883
1982__	6 196 310	40 361	49 046	35 579	90 983	81 832	39 490
Corporation:							
Family held _____ farms, 1987__	1 942	5	7	14	12	21	16
1982__	1 695	7	3	8	11	14	8
acres, 1987__	3 446 745	(D)	8 511	(D)	(D)	(D)	13 444
1982__	3 206 051	(D)	(D)	11 378	25 815	(D)	19 207
Other than family held _____ farms, 1987__	158	1	1	2	2	2	1
1982__	181	1	1	-	2	1	-
acres, 1987__	159 976	(D)	(D)	(D)	(D)	(D)	(D)
1982__	246 736	(D)	(D)	-	(D)	(D)	-
Other—cooperative, estate or trust,							
institutional, etc. _____ farms, 1987__	386	-	1	4	5	8	1
1982__	424	3	1	4	2	6	-
acres, 1987__	450 347	-	(D)	842	1 620	3 085	(D)
1982__	517 810	392	(D)	680	(D)	3 378	-

Table 10. Tenure and Characteristics of Operator and Type of Organization: 1987 and 1982—Con.

[For meaning of abbreviations and symbols, see introductory text]

Characteristics	Brown	Butler	Chase	Chautauqua	Cherokee	Cheyenne	Clark
OPERATOR CHARACTERISTICS—Con.							
Operators by age group:							
Under 25 years .... 1987..	29	16	2	8	21	8	-
1982..	46	23	5	5	37	21	10
25 to 34 years .... 1987..	98	146	42	49	99	73	49
1982..	139	193	44	41	124	87	43
35 to 44 years .... 1987..	153	216	57	69	159	79	51
1982..	133	219	41	81	201	84	40
45 to 54 years .... 1987..	117	261	46	92	194	72	41
1982..	117	275	55	90	169	101	56
55 to 64 years .... 1987..	157	299	57	83	163	142	80
1982..	206	369	61	69	215	157	93
55 to 59 years .... 1987..	67	153	30	40	87	67	35
60 to 64 years .... 1987..	90	146	27	43	76	75	45
65 years and over .... 1987..	174	362	84	120	205	119	69
1982..	183	307	69	115	193	116	66
65 to 69 years .... 1987..	71	140	36	46	87	53	32
70 years and over .... 1987..	103	222	48	74	118	66	37
Average age .... 1987..	51.2	53.2	52.7	53.5	51.9	53.2	52.6
1982..	50.4	52.1	53.4	53.5	50.6	51.8	52.1
Operators by sex:							
Male .... farms, 1987..	696	1 228	273	396	811	468	275
1982..	787	1 313	276	401	904	519	292
acres, 1987..	332 860	684 411	309 935	311 408	276 448	606 605	575 664
1982..	336 515	680 438	396 332	320 962	288 730	583 773	573 945
Female .... farms, 1987..	32	72	15	25	30	25	15
1982..	38	63	19	30	35	27	16
acres, 1987..	6 993	15 076	18 970	3 546	4 256	13 265	11 910
1982..	9 825	10 843	18 573	12 996	7 968	18 953	14 343
TYPE OF ORGANIZATION							
Individual or family (sole proprietorship) .... farms, 1987..	580	1 173	252	380	758	429	242
1982..	664	1 226	241	368	858	473	262
acres, 1987..	230 508	553 142	222 733	249 208	230 542	474 045	387 675
1982..	240 637	521 328	244 468	252 960	243 641	490 431	405 027
Partnership .... farms, 1987..	84	86	20	31	67	40	24
1982..	117	119	33	34	67	46	25
acres, 1987..	39 238	78 149	63 031	39 469	36 335	74 621	(D)
1982..	55 889	102 073	91 956	56 096	39 144	(D)	85 570
Corporation:							
Family held .... farms, 1987..	53	31	13	8	13	22	18
1982..	37	23	15	5	11	24	18
acres, 1987..	60 489	40 759	29 031	27 506	(D)	(D)	94 197
1982..	(D)	49 987	(D)	24 072	(D)	(D)	89 392
Other than family held .... farms, 1987..	3	5	-	1	-	-	4
1982..	2	3	1	2	-	1	2
acres, 1987..	3 293	11 414	(D)	(D)	-	-	21 270
1982..	(D)	2 354	(D)	(D)	-	(D)	(D)
Other—cooperative, estate or trust, institutional, etc. .... farms, 1987..	8	5	2	1	3	2	2
1982..	8	5	6	2	3	2	1
acres, 1987..	6 325	16 023	(D)	(D)	(D)	(D)	(D)
1982..	5 080	15 539	10 592	(D)	(D)	(D)	(D)

Table 10. **Tenure and Characteristics of Operator and Type of Organization: 1987 and 1982**—Con.

[For meaning of abbreviations and symbols, see introductory text]

Characteristics	Clay	Cloud	Coffey	Comanche	Cowley	Crawford	Decatur
OPERATOR CHARACTERISTICS—Con.							
Operators by age group:							
Under 25 years ...1987	31	20	16	2	13	18	16
1982	39	41	21	7	47	38	31
25 to 34 years 1987	103	112	78	39	123	105	83
1982	106	127	118	45	156	122	93
35 to 44 years 1987	116	134	128	47	181	126	77
1982	99	126	115	38	180	151	71
45 to 54 years 1987	90	113	111	44	203	163	82
1982	130	126	118	54	230	172	99
55 to 64 years 1987	160	130	131	56	231	185	104
1982	190	158	143	50	258	245	114
55 to 59 years 1987	80	51	71	33	112	95	45
60 to 64 years 1987	100	79	60	23	119	90	59
65 years and over 1987	172	150	142	89	246	212	124
1982	155	148	158	65	230	186	108
65 to 69 years 1987	73	63	60	24	96	86	56
70 years and over 1987	99	87	82	65	150	126	68
Average age 1987	51.6	50.6	51.4	54.3	52.9	52.9	51.3
1982	50.9	49.4	50.9	51.0	50.8	51.2	50.0
Operators by sex:							
Male farms, 1987	648	629	595	264	957	773	472
1982	709	699	653	251	1 071	874	500
acres, 1987	381 551	390 093	329 007	466 209	604 137	276 885	538 299
1982	363 600	388 673	321 401	446 863	690 878	318 578	528 373
Female farms, 1987	24	30	11	13	40	36	14
1982	10	27	18	8	30	41	16
acres, 1987	10 770	7 290	1 428	14 927	15 610	6 704	5 167
1982	1 474	14 417	3 841	15 871	8 800	6 504	6 694
TYPE OF ORGANIZATION							
Individual or family (sole proprietorship) farms, 1987	584	564	568	228	906	755	397
1982	653	616	617	213	979	844	421
acres, 1987	314 613	332 255	295 326	335 407	480 652	260 823	398 151
1982	319 828	326 955	283 392	296 427	535 924	285 418	400 218
Partnership farms, 1987	72	73	28	40	71	38	42
1982	53	98	40	36	94	64	58
acres, 1987	60 600	42 310	18 752	100 498	89 206	16 405	49 116
1982	36 282	61 926	36 908	109 152	110 461	29 563	64 534
Corporation:							
Family held farms, 1987	13	19	10	6	14	14	41
1982	8	9	10	6	16	7	34
acres, 1987	16 841	19 320	16 357	(D)	(D)	(D)	(D)
1982	7 990	13 569	(D)	(D)	42 640	10 101	(D)
Other than family held farms, 1987	1	-	1	2	1	-	1
1982	3	-	-	-	5	-	(D)
acres, 1987	(D)	(D)	(D)	(D)	(D)	-	(D)
1982	(D)	-	-	-	7 068	-	(D)
Other—cooperative, estate or trust, institutional, etc. farms, 1987	2	2	-	3	5	2	5
1982	2	3	3	2	7	-	4
acres, 1987	(D)	(D)	-	(D)	2 742	(D)	1 097
1982	(D)	840	446	(D)	3 585	-	744

Table 10. **Tenure and Characteristics of Operator and Type of Organization: 1987 and 1982**—Con.

[For meaning of abbreviations and symbols, see introductory text]

Characteristics	Dickinson	Doniphan	Douglas	Edwards	Elk	Ellis	Ellsworth
OPERATOR CHARACTERISTICS— Con.							
Operators by age group:							
Under 25 years ...... 1987..	25	15	11	12	5	15	9
1982..	40	26	21	23	10	20	33
25 to 34 years ...... 1987..	164	86	82	57	43	103	61
1982..	165	122	87	63	57	116	77
35 to 44 years ...... 1987..	136	108	158	57	44	161	82
1982..	162	120	192	55	57	136	73
45 to 54 years ...... 1987..	159	91	198	51	77	152	81
1982..	232	119	171	62	105	155	78
55 to 64 years ...... 1987..	232	122	172	84	93	204	126
1982..	262	134	213	96	109	232	134
55 to 59 years ...... 1987..	108	42	74	44	43	86	51
60 to 64 years ...... 1987..	124	80	98	40	50	118	77
65 years and over ...... 1987..	252	108	231	100	147	160	136
1982..	266	100	212	101	129	131	132
65 to 69 years ...... 1987..	109	52	91	33	58	73	47
70 years and over ...... 1987..	143	56	140	67	89	87	91
Average age ...... 1987..	51.7	50.4	53.8	52.6	56.7	51.3	54.3
1982..	52.1	46.0	52.4	51.3	54.0	50.3	51.6
Operators by sex:							
Male ...... farms, 1987..	1 007	510	797	336	387	762	476
1982..	1 122	608	857	364	451	760	506
acres, 1987..	507 795	210 705	216 202	365 998	334 305	550 850	410 064
1982..	523 277	221 909	216 013	371 177	357 061	495 659	381 807
Female ...... farms, 1987..	21	20	55	25	22	33	28
1982..	27	14	39	18	16	30	21
acres, 1987..	6 151	5 474	7 224	21 311	6 594	16 284	13 591
1982..	4 174	2 610	4 846	11 300	7 821	13 391	5 766
TYPE OF ORGANIZATION							
Individual or family (sole proprietorship) ...... farms, 1987..	918	431	765	319	365	703	456
1982..	1 019	469	800	351	417	699	479
acres, 1987..	433 972	144 402	166 759	325 003	266 865	470 171	338 979
1982..	436 520	145 040	176 738	314 796	299 666	450 281	322 217
Partnership ...... farms, 1987..	83	62	64	32	34	75	24
1982..	106	92	71	41	40	72	32
acres, 1987..	53 713	(D)	41 173	44 936	57 121	50 711	39 933
1982..	66 442	33 412	28 375	46 957	39 816	45 937	37 472
Corporation:							
Family held ...... farms, 1987..	15	34	17	9	7	8	10
1982..	18	34	20	8	8	9	6
acres, 1987..	19 029	(D)	(D)	(D)	6 350	(D)	26 181
1982..	(D)	(D)	(D)	(D)	(D)	4 812	(D)
Other than family held ...... farms, 1987..	3	2	2	1	-	1	1
1982..	-	2	1	2	1	4	2
acres, 1987..	297	(D)	(D)	(D)	-	(D)	-
1982..	-	(D)	(D)	(D)	(D)	926	(D)
Other—cooperative, estate or trust, institutional, etc. ...... farms, 1987..	9	1	4	-	3	8	7
1982..	4	3	4	-	1	6	6
acres, 1987..	6 945	(D)	388	-	6 563	13 895	18 562
1982..	(D)	1 767	282	-	(D)	7 094	1 122

Table 10. **Tenure and Characteristics of Operator and Type of Organization: 1987 and 1982**—Con.

[For meaning of abbreviations and symbols, see introductory text]

Characteristics	Finney	Ford	Franklin	Geary	Gove	Graham	Grant
OPERATOR CHARACTERISTICS— Con.							
Operators by age group:							
Under 25 years ....1987..	7	21	15	5	20	12	18
1982..	21	40	36	11	36	21	7
25 to 34 years ....1987..	72	109	116	44	114	60	43
1982..	91	109	143	43	115	80	52
35 to 44 years ....1987..	126	163	169	39	88	68	61
1982..	92	147	212	47	88	60	59
45 to 54 years ....1987..	104	147	229	54	92	86	54
1982..	113	166	235	52	125	127	62
55 to 64 years ....1987..	115	181	231	65	115	127	57
1982..	151	203	227	75	102	102	65
55 to 59 years ....1987..	46	89	98	28	48	73	31
60 to 64 years ....1987..	69	92	133	37	67	54	26
65 years and over ....1987..	110	191	219	86	105	99	70
1982..	90	171	234	71	62	105	31
65 to 69 years ....1987..	54	82	76	27	37	41	32
70 years and over ....1987..	56	109	143	61	68	58	38
Average age ....1987..	50.8	51.8	52.6	54.0	49.7	52.6	50.0
1982..	50.2	50.7	51.1	51.7	47.0	51.0	47.8
Operators by sex:							
Male ....farms, 1987..	519	764	921	283	511	422	295
1982..	540	790	1 044	289	526	485	269
acres, 1987..	696 531	649 441	302 832	162 835	666 908	483 494	318 657
1982..	702 766	670 384	297 999	153 290	656 244	516 022	329 194
Female.......................farms, 1987..	15	48	68	12	23	30	6
1982..	18	46	43	10	22	10	7
acres, 1987..	24 215	25 545	9 951	7 504	9 667	20 095	4 481
1982..	18 856	21 549	6 872	3 372	18 439	7 080	3 799
TYPE OF ORGANIZATION							
Individual or family (sole proprietorship) ....farms, 1987..	403	665	883	254	471	396	254
1982..	446	677	975	248	478	427	235
acres, 1987..	457 027	499 916	247 552	136 733	572 360	447 560	239 878
1982..	484 025	503 143	250 826	126 282	557 917	438 096	248 866
Partnership ....farms, 1987..	70	107	74	18	41	44	33
1982..	60	119	93	35	45	59	20
acres, 1987..	155 451	119 304	41 436	(D)	56 159	37 541	53 635
1982..	126 931	119 578	39 360	17 040	58 486	73 942	48 513
Corporation:							
Family held ....farms, 1987..	50	32	14	12	19	7	15
1982..	36	32	9	10	22	6	18
acres, 1987..	100 072	50 101	21 871	23 382	(D)	(D)	(D)
1982..	77 089	(D)	10 261	(D)	54 671	9 360	30 176
Other than family held ....farms, 1987..	6	1	-	1	-	-	1
1982..	9	2	4	1	-	-	2
acres, 1987..	4 261	(D)	-	(D)	-	-	(D)
1982..	(D)	(D)	(D)	(D)	-	-	(D)
Other—cooperative, estate or trust,							
institutional, etc. ....farms, 1987..	5	2	8	1	3	5	-
1982..	7	6	6	5	3	3	1
acres, 1987..	5 935	(D)	1 924	(D)	(D)	(D)	-
1982..	(D)	6 090	(D)	2 552	3 609	1 704	(D)

[For meaning of abbreviations and symbols, see introductory text]

Characteristics	Gray	Greeley	Greenwood	Hamilton	Harper	Harvey	Haskell
OPERATOR CHARACTERISTICS—Con.							
Operators by age group:							
Under 25 years ... 1987	35	4	7	12	12	33	9
1982	35	10	16	8	14	29	13
25 to 34 years 1987	100	42	55	46	87	114	62
1982	113	35	63	36	80	129	75
35 to 44 years 1987	134	53	90	58	98	162	71
1982	109	49	114	58	110	176	69
45 to 54 years 1987	87	48	106	60	117	158	49
1982	117	43	122	49	138	199	62
55 to 64 years 1987	101	75	151	51	166	215	84
1982	104	81	171	67	165	222	66
55 to 59 years 1987	49	28	76	20	83	109	30
60 to 64 years 1987	52	47	75	31	83	106	54
65 years and over 1987	90	72	178	52	168	192	40
1982	74	59	165	52	153	166	39
65 to 69 years 1987	34	23	56	23	75	96	11
70 years and over 1987	56	49	122	29	93	96	29
Average age 1987	47.6	53.1	55.5	49.2	53.4	51.3	48.5
1982	46.4	51.6	53.6	50.6	52.6	50.5	46.4
Operators by sex:							
Male farms, 1987	524	270	562	267	614	854	308
1982	531	255	617	258	639	896	311
acres, 1987	511 780	455 986	537 363	525 120	470 736	307 266	366 797
1982	520 715	437 798	586 228	535 124	483 787	314 614	356 822
Female farms, 1987	23	24	25	12	34	20	7
1982	21	22	34	12	22	27	13
acres, 1987	20 504	19 292	12 144	13 329	13 735	1 857	3 053
1982	16 254	8 184	15 595	9 792	6 668	6 421	4 479
TYPE OF ORGANIZATION							
Individual or family (sole proprietorship) farms, 1987	431	224	536	224	545	787	233
1982	442	225	585	223	572	829	252
acres, 1987	364 981	286 430	439 176	394 326	360 686	254 563	246 979
1982	360 977	297 554	490 273	436 149	396 620	260 427	264 165
Partnership farms, 1987	60	30	37	33	67	66	52
1982	64	36	56	26	64	71	43
acres, 1987	(D)	102 335	69 129	83 398	76 352	35 837	(D)
1982	(D)	102 963	72 810	59 209	53 873	40 587	52 597
Corporation:							
Family held farms, 1987	51	35	11	18	26	16	23
1982	41	12	7	15	17	15	20
acres, 1987	90 072	(D)	36 362	58 120	43 114	(D)	42 628
1982	97 731	38 715	20 060	47 456	(D)	14 963	39 781
Other than family held farms, 1987	4	-	1	4	3	2	5
1982	3	1	1	3	1	5	4
acres, 1987	9 939	-	(D)	2 605	1 240	(D)	4 167
1982	8 206	(D)	(D)	(D)	(D)	(D)	2 220
Other—cooperative, estate or trust, institutional, etc. farms, 1987	1	5	2	-	7	3	2
1982	2	3	2	3	6	3	5
acres, 1987	(D)	(D)	(D)	-	3 079	381	(D)
1982	(D)	(D)	(D)	(D)	3 625	(D)	2 536

Table 10. **Tenure and Characteristics of Operator and Type of Organization: 1987 and 1982**—Con.

[For meaning of abbreviations and symbols, see introductory text]

Characteristics	Hodgeman	Jackson	Jefferson	Jewell	Johnson	Kearny	Kingman	Kiowa
OPERATOR CHARACTERISTICS—Con.								
Operators by age group:								
Under 25 years .... 1987..	23	25	22	27	12	6	19	4
1982..	24	48	23	33	9	10	29	16
25 to 34 years .... 1987..	79	127	101	120	53	40	131	42
1982..	72	169	153	120	72	33	132	45
35 to 44 years .... 1987..	77	236	212	128	122	61	152	52
1982..	83	247	193	132	160	53	147	59
45 to 54 years .... 1987..	64	193	216	116	160	65	140	47
1982..	72	220	228	158	166	74	178	66
55 to 64 years .... 1987..	95	276	242	183	151	69	178	81
1982..	112	284	251	196	181	74	194	90
55 to 59 years .... 1987..	32	124	110	89	84	35	96	40
60 to 64 years .... 1987..	63	152	132	94	67	34	82	41
65 years and over .... 1987..	85	225	224	162	161	50	198	84
1982..	103	188	199	169	158	53	180	78
65 to 69 years .... 1987..	23	95	98	61	69	22	70	45
70 years and over .... 1987..	62	130	126	101	92	28	128	39
Average age .... 1987..	49.7	51.7	52.2	51.2	53.4	50.4	51.3	53.1
1982..	50.0	49.5	51.2	50.9	52.3	50.8	50.4	51.9
Operators by sex:								
Male .... farms, 1987..	398	1 032	969	717	605	272	800	300
1982..	448	1 100	1 006	787	728	275	846	339
acres, 1987..	475 100	327 565	249 748	499 102	144 830	525 250	515 167	389 469
1982..	471 320	365 563	266 669	505 950	166 637	509 244	489 635	417 231
Female .... farms, 1987..	25	50	48	19	54	19	18	10
1982..	18	56	41	21	38	22	14	15
acres, 1987..	19 980	7 577	13 844	3 004	6 933	24 121	2 485	2 776
1982..	11 419	10 767	5 022	4 497	3 349	22 833	2 562	5 621
TYPE OF ORGANIZATION								
Individual or family (sole proprietorship) .... farms, 1987..	360	1 002	938	648	577	226	747	262
1982..	396	1 055	952	718	663	235	781	310
acres, 1987..	374 178	292 771	230 259	410 764	117 823	319 625	428 870	288 845
1982..	371 690	332 051	231 625	417 632	120 955	327 025	424 059	308 034
Partnership .... farms, 1987..	43	69	67	72	51	34	63	35
1982..	41	92	78	73	73	39	70	37
acres, 1987..	75 556	34 155	23 344	66 463	17 484	149 427	78 331	75 051
1982..	65 242	39 545	26 553	67 665	24 088	118 426	60 956	99 532
Corporation:								
Family held .... farms, 1987..	17	8	8	14	22	26	6	12
1982..	19	3	10	13	23	16	6	4
acres, 1987..	43 160	7 032	9 414	22 473	(D)	79 957	(D)	(D)
1982..	37 903	1 440	(D)	(D)	18 543	65 414	6 940	10 110
Other than family held .... farms, 1987..	3	-	2	1	1	3	-	-
1982..	3	1	2	-	3	4	-	-
acres, 1987..	2 186	-	(D)	(D)	(D)	362	-	-
1982..	(D)	(D)	(D)	-	6 297	(D)	-	-
Other—cooperative, estate or trust,								
institutional, etc. .... farms, 1987..	-	3	2	1	8	-	2	1
1982..	7	5	5	4	4	1	3	3
acres, 1987..	-	1 184	(D)	(D)	1 131	-	(D)	(D)
1982..	(D)	(D)	1 719	(D)	103	(D)	242	5 176

[For meaning of abbreviations and symbols, see introductory text]

Characteristics		Labette	Lane	Leavenworth	Lincoln	Linn	Logan	Lyon	McPherson
OPERATOR CHARACTERISTICS—Con.									
Operators by age group:									
Under 25 years	1987...	23	5	20	4	4	11	13	40
	1982...	42	7	26	17	20	18	45	55
25 to 34 years	1987...	122	35	119	82	50	65	142	191
	1982...	159	55	133	116	81	67	118	219
35 to 44 years	1987...	185	72	199	118	130	79	150	249
	1982...	201	57	225	73	146	56	169	243
45 to 54 years	1987...	184	57	273	74	137	55	169	241
	1982...	221	69	310	118	157	80	183	303
55 to 64 years	1987...	230	73	286	165	182	96	173	330
	1982...	226	85	306	162	203	100	215	366
55 to 59 years	1987...	126	38	131	64	85	52	94	162
60 to 64 years	1987...	104	35	155	101	97	44	79	168
65 years and over	1987...	227	80	247	135	185	76	225	306
	1982...	213	61	237	129	165	58	215	290
65 to 69 years	1987...	78	33	97	57	76	34	68	138
70 years and over	1987...	149	47	150	78	109	42	157	168
Average age	1987...	52.2	52.5	52.7	52.7	55.1	50.3	52.1	51.5
	1982...	50.3	50.5	51.8	51.1	52.2	49.3	51.7	50.7
Operators by sex:									
Male	farms, 1987...	929	307	1 090	552	660	357	830	1 320
	1982...	1 035	314	1 177	590	736	364	899	1 448
	acres, 1987...	342 620	450 490	204 555	442 194	267 541	591 529	459 851	527 718
	1982...	348 650	433 672	222 399	432 903	270 314	576 582	492 376	550 839
Female	farms	42	15	54	26	28	25	42	37
	1982...	29	21	60	25	36	15	46	28
	acres, 1987...	7 390	16 515	6 615	12 147	5 670	18 951	10 057	5 714
	1982...	6 072	29 306	4 932	7 617	10 323	6 732	8 298	6 318
TYPE OF ORGANIZATION									
Individual or family (sole proprietorship)	farms, 1987...	888	258	1 039	506	638	324	774	1 233
	1982...	971	285	1 117	534	735	345	843	1 328
	acres, 1987...	295 963	327 381	167 118	355 772	250 457	495 930	358 345	450 586
	1982...	302 070	357 112	177 982	357 514	253 737	491 467	361 378	482 423
Partnership	farms, 1987...	72	43	92	49	34	32	80	107
	1982...	80	28	106	58	30	23	74	113
	acres, 1987...	42 413	95 308	32 493	63 787	13 793	53 080	73 746	60 368
	1982...	43 617	61 230	34 162	53 730	21 892	53 421	63 469	54 351
Corporation:									
Family held	farms, 1987...	7	19	11	12	11	17	14	12
	1982...	6	18	9	8	5	7	16	26
	acres, 1987...	6 648	(D)	(D)	26 841	8 074	44 027	37 345	(D)
	1982...	(D)	(D)	10 190	(D)	(D)	24 746	50 943	(D)
Other than family held	farms, 1987...	1	-	-	-	-	4	-	1
	1982...	2	1	-	2	1	-	5	2
	acres, 1987...	(D)	-	-	-	-	2 040	-	(D)
	1982...	(D)	(D)	-	(D)	(D)	-	4 253	(D)
Other—cooperative, estate or trust, institutional, etc.	farms, 1987...	3	2	2	11	6	5	4	4
	1982...	5	3	5	13	1	4	7	7
	acres, 1987...	(D)	(D)	(D)	7 971	887	15 423	470	846
	1982...	3 616	3 955	4 997	7 327	(D)	13 680	631	4 219

[For meaning of abbreviations and symbols, see introductory text]

Characteristics		Marion	Marshall	Meade	Miami	Mitchell	Montgomery	Morris	Morton
OPERATOR CHARACTERISTICS—Con.									
Operators by age group:									
Under 25 years	1987	34	40	10	30	28	10	14	7
	1982	74	65	29	22	31	16	29	11
25 to 34 years	1987	162	210	71	121	91	99	66	30
	1982	171	209	55	123	109	112	68	35
35 to 44 years	1987	210	164	62	217	129	162	83	56
	1982	190	146	72	270	84	186	89	44
45 to 54 years	1987	190	194	89	286	89	196	83	51
	1982	216	244	114	287	127	214	100	54
55 to 64 years	1987	240	265	120	283	160	243	133	45
	1982	323	281	126	288	147	244	154	57
55 to 59 years	1987	93	128	67	129	86	111	54	20
60 to 64 years	1987	147	137	53	154	74	132	79	25
65 years and over	1987	283	188	112	214	125	264	171	37
	1982	210	204	93	235	144	249	131	34
65 to 69 years	1987	133	75	48	77	38	115	63	15
70 years and over	1987	150	113	64	137	87	149	108	22
Average age	1987	51.7	49.6	52.5	51.8	50.4	54.3	54.3	49.8
	1982	49.8	49.3	51.0	51.5	50.7	53.0	51.8	48.9
Operators by sex:									
Male	farms, 1987	1 094	1 043	445	1 094	598	916	526	214
	1982	1 158	1 113	476	1 180	632	964	552	226
	acres, 1987	568 271	547 255	562 310	259 269	465 747	318 964	375 984	446 167
	1982	552 878	519 310	584 991	301 078	444 867	317 422	396 029	421 488
Female	farms, 1987	25	18	19	57	24	58	24	12
	1982	26	36	13	43	10	57	19	9
	acres, 1987	9 429	6 181	20 144	13 021	8 082	10 229	20 572	11 273
	1982	18 829	9 439	8 534	7 663	3 027	7 585	6 919	8 551
TYPE OF ORGANIZATION									
Individual or family (sole proprietorship)	farms, 1987	1 021	940	378	1 070	539	911	483	180
	1982	1 077	1 043	423	1 095	552	939	498	195
	acres, 1987	493 891	479 437	426 417	229 893	383 052	274 873	307 798	252 091
	1982	466 513	464 704	446 113	250 969	345 682	262 144	333 823	254 444
Partnership	farms, 1987	79	85	62	62	48	44	59	30
	1982	92	86	48	104	61	70	65	35
	acres, 1987	59 250	46 955	78 904	31 253	43 491	22 798	80 176	65 670
	1982	79 659	47 751	88 562	41 383	57 780	46 857	64 447	49 444
Corporation:									
Family held	farms, 1987	16	26	20	11	27	12	7	8
	1982	13	13	13	13	24	9	3	4
	acres, 1987	24 033	22 546	72 653	(D)	44 711	(D)	(D)	24 200
	1982	(D)	(D)	52 306	12 207	(D)	14 941	3 680	(D)
Other than family held	farms, 1987	1	1	4	1	4	2	-	1
	1982	-	1	-	4	2	-	-	-
	acres, 1987	(D)	1 749	(D)	(D)	753	(D)	-	(D)
	1982	-	(D)	(D)	904	(D)	-	-	-
Other—cooperative, estate or trust, institutional, etc.	farms, 1987	2	7	4	7	4	5	1	7
	1982	2	6	1	7	3	3	5	1
	acres, 1987	(D)	749	4 480	1 120	1 822	891	(D)	(D)
	1982	(D)	1 836	(D)	3 278	2 240	1 065	998	(D)

Table 10. Tenure and Characteristics of Operator and Type of Organization: 1987 and 1982—Con.

[For meaning of abbreviations and symbols, see introductory text]

Characteristics		Nemaha	Neosho	Ness	Norton	Osage	Osborne	Ottawa	Pawnee
OPERATOR CHARACTERISTICS—Con.									
Operators by age group:									
Under 25 years	1987	44	18	13	5	20	24	11	15
	1982	80	39	36	31	41	25	26	15
25 to 34 years	1987	230	103	95	79	122	90	85	61
	1982	226	109	101	75	134	115	82	69
35 to 44 years	1987	197	126	92	80	148	106	89	99
	1982	171	142	88	74	206	69	85	88
45 to 54 years	1987	202	142	97	90	197	96	114	74
	1982	235	138	117	94	210	130	131	99
55 to 64 years	1987	258	166	155	101	208	136	109	121
	1982	268	196	151	125	227	158	137	147
55 to 59 years	1987	135	77	82	44	106	69	53	59
60 to 64 years	1987	123	89	73	57	102	67	56	62
65 years and over	1987	196	196	145	116	190	155	136	160
	1982	168	178	149	116	171	140	128	150
65 to 69 years	1987	63	88	61	45	81	58	58	56
70 years and over	1987	133	108	84	70	109	97	77	104
Average age	1987	48.7	52.6	52.3	51.9	51.7	51.7	52.8	53.5
	1982	47.4	51.1	51.1	51.1	49.8	51.1	51.2	53.7
Operators by sex:									
Male	farms, 1987	1 101	708	579	458	850	584	495	512
	1982	1 138	772	623	507	965	619	571	550
	acres, 1987	430 881	295 082	659 906	499 716	350 540	533 805	373 475	475 799
	1982	410 818	312 633	669 367	506 172	374 945	504 831	386 309	457 398
Female	farms, 1987	26	43	18	12	36	23	28	18
	1982	20	30	21	10	24	18	18	18
	acres, 1987	5 880	10 410	13 283	7 910	6 659	11 612	12 067	11 201
	1982	3 492	5 584	9 741	7 093	5 021	6 713	7 124	11 242
TYPE OF ORGANIZATION									
Individual or family (sole proprietorship)	farms, 1987	998	690	522	420	904	540	461	446
	1982	1 003	730	565	465	905	565	506	480
	acres, 1987	359 750	256 698	583 547	425 562	284 366	470 342	310 428	371 916
	1982	346 362	252 996	556 821	435 003	313 820	441 485	320 586	376 021
Partnership	farms, 1987	118	39	65	21	75	51	36	62
	1982	118	57	86	22	62	57	55	67
	acres, 1987	63 565	24 094	73 385	(D)	67 797	53 812	26 403	77 358
	1982	47 215	47 485	94 978	19 996	(D)	44 643	37 034	70 999
Corporation:									
Family held	farms, 1987	21	10	8	26	3	7	22	16
	1982	25	11	8	20	2	8	21	14
	acres, 1987	13 446	17 555	(D)	(D)	4 325	(D)	42 959	34 216
	1982	(D)	(D)	(D)	(D)	-	(D)	33 494	17 462
Other than family held	farms, 1987	-	5	-	1	-	2	-	3
	1982	1	1	-	2	-	1	-	3
	acres, 1987	-	5 561	-	(D)	-	(D)	-	(D)
	1982	(D)	(D)	-	(D)	-	-	-	(D)
Other—cooperative, estate or trust, institutional, etc.	farms, 1987	-	7	2	2	3	7	4	3
	1982	11	3	5	8	-	6	7	4
	acres, 1987	-	1 594	(D)	(D)	711	2 997	3 752	(D)
	1982	5 090	1 132	(D)	11 641	-	5 286	2 219	(D)

Table 10. **Tenure and Characteristics of Operator and Type of Organization: 1987 and 1982** —Con.

[For meaning of abbreviations and symbols, see introductory text]

Characteristics	Phillips	Pottawatomie	Pratt	Rawlins	Reno	Republic	Rice	Riley
OPERATOR CHARACTERISTICS—Con.								
Operators by age group:								
Under 25 years .... 1987..	19	22	12	10	36	34	15	9
1982..	29	26	17	27	47	62	18	25
25 to 34 years .... 1987..	79	88	63	83	201	158	92	69
1982..	102	121	81	109	211	158	95	82
35 to 44 years .... 1987..	100	156	106	101	331	154	104	99
1982..	94	157	98	84	310	150	112	100
45 to 54 years .... 1987..	108	145	91	107	293	138	121	108
1982..	104	165	100	129	315	204	129	137
55 to 64 years .... 1987..	126	175	100	122	361	179	128	120
1982..	173	203	130	163	412	164	154	126
55 to 59 years .... 1987..	49	86	52	62	151	95	54	56
60 to 64 years .... 1987..	77	89	48	60	210	84	74	64
65 years and over .... 1987..	159	204	145	118	345	169	144	146
1982..	145	197	121	110	343	185	135	111
65 to 69 years .... 1987..	77	91	64	54	149	67	55	66
70 years and over .... 1987..	82	113	81	64	196	102	89	78
Average age .... 1987..	52.1	52.6	52.5	51.3	51.5	49.6	51.9	52.9
1982..	51.6	51.7	51.5	50.2	51.5	48.7	51.1	50.0
Operators by sex								
Male .... farms, 1987..	575	752	497	523	1 504	800	587	528
1982..	633	848	532	603	1 584	902	632	572
acres, 1987..	534 650	435 543	455 437	630 266	705 893	431 859	427 244	245 004
1982..	536 619	455 332	433 173	673 910	686 285	430 407	428 449	250 329
Female .... farms, 1987..	16	38	20	18	53	33	17	18
1982..	14	21	15	18	54	21	11	11
acres, 1987..	7 928	8 117	10 808	11 544	11 871	8 356	1 821	2 605
1982..	7 713	9 407	5 328	12 561	15 150	10 711	1 432	2 574
TYPE OF ORGANIZATION								
Individual or family (sole proprietorship) .... farms, 1987..	520	680	433	446	1 366	739	533	473
1982..	558	746	472	507	1 419	814	556	500
acres, 1987..	434 522	324 994	370 762	499 197	579 318	378 025	363 279	188 447
1982..	412 792	347 268	366 212	509 740	581 976	369 070	350 190	195 357
Partnership .... farms, 1987..	51	88	53	74	126	71	39	57
1982..	66	96	43	81	157	84	59	66
acres, 1987..	70 484	77 848	52 587	108 407	84 741	41 140	30 808	38 946
1982..	77 044	67 112	39 750	115 369	73 725	48 557	42 360	32 594
Corporation:								
Family held .... farms, 1987..	17	18	25	17	50	17	27	12
1982..	16	19	27	21	49	22	24	12
acres, 1987..	35 265	(D)	39 467	(D)	(D)	20 067	(D)	14 408
1982..	(D)	(D)	(D)	(D)	43 111	(D)	34 716	(D)
Other than family held .... farms, 1987..	–	2	1	2	8	3	1	2
1982..	–	2	1	–	8	–	3	2
acres, 1987..	–	(D)	(D)	–	(D)	655	(D)	(D)
1982..	–	(D)	(D)	(D)	1 343	–	(D)	(D)
Other—cooperative, estate or trust,								
institutional, etc. .... farms, 1987..	3	3	4	2	7	3	4	2
1982..	5	6	4	10	5	3	1	3
acres, 1987..	2 307	221	(D)	(D)	4 442	326	3 470	(D)
1982..	(D)	8 305	2 520	11 773	1 280	(D)	(D)	5 481

Table 10. **Tenure and Characteristics of Operator and Type of Organization: 1987 and 1982**—Con.

[For meaning of abbreviations and symbols, see introductory text]

Characteristics	Rooks	Rush	Russell	Saline	Scott	Sedgwick	Seward	Shawnee
OPERATOR CHARACTERISTICS— Con.								
Operators by age group:								
Under 25 years .... 1987..	11	19	7	15	6	22	17	16
1982..	15	27	8	32	13	44	15	19
25 to 34 years .... 1987..	77	72	68	111	62	203	52	74
1982..	69	76	81	115	67	250	49	90
35 to 44 years .... 1987..	89	70	88	128	87	302	61	140
1982..	85	80	91	95	69	281	50	171
45 to 54 years .... 1987..	85	83	75	145	64	318	53	200
1982..	104	108	123	170	94	356	57	234
55 to 64 years .... 1987..	100	144	141	153	94	377	57	209
1982..	134	161	135	182	107	448	59	223
55 to 59 years .... 1987..	42	66	62	75	48	177	26	117
60 to 64 years .... 1987..	58	78	59	78	46	200	31	92
65 years and over .... 1987..	111	149	155	191	78	387	45	214
1982..	121	130	152	169	66	286	47	200
65 to 69 years .... 1987..	35	61	51	83	31	186	15	96
70 years and over .... 1987..	76	88	104	108	47	181	30	118
Average age .... 1987..	51.8	53.6	54.2	52.1	50.5	52.0	47.6	53.8
1982..	51.9	51.9	52.8	51.6	49.8	50.4	49.2	52.5
Operators by sex:								
Male .... farms, 1987..	460	523	515	724	372	1 503	266	613
1982..	501	567	572	734	404	1 586	270	852
acres, 1987..	536 937	413 065	450 252	401 045	459 667	503 654	321 810	215 806
1982..	513 623	418 770	456 447	388 280	468 566	505 409	320 635	221 921
Female .... farms, 1987..	13	23	19	19	19	86	19	39
1982..	27	17	18	29	12	79	7	45
acres, 1987..	8 602	9 761	10 762	2 753	11 087	19 926	9 587	5 292
1982..	18 566	5 348	15 012	8 496	21 040	17 265	4 693	7 926
TYPE OF ORGANIZATION								
Individual or family (sole proprietorship) .... farms, 1987..	402	469	453	666	279	1 400	243	776
1982..	468	503	512	673	302	1 459	234	852
acres, 1987..	439 468	340 897	354 822	323 349	291 669	422 917	259 836	187 974
1982..	449 910	345 787	376 264	330 363	319 535	423 953	251 847	190 697
Partnership .... farms, 1987..	59	47	68	52	58	130	25	58
1982..	48	60	64	71	66	143	26	58
acres, 1987..	93 127	36 719	76 496	47 179	93 749	88 396	32 603	24 532
1982..	66 080	(D)	63 401	46 584	84 750	66 173	36 503	26 763
Corporation:								
Family held .... farms, 1987..	7	26	12	20	44	44	13	11
1982..	5	18	10	11	40	49	8	20
acres, 1987..	10 199	42 281	(D)	(D)	76 901	28 997	23 291	(D)
1982..	10 507	(D)	31 642	(D)	97 202	30 783		8 990
Other than family held .... farms, 1987..	-	2	-	1	5	7	1	2
1982..	1		-	2	4	5	4	
acres, 1987..	-	-	-	(D)	772	1 546	(D)	(D)
1982..	(D)	(D)	-	(D)	1 047	390	7 350	-
Other—cooperative, estate or trust, institutional, etc. .... farms, 1987..	5	4	1	4	5	8	3	5
1982..	6	1	4	6	4	9	3	7
acres, 1987..	4 751	2 929	(D)	1 645	7 683	1 724	9 753	509
1982..	(D)	(D)	152	1 023	7 072	1 375	6 337	9 397

Table 10. **Tenure and Characteristics of Operator and Type of Organization: 1987 and 1982**—Con.

[For meaning of abbreviations and symbols, see introductory text]

Characteristics	Sheridan	Sherman	Smith	Stafford	Stanton	Stevens	Sumner	Thomas
OPERATOR CHARACTERISTICS— Con.								
Operators by age group:								
Under 25 years ... 1987..	10	17	24	14	9	5	27	21
1982..	23	32	49	24	9	8	54	23
25 to 34 years ... 1987..	97	82	113	76	56	44	173	94
1982..	94	80	127	90	48	61	208	100
35 to 44 years ... 1987..	92	79	126	106	55	63	239	117
1982..	81	78	100	92	42	60	217	97
45 to 54 years ... 1987..	93	99	104	105	54	56	274	129
1982..	129	113	160	104	50	59	280	137
55 to 64 years ... 1987..	131	134	171	113	74	71	277	124
1982..	152	134	188	109	51	85	342	116
55 to 59 years ... 1987..	65	59	74	53	32	34	123	62
60 to 64 years ... 1987..	66	75	97	60	42	37	154	62
65 years and over ... 1987..	95	113	154	126	32	59	281	159
1982..	92	113	137	138	32	52	285	155
65 to 69 years ... 1987..	46	32	63	39	13	34	124	59
70 years and over ... 1987..	49	81	91	87	19	25	157	100
Average age ... 1987..	50.1	52.0	50.9	51.7	48.4	50.7	51.5	51.7
1982..	49.8	50.5	49.3	50.7	47.4	49.4	50.8	51.6
Operators by sex:								
Male ... farms, 1987..	499	481	659	520	268	288	1 229	901
1982..	547	518	744	543	229	322	1 341	573
acres, 1987..	495 274	594 410	545 993	455 008	419 419	447 174	692 378	651 940
1982..	501 803	634 220	541 724	456 315	(D)	455 487	720 679	625 875
Female ... farms, 1987..	19	43	33	20	12	12	42	43
1982..	24	32	17	14	2	3	45	55
acres, 1987..	8 308	31 532	9 685	6 205	5 731	13 800	12 410	25 259
1982..	11 655	38 034	4 344	2 066	(D)	1 108	13 899	32 683
TYPE OF ORGANIZATION								
Individual or family (sole proprietorship) ... farms, 1987..	449	443	613	453	215	225	1 138	545
1982..	493	436	658	455	181	264	1 255	522
acres, 1987..	426 295	490 593	436 423	345 378	291 550	310 102	583 195	497 451
1982..	429 057	487 191	414 836	335 609	305 195	338 535	637 642	477 990
Partnership ... farms, 1987..	37	33	46	49	35	55	104	40
1982..	50	68	65	68	36	44	104	54
acres, 1987..	36 476	60 332	(D)	66 583	81 635	115 484	96 308	64 296
1982..	45 545	93 646	55 286	74 896	(D)	80 243	69 024	59 996
Corporation:								
Family held ... farms, 1987..	25	37	31	31	28	13	21	47
1982..	23	40	35	27	12	14	19	40
acres, 1987..	34 388	(D)	71 637	45 466	(D)	30 377	(D)	80 454
1982..		(D)	72 982		60 548	28 437	(D)	(D)
Other than family held ... farms, 1987..	1	2	3	3	-	2	3	2
1982..	2	2	1	1	2	1	2	2
acres, 1987..	(D)	(D)	(D)	961	-	(D)	(D)	(D)
1982..	(D)	(D)	2 964	(D)	(D)	(D)	(D)	(D)
Other—cooperative, estate or trust, institutional, etc. ... farms, 1987..	6	9	2	4	2	5	6	10
1982..	3	4	-	6	-	2	6	10
acres, 1987..	2 621	3 903	(D)	805	(D)	(D)	4 976	(D)
1982..	(D)	12 003	-	7 211	-	(D)	5 361	27 145

Table 10. Tenure and Characteristics of Operator and Type of Organization: 1987 and 1982—Con.

[For meaning of abbreviations and symbols, see introductory text]

Characteristics	Trego	Wabaunsee	Wallace	Washington	Wichita	Wilson	Woodson	Wyandotte
OPERATOR CHARACTERISTICS—Con.								
Operators by age group:								
Under 25 years 1987..	13	21	8	43	12	10	9	6
1982..	18	30	15	60	17	26	5	2
25 to 34 years 1987..	75	70	71	167	75	74	51	10
1982..	76	87	62	133	72	107	56	14
35 to 44 years 1987..	92	118	51	148	62	95	70	36
1982..	66	104	45	187	63	120	62	45
45 to 54 years 1987..	87	99	52	140	77	119	55	35
1982..	125	143	74	205	67	127	78	43
55 to 64 years 1987..	116	158	70	226	84	153	92	52
1982..	119	156	76	240	80	169	102	63
55 to 59 years 1987..	50	74	31	122	40	67	44	27
60 to 64 years 1987..	66	84	39	104	44	86	48	25
65 years and over 1987..	99	167	78	215	45	159	92	60
1982..	93	158	65	206	42	131	99	49
65 to 69 years 1987..	43	57	33	82	21	71	40	22
70 years and over 1987..	56	110	45	133	24	88	52	38
Average age 1987..	51.2	53.4	50.8	50.7	48.3	53.4	52.3	55.6
1982..	51.1	51.7	49.9	50.4	47.0	50.6	52.6	54.3
Operators by sex:								
Male farms, 1987..	459	594	308	913	349	585	351	184
1982..	480	655	317	1 000	338	656	388	207
acres, 1987..	467 004	481 282	506 292	510 778	436 146	291 030	248 108	23 136
1982..	491 264	432 985	474 763	522 203	424 622	328 478	272 841	(D)
Female farms, 1987..	23	39	22	26	6	25	16	15
1982..	17	23	21	32	3	24	14	9
acres, 1987..	13 155	9 022	23 457	7 723	2 321	8 432	5 859	800
1982..	8 507	9 504	31 153	8 000	2 920	4 424	3 240	(D)
TYPE OF ORGANIZATION								
Individual or family (sole proprietorship) farms, 1987..	427	576	283	808	281	552	340	184
1982..	444	601	285	912	274	613	376	189
acres, 1987..	416 423	313 779	393 391	405 181	310 767	243 195	233 511	16 474
1982..	406 653	313 822	365 652	443 782	319 038	271 179	214 569	19 917
Partnership farms, 1987..	50	42	19	100	34	44	25	8
1982..	43	61	28	88	36	61	19	17
acres, 1987..	46 724	100 010	45 941	65 555	64 237	35 516	16 612	(D)
1982..	68 398	114 282	54 797	42 400	50 278	53 533	36 476	3 730
Corporation:								
Family held farms, 1987..	4	11	19	28	31	12	2	5
1982..	5	11	18	24	28	4	4	7
acres, 1987..	(D)	40 216	(D)	(D)	(D)	20 656	(D)	(D)
1982..	17 307	(D)	78 721	(D)	56 705	(D)	(D)	1 244
Other than family held farms, 1987..	2	1	–	1	1	2	–	1
1982..	–	1	–	2	3	–	–	1
acres, 1987..	–	(D)	(D)	(D)	(D)	(D)	(D)	(D)
1982..	–	(D)	–	(D)	1 521	(D)	–	(D)
Other—cooperative, estate or trust, institutional, etc. farms, 1987..	1	2	8	4	8	1	1	1
1982..	5	4	7	6	–	3	3	2
acres, 1987..	(D)	(D)	8 671	412	4 133	(D)	(D)	(D)
1982..	7 415	572	6 546	976	–	–	(D)	(D)

Table 11. Cattle and Calves—Inventory and Sales: 1987 and 1982

[For meaning of abbreviations and symbols, see introductory text]

Item	Kansas	Allen	Anderson	Atchison	Barber	Barton	Bourbon
INVENTORY							
Cattle and calves ... farms, 1987..	40 785	492	522	456	386	540	635
1982..	47 008	568	607	540	378	570	717
number, 1987..	5 539 292	30 062	35 758	29 344	89 515	85 041	46 580
1982..	5 800 138	35 484	43 833	33 846	92 236	82 712	48 749
Farms by inventory:							
1 to 9 ... farms, 1987..	4 367	52	63	36	14	65	80
1982..	4 715	52	74	68	13	69	77
number, 1987..	23 155	301	366	201	89	362	444
1982..	25 526	296	468	401	75	363	455
10 to 19 ... farms, 1987..	5 573	90	84	93	29	88	121
1982..	6 086	92	75	93	27	70	110
number, 1987..	77 961	1 257	1 036	1 299	422	1 206	1 710
1982..	84 785	1 278	1 238	1 332	378	989	1 524
20 to 49 ... farms, 1987..	11 268	146	154	143	71	172	191
1982..	13 181	193	188	171	69	184	253
number, 1987..	360 946	4 767	5 002	4 620	2 259	5 437	5 984
1982..	422 804	6 050	5 933	5 310	2 226	5 901	8 363
50 to 99 ... farms, 1987..	8 529	112	123	95	68	118	137
1982..	10 146	130	124	117	68	155	141
number, 1987..	589 156	7 594	8 474	6 672	4 084	8 083	9 389
1982..	703 817	9 182	8 759	7 620	4 660	10 527	9 662
100 to 199 ... farms, 1987..	6 150	69	73	62	78	77	58
1982..	7 336	65	88	65	69	67	61
number, 1987..	830 820	9 077	9 619	8 026	10 807	(D)	7 632
1982..	990 498	(D)	12 092	8 697	9 446	8 666	11 808
200 to 499 ... farms, 1987..	3 580	18	31	21	90	16	41
1982..	4 163	34	44	20	65	18	38
number, 1987..	1 046 310	4 672	8 571	5 625	26 032	(D)	11 912
1982..	1 198 771	8 616	12 470	5 935	25 695	5 327	10 949
500 or more ... farms, 1987..	1 318	3	3	4	46	6	7
1982..	1 381	2	5	6	47	7	7
number, 1987..	2 611 144	2 394	2 791	2 701	43 822	54 985	9 509
1982..	2 373 957	(D)	2 873	4 353	49 556	50 939	5 988
Cows and heifers that had calved ... farms, 1987..	33 157	458	465	394	276	487	547
1982..	38 955	527	526	460	280	485	613
number, 1987..	1 451 324	15 218	16 576	12 302	29 146	16 651	18 955
1982..	1 646 706	17 968	19 420	12 927	26 441	15 503	18 976
Beef cows ... farms, 1987..	31 475	423	432	368	269	468	515
1982..	36 497	484	479	420	263	474	569
number, 1987..	1 354 649	12 799	14 924	10 970	28 337	14 700	17 494
1982..	1 523 697	15 256	17 385	11 396	27 623	14 790	16 717
1987 farms by inventory:							
1 to 9 ... farms..	8 299	105	89	75	26	97	118
number..	32 616	585	450	383	161	512	611
10 to 19 ... farms..	8 677	96	100	111	40	109	134
number..	91 238	1 301	1 379	1 540	519	1 494	1 819
20 to 49 ... farms..	10 446	152	152	132	58	166	170
number..	320 969	4 681	4 701	4 095	1 816	5 046	5 255
50 to 99 ... farms..	5 108	52	65	34	55	79	63
number..	339 951	3 299	4 107	2 185	3 725	5 061	3 847
100 to 199 ... farms..	2 115	15	20	13	49	12	21
number..	271 669	1 820	2 523	1 705	(D)	1 361	2 666
200 to 499 ... farms..	714	2	5	5	36	5	8
number..	196 616	(D)	(D)	1 062	(D)	1 226	(D)
500 or more ... farms..	116	1	1	1	5	–	1
number..	101 591	(D)	(D)	–	4 920	–	(D)
Milk cows ... farms, 1987..	3 093	54	53	49	13	36	59
1982..	4 831	83	83	74	22	44	94
number, 1987..	96 675	2 419	1 655	1 332	811	951	1 461
1982..	123 009	2 712	2 035	1 531	818	713	2 259
1987 farms by inventory:							
1 to 9 ... farms..	1 345	18	19	20	2	15	19
number..	2 871	51	31	40	(D)	45	40
10 to 19 ... farms..	254	3	5	4	1	8	8
number..	3 551	49	80	42	(D)	98	113
20 to 49 ... farms..	725	10	19	13	4	10	24
number..	23 698	348	665	407	140	313	732
50 to 99 ... farms..	582	17	5	9	4	4	7
number..	38 874	1 176	298	523	313	(D)	(D)
100 to 199 ... farms..	163	6	5	3	1	–	1
number..	20 491	795	581	320	(D)	–	(D)
200 to 499 ... farms..	21	–	–	–	1	1	–
number..	5 540	–	–	–	(D)	(D)	–
500 or more ... farms..	3	–	–	–	–	–	–
number..	1 650	–	–	–	–	–	–
Heifers and heifer calves ... farms, 1987..	31 410	413	434	349	265	436	483
1982..	37 146	479	506	448	262	463	582
number, 1987..	1 632 193	8 239	10 200	6 439	23 404	33 304	11 497
1982..	1 610 349	8 815	10 037	9 794	19 312	30 116	11 115
Steers, steer calves, bulls, and bull calves ... farms, 1987..	35 035	441	455	400	323	479	539
1982..	41 395	509	538	470	337	508	629
number, 1987..	2 455 775	6 605	8 979	8 603	36 963	36 086	16 128
1982..	2 543 083	8 701	14 376	11 127	44 483	37 093	16 658

Table 11. **Cattle and Calves—Inventory and Sales: 1987 and 1982**—Con.

[For meaning of abbreviations and symbols, see introductory text]

Item	Brown	Butler	Chase	Chautauqua	Cherokee	Cheyenne	Clark
INVENTORY							
Cattle and calves .... farms, 1987..	442	788	197	328	551	254	197
1982..	566	897	224	369	642	307	200
number, 1987..	39 705	107 777	39 591	34 230	22 329	42 329	66 325
1982..	49 409	125 610	38 742	41 215	24 909	45 923	66 490
Farms by inventory:							
1 to 9 .... farms, 1987..	36	113	13	36	102	12	7
1982..	50	126	15	26	132	17	10
number, 1987..	189	615	61	206	598	47	31
1982..	262	685	61	151	774	76	49
10 to 19 .... farms, 1987..	63	125	19	44	145	20	14
1982..	58	127	17	44	157	34	6
number, 1987..	844	1 696	289	638	2 079	281	206
1982..	794	1 683	225	611	2 098	485	102
20 to 49 .... farms, 1987..	149	217	41	102	175	62	27
1982..	168	241	54	108	202	69	34
number, 1987..	4 651	6 735	1 202	3 227	5 461	2 050	780
1982..	5 933	7 458	1 629	3 545	6 439	2 319	1 077
50 to 99 .... farms, 1987..	91	101	41	58	83	54	32
1982..	120	170	54	92	97	64	27
number, 1987..	6 251	6 705	3 024	4 098	5 671	3 669	2 354
1982..	8 261	11 856	3 885	6 502	6 663	4 524	1 867
100 to 199 .... farms, 1987..	63	113	35	45	33	58	34
1982..	114	114	32	49	42	77	47
number, 1987..	8 416	15 083	4 775	6 604	4 338	7 872	4 697
1982..	12 386	15 508	4 281	6 947	5 524	10 483	6 077
200 to 499 .... farms, 1987..	31	80	34	28	11	34	43
1982..	44	80	31	34	12	35	40
number, 1987..	8 868	24 212	9 668	7 960	(D)	9 921	13 754
1982..	11 870	29 882	9 997	10 195	3 411	10 084	12 440
500 or more .... farms, 1987..	9	39	14	15	2	14	40
1982..	14	39	21	16	1	11	41
number, 1987..	10 486	52 731	20 572	11 497	(D)	18 589	44 504
1982..	9 903	64 538	18 664	13 264	–	17 952	44 878
Cows and heifers that had calved .... farms, 1987..	366	607	154	296	489	210	99
1982..	456	701	182	340	565	260	114
number, 1987	13 797	26 113	9 801	18 363	10 708	15 321	10 004
1982..	16 879	28 553	14 509	21 432	12 123	16 059	13 005
Beef cows .... farms, 1987..	336	581	147	286	484	210	97
1982..	408	649	176	329	551	252	110
number, 1987..	12 065	24 898	9 452	15 854	10 566	15 303	(D)
1982..	14 210	25 563	14 255	21 012	11 835	15 550	12 991
1987 farms by inventory:							
1 to 9 .... farms..	57	164	18	50	169	11	12
number..	267	634	81	258	954	51	(D)
10 to 19 .... farms..	101	134	30	62	134	25	13
number..	1 300	1 794	397	826	1 847	336	181
20 to 49 .... farms..	109	152	44	95	139	69	22
number..	3 235	4 599	1 497	2 834	4 021	2 221	676
50 to 99 .... farms..	48	76	28	40	29	55	18
number..	3 239	5 020	1 880	2 781	1 720	3 759	1 249
100 to 199 .... farms..	18	32	19	25	11	38	19
number..	2 271	4 247	2 360	3 393	(D)	4 912	2 940
200 to 499 .... farms..	1	19	10	12	2	10	10
number..	(D)	5 131	3 237	3 624	(D)	(D)	2 855
500 or more .... farms..	2	4	–	2	–	2	4
number..	(D)	3 273	–	2 138	–	(D)	2 366
Milk cows .... farms, 1987..	55	52	15	18	13	8	2
1982..	78	97	21	33	23	21	7
number, 1987..	1 732	1 214	349	496	138	18	(D)
1982..	2 669	1 990	254	420	288	509	14
1987 farms by inventory:							
1 to 9 .... farms..	22	32	8	10	10	8	2
number..	60	57	10	20	31	18	(D)
10 to 19 .... farms..	5	4	1	–	–	–	–
number..	62	55	(D)	–	–	–	–
20 to 49 .... farms..	11	6	3	4	3	–	–
number..	345	221	87	108	107	–	–
50 to 99 .... farms..	15	7	2	3	–	–	–
number..	(D)	371	(D)	(D)	–	–	–
100 to 199 .... farms..	2	2	1	1	–	–	–
number..	(D)	(D)	(D)	(D)	–	–	–
200 to 499 .... farms..	–	1	–	–	–	–	–
number..	–	(D)	–	–	–	–	–
500 or more .... farms..	–	–	–	–	–	–	–
number..	–	–	–	–	–	–	–
Heifers and heifer calves .... farms, 1987..	344	600	153	276	417	184	122
1982..	433	664	172	309	497	235	150
number, 1987..	8 587	35 557	10 060	9 531	5 796	9 664	17 022
1982..	11 203	39 441	10 409	8 541	6 267	13 124	26 379
Steers, steer calves, bulls, and bull calves ... farms, 1987..	372	670	178	295	469	213	169
1982..	498	790	188	325	552	273	154
number, 1987..	17 321	46 108	19 730	8 347	5 827	17 344	36 969
1982..	21 327	57 616	13 824	11 242	6 519	16 740	27 106

1987 CENSUS OF AGRICULTURE—COUNTY DATA

Table 11. **Cattle and Calves—Inventory and Sales: 1987 and 1982**—Con.

[For meaning of abbreviations and symbols, see introductory text]

Item	Clay	Cloud	Coffey	Comanche	Cowley	Crawford	Decatur
INVENTORY							
Cattle and calves .... farms, 1987..	446	374	363	203	614	574	302
1982..	515	439	442	204	723	699	368
number, 1987..	39 466	31 448	31 584	50 945	61 062	31 162	57 326
1982..	46 247	37 868	38 704	38 669	91 038	43 046	58 215
Farms by inventory:							
1 to 9 .... farms, 1987..	34	33	43	13	75	78	13
1982..	35	38	44	15	83	97	18
number, 1987..	161	169	233	59	426	437	56
1982..	188	182	253	73	432	555	67
10 to 19 .... farms, 1987..	46	31	43	12	99	116	14
1982..	45	47	58	18	124	126	16
number, 1987..	690	458	603	180	1 420	1 621	206
1982..	681	675	792	271	1 707	1 732	226
20 to 49 .... farms, 1987..	130	124	99	24	199	194	57
1982..	144	114	132	20	207	222	89
number, 1987..	4 117	3 835	3 195	893	6 168	6 000	1 850
1982..	4 938	3 784	4 306	662	6 277	7 039	2 859
50 to 99 .... farms, 1987..	83	83	67	37	125	104	81
1982..	140	112	103	49	127	137	88
number, 1987..	6 488	5 918	6 001	2 454	8 836	6 603	5 635
1982..	9 661	7 217	7 012	3 574	8 908	9 543	6 231
100 to 199 .... farms, 1987..	93	71	55	40	56	53	82
1982..	94	91	52	43	97	79	93
number, 1987..	11 871	9 597	7 571	5 258	7 518	6 733	11 553
1982..	12 366	11 989	6 915	5 728	13 678	10 391	13 184
200 to 499 .... farms, 1987..	42	29	29	29	39	26	43
1982..	49	29	43	44	55	32	48
number, 1987..	11 874	9 248	8 981	13 855	10 741	7 828	11 692
1982..	12 846	8 308	12 820	10 995	16 801	8 897	13 691
500 or more .... farms, 1987..	6	3	7	33	21	3	12
1982..	8	8	10	22	30	6	16
number, 1987..	4 465	2 223	5 000	28 236	26 155	1 940	26 334
1982..	5 567	5 713	6 606	17 366	43 235	4 889	31 957
Cows and heifers that had calved .... farms, 1987..	385	332	270	135	514	529	259
1982..	419	385	353	146	611	634	294
number, 1987..	15 169	14 251	8 552	15 226	21 295	15 274	16 847
1982..	16 574	16 571	11 752	14 828	29 640	18 727	17 727
Beef cows .... farms, 1987..	367	325	265	131	505	513	254
1982..	395	364	343	138	594	616	293
number, 1987..	14 394	13 958	8 335	14 951	20 584	14 508	16 631
1982..	15 510	15 733	11 294	14 810	28 750	17 708	16 898
1987 farms by inventory:							
1 to 9 .... farms..	54	45	61	15	107	131	15
number..	255	221	315	64	533	664	86
10 to 19 .... farms..	79	68	64	9	137	139	26
number..	1 122	945	879	111	1 832	1 844	354
20 to 49 .... farms..	125	106	92	42	155	164	87
number..	3 956	3 249	2 740	1 330	4 780	4 874	2 880
50 to 99 .... farms..	83	78	37	26	67	53	68
number..	5 411	5 207	2 416	1 823	4 236	3 403	4 544
100 to 199 .... farms..	22	21	8	14	24	23	46
number..	2 570	2 696	1 005	1 837	3 423	2 772	5 779
200 to 499 .... farms..	4	7	2	21	11	2	12
number..	1 080	1 640	(D)	6 878	2 872	(D)	2 988
500 or more .... farms..	-	-	1	4	4	1	-
number..	-	-	(D)	2 908	2 908	(D)	-
Milk cows .... farms, 1987..	38	16	17	8	33	35	11
1982..	47	37	38	13	47	36	23
number, 1987..	775	293	217	277	711	766	216
1982..	1 064	838	458	218	890	1 019	829
1987 farms by inventory:							
1 to 9 .... farms..	18	11	12	3	23	15	6
number..	38	36	25	6	48	32	14
10 to 19 .... farms..	7	-	-	-	-	8	2
number..	106	-	-	-	-	108	(D)
20 to 49 .... farms..	6	4	4	2	4	8	2
number..	207	(D)	(D)	(D)	131	196	(D)
50 to 99 .... farms..	7	1	-	3	4	3	1
number..	424	(D)	-	(D)	(D)	(D)	(D)
100 to 199 .... farms..	-	1	-	-	2	1	-
number..	-	(D)	-	-	(D)	(D)	-
200 to 499 .... farms..	-	-	-	-	-	-	-
number..	-	-	-	-	-	-	-
500 or more .... farms..	-	-	-	-	-	-	-
number..	-	-	-	-	-	-	-
Heifers and heifer calves .... farms, 1987..	368	298	285	134	494	433	237
1982..	440	350	346	133	577	558	290
number, 1987..	11 472	7 295	8 653	10 327	15 068	6 990	18 073
1982..	13 263	8 421	8 631	8 349	27 398	10 128	22 549
Steers, steer calves, bulls, and bull calves ... farms, 1987..	395	326	316	186	526	501	265
1982..	470	393	414	183	619	617	334
number, 1987..	12 825	9 902	14 379	25 390	24 699	8 898	22 406
1982..	16 410	12 876	18 121	15 492	34 000	14 191	27 939

Table 11. **Cattle and Calves—Inventory and Sales: 1987 and 1982**—Con.

[For meaning of abbreviations and symbols, see introductory text]

Item	Dickinson	Doniphan	Douglas	Edwards	Elk	Ellis	Ellsworth
INVENTORY							
Cattle and calves — farms, 1987	635	299	512	194	321	528	344
1982	743	337	612	206	379	568	370
number, 1987	73 786	20 301	27 845	51 127	37 023	55 888	36 868
1982	78 683	22 705	33 654	54 321	42 858	61 283	34 452
Farms by inventory:							
1 to 9 — farms, 1987	49	37	85	13	18	47	19
1982	78	33	91	6	22	48	19
number, 1987	249	185	488	70	108	266	121
1982	429	166	511	48	128	281	103
10 to 19 — farms, 1987	79	54	113	14	37	65	38
1982	78	52	129	18	46	73	36
number, 1987	1 077	760	1 573	184	530	891	510
1982	1 083	737	1 761	239	635	1 105	485
20 to 49 — farms, 1987	182	102	153	39	88	184	79
1982	193	109	208	38	109	186	104
number, 1987	5 777	3 368	4 917	1 311	2 754	5 913	2 628
1982	6 206	3 467	6 578	1 215	3 488	5 782	3 345
50 to 99 — farms, 1987	127	52	91	43	76	115	92
1982	174	84	95	50	81	147	101
number, 1987	8 727	3 682	6 173	3 057	5 250	7 861	6 757
1982	11 990	5 613	6 565	3 604	5 750	9 884	7 175
100 to 199 — farms, 1987	93	33	47	33	52	83	69
1982	125	38	47	47	58	74	80
number, 1987	12 796	4 156	6 356	4 681	6 830	11 038	9 390
1982	16 807	4 972	7 556	6 057	9 341	9 664	11 112
200 to 499 — farms, 1987	78	17	19	30	39	22	41
1982	71	18	24	32	41	27	22
number, 1987	24 247	5 668	5 075	9 785	12 479	5 837	12 207
1982	21 430	5 811	6 518	9 210	12 710	7 753	6 133
500 or more — farms, 1987	27	4	4	22	11	12	6
1982	24	3	6	17	12	13	8
number, 1987	20 913	2 482	3 263	32 059	9 072	24 082	5 255
1982	20 738	1 939	4 163	33 948	10 606	26 814	6 099
Cows and heifers that had calved — farms, 1987	454	251	421	118	285	483	306
1982	585	277	538	144	354	498	333
number, 1987	16 502	8 276	10 680	4 954	16 790	23 263	17 869
1982	18 173	8 828	13 894	6 981	21 180	25 788	15 604
Beef cows — farms, 1987	422	246	394	112	282	462	305
1982	518	266	489	138	352	472	325
number, 1987	14 853	7 716	8 587	4 670	16 665	21 957	17 434
1982	16 189	8 181	10 891	6 443	21 048	24 504	15 150
1987 farms by inventory:							
1 to 9 — farms	81	83	121	18	36	69	37
number	443	349	670	99	203	370	229
10 to 19 — farms	97	57	104	20	49	94	38
number	1 300	793	1 415	250	690	1 271	547
20 to 49 — farms	147	90	131	50	109	180	113
number	4 407	2 687	3 808	1 549	3 489	5 464	3 740
50 to 99 — farms	75	20	30	14	39	78	72
number	4 876	1 209	1 800	880	2 591	5 240	4 970
100 to 199 — farms	15	13	8	6	27	25	33
number	2 112	1 578	894	767	3 373	3 230	4 131
200 to 499 — farms	7	3	-	4	20	14	11
number	1 715	1 100	-	1 125	(D)	(D)	(D)
500 or more — farms	-	-	-	-	2	2	1
number	-	-	-	-	(D)	(D)	(D)
Milk cows — farms, 1987	50	15	43	9	10	31	12
1982	75	30	69	13	21	40	24
number, 1987	1 649	560	2 093	184	125	1 306	135
1982	1 984	647	2 803	538	132	1 284	454
1987 farms by inventory:							
1 to 9 — farms	18	8	10	5	7	9	10
number	28	10	34	12	7	(D)	(D)
10 to 19 — farms	3	-	4	1	1	1	-
number	38	-	60	(D)	(D)	(D)	-
20 to 49 — farms	13	1	10	2	1	7	1
number	425	(D)	318	(D)	(D)	290	(D)
50 to 99 — farms	13	4	14	1	-	11	1
number	848	225	1 083	(D)	-	646	(D)
100 to 199 — farms	3	2	5	-	-	3	-
number	310	(D)	598	-	-	341	-
200 to 499 — farms	-	-	-	-	-	-	-
number	-	-	-	-	-	-	-
500 or more — farms	-	-	-	-	-	-	-
number	-	-	-	-	-	-	-
Heifers and heifer calves — farms, 1987	460	235	384	136	257	386	282
1982	563	261	491	143	302	436	322
number, 1987	20 558	5 480	8 495	16 332	9 812	14 370	9 027
1982	22 921	5 753	8 822	16 807	9 460	16 840	8 380
Steers, steer calves, bulls and bull calves — farms, 1987	544	255	442	156	281	456	305
1982	666	299	531	179	345	481	335
number, 1987	36 626	6 545	8 670	29 941	10 421	18 255	10 272
1982	37 589	6 124	11 338	30 533	12 216	18 655	10 466

1987 CENSUS OF AGRICULTURE—COUNTY DATA

Table 11. **Cattle and Calves—Inventory and Sales: 1987 and 1982**—Con.

[For meaning of abbreviations and symbols, see introductory text]

Item	Finney	Ford	Franklin	Geary	Gove	Graham	Grant
INVENTORY							
Cattle and calves .... farms, 1987..	171	423	653	209	310	281	120
1982..	206	440	745	214	349	325	119
number, 1987..	193 533	137 745	35 740	22 321	81 975	36 291	149 230
1982..	148 106	148 090	44 946	19 659	87 686	43 101	76 503
Farms by inventory:							
1 to 9 .... farms, 1987..	24	36	131	23	12	16	13
1982..	23	44	132	19	10	15	13
number, 1987..	94	168	677	111	77	76	76
1982..	110	230	735	110	60	67	68
10 to 19 .... farms, 1987..	10	47	129	25	19	15	7
1982..	18	45	150	31	19	22	7
number, 1987..	132	630	1 777	348	289	218	94
1982..	205	628	2 045	457	266	308	115
20 to 49 .... farms, 1987..	19	106	221	61	62	67	37
1982..	32	102	222	45	65	66	28
number, 1987..	650	3 456	7 184	1 895	2 038	2 182	1 161
1982..	1 050	3 384	6 801	1 387	2 082	2 126	895
50 to 99 .... farms, 1987..	30	88	84	38	69	62	20
1982..	35	116	124	50	72	68	21
number, 1987..	1 951	5 801	5 909	2 486	4 854	4 152	1 417
1982..	2 542	7 790	8 396	3 606	4 897	4 597	1 448
100 to 199 .... farms, 1987..	31	88	66	36	67	76	19
1982..	35	58	74	45	91	100	19
number, 1987..	4 211	9 052	9 001	5 162	9 006	11 003	2 502
1982..	4 915	7 432	10 235	6 223	12 469	13 815	2 496
200 to 499 .... farms, 1987..	24	47	17	24	53	40	13
1982..	33	44	34	21	62	50	21
number, 1987..	6 520	14 167	5 610	6 839	16 575	11 680	3 792
1982..	9 415	12 971	9 300	5 839	19 047	14 170	5 898
500 or more .... farms, 1987..	33	31	5	4	28	5	11
1982..	32	33	9	3	30	4	10
number, 1987..	179 975	104 471	5 582	5 460	49 136	6 980	140 188
1982..	129 769	113 655	7 434	2 037	48 863	8 018	65 585
Cows and heifers that had calved .... farms, 1987..	93	220	568	182	246	257	77
1982..	113	242	613	197	279	290	87
number, 1987..	6 239	14 693	16 140	9 617	17 638	17 043	3 950
1982..	5 520	10 214	18 140	9 050	21 316	18 929	6 187
Beef cows .... farms, 1987..	91	210	514	170	239	247	76
1982..	110	232	562	181	270	284	82
number, 1987..	6 224	14 024	12 776	8 819	16 992	16 306	3 872
1982..	5 505	9 366	14 788	8 149	20 587	18 307	6 091
1987 farms by inventory:							
1 to 9 .... farms..	19	43	168	37	28	22	7
number..	61	208	907	199	121	103	36
10 to 19 .... farms..	13	47	151	36	25	23	15
number..	175	637	2 063	524	317	295	207
20 to 49 .... farms..	25	80	133	48	86	79	32
number..	849	2 418	3 797	1 497	2 772	2 472	924
50 to 99 .... farms..	18	30	46	29	54	66	10
number..	1 393	2 006	3 074	1 905	3 560	4 571	679
100 to 199 .... farms..	9	8	12	15	31	43	10
number..	1 276	745	1 503	1 922	4 189	5 536	(D)
200 to 499 .... farms..	6	2	3	3	13	14	1
number..	(D)	(D)	(D)	(D)	(D)	3 327	(D)
500 or more .... farms..	1	2	1	2	4	–	1
number..	(D)	(D)	(D)	(D)	(D)	–	(D)
Milk cows .... farms, 1987..	7	17	81	18	21	23	9
1982..	10	25	92	28	23	22	14
number, 1987..	15	609	3 364	798	646	737	78
1982..	15	848	3 352	901	729	622	96
1987 farms by inventory:							
1 to 9 .... farms..	7	12	33	5	14	9	6
number..	15	18	80	(D)	32	23	8
10 to 19 .... farms..	–	–	8	1	–	5	–
number..	–	–	85	(D)	–	66	–
20 to 49 .... farms..	–	–	12	4	3	5	3
number..	–	–	405	156	110	157	70
50 to 99 .... farms..	–	4	24	7	–	2	–
number..	–	(D)	1 552	474	–	(D)	–
100 to 199 .... farms..	–	–	5	1	4	1	–
number..	–	–	(D)	(D)	504	(D)	–
200 to 499 .... farms..	–	–	1	–	–	1	–
number..	–	–	(D)	–	–	(D)	–
500 or more .... farms..	–	–	1	–	–	–	–
number..	–	–	(D)	–	–	–	–
Heifers and heifer calves .... farms, 1987..	126	268	521	167	243	232	98
1982..	152	293	597	185	267	260	92
number, 1987..	48 542	55 637	11 175	5 609	27 044	11 572	69 466
1982..	28 338	55 998	11 802	4 709	21 185	12 648	16 655
Steers, steer calves, bulls, and bull calves ... farms, 1987..	141	352	530	189	272	232	102
1982..	179	366	645	197	314	292	102
number, 1987..	138 752	67 475	8 425	7 095	37 293	7 676	75 814
1982..	114 248	79 878	15 004	5 900	45 185	11 524	53 661

Item	Gray	Greeley	Greenwood	Hamilton	Harper	Harvey	Haskell
INVENTORY							
Cattle and calves .... farms, 1987...	265	85	440	105	410	422	103
1982...	248	87	520	122	448	458	111
number, 1987...	148 260	52 354	63 675	58 221	70 210	33 335	134 363
1982...	99 848	39 691	78 736	41 895	60 073	36 805	160 068
Farms by inventory:							
1 to 9 .... farms, 1987...	15	5	47	4	23	87	6
1982...	21	1	35	7	19	76	4
number, 1987...	70	22	265	22	100	437	40
1982...	108	(D)	191	31	107	385	(D)
10 to 19 .... farms, 1987...	27	4	45	7	45	61	7
1982...	19	11	61	4	48	84	3
number, 1987...	383	40	656	84	639	878	77
1982...	281	(D)	867	55	647	1 127	(D)
20 to 49 .... farms, 1987...	30	7	111	23	94	132	10
1982...	37	21	112	19	117	142	13
number, 1987...	990	242	3 654	908	3 255	4 072	359
1982...	1 174	648	3 555	660	3 929	4 613	402
50 to 99 .... farms, 1987...	50	18	91	25	82	62	6
1982...	40	9	107	33	103	64	20
number, 1987...	3 401	1 307	6 459	1 974	5 840	4 327	598
1982...	2 663	664	7 471	2 392	7 327	4 542	1 377
100 to 199 .... farms, 1987...	49	19	82	23	66	39	26
1982...	41	14	98	28	75	50	26
number, 1987...	6 477	2 789	8 611	2 902	8 776	5 325	3 470
1982...	5 704	1 986	13 513	3 774	9 890	6 401	3 776
200 to 499 .... farms, 1987...	58	16	51	16	66	30	23
1982...	61	14	78	20	65	29	22
number, 1987...	17 195	4 826	14 858	5 089	20 624	8 634	7 056
1982...	18 803	4 363	23 800	5 951	19 366	8 092	5 783
500 or more .... farms, 1987...	36	16	32	7	34	11	21
1982...	29	17	29	11	21	13	23
number, 1987...	119 734	43 128	29 172	47 242	30 974	9 662	122 763
1982...	71 095	31 853	27 338	29 032	18 607	11 945	148 669
Cows and heifers that had calved .... farms, 1987...	94	44	361	75	253	306	44
1982...	108	58	454	85	326	344	49
number, 1987...	5 851	6 901	26 718	5 001	12 039	7 679	2 839
1982...	4 998	3 665	32 243	5 940	14 490	9 393	2 814
Beef cows .... farms, 1987...	90	43	352	75	245	264	40
1982...	106	54	442	83	315	291	46
number, 1987...	5 832	6 888	25 751	5 057	11 560	6 314	2 832
1982...	4 973	3 651	31 005	5 937	13 825	7 435	(D)
1987 farms by inventory:							
1 to 9 .... farms...	26	7	54	8	32	102	6
number...	116	31	334	32	188	518	35
10 to 19 .... farms...	13	3	49	11	60	64	3
number...	192	44	685	168	843	872	39
20 to 49 .... farms...	20	17	100	20	77	74	10
number...	685	552	2 991	696	2 524	2 092	329
50 to 99 .... farms...	15	9	75	24	44	14	13
number...	1 042	600	5 289	1 753	2 846	904	(D)
100 to 199 .... farms...	9	4	34	8	23	8	2
number...	1 224	550	4 588	1 138	2 919	(D)	(D)
200 to 499 .... farms...	5	1	23	3	9	1	1
number...	(D)	(D)	6 687	(D)	2 240	(D)	1 028
500 or more .... farms...	2	2	7	-	1	1	-
number...	(D)	(D)	5 177	(D)	-	(D)	-
Milk cows .... farms, 1987...	6	7	32	4	15	56	5
1982...	11	9	48	3	26	74	3
number, 1987...	19	13	957	4	479	1 365	7
1982...	25	14	1 238	3	665	1 958	(D)
1987 farms by inventory:							
1 to 9 .... farms...	5	7	18	4	7	26	5
number...	(D)	13	(D)	4	(D)	61	7
10 to 19 .... farms...	1	-	1	-	1	6	-
number...	(D)	-	(D)	-	(D)	85	-
20 to 49 .... farms...	-	-	7	-	3	13	-
number...	-	-	253	-	111	420	-
50 to 99 .... farms...	-	-	5	-	3	10	-
number...	-	-	330	-	218	(D)	-
100 to 199 .... farms...	-	-	-	-	1	1	-
number...	-	-	-	-	(D)	(D)	-
200 to 499 .... farms...	-	-	1	-	-	-	-
number...	-	-	(D)	-	-	-	-
500 or more .... farms...	-	-	-	-	-	-	-
number...	-	-	-	-	-	-	-
Heifers and heifer calves .... farms, 1987...	145	56	329	77	286	317	67
1982...	131	57	420	96	324	345	78
number, 1987...	34 249	16 718	17 488	17 178	18 161	8 528	42 935
1982...	19 402	10 245	20 209	18 648	13 363	8 517	50 858
Steers, steer calves, bulls, and bull calves ... farms, 1987...	228	71	376	95	346	358	74
1982...	230	73	474	104	401	394	86
number, 1987...	108 150	28 735	19 469	35 962	40 010	17 028	88 909
1982...	75 448	25 781	24 284	17 307	32 220	18 895	106 396

Table 11. **Cattle and Calves—Inventory and Sales: 1987 and 1982**—Con.

[For meaning of abbreviations and symbols, see introductory text]

Item	Hodgeman	Jackson	Jefferson	Jewell	Johnson	Kearny	Kingman	Kiowa
INVENTORY								
Cattle and calves .... farms, 1987..	253	799	663	472	357	123	531	167
1982..	313	910	757	542	437	137	592	214
number, 1987..	83 072	43 136	32 679	44 080	19 542	77 869	51 395	31 041
1982..	75 917	56 854	41 277	56 553	22 955	80 725	46 972	35 451
Farms by inventory:								
1 to 9 .... farms, 1987..	9	93	104	36	65	12	34	10
1982..	14	87	125	31	66	14	52	11
number, 1987..	59	512	506	167	343	60	183	64
1982..	54	498	672	177	389	65	242	58
10 to 19 .... farms, 1987..	11	146	142	43	64	12	56	12
1982..	13	153	154	49	81	8	60	21
number, 1987..	163	2 019	1 856	610	683	157	899	167
1982..	209	2 149	2 159	695	1 096	97	845	321
20 to 49 .... farms, 1987..	45	261	231	136	110	20	148	31
1982..	56	310	236	147	164	26	193	47
number, 1987..	1 606	9 087	7 264	4 451	3 344	652	4 885	1 030
1982..	1 776	10 395	7 480	4 850	5 101	853	6 223	1 468
50 to 99 .... farms, 1987..	48	175	106	111	64	18	123	36
1982..	74	202	134	136	74	32	128	47
number, 1987..	3 357	11 771	7 014	7 678	4 133	1 277	8 560	2 631
1982..	5 059	13 826	9 340	9 725	4 670	2 099	8 603	3 454
100 to 199 .... farms, 1987..	53	70	52	88	40	28	94	32
1982..	70	109	72	109	30	26	97	46
number, 1987..	7 432	9 377	6 846	11 600	5 354	3 754	12 389	4 575
1982..	9 714	14 301	9 463	14 591	4 027	3 498	13 476	6 048
200 to 499 .... farms, 1987..	67	30	24	48	11	20	55	33
1982..	60	45	32	60	18	21	56	29
number, 1987..	20 726	7 620	6 643	14 290	3 035	5 976	16 488	10 321
1982..	17 530	12 615	9 649	17 766	4 647	6 375	15 471	9 280
500 or more .... farms, 1987..	19	4	4	8	3	13	11	13
1982..	26	4	4	10	4	11	6	13
number, 1987..	49 725	2 750	2 448	5 284	2 450	65 993	7 991	12 253
1982..	41 575	3 100	2 514	8 749	2 825	67 738	4 112	14 822
Cows and heifers that had calved .... farms, 1987..	142	699	563	398	298	94	432	108
1982..	198	797	643	469	365	108	469	155
number, 1987..	8 393	19 958	15 452	19 232	6 161	8 220	21 321	8 164
1982..	9 807	26 041	17 308	21 466	9 088	5 714	20 237	11 572
Beef cows .... farms, 1987..	134	657	533	387	284	93	415	105
1982..	186	748	598	454	354	106	460	152
number, 1987..	7 702	18 554	13 793	18 427	7 377	8 038	20 005	8 156
1982..	9 018	23 671	15 149	20 422	8 319	5 570	18 572	11 437
1987 farms by inventory:								
1 to 9 .... farms..	17	165	150	56	86	17	56	15
number..	91	804	764	267	428	82	336	86
10 to 19 .... farms..	12	171	157	72	59	11	82	18
number..	175	2 326	2 150	1 008	933	166	1 109	232
20 to 49 .... farms..	47	215	163	136	88	19	141	27
number..	1 431	6 529	4 878	4 080	2 531	661	4 395	834
50 to 99 .... farms..	34	76	45	62	31	25	87	23
number..	2 418	5 052	3 094	5 577	2 050	1 814	6 098	1 508
100 to 199 .... farms..	20	26	14	27	9	10	39	14
number..	2 517	(D)	1 598	3 548	(D)	1 189	5 083	1 839
200 to 499 .... farms..	4	2	4	11	1	8	9	6
number..	1 070	(D)	1 249	(D)	(D)	1 995	(D)	(D)
500 or more .... farms..	–	–	–	1	–	3	1	2
number..	–	–	–	(D)	–	2 131	(D)	(D)
Milk cows .... farms, 1987..	17	75	52	38	19	8	29	4
1982..	20	114	103	47	23	12	54	6
number, 1987..	691	1 404	1 719	805	784	182	1 316	8
1982..	789	2 370	2 159	1 044	769	144	1 665	135
1987 farms by inventory:								
1 to 9 .... farms..	9	34	21	19	9	5	11	4
number..	16	67	48	(D)	23	8	(D)	8
10 to 19 .... farms..	1	9	4	2	–	–	1	–
number..	(D)	115	67	(D)	–	–	(D)	–
20 to 49 .... farms..	1	25	11	11	2	1	7	–
number..	(D)	756	332	297	(D)	(D)	252	–
50 to 99 .... farms..	4	7	13	6	6	2	5	–
number..	365	466	899	443	461	(D)	385	–
100 to 199 .... farms..	2	–	3	–	2	–	3	–
number..	(D)	–	373	–	(D)	–	370	–
200 to 499 .... farms..	–	–	–	–	–	–	1	–
number..	–	–	–	–	–	–	(D)	–
500 or more .... farms..	–	–	–	–	–	–	–	–
number..	–	–	–	–	–	–	–	–
Heifers and heifer calves .... farms, 1987..	189	623	510	397	272	91	390	115
1982..	207	756	622	445	356	105	449	150
number, 1987..	30 503	10 308	8 712	11 143	7 354	17 390	13 186	9 013
1982..	27 901	14 093	11 217	15 261	7 530	16 857	12 261	10 317
Steers, steer calves, bulls, and bull calves .... farms, 1987..	203	697	578	426	277	99	450	143
1982..	261	810	659	489	371	124	520	183
number, 1987..	44 176	12 670	8 515	13 705	4 027	52 256	16 888	13 664
1982..	38 209	16 750	12 752	19 826	6 337	58 154	16 474	13 562

Table 11. Cattle and Calves—Inventory and Sales: 1987 and 1982—Con.

[For meaning of abbreviations and symbols, see introductory text]

Item	Labette	Lane	Leavenworth	Lincoln	Linn	Logan	Lyon	McPherson
INVENTORY								
Cattle and calves ... farms, 1987	704	129	781	357	483	180	535	670
1982	815	171	895	410	589	210	619	776
number, 1987	56 329	59 727	30 300	53 344	35 037	31 593	75 525	56 946
1982	59 474	64 597	36 944	50 733	40 984	33 054	76 291	58 759
Farms by inventory:								
1 to 9 ... farms, 1987	84	9	158	16	60	12	70	104
1982	84	11	170	14	68	15	63	113
number, 1987	490	(D)	913	89	278	77	365	542
1982	502	61	923	78	361	89	280	630
10 to 19 ... farms, 1987	130	1	185	32	81	10	75	101
1982	140	14	215	28	73	14	84	124
number, 1987	1 895	(D)	2 623	462	1 106	136	1 028	1 411
1982	1 969	203	2 861	384	994	184	1 217	1 683
20 to 49 ... farms, 1987	250	36	256	85	134	31	160	200
1982	277	28	278	103	194	51	176	236
number, 1987	7 778	1 214	7 969	2 850	4 367	1 004	4 961	6 354
1982	8 869	986	8 636	3 408	6 193	1 715	5 583	7 449
50 to 99 ... farms, 1987	115	25	121	80	115	53	118	120
1982	182	27	145	113	136	39	134	140
number, 1987	7 921	(D)	7 938	5 366	7 940	3 637	8 167	8 079
1982	12 309	1 939	9 411	7 053	9 399	2 614	9 367	9 832
100 to 199 ... farms, 1987	88	15	48	74	55	30	64	92
1982	87	34	70	73	81	48	90	94
number, 1987	11 932	(D)	6 348	9 965	7 165	4 021	8 567	12 895
1982	11 712	4 695	9 125	10 668	11 084	6 649	12 167	12 462
200 to 499 ... farms, 1987	34	29	11	57	32	32	30	43
1982	40	45	14	62	31	34	55	60
number, 1987	10 275	8 083	(D)	16 292	8 402	9 810	8 835	12 435
1982	11 084	13 505	3 808	16 693	9 041	10 240	15 624	17 210
500 or more ... farms, 1987	3	14	2	13	6	12	18	10
1982	5	12	3	17	8	0	17	9
number, 1987	16 100	46 531	(D)	18 330	5 789	12 909	43 602	15 230
1982	13 029	43 208	2 150	11 549	3 892	11 563	32 053	9 493
Cows and heifers that had calved ... farms, 1987	612	82	705	325	420	155	412	508
1982	724	113	799	373	529	173	488	611
number, 1987	19 087	5 607	15 747	20 046	14 703	11 302	19 143	15 399
1982	22 951	7 367	17 762	22 132	18 416	13 022	18 839	17 813
Beef cows ... farms, 1987	595	79	651	321	403	153	398	449
1982	693	112	735	361	510	171	464	533
number, 1987	17 913	5 587	12 250	19 348	14 000	11 127	18 555	12 831
1982	20 834	7 355	13 343	21 206	17 017	12 987	17 558	14 589
1987 farms by inventory:								
1 to 9 ... farms	122	4	249	41	97	19	94	131
number	637	15	1 278	254	480	84	467	702
10 to 19 ... farms	170	10	185	42	76	18	84	110
number	2 349	137	2 631	584	1 018	231	1 124	1 536
20 to 49 ... farms	195	26	172	105	131	44	142	139
number	5 547	732	5 114	3 359	4 057	1 425	4 407	4 185
50 to 99 ... farms	77	18	36	67	70	36	53	49
number	4 914	1 211	2 221	4 593	4 190	2 410	3 487	3 215
100 to 199 ... farms	23	15	9	51	25	23	16	15
number	2 746	1 902	1 108	6 487	3 009	2 852	2 035	1 951
200 to 499 ... farms	8	6	-	15	4	11	7	5
number	1 720	1 580	-	4 071	1 246	(D)	(D)	1 240
500 or more ... farms	-	-	-	-	-	2	2	-
number	-	-	-	-	-	(D)	(D)	-
Milk cows ... farms, 1987	31	7	86	26	29	18	36	80
1982	70	8	118	35	47	19	66	114
number, 1987	1 184	20	3 497	698	763	175	588	2 568
1982	2 117	12	4 419	926	1 399	35	981	3 224
1987 farms by inventory:								
1 to 9 ... farms	13	7	30	12	16	15	24	32
number	28	20	89	20	40	25	41	79
10 to 19 ... farms	3	-	6	(D)	2	-	4	4
number	47	-	102	(D)	(D)	-	55	58
20 to 49 ... farms	7	-	29	6	6	1	(D)	23
number	(D)	-	886	270	217	(D)	(D)	603
50 to 99 ... farms	2	-	9	3	3	2	1	19
number	(D)	-	549	187	218	(D)	(D)	(D)
100 to 199 ... farms	6	-	9	2	2	-	-	2
number	714	-	969	(D)	(D)	-	-	(D)
200 to 499 ... farms	-	-	3	-	-	-	(D)	-
number	-	-	902	-	-	-	(D)	-
500 or more ... farms	-	-	-	-	-	-	-	-
number	-	-	-	-	-	-	-	-
Heifers and heifer calves ... farms, 1987	543	92	602	284	397	135	404	519
1982	659	118	728	349	471	150	509	626
number, 1987	17 379	16 599	7 878	14 874	9 451	7 734	25 441	18 868
1982	15 997	8 935	9 498	13 062	10 523	9 869	21 502	20 372
Steers, steer calves, bulls, and bull calves ... farms, 1987	606	114	649	314	426	149	443	552
1982	734	149	771	376	512	183	543	660
number, 1987	19 853	37 521	6 675	18 424	10 823	12 557	30 941	22 679
1982	20 526	46 295	9 684	15 539	12 045	10 163	35 850	20 574

Table 11. **Cattle and Calves—Inventory and Sales: 1987 and 1982**—Con.

[For meaning of abbreviations and symbols, see introductory text]

Item	Marion	Marshall	Meade	Miami	Mitchell	Montgomery	Morris	Morton
INVENTORY								
Cattle and calves ..... farms, 1987..	680	668	213	771	312	695	391	103
1982..	789	781	239	904	373	777	440	120
number, 1987..	66 026	49 806	50 379	33 569	47 246	32 459	55 338	15 115
1982..	76 608	50 674	46 384	44 848	47 866	39 845	62 002	17 228
Farms by inventory:								
1 to 9 ..... farms, 1987..	63	62	10	140	19	112	29	8
1982	80	55	15	161	33	107	23	4
number, 1987..	328	330	41	778	81	664	123	30
1982..	396	312	78	887	208	639	134	15
10 to 19 ..... farms, 1987..	91	75	13	164	30	151	33	7
1982..	83	108	19	185	45	148	34	8
number, 1987..	1 279	1 045	206	2 347	414	2 063	459	89
1982..	1 201	1 443	257	2 611	588	2 081	499	111
20 to 49 ..... farms, 1987..	193	203	50	257	74	234	86	19
1982..	219	254	53	270	94	277	114	35
number, 1987..	6 231	6 309	1 657	7 884	2 387	7 383	2 829	626
1982..	6 906	8 373	1 727	8 333	2 970	8 728	3 795	1 099
50 to 99 ..... farms, 1987..	156	196	39	120	81	120	120	23
1982..	176	200	46	158	91	146	113	22
number, 1987..	11 015	13 383	2 683	8 168	5 435	7 797	8 533	1 618
1982..	12 466	13 783	3 276	10 669	6 172	9 944	8 107	1 658
100 to 199 ..... farms, 1987..	103	89	41	68	71	80	63	24
1982..	143	91	56	103	57	98	74	28
number, 1987..	14 161	11 802	5 272	8 644	9 571	8 108	8 544	3 144
1982..	18 980	11 833	7 466	(D)	7 540	(D)	9 988	3 711
200 to 499 ..... farms, 1987..	55	40	38	21	26	16	41	19
1982..	69	40	34	25	39	29	62	18
number, 1987..	15 529	11 779	11 023	(D)	7 758	(D)	12 136	4 713
1982..	20 359	10 930	10 411	6 481	10 927	6 427	18 201	5 511
500 or more ..... farms, 1987..	19	3	22	1	11	2	19	5
1982..	19	3	16	2	14	2	20	5
number, 1987..	17 483	5 156	29 497	(D)	21 500	(D)	22 714	4 895
1982..	16 416	4 200	23 171	(D)	19 460	(D)	21 278	5 123
Cows and heifers that had calved ..... farms, 1987..	510	585	126	691	261	609	333	86
1982..	596	664	167	795	298	704	372	90
number, 1987..	20 866	18 939	9 115	17 178	12 856	16 598	19 708	5 281
1982..	24 156	20 461	11 596	20 027	13 220	19 415	20 517	5 645
Beef cows ..... farms, 1987..	432	542	122	660	254	592	311	84
1982..	496	614	162	766	298	674	344	88
number, 1987..	16 960	16 259	(D)	15 513	12 215	15 636	17 055	5 271
1982..	19 286	17 559	11 283	17 913	12 741	18 197	19 881	5 638
1987 farms by inventory:								
1 to 9 ..... farms..	103	111	11	206	32	155	32	4
number..	533	562	53	1 097	161	822	129	19
10 to 19 ..... farms..	96	133	22	174	35	183	53	7
number..	1 372	1 775	323	2 300	489	2 480	724	96
20 to 49 ..... farms..	151	197	36	204	98	183	132	27
number..	4 562	6 096	1 139	5 969	3 102	5 369	4 246	786
50 to 99 ..... farms..	62	80	33	55	62	50	53	34
number..	4 195	5 044	2 214	3 529	3 971	3 374	3 459	2 334
100 to 199 ..... farms..	14	19	11	20	22	16	25	10
number..	(D)	(D)	1 530	(D)	2 742	2 041	3 317	(D)
200 to 499 ..... farms..	2	2	8	1	4	4	14	1
number..	(D)	(D)	2 200	(D)	(D)	(D)	(D)	(D)
500 or more ..... farms..	4	–	1	–	1	1	2	1
number..	4 072	–	(D)	–	(D)	(D)	(D)	(D)
Milk cows ..... farms, 1987..	103	77	6	58	15	25	52	6
1982..	148	97	13	67	25	50	81	3
number, 1987..	3 906	2 680	(D)	1 665	441	950	1 653	10
1982..	4 870	2 902	313	2 114	479	1 218	1 636	7
1987 farms by inventory:								
1 to 9 ..... farms..	25	22	4	29	7	9	15	6
number..	64	65	6	63	25	16	34	10
10 to 19 ..... farms..	14	10	–	4	–	4	3	–
number..	194	119	–	(D)	–	62	36	–
20 to 49 ..... farms..	32	27	–	11	4	2	23	–
number..	1 075	875	–	(D)	97	(D)	815	–
50 to 99 ..... farms..	25	13	2	9	3	6	10	–
number..	1 725	833	(D)	601	(D)	529	(D)	–
100 to 199 ..... farms..	7	5	–	5	1	2	1	–
number..	848	788	–	615	(D)	(D)	(D)	–
200 to 499 ..... farms..	–	–	–	–	–	–	–	–
number..	–	–	–	–	–	–	–	–
500 or more ..... farms..	–	–	–	–	–	–	–	–
number..	–	–	–	–	–	–	–	–
Heifers and heifer calves ..... farms, 1987..	515	527	148	601	237	564	316	73
1982..	617	610	180	723	293	672	371	94
number, 1987..	16 893	16 015	13 192	7 748	12 094	8 550	13 144	2 536
1982..	21 148	16 056	13 945	11 681	14 670	10 752	21 588	3 644
Steers, steer calves, bulls, and bull calves ..... farms, 1987..	570	585	184	653	276	614	352	91
1982..	665	653	205	798	324	703	396	111
number, 1987..	28 265	14 852	28 072	8 843	22 496	7 323	23 486	7 298
1982..	31 304	14 357	20 843	13 140	19 976	9 676	19 897	7 939

Table 11. **Cattle and Calves—Inventory and Sales: 1987 and 1982**—Con.

[For meaning of abbreviations and symbols, see introductory text]

Item	Nemaha	Neosho	Ness	Norton	Osage	Osborne	Ottawa	Pawnee
INVENTORY								
Cattle and calves .... farms, 1987__	746	528	362	310	517	372	301	232
1982__	872	594	433	362	645	436	341	263
number, 1987__	60 317	34 652	42 710	38 256	34 842	47 252	40 760	57 425
1982__	70 793	42 145	46 789	50 324	44 803	53 546	45 728	46 372
Farms by inventory:								
1 to 9 .... farms, 1987__	57	56	12	19	73	24	27	14
1982__	43	62	26	9	88	22	21	16
number, 1987__	293	311	71	109	396	111	106	83
1982__	215	364	122	49	504	110	104	98
10 to 19 .... farms, 1987__	75	86	27	25	90	28	27	22
1982__	87	92	21	19	100	52	23	19
number, 1987__	1 049	1 231	390	335	1 302	383	371	309
1982__	1 253	1 292	288	268	1 370	697	317	251
20 to 49 .... farms, 1987__	214	193	86	74	160	69	58	66
1982__	295	201	119	76	220	79	89	74
number, 1987__	6 810	6 198	2 798	2 643	5 125	2 167	2 000	2 226
1982__	9 529	6 279	3 995	2 736	7 107	2 567	2 826	2 459
50 to 99 .... farms, 1987__	205	116	88	85	103	95	83	40
1982__	216	134	105	98	126	117	83	61
number, 1987__	14 507	8 151	6 111	5 517	6 940	6 657	4 261	2 741
1982__	14 485	9 255	7 147	6 956	8 795	8 318	5 855	4 295
100 to 199 .... farms, 1987__	136	46	89	67	56	78	52	42
1982__	159	67	99	92	68	95	96	52
number, 1987__	18 036	6 367	12 369	8 770	7 157	10 843	8 393	5 387
1982__	20 494	9 350	13 480	12 431	9 169	13 172	9 242	6 582
200 to 499 .... farms, 1987__	53	22	53	35	26	69	45	27
1982__	65	28	56	50	30	58	47	28
number, 1987__	14 207	6 055	14 923	9 651	7 728	18 736	13 509	7 951
1982__	17 577	7 805	16 545	13 845	9 333	16 584	13 502	7 854
500 or more .... farms, 1987__	6	9	9	12	9	9	9	19
1982__	7	10	7	16	13	11	12	13
number, 1987__	5 415	6 339	6 048	11 231	6 194	8 355	12 120	39 326
1982__	7 240	7 800	5 212	14 039	8 525	12 096	13 782	24 833
Cows and heifers that had calved ....farms, 1987__	575	470	273	268	418	328	238	166
1982__	721	543	325	325	498	384	271	202
number, 1987__	20 844	15 080	15 973	16 403	12 181	19 712	14 062	10 409
1982__	24 808	17 575	18 207	21 510	14 375	23 110	14 080	11 535
Beef cows .... farms, 1987__	461	452	269	265	405	324	231	164
1982__	589	514	320	307	485	374	261	197
number, 1987__	14 864	13 699	15 690	16 197	11 706	19 139	13 579	(D)
1982__	16 301	15 025	17 815	20 478	13 757	22 397	13 410	11 346
1987 farms by inventory:								
1 to 9 .... farms	67	86	25	22	98	41	23	18
number	332	452	159	122	537	228	93	92
10 to 19 .... farms	124	130	36	35	117	34	39	31
number	1 733	1 708	504	496	1 631	473	509	433
20 to 49 .... farms	164	166	102	101	121	103	78	56
number	5 641	4 864	3 397	3 226	3 594	3 326	2 410	1 762
50 to 99 .... farms	70	49	60	59	58	83	53	35
number	4 517	3 285	4 118	3 887	3 807	5 633	3 559	2 338
100 to 199 .... farms	13	18	32	34	8	51	28	15
number	1 706	2 386	4 065	4 311	898	6 613	3 938	1 864
200 to 499 .... farms	3	3	14	13	2	12	9	5
number	935	1 004	3 447	(D)	(D)	2 864	(D)	1 720
500 or more .... farms	–	–	–	3	1	–	1	2
number	–	–	–	(D)	(D)	–	(D)	(D)
Milk cows.. farms, 1987__	145	42	14	14	26	20	23	3
1982__	188	69	15	34	34	37	23	10
number, 1987__	5 980	1 381	283	206	475	573	503	(D)
1982__	6 507	2 550	392	1 032	618	713	670	189
1987 farms by inventory:								
1 to 9 .... farms	25	16	9	7	13	5	15	2
number	37	53	21	(D)	20	(D)	37	(D)
10 to 19 .... farms	8	6	–	(D)	5	6	1	–
number	87	82	–	(D)	54	(D)	(D)	–
20 to 49 .... farms	55	6	3	181	4	4	2	–
number	1 875	194	(D)		111	118	(D)	–
50 to 99 .... farms	50	12	2	–	4	6	4	1
number	3 132	(D)	(D)	–	290	369	270	(D)
100 to 199 .... farms	7	2	–	–	–	–	1	–
number	849	(D)	–	–	–	–	(D)	–
200 to 499 .... farms	–	–	–	–	–	–	–	–
number	–	–	–	–	–	–	–	–
500 or more .... farms	–	–	–	–	–	–	–	–
number	–	–	–	–	–	–	–	–
Heifers and heifer calves .... farms, 1987__	572	436	262	246	412	311	237	190
1982__	676	501	296	298	509	340	260	201
number, 1987__	19 102	10 053	12 283	10 541	10 948	13 358	12 795	15 316
1982__	19 257	12 316	9 972	12 891	12 163	13 551	12 021	12 274
Steers, steer calves, bulls, and bull calves ....farms, 1987__	605	461	308	271	437	335	262	199
1982__	761	518	383	321	578	382	309	236
number, 1987__	20 371	9 519	14 454	11 312	11 713	14 162	13 883	31 700
1982__	26 728	12 254	18 610	15 923	18 265	16 885	19 627	22 563

Table 11. **Cattle and Calves—Inventory and Sales: 1987 and 1982**—Con.

[For meaning of abbreviations and symbols, see introductory text]

Item	Phillips	Pottawatomie	Pratt	Rawlins	Reno	Republic	Rice	Riley
INVENTORY								
Cattle and calves .... farms, 1987__	421	544	276	321	795	498	320	352
1982__	484	622	283	398	935	636	362	403
number, 1987__	51 554	56 613	61 095	44 947	68 838	58 209	50 618	31 205
1982__	65 615	69 985	57 637	47 413	75 853	60 852	56 620	35 830
Farms by inventory:								
1 to 9 .... farms, 1987__	17	60	30	8	125	61	31	34
1982__	20	51	21	8	148	43	32	56
number, 1987__	84	281	152	51	666	319	152	159
1982__	108	294	124	44	735	234	171	292
10 to 19 .... farms, 1987__	33	65	36	26	106	67	32	52
1982__	22	65	27	16	162	80	46	47
number, 1987__	512	876	508	381	1 469	944	464	738
1982__	318	871	382	230	2 250	1 118	638	654
20 to 49 .... farms, 1987__	95	130	66	50	234	143	88	94
1982__	103	175	72	90	245	207	88	107
number, 1987__	3 164	4 279	2 155	1 591	7 426	4 704	3 025	3 217
1982__	3 474	5 913	2 262	2 860	7 754	6 914	2 939	3 441
50 to 99 .... farms, 1987__	93	124	65	89	173	119	67	80
1982__	104	138	73	103	191	180	62	70
number, 1987__	6 559	8 579	4 603	6 578	11 882	8 173	4 698	5 737
1982__	7 715	10 007	5 115	7 193	13 300	12 107	5 604	5 082
100 to 199 .... farms, 1987__	117	100	38	93	101	82	63	56
1982__	138	117	43	121	129	88	57	80
number, 1987__	15 946	13 245	5 363	13 083	13 700	11 110	8 344	7 979
1982__	18 974	15 871	6 029	16 905	16 954	11 684	7 620	10 700
200 to 499 .... farms, 1987__	53	46	25	45	47	22	26	30
1982__	60	55	36	53	40	31	32	35
number, 1987__	16 041	13 752	8 083	13 891	14 206	5 560	8 637	8 323
1982__	22 185	16 169	9 943	15 271	10 472	7 800	9 397	8 759
500 or more .... farms, 1987__	13	19	16	10	9	4	13	6
1982__	17	21	11	7	20	7	25	8
number, 1987__	9 248	15 601	40 231	9 372	19 489	27 299	25 298	5 052
1982__	12 841	20 860	33 782	4 910	24 388	20 995	29 251	6 902
Cows and heifers that had calved .... farms, 1987__	391	474	182	289	634	441	248	291
1982__	454	548	208	359	758	566	263	345
number, 1987__	25 833	22 414	6 900	19 561	21 507	14 262	9 700	12 805
1982__	30 023	24 983	7 482	23 492	24 726	17 491	10 431	12 448
Beef cows .... farms, 1987__	387	456	176	292	535	433	235	277
1982__	449	527	197	344	640	552	243	323
number, 1987__	25 421	21 027	5 627	19 207	17 232	13 418	8 824	11 697
1982__	29 613	22 992	7 021	21 897	20 421	16 750	9 246	11 056
1987 farms by inventory:								
1 to 9 .... farms__	42	85	45	24	131	77	39	57
number__	202	417	260	160	699	371	197	292
10 to 19 .... farms__	42	79	36	27	123	108	41	47
number__	609	1 055	485	384	1 668	1 506	584	620
20 to 49 .... farms__	122	149	58	71	176	176	94	109
number__	3 942	4 393	1 737	2 417	5 299	5 244	2 975	3 391
50 to 99 .... farms__	104	99	29	106	78	63	48	43
number__	7 153	6 686	1 842	7 492	5 037	4 040	3 257	2 992
100 to 199 .... farms__	56	30	9	38	20	15	11	16
number__	7 453	3 851	(D)	4 794	. 2 769	(D)	(D)	2 014
200 to 499 .... farms__	19	13	1	15	7	2	2	3
number__	(D)	(D)	(D)	(D)	1 860	(D)	(D)	(D)
500 or more .... farms__	2	1	–	1	–	–	–	2
number__	(D)	(D)	–	(D)	–	–	–	(D)
Milk cows .... farms, 1987__	28	63	10	15	145	22	23	31
1982__	38	87	23	39	168	38	39	56
number, 1987__	412	1 387	273	354	4 275	844	876	1 108
1982__	410	1 991	461	1 595	4 305	741	1 183	1 392
1987 farms by inventory:								
1 to 9 .... farms__	17	29	5	6	54	10	6	13
number__	35	66	8	9	97	15	7	41
10 to 19 .... farms__	2	12	1	4	15	1	5	–
number__	(D)	179	(D)	(D)	204	(D)	86	–
20 to 49 .... farms__	8	19	2	2	44	–	4	11
number__	300	601	(D)	(D)	1 427	–	109	403
50 to 99 .... farms__	(D)	2	–	227	27	9	6	6
number__	(D)	(D)	(D)		1 833	615	(D)	(D)
100 to 199 .... farms__	–	–	1	–	5	2	2	–
number__			(D)		714	(D)	(D)	
200 to 499 .... farms__	–	1	–	–	–	–	–	1
number__		(D)						(D)
500 or more .... farms__	–	–	–	–	–	–	–	–
number__	–	–	–	–	–	–	–	–
Heifers and heifer calves .... farms, 1987__	335	432	167	253	587	398	243	296
1982__	399	507	205	316	758	523	291	343
number, 1987__	12 792	15 595	17 995	10 606	17 772	12 910	19 371	8 446
1982__	14 837	17 381	14 566	12 050	21 759	17 003	20 194	10 056
Steers, steer calves, bulls, and bull calves .... farms, 1987__	374	477	236	290	647	449	281	317
1982__	445	557	259	340	808	583	309	348
number, 1987__	12 929	18 604	37 200	14 780	29 559	31 037	21 547	9 954
1982__	20 755	27 621	35 569	11 871	29 368	26 358	24 995	13 326

Table 11. **Cattle and Calves—Inventory and Sales: 1987 and 1982**—Con.

[For meaning of abbreviations and symbols, see introductory text]

Item	Rooks	Rush	Russell	Saline	Scott	Sedgwick	Seward	Shawnee
INVENTORY								
Cattle and calves .... farms, 1987__	290	298	331	373	131	673	108	459
1982__	326	360	388	431	163	790	113	555
number, 1987__	35 999	23 531	34 604	36 119	169 825	41 135	86 120	19 849
1982__	39 210	33 498	37 253	45 060	143 662	46 586	78 679	23 788
Farms by inventory:								
1 to 9 .... farms, 1987__	13	14	23	51	10	118	12	93
1982__	21	7	27	58	12	164	8	120
number, 1987__	34	91	112	270	68	621	48	480
1982__	92	28	150	297	42	847	28	630
10 to 19 .... farms, 1987__	20	33	38	62	7	142	13	116
1982__	31	29	33	55	8	160	15	128
number, 1987__	283	434	550	830	94	1 966	176	1 637
1982__	449	420	450	746	99	2 170	205	1 845
20 to 49 .... farms, 1987__	62	95	98	85	15	181	19	137
1982__	74	129	118	121	21	217	21	186
number, 1987__	1 929	3 158	3 216	2 784	491	5 738	666	4 122
1982__	2 447	4 208	3 855	3 945	724	6 761	645	5 611
50 to 99 .... farms, 1987__	62	89	63	73	17	113	15	71
1982__	73	91	102	81	23	135	19	72
number, 1987__	5 633	6 246	4 531	5 117	1 154	7 452	1 033	4 817
1982__	4 972	6 550	7 107	5 713	1 770	9 312	1 448	4 890
100 to 199 .... farms, 1987__	63	44	64	51	18	73	21	27
1982__	76	67	64	67	24	72	16	27
number, 1987__	8 522	(D)	8 766	7 029	2 409	9 806	2 976	3 809
1982__	9 944	9 148	8 828	9 226	3 241	9 899	2 361	(D)
200 to 499 .... farms, 1987__	43	19	37	40	17	40	14	13
1982__	41	30	35	40	35	37	18	20
number, 1987__	13 575	(D)	11 014	11 779	5 611	10 857	4 271	(D)
1982__	12 598	8 031	9 908	12 112	10 277	11 037	5 239	(D)
500 or more .... farms, 1987__	7	4	8	11	47	8	14	2
1982__	10	7	9	9	40	5	14	2
number, 1987__	6 023	(D)	6 393	8 310	159 998	4 695	76 948	(D)
1982__	8 708	5 110	6 955	13 021	127 509	6 560	68 753	(D)
Cows and heifers that had calved .... farms, 1987__	260	257	303	303	44	517	70	380
1982__	286	291	340	356	82	598	79	448
number, 1987__	17 644	10 448	17 266	16 857	5 096	17 333	3 354	8 134
1982__	17 896	12 245	16 583	15 421	5 053	18 294	5 472	9 736
Beef cows .... farms, 1987__	249	250	285	279	44	430	69	369
1982__	274	289	318	325	76	499	77	421
number, 1987__	16 746	10 168	16 436	13 844	(D)	10 344	3 348	7 784
1982__	16 650	12 031	15 570	13 792	5 008	11 441	5 466	9 002
1987 farms by inventory:								
1 to 9 .... farms	19	31	32	67	10	140	16	139
number	92	197	175	338	51	690	56	759
10 to 19 .... farms	37	41	56	31	6	115	11	93
number	511	576	779	411	75	1 606	143	1 215
20 to 49 .... farms	92	113	88	99	9	136	19	104
number	2 404	3 544	2 866	3 133	271	3 950	613	3 119
50 to 99 .... farms	70	41	63	47	6	26	14	23
number	4 777	2 614	4 268	3 177	555	1 834	918	1 451
100 to 199 .... farms	34	22	32	24	7	9	5	10
number	4 399	(D)	4 237	3 117	921	1 060	666	1 220
200 to 499 .... farms	13	2	14	10	2	5	4	-
number	(D)	(D)	4 091	(D)	(D)	1 404	952	-
500 or more .... farms	1	-	-	(D)	2	-	-	-
number	(D)	-	-	(D)	(D)	-	-	-
Milk cows .... farms, 1987__	23	12	26	38	1	104	5	20
1982__	34	11	37	58	9	126	4	45
number, 1987__	798	278	822	1 413	(D)	6 989	6	370
1982__	1 246	214	1 013	1 629	45	6 853	6	734
1987 farms by inventory:								
1 to 9 .... farms	12	4	6	21	-	21	5	11
number	39	10	13	(D)	-	79	6	(D)
10 to 19 .... farms	-	2	3	3	-	4	-	(D)
number	-	(D)	42	(D)	-	58	-	(D)
20 to 49 .... farms	5	4	10	4	1	24	-	4
number	(D)	115	330	102	(D)	784	-	130
50 to 99 .... farms	2	2	7	8	-	31	-	3
number	(D)	(D)	437	608	-	2 166	-	192
100 to 199 .... farms	4	-	-	3	-	19	-	-
number	470	-	-	425	-	2 340	-	-
200 to 499 .... farms	-	-	-	1	-	4	-	-
number	-	-	-	(D)	-	(D)	-	-
500 or more .... farms	-	-	-	-	-	1	-	-
number	-	-	-	-	-	(D)	-	-
Heifers and heifer calves .... farms, 1987__	230	235	249	290	99	503	91	348
1982__	262	290	310	351	123	585	84	417
number, 1987__	8 559	6 179	9 054	9 465	76 574	12 543	29 453	4 709
1982__	10 229	10 321	9 728	11 955	62 623	14 395	31 722	6 212
Steers, steer calves, bulls, and bull calves .... farms, 1987__	258	259	297	325	95	547	95	396
1982__	287	309	346	362	126	673	98	482
number, 1987__	9 896	6 906	8 292	11 397	86 155	11 159	53 313	7 006
1982__	11 085	10 929	10 942	17 684	75 986	13 897	41 485	7 841

Table 11. Cattle and Calves—Inventory and Sales: 1987 and 1982—Con.

[For meaning of abbreviations and symbols, see introductory text]

Item	Sheridan	Sherman	Smith	Stafford	Stanton	Stevens	Sumner	Thomas
INVENTORY								
Cattle and calves ... farms, 1987..	291	167	451	255	101	113	598	217
1982..	339	210	550	278	78	131	740	239
number, 1987..	43 899	33 721	54 892	62 373	49 389	52 216	41 742	36 649
1982..	58 147	37 469	69 002	53 862	44 706	19 417	44 750	43 537
Farms by inventory:								
1 to 9 ... farms, 1987..	12	14	19	22	10	10	68	16
1982..	8	18	24	17	5	13	69	15
number, 1987..	46	(D)	91	105	46	46	328	80
1982..	43	86	126	99	13	70	466	76
10 to 19 ... farms, 1987..	12	7	34	14	13	13	111	20
1982..	15	15	32	23	6	17	128	11
number, 1987..	173	(D)	500	159	156	212	1 571	267
1982..	226	221	444	327	91	260	1 801	158
20 to 49 ... farms, 1987..	69	34	100	39	18	26	198	56
1982..	62	43	108	61	8	31	252	60
number, 1987..	2 325	1 079	3 258	1 296	542	821	6 058	1 866
1982..	2 130	1 452	3 691	2 013	272	972	7 673	1 988
50 to 99 ... farms, 1987..	85	46	122	57	16	16	93	48
1982..	89	42	144	56	9	19	149	59
number, 1987..	5 899	3 335	8 690	3 940	1 215	983	5 974	3 495
1982..	6 477	2 921	10 151	3 906	723	1 331	10 041	4 062
100 to 199 ... farms, 1987..	66	35	103	54	22	23	79	40
1982..	91	48	146	53	22	33	80	49
number, 1987..	9 140	4 656	14 213	7 444	2 990	3 034	10 442	5 088
1982..	12 406	6 855	19 675	7 126	3 112	4 713	10 554	6 560
200 to 499 ... farms, 1987..	37	20	60	46	10	20	39	27
1982..	57	32	81	46	19	13	35	32
number, 1987..	10 205	5 865	16 109	13 590	2 868	6 559	10 022	7 558
1982..	15 314	9 623	22 410	12 917	5 546	3 680	9 135	9 242
500 or more ... farms, 1987..	10	12	13	23	12	6	10	10
1982..	17	12	15	22	9	6	7	13
number, 1987..	16 111	18 630	12 031	35 839	41 572	40 561	7 347	18 275
1982..	21 551	16 311	12 505	27 474	34 949	8 391	5 080	21 451
Cows and heifers that had calved ... farms, 1987..	238	131	394	181	54	90	446	174
1982..	304	164	489	212	47	111	571	189
number, 1987..	14 770	8 372	21 800	12 896	1 507	5 332	13 448	9 272
1982..	17 227	10 182	29 087	14 070	3 605	5 451	13 865	10 186
Beef cows ... farms, 1987..	233	128	379	181	53	90	421	173
1982..	297	154	468	207	47	109	546	186
number, 1987..	(D)	8 262	20 908	(D)	1 504	5 332	12 183	9 257
1982..	16 205	9 750	28 231	(D)	(D)	5 374	12 603	10 139
1987 farms by inventory:								
1 to 9 ... farms..	13	12	29	25	20	13	102	25
number..	82	46	143	92	104	66	571	102
10 to 19 ... farms..	42	16	55	19	6	20	127	23
number..	616	223	790	284	78	260	1 748	335
20 to 49 ... farms..	82	44	134	59	18	18	127	65
number..	2 814	1 404	4 222	1 952	584	516	3 706	2 171
50 to 99 ... farms..	62	33	106	41	8	21	49	33
number..	4 360	2 236	7 100	2 802	(D)	1 365	3 174	2 203
100 to 199 ... farms..	26	16	49	26	-	14	13	23
number..	3 414	2 102	5 930	3 487	-	1 895	1 594	3 037
200 to 499 ... farms..	7	6	3	9	1	4	1	4
number..	1 986	(D)	1 010	2 336	(D)	1 196	(D)	1 409
500 or more ... farms..	1	1	3	2	-	-	2	-
number..	(D)	(D)	1 713	(D)	-	-	(D)	-
Milk cows ... farms, 1987..	14	11	42	4	3	-	36	12
1982..	43	21	45	11	2	10	46	12
number, 1987..	(D)	110	892	(D)	3	-	1 265	15
1982..	1 022	432	856	(D)	(D)	77	1 262	47
1987 farms by inventory:								
1 to 9 ... farms..	10	8	28	2	3	-	18	12
number..	11	17	69	(D)	3	-	26	15
10 to 19 ... farms..	1	1	2	-	-	-	3	-
number..	(D)	(D)	(D)	-	-	-	38	-
20 to 49 ... farms..	1	-	7	2	-	-	3	-
number..	(D)	(D)	276	(D)	-	-	123	-
50 to 99 ... farms..	-	(D)	3	-	-	-	8	-
number..	-	(D)	220	-	-	-	558	-
100 to 199 ... farms..	1	-	2	-	-	-	3	-
number..	(D)	-	(D)	-	-	-	410	-
200 to 499 ... farms..	-	-	-	-	-	-	-	-
number..	-	-	-	-	-	-	-	-
500 or more ... farms..	1	-	-	-	-	-	-	-
number..	(D)	-	-	-	-	-	-	-
Heifers and heifer calves ... farms, 1987..	208	131	363	196	70	87	442	173
1982..	277	164	468	214	56	109	543	192
number, 1987..	12 014	7 569	13 185	19 547	28 112	14 347	11 046	8 840
1982..	15 126	7 945	18 933	18 878	13 303	7 651	12 183	13 237
Steers, steer calves, bulls, and bull calves ... farms, 1987..	259	139	407	219	70	99	506	174
1982..	317	192	497	240	67	115	667	206
number, 1987..	17 115	17 780	19 907	29 930	19 770	32 537	17 248	18 537
1982..	25 792	19 342	20 982	21 114	27 798	6 315	18 702	20 114

Table 11. Cattle and Calves—Inventory and Sales: 1987 and 1982—Con.

[For meaning of abbreviations and symbols, see introductory text]

Item	Trego	Wabaunsee	Wallace	Washington	Wichita	Wilson	Woodson	Wyandotte
INVENTORY								
Cattle and calves _____ farms, 1987__	340	412	161	668	136	426	266	94
1982__	352	490	182	752	165	493	326	116
number, 1987__	36 838	51 672	22 920	57 997	90 559	26 333	22 297	1 887
1982__	44 415	76 107	31 771	72 273	81 938	36 540	37 670	4 160
Farms by inventory:								
1 to 9 _____ farms, 1987__	26	43	10	37	13	56	34	42
1982__	23	47	12	46	8	51	23	42
number, 1987__	136	238	39	228	60	309	172	231
1982__	116	232	61	259	38	278	119	234
10 to 19 _____ farms, 1987__	26	53	15	77	12	69	34	24
1982__	18	58	16	73	17	75	44	35
number, 1987__	371	772	187	1 027	164	968	478	339
1982__	236	771	239	1 039	236	1 090	622	484
20 to 49 _____ farms, 1987__	75	110	42	193	22	117	67	20
1982__	69	132	38	205	37	144	62	22
number, 1987__	2 487	3 516	1 325	6 417	628	3 815	2 276	544
1982__	2 331	4 356	1 260	6 597	1 069	4 695	2 654	628
50 to 99 _____ farms, 1987__	118	88	32	169	26	104	71	3
1982__	113	98	37	209	33	109	87	12
number, 1987__	7 964	6 297	2 016	11 615	1 617	7 266	5 147	(D)
1982__	7 651	6 947	2 369	14 421	2 373	7 666	6 200	745
100 to 199 _____ farms, 1987__	58	52	24	136	26	56	38	4
1982__	52	62	33	130	27	77	50	2
number, 1987__	7 667	7 151	3 469	18 775	3 817	7 703	5 561	(D)
1982__	11 249	11 347	4 438	17 051	3 685	10 793	6 675	(D)
200 to 499 _____ farms, 1987__	30	50	24	46	21	19	17	1
1982__	36	58	29	70	30	34	33	2
number, 1987__	7 864	13 458	6 615	13 291	6 190	4 943	4 913	(D)
1982__	10 515	16 519	8 754	19 752	9 095	9 625	8 904	(D)
500 or more _____ farms, 1987__	5	16	14	10	16	3	5	–
1982__	9	15	18	19	13	3	7	1
number, 1987__	12 349	20 440	9 069	6 441	78 063	3 339	3 750	–
1982__	12 317	35 935	14 630	13 154	65 422	2 373	12 496	(D)
Cows and heifers that had calved _____ farms, 1987__	301	333	134	545	91	361	222	78
1982__	309	409	130	529	118	442	294	94
number, 1987__	16 363	10 378	10 545	22 247	5 934	12 735	6 476	962
1982__	18 205	21 190	12 491	24 408	7 106	16 912	14 507	1 905
Beef cows _____ farms, 1987__	277	316	127	516	91	352	221	77
1982__	285	365	125	574	112	490	264	91
number, 1987__	15 468	16 420	10 441	20 017	5 934	12 076	(D)	(D)
1982__	17 136	20 070	12 393	21 576	6 887	16 040	14 081	1 658
1987 farms by inventory:								
1 to 9 _____ farms__	25	52	17	74	11	75	44	42
number__	141	306	69	388	55	391	205	(D)
10 to 19 _____ farms__	29	59	19	94	17	62	32	25
number__	418	798	269	1 299	208	1 115	454	309
20 to 49 _____ farms__	107	111	40	219	29	125	90	7
number__	3 376	3 389	1 292	6 624	887	3 861	2 833	174
50 to 99 _____ farms__	72	54	20	97	18	54	42	3
number__	4 973	3 622	1 335	6 405	1 214	3 581	2 879	202
100 to 199 _____ farms__	40	25	18	24	12	15	11	–
number__	5 186	3 332	2 508	3 044	1 466	1 856	1 508	–
200 to 499 _____ farms__	3	13	10	6	3	2	2	–
number__	(D)	(D)	2 958	2 257	(D)	(D)	(D)	–
500 or more _____ farms__	1	2	3	–	1	1	–	–
number__	(D)	(D)	1 990	–	(D)	(D)	–	–
Milk cows _____ farms, 1987__	36	37	16	47	–	20	6	3
1982__	51	59	23	94	8	54	29	(D)
number, 1987__	864	958	104	2 230	–	659	(D)	(D)
1982__	1 069	1 120	98	2 832	219	872	426	247
1987 farms by inventory:								
1 to 9 _____ farms__	15	22	15	8	–	11	5	1
number__	27	51	(D)	14	–	34	7	(D)
10 to 19 _____ farms__	5	1	–	5	–	–	–	1
number__	70	(D)	–	69	–	–	–	(D)
20 to 49 _____ farms__	5	7	–	14	–	4	–	–
number__	149	221	–	421	–	135	–	–
50 to 99 _____ farms__	11	5	1	15	–	3	–	1
number__	638	347	(D)	996	–	(D)	–	(D)
100 to 199 _____ farms__	–	1	–	3	–	2	1	–
number__	–	(D)	–	(D)	–	(D)	(D)	–
200 to 499 _____ farms__	–	1	–	2	–	–	–	–
number__	–	(D)	–	(D)	–	–	–	–
500 or more _____ farms__	–	–	–	–	–	–	–	–
number__	–	–	–	–	–	–	–	–
Heifers and heifer calves _____ farms, 1987__	228	308	126	524	104	357	217	61
1982__	296	398	131	616	130	407	267	76
number, 1987__	10 166	13 292	5 851	16 010	26 798	7 856	6 769	491
1982__	10 566	16 826	6 269	20 870	15 401	10 015	9 064	1 153
Steers, steer calves, bulls, and bull calves ____ farms, 1987__	290	381	140	583	115	385	234	77
1982__	315	432	162	679	133	436	296	104
number, 1987__	12 300	19 202	6 524	19 740	57 827	7 742	7 050	434
1982__	15 644	38 091	12 991	26 995	59 431	9 613	14 099	1 102

Table 11. **Cattle and Calves—Inventory and Sales: 1987 and 1982**—Con.

[For meaning of abbreviations and symbols, see introductory text]

Item	Kansas	Allen	Anderson	Atchison	Barber	Barton	Bourbon
SALES							
Dairy products sold ... farms, 1987	2 004	40	37	28	10	23	49
1982	2 867	63	57	47	10	25	80
$1,000, 1987	140 232	2 950	2 131	1 712	1 278	1 164	1 899
1982	162 232	3 655	2 357	1 940	1 166	822	2 744
Cattle and calves sold ... farms, 1987	41 498	488	525	463	393	536	845
1982	47 032	566	593	530	383	547	696
number, 1987	7 310 338	16 932	26 577	15 993	69 121	150 497	32 536
1982	6 519 159	17 955	21 893	19 475	72 168	131 211	35 005
$1,000, 1987	4 305 335	7 038	13 085	7 102	33 934	97 664	13 876
1982	3 516 670	6 417	9 078	8 148	30 107	80 795	13 257
1987 farms by number sold:							
1 to 9 ... farms	8 828	125	128	119	40	129	160
number	44 436	666	652	579	215	648	827
10 to 19 ... farms	8 136	126	137	127	46	132	150
number	112 031	1 689	1 889	1 753	627	1 839	1 988
20 to 49 ... farms	11 824	146	146	133	70	173	210
number	367 698	4 365	4 576	4 017	2 120	5 247	6 201
50 to 99 ... farms	6 086	67	72	54	77	66	67
number	415 257	4 520	4 978	3 668	5 430	4 211	4 280
100 to 199 ... farms	3 224	17	24	19	68	19	26
number	433 691	2 071	3 080	2 408	9 122	2 488	3 544
200 to 499 ... farms	2 125	4	14	11	65	9	23
number	631 044	1 283	4 130	3 568	17 218	2 568	6 396
500 or more ... farms	1 275	3	4	-	37	8	8
number	5 306 181	2 338	9 272	-	34 369	133 498	9 300
Calves sold ... farms, 1987	18 518	287	256	216	151	297	371
1982	22 120	319	296	296	155	352	400
number, 1987	468 328	5 422	5 404	4 350	8 292	6 466	8 412
1982	583 219	6 641	6 337	5 009	10 641	6 765	10 347
$1,000, 1987	145 961	1 653	1 700	1 317	2 627	2 053	2 448
1982	155 547	1 788	1 586	1 248	2 988	1 706	2 627
1987 farms by number sold:							
1 to 9 ... farms	7 205	117	87	73	28	118	139
number	31 769	539	398	319	126	521	655
10 to 19 ... farms	4 501	82	91	75	26	75	106
number	59 950	1 079	1 253	1 018	371	997	1 342
20 to 49 ... farms	4 744	63	63	51	44	76	94
number	139 558	1 844	1 830	1 451	1 304	2 275	2 722
50 to 99 ... farms	1 368	23	8	10	26	19	18
number	89 246	(D)	480	631	1 670	1 225	1 142
100 to 199 ... farms	488	1	3	7	20	8	8
number	62 624	(D)	354	931	2 567	(D)	1 117
200 to 499 ... farms	175	1	4	-	7	1	6
number	50 782	(D)	1 069	-	2 254	(D)	1 434
500 or more ... farms	37	-	-	-	-	-	-
number	34 499	-	-	-	-	-	-
Cattle sold ... farms, 1987	34 216	393	413	351	327	411	471
1982	37 556	447	448	389	316	368	507
number, 1987	6 842 010	11 510	23 173	11 643	60 829	144 031	24 124
1982	5 935 940	11 114	15 556	14 466	61 527	124 446	24 658
$1,000, 1987	4 159 374	5 354	11 384	5 784	31 107	95 581	11 428
1982	3 361 124	4 629	7 493	6 900	27 120	79 089	10 630
1987 farms by number sold:							
1 to 9 ... farms	9 697	147	126	123	49	141	158
number	42 993	616	579	490	232	623	701
10 to 19 ... farms	6 135	92	97	80	33	100	106
number	82 997	1 204	1 309	1 083	410	1 332	1 384
20 to 49 ... farms	8 254	102	104	89	51	109	123
number	255 986	2 961	3 226	2 719	1 614	3 265	3 714
50 to 99 ... farms	4 434	36	51	37	62	36	43
number	303 172	2 384	3 482	2 648	4 467	2 324	2 905
100 to 199 ... farms	2 586	10	20	12	50	11	18
number	348 357	1 236	2 664	1 515	6 476	1 412	2 265
200 to 499 ... farms	1 902	3	12	10	47	6	14
number	564 770	831	3 489	3 188	14 448	1 634	3 855
500 or more ... farms	1 208	3	3	-	35	8	9
number	5 243 772	2 278	8 422	-	33 180	133 441	9 300
Cattle fattened on grain and concentrates sold ... farms, 1987	4 620	39	39	64	17	41	54
1982	6 853	69	56	94	23	31	65
number, 1987	4 551 726	1 119	2 616	3 845	5 444	(D)	5 291
1982	3 879 210	2 512	2 339	6 019	5 363	112 889	3 700
$1,000, 1987	3 041 622	636	1 649	2 299	3 409	88 665	2 998
1982	2 488 360	1 396	1 750	3 678	3 302	74 189	2 159
1987 farms by number sold:							
1 to 9 ... farms	1 554	13	14	16	6	23	22
number	5 563	43	58	71	17	85	103
10 to 19 ... farms	539	7	5	16	1	10	12
number	7 278	99	65	210	(D)	140	162
20 to 49 ... farms	799	13	4	4	(D)	4	6
number	24 533	384	105	299	84	139	217
50 to 99 ... farms	528	4	8	12	9	-	7
number	36 731	(D)	523	787	220	-	504
100 to 199 ... farms	395	1	5	7	-	1	2
number	53 844	(D)	650	832	-	(D)	(D)
200 to 499 ... farms	372	1	3	5	2	-	(D)
number	109 970	(D)	1 217	1 846	(D)	-	(D)
500 or more ... farms	433	-	-	-	(D)	3	2
number	4 313 687	-	-	-	(D)	(D)	(D)

Table 11. **Cattle and Calves—Inventory and Sales: 1987 and 1982**—Con.

[For meaning of abbreviations and symbols, see introductory text]

Item	Brown	Butler	Chase	Chautauqua	Cherokee	Cheyenne	Clark
SALES							
Dairy products sold ... farms, 1987	40	30	8	8	4	1	-
1982	57	50	10	8	14	(D)	1
$1,000, 1987	2 645	1 773	417	660	147	(D)	-
1982	3 919	2 738	269	462	342	294	(D)
Cattle and calves sold ... farms, 1987	447	831	219	324	528	259	214
1982	565	893	231	368	615	317	215
number, 1987	43 045	137 769	57 451	21 126	(D)	55 568	90 994
1982	38 813	142 430	52 883	25 374	14 492	48 348	85 809
$1,000, 1987	25 265	75 616	27 990	9 132	5 447	31 650	48 797
1982	20 640	75 880	23 158	9 343	4 597	25 654	41 313
1987 farms by number sold:							
1 to 9 ... farms	91	207	23	65	212	26	18
number	486	997	102	319	1 105	119	72
10 to 19 ... farms	106	147	27	62	130	33	12
number	1 393	1 896	364	859	1 756	433	194
20 to 49 ... farms	133	188	63	104	139	72	39
number	4 124	5 724	1 914	3 130	4 016	2 315	1 293
50 to 99 ... farms	63	107	39	42	26	68	34
number	4 340	7 409	2 768	2 906	1 706	4 682	2 576
100 to 199 ... farms	28	80	25	29	11	34	28
number	3 763	11 273	3 626	4 151	(D)	4 292	4 111
200 to 499 ... farms	15	60	25	13	7	18	43
number	4 385	17 598	7 408	3 988	(D)	5 480	13 054
500 or more ... farms	11	42	17	9	3	8	40
number	24 574	92 772	41 267	5 773	2 259	38 047	69 694
Calves sold ... farms, 1987	168	360	70	184	358	112	43
1982	215	410	97	202	438	134	65
number, 1987	3 497	13 161	3 405	4 109	6 725	4 886	8 488
1982	4 656	12 594	5 509	6 068	6 982	5 694	9 041
$1,000, 1987	1 016	4 227	1 203	1 327	1 960	1 613	1 707
1982	1 163	3 689	1 445	1 708	1 758	1 518	2 079
1987 farms by number sold:							
1 to 9 ... farms	54	158	26	73	178	15	16
number	246	687	127	333	810	61	59
10 to 19 ... farms	50	77	14	48	83	32	6
number	663	1 021	167	609	1 073	446	116
20 to 49 ... farms	50	78	14	50	75	30	5
number	1 401	2 275	492	1 497	2 070	989	125
50 to 99 ... farms	11	23	8	8	13	21	5
number	687	1 449	622	583	784	1 321	438
100 to 199 ... farms	2	9	4	3	5	11	3
number	(D)	1 221	541	(D)	625	1 374	300
200 to 499 ... farms	1	14	3	2	3	3	3
number	(D)	(D)	(D)	(D)	(D)	695	(D)
500 or more ... farms	-	2	1	-	1	-	2
number	-	(D)	(D)	-	(D)	-	(D)
Cattle sold ... farms, 1987	363	726	199	257	353	208	198
1982	463	736	184	296	394	258	180
number, 1987	39 548	124 608	54 046	17 017	7 902	50 682	82 506
1982	34 157	129 836	47 374	19 306	7 510	42 654	76 768
$1,000, 1987	24 249	71 391	26 787	7 805	3 487	30 436	47 090
1982	19 477	72 171	21 710	7 637	2 840	24 136	39 234
1987 farms by number sold:							
1 to 9 ... farms	94	230	25	73	197	42	17
number	436	1 024	92	315	776	188	46
10 to 19 ... farms	89	126	21	43	69	26	7
number	1 202	1 668	287	590	916	319	112
20 to 49 ... farms	83	130	69	62	64	48	38
number	2 683	3 946	1 747	1 721	1 803	1 522	1 274
50 to 99 ... farms	49	83	35	34	9	47	31
number	3 416	5 616	2 396	2 308	617	3 386	2 366
100 to 199 ... farms	23	71	22	25	7	23	27
number	3 162	10 185	3 079	3 547	955	2 857	3 938
200 to 499 ... farms	14	48	20	13	6	14	39
number	4 075	13 912	5 906	3 911	(D)	4 363	11 946
500 or more ... farms	11	38	17	7	1	8	39
number	24 574	88 257	40 539	4 625	(D)	38 047	62 824
Cattle fattened on grain and concentrates sold ... farms, 1987	101	147	22	17	35	27	22
1982	159	143	19	15	61	95	16
number, 1987	26 102	73 797	4 531	561	501	31 395	31 763
1982	23 074	91 900	2 490	289	1 143	268	32 005
$1,000, 1987	17 329	45 708	2 664	307	(D)	(D)	21 881
1982	14 274	55 591	1 310	138	701	19 653	19 297
1987 farms by number sold:							
1 to 9 ... farms	22	52	7	8	20	5	1
number	65	174	20	(D)	80	13	(D)
10 to 19 ... farms	9	13	2	1	7	3	-
number	127	172	(D)	(D)	80	33	(D)
20 to 49 ... farms	19	11	3	3	7	2	5
number	659	419	80	70	(D)	(D)	6
50 to 99 ... farms	16	16	6	4	-	6	7
number	1 084	1 098	453	303	-	588	490
100 to 199 ... farms	15	25	-	1	1	4	-
number	2 071	3 620	-	(D)	(D)	508	-
200 to 499 ... farms	12	10	2	-	-	3	3
number	3 391	2 928	(D)	-	-	664	734
500 or more ... farms	8	20	2	-	-	2	5
number	18 705	65 386	(D)	-	-	(D)	30 340

1987 CENSUS OF AGRICULTURE—COUNTY DATA

Table 11. **Cattle and Calves—Inventory and Sales: 1987 and 1982**—Con.

[For meaning of abbreviations and symbols, see introductory text]

Item	Clay	Cloud	Coffey	Comanche	Cowley	Crawford	Decatur
SALES							
Dairy products sold .... farms, 1987..	21	7	7	5	13	23	8
1982..	29	23	21	5	20	28	10
$1,000, 1987..	893	379	228	523	1 007	725	244
1982..	1 164	1 090	528	315	1 195	1 247	1 122
Cattle and calves sold .... farms, 1987..	455	381	371	218	628	578	315
1982..	526	437	455	210	714	676	374
number, 1987..	25 540	20 930	27 790	48 538	71 875	21 806	85 340
1982..	26 131	25 700	24 610	31 065	102 273	26 358	83 838
$1,000, 1987..	12 786	10 027	15 600	22 648	98 289	10 047	52 158
1982..	11 226	10 839	12 696	12 025	52 189	10 361	48 419
1987 farms by number sold:							
1 to 9 .... farms..	76	66	73	25	152	154	17
number..	387	355	376	119	768	797	97
10 to 19 .... farms..	102	80	82	19	152	171	42
number..	1 449	1 097	827	259	2 050	2 231	631
20 to 49 .... farms..	140	121	106	33	169	166	93
number..	4 565	3 897	3 176	1 195	5 214	5 059	2 937
50 to 99 .... farms..	94	71	66	45	79	54	80
number..	6 516	4 746	4 601	3 003	5 330	3 699	5 731
100 to 199 .... farms..	19	27	31	30	25	20	49
number..	2 352	3 579	4 325	4 233	3 300	2 483	6 661
200 to 499 .... farms..	17	10	18	40	27	8	24
number..	5 499	3 266	5 189	12 895	8 042	1 627	7 123
500 or more .... farms..	5	6	13	26	24	5	10
number..	4 770	3 990	9 296	24 834	46 971	5 710	62 160
Calves sold .... farms, 1987..	127	161	96	64	337	352	116
1982..	201	220	134	76	341	422	159
number, 1987..	3 923	3 722	1 525	3 310	7 302	5 722	4 740
1982..	4 578	6 452	2 003	5 959	10 416	7 829	6 636
$1,000, 1987..	1 034	1 210	492	1 234	2 488	1 724	1 584
1982..	1 272	1 750	526	1 592	2 695	1 866	1 770
1987 farms by number sold:							
1 to 9 .... farms..	50	57	48	19	137	155	21
number..	186	270	218	112	564	721	124
10 to 19 .... farms..	37	35	19	9	96	97	25
number..	539	456	255	112	1 290	1 238	359
20 to 49 .... farms..	28	51	24	16	72	85	38
number..	826	1 513	664	472	2 075	2 590	1 198
50 to 99 .... farms..	8	15	3	8	23	12	22
number..	506	943	(D)	466	1 566	801	1 634
100 to 199 .... farms..	1	2	1	9	6	3	9
number..	(D)	(D)	(D)	1 148	907	372	(D)
200 to 499 .... farms..	2	1	-	2	3	-	1
number..	(D)	(D)	-	(D)	900	-	(D)
500 or more .... farms..	1	-	-	1	-	-	-
number..	(D)	-	-	(D)	-	-	-
Cattle sold .... farms, 1987..	406	324	337	195	471	426	273
1982..	456	337	385	180	591	456	298
number, 1987..	21 617	17 208	26 265	43 228	64 373	15 884	80 800
1982..	21 553	19 248	22 607	25 106	91 857	18 529	77 200
$1,000, 1987..	11 752	8 817	15 108	21 414	35 800	8 323	50 575
1982..	9 958	9 089	12 172	10 433	49 494	8 495	46 649
1987 farms by number sold:							
1 to 9 .... farms..	79	82	84	32	159	171	40
number..	353	350	415	146	724	690	175
10 to 19 .... farms..	92	65	48	13	95	111	35
number..	1 287	878	636	170	1 226	1 405	526
20 to 49 .... farms..	118	88	85	28	100	82	66
number..	3 808	2 830	2 577	966	3 185	2 343	2 054
50 to 99 .... farms..	81	52	62	34	51	40	63
number..	5 634	3 461	4 423	2 203	3 492	2 547	4 465
100 to 199 .... farms..	17	22	27	28	18	13	39
number..	2 132	2 826	3 729	4 063	2 280	1 562	5 378
200 to 499 .... farms..	15	10	18	35	26	8	20
number..	4 433	3 393	5 189	11 444	7 595	1 627	5 842
500 or more .... farms..	4	5	13	25	22	5	10
number..	3 970	3 470	9 296	24 234	45 871	5 710	62 160
Cattle fattened on grain and concentrates							
sold .... farms, 1987..	62	26	68	16	67	33	61
1982..	69	40	99	21	86	70	75
number, 1987..	7 237	4 160	8 656	4 807	21 040	809	62 517
1982..	7 442	6 197	8 769	2 841	(D)	2 126	55 139
$1,000, 1987..	4 850	2 752	5 581	2 988	14 242	311	41 471
1982..	4 509	3 833	5 611	1 679	(D)	1 081	35 915
1987 farms by number sold:							
1 to 9 .... farms..	13	6	17	6	24	14	4
number..	58	21	82	24	74	57	(D)
10 to 19 .... farms..	9	6	7	-	7	6	7
number..	122	90	92	-	81	79	(D)
20 to 49 .... farms..	19	3	14	-	8	11	15
number..	599	(D)	392	-	251	(D)	505
50 to 99 .... farms..	8	2	12	1	7	1	19
number..	547	(D)	905	(D)	451	(D)	1 403
100 to 199 .... farms..	3	3	4	1	4	1	8
number..	427	420	559	(D)	452	(D)	1 116
200 to 499 .... farms..	6	3	6	3	3	-	8
number..	1 684	1 008	1 701	(D)	953	-	2 297
500 or more .... farms..	4	4	8	5	4	-	6
number..	3 800	2 380	4 924	3 700	18 778	-	57 160

Table 11. Cattle and Calves—Inventory and Sales: 1987 and 1982—Con.

[For meaning of abbreviations and symbols, see introductory text]

Item	Dickinson	Doniphan	Douglas	Edwards	Elk	Ellis	Ellsworth
SALES							
Dairy products sold — farms, 1987	34	7	38	5	3	24	5
1982	58	11	52	9	3	30	6
$1,000, 1987	2 528	818	2 807	261	135	1 827	(D)
1982	2 826	966	3 517	574	(D)	1 757	634
Cattle and calves sold — farms, 1987	658	303	517	201	339	537	346
1982	740	344	600	219	392	571	378
number, 1987	77 223	15 426	21 697	61 840	29 016	64 199	22 831
1982	67 189	15 411	24 319	89 826	23 694	46 813	17 994
$1,000, 1987	40 616	7 942	10 957	32 958	13 713	34 845	10 611
1982	31 409	7 015	10 914	37 528	9 187	22 453	6 575
1987 farms by number sold:							
1 to 9 — farms	116	76	180	25	48	115	44
number	605	358	845	167	243	580	276
10 to 19 — farms	131	61	115	24	69	105	53
number	1 801	845	1 549	314	979	1 437	729
20 to 49 — farms	187	103	152	61	101	183	117
number	5 054	3 091	4 464	1 703	3 151	5 377	3 728
50 to 99 — farms	89	30	45	24	54	81	86
number	6 100	2 005	3 068	1 690	3 670	5 576	5 377
100 to 199 — farms	73	14	12	29	37	28	30
number	9 608	1 782	1 593	3 939	5 195	3 694	4 263
200 to 499 — farms	50	13	7	24	19	17	19
number	14 790	3 782	1 990	7 575	5 304	4 875	5 658
500 or more — farms	32	6	8	24	11	8	8
number	39 265	3 563	8 190	46 452	10 474	42 680	2 800
Calves sold — farms, 1987	195	132	271	88	130	356	152
1982	247	144	287	97	196	378	189
number, 1987	3 818	2 550	3 837	2 463	3 701	9 307	4 510
1982	4 859	3 191	5 166	4 325	6 380	9 881	3 911
$1,000, 1987	1 228	799	1 091	819	1 108	2 877	1 489
1982	1 344	884	1 311	1 242	1 732	2 459	1 018
1987 farms by number sold:							
1 to 9 — farms	85	57	139	26	37	113	48
number	382	242	636	162	161	513	219
10 to 19 — farms	51	30	71	21	39	79	40
number	626	405	980	263	485	1 049	573
20 to 49 — farms	44	36	48	31	31	119	43
number	1 376	967	1 428	902	881	3 384	1 227
50 to 99 — farms	13	6	12	5	15	32	14
number	(D)	295	793	348	963	2 206	999
100 to 199 — farms	–	3	–	4	6	9	5
number	–	(D)	–	(D)	(D)	1 171	(D)
200 to 499 — farms	2	1	–	(D)	2	4	2
number	(D)	(D)	–	(D)	(D)	984	(D)
500 or more — farms	–	–	–	–	–	–	–
number	–	–	–	–	–	–	–
Cattle sold — farms, 1987	583	256	412	160	298	387	286
1982	633	275	484	168	332	396	308
number, 1987	73 405	12 876	17 860	59 377	25 315	54 892	18 321
1982	62 330	12 220	19 153	85 501	17 514	36 932	14 083
$1,000, 1987	39 388	7 143	9 865	32 139	12 607	31 968	9 122
1982	30 065	6 131	9 603	36 286	7 454	19 994	5 557
1987 farms by number sold:							
1 to 9 — farms	110	81	180	22	52	135	51
number	485	344	716	124	248	542	272
10 to 19 — farms	122	59	86	19	62	83	37
number	1 656	762	1 155	255	886	1 090	499
20 to 49 — farms	135	66	98	29	89	98	90
number	4 179	2 009	2 910	1 005	2 866	2 899	2 871
50 to 99 — farms	66	21	25	20	39	31	89
number	4 472	1 388	1 596	1 365	2 674	2 123	4 750
100 to 199 — farms	70	12	10	23	29	22	21
number	9 271	1 566	1 303	3 051	4 002	2 831	2 800
200 to 499 — farms	48	12	7	23	17	10	15
number	14 090	3 244	1 990	7 105	4 740	2 760	4 329
500 or more — farms	32	6	6	24	10	8	3
number	39 252	3 563	8 190	46 452	9 899	42 657	2 800
Cattle fattened on grain and concentrates sold — farms, 1987	87	73	82	16	24	35	17
1982	135	105	100	18	37	30	20
number, 1987	19 265	8 047	7 038	25 706	3 829	(D)	967
1982	24 195	7 672	8 269	(D)	1 270	(D)	1 002
$1,000, 1987	12 441	5 104	4 447	15 209	1 909	(D)	430
1982	13 326	4 383	5 489	(D)	828	(D)	490
1987 farms by number sold:							
1 to 9 — farms	9	13	44	2	12	17	5
number	42	53	176	(D)	40	43	14
10 to 19 — farms	13	7	12	–	5	4	–
number	181	94	149	–	68	45	–
20 to 49 — farms	16	24	15	–	3	5	4
number	492	714	419	–	86	127	97
50 to 99 — farms	11	8	1	1	(D)	2	9
number	772	504	(D)	(D)	(D)	8	394
100 to 199 — farms	15	7	2	2	1	2	3
number	2 010	836	(D)	(D)	(D)	(D)	462
200 to 499 — farms	13	9	5	4	1	3	–
number	3 377	2 796	1 221	1 256	(D)	759	–
500 or more — farms	10	5	3	6	1	2	–
number	12 391	3 050	4 700	24 092	(D)	(D)	–

Table 11. Cattle and Calves—Inventory and Sales: 1987 and 1982—Con.

[For meaning of abbreviations and symbols, see introductory text]

Item	Finney	Ford	Franklin	Geary	Gove	Graham	Grant
SALES							
Dairy products sold .... farms, 1987..	1	5	50	16	9	14	5
1982..	2	13	67	16	12	15	4
$1,000, 1987..	(D)	914	5 126	1 161	939	1 115	35
1982..	(D)	1 248	5 129	1 416	996	913	(D)
Cattle and calves sold .... farms, 1987..	174	442	646	207	324	282	117
1982..	208	451	729	210	360	326	116
number, 1987..	484 784	333 262	24 035	14 246	124 523	27 797	307 689
1982..	274 193	274 334	26 595	(D)	93 891	30 644	(D)
$1,000, 1987..	337 030	197 377	11 277	7 212	75 809	13 951	210 294
1982..	163 139	164 596	11 359	3 650	58 634	13 906	(D)
1987 farms by number sold:							
1 to 9 .... farms..	29	79	231	46	36	34	21
number..	111	363	1 059	252	174	194	117
10 to 19 .... farms..	9	58	156	40	20	35	22
number..	119	766	2 171	594	266	518	302
20 to 49 .... farms..	32	115	167	49	99	87	26
number..	1 000	3 548	5 221	1 532	3 206	2 777	805
50 to 99 .... farms..	22	51	62	44	62	71	19
number..	1 462	3 427	4 110	3 009	4 197	4 925	(D)
100 to 199 .... farms..	33	57	17	17	42	41	10
number..	4 333	8 099	2 181	2 369	5 622	5 731	(D)
200 to 499 .... farms..	16	50	8	9	39	12	5
number..	4 274	15 386	2 450	(D)	11 460	(D)	1 435
500 or more .... farms..	34	32	5	2	26	2	14
number..	473 385	301 673	6 843	(D)	99 598	(D)	302 426
Calves sold .... farms, 1987..	48	122	318	94	128	150	36
1982..	77	128	344	87	158	171	44
number, 1987..	1 864	3 220	5 875	1 865	7 584	5 309	958
1982..	5 324	5 136	4 763	1 719	6 219	5 757	3 249
$1,000, 1987..	678	982	1 574	583	2 505	1 698	280
1982..	1 529	1 236	1 039	401	1 683	1 727	786
1987 farms by number sold:							
1 to 9 .... farms..	10	49	158	39	33	36	10
number..	34	211	710	176	155	181	48
10 to 19 .... farms..	9	19	74	19	22	25	10
number..	123	243	1 011	235	299	364	137
20 to 49 .... farms..	16	39	67	28	48	56	11
number..	471	1 180	2 047	836	1 551	1 730	342
50 to 99 .... farms..	6	10	15	9	14	20	3
number..	393	627	1 045	638	852	1 410	(D)
100 to 199 .... farms..	6	4	3	-	10	11	2
number..	(D)	(D)	(D)	-	(D)	(D)	(D)
200 to 499 .... farms..	1	1	-	-	-	1	-
number..	(D)	(D)	-	-	-	(D)	-
500 or more .... farms..	-	-	1	-	1	-	-
number..	-	-	(D)	-	(D)	-	-
Cattle sold .... farms, 1987..	148	372	534	166	271	204	104
1982..	169	379	598	183	301	247	100
number, 1987..	482 920	330 042	18 160	12 361	116 939	22 488	306 731
1982..	268 869	269 198	21 832	(D)	87 672	24 887	(D)
$1,000, 1987..	336 352	196 395	9 703	6 649	73 304	12 253	210 014
1982..	161 611	163 360	10 321	(D)	57 251	12 179	(D)
1987 farms by number sold:							
1 to 9 .... farms..	33	75	238	60	40	41	28
number..	139	342	934	297	196	238	129
10 to 19 .... farms..	7	40	112	35	21	29	18
number..	107	544	1 543	470	290	402	229
20 to 49 .... farms..	18	82	123	36	71	44	18
number..	537	2 540	3 723	1 067	2 258	1 359	550
50 to 99 .... farms..	14	43	39	30	45	49	13
number..	895	2 909	2 599	2 091	2 893	3 347	872
100 to 199 .... farms..	27	51	12	14	34	29	6
number..	3 895	7 078	1 464	1 946	4 628	4 095	1 090
200 to 499 .... farms..	15	49	6	9	36	11	5
number..	4 194	14 956	1 954	(D)	10 847	(D)	1 435
500 or more .... farms..	34	32	4	2	24	1	14
number..	473 383	301 673	6 043	(D)	95 727	(D)	302 426
Cattle fattened on grain and concentrates sold .... farms, 1987..	46	51	85	23	54	14	15
1982..	40	52	86	23	48	15	26
number, 1987..	455 331	294 269	6 916	1 614	87 180	(D)	(D)
1982..	246 250	217 430	6 880	927	45 641	(D)	(D)
$1,000, 1987..	321 509	179 351	4 345	1 051	58 743	(D)	205 (D)
1982..	152 280	140 950	4 274	516	40 473	(D)	(D)
1987 farms by number sold:							
1 to 9 .... farms..	9	11	49	8	12	5	2
number..	30	53	152	36	(D)	18	(D)
10 to 19 .... farms..	1	2	8	2	2	-	1
number..	(D)	(D)	100	(D)	(D)	-	(D)
20 to 49 .... farms..	6	3	17	3	8	4	-
number..	185	75	586	91	176	148	-
50 to 99 .... farms..	3	2	5	8	6	-	1
number..	199	(D)	419	453	374	-	(D)
100 to 199 .... farms..	5	8	-	2	4	5	(D)
number..	702	1 124	-	(D)	450	514	(D)
200 to 499 .... farms..	2	8	2	1	8	-	2
number..	(D)	2 372	(D)	(D)	2 446	-	(D)
500 or more .... farms..	20	17	4	1	16	-	8
number..	453 792	290 498	(D)	(D)	83 673	(D)	(D)

Table 11. **Cattle and Calves—Inventory and Sales: 1987 and 1982**—Con.

[For meaning of abbreviations and symbols, see introductory text]

Item	Gray	Greeley	Greenwood	Hamilton	Harper	Harvey	Haskell
SALES							
Dairy products sold _____ farms, 1987__	2	-	17	-	9	41	-
1982__	4	-	17	1	13	55	1
$1,000, 1987__	(D)	-	1 729	-	619	2 649	-
1982__	(D)	-	1 844	(D)	784	2 977	(D)
Cattle and calves sold _____ farms, 1987__	274	89	457	116	422	408	112
1982__	250	93	533	122	455	449	119
number, 1987__	314 237	90 929	58 628	110 524	69 401	37 716	329 026
1982__	172 238	155 617	54 391	67 150	59 505	35 511	492 161
$1,000, 1987__	197 008	64 851	28 689	66 995	32 500	21 393	216 725
1982__	104 871	94 026	23 922	40 743	26 413	20 336	293 826
1987 farms by number sold:							
1 to 9 _____ farms__	24	11	71	9	68	127	10
number__	123	51	330	49	310	561	53
10 to 19 _____ farms__	27	6	78	10	48	93	9
number__	351	95	1 094	147	678	1 292	114
20 to 49 _____ farms__	46	15	120	32	98	92	17
number__	1 575	(D)	3 858	1 074	3 104	2 799	(D)
50 to 99 _____ farms__	39	4	87	26	61	40	13
number__	2 720	(D)	6 105	1 813	4 184	2 720	(D)
100 to 199 _____ farms__	44	11	42	17	53	19	16
number__	5 936	1 578	5 809	2 270	7 071	2 647	2 177
200 to 499 _____ farms__	54	20	36	14	61	21	23
number__	16 554	6 023	10 599	4 406	18 811	6 170	7 204
500 or more _____ farms__	40	17	23	6	35	16	24
number__	286 978	82 012	29 035	100 763	35 243	21 527	317 948
Calves sold _____ farms, 1987__	68	14	173	45	116	177	25
1982__	76	32	215	34	160	206	32
number, 1987__	3 743	483	7 397	1 425	4 075	2 107	1 418
1982__	3 683	858	7 487	1 373	3 858	2 536	1 237
$1,000, 1987__	1 301	175	2 243	549	1 285	499	462
1982__	1 006	228	1 979	330	1 116	627	244
1987 farms by number sold:							
1 to 9 _____ farms__	28	6	59	7	39	108	7
number__	140	23	277	32	150	450	29
10 to 19 _____ farms__	11	3	38	8	26	34	6
number__	135	(D)	490	113	344	449	82
20 to 49 _____ farms__	15	2	43	20	27	30	5
number__	493	(D)	1 219	601	874	752	133
50 to 99 _____ farms__	4	-	19	10	14	4	4
number__	290	-	1 197	679	868	(D)	274
100 to 199 _____ farms__	5	3	8	-	6	-	-
number__	717	361	1 170	-	729	-	-
200 to 499 _____ farms__	3	-	4	-	4	1	3
number__	(D)	-	(D)	-	1 090	(D)	900
500 or more _____ farms__	2	-	2	-	-	-	-
number__	(D)	-	(D)	-	-	-	-
Cattle sold _____ farms, 1987__	242	82	396	93	363	350	100
1982__	203	79	442	105	403	365	110
number, 1987__	310 494	90 446	49 231	109 099	65 326	35 609	327 608
1982__	168 555	154 759	46 904	65 777	55 649	32 975	490 924
$1,000, 1987__	195 707	64 676	26 446	66 446	31 215	20 894	216 263
1982__	103 866	93 798	21 943	40 412	25 297	19 709	293 361
1987 farms by number sold:							
1 to 9 _____ farms__	21	8	86	11	51	126	6
number__	81	38	367	56	275	548	51
10 to 19 _____ farms__	21	7	66	8	37	71	9
number__	271	105	969	108	570	970	124
20 to 49 _____ farms__	37	13	85	22	78	65	14
number__	1 228	461	2 692	793	2 407	1 969	462
50 to 99 _____ farms__	36	9	68	15	48	33	10
number__	2 530	643	4 618	1 060	3 242	2 249	722
100 to 199 _____ farms__	40	8	36	16	50	19	15
number__	5 432	1 179	4 893	2 230	6 694	2 703	1 997
200 to 499 _____ farms__	49	20	32	13	58	20	20
number__	15 288	6 006	9 674	4 067	18 154	5 936	6 304
500 or more _____ farms__	38	17	23	8	33	16	24
number__	285 686	82 012	25 818	100 763	33 984	21 234	317 948
Cattle fattened on grain and concentrates sold _____ farms, 1987__	26	28	47	11	18	76	21
1982__	26	18	93	13	37	103	18
number, 1987__	259 938	78 148	7 149	(D)	6 314	17 884	302 285
1982__	130 740	141 976	8 650	52 566	2 263	17 318	471 520
$1,000, 1987__	168 244	57 445	4 132	60 692	3 242	11 523	204 278
1982__	86 622	88 710	5 341	34 432	1 253	11 135	284 541
1987 farms by number sold:							
1 to 9 _____ farms__	3	1	17	-	5	33	4
number__	11	(D)	(D)	-	21	110	9
10 to 19 _____ farms__	-	1	(D)	-	2	9	-
number__	-	(D)	(D)	1	2	113	-
20 to 49 _____ farms__	1	-	8	1	(D)	8	-
number__	(D)	-	268	(D)	(D)	207	-
50 to 99 _____ farms__	2	1	7	2	(D)	7	2
number__	(D)	(D)	596	(D)	(D)	449	(D)
100 to 199 _____ farms__	-	4	6	1	3	7	3
number__	-	556	848	(D)	377	977	418
200 to 499 _____ farms__	4	11	4	4	4	6	2
number__	1 100	3 180	1 139	1 168	1 197	1 579	(D)
500 or more _____ farms__	16	10	3	3	2	9	10
number__	258 303	74 297	4 235	(D)	(D)	14 449	301 106

Table 11. Cattle and Calves—Inventory and Sales: 1987 and 1982—Con.

[For meaning of abbreviations and symbols, see introductory text]

Item	Hodgeman	Jackson	Jefferson	Jewell	Johnson	Kearny	Kingman	Kiowa
SALES								
Dairy products sold ... farms, 1987..	10	41	33	19	12	4	18	1
1982..	12	66	56	24	12	3	35	4
$1,000, 1987..	1 046	2 049	2 655	972	1 359	270	2 136	(D)
1982..	1 010	2 574	2 902	1 238	1 006	(D)	2 774	197
Cattle and calves sold ... farms, 1987..	260	615	668	488	361	125	541	172
1982..	318	910	721	554	447	139	597	228
number, 1987..	122 505	30 393	21 053	30 448	17 123	136 995	36 725	23 981
1982..	113 213	31 228	23 608	34 519	18 419	(D)	33 959	23 240
$1,000, 1987..	74 986	13 915	8 549	14 681	8 587	91 659	15 738	11 097
1982..	56 623	11 609	9 177	15 844	9 088	(D)	12 645	9 330
1987 farms by number sold:								
1 to 9 ... farms..	24	219	215	87	110	17	99	20
number..	109	1 134	1 037	427	523	79	508	107
10 to 19 ... farms..	14	211	173	81	97	17	75	16
number..	193	2 928	2 295	1 099	1 310	225	1 060	225
20 to 49 ... farms..	67	248	178	155	85	24	181	35
number..	2 155	7 849	5 218	4 804	2 526	774	5 699	1 062
50 to 99 ... farms..	48	96	69	92	41	23	94	33
number..	3 314	6 533	4 671	6 447	2 891	1 541	6 275	2 287
100 to 199 ... farms..	39	26	20	50	18	17	49	32
number..	5 290	(D)	2 532	6 587	587	2 312	6 583	4 756
200 to 499 ... farms..	46	11	10	16	4	16	34	25
number..	13 383	(D)	3 459	4 507	(D)	4 608	9 843	7 364
500 or more ... farms..	22	4	3	8	6	9	9	11
number..	98 061	5 319	1 841	6 577	6 181	127 456	6 757	8 158
Calves sold ... farms, 1987..	61	435	362	202	188	59	242	59
1982..	112	443	380	230	202	72	273	102
number, 1987..	2 497	6 361	7 016	4 369	3 737	3 414	6 735	4 026
1982..	5 699	8 489	6 776	5 722	6 911	2 629	8 757	4 767
$1,000, 1987..	776	2 240	1 808	1 476	1 081	1 166	2 181	1 377
1982..	1 537	2 210	1 671	1 636	4 005	664	2 388	1 354
1987 farms by number sold:								
1 to 9 ... farms..	14	203	182	80	74	10	87	19
number..	55	865	836	351	326	47	397	92
10 to 19 ... farms..	12	112	84	49	55	15	49	9
number..	181	1 457	1 092	642	747	207	638	117
20 to 49 ... farms..	19	91	76	52	43	13	75	13
number..	549	2 669	2 236	1 619	1 281	391	2 346	340
50 to 99 ... farms..	9	23	13	13	12	6	17	4
number..	684	1 425	795	781	791	396	1 030	389
100 to 199 ... farms..	5	3	3	8	3	12	11	6
number..	(D)	302	336	976	(D)	1 685	1 324	773
200 to 499 ... farms..	2	2	4	-	1	3	3	4
number..	(D)	(O)	1 719	-	(D)	688	1 000	2
500 or more ... farms..	-	1	-	-	-	-	-	2
number..	-	(D)	-	-	-	-	-	(D)
Cattle sold ... farms, 1987..	227	676	532	419	264	99	438	148
1982..	272	742	565	450	354	113	483	189
number, 1987..	120 008	22 032	14 037	26 079	13 386	133 581	29 990	19 955
1982..	107 514	22 739	16 832	28 797	11 508	(D)	25 202	18 473
$1,000, 1987..	74 210	11 676	6 742	13 205	7 486	90 493	13 557	9 720
1982..	55 086	9 399	7 505	14 208	5 083	(D)	10 257	7 976
1987 farms by number sold:								
1 to 9 ... farms..	19	258	234	102	114	25	98	20
number..	85	1 181	1 034	391	464	95	414	77
10 to 19 ... farms..	18	158	113	57	57	11	69	9
number..	241	2 163	1 515	816	768	133	953	141
20 to 49 ... farms..	51	163	123	128	40	22	122	33
number..	1 682	4 673	3 521	3 867	1 150	697	3 726	971
50 to 99 ... farms..	38	68	36	67	22	11	73	30
number..	2 625	4 696	2 391	4 746	2 110	775	4 959	2 051
100 to 199 ... farms..	35	19	16	42	13	7	42	25
number..	4 811	2 618	1 932	5 384	(D)	677	5 849	3 822
200 to 499 ... farms..	44	7	8	17	4	12	25	23
number..	12 503	2 281	(D)	4 861	(D)	3 546	7 330	6 727
500 or more ... farms..	22	3	2	6	6	11	9	8
number..	98 061	4 220	(D)	6 012	5 881	127 456	6 757	6 166
Cattle fattened on grain and concentrates sold ... farms, 1987..	28	95	67	62	58	14	34	8
1982..	21	84	102	82	92	17	39	20
number, 1987..	89 787	4 230	2 587	6 993	3 410	118 113	1 234	155
1982..	65 377	2 910	3 041	11 688	2 627	152 136	1 238	1 288
$1,000, 1987..	60 087	2 600	1 563	4 543	1 889	82 714	874	75
1982..	36 267	1 669	1 697	7 013	1 325	109 226	613	600
1987 farms by number sold:								
1 to 9 ... farms..	1	44	50	36	36	4	19	5
number..	(D)	133	186	53	128	13	(D)	10
10 to 19 ... farms..	1	14	12	12	6	-	1	-
number..	(D)	230	176	172	92	1	-	1
20 to 49 ... farms..	4	21	14	11	4	(D)	4	(D)
number..	139	624	416	340	117	1	143	1
50 to 99 ... farms..	5	8	6	11	6	(D)	1	2
number..	335	561	407	753	464	(D)	359	(D)
100 to 199 ... farms..	2	4	3	5	4	2	5	-
number..	(D)	540	(D)	641	(D)	(D)	657	-
200 to 499 ... farms..	6	2	1	4	-	-	-	-
number..	1 793	(D)	(D)	1 022	-	-	-	-
500 or more ... farms..	9	2	1	4	2	6	-	-
number..	87 230	(D)	(D)	4 012	(D)	117 801	-	-

Table 11. **Cattle and Calves—Inventory and Sales: 1987 and 1982**—Con.

[For meaning of abbreviations and symbols, see introductory text]

Item	Labette	Lane	Leavenworth	Lincoln	Linn	Logan	Lyon	McPherson
SALES								
Dairy products sold .... farms, 1987..	23	–	70	17	15	3	15	58
1982..	48	–	88	24	27	3	28	91
$1,000, 1987..	1 641	–	4 938	1 304	1 197	(D)	786	4 259
1982..	2 985	–	5 359	1 086	1 949	(D)	801	4 926
Cattle and calves sold .... farms, 1987..	708	142	745	371	472	191	554	677
1982..	816	179	839	427	566	218	522	776
number, 1987..	57 624	114 170	14 862	47 799	22 610	22 537	79 945	62 079
1982..	49 317	106 816	16 891	25 692	21 462	22 458	67 698	46 578
$1,000, 1987..	32 556	73 772	5 558	24 106	9 510	10 341	42 482	35 541
1982..	32 221	62 388	6 141	11 094	7 324	9 930	34 675	20 425
1987 farms by number sold:								
1 to 9 .... farms..	184	8	311	53	95	20	129	182
number..	945	37	1 596	314	481	82	645	904
10 to 19 .... farms..	183	16	199	53	105	16	122	133
number..	2 541	233	2 717	699	1 399	213	1 666	1 812
20 to 49 .... farms..	224	28	177	116	162	56	166	194
number..	6 783	902	5 264	3 702	5 215	1 883	5 162	5 920
50 to 99 .... farms..	67	22	37	74	63	42	61	87
number..	4 424	1 426	2 464	5 176	3 894	3 134	4 328	5 623
100 to 199........................ farms..	33	26	20	44	29	26	35	42
number..	(D)	3 917	(D)	6 044	4 002	3 650	5 019	5 916
200 to 499........................ farms..	11	24	1	23	15	23	22	27
number..	(D)	7 199	(D)	6 381	4 041	6 950	6 571	7 996
500 or more .... farms..	6	18	–	8	3	8	19	12
number..	35 792	101 065	–	25 483	3 576	6 626	56 754	33 908
Calves sold .... farms, 1987..	407	42	452	136	252	94	215	266
1982..	502	54	469	179	325	96	231	360
number, 1987..	6 909	2 152	6 235	4 528	4 836	5 052	3 824	5 268
1982..	9 664	2 059	6 483	5 887	6 119	5 162	5 474	7 963
$1,000, 1987..	2 054	819	1 624	1 326	1 387	1 709	1 124	1 631
1982..	2 373	493	1 632	1 594	1 959	1 286	1 460	1 786
1987 farms by number sold:								
1 to 9 .... farms..	177	10	242	46	92	22	104	137
number..	784	23	1 119	253	393	89	436	596
10 to 19 .... farms..	104	8	108	26	71	16	61	71
number..	1 450	120	1 585	330	940	264	830	913
20 to 49 .... farms..	104	11	88	38	71	34	40	64
number..	2 825	301	2 544	1 096	2 099	1 012	1 174	1 780
50 to 99 .... farms..	17	7	10	33	14	10	6	6
number..	1 123	406	607	1 458	966	756	401	363
100 to 199........................ farms..	5	3	4	2	4	4	3	5
number..	727	302	580	(D)	440	515	(D)	636
200 to 499........................ farms..	–	2	–	1	–	4	–	2
number..	–	(D)	–	(D)	–	(D)	–	(D)
500 or more .... farms..	–	1	–	–	–	2	1	1
number..	–	(D)	–	(D)	–	(D)	(D)	(D)
Cattle sold .... farms, 1987..	562	122	558	322	380	148	464	585
1982..	599	159	652	335	410	167	528	620
number, 1987..	50 915	112 027	8 627	43 271	17 772	17 485	76 121	56 791
1982..	39 653	104 757	10 428	19 805	13 344	17 296	62 224	39 615
$1,000, 1987..	30 501	72 952	3 931	22 777	8 123	8 631	41 357	33 911
1982..	29 848	61 895	4 509	9 500	5 365	8 644	33 414	18 638
1987 farms by number sold:								
1 to 9 .... farms..	226	7	299	59	115	26	129	189
number..	969	30	1 260	260	543	118	559	814
10 to 19 .... farms..	118	17	138	50	70	11	89	116
number..	1 600	237	1 838	642	924	141	1 203	1 534
20 to 49 .... farms..	136	26	91	86	111	35	123	136
number..	4 051	669	2 606	2 766	3 537	1 210	3 808	4 290
50 to 99 .... farms..	46	18	20	63	50	30	51	70
number..	3 164	1 153	1 468	4 316	3 269	2 014	3 681	4 744
100 to 199........................ farms..	21	20	12	35	17	21	33	36
number..	(D)	2 694	1 453	4 878	2 250	3 015	4 747	5 236
200 to 499........................ farms..	9	22	–	23	14	19	21	27
number..	(D)	6 799	–	6 329	3 721	5 702	6 127	7 763
500 or more .... farms..	6	18	–	8	3	6	18	9
number..	35 792	100 445	–	24 076	3 528	5 285	56 002	32 406
Cattle fattened on grain and concentrates sold .... farms, 1987..	31	21	78	26	52	16	100	68
1982..	67	28	102	61	48	17	123	91
number, 1987..	(D)	(D)	1 208	3 641	2 572	1 836	33 962	(D)
1982..	(D)	(D)	1 797	5 591	1 586	5 065	33 220	13 726
$1,000, 1987..	(D)	82 813	670	2 584	1 366	1 219	20 564	(D)
1982..	(D)	(D)	1 001	3 571	779	2 948	20 490	7 980
1987 farms by number sold:								
1 to 9 .... farms..	11	2	48	6	16	1	26	34
number..	43	(D)	135	20	47	(D)	79	119
10 to 19 .... farms..	5	1	16	4	3	3	10	11
number..	64	(D)	202	59	46	(D)	(D)	133
20 to 49 .... farms..	6	–	8	6	21	5	20	9
number..	237	–	161	225	643	127	(D)	285
50 to 99 .... farms..	5	–	5	5	4	–	14	9
number..	325	383	360	339	246	–	1 048	329
100 to 199........................ farms..	–	4	3	1	5	3	14	4
number..	–	551	350	(D)	679	379	2 127	654
200 to 499........................ farms..	2	5	–	4	3	4	10	3
number..	(D)	1 733	–	1 316	911	1 282	2 840	977
500 or more .... farms..	2	4	–	2	–	–	6	2
number..	(D)	(D)	–	(D)	–	–	27 120	(D)

Item	Marion	Marshall	Meade	Miami	Mitchell	Montgomery	Morris	Morton
SALES								
Dairy products sold ... farms, 1987	88	59	3	33	9	16	40	-
1982	114	67	4	43	15	35	44	-
$1,000, 1987	6 296	3 738	(D)	1 885	616	1 484	2 296	-
1982	6 910	3 591	591	2 850	(D)	1 784	2 138	-
Cattle and calves sold ... farms, 1987	690	676	226	783	320	701	402	111
1982	791	771	244	860	368	769	453	124
number, 1987	55 595	35 633	56 100	19 583	54 604	16 690	52 164	17 774
1982	54 512	32 612	50 809	21 962	49 808	22 588	59 156	15 062
$1,000, 1987	27 560	17 343	31 493	7 845	33 262	7 234	26 189	10 335
1982	24 135	14 239	23 880	8 173	21 388	7 455	30 734	8 927
1987 farms by number sold:								
1 to 9 ... farms	168	144	13	304	53	212	64	17
number	921	722	73	1 474	288	1 115	291	79
10 to 19 ... farms	130	148	36	177	66	213	72	14
number	1 833	2 055	538	2 347	904	2 904	962	200
20 to 49 ... farms	192	233	56	204	100	189	134	24
number	5 915	7 141	1 862	6 123	3 128	5 739	4 349	809
50 to 99 ... farms	94	95	47	71	43	57	71	24
number	6 310	6 329	3 212	4 553	2 828	3 831	4 610	1 741
100 to 199 ... farms	44	38	21	17	28	22	39	18
number	5 697	5 182	2 612	2 395	3 825	(D)	5 026	2 145
200 to 499 ... farms	41	15	31	10	16	8	20	9
number	12 507	4 097	9 650	2 591	5 044	(D)	5 936	2 500
500 or more ... farms	3	3	20	14	14	-	12	5
number	22 402	10 107	36 153	-	38 587	-	30 688	10 300
Calves sold ... farms, 1987	270	273	75	378	107	438	148	45
1982	291	326	84	442	142	486	162	60
number, 1987	7 202	5 468	3 667	5 827	2 571	6 989	3 720	1 176
1982	6 063	5 877	3 374	6 328	4 144	8 662	8 392	2 559
$1,000, 1987	2 100	1 680	1 124	1 596	828	2 052	1 144	410
1982	1 516	1 483	906	1 577	1 083	2 266	2 666	741
1987 farms by number sold:								
1 to 9 ... farms	122	112	20	204	42	198	46	15
number	564	504	95	797	198	870	183	69
10 to 19 ... farms	56	70	16	79	19	135	39	11
number	757	957	236	1 046	271	1 724	515	163
20 to 49 ... farms	68	68	16	75	32	89	46	11
number	1 983	1 992	488	2 093	952	2 626	1 434	364
50 to 99 ... farms	13	16	13	13	11	11	10	7
number	882	1 064	913	785	581	(D)	658	(D)
100 to 199 ... farms	6	6	5	6	2	5	6	1
number	740	(D)	558	(D)	(D)	(D)	(D)	(D)
200 to 499 ... farms	4	1	2	1	1	2	1	-
number	(D)	(D)	(D)	(D)	(D)	(D)	(D)	-
500 or more ... farms	1	-	1	-	-	-	-	-
number	(D)	-	(D)	-	-	-	-	-
Cattle sold ... farms, 1987	592	669	187	631	272	544	350	101
1982	699	645	219	683	298	564	375	67
number, 1987	48 383	30 165	52 433	13 756	52 033	11 701	48 464	16 598
1982	48 449	26 735	47 435	15 634	45 664	13 926	50 764	12 503
$1,000, 1987	25 459	15 663	30 370	6 249	32 434	5 182	27 045	9 925
1982	22 620	12 756	22 971	6 596	20 305	5 189	26 068	6 186
1987 farms by number sold:								
1 to 9 ... farms	191	165	17	297	52	264	71	16
number	925	760	84	1 336	242	1 142	371	60
10 to 19 ... farms	98	119	28	130	63	111	65	13
number	1 325	1 669	376	1 734	825	1 455	854	190
20 to 49 ... farms	139	166	45	135	73	111	102	21
number	4 348	5 034	1 539	3 998	2 290	3 309	3 421	659
50 to 99 ... farms	71	69	34	49	29	40	51	25
number	4 717	4 512	2 264	3 100	1 950	2 642	3 311	1 773
100 to 199 ... farms	38	35	14	15	26	13	30	15
number	4 797	4 691	1 744	2 144	3 499	1 628	3 844	1 609
200 to 499 ... farms	37	12	30	5	15	5	19	6
number	11 278	3 392	9 229	1 454	4 640	1 325	5 677	1 807
500 or more ... farms	20	3	19	-	14	-	12	5
number	20 993	10 107	37 203	-	36 587	-	30 986	10 300
Cattle fattened on grain and concentrates sold ... farms, 1987	109	65	13	74	30	53	56	9
1982	123	84	15	104	53	79	67	4
number, 1987	7 331	10 729	26 215	972	33 363	1 123	23 785	(D)
1982	8 908	10 181	(D)	1 604	29 949	1 782	25 425	(D)
$1,000, 1987	5 054	6 565	(D)	504	(D)	698	14 779	(D)
1982	5 276	6 051	(D)	866	13 856	758	16 673	(D)
1987 farms by number sold:								
1 to 9 ... farms	41	27	1	45	11	31	14	6
number	161	106	(D)	175	60	103	57	20
10 to 19 ... farms	21	11	1	10	2	10	5	-
number	264	144	(D)	118	10	125	67	-
20 to 49 ... farms	17	10	1	16	2	2	6	-
number	556	321	(D)	481	(D)	(D)	431	-
50 to 99 ... farms	13	6	3	2	(D)	1	8	-
number	867	414	203	(D)	(D)	(D)	551	-
100 to 199 ... farms	8	7	-	1	3	3	5	2
number	1 040	1 002	-	(D)	752	392	685	(D)
200 to 499 ... farms	6	3	2	-	3	1	3	-
number	1 925	(D)	(D)	-	1 080	(D)	814	-
500 or more ... farms	3	1	13	-	4	-	4	1
number	2 496	(D)	25 433	-	31 274	-	21 180	(D)

Table 11. Cattle and Calves—Inventory and Sales: 1987 and 1982—Con.

[For meaning of abbreviations and symbols, see introductory text]

Item	Nemaha	Neosho	Ness	Norton	Osage	Osborne	Ottawa	Pawnee
SALES								
Dairy products sold ... farms, 1987	126	29	6	11	14	16	10	2
1982	153	51	10	24	18	19	13	6
$1,000, 1987	8 976	1 744	360	336	491	885	676	(D)
1982	8 868	3 318	406	(D)	864	(D)	885	253
Cattle and calves sold ... farms, 1987	741	532	387	316	532	379	307	240
1982	895	591	458	368	637	441	352	260
number, 1987	39 541	21 342	30 993	31 830	27 683	35 512	45 524	130 566
1982	47 169	21 530	36 651	32 517	32 900	34 277	42 097	61 971
$1,000, 1987	19 934	9 119	13 708	16 382	14 511	15 768	24 599	54 244
1982	22 040	8 016	13 794	12 800	14 967	15 191	19 442	32 998
1987 farms by number sold:								
1 to 9 ... farms	113	136	38	37	130	49	49	44
number	563	659	201	174	664	222	267	264
10 to 19 ... farms	160	147	50	44	140	48	49	35
number	2 282	1 980	678	616	1 935	626	669	477
20 to 49 ... farms	252	160	107	125	150	103	73	71
number	7 600	4 739	3 524	4 117	4 600	3 560	2 250	2 266
50 to 99 ... farms	132	45	92	57	65	84	60	36
number	9 033	2 944	6 097	4 035	4 167	5 726	4 121	2 475
100 to 199 ... farms	55	30	61	29	13	66	37	22
number	7 623	3 656	8 075	3 756	1 731	8 754	5 336	2 980
200 to 499 ... farms	25	8	34	18	21	24	26	17
number	7 625	2 644	9 303	5 113	6 140	7 129	7 284	5 894
500 or more ... farms	4	6	6	8	13	7	13	16
number	4 715	4 520	3 115	14 019	8 456	9 495	25 595	116 407
Calves sold ... farms, 1987	263	296	162	159	199	150	122	102
1982	387	388	230	196	245	186	140	112
number, 1987	5 281	5 494	5 834	4 839	3 136	5 496	4 384	3 634
1982	7 320	6 605	9 020	7 741	5 553	5 451	4 094	3 966
$1,000, 1987	1 367	1 749	1 653	1 652	906	1 907	1 479	1 374
1982	1 693	1 698	2 257	1 910	1 330	1 426	1 059	1 052
1987 farms by number sold:								
1 to 9 ... farms	87	124	40	31	97	30	46	44
number	371	579	193	120	443	147	231	176
10 to 19 ... farms	77	89	40	32	52	38	31	11
number	1 041	1 137	567	457	665	499	402	159
20 to 49 ... farms	82	68	44	68	41	45	22	28
number	2 350	1 838	1 223	1 966	1 267	1 449	642	878
50 to 99 ... farms	13	11	26	21	7	27	11	12
number	745	687	1 856	1 376	(D)	1 974	725	779
100 to 199 ... farms	3	5	9	6	1	9	5	4
number	(D)	(D)	1 070	(D)	(D)	(D)	793	442
200 to 499 ... farms	1	-	3	1	-	-	4	2
number	(D)	-	626	(D)	-	-	(D)	(D)
500 or more ... farms	-	1	-	-	-	-	1	1
number	-	(D)	-	-	-	-	(D)	(D)
Cattle sold ... farms, 1987	629	437	324	237	456	331	267	207
1982	688	449	347	293	529	363	305	208
number, 1987	34 260	15 848	25 459	26 991	24 547	30 016	41 140	126 932
1982	39 849	14 925	27 631	24 776	27 347	28 826	38 003	58 015
$1,000, 1987	18 567	7 370	11 854	14 730	13 604	13 862	23 120	62 870
1982	20 147	6 318	11 597	10 890	13 636	13 766	18 383	31 944
1987 farms by number sold:								
1 to 9 ... farms	129	180	50	54	138	54	50	54
number	651	736	264	255	638	236	219	263
10 to 19 ... farms	123	97	43	27	112	41	42	28
number	1 730	1 317	593	359	1 523	536	559	376
20 to 49 ... farms	190	98	77	74	108	91	61	50
number	5 988	2 865	2 690	2 422	3 226	2 929	1 876	1 515
50 to 99 ... farms	112	30	71	39	52	80	49	28
number	7 620	1 938	4 659	2 755	3 226	5 681	3 309	1 886
100 to 199 ... farms	47	20	48	21	14	39	29	15
number	6 407	2 608	6 241	2 703	1 837	5 062	3 992	2 244
200 to 499 ... farms	24	9	31	16	19	21	26	17
number	7 169	2 944	8 437	4 576	5 643	6 212	7 218	5 542
500 or more ... farms	4	5	4	6	13	5	10	15
number	4 715	3 440	2 575	13 919	8 454	9 360	23 987	115 107
Cattle fattened on grain and concentrates sold ... farms, 1987	136	38	19	25	62	40	29	22
1982	212	39	17	46	90	50	34	25
number, 1987	12 672	1 741	1 287	13 610	5 671	9 871	(D)	(D)
1982	19 212	2 351	1 649	10 352	7 065	8 026	(D)	(D)
$1,000, 1987	8 119	1 036	615	8 377	3 919	4 426	(D)	52 683
1982	11 422	1 267	942	5 343	4 756	(D)	6 766	(D)
1987 farms by number sold:								
1 to 9 ... farms	20	17	8	8	27	9	11	4
number	65	94	34	30	98	24	37	5
10 to 19 ... farms	17	2	1	-	9	3	(D)	5
number	235	(D)	(D)	-	124	36	(D)	(D)
20 to 49 ... farms	46	10	5	4	10	11	5	3
number	1 388	283	192	(D)	302	306	160	99
50 to 99 ... farms	30	3	2	(D)	(D)	8	7	1
number	1 992	(D)	(D)	(D)	(D)	620	454	(D)
100 to 199 ... farms	7	4	1	6	2	3	-	4
number	1 015	516	(D)	791	(D)	355	-	619
200 to 499 ... farms	13	2	1	3	6	3	3	4
number	3 762	(D)	(D)	882	1 620	(D)	881	1 428
500 or more ... farms	3	-	(D)	3	5	2	2	5
number	4 215	-	(D)	11 741	3 111	(D)	(D)	(D)

Table 11. Cattle and Calves—Inventory and Sales: 1987 and 1982—Con.

[For meaning of abbreviations and symbols, see introductory text]

Item	Phillips	Pottawatomie	Pratt	Rawlins	Reno	Republic	Rice	Riley
SALES								
Dairy products sold .... farms, 1987..	11	40	5	11	105	12	19	22
1982..	15	65	9	26	125	19	29	32
$1,000, 1987..	435	1 345	529	590	6 315	1 176	1 171	1 622
1982..	293	2 024	587	2 022	5 719	903	1 478	1 887
Cattle and calves sold .... farms, 1987..	426	550	278	325	783	513	323	363
1982..	491	619	281	413	897	642	376	393
number, 1987..	28 308	40 874	104 585	24 064	79 028	95 611	69 919	21 457
1982..	33 064	45 195	76 616	23 666	69 145	66 579	57 170	22 565
$1,000, 1987..	12 418	20 667	66 769	11 862	36 531	62 420	44 587	11 059
1982..	12 327	19 247	43 747	9 306	37 608	41 242	29 528	11 127
1987 farms by number sold:								
1 to 9 .... farms..	43	107	48	28	203	111	53	77
number..	215	491	241	142	1 027	561	272	362
10 to 19 .... farms..	57	99	41	41	188	120	63	66
number..	915	1 362	641	569	2 601	1 700	823	940
20 to 49 .... farms..	136	169	72	99	214	165	101	114
number..	4 375	4 937	2 234	3 221	6 747	5 085	3 248	3 627
50 to 99 .... farms..	102	104	51	101	99	77	46	64
number..	7 112	7 358	3 442	6 911	8 490	5 112	3 171	4 496
100 to 199 .... farms..	49	42	22	40	40	28	28	23
number..	6 112	5 868	2 733	5 368	5 226	3 652	4 010	3 113
200 to 499 .... farms..	25	25	19	12	30	8	18	14
number..	7 097	7 959	6 024	3 259	8 829	1 888	5 897	3 888
500 or more .... farms..	14	14	17	4	17	9	14	5
number..	2 482	12 879	89 270	4 594	48 108	77 613	52 398	5 011
Calves sold .... farms, 1987..	189	290	114	172	406	203	137	138
1982..	260	310	122	263	480	268	183	156
number, 1987..	5 859	6 244	4 268	5 772	8 020	3 500	3 964	2 501
1982..	8 443	7 967	3 842	9 125	9 131	5 520	4 279	2 901
$1,000, 1987..	1 913	2 179	1 135	1 977	2 142	1 214	1 308	792
1982..	2 259	2 118	1 116	2 444	2 300	1 616	1 106	767
1987 farms by number sold:								
1 to 9 .... farms..	53	68	37	40	170	83	45	57
number..	232	297	154	203	720	345	228	219
10 to 19 .... farms..	36	55	21	24	93	52	42	29
number..	487	707	272	312	1 247	680	555	339
20 to 49 .... farms..	68	71	40	62	115	53	32	42
number..	2 013	2 081	1 169	1 832	3 307	1 452	1 051	1 208
50 to 99 .... farms..	21	31	10	41	22	13	13	9
number..	1 369	2 014	656	2 654	1 396	(D)	905	(D)
100 to 199 .... farms..	8	4	3	5	4	2	3	1
number..	(D)	(D)	417	771	(D)	(D)	(D)	(D)
200 to 499 .... farms..	2	-	2	-	2	2	2	-
number..	(D)	-	(D)	-	(D)	(D)	(D)	-
500 or more .... farms..	-	1	(D)	-	-	-	-	-
number..	-	(D)	(D)	-	-	-	-	-
Cattle sold .... farms, 1987..	360	465	229	257	644	443	264	320
1982..	354	524	229	293	703	516	295	337
number, 1987..	22 449	34 630	100 317	18 292	71 008	92 111	65 955	18 956
1982..	24 621	37 228	72 774	14 541	60 014	63 059	52 891	19 664
$1,000, 1987..	10 505	18 488	65 634	9 884	34 388	61 206	43 279	10 267
1982..	10 069	17 129	42 632	8 862	35 307	39 626	28 420	10 361
1987 farms by number sold:								
1 to 9 .... farms..	53	140	68	47	237	130	61	66
number..	229	591	257	207	1 142	638	269	390
10 to 19 .... farms..	65	71	39	34	149	95	41	65
number..	891	968	493	467	1 993	1 306	557	771
20 to 49 .... farms..	107	112	43	72	127	124	72	89
number..	3 393	3 413	1 433	2 334	3 904	3 957	2 217	2 817
50 to 99 .... farms..	72	68	36	63	66	63	36	53
number..	5 012	4 737	2 384	4 171	4 321	4 198	2 513	3 586
100 to 199 .... farms..	39	38	20	25	30	19	24	18
number..	4 792	5 980	2 301	3 260	4 085	2 522	3 377	2 743
200 to 499 .... farms..	20	23	18	12	26	8	16	13
number..	5 650	7 433	5 909	3 259	7 455	1 877	5 210	3 680
500 or more .... farms..	4	13	15	4	9	9	14	5
number..	2 482	12 108	87 540	4 594	48 108	77 613	51 782	4 967
Cattle fattened on grain and concentrates sold .... farms, 1987..	35	64	36	41	72	45	29	72
1982..	50	75	29	36	75	48	48	72
number, 1987..	1 616	6 332	(D)	7 284	46 929	(D)	46 991	8 399
1982..	5 189	9 022	(D)	3 572	(D)	(D)	30 741	7 781
$1,000, 1987..	970	4 193	54 100	4 841	23 518	55 004	34 001	4 655
1982..	2 778	5 585	(D)	2 442	(D)	(D)	18 569	4 996
1987 farms by number sold:								
1 to 9 .... farms..	8	25	13	4	37	12	10	12
number..	33	78	40	(D)	120	45	31	57
10 to 19 .... farms..	5	8	2	2	9	4	1	8
number..	86	108	(D)	(D)	120	60	6	103
20 to 49 .... farms..	11	14	7	7	12	12	4	25
number..	333	372	212	363	265	337	139	789
50 to 99 .... farms..	7	7	5	7	6	7	3	6
number..	593	430	367	463	445	440	205	397
100 to 199 .... farms..	4	3	3	3	1	(D)	4	12
number..	571	330	377	1 182	(D)	480	(D)	1 877
200 to 499 .... farms..	-	3	4	5	5	3	2	5
number..	-	735	1 365	1 240	(D)	708	1 304	1 300
500 or more .... farms..	-	4	2	3	4	3	5	4
number..	-	4 281	(D)	4 012	44 198	(D)	44 962	3 876

Table 11. Cattle and Calves—Inventory and Sales: 1987 and 1982—Con.

[For meaning of abbreviations and symbols, see introductory text]

Item	Rooks	Rush	Russell	Saline	Scott	Sedgwick	Seward	Shawnee
SALES								
Dairy products sold ... farms, 1987..	15	8	22	24	1	93	-	10
1982..	25	7	25	40	2	100	-	23
$1,000, 1987..	1 088	403	909	2 515	(D)	12 020	-	520
1982..	1 530	216	986	2 349	(D)	10 873	-	907
Cattle and calves sold ... farms, 1987..	298	312	336	382	143	677	113	466
1982..	335	374	401	421	176	738	117	551
number, 1987..	23 034	15 492	21 249	25 262	393 502	25 327	145 857	14 737
1982..	29 116	23 906	24 082	37 232	311 271	26 529	164 752	16 525
$1,000, 1987..	10 504	6 655	9 182	11 774	255 682	11 037	95 689	6 994
1982..	11 159	9 708	8 719	17 623	194 293	12 129	104 596	6 843
1987 farms by number sold:								
1 to 9 ... farms..	28	44	51	99	12	219	24	170
number..	157	264	273	486	63	1 080	112	854
10 to 19 ... farms..	50	63	59	62	8	162	8	114
number..	672	938	851	861	119	2 215	107	1 529
20 to 49 ... farms..	99	118	111	113	21	185	24	118
number..	3 109	3 659	3 685	3 538	740	5 505	717	3 530
50 to 99 ... farms..	65	53	60	47	13	57	12	43
number..	4 287	3 581	4 007	3 183	855	3 865	860	2 916
100 to 199 ... farms..	32	20	35	30	18	32	19	15
number..	4 130	2 564	4 499	4 296	2 465	4 066	2 727	1 966
200 to 499 ... farms..	20	13	16	24	19	17	7	7
number..	5 951	(D)	4 554	6 259	6 545	4 429	2 296	(D)
500 or more ... farms..	4	1	4	7	52	5	19	2
number..	4 718	(D)	3 480	6 639	382 715	4 167	139 038	(D)
Calves sold ... farms, 1987..	156	165	200	160	30	361	35	225
1982..	151	199	244	168	38	369	47	282
number, 1987..	5 377	3 231	5 379	4 469	914	7 161	2 256	2 837
1982..	5 177	6 577	6 847	2 754	2 743	5 640	4 549	3 724
$1,000, 1987..	1 748	1 058	1 818	1 473	340	2 081	871	934
1982..	1 465	1 753	1 776	740	741	1 271	1 213	1 001
1987 farms by number sold:								
1 to 9 ... farms..	36	49	64	67	8	153	9	130
number..	144	212	279	288	40	592	43	487
10 to 19 ... farms..	34	61	52	30	9	97	3	43
number..	410	810	739	403	120	1 292	(D)	558
20 to 49 ... farms..	56	42	49	44	7	88	15	44
number..	1 749	1 178	1 500	1 337	220	2 539	437	1 196
50 to 99 ... farms..	19	10	20	11	5	15	3	6
number..	1 192	670	1 533	684	(D)	958	205	(D)
100 to 199 ... farms..	8	3	12	4	1	8	3	2
number..	919	361	1 328	542	(D)	(D)	(D)	(D)
200 to 499 ... farms..	3	-	-	2	-	1	-	-
number..	963	-	-	1 515	-	(D)	-	-
500 or more ... farms..	-	-	-	-	-	1	2	-
number..	-	-	-	-	-	(D)	(D)	-
Cattle sold ... farms, 1987..	233	259	258	317	126	533	97	398
1982..	272	290	302	363	159	588	95	452
number, 1987..	17 657	12 261	15 870	20 793	392 588	18 166	143 601	11 900
1982..	23 941	17 329	17 235	34 478	306 526	22 869	160 203	12 801
$1,000, 1987..	8 756	5 596	7 364	10 302	255 342	8 956	95 017	6 061
1982..	9 694	7 955	6 943	17 083	193 552	10 858	103 385	5 842
1987 farms by number sold:								
1 to 9 ... farms..	35	89	65	92	11	249	22	171
number..	173	357	273	410	71	1 065	104	753
10 to 19 ... farms..	48	47	41	56	3	103	8	80
number..	654	602	555	740	42	1 391	101	1 077
20 to 49 ... farms..	70	76	76	82	18	111	19	100
number..	2 126	2 523	2 512	2 506	617	3 469	531	3 040
50 to 99 ... farms..	35	37	39	37	8	25	9	29
number..	2 314	2 521	2 564	2 542	547	1 729	558	1 978
100 to 199 ... farms..	25	14	19	26	15	27	16	10
number..	3 141	1 794	2 482	(D)	2 061	3 552	2 311	1 330
200 to 499 ... farms..	16	13	15	19	19	14	6	5
number..	4 531	(D)	4 584	(D)	6 545	3 603	2 096	(D)
500 or more ... farms..	4	1	3	6	52	4	17	2
number..	4 718	(D)	2 900	6 089	382 715	3 377	137 900	(D)
Cattle fattened on grain and concentrates sold ... farms, 1987..	17	8	30	19	46	126	19	44
1982..	24	27	23	44	54	137	20	95
number, 1987..	4 202	288	1 733	740	309 059	2 872	(D)	1 929
1982..	5 745	4 347	1 530	14 694	281 962	7 524	(D)	3 635
$1,000, 1987..	2 495	203	932	446	216 131	1 508	83 853	1 209
1982..	2 407	2 626	875	8 860	181 342	4 190	(D)	1 950
1987 farms by number sold:								
1 to 9 ... farms..	8	4	10	8	-	74	1	23
number..	27	19	27	27	-	271	(D)	70
10 to 19 ... farms..	(D)	1	6	3	-	26	-	8
number..	(D)	(D)	72	36	-	338	-	111
20 to 49 ... farms..	-	(D)	8	64	(D)	13	2	5
number..	-	(D)	240	(D)	(D)	367	(D)	143
50 to 99 ... farms..	3	-	3	3	3	6	3	2
number..	189	-	(D)	(D)	(D)	449	170	(D)
100 to 199 ... farms..	2	1	2	1	6	4	1	4
number..	(D)	(D)	(D)	(D)	821	583	(D)	501
200 to 499 ... farms..	2	-	2	-	7	3	2	1
number..	(D)	-	(D)	(D)	2 173	894	(D)	(D)
500 or more ... farms..	(D)	-	-	-	28	-	3	1
number..	(D)	-	-	-	305 826	-	(D)	(D)

Item	Sheridan	Sherman	Smith	Stafford	Stanton	Stevens	Sumner	Thomas
SALES								
Dairy products sold .... farms, 1987..	4	4	18	3	1	-	23	-
1982..	15	13	25	3	-	1	21	3
$1,000, 1987..	(D)	104	1 041	48	(D)	-	2 063	-
1982..	1 084	315	910	(D)	-	(D)	1 921	(D)
Cattle and calves sold .... farms, 1987..	297	172	468	260	105	118	800	231
1982..	354	213	569	286	84	128	740	249
number, 1987..	48 624	54 185	43 689	86 803	99 059	(D)	33 680	55 597
1982..	50 208	39 466	50 056	59 120	76 809	(D)	33 215	54 719
$1,000, 1987..	29 822	36 193	23 072	47 341	63 188	71 166	15 385	37 357
1982..	26 879	24 339	23 301	29 472	48 813	(D)	13 026	32 657
1987 farms by number sold:								
1 to 9 .... farms..	36	19	58	26	17	20	160	40
number..	188	68	270	113	95	115	788	178
10 to 19 .... farms..	26	21	63	37	14	14	138	37
number..	378	329	938	534	205	200	1 957	514
20 to 49 .... farms..	107	52	149	48	12	26	162	70
number..	3 614	1 808	4 904	1 592	340	942	4 794	2 208
50 to 99 .... farms..	71	27	110	51	16	25	84	34
number..	5 053	1 899	7 705	3 697	1 170	1 759	4 192	2 339
100 to 199 .... farms..	33	24	45	38	20	19	39	23
number..	4 376	3 255	5 594	4 992	2 960	2 446	5 082	2 843
200 to 499 .... farms..	13	16	26	31	14	8	27	16
number..	3 565	4 793	7 419	8 696	4 452	2 757	7 452	4 805
500 or more .... farms..	11	13	17	27	12	4	10	11
number..	31 450	42 033	16 859	67 177	89 828	(D)	9 415	42 550
Calves sold .... farms, 1987..	103	79	167	71	34	39	268	95
1982..	135	104	210	121	26	58	322	103
number, 1987..	3 253	3 527	4 379	3 666	656	(D)	4 080	2 307
1982..	4 953	4 626	5 315	3 159	1 095	2 002	5 687	3 464
$1,000, 1987..	1 041	1 107	1 501	1 301	203	621	1 232	746
1982..	1 369	1 238	1 771	902	272	550	1 382	964
1987 farms by number sold:								
1 to 9 .... farms..	29	14	40	17	13	8	135	29
number..	125	45	154	48	44	34	609	132
10 to 19 .... farms..	17	22	50	13	9	6	62	21
number..	253	307	717	182	107	86	819	301
20 to 49 .... farms..	39	25	55	16	10	13	57	34
number..	1 214	785	1 820	466	(D)	396	1 606	1 067
50 to 99 .... farms..	13	12	15	19	1	6	11	8
number..	762	840	948	1 286	(D)	621	678	(D)
100 to 199 .... farms..	5	4	6	2	1	-	3	2
number..	(D)	(D)	(D)	(D)	(D)	-	369	(D)
200 to 499 .... farms..	1	1	1	3	-	2	-	-
number..	(D)	(D)	(D)	964	-	(D)	-	-
500 or more .... farms..	-	1	-	1	-	-	-	-
number..	-	(D)	-	(D)	-	(D)	-	-
Cattle sold .... farms, 1987..	249	143	418	226	97	98	456	186
1982..	296	164	485	222	71	97	589	196
number, 1987..	45 371	50 658	39 310	83 137	98 403	(D)	29 600	53 290
1982..	45 255	34 840	43 741	55 961	75 714	(D)	27 548	51 255
$1,000, 1987..	28 581	35 086	21 571	44 041	62 985	70 546	14 153	36 612
1982..	25 509	23 101	21 530	28 570	48 541	(D)	11 644	31 694
1987 farms by number sold:								
1 to 9 .... farms..	46	27	82	33	22	19	117	41
number..	238	94	332	125	117	109	491	179
10 to 19 .... farms..	22	19	54	26	5	11	107	24
number..	305	283	712	369	80	150	1 491	341
20 to 49 .... farms..	75	32	111	43	13	23	117	51
number..	2 551	1 035	3 575	1 339	403	780	3 350	1 585
50 to 99 .... farms..	57	19	92	34	13	23	45	27
number..	4 191	1 376	6 362	2 437	930	1 633	3 022	1 799
100 to 199 .... farms..	27	20	37	35	18	13	33	18
number..	3 555	2 687	4 561	4 648	2 648	1 673	4 381	2 209
200 to 499 .... farms..	11	13	25	29	14	8	27	17
number..	3 084	3 950	7 169	7 865	4 397	2 135	7 450	5 070
500 or more .... farms..	11	13	17	26	12	3	10	10
number..	31 447	41 233	15 599	66 383	89 828	(D)	9 415	42 107
Cattle fattened on grain and concentrates								
sold .... farms, 1987..	51	32	52	37	19	5	66	46
1982..	68	36	68	33	12	8	71	46
number, 1987..	30 218	41 768	10 877	44 075	85 259	(D)	4 170	44 834
1982..	26 821	25 285	15 822	(D)	66 861	(D)	5 076	38 398
$1,000, 1987..	20 518	30 596	7 455	26 494	56 565	67 757	2 555	32 791
1982..	18 059	18 463	9 951	(D)	45 034	(D)	2 812	25 636
1987 farms by number sold:								
1 to 9 .... farms..	7	5	12	11	4	-	31	11
number..	(D)	10	47	33	21	-	113	(D)
10 to 19 .... farms..	6	1	5	2	2	-	16	2
number..	(D)	(D)	71	(D)	(D)	-	230	(D)
20 to 49 .... farms..	11	2	7	1	-	-	5	7
number..	369	(D)	221	151	-	-	85	225
50 to 99 .... farms..	7	2	13	2	-	-	8	6
number..	644	(D)	865	(D)	-	-	591	409
100 to 199 .... farms..	9	5	3	7	3	-	(D)	4
number..	1 294	614	421	1 089	(D)	-	(D)	492
200 to 499 .... farms..	3	5	6	6	3	2	2	10
number..	768	1 752	1 705	1 811	1 047	(D)	(D)	3 171
500 or more .... farms..	6	12	6	5	7	3	3	8
number..	27 003	39 163	7 527	40 816	83 741	(D)	2 190	40 483

Table 11. **Cattle and Calves—Inventory and Sales: 1987 and 1982**—Con.

[For meaning of abbreviations and symbols, see introductory text]

Item	Trego	Wabaunsee	Wallace	Washington	Wichita	Wilson	Woodson	Wyandotte
SALES								
Dairy products sold .... farms, 1987	22	18	3	41	–	13	2	2
1982	29	30	2	68	4	19	13	5
$1,000, 1987	1 123	1 152	(D)	3 295	–	684	(D)	(D)
1982	1 164	1 330	(D)	4 006	207	867	488	277
Cattle and calves sold .... farms, 1987	343	430	173	676	140	420	269	85
1982	349	500	184	752	165	483	327	98
number, 1987	43 119	42 728	22 503	41 984	294 835	15 095	26 356	(D)
1982	69 258	56 084	21 929	47 144	204 147	18 859	34 369	1 803
$1,000, 1987	23 211	21 315	12 535	21 919	202 946	6 206	13 310	855
1982	41 549	27 782	10 185	22 033	131 207	6 527	14 764	746
1987 farms by number sold:								
1 to 9 .... farms	44	88	24	112	15	100	58	50
number	220	492	126	625	99	535	251	251
10 to 19 .... farms	55	90	28	132	20	101	51	19
number	767	1 248	398	1 880	262	1 376	733	245
20 to 49 .... farms	133	116	33	222	34	135	80	12
number	4 221	3 614	1 042	6 872	1 016	4 136	2 499	(D)
50 to 99 .... farms	68	59	34	121	18	54	37	2
number	4 707	3 997	2 381	8 071	1 278	3 690	2 649	(D)
100 to 199 .... farms	30	40	30	48	18	22	26	–
number	3 802	5 631	4 146	6 503	2 589	2 927	(D)	–
200 to 499 .... farms	10	23	15	29	16	7	12	1
number	2 772	6 676	4 480	9 081	4 579	(D)	(D)	(D)
500 or more .... farms	3	14	9	12	19	1	5	1
number	26 630	21 070	9 948	9 952	285 012	(D)	13 148	(D)
Calves sold .... farms, 1987	196	158	95	245	54	201	98	50
1982	200	216	104	276	59	268	159	55
number, 1987	6 454	4 896	3 764	4 960	1 905	3 336	2 635	(D)
1982	7 951	4 791	4 837	5 768	2 489	6 126	3 627	482
$1,000, 1987	1 994	1 713	1 357	1 575	709	896	919	180
1982	2 123	1 278	1 258	1 599	704	1 665	1 080	102
1987 farms by number sold:								
1 to 9 .... farms	54	60	29	96	16	95	44	35
number	233	245	133	438	89	418	153	175
10 to 19 .... farms	52	43	23	60	9	52	19	8
number	520	577	303	786	110	684	274	91
20 to 49 .... farms	63	30	19	63	18	40	28	5
number	1 905	910	635	1 747	515	1 184	867	122
50 to 99 .... farms	34	17	10	31	4	10	2	1
number	2 183	1 194	819	1 325	226	612	(D)	(D)
100 to 199 .... farms	6	4	9	4	6	4	3	–
number	(D)	465	(D)	(D)	(D)	438	350	–
200 to 499 .... farms	2	3	2	1	1	–	1	1
number	(D)	(D)	(D)	(D)	(D)	–	(D)	(D)
500 or more .... farms	–	1	–	–	–	–	1	–
number	–	(D)	–	–	–	–	(D)	–
Cattle sold .... farms, 1987	267	376	142	581	118	350	232	63
1982	286	423	137	645	132	357	254	71
number, 1987	36 665	37 832	18 739	37 024	292 930	11 759	23 721	(D)
1982	61 307	53 293	17 092	41 376	201 658	12 733	30 542	1 321
$1,000, 1987	21 217	19 602	11 177	20 344	202 236	5 209	12 392	675
1982	39 426	26 504	8 926	20 434	130 504	4 862	13 684	643
1987 farms by number sold:								
1 to 9 .... farms	67	91	30	132	27	108	50	41
number	317	483	124	609	139	491	219	170
10 to 19 .... farms	47	83	18	102	8	77	47	14
number	647	1 140	235	1 421	96	1 029	657	163
20 to 49 .... farms	90	98	29	176	20	104	64	6
number	2 609	3 047	893	5 349	855	3 224	2 019	191
50 to 99 .... farms	30	37	22	89	10	36	35	–
number	2 121	2 616	1 592	6 097	707	2 482	2 505	–
100 to 199 .... farms	24	37	22	42	15	18	21	–
number	3 086	5 079	2 974	5 751	2 316	2 306	2 834	–
200 to 499 .... farms	7	19	13	28	13	6	12	1
number	(D)	5 437	3 815	8 845	3 825	(D)	3 498	(D)
500 or more .... farms	2	13	8	12	19	1	3	1
number	(D)	20 060	9 106	8 952	284 992	(D)	11 989	(D)
Cattle fattened on grain and concentrates sold .... farms, 1987	9	48	14	95	24	24	28	19
1982	27	48	21	120	33	30	30	21
number, 1987	(D)	4 128	5 575	11 964	277 148	890	1 390	374
1982	(D)	(D)	7 231	17 108	191 811	979	11 232	504
$1,000, 1987	(D)	2 731	4 565	8 246	194 206	558	837	249
1982	(D)	(D)	4 843	10 173	126 404	504	6 904	291
1987 farms by number sold:								
1 to 9 .... farms	5	21	–	17	1	7	10	12
number	22	90	–	86	(D)	33	39	30
10 to 19 .... farms	–	4	–	16	–	7	5	5
number	–	55	–	215	–	96	(D)	(D)
20 to 49 .... farms	3	12	3	24	2	5	6	1
number	87	375	85	681	(D)	156	272	(D)
50 to 99 .... farms	–	6	3	13	2	2	2	–
number	–	(D)	227	905	(D)	(D)	199	–
100 to 199 .... farms	–	3	3	6	2	2	2	–
number	–	(D)	434	922	(D)	(D)	(D)	–
200 to 499 .... farms	–	4	3	11	5	1	2	1
number	–	1 170	(D)	4 071	1 545	(D)	(U)	(D)
500 or more .... farms	1	1	2	8	12	–	–	–
number	(D)	(D)	(D)	5 084	275 118	–	–	–

Table 12. Hogs and Pigs—Inventory, Litters, and Sales: 1987 and 1982

[For meaning of abbreviations and symbols, see introductory text]

Item	Kansas	Allen	Anderson	Atchison	Barber	Barton	Bourbon
INVENTORY							
Hogs and pigs ... farms, 1987..	6 768	59	60	134	29	67	71
1982..	9 241	85	87	200	26	83	105
number, 1987..	1 516 878	6 612	10 240	17 675	3 900	5 473	7 261
1982..	1 708 770	9 210	14 277	24 328	3 185	6 405	10 464
Farms by inventory:							
1 to 24 ... farms, 1987..	1 916	23	27	32	12	26	31
1982..	2 812	33	37	54	14	47	29
number, 1987..	19 902	244	210	375	159	272	318
1982..	27 953	319	413	507	119	481	268
25 to 49 ... farms, 1987..	826	4	10	21	2	15	10
1982..	1 144	12	12	25	-	8	21
number, 1987..	29 265	115	302	749	(D)	500	338
1982..	40 471	445	401	854	-	180	758
50 to 99 ... farms, 1987..	1 087	12	8	17	3	11	10
1982..	1 582	12	13	46	6	11	22
number, 1987..	74 756	744	547	1 207	(D)	711	649
1982..	109 247	851	845	3 187	403	740	1 499
100 to 199 ... farms, 1987..	1 092	11	5	27	7	10	9
1982..	1 551	14	6	39	-	8	13
number, 1987..	147 160	594	1 121	3 163	896	1 484	1 207
1982..	209 570	1 768	1 757	5 432	-	1 155	(D)
200 to 499 ... farms, 1987..	1 226	7	4	34	4	3	8
1982..	1 415	9	9	28	4	7	18
number, 1987..	366 822	(D)	(D)	9 481	(D)	(D)	2 351
1982..	420 095	2 252	2 953	7 928	(D)	1 839	5 113
500 to 999 ... farms, 1987..	372	2	2	1	-	2	2
1982..	490	4	3	7	1	3	2
number, 1987..	243 374	(D)	(D)	(D)	-	(D)	(D)
1982..	319 600	(D)	2 115	(D)	1	2 010	(D)
1,000 or more ... farms, 1987..	247	-	4	2	1	-	1
1982..	247	1	5	1	1	-	-
number, 1987..	629 597	-	5 999	(D)	(D)	-	(D)
1982..	581 834	(D)	6 429	(D)	(D)	-	-
Hogs and pigs used or to be used for breeding ... farms, 1987..	4 596	45	35	100	22	39	58
1982..	6 360	66	61	152	12	48	81
number, 1987..	191 079	935	921	2 232	603	1 042	1 118
1982..	207 873	1 386	1 152	2 900	466	897	1 322
1987 farms by inventory:							
1 to 24	2 741	34	26	69	15	28	43
25 to 49	898	6	6	19	3	6	11
50 to 99	572	4	5	10	3	3	2
100 or more ... farms	385	1	2	2	1	2	2
number	94 186	(D)	(D)	(D)	(D)	(D)	(D)
Other hogs and pigs ... farms, 1987..	6 286	56	56	123	27	62	64
1982..	8 501	78	80	185	25	69	96
number, 1987..	1 325 799	5 677	9 319	15 443	3 297	4 431	6 143
1982..	1 500 897	7 824	13 125	21 428	2 719	5 508	9 142
LITTERS							
Litters of pigs farrowed between—							
Dec. 1 of preceding year and Nov. 30 ... farms, 1987..	4 819	48	36	106	23	40	59
1982..	6 713	66	69	158	12	53	86
number, 1987..	295 974	1 490	1 449	3 281	738	1 567	1 483
1982..	322 969	2 230	1 868	4 391	661	1 472	2 096
Dec. 1 of preceding year and May 31 ... farms, 1987..	4 455	43	32	97	18	38	49
1982..	6 140	60	61	146	8	51	82
number, 1987..	149 414	755	670	1 642	372	764	774
1982..	164 086	1 140	960	2 247	297	789	1 141
June 1 and Nov. 30 ... farms, 1987..	4 403	41	31	95	21	39	50
1982..	5 907	60	56	146	12	45	66
number, 1987..	146 560	735	779	1 639	366	603	709
1982..	158 903	1 090	928	2 144	364	683	955
SALES							
Hogs and pigs sold ... farms, 1987..	7 090	62	60	144	32	71	74
1982..	9 778	85	90	209	24	86	115
number, 1987..	2 759 676	12 015	16 843	28 541	5 509	14 919	11 596
1982..	3 038 205	17 085	23 811	36 602	5 094	15 198	16 988
$1,000, 1987..	284 375	1 234	1 705	3 119	539	1 276	1 128
1982..	316 882	1 760	2 616	3 903	586	1 294	1 765
1987 farms by number sold:							
1 to 24 ... farms	1 265	17	24	15	5	18	26
number	13 716	179	284	201	50	216	207
25 to 49 ... farms	844	3	10	24	6	11	10
number	29 704	101	374	863	211	380	360
50 to 99 ... farms	1 060	15	3	25	11	7	6
number	74 489	1 093	212	1 847	806	471	555
100 to 199 ... farms	1 143	9	8	24	5	13	12
number	157 706	1 193	1 153	3 324	662	1 632	1 635
200 to 499 ... farms	1 466	12	6	45	3	13	13
number	448 491	3 952	1 778	13 303	(D)	3 537	3 921
500 to 999 ... farms	729	5	3	9	(D)	5	(D)
number	492 919	(D)	2 592	(D)	(D)	3 931	(D)
1,000 or more ... farms	583	1	2	(D)	2	4	2
number	1 542 651	(D)	10 450	(D)	(D)	4 752	(D)
Feeder pigs sold ... farms, 1987..	1 869	13	13	41	8	32	13
1982..	2 741	32	22	59	6	33	21
number, 1987..	514 364	1 376	2 118	3 494	837	6 525	2 849
1982..	555 066	3 102	1 265	6 252	364	6 529	3 052
$1,000, 1987..	23 029	53	86	146	41	302	138
1982..	24 918	136	53	271	13	250	140
Hogs and pigs other than feeder pigs sold ... farms, 1987..	6 596	58	62	137	27	63	70
1982..	9 006	75	86	192	23	77	107
number, 1987..	2 245 262	10 639	14 725	25 047	4 672	8 394	8 747
1982..	2 481 139	13 983	22 546	30 350	4 790	8 669	13 936
$1,000, 1987..	261 346	1 181	1 619	2 973	498	974	990
1982..	291 965	1 625	2 562	3 632	573	1 044	1 625

Table 12. **Hogs and Pigs—Inventory, Litters, and Sales: 1987 and 1982**—Con.

[For meaning of abbreviations and symbols, see introductory text]

Item	Brown	Butler	Chase	Chautauqua	Cherokee	Cheyenne	Clark
INVENTORY							
Hogs and pigs ---------------------------- farms, 1987__	135	130	36	40	51	35	5
1982__	173	167	39	47	79	56	9
number, 1987__	42 810	37 102	7 829	7 682	6 217	5 134	(D)
1982__	43 984	32 479	6 988	5 855	5 632	9 047	343
Farms by inventory:							
1 to 24 ------------------------------- farms, 1987__	16	38	10	7	24	9	3
1982__	19	59	13	16	39	21	4
number, 1987__	172	395	60	86	193	127	9
1982__	202	590	138	153	327	270	(D)
25 to 49 ------------------------------- farms, 1987__	9	12	4	10	2	5	1
1982__	21	12	7	9	7	5	2
number, 1987__	(D)	395	149	399	(D)	180	(D)
1982__	736	413	237	305	205	188	(D)
50 to 99 ------------------------------- farms, 1987__	27	14	7	8	6	11	1
1982__	28	21	3	8	14	11	3
number, 1987__	1 796	954	564	417	(D)	777	(D)
1982__	1 907	1 422	227	610	870	734	235
100 to 199 ------------------------------ farms, 1987__	19	13	5	6	9	6	-
1982__	38	17	5	5	13	5	-
number, 1987__	(D)	1 911	817	722	1 126	(D)	-
1982__	4 853	2 345	(D)	598	(D)	533	-
200 to 499 ------------------------------ farms, 1987__	38	26	6	8	4	2	-
1982__	43	39	9	5	4	9	-
number, 1987__	12 068	8 536	1 399	2 639	1 051	(D)	-
1982__	12 344	12 644	2 374	1 460	1 254	2 752	-
500 to 999 ------------------------------ farms, 1987__	13	20	2	3	6	3	-
1982__	14	16	3	3	6	3	-
number, 1987__	8 975	13 939	(D)	(D)	3 360	2 746	-
1982__	9 223	10 965	-	(D)	(D)	(D)	-
1,000 or more -------------------------- farms, 1987__	11	7	2	1	-	2	-
1982__	10	3	1	1	-	-	-
number, 1987__	17 046	10 670	(D)	(D)	-	2	-
1982__	14 719	4 100	(D)	(D)	-	(D)	-
Hogs and pigs used or to be used for breeding ------------------------------- farms, 1987__	96	78	24	35	37	25	3
1982__	123	111	27	37	57	25	6
number, 1987__	5 473	3 588	645	1 447	743	615	27
1982__	5 257	3 300	489	858	631	757	62
1987 farms by inventory:							
1 to 24 ---	42	34	17	14	29	18	3
25 to 49 ---	18	14	3	15	3	3	-
50 to 99 ---	17	18	2	4	4	1	-
100 or more ------------------------------- farms__	19	12	2	2	1	3	-
number__	3 316	1 722	(D)	(D)	(D)	312	-
Other hogs and pigs --------------------- farms, 1987__	126	125	33	38	47	34	5
1982__	163	149	37	41	72	56	7
number, 1987__	37 337	33 214	7 184	6 559	5 474	4 519	(D)
1982__	38 727	29 179	6 499	4 997	4 801	8 290	281
LITTERS							
Litters of pigs farrowed between—							
Dec. 1 of preceding year and Nov. 30 ------ farms, 1987__	98	81	25	35	37	25	3
1982__	128	120	27	40	66	25	8
number, 1987__	8 586	6 080	958	1 447	1 073	899	18
1982__	8 213	5 555	623	1 672	1 120	1 211	152
Dec. 1 of preceding year and May 31 ------ farms, 1987__	93	74	25	32	33	25	3
1982__	117	110	25	35	58	22	8
number, 1987__	4 311	2 972	379	762	534	482	3
1982__	4 149	2 866	304	934	583	603	106
June 1 and Nov. 30 --------------------- farms, 1987__	92	77	23	32	31	24	3
1982__	116	104	24	36	57	24	4
number, 1987__	4 277	3 108	579	685	539	407	9
1982__	4 064	2 689	319	738	537	608	46
SALES							
Hogs and pigs sold --------------------- farms, 1987__	142	142	35	39	51	36	4
1982__	185	179	40	49	79	54	14
number, 1987__	77 802	60 680	15 809	11 334	10 054	8 566	(D)
1982__	76 143	57 975	14 821	12 704	9 128	16 196	1 347
$1,000, 1987__	7 768	6 455	1 865	963	1 075	749	(D)
1982__	7 603	6 493	1 572	1 055	900	1 822	196
1987 farms by number sold:							
1 to 24 ------------------------------------- farms__	7	35	8	28	16	3	2
number__	82	295	68	28	156	25	(D)
25 to 49 ----------------------------------- farms__	8	11	5	3	5	7	-
number__	272	362	189	87	169	290	(D)
50 to 99 ----------------------------------- farms__	17	15	6	9	4	11	1
number__	1 143	1 004	360	508	239	594	(D)
100 to 199 --------------------------------- farms__	26	11	4	4	11	8	-
number__	3 250	1 479	543	647	1 312	1 090	-
200 to 499 --------------------------------- farms__	37	28	7	12	9	4	-
number__	11 189	9 483	(D)	3 807	1 998	(D)	-
500 to 999 --------------------------------- farms__	21	26	2	6	3	2	-
number__	13 643	18 927	(D)	(D)	2 860	(D)	-
1,000 or more ------------------------------ farms__	26	16	3	2	3	3	-
number__	48 223	29 130	11 312	(D)	3 320	4 230	-
Feeder pigs sold ----------------------- farms, 1987__	35	18	9	20	13	11	1
1982__	51	43	9	23	26	12	2
number, 1987__	15 241	4 354	2 739	4 593	1 161	3 336	(D)
1982__	17 469	5 502	672	5 597	2 603	1 125	(D)
$1,000, 1987__	701	177	(D)	183	52	145	(D)
1982__	812	261	29	238	119	47	(D)
Hogs and pigs other than feeder pigs sold --- farms, 1987__	132	139	32	31	48	34	4
1982__	169	172	36	44	69	50	14
number, 1987__	62 561	56 326	13 070	6 741	8 893	5 230	89
1982__	58 674	52 473	14 149	7 107	8 525	15 070	(D)
$1,000, 1987__	7 066	6 278	(D)	780	1 023	603	(D)
1982__	6 791	6 232	1 543	818	781	1 775	(D)

Table 12. Hogs and Pigs—Inventory, Litters, and Sales: 1987 and 1982—Con.

[For meaning of abbreviations and symbols, see introductory text]

Item	Clay	Cloud	Coffey	Comanche	Cowley	Crawford	Decatur
INVENTORY							
Hogs and pigs .... farms, 1987..	147	71	51	17	119	44	68
1982..	153	103	88	25	129	107	71
number, 1987..	42 511	16 703	5 827	2 035	24 287	2 859	12 545
1982..	35 206	15 878	9 459	1 597	33 170	12 358	17 489
Farms by inventory:							
1 to 24 .... farms, 1987..	19	17	25	3	46	25	21
1982..	25	31	31	9	45	41	15
number, 1987..	193	170	326	24	419	230	290
1982..	232	301	336	101	408	425	161
25 to 49 .... farms, 1987..	16	7	6	6	17	6	8
1982..	12	13	17	6	22	9	7
number, 1987..	648	240	210	(D)	647	(D)	328
1982..	451	440	616	227	857	302	284
50 to 99 .... farms, 1987..	16	12	3	3	13	4	6
1982..	26	20	16	6	21	14	8
number, 1987..	1 175	804	209	(D)	847	(D)	437
1982..	1 887	1 233	1 087	405	1 516	1 017	599
100 to 199 .... farms, 1987..	30	14	9	2	17	7	10
1982..	39	13	12	2	11	19	14
number, 1987..	4 235	1 704	1 112	(D)	2 225	(D)	1 278
1982..	5 556	1 798	1 543	(D)	1 529	2 338	1 964
200 to 499 .... farms, 1987..	45	18	6	2	14	1	19
1982..	36	20	7	2	15	20	22
number, 1987..	12 413	4 836	(D)	(D)	4 160	(D)	5 246
1982..	10 734	6 249	2 697	(D)	4 308	5 626	6 659
500 to 999 .... farms, 1987..	14	3	1	1	7	1	3
1982..	9	5	5	-	8	4	4
number, 1987..	9 564	(D)	(D)	(D)	4 517	(D)	(D)
1982..	6 078	(D)	3 180	-	5 318	2 650	(D)
1,000 or more .... farms, 1987..	7	2	1	-	5	-	1
1982..	6	1	-	-	7	-	1
number, 1987..	14 283	(D)	(D)	-	11 452	-	(D)
1982..	10 270	(D)	-	-	19 234	-	(D)
Hogs and pigs used or to be used for breeding .... farms, 1987..	127	54	32	10	81	28	50
1982..	114	67	63	10	92	84	48
number, 1987..	5 228	2 237	660	382	3 294	551	2 044
1982..	4 638	2 085	1 437	197	3 542	1 784	2 064
1987 farms by inventory:							
1 to 24	71	33	23	6	53	22	26
25 to 49	25	8	6	1	12	3	11
50 to 99	16	6	1	2	8	1	10
100 or more .... farms..	15	7	2	1	8	2	3
number..	2 390	1 273	(D)	(D)	1 902	(D)	805
Other hogs and pigs .... farms, 1987..	142	65	48	17	107	40	60
1982..	146	97	81	24	111	98	68
number, 1987..	37 283	14 466	4 967	1 653	20 973	2 308	10 501
1982..	30 568	13 793	8 022	1 400	29 628	10 594	15 425
LITTERS							
Litters of pigs farrowed between—							
Dec. 1 of preceding year and Nov. 30 .... farms, 1987..	130	60	34	10	89	30	50
1982..	117	69	66	10	102	85	53
number, 1987..	8 790	3 359	1 190	443	4 829	803	3 542
1982..	6 874	3 658	2 646	309	6 201	2 570	3 370
Dec. 1 of preceding year and May 31 .... farms, 1987..	122	53	31	10	75	26	43
1982..	111	63	62	10	101	76	44
number, 1987..	4 355	1 651	582	193	2 493	423	1 746
1982..	3 360	1 809	1 325	151	3 395	1 292	1 619
June 1 and Nov. 30 .... farms, 1987..	127	58	34	10	72	22	48
1982..	111	66	56	10	90	75	50
number, 1987..	4 435	1 708	608	250	2 336	380	1 796
1982..	3 494	1 849	1 321	158	2 806	1 278	1 751
SALES							
Hogs and pigs sold .... farms, 1987..	156	77	55	17	117	41	73
1982..	156	111	94	28	139	108	75
number, 1987..	75 529	33 133	11 755	3 406	48 321	6 365	29 881
1982..	61 028	33 827	24 077	3 253	67 117	21 589	31 105
$1,000, 1987..	8 014	3 112	1 003	328	4 805	464	2 627
1982..	6 334	3 140	2 040	317	6 480	2 083	2 924
1987 farms by number sold:							
1 to 24 .... farms..	7	8	21	2	28	20	9
number..	62	63	256	(D)	321	262	134
25 to 49 .... farms..	14	10	4	3	18	3	9
number..	507	360	147	100	592	106	318
50 to 99 .... farms..	17	11	12	4	14	4	7
number..	1 257	784	883	244	1 009	336	482
100 to 199 .... farms..	30	15	8	1	17	5	18
number..	4 321	1 954	818	(D)	2 380	647	2 381
200 to 499 .... farms..	47	13	6	6	18	7	14
number..	14 680	3 470	2 083	2 013	5 599	(D)	4 512
500 to 999 .... farms..	17	5	4	1	13	1	12
number..	11 870	4 594	(D)	(D)	8 576	(D)	8 042
1,000 or more .... farms..	24	12	2	-	9	1	4
number..	42 632	21 928	(D)	-	29 844	(D)	14 012
Feeder pigs sold .... farms, 1987..	41	28	13	4	35	10	20
1982..	50	29	34	4	45	28	22
number, 1987..	13 291	9 782	5 093	724	11 074	2 205	11 628
1982..	13 515	8 422	10 546	(D)	5 483	7 671	8 295
$1,000, 1987..	529	443	212	28	521	84	514
1982..	635	340	495	(D)	206	341	371
Hogs and pigs other than feeder pigs sold ... farms, 1987..	144	70	53	16	104	38	67
1982..	140	99	87	26	124	89	70
number, 1987..	62 238	23 351	6 662	2 682	37 247	3 160	18 253
1982..	47 513	25 405	13 431	(D)	61 634	13 918	22 810
$1,000, 1987..	7 385	2 670	791	302	4 284	379	2 113
1982..	5 699	2 800	1 544	(D)	6 275	1 741	2 553

Table 12. Hogs and Pigs—Inventory, Litters, and Sales: 1987 and 1982—Con.

[For meaning of abbreviations and symbols, see introductory text]

Item	Dickinson	Doniphan	Douglas	Edwards	Elk	Ellis	Ellsworth
INVENTORY							
Hogs and pigs ... farms, 1987..	137	113	51	12	40	40	45
1982..	173	176	80	15	63	47	49
number, 1987..	19 456	16 432	8 120	1 333	9 613	4 096	6 985
1982..	24 266	23 106	16 779	1 105	14 260	4 314	8 711
Farms by inventory:							
1 to 24 ... farms, 1987..	26	28	18	3	13	19	14
1982..	53	39	30	6	20	22	12
number, 1987..	248	351	145	25	111	140	106
1982..	578	467	253	(D)	217	238	106
25 to 49 ... farms, 1987..	22	14	8	3	7	-	2
1982..	24	24	12	1	4	6	8
number, 1987..	700	452	301	(D)	260	-	(D)
1982..	864	903	486	(D)	118	240	270
50 to 99 ... farms, 1987..	34	27	10	1	7	5	13
1982..	33	37	16	3	10	7	11
number, 1987..	2 521	1 732	752	(D)	505	296	(D)
1982..	2 134	2 579	1 006	165	671	521	732
100 to 199 ... farms, 1987..	24	22	6	1	5	4	10
1982..	23	40	8	3	12	4	7
number, 1987..	3 240	2 862	782	(D)	610	1 090	1 372
1982..	3 155	5 516	1 091	(D)	1 480	525	(D)
200 to 499 ... farms, 1987..	23	14	7	4	5	7	3
1982..	29	30	8	2	8	8	6
number, 1987..	5 923	4 063	(D)	1 060	1 597	(D)	700
1982..	8 263	6 633	1 870	(D)	1 920	2 790	1 860
500 to 999 ... farms, 1987..	4	5	5	1	-	7	1
1982..	6	8	4	-	7	-	2
number, 1987..	2 430	3 068	(D)	-	-	(D)	(D)
1982..	3 515	5 010	(D)	-	(D)	-	(D)
1,000 or more ... farms, 1987..	4	3	1	-	3	-	2
1982..	5	-	2	-	2	-	3
number, 1987..	4 394	5 884	(D)	-	6 530	-	(D)
1982..	5 757	-	(D)	-	(D)	-	3 707
Hogs and pigs used or to be used for breeding ... farms, 1987..	97	73	35	9	24	21	22
1982..	122	104	54	9	53	25	37
number, 1987..	2 513	2 552	1 197	169	620	620	965
1982..	2 922	2 290	1 930	90	1 103	822	1 169
1987 farms by inventory:							
1 to 24 ...	54	49	27	5	15	13	11
25 to 49 ...	21	10	5	4	7	3	6
50 to 99 ...	8	9	1	-	1	3	3
100 or more ... farms..	4	5	2	-	1	2	2
number..	601	1 199	(D)	-	(D)	(D)	(D)
Other hogs and pigs ... farms, 1987..	133	107	47	12	37	36	45
1982..	162	171	74	13	58	46	45
number, 1987..	16 943	15 880	6 923	1 164	8 993	3 343	6 020
1982..	21 344	20 818	16 849	1 015	13 157	3 492	7 542
LITTERS							
Litters of pigs farrowed between—							
Dec. 1 of preceding year and Nov. 30 ... farms, 1987..	106	75	35	12	25	21	22
1982..	128	114	57	9	54	27	37
number, 1987..	3 790	3 920	1 923	301	988	1 263	1 582
1982..	4 411	3 185	3 246	110	1 580	1 267	1 736
Dec. 1 of preceding year and May 31 ... farms, 1987..	97	65	33	12	24	20	21
1982..	111	105	54	8	50	27	31
number, 1987..	1 935	1 954	985	141	534	627	757
1982..	2 250	1 635	1 356	63	850	646	824
June 1 and Nov. 30 ... farms, 1987..	97	65	34	12	24	21	21
1982..	119	92	51	7	46	23	36
number, 1987..	1 855	1 966	938	160	454	636	825
1982..	2 161	1 550	1 890	47	730	621	912
SALES							
Hogs and pigs sold ... farms, 1987..	144	116	50	15	40	35	41
1982..	186	198	96	16	72	46	50
number, 1987..	36 541	33 669	12 945	2 185	18 624	9 577	14 020
1982..	41 512	36 902	28 396	1 243	24 390	10 152	14 826
$1,000, 1987..	3 765	3 638	1 428	200	1 891	852	1 390
1982..	4 308	4 116	3 034	146	2 776	729	1 540
1987 farms by number sold:							
1 to 24 ... farms..	24	17	11	3	9	9	8
number..	266	207	91	(D)	76	83	71
25 to 49 ... farms..	13	11	6	1	4	1	2
number..	466	392	209	(D)	117	(D)	(D)
50 to 99 ... farms..	23	27	9	4	5	7	5
number..	1 546	1 835	632	306	391	468	250
100 to 199 ... farms..	28	26	8	1	9	6	10
number..	3 913	3 391	1 180	(D)	1 225	775	1 395
200 to 499 ... farms..	38	19	10	6	7	7	10
number..	11 412	5 610	2 673	1 715	2 142	(D)	(D)
500 to 999 ... farms..	11	7	3	-	3	-	2
number..	8 030	4 970	1 600	-	2 168	(D)	(D)
1,000 or more ... farms..	7	9	3	-	3	5	4
number..	11 008	17 254	6 560	-	12 505	5 520	7 488
Feeder pigs sold ... farms, 1987..	36	23	17	8	12	10	14
1982..	51	39	28	3	19	15	18
number, 1987..	7 130	3 963	4 055	677	1 587	4 848	4 602
1982..	7 095	4 964	6 083	53	3 495	5 964	3 383
$1,000, 1987..	361	174	190	23	65	199	230
1982..	335	204	298	2	156	233	178
Hogs and pigs other than feeder pigs sold ... farms, 1987..	126	114	40	12	37	31	38
1982..	167	194	78	16	65	42	47
number, 1987..	29 511	29 696	8 890	1 508	17 037	4 729	9 418
1982..	34 417	31 938	22 313	1 190	20 895	4 188	11 545
$1,000, 1987..	3 404	3 464	1 239	177	1 826	453	1 161
1982..	3 974	3 911	2 736	143	2 618	496	1 362

Table 12. **Hogs and Pigs—Inventory, Litters, and Sales: 1987 and 1982**—Con.

[For meaning of abbreviations and symbols, see introductory text]

Item	Finney	Ford	Franklin	Geary	Gove	Graham	Grant
INVENTORY							
Hogs and pigs .... farms, 1987..	34	37	84	44	39	17	30
1982..	34	50	143	60	44	36	28
number, 1987..	6 046	4 936	17 076	19 063	6 628	2 239	3 797
1982..	5 331	7 156	24 376	18 654	11 385	4 384	3 715
Farms by inventory:							
1 to 24 .... farms, 1987..	19	21	33	11	9	9	17
1982..	20	19	54	13	16	12	12
number, 1987..	160	183	290	72	116	108	181
1982..	160	130	406	149	150	104	(D)
25 to 49 .... farms, 1987..	4	5	8	3	7	3	5
1982..	4	7	21	7	6	3	2
number, 1987..	(D)	180	303	90	271	(D)	145
1982..	165	247	722	252	(D)	104	(D)
50 to 99 .... farms, 1987..	2	4	13	9	3	2	4
1982..	3	9	25	10	2	8	10
number, 1987..	(D)	261	959	669	161	(D)	316
1982..	222	670	1 846	739	(D)	522	659
100 to 199 .... farms, 1987..	3	2	14	5	5	1	3
1982..	3	6	18	13	8	10	2
number, 1987..	360	(D)	1 898	765	748	(D)	(D)
1982..	(D)	794	2 437	(D)	(D)	1 149	(D)
200 to 499 .... farms, 1987..	2	3	7	11	11	1	-
1982..	1	6	15	11	8	1	-
number, 1987..	(D)	802	2 193	(D)	3 077	(D)	-
1982..	(D)	1 595	4 182	3 548	2 495	-	-
500 to 999 .... farms, 1987..	1	1	5	1	4	-	-
1982..	1	2	7	2	2	2	-
number, 1987..	1 870	(D)	3 133	(D)	(D)	(D)	-
1982..	(D)	(D)	4 925	(D)	2 235	(D)	-
1,000 or more .... farms, 1987..	1	1	4	4	-	1	1
1982..	2	1	3	4	3	1	2
number, 1987..	(D)	(D)	8 300	13 254	-	(D)	(D)
1982..	(D)	(D)	9 856	10 887	6 800	(D)	(D)
Hogs and pigs used or to be used for							
breeding .... farms, 1987..	17	22	59	31	25	12	13
1982..	15	27	103	44	21	21	15
number, 1987..	740	575	2 298	4 545	858	340	466
1982..	504	790	3 195	2 277	634	583	535
1987 farms by inventory:							
1 to 24 .... farms..	10	18	46	14	13	10	10
25 to 49	4	2	6	5	7	1	2
50 to 99	1	-	5	6	3	1	-
100 or more .... farms..	2	2	2	6	2	-	1
number..	(D)	(D)	(D)	3 886	(D)	(D)	(D)
Other hogs and pigs .... farms, 1987..	26	29	77	42	35	14	29
1982..	33	47	128	57	43	32	28
number, 1987..	5 306	4 361	14 778	14 518	5 770	1 899	3 331
1982..	4 827	6 366	21 181	16 377	10 751	3 801	3 180
LITTERS							
Litters of pigs farrowed between—							
Dec. 1 of preceding year and Nov. 30 .... farms, 1987..	17	22	64	32	25	14	13
1982..	15	28	111	47	24	21	19
number, 1987..	1 113	900	3 508	4 462	1 055	564	696
1982..	847	1 305	5 175	3 979	1 290	919	905
Dec. 1 of preceding year and May 31 .... farms, 1987..	16	20	56	32	23	14	13
1982..	13	24	91	44	19	21	19
number, 1987..	552	444	1 786	2 221	488	285	344
1982..	419	657	2 576	2 014	712	451	479
June 1 and Nov. 30 .... farms, 1987..	16	20	58	31	24	13	10
1982..	15	26	96	46	24	17	15
number, 1987..	561	456	1 722	2 241	567	279	352
1982..	428	648	2 599	1 965	578	468	426
SALES							
Hogs and pigs sold .... farms, 1987..	33	38	90	44	44	23	27
1982..	32	46	145	66	46	42	31
number, 1987..	10 917	10 295	33 393	35 803	11 069	5 034	5 802
1982..	8 580	12 022	45 621	36 703	15 259	9 789	7 251
$1,000, 1987..	1 296	1 109	2 792	3 900	1 116	623	583
1982..	988	1 303	4 312	3 895	1 565	1 074	732
1987 farms by number sold:							
1 to 24 .... farms..	9	13	28	2	2	1	9
number..	90	133	258	(D)	149	(D)	120
25 to 49 .... farms..	10	10	12	6	6	7	8
number..	371	355	396	(D)	(D)	276	270
50 to 99 .... farms..	5	5	12	3	4	5	2
number..	407	371	902	175	(D)	368	(D)
100 to 199 .... farms..	1	3	13	9	3	3	2
number..	(D)	368	1 713	1 375	688	300	(D)
200 to 499 .... farms..	3	4	12	12	10	8	5
number..	950	1 538	(D)	4 092	2 791	(D)	1 414
500 to 999 .... farms..	2	1	6	6	4	-	-
number..	(D)	(D)	(D)	4 256	2 216	-	-
1,000 or more .... farms..	3	2	5	6	3	1	1
number..	7 989	(D)	20 300	25 656	4 500	(D)	(D)
Feeder pigs sold .... farms, 1987..	9	9	23	18	10	5	5
1982..	9	14	49	26	13	6	13
number, 1987..	923	392	13 719	3 987	3 179	565	481
1982..	1 280	1 065	19 126	6 080	2 559	2 402	1 168
$1,000, 1987..	50	12	477	218	166	24	21
1982..	66	42	977	265	117	103	44
Hogs and pigs other than feeder pigs sold ... farms, 1987..	32	34	80	41	41	22	23
1982..	30	44	132	59	41	41	28
number, 1987..	9 994	9 903	19 674	31 816	7 890	4 469	5 321
1982..	7 300	10 957	26 700	30 623	12 700	7 387	6 083
$1,000, 1987..	1 248	1 097	2 315	3 682	950	599	563
1982..	922	1 261	3 336	3 630	1 447	971	668

Table 12. **Hogs and Pigs—Inventory, Litters, and Sales: 1987 and 1982**—Con.

[For meaning of abbreviations and symbols, see introductory text]

Item	Gray	Greeley	Greenwood	Hamilton	Harper	Harvey	Haskell
INVENTORY							
Hogs and pigs .... farms, 1987..	19	9	37	10	31	116	11
1982..	40	16	57	17	45	129	14
number, 1987..	4 607	1 030	5 848	1 007	4 205	30 478	4 882
1982..	6 574	1 700	7 709	1 582	4 485	26 442	9 887
Farms by inventory:							
1 to 24 .... farms, 1987..	9	2	17	4	12	25	3
1982..	18	6	18	12	19	29	4
number, 1987..	86	(D)	163	39	119	247	20
1982..	205	(D)	162	125	179	279	(D)
25 to 49 .... farms, 1987..	1	4	2	2	2	15	-
1982..	3	1	7	1	8	17	-
number, 1987..	(D)	(D)	(D)	(D)	(D)	574	-
1982..	107	(D)	234	(D)	291	599	-
50 to 99 .... farms, 1987..	1	1	5	3	6	16	-
1982..	3	3	9	2	7	19	1
number, 1987..	(D)	(D)	(D)	236	(D)	1 095	-
1982..	177	200	540	(D)	504	1 337	(D)
100 to 199..................... farms, 1987..	2	1	6	-	4	26	4
1982..	5	4	9	1	4	23	2
number, 1987..	(D)	(D)	721	-	591	3 574	481
1982..	727	440	(D)	(D)	(D)	3 145	(D)
200 to 499..................... farms, 1987..	4	-	3	-	6	18	3
1982..	6	1	12	-	5	28	5
number, 1987..	1 313	-	780	-	(D)	(D)	(D)
1982..	2 338	(D)	3 417	-	1 421	8 169	1 965
500 to 999..................... farms, 1987..	-	1	3	1	1	11	-
1982..	1	1	1	-	2	10	1
number, 1987..	(D)	(D)	(D)	(D)	(D)	(D)	-
1982..	(D)	(D)	(D)	-	(D)	6 833	(D)
1,000 or more .... farms, 1987..	2	-	1	-	-	5	1
1982..	2	-	1	1	-	3	1
number, 1987..	(D)	-	(D)	(D)	-	12 382	(D)
1982..	(D)	-	(D)	(D)	-	6 080	(D)
Hogs and pigs used or to be used for breeding.................... farms, 1987..	8	6	20	3	22	59	7
1982..	20	11	39	9	39	71	9
number, 1987..	460	86	768	(D)	484	2 328	1 046
1982..	574	121	819	133	905	2 752	1 079
1987 farms by inventory:							
1 to 24	4	5	14	2	14	29	4
25 to 49	-	-	1	-	7	15	-
50 to 99	2	1	1	1	-	11	2
100 or more .... farms..	2	-	4	-	1	4	1
number..	(D)	-	480	-	(D)	640	(D)
Other hogs and pigs .... farms, 1987..	19	9	34	10	30	115	10
1982..	36	16	54	14	37	122	14
number, 1987..	4 147	944	5 080	(D)	3 721	28 150	3 836
1982..	6 000	1 579	6 890	1 449	3 580	23 690	8 808
LITTERS							
Litters of pigs farrowed between—							
Dec. 1 of preceding year and Nov. 30 .... farms, 1987..	8	7	21	3	25	61	8
1982..	22	11	43	9	41	75	9
number, 1987..	692	178	1 123	(D)	736	3 622	1 777
1982..	875	192	1 546	(D)	1 397	4 052	1 910
Dec. 1 of preceding year and May 31 .... farms, 1987..	7	6	21	3	21	54	8
1982..	21	10	38	7	37	70	9
number, 1987..	336	81	575	(D)	364	1 790	908
1982..	444	92	845	(D)	709	2 074	956
June 1 and Nov. 30 .... farms, 1987..	6	6	19	3	22	59	6
1982..	21	10	36	7	32	65	6
number, 1987..	356	97	548	(D)	372	1 832	869
1982..	431	100	701	(D)	688	1 988	952
SALES							
Hogs and pigs sold .... farms, 1987..	23	10	36	11	29	121	12
1982..	45	17	60	16	49	139	18
number, 1987..	9 771	1 571	7 687	2 529	5 678	51 767	16 039
1982..	11 271	2 338	14 427	2 592	9 465	54 766	15 013
$1,000, 1987..	1 086	181	794	306	829	5 375	1 635
1982..	1 230	241	1 428	314	772	5 749	1 566
1987 farms by number sold:							
1 to 24 .... farms..	6	4	10	5	7	19	4
number..	68	44	70	27	104	157	56
25 to 49 .... farms..	2	1	7	-	1	13	-
number..	(D)	(D)	255	-	(D)	439	-
50 to 99 .... farms..	3	2	2	2	2	6	-
number..	(D)	(D)	(D)	(D)	378	487	-
100 to 199..................... farms..	1	-	8	-	5	24	-
number..	(D)	(D)	962	(D)	689	3 476	-
200 to 499..................... farms..	5	1	5	1	8	34	4
number..	1 611	(D)	1 890	(D)	2 520	10 379	926
500 to 999..................... farms..	3	1	1	(D)	1	13	3
number..	1 739	(D)	(D)	(D)	(D)	9 085	(D)
1,000 or more .... farms..	3	-	3	1	1	12	1
number..	5 875	-	3 800	(D)	(D)	27 744	(D)
Feeder pigs sold .... farms, 1987..	1	2	7	-	9	23	4
1982..	12	(D)	20	5	9	33	-
number, 1987..	(D)	(D)	589	-	415	4 157	(D)
1982..	1 087	(D)	3 218	104	4 264	13 058	-
$1,000, 1987..	(D)	(D)	26	-	15	182	5
1982..	43	(D)	132	4	165	813	-
Hogs and pigs other than feeder pigs sold ... farms, 1987..	23	10	33	11	28	114	10
1982..	44	16	54	12	43	132	18
number, 1987..	(D)	(D)	7 098	2 529	5 263	47 610	(D)
1982..	10 214	(D)	11 209	2 488	5 201	41 708	15 013
$1,000, 1987..	(D)	(D)	768	306	614	5 193	1 630
1982..	1 187	(D)	1 296	310	607	5 136	1 566

Table 12. **Hogs and Pigs—Inventory, Litters, and Sales: 1987 and 1982**—Con.

[For meaning of abbreviations and symbols, see introductory text]

Item	Hodgeman	Jackson	Jefferson	Jewell	Johnson	Kearny	Kingman	Kiowa
INVENTORY								
Hogs and pigs .... farms, 1987..	18	133	106	159	40	14	96	13
1982..	25	214	171	206	50	24	100	21
number, 1987..	672	16 634	11 369	49 577	8 292	1 457	9 076	1 840
1982..	1 519	21 332	21 079	55 067	11 456	2 245	10 112	5 720
Farms by inventory:								
1 to 24 .... farms, 1987..	11	45	51	19	14	9	28	5
1982..	11	82	75	41	19	7	28	4
number, 1987..	99	480	573	195	137	117	333	58
1982..	124	729	732	520	169	91	240	(D)
25 to 49 .... farms, 1987..	3	21	17	19	5	–	17	3
1982..	4	25	22	19	4	3	21	2
number, 1987..	86	716	554	707	190	–	600	120
1982..	147	910	781	657	132	96	773	(D)
50 to 99 .... farms, 1987..	3	22	11	28	6	1	18	–
1982..	3	43	17	46	9	4	16	5
number, 1987..	(D)	1 395	728	1 915	382	(D)	1 266	–
1982..	169	2 923	1 189	3 139	645	274	1 042	367
100 to 199 .... farms, 1987..	–	23	16	21	7	2	16	3
1982..	6	38	26	36	7	5	17	3
number, 1987..	–	2 955	2 014	2 979	958	(D)	2 018	(D)
1982..	(D)	5 014	3 340	5 042	970	646	(D)	(D)
200 to 499 .... farms, 1987..	1	15	6	46	3	1	17	1
1982..	1	17	21	31	4	5	16	2
number, 1987..	(D)	4 428	2 026	12 378	(D)	(D)	4 839	(D)
1982..	(D)	5 241	6 249	10 013	1 100	1 138	4 236	(D)
500 to 999 .... farms, 1987..	–	5	3	16	2	1	–	1
1982..	–	8	6	22	5	–	2	4
number, 1987..	–	(D)	(D)	11 213	(D)	(D)	–	(D)
1982..	–	(D)	3 457	14 498	(D)	(D)	(D)	(D)
1,000 or more .... farms, 1987..	–	1	2	10	3	–	–	–
1982..	–	1	4	11	2	–	–	1
number, 1987..	–	(D)	(D)	20 190	4 180	–	–	–
1982..	–	(D)	5 331	21 200	(D)	–	–	(D)
Hogs and pigs used or to be used for breeding .... farms, 1987..	7	95	71	132	28	9	59	10
1982..	10	152	117	169	37	11	66	15
number, 1987..	108	2 177	1 597	6 668	1 397	215	1 189	274
1982..	173	2 899	2 524	7 944	1 559	262	1 017	512
1987 farms by inventory:								
1 to 24	6	79	54	57	15	7	37	7
25 to 49	–	10	10	34	5	1	21	–
50 to 99	1	5	4	21	3	–	–	3
100 or more .... farms..	–	1	3	20	5	–	1	–
number..	–	(D)	462	3 407	935	(D)	(D)	–
Other hogs and pigs .... farms, 1987..	14	114	96	148	36	12	80	11
1982..	24	191	152	190	47	24	91	21
number, 1987..	564	14 457	9 772	42 911	6 895	1 242	7 887	1 366
1982..	1 346	18 433	18 555	47 123	9 897	1 983	9 095	5 208
LITTERS								
Litters of pigs farrowed between—								
Dec. 1 of preceding year and Nov. 30 .... farms, 1987..	8	95	75	136	31	9	61	10
1982..	12	158	128	178	39	15	66	17
number, 1987..	169	3 359	2 362	9 983	2 404	300	1 532	325
1982..	250	4 468	3 619	11 941	2 654	390	1 530	972
Dec. 1 of preceding year and May 31 .... farms, 1987..	6	84	68	128	30	9	59	10
1982..	11	143	113	168	36	15	58	15
number, 1987..	80	1 636	1 158	5 251	1 272	157	792	191
1982..	161	2 343	1 738	6 098	1 293	223	790	516
June 1 and Nov. 30 .... farms, 1987..	8	88	68	120	22	7	52	8
1982..	9	130	109	159	38	11	53	14
number, 1987..	89	1 723	1 204	4 732	1 132	143	740	134
1982..	89	2 125	1 881	5 653	1 361	187	740	456
SALES								
Hogs and pigs sold .... farms, 1987..	17	137	111	164	48	14	101	15
1982..	25	220	179	230	54	28	101	26
number, 1987..	1 934	33 122	19 935	85 126	16 839	2 291	18 368	3 041
1982..	4 103	38 648	34 599	84 704	19 264	5 547	14 794	(D)
$1,000, 1987..	184	3 438	1 955	9 145	1 209	240	1 783	347
1982..	427	3 871	3 654	9 018	1 629	594	1 545	(D)
1987 farms by number sold:								
1 to 24 .... farms..	5	30	29	11	12	6	17	2
number..	41	383	239	158	136	79	203	(D)
25 to 49 .... farms..	3	20	19	13	5	–	11	4
number..	93	703	679	483	283	–	398	128
50 to 99 .... farms..	6	24	22	19	10	2	13	1
number..	382	1 741	1 475	1 242	721	(D)	1 011	(O)
100 to 199 .... farms..	1	26	18	26	3	4	30	3
number..	(D)	3 806	2 500	3 871	381	490	4 455	362
200 to 499 .... farms..	1	25	14	51	8	–	18	3
number..	(D)	7 271	3 560	15 581	(D)	–	4 955	1 150
500 to 999 .... farms..	–	6	3	21	2	1	12	2
number..	(D)	4 399	1 943	13 092	(D)	(D)	7 341	(O)
1,000 or more .... farms..	–	6	6	23	4	1	–	–
number..	–	14 819	9 539	50 721	12 113	(D)	–	–
Feeder pigs sold .... farms, 1987..	4	37	39	40	12	5	24	4
1982..	7	76	64	51	14	4	24	7
number, 1987..	(D)	5 098	5 763	5 892	10 165	386	4 626	(D)
1982..	546	9 605	6 430	11 953	10 136	(D)	2 432	(D)
$1,000, 1987..	(D)	224	269	272	465	13	184	(D)
1982..	19	453	273	549	496	(D)	102	(D)
Hogs and pigs other than feeder pigs sold .... farms, 1987..	17	125	95	157	44	14	91	14
1982..	24	206	161	206	52	26	92	26
number, 1987..	(D)	28 024	14 172	79 234	6 674	1 875	13 740	(D)
1982..	3 557	28 943	28 179	72 751	9 128	(D)	12 362	9 306
$1,000, 1987..	(D)	3 214	1 687	8 873	745	228	1 599	(D)
1982..	408	3 418	3 381	8 469	1 134	(D)	1 443	1 042

Table 12. **Hogs and Pigs—Inventory, Litters, and Sales: 1987 and 1982**—Con.

[For meaning of abbreviations and symbols, see introductory text]

Item	Labette	Lane	Leavenworth	Lincoln	Linn	Logan	Lyon	McPherson
INVENTORY								
Hogs and pigs ... farms, 1987	61	14	145	52	45	20	106	129
1982	112	24	168	61	87	25	181	186
number, 1987	14 152	1 922	17 890	6 635	15 530	1 883	11 099	22 117
1982	20 573	2 702	15 156	8 110	19 170	3 032	17 612	25 487
Farms by inventory:								
1 to 24 ... farms, 1987	27	5	64	15	12	4	36	33
1982	47	12	82	20	34	10	63	49
number, 1987	317	(D)	681	123	101	38	383	394
1982	475	111	778	207	295	74	679	427
25 to 49 ... farms, 1987	12	1	19	9	5	6	16	13
1982	21	3	16	10	4	3	34	19
number, 1987	440	(D)	669	306	174	222	556	472
1982	787	125	535	378	272	111	1 260	670
50 to 99 ... farms, 1987	6	1	27	4	6	3	24	19
1982	16	3	30	6	6	5	33	47
number, 1987	420	(D)	1 931	273	403	220	1 586	1 259
1982	1 260	170	1 903	382	403	337	2 372	3 200
100 to 199 ... farms, 1987	5	3	11	12	3	3	11	18
1982	10	2	13	8	15	2	25	31
number, 1987	675	410	1 550	1 681	380	370	1 332	2 434
1982	1 289	(D)	1 999	924	1 936	(D)	3 353	4 201
200 to 499 ... farms, 1987	6	4	17	10	3	3	15	38
1982	12	3	24	14	8	3	21	30
number, 1987	1 459	1 391	5 712	(D)	1 208	1 033	3 959	12 585
1982	3 839	1 126	6 727	4 263	2 215	1 160	5 778	9 784
500 to 999 ... farms, 1987	3	-	4	2	3	2	3	8
1982	4	1	2	3	14	2	4	8
number, 1987	(D)	-	3 008	(D)	7 944	(D)	(D)	4 973
1982	(D)	(D)	(D)	1 956	(D)	(D)	(D)	(D)
1,000 or more ... farms, 1987	2	-	3	-	4	-	1	-
1982	2	-	1	-	2	-	1	1
number, 1987	(D)	-	4 359	-	5 320	-	(D)	1
1982	(D)	-	(D)	-	(D)	-	(D)	(D)
Hogs and pigs used or to be used for breeding ... farms, 1987	38	7	98	30	30	14	76	77
1982	80	15	129	42	65	11	123	109
number, 1987	828	149	2 412	946	1 527	250	1 629	2 427
1982	1 513	624	2 133	1 046	2 117	411	2 424	2 703
1987 farms by inventory:								
1 to 24	29	4	70	14	15	11	60	39
25 to 49	3	2	17	12	4	2	8	16
50 to 99	4	1	7	1	5	1	8	20
100 or more ... farms	2	-	4	3	6	-	2	2
number	(D)	-	704	321	876	-	(D)	(U)
Other hogs and pigs ... farms, 1987	56	14	135	49	43	19	97	125
1982	100	21	149	55	71	25	165	172
number, 1987	13 324	1 773	15 478	5 689	14 003	1 633	9 470	19 690
1982	19 060	2 078	13 023	7 062	17 053	2 621	15 188	22 754
LITTERS								
Litters of pigs farrowed between—								
Dec. 1 of preceding year and Nov. 30 ... farms, 1987	39	8	105	31	31	14	79	82
1982	80	15	134	43	70	12	137	114
number, 1987	1 163	197	3 976	1 457	2 557	538	2 239	3 737
1982	1 980	1 011	3 221	1 488	3 233	775	3 585	4 162
Dec. 1 of preceding year and May 31 ... farms, 1987	36	7	96	29	31	12	76	71
1982	71	12	113	40	80	10	124	108
number, 1987	612	100	2 006	755	1 319	285	1 104	1 948
1982	1 006	508	1 565	766	1 669	573	1 851	2 121
June 1 and Nov. 30 ... farms, 1987	35	7	96	30	26	13	68	78
1982	72	14	118	38	57	9	116	102
number, 1987	551	97	1 970	702	1 238	253	1 135	1 789
1982	974	503	1 656	722	1 564	202	1 734	2 041
SALES								
Hogs and pigs sold ... farms, 1987	65	15	146	51	48	20	107	140
1982	116	23	173	72	89	22	188	195
number, 1987	26 029	2 180	32 772	14 066	26 842	4 601	18 004	40 812
1982	45 662	8 838	23 897	17 559	26 836	5 105	35 008	52 742
$1,000, 1987	3 309	215	3 297	1 331	2 914	480	1 882	4 139
1982	6 016	1 055	2 431	1 819	2 926	604	3 404	5 345
1987 farms by number sold:								
1 to 24 ... farms	20	5	42	12	11	3	22	24
number	148	57	446	(D)	123	27	162	296
25 to 49 ... farms	9	1	20	2	7	5	18	16
number	323	(D)	737	(D)	256	170	666	579
50 to 99 ... farms	14	1	26	8	6	6	20	19
number	1 023	(D)	1 886	531	280	328	1 416	1 370
100 to 199 ... farms	8	4	23	9	9	-	20	16
number	1 148	590	3 204	1 164	472	-	2 627	2 451
200 to 499 ... farms	4	3	21	10	3	3	20	35
number	1 120	902	6 327	2 921	978	770	5 855	11 337
500 to 999 ... farms	8	1	5	6	6	3	3	24
number	3 648	(D)	2 919	3 966	5 735	(D)	2 126	17 449
1,000 or more ... farms	4	-	9	4	11	1	4	6
number	20 819	-	17 253	5 301	18 998	(D)	5 152	7 330
Feeder pigs sold ... farms, 1987	23	3	40	18	18	9	22	37
1982	37	6	53	20	33	4	52	41
number, 1987	3 257	432	4 745	4 160	(D)	(D)	2 632	7 294
1982	5 121	(D)	4 862	3 924	4 173	(D)	8 731	11 936
$1,000, 1987	134	(D)	207	195	(D)	(D)	119	318
1982	251	(D)	236	196	197	(D)	315	609
Hogs and pigs other than feeder pigs sold ... farms, 1987	59	14	132	40	40	19	100	132
1982	99	22	160	63	82	22	179	189
number, 1987	24 772	1 748	28 027	9 926	(D)	(D)	15 372	33 518
1982	40 541	(D)	19 035	13 635	22 663	(D)	26 277	40 806
$1,000, 1987	3 175	(D)	3 091	1 136	(D)	(D)	1 763	3 815
1982	5 765	(D)	2 195	1 623	2 729	(D)	3 069	4 735

[For meaning of abbreviations and symbols, see introductory text]

Item	Marion	Marshall	Meade	Miami	Mitchell	Montgomery	Morris	Morton
INVENTORY								
Hogs and pigs _____ farms, 1987__	158	267	13	62	84	60	81	7
1982__	210	278	30	103	106	104	119	7
number, 1987__	30 622	44 970	2 728	11 243	23 109	20 969	10 777	80
1982__	29 771	52 319	(D)	12 698	28 393	24 323	17 911	610
Farms by inventory:								
1 to 24 _____ farms, 1987__	29	42	5	25	17	16	20	7
1982__	58	36	7	34	22	49	35	1
number, 1987__	359	537	38	199	144	137	181	80
1982__	700	488	73	337	248	402	367	(D)
25 to 49 _____ farms, 1987__	13	31	-	2	7	9	15	-
1982__	34	27	6	22	9	7	14	2
number, 1987__	470	1 129	-	(D)	(D)	275	518	-
1982__	1 196	889	237	774	312	264	551	(D)
50 to 99 _____ farms, 1987__	28	49	2	12	11	7	18	-
1982__	35	57	5	13	19	12	22	2
number, 1987__	1 899	3 605	(D)	(D)	759	471	1 298	-
1982__	2 537	3 806	384	905	1 230	846	1 563	(D)
100 to 199 _____ farms, 1987__	34	63	1	7	19	10	13	-
1982__	36	74	4	17	18	9	21	1
number, 1987__	4 446	8 451	(D)	838	(D)	1 299	1 927	-
1982__	5 409	9 911	750	2 051	2 364	1 298	2 707	(D)
200 to 499 _____ farms, 1987__	36	69	1	12	20	8	11	-
1982__	28	56	6	12	23	13	18	1
number, 1987__	10 207	20 670	(D)	4 063	6 138	(D)	3 554	-
1982__	9 361	16 623	1 858	3 866	7 330	3 640	5 153	(D)
500 to 999 _____ farms, 1987__	15	8	1	2	4	2	3	-
1982__	17	20	1	3	9	7	7	-
number, 1987__	10 226	4 778	2 225	(D)	2 625	(D)	(D)	-
1982__	10 568	12 129	(D)	(D)	6 183	4 337	(D)	-
1,000 or more _____ farms, 1987__	3	5	-	2	6	8	1	-
1982__	28	6	1	2	6	7	2	-
number, 1987__	3 015	5 800	-	(D)	10 636	14 679	(D)	-
1982__	-	8 473	(D)	(D)	10 726	13 546	(D)	-
Hogs and pigs used or to be used for breeding _____ farms, 1987__	109	195	10	44	69	45	55	2
1982__	155	202	19	71	73	76	92	4
number, 1987__	4 446	5 949	400	1 321	2 649	2 369	2 519	(D)
1982__	3 926	5 805	(D)	1 562	2 684	2 339	2 453	99
1987 farms by inventory:								
1 to 24 _____ farms__	54	100	4	27	37	30	33	2
25 to 49 _____ farms__	19	56	2	8	13	5	7	-
50 to 99 _____ farms__	20	35	3	5	15	4	11	-
100 or more _____ farms__	16	4	1	4	4	6	4	-
number__	1 802	490	(D)	594	660	1 643	1 283	-
Other hogs and pigs _____ farms, 1987__	149	251	13	55	77	56	76	7
1982__	186	261	29	97	99	85	109	7
number, 1987__	26 174	39 021	2 328	9 922	20 460	18 600	8 258	(D)
1982__	25 845	46 514	(D)	11 136	25 709	21 984	15 458	511
LITTERS								
Litters of pigs farrowed between—								
Dec. 1 of preceding year and Nov. 30 _____ farms, 1987__	113	206	10	45	73	48	61	2
1982__	162	209	19	81	81	85	96	4
number, 1987__	6 618	8 978	576	1 983	3 778	4 175	2 495	(D)
1982__	6 583	9 252	(D)	2 427	4 719	3 956	3 306	142
Dec. 1 of preceding year and May 31 _____ farms, 1987__	105	182	10	41	71	48	57	2
1982__	145	193	18	73	74	78	86	4
number, 1987__	3 339	4 449	289	1 010	1 839	2 082	1 326	(D)
1982__	3 325	4 777	(D)	1 222	2 350	2 017	1 668	(D)
June 1 and Nov. 30 _____ farms, 1987__	107	193	10	40	66	45	51	2
1982__	160	196	18	68	69	75	83	4
number, 1987__	3 279	4 529	287	973	1 939	2 093	1 169	(D)
1982__	3 258	4 475	(D)	1 205	2 369	1 939	1 638	(D)
SALES								
Hogs and pigs sold _____ farms, 1987__	173	279	14	57	88	62	81	5
1982__	222	291	31	111	113	119	128	9
number, 1987__	57 777	85 900	5 972	16 471	42 278	43 551	21 411	(D)
1982__	53 217	98 761	(D)	20 221	47 892	51 611	30 230	1 109
$1,000, 1987__	5 544	8 392	647	1 730	4 073	4 662	2 063	(D)
1982__	5 426	9 641	(D)	2 158	4 843	5 536	3 145	112
1987 farms by number sold:								
1 to 24 _____ farms__	21	18	2	12	7	8	7	4
number__	264	250	(D)	117	85	55	91	34
25 to 49 _____ farms__	23	23	-	5	8	7	15	-
number__	868	843	-	141	296	275	558	-
50 to 99 _____ farms__	19	49	2	12	13	14	19	-
number__	1 430	3 390	(D)	896	974	956	1 325	-
100 to 199 _____ farms__	39	56	-	9	16	6	8	1
number__	5 392	8 116	-	1 171	2 146	721	1 017	(D)
200 to 499 _____ farms__	30	71	6	10	23	10	20	-
number__	8 971	22 085	1 769	3 561	7 388	2 896	6 804	-
500 to 999 _____ farms__	23	47	1	5	10	8	9	-
number__	15 635	30 986	(D)	3 855	7 054	5 240	6 620	-
1,000 or more _____ farms__	18	15	3	4	11	9	3	-
number__	25 217	20 228	3 100	6 730	24 335	33 408	4 996	-
Feeder pigs sold _____ farms, 1987__	48	93	5	8	32	19	23	3
1982__	72	90	6	25	31	43	35	3
number, 1987__	16 565	18 841	361	1 680	10 774	2 568	6 127	-
1982__	11 261	19 803	921	2 516	10 284	5 573	4 843	(D)
$1,000, 1987__	797	849	14	79	508	110	261	-
1982__	509	817	37	106	511	215	216	(D)
Hogs and pigs other than feeder pigs sold _____ farms, 1987__	158	259	14	54	81	61	75	5
1982__	201	267	31	105	106	102	113	8
number, 1987__	41 112	67 059	5 611	14 791	31 504	40 983	15 284	(D)
1982__	41 956	78 958	(D)	17 705	37 608	46 038	25 287	(D)
$1,000, 1987__	4 747	7 544	633	1 651	3 565	4 552	1 802	(D)
1982__	4 916	8 824	(D)	2 051	4 332	5 321	2 929	(D)

Table 12. Hogs and Pigs—Inventory, Litters, and Sales: 1987 and 1982—Con.

[For meaning of abbreviations and symbols, see introductory text]

Item	Nemaha	Neosho	Ness	Norton	Osage	Osborne	Ottawa	Pawnee
INVENTORY								
Hogs and pigs _____ farms, 1987__	308	51	18	60	82	53	34	36
1982__	353	91	24	60	135	70	47	54
number, 1987__	86 022	23 529	1 870	16 293	6 067	7 984	3 809	10 136
1982__	76 480	27 291	1 187	11 917	14 354	8 343	7 813	12 022
Farms by inventory:								
1 to 24 _____ farms, 1987__	27	14	7	12	32	4	18	6
1982__	45	24	13	13	44	16	22	13
number, 1987__	384	111	73	93	327	30	163	58
1982__	491	293	96	136	471	185	201	192
25 to 49 _____ farms, 1987__	27	5	1	7	12	11	5	2
1982__	31	15	3	5	23	8	3	6
number, 1987__	918	173	(D)	228	368	403	212	(D)
1982__	1 112	486	105	166	895	308	99	276
50 to 99 _____ farms, 1987__	53	11	6	11	11	11	3	5
1982__	59	15	3	4	24	16	5	13
number, 1987__	3 585	744	(D)	798	778	858	196	(D)
1982__	4 151	1 119	170	240	1 633	1 121	282	862
100 to 199 _____ farms, 1987__	73	8	2	12	17	13	1	9
1982__	96	18	3	11	27	15	7	5
number, 1987__	9 414	735	(D)	1 551	2 268	1 768	(D)	1 211
1982__	13 032	2 027	(D)	(D)	3 563	2 134	1 139	(D)
200 to 499 _____ farms, 1987__	92	8	2	12	7	12	5	9
1982__	83	10	2	12	14	10	5	8
number, 1987__	28 216	2 691	(D)	3 425	2 132	(D)	1 226	2 660
1982__	25 420	3 459	(D)	3 875	4 319	2 952	1 316	2 230
500 to 999 _____ farms, 1987__	22	5	-	4	3	2	3	5
1982__	28	7	-	2	2	3	2	3
number, 1987__	15 626	(D)	-	(D)	2 174	(D)	(D)	(D)
1982__	17 991	5 572	-	(D)	(D)	1 643	(D)	(D)
1,000 or more _____ farms, 1987__	14	2	-	2	1	-	1	2
1982__	9	4	-	3	1	-	2	2
number, 1987__	27 877	(D)	-	(D)	(D)	-	(D)	(D)
1982__	14 283	14 335	-	4 710	(D)	-	(D)	6 800
Hogs and pigs used or to be used for breeding _____ farms, 1987__	224	31	11	33	53	41	23	25
1982__	235	72	14	43	109	44	37	37
number, 1987__	9 917	2 743	215	2 494	1 406	1 545	543	1 263
1982__	8 171	3 611	175	2 260	2 106	976	867	1 711
1987 farms by inventory:								
1 to 24 _____	90	17	9	19	40	23	17	11
25 to 49 _____	74	4	2	7	5	10	2	6
50 to 99 _____	41	6	2	2	4	7	3	5
100 or more _____ farms	19	4	-	5	4	1	1	3
number	3 514	2 075	-	1 879	622	(D)	(D)	567
Other hogs and pigs _____ farms, 1987__	293	46	18	57	69	49	26	34
1982__	336	88	22	44	120	65	46	50
number, 1987__	76 105	20 786	1 652	13 799	6 661	6 439	3 266	8 873
1982__	68 309	23 780	1 012	9 657	12 246	7 367	6 946	10 311
LITTERS								
Litters of pigs farrowed between—								
Dec. 1 of preceding year and Nov. 30 _____ farms, 1987__	236	32	11	35	54	45	24	25
1982__	236	78	14	43	112	50	26	37
number, 1987__	17 388	3 800	237	3 804	1 649	1 566	808	2 183
1982__	12 498	5 236	263	2 969	2 530	1 542	1 247	2 621
Dec. 1 of preceding year and May 31 _____ farms, 1987__	225	31	9	33	50	42	19	24
1982__	221	70	10	38	100	43	21	36
number, 1987__	8 767	1 903	112	1 814	808	718	400	1 090
1982__	6 433	2 636	147	1 521	1 185	772	598	1 321
June 1 and Nov. 30 _____ farms, 1987__	227	24	11	33	48	41	22	22
1982__	221	70	11	11	99	42	25	34
number, 1987__	8 619	1 897	125	1 990	841	846	406	1 093
1982__	6 465	2 602	116	1 448	1 345	770	649	1 300
SALES								
Hogs and pigs sold _____ farms, 1987__	327	57	17	60	85	61	35	42
1982__	363	103	25	56	136	76	51	55
number, 1987__	151 416	33 580	2 322	34 919	16 834	13 912	6 862	17 760
1982__	121 997	45 994	2 383	22 696	23 343	15 566	18 158	20 449
$1,000, 1987__	15 731	3 959	193	2 869	1 620	1 284	872	1 738
1982__	13 278	4 774	275	2 263	2 436	1 421	1 751	2 170
1987 farms by number sold:								
1 to 24 _____ farms	22	11	4	8	24	2	10	3
number	309	88	(D)	64	317	(D)	122	44
25 to 49 _____ farms	25	11	1	10	13	7	1	1
number	644	403	(D)	321	444	264	395	135
50 to 99 _____ farms	38	11	5	3	11	19	3	7
number	2 614	732	380	260	811	1 360	193	428
100 to 199 _____ farms	51	12	-	12	17	11	4	6
number	7 328	594	-	1 584	2 399	1 560	572	901
200 to 499 _____ farms	103	7	7	13	10	14	4	10
number	32 828	1 911	1 680	3 420	3 265	4 745	1 204	3 400
500 to 999 _____ farms	55	8	-	8	8	6	-	7
number	37 359	6 169	-	5 513	3 639	(D)	(D)	4 373
1,000 or more _____ farms	53	8	-	4	2	2	-	8
number	70 124	23 683	-	23 767	5 969	(D)	(D)	8 479
Feeder pigs sold _____ farms, 1987__	87	9	5	13	22	21	18	6
1982__	76	33	8	8	43	28	13	18
number, 1987__	29 100	1 734	680	17 930	4 522	4 312	746	3 405
1982__	15 694	6 351	372	(D)	5 578	4 567	2 607	3 096
$1,000, 1987__	1 339	80	39	662	202	204	33	140
1982__	713	307	15	(D)	222	202	119	140
Hogs and pigs other than feeder pigs sold _____ farms, 1987__	303	53	14	56	77	56	25	41
1982__	337	88	25	55	126	66	47	45
number, 1987__	122 316	31 846	1 342	16 989	12 312	9 600	6 116	14 355
1982__	105 703	39 643	2 011	(D)	17 765	11 009	15 551	17 363
$1,000, 1987__	14 392	3 879	154	2 007	1 418	1 080	639	1 599
1982__	12 565	4 467	260	(D)	2 214	1 220	1 632	2 030

Table 12. Hogs and Pigs—Inventory, Litters, and Sales: 1987 and 1982—Con.

For meaning of abbreviations and symbols, see introductory text]

Item	Phillips	Pottawatomie	Pratt	Rawlins	Reno	Republic	Rice	Riley
INVENTORY								
Hogs and pigs ... farms, 1987..	101	186	29	68	140	110	30	99
1982..	116	241	26	80	205	165	60	145
number, 1987..	41 030	36 063	18 001	11 548	21 871	19 475	17 285	29 764
1982..	34 967	43 901	19 210	10 517	23 053	32 827	20 629	23 531
Farms by inventory:								
1 to 24 ... farms, 1987..	17	37	12	17	61	24	6	14
1982..	24	40	8	25	87	27	18	31
number, 1987..	161	416	122	218	569	271	74	135
1982..	232	326	41	262	807	319	183	385
25 to 49 ... farms, 1987..	11	22	5	6	24	12	-	9
1982..	8	29	-	12	34	23	7	19
number, 1987..	415	639	(D)	184	831	464	-	311
1982..	251	985	-	470	1 111	841	247	664
50 to 99 ... farms, 1987..	16	30	2	11	23	23	10	19
1982..	21	52	4	13	34	32	5	25
number, 1987..	1 326	2 083	(D)	698	1 577	1 499	693	1 274
1982..	1 352	3 735	294	982	2 309	2 399	427	1 849
100 to 199 ... farms, 1987..	20	41	6	14	11	23	3	10
1982..	32	55	4	16	31	36	11	32
number, 1987..	2 745	5 490	733	1 992	1 383	3 536	369	1 417
1982..	4 160	8 102	(D)	2 106	3 946	4 865	1 410	4 568
200 to 499 ... farms, 1987..	17	36	4	16	12	21	5	33
1982..	15	50	8	9	10	33	7	26
number, 1987..	5 234	10 345	(D)	5 391	(D)	6 592	(D)	9 114
1982..	3 891	14 554	2 714	2 243	2 704	8 833	1 975	7 190
500 to 999 ... farms, 1987..	6	12	-	3	2	4	1	5
1982..	5	8	-	5	3	11	6	9
number, 1987..	4 062	7 897	-	(D)	(D)	2 873	(D)	3 399
1982..	3 446	4 862	-	(D)	2 020	7 410	3 530	5 457
1,000 or more ... farms, 1987..	12	6	1	1	7	3	5	5
1982..	11	7	2	1	6	4	6	3
number, 1987..	27 087	8 993	(D)	(D)	12 665	4 240	14 110	14 114
1982..	21 635	11 237	(D)	(D)	10 156	8 160	12 857	3 378
Hogs and pigs used or to be used for breeding ... farms, 1987..	67	147	20	58	83	65	26	77
1982..	84	193	16	55	127	113	36	107
number, 1987..	5 086	4 700	1 752	2 036	3 126	2 242	2 104	3 026
1982..	3 975	6 460	1 625	2 078	3 167	3 526	2 468	3 274
1987 farms by inventory:								
1 to 24 ...	29	88	13	30	63	32	14	42
25 to 49 ...	15	36	1	16	7	22	4	21
50 to 99 ...	9	13	5	8	8	7	1	7
100 or more ... farms..	14	10	1	4	5	4	-	7
number..	3 676	1 733	(D)	582	1 694	649	1 717	1 312
Other hogs and pigs ... farms, 1987..	94	173	26	57	125	104	27	96
1982..	108	226	25	71	183	156	54	136
number, 1987..	35 944	31 363	16 249	9 512	18 745	17 233	15 181	26 738
1982..	30 992	37 341	17 585	8 439	19 886	29 301	18 160	20 257
LITTERS								
Litters of pigs farrowed between—								
Dec. 1 of preceding year and Nov. 30 ... farms, 1987..	75	154	20	58	87	73	26	80
1982..	87	203	19	56	135	115	41	115
number, 1987..	7 560	7 575	3 085	3 146	4 709	3 094	3 430	5 256
1982..	6 544	9 767	3 048	2 833	5 530	5 824	4 369	4 940
Dec. 1 of preceding year and May 31 ... farms, 1987..	70	144	18	54	79	70	26	75
1982..	83	192	17	48	130	107	37	109
number, 1987..	4 112	3 808	1 541	1 510	2 315	1 574	1 663	2 844
1982..	3 297	5 049	1 518	1 424	2 820	2 965	2 094	2 512
June 1 and Nov. 30 ... farms, 1987..	65	140	17	55	81	66	26	76
1982..	74	183	18	51	116	106	36	98
number, 1987..	3 448	3 767	1 544	1 636	2 394	1 520	1 767	2 412
1982..	3 247	4 716	1 530	1 409	2 710	2 859	2 275	2 428
SALES								
Hogs and pigs sold ... farms, 1987..	111	196	31	69	150	123	38	113
1982..	126	256	31	79	215	179	62	162
number, 1987..	67 272	64 890	25 403	25 292	41 754	33 206	26 149	50 123
1982..	56 387	65 548	27 789	25 470	44 793	50 613	34 980	41 230
$1,000, 1987..	7 926	6 845	2 880	2 055	4 167	3 490	3 030	5 231
1982..	6 029	6 867	3 161	1 779	4 401	5 216	3 675	4 594
1987 farms by number sold:								
1 to 24 ... farms..	18	21	12	5	45	22	6	15
number..	213	265	113	51	460	252	36	191
25 to 49 ... farms..	11	17	2	10	17	10	2	9
number..	390	586	(D)	357	608	312	(D)	292
50 to 99 ... farms..	14	27	4	7	36	15	4	12
number..	933	1 812	351	460	2 552	(D)	230	919
100 to 199 ... farms..	12	49	5	9	17	21	12	18
number..	1 580	6 891	796	1 170	2 392	(D)	1 793	2 291
200 to 499 ... farms..	28	40	4	21	17	36	6	32
number..	8 268	10 890	(D)	6 082	4 716	11 384	(D)	9 741
500 to 999 ... farms..	10	25	1	7	9	7	2	15
number..	6 106	16 414	(D)	5 612	4 307	8 501	(D)	9 361
1,000 or more ... farms..	18	17	3	8	9	6	6	12
number..	49 773	28 132	22 000	11 560	26 719	8 702	20 959	27 328
Feeder pigs sold ... farms, 1987..	13	40	5	36	42	16	11	28
1982..	25	56	6	35	66	38	25	42
number, 1987..	4 532	9 428	200	12 039	7 118	5 172	1 765	8 250
1982..	4 945	12 081	549	16 056	9 555	6 335	7 474	6 795
$1,000, 1987..	223	432	8	497	273	239	76	386
1982..	218	576	24	666	396	308	337	320
Hogs and pigs other than feeder pigs sold ... farms, 1987..	106	180	28	56	141	118	36	104
1982..	124	251	31	56	204	169	56	153
number, 1987..	62 740	55 462	25 203	13 253	34 636	28 034	24 384	41 873
1982..	51 442	53 467	27 240	9 412	35 238	44 278	27 506	34 435
$1,000, 1987..	7 703	6 413	2 873	1 558	3 894	3 252	2 954	4 845
1982..	5 811	6 291	3 138	1 113	4 006	4 908	3 339	4 274

[For meaning of abbreviations and symbols, see introductory text]

Item	Rooks	Rush	Russell	Saline	Scott	Sedgwick	Seward	Shawnee
INVENTORY								
Hogs and pigs --- farms, 1987..	37	10	38	36	25	101	17	52
1982..	38	21	36	46	34	147	18	93
number, 1987..	2 903	581	4 125	21 121	29 994	15 370	(D)	4 620
1982..	5 831	1 586	3 331	25 136	25 717	17 760	10 412	9 125
Farms by inventory:								
1 to 24 --- farms, 1987..	16	5	13	10	4	32	6	26
1982..	12	11	14	19	9	70	8	46
number, 1987..	175	54	132	120	33	294	80	248
1982..	119	100	(D)	197	72	728	(D)	421
25 to 49 --- farms, 1987..	9	1	3	4	1	14	3	2
1982..	4	2	2	6	3	19	–	9
number, 1987..	343	(D)	95	138	(D)	495	105	(D)
1982..	144	(D)	(D)	180	(D)	648	–	324
50 to 99 --- farms, 1987..	5	2	10	8	4	16	–	11
1982..	8	2	11	10	1	20	–	17
number, 1987..	352	(D)	618	491	289	1 143	–	(D)
1982..	511	(D)	777	620	(D)	1 321	–	1 081
100 to 199 --- farms, 1987..	2	2	3	6	1	14	2	6
1982..	3	4	5	4	3	16	1	4
number, 1987..	(D)	(D)	450	795	(D)	1 810	(D)	769
1982..	410	(D)	(D)	507	390	2 020	(D)	566
200 to 499 --- farms, 1987..	3	–	8	5	7	20	2	5
1982..	5	2	3	6	7	15	–	12
number, 1987..	713	–	(D)	1 477	2 621	5 416	(D)	(D)
1982..	1 776	(D)	1 075	1 424	2 190	4 393	–	3 403
500 to 999 --- farms, 1987..	2	–	1	1	3	4	1	2
1982..	3	–	1	–	4	5	5	4
number, 1987..	(D)	–	(D)	(D)	2 330	(D)	(D)	(D)
1982..	(D)	–	(D)	–	2 675	3 000	3 708	(D)
1,000 or more --- farms, 1987..	–	–	–	2	5	1	3	–
1982..	1	–	–	3	7	3	4	1
number, 1987..	–	–	–	(D)	24 558	(D)	(D)	–
1982..	(D)	–	–	22 208	20 233	5 650	6 480	(D)
Hogs and pigs used or to be used for breeding --- farms, 1987..	20	4	29	23	15	57	12	29
1982..	23	11	21	26	24	91	13	60
number, 1987..	306	(D)	725	2 048	2 947	1 295	(D)	574
1982..	793	146	615	2 368	2 981	1 149	1 375	1 259
1987 farms by inventory:								
1 to 24 ---	17	3	18	12	3	39	5	24
25 to 49 ---	2	–	9	7	–	11	1	3
50 to 99 ---	1	1	–	3	5	5	3	1
100 or more --- farms..	–	–	2	1	7	2	3	1
number..	–	–	(D)	(D)	2 523	(D)	(D)	(D)
Other hogs and pigs --- farms, 1987..	31	10	35	35	23	97	16	48
1982..	31	19	31	46	31	129	18	63
number, 1987..	2 595	(D)	3 400	19 073	27 047	14 075	(D)	4 046
1982..	5 038	1 440	2 716	22 768	22 736	16 611	9 037	7 866
LITTERS								
Litters of pigs farrowed between—								
Dec. 1 of preceding year and Nov. 30 --- farms, 1987..	21	4	29	24	15	61	13	30
1982..	26	11	22	30	25	99	13	66
number, 1987..	470	(D)	1 343	4 483	5 074	2 003	(D)	968
1982..	1 284	221	874	4 481	5 642	1 866	1 550	1 880
Dec. 1 of preceding year and May 31 --- farms, 1987..	21	4	25	23	14	57	13	30
1982..	23	11	20	28	21	92	13	59
number, 1987..	244	(D)	682	2 213	2 546	1 037	(D)	521
1982..	669	113	452	2 301	2 921	894	837	956
June 1 and Nov. 30 --- farms, 1987..	20	4	23	22	15	54	12	25
1982..	22	9	18	27	23	76	12	56
number, 1987..	226	(D)	681	2 270	2 528	966	(D)	447
1982..	615	108	422	2 180	2 721	771	713	924
SALES								
Hogs and pigs sold --- farms, 1987..	37	10	37	39	24	107	17	54
1982..	41	20	39	56	31	162	21	102
number, 1987..	5 295	1 267	9 305	43 610	45 761	30 510	(D)	15 245
1982..	12 149	2 335	9 164	41 720	42 994	39 772	19 528	18 124
$1,000, 1987..	397	106	687	3 977	5 501	2 993	(D)	1 381
1982..	1 293	171	919	4 821	4 863	4 174	2 012	1 716
1987 farms by number sold:								
1 to 24 ---	6	1	7	8	1	22	3	15
number..	55	(D)	78	89	(D)	213	21	172
25 to 49 ---	9	3	3	11	2	14	3	11
number..	334	105	91	373	(D)	502	101	345
50 to 99 ---	7	2	8	3	4	21	4	4
number..	467	(D)	461	(D)	359	1 476	286	239
100 to 199 ---	9	(D)	3	3	1	15	–	10
number..	1 230	(D)	407	(D)	(D)	2 025	(D)	1 349
200 to 499 ---	3	2	9	9	5	21	2	5
number..	904	(D)	2 620	2 632	1 870	5 738	(D)	1 216
500 to 999 ---	2	–	6	3	5	10	3	3
number..	(D)	–	(D)	2 075	3 900	7 159	(D)	3 770
1,000 or more ---	1	–	1	3	6	4	3	8
number..	(D)	–	(D)	37 961	39 407	13 397	(D)	8 154
Feeder pigs sold --- farms, 1987..	9	2	15	11	4	36	4	16
1982..	9	5	7	14	9	51	9	31
number, 1987..	2 435	(D)	4 893	5 346	(D)	4 892	(D)	3 835
1982..	1 312	1 406	1 171	1 303	4 100	4 137	2 088	5 249
$1,000, 1987..	83	(D)	174	268	(D)	206	(D)	187
1982..	65	57	49	54	204	153	76	252
Hogs and pigs other than feeder pigs sold --- farms, 1987..	38	10	32	36	23	101	16	52
1982..	38	18	38	38	25	145	20	94
number, 1987..	2 850	(D)	4 412	38 264	(D)	25 618	(D)	11 410
1982..	10 837	929	8 013	40 417	38 894	35 635	17 440	12 875
$1,000, 1987..	314	(D)	513	3 710	(D)	2 788	(D)	1 194
1982..	1 228	114	870	4 767	4 659	4 021	1 934	1 464

Table 12. Hogs and Pigs—Inventory, Litters, and Sales: 1987 and 1982—Con.

[For meaning of abbreviations and symbols, see introductory text]

Item	Sheridan	Sharman	Smith	Stafford	Stanton	Stevens	Sumner	Thomas
INVENTORY								
Hogs and pigs ... farms, 1987..	59	24	103	28	12	9	97	24
1982..	91	49	155	28	14	10	119	36
number, 1987..	7 319	1 960	28 020	4 160	185	3 663	20 817	5 896
1982..	10 949	6 607	29 635	3 395	(D)	3 539	22 189	8 694
Farms by inventory:								
1 to 24 ... farms, 1987..	22	12	21	5	10	3	32	10
1982..	28	21	23	10	9	1	36	11
number, 1987..	273	168	277	48	(D)	30	302	94
1982..	298	219	263	58	122	(D)	284	105
25 to 49 ... farms, 1987..	5	4	14	2	2	-	12	8
1982..	14	3	27	4	2	3	24	9
number, 1987..	180	131	514	(D)	(D)	-	429	(D)
1982..	462	112	906	(D)	(D)	(D)	794	321
50 to 99 ... farms, 1987..	8	4	19	8	1	3	13	2
1982..	8	8	32	1	1	-	11	5
number, 1987..	457	(D)	1 272	(D)	-	175	870	(D)
1982..	594	505	2 048	(D)	(D)	-	849	296
100 to 199 ... farms, 1987..	15	1	36	4	-	2	16	1
1982..	24	6	36	4	2	2	14	2
number, 1987..	2 161	(D)	659	538	-	(D)	2 301	(D)
1982..	2 970	759	5 232	680	(D)	(D)	2 013	(D)
200 to 499 ... farms, 1987..	5	3	29	8	-	1	14	1
1982..	12	7	23	9	-	-	23	1
number, 1987..	1 681	1 295	9 158	(D)	-	(D)	4 060	(D)
1982..	2 927	2 274	7 655	2 435	-	-	6 300	(D)
500 to 999 ... farms, 1987..	4	-	11	1	-	-	5	-
1982..	4	3	7	-	-	3	5	8
number, 1987..	2 567	(D)	7 475	(D)	-	1 640	3 425	-
1982..	(D)	(D)	4 057	-	-	-	3 445	(D)
1,000 or more ... farms, 1987..	-	-	4	-	-	-	5	2
1982..	1	1	7	-	-	2	1	2
number, 1987..	-	-	8 665	-	-	(D)	9 430	(D)
1982..	(D)	(D)	9 474	-	-	(D)	8 495	(D)
Hogs and pigs used or to be used for breeding ... farms, 1987..	34	17	78	17	7	8	66	10
1982..	47	26	125	15	6	8	83	20
number, 1987..	954	650	3 782	508	54	475	2 595	(D)
1982..	1 470	750	4 153	407	(D)	282	2 301	924
1987 farms by inventory:								
1 to 24 ...	22	15	34	6	7	5	40	8
25 to 49 ...	5	1	22	6	-	5	12	-
50 to 99 ...	6	-	11	1	-	-	7	1
100 or more ... farms..	1	1	11	2	-	2	7	1
number..	(D)	(D)	1 855	(D)	-	(D)	1 444	(D)
Other hogs and pigs ... farms, 1987..	59	23	100	26	9	8	90	21
1982..	86	47	142	28	14	10	103	33
number, 1987..	6 365	1 310	24 238	3 552	131	3 188	18 222	(D)
1982..	9 479	5 857	25 482	2 988	(D)	3 257	19 888	7 770
LITTERS								
Litters of pigs farrowed between—								
Dec. 1 of preceding year and Nov. 30 ... farms, 1987..	37	18	80	17	7	8	72	10
1982..	47	30	130	15	8	8	85	22
number, 1987..	1 278	1 185	6 894	874	44	811	4 744	(D)
1982..	1 931	1 023	6 266	546	112	481	4 096	1 352
Dec. 1 of preceding year and May 31 ... farms, 1987..	26	17	76	17	6	8	66	8
1982..	43	28	116	14	7	8	80	21
number, 1987..	655	820	3 025	427	32	365	2 414	(D)
1982..	973	526	3 255	288	68	254	2 062	849
June 1 and Nov. 30 ... farms, 1987..	35	16	77	14	5	8	66	10
1982..	41	29	107	13	8	8	78	15
number, 1987..	623	565	3 869	447	12	446	2 330	(D)
1982..	958	497	3 011	272	44	227	2 034	503
SALES								
Hogs and pigs sold ... farms, 1987..	56	27	113	33	11	9	102	26
1982..	91	55	162	27	14	13	119	43
number, 1987..	12 218	12 480	64 014	8 369	291	5 352	46 307	12 581
1982..	20 113	18 466	(D)	5 626	1 023	4 957	37 445	17 419
$1,000, 1987..	1 136	741	6 545	(D)	26	592	4 410	1 229
1982..	2 134	1 349	(D)	890	89	502	3 639	2 120
1987 farms by number sold:								
1 to 24 ... farms..	14	8	15	8	6	-	26	7
number..	182	96	178	72	34	-	288	67
25 to 49 ... farms..	5	5	9	2	2	1	13	5
number..	168	192	333	(D)	(D)	3	446	169
50 to 99 ... farms..	9	7	14	4	3	3	11	2
number..	574	518	1 098	293	(D)	220	766	525
100 to 199 ... farms..	12	1	22	7	-	1	15	2
number..	1 468	357	3 336	1 042	-	(D)	1 869	(D)
200 to 499 ... farms..	9	1	21	6	-	(D)	18	2
number..	2 531	(D)	7 073	1 996	-	(D)	6 266	(D)
500 to 999 ... farms..	5	(D)	13	5	-	-	10	-
number..	(D)	(D)	6 756	(D)	-	-	6 742	-
1,000 or more ... farms..	2	2	19	1	-	2	9	2
number..	(D)	(D)	43 240	(D)	-	(D)	31 930	(D)
Feeder pigs sold ... farms, 1987..	15	7	32	7	2	4	26	5
1982..	22	9	54	(D)	5	5	34	8
number, 1987..	4 025	(D)	10 008	2 890	(D)	361	13 631	(D)
1982..	2 424	(D)	(D)	781	320	(D)	7 468	1 374
$1,000, 1987..	184	(D)	435	129	(D)	14	412	(D)
1982..	109	(D)	(D)	34	13	(D)	261	64
Hogs and pigs other than feeder pigs sold ... farms, 1987..	48	25	105	50	10	6	97	22
1982..	82	54	(D)	26	12	10	109	41
number, 1987..	8 193	(D)	54 006	5 479	(D)	4 991	34 676	(D)
1982..	17 689	(D)	42 655	4 845	703	(D)	29 977	16 045
$1,000, 1987..	952	(D)	6 110	649	(D)	578	3 998	(D)
1982..	2 025	(D)	5 014	656	76	(D)	3 358	2 056

[For meaning of abbreviations and symbols, see introductory text]

Item	Trego	Wabaunsee	Wallace	Washington	Wichita	Wilson	Woodson	Wyandotte
INVENTORY								
Hogs and pigs ... farms, 1987..	37	70	28	246	16	44	27	13
1982..	52	117	32	279	40	83	61	20
number, 1987..	2 771	19 702	2 528	92 927	1 600	12 236	2 585	1 052
1982..	5 413	17 369	2 100	78 488	4 893	17 742	5 703	876
Farms by inventory:								
1 to 24 ... farms, 1987..	15	15	15	30	8	13	12	6
1982..	15	41	18	43	11	24	22	16
number, 1987..	153	128	189	469	83	90	131	61
1982..	147	392	111	527	(D)	198	181	115
25 to 49 ... farms, 1987..	5	16	2	24	-	-	3	4
1982..	4	11	3	21	2	10	6	1
number, 1987..	152	563	(D)	876	-	-	96	145
1982..	127	382	96	761	(D)	339	223	(D)
50 to 99 ... farms, 1987..	8	9	1	38	2	6	4	-
1982..	18	27	5	51	7	9	15	1
number, 1987..	416	668	(D)	2 682	(D)	490	273	-
1982..	1 122	1 898	383	3 634	515	673	1 077	(D)
100 to 199 ... farms, 1987..	8	13	3	43	4	7	5	2
1982..	9	20	4	56	13	7	9	1
number, 1987..	1 262	1 874	300	6 060	523	1 097	752	(D)
1982..	(D)	2 649	(D)	7 630	(D)	975	(D)	(D)
200 to 499 ... farms, 1987..	3	8	7	70	1	9	1	-
1982..	6	10	1	70	6	21	8	-
number, 1987..	788	2 613	1 896	21 013	(D)	2 745	(D)	-
1982..	1 765	3 023	(D)	21 532	1 696	6 033	2 597	-
500 to 999 ... farms, 1987..	-	3	-	21	1	1	1	-
1982..	-	5	1	23	1	7	2	1
number, 1987..	2	1 600	(D)	13 342	(D)	10	1	(D)
1982..	(D)	3 325	(D)	15 491	(D)	(D)	(D)	(D)
1,000 or more ... farms, 1987..	-	6	-	20	-	2	-	-
1982..	-	3	1	15	-	2	-	-
number, 1987..	-	12 256	-	48 485	-	(D)	-	-
1982..	-	5 700	-	28 913	-	(D)	-	-
Hogs and pigs used or to be used for breeding ... farms, 1987..	21	46	13	168	9	29	17	12
1982..	25	80	21	203	20	53	49	14
number, 1987..	371	2 745	166	9 928	160	1 676	336	322
1982..	525	2 493	445	9 659	561	2 215	705	172
1987 farms by inventory:								
1 to 24	15	25	12	83	7	9	11	8
25 to 49	4	5	1	29	2	6	4	2
50 to 99	2	8	-	28	-	11	2	1
100 or more ... farms..	-	7	-	26	-	3	-	1
number..	-	1 772	-	6 258	-	837	-	(U)
Other hogs and pigs ... farms, 1987..	36	64	24	236	14	43	24	9
1982..	48	105	25	261	40	79	54	18
number, 1987..	2 400	16 957	2 362	82 999	1 440	10 558	2 247	730
1982..	4 888	14 876	1 655	68 829	4 312	15 527	4 998	704
LITTERS								
Litters of pigs farrowed between—								
Dec. 1 of preceding year and Nov. 30 ... farms, 1987..	23	49	16	168	9	33	18	13
1982..	25	64	23	209	22	61	53	14
number, 1987..	425	4 572	225	15 822	181	2 844	370	282
1982..	793	3 729	622	14 859	963	3 428	1 028	210
Dec. 1 of preceding year and May 31 ... farms, 1987..	23	47	14	157	9	31	17	12
1982..	22	77	21	199	21	60	51	13
number, 1987..	241	2 998	121	7 995	88	1 579	181	137
1982..	368	1 918	312	7 515	520	1 667	577	114
June 1 and Nov. 30 ... farms, 1987..	21	43	11	158	8	30	17	9
1982..	24	74	17	191	19	58	40	9
number, 1987..	184	1 574	104	7 827	93	1 265	189	145
1982..	425	1 811	310	7 344	443	1 761	448	96
SALES								
Hogs and pigs sold ... farms, 1987..	36	75	34	254	17	44	31	14
1982..	53	126	32	295	43	65	61	14
number, 1987..	4 602	37 551	5 414	165 832	3 124	22 188	4 908	2 096
1982..	9 754	34 176	6 749	148 890	(D)	34 499	10 289	(D)
$1,000, 1987..	451	3 910	554	17 487	351	2 048	457	189
1982..	1 024	3 255	787	15 189	(D)	3 384	1 037	(D)
1987 farms by number sold:								
1 to 24 ... farms..	10	7	14	17	4	10	11	6
number..	115	105	141	255	57	(D)	122	81
25 to 49 ... farms..	4	14	4	26	2	2	7	3
number..	124	449	136	835	(D)	(D)	251	86
50 to 99 ... farms..	7	14	5	35	2	4	3	3
number..	499	977	343	2 720	(D)	316	210	(D)
100 to 199 ... farms..	6	11	3	36	4	4	3	-
number..	790	1 384	360	4 911	500	692	417	-
200 to 499 ... farms..	7	14	7	56	3	11	4	1
number..	(D)	4 319	(D)	17 493	785	3 596	1 320	(D)
500 to 999 ... farms..	2	8	-	49	2	8	2	-
number..	(D)	3 600	-	33 783	(D)	6 060	(D)	-
1,000 or more ... farms..	-	10	1	35	-	5	1	1
number..	-	27 017	(D)	105 731	-	11 374	(D)	(D)
Feeder pigs sold ... farms, 1987..	10	25	10	63	1	11	12	5
1982..	15	48	7	76	7	26	20	5
number, 1987..	1 124	9 539	(D)	30 192	(D)	6 335	822	700
1982..	1 215	10 720	1 362	26 466	(D)	11 321	1 913	26
$1,000, 1987..	44	53	31	1 497	(D)	230	36	(D)
1982..	53	485	46	1 240	(D)	557	75	12
Hogs and pigs other than feeder pigs sold ... farms, 1987..	38	67	27	236	17	42	27	12
1982..	50	109	32	274	41	78	58	13
number, 1987..	3 678	28 312	(D)	135 640	(D)	15 853	4 086	1 396
1982..	8 538	23 456	5 397	122 424	7 912	23 178	8 358	713
$1,000, 1987..	407	3 479	523	15 990	(D)	1 819	421	161
1982..	971	2 770	741	13 929	933	2 526	961	103

Table 13. **Sheep and Horses—Inventory and Sales: 1987 and 1982**

[For meaning of abbreviations and symbols, see introductory text]

Item	Kansas	Allen	Anderson	Atchison	Barber	Barton	Bourbon
Sheep and lambs inventory .... farms, 1987	2 400	15	29	14	19	17	24
1982	2 478	26	35	19	15	23	27
number, 1987	249 303	421	1 171	1 718	5 455	1 515	721
1982	278 616	1 365	1 563	2 319	4 073	2 566	1 959
1987 farms by inventory:							
1 to 24	1 050	11	12	9	5	4	14
25 to 99	850	3	15	3	5	9	9
100 to 299	342	1	-	2	4	3	1
300 to 999	123	-	-	2	3	1	-
1,000 or more	35	-	-	-	2	-	-
Ewes 1 year old or older .... farms, 1987	2 195	14	24	14	18	15	20
1982	2 247	25	34	15	13	20	27
number, 1987	129 607	297	824	1 451	1 777	971	500
1982	150 502	1 003	1 144	1 857	2 300	1 633	1 150
Sheep and lambs shorn .... farms, 1987	2 183	13	23	13	18	14	19
1982	2 220	25	33	16	13	21	23
number, 1987	218 960	339	1 024	2 106	2 079	1 300	504
1982	231 016	1 165	1 240	2 407	2 769	1 847	827
pounds of wool, 1987	1 510 663	2 339	8 180	19 712	16 061	9 997	3 325
1982	1 607 200	9 047	8 495	21 458	19 462	17 133	5 995
Sheep and lambs sold .... farms, 1987	2 396	13	26	14	19	15	23
1982	2 462	30	34	17	13	22	24
number, 1987	267 152	319	1 077	1 165	2 351	856	576
1982	262 947	992	1 113	1 575	2 272	1 311	771
Sheep, lambs, and wool sold .... farms, 1987	2 456	14	28	14	20	15	25
1982	2 535	30	34	17	14	23	26
$1,000, 1987	18 561	27	68	96	160	(D)	41
1982	15 502	81	55	108	141	113	36
Horses and ponies inventory .... farms, 1987	12 879	127	146	84	180	114	196
1982	14 069	142	152	85	188	114	201
number, 1987	55 598	435	550	291	948	470	790
1982	60 285	535	623	221	889	472	734
Horses and ponies sold .... farms, 1987	2 260	17	16	14	22	25	36
1982	2 353	33	20	17	33	19	33
number, 1987	8 467	56	74	41	67	99	120
1982	8 743	88	50	31	81	60	122
$1,000, 1987	5 496	19	29	12	41	183	43
1982	8 490	53	37	17	72	53	89

Item	Brown	Butler	Chase	Chautauqua	Cherokee	Cheyenne	Clark
Sheep and lambs inventory .... farms, 1987	31	63	17	27	10	14	7
1982	35	55	9	16	9	6	6
number, 1987	1 997	2 336	1 993	1 094	153	677	132
1982	2 126	2 700	517	1 053	108	333	136
1987 farms by inventory:							
1 to 24	11	37	10	15	8	2	4
25 to 99	13	21	2	7	2	10	3
100 to 299	7	5	4	5	-	2	-
300 to 999	7	-	-	-	-	-	-
1,000 or more	-	-	1	-	-	-	-
Ewes 1 year old or older .... farms, 1987	29	56	12	23	8	14	6
1982	32	48	9	14	7	7	5
number, 1987	1 477	1 695	1 292	770	95	821	108
1982	1 205	1 697	374	615	56	242	92
Sheep and lambs shorn .... farms, 1987	30	55	11	24	7	14	6
1982	32	45	8	13	6	6	6
number, 1987	1 923	2 350	1 356	662	100	799	107
1982	1 866	2 171	353	783	73	236	116
pounds of wool, 1987	13 814	14 898	9 365	5 720	686	5 974	1 001
1982	14 087	15 092	2 604	5 070	417	1 679	754
Sheep and lambs sold .... farms, 1987	32	60	15	27	8	14	6
1982	33	47	8	16	8	10	6
number, 1987	1 719	2 297	1 711	551	87	787	101
1982	1 346	1 625	261	637	139	428	131
Sheep, lambs, and wool sold .... farms, 1987	32	62	15	28	8	14	6
1982	34	51	9	16	9	10	6
$1,000, 1987	127	(D)	91	39	5	63	(D)
1982	87	97	13	41	7	26	7
Horses and ponies inventory .... farms, 1987	75	437	111	176	157	77	99
1982	91	458	119	183	147	91	100
number, 1987	179	2 029	615	610	527	308	437
1982	281	1 994	615	720	515	361	453
Horses and ponies sold .... farms, 1987	14	77	26	19	22	8	11
1982	6	77	23	18	18	10	19
number, 1987	36	287	99	30	63	12	21
1982	15	235	123	35	51	33	74
$1,000, 1987	30	298	58	12	28	(D)	10
1982	13	229	93	39	30	18	69

Table 13. Sheep and Horses—Inventory and Sales: 1987 and 1982—Con.

[For meaning of abbreviations and symbols, see introductory text]

Item	Clay	Cloud	Coffey	Comanche	Cowley	Crawford	Decatur
Sheep and lambs inventory ___ farms, 1987__	21	25	21	5	41	18	8
1982__	23	16	12	10	58	22	10
number, 1987__	1 496	2 261	1 287	133	5 692	1 003	785
1982__	2 679	2 167	482	310	5 079	2 011	681
1987 farms by inventory:							
1 to 24	6	15	13	2	14	9	2
25 to 99	10	8	4	3	17	6	4
100 to 299	4	1	3	-	3	2	1
300 to 999	1	-	1	-	6	1	1
1,000 or more	-	1	-	-	1	-	-
Ewes 1 year old or older ___ farms, 1987__	21	25	17	5	38	16	6
1982__	21	14	8	8	55	19	10
number, 1987__	1 181	1 469	975	105	2 697	742	468
1982__	1 700	1 364	320	235	3 042	587	384
Sheep and lambs shorn ___ farms, 1987__	24	26	18	4	39	14	9
1982__	22	14	9	9	52	21	10
number, 1987__	1 303	1 185	902	121	2 898	958	372
1982__	1 397	1 028	393	250	3 207	1 901	409
pounds of wool, 1987__	10 678	8 218	6 125	1 305	23 485	5 587	3 086
1982__	10 162	7 282	3 144	2 088	20 845	8 928	2 745
Sheep and lambs sold ___ farms, 1987__	24	27	20	4	43	15	13
1982__	25	17	11	10	58	21	12
number, 1987__	1 388	1 182	816	90	3 622	843	708
1982__	920	1 051	337	189	3 187	1 721	358
Sheep, lambs, and wool sold ___ farms, 1987__	24	27	24	6	46	17	13
1982__	25	17	13	10	60	22	12
$1,000, 1987__	114	66	62	(D)	306	68	40
1982__	62	70	20	11	177	84	20
Horses and ponies inventory ___ farms, 1987__	70	90	114	102	262	135	51
1982__	71	113	129	110	293	154	92
number, 1987__	252	301	466	328	1 238	504	218
1982__	235	370	434	402	1 374	523	591
Horses and ponies sold ___ farms, 1987__	10	6	17	12	45	28	5
1982__	12	19	14	13	50	22	9
number, 1987__	14	13	45	30	153	104	8
1982__	22	46	24	73	272	52	166
$1,000, 1987__	8	7	19	12	69	151	3
1982__	14	25	12	38	283	40	96

Item	Dickinson	Doniphan	Douglas	Edwards	Elk	Ellis	Ellsworth
Sheep and lambs inventory ___ farms, 1987__	61	22	41	7	10	15	10
1982__	44	28	28	10	12	14	4
number, 1987__	3 800	1 054	1 296	(D)	468	1 797	1 120
1982__	4 309	1 341	1 369	3 062	1 151	2 369	246
1987 farms by inventory:							
1 to 24	23	11	22	4	6	8	2
25 to 99	27	6	17	1	3	1	3
100 to 299	8	5	2	1	1	4	4
300 to 999	3	-	-	1	-	2	1
1,000 or more	-	-	-	-	-	-	-
Ewes 1 year old or older ___ farms, 1987__	56	20	37	7	10	14	6
1982__	41	27	25	9	8	10	4
number, 1987__	2 329	668	872	790	411	1 121	855
1982__	2 539	893	911	1 391	638	1 199	214
Sheep and lambs shorn ___ farms, 1987__	57	17	37	6	10	13	9
1982__	40	29	27	27	10	8	4
number, 1987__	2 994	817	1 185	800	696	1 396	796
1982__	3 328	1 358	1 688	2 156	876	1 228	161
pounds of wool, 1987__	22 678	6 344	5 203	5 599	4 988	9 042	5 976
1982__	25 730	8 484	8 660	16 309	7 839	9 134	1 237
Sheep and lambs sold ___ farms, 1987__	61	22	39	7	10	14	9
1982__	46	31	27	8	15	11	4
number, 1987__	2 686	761	911	787	405	1 279	841
1982__	3 088	980	1 350	2 407	1 354	1 030	193
Sheep, lambs, and wool sold ___ farms, 1987__	61	22	40	7	10	14	9
1982__	46	31	27	10	15	11	4
$1,000, 1987__	211	59	46	(D)	31	103	65
1982__	188	55	82	87	56	8	8
Horses and ponies inventory ___ farms, 1987__	133	74	179	65	140	106	87
1982__	184	60	180	56	161	105	86
number, 1987__	488	209	908	188	684	527	306
1982__	566	175	883	164	755	533	298
Horses and ponies sold ___ farms, 1987__	22	10	38	7	19	20	21
1982__	20	5	36	10	20	20	16
number, 1987__	54	33	119	22	50	75	29
1982__	38	27	133	28	64	47	40
$1,000, 1987__	44	9	81	5	29	32	31
1982__	42	15	246	30	78	78	32

1987 CENSUS OF AGRICULTURE—COUNTY DATA

Table 13. Sheep and Horses—Inventory and Sales: 1987 and 1982—Con.

[For meaning of abbreviations and symbols, see introductory text]

Item	Finney	Ford	Franklin	Geary	Gove	Graham	Grant
Sheep and lambs inventory ... farms, 1987..	19	22	34	7	12	7	10
1982..	13	16	33	7	14	10	13
number, 1987..	691	539	1 123	281	4 292	419	218
1982..	661	575	2 179	350	3 771	849	463
1987 farms by inventory:							
1 to 24	7	10	22	3	4	3	7
25 to 99	10	12	8	3	3	3	3
100 to 299	2	-	4	1	2	1	-
300 to 999	-	-	-	-	2	-	-
1,000 or more	-	-	-	-	1	-	-
Ewes 1 year old or older ... farms, 1987..	17	19	28	6	8	7	9
1982..	11	18	26	7	12	9	12
number, 1987..	531	430	818	225	1 046	259	145
1982..	390	355	1 027	260	2 621	524	337
Sheep and lambs shorn ... farms, 1987..	20	20	28	7	9	7	7
1982..	7	16	27	8	14	11	10
number, 1987..	1 388	615	1 306	212	(D)	296	257
1982..	462	393	2 060	258	2 997	454	586
pounds of wool, 1987..	6 434	3 586	11 116	1 408	18 058	2 451	1 046
1982..	3 093	2 853	14 849	2 075	20 379	4 423	3 544
Sheep and lambs sold ... farms, 1987..	21	22	34	6	13	7	8
1982..	17	17	33	7	18	13	12
number, 1987..	1 661	633	1 049	448	3 344	305	383
1982..	417	364	3 083	193	3 084	503	433
Sheep, lambs, and wool sold ... farms, 1987..	23	22	35	7	13	7	8
1982..	17	17	36	7	18	13	14
$1,000, 1987..	157	(D)	82	34	305	(D)	22
1982..	22	18	150	12	203	25	25
Horses and ponies inventory ... farms, 1987..	100	122	218	79	64	86	63
1982..	112	120	244	62	76	84	70
number, 1987..	382	652	918	323	264	310	280
1982..	543	622	1 083	528	261	297	237
Horses and ponies sold ... farms, 1987..	17	26	38	9	9	17	17
1982..	22	17	38	18	7	6	10
number, 1987..	30	98	101	63	84	75	56
1982..	66	37	106	113	15	19	25
$1,000, 1987..	45	60	54	16	20	(D)	25
1982..	132	36	97	49	4	7	45

Item	Gray	Greeley	Greenwood	Hamilton	Harper	Harvey	Haskell
Sheep and lambs inventory ... farms, 1987..	16	5	24	5	26	68	9
1982..	12	6	31	6	22	92	9
number, 1987..	4 535	477	891	(D)	33 724	7 858	(D)
1982..	3 255	153	1 349	89	2 349	13 765	761
1987 farms by inventory:							
1 to 24	4	2	6	3	13	22	5
25 to 99	8	1	18	-	2	24	3
100 to 299	2	2	-	2	5	17	-
300 to 999	1	-	-	-	5	4	-
1,000 or more	1	-	-	-	3	1	1
Ewes 1 year old or older ... farms, 1987..	16	5	23	5	26	65	6
1982..	9	4	31	5	20	86	8
number, 1987..	2 233	431	648	159	3 474	5 135	465
1982..	1 794	76	862	42	1 356	8 022	407
Sheep and lambs shorn ... farms, 1987..	15	5	23	3	26	68	7
1982..	9	4	26	4	18	87	7
number, 1987..	2 259	195	725	(D)	47 223	7 963	(D)
1982..	1 925	(D)	1 009	52	1 199	8 425	761
pounds of wool, 1987..	19 651	892	4 411	(D)	281 823	50 889	(D)
1982..	18 960	(D)	7 569	631	10 991	61 357	6 086
Sheep and lambs sold ... farms, 1987..	16	5	24	5	31	69	9
1982..	8	8	31	5	21	94	8
number, 1987..	2 311	212	692	215	(D)	6 494	(D)
1982..	1 303	129	874	102	1 373	8 315	735
Sheep, lambs, and wool sold ... farms, 1987..	16	5	24	5	31	70	9
1982..	9	8	31	5	21	95	8
$1,000, 1987..	187	18	51	19	5 247	538	(D)
1982..	84	8	50	6	79	496	49
Horses and ponies inventory ... farms, 1987..	84	34	191	55	116	143	55
1982..	84	31	247	48	139	134	58
number, 1987..	336	147	837	380	359	616	254
1982..	286	134	968	352	467	504	232
Horses and ponies sold ... farms, 1987..	14	3	27	12	11	29	6
1982..	19	3	40	15	17	35	12
number, 1987..	51	(D)	87	50	26	117	12
1982..	62	(D)	261	79	25	105	22
$1,000, 1987..	24	(D)	34	(D)	40	141	10
1982..	65	(D)	138	49	23	56	24

Table 13. **Sheep and Horses—Inventory and Sales: 1987 and 1982**—Con.

[For meaning of abbreviations and symbols, see introductory text]

Item	Hodgeman	Jackson	Jefferson	Jewell	Johnson	Kearny	Kingman	Kiowa
Sheep and lambs inventory ... farms, 1987	8	37	29	39	16	8	32	2
1982	8	27	30	40	24	6	31	2
number, 1987	1 577	3 141	689	6 180	1 890	1 976	1 838	(D)
1982	883	2 584	611	8 187	1 497	(D)	1 517	(D)
1987 farms by inventory:								
1 to 24	3	18	22	16	8	3	10	1
25 to 99	2	16	5	10	3	4	16	1
100 to 299	1	-	2	5	4	-	6	-
300 to 999	2	2	-	5	-	-	-	-
1,000 or more	-	1	-	3	1	1	-	-
Ewes 1 year old or older ... farms, 1987	7	35	25	36	15	8	26	2
1982	5	26	24	36	22	5	27	2
number, 1987	1 190	1 982	631	4 646	1 144	844	1 057	(D)
1982	526	1 417	538	5 210	940	(D)	873	(D)
Sheep and lambs shorn ... farms, 1987	7	31	28	35	15	8	27	2
1982	8	25	22	38	19	5	29	2
number, 1987	1 235	2 149	684	6 430	1 710	(D)	1 540	(D)
1982	591	2 521	647	5 606	1 404	(D)	1 092	(D)
pounds of wool, 1987	6 222	13 995	4 343	51 789	17 538	(D)	12 401	(D)
1982	4 901	15 480	4 825	51 812	8 824	(D)	6 997	(D)
Sheep and lambs sold ... farms, 1987	9	37	33	42	17	8	33	2
1982	13	29	28	38	23	5	32	2
number, 1987	1 106	2 431	651	7 026	342	862	3 309	(D)
1982	614	2 393	542	5 381	635	(D)	1 250	(D)
Sheep, lambs, and wool sold ... farms, 1987	9	38	33	42	18	8	34	2
1982	13	28	28	41	23	5	34	2
$1,000, 1987	84	204	54	608	45	62	177	(D)
1982	32	135	27	336	39	(D)	66	(D)
Horses and ponies inventory ... farms, 1987	65	269	203	104	195	71	156	72
1982	61	265	224	110	208	80	169	105
number, 1987	288	1 056	875	334	1 424	480	713	312
1982	251	831	801	361	1 263	558	536	463
Horses and ponies sold ... farms, 1987	13	40	37	10	61	15	30	10
1982	9	40	31	15	63	13	21	18
number, 1987	27	105	96	39	326	86	158	16
1982	44	73	102	45	173	83	59	65
$1,000, 1987	(D)	53	94	27	366	63	82	(D)
1982	90	89	70	42	208	046	45	40

Item	Labette	Lane	Leavenworth	Lincoln	Linn	Logan	Lyon	McPherson
Sheep and lambs inventory ... farms, 1987	32	6	31	26	12	12	29	63
1982	35	13	33	35	17	12	23	66
number, 1987	1 088	261	1 075	5 137	224	(D)	857	8 899
1982	1 486	750	673	6 625	505	1 000	915	8 693
1987 farms by inventory:								
1 to 24	12	1	19	4	9	3	17	20
25 to 99	18	5	9	14	3	-	10	21
100 to 299	2	-	3	6	-	1	2	13
300 to 999	-	-	-	5	-	1	-	7
1,000 or more	-	-	-	-	-	-	-	2
Ewes 1 year old or older ... farms, 1987	30	6	29	28	9	5	28	56
1982	34	11	27	35	15	10	21	59
number, 1987	806	177	577	2 501	111	(D)	606	5 329
1982	1 046	372	509	4 380	249	530	607	4 226
Sheep and lambs shorn ... farms, 1987	31	6	27	30	8	5	24	56
1982	34	11	27	36	16	12	27	63
number, 1987	887	209	796	3 964	134	(D)	793	6 220
1982	1 314	552	630	4 597	331	671	851	7 592
pounds of wool, 1987	5 058	1 081	5 874	27 225	1 052	1 600	5 313	48 591
1982	8 565	4 087	4 191	39 539	1 823	3 989	5 703	48 475
Sheep and lambs sold ... farms, 1987	32	8	31	30	11	5	27	59
1982	39	13	29	38	18	27	26	67
number, 1987	657	274	653	5 135	173	115	715	6 045
1982	1 070	562	508	4 207	449	1 042	743	15 344
Sheep, lambs, and wool sold ... farms, 1987	32	8	31	30	11	6	27	60
1982	39	13	32	38	18	14	28	69
$1,000, 1987	44	19	48	411	12	10	48	548
1982	58	26	23	271	26	41	34	668
Horses and ponies inventory ... farms, 1987	205	62	196	69	154	69	240	222
1982	255	61	210	84	158	93	270	242
number, 1987	791	296	815	210	662	278	963	1 075
1982	918	372	830	245	1 029	468	1 106	1 197
Horses and ponies sold ... farms, 1987	34	9	38	11	27	8	43	47
1982	46	14	44	14	17	13	30	53
number, 1987	192	74	139	23	67	89	167	183
1982	116	73	138	35	89	52	166	295
$1,000, 1987	81	45	91	(D)	43	36	64	106
1982	116	47	111	29	42	28	130	342

Table 13. **Sheep and Horses—Inventory and Sales: 1987 and 1982**—Con.

[For meaning of abbreviations and symbols, see introductory text]

Item	Marion	Marshall	Meade	Miami	Mitchell	Montgomery	Morris	Morton
Sheep and lambs inventory...farms, 1987	62	27	6	41	39	21	19	4
1982	50	30	10	29	42	27	20	5
number, 1987	4 454	1 529	514	904	5 400	491	599	(D)
1982	3 564	1 683	769	1 145	6 176	967	859	71
1987 farms by inventory:								
1 to 24	25	10	3	26	10	14	11	-
25 to 99	21	13	1	15	13	7	6	2
100 to 299	13	3	2	-	12	-	2	-
300 to 999	3	1	-	-	3	-	-	2
1,000 or more	-	-	-	-	1	-	-	-
Ewes 1 year old or older...farms, 1987	59	25	6	36	38	19	18	4
1982	46	27	8	26	38	27	17	5
number, 1987	3 101	1 028	319	692	3 658	351	480	288
1982	2 390	1 249	437	757	5 641	688	565	44
Sheep and lambs shorn...farms, 1987	60	26	7	33	36	19	18	4
1982	48	27	9	23	39	24	15	5
number, 1987	3 715	1 246	571	637	4 557	507	650	302
1982	3 027	1 412	458	910	6 919	681	619	57
pounds of wool, 1987	27 240	6 600	3 005	5 914	29 013	3 216	3 859	2 967
1982	17 803	10 384	3 801	6 768	51 918	4 270	4 680	542
Sheep and lambs sold...farms, 1987	62	28	7	37	40	21	16	4
1982	53	29	11	27	42	28	17	5
number, 1987	2 984	1 050	682	860	3 981	544	480	(D)
1982	3 159	1 294	805	717	6 235	625	559	(D)
Sheep, lambs, and wool sold...farms, 1987	63	29	7	39	40	21	18	4
1982	54	29	11	29	42	29	17	5
$1,000, 1987	237	93	48	53	280	35	93	(D)
1982	170	59	(D)	42	347	26	27	5
Horses and ponies inventory...farms, 1987	176	127	71	296	60	247	148	62
1982	197	152	75	309	66	258	167	49
number, 1987	554	408	361	1 562	353	1 179	571	249
1982	613	678	314	1 374	274	1 372	585	143
Horses and ponies sold...farms, 1987	33	14	16	52	7	44	18	14
1982	24	22	12	53	9	49	21	8
number, 1987	59	55	73	226	(D)	228	46	22
1982	87	75	43	167	31	294	54	16
$1,000, 1987	44	40	(D)	150	86	164	49	(D)
1982	47	63	47	195	51	508	48	10

Item	Nemaha	Neosho	Ness	Norton	Osage	Osborne	Ottawa	Pawnee
Sheep and lambs inventory...farms, 1987	41	17	12	15	15	43	21	14
1982	34	22	17	29	18	37	17	16
number, 1987	1 997	644	1 352	1 354	284	3 491	2 537	2 177
1982	1 506	739	1 593	3 001	649	3 331	2 355	2 018
1987 farms by inventory:								
1 to 24	16	10	5	5	10	19	7	2
25 to 99	17	5	2	6	5	17	10	6
100 to 299	8	1	3	3	-	2	3	5
300 to 999	-	1	2	1	-	5	-	-
1,000 or more	-	-	-	-	-	-	1	1
Ewes 1 year old or older...farms, 1987	39	15	10	14	15	38	19	12
1982	29	19	14	26	15	37	16	13
number, 1987	1 470	240	949	948	221	2 178	1 518	1 274
1982	1 219	478	1 120	1 966	479	1 874	1 717	1 164
Sheep and lambs shorn...farms, 1987	36	14	12	14	11	38	19	12
1982	34	16	15	24	17	36	17	15
number, 1987	1 833	293	996	1 221	244	2 101	1 980	1 370
1982	1 605	573	1 120	1 853	559	2 133	1 853	1 148
pounds of wool, 1987	11 854	2 301	6 415	10 392	1 399	16 454	17 978	8 614
1982	10 812	2 348	7 809	13 799	4 083	16 524	12 964	8 709
Sheep and lambs sold...farms, 1987	41	16	14	15	12	44	23	14
1982	35	16	16	25	17	33	18	18
number, 1987	1 960	525	1 012	1 365	202	2 920	1 526	1 611
1982	1 412	577	1 083	2 064	530	2 286	1 740	1 506
Sheep, lambs, and wool sold...farms, 1987	41	18	15	15	12	45	23	14
1982	35	18	17	25	20	36	18	18
$1,000, 1987	163	29	76	112	(D)	252	114	81
1982	69	29	67	103	35	154	81	83
Horses and ponies inventory...farms, 1987	90	147	67	73	184	92	108	49
1982	97	137	76	80	214	86	105	72
number, 1987	268	588	269	251	717	365	359	212
1982	323	540	361	307	899	364	408	360
Horses and ponies sold...farms, 1987	6	27	13	14	35	24	23	8
1982	11	20	18	13	33	16	19	13
number, 1987	15	51	45	33	401	88	49	16
1982	17	80	35	82	499	28	59	69
$1,000, 1987	7	27	13	13	121	66	13	6
1982	12	36	35	40	225	15	60	33

Table 13. **Sheep and Horses—Inventory and Sales: 1987 and 1982**—Con.

[For meaning of abbreviations and symbols, see introductory text]

Item	Phillips	Pottawatomie	Pratt	Rawlins	Reno	Republic	Rice	Riley
Sheep and lambs inventory ... farms, 1987...	18	21	17	11	140	34	15	24
1982...	21	19	12	17	151	32	11	24
number, 1987...	1 025	460	1 221	2 438	13 858	3 951	1 217	2 893
1982...	648	726	973	3 811	19 186	4 419	672	6 168
1987 farms by inventory:								
1 to 24 ...	4	15	5	4	55	13	6	11
25 to 99 ...	12	6	5	3	47	10	3	7
100 to 299 ...	2	–	7	2	24	7	6	3
300 to 999 ...	–	–	–	1	14	4	–	2
1,000 or more ...	–	–	–	1	–	–	–	1
Ewes 1 year old or older ... farms, 1987...	18	20	17	9	131	34	14	23
1982...	20	16	11	15	136	29	11	24
number, 1987...	610	320	753	1 104	8 772	2 403	786	1 649
1982...	513	428	534	2 838	9 955	3 039	468	3 555
Sheep and lambs shorn ... farms, 1987...	19	18	16	9	130	33	15	24
1982...	23	18	10	15	135	29	13	23
number, 1987...	676	409	830	1 086	10 123	3 342	1 074	2 661
1982...	624	832	516	3 105	11 963	3 622	705	3 565
pounds of wool, 1987...	5 653	3 069	7 131	8 329	76 623	24 094	8 895	14 877
1982...	5 332	5 941	4 870	25 385	98 392	41 465	5 406	21 136
Sheep and lambs sold ... farms, 1987...	20	20	16	10	140	37	16	23
1982...	26	18	12	20	146	35	14	20
number, 1987...	859	554	717	995	8 777	3 032	690	2 531
1982...	614	1 097	366	2 454	11 219	2 952	689	2 058
Sheep, lambs, and wool sold ... farms, 1987...	20	20	16	10	143	37	16	24
1982...	26	19	12	22	150	35	14	23
$1,000, 1987...	65	(D)	55	(D)	662	261	54	242
1982...	30	67	21	133	639	192	37	106
Horses and ponies inventory ... farms, 1987...	124	217	82	86	328	100	97	123
1982...	142	204	79	111	341	116	93	122
number, 1987...	583	840	349	311	1 524	346	456	522
1982...	742	697	359	603	1 554	290	320	490
Horses and ponies sold ... farms, 1987...	26	29	17	18	68	14	24	16
1982...	30	29	13	19	76	15	15	15
number, 1987...	62	62	38	59	541	51	70	44
1982...	133	91	37	59	313	32	36	60
$1,000, 1987...	26	52	38	20	213	(D)	(D)	24
1982...	71	64	81	90	241	15	23	38

Item	Rooks	Rush	Russell	Saline	Scott	Sedgwick	Seward	Shawnee
Sheep and lambs inventory ... farms, 1987...	16	9	12	20	3	86	5	5
1982...	8	12	12	22	14	66	7	12
number, 1987...	478	1 517	1 033	1 296	(D)	15 254	117	(D)
1982...	337	3 256	936	1 993	2 210	34 054	139	465
1987 farms by inventory:								
1 to 24 ...	8	3	5	10	1	34	4	3
25 to 99 ...	8	1	3	6	1	31	1	2
100 to 299 ...	–	3	3	3	1	12	–	–
300 to 999 ...	–	2	1	1	–	4	–	–
1,000 or more ...	–	–	–	–	–	5	–	–
Ewes 1 year old or older ... farms, 1987...	16	8	11	18	2	77	4	5
1982...	8	17	12	22	13	78	7	11
number, 1987...	451	950	659	945	(D)	7 469	82	49
1982...	215	1 900	732	1 662	1 535	8 949	52	345
Sheep and lambs shorn ... farms, 1987...	15	8	10	16	14	77	4	5
1982...	8	14	10	22	14	74	4	10
number, 1987...	338	1 168	730	1 012	300	12 905	65	58
1982...	267	2 635	773	1 774	2 276	40 437	56	525
pounds of wool, 1987...	2 639	11 021	6 309	6 232	1 986	102 482	287	301
1982...	2 385	22 848	6 806	12 511	10 883	237 406	284	2 947
Sheep and lambs sold ... farms, 1987...	16	9	12	18	5	85	4	6
1982...	8	15	10	23	15	67	6	10
number, 1987...	395	1 184	511	967	399	15 115	71	47
1982...	322	2 392	684	1 306	1 044	44 225	101	351
Sheep, lambs, and wool sold ... farms, 1987...	16	9	12	20	5	88	4	6
1982...	8	15	10	23	16	87	6	10
$1,000, 1987...	25	86	40	77	(D)	965	6	4
1982...	20	141	38	86	52	2 894	5	20
Horses and ponies inventory ... farms, 1987...	79	33	66	153	53	300	74	202
1982...	97	52	81	145	83	325	68	220
number, 1987...	297	98	214	618	376	1 983	374	967
1982...	431	186	327	570	443	2 287	343	1 025
Horses and ponies sold ... farms, 1987...	17	6	9	25	8	90	13	43
1982...	18	7	15	24	14	80	11	49
number, 1987...	53	13	38	60	85	292	30	130
1982...	84	(D)	50	63	39	410	34	139
$1,000, 1987...	23	(D)	(D)	50	(D)	441	(D)	101
1982...	58	(D)	28	49	52	1 232	32	156

Table 13. Sheep and Horses—Inventory and Sales: 1987 and 1982—Con.

[For meaning of abbreviations and symbols, see introductory text]

Item	Sheridan	Sherman	Smith	Stafford	Stanton	Stevens	Sumner	Thomas
Sheep and lambs inventory .... farms, 1987	9	11	41	16	9	7	65	19
1982	14	14	51	17	4	4	65	19
number, 1987	1 294	1 382	2 755	1 112	147	699	9 493	1 758
1982	2 361	1 797	5 654	1 710	48	197	9 045	4 188
1987 farms by inventory:								
1 to 24	2	2	14	10	7	4	23	7
25 to 99	3	5	16	3	2	2	23	10
100 to 299	2	2	8	1	-	-	9	1
300 to 999	2	2	1	2	-	1	7	1
1,000 or more	-	-	-	-	-	-	3	-
Ewes 1 year old or older .... farms, 1987	9	11	39	16	6	6	60	16
1982	12	14	49	14	4	4	57	16
number, 1987	850	920	2 151	704	100	159	4 559	997
1982	1 051	1 342	2 076	535	28	169	4 701	2 152
Sheep and lambs shorn .... farms, 1987	10	14	40	15	9	3	64	13
1982	14	15	51	11	4	3	60	16
number, 1987	813	1 366	2 317	1 612	137	(D)	7 468	1 373
1982	2 406	1 614	9 521	572	27	142	7 269	3 766
pounds of wool, 1987	6 183	10 604	16 188	8 074	1 119	(D)	48 432	9 844
1982	14 979	11 079	37 391	4 749	99	675	64 612	26 580
Sheep and lambs sold .... farms, 1987	10	14	42	15	11	5	63	19
1982	16	16	51	14	4	4	63	20
number, 1987	739	1 539	1 905	1 922	121	(D)	7 254	1 166
1982	2 978	1 249	(D)	1 220	30	169	6 471	4 213
Sheep, lambs, and wool sold .... farms, 1987	10	14	42	15	12	5	67	20
1982	16	16	51	14	4	4	65	20
$1,000, 1987	66	123	136	127	8	(D)	604	119
1982	215	81	(D)	56	1	(D)	403	243
Horses and ponies inventory .... farms, 1987	48	63	89	87	49	85	193	88
1982	72	90	113	117	43	63	211	91
number, 1987	146	313	291	316	326	324	675	451
1982	233	472	397	483	248	217	698	614
Horses and ponies sold .... farms, 1987	8	16	8	15	8	11	39	23
1982	5	15	19	20	6	8	35	25
number, 1987	24	131	15	31	71	32	125	116
1982	27	47	37	53	10	13	102	127
$1,000, 1987	(D)	80	6	9	42	(D)	68	56
1982	10	57	28	33	6	11	71	99

Item	Trego	Wabaunsee	Wallace	Washington	Wichita	Wilson	Woodson	Wyandotte
Sheep and lambs inventory .... farms, 1987	14	21	18	43	15	17	22	4
1982	14	18	15	54	14	19	26	4
number, 1987	972	3 746	2 953	3 056	890	905	1 606	(D)
1982	1 793	2 451	6 879	5 260	5 562	877	1 595	38
1987 farms by inventory:								
1 to 24	7	12	9	17	6	10	6	2
25 to 99	4	5	5	11	4	5	9	2
100 to 299	3	1	2	14	5	1	7	-
300 to 999	-	2	1	1	-	1	-	-
1,000 or more	-	1	1	-	-	-	-	-
Ewes 1 year old or older .... farms, 1987	10	20	17	41	12	15	19	4
1982	14	15	12	48	12	18	24	4
number, 1987	644	2 477	646	2 098	682	610	1 190	(D)
1982	1 144	1 865	1 040	2 323	1 466	729	1 197	31
Sheep and lambs shorn .... farms, 1987	12	20	16	43	12	13	19	3
1982	13	13	11	45	12	17	24	1
number, 1987	1 024	3 338	1 698	1 658	952	477	1 711	58
1982	1 402	2 320	1 543	2 656	10 973	1 154	1 267	(D)
pounds of wool, 1987	7 011	19 853	10 260	12 947	7 723	4 555	10 410	(D)
1982	9 517	18 477	13 264	25 147	48 675	7 512	9 208	(D)
Sheep and lambs sold .... farms, 1987	15	21	19	42	13	15	21	4
1982	12	15	13	51	13	20	25	2
number, 1987	677	3 501	4 366	1 896	(D)	(D)	1 385	(D)
1982	1 073	1 855	6 950	3 091	(D)	845	1 144	(D)
Sheep, lambs, and wool sold .... farms, 1987	15	21	19	44	14	15	22	4
1982	13	15	13	53	13	22	26	2
$1,000, 1987	50	267	344	155	(D)	33	106	5
1982	74	111	410	165	(D)	39	68	(D)
Horses and ponies inventory .... farms, 1987	66	152	69	113	56	115	89	50
1982	74	190	90	130	75	142	106	55
number, 1987	212	711	498	474	274	354	304	256
1982	323	776	470	608	376	389	348	332
Horses and ponies sold .... farms, 1987	11	22	10	20	11	14	14	14
1982	20	15	17	30	8	25	18	11
number, 1987	22	50	60	49	24	41	28	51
1982	43	46	147	53	43	42	55	23
$1,000, 1987	(D)	36	(D)	16	10	15	13	56
1982	26	30	67	33	19	17	43	30

Table 14. Poultry—Inventory and Sales: 1987 and 1982

[For meaning of abbreviations and symbols, see introductory text]

Item	Kansas	Allen	Anderson	Atchison	Barber	Barton	Bourbon
INVENTORY							
Any poultry ... farms, 1987	4 691	58	77	42	35	89	50
1982	6 535	74	110	74	34	119	94
Chickens 3 months old or older ... farms, 1987	4 206	54	68	38	30	78	48
1982	6 044	70	100	71	31	111	86
number, 1987	2 094 810	1 686	21 814	(D)	692	(D)	2 247
1982	2 093 245	3 187	23 542	10 277	875	(D)	4 265
Hens and pullets of laying age ... farms, 1987	4 150	54	66	37	29	75	46
1982	5 988	70	100	71	31	111	84
number, 1987	1 797 313	1 609	21 045	7 246	(D)	(D)	2 058
1982	1 794 873	2 718	23 308	(D)	(D)	(D)	3 837
1987 farms by inventory:							
1 to 99	3 824	52	54	33	29	70	39
100 to 399	246	2	9	2	-	4	7
400 to 3,199	26	-	2	1	-	-	-
3,200 to 9,999	14	-	-	1	-	-	-
10,000 to 19,999	14	-	1	-	-	-	-
20,000 to 49,999	16	-	-	-	-	1	-
50,000 to 99,999	7	-	-	-	-	-	-
100,000 or more ... farms	2	-	-	-	-	-	-
number	(D)	-	-	-	-	-	-
Pullets 3 months old or older not of laying age ... farms, 1987	415	5	12	7	1	7	8
1982	521	8	7	8	1	6	10
number, 1987	297 297	77	759	(D)	(D)	156	169
1982	298 572	469	234	(D)	(D)	151	448
Pullet chicks and pullets under 3 months old ... farms, 1987	98	-	4	2	1	3	1
1982	121	2	2	-	-	4	-
number, 1987	273 671	(D)	(D)	(D)	(D)	(D)	(D)
1982	159 417	(D)	(D)	-	-	155	-
Broilers and other meat-type chickens ... farms, 1987	592	7	10	4	5	9	4
1982	954	10	14	11	-	17	7
number, 1987	49 559	168	452	(D)	375	2 226	41
1982	64 603	276	962	(D)	-	3 620	217
Turkeys ... farms, 1987	331	1	7	4	2	8	1
1982	368	6	8	5	2	5	4
number, 1987	112 661	(D)	15	(D)	(D)	57	(D)
1982	35 556	63	100	3	19	73	72
Turkey hens kept for breeding ... farms, 1987	194	1	4	3	-	6	1
1982	237	3	6	3	2	3	4
number, 1987	(D)	(D)	10	5	-	(D)	(D)
1982	35 793	10	(D)	(D)	(D)	5	(D)
Ducks, geese, and other poultry ... farms, 1987	1 084	11	8	8	5	26	13
1982	1 183	22	13	7	5	17	19
SALES							
Any poultry sold ... farms, 1987	1 550	23	35	16	3	29	19
1982	2 385	23	41	19	4	42	29
$1,000, 1987	25 284	6	(D)	(D)	(D)	(D)	14
1982	25 755	11	214	119	(D)	719	16
Hens and pullets sold ... farms, 1987	363	1	7	4	1	6	3
1982	692	7	13	(D)	2	8	8
number, 1987	2 380 936	(D)	(D)	(D)	(D)	(D)	(D)
1982	2 714 323	531	(D)	(D)	(D)	6	536
Hens and pullets of laying age sold ... farms, 1987	336	1	6	4	2	5	3
1982	674	6	13	7	1	3	8
number, 1987	1 384 767	(D)	(D)	(D)	(D)	(D)	(D)
1982	1 312 177	(D)	(D)	(D)	(D)	(D)	536
Pullets not of laying age sold ... farms, 1987	39	1	1	1	-	1	-
1982	33	1	-	-	-	-	-
number, 1987	996 169	(D)	(D)	(D)	-	(D)	-
1982	1 402 146	(D)	(D)	-	-	-	-
Broilers and other meat-type chickens sold ... farms, 1987	132	2	2	2	2	4	-
1982	210	1	2	1	-	1	-
number, 1987	176 061	(D)	(D)	(D)	-	(D)	-
1982	94 543	(D)	(D)	(D)	(D)	3 509	-
1987 farms by number sold:							
1 to 1,999	123	2	2	1	-	3	-
2,000 to 59,999	7	-	-	1	-	1	-
60,000 to 99,999	2	-	-	-	-	-	-
100,000 to 199,999	-	-	-	-	-	-	-
200,000 to 499,999	-	-	-	-	-	-	-
500,000 or more ... farms	-	-	-	-	-	-	-
number	-	-	-	-	-	-	-
Turkeys sold ... farms, 1987	86	-	-	2	3	1	-
1982	57	-	1	2	2	-	-
number, 1987	230 719	-	(D)	(D)	12 437	(D)	-
1982	65 161	-	(D)	(D)	(D)	-	-
Turkeys for slaughter sold ... farms, 1987	76	-	1	1	3	1	-
1982	43	-	1	1	-	-	-
number, 1987	(D)	-	(D)	(D)	(D)	(D)	-
1982	(D)	-	(D)	(D)	-	-	-
Ducks, geese, and other poultry sold ... farms, 1987	167	2	2	-	-	5	1
1982	207	5	2	-	-	1	2

Table 14. **Poultry—Inventory and Sales: 1987 and 1982**—Con.

[For meaning of abbreviations and symbols, see introductory text]

Item	Brown	Butler	Chase	Chautauqua	Cherokee	Cheyenne	Clark
INVENTORY							
Any poultry .... farms, 1987..	39	121	14	44	46	31	11
1982..	49	174	26	40	62	45	14
Chickens 3 months old or older .... farms, 1987..	35	110	13	42	39	24	9
1982..	47	161	23	37	59	41	14
number, 1987..	1 709	(D)	(D)	1 039	1 163	896	229
1982..	2 788	34 662	(D)	1 341	2 104	1 032	440
Hens and pullets of laying age .... farms, 1987..	34	104	13	41	37	24	9
1982..	47	161	23	36	57	41	14
number, 1987..	1 661	(D)	(D)	1 002	1 002	553	(D)
1982..	2 596	34 556	(D)	1 209	1 939	957	(D)
1987 farms by inventory:							
1 to 99	26	99	10	39	33	24	9
100 to 399	8	4	2	2	4	–	–
400 to 3,199	–	–	–	–	–	–	–
3,200 to 9,999	–	–	1	–	–	–	–
10,000 to 19,999	–	–	–	–	–	–	–
20,000 to 49,999	–	1	–	–	–	–	–
50,000 to 99,999	–	–	–	–	–	–	–
100,000 or more .... farms..	–	–	–	–	–	–	–
number..	–	–	–	–	–	–	–
Pullets 3 months old or older not of laying age .... farms, 1987..	3	7	1	2	6	3	1
1982..	4	10	2	6	8	5	2
number, 1987..	48	226	(D)	(D)	161	43	(D)
1982..	190	106	(D)	132	165	75	(D)
Pullet chicks and pullets under 3 months old .... farms, 1987..	–	1	–	1	2	–	–
1982..	1	–	–	–	1	–	–
number, 1987..	(D)	(D)	–	(D)	(D)	–	–
1982..	(D)	–	–	–	(D)	–	–
Broilers and other meat-type chickens .... farms, 1987..	6	6	1	–	6	5	1
1982..	10	27	2	7	7	8	3
number, 1987..	66	320	(D)	–	195	179	(D)
1982..	680	1 368	(D)	197	(D)	825	46
Turkeys .... farms, 1987..	–	8	–	4	7	–	2
1982..	1	7	1	5	–	1	–
number, 1987..	–	94	–	19	60 006	–	(D)
1982..	(D)	18	(D)	25	–	(D)	1
Turkey hens kept for breeding .... farms, 1987..	–	7	–	3	4	–	1
1982..	1	3	1	4	–	–	–
number, 1987..	–	(D)	–	(D)	(D)	–	(D)
1982..	(D)	9	(D)	14	–	–	–
Ducks, geese, and other poultry .... farms, 1987..	10	34	3	8	14	9	1
1982..	10	39	7	9	6	4	1
SALES							
Any poultry sold .... farms, 1987..	15	36	7	7	13	6	–
1982..	24	64	7	9	17	14	4
$1,000, 1987..	11	(D)	(D)	2	772	(D)	–
1982..	17	333	114	4	14	1	(Z)
Hens and pullets sold .... farms, 1987..	4	10	2	1	3	1	–
1982..	7	13	3	2	9	4	–
number, 1987..	242	(D)	(D)	(D)	(D)	(D)	–
1982..	592	(D)	(D)	(D)	483	158	–
Hens and pullets of laying age sold .... farms, 1987..	3	10	2	2	3	1	–
1982..	7	13	3	3	9	4	–
number, 1987..	(D)	(D)	(D)	(D)	98	(D)	–
1982..	592	(D)	(D)	(D)	(D)	(D)	–
Pullets not of laying age sold .... farms, 1987..	1	–	–	–	1	1	–
1982..	–	2	–	–	1	–	–
number, 1987..	(D)	–	–	–	(D)	(D)	–
1982..	–	(D)	–	–	(D)	(D)	–
Broilers and other meat-type chickens sold .... farms, 1987..	–	2	2	–	1	1	–
1982..	1	5	1	–	1	5	–
number, 1987..	–	(D)	(D)	–	(D)	(D)	–
1982..	(D)	706	(D)	–	(D)	269	–
1987 farms by number sold:							
1 to 1,999	–	2	2	–	1	1	–
2,000 to 59,999	–	–	–	–	–	–	–
60,000 to 99,999	–	–	–	–	–	–	–
100,000 to 199,999	–	–	–	–	–	–	–
200,000 to 499,999	–	–	–	–	–	–	–
500,000 or more .... farms..	–	–	–	–	–	–	–
number..	–	–	–	–	–	–	–
Turkeys sold .... farms, 1987..	–	1	–	–	4	–	–
1982..	–	–	–	–	–	–	–
number, 1987..	–	(D)	–	–	109 002	–	–
1982..	–	–	–	–	–	–	–
Turkeys for slaughter sold .... farms, 1987..	–	1	–	–	3	–	–
1982..	–	–	–	–	–	–	–
number, 1987..	–	(D)	–	–	(D)	–	–
1982..	–	–	–	–	–	–	–
Ducks, geese, and other poultry sold .... farms, 1987..	1	4	–	–	3	1	–
1982..	2	9	–	–	–	–	–

Table 14. Poultry—Inventory and Sales: 1987 and 1982—Con.

[For meaning of abbreviations and symbols, see introductory text]

Item	Clay	Cloud	Coffey	Comanche	Cowley	Crawford	Decatur
INVENTORY							
Any poultry .... farms, 1987	38	30	48	12	76	39	40
1982	59	42	60	25	96	62	54
Chickens 3 months old or older .... farms, 1987	35	28	45	9	68	36	37
1982	53	37	53	25	93	57	45
number, 1987	(D)	978	(D)	194	1 697	1 059	1 526
1982	(D)	1 563	(D)	434	2 892	1 847	2 231
Hens and pullets of laying age .... farms, 1987	35	28	45	9	68	36	37
1982	53	37	53	25	92	57	45
number, 1987	(D)	(D)	(D)	(D)	1 593	(D)	(D)
1982	(D)	(D)	(D)	(D)	2 707	1 717	2 187
1987 farms by inventory:							
1 to 99	29	26	40	9	67	34	33
100 to 399	4	2	1	-	1	2	4
400 to 3,199	1	-	2	-	-	-	-
3,200 to 9,999	-	-	-	-	-	-	-
10,000 to 19,999	-	-	1	-	-	-	-
20,000 to 49,999	-	-	-	-	-	-	-
50,000 to 99,999	-	-	1	-	-	-	-
100,000 or more .... farms	1	-	1	-	-	-	-
number	(D)	-	-	-	-	-	-
Pullets 3 months old or older not of laying age .... farms, 1987	5	1	4	2	6	1	2
1982	7	2	7	2	11	10	3
number, 1987	37	(D)	(D)	(D)	104	(D)	(D)
1982	311	(D)	(D)	(D)	185	130	44
Pullet chicks and pullets under 3 months old .... farms, 1987	4	-	3	1	3	1	1
1982	-	-	1	-	2	-	-
number, 1987	34	-	67	(D)	(D)	(D)	(D)
1982	-	-	(D)	-	(D)	-	-
Broilers and other meat-type chickens .... farms, 1987	4	5	7	1	11	3	4
1982	6	6	9	1	14	10	12
number, 1987	134	432	245	(D)	1 448	(D)	625
1982	525	656	377	(D)	371	456	1 177
Turkeys .... farms, 1987	2	5	6	1	4	1	2
1982	1	3	2	-	10	4	7
number, 1987	(D)	14	15	(D)	26	(D)	(D)
1982	(D)	22	(D)	-	69	18	69
Turkey hens kept for breeding .... farms, 1987	2	2	6	1	3	1	-
1982	1	2	1	-	7	2	1
number, 1987	(D)	(D)	15	(D)	(D)	(D)	(D)
1982	(D)	(D)	(D)	-	32	(D)	(D)
Ducks, geese, and other poultry .... farms, 1987	11	6	10	6	17	11	2
1982	8	9	13	2	17	14	10
SALES							
Any poultry sold .... farms, 1987	12	11	18	2	21	12	14
1982	35	14	24	4	29	18	11
$1,000, 1987	(D)	5	(D)	(D)	8	5	9
1982	2 049	12	923	(Z)	11	10	13
Hens and pullets sold .... farms, 1987	1	2	5	-	4	1	-
1982	15	6	5	1	8	9	3
number, 1987	(D)	(D)	(D)	-	145	(D)	-
1982	(D)	1 041	(D)	(D)	459	114	(D)
Hens and pullets of laying age sold .... farms, 1987	1	2	5	-	4	1	-
1982	15	6	5	1	8	6	3
number, 1987	(D)	(D)	(D)	-	145	(D)	(D)
1982	(D)	1 041	(D)	(D)	459	(D)	(D)
Pullets not of laying age sold .... farms, 1987	-	-	2	-	-	-	-
1982	1	-	-	-	-	1	-
number, 1987	(D)	-	(D)	-	-	(D)	-
Broilers and other meat-type chickens sold .... farms, 1987	-	1	1	-	2	-	1
1982	3	3	2	-	-	-	(D)
number, 1987	(D)	(D)	(D)	-	(D)	-	(D)
1982	(D)	(D)	(D)	-	-	-	(D)
1987 farms by number sold:							
1 to 1,999	-	1	1	-	2	-	1
2,000 to 59,999	-	-	-	-	-	-	-
60,000 to 199,999	-	-	-	-	-	-	-
100,000 to 499,999	-	-	-	-	-	-	-
200,000 to 499,999	-	-	-	-	-	-	-
500,000 or more .... farms	-	-	-	-	-	-	-
number	-	-	-	-	-	-	-
Turkeys sold .... farms, 1987	-	-	-	1	2	-	-
1982	-	1	-	-	2	-	-
number, 1987	-	(D)	-	(D)	(D)	-	-
1982	-	-	-	-	(D)	-	-
Turkeys for slaughter sold .... farms, 1987	-	1	-	1	2	-	-
1982	-	-	-	-	-	-	-
number, 1987	-	(D)	-	(D)	(D)	-	-
1982	-	(D)	-	-	-	-	-
Ducks, geese, and other poultry sold .... farms, 1987	1	2	-	1	4	-	-
1982	3	3	3	-	4	3	-

Table 14. **Poultry—Inventory and Sales: 1987 and 1982**—Con.

[For meaning of abbreviations and symbols, see introductory text]

Item	Dickinson	Doniphan	Douglas	Edwards	Elk	Ellis	Ellsworth
INVENTORY							
Any poultry ----------------------------------- farms, 1987..	61	45	71	11	29	84	64
1982..	97	59	105	22	42	111	57
Chickens 3 months old or older ------------ farms, 1987..	54	41	60	10	29	82	61
1982..	87	54	95	22	39	106	56
number, 1987..	18 274	1 441	2 634	892	1 071	2 762	2 356
1982..	19 891	2 352	3 660	1 517	1 501	4 045	3 255
Hens and pullets of laying age ------------- farms, 1987..	54	41	58	10	28	82	61
1982..	87	53	93	22	39	106	55
number, 1987..	18 160	(D)	2 543	(D)	689	2 476	(D)
1982..	19 765	(D)	3 471	1 517	(D)	(D)	3 157
1987 farms by inventory:							
1 to 99 ---	47	37	56	9	26	79	56
100 to 399 ---	5	4	1	1	2	3	5
400 to 3,199 --	1	-	1	-	-	-	-
3,200 to 9,999 --	-	-	-	-	-	-	-
10,000 to 19,999 --	1	-	-	-	-	-	-
20,000 to 49,999 --	-	-	-	-	-	-	-
50,000 to 99,999 --	-	-	-	-	-	-	-
100,000 or more ------------------------------- farms..	-	-	-	-	-	-	-
number..	-	-	-	-	-	-	-
Pullets 3 months old or older not of							
laying age ----------------------------------- farms, 1987..	5	2	6	2	6	11	3
1982..	2	4	9	-	3	2	6
number, 1987..	114	(D)	91	(D)	182	286	(D)
1982..	126	(D)	189	-	(D)	(D)	98
Pullet chicks and pullets under 3 months							
old -- farms, 1987..	1	2	1	-	1	-	-
1982..	1	1	1	-	1	2	-
number, 1987..	(D)	(D)	(D)	-	(D)	(D)	-
1982..	(D)	(D)	(D)	2	(D)	(D)	3
Broilers and other meat-type chickens ------- farms, 1987..	7	9	6	2	3	6	9
1982..	9	11	21	4	4	11	(D)
number, 1987..	261	438	503	(D)	45	633	733
1982..	503	664	773	(D)	227	493	
Turkeys -- farms, 1987..	2	3	7	-	4	7	4
1982..	2	2	5	-	3	6	1
number, 1987..	(D)	9	75	-	17	37	35
1982..	(D)	(D)	22	-	13	44	(D)
Turkey hens kept for breeding ------------- farms, 1987..	-	2	4	-	2	4	-
1982..	-	2	2	-	1	1	1
number, 1987..	-	(D)	37	-	(D)	13	(D)
1982..	-	(D)	(D)	-	(D)	(D)	
Ducks, geese, and other poultry ------------- farms, 1987..	17	12	18	2	5	9	11
1982..	18	5	20	2	9	10	7
SALES							
Any poultry sold ---------------------------- farms, 1987..	27	17	35	4	8	22	31
1982..	34	17	45	9	11	34	27
$1,000, 1987..	(D)	6	159	(D)	5	6	9
1982..	279	9	22	7	40	13	11
Hens and pullets sold --------------------- farms, 1987..	4	2	12	1	2	1	2
1982..	15	5	10	5	3	7	5
number, 1987..	(D)	(D)	707	(D)	(D)	(D)	(D)
1982..	(D)	249	1 253	400	(D)	902	561
Hens and pullets of laying age sold ------- farms, 1987..	4	2	11	1	2	1	2
1982..	14	6	10	5	3	7	5
number, 1987..	(D)	(D)	(D)	(D)	(D)	(D)	(D)
1982..	(D)	249	1 253	400	(D)	902	561
Pullets not of laying age sold ------------ farms, 1987..	1	-	1	-	1	-	-
1982..	1	-	-	-	1	-	-
number, 1987..	(D)	-	(D)	-	(D)	-	-
1982..	(D)	-	-	-	(D)	-	-
Broilers and other meat-type chickens sold--- farms, 1987..	2	-	2	-	-	1	2
1982..	2	1	1	2	1	-	1
number, 1987..	(D)	-	(D)	2	1	(D)	(D)
1982..	(D)	-	404	(D)	(D)	-	(D)
1987 farms by number sold:							
1 to 1,999 --	2	-	-	-	-	1	2
2,000 to 59,999 ---	-	-	-	-	-	-	-
60,000 to 99,999 --	-	-	2	-	-	-	-
100,000 to 199,999 --------------------------------------	-	-	-	-	-	-	-
200,000 to 499,999 --------------------------------------	-	-	-	-	-	-	-
500,000 or more --------------------------------- farms..	-	-	-	-	-	-	-
number..	-	-	-	-	-	-	-
Turkeys sold --------------------------------- farms, 1987..	1	-	4	-	1	-	-
1982..	-	-	1	-	2	-	-
number, 1987..	(D)	-	35	-	(D)	-	-
1982..	-	-	(D)	-	(D)	-	-
Turkeys for slaughter sold ----------------- farms, 1987..	1	-	4	-	1	-	-
1982..	-	-	1	-	2	-	-
number, 1987..	(D)	-	35	-	(D)	-	-
1982..	-	-	(D)	-	(D)	-	-
Ducks, geese, and other poultry sold -------- farms, 1987..	2	1	6	2	-	1	2
1982..	2	-	3	1	3	1	1

Table 14. **Poultry—Inventory and Sales: 1987 and 1982**—Con.

[For meaning of abbreviations and symbols, see introductory text]

Item	Finney	Ford	Franklin	Geary	Gove	Graham	Grant
INVENTORY							
Any poultry — farms, 1987..	36	33	61	24	32	20	31
1982..	22	39	142	26	45	33	34
Chickens 3 months old or older — farms, 1987..	30	29	59	23	28	20	29
1982..	20	37	134	25	45	30	34
number, 1987..	607	825	3 367	2 316	834	661	850
1982..	816	1 063	4 933	1 863	1 238	986	1 131
Hens and pullets of laying age — farms, 1987..	30	29	69	22	28	20	28
1982..	20	37	131	24	45	30	34
number, 1987..	(D)	(D)	3 213	(D)	(D)	572	625
1982..	616	(D)	4 677	1 682	(D)	(D)	1 001
1987 farms by inventory:							
1 to 99	30	29	63	16	26	20	28
100 to 399	-	-	4	4	2	-	-
400 to 3,199	-	-	2	2	-	-	-
3,200 to 9,999	-	-	-	-	-	-	-
10,000 to 19,999	-	-	-	-	-	-	-
20,000 to 49,999	-	-	-	-	-	-	-
50,000 to 99,999	-	-	-	-	-	-	-
100,000 or more — farms.. number..	-	-	-	-	-	-	-
Pullets 3 months old or older not of laying age — farms, 1987..	1	3	11	3	1	5	4
1982..	5	3	16	5	1	1	5
number, 1987..	(D)	(D)	154	(D)	(D)	89	25
1982..	200	(D)	256	181	(D)	(D)	130
Pullet chicks and pullets under 3 months old — farms, 1987..	1	1	3	-	-	-	1
1982..	1	3	2	-	-	-	2
number, 1987..	(D)	(D)	9	-	-	-	(D)
1982..	(D)	(D)	(D)	-	-	-	(D)
Broilers and other meat-type chickens — farms, 1987..	6	3	10	3	5	3	9
1982..	7	4	19	6	9	3	11
number, 1987..	90	(D)	350	200	550	86	657
1982..	207	505	561	217	277	325	1 318
Turkeys — farms, 1987..	1	2	4	1	2	-	1
1982..	2	1	12	2	5	4	4
number, 1987..	(D)	(D)	17	(D)	(D)	-	(D)
1982..	(D)	(D)	114	(D)	8	17	(D)
Turkey hens kept for breeding — farms, 1987..	1	-	3	1	-	-	1
1982..	1	-	10	2	4	1	3
number, 1987..	(D)	(D)	(D)	(D)	(D)	-	(D)
1982..	(D)	-	46	(D)	4	(D)	(D)
Ducks, geese, and other poultry — farms, 1987..	12	13	30	4	2	4	8
1982..	7	6	36	9	6	6	3
SALES							
Any poultry sold — farms, 1987..	11	14	39	13	12	3	12
1982..	5	14	54	16	8	10	13
$1,000, 1987..	(Z)	(D)	18	16	3	(D)	2
1982..	2	2	18	11	(Z)	3	5
Hens and pullets sold — farms, 1987..	5	5	12	2	2	1	1
1982..	7	4	20	2	1	-	4
number, 1987..	95	(D)	329	(D)	(D)	(D)	(D)
1982..	-	44	1 093	(D)	(D)	93	94
Hens and pullets of laying age sold — farms, 1987..	3	4	12	2	1	3	1
1982..	-	4	20	2	-	-	4
number, 1987..	(D)	215	329	(D)	(D)	-	(D)
1982..	-	44	1 093	(D)	(D)	(D)	94
Pullets not of laying age sold — farms, 1987..	2	1	-	-	1	1	-
1982..	-	-	-	-	-	1	-
number, 1987..	(D)	(D)	-	-	(D)	(D)	-
1982..	-	-	-	-	-	(D)	-
Broilers and other meat-type chickens sold — farms, 1987..	-	2	4	1	4	1	4
1982..	-	1	1	1	-	-	1
number, 1987..	-	(D)	180	(D)	350	(D)	750
1982..	-	(D)	442	(D)	(D)	(D)	835
1987 farms by number sold:							
1 to 1,999	-	1	4	1	4	1	4
2,000 to 59,999	-	1	-	-	-	-	-
60,000 to 99,999	-	-	-	-	-	-	-
100,000 to 199,999	-	-	-	-	-	-	-
200,000 to 499,999	-	-	-	-	-	-	-
500,000 or more — farms.. number..	-	-	-	-	-	-	-
Turkeys sold — farms, 1987..	-	1	1	2	2	-	1
1982..	-	1	2	-	-	1	1
number, 1987..	-	(D)	(D)	(D)	(D)	(D)	(D)
1982..	-	(D)	(D)	-	-	(D)	(D)
Turkeys for slaughter sold — farms, 1987..	-	1	2	-	2	-	1
1982..	-	1	-	2	-	2	1
number, 1987..	-	(D)	(D)	(D)	(D)	(D)	(D)
1982..	-	(D)	(D)	-	-	(D)	(D)
Ducks, geese, and other poultry sold — farms, 1987..	2	2	9	2	-	1	2
1982..	-	1	16	2	1	-	1

Table 14. **Poultry—Inventory and Sales: 1987 and 1982**—Con.

[For meaning of abbreviations and symbols, see introductory text]

Item	Gray	Greeley	Greenwood	Hamilton	Harper	Harvey	Haskell
INVENTORY							
Any poultry .... farms, 1987..	29	9	39	14	26	64	12
1982..	42	15	59	20	43	79	7
Chickens 3 months old or older ...... farms, 1987..	23	9	38	10	23	57	11
1982..	31	13	58	19	42	67	7
number, 1987..	678	370	1 048	266	496	242 016	708
1982..	781	394	1 679	655	805	207 812	205
Hens and pullets of laying age .... farms, 1987..	23	9	38	10	23	55	11
1982..	30	13	56	19	42	65	7
number, 1987..	(D)	(D)	1 002	(D)	387	(D)	(D)
1982..	758	(D)	1 777	496	(D)	(D)	205
1987 farms by inventory:							
1 to 99	22	8	34	10	23	47	8
100 to 399	1	1	2	-	-	-	3
400 to 3,199	-	-	-	-	-	2	-
3,200 to 9,999	-	-	-	-	-	1	-
10,000 to 19,999	-	-	-	-	-	3	-
20,000 to 49,999	-	-	-	-	-	-	-
50,000 to 99,999 ...... farms..	-	-	-	-	-	2	-
100,000 or more ...... farms..	-	-	-	-	-	-	-
number..	-	-	-	-	-	-	-
Pullets 3 months old or older not of laying age ...... farms, 1987..	2	2	4	1	5	6	1
1982..	3	1	4	4	2	5	-
number, 1987..	(D)	(D)	46	(D)	109	(D)	(D)
1982..	23	(D)	102	159	(D)	(D)	-
Pullet chicks and pullets under 3 months old ...... farms, 1987..	1	-	1	2	-	1	-
1982..	2	-	-	-	-	4	-
number, 1987..	(D)	-	(D)	(D)	-	(D)	-
1982..	(D)	-	-	-	-	25 050	-
Broilers and other meat-type chickens .... farms, 1987..	5	2	8	3	4	8	-
1982..	13	2	9	3	4	15	-
number, 1987..	925	(D)	424	(D)	523	759	-
1982..	1 659	(D)	380	62	231	1 343	-
Turkeys ...... farms, 1987..	1	-	5	-	2	7	2
1982..	2	1	2	-	1	5	(D)
number, 1987..	(D)	-	55	-	(D)	(D)	(D)
1982..	(D)	(D)	(D)	-	(D)	(D)	-
Turkey hens kept for breeding .... farms, 1987..	-	1	2	-	2	2	1
1982..	-	1	1	-	1	3	-
number, 1987..	-	(D)	(D)	-	(D)	(D)	(D)
1982..	-	(D)	(D)	-	(D)	(D)	-
Ducks, geese, and other poultry .... farms, 1987..	7	2	11	3	4	11	4
1982..	6	3	7	5	4	13	2
SALES							
Any poultry sold ...... farms, 1987..	6	2	14	5	8	36	4
1982..	23	2	20	9	11	42	3
$1,000, 1987..	2	(D)	4	(Z)	1	2 813	3
1982..	3	(D)	9	1	12	2 718	1
Hens and pullets sold ...... farms, 1987..	1	2	2	3	3	11	-
1982..	2	-	2	2	2	20	1
number, 1987..	(D)	(D)	(D)	62	36	348 446	-
1982..	49	-	565	(D)	(D)	259 495	(D)
Hens and pullets of laying age sold .... farms, 1987..	1	2	2	1	2	8	-
1982..	3	-	6	2	2	18	1
number, 1987..	(D)	(D)	(D)	(D)	36	147 446	-
1982..	49	-	565	(D)	(D)	146 495	(D)
Pullets not of laying age sold .... farms, 1987..	-	-	1	2	-	3	-
1982..	-	-	-	-	-	4	-
number, 1987..	-	-	(D)	(D)	-	201 000	-
1982..	-	-	-	-	-	113 000	-
Broilers and other meat-type chickens sold... farms, 1987..	4	-	-	2	1	8	1
1982..	12	-	1	-	1	3	1
number, 1987..	610	-	-	(D)	(D)	666	-
1982..	1 381	-	(D)	-	(D)	575	(D)
1987 farms by number sold:							
1 to 1,999	4	-	-	2	1	4	-
2,000 to 59,999	-	-	-	-	-	-	-
60,000 to 99,999	-	-	-	-	-	-	-
100,000 to 199,999	-	-	-	-	-	-	-
200,000 to 499,999	-	-	-	-	-	-	-
500,000 or more ...... farms..	-	-	-	-	-	-	-
number..	-	-	-	-	-	-	-
Turkeys sold ...... farms, 1987..	-	-	2	-	-	3	1
1982..	-	-	3	-	-	3	(D)
number, 1987..	-	-	(D)	-	-	(D)	(D)
1982..	-	-	(D)	-	-	(D)	-
Turkeys for slaughter sold .... farms, 1987..	-	-	1	-	-	3	1
1982..	-	-	1	-	-	2	(D)
number, 1987..	-	-	(D)	-	-	(D)	(D)
1982..	-	-	(D)	-	-	(D)	-
Ducks, geese, and other poultry sold .... farms, 1987..	-	-	3	-	-	3	-
1982..	1	-	1	-	1	1	-

Table 14. **Poultry—Inventory and Sales: 1987 and 1982**—Con.

[For meaning of abbreviations and symbols, see introductory text]

Item	Hodgeman	Jackson	Jefferson	Jewell	Johnson	Kearny	Kingman	Kiowa
INVENTORY								
Any poultry _____ farms, 1987__	29	79	88	51	35	21	65	7
1982__	27	132	135	82	63	31	84	16
Chickens 3 months old or older _____ farms, 1987__	26	70	82	46	31	21	57	4
1982__	25	119	126	76	52	31	80	15
number, 1987__	772	(D)	2 473	2 024	2 305	838	2 049	91
1982__	1 059	(D)	5 213	3 300	11 961	1 107	3 632	491
Hens and pullets of laying age _____ farms, 1987__	26	69	81	46	31	21	56	4
1982__	25	118	126	75	52	30	79	15
number, 1987__	(D)	(D)	2 352	1 960	2 223	779	1 919	91
1982__	(D)	(D)	5 053	2 857	11 886	(D)	3 328	(D)
1987 farms by inventory:								
1 to 99 _____	24	65	78	43	26	20	52	4
100 to 399_____	2	3	5	2	4	1	4	-
400 to 3,199 _____	-	-	-	1	1	-	-	-
3,200 to 9,999 _____	-	-	-	-	-	-	-	-
10,000 to 19,999 _____	-	-	-	-	-	-	-	-
20,000 to 49,999 _____	-	1	-	-	-	-	-	-
50,000 to 99,999 _____	-	-	-	-	-	-	-	-
100,000 or more _____ farms__	-	-	-	-	-	-	-	-
number__	-	-	-	-	-	-	-	-
Pullets 3 months old or older not of laying age _____ farms, 1987__	2	7	6	3	7	4	4	-
1982__	2	11	12	8	7	2	9	1
number, 1987__	(D)	80	121	64	82	59	130	-
1982__	(D)	(D)	160	443	75	(D)	304	(D)
Pullet chicks and pullets under 3 months old _____ farms, 1987__	1	1	-	3	-	3	1	2
1982__	(D)	2	1	2	1	(D)	(D)	(D)
number, 1987__	(D)	(D)	(D)	350	(D)	-	(D)	(D)
1982__	(D)	(D)	-	(D)	(D)	3	15	3
Broilers and other meat-type chickens _____ farms, 1987__	4	12	9	8	4	2	17	3
number, 1987__	6	25	23	16	9	(D)	1 255	172
1982__	(D)	322	317	979	210	(D)	904	110
1982__	613	1 137	971	1 088	245			
Turkeys _____ farms, 1987__	2	7	7	4	4	4	2	-
1982__	1	8	10	3	4	6	1	-
number, 1987__	(D)	38	81	26	14	19	(D)	-
1982__	(D)	66	43	7	7	21	(f)	-
Turkey hens kept for breeding _____ farms, 1987__	1	5	8	3	3	4	2	-
1982__	1	7	8	2	2	3	1	-
number, 1987__	(D)	(D)	35	(D)	(D)	19	(D)	-
1982__	(D)	18	(D)	(D)	(D)	(D)	(D)	-
Ducks, geese, and other poultry _____ farms, 1987__	8	10	20	6	8	9	11	2
1982__	6	29	34	7	26	7	10	4
SALES								
Any poultry sold _____ farms, 1987__	8	27	20	17	15	6	19	2
1982__	11	51	46	31	19	11	29	5
$1,000, 1987__	2	(D)	16	13	17	6	8	(D)
1982__	5	405	30	17	111	3	19	3
Hens and pullets sold _____ farms, 1987__	-	5	6	5	4	2	5	-
1982__	2	17	15	12	7	1	8	-
number, 1987__	-	(D)	138	319	(D)	(D)	429	-
1982__	(D)	(D)	1 633	822	(D)	(D)	793	-
Hens and pullets of laying age sold _____ farms, 1987__	-	5	6	5	4	2	4	-
1982__	2	17	15	12	7	1	6	-
number, 1987__	-	(D)	138	319	(D)	(D)	(D)	-
1982__	(D)	(D)	1 633	822	(D)	(D)	793	-
Pullets not of laying age sold _____ farms, 1987__	-	1	-	-	-	-	1	-
number, 1987__	-	(D)	-	-	-	(D)	(D)	-
1982__	-	-	-	-	-	-	-	-
Broilers and other meat-type chickens sold____ farms, 1987__	-	2	1	1	1	1	2	2
1982__	1	6	3	2	2	2	2	(D)
number, 1987__	(D)	(D)	(D)	(D)	(D)	(D)	(D)	(D)
1982__		338						
1987 farms by number sold:								
1 to 1,999 _____	-	2	1	1	1	1	2	-
2,000 to 59,999 _____	-	-	-	-	-	-	-	-
60,000 to 99,999 _____	-	-	-	-	-	-	-	-
100,000 to 199,999 _____	-	-	-	-	-	-	-	-
200,000 to 499,999 _____	-	-	-	-	-	-	-	-
500,000 or more _____ farms__	-	-	-	-	-	-	-	-
number__	-	-	-	-	-	-	-	-
Turkeys sold _____ farms, 1987__	1	2	1	2	-	1	-	-
1982__	1	1	1	-	-	-	-	-
number, 1987__	(D)	(D)	(D)	(D)	-	(D)	-	-
1982__	(D)	-	-	-	-	-	-	-
Turkeys for slaughter sold _____ farms, 1987__	1	2	-	1	-	1	-	-
1982__	1	-	-	-	-	-	-	-
number, 1987__	(D)	(D)	-	(D)	-	(D)	-	-
1982__	(D)	-	-	-	-	-	-	-
Ducks, geese, and other poultry sold _____ farms, 1987__	1	2	2	-	2	4	1	1
1982__	1	5	2	1	4	3	1	-

Item	Labette	Lane	Leavenworth	Lincoln	Linn	Logan	Lyon	McPherson
INVENTORY								
Any poultry .... farms, 1987..	53	16	111	43	55	25	65	93
1982..	96	22	142	54	63	34	96	156
Chickens 3 months old or older .... farms, 1987..	47	15	95	39	47	23	55	88
1982..	84	22	129	50	53	33	84	142
number, 1987..	999	550	2 818	1 151	1 506	747	(D)	364 291
1982..	5 593	1 098	6 645	2 075	2 360	1 035	(D)	218 100
Hens and pullets of laying age .... farms, 1987..	47	15	95	39	47	23	54	87
1982..	83	22	123	50	49	33	84	137
number, 1987..	(D)	550	2 496	1 040	1 467	(D)	(D)	(D)
1982..	5 494	(D)	5 890	1 978	2 255	(D)	(D)	(D)
1987 farms by inventory:								
1 to 99	47	14	93	38	44	22	50	75
100 to 399	-	1	2	1	3	1	2	3
400 to 3,199	-	-	-	-	-	-	-	-
3,200 to 9,999	-	-	-	-	-	-	-	1
10,000 to 19,999	-	-	-	-	-	-	-	1
20,000 to 49,999	-	-	-	-	-	-	-	1
50,000 to 99,999	-	-	-	-	-	-	2	5
100,000 or more .... farms..	-	-	-	-	-	-	-	2
number..	-	-	-	-	-	-	-	-
Pullets 3 months old or older not of laying age .... farms, 1987..	4	-	6	5	3	3	1	3
1982..	8	2	23	5	6	1	9	15
number, 1987..	(D)	-	122	111	39	(D)	(D)	(D)
1982..	99	(D)	755	97	105	(D)	128	(D)
Pullet chicks and pullets under 3 months old .... farms, 1987..	1	-	3	-	-	1	3	3
1982..	4	1	6	3	2	-	5	5
number, 1987..	(D)	-	73	-	-	(D)	(D)	(D)
1982..	(D)	(D)	511	(D)	(D)	-	(D)	(D)
Broilers and other meat-type chickens .... farms, 1987..	7	4	14	4	5	2	5	11
1982..	11	8	19	6	9	3	15	21
number, 1987..	294	360	730	249	89	(D)	35	1 832
1982..	233	280	808	199	409	(D)	481	1 371
Turkeys .... farms, 1987..	5	2	13	4	3	3	6	6
1982..	15	1	6	4	4	8	6	7
number, 1987..	40	(D)	1 029	-	14	18	48	342
1982..	63	(D)	17	15	25	25	34	42
Turkey hens kept for breeding .... farms, 1987..	3	-	8	-	2	2	6	1
1982..	14	-	4	4	3	4	4	4
number, 1987..	(D)	-	(D)	-	(D)	(D)	(D)	(D)
1982..	42	-	(D)	(D)	(D)	8	12	7
Ducks, geese, and other poultry .... farms, 1987..	12	7	35	5	17	4	19	22
1982..	25	2	35	10	12	9	24	16
SALES								
Any poultry sold .... farms, 1987..	16	5	36	9	12	5	22	44
1982..	24	8	55	18	21	7	24	77
$1,000, 1987..	4	2	29	4	15	2	936	6 509
1982..	50	9	46	7	11	1	1 103	4 161
Hens and pullets sold .... farms, 1987..	4	-	9	3	1	2	4	17
1982..	10	1	14	4	4	4	6	33
number, 1987..	86	1	199	(D)	(D)	(D)	151 980	381 266
1982..	968	(D)	1 484	561	905	155	164 198	211 034
Hens and pullets of laying age sold .... farms, 1987..	4	-	9	3	-	2	3	14
1982..	10	1	14	4	5	4	5	31
number, 1987..	86	-	199	(D)	905	(D)	(D)	273 866
1982..	(D)	(D)	1 484	561	155	(D)	(D)	(D)
Pullets not of laying age sold .... farms, 1987..	-	-	-	-	-	1	-	3
1982..	1	-	-	-	1	-	2	2
number, 1987..	-	-	-	-	(D)	-	(D)	107 400
1982..	(D)	-	-	-	-	-	(D)	(D)
Broilers and other meat-type chickens sold .... farms, 1987..	-	-	3	1	-	1	-	5
1982..	1	-	-	-	3	-	1	10
number, 1987..	-	-	110	(D)	-	(D)	-	1 410
1982..	(D)	-	-	-	(D)	(D)	(D)	1 375
1987 farms by number sold:								
1 to 1,999	-	-	3	1	-	1	-	5
2,000 to 59,999	-	-	-	-	-	-	-	-
60,000 to 99,999	-	-	-	-	-	-	-	-
100,000 to 199,999	-	-	-	-	-	-	-	-
200,000 to 499,999	-	-	-	-	-	-	-	-
500,000 or more .... farms..	-	-	-	-	-	-	-	-
number..	-	-	-	-	-	-	-	-
Turkeys sold .... farms, 1987..	2	-	1	-	1	1	1	5
1982..	2	-	-	-	1	2	-	2
number, 1987..	(D)	-	(D)	-	(D)	(D)	(D)	(D)
1982..	(D)	-	-	-	-	(D)	-	(D)
Turkeys for slaughter sold .... farms, 1987..	2	-	1	-	1	1	1	5
1982..	1	-	-	-	-	2	-	2
number, 1987..	(D)	-	(D)	-	(D)	(D)	(D)	(D)
1982..	(D)	-	-	-	-	(D)	-	(D)
Ducks, geese, and other poultry sold .... farms, 1987..	4	-	8	-	1	-	5	3
1982..	4	-	7	2	2	-	5	6

Table 14. **Poultry—Inventory and Sales: 1987 and 1982**—Con.

[For meaning of abbreviations and symbols, see introductory text]

Item	Marion	Marshall	Meade	Miami	Mitchell	Montgomery	Morris	Morton
INVENTORY								
Any poultry ------ farms, 1987--	60	63	17	95	35	68	43	11
1982--	119	77	26	125	37	104	43	26
Chickens 3 months old or older ----- farms, 1987--	73	55	16	86	32	56	40	10
1982--	109	73	23	112	37	96	39	26
number, 1987--	165 871	3 756	535	1 953	1 330	1 474	1 531	359
1982--	159 661	14 049	489	4 356	1 355	2 621	1 845	832
Hens and pullets of laying age ------ farms, 1987--	73	55	16	61	32	54	40	10
1982--	109	72	23	111	37	95	39	26
number, 1987--	(D)	3 205	(D)	1 704	(D)	1 343	(D)	(D)
1982--	159 491	13 444	489	3 801	(D)	2 350	1 789	(D)
1987 farms by inventory:								
1 to 99 -----	56	43	14	60	29	53	36	8
100 to 399 -----	6	11	2	1	3	1	4	2
400 to 3,199 -----	2	1	-	-	-	-	-	-
3,200 to 9,999 -----	3	-	-	-	-	-	-	-
10,000 to 19,999 -----	2	-	-	-	-	-	-	-
20,000 to 49,999 -----	4	-	-	-	-	-	-	-
50,000 to 99,999 ----- farms--	-	-	-	-	-	-	-	-
100,000 or more ----- number--	-	-	-	-	-	-	-	-
Pullets 3 months old or older not of								
laying age ----- farms, 1987--	3	5	1	14	4	6	3	1
1982--	7	7	-	11	-	11	4	1
number, 1987--	(D)	551	(D)	249	(D)	131	(D)	(D)
1982--	170	605	-	555	(D)	262	56	(D)
Pullet chicks and pullets under 3 months								
old ----- farms, 1987--	1	1	1	2	-	3	-	-
1982--	3	4	-	1	-	3	-	-
number, 1987--	140	300	(D)	(D)	-	(D)	-	-
1982--	12	18	-	6	5	6	2	1
Broilers and other meat-type chickens -------- farms, 1987--	12	18	-	19	4	14	7	5
1982--	14	17	5	(D)	232	206	(D)	(D)
number, 1987--	673	1 259	-	(D)	332	351	454	192
1982--	1 044	910	345	509				
Turkeys ----- farms, 1987--	4	7	2	8	-	1	6	1
1982--	6	5	-	6	-	4	-	5
number, 1987--	47	53	(D)	526	-	(D)	10	(D)
1982--	70	94	-	(D)	-	26	-	67
Turkey hens kept for breeding ----- farms, 1987--	3	4	1	5	-	1	6	-
1982--	4	3	-	1	-	3	-	3
number, 1987--	(D)	22	(D)	(D)	-	(D)	10	-
1982--	6	8	-	(D)	-	(D)	-	11
Ducks, geese, and other poultry ----- farms, 1987--	15	18	1	23	3	26	9	4
1982--	10	13	3	30	2	25	4	9
SALES								
Any poultry sold ----- farms, 1987--	35	20	6	35	7	17	14	3
1982--	61	42	11	43	9	26	14	6
$1,000, 1987--	1 593	152	(D)	14	3	3	7	(D)
1982--	1 739	141	1	151	5	9	6	2
Hens and pullets sold ----- farms, 1987--	15	2	3	9	1	5	2	-
1982--	22	23	3	10	-	6	(D)	-
number, 1987--	148 825	(D)	207	175	(D)	62	(D)	1
1982--	152 176	8 906	(D)	(D)	(D)	113	(D)	(D)
Hens and pullets of laying age sold -------- farms, 1987--	15	2	3	9	1	5	2	-
1982--	22	23	3	10	-	7	(D)	1
number, 1987--	148 825	(D)	207	175	(D)	62	(D)	-
1982--	152 176	8 906	(D)	(D)	(D)	113	(D)	(D)
Pullets not of laying age sold ----- farms, 1987--	-	-	-	-	-	-	-	-
1982--	-	-	-	-	-	-	-	-
number, 1987--	-	-	-	-	-	-	-	-
1982--	-	-	-	-	-	-	-	-
Broilers and other meat-type chickens sold ----- farms, 1987--	2	3	1	-	1	4	-	-
1982--	7	3	4	8	-	1	-	-
number, 1987--	(D)	-	(D)	-	(D)	267	-	-
1982--	202	(D)	(D)	277	-	(D)	-	-
1987 farms by number sold:								
1 to 1,999 -----	2	-	1	-	1	4	-	-
2,000 to 59,999 -----	-	-	-	-	-	-	-	-
60,000 to 99,999 -----	-	-	-	-	-	-	-	-
100,000 to 199,999 -----	-	-	-	-	-	-	-	-
200,000 to 499,999 -----	-	-	-	-	-	-	-	-
500,000 or more ----- farms--	-	-	-	-	-	-	-	-
number--								
Turkeys sold ----- farms, 1987--	1	-	2	4	-	2	-	2
1982--	2	-	-	2	-	-	-	-
number, 1987--	(D)	-	(D)	(D)	-	(D)	-	(D)
1982--	(D)	-	-	(D)	-	-	-	-
Turkeys for slaughter sold ----- farms, 1987--	1	-	2	4	-	1	-	2
1982--	2	-	-	2	-	-	-	-
number, 1987--	(D)	-	(D)	(D)	-	(D)	-	(D)
1982--	(D)	-	-	(D)	-	-	-	-
Ducks, geese, and other poultry sold --------- farms, 1987--	5	1	1	7	2	2	2	-
1982--	3	1	-	5	1	2	1	1

Table 14. **Poultry—Inventory and Sales: 1987 and 1982**—Con.

[For meaning of abbreviations and symbols, see introductory text]

Item	Nemaha	Neosho	Ness	Norton	Osage	Osborne	Ottawa	Pawnee
INVENTORY								
Any poultry .... farms, 1987..	54	52	34	34	63	44	43	19
1982..	78	63	32	40	95	59	49	31
Chickens 3 months old or older .... farms, 1987..	49	47	32	34	55	41	40	16
1982..	74	57	31	40	88	59	43	30
number, 1987..	91 184	2 431	819	865	1 473	1 901	2 007	570
1982..	110 073	3 282	1 004	1 891	4 694	1 966	2 056	1 321
Hens and pullets of laying age .... farms, 1987..	48	47	31	34	52	41	38	16
1982..	72	55	31	40	87	59	43	30
number, 1987..	45 947	2 095	776	(D)	1 351	1 837	1 932	(D)
1982..	(D)	2 766	1 004	1 814	4 387	(D)	1 984	(D)
1987 farms by inventory:								
1 to 99	35	43	31	34	50	37	32	15
100 to 399	8	2	-	-	2	3	5	1
400 to 3,199	-	2	-	-	-	1	1	-
3,200 to 9,999	4	-	-	-	-	-	-	-
10,000 to 19,999	1	-	-	-	-	-	-	-
20,000 to 49,999	-	-	-	-	-	-	-	-
50,000 to 99,999	-	-	-	-	-	-	-	-
100,000 or more .... farms..	-	-	-	-	-	-	-	-
number..	-	-	-	-	-	-	-	-
Pullets 3 months old or older not of								
laying age .... farms, 1987..	11	7	3	1	6	5	3	1
1982..	5	10	-	4	11	1	5	1
number, 1987..	45 237	336	43	(D)	122	64	75	(D)
1982..	(D)	516	-	77	307	(D)	72	(D)
Pullet chicks and pullets under 3 months								
old .... farms, 1987..	-	-	1	1	2	-	-	-
1982..	1	1	-	-	-	-	1	-
number, 1987..	-	-	(D)	(D)	2	-	-	-
1982..	(D)	(D)	-	-	(D)	-	(D)	-
Broilers and other meat-type chickens .... farms, 1987..	8	3	5	5	11	4	4	3
1982..	12	7	4	5	10	7	7	5
number, 1987..	543	(D)	(D)	38	442	525	328	(D)
1982..	751	331	(D)	172	646	300	538	392
Turkeys .... farms, 1987..	4	2	1	4	7	3	5	1
1982..	2	9	1	-	4	3	-	1
number, 1987..	30	(D)	(D)	8	93	36	37	(D)
1982..	(D)	65	(D)	-	46	8	-	(D)
Turkey hens kept for breeding .... farms, 1987..	-	1	1	4	4	1	2	1
1982..	2	8	-	-	3	2	-	-
number, 1987..	-	(D)	(D)	8	(D)	(D)	(D)	(D)
1982..	(D)	(D)	-	-	(D)	(D)	-	-
Ducks, geese, and other poultry .... farms, 1987..	8	16	11	2	22	11	18	4
1982..	3	21	5	6	18	7	11	9
SALES								
Any poultry sold .... farms, 1987..	22	12	11	5	16	17	15	6
1982..	39	16	10	16	28	12	24	10
$1,000, 1987..	521	12	2	2	9	10	62	3
1982..	812	27	2	6	29	5	54	6
Hens and pullets sold .... farms, 1987..	12	3	1	-	1	4	3	2
1982..	20	9	-	2	12	4	4	-
number, 1987..	73 465	78	(D)	(D)	(D)	104	(D)	(D)
1982..	150 742	586	-	(D)	1 059	240	(D)	(D)
Hens and pullets of laying age sold .... farms, 1987..	11	3	1	-	1	4	3	2
1982..	20	9	-	2	12	4	4	-
number, 1987..	(D)	78	(D)	-	(D)	104	(D)	(D)
1982..	(D)	586	-	(D)	(D)	240	(D)	(D)
Pullets not of laying age sold .... farms, 1987..	1	-	-	-	1	-	-	-
1982..	1	-	-	-	-	-	-	-
number, 1987..	(D)	-	-	-	(D)	-	-	-
1982..	(D)	-	-	-	-	-	-	-
Broilers and other meat-type chickens sold .... farms, 1987..	1	-	2	-	2	2	-	-
1982..	4	1	1	-	4	-	-	-
number, 1987..	(D)	-	(D)	-	(D)	(D)	-	-
1982..	155	(D)	(D)	-	(D)	-	-	-
1987 farms by number sold:								
1 to 1,999	1	-	2	-	2	2	-	-
2,000 to 59,999	-	-	-	-	-	-	-	-
60,000 to 99,999	-	-	-	-	-	-	-	-
100,000 to 199,999	-	-	-	-	-	-	-	-
200,000 to 499,999	-	-	-	-	-	-	-	-
500,000 or more .... farms..	-	-	-	-	-	-	-	-
number..	-	-	-	-	-	-	-	-
Turkeys sold .... farms, 1987..	-	-	-	-	-	1	4	-
1982..	-	1	-	-	-	(D)	14	-
number, 1987..	-	(D)	-	-	-	(D)	4	-
1982..	-	1	-	-	-	-	14	-
number, 1987..	-	(D)	-	-	-	-	-	-
1982..	-	-	-	-	-	-	-	-
Ducks, geese, and other poultry sold .... farms, 1987..	-	-	2	-	3	2	2	-
1982..	-	4	1	-	2	-	2	1

Table 14. Poultry—Inventory and Sales: 1987 and 1982—Con.

[For meaning of abbreviations and symbols, see introductory text]

Item	Phillips	Pottawatomie	Pratt	Rawlins	Reno	Republic	Rice	Riley
INVENTORY								
Any poultry .... farms, 1987..	54	70	27	46	154	51	30	43
1982..	71	83	39	73	229	59	39	63
Chickens 3 months old or older ..... farms, 1987..	46	61	21	43	129	47	25	38
1982..	68	74	34	68	215	54	35	60
number, 1987..	1 109	(D)	425	2 057	139 418	1 664	730	7 996
1982..	3 794	(D)	5 643	5 199	176 823	4 437	1 736	8 810
Hens and pullets of laying age .... farms, 1987..	46	56	21	43	126	47	25	38
1982..	66	73	33	66	215	54	34	59
number, 1987..	(D)	3 249	(D)	1 995	139 254	1 573	(D)	(D)
1982..	3 108	3 974	(D)	5 199	176 242	4 187	1 636	(D)
1987 farms by inventory:								
1 to 99	45	47	20	42	103	43	23	35
100 to 399	1	8	1	-	17	4	2	2
400 to 3,199	-	1	-	1	1	-	-	-
3,200 to 9,999	-	-	-	-	1	-	-	1
10,000 to 19,999	-	-	-	-	4	-	-	-
20,000 to 49,999	-	-	-	-	2	-	-	-
50,000 to 99,999 .... farms..	-	-	-	-	-	-	-	-
100,000 or more .... farms..	-	-	-	-	-	-	-	-
number..	-	-	-	-	-	-	-	-
Pullets 3 months old or older not of laying age .... farms, 1987..	3	6	2	4	9	4	1	3
1982..	4	6	2	2	15	6	3	4
number, 1987..	(D)	(D)	(D)	62	164	91	(D)	(D)
1982..	686	(D)	(D)	-	581	250	100	(D)
Pullet chicks and pullets under 3 months old .... farms, 1987..	-	2	-	-	3	-	2	1
1982..	-	2	-	-	4	-	2	(D)
number, 1987..	-	(D)	-	-	50	-	(D)	(D)
1982..	-	(D)	-	-	19	-	-	-
Broilers and other meat-type chickens ...... farms, 1987..	10	9	5	6	22	7	6	8
1982..	9	16	8	15	36	7	6	9
number, 1987..	623	301	500	270	4 042	274	348	454
1982..	386	1 282	613	1 535	1 622	520	333	217
Turkeys .... farms, 1987..	1	3	4	1	8	3	-	1
1982..	2	4	3	1	14	4	2	3
number, 1987..	(D)	8	10	(D)	5 739	(D)	(D)	(D)
1982..	(D)	41	31	(D)	101	20	(D)	16
Turkey hens kept for breeding .... farms, 1987..	-	2	3	-	3	-	-	-
1982..	1	2	3	1	10	-	2	2
number, 1987..	-	(D)	(D)	-	(D)	-	-	-
1982..	(D)	(D)	31	(D)	46	-	(D)	(D)
Ducks, geese, and other poultry .... farms, 1987..	6	10	12	4	29	15	8	6
1982..	7	8	11	8	35	12	4	14
SALES								
Any poultry sold .... farms, 1987..	12	26	6	12	83	20	7	14
1982..	19	34	20	17	118	26	16	26
$1,000, 1987..	2	(D)	(D)	10	1 777	6	2	(D)
1982..	10	2 081	441	29	1 920	24	8	87
Hens and pullets sold .... farms, 1987..	3	6	2	3	27	1	1	2
1982..	8	9	8	5	40	7	6	8
number, 1987..	(D)	(D)	(D)	(D)	117 631	(D)	(D)	(D)
1982..	1 050	(D)	2 812	(D)	161 830	1 519	369	(D)
Hens and pullets of laying age sold .... farms, 1987..	3	6	2	3	25	1	1	2
1982..	8	7	8	5	39	7	4	8
number, 1987..	(D)	317	(D)	(D)	(D)	(D)	(D)	(D)
1982..	1 050	1 084	2 812	(D)	(D)	1 519	369	(D)
Pullets not of laying age sold .... farms, 1987..	-	1	-	-	2	-	-	-
1982..	-	2	-	-	2	-	-	-
number, 1987..	-	(D)	-	-	(D)	-	-	-
1982..	-	(D)	-	-	(D)	-	-	-
Broilers and other meat-type chickens sold .... farms, 1987..	2	1	-	2	11	-	1	2
1982..	2	4	-	2	10	-	-	(D)
number, 1987..	(D)	(D)	-	(D)	25 405	-	(D)	(D)
1982..	(D)	230	(D)	(D)	1 690	-	(D)	-
1987 farms by number sold:								
1 to 1,999	2	1	-	-	7	-	1	2
2,000 to 59,999	-	-	-	-	4	-	-	-
60,000 to 99,999	-	-	-	-	-	-	-	-
100,000 to 199,999	-	-	-	-	-	-	-	-
200,000 to 499,999	-	-	-	-	-	-	-	-
500,000 or more .... farms..	-	-	-	-	-	-	-	-
number..	-	-	-	-	-	-	-	-
Turkeys sold .... farms, 1987..	-	2	1	1	2	1	-	-
1982..	-	(D)	3	(D)	3	(D)	-	-
number, 1987..	-	(D)	(D)	(D)	(D)	(D)	-	-
1982..	-	-	27	-	(D)	-	-	-
Turkeys for slaughter sold .... farms, 1987..	-	-	1	1	2	1	-	-
1982..	-	-	1	-	2	-	-	-
number, 1987..	-	-	(D)	(D)	(D)	(D)	-	-
1982..	-	-	(D)	-	(D)	-	-	-
Ducks, geese, and other poultry sold .... farms, 1987..	2	1	-	1	5	3	-	-
1982..	-	3	2	1	12	4	1	2

Table 14. **Poultry—Inventory and Sales: 1987 and 1982**—Con.

[For meaning of abbreviations and symbols, see introductory text]

Item	Rooks	Rush	Russell	Saline	Scott	Sedgwick	Seward	Shawnee
INVENTORY								
Any poultry .... farms, 1987..	36	32	34	44	11	87	16	67
1982..	40	45	46	78	21	140	21	89
Chickens 3 months old or older .... farms, 1987..	30	28	32	40	11	75	15	59
1982..	40	45	41	75	20	120	21	78
number, 1987..	965	5 743	903	3 506	248	115 757	275	1 181
1982..	1 132	7 629	1 747	3 778	1 005	174 727	678	13 869
Hens and pullets of laying age .... farms, 1987..	30	28	32	40	11	73	15	59
1982..	40	44	41	74	20	119	21	78
number, 1987..	764	5 743	(D)	3 493	248	(D)	275	1 110
1982..	(D)	(D)	1 698	3 444	(D)	(D)	678	(D)
1987 farms by inventory:								
1 to 99	30	27	32	38	11	72	15	59
100 to 399	-	-	-	1	-	-	-	-
400 to 3,199	-	-	-	1	-	-	-	-
3,200 to 9,999	-	1	-	-	-	-	-	-
10,000 to 19,999	-	-	-	-	-	-	-	-
20,000 to 49,999	-	-	-	-	-	-	-	-
50,000 to 99,999 .... farms..	-	-	-	-	-	1	-	-
100,000 or more .... number..	-	-	-	-	-	-	-	-
Pullets 3 months old or older not of								
laying age .... farms, 1987..	7	-	2	3	-	9	-	6
1982..	3	2	3	7	2	7	-	2
number, 1987..	201	-	(D)	13	(D)	(D)	-	71
1982..	(D)	(D)	49	334	(D)	(D)	-	(D)
Pullet chicks and pullets under 3 months								
old .... farms, 1987..	1	-	3	-	1	4	-	-
1982..	1	-	-	1	-	7	-	3
number, 1987..	(D)	-	(D)	-	(D)	(D)	-	-
1982..	(D)	-	-	(D)	-	22 256	-	(D)
Broilers and other meat-type chickens .... farms, 1987..	11	5	5	6	1	19	1	6
1982..	4	5	8	10	3	5	1	13
number, 1987..	432	865	438	150	(D)	311	(D)	198
1982..	200	370	701	344	330	796	(D)	477
Turkeys .... farms, 1987..	4	1	1	4	-	6	3	6
1982..	2	1	3	6	2	9	2	8
number, 1987..	14	(D)	(D)	41	-	(D)	8	35
1982..	(D)	(D)	(D)	20	(D)	(D)	6	36
Turkey hens kept for breeding .... farms, 1987..	-	-	1	2	-	4	-	5
1982..	1	-	2	2	1	7	2	5
number, 1987..	-	-	(D)	(D)	-	(D)	(D)	(D)
1982..	(D)	-	(D)	(D)	(D)	(D)	(D)	6
Ducks, geese, and other poultry .... farms, 1987..	6	5	6	9	1	31	6	27
1982..	8	3	10	17	1	38	3	27
SALES								
Any poultry sold .... farms, 1987..	11	12	9	16	5	29	2	13
1982..	15	17	16	36	9	66	7	35
$1,000, 1987..	2	(D)	1	43	1	1 260	(D)	21
1982..	2	76	5	32	7	2 599	2	120
Hens and pullets sold .... farms, 1987..	4	2	5	3	-	7	-	6
1982..	2	2	3	5	1	29	2	10
number, 1987..	156	(D)	137	(D)	(D)	133 968	-	566
1982..	(D)	(D)	200	447	(D)	150 696	(D)	(D)
Hens and pullets of laying age sold .... farms, 1987..	4	2	5	3	-	6	2	6
1982..	2	2	3	5	1	25	2	10
number, 1987..	156	(D)	137	(D)	-	(D)	-	(D)
1982..	(D)	(D)	200	447	(D)	103 636	(D)	(D)
Pullets not of laying age sold .... farms, 1987..	-	-	-	-	-	2	-	1
1982..	-	-	-	-	-	4	-	-
number, 1987..	-	-	-	-	-	(D)	-	(D)
1982..	-	-	-	-	-	47 060	-	-
Broilers and other meat-type chickens sold .... farms, 1987..	1	3	1	-	-	4	1	2
1982..	-	-	-	4	-	4	1	2
number, 1987..	(D)	265	(D)	-	-	375	(D)	(D)
1982..	-	-	-	200	-	255	(D)	(D)
1987 farms by number sold:								
1 to 1,999	1	3	1	-	-	4	1	2
2,000 to 59,999	-	-	-	-	-	-	-	-
60,000 to 99,999	-	-	-	-	-	-	-	-
100,000 to 199,999	-	-	-	-	-	-	-	-
200,000 to 499,999	-	-	-	-	-	-	-	-
500,000 or more .... farms..	-	-	-	-	-	-	-	-
number..	-	-	-	-	-	-	-	-
Turkeys sold .... farms, 1987..	-	-	-	-	-	3	-	3
1982..	-	-	-	1	-	5	-	3
number, 1987..	-	-	-	-	-	29 913	-	1 432
1982..	-	-	-	(D)	-	(D)	-	(D)
Turkeys for slaughter sold .... farms, 1987..	-	-	-	1	-	2	-	3
1982..	-	-	-	-	-	1	-	3
number, 1987..	-	-	-	(D)	-	(D)	-	(D)
1982..	-	-	-	(D)	-	(D)	-	(D)
Ducks, geese, and other poultry sold .... farms, 1987..	-	2	1	1	-	5	1	3
1982..	1	1	2	-	-	12	-	4

Table 14. **Poultry—Inventory and Sales: 1987 and 1982**—Con.

[For meaning of abbreviations and symbols, see introductory text]

Item	Sheridan	Sherman	Smith	Stafford	Stanton	Stevens	Sumner	Thomas
INVENTORY								
Any poultry .... farms, 1987..	28	34	61	28	13	15	56	36
1982..	44	38	73	34	16	26	89	30
Chickens 3 months old or older .... farms, 1987..	26	31	60	25	6	11	54	32
1982..	39	36	71	32	16	24	86	26
number, 1987..	819	903	2 209	677	382	283	2 068	757
1982..	1 405	1 298	2 813	1 111	658	735	2 289	1 011
Hens and pullets of laying age .... farms, 1987..	26	29	60	25	9	11	54	32
1982..	39	36	71	31	16	23	84	26
number, 1987..	(D)	800	1 900	(D)	(D)	(D)	(D)	735
1982..	(D)	(D)	2 721	1 037	(D)	(D)	1 956	1 011
1987 farms by inventory:								
1 to 99	27	29	55	26	8	11	50	32
100 to 399	1	-	5	-	1	-	4	-
400 to 3,199	-	-	-	-	-	-	-	-
3,200 to 9,999	-	-	-	-	-	-	-	-
10,000 to 19,999	-	-	-	-	-	-	-	-
20,000 to 49,999	-	-	-	-	-	-	-	-
50,000 to 99,999	-	-	-	-	-	-	-	-
100,000 or more .... farms..	-	-	-	-	-	-	-	-
number..	-	-	-	-	-	-	-	-
Pullets 3 months old or older not of laying age .... farms, 1987..	1	7	6	1	2	2	2	3
1982..	2	2	9	4	3	2	6	-
number, 1987..	(D)	103	309	(D)	(D)	(D)	(D)	22
1982..	(D)	(D)	92	74	(D)	(D)	333	-
Pullet chicks and pullets under 3 months old .... farms, 1987..	-	1	1	-	-	-	-	-
1982..	1	2	2	-	-	1	4	-
number, 1987..	-	(D)	(D)	-	-	-	-	-
1982..	(D)	(D)	(D)	-	-	(D)	27	-
Broilers and other meat-type chickens .... farms, 1987..	4	9	6	3	2	1	2	3
1982..	8	3	13	1	3	-	7	(D)
number, 1987..	127	492	433	(D)	(D)	-	(D)	(D)
1982..	497	125	628	(D)	(D)	(D)	456	(D)
Turkeys .... farms, 1987..	-	3	7	3	2	1	3	1
1982..	2	2	5	2	3	3	3	3
number, 1987..	-	35	14	120	(D)	(D)	32	(D)
1982..	(D)	(D)	32	(D)	11	(D)	28	(D)
Turkey hens kept for breeding .... farms, 1987..	-	2	7	2	2	-	3	1
1982..	-	2	5	1	3	3	2	-
number, 1987..	-	(D)	14	(D)	2	-	(D)	(D)
1982..	-	(D)	8	(D)	11	(D)	(D)	(D)
Ducks, geese, and other poultry .... farms, 1987..	2	5	16	7	6	6	13	6
1982..	5	9	9	8	2	9	16	6
SALES								
Any poultry sold .... farms, 1987..	5	7	21	9	3	2	18	10
1982..	9	13	26	12	4	6	31	9
$1,000, 1987..	(D)	1	7	(D)	(D)	(D)	10	2
1982..	6	5	11	4	1	4	77	5
Hens and pullets sold .... farms, 1987..	4	-	2	-	2	1	6	4
1982..	2	2	6	6	-	(D)	3	-
number, 1987..	173	-	(D)	-	(D)	(D)	114	169
1982..	(D)	(D)	183	220	-	(D)	46	-
Hens and pullets of laying age sold .... farms, 1987..	4	-	2	-	-	1	6	4
1982..	2	2	5	6	-	2	3	-
number, 1987..	173	-	(D)	-	-	(D)	114	169
1982..	(D)	(D)	(D)	220	-	(D)	46	-
Pullets not of laying age sold .... farms, 1987..	-	-	1	-	2	-	-	-
1982..	-	-	-	-	(D)	-	-	-
number, 1987..	-	-	(D)	-	(D)	-	-	-
1982..	-	-	-	-	-	-	-	-
Broilers and other meat-type chickens sold .... farms, 1987..	-	1	6	-	-	2	4	2
1982..	-	2	2	-	-	-	4	2
number, 1987..	-	(D)	740	-	-	-	289	(D)
1982..	-	(D)	(D)	-	-	(D)	(D)	(D)
1987 farms by number sold:								
1 to 1,999	-	1	6	-	-	-	4	2
2,000 to 59,999	-	-	-	-	-	-	-	-
60,000 to 99,999	-	-	-	-	-	-	-	-
100,000 to 199,999	-	-	-	-	-	-	-	-
200,000 to 499,999	-	-	-	-	-	-	-	-
500,000 or more .... farms..	-	-	-	-	-	-	-	-
number..	-	-	-	-	-	-	-	-
Turkeys sold .... farms, 1987..	-	1	2	1	-	-	2	-
1982..	2	-	1	-	-	-	1	-
number, 1987..	-	(D)	(D)	(D)	-	-	(D)	-
1982..	(D)	-	(D)	-	-	-	(D)	-
Turkeys for slaughter sold .... farms, 1987..	-	1	1	-	-	-	2	-
1982..	2	-	1	-	-	-	1	-
number, 1987..	-	(D)	(D)	(D)	-	-	(D)	-
1982..	(D)	-	-	-	-	-	(D)	-
Ducks, geese, and other poultry sold .... farms, 1987..	-	-	2	2	-	-	3	1
1982..	1	2	2	1	1	2	1	-

Table 14. **Poultry—Inventory and Sales: 1987 and 1982**—Con.

[For meaning of abbreviations and symbols, see introductory text]

Item	Trego	Wabaunsee	Wallace	Washington	Wichita	Wilson	Woodson	Wyandotte
INVENTORY								
Any poultry .... farms, 1987..	45	42	25	62	19	36	27	16
1982..	56	73	46	68	40	50	35	29
Chickens 3 months old or older .... farms, 1987..	41	37	24	56	16	34	26	16
1982..	53	69	42	64	38	47	33	26
number, 1987..	1 102	(D)	704	4 251	407	847	535	306
1982..	2 163	(D)	959	4 843	992	1 788	990	5 175
Hens and pullets of laying age .... farms, 1987..	41	37	24	56	16	32	25	16
1982..	53	69	41	64	38	47	33	26
number, 1987..	964	(D)	641	3 918	(D)	722	(D)	(D)
1982..	1 994	(D)	908	(D)	965	1 677	(D)	4 975
1987 farms by inventory:								
1 to 99	41	32	24	44	16	30	24	16
100 to 399	-	4	-	11	-	2	1	-
400 to 3,199	-	-	-	1	-	-	-	-
3,200 to 9,999	-	-	-	-	-	-	-	-
10,000 to 19,999	-	-	-	-	-	-	-	-
20,000 to 49,999	-	-	-	-	-	-	-	-
50,000 to 99,999	-	-	-	-	-	-	-	-
100,000 or more .... farms..	-	1	-	-	-	-	-	-
number..	-	(D)	-	-	-	-	-	-
Pullets 3 months old or older not of laying age .... farms, 1987..	4	1	4	7	2	6	2	2
1982..	8	2	4	3	4	6	2	3
number, 1987..	138	(D)	63	333	(D)	125	(D)	(D)
1982..	169	(D)	151	(D)	37	111	(D)	200
Pullet chicks and pullets under 3 months old .... farms, 1987..	3	-	2	1	-	1	-	-
1982..	1	1	2	-	1	1	-	-
number, 1987..	46	-	(D)	(D)	-	(D)	-	-
1982..	(D)	(D)	(D)	-	(D)	(D)	-	-
Broilers and other meat-type chickens .... farms, 1987..	6	4	2	13	6	3	7	-
1982..	6	4	8	12	10	8	5	4
number, 1987..	(D)	129	(D)	992	390	(D)	208	-
1982..	134	101	995	1 561	794	337	363	(D)
Turkeys .... farms, 1987..	3	1	4	5	2	2	2	2
1982..	2	2	3	4	2	4	-	-
number, 1987..	23	(D)	20	34	(D)	(D)	(D)	(D)
1982..	(D)	(D)	5	45	(D)	4	-	-
Turkey hens kept for breeding .... farms, 1987..	1	-	1	1	-	-	2	-
1982..	-	2	2	1	1	4	-	-
number, 1987..	(D)	(D)	(D)	(D)	-	-	(D)	-
1982..	-	(D)	(D)	(D)	(D)	4	-	-
Ducks, geese, and other poultry .... farms, 1987..	2	8	6	12	5	10	7	2
1982..	12	6	8	12	4	12	7	5
SALES								
Any poultry sold .... farms, 1987..	5	11	3	30	4	9	5	5
1982..	21	26	12	43	5	12	11	15
$1,000, 1987..	1	(D)	(D)	20	(Z)	5	2	(D)
1982..	4	1 373	1	35	1	7	2	52
Hens and pullets sold .... farms, 1987..	2	3	1	2	-	3	2	1
1982..	3	8	-	10	2	3	1	2
number, 1987..	(D)	(D)	(D)	(D)	-	72	(D)	(D)
1982..	(D)	(D)	-	1 942	(D)	(D)	(D)	(D)
Hens and pullets of laying age sold .... farms, 1987..	2	3	1	2	-	3	2	1
1982..	3	8	-	10	2	3	1	2
number, 1987..	(D)	(D)	(D)	(D)	-	72	(D)	(D)
1982..	(D)	(D)	-	1 942	(D)	(D)	(D)	(D)
Pullets not of laying age sold .... farms, 1987..	-	-	-	-	-	1	-	-
1982..	-	-	-	-	-	1	-	-
number, 1987..	-	-	-	-	-	(D)	-	-
Broilers and other meat-type chickens sold..... farms, 1987..	1	1	-	1	-	1	-	1
1982..	3	2	1	4	1	1	1	1
number, 1987..	(D)	(D)	-	(D)	-	(D)	(D)	(D)
1982..	75	(D)	(D)	210	(D)	(D)	(D)	(D)
1987 farms by number sold:								
1 to 1,999	1	1	-	1	-	-	-	-
2,000 to 59,999	-	-	-	-	-	-	-	-
60,000 to 99,999	-	-	-	-	-	-	-	-
100,000 to 199,999	-	-	-	-	-	-	-	-
200,000 to 499,999	-	-	-	-	-	-	-	-
500,000 or more .... farms..	-	-	-	-	-	-	-	-
number..	-	-	-	-	-	-	-	-
Turkeys sold .... farms, 1987..	1	-	1	3	2	-	-	-
1982..	-	-	-	1	-	-	-	-
number, 1987..	(D)	-	(D)	20	(D)	-	-	-
1982..	-	-	-	(D)	-	-	-	-
Turkeys for slaughter sold .... farms, 1987..	1	-	1	3	2	-	-	-
1982..	-	-	-	1	-	-	-	-
number, 1987..	(D)	-	(D)	20	(D)	-	-	-
1982..	-	-	-	(D)	-	-	-	-
Ducks, geese, and other poultry sold .... farms, 1987..	-	-	1	1	-	1	3	-
1982..	2	-	1	2	-	2	1	4

Crop		Kansas	Allen	Anderson	Atchison	Barber	Barton	Bourbon
Harvested cropland	farms, 1987	57 822	564	611	589	415	806	645
	1982	62 860	614	667	637	445	871	705
	acres, 1987	17 729 394	125 078	161 985	122 717	149 449	262 050	90 939
	1982	20 186 974	137 642	167 000	129 487	190 605	314 881	121 086
Irrigated	farms, 1987	7 268	7	9	11	27	111	8
	1982	7 211	6	10	-	25	131	9
	acres, 1987	2 408 176	(D)	(D)	478	2 954	26 168	(D)
	1982	2 639 024	(D)	(D)	-	(D)	39 499	(D)
Corn for grain or seed	farms, 1987	8 944	103	199	285	-	43	105
	1982	8 346	100	232	248	6	33	101
	acres, 1987	1 243 969	7 562	13 596	22 627	-	9 382	5 937
	1982	1 161 875	4 855	15 289	16 396	1 218	6 679	5 501
	bushels, 1987	144 133 581	600 173	1 111 323	1 910 556	-	1 166 648	482 711
	1982	130 862 235	324 550	1 115 829	1 385 378	142 250	876 725	395 711
Irrigated	farms, 1987	3 647	-	7	4	-	37	5
	1982	3 007	1	6	5	5	29	6
	acres, 1987	816 992	(D)	773	192	-	8 731	379
	1982	755 272	(D)	620	-	(D)	5 582	(D)
1987 farms by acres harvested:								
1 to 24 acres		1 984	47	55	72	-	1	43
25 to 99 acres		3 279	34	107	131	-	14	46
100 to 249 acres		2 195	13	27	70	-	15	11
250 acres or more		1 485	9	10	12	-	13	5
Sorghum for grain or seed	farms, 1987	32 492	294	330	381	104	501	213
	1982	26 908	254	295	355	72	484	225
	acres, 1987	3 399 564	19 291	22 705	32 153	6 932	41 882	12 311
	1982	3 187 148	17 669	17 966	27 756	5 359	49 779	14 386
	bushels, 1987	228 045 100	1 392 031	1 701 589	2 555 518	348 987	2 893 658	707 820
	1982	192 400 229	1 075 727	1 224 904	1 783 258	239 986	2 747 676	894 551
Irrigated	farms, 1987	3 137	-	1	1	8	71	-
	1982	3 474	-	4	-	6	86	-
	acres, 1987	464 119	-	(D)	(D)	746	7 967	-
	1982	643 658	(D)	(D)	-	500	12 924	-
1987 farms by acres harvested:								
1 to 24 acres		7 280	90	89	94	27	118	68
25 to 99 acres		14 139	141	169	180	52	240	111
100 to 249 acres		7 830	50	61	86	22	113	31
250 acres or more		3 243	13	11	21	3	30	3
Wheat for grain	farms, 1987	38 638	141	135	133	375	750	65
	1982	49 231	403	386	397	411	781	315
	acres, 1987	8 679 588	9 519	6 676	5 160	121 445	167 857	3 442
	1982	11 664 008	38 549	26 129	22 948	161 844	216 460	27 231
	bushels, 1987	292 999 442	273 355	197 151	137 915	3 341 963	5 428 175	85 667
	1982	373 590 046	1 011 698	635 014	467 804	5 813 295	6 985 195	608 942
Irrigated	farms, 1987	3 046	1	-	-	5	37	-
	1982	3 111	1	-	-	4	52	-
	acres, 1987	635 524	(D)	-	-	416	3 859	-
	1982	715 446	6	-	-	275	9 990	-
1987 farms by acres harvested:								
1 to 24 acres		4 230	51	60	67	18	36	26
25 to 99 acres		11 451	63	54	55	70	207	31
100 to 249 acres		11 111	21	18	10	112	266	6
250 acres or more		11 846	6	3	1	175	241	2
Oats for grain	farms, 1987	5 313	77	84	107	14	52	63
	1982	8 644	92	120	100	38	27	91
	acres, 1987	126 091	1 965	2 144	2 589	779	880	1 434
	1982	168 982	2 042	2 618	1 829	1 360	381	737
	bushels, 1987	4 775 729	76 541	60 947	127 246	29 834	39 723	45 437
	1982	7 799 056	111 540	108 158	78 244	47 082	15 391	77 622
Irrigated	farms, 1987	48	-	-	-	-	-	-
	1982	108	-	-	-	-	2	-
	acres, 1987	2 278	-	-	-	-	-	-
	1982	7 176	-	-	-	-	(D)	-
1987 farms by acres harvested:								
1 to 24 acres		3 728	55	64	70	5	42	45
25 to 99 acres		1 440	20	19	34	6	10	17
100 to 249 acres		131	1	-	2	3	-	1
250 acres or more		14	1	1	1	-	-	-
Soybeans for beans	farms, 1987	18 854	398	449	435	16	77	317
	1982	17 116	423	478	439	8	38	392
	acres, 1987	1 878 978	61 809	80 630	43 701	1 416	6 945	32 777
	1982	1 692 288	52 354	66 391	41 718	1 358	5 675	42 966
	bushels, 1987	55 789 994	1 787 211	2 618 386	1 474 034	45 929	266 240	817 832
	1982	43 042 471	1 205 004	1 701 311	1 091 792	52 860	260 007	932 787
Irrigated	farms, 1987	1 639	1	4	3	11	52	1
	1982	1 725	-	7	-	7	32	6
	acres, 1987	175 053	(D)	285	308	1 098	5 239	(D)
	1982	199 270	(D)	530	-	1 270	5 277	250
1987 farms by acres harvested:								
1 to 24 acres		5 008	65	69	87	3	12	87
25 to 99 acres		8 253	154	144	204	8	40	134
100 to 249 acres		3 775	100	129	104	4	18	69
250 acres or more		1 828	79	107	40	1	7	27
Hay—alfalfa, other tame, small grain, wild, grass silage, green chop, etc. (see text)	farms, 1987	33 964	435	463	395	222	492	522
	1982	37 341	460	498	457	216	560	543
	acres, 1987	2 254 082	30 385	39 800	19 182	18 355	37 437	36 721
	1982	2 233 631	27 383	40 901	19 595	17 185	37 622	32 187
	tons, dry, 1987	5 080 847	48 927	62 070	36 644	51 611	106 817	61 439
	1982	5 092 039	48 867	66 176	44 666	41 672	107 071	56 390
Irrigated	farms, 1987	1 492	-	1	-	10	26	1
	1982	1 841	1	-	-	10	39	-
	acres, 1987	205 951	-	-	-	454	1 777	(D)
	1982	187 173	(D)	-	(D)	473	4 596	-
1987 farms by acres harvested:								
1 to 24 acres		11 391	140	105	153	48	154	166
25 to 99 acres		16 111	201	228	194	106	240	240
100 to 249 acres		5 297	78	102	45	57	71	94
250 acres or more		1 165	18	28	3	11	27	22

Table 15. Selected Crops: 1987 and 1982—Con.

[For meaning of abbreviations and symbols, see introductory text]

Crop	Brown	Butler	Chase	Chautauqua	Cherokee	Cheyenne	Clark
Harvested cropland ... farms, 1987	637	934	223	248	657	426	233
1982	732	1 053	238	294	729	491	254
acres, 1987	197 847	210 975	45 580	35 741	156 409	176 293	92 271
1982	226 953	225 388	49 790	40 561	186 648	197 174	113 399
irrigated ... farms, 1987	3	19	-	3	7	149	28
1982	-	17	2	2	9	159	27
acres, 1987	(D)	(D)	-	31	376	40 555	(D)
1982	-	614	(D)	(D)	394	44 281	5 605
Corn for grain or seed ... farms, 1987	349	43	38	12	80	98	-
1982	412	16	40	11	46	102	2
acres, 1987	48 227	3 180	2 323	658	5 166	18 604	-
1982	52 287	1 195	1 703	588	2 986	17 710	(D)
bushels, 1987	4 726 726	250 012	183 141	42 190	502 149	2 367 733	-
1982	5 180 537	81 609	82 895	29 755	227 140	1 937 921	(D)
Irrigated ... farms, 1987	-	2	-	-	4	88	-
1982	-	2	-	-	3	95	-
acres, 1987	-	(D)	-	-	169	17 474	-
1982	-	(D)	-	-	133	18 645	-
1987 farms by acres harvested:							
1 to 24 acres	57	14	12	2	32	10	-
25 to 99 acres	139	20	19	7	28	26	-
100 to 249 acres	90	6	6	3	17	39	-
250 acres or more	63	3	1	-	3	23	-
Sorghum for grain or seed ... farms, 1987	354	496	122	65	248	131	108
1982	310	401	114	42	121	94	66
acres, 1987	28 762	68 302	7 794	5 308	20 936	11 063	9 362
1982	24 208	50 154	8 688	4 654	9 222	11 420	7 888
bushels, 1987	2 296 531	4 789 767	521 325	265 900	1 445 829	707 778	521 390
1982	1 850 117	2 919 375	375 443	194 849	590 433	730 686	292 140
Irrigated ... farms, 1987	-	3	-	-	-	34	17
1982	-	4	-	-	-	37	12
acres, 1987	-	260	-	-	-	3 689	1 556
1982	-	(D)	-	-	-	5 713	1 548
1987 farms by acres harvested:							
1 to 24 acres	68	94	34	14	47	32	17
25 to 99 acres	192	181	65	26	127	58	55
100 to 249 acres	76	136	20	23	61	31	30
250 acres or more	18	85	3	2	13	10	6
Wheat for grain ... farms, 1987	367	488	136	78	158	409	213
1982	566	651	178	144	523	459	237
acres, 1987	26 577	63 948	11 898	8 028	16 295	109 225	70 665
1982	54 046	87 703	17 804	19 411	83 914	145 981	94 556
bushels, 1987	1 030 105	1 865 760	330 110	179 242	372 571	4 063 922	2 097 680
1982	1 504 957	2 789 142	477 274	639 762	2 260 391	5 255 519	2 683 999
Irrigated ... farms, 1987	-	1	-	-	-	-	-
1982	-	2	-	-	-	1	14
acres, 1987	-	(D)	-	-	-	-	1 857
1982	-	(D)	-	-	-	5 127	2 544
1987 farms by acres harvested:							
1 to 24 acres	109	75	28	10	42	7	3
25 to 99 acres	169	198	72	43	68	97	30
100 to 249 acres	72	141	24	21	31	133	80
250 acres or more	17	74	12	4	17	172	100
Oats for grain ... farms, 1987	114	49	31	14	50	25	7
1982	163	103	64	44	75	12	2
acres, 1987	2 277	951	527	793	1 186	1 107	260
1982	3 089	2 729	1 112	1 048	1 731	1 153	(D)
bushels, 1987	101 458	27 956	20 226	25 175	34 397	58 106	7 718
1982	167 930	113 865	47 674	46 677	105 011	37 817	(D)
Irrigated ... farms, 1987	-	1	-	-	-	5	-
1982	-	-	-	-	-	3	1
acres, 1987	-	-	-	-	-	257	-
1982	-	(D)	-	-	-	191	(D)
1987 farms by acres harvested:							
1 to 24 acres	91	35	25	2	36	8	3
25 to 99 acres	22	14	6	9	13	14	4
100 to 249 acres	1	-	-	3	1	3	-
250 acres or more	-	-	-	-	-	-	-
Soybeans for beans ... farms, 1987	539	279	121	48	457	33	3
1982	567	181	111	29	556	26	3
acres, 1987	78 311	23 825	9 639	8 401	100 264	4 029	(D)
1982	71 005	12 798	7 422	3 295	104 013	2 872	(D)
bushels, 1987	2 532 198	714 366	339 233	225 752	2 089 323	167 976	(D)
1982	2 065 005	211 960	163 247	62 838	1 807 194	91 162	(D)
Irrigated ... farms, 1987	-	1	-	2	-	30	2
1982	-	-	-	-	-	21	2
acres, 1987	-	(D)	-	(D)	-	3 785	(D)
1982	-	(D)	-	(D)	-	2 460	(D)
1987 farms by acres harvested:							
1 to 24 acres	62	73	36	9	40	1	1
25 to 99 acres	242	126	50	22	154	14	1
100 to 249 acres	140	65	30	8	122	16	1
250 acres or more	95	15	5	9	141	2	-
Hay—alfalfa, other tame, small grain, wild, grass silage, green chop, etc. (see text) ... farms, 1987	354	676	180	208	411	156	110
1982	475	774	190	239	431	158	100
acres, 1987	16 003	54 005	12 737	13 125	18 011	11 353	11 181
1982	21 667	63 362	13 566	13 693	17 936	10 220	8 864
tons, 1987	36 477	86 301	26 011	21 664	27 319	31 388	31 085
1982	51 561	100 627	27 834	22 521	22 949	33 757	22 374
Irrigated ... farms, 1987	-	2	-	-	1	46	12
1982	-	3	1	-	2	57	7
acres, 1987	-	(D)	-	-	(D)	3 299	1 197
1982	-	138	(D)	-	(D)	4 194	337
1987 farms by acres harvested:							
1 to 24 acres	146	203	53	58	184	34	30
25 to 99 acres	163	295	86	103	176	88	51
100 to 249 acres	43	144	36	40	47	30	21
250 acres or more	2	34	5	7	4	4	8

Table 15. **Selected Crops: 1987 and 1982**—Con.

[For meaning of abbreviations and symbols, see introductory text]

Crop	Clay	Cloud	Coffey	Comanche	Cowley	Crawford	Decatur
Harvested cropland .... farms, 1987...	586	583	515	209	760	649	438
1982...	647	642	572	215	885	725	459
acres, 1987...	176 217	184 007	142 668	93 062	160 651	116 714	178 861
1982...	189 827	214 074	157 589	118 916	212 326	155 932	172 683
Irrigated .... farms, 1987...	49	76	8	26	18	11	91
1982...	60	70	10	26	13	16	93
acres, 1987...	10 626	10 139	466	(D)	(D)	1 447	(D)
1982...	11 090	9 146	288	(D)	(D)	2 047	(D)
Corn for grain or seed .... farms, 1987...	75	59	136	7	12	108	114
1982...	92	66	143	1	3	110	71
acres, 1987...	7 405	7 338	7 662	809	612	7 737	17 038
1982...	8 660	8 293	7 227	(D)	(D)	6 725	8 005
bushels, 1987...	888 470	880 934	620 771	127 386	46 912	675 502	1 741 211
1982...	844 478	817 845	536 151	(D)	(D)	486 704	761 611
Irrigated .... farms, 1987...	36	45	1	7	1	9	72
1982...	45	43	4	1	–	7	53
acres, 1987...	5 236	6 283	(D)	809	(D)	1 004	7 217
1982...	5 524	5 483	(D)	(D)	–	671	5 017
1987 farms by acres harvested:							
1 to 24 acres	16	6	38	2	5	30	10
25 to 99 acres	33	26	73	1	5	49	52
100 to 249 acres	20	20	22	3	2	26	28
250 acres or more	6	7	3	1	–	3	24
Sorghum for grain or seed..................... farms, 1987...	464	410	342	78	385	345	326
1982...	357	273	256	64	283	313	233
acres, 1987...	41 625	37 418	24 607	7 311	29 662	26 330	37 248
1982...	30 682	24 003	20 346	8 434	25 101	24 778	28 712
bushels, 1987...	2 954 750	3 004 763	1 592 593	333 660	1 795 900	1 787 148	2 567 910
1982...	2 127 030	1 646 295	1 297 139	290 501	1 165 622	1 580 774	1 648 332
Irrigated .... farms, 1987...	13	31	3	8	9	4	15
1982...	16	22	–	14	5	7	25
acres, 1987...	579	1 865	80	732	826	(D)	763
1982...	(D)	1 083	–	1 239	800	(D)	1 445
1987 farms by acres harvested:							
1 to 24 acres	109	99	106	8	118	108	35
25 to 99 acres	209	177	153	43	168	153	154
100 to 249 acres	110	103	69	24	77	61	99
250 acres or more	36	31	14	3	24	23	38
Wheat for grain .... farms, 1987...	519	501	182	182	549	89	396
1982...	598	576	404	202	730	411	428
acres, 1987...	79 221	109 697	11 740	71 867	95 945	3 999	93 716
1982...	111 394	149 400	38 862	96 249	147 415	34 510	117 804
bushels, 1987...	2 715 122	3 909 381	313 311	1 848 967	2 695 979	121 569	3 999 819
1982...	3 104 666	4 046 694	832 139	3 058 969	4 662 442	677 364	4 790 172
Irrigated .... farms, 1987...	7	4	–	10	3	1	8
1982...	6	5	–	12	3	1	9
acres, 1987...	520	230	–	1 007	220	–	1 110
1982...	700	280	–	2 149	350	(D)	775
1987 farms by acres harvested:							
1 to 24 acres	40	42	52	6	67	31	17
25 to 99 acres	198	152	103	32	197	29	92
100 to 249 acres	173	134	21	48	149	6	134
250 acres or more	108	173	6	102	136	3	153
Oats for grain .... farms, 1987...	135	82	36	2	33	98	42
1982...	129	91	46	6	74	159	35
acres, 1987...	2 298	1 769	629	(D)	667	3 003	1 448
1982...	2 360	2 646	820	865	1 865	4 294	932
bushels, 1987...	106 359	80 251	18 793	28 709	141 824	109 140	57 297
1982...	99 640	126 326	25 733	23 341	88 729	245 432	53 635
Irrigated .... farms, 1987...	–	–	–	2	–	–	–
1982...	–	–	–	2	–	–	–
acres, 1987...	–	–	–	(D)	–	–	–
1982...	–	–	–	(D)	–	–	–
1987 farms by acres harvested:							
1 to 24 acres	104	57	30	2	23	57	20
25 to 99 acres	30	25	5	–	9	37	19
100 to 249 acres	1	–	1	–	1	4	3
250 acres or more	–	–	–	–	–	–	–
Soybeans for beans .... farms, 1987...	349	231	434	9	123	475	12
1982...	276	158	446	4	50	545	4
acres, 1987...	23 155	12 176	70 461	774	5 627	58 552	954
1982...	15 839	8 615	61 131	1 469	2 350	69 213	259
bushels, 1987...	743 382	357 497	2 150 726	28 709	141 824	1 259 435	23 712
1982...	494 782	251 608	1 440 911	(D)	48 639	1 449 138	2 700
Irrigated .... farms, 1987...	34	38	3	7	4	4	8
1982...	35	26	4	2	1	4	1
acres, 1987...	3 196	1 571	275	626	216	333	204
1982...	2 437	1 137	145	(D)	(D)	909	(D)
1987 farms by acres harvested:							
1 to 24 acres	99	84	58	4	47	100	8
25 to 99 acres	168	110	163	–	60	188	2
100 to 249 acres	76	35	118	5	15	120	1
250 acres or more	6	2	95	–	1	67	1
Hay—alfalfa, other tame, small grain, wild,							
grass silage, green chop, etc. (see text) .... farms, 1987...	424	328	330	119	500	439	228
1982...	451	413	390	99	607	495	247
acres, 1987...	25 074	18 121	31 082	9 870	31 618	21 593	13 517
1982...	22 187	20 430	33 163	8 664	38 093	21 813	13 633
tons, dry, 1987...	50 497	39 301	41 420	27 747	61 034	36 858	42 846
1982...	50 066	51 946	47 073	20 277	76 682	36 377	42 845
Irrigated .... farms, 1987...	1	5	–	15	2	–	16
1982...	6	10	–	11	–	–	27
acres, 1987...	(D)	175	–	1 054	(D)	–	529
1982...	(D)	594	–	697	–	–	1 271
1987 farms by acres harvested:							
1 to 24 acres	130	111	80	21	190	161	80
25 to 99 acres	225	168	145	69	216	224	129
100 to 249 acres	59	42	75	33	79	48	37
250 acres or more	10	5	30	6	15	6	2

Table 15. **Selected Crops: 1987 and 1982**—Con.

[For meaning of abbreviations and symbols, see introductory text]

Crop		Dickinson	Doniphan	Douglas	Edwards	Elk	Ellis	Ellsworth
Harvested cropland	farms, 1987..	908	454	691	328	293	691	450
	1982..	1 012	543	740	373	346	695	471
	acres, 1987..	245 504	127 686	108 864	186 513	40 040	147 980	128 533
	1982..	297 527	150 592	112 306	206 856	54 719	162 248	146 178
Irrigated	farms, 1987..	33	2	13	154	1	13	6
	1982..	23	3	14	161	-	30	8
	acres, 1987..	(D)	(D)	(D)	82 708	(D)	(D)	896
	1982..	(D)	(D)	(D)	(D)	(D)	2 582	851
Corn for grain or seed	farms, 1987..	44	362	175	100	8	4	6
	1982..	96	383	186	51	11	9	3
	acres, 1987..	1 915	56 130	15 643	38 522	307	207	231
	1982..	3 291	56 482	14 746	16 525	(D)	1 445	(D)
	bushels, 1987..	148 123	6 228 898	1 513 650	4 203 683	21 270	9 840	16 945
	1982..	229 442	6 727 207	1 309 935	2 446 103	12 005	127 653	(D)
Irrigated	farms, 1987..	10	-	5	96	-	-	1
	1982..	5	1	3	48	-	4	-
	acres, 1987..	824	-	580	36 963	-	-	(D)
	1982..	341	(D)	(D)	15 225	-	(D)	-
1987 farms by acres harvested:								
1 to 24 acres		19	51	49	1	5	1	2
25 to 99 acres		21	130	72	13	2	2	4
100 to 249 acres		4	108	43	27	1	1	-
250 acres or more		-	73	11	59	-	-	-
Sorghum for grain or seed	farms, 1987..	619	80	242	194	104	314	291
	1982..	465	102	203	193	77	186	212
	acres, 1987..	47 319	4 352	16 903	20 630	5 465	21 586	18 469
	1982..	35 952	5 999	14 111	34 666	5 650	17 316	15 416
	bushels, 1987..	2 702 408	378 074	1 374 994	1 290 566	290 331	1 182 640	1 227 419
	1982..	2 180 955	435 442	858 675	1 966 382	288 866	836 178	832 497
Irrigated	farms, 1987..	16	-	-	53	-	6	4
	1982..	9	-	-	91	1	8	2
	acres, 1987..	825	-	-	5 309	-	598	186
	1982..	(D)	-	-	14 624	(D)	334	(D)
1987 farms by acres harvested:								
1 to 24 acres		154	29	82	39	38	113	107
25 to 99 acres		302	40	99	78	51	131	120
100 to 249 acres		136	9	44	55	14	50	51
250 acres or more		27	2	17	22	1	20	13
Wheat for grain	farms, 1987..	816	118	76	296	99	611	405
	1982..	927	329	363	338	181	611	439
	acres, 1987..	135 344	7 949	2 844	87 995	6 405	99 562	85 816
	1982..	194 101	28 108	24 460	114 098	19 781	118 060	111 611
	bushels, 1987..	4 377 284	326 510	92 999	2 921 112	148 994	3 181 838	2 976 878
	1982..	5 980 097	756 627	539 068	3 467 145	606 202	3 735 127	3 674 534
Irrigated	farms, 1987..	-	-	-	61	-	2	2
	1982..	-	-	1	71	-	4	3
	acres, 1987..	-	-	-	11 093	-	(D)	(D)
	1982..	-	-	(D)	13 147	-	368	335
1987 farms by acres harvested:								
1 to 24 acres		81	56	46	3	26	42	21
25 to 99 acres		287	38	22	67	52	248	120
100 to 249 acres		260	18	8	91	19	209	121
250 acres or more		188	6	-	135	2	112	143
Oats for grain	farms, 1987..	201	34	82	9	24	25	51
	1982..	294	36	102	5	40	9	19
	acres, 1987..	4 012	425	1 611	355	507	650	1 046
	1982..	8 273	1 036	1 711	203	1 068	192	582
	bushels, 1987..	129 951	22 486	49 741	10 060	13 300	20 211	34 586
	1982..	319 736	56 697	78 925	(D)	41 226	7 688	27 570
Irrigated	farms, 1987..	2	-	-	1	-	-	-
	1982..	1	-	-	3	-	-	-
	acres, 1987..	-	-	-	(D)	-	-	-
	1982..	(D)	-	-	(D)	-	-	-
1987 farms by acres harvested:								
1 to 24 acres		151	31	63	6	18	15	38
25 to 99 acres		47	3	19	2	6	10	12
100 to 249 acres		3	-	-	1	-	-	1
250 acres or more		-	-	-	-	-	-	-
Soybeans for beans	farms, 1987..	336	376	373	90	98	3	31
	1982..	259	423	328	84	82	-	15
	acres, 1987..	14 637	52 547	42 051	21 083	9 348	-	1 582
	1982..	10 798	53 287	31 700	24 177	5 462	695	688
	bushels, 1987..	413 709	1 931 717	1 399 719	806 146	269 817	-	45 930
	1982..	262 516	1 772 646	748 167	918 274	123 578	16 400	23 823
Irrigated	farms, 1987..	-	-	3	83	-	-	3
	1982..	6	1	4	78	-	-	4
	acres, 1987..	420	-	509	16 363	-	-	281
	1982..	310	(D)	390	19 336	-	-	335
1987 farms by acres harvested:								
1 to 24 acres		145	66	117	5	21	-	10
25 to 99 acres		170	138	135	31	53	-	16
100 to 249 acres		15	100	71	30	12	-	5
250 acres or more		6	72	50	24	12	-	-
Hay—alfalfa, other tame, small grain, wild, grass silage, green chop, etc. (see text)	farms, 1987..	650	210	540	145	250	358	312
	1982..	692	250	574	165	295	335	315
	acres, 1987..	39 964	6 512	27 405	19 249	19 341	22 783	23 590
	1982..	37 823	6 137	26 060	22 460	23 589	20 672	18 327
	tons, dry, 1987..	90 833	16 496	50 418	76 879	27 887	51 546	48 605
	1982..	96 419	15 976	50 596	87 712	36 835	49 224	38 455
Irrigated	farms, 1987..	9	1	-	50	1	6	-
	1982..	2	2	2	63	-	17	4
	acres, 1987..	279	-	(D)	12 517	(D)	(D)	147
	1982..	(D)	(D)	-	13 501	(D)	546	146
1987 farms by acres harvested:								
1 to 24 acres		202	126	216	37	57	137	80
25 to 99 acres		343	75	248	59	134	163	153
100 to 249 acres		90	9	69	28	48	47	63
250 acres or more		15	-	7	21	11	11	16

Crop	Finney	Ford	Franklin	Geary	Gove	Graham	Grant
Harvested cropland .... farms, 1987..	463	703	799	239	454	403	258
1982..	494	730	895	250	485	464	236
acres, 1987..	323 607	284 042	135 097	48 216	194 728	148 177	156 356
1982..	384 552	301 832	142 823	50 306	195 149	161 560	199 136
Irrigated .... farms, 1987..	279	208	16	22	87	53	189
1982..	297	213	16	17	95	70	171
acres, 1987..	175 045	75 306	1 503	1 616	(D)	(D)	97 129
1982..	197 003	79 926	1 036	(D)	(D)	13 074	119 648
Corn for grain or seed .... farms, 1987..	142	81	182	22	37	25	110
1982..	135	60	205	29	36	29	83
acres, 1987..	50 415	19 058	11 765	952	5 013	3 302	28 236
1982..	66 191	16 540	12 143	1 159	6 063	4 491	29 204
bushels, 1987..	6 724 251	2 317 718	920 810	84 624	547 514	375 964	4 104 121
1982..	8 878 132	1 997 690	960 559	96 162	722 974	456 266	4 007 668
Irrigated .... farms, 1987..	140	78	4	6	36	19	105
1982..	131	56	6	9	32	25	82
acres, 1987..	49 215	19 532	(D)	321	4 721	2 675	27 776
1982..	65 311	15 719	(D)	(D)	5 571	4 201	29 129
1987 farms by acres harvested:							
1 to 24 acres	3	2	65	10	1	2	–
25 to 99 acres	26	19	78	10	14	13	21
100 to 249 acres	47	29	32	2	17	7	43
250 acres or more...............................	66	31	7	–	5	3	46
Sorghum for grain or seed............. farms, 1987..	268	428	322	168	308	287	174
1982..	265	289	249	132	300	201	183
acres, 1987..	55 632	52 001	21 469	10 601	40 514	30 316	42 463
1982..	54 674	44 701	14 188	9 361	46 482	22 608	65 933
bushels, 1987..	3 950 620	3 911 021	1 523 437	706 133	2 505 504	1 838 475	2 350 816
1982..	4 108 566	2 878 152	883 396	693 798	2 732 785	1 134 143	4 066 037
Irrigated .... farms, 1987..	140	115	2	6	49	27	107
1982..	174	121	3	6	46	24	130
acres, 1987..	28 229	17 879	(D)	305	4 864	2 557	20 910
1982..	36 103	23 192	(D)	(D)	5 017	2 386	36 736
1987 farms by acres harvested:							
1 to 24 acres	17	71	119	49	44	45	8
25 to 99 acres	75	192	134	83	115	127	58
100 to 249 acres	100	105	57	34	109	91	47
250 acres or more...............................	76	60	12	2	40	24	61
Wheat for grain .... farms, 1987..	431	644	87	170	435	379	232
1982..	463	667	378	189	416	425	209
acres, 1987..	174 488	181 190	4 832	16 731	117 701	91 909	72 047
1982..	214 825	214 227	22 532	23 265	116 232	114 914	92 689
bushels, 1987..	7 146 392	6 427 347	136 448	603 083	4 496 191	3 548 458	2 628 269
1982..	7 047 679	6 779 134	442 477	744 946	3 383 960	3 710 398	3 609 301
Irrigated .... farms, 1987..	229	111	–	2	19	14	156
1982..	233	111	1	2	18	30	141
acres, 1987..	61 592	22 320	–	(D)	2 389	1 784	36 744
1982..	62 464	25 597	(D)	(D)	1 917	3 575	44 853
1987 farms by acres harvested:							
1 to 24 acres	26	27	37	41	11	19	7
25 to 99 acres	54	139	41	68	93	101	42
100 to 249 acres	109	214	7	48	154	123	72
250 acres or more...............................	242	264	2	13	177	136	111
Oats for grain .... farms, 1987..	7	24	113	62	16	22	3
1982..	5	9	202	53	18	17	3
acres, 1987..	372	976	1 891	1 168	1 005	776	(D)
1982..	375	649	3 029	965	1 371	1 124	45
bushels, 1987..	13 836	24 292	67 971	40 286	32 069	31 190	4 200
1982..	16 070	23 438	192 941	44 930	35 528	49 744	2 450
Irrigated .... farms, 1987..	1	1	–	1	1	1	2
1982..	3	4	–	1	4	4	2
acres, 1987..	(D)	(D)	–	1	(D)	–	(D)
1982..	335	267	–	(D)	330	500	(D)
1987 farms by acres harvested:							
1 to 24 acres	3	11	89	46	6	8	1
25 to 99 acres	2	10	23	15	9	12	2
100 to 249 acres	2	3	1	1	1	2	–
250 acres or more...............................	–	–	–	–	–	–	–
Soybeans for beans .... farms, 1987..	87	65	498	113	3	3	43
1982..	45	61	521	67	10	2	26
acres, 1987..	8 544	6 586	62 225	5 462	(D)	205	3 793
1982..	4 359	7 146	57 240	3 296	458	(D)	3 576
bushels, 1987..	263 194	233 727	1 871 238	163 290	15 294	(D)	106 002
1982..	141 354	280 610	1 226 234	93 238	14 089	(D)	116 842
Irrigated .... farms, 1987..	80	55	6	9	2	1	38
1982..	42	53	5	7	7	1	27
acres, 1987..	7 773	5 960	643	504	(D)	(D)	3 409
1982..	4 104	6 044	347	307	410	(D)	3 076
1987 farms by acres harvested:							
1 to 24 acres	19	10	115	39	–	–	8
25 to 99 acres	35	29	214	64	1	2	25
100 to 249 acres	26	23	97	8	1	1	7
250 acres or more...............................	7	3	72	2	1	–	3
Hay—alfalfa, other tame, small grain, wild,							
grass silage, green chop, etc. (see text) ...... farms, 1987..	169	273	613	189	162	165	64
1982..	193	212	657	164	189	205	66
acres, 1987..	30 042	19 770	33 840	13 587	14 985	11 912	7 349
1982..	39 690	15 266	33 947	12 120	14 177	12 141	6 668
tons, dry, 1987..	130 942	67 181	57 077	24 346	39 347	32 560	34 351
1982..	155 955	50 665	51 504	26 057	42 646	33 592	24 713
Irrigated .... farms, 1987..	117	54	2	5	13	11	40
1982..	156	52	1	9	18	21	44
acres, 1987..	25 700	8 778	(D)	243	862	862	5 883
1982..	24 688	7 379	(D)	(D)	1 154	1 318	4 253
1987 farms by acres harvested:							
1 to 24 acres	23	101	240	72	41	47	11
25 to 99 acres	67	128	277	71	86	76	30
100 to 249 acres	45	26	78	41	24	35	16
250 acres or more...............................	34	18	18	5	12	7	7

Table 15. Selected Crops: 1987 and 1982—Con.

[For meaning of abbreviations and symbols, see introductory text]

Crop	Gray	Greeley	Greenwood	Hamilton	Harper	Harvey	Haskell
Harvested cropland .... farms, 1987..	480	266	409	225	595	740	284
1982..	502	259	498	237	617	826	290
acres, 1987..	258 379	196 152	73 937	160 504	233 900	197 917	200 065
1982..	325 993	193 327	81 686	204 376	288 416	232 904	249 122
Irrigated .... farms, 1987..	303	57	8	58	10	118	222
1982..	327	39	6	61	18	122	238
acres, 1987..	149 840	(D)	819	18 554	584	20 827	150 442
1982..	189 847	(D)	244	23 252	(D)	(D)	177 420
Corn for grain or seed .... farms, 1987..	196	38	29	22	1	82	157
1982..	203	19	26	10	2	59	158
acres, 1987..	51 161	12 977	1 119	4 574	(D)	11 053	55 966
1982..	62 515	7 255	1 167	2 305	(D)	6 519	60 411
bushels, 1987..	6 327 646	1 678 904	90 870	624 772	(D)	1 370 794	7 401 004
1982..	8 720 968	799 353	72 786	323 790	(D)	840 834	8 413 068
Irrigated .... farms, 1987..	194	37	2	21	-	56	152
1982..	193	17	4	10	2	50	157
acres, 1987..	50 995	12 965	(D)	4 466	-	9 806	55 319
1982..	59 515	6 639	156	2 305	(D)	6 254	59 986
1987 farms by acres harvested:							
1 to 24 acres	2	3	14	2	-	10	4
25 to 99 acres	29	5	11	3	1	42	24
100 to 249 acres	80	12	4	10	-	17	34
250 acres or more	85	18	-	7	-	13	95
Sorghum for grain or seed .... farms, 1987..	275	124	174	127	79	520	151
1982..	233	53	151	86	44	487	168
acres, 1987..	47 462	16 705	12 603	18 681	(D)	55 624	32 584
1982..	51 785	16 951	11 826	14 927	3 329	64 182	44 207
bushels, 1987..	4 043 766	745 922	723 755	724 726	(D)	4 377 977	2 843 263
1982..	4 853 670	1 137 342	563 702	710 637	164 334	3 478 461	4 001 362
Irrigated .... farms, 1987..	141	19	1	17	1	49	97
1982..	180	22	-	36	2	52	135
acres, 1987..	28 627	3 214	(D)	1 264	(D)	3 514	23 034
1982..	40 919	10 612	-	5 091	(D)	4 279	35 148
1987 farms by acres harvested:							
1 to 24 acres	31	23	64	8	38	133	2
25 to 99 acres	97	53	74	51	31	201	55
100 to 249 acres	92	28	27	48	9	138	47
250 acres or more	55	20	9	20	1	48	47
Wheat for grain .... farms, 1987..	453	252	160	207	579	602	259
1982..	466	252	293	219	596	597	267
acres, 1987..	133 609	145 703	9 895	125 546	212 192	103 013	99 081
1982..	185 813	161 289	23 006	176 830	267 854	128 828	127 700
bushels, 1987..	4 994 017	4 553 923	249 303	3 977 998	6 247 571	3 078 624	3 800 254
1982..	7 107 376	4 204 599	629 403	4 155 467	9 640 603	4 256 279	5 032 452
Irrigated .... farms, 1987..	237	31	1	32	1	10	165
1982..	248	22	1	33	3	20	194
acres, 1987..	47 179	5 651	(D)	6 878	(D)	874	60 292
1982..	67 307	7 557	(D)	9 343	380	1 702	66 589
1987 farms by acres harvested:							
1 to 24 acres	15	7	50	8	41	65	7
25 to 99 acres	97	43	88	20	100	207	38
100 to 249 acres	168	67	15	36	142	214	64
250 acres or more	173	135	7	143	296	116	150
Oats for grain .... farms, 1987..	4	4	36	4	20	33	3
1982..	8	1	60	2	36	65	2
acres, 1987..	105	306	691	132	1 045	854	37
1982..	980	(D)	1 498	-	961	1 445	(D)
bushels, 1987..	2 450	6 187	24 087	2 492	29 335	25 612	1 300
1982..	70 975	(D)	54 182	-	34 713	76 885	(D)
Irrigated .... farms, 1987..	2	-	-	4	-	-	2
1982..	8	-	-	-	-	2	2
acres, 1987..	(D)	-	-	132	-	-	(D)
1982..	910	-	-	-	-	(D)	(D)
1987 farms by acres harvested:							
1 to 24 acres	1	-	24	2	14	21	2
25 to 99 acres	3	3	11	2	5	10	1
100 to 249 acres	-	1	1	-	-	2	-
250 acres or more	-	-	-	-	1	-	-
Soybeans for beans .... farms, 1987..	68	9	197	2	3	217	53
1982..	84	1	175	2	1	198	71
acres, 1987..	5 462	499	17 664	(D)	(D)	12 996	3 719
1982..	10 084	(D)	12 204	(D)	(D)	14 858	6 937
bushels, 1987..	208 432	13 450	500 533	(D)	(D)	479 136	110 636
1982..	394 216	(D)	265 629	(D)	(D)	425 503	259 871
Irrigated .... farms, 1987..	60	7	1	2	2	58	49
1982..	76	1	9	2	3	78	68
acres, 1987..	4 970	479	(D)	(D)	(D)	6 058	3 561
1982..	8 826	(D)	-	(D)	(D)	7 586	6 827
1987 farms by acres harvested:							
1 to 24 acres	16	3	34	2	1	84	11
25 to 99 acres	32	5	109	-	1	96	24
100 to 249 acres	17	1	43	-	1	30	11
250 acres or more	3	-	11	-	-	7	2
Hay—alfalfa, other tame, small grain, wild, grass silage, green chop, etc. (see text) ...... farms, 1987..	131	65	331	63	294	401	58
1982..	125	41	415	62	317	488	59
acres, 1987..	20 644	4 570	35 069	8 479	17 327	14 908	6 126
1982..	14 442	2 943	32 077	7 617	15 378	18 694	6 049
tons, dry, 1987..	103 541	11 021	51 958	26 944	41 069	36 505	23 904
1982..	61 686	6 734	51 455	24 849	35 103	37 964	22 335
Irrigated .... farms, 1987..	76	4	2	28	3	11	48
1982..	79	9	-	32	10	16	44
acres, 1987..	17 966	(D)	(D)	5 148	10	570	5 565
1982..	10 624	1 003	-	4 943	514	944	4 637
1987 farms by acres harvested:							
1 to 24 acres	44	19	61	9	95	206	12
25 to 99 acres	49	32	154	25	155	167	33
100 to 249 acres	19	13	80	17	36	28	9
250 acres or more	20	1	36	12	6	-	8

Table 15. Selected Crops: 1987 and 1982—Con.

[For meaning of abbreviations and symbols, see introductory text]

Crop	Hodgeman	Jackson	Jefferson	Jewell	Johnson	Kearny	Kingman	Kiowa
Harvested cropland ... farms, 1987	382	844	836	647	486	247	718	276
1982	417	951	855	718	555	242	772	317
acres, 1987	159 903	114 691	112 895	208 645	69 445	202 166	219 448	128 425
1982	164 424	139 408	128 243	249 175	89 698	216 509	265 252	144 836
Irrigated ... farms, 1987	125	7	7	20	17	109	65	91
1982	126	6	7	52	20	113	65	96
acres, 1987	21 712	2 276	(D)	(D)	165	78 112	14 763	36 599
1982	(D)	2 445	1 176	7 074	(D)	86 819	(D)	(D)
Corn for grain or seed ... farms, 1987	35	205	262	67	104	39	26	52
1982	14	187	251	63	110	33	11	21
acres, 1987	2 826	12 664	23 174	6 361	6 787	24 651	5 130	13 151
1982	1 546	12 193	21 860	6 917	7 716	37 732	1 529	5 114
bushels, 1987	343 924	858 889	2 053 312	742 577	759 913	3 148 328	574 524	1 742 065
1982	161 916	819 839	1 780 456	689 861	705 743	5 118 081	150 521	670 085
Irrigated ... farms, 1987	33	1	5	47	1	36	22	52
1982	12	1	4	39	-	30	9	20
acres, 1987	2 779	(D)	842	5 113	(D)	24 631	4 472	13 091
1982	1 386	(D)	706	4 693	-	37 549	1 323	5 099
1987 farms by acres harvested:								
1 to 24 acres	3	77	87	15	32	2	2	-
25 to 99 acres	24	92	118	31	46	9	7	10
100 to 249 acres	5	27	31	16	18	9	8	19
250 acres or more	3	9	26	6	8	19	9	23
Sorghum for grain or seed ... farms, 1987	282	365	279	523	103	145	231	180
1982	171	304	225	438	95	120	189	168
acres, 1987	31 439	23 760	17 596	58 469	4 799	25 436	11 934	21 760
1982	21 644	17 746	12 529	48 073	5 086	21 991	12 527	26 727
bushels, 1987	1 923 912	1 382 502	1 219 455	4 277 975	346 106	1 241 764	622 839	1 501 690
1982	1 068 834	899 661	733 212	3 010 074	308 045	1 172 509	591 613	1 438 103
Irrigated ... farms, 1987	72	1	4	3	-	44	27	41
1982	68	2	-	13	-	66	30	56
acres, 1987	5 669	(D)	377	175	-	7 230	2 317	5 776
1982	7 036	(D)	-	812	-	10 117	3 424	10 728
1987 farms by acres harvested:								
1 to 24 acres	46	111	90	94	37	21	85	22
25 to 99 acres	139	181	136	228	56	46	107	78
100 to 249 acres	64	63	41	149	10	40	33	52
250 acres or more	33	10	12	52	-	38	5	28
Wheat for grain ... farms, 1987	370	155	83	566	50	226	661	252
1982	402	459	367	640	231	230	713	288
acres, 1987	105 731	9 222	3 836	109 628	2 575	121 394	176 798	74 813
1982	126 997	34 356	25 522	160 165	19 687	138 241	221 474	90 420
bushels, 1987	3 854 253	240 021	126 760	4 379 120	74 630	4 521 316	4 985 931	2 338 400
1982	4 369 244	555 197	516 448	5 340 637	577 691	4 732 102	7 020 389	2 586 716
Irrigated ... farms, 1987	55	1	-	3	-	84	15	49
1982	54	3	-	7	-	89	12	55
acres, 1987	5 220	(D)	-	260	-	23 260	3 945	7 715
1982	5 497	650	-	495	-	22 406	1 502	9 534
1987 farms by acres harvested:								
1 to 24 acres	7	58	39	57	18	6	42	4
25 to 99 acres	85	72	30	201	24	32	152	50
100 to 249 acres	118	20	14	141	6	49	201	83
250 acres or more	160	5	-	167	1	139	266	115
Oats for grain ... farms, 1987	4	95	97	116	52	7	33	10
1982	2	121	119	97	57	2	58	5
acres, 1987	131	2 186	1 945	2 973	928	516	1 540	717
1982	704	2 707	2 521	3 099	1 024	(D)	2 387	1 187
bushels, 1987	3 670	89 656	68 835	132 963	93 361	12 519	51 915	18 010
1982	(D)	111 342	102 349	124 515	42 305		107 413	29 100
Irrigated ... farms, 1987	-	-	-	-	-	2	1	-
1982	-	3	-	-	-	2	1	(D)
acres, 1987	-	(D)	-	-	-	(D)	(D)	(D)
1982	-	(D)	-	-	-	(D)	(D)	-
1987 farms by acres harvested:								
1 to 24 acres	1	81	65	77	41	1	29	6
25 to 99 acres	3	12	31	37	11	3	22	3
100 to 249 acres	-	1	1	2	-	3	2	-
250 acres or more	-	1	-	-	-	-	-	1
Soybeans for beans ... farms, 1987	31	369	365	164	239	14	43	60
1982	12	378	374	77	256	9	17	49
acres, 1987	1 918	25 243	36 268	8 942	33 097	1 596	3 644	6 696
1982	704	25 830	35 778	9 865	35 614	865	1 729	9 320
bushels, 1987	59 874	666 413	1 155 963	254 175	1 030 735	32 278	146 047	270 986
1982	28 632	559 109	917 153	110 101	997 403	33 206	73 600	388 151
Irrigated ... farms, 1987	23	1	1	23	1	12	27	42
1982	11	2	(D)	15	1	7	14	45
acres, 1987	1 516	-	(D)	1 282	(D)	1 386	3 037	5 220
1982	682	(D)	(D)	1 064	(D)	585	1 585	8 760
1987 farms by acres harvested:								
1 to 24 acres	9	124	100	57	57	-	13	2
25 to 99 acres	16	156	159	82	87	5	18	36
100 to 249 acres	5	76	64	24	51	9	9	15
250 acres or more	1	13	42	1	44	-	3	7
Hay—alfalfa, other tame, small grain, wild, grass silage, green chop, etc. (see text) ... farms, 1987	170	706	638	420	336	100	426	102
1982	152	762	656	493	398	80	458	120
acres, 1987	10 680	43 661	32 019	22 884	17 728	20 561	26 671	11 051
1982	7 993	50 122	32 429	25 469	18 774	14 339	23 089	11 937
tons, 1987	27 556	71 748	56 692	57 762	30 035	89 250	62 799	36 268
1982	22 578	94 726	59 660	66 933	33 366	56 068	49 194	37 778
Irrigated ... farms, 1987	35	3	3	5	5	2	17	25
1982	51	1	1	2	3	5	27	42
acres, 1987	1 609	364	56	65	(D)	17 589	937	5 190
1982	2 190	(D)	(D)	(D)	86	12 199	1 067	5 025
1987 farms by acres harvested:								
1 to 24 acres	44	216	235	131	136	11	153	20
25 to 99 acres	92	354	323	226	146	47	190	54
100 to 249 acres	32	122	67	55	47	23	70	15
250 acres or more	2	16	13	5	7	19	13	13

Crop	Labette	Lane	Leavenworth	Lincoln	Linn	Logan	Lyon	McPherson
Harvested cropland .... farms, 1987..	767	291	892	510	551	334	709	1 210
1982..	840	300	956	552	642	329	796	1 331
acres, 1987..	136 983	154 879	96 700	153 709	93 665	160 236	153 982	283 623
1982..	170 902	159 352	108 423	174 863	120 739	166 407	165 108	345 140
Irrigated .... farms, 1987..	18	46	16	7	2	46	6	162
1982..	17	57	8	11	2	58	5	161
acres, 1987..	(D)	14 902	(D)	699	(D)	(D)	(D)	23 993
1982..	1 374	17 895	(D)	703	(D)	(D)	402	(D)
Corn for grain or seed .... farms, 1987..	47	8	292	9	92	16	180	106
1982..	56	14	232	10	89	17	149	86
acres, 1987..	2 261	643	17 320	1 131	6 544	3 448	11 007	11 579
1982..	2 573	2 036	11 835	266	5 723	4 578	6 975	8 079
bushels, 1987..	175 848	66 966	1 525 704	37 506	485 739	368 647	805 657	1 498 266
1982..	166 778	165 724	1 000 720	27 769	448 443	527 785	442 752	954 942
Irrigated .... farms, 1987..	5	6	–	–	–	16	2	92
1982..	6	9	–	6	–	13	2	72
acres, 1987..	444	379	–	–	–	3 438	(D)	10 935
1982..	(D)	1 202	–	142	–	(D)	(D)	7 539
1987 farms by acres harvested:								
1 to 24 acres	22	1	121	3	42	–	58	16
25 to 99 acres	16	4	114	3	27	4	95	46
100 to 249 acres	8	3	48	–	18	7	19	32
250 acres or more	1	–	9	3	5	5	8	10
Sorghum for grain or seed................... farms, 1987..	342	176	260	350	241	184	459	683
1982..	210	96	266	245	209	133	408	553
acres, 1987..	25 624	26 210	14 487	24 531	16 867	21 236	35 421	44 923
1982..	13 952	15 993	16 905	15 157	17 879	24 955	30 521	44 882
bushels, 1987..	1 819 205	1 400 041	1 030 845	1 624 769	1 144 733	1 019 214	2 360 796	3 602 374
1982..	784 421	896 652	1 042 078	966 035	1 019 030	1 229 282	1 594 448	3 047 246
Irrigated .... farms, 1987..	5	27	–	4	–	19		80
1982..	3	40	–	1	–	23	1	84
acres, 1987..	372	4 030	–	202	–	2 923	–	5 602
1982..	300	6 455	–	(D)	–	3 313	(D)	6 452
1987 farms by acres harvested:								
1 to 24 acres	104	26	101	106	88	32	165	229
25 to 99 acres	162	69	119	171	95	79	180	308
100 to 249 acres	51	52	33	59	46	47	84	124
250 acres or more	25	29	7	14	12	26	30	22
Wheat for grain .... farms, 1987..	171	280	74	480	73	322	274	1 077
1982..	595	291	390	520	299	292	553	1 213
acres, 1987..	11 815	111 527	3 049	99 912	2 608	111 896	17 625	184 434
1982..	82 529	128 244	20 703	128 675	22 360	126 792	41 908	244 679
bushels, 1987..	252 913	4 240 788	86 850	3 442 697	70 864	3 567 380	498 181	6 198 954
1982..	2 225 675	4 186 591	421 059	4 275 564	502 544	3 744 938	884 017	7 509 966
Irrigated .... farms, 1987..	–	26	–	1	–	18	–	9
1982..	1	37	–	1	–	11	1	6
acres, 1987..	–	3 904	–	(D)	–	2 176	–	1 133
1982..	(D)	5 695	–	(D)	–	1 919	(D)	730
1987 farms by acres harvested:								
1 to 24 acres	63	7	42	19	39	5	118	81
25 to 99 acres	73	54	23	133	27	55	110	352
100 to 249 acres	26	62	7	184	7	107	35	394
250 acres or more	9	157	2	144	–	157	11	250
Oats for grain .... farms, 1987..	179	13	90	77	61	21	47	53
1982..	247	3	85	67	99	7	105	92
acres, 1987..	5 485	645	1 647	1 845	1 225	1 329	1 332	675
1982..	7 155	(D)	1 094	2 020	1 929	328	1 655	1 541
bushels, 1987..	172 356	21 415	55 135	71 466	44 681	46 655	43 923	27 692
1982..	376 383	(D)	42 429	96 538	82 412	12 975	68 082	59 434
Irrigated .... farms, 1987..	7	1	1	–	–	–	3	9
1982..	1	2	–	1	–	–	3	10
acres, 1987..	–	(D)	(D)	–	–	–	(D)	101
1982..	–	(D)	–	–	–	(D)	–	(D)
1987 farms by acres harvested:								
1 to 24 acres	101	9	66	51	47	8	39	45
25 to 99 acres	71	1	24	25	13	8	7	8
100 to 249 acres	7	2	–	1	1	4	1	–
250 acres or more	–	1	–	–	–	1	–	–
Soybeans for beans .... farms, 1987..	482	4	361	44	297	2	492	352
1982..	464	11	392	42	358	3	489	295
acres, 1987..	66 168	174	31 563	1 896	40 829	(D)	43 599	16 498
1982..	58 200	924	29 060	1 968	46 800	425	36 664	18 290
bushels, 1987..	1 538 005	5 240	974 966	48 261	1 208 979	(D)	1 340 496	554 623
1982..	917 753	30 170	833 186	52 203	1 135 792	(D)	779 657	548 366
Irrigated .... farms, 1987..	7	4	2	2	–	–	3	80
1982..	4	9	1	3	–	–	3	101
acres, 1987..	572	164	(D)	(D)	–	(D)	(D)	5 299
1982..	315	848	(D)	120	–	–	122	7 915
1987 farms by acres harvested:								
1 to 24 acres	104	1	132	19	64	–	144	150
25 to 99 acres	197	3	158	21	115	1	220	163
100 to 249 acres	110	–	65	3	75	1	90	36
250 acres or more	71	–	6	1	43	–	38	3
Hay—alfalfa, other tame, small grain, wild, grass silage, green chop, etc, (see text) .... farms, 1987..	545	75	677	326	438	117	492	654
1982..	587	70	744	375	483	113	562	722
acres, 1987..	26 555	4 653	29 970	26 059	27 364	7 713	44 903	26 779
1982..	24 601	3 616	29 580	25 322	28 424	6 596	44 655	25 947
tons, dry, 1987..	47 709	8 716	55 874	57 949	46 141	15 478	59 188	66 796
1982..	39 657	8 774	60 423	67 577	45 068	17 182	64 654	65 411
Irrigated .... farms, 1987..	4	12	2	1	–	15	1	11
1982..	4	15	–	2	–	20	1	14
acres, 1987..	–	372	(D)	(D)	–	592	(D)	367
1982..	51	389	–	(D)	–	904	(D)	339
1987 farms by acres harvested:								
1 to 24 acres	219	23	300	89	132	25	140	296
25 to 99 acres	248	40	312	147	215	66	217	297
100 to 249 acres	69	11	59	75	80	24	98	58
250 acres or more	9	1	6	16	11	2	37	3

Table 15. **Selected Crops: 1987 and 1982** — Con.

[For meaning of abbreviations and symbols, see introductory text]

Crop	Marion	Marshall	Meade	Miami	Mitchell	Montgomery	Morris	Morton
Harvested cropland .... farms, 1987..	994	944	413	902	570	674	472	192
1982..	1 072	1 045	436	972	683	696	494	210
acres, 1987..	252 314	261 802	200 706	116 217	237 322	111 306	112 525	139 398
1982..	292 672	279 758	215 390	126 669	246 161	129 397	117 842	170 522
Irrigated .... farms, 1987..	26	20	190	14	38	21	4	78
1982..	25	12	187	6	36	19	5	60
acres, 1987..	2 188	2 159	99 161	437	(D)	(D)	(D)	(D)
1982..	(D)	(D)	101 522	449	3 860	(D)	311	(D)
Corn for grain or seed .... farms, 1987..	85	114	80	156	32	73	65	10
1982..	90	138	50	127	24	70	88	11
acres, 1987..	3 765	6 075	21 643	9 976	2 516	7 980	2 657	2 658
1982..	3 618	6 796	13 834	9 004	1 886	6 171	2 752	2 958
bushels, 1987..	319 364	516 618	2 651 087	857 078	265 085	717 163	205 977	361 116
1982..	231 038	559 889	1 907 057	766 364	211 373	478 909	222 855	335 863
Irrigated .... farms, 1987..	14	10	79	–	20	6	–	6
1982..	12	8	49	1	16	6	1	7
acres, 1987..	1 189	1 307	21 543	–	2 141	1 597	–	2 475
1982..	743	(D)	13 575	(D)	1 401	722	(D)	2 653
1987 farms by acres harvested:								
1 to 24 acres	44	39	3	65	10	18	27	1
25 to 99 acres	32	64	17	63	9	30	30	1
100 to 249 acres	8	8	26	18	11	16	8	3
250 acres or more	1	3	34	9	2	9	–	5
Sorghum for grain or seed .... farms, 1987..	739	824	269	282	429	263	347	148
1982..	676	720	204	259	283	189	284	145
acres, 1987..	68 973	91 784	56 143	17 421	48 087	28 613	27 744	58 159
1982..	67 848	74 616	61 501	14 174	30 793	19 516	21 146	76 801
bushels, 1987..	4 561 421	6 350 013	4 632 670	1 208 594	3 559 899	1 921 024	1 494 922	2 548 003
1982..	3 440 263	5 088 555	5 126 686	850 254	1 990 375	1 130 559	1 029 188	2 710 914
Irrigated .... farms, 1987..	9	2	141	1	8	2	1	57
1982..	7	2	140	3	8	2	1	47
acres, 1987..	652	(D)	36 130	(D)	305	(D)	(D)	13 856
1982..	475	(D)	49 606	112	797	(D)	(D)	15 296
1987 farms by acres harvested:								
1 to 24 acres	146	88	25	107	100	59	88	7
25 to 99 acres	351	384	92	100	171	115	159	20
100 to 249 acres	184	272	73	46	111	51	83	37
250 acres or more	58	80	79	9	47	23	17	84
Wheat for grain .... farms, 1987..	857	766	391	46	529	177	326	167
1982..	969	901	410	340	548	423	398	174
acres, 1987..	118 472	75 311	106 765	1 631	164 343	16 023	36 194	74 500
1982..	156 067	101 052	125 027	19 181	196 397	62 293	49 490	88 260
bushels, 1987..	3 717 501	2 580 342	3 452 545	44 393	6 254 876	365 771	1 020 099	2 058 361
1982..	4 900 608	3 010 208	3 861 634	491 170	6 139 739	1 772 173	1 067 703	2 042 541
Irrigated .... farms, 1987..	–	1	152	–	4	1	–	64
1982..	2	1	130	–	–	–	–	47
acres, 1987..	–	(D)	31 487	–	644	–	–	17 937
1982..	(D)	(D)	29 088	–	–	(D)	–	14 895
1987 farms by acres harvested:								
1 to 24 acres	82	120	7	33	33	51	55	4
25 to 99 acres	324	362	90	12	109	79	158	36
100 to 249 acres	315	224	138	3	160	32	74	37
250 acres or more	136	60	156	–	227	15	39	91
Oats for grain .... farms, 1987..	148	145	2	89	79	64	83	4
1982..	271	215	2	67	54	110	131	–
acres, 1987..	2 925	2 320	(D)	1 520	1 503	1 552	1 759	288
1982..	6 151	4 852	(D)	2 188	1 572	2 823	2 789	–
bushels, 1987..	85 026	112 692	(D)	53 856	71 496	48 806	48 007	12 340
1982..	231 647	256 400	(D)	103 223	78 372	132 680	101 938	–
Irrigated .... farms, 1987..	–	–	–	–	2	1	–	2
1982..	–	–	–	–	1	–	–	–
acres, 1987..	–	–	–	–	(D)	1	–	(D)
1982..	–	–	–	–	–	(D)	–	–
1987 farms by acres harvested:								
1 to 24 acres	106	124	1	68	65	39	60	–
25 to 99 acres	41	19	1	21	12	24	22	3
100 to 249 acres	1	2	–	–	2	1	1	1
250 acres or more	–	–	–	–	–	–	–	–
Soybeans for beans .... farms, 1987..	321	741	54	393	114	280	212	3
1982..	218	683	32	428	32	218	181	2
acres, 1987..	11 732	61 942	5 222	46 043	7 764	34 604	12 488	(D)
1982..	10 745	63 888	5 416	46 033	2 934	31 853	9 134	(D)
bushels, 1987..	301 506	1 639 663	202 830	1 462 632	194 245	913 282	329 534	(D)
1982..	218 155	1 761 294	183 530	1 119 469	101 227	402 931	215 488	(D)
Irrigated .... farms, 1987..	5	7	45	3	16	2	3	3
1982..	8	8	49	–	8	2	4	1
acres, 1987..	166	403	4 999	(D)	1 373	172	(D)	(D)
1982..	249	373	5 196	–	1 011	(D)	156	(D)
1987 farms by acres harvested:								
1 to 24 acres	151	185	11	104	41	58	66	1
25 to 99 acres	152	347	24	179	50	121	110	1
100 to 249 acres	15	169	15	62	18	64	28	–
250 acres or more	3	40	4	48	5	37	8	1
Hay—alfalfa, other tame, small grain, wild,								
grass silage, green chop, etc. (see text) .... farms, 1987..	710	617	125	748	285	524	348	39
1982..	782	728	112	796	306	511	380	32
acres, 1987..	45 711	29 463	9 848	40 425	14 427	25 547	31 649	3 273
1982..	43 651	32 231	10 475	40 966	13 705	23 320	32 154	1 558
tons, dry, 1987..	91 483	58 624	25 891	70 017	36 215	40 851	60 014	6 166
1982..	85 464	77 057	27 169	74 032	35 378	99 202	62 217	4 711
Irrigated .... farms, 1987..	2	3	36	1	2	1	–	9
1982..	6	2	57	–	4	2	–	10
acres, 1987..	(D)	60	2 976	(D)	(D)	(D)	–	766
1982..	131	(D)	4 856	–	301	6	–	690
1987 farms by acres harvested:								
1 to 24 acres	230	228	34	263	99	220	81	10
25 to 99 acres	359	320	65	342	154	232	159	17
100 to 249 acres	102	65	20	110	28	63	81	9
250 acres or more	19	4	6	13	4	9	27	3

Table 15. Selected Crops: 1987 and 1982—Con.

[For meaning of abbreviations and symbols, see introductory text]

Crop	Nemaha	Neosho	Ness	Norton	Osage	Osborne	Ottawa	Pawnee
Harvested cropland .... farms, 1987..	994	611	542	415	729	554	476	475
1982..	1 024	662	577	458	825	572	514	519
acres, 1987..	203 290	126 121	193 380	154 827	140 377	182 056	149 879	223 904
1982..	215 292	142 932	216 742	170 487	158 633	179 133	185 635	256 255
Irrigated .... farms, 1987..	7	6	29	54	5	76	24	180
1982..	1	6	34	64	11	48	25	173
acres, 1987..	(D)	(D)	2 662	(D)	(D)	(D)	(D)	64 081
1982..	(D)	(D)	3 865	(D)	(D)	(D)	(D)	64 641
Corn for grain or seed .... farms, 1987..	243	88	2	70	98	26	11	52
1982..	286	62	4	36	107	22	18	27
acres, 1987..	10 685	5 010	(D)	9 097	4 676	1 180	2 232	13 077
1982..	13 878	3 321	693	3 825	4 662	975	1 913	7 163
bushels, 1987..	711 109	443 841	(D)	681 532	360 132	121 174	301 182	1 819 964
1982..	1 105 065	211 436	(D)	472 768	292 600	107 752	119 637	861 714
Irrigated .... farms, 1987..	-	1	1	39	-	16	6	52
1982..	-	2	2	33	1	14	11	24
acres, 1987..	-	(D)	(D)	4 656	-	761	354	13 007
1982..	-	-	(D)	3 132	(D)	562	1 070	6 672
1987 farms by acres harvested:								
1 to 24 acres	101	35	-	9	46	11	4	-
25 to 99 acres	117	34	1	26	38	12	4	19
100 to 249 acres	22	18	1	26	12	3	2	22
250 acres or more	3	1	-	9	2	-	1	11
Sorghum for grain or seed .... farms, 1987..	622	318	362	242	435	417	211	337
1982..	730	211	193	208	409	291	147	297
acres, 1987..	90 325	26 847	32 270	23 991	39 997	35 210	12 192	46 236
1982..	82 005	15 915	17 957	23 987	33 514	23 290	8 065	49 953
bushels, 1987..	6 296 279	2 130 009	1 744 228	1 713 245	2 864 632	2 602 595	860 169	3 497 382
1982..	5 651 871	1 038 440	805 964	1 328 086	2 002 085	1 431 002	481 779	3 313 821
Irrigated .... farms, 1987..	2	-	20	6	2	58	11	117
1982..	-	-	19	13	3	24	3	135
acres, 1987..	(D)	-	1 177	409	(D)	4 190	615	16 439
1982..	-	-	1 300	847	(D)	1 400	(D)	22 090
1987 farms by acres harvested:								
1 to 24 acres	109	88	92	40	121	120	73	57
25 to 99 acres	368	137	160	126	187	182	106	124
100 to 249 acres	267	70	83	50	85	88	24	101
250 acres or more	78	23	27	26	42	27	8	55
Wheat for grain .... farms, 1987..	654	136	519	376	160	517	424	433
1982..	755	475	557	421	528	528	476	481
acres, 1987..	35 303	13 064	135 612	96 466	7 688	117 191	111 270	125 758
1982..	53 302	58 446	180 164	121 570	37 407	129 846	153 160	158 657
bushels, 1987..	1 080 837	335 523	4 654 376	3 942 685	205 292	4 308 743	3 482 863	4 295 992
1982..	1 522 644	1 575 703	6 279 479	4 720 905	711 880	4 195 634	4 588 654	5 142 355
Irrigated .... farms, 1987..	-	-	14	2	1	2	3	94
1982..	-	(D)	17	6	(D)	4	-	95
acres, 1987..	-	-	745	(D)	(D)	1 621	485	11 786
1982..	-	-	1 300	1 037	(D)		485	15 083
1987 farms by acres harvested:								
1 to 24 acres	222	48	18	11	70	21	42	26
25 to 99 acres	341	61	123	94	72	148	89	86
100 to 249 acres	80	16	161	130	15	177	133	137
250 acres or more	11	11	217	141	3	171	160	184
Oats for grain .... farms, 1987..	120	147	12	62	63	61	40	12
1982..	171	162	9	42	9	24	23	11
acres, 1987..	2 034	4 216	297	2 996	1 040	1 344	625	324
1982..	2 825	5 260	258	1 798	1 713	701	369	698
bushels, 1987..	84 605	168 894	5 780	103 836	34 658	66 886	25 481	10 876
1982..	134 916	291 000	15 810	88 502	69 534	36 062	17 169	33 820
Irrigated .... farms, 1987..	-	-	-	1	-	-	1	-
1982..	-	-	-	(D)	-	-	-	-
acres, 1987..	-	-	-	1	-	-	1	-
1982..	-	-	-	(D)	-	-	(D)	-
1987 farms by acres harvested:								
1 to 24 acres	97	77	9	29	50	43	32	7
25 to 99 acres	23	67	3	27	13	17	8	5
100 to 249 acres	-	3	-	5	-	1	-	-
250 acres or more	-	-	-	1	-	-	-	-
Soybeans for beans .... farms, 1987..	613	406	11	9	481	74	117	98
1982..	479	397	3	4	543	40	55	91
acres, 1987..	31 953	50 660	969	344	50 704	3 224	5 250	11 666
1982..	27 259	43 652	262	182	46 896	2 122	2 534	11 878
bushels, 1987..	839 157	1 290 328	9 850	4 846	1 608 243	84 719	155 104	461 282
1982..	667 201	844 057	4 484	(D)	1 020 408	84 453	68 566	458 598
Irrigated .... farms, 1987..	1	1	1	-	2	1	1	9
1982..	-	2	2	1	4	2	7	77
acres, 1987..	(D)	(D)	(D)	-	(D)	852	588	10 000
1982..	-	(D)	(D)	1	235	408	571	11 042
1987 farms by acres harvested:								
1 to 24 acres	230	86	4	2	123	27	43	21
25 to 99 acres	290	161	5	4	194	37	61	36
100 to 249 acres	84	96	4	1	110	10	13	29
250 acres or more	9	65	-	-	54	-	-	12
Hay—alfalfa, other tame, small grain, wild, grass silage, green chop, etc. (see text) ...... farms, 1987..	662	462	272	220	489	331	293	220
1982..	739	440	254	272	559	318	323	265
acres, 1987..	33 071	26 155	18 306	12 510	37 588	20 527	18 533	27 298
1982..	32 666	21 837	13 853	15 306	38 207	19 191	17 722	29 925
tons, dry, 1987..	70 183	45 326	43 749	34 952	52 307	50 319	43 177	96 658
1982..	79 326	35 817	30 019	41 469	54 892	51 295	42 496	103 807
Irrigated .... farms, 1987..	2	-	13	11	7	7	2	69
1982..	-	-	21	14	2	8	-	79
acres, 1987..	(D)	(D)	385	358	(D)	422	(D)	12 465
1982..	-	-	732	376	(D)	398	281	9 923
1987 farms by acres harvested:								
1 to 24 acres	253	161	66	73	161	109	88	55
25 to 99 acres	320	221	150	109	215	182	150	97
100 to 249 acres	82	68	47	33	89	52	49	51
250 acres or more	7	12	9	8	24	8	6	27

Table 15. **Selected Crops: 1987 and 1982**—Con.

[For meaning of abbreviations and symbols, see introductory text]

Crop	Phillips	Pottawatomie	Pratt	Rawlins	Reno	Republic	Rice	Riley
Harvested cropland .... farms, 1987..	527	614	465	497	1 346	736	541	462
1982..	596	732	511	579	1 438	831	586	466
acres, 1987..	162 736	118 376	242 460	196 707	374 679	230 517	214 092	80 307
1982..	173 288	134 722	249 755	217 218	446 428	259 275	248 311	84 221
Irrigated .... farms, 1987..	37	48	160	72	154	232	67	25
1982..	42	47	152	95	135	208	64	23
acres, 1987..	4 910	(D)	69 512	(D)	(D)	44 869	15 058	1 851
1982..	(D)	7 796	52 822	(D)	23 434	(D)	18 232	(D)
Corn for grain or seed .... farms, 1987..	38	133	112	54	69	265	36	56
1982..	36	140	57	46	45	256	32	57
acres, 1987..	5 261	11 352	29 531	6 047	11 147	39 494	7 833	2 892
1982..	4 942	10 913	16 479	7 684	5 291	37 203	5 343	3 506
bushels, 1987..	604 232	1 167 310	2 996 866	639 516	1 243 297	5 110 811	1 015 410	263 926
1982..	635 845	964 007	2 415 470	747 659	556 907	3 853 235	646 360	305 181
Irrigated .... farms, 1987..	28	36	107	34	50	211	35	8
1982..	24	34	63	34	35	167	29	10
acres, 1987..	3 729	6 305	27 173	3 925	8 847	36 391	7 603	633
1982..	3 051	4 387	15 921	5 965	3 355	30 091	5 195	(D)
1987 farms by acres harvested:								
1 to 24 acres	8	46	1	6	14	37	2	29
25 to 99 acres	18	56	25	25	16	86	8	19
100 to 249 acres	9	22	51	19	22	95	12	7
250 acres or more	5	9	35	4	17	47	14	1
Sorghum for grain or seed .... farms, 1987..	366	382	292	354	785	536	416	312
1982..	344	409	280	245	754	500	393	263
acres, 1987..	36 063	27 721	36 214	40 057	80 060	64 091	53 304	25 050
1982..	33 627	25 128	41 923	26 618	87 852	56 484	52 500	21 156
bushels, 1987..	2 650 230	1 707 764	2 301 925	2 357 618	5 271 312	5 252 036	4 174 853	1 717 217
1982..	1 762 323	1 556 706	2 434 254	1 452 559	4 932 141	4 021 235	3 267 617	1 476 890
Irrigated .... farms, 1987..	9	7	72	40	78	25	31	3
1982..	7		73	40	70	29	22	3
acres, 1987..	(D)	397	8 625	3 223	7 851	1 148	2 779	63
1982..	507	(D)	10 836	4 344	8 034	1 601	3 094	(D)
1987 farms by acres harvested:								
1 to 24 acres	86	104	39	51	168	100	62	67
25 to 99 acres	162	202	125	171	338	215	159	156
100 to 249 acres	84	59	92	93	202	156	141	74
250 acres or more	34	17	36	39	79	67	56	15
Wheat for grain .... farms, 1987..	473	301	426	467	1 140	638	484	302
1982..	532	465	465	541	1 232	723	533	360
acres, 1987..	84 316	16 968	143 482	123 069	237 738	83 080	130 672	21 023
1982..	97 804	35 486	165 792	162 641	298 224	116 066	165 617	29 744
bushels, 1987..	3 467 434	524 558	4 258 896	4 776 125	6 846 396	3 356 029	4 465 243	723 631
1982..	3 610 023	908 002	4 997 093	5 234 484	9 448 664	3 560 207	5 436 911	912 477
Irrigated .... farms, 1987..	3	1	47	14	19	15	7	1
1982..			38	22	33	11	10	3
acres, 1987..	(D)	(D)	6 499	1 605	2 999	769	321	(D)
1982..	(D)	(D)	6 327	2 483	3 947	1 844	1 223	210
1987 farms by acres harvested:								
1 to 24 acres	34	130	21	21	120	103	38	74
25 to 99 acres	165	118	57	99	349	238	104	161
100 to 249 acres	161	44	114	153	332	204	147	55
250 acres or more	113	9	226	194	339	93	195	12
Oats for grain .... farms, 1987..	77	95	12	59	55	111	22	68
1982..	78	109	23	24	119	191	15	78
acres, 1987..	1 834	1 421	464	2 150	1 157	2 162	889	1 027
1982..	1 871	1 643	1 048	859	4 444	4 120	853	1 342
bushels, 1987..	63 457	56 179	16 979	100 025	36 090	109 378	29 124	43 598
1982..	62 750	63 992	49 241	46 497	224 787	212 050	49 463	60 657
Irrigated .... farms, 1987..	-	-	2	-	5	2	-	-
1982..	-	-	4	3	2	7	2	-
acres, 1987..	-	-	(D)	-	(D)	(D)	(D)	-
1982..	-	-	300	110	328	-	-	-
1987 farms by acres harvested:								
1 to 24 acres	49	80	6	32	41	83	16	59
25 to 99 acres	28	15	5	21	11	26	5	8
100 to 249 acres	-	-	1	6	3	-	1	1
250 acres or more	-	-	-	-	-	-	-	-
Soybeans for beans .... farms, 1987..	20	311	80	11	132	434	117	206
1982..	4	282	69	5	112	394	79	162
acres, 1987..	904	18 726	8 871	461	6 400	24 503	7 475	10 911
1982..	75	15 180	11 746	(D)	6 473	24 208	6 953	7 707
bushels, 1987..	26 818	584 261	334 145	8 451	297 067	852 680	253 945	341 081
1982..	2 502	396 678	492 824	(D)	268 331	783 548	254 623	237 292
Irrigated .... farms, 1987..	2	23	23	2	60	114	29	11
1982..	(D)	10	63	1	48	113	29	10
acres, 1987..	(D)	1 719	7 744		3 905	5 783	2 506	464
1982..	(D)	1 043	10 970	(D)	4 927	7 296	3 892	767
1987 farms by acres harvested:								
1 to 24 acres	9	125	14	2	36	151	28	66
25 to 99 acres	7	131	34	9	66	217	66	108
100 to 249 acres	4	44	22	-	26	52	22	28
250 acres or more	-	11	10	-	2	14	1	4
Hay—alfalfa, other tame, small grain, wild, grass silage, green chop, etc. (see text) .... farms, 1987..	368	469	154	233	734	455	287	333
1982..	407	540	177	260	811	559	330	339
acres, 1987..	27 505	43 089	28 831	15 764	40 161	19 993	16 076	17 945
1982..	26 768	45 063	16 190	15 707	42 476	22 059	17 067	18 797
tons, dry, 1987..	74 247	71 446	127 661	48 473	106 117	52 593	45 925	34 521
1982..	71 306	85 774	54 310	50 306	109 787	61 834	50 490	41 976
Irrigated .... farms, 1987..	10	5	20	26	26	23	13	4
1982..	9	-	22	47	27	18	9	3
acres, 1987..	251	342	(D)	1 434	1 861	444	838	110
1982..	193	-	9 366	2 834	1 663	421	825	(D)
1987 farms by acres harvested:								
1 to 24 acres	94	120	53	49	294	216	97	118
25 to 99 acres	192	197	72	129	339	204	141	173
100 to 249 acres	70	120	21	51	83	33	43	38
250 acres or more	12	32	8	4	16	2	6	4

Crop	Rooks	Rush	Russell	Saline	Scott	Sedgwick	Seward	Shawnee
Harvested cropland .... farms, 1987..	431	494	469	549	330	1 345	229	659
1982..	463	525	517	594	356	1 423	228	726
acres, 1987..	157 823	160 253	135 417	173 828	180 540	319 625	141 650	101 139
1982..	168 987	172 379	163 585	205 872	209 383	363 417	159 542	103 231
Irrigated .... farms, 1987..	22	74	6	50	162	176	139	66
1982..	27	86	5	33	195	182	127	59
acres, 1987..	(D)	7 780	434	(D)	54 147	29 446	75 210	(D)
1982..	(D)	(D)	(D)	(D)	67 377	28 560	76 212	(D)
Corn for grain or seed .... farms, 1987..	11	15	8	27	53	79	51	176
1982..	10	18	9	36	49	65	33	154
acres, 1987..	1 303	966	102	1 324	6 948	13 005	11 367	20 588
1982..	1 678	1 446	(D)	1 575	11 902	8 341	8 805	19 857
bushels, 1987..	134 750	104 265	6 047	115 318	1 137 275	1 568 412	1 340 010	2 194 933
1982..	106 081	133 260	(D)	116 340	1 444 365	963 198	1 109 932	1 904 940
Irrigated .... farms, 1987..	8	12	-	7	52	67	51	41
1982..	6	10	1	10	46	56	32	41
acres, 1987..	971	849	-	305	6 801	11 542	11 367	7 110
1982..	296	704	(D)	276	11 600	7 493	8 750	(D)
1987 farms by acres harvested:								
1 to 24 acres	3	4	6	12	1	9	-	56
25 to 99 acres	4	10	2	11	16	19	18	55
100 to 249 acres	3	-	-	4	22	38	19	43
250 acres or more...............	1	1	-	-	14	13	14	22
Sorghum for grain or seed.................... farms, 1987..	264	337	253	303	203	709	165	260
1982..	201	241	193	194	184	516	157	189
acres, 1987..	30 101	30 125	21 517	16 514	35 551	63 831	49 622	20 453
1982..	20 266	22 367	16 688	10 539	34 864	57 696	61 383	14 800
bushels, 1987..	1 624 566	1 736 580	1 336 856	1 098 936	2 314 111	4 162 363	3 281 751	1 279 717
1982..	988 040	1 116 218	949 603	596 827	2 463 626	3 380 245	3 471 353	774 951
Irrigated .... farms, 1987..	9	57	1	16	97	46	100	6
1982..	8	60	1	8	117	61	86	3
acres, 1987..	449	4 247	(D)	1 197	17 556	4 030	25 160	147
1982..	(D)	4 746	(D)	286	21 038	7 934	30 557	(D)
1987 farms by acres harvested:								
1 to 24 acres	54	70	61	99	29	179	4	105
25 to 99 acres	132	161	117	156	71	327	24	91
100 to 249 acres	64	79	58	41	59	147	66	45
250 acres or more...............	34	27	17	5	44	56	71	19
Wheat for grain .... farms, 1987..	408	481	414	541	315	1 041	208	148
1982..	455	494	466	606	336	1 108	195	355
acres, 1987..	100 707	113 315	92 100	126 775	115 140	189 806	68 948	7 719
1982..	126 985	135 359	123 359	166 557	141 976	242 204	79 668	27 231
bushels, 1987..	3 769 144	3 615 969	2 995 383	3 770 758	4 521 675	5 504 665	2 317 037	233 770
1982..	4 533 142	4 619 455	4 217 092	5 039 990	4 626 370	8 445 246	2 613 642	538 936
Irrigated .... farms, 1987..	6	30	2	5	88	21	123	-
1982..	(D)	24	2	1	111	25	90	4
acres, 1987..	(D)	1 481	(D)	198	16 013	2 162	30 213	-
1982..	1 217	1 300	(D)	(D)	18 083	2 679	29 436	194
1987 farms by acres harvested:								
1 to 24 acres	17	19	15	54	7	125	1	64
25 to 99 acres	108	100	140	158	56	365	42	58
100 to 249 acres	137	177	131	149	80	284	67	22
250 acres or more...............	146	165	128	180	172	267	98	4
Oats for grain .... farms, 1987..	22	50	39	33	3	27	3	73
1982..	21	29	28	9	6	65	1	64
acres, 1987..	736	1 569	827	703	122	560	123	1 066
1982..	1 415	1 919	909	1 244	220	2 947	(D)	894
bushels, 1987..	23 120	46 850	30 517	25 825	6 500	15 865	3 777	30 440
1982..	65 875	83 902	31 256	52 017	11 302	109 766	(D)	29 082
Irrigated .... farms, 1987..	-	-	-	-	1	-	2	-
1982..	1	5	-	-	4	-	1	-
acres, 1987..	-	(D)	-	-	(D)	-	(D)	-
1982..	(D)	116	-	-	197	-	(D)	-
1987 farms by acres harvested:								
1 to 24 acres	12	30	30	26	-	17	-	65
25 to 99 acres	9	17	8	6	3	10	3	8
100 to 249 acres	1	3	1	1	-	-	-	-
250 acres or more...............	-	-	-	-	-	-	-	-
Soybeans for beans .... farms, 1987..	9	36	17	183	14	240	16	323
1982..	5	23	3	111	24	166	21	271
acres, 1987..	880	3 179	669	7 565	1 046	21 042	824	30 060
1982..	746	690	70	4 396	4 352	13 902	3 153	17 363
bushels, 1987..	11 685	40 534	17 750	199 976	39 512	779 026	29 413	913 322
1982..	5 189	24 077	1 038	108 781	155 475	418 537	92 079	413 603
Irrigated .... farms, 1987..	3	12	1	15	13	79	16	33
1982..	3	18	-	2	21	80	18	18
acres, 1987..	(D)	318	(D)	715	1 006	9 437	824	3 077
1982..	(D)	463	-	(D)	3 097	7 926	2 629	1 681
1987 farms by acres harvested:								
1 to 24 acres	3	16	7	82	7	58	4	105
25 to 99 acres	4	10	9	80	2	122	10	119
100 to 249 acres	1	6	1	20	5	45	2	64
250 acres or more...............	1	4	-	1	-	15	-	35
Hay—alfalfa, other tame, small grain, wild, grass silage, green chop, etc. (see text) .... farms, 1987..	208	213	265	362	86	669	59	443
1982..	232	220	301	393	76	800	58	515
acres, 1987..	18 051	12 056	20 371	22 883	6 975	35 692	9 878	23 711
1982..	14 961	9 826	17 725	19 167	5 181	38 277	6 918	25 510
tons, dry, 1987..	46 623	28 721	44 657	54 221	19 126	84 452	37 342	34 650
1982..	41 007	24 760	39 468	53 219	15 775	75 626	25 991	45 326
Irrigated .... farms, 1987..	4	23	2	6	32	12	29	4
1982..	11	40	2	10	43	24	29	4
acres, 1987..	(D)	517	(D)	162	2 364	478	7 530	14
1982..	461	1 234	(D)	263	2 485	846	4 371	41
1987 farms by acres harvested:								
1 to 24 acres	58	78	70	149	25	280	10	192
25 to 99 acres	104	98	123	139	39	298	25	183
100 to 249 acres	36	34	62	62	16	73	14	57
250 acres or more...............	10	3	10	12	6	18	10	11

Table 15. Selected Crops: 1987 and 1982—Con.

[For meaning of abbreviations and symbols, see introductory text]

Crop	Sheridan	Sherman	Smith	Stafford	Stanton	Stevens	Sumner	Thomas
Harvested cropland ...... farms, 1987..	461	470	630	488	241	260	1 137	592
1982..	521	512	675	526	209	292	1 271	575
acres, 1987..	183 013	251 334	211 337	230 807	184 701	238 568	415 440	296 047
1982..	200 637	296 853	216 933	266 542	220 929	298 655	519 906	307 900
Irrigated ...... farms, 1987..	167	241	61	196	168	161	28	214
1982..	208	261	49	170	147	161	21	196
acres, 1987..	49 232	82 671	(D)	65 784	110 331	115 787	(D)	72 347
1982..	65 255	(D)	8 618	60 765	120 784	115 696	1 764	(D)
Corn for grain or seed ...... farms, 1987..	130	168	50	106	96	65	17	184
1982..	141	177	39	57	76	48	4	141
acres, 1987..	26 533	35 617	3 029	29 798	30 940	25 418	997	48 965
1982..	37 152	44 346	3 098	15 638	31 895	15 870	277	46 137
bushels, 1987..	4 061 477	5 066 990	353 379	3 786 704	4 387 760	3 303 471	69 170	7 122 349
1982..	4 728 234	4 896 661	251 513	2 002 090	4 269 541	2 058 099	20 110	5 958 506
Irrigated ...... farms, 1987..	124	182	37	100	95	64	3	174
1982..	138	171	24	49	74	48	1	136
acres, 1987..	27 485	34 781	2 270	29 140	30 360	25 408	432	45 449
1982..	36 419	43 584	1 705	14 181	31 542	15 670	(D)	45 721
1987 farms by acres harvested:								
1 to 24 acres	3	11	20	3	-	1	5	4
25 to 99 acres	33	58	17	24	15	9	9	39
100 to 249 acres	52	74	12	37	42	17	2	74
250 acres or more	42	45	1	42	39	38	1	67
Sorghum for grain or seed ...... farms, 1987..	304	115	507	328	146	225	412	322
1982..	241	96	473	338	131	266	246	184
acres, 1987..	35 704	10 329	61 188	47 264	31 419	114 832	31 913	36 435
1982..	26 324	9 199	54 710	60 986	39 102	180 500	17 557	27 679
bushels, 1987..	2 549 462	620 776	5 249 221	3 023 173	1 937 190	5 595 676	1 506 504	2 357 796
1982..	1 968 008	530 600	3 564 954	3 631 977	2 933 275	7 880 269	763 645	1 871 603
Irrigated ...... farms, 1987..	71	42	49	90	95	124	5	56
1982..	92	51	26	102	103	135	8	79
acres, 1987..	8 434	4 033	2 962	11 350	20 217	35 128	460	8 268
1982..	11 220	4 826	1 571	16 401	27 637	48 974	(D)	11 815
1987 farms by acres harvested:								
1 to 24 acres	43	19	67	42	11	1	115	57
25 to 99 acres	134	63	227	116	33	29	174	147
100 to 249 acres	95	28	150	112	53	39	103	72
250 acres or more	32	5	63	58	49	156	20	46
Wheat for grain ...... farms, 1987..	421	445	579	438	233	224	1 040	551
1982..	458	478	613	462	205	237	1 168	538
acres, 1987..	94 689	155 862	107 735	124 760	113 050	89 747	356 942	161 694
1982..	112 641	198 634	128 944	153 438	137 229	98 712	476 013	217 872
bushels, 1987..	3 742 447	5 887 056	4 438 271	3 532 057	4 138 357	3 172 411	10 409 785	6 513 764
1982..	4 419 761	7 112 127	4 704 127	6 096 084	4 469 170	3 486 470	16 610 060	7 604 667
Irrigated ...... farms, 1987..	54	120	1	5	87	157	7	76
1982..	58	122	6	76	127	134	3	80
acres, 1987..	5 811	17 196	(D)	11 272	51 671	48 869	418	6 745
1982..	5 634	21 346	519	12 216	49 338	45 484	(D)	15 731
1987 farms by acres harvested:								
1 to 24 acres	18	14	31	22	1	2	89	20
25 to 99 acres	99	84	184	86	28	20	212	107
100 to 249 acres	163	124	219	128	56	63	259	178
250 acres or more	141	223	145	202	148	139	480	246
Oats for grain ...... farms, 1987..	26	20	110	16	-	2	11	36
1982..	24	30	81	24	1	-	36	27
acres, 1987..	1 038	959	2 874	792	-	(D)	538	2 369
1982..	1 103	2 479	1 843	1 222	(D)	-	1 144	2 131
bushels, 1987..	33 054	49 845	123 453	21 879	-	(D)	13 000	113 468
1982..	57 286	159 884	110 777	64 388	(D)	-	47 144	105 113
Irrigated ...... farms, 1987..	3	3	-	-	-	-	-	1
1982..	7	7	-	2	-	-	-	10
acres, 1987..	(D)	212	-	(D)	-	-	-	(D)
1982..	(D)	362	-	(D)	-	-	-	784
1987 farms by acres harvested:								
1 to 24 acres	12	9	70	9	-	1	8	11
25 to 99 acres	11	9	37	5	-	1	4	19
100 to 249 acres	3	2	3	1	-	-	-	5
250 acres or more	-	-	-	1	-	-	1	1
Soybeans for beans ...... farms, 1987..	55	46	175	86	19	16	196	70
1982..	39	41	34	89	31	11	39	39
acres, 1987..	3 899	5 071	10 697	8 721	2 380	890	14 494	5 742
1982..	5 068	4 315	1 225	6 524	5 594	652	1 620	4 742
bushels, 1987..	169 748	211 544	307 315	324 309	75 869	26 397	305 850	183 971
1982..	189 277	130 979	35 803	838 926	214 535	20 265	38 298	172 249
Irrigated ...... farms, 1987..	47	43	20	66	18	14	9	49
1982..	33	33	12	76	30	10	3	37
acres, 1987..	3 637	4 656	1 200	7 390	2 310	745	1 263	3 710
1982..	4 155	3 686	446	14 692	5 534	642	(D)	4 361
1987 farms by acres harvested:								
1 to 24 acres	13	3	50	10	2	4	64	9
25 to 99 acres	29	26	95	36	7	10	82	39
100 to 249 acres	11	12	26	35	8	2	39	21
250 acres or more	2	5	4	5	2	-	11	1
Hay—alfalfa, other tame, small grain, wild, grass silage, green chop, etc. (see text) ...... farms, 1987..	180	113	401	215	40	47	489	122
1982..	197	136	449	255	33	49	585	99
acres, 1987..	10 891	9 169	22 323	20 966	3 734	7 048	22 686	6 733
1982..	10 640	8 548	24 089	23 009	3 567	6 676	24 890	4 756
tons, dry, 1987..	31 916	23 389	63 066	63 614	11 454	33 777	49 487	18 031
1982..	36 492	26 808	65 095	66 542	15 969	33 068	50 358	14 585
Irrigated ...... farms, 1987..	18	54	9	34	22	28	2	10
1982..	36	71	12	25	25	36	8	15
acres, 1987..	1 145	3 007	737	4 642	2 477	5 957	(D)	754
1982..	1 886	4 302	892	4 079	3 149	6 216	152	1 005
1987 farms by acres harvested:								
1 to 24 acres	59	16	133	50	10	9	204	38
25 to 99 acres	96	67	201	95	16	21	224	64
100 to 249 acres	32	22	61	56	11	12	58	19
250 acres or more	2	8	6	14	3	5	3	1

Crop		Trego	Wabaunsee	Wallace	Washington	Wichita	Wilson	Woodson	Wyandotte
Harvested cropland	farms, 1987..	426	488	283	794	307	505	303	125
	1982..	443	551	261	907	294	574	318	148
	acres, 1987..	139 788	90 028	146 695	239 242	182 673	114 733	85 309	12 112
	1982..	142 586	103 331	162 334	272 022	195 601	143 416	87 002	14 095
Irrigated	farms, 1987..	29	32	115	115	61	169	3	7
	1982..	33	19	116	116	41	178	2	2
	acres, 1987..	(D)	(D)	45 435	(D)	72 611	(D)	(D)	14
	1982..	(D)	(D)	63 954	(D)	95 738	895	(D)	(D)
Corn for grain or seed	farms, 1987..	10	75	96	129	94	38	28	21
	1982..	7	82	83	152	87	45	24	16
	acres, 1987..	520	6 814	22 478	8 272	16 401	2 231	1 515	2 104
	1982..	862	5 881	24 670	10 151	20 289	2 336	1 148	1 504
	bushels, 1987..	66 335	701 730	3 210 151	785 743	2 291 617	176 995	94 015	229 180
	1982..	87 010	471 383	2 763 152	932 186	2 515 016	188 458	66 895	134 923
Irrigated	farms, 1987..	6	17	95	45	88	4	-	-
	1982..	5	8	74	31	84	3	-	-
	acres, 1987..	425	2 647	22 148	3 716	15 870	272	-	-
	1982..	707	(D)	23 975	3 540	20 103	(D)	-	-
1987 farms by acres harvested:									
1 to 24 acres		6	27	2	30	8	16	12	11
25 to 99 acres		3	30	26	73	31	12	10	7
100 to 249 acres		1	11	33	21	32	9	5	1
250 acres or more		-	7	35	5	23	1	1	2
Sorghum for grain or seed	farms, 1987..	273	292	81	689	187	269	191	6
	1982..	186	294	85	690	168	253	163	13
	acres, 1987..	26 500	19 382	9 731	96 823	24 374	26 603	17 603	(D)
	1982..	19 430	21 507	18 732	82 730	30 202	20 886	13 370	511
	bushels, 1987..	1 507 727	1 274 145	463 198	7 110 326	1 693 699	1 796 323	1 250 906	(D)
	1982..	851 440	1 139 425	1 382 213	5 853 379	2 419 424	1 312 404	873 354	39 956
Irrigated	farms, 1987..	12	6	28	26	115	2	-	-
	1982..	16	-	50	10	131	1	-	-
	acres, 1987..	1 198	470	3 100	3 021	14 259	(D)	-	-
	1982..	1 399	-	14 278	(D)	24 204	(D)	-	-
1987 farms by acres harvested:									
1 to 24 acres		47	90	11	80	28	74	49	3
25 to 99 acres		131	136	39	281	71	113	79	2
100 to 249 acres		84	53	20	229	61	81	43	-
250 acres or more		11	13	11	99	27	21	20	1
Wheat for grain	farms, 1987..	413	222	267	652	300	210	114	9
	1982..	411	355	255	784	288	439	206	36
	acres, 1987..	91 726	11 153	93 419	74 196	118 864	16 950	7 522	482
	1982..	105 559	24 503	96 463	109 298	126 266	61 262	21 000	3 473
	bushels, 1987..	3 380 637	330 170	3 009 097	2 638 117	4 477 060	394 873	171 930	14 156
	1982..	3 267 173	572 873	3 392 212	3 356 641	4 440 890	1 692 195	559 055	103 314
Irrigated	farms, 1987..	6	2	69	1	135	-	-	-
	1982..	8	3	67	4	152	2	-	-
	acres, 1987..	400	(D)	12 340	(D)	29 168	-	-	-
	1982..	313	(D)	16 220	207	34 858	(D)	-	-
1987 farms by acres harvested:									
1 to 24 acres		16	89	9	94	6	65	42	3
25 to 99 acres		96	96	33	307	55	82	50	5
100 to 249 acres		171	35	89	177	73	55	18	1
250 acres or more		130	2	136	74	166	8	4	-
Oats for grain	farms, 1987..	28	66	12	155	11	31	38	4
	1982..	6	65	3	81	7	72	51	5
	acres, 1987..	675	1 122	752	2 775	757	318	740	51
	1982..	251	1 067	157	4 585	432	1 244	863	60
	bushels, 1987..	24 243	42 866	25 950	143 002	32 630	29 093	27 145	1 730
	1982..	11 769	42 862	10 480	219 260	(D)	66 771	37 292	2 320
Irrigated	farms, 1987..	1	-	-	-	2	-	-	-
	1982..	1	-	-	-	1	-	-	-
	acres, 1987..	(D)	-	-	-	(D)	-	-	-
	1982..	(D)	-	-	-	(D)	-	-	-
1987 farms by acres harvested:									
1 to 24 acres		21	50	3	133	5	20	30	4
25 to 99 acres		6	16	6	17	6	9	8	-
100 to 249 acres		1	-	3	5	-	2	-	-
250 acres or more		-	-	-	-	-	-	-	-
Soybeans for beans	farms, 1987..	-	227	13	475	23	329	210	35
	1982..	2	192	3	460	34	358	206	37
	acres, 1987..	(D)	14 271	845	30 869	1 295	52 601	30 000	5 417
	1982..	(D)	9 969	152	31 776	1 760	44 558	22 881	3 611
	bushels, 1987..	(D)	434 517	28 159	902 105	37 428	1 505 453	905 137	204 728
	1982..	(D)	230 553	(D)	962 189	61 533	963 660	538 229	117 513
Irrigated	farms, 1987..	1	14	2	22	20	7	-	-
	1982..	-	8	2	12	31	4	-	-
	acres, 1987..	(D)	557	759	879	1 147	697	-	-
	1982..	(D)	522	(D)	1 346	1 624	279	-	-
1987 farms by acres harvested:									
1 to 24 acres		-	83	2	156	8	64	38	7
25 to 99 acres		-	107	8	238	12	95	76	19
100 to 249 acres		-	26	3	62	2	98	58	4
250 acres or more		-	11	-	19	1	72	38	5
Hay—alfalfa, other tame, small grain, wild, grass silage, green chop, etc, (see text)	farms, 1987..	225	360	105	581	87	353	240	66
	1982..	220	457	91	663	87	397	240	69
	acres, 1987..	13 979	36 781	10 267	29 903	6 973	20 675	31 246	2 063
	1982..	11 879	40 214	8 678	34 928	6 237	23 016	31 537	3 180
	tons, dry, 1987..	32 250	62 976	22 017	64 736	20 717	34 169	38 745	3 215
	1982..	31 021	67 635	21 278	82 357	20 022	43 556	46 695	5 929
Irrigated	farms, 1987..	12	6	23	8	50	7	1	-
	1982..	13	8	30	8	55	3	-	-
	acres, 1987..	526	2 670	1 914	255	4 492	260	(D)	-
	1982..	826	2 185	2 937	431	4 393	74	(D)	-
1987 farms by acres harvested:									
1 to 24 acres		66	78	20	197	19	115	53	37
25 to 99 acres		116	163	53	304	52	174	94	26
100 to 249 acres		38	92	24	74	12	61	62	1
250 acres or more		5	27	8	6	4	3	31	-

Table 16. Farms With Sales of $10,000 or More: 1987 and 1982

[Data for 1987 include abnormal farms. For meaning of abbreviations and symbols, see introductory text]

Item	Kansas	Allen	Anderson	Atchison	Barber	Barton	Bourbon
FARMS AND LAND IN FARMS							
Land in farms ... farms, 1987..	42 728	356	444	431	381	617	377
1982..	47 695	404	453	450	417	704	412
acres, 1987..	42 828 070	234 752	317 445	208 974	652 875	512 126	251 798
1982..	43 660 307	244 927	324 623	207 901	660 968	527 871	270 000
Average size of farm ...acres, 1987..	1 002	659	715	485	1 714	830	668
1982..	912	606	701	462	1 633	750	656
Value of land and buildings[1]:							
Average per farm ...dollars, 1987..	392 590	264 666	240 610	248 963	467 227	352 273	219 255
1982..	529 905	380 666	376 402	349 240	853 832	505 260	324 047
Average per acre ...dollars, 1987..	397	424	337	546	289	436	334
1982..	587	603	593	737	517	686	524
Total cropland ... farms, 1987..	40 638	348	425	413	343	596	353
1982..	46 005	392	461	431	397	692	368
acres, 1987..	29 090 488	166 082	212 220	163 490	236 651	450 152	136 606
1982..	28 733 772	167 200	199 809	156 118	242 588	446 151	151 958
Harvested cropland ... farms, 1987..	39 574	340	419	401	329	588	337
1982..	45 244	363	456	428	388	683	376
acres, 1987..	16 756 210	114 501	152 696	115 188	143 078	246 672	77 153
1982..	19 296 968	127 567	156 131	121 091	187 467	303 559	105 826
Irrigated land ... farms, 1987..	6 788	3	8	6	23	104	7
1982..	6 846	4	10	-	25	124	9
acres, 1987..	2 447 138	(D)	(D)	364	2 702	29 002	(D)
1982..	2 665 337	(D)	(D)	-	3 516	39 488	(D)
MARKET VALUE OF AGRICULTURAL PRODUCTS SOLD							
Total sales (see text) ... $1,000, 1987..	6 373 092	21 776	33 067	25 106	45 116	123 831	21 205
1982..	6 087 109	22 357	28 317	25 540	51 969	115 771	24 826
Average per farm ...dollars, 1987..	149 155	61 170	74 475	58 250	118 415	200 699	56 247
1982..	127 093	55 339	61 161	56 755	124 626	165 867	60 258
1987 sales by commodity or commodity group:							
Crops, including nursery and greenhouse crops ... farms..	37 640	297	386	363	316	580	269
$1,000..	1 641 827	11 254	16 300	13 589	9 363	23 195	5 466
Grains ... farms..	36 577	290	380	375	310	574	237
$1,000..	1 504 937	10 721	15 760	13 156	8 902	19 997	5 132
Corn for grain ... farms..	6 776	66	138	203	-	41	59
$1,000..	254 432	951	1 546	2 643	-	2 168	626
Wheat ... farms..	30 471	115	113	111	305	564	48
$1,000..	669 098	601	424	306	8 224	12 243	205
Soybeans ... farms..	14 988	264	358	352	15	77	206
$1,000..	253 858	7 554	11 562	6 721	(D)	1 366	3 534
Sorghum for grain ... farms..	23 980	194	251	280	71	410	123
$1,000..	302 969	1 565	2 167	3 405	378	4 169	748
Barley ... farms..	1 598	-	-	1	1	9	-
$1,000..	3 881	-	-	(D)	(D)	(D)	(D)
Oats ... farms..	2 033	26	26	36	6	26	13
$1,000..	3 093	(D)	(D)	(D)	(D)	26	(D)
Other grains ... farms..	1 553	1	2	1	-	4	-
$1,000..	17 606	(D)	(D)	(D)	-	(D)	-
Cotton and cottonseed ... farms..	10	-	-	-	-	-	-
$1,000..	186	-	-	-	-	-	-
Tobacco ... farms..	10	-	-	4	-	-	-
$1,000..	73	-	-	(D)	-	-	-
Hay, silage, and field seeds ... farms..	9 398	84	108	83	51	182	92
$1,000..	104 350	527	538	277	461	(D)	(D)
Vegetables, sweet corn, and melons ... farms..	223	9	2	2	-	-	-
$1,000..	3 664	(D)	(D)	(D)	-	-	-
Fruits, nuts, and berries ... farms..	125	3	2	2	-	-	1
$1,000..	1 442	(D)	(D)	(D)	-	-	(D)
Nursery and greenhouse crops ... farms..	171	-	-	1	-	1	1
$1,000..	26 474	-	-	(D)	-	(D)	(D)
Other crops ... farms..	57	-	-	1	-	-	-
$1,000..	701	-	-	(D)	-	-	-
Livestock, poultry, and their products ... farms..	31 350	296	373	327	338	442	340
$1,000..	4 731 265	10 522	16 767	11 517	35 753	100 636	15 720
Poultry and poultry products ... farms..	881	10	25	7	2	17	8
$1,000..	24 998	5	(D)	(D)	(D)	(D)	8
Dairy products ... farms..	1 901	36	36	27	10	23	44
$1,000..	139 998	(D)	(D)	(D)	1 278	1 164	1 882
Cattle and calves ... farms..	29 287	290	353	305	331	414	333
$1,000..	4 261 066	6 325	12 458	6 666	33 670	97 300	12 699
Hogs and pigs ... farms..	5 791	49	43	117	27	56	47
$1,000..	281 062	1 208	1 685	3 056	522	1 250	1 079
Sheep, lambs, and wool ... farms..	1 430	4	15	7	13	9	12
$1,000..	16 929	16	54	(D)	143	65	29
Other livestock and livestock products (see text) ... farms..	1 273	13	15	6	17	10	19
$1,000..	7 212	(D)	26	7	(D)	(D)	23

See footnotes at end of table.

Table 16. Farms With Sales of $10,000 or More: 1987 and 1982—Con.

[Data for 1987 include abnormal farms. For meaning of abbreviations and symbols, see introductory text]

Item	Brown	Butler	Chase	Chautauqua	Cherokee	Cheyenne	Clark
FARMS AND LAND IN FARMS							
Land in terms .... farms, 1987..	543	650	211	190	374	384	229
1982..	616	657	208	223	443	456	246
acres, 1987..	325 430	615 061	316 162	269 262	238 747	591 443	570 968
1982..	327 591	603 505	389 331	291 609	253 236	583 860	583 686
Average size of farm ...... acres, 1987..	599	946	1 498	1 417	633	1 540	2 493
1982..	532	919	1 872	1 308	572	1 280	2 291
Value of land and buildings[1]:							
Average per farm ...... dollars, 1987..	399 222	402 489	400 249	320 326	285 524	469 052	592 148
1982..	566 346	518 507	719 303	550 170	407 809	534 787	841 203
Average per acre ...... dollars, 1987..	652	450	274	227	467	302	240
1982..	1 053	576	396	427	645	445	364
Total cropland .... farms, 1987..	524	586	183	157	362	367	208
1982..	605	597	164	193	431	445	224
acres, 1987..	262 926	302 442	79 126	57 434	185 084	384 768	185 871
1982..	267 143	269 387	64 734	57 101	195 208	381 014	181 427
Harvested cropland ...... farms, 1987..	517	551	164	137	356	355	192
1982..	595	562	176	162	428	441	220
acres, 1987..	192 429	194 602	42 600	31 258	142 571	169 821	88 792
1982..	220 347	202 981	46 031	37 051	172 025	194 097	110 259
Irrigated land .... farms, 1987..	2	14	-	3	4	142	25
1982..	-	6	1	1	7	157	26
acres, 1987..	(D)	1 535	-	31	(D)	40 413	5 995
1982..	-	566	(D)	(D)	(D)	44 361	(D)
MARKET VALUE OF AGRICULTURAL PRODUCTS SOLD							
Total sales (see text) .... $1,000, 1987..	61 732	97 263	33 699	14 819	20 385	51 043	54 694
1982..	59 513	99 549	28 134	14 971	22 936	51 444	50 295
Average per farm ...... dollars, 1987..	113 687	149 636	159 709	77 997	54 506	132 925	238 837
1982..	96 611	151 521	135 257	67 136	51 775	112 815	204 453
1987 sales by commodity or commodity group:							
Crops, including nursery and greenhouse crops .... farms..	505	462	137	79	329	349	186
$1,000..	26 271	13 782	3 533	4 742	13 872	18 433	5 965
Grains .... farms..	494	448	132	68	317	346	182
$1,000..	25 727	12 450	3 124	1 910	12 591	17 704	5 512
Corn for grain .... farms..	286	24	29	8	57	85	-
$1,000..	7 878	(D)	(D)	(D)	690	4 163	-
Wheat .... farms..	332	367	109	54	118	342	181
$1,000..	2 535	4 145	722	428	760	9 491	4 719
Soybeans .... farms..	464	232	101	38	306	33	3
$1,000..	12 165	3 277	1 557	1 100	9 249	833	(D)
Sorghum for grain .... farms..	273	323	73	32	187	107	91
$1,000..	3 075	4 821	605	316	1 872	913	704
Barley .... farms..	-	-	1	-	-	42	2
$1,000..	-	-	(D)	-	-	(D)	(D)
Oats .... farms..	42	8	6	3	19	15	5
$1,000..	(D)	17	(D)	(D)	19	(D)	8
Other grains .... farms..	1	2	1	-	-	126	4
$1,000..	(D)	(D)	(D)	-	-	2 150	31
Cotton and cottonseed .... farms..	-	1	-	-	-	-	-
$1,000..	-	(D)	-	-	-	-	-
Tobacco .... farms..	-	-	-	-	-	-	-
$1,000..	-	-	-	-	-	-	-
Hay, silage, and field seeds .... farms..	133	181	53	26	65	63	44
$1,000..	460	1 188	409	185	224	(D)	(D)
Vegetables, sweet corn, and melons .... farms..	1	1	-	2	1	1	-
$1,000..	(D)	(D)	-	(D)	(D)	(D)	-
Fruits, nuts, and berries .... farms..	-	2	-	2	6	-	-
$1,000..	-	(D)	-	(D)	(D)	-	-
Nursery and greenhouse crops .... farms..	2	4	1	1	1	1	-
$1,000..	(D)	104	(D)	(D)	(D)	(D)	-
Other crops .... farms..	-	-	-	-	-	-	1
$1,000..	-	-	-	-	-	-	(D)
Livestock, poultry, and their products .... farms..	409	559	188	177	258	237	189
$1,000..	35 462	83 481	30 166	10 078	6 513	32 610	48 729
Poultry and poultry products .... farms..	9	23	6	2	6	5	-
$1,000..	7	(D)	(D)	(D)	767	(D)	-
Dairy products .... farms..	40	27	8	8	4	1	-
$1,000..	2 645	1 773	417	660	147	(D)	-
Cattle and calves .... farms..	362	517	180	170	245	226	188
$1,000..	24 959	74 472	27 848	8 449	4 551	31 822	48 696
Hogs and pigs .... farms..	131	109	11	33	37	31	4
$1,000..	7 718	6 405	1 661	949	1 039	734	(D)
Sheep, lambs, and wool .... farms..	18	18	11	9	2	10	4
$1,000..	(D)	(D)	86	12	(D)	41	(D)
Other livestock and livestock products (see text) .... farms..	11	31	25	9	5	4	9
$1,000..	(D)	429	(D)	(D)	(D)	(D)	(D)

See footnotes at end of table.

Table 16. **Farms With Sales of $10,000 or More: 1987 and 1982**—Con.

[Data for 1987 include abnormal farms. For meaning of abbreviations and symbols, see introductory text]

Item	Clay	Cloud	Coffey	Comanche	Cowley	Crawford	Decatur
FARMS AND LAND IN FARMS							
Land in farms .... farms, 1987..	488	436	404	204	499	376	391
1982..	533	509	416	209	666	439	433
acres, 1987..	365 392	369 168	307 915	448 053	542 410	226 660	519 348
1982..	343 694	380 084	307 545	443 804	648 874	266 705	521 333
Average size of farm .... acres, 1987..	749	847	762	2 196	1 087	603	1 328
1982..	645	747	739	2 123	974	608	1 204
Value of land and buildings[1]:							
Average per farm .... dollars, 1987..	316 747	385 916	268 129	523 673	369 692	235 623	416 849
1982..	352 324	453 847	358 651	672 765	516 856	414 968	605 598
Average per acre .... dollars, 1967..	428	405	347	259	348	393	292
1982..	565	622	527	356	537	727	492
Total cropland .... farms, 1987..	457	416	383	181	456	361	374
1982..	520	486	400	197	628	418	415
acres, 1987..	265 648	273 756	194 248	173 799	227 460	152 434	340 226
1982..	239 762	263 460	181 854	174 562	245 088	174 389	329 877
Harvested cropland .... farms, 1987..	449	410	374	173	432	349	369
1982..	513	480	392	193	600	411	410
acres, 1987..	168 818	175 207	136 083	90 611	142 393	103 271	170 285
1982..	181 329	204 606	147 982	117 281	199 439	139 008	169 686
Irrigated land .... farms, 1987..	47	72	8	27	17	11	89
1982..	56	70	8	26	10	16	90
acres, 1987..	(D)	9 896	466	(D)	(D)	1 447	10 345
1982..	11 061	9 146	(D)	(D)	1 186	2 047	9 444
MARKET VALUE OF AGRICULTURAL PRODUCTS SOLD							
Total sales (see text) .... $1,000, 1987..	38 876	29 884	31 611	28 898	53 986	19 902	72 090
1982..	37 722	33 702	28 495	23 686	77 902	25 900	71 142
Average per farm .... dollars, 1987..	79 663	68 542	78 245	141 657	108 187	52 931	184 373
1982..	70 773	66 213	68 497	113 330	116 971	58 998	164 299
1987 sales by commodity or commodity group:							
Crops, including nursery and greenhouse crops .... farms..	447	403	358	165	389	318	364
$1,000..	15 633	16 652	13 724	5 508	10 555	9 540	17 177
Grains .... farms..	445	399	354	160	384	315	356
$1,000..	14 990	15 908	12 984	5 170	8 866	9 256	16 591
Corn for grain .... farms..	56	53	96	7	8	79	83
$1,000..	1 420	(D)	886	253	85	1 047	2 453
Wheat .... farms..	424	384	155	159	353	49	343
$1,000..	6 223	8 751	643	4 359	6 041	314	9 274
Soybeans .... farms..	304	203	344	6	98	306	12
$1,000..	3 569	1 672	9 516	(D)	618	5 509	123
Sorghum for grain .... farms..	340	319	262	52	217	232	261
$1,000..	3 613	4 188	1 915	(D)	2 069	2 293	3 600
Barley .... farms..	1	1	2	-	9	-	35
$1,000..	(D)	(D)	(D)	-	(D)	-	31
Oats .... farms..	53	42	12	-	9	42	19
$1,000..	62	69	11	-	7	(D)	(D)
Other grains .... farms..	5	5	2	1	2	1	102
$1,000..	(D)	(D)	(D)	(D)	(D)	(D)	(D)
Cotton and cottonseed .... farms..	-	-	-	-	3	-	-
$1,000..	-	-	-	-	(D)	-	-
Tobacco .... farms..	-	-	-	-	-	-	-
$1,000..	-	-	-	-	-	-	-
Hay, silage, and field seeds .... farms..	119	81	84	44	121	69	76
$1,000..	(D)	563	507	(D)	1 208	231	(D)
Vegetables, sweet corn, and melons .... farms..	-	3	2	1	8	2	-
$1,000..	-	(D)	(D)	(D)	90	(D)	-
Fruits, nuts, and berries .... farms..	-	1	-	-	4	-	-
$1,000..	-	(D)	-	-	(D)	-	-
Nursery and greenhouse crops .... farms..	1	2	3	-	5	1	-
$1,000..	(D)	(D)	(D)	-	295	(D)	-
Other crops .... farms..	-	-	-	-	3	-	1
$1,000..	-	-	-	-	(D)	-	(D)
Livestock, poultry, and their products .... farms..	417	304	292	190	410	302	301
$1,000..	23 243	13 233	17 887	23 390	43 431	10 362	54 913
Poultry and poultry products .... farms..	9	5	9	1	7	4	12
$1,000..	(D)	4	(D)	(D)	11	3	(D)
Dairy products .... farms..	21	6	7	5	11	22	6
$1,000..	893	(D)	228	523	(D)	(D)	(D)
Cattle and calves .... farms..	379	283	271	187	379	295	283
$1,000..	12 496	9 634	15 213	22 546	37 378	9 005	52 015
Hogs and pigs .... farms..	145	64	40	13	79	24	64
$1,000..	7 974	3 060	988	315	4 718	435	2 603
Sheep, lambs, and wool .... farms..	19	15	17	2	23	7	12
$1,000..	109	68	49	(D)	276	47	(D)
Other livestock and livestock products (see text) .... farms..	12	11	13	6	17	10	6
$1,000..	(D)	(D)	(D)	4	(D)	(D)	(D)

See footnotes at end of table.

Table 16. **Farms With Sales of $10,000 or More: 1987 and 1982**—Con.

[Data for 1987 include abnormal farms. For meaning of abbreviations and symbols, see introductory text]

Item	Dickinson	Doniphan	Douglas	Edwards	Elk	Ellis	Ellsworth
FARMS AND LAND IN FARMS							
Land in terms .... farms, 1987..	660	369	333	283	226	440	355
1982..	768	447	358	337	250	511	390
acres, 1987..	463 147	204 498	174 764	369 313	290 909	498 237	397 936
1982..	486 536	213 250	173 267	369 690	312 185	460 799	352 271
Average size of farm .... acres, 1987..	702	554	525	1 305	1 287	1 132	1 121
1982..	617	477	484	1 098	1 249	902	929
Value of land and buildings[1]:							
Average per term .... dollars, 1987..	285 164	366 268	347 639	524 089	349 146	369 751	363 170
1982..	346 184	465 190	446 728	692 582	494 372	510 775	422 790
Average per acre .... dollars, 1987..	427	695	706	425	266	344	337
1982..	609	998	871	615	418	502	493
Total cropland .... farms, 1987..	633	352	325	270	204	421	342
1982..	762	426	348	327	225	486	361
acres, 1987..	358 892	162 482	128 754	303 267	67 712	284 937	227 944
1982..	365 011	167 035	123 023	304 687	76 738	258 328	219 412
Harvested cropland .... farms, 1987..	623	349	321	266	192	416	333
1982..	750	417	340	326	218	478	379
acres, 1987..	228 903	124 762	95 332	181 498	35 161	131 735	120 632
1982..	291 954	146 340	96 621	203 609	47 765	148 022	140 263
Irrigated land .... farms, 1987..	33	2	9	153	-	12	5
1982..	21	3	7	160	1	27	8
acres, 1987..	(D)	(D)	1 423	(D)	-	(D)	(D)
1982..	(D)	(D)	1 166	(D)	(D)	2 890	861
MARKET VALUE OF AGRICUL-TURAL PRODUCTS SOLD							
Total sales (see text) .... $1,000, 1987..	63 584	33 925	26 267	57 517	17 078	45 474	20 699
1982..	63 037	37 094	26 354	67 019	14 715	35 873	21 695
Average per farm .... dollars, 1987..	96 339	91 937	78 879	203 239	75 565	103 349	58 306
1982..	79 996	82 985	73 614	198 868	58 862	70 202	55 628
1987 sales by commodity or commodity group:							
Crops, including nursery and greenhouse crops .... farms..	607	341	287	260	135	404	322
$1,000..	16 887	21 824	11 669	24 107	1 930	8 679	8 710
Grains .... farms..	598	337	263	259	119	399	318
$1,000..	15 003	21 189	10 708	20 686	1 759	8 223	8 396
Corn for grain .... farms..	26	298	122	98	4	1	3
$1,000..	(D)	10 662	2 424	8 176	(D)	(D)	(D)
Wheat .... farms..	593	112	61	246	75	394	312
$1,000..	9 724	834	205	6 618	326	6 692	6 453
Soybeans .... farms..	296	324	241	90	75	-	26
$1,000..	1 944	9 154	5 197	4 011	1 195	-	222
Sorghum for grain .... farms..	417	63	153	153	58	219	221
$1,000..	2 998	522	1 799	1 745	228	1 492	1 644
Barley .... farms..	21	-	1	36	-	6	4
$1,000..	21	-	(D)	82	-	(D)	(D)
Oats .... farms..	81	15	40	3	-	5	20
$1,000..	85	(D)	43	11	-	(D)	25
Other grains .... farms..	3	2	6	7	1	8	6
$1,000..	(D)	(D)	(D)	41	(D)	(D)	(D)
Cotton and cottonseed .... farms..	-	-	-	-	-	-	-
$1,000..	-	-	-	-	-	-	-
Tobacco .... farms..	-	2	-	-	-	-	-
$1,000..	-	(D)	-	-	-	-	-
Hay, silage, and field seeds .... farms..	201	43	108	74	41	75	62
$1,000..	1 837	194	545	(D)	172	378	(D)
Vegetables, sweet corn, and melons .... farms..	1	4	10	1	-	3	-
$1,000..	(D)	(D)	88	(D)	-	(D)	-
Fruits, nuts, and berries .... farms..	1	8	4	-	-	-	-
$1,000..	(D)	397	(D)	-	-	-	-
Nursery and greenhouse crops .... farms..	2	-	5	1	-	-	-
$1,000..	(D)	-	90	(D)	-	-	-
Other crops .... farms..	-	-	2	-	-	1	1
$1,000..	-	-	(D)	-	-	(D)	(D)
Livestock, poultry, and their products .... farms..	546	252	263	190	216	376	293
$1,000..	46 696	12 101	14 598	33 410	15 147	36 795	11 988
Poultry and poultry products .... farms..	20	11	7	3	9	17	23
$1,000..	(D)	4	147	(D)	(D)	5	8
Dairy products .... farms..	33	7	36	5	3	24	4
$1,000..	(D)	818	(D)	261	135	1 827	(D)
Cattle and calves .... farms..	504	218	248	182	212	362	287
$1,000..	40 051	7 637	10 036	32 887	13 088	34 219	10 358
Hogs and pigs .... farms..	117	97	37	13	30	29	32
$1,000..	3 692	3 571	1 398	(D)	1 874	630	1 361
Sheep, lambs, and wool .... farms..	33	16	18	5	7	10	7
$1,000..	168	50	22	(D)	29	91	(D)
Other livestock and livestock products (see text) .... farms..	20	7	9	9	15	16	15
$1,000..	51	21	(D)	(D)	(D)	22	31

See footnotes at end of table.

Table 16. **Farms With Sales of $10,000 or More: 1987 and 1982**—Con.

[Data for 1987 include abnormal farms. For meaning of abbreviations and symbols, see introductory text.]

Item	Finney	Ford	Franklin	Geary	Gove	Graham	Grant
FARMS AND LAND IN FARMS							
Land in farms _____ farms, 1987__	421	579	410	178	410	332	240
1982__	475	629	467	183	432	354	238
acres, 1987__	702 252	642 344	253 720	154 612	645 282	479 953	311 150
1982__	712 656	656 894	245 971	141 546	645 530	491 863	326 181
Average size of farm_____acres, 1987__	1 668	1 109	619	869	1 574	1 446	1 296
1982__	1 500	1 044	527	773	1 497	1 351	1 379
Value of land and buildings[1]:							
Average per farm_____dollars, 1987__	805 567	436 535	332 152	331 472	443 807	479 491	659 517
1982__	1 020 027	536 447	352 687	367 973	738 544	526 104	1 038 055
Average per acre _____dollars, 1987__	499	405	533	396	267	316	505
1982__	683	519	686	501	448	393	779
Total cropland_____ farms, 1987__	404	549	398	166	387	323	224
1982__	452	590	448	172	423	362	222
acres, 1987__	565 474	524 282	175 928	69 553	418 706	304 037	269 410
1982__	584 314	500 509	165 329	64 693	391 883	301 822	291 541
Harvested cropland _____ farms, 1987__	393	541	387	163	378	316	223
1982__	445	581	435	168	412	356	216
acres, 1987__	318 589	274 672	120 483	44 758	189 358	142 921	152 971
1982__	382 357	291 844	126 173	47 182	190 016	153 877	198 077
Irrigated land_____ farms, 1987__	264	200	15	19	65	51	177
1982__	282	207	13	14	84	87	168
acres, 1987__	183 208	77 444	(D)	1 587	(D)	(D)	98 631
1982__	206 881	81 138	1 006	1 907	(D)	13 356	120 829
MARKET VALUE OF AGRICUL- TURAL PRODUCTS SOLD							
Total sales (see text) _____ $1,000, 1987__	381 118	228 158	30 976	16 031	93 358	27 012	231 146
1982__	224 368	201 241	30 925	13 472	78 547	29 872	140 123
Average per farm_____dollars, 1987__	905 269	394 054	75 550	90 060	227 703	81 361	963 110
1982__	472 353	319 938	66 220	73 618	181 822	82 066	588 751
1987 sales by commodity or commodity group:							
Crops, including nursery and greenhouse crops_____ farms__	390	532	347	151	373	310	221
$1,000__	42 708	28 999	12 865	4 014	15 399	11 418	20 267
Grains_____ farms__	381	524	336	143	372	309	215
$1,000__	36 385	26 788	11 999	3 076	14 606	11 111	18 420
Corn for grain _____ farms__	135	79	113	14	32	23	98
$1,000__	12 652	4 964	1 216	95	801	545	(D)
Wheat _____ farms__	370	517	72	132	369	305	206
$1,000__	16 017	14 484	297	168	10 109	7 725	6 406
Soybeans _____ farms__	83	84	321	96	3	3	41
$1,000__	(D)	1 078	8 586	700	77	(D)	(D)
Sorghum for grain _____ farms__	245	367	204	112	231	229	154
$1,000__	6 178	5 853	1 655	808	3 253	2 497	3 709
Barley _____ farms__	42	72	2	1	67	22	22
$1,000__	116	102	(D)	(D)	209	(D)	51
Oats _____ farms__	3	11	39	27	8	10	3
$1,000__	(D)	(D)	42	(D)	(D)	(D)	5
Other grains _____ farms__	21	26	1	-	23	32	19
$1,000__	202	(D)	(D)	-	(D)	(D)	373
Cotton and cottonseed_____ farms__	-	-	-	-	-	-	-
$1,000__	-	-	-	-	-	-	-
Tobacco _____ farms__	-	-	-	-	-	-	-
$1,000__	-	-	-	-	-	-	-
Hay, silage, and field seeds _____ farms__	127	95	110	44	74	43	47
$1,000__	5 988	2 099	469	(D)	(D)	(D)	(D)
Vegetables, sweet corn, and melons _____ farms__	1	1	3	-	-	-	4
$1,000__	(D)	(D)	(D)	-	-	-	(D)
Fruits, nuts, and berries _____ farms__	-	-	2	-	-	-	-
$1,000__	-	-	(D)	-	-	-	-
Nursery and greenhouse crops_____ farms__	1	2	4	3	1	1	-
$1,000__	(D)	(D)	(D)	(D)	(D)	(D)	-
Other crops _____ farms__	(D)	-	1	-	-	-	1
$1,000__	(D)	-	(D)	-	-	-	(D)
Livestock, poultry, and their products _____ farms__	165	366	333	149	281	250	120
$1,000__	338 410	199 159	18 111	12 017	77 959	15 594	210 860
Poultry and poultry products _____ farms__	6	7	21	8	12	1	10
$1,000__	(Z)	(D)	12	10	3	(D)	(D)
Dairy products _____ farms__	1	5	49	14	8	14	5
$1,000__	(D)	914	(D)	(D)	(D)	1 115	35
Cattle and calves_____ farms__	151	356	316	139	270	246	98
$1,000__	336 965	197 095	10 183	6 941	75 613	13 823	210 224
Hogs and pigs _____ farms__	25	23	60	36	35	21	23
$1,000__	1 276	1 068	2 728	3 874	1 092	(D)	576
Sheep, lambs, and wool_____ farms__	11	7	16	1	9	5	4
$1,000__	140	(D)	52	(D)	297	(D)	(D)
Other livestock and livestock products (see text) _____ farms__	5	12	13	5	10	10	11
$1,000__	(D)	40	(D)	9	(D)	15	13

See footnotes at end of table.

Table 16. Farms With Sales of $10,000 or More: 1987 and 1982—Con.

[Data for 1987 include abnormal farms. For meaning of abbreviations and symbols, see introductory text]

Item	Gray	Greeley	Greenwood	Hamilton	Harper	Harvey	Haskell
FARMS AND LAND IN FARMS							
Land in farms .... farms, 1987..	448	216	355	214	472	506	269
1982..	473	208	380	223	543	612	299
acres, 1987..	513 016	456 352	503 857	509 735	458 863	282 016	357 382
1982..	524 033	426 672	544 015	528 342	477 967	296 591	358 189
Average size of farm .... acres, 1987..	1 145	2 113	1 419	2 382	972	557	1 329
1982..	1 108	2 051	1 432	2 369	860	485	1 198
Value of land and buildings¹:							
Average per farm .... dollars, 1987..	550 933	861 255	477 957	707 384	410 934	390 215	813 096
1982..	763 097	1 005 601	585 116	915 278	685 674	427 923	1 023 576
Average per acre .... dollars, 1987..	502	420	310	306	423	631	662
1982..	682	481	413	390	789	976	872
Total cropland .... farms, 1987..	420	208	295	200	454	483	257
1982..	462	202	344	212	531	594	284
acres, 1987..	447 534	413 443	107 386	381 925	333 051	253 727	321 918
1982..	450 963	385 222	109 463	411 334	335 156	255 764	327 244
Harvested cropland .... farms, 1987..	409	199	271	187	448	477	254
1982..	459	197	321	207	530	586	282
acres, 1987..	252 030	189 270	66 743	157 349	222 542	185 362	197 582
1982..	321 948	186 687	71 944	201 036	283 371	220 347	248 009
Irrigated land .... farms, 1987..	297	56	8	51	10	102	214
1982..	325	36	6	56	18	116	238
acres, 1987..	154 083	(D)	819	18 508	584	20 640	154 015
1982..	191 086	26 519	244	23 267	1 440	20 677	180 643
MARKET VALUE OF AGRICULTURAL PRODUCTS SOLD							
Total sales (see text) .... $1,000, 1987..	235 941	81 194	34 438	79 888	54 567	50 934	248 781
1982..	160 980	111 721	30 417	57 349	58 752	55 794	344 054
Average per farm .... dollars, 1987..	526 653	375 897	97 009	373 310	115 608	100 660	924 836
1982..	340 338	537 122	80 045	257 168	108 198	91 167	1 150 682
1987 sales by commodity or commodity group:							
Crops, including nursery and greenhouse crops .... farms..	408	198	212	181	443	471	253
$1,000..	37 761	16 167	3 804	12 656	15 724	18 505	30 208
Grains .... farms..	403	198	198	179	442	462	251
$1,000..	32 132	15 573	3 297	11 548	15 236	17 434	29 084
Corn for grain .... farms..	190	36	15	21	-	75	150
$1,000..	(D)	(D)	(D)	1 264	-	2 491	15 130
Wheat .... farms..	366	189	132	174	442	445	237
$1,000..	11 763	10 912	472	9 090	14 956	6 940	8 716
Soybeans .... farms..	65	9	154	2	(D)	51	51
$1,000..	1 010	47	2 086	(D)	(D)	2 371	(D)
Sorghum for grain .... farms..	242	102	100	112	53	378	142
$1,000..	6 430	1 000	641	1 073	(D)	5 581	4 450
Barley .... farms..	6	63	-	18	4	10	7
$1,000..	5	384	-	(D)	10	(D)	(D)
Oats .... farms..	4	4	12	2	12	12	-
$1,000..	3	(D)	(D)	(D)	10	(D)	-
Other grains .... farms..	12	40	-	5	3	10	9
$1,000..	(D)	279	-	(D)	(D)	(D)	207
Cotton and cottonseed .... farms..	-	-	-	-	-	1	-
$1,000..	-	-	-	-	-	(D)	-
Tobacco .... farms..	-	-	-	-	-	-	-
$1,000..	-	-	-	-	-	-	-
Hay, silage, and field seeds .... farms..	57	39	79	36	75	138	39
$1,000..	(D)	(D)	(D)	1 107	488	702	1 105
Vegetables, sweet corn, and melons .... farms..	1	-	-	-	-	12	2
$1,000..	(D)	-	-	-	-	110	(D)
Fruits, nuts, and berries .... farms..	-	-	1	-	-	1	1
$1,000..	-	-	(D)	-	-	(D)	(D)
Nursery and greenhouse crops .... farms..	-	-	1	-	-	1	-
$1,000..	-	(D)	(D)	-	-	(D)	-
Other crops .... farms..	-	-	-	-	-	3	-
$1,000..	-	-	-	-	-	(D)	-
Livestock, poultry, and their products .... farms..	267	90	325	100	376	357	112
$1,000..	198 180	65 007	30 634	67 233	38 843	32 429	218 573
Poultry and poultry products .... farms..	5	1	4	1	4	24	3
$1,000..	(D)	(D)	1	(D)	(D)	2 810	(D)
Dairy products .... farms..	2	-	17	-	9	39	-
$1,000..	(D)	-	1 729	-	619	(D)	-
Cattle and calves .... farms..	245	82	319	97	362	283	100
$1,000..	196 898	64 815	28 084	66 909	32 326	20 990	216 674
Hogs and pigs .... farms..	20	8	28	10	25	95	12
$1,000..	1 083	171	776	(D)	619	5 314	1 635
Sheep, lambs, and wool .... farms..	12	4	13	2	25	40	8
$1,000..	178	(D)	26	(D)	5 243	468	(D)
Other livestock and livestock products (see text) .... farms..	8	3	14	9	10	15	5
$1,000..	16	(D)	17	9	(D)	(D)	(D)

See footnotes at end of table.

Table 16. **Farms With Sales of $10,000 or More: 1987 and 1982** — Con.

[Data for 1987 include abnormal farms. For meaning of abbreviations and symbols, see introductory text]

Item	Hodgeman	Jackson	Jefferson	Jewell	Johnson	Kearny	Kingman	Kiowa
FARMS AND LAND IN FARMS								
Land in farms ... farms, 1987	334	518	422	543	261	226	537	234
1982	377	540	448	630	303	235	636	291
acres, 1987	477 937	265 664	204 317	472 361	122 384	537 602	470 487	369 763
1982	465 232	305 673	214 083	484 639	134 622	521 201	465 823	413 035
Average size of farm ... acres, 1987	1 431	513	484	870	469	2 358	876	1 580
1982	1 234	566	478	769	444	2 218	732	1 419
Value of land and buildings[1]:								
Average per farm ... dollars, 1987	466 967	179 318	311 265	306 693	607 172	933 314	355 816	490 906
1982	601 689	325 974	393 715	429 759	693 033	1 003 094	498 226	549 679
Average per acre ... dollars, 1987	308	375	605	387	1 174	380	411	338
1982	484	555	823	538	1 541	423	682	437
Total cropland ... farms, 1987	318	493	398	519	238	218	515	226
1982	364	511	437	602	260	223	618	281
acres, 1987	329 858	170 816	144 207	334 852	89 036	364 866	329 445	243 747
1982	311 905	184 400	149 610	333 190	98 482	378 406	330 977	240 268
Harvested cropland ... farms, 1987	313	465	391	511	224	211	495	221
1982	358	499	427	597	272	213	613	260
acres, 1987	154 698	97 931	97 127	199 822	60 731	198 492	201 630	124 067
1982	159 584	120 092	112 453	242 329	79 997	214 792	256 474	142 439
Irrigated land ... farms, 1987	121	7	11	49	14	98	61	69
1982	118	5	6	46	15	106	59	94
acres, 1987	22 724	2 276	1 656	6 992	144	82 568	14 524	(D)
1982	21 694		(D)	(D)	6 939	1 408	87 387	9 528	(D)
MARKET VALUE OF AGRICULTURAL PRODUCTS SOLD								
Total sales (see text) ... $1,000, 1987	89 120	25 564	23 028	43 079	21 589	118 718	34 654	24 265
1982	74 079	24 465	24 970	49 160	23 325	148 473	40 965	26 151
Average per farm ... dollars, 1987	266 827	49 352	54 570	79 335	82 717	520 695	64 532	103 698
1982	196 495	45 306	55 737	78 031	76 979	631 802	64 411	89 866
1987 sales by commodity or commodity group:								
Crops, including nursery and greenhouse crops ... farms	310	372	320	489	204	207	479	216
$1,000	12 895	7 191	11 217	18 068	10 090	26 523	15 066	12 912
Grains ... farms	310	332	291	489	167	198	472	213
$1,000	11 770	6 447	10 532	17 616	6 494	20 865	14 415	11 946
Corn for grain ... farms	26	116	157	53	75	38	23	49
$1,000	(D)	1 230	3 198	(D)	1 177	(D)	1 064	3 200
Wheat ... farms	308	118	72	466	38	193	464	208
$1,000	8 170	497	261	9 963	153	10 376	11 852	5 101
Soybeans ... farms	30	276	251	152	160	14	42	60
$1,000	(D)	3 045	5 425	1 204	4 783	163	(D)	1 326
Sorghum for grain ... farms	226	221	164	399	69	125	143	141
$1,000	2 563	1 597	1 556	5 195	396	2 120	725	2 271
Barley ... farms	54	1	-	10	-	47	8	6
$1,000	92	(D)		61	-	267	(D)	5
Oats ... farms	3	27	33	42	15	6	21	6
$1,000	3	43	47	70	(D)	(D)	(D)	22
Other grains ... farms	9	2	4	18	2	11	6	7
$1,000	26	(D)	23	(D)	(D)	(D)	11	22
Cotton and cottonseed ... farms	-	-	-	-	-	-	-	-
$1,000	-	-	-	-	-	-	-	-
Tobacco ... farms	-	-	-	-	-	-	-	-
$1,000	-	-	-	-	-	-	-	-
Hay, silage, and field seeds ... farms	66	143	103	112	69	74	98	32
$1,000	1 117	741	445	452	334	5 668	816	(D)
Vegetables, sweet corn, and melons ... farms	2	2	6	-	9	-	3	-
$1,000	(D)	(D)	(D)	-	93	-	(D)	-
Fruits, nuts, and berries ... farms	-	-	3	-	3	-	3	-
$1,000	-	-	(D)	-	(D)	-	(D)	-
Nursery and greenhouse crops ... farms	-	1	2	-	19	-	2	1
$1,000	-	(D)	(D)	-	3 145	-	(D)	(D)
Other crops ... farms	2	-	1	-	4	-	-	-
$1,000	(D)	-	(D)	-	(D)	-	-	-
Livestock, poultry, and their products ... farms	240	470	331	439	193	113	440	155
$1,000	76 225	18 373	11 812	25 011	11 499	92 195	19 587	11 353
Poultry and poultry products ... farms	6	10	6	13	6	3	11	2
$1,000	(D)	(D)	9	13	13	1	3	(D)
Dairy products ... farms	10	41	31	19	12	4	18	4
$1,000	1 046	2 049	(D)	972	1 359	270	2 196	(D)
Cattle and calves ... farms	233	454	306	396	177	106	422	150
$1,000	74 890	12 504	7 200	14 335	7 956	91 587	15 319	11 002
Hogs and pigs ... farms	16	108	63	146	37	8	89	12
$1,000	(D)	3 358	1 845	9 086	1 187	216	1 719	336
Sheep, lambs, and wool ... farms	8	14	11	27	6	6	25	2
$1,000	(D)	189	(D)	(D)	(D)	(D)	164	(D)
Other livestock and livestock products (see text) ... farms	11	21	14	11	20	13	23	9
$1,000	21	(D)	73	(D)	(D)	(D)	251	(D)

See footnotes at end of table.

Table 16. **Farms With Sales of $10,000 or More: 1987 and 1982**—Con.

[Data for 1987 include abnormal farms. For meaning of abbreviations and symbols, see introductory text]

Item	Labette	Lane	Leavenworth	Lincoln	Linn	Logan	Lyon	McPherson
FARMS AND LAND IN FARMS								
Land in farms .... farms, 1987..	457	246	390	415	348	286	477	854
1982..	524	278	411	491	350	284	513	1 057
acres, 1987..	286 341	448 652	154 742	423 807	226 712	565 949	416 506	481 283
1982..	297 345	451 739	160 429	422 907	223 348	541 804	445 422	513 400
Average size of farm .... acres, 1987..	627	1 824	397	1 021	651	1 979	873	564
1982..	567	1 637	390	861	638	1 908	868	486
Value of land and buildings[1]:								
Average per farm .... dollars, 1987..	258 366	721 568	320 661	330 210	233 293	480 481	250 736	302 423
1982..	301 403	781 953	366 102	416 240	371 551	858 394	425 064	358 057
Average per acre .... dollars, 1987..	407	369	780	325	362	241	288	539
1982..	592	487	936	469	533	447	523	821
Total cropland .... farms, 1987..	429	234	373	399	332	274	439	820
1982..	498	263	392	479	339	273	491	1 015
acres, 1987..	191 582	329 136	111 664	249 543	132 189	328 492	216 283	392 016
1982..	195 152	310 272	113 426	261 531	142 542	318 738	200 642	397 572
Harvested cropland .... farms, 1987..	413	233	366	388	318	262	426	814
1982..	480	260	382	473	331	260	474	1 008
acres, 1987..	120 511	151 128	80 183	144 945	84 231	143 798	139 742	259 675
1982..	155 119	157 056	89 277	169 999	107 120	161 261	148 566	326 543
Irrigated land .... farms, 1987..	12	44	10	7	1	43	4	152
1982..	11	57	4	11	1	56	3	154
acres, 1987..	1 862	(D)	239	699	(D)	10 908	(D)	23 863
1982..	1 353	17 895	(D)	703	(D)	12 357	(D)	23 652
MARKET VALUE OF AGRICUL-TURAL PRODUCTS SOLD								
Total sales (see text) ....$1,000, 1987..	46 807	87 880	24 231	37 897	20 511	21 960	56 603	75 657
1982..	53 074	79 501	20 662	29 772	20 297	26 113	48 774	69 212
Average per farm .... dollars, 1987..	102 422	357 237	62 130	91 318	58 939	76 782	118 665	88 591
1982..	101 287	288 048	50 273	60 635	57 991	91 949	95 075	65 479
1987 sales by commodity or commodity group:								
Crops, including nursery and greenhouse crops..................................... farms..	369	230	312	381	257	260	391	907
$1,000..	10 524	13 885	11 900	10 864	7 605	11 055	11 235	25 046
Grains .... farms..	345	229	298	379	234	259	374	798
$1,000..	9 926	12 133	7 593	10 061	7 223	10 817	10 337	23 894
Corn for grain .... farms..	28	7	159	5	48	15	126	91
$1,000..	244	80	1 898	(D)	605	838	1 101	2 628
Wheat .... farms..	126	226	49	374	48	258	209	774
$1,000..	542	9 732	166	7 870	144	8 240	1 057	13 747
Soybeans .... farms..	310	4	258	42	223	2	348	304
$1,000..	6 683	25	4 202	(D)	5 231	(D)	5 507	2 632
Sorghum for grain .... farms..	221	147	145	272	155	133	286	617
$1,000..	2 300	2 049	1 183	1 838	1 236	1 484	2 609	4 844
Barley .... farms..	1	72	1	4	–	35	1	7
$1,000..	(D)	200	(D)	18	–	65	(D)	9
Oats .... farms..	71	6	26	49	11	10	15	13
$1,000..	115	9	27	(D)	8	(D)	11	16
Other grains .... farms..	4	6	5	5	–	12	2	6
$1,000..	(D)	37	(D)	14	–	(D)	(D)	19
Cotton and cottonseed .... farms..	–	–	–	–	–	–	–	2
$1,000..	–	–	–	–	–	–	–	(D)
Tobacco .... farms..	–	–	4	–	–	–	–	–
$1,000..	–	–	(D)	–	–	–	–	–
Hay, silage, and field seeds .... farms..	111	46	86	112	93	44	128	221
$1,000..	460	1 753	394	802	305	239	893	1 079
Vegetables, sweet corn, and melons .... farms..	–	–	10	–	3	–	2	3
$1,000..	–	–	165	–	(D)	–	(D)	(D)
Fruits, nuts, and berries .... farms..	5	–	2	–	8	–	1	1
$1,000..	31	–	(D)	–	34	–	–	(D)
Nursery and greenhouse crops................... farms..	2	–	2	–	1	–	–	5
$1,000..	(D)	–	(D)	–	(D)	–	–	(D)
Other crops .... farms..	2	–	2	–	–	–	1	1
$1,000..	(D)	–	(D)	–	–	–	(D)	(D)
Livestock, poultry, and their products .... farms..	390	136	332	331	300	173	388	577
$1,000..	36 283	73 996	12 331	27 033	12 906	10 904	45 368	50 611
Poultry and poultry products .... farms..	3	4	7	6	6	5	12	28
$1,000..	(Z)	(D)	(D)	(D)	(D)	2	934	6 495
Dairy products .... farms..	21	–	61	17	14	3	14	55
$1,000..	(D)	–	4 914	1 304	(D)	(D)	(D)	4 244
Cattle and calves .... farms..	372	130	311	320	283	166	365	496
$1,000..	31 285	73 725	4 194	23 926	8 779	10 242	41 766	34 936
Hogs and pigs .... farms..	47	14	90	41	42	20	84	115
$1,000..	3 277	(D)	3 142	1 309	2 902	480	1 818	4 060
Sheep, lambs, and wool .... farms..	12	4	9	22	6	3	10	43
$1,000..	(D)	10	(D)	384	8	(D)	(D)	519
Other livestock and livestock products (see text) .... farms..	18	9	8	8	8	5	22	28
$1,000..	59	45	37	(D)	7	5	37	357

See footnotes at end of table.

Table 16. Farms With Sales of $10,000 or More: 1987 and 1982—Con.

[Data for 1987 include abnormal farms. For meaning of abbreviations and symbols, see introductory text.]

Item	Marion	Marshall	Meade	Miami	Mitchell	Montgomery	Morris	Morton
FARMS AND LAND IN FARMS								
Land in farms ... farms, 1987	731	791	372	402	476	350	364	162
1982	836	863	389	427	492	396	402	180
acres, 1987	527 838	518 606	555 207	199 013	457 026	247 376	364 062	328 579
1982	534 205	491 277	562 451	226 699	428 976	252 162	372 169	308 255
Average size of farm ... acres, 1987	722	656	1 492	495	960	707	1 000	2 028
1982	639	569	1 446	531	872	837	926	1 713
Value of land and buildings[1]:								
Average per farm ... dollars, 1987	296 266	293 223	574 341	341 583	425 207	283 972	325 475	754 170
1982	389 468	402 346	780 990	468 747	540 606	477 215	453 851	629 717
Average per acre ... dollars, 1987	425	450	412	757	436	421	332	333
1982	610	677	500	875	639	706	463	378
Total cropland ... farms, 1987	702	766	356	385	462	330	348	156
1982	809	837	375	414	476	360	379	175
acres, 1987	354 068	386 610	377 714	139 542	368 918	147 657	178 431	272 433
1982	358 149	355 184	326 865	153 080	324 086	143 725	171 265	271 654
Harvested cropland ... farms, 1987	692	758	347	369	455	312	339	152
1982	802	832	369	402	473	348	388	172
acres, 1987	233 657	251 907	195 727	97 480	230 968	97 122	104 918	132 551
1982	276 378	268 731	209 686	109 422	238 740	115 228	110 325	166 846
Irrigated land ... farms, 1987	23	16	186	6	33	15	4	69
1982	19	14	184	5	33	15	4	69
acres, 1987	2 169	2 153	100 026	(D)	4 802	2 249	(D)	35 074
1982	1 995	985	102 089	(D)	3 843	1 804	(D)	(D)
MARKET VALUE OF AGRICULTURAL PRODUCTS SOLD								
Total sales (see text) ... $1,000, 1987	56 965	52 562	54 872	22 438	59 312	20 707	38 415	19 902
1982	58 176	55 345	70 322	22 316	50 810	24 656	41 708	20 951
Average per farm ... dollars, 1987	77 928	66 450	147 504	55 817	124 604	59 164	105 535	122 849
1982	69 588	64 131	180 777	52 261	103 272	62 262	103 752	116 396
1987 sales by commodity or commodity group:								
Crops, including nursery and greenhouse crops ... farms	672	744	344	305	449	261	296	152
$1,000	16 350	23 357	22 489	12 428	21 162	8 810	6 202	9 569
Grains ... farms	657	738	339	287	444	233	287	162
$1,000	15 173	22 413	21 785	9 632	20 593	8 024	5 416	(D)
Corn for grain ... farms	54	69	72	88	22	52	35	7
$1,000	392	710	(D)	1 226	397	1 114	224	(D)
Wheat ... farms	640	671	335	30	442	126	248	135
$1,000	8 147	5 736	6 005	86	14 677	837	2 197	4 641
Soybeans ... farms	271	648	49	252	105	183	171	3
$1,000	1 357	7 723	1 029	6 772	907	3 705	1 390	(D)
Sorghum for grain ... farms	517	635	232	175	344	171	209	125
$1,000	5 187	6 160	7 616	1 500	4 519	2 331	1 589	4 001
Barley ... farms	20	-	21	-	4	2	1	10
$1,000	(D)	-	(D)	-	(D)	(D)	(D)	32
Oats ... farms	60	75	-	25	36	19	13	3
$1,000	41	79	-	(D)	50	33	11	(D)
Other grains ... farms	4	3	10	1	6	1	2	7
$1,000	(D)	5	53	(D)	(D)	(D)	(D)	21
Cotton and cottonseed ... farms	-	-	-	-	-	-	-	-
$1,000	-	-	-	-	-	-	-	-
Tobacco ... farms	-	-	-	-	-	-	-	-
$1,000	-	-	-	-	-	-	-	-
Hay, silage, and field seeds ... farms	222	156	54	117	85	80	87	11
$1,000	1 093	(D)	(D)	740	514	327	(D)	(D)
Vegetables, sweet corn, and melons ... farms	1	2	-	1	3	4	-	-
$1,000	(D)	(D)	-	(D)	(D)	50	-	-
Fruits, nuts, and berries ... farms	-	-	1	2	-	4	-	-
$1,000	-	-	(D)	(D)	-	(D)	-	-
Nursery and greenhouse crops ... farms	3	-	1	1	2	4	1	-
$1,000	(D)	-	(D)	10	(D)	(D)	(D)	-
Other crops ... farms	-	-	-	-	-	-	-	-
$1,000	-	-	-	-	-	-	-	-
Livestock, poultry, and their products ... farms	594	611	208	337	307	304	318	97
$1,000	40 615	29 175	32 382	10 010	38 150	11 897	32 213	10 332
Poultry and poultry products ... farms	28	13	6	7	5	3	6	-
$1,000	1 591	148	(D)	9	(D)	(D)	6	(D)
Dairy products ... farms	82	58	3	29	8	16	39	-
$1,000	6 265	(D)	(D)	1 867	(D)	(D)	(D)	-
Cattle and calves ... farms	534	538	199	326	277	294	310	93
$1,000	27 052	16 872	31 348	8 345	33 140	5 662	27 814	10 266
Hogs and pigs ... farms	153	257	12	43	81	49	70	3
$1,000	5 491	8 308	(D)	1 696	4 058	4 628	2 036	(D)
Sheep, lambs, and wool ... farms	44	18	6	14	27	8	8	9
$1,000	192	79	(D)	16	250	22	(D)	(D)
Other livestock and livestock products (see text) ... farms	19	11	9	11	10	11	14	8
$1,000	24	(D)	22	77	86	110	41	10

See footnotes at end of table.

Table 16. Farms With Sales of $10,000 or More: 1987 and 1982—Con.

[Data for 1987 include abnormal farms. For meaning of abbreviations and symbols, see introductory text]

Item	Nemaha	Neosho	Ness	Norton	Osage	Osborne	Ottawa	Pawnee
FARMS AND LAND IN FARMS								
Land in farms .... farms, 1987..	836	379	431	370	432	458	354	403
1982..	865	398	502	421	478	482	440	461
acres, 1987..	397 662	257 707	631 772	487 062	301 306	520 148	360 922	481 166
1982..	379 712	270 814	649 400	492 069	314 026	488 882	376 756	453 471
Average size of farm .... acres, 1987..	476	680	1 466	1 316	697	1 136	1 020	1 144
1982..	439	680	1 294	1 169	657	1 014	856	984
Value of land and buildings[1]:								
Average per farm .... dollars, 1987..	205 063	248 775	361 727	407 154	257 459	350 617	353 938	490 775
1982..	313 047	458 691	540 944	499 323	375 361	465 212	477 333	696 203
Average per acre .... dollars, 1987..	449	363	254	315	374	303	388	416
1982..	735	685	419	447	588	484	607	660
Total cropland .... farms, 1987..	797	370	417	355	418	443	343	388
1982..	822	387	486	400	450	466	421	452
acres, 1987..	304 453	170 326	434 335	307 783	186 306	328 606	226 167	364 235
1982..	271 588	170 423	430 544	295 916	180 456	299 731	226 104	384 235
Harvested cropland .... farms, 1987..	782	352	412	345	408	441	340	376 923
1982..	813	383	482	399	440	462	409	381
acres, 1987..	190 555	114 915	182 690	150 250	126 837	174 458	141 578	217 144
1982..	204 105	129 997	210 243	166 689	139 327	172 719	179 521	250 814
Irrigated land .... farms, 1987..	7	5	21	52	3	72	20	176
1982..	1	2	33	61	9	45	23	170
acres, 1987..	(D)	(D)	2 440	(D)	(O)	8 394	1 613	64 712
1982..	(D)	(D)	(D)	6 202	1 314	3 232	(O)	65 037
MARKET VALUE OF AGRICUL-TURAL PRODUCTS SOLD								
Total sales (see text) .... $1,000, 1987..	60 123	24 662	27 195	32 930	28 987	32 607	36 860	90 881
1982..	62 295	26 815	34 709	34 256	29 583	33 487	38 714	65 455
Average per farm .... dollars, 1987..	71 917	65 072	63 096	89 001	67 099	71 195	104 125	225 511
1982..	72 017	67 374	59 142	81 367	59 796	69 476	87 986	141 986
1987 sales by commodity or commodity group:								
Crops, including nursery and greenhouse crops .... farms..	719	319	408	329	370	432	330	377
$1,000..	15 297	10 677	13 098	13 405	12 313	14 536	10 980	24 905
Grains .... farms..	705	308	406	326	355	429	325	368
$1,000..	14 407	9 856	12 654	12 991	11 609	13 991	10 311	20 590
Corn for grain .... farms..	122	54	2	58	66	16	9	48
$1,000..	869	540	(D)	1 440	550	164	527	2 920
Wheat .... farms..	573	110	400	320	129	425	319	354
$1,000..	2 391	855	10 071	8 912	454	9 784	7 960	9 926
Soybeans .... farms..	516	288	11	7	338	71	103	93
$1,000..	3 767	5 757	47	(D)	7 013	417	726	2 144
Sorghum for grain .... farms..	572	225	266	189	292	327	149	264
$1,000..	7 332	2 616	2 317	2 103	3 565	3 410	1 057	5 434
Barley .... farms..	-	-	73	41	1	8	1	16
$1,000..	-	-	113	89	(D)	(D)	(D)	31
Oats .... farms..	29	59	6	36	16	27	22	7
$1,000..	39	(D)	(O)	(O)	(D)	43	(O)	(O)
Other grains .... farms..	3	1	21	44	1	16	6	25
$1,000..	8	(D)	56	346	(D)	(D)	21	(D)
Cotton and cottonseed .... farms..	-	-	-	-	-	-	-	-
$1,000..	-	-	-	-	-	-	-	-
Tobacco .... farms..	-	-	-	-	-	-	-	-
$1,000..	-	-	-	-	-	-	-	-
Hay, silage, and field seeds .... farms..	187	99	82	63	104	102	96	127
$1,000..	(D)	479	(D)	(O)	654	482	(D)	4 231
Vegetables, sweet corn, and melons ..... farms..	-	7	1	1	-	3	-	3
$1,000..	-	(D)	(D)	(O)	-	(D)	-	(D)
Fruits, nuts, and berries .... farms..	-	6	1	-	2	1	-	1
$1,000..	-	96	(D)	-	(D)	(D)	-	(D)
Nursery and greenhouse crops .... farms..	1	1	-	-	2	-	2	1
$1,000..	(D)	(D)	-	(D)	(D)	-	(D)	(D)
Other crops .... farms..	-	-	-	-	-	1	-	-
$1,000..	-	-	-	-	-	(D)	-	-
Livestock, poultry, and their products ..... farms..	706	310	335	283	326	345	262	224
$1,000..	44 826	13 986	14 096	19 526	16 674	18 071	25 880	65 976
Poultry and poultry products .... farms..	18	8	8	9	8	13	11	3
$1,000..	517	4	1	2	4	9	(D)	(D)
Dairy products .... farms..	127	29	6	11	12	15	10	1
$1,000..	(D)	1 744	360	336	(D)	(D)	676	(D)
Cattle and calves .... farms..	613	302	327	269	309	329	246	203
$1,000..	19 475	8 277	13 467	16 212	13 606	15 634	24 388	64 103
Hogs and pigs .... farms..	304	46	15	56	61	56	19	35
$1,000..	15 661	3 933	(D)	2 864	1 556	1 254	642	1 710
Sheep, lambs, and wool .... farms..	34	8	12	9	4	34	18	10
$1,000..	153	20	63	89	4	235	108	72
Other livestock and livestock products (see text) .... farms..	8	12	12	12	15	22	11	4
$1,000..	(D)	6	(D)	21	(D)	(D)	(D)	8

See footnotes at end of table.

Table 16. Farms With Sales of $10,000 or More: 1987 and 1982—Con.

[Data for 1987 include abnormal farms. For meaning of abbreviations and symbols, see introductory text]

Item	Phillips	Pottawatomie	Pratt	Rawlins	Reno	Republic	Rice	Riley
FARMS AND LAND IN FARMS								
Land in farms .... farms, 1987	428	456	391	423	906	627	417	325
1982	486	525	437	512	1 091	679	482	344
acres, 1987	512 287	397 919	442 192	515 033	643 978	420 278	404 848	220 638
1982	516 180	413 140	423 435	657 794	659 132	414 671	412 690	222 410
Average size of farm .... acres, 1987	1 197	873	1 131	1 454	711	670	971	679
1982	1 062	787	969	1 285	804	611	856	647
Value of land and buildings[1]:								
Average per farm .... dollars, 1987	350 125	298 026	526 870	397 075	395 816	334 280	415 067	258 917
1982	504 747	416 734	611 059	558 041	523 697	499 516	559 585	417 401
Average per acre .... dollars, 1987	318	351	462	272	552	483	435	420
1982	486	536	562	483	854	775	658	605
Total cropland .... farms, 1987	415	423	379	407	878	627	405	307
1982	475	501	428	495	1 062	662	465	320
acres, 1987	316 896	170 313	375 695	394 854	527 995	328 963	330 378	120 559
1982	308 040	176 600	339 981	421 417	538 695	313 403	338 012	111 831
Harvested cropland .... farms, 1987	404	409	372	402	865	600	400	301
1982	471	488	424	491	1 048	661	463	314
acres, 1987	156 706	110 047	235 292	189 631	345 421	223 760	205 682	74 259
1982	166 598	123 559	244 407	209 527	428 255	250 752	240 749	78 688
Irrigated land .... farms, 1987	35	45	158	71	135	217	51	18
1982	41	44	148	92	121	202	59	20
acres, 1987	(D)	9 557	71 361	(D)	25 408	44 726	14 919	1 859
1982	(D)	7 769	53 012	17 595	23 457	42 585	16 058	2 084
MARKET VALUE OF AGRICULTURAL PRODUCTS SOLD								
Total sales (see text) $1,000, 1987	33 938	38 160	97 098	31 306	80 286	96 433	68 859	24 608
1982	34 227	38 765	78 311	33 595	95 666	77 264	60 800	25 030
Average per farm .... dollars, 1987	79 293	83 683	248 334	74 009	88 616	153 801	165 130	75 716
1982	70 425	73 839	179 202	65 616	87 705	113 621	125 728	72 761
1987 sales by commodity or commodity group:								
Crops, including nursery and greenhouse crops .... farms	391	359	352	399	847	594	392	272
$1,000	13 362	8 859	26 686	16 728	31 579	29 434	20 230	6 779
Grains .... farms	383	335	358	397	825	586	390	263
$1,000	12 462	7 449	20 562	15 926	27 014	28 307	19 266	5 249
Corn for grain .... farms	30	76	105	46	53	222	48	27
$1,000	982	1 730	5 395	1 061	2 158	8 933	1 579	365
Wheat .... farms	374	244	349	392	805	546	379	238
$1,000	7 788	1 124	9 975	10 850	15 902	7 557	10 311	1 681
Soybeans .... farms	18	257	80	11	121	399	109	173
$1,000	(D)	2 801	1 677	(D)	1 464	3 986	1 239	1 593
Sorghum for grain .... farms	262	193	253	286	574	446	344	186
$1,000	3 125	1 763	3 490	3 236	7 432	7 612	6 067	1 569
Barley .... farms	20	-	15	40	10	-	4	3
$1,000	19	-	(D)	(D)	(D)	-	4	3
Oats .... farms	44	19	3	26	16	54	11	21
$1,000	41	31	(D)	79	(D)	69	46	38
Other grains .... farms	35	-	-	72	9	30	5	-
$1,000	(D)	-	(D)	588	(D)	149	22	-
Cotton and cottonseed .... farms	-	-	-	-	-	-	2	-
$1,000	-	-	-	-	-	-	(D)	-
Tobacco .... farms	-	-	-	-	-	-	-	-
$1,000	-	-	-	-	-	-	-	-
Hay, silage, and field seeds .... farms	104	86	46	71	263	120	108	87
$1,000	882	606	(D)	802	1 895	933	849	408
Vegetables, sweet corn, and melons .... farms	3	4	-	-	13	5	2	6
$1,000	(D)	(D)	-	-	127	(D)	(D)	295
Fruits, nuts, and berries .... farms	-	1	-	-	2	3	-	5
$1,000	-	(D)	-	-	(D)	(D)	-	14
Nursery and greenhouse crops .... farms	-	3	1	-	6	-	1	4
$1,000	-	(D)	(D)	-	2 507	-	(D)	(D)
Other crops .... farms	1	-	-	-	2	-	-	3
$1,000	(D)	-	-	-	(D)	-	(D)	(D)
Livestock, poultry, and their products .... farms	378	409	235	304	828	448	272	261
$1,000	20 575	29 301	70 412	14 578	48 707	66 999	48 629	17 829
Poultry and poultry products .... farms	9	18	5	7	44	14	2	10
$1,000	2	(D)	(D)	(D)	1 751	5	(D)	(D)
Dairy products .... farms	11	35	5	10	95	12	16	6
$1,000	435	1 334	529	(D)	6 294	1 176	(D)	1 622
Cattle and calves .... farms	359	379	224	287	554	416	263	257
$1,000	12 168	20 042	66 575	11 833	35 788	62 098	44 381	10 700
Hogs and pigs .... farms	100	168	22	62	106	111	34	97
$1,000	7 909	6 767	2 865	2 037	4 042	3 489	3 022	5 191
Sheep, lambs, and wool .... farms	14	6	11	4	90	28	10	13
$1,000	45	(D)	48	(D)	581	247	46	228
Other livestock and livestock products (see text) .... farms	19	9	15	17	40	8	8	14
$1,000	16	29	(D)	(D)	251	4	8	(D)

See footnotes at end of table.

Table 16. **Farms With Sales of $10,000 or More: 1987 and 1982**—Con.

[Data for 1987 include abnormal farms. For meaning of abbreviations and symbols, see introductory text.]

Item	Rooks	Rush	Russell	Saline	Scott	Sedgwick	Seward	Shawnee
FARMS AND LAND IN FARMS								
Land in farms .... farms, 1987..	336	369	341	399	316	789	208	339
1982..	402	456	423	488	335	928	215	311
acres, 1987..	512 775	363 155	416 568	364 369	452 781	457 632	311 745	175 303
1982..	504 391	400 607	442 870	364 921	496 585	475 038	312 012	172 982
Average size of farm .... acres, 1987..	1 526	1 038	1 222	913	1 433	580	1 499	517
1982..	1 255	879	1 047	748	1 482	512	1 451	556
Value of land and buildings[1]:								
Average per farm .... dollars, 1987..	371 053	309 692	325 451	401 584	519 859	472 479	624 913	314 389
1982..	610 124	472 985	500 889	486 352	776 338	593 335	866 488	466 230
Average per acre .... dollars, 1987..	269	318	273	450	368	806	458	705
1982..	482	553	504	692	522	1 164	614	864
Total cropland............................ farms, 1987..	326	356	327	388	283	758	194	306
1982..	395	437	414	476	306	889	198	295
acres, 1987..	299 247	313 937	256 289	261 148	362 384	396 128	235 211	124 224
1982..	291 019	313 683	257 974	248 034	372 760	403 778	229 030	116 206
Harvested cropland .... farms, 1987..	321	353	316	384	278	751	191	294
1982..	385	432	404	468	303	883	194	279
acres, 1987..	150 329	148 272	124 897	160 290	176 785	289 111	138 174	87 795
1982..	162 281	165 542	156 633	193 355	206 282	340 041	157 079	87 071
Irrigated land............................ farms, 1987..	18	65	4	39	152	132	136	57
1982..	26	80	5	25	175	143	121	49
acres, 1987..	2 773	7 709	(D)	3 016	54 020	29 035	77 593	11 178
1982..	(D)	9 113	(D)	1 835	67 145	29 011	77 227	9 698
MARKET VALUE OF AGRICUL-								
TURAL PRODUCTS SOLD								
Total sales (see text) .... $1,000, 1987..	24 295	19 115	19 366	29 507	279 907	56 542	130 099	20 137
1982..	29 778	26 742	25 414	42 786	225 491	72 976	125 931	21 081
Average per farm .... dollars, 1987..	72 278	51 801	56 791	73 952	885 782	71 663	625 475	59 400
1982..	74 076	58 644	60 081	87 676	673 108	78 640	585 725	67 783
1987 sales by commodity or commodity group:								
Crops, including nursery and greenhouse crops.............................. farms..	321	352	302	366	277	738	187	260
$1,000..	12 476	12 118	8 866	11 500	16 615	28 732	15 217	12 083
Grains.............................. farms..	319	352	302	356	274	704	186	235
$1,000..	11 785	11 436	8 346	10 461	16 609	23 832	13 438	9 743
Corn for grain .... farms..	8	14	1	14	48	66	49	119
$1,000..	169	162	(D)	90	(D)	2 707	2 566	3 488
Wheat.............................. farms..	317	351	294	347	270	675	180	101
$1,000..	6 685	8 524	6 489	8 241	10 446	12 005	5 426	531
Soybeans.......................... farms..	8	33	17	157	14	220	16	205
$1,000..	59	194	65	835	212	3 778	136	4 089
Sorghum for grain .... farms..	225	260	202	211	174	483	149	152
$1,000..	2 464	2 412	1 728	1 258	3 463	5 319	5 220	1 619
Barley.............................. farms..	19	42	6	6	6	5	13	-
$1,000..	(D)	(D)	(D)	(D)	77	3	31	-
Oats................................ farms..	13	27	16	9	247	11	3	18
$1,000..	(D)	41	(D)	22	2	12	6	16
Other grains .... farms..	36	15	3	2	(D)	5	10	-
$1,000..	164	(D)	(D)	(D)	196	9	54	-
Cotton and cottonseed.............. farms..	-	-	-	-	-	-	-	-
$1,000..	-	-	-	-	-	-	-	-
Tobacco............................ farms..	-	-	-	-	-	-	-	-
$1,000..	-	-	-	-	-	-	-	-
Hay, silage, and field seeds .... farms..	62	67	86	114	97	225	22	77
$1,000..	(D)	682	(D)	890	(D)	1 837	(D)	319
Vegetables, sweet corn, and melons .... farms..	-	-	1	3	1	10	-	6
$1,000..	-	-	(D)	(D)	(D)	145	-	(D)
Fruits, nuts, and berries .... farms..	-	-	-	1	-	5	-	4
$1,000..	-	-	-	(D)	-	(D)	-	(D)
Nursery and greenhouse crops.......... farms..	1	-	1	4	-	15	-	8
$1,000..	(D)	-	(D)	(D)	-	2 879	-	1 462
Other crops .... farms..	-	-	-	1	-	2	1	6
$1,000..	-	-	-	(D)	-	(D)	(D)	25
Livestock, poultry, and their products .... farms..	260	248	266	289	162	498	93	235
$1,000..	11 809	6 996	10 479	18 007	261 292	27 810	114 882	8 053
Poultry and poultry products .... farms..	8	8	7	6	2	13	1	4
$1,000..	2	(D)	(D)	(D)	(D)	1 271	(D)	(D)
Dairy products .... farms..	14	8	21	20	1	89	-	9
$1,000..	(D)	403	(D)	2 506	(D)	12 013	-	(D)
Cattle and calves.................. farms..	254	241	256	264	131	434	87	219
$1,000..	10 316	6 352	8 857	11 410	255 636	10 306	95 591	6 118
Hogs and pigs .... farms..	33	9	29	29	21	74	(D)	34
$1,000..	386	(D)	671	3 969	5 465	2 914	(D)	1 335
Sheep, lambs, and wool............ farms..	10	6	7	12	2	44	-	-
$1,000..	(D)	75	33	71	(D)	894	-	-
Other livestock and livestock products (see text) .... farms..	13	3	5	13	6	37	8	10
$1,000..	25	2	9	(D)	(D)	411	6	71

See footnotes at end of table.

Table 16. **Farms With Sales of $10,000 or More: 1987 and 1982**—Con.

[Data for 1987 include abnormal farms. For meaning of abbreviations and symbols, see introductory text]

Item	Sheridan	Sherman	Smith	Stafford	Stanton	Stevens	Sumner	Thomas
FARMS AND LAND IN FARMS								
Land in farms .... farms, 1987..	422	409	555	394	220	241	772	493
1982..	495	459	622	480	203	277	1 017	519
acres, 1987..	487 846	595 726	536 006	432 148	410 260	443 063	846 740	646 871
1982..	497 233	648 658	523 697	448 485	440 055	448 485	597 827	638 256
Average size of farm .... acres, 1987..	1 156	1 457	966	1 097	1 865	1 838	838	1 312
1982..	1 005	1 413	842	936	2 168	1 612	686	1 230
Value of land and buildings[1]:								
Average per farm .... dollars, 1987..	426 524	486 961	336 052	548 542	688 137	820 955	434 021	505 939
1982..	604 552	843 930	421 257	807 190	1 050 108	873 241	621 716	773 378
Average per acre .... dollars, 1987..	369	355	342	490	401	444	514	393
1982..	576	572	495	665	500	576	867	635
Total cropland .... farms, 1987..	397	390	533	383	210	234	749	479
1982..	478	449	595	475	196	279	997	507
acres, 1987..	361 968	472 309	367 967	354 223	368 033	377 821	557 454	561 225
1982..	366 606	526 314	333 826	357 762	361 065	378 501	550 803	543 800
Harvested cropland .... farms, 1987..	394	384	528	379	209	230	746	477
1982..	472	444	588	473	192	268	995	504
acres, 1987..	176 583	242 632	206 206	221 722	181 302	234 782	390 415	265 632
1982..	197 455	291 450	212 460	262 924	219 185	295 878	505 452	303 580
Irrigated land .... farms, 1987..	178	238	73	180	162	162	20	212
1982..	205	257	48	168	144	158	12	188
acres, 1987..	50 074	83 025	7 683	66 363	112 460	119 112	2 667	73 212
1982..	65 491	103 949	(D)	(D)	123 624	116 820	1 701	83 942
MARKET VALUE OF AGRICUL-								
TURAL PRODUCTS SOLD								
Total sales (see text) .... $1,000, 1987..	53 625	66 857	50 179	71 458	86 682	96 416	51 408	73 434
1982..	58 543	68 972	53 801	63 570	79 207	89 974	70 332	77 266
Average per farm .... dollars, 1987..	127 072	163 464	90 413	181 365	394 010	400 067	66 590	148 953
1982..	118 269	150 266	86 497	132 438	390 181	252 614	69 156	148 876
1987 sales by commodity or commodity group:								
Crops, including nursery and greenhouse crops .... farms..	388	381	517	376	208	220	764	479
$1,000..	21 813	29 715	19 661	23 272	23 518	24 631	29 510	34 800
Grains .... farms..	382	380	510	369	209	225	728	471
$1,000..	20 999	28 964	18 882	21 358	22 755	23 200	28 511	34 127
Corn for grain .... farms..	121	174	42	100	93	61	14	777
$1,000..	(D)	8 986	(D)	6 903	9 023	6 523	106	13 017
Wheat .... farms..	366	364	505	350	206	206	722	454
$1,000..	8 202	13 764	9 719	8 334	9 447	7 220	25 035	15 769
Soybeans .... farms..	52	44	165	85	19	16	157	69
$1,000..	(D)	(D)	1 463	1 654	386	128	1 438	883
Sorghum for grain .... farms..	251	98	428	267	127	204	308	269
$1,000..	3 425	876	6 926	4 414	3 069	8 998	1 796	3 262
Barley .... farms..	49	51	24	11	31	23	19	47
$1,000..	77	(D)	(D)	(D)	100	(D)	10	(D)
Oats .... farms..	15	12	41	7	-	1	4	21
$1,000..	29	(D)	95	(D)	-	(D)	(D)	(D)
Other grains .... farms..	65	178	28	16	23	14	13	78
$1,000..	(D)	4 044	117	(D)	730	(D)	(D)	952
Cotton and cottonseed .... farms..	-	-	-	1	-	-	-	-
$1,000..	-	-	-	(D)	-	-	-	-
Tobacco .... farms..	-	-	-	-	-	-	-	-
$1,000..	-	-	-	-	-	-	-	-
Hay, silage, and field seeds .... farms..	84	62	122	116	26	27	167	63
$1,000..	(D)	751	(D)	1 739	(D)	1 430	922	(D)
Vegetables, sweet corn, and melons .... farms..	1	-	-	3	-	-	3	1
$1,000..	(D)	-	-	(D)	-	-	(D)	(D)
Fruits, nuts, and berries .... farms..	-	-	2	2	1	-	3	-
$1,000..	-	-	(D)	(D)	(D)	-	(D)	-
Nursery and greenhouse crops .... farms..	1	-	-	1	-	-	2	1
$1,000..	(D)	-	-	(D)	-	-	(D)	(D)
Other crops .... farms..	-	-	-	3	-	-	3	-
$1,000..	-	-	-	(D)	-	-	(D)	-
Livestock, poultry, and their products .... farms..	276	168	447	239	87	107	484	212
$1,000..	31 812	37 142	30 518	48 166	63 164	71 785	21 898	38 634
Poultry and poultry products .... farms..	5	6	14	4	3	1	10	7
$1,000..	(D)	(D)	6	(D)	(D)	(D)	9	1
Dairy products .... farms..	4	4	18	3	-	-	18	-
$1,000..	(D)	104	1 041	48	-	-	2 061	-
Cattle and calves .... farms..	266	147	414	224	84	103	435	197
$1,000..	29 490	36 099	22 855	47 222	63 097	71 116	14 902	37 269
Hogs and pigs .... farms..	49	21	102	26	5	6	74	19
$1,000..	1 114	720	6 497	768	24	579	4 340	12
Sheep, lambs, and wool .... farms..	9	12	33	9	4	3	44	109
$1,000..	(D)	(D)	(D)	121	3	(D)	572	
Other livestock and livestock products (see text) .... farms..	7	16	10	12	3	6	16	14
$1,000..	(D)	97	(D)	(D)	(D)	5	14	(D)

See footnotes at end of table.

Table 16. **Farms With Sales of $10,000 or More: 1987 and 1982** —Con.

[Data for 1987 include abnormal farms. For meaning of abbreviations and symbols, see introductory text]

Item	Trego	Wabaunsee	Wallace	Washington	Wichita	Wilson	Woodson	Wyandotte
FARMS AND LAND IN FARMS								
Land in farms .... farms, 1987..	381	357	257	706	282	343	223	41
1982..	375	406	260	765	291	410	227	46
acres, 1987..	459 525	411 539	511 288	491 881	428 590	257 470	230 799	16 489
1982..	468 470	395 091	490 608	500 801	415 321	293 572	247 064	18 160
Average size of farm .... acres, 1987..	1 206	1 153	1 989	897	1 520	751	1 035	402
1982..	1 249	973	1 887	838	1 427	716	1 088	395
Value of land and buildings[1]:								
Average per farm .... dollars, 1987..	289 192	426 131	693 331	272 453	555 588	251 093	303 996	503 000
1982..	507 229	425 515	837 632	397 447	733 523	421 912	545 925	426 740
Average per acre .... dollars, 1987..	254	371	350	406	374	339	289	1 358
1982..	398	458	468	637	530	593	542	1 135
Total cropland .... farms, 1987..	366	324	242	655	264	336	211	36
1982..	367	376	253	761	276	395	214	43
acres, 1987..	309 563	130 006	286 803	362 123	359 221	163 988	110 689	12 663
1982..	289 324	131 493	294 665	333 400	350 238	170 967	109 640	14 048
Harvested cropland .... farms, 1987..	360	310	237	634	263	323	202	33
1982..	356	365	247	750	270	386	205	43
acres, 1987..	134 760	82 027	142 816	230 586	179 593	107 210	79 362	10 005
1982..	135 696	94 278	159 610	264 078	193 240	134 811	81 117	11 964
Irrigated land .... farms, 1987..	30	28	115	60	166	12	1	4
1982..	30	17	116	41	173	10	-	2
acres, 1987..	3 076	6 714	(D)	(D)	73 216	1 283	(D)	10
1982..	4 460	4 045	(D)	6 552	95 620	(D)	-	(D)
MARKET VALUE OF AGRICUL-								
TURAL PRODUCTS SOLD								
Total sales (see text) .... $1,000, 1987..	35 091	33 207	28 251	61 698	222 911	19 164	20 443	4 555
1982..	55 728	39 380	32 740	67 067	158 986	23 247	21 982	6 459
Average per farm .... dollars, 1987..	92 102	93 018	109 926	87 391	790 466	55 930	91 674	111 103
1982..	148 607	96 996	125 922	85 422	546 345	56 700	96 836	140 421
1987 sales by commodity or commodity								
group:								
Crops, including nursery and greenhouse								
crops .... farms..	354	260	231	615	262	283	183	29
$1,000..	10 419	5 943	14 870	19 203	19 339	10 860	6 793	3 600
Grains .... farms..	353	242	231	613	261	274	175	22
$1,000..	9 962	5 144	14 415	18 726	18 016	10 444	6 113	(D)
Corn for grain .... farms..	9	50	94	86	88	29	16	12
$1,000..	102	1 092	(D)	965	(D)	(D)	91	354
Wheat .... farms..	352	164	226	559	256	166	100	6
$1,000..	7 605	731	6 912	5 606	10 510	917	360	34
Soybeans .... farms..	-	175	13	425	23	251	166	20
$1,000..	-	1 842	117	3 984	172	6 770	4 046	940
Sorghum for grain .... farms..	225	167	74	514	162	215	141	2
$1,000..	2 105	1 481	712	8 019	2 485	2 499	1 607	(D)
Barley .... farms..	36	-	32	1	69	1	-	-
$1,000..	(D)	-	51	(D)	231	(D)	-	-
Oats .... farms..	12	24	7	61	8	9	9	2
$1,000..	(D)	(D)	(D)	(D)	(D)	14	(D)	(D)
Other grains .... farms..	19	2	52	12	60	-	1	-
$1,000..	(D)	(D)	894	79	927	-	(D)	-
Cotton and cottonseed .... farms..	-	-	-	-	-	-	-	-
$1,000..	-	-	-	-	-	-	-	-
Tobacco .... farms..	-	-	-	-	-	-	-	-
$1,000..	-	-	-	-	-	-	-	-
Hay, silage, and field seeds .... farms..	65	100	40	127	66	64	74	5
$1,000..	(D)	756	455	457	(D)	316	645	46
Vegetables, sweet corn, and melons .... farms..	-	2	-	2	1	5	3	10
$1,000..	-	(D)	-	(D)	(D)	(D)	(D)	874
Fruits, nuts, and berries .... farms..	2	1	-	-	-	4	1	3
$1,000..	(D)	(D)	-	-	-	(D)	(D)	(D)
Nursery and greenhouse crops .... farms..	-	-	-	1	-	-	-	6
$1,000..	-	-	-	(D)	-	-	-	(D)
Other crops .... farms..	-	3	-	-	1	-	-	2
$1,000..	-	(D)	-	-	(D)	-	-	(D)
Livestock, poultry, and their products .... farms..	301	311	152	606	137	272	184	20
$1,000..	24 672	27 264	13 381	42 495	203 572	8 324	13 650	955
Poultry and poultry products .... farms..	6	2	2	24	3	3	1	4
$1,000..	(D)	(D)	(D)	16	(D)	(D)	(D)	(D)
Dairy products .... farms..	21	16	3	40	-	12	2	2
$1,000..	(D)	1 152	(D)	(D)	-	(D)	(D)	(D)
Cattle and calves .... farms..	298	285	141	548	121	256	181	18
$1,000..	23 068	20 705	12 408	21 414	202 852	5 576	12 961	644
Hogs and pigs .... farms..	34	60	23	239	14	37	24	4
$1,000..	(D)	3 860	537	17 450	337	2 032	444	(D)
Sheep, lambs, and wool .... farms..	9	13	14	34	9	8	13	2
$1,000..	28	259	337	(D)	(D)	28	88	(D)
Other livestock and livestock products								
(see text) .... farms..	7	12	8	17	9	10	9	2
$1,000..	3	(D)	18	186	9	(D)	8	(D)

See footnotes at end of table.

Table 16. Farms With Sales of $10,000 or More: 1987 and 1982—Con.

[Data for 1987 include abnormal farms. For meaning of abbreviations and symbols, see introductory text]

Item	Kansas	Allen	Anderson	Atchison	Barber	Barton	Bourbon
1987 FARMS BY STANDARD INDUSTRIAL CLASSIFICATION							
Cash grains (011)	22 225	190	252	242	96	414	96
Field crops, except cash grains (013)	569	2	4	1	3	30	5
Cotton (0131)	1	-	-	-	-	-	-
Tobacco (0132)	-	-	-	-	-	-	-
Sugarcane and sugar beets; Irish potatoes; field crops, except cash grains, n.e.c. (0133, 0134, 0139)	568	2	4	1	3	30	5
Vegetables and melons (016)	59	-	-	-	-	-	-
Fruits and tree nuts (017)	24	-	-	2	-	-	-
Horticultural specialties (018)	145	-	-	1	-	-	1
General farms, primarily crop (019)	718	5	10	9	7	23	3
Livestock, except dairy, poultry, and animal specialties (021)	17 179	126	144	151	265	131	237
Beef cattle, except feedlots (0212)	12 004	90	115	65	244	97	196
Dairy farms (024)	1 348	28	24	17	6	12	32
Poultry and eggs (025)	83	-	2	2	1	1	-
Animal specialties (027)	104	1	-	-	-	1	-
General farms, primarily livestock and animal specialties (029)	274	4	8	6	-	5	3
FARMS BY SIZE							
1 to 9 acres 1987	1 104	1	4	13	21	16	9
1982	995	3	2	12	9	8	5
10 to 49 acres 1987	578	4	8	13	1	10	7
1982	637	4	1	5	1	11	2
50 to 69 acres 1987	218	2	3	6	1	3	3
1982	261	3	4	4	1	2	5
70 to 99 acres 1987	687	9	7	9	7	10	21
1982	895	11	11	22	9	7	11
100 to 139 acres 1987	863	5	15	18	4	5	16
1982	1 079	12	15	32	8	14	20
140 to 179 acres 1987	2 044	19	30	51	7	19	24
1982	2 831	18	22	41	20	50	21
180 to 219 acres 1987	1 168	21	22	22	7	6	15
1982	1 417	10	25	26	9	18	22
220 to 259 acres 1987	1 603	23	23	35	8	19	19
1982	2 132	36	33	29	16	30	17
260 to 499 acres 1987	8 949	119	103	119	43	160	93
1982	10 823	125	120	122	56	174	121
500 to 999 acres 1987	11 352	80	130	103	66	204	102
1982	13 072	122	136	113	88	211	110
1,000 to 1,999 acres 1987	9 152	60	76	35	122	116	47
1982	9 306	49	69	37	100	134	62
2,000 acres or more 1987	5 020	13	23	7	7	49	21
1982	4 468	11	25	4	100	36	16
TENURE OF OPERATOR							
Full owners farms, 1987	11 862	110	139	181	99	122	154
1982	14 006	129	149	159	110	169	145
acres, 1987	6 717 881	44 369	53 916	56 674	87 531	68 616	60 854
1982	8 552 196	47 418	73 129	48 970	120 146	84 673	56 479
Part owners farms, 1987	23 793	220	249	188	181	352	194
1982	25 981	238	261	224	200	400	239
acres, 1987	29 906 320	175 575	237 343	128 810	426 516	354 214	159 460
1982	29 554 529	178 991	230 872	135 764	429 876	364 045	194 098
Tenants farms, 1987	7 073	26	56	62	101	143	29
1982	7 806	37	63	67	107	135	28
acres, 1987	6 204 869	14 808	26 186	23 480	138 828	89 196	31 484
1982	5 583 582	16 518	20 622	23 167	130 966	79 153	17 423
OPERATOR CHARACTERISTICS							
Operators by place of residence:							
On farm operated 1987	30 071	282	346	328	207	437	302
1982	32 866	314	364	337	213	479	321
Not on farm operated 1987	9 806	61	64	82	144	142	51
1982	10 163	56	61	77	157	165	60
Not reported 1987	2 849	13	34	21	30	38	24
1982	4 866	34	38	36	47	60	31
Operators by principal occupation:							
Farming 1987	33 778	274	344	322	312	486	265
1982	38 661	316	393	367	353	560	335
Other 1987	8 950	82	100	109	69	121	112
1982	9 234	88	70	83	64	144	77
Operators by days of work off farm:							
None 1987	22 573	172	217	228	197	322	189
1982	24 034	203	232	237	202	332	221
Any 1987	17 268	153	186	166	147	248	163
1982	18 444	144	173	170	164	284	155
1 to 49 days 1987	4 031	33	34	29	39	65	21
1982	4 964	41	45	42	38	55	42
50 to 99 days 1987	1 768	14	24	11	18	25	8
1982	1 767	7	22	13	16	36	19
100 to 149 days 1987	1 466	13	16	7	11	27	15
1982	1 531	8	17	10	20	28	10

See footnotes at end of table.

Table 16. **Farms With Sales of $10,000 or More: 1987 and 1982**—Con.

[Data for 1987 include abnormal farms. For meaning of abbreviations and symbols, see introductory text.]

Item	Brown	Butler	Chase	Chautauqua	Cherokee	Cheyenne	Clark
1987 FARMS BY STANDARD INDUSTRIAL CLASSIFICATION							
Cash grains (011)	338	173	51	18	260	241	56
Field crops, except cash grains (013)	2	7	2	2	1	1	4
Cotton (0131)	-	-	-	-	-	-	-
Tobacco (0132)	-	-	-	-	-	-	-
Sugarcane and sugar beets; Irish potatoes; field crops, except cash grains, n.e.c. (0133, 0134, 0139)	2	7	2	2	1	1	4
Vegetables and melons (016)	-	-	-	-	-	-	-
Fruits and tree nuts (017)	-	-	-	-	3	-	-
Horticultural specialties (018)	2	3	-	1	1	-	-
General farms, primarily crop (019)	7	14	2	2	2	3	2
Livestock, except dairy, poultry, and animal specialties (021)	165	430	146	162	99	138	167
Beef cattle, except feedlots (0212)	53	294	122	133	77	105	148
Dairy farms (024)	23	15	4	5	2	-	-
Poultry and eggs (025)	-	1	1	-	3	-	-
Animal specialties (027)	1	4	-	-	-	-	-
General farms, primarily livestock and animal specialties (029)	7	3	5	-	3	1	-
FARMS BY SIZE							
1 to 9 acres ... 1987	16	21	7	8	6	7	6
1982	6	17	2	5	1	10	6
10 to 49 acres ... 1987	4	8	2	3	2	2	3
1982	12	11	1	2	3	2	2
50 to 69 acres ... 1987	3	3	2	-	4	-	-
1982	7	6	2	-	4	2	-
70 to 99 acres ... 1987	13	17	2	-	8	3	-
1982	20	11	2	2	15	3	3
100 to 139 acres ... 1987	22	18	5	3	15	-	-
1982	18	18	10	6	26	4	3
140 to 179 acres ... 1987	55	39	6	9	29	6	10
1982	57	41	9	10	35	13	7
180 to 219 acres ... 1987	22	19	9	1	18	4	2
1982	28	29	3	4	26	4	3
220 to 259 acres ... 1987	39	38	6	2	27	1	-
1982	45	42	6	8	29	9	1
260 to 499 acres ... 1987	146	131	38	33	90	54	31
1982	181	131	42	34	105	85	31
500 to 999 acres ... 1987	129	156	61	47	104	87	45
1982	158	172	49	67	139	106	54
1,000 to 1,999 acres ... 1987	76	137	42	46	57	134	55
1982	74	120	40	44	52	139	58
2,000 acres or more ... 1987	18	63	31	38	14	86	77
1982	8	59	42	42	10	79	78
TENURE OF OPERATOR							
Full owners ... farms, 1987	214	204	72	75	103	108	56
1982	236	201	64	84	119	161	60
acres, 1987	75 429	114 920	53 783	78 906	33 457	118 979	85 150
1982	90 360	108 280	90 119	86 924	44 596	174 375	107 406
Part owners ... farms, 1987	235	371	93	95	233	212	114
1982	257	377	109	112	275	228	127
acres, 1987	203 543	440 961	169 631	170 794	183 810	404 288	381 793
1982	188 351	434 608	217 409	181 529	192 118	367 849	327 324
Tenants ... farms, 1987	94	75	46	20	38	64	59
1982	123	79	35	27	49	87	59
acres, 1987	46 458	59 180	92 748	19 582	19 480	66 176	124 045
1982	48 880	60 417	81 803	23 156	16 522	41 636	128 956
OPERATOR CHARACTERISTICS							
Operators by place of residence:							
On farm operated ... 1987	401	500	138	145	296	253	114
1982	459	474	145	154	347	264	121
Not on farm operated ... 1987	107	122	60	39	53	98	101
1982	112	124	41	44	58	135	96
Not reported ... 1987	35	28	13	6	25	33	14
1982	45	59	22	25	38	57	29
Operators by principal occupation:							
Farming ... 1987	459	479	156	145	295	329	173
1982	532	466	179	176	344	374	203
Other ... 1987	84	171	55	45	79	55	56
1982	84	191	29	47	99	82	43
Operators by days of work off farm:							
None ... 1987	334	325	104	98	192	213	113
1982	372	281	99	101	229	242	126
Any ... 1987	175	295	94	84	160	139	105
1982	176	326	86	95	172	161	91
1 to 49 days ... 1987	45	60	19	13	26	45	23
1982	67	84	34	17	36	57	29
50 to 99 days ... 1987	24	30	11	9	21	13	16
1982	16	26	9	9	22	20	6
100 to 149 days ... 1987	14	24	9	9	13	12	3
1982	10	21	7	7	15	11	10

See footnotes at end of table.

Table 16. **Farms With Sales of $10,000 or More: 1987 and 1982**—Con.

[Data for 1987 include abnormal farms. For meaning of abbreviations and symbols, see introductory text]

Item	Clay	Cloud	Coffey	Comanche	Cowley	Crawford	Decatur
1987 FARMS BY STANDARD INDUSTRIAL CLASSIFICATION							
Cash grains (011)	239	295	222	46	186	212	215
Field crops, except cash grains (013)	2	3	4	-	9	2	5
Cotton (0131)	-	-	-	-	1	-	-
Tobacco (0132)	-	-	-	-	-	-	-
Sugarcane and sugar beets; Irish potatoes; field crops, except cash grains, n.e.c. (0133, 0134, 0139)	2	3	4	-	8	2	6
Vegetables and melons (016)	-	-	-	-	3	-	-
Fruits and tree nuts (017)	-	-	-	-	-	-	-
Horticultural specialties (018)	-	1	3	-	4	1	-
General farms, primarily crop (019)	12	8	5	2	12	7	4
Livestock, except dairy, poultry, and animal specialties (021)	214	135	162	151	275	137	162
Beef cattle, except feedlots (0212)	76	86	110	137	200	112	89
Dairy farms (024)	13	4	-	5	9	13	2
Poultry and eggs (025)	1	-	2	-	-	-	-
Animal specialties (027)	2	1	-	-	-	2	-
General farms, primarily livestock and animal specialties (029)	5	1	6	-	1	2	3
FARMS BY SIZE							
1 to 9 acres ... 1987	20	16	3	11	10	6	11
1982	8	21	6	1	10	9	9
10 to 49 acres ... 1987	2	2	6	-	16	4	6
1982	6	11	13	-	12	8	1
50 to 69 acres ... 1987	-	-	1	-	4	-	-
1982	1	2	1	-	4	2	-
70 to 99 acres ... 1987	10	2	13	2	6	10	4
1982	9	6	7	1	10	13	4
100 to 139 acres ... 1987	8	9	11	1	5	16	1
1982	11	7	9	4	21	15	3
140 to 179 acres ... 1987	26	19	29	6	18	24	16
1982	36	22	22	5	41	38	11
180 to 219 acres ... 1987	8	10	20	4	5	19	6
1982	15	13	18	4	21	22	7
220 to 259 acres ... 1987	22	18	24	2	13	37	3
1982	35	32	22	-	44	36	6
260 to 499 acres ... 1987	104	98	79	14	113	112	41
1982	139	113	108	23	148	94	60
500 to 999 acres ... 1987	156	119	125	49	161	90	69
1982	163	151	121	54	175	138	122
1,000 to 1,999 acres ... 1987	107	111	63	37	90	42	139
1982	93	109	55	52	114	47	140
2,000 acres or more ... 1987	23	32	30	78	58	16	75
1982	15	22	31	65	66	17	70
TENURE OF OPERATOR							
Full owners ... farms, 1987	126	119	98	68	140	137	101
1982	168	140	119	56	191	142	102
acres, 1987	49 593	56 318	33 344	100 688	90 783	49 756	78 719
1982	64 728	74 721	42 018	125 012	134 504	50 430	98 161
Part owners ... farms, 1987	293	241	245	105	291	200	215
1982	276	258	242	101	362	265	256
acres, 1987	261 748	280 486	245 242	294 073	379 505	158 837	361 240
1982	238 903	250 657	238 875	239 200	448 573	203 934	372 393
Tenants ... farms, 1987	79	76	61	31	68	39	75
1982	89	111	55	52	113	32	75
acres, 1987	54 051	52 364	28 329	53 292	72 122	18 067	79 389
1982	40 063	54 706	26 652	79 592	65 797	12 341	50 779
OPERATOR CHARACTERISTICS							
Operators by place of residence:							
On farm operated ... 1987	365	308	300	124	393	295	257
1982	393	335	326	125	523	349	261
Not on farm operated ... 1987	82	103	76	62	86	53	109
1982	72	129	53	62	97	56	112
Not reported ... 1987	41	25	28	18	20	26	25
1982	68	45	37	22	46	34	40
Operators by principal occupation:							
Farming ... 1987	413	366	296	156	375	293	337
1982	465	420	331	179	489	345	368
Other ... 1987	75	70	108	48	124	83	54
1982	68	89	85	30	177	94	64
Operators by days of work off farm:							
None ... 1987	280	233	204	108	239	202	213
1982	292	273	205	108	271	246	221
Any ... 1987	168	170	180	74	235	155	155
1982	167	189	163	71	336	166	165
1 to 49 days ... 1987	50	55	31	23	41	26	63
1982	50	56	46	18	71	29	67
50 to 99 days ... 1987	19	17	25	6	22	28	20
1982	28	19	10	6	37	12	16
100 to 149 days ... 1987	10	15	12	5	22	8	12
1982	12	17	14	10	29	14	14

See footnotes at end of table.

Table 16. **Farms With Sales of $10,000 or More: 1987 and 1982**—Con.

[Data for 1987 include abnormal farms. For meaning of abbreviations and symbols, see introductory text.]

Item	Dickinson	Doniphan	Douglas	Edwards	Elk	Ellis	Ellsworth
1987 FARMS BY STANDARD INDUSTRIAL CLASSIFICATION							
Cash grains (011)	264	267	146	162	23	211	179
Field crops, except cash grains (013)	11	-	7	10	3	4	1
Cotton (0131)	-	-	-	-	-	-	-
Tobacco (0132)	-	-	-	-	-	-	-
Sugarcane and sugar beets; Irish potatoes; field crops, except cash grains, n.e.c. (0133, 0134, 0139)	11	-	7	10	3	4	1
Vegetables and melons (016)	-	2	1	-	-	-	-
Fruits and tree nuts (017)	-	2	-	-	-	-	-
Horticultural specialties (018)	2	-	2	1	-	-	-
General farms, primarily crop (019)	21	2	8	11	1	5	3
Livestock, except dairy, poultry, and animal specialties (021)	334	91	134	95	197	198	170
Beef cattle, except feedlots (0212)	219	23	95	82	180	168	145
Dairy farms (024)	24	4	25	3	2	19	2
Poultry and eggs (025)	1	-	3	-	-	-	-
Animal specialties (027)	-	1	2	-	-	1	-
General farms, primarily livestock and animal specialties (029)	3	-	5	1	-	2	-
FARMS BY SIZE							
1 to 9 acres - - - 1987	22	15	3	5	3	9	6
1982	18	15	4	6	5	15	3
10 to 49 acres - - - 1987	11	6	5	1	-	6	4
1982	9	13	8	4	2	7	6
50 to 69 acres - - - 1987	3	8	4	-	2	-	1
1982	2	7	8	-	1	-	-
70 to 99 acres - - - 1987	8	17	12	3	1	1	3
1982	20	28	16	-	5	4	6
100 to 139 acres - - - 1987	13	20	22	-	1	6	7
1982	25	23	19	2	4	8	4
140 to 179 acres - - - 1987	31	29	42	4	11	7	4
1982	59	38	36	20	7	30	9
180 to 219 acres - - - 1987	21	18	29	2	5	4	6
1982	20	15	20	6	2	7	10
220 to 259 acres - - - 1987	26	15	16	11	5	7	6
1982	38	23	30	4	5	11	14
260 to 499 acres - - - 1987	174	94	88	51	49	103	63
1982	234	141	102	73	43	124	84
500 to 999 acres - - - 1987	200	89	67	63	63	156	98
1982	242	94	74	89	84	181	127
1,000 to 1,999 acres - - - 1987	124	51	37	84	46	95	115
1982	100	43	35	86	59	78	97
2,000 acres or more - - - 1987	27	7	8	59	40	46	40
1982	21	7	6	47	33	45	30
TENURE OF OPERATOR							
Full owners - - - farms, 1987	171	130	128	57	85	105	66
1982	246	153	134	79	85	185	78
acres, 1987	64 410	36 282	34 074	49 039	80 825	79 404	37 219
1982	93 368	51 150	40 753	74 706	86 087	101 748	48 652
Part owners - - - farms, 1987	393	163	163	178	117	273	222
1982	434	187	178	180	144	258	230
acres, 1987	340 872	135 937	125 109	274 486	185 753	371 616	302 578
1982	343 141	124 566	115 927	238 752	200 606	301 867	252 809
Tenants - - - farms, 1987	96	76	42	50	24	62	65
1982	108	107	46	78	21	88	82
acres, 1987	57 865	32 278	15 581	45 798	24 331	47 217	58 139
1982	50 027	37 534	16 587	56 432	23 492	57 184	60 810
OPERATOR CHARACTERISTICS							
Operators by place of residence:							
On farm operated - - - 1987	507	273	258	176	145	284	248
1982	502	295	281	189	164	321	272
Not on farm operated - - - 1987	112	72	54	82	60	109	77
1982	107	103	50	108	70	114	84
Not reported - - - 1987	41	24	21	25	21	47	30
1982	79	49	27	40	16	78	34
Operators by principal occupation:							
Farming - - - 1987	523	304	224	250	164	326	292
1982	673	362	261	287	187	378	341
Other - - - 1987	137	65	109	33	62	114	63
1982	115	85	97	50	63	133	49
Operators by days of work off farm:							
None - - - 1987	365	221	148	163	107	182	195
1982	429	241	177	174	111	218	197
Any - - - 1987	261	118	157	86	97	220	136
1982	262	164	146	118	115	237	145
1 to 49 days - - - 1987	43	37	21	32	15	49	31
1982	91	47	27	40	25	27	53
50 to 99 days - - - 1987	45	10	13	11	7	22	16
1982	23	16	10	13	8	21	16
100 to 149 days - - - 1987	29	6	15	5	4	17	7
1982	21	6	11	16	11	30	6

See footnotes at end of table.

Table 16. **Farms With Sales of $10,000 or More: 1987 and 1982**—Con.

[Data for 1987 include abnormal farms. For meaning of abbreviations and symbols, see introductory text]

Item	Finney	Ford	Franklin	Geary	Gove	Graham	Grant
1987 FARMS BY STANDARD INDUSTRIAL CLASSIFICATION							
Cash grains (011)	292	347	194	56	225	209	185
Field crops, except cash grains (013)	18	9	3	4	-	3	9
Cotton (0131)	-	-	-	-	-	-	-
Tobacco (0132)	-	-	-	-	-	-	-
Sugarcane and sugar beets; Irish potatoes; field crops, except cash grains, n.e.c. (0133, 0134, 0139)	18	9	3	4	-	3	9
Vegetables and melons (016)	1	-	-	-	-	-	-
Fruits and tree nuts (017)	-	-	-	-	-	-	-
Horticultural specialties (018)	1	2	4	3	-	1	-
General farms, primarily crop (019)	9	6	7	5	4	4	1
Livestock, except dairy, poultry, and animal specialties (021)	99	208	156	98	175	101	41
Beef cattle, except feedlots (0212)	61	163	108	60	123	89	26
Dairy farms (024)	-	5	43	10	5	13	3
Poultry and eggs (025)	-	1	-	-	-	-	-
Animal specialties (027)	1	-	-	-	-	-	-
General farms, primarily livestock and animal specialties (029)	-	1	3	2	1	1	1
FARMS BY SIZE							
1 to 9 acres ___ 1987	8	19	8	10	18	8	7
1982	13	26	10	11	2	1	7
10 to 49 acres ___ 1987	9	6	6	4	5	1	2
1982	4	6	22	6	3	2	8
50 to 69 acres ___ 1987	-	2	8	1	1	-	1
1982	1	2	7	1	2	1	-
70 to 99 acres ___ 1987	4	7	7	4	4	-	2
1982	3	5	25	2	4	-	2
100 to 139 acres ___ 1987	2	4	23	8	2	1	2
1982	3	16	25	6	1	3	-
140 to 179 acres ___ 1987	9	16	31	2	4	5	7
1982	19	24	36	5	8	13	13
180 to 219 acres ___ 1987	6	5	29	5	3	4	2
1982	8	7	20	6	1	5	2
220 to 259 acres ___ 1987	9	9	21	10	-	3	-
1982	8	14	22	10	11	4	-
260 to 499 acres ___ 1987	53	107	115	35	54	50	41
1982	60	121	117	33	65	56	23
500 to 999 acres ___ 1987	76	162	94	43	94	78	50
1982	115	176	120	51	116	87	56
1,000 to 1,999 acres ___ 1987	123	135	55	41	121	104	81
1982	140	155	50	40	121	119	74
2,000 acres or more ___ 1987	122	87	15	15	104	78	45
1982	104	76	13	14	99	74	53
TENURE OF OPERATOR							
Full owners ___ farms, 1987	96	166	144	58	114	67	43
1982	120	208	158	50	121	79	46
acres, 1987	134 611	114 472	49 295	36 815	118 167	50 476	29 684
1982	123 383	157 294	52 544	18 209	135 224	72 705	45 955
Part owners ___ farms, 1987	214	296	296	85	231	200	115
1982	227	295	278	97	238	245	122
acres, 1987	405 281	405 557	179 817	94 314	483 756	374 693	193 896
1982	443 145	402 256	178 681	101 759	450 163	393 127	211 697
Tenants ___ farms, 1987	109	117	36	35	65	65	82
1982	128	126	33	36	75	40	70
acres, 1987	162 360	122 315	24 608	23 683	63 359	54 784	87 570
1982	146 128	97 344	14 766	21 576	61 143	26 031	70 529
OPERATOR CHARACTERISTICS							
Operators by place of residence:							
On farm operated ___ 1987	251	346	323	135	267	205	148
1982	245	339	365	137	263	212	155
Not on farm operated ___ 1987	138	191	60	31	112	99	72
1982	152	203	63	27	105	114	58
Not reported ___ 1987	32	42	27	12	31	28	20
1982	78	87	39	19	64	38	25
Operators by principal occupation:							
Farming ___ 1987	349	432	284	129	340	281	208
1982	398	460	340	143	366	282	204
Other ___ 1987	72	147	126	49	70	51	32
1982	77	169	127	40	66	82	34
Operators by days of work off farm:							
None ___ 1987	256	261	202	91	237	187	148
1982	278	262	211	98	209	156	153
Any ___ 1987	133	236	179	73	140	127	68
1982	136	289	219	66	164	154	59
1 to 49 days ___ 1987	32	48	25	11	31	31	22
1982	35	78	63	19	43	43	20
50 to 99 days ___ 1987	18	17	8	9	12	20	7
1982	11	18	19	4	15	19	5
100 to 149 days ___ 1987	9	25	12	2	15	10	4
1982	8	23	14	9	18	5	5

See footnotes at end of table.

Table 16. **Farms With Sales of $10,000 or More: 1987 and 1982**—Con.

[Data for 1987 include abnormal farms. For meaning of abbreviations and symbols, see introductory text]

Item	Gray	Greeley	Greenwood	Hamilton	Harper	Harvey	Haskell
1987 FARMS BY STANDARD INDUSTRIAL CLASSIFICATION							
Cash grains (011)	266	161	56	142	223	266	211
Field crops, except cash grains (013)	9	4	4	5	1	2	4
Cotton (0131)	-	-	-	-	-	-	-
Tobacco (0132)	-	-	-	-	-	-	-
Sugarcane and sugar beets; Irish potatoes; field crops, except cash grains, n.e.c. (0133, 0134, 0139)	9	4	4	5	1	2	4
Vegetables and melons (016)	-	-	-	-	-	3	1
Fruits and tree nuts (017)	-	-	-	-	-	-	-
Horticultural specialties (018)	-	-	1	-	-	1	-
General farms, primarily crop (019)	9	1	5	3	4	8	1
Livestock, except dairy, poultry, and animal specialties (021)	142	50	278	64	237	160	52
Beef cattle, except feedlots (0212)	107	25	249	52	210	59	32
Dairy farms (024)	-	-	8	-	4	22	-
Poultry and eggs (025)	-	-	-	-	-	12	-
Animal specialties (027)	1	-	-	-	3	6	-
General farms, primarily livestock and animal specialties (029)	1	-	3	-	-	4	-
FARMS BY SIZE							
1 to 9 acres ... 1987	22	9	21	-	12	22	9
1982	2	6	2	3	12	12	9
10 to 49 acres ... 1987	2	-	6	4	2	15	1
1982	3	-	7	1	3	11	1
50 to 69 acres ... 1987	4	-	2	-	-	7	-
1982	1	-	1	-	-	7	-
70 to 99 acres ... 1987	7	1	3	1	2	14	-
1982	5	-	3	2	9	26	3
100 to 139 acres ... 1987	6	-	9	-	7	8	2
1982	3	2	5	1	10	19	3
140 to 179 acres ... 1987	19	2	17	1	24	36	10
1982	29	6	16	10	48	65	12
180 to 219 acres ... 1987	2	1	12	1	9	17	-
1982	1	-	12	2	11	30	5
220 to 259 acres ... 1987	5	2	9	-	16	28	2
1982	8	3	10	-	20	51	2
260 to 499 acres ... 1987	84	30	74	17	93	156	36
1982	114	23	72	16	97	182	54
500 to 999 acres ... 1987	115	43	77	38	135	146	72
1982	136	31	97	25	162	146	76
1,000 to 1,999 acres ... 1987	112	43	66	47	121	49	88
1982	105	62	87	58	122	53	89
2,000 acres or more ... 1987	70	65	59	105	105	14	49
1982	64	75	68	105	105	10	45
TENURE OF OPERATOR							
Full owners ... farms, 1987	119	55	124	38	105	109	64
1982	100	49	112	51	129	146	85
acres, 1987	79 344	43 011	96 155	59 080	55 387	25 307	63 676
1982	81 775	57 498	79 874	57 713	60 545	41 868	(D)
Part owners ... farms, 1987	219	108	187	129	268	323	127
1982	244	115	221	136	297	379	126
acres, 1987	322 192	326 520	359 359	378 743	317 560	220 614	204 570
1982	362 677	292 004	422 189	414 130	340 342	220 128	(D)
Tenants ... farms, 1987	110	53	44	47	99	74	78
1982	129	44	47	36	117	87	86
acres, 1987	111 480	84 621	48 343	71 912	85 916	36 095	89 138
1982	79 581	77 170	41 952	56 499	77 080	34 595	83 488
OPERATOR CHARACTERISTICS							
Operators by place of residence:							
On farm operated ... 1987	255	120	243	111	292	427	152
1982	258	106	269	111	337	483	144
Not on farm operated ... 1987	142	82	93	81	154	63	85
1982	174	77	85	81	150	83	98
Not reported ... 1987	51	14	19	22	26	16	32
1982	41	25	26	31	56	46	57
Operators by principal occupation:							
Farming ... 1987	382	177	250	178	376	380	232
1982	398	183	282	196	454	447	266
Other ... 1987	66	39	105	36	96	126	37
1982	75	25	98	27	89	165	33
Operators by days of work off farm:							
None ... 1987	237	114	165	125	241	244	161
1982	258	118	177	126	281	248	167
Any ... 1987	179	87	158	74	195	238	79
1982	177	64	171	74	196	317	73
1 to 49 days ... 1987	55	25	32	23	42	70	32
1982	54	22	31	19	50	72	22
50 to 99 days ... 1987	21	7	7	10	15	17	7
1982	15	2	16	5	23	30	6
100 to 149 days ... 1987	17	9	11	8	22	18	2
1982	14	10	15	8	22	30	2

See footnotes at end of table.

Table 16. **Farms With Sales of $10,000 or More: 1987 and 1982**—Con.

[Data for 1987 include abnormal farms. For meaning of abbreviations and symbols, see introductory text]

Item	Hodgeman	Jackson	Jefferson	Jewell	Johnson	Kearny	Kingman	Kiowa
1987 FARMS BY STANDARD INDUSTRIAL CLASSIFICATION								
Cash grains (011)	168	131	168	261	104	153	245	130
Field crops, except cash grains (013)	4	14	6	2	6	20	4	5
Cotton (0131)	-	-	-	-	-	-	-	-
Tobacco (0132)	-	-	-	-	-	-	-	-
Sugarcane and sugar beets; Irish potatoes; field crops, except cash grains, n.e.c. (0133, 0134, 0139)	4	14	6	2	6	20	4	5
Vegetables and melons (016)	-	-	2	-	2	-	-	-
Fruits and tree nuts (017)	-	-	2	-	2	-	1	-
Horticultural specialties (018)	-	-	2	-	19	-	1	1
General farms, primarily crop (019)	1	24	8	7	6	4	6	3
Livestock, except dairy, poultry, and animal specialties (021)	152	308	201	255	103	49	258	95
Beef cattle, except feedlots (0212)	127	219	147	124	75	36	193	87
Dairy farms (024)	6	37	29	13	9	1	15	..
Poultry and eggs (025)	-	1	-	1	-	-	-	-
Animal specialties (027)	-	1	2	-	10	-	3	-
General farms, primarily livestock and animal specialties (029)	3	2	2	4	-	1	4	-
FARMS BY SIZE								
1 to 9 acres ... 1987	7	12	6	17	13	5	11	6
1982	4	8	2	19	9	5	9	4
10 to 49 acres ... 1987	1	8	8	5	22	-	10	1
1982	1	10	11	3	20	5	7	2
50 to 69 acres ... 1987	1	5	6	1	6	-	3	-
1982	1	4	6	10	6	-	3	-
70 to 99 acres ... 1987	1	34	19	3	15	-	4	1
1982	-	25	27	7	20	-	5	2
100 to 139 acres ... 1987	1	22	26	10	16	1	6	2
1982	5	11	22	8	20	4	13	4
140 to 179 acres ... 1987	9	49	51	21	18	13	18	5
1982	20	43	45	38	25	15	39	7
180 to 219 acres ... 1987	2	25	27	18	15	3	19	3
1982	4	30	29	22	25	3	15	-
220 to 259 acres ... 1987	1	32	26	23	13	1	22	3
1982	1	47	32	32	23	2	44	6
260 to 499 acres ... 1987	50	140	112	123	64	18	119	21
1982	52	117	120	146	66	28	180	40
500 to 999 acres ... 1987	75	126	88	148	48	37	157	62
1982	107	168	103	174	61	39	170	81
1,000 to 1,999 acres ... 1987	104	55	44	129	27	60	128	68
1982	113	66	44	128	21	60	115	67
2,000 acres or more ... 1987	82	10	9	46	4	90	40	62
1982	89	11	7	43	5	64	36	50
TENURE OF OPERATOR								
Full owners ... farms, 1987	79	213	166	146	85	48	116	47
1982	84	216	178	211	107	58	159	66
acres, 1987	51 028	66 931	42 262	55 748	16 664	71 109	46 076	35 232
1982	68 737	63 525	55 748	114 648	24 865	101 733	68 146	55 365
Part owners ... farms, 1987	208	267	214	299	138	127	319	141
1982	222	282	219	312	145	125	359	160
acres, 1987	364 203	178 767	148 093	321 941	86 746	351 486	342 739	254 181
1982	335 666	202 918	137 104	309 277	81 334	304 313	338 464	282 474
Tenants ... farms, 1987	47	38	42	98	38	53	102	46
1982	71	42	51	107	51	52	118	65
acres, 1987	62 706	19 966	13 962	61 202	18 974	115 007	81 672	80 350
1982	60 629	19 230	21 231	60 714	26 423	115 155	59 213	75 196
OPERATOR CHARACTERISTICS								
Operators by place of residence:								
On farm operated ... 1987	215	429	331	380	194	127	411	153
1982	230	437	344	427	214	126	449	170
Not on farm operated ... 1987	101	64	72	129	55	85	102	64
1982	111	57	82	142	63	76	113	86
Not reported ... 1987	18	25	19	34	12	16	24	17
1982	36	46	42	61	26	33	74	36
Operators by principal occupation:								
Farming ... 1987	280	351	304	477	171	193	437	200
1982	310	394	330	545	220	200	512	247
Other ... 1987	54	167	118	66	90	35	100	34
1982	67	146	118	85	83	35	124	44
Operators by days of work off farm:								
None ... 1987	188	227	206	316	121	144	251	131
1982	176	268	205	347	159	137	292	151
Any ... 1987	115	255	193	180	127	75	262	88
1982	146	226	188	204	112	65	258	102
1 to 49 days ... 1987	36	36	27	48	17	16	74	24
1982	43	29	29	68	17	24	57	31
50 to 99 days ... 1987	10	22	18	25	7	6	22	9
1982	16	27	13	20	4	6	34	16
100 to 149 days ... 1987	9	19	10	12	11	6	33	10
1982	9	14	10	13	12	6	25	3

See footnotes at end of table.

1987 CENSUS OF AGRICULTURE—COUNTY DATA

Table 16. Farms With Sales of $10,000 or More: 1987 and 1982—Con.

[Data for 1987 include abnormal farms. For meaning of abbreviations and symbols, see introductory text]

Item	Labette	Lane	Leavenworth	Lincoln	Linn	Logan	Lyon	McPherson
1987 FARMS BY STANDARD INDUSTRIAL CLASSIFICATION								
Cash grains (011)	188	155	140	188	116	176	183	505
Field crops, except cash grains (013)	5	6	4	9	1	1	9	7
Cotton (0131)	-	-	-	-	-	-	-	-
Tobacco (0132)	-	-	-	-	-	-	-	-
Sugarcane and sugar beets; Irish potatoes; field crops, except cash grains, n.e.c. (0133, 0134, 0139)	5	6	4	9	1	1	9	7
Vegetables and melons (016)	-	-	4	-	-	-	-	-
Fruits and tree nuts (017)	-	-	-	-	2	-	-	-
Horticultural specialties (018)	2	-	7	-	1	-	-	5
General farms, primarily crop (019)	8	4	6	20	3	5	9	16
Livestock, except dairy, poultry, and animal specialties (021)	234	81	171	182	212	101	262	262
Beef cattle, except feedlots (0212)	196	62	106	136	162	84	173	170
Dairy farms (024)	17	-	50	12	9	2	9	35
Poultry and eggs (025)	-	-	1	-	1	-	3	10
Animal specialties (027)	-	-	2	1	-	1	-	4
General farms, primarily livestock and animal specialties (029)	2	-	5	3	3	-	2	9
FARMS BY SIZE								
1 to 9 acres 1987	14	8	10	8	5	6	8	21
1982	12	8	5	9	2	7	4	27
10 to 49 acres 1987	3	-	13	5	7	-	9	11
1982	9	1	12	-	3	1	8	26
50 to 69 acres 1987	6	-	4	-	5	-	1	5
1982	4	-	7	1	3	-	1	7
70 to 99 acres 1987	20	-	21	1	7	-	11	18
1982	11	3	16	9	11	-	14	21
100 to 139 acres 1987	17	1	21	7	14	5	27	20
1982	12	-	19	11	10	2	22	42
140 to 179 acres 1987	31	4	56	19	23	2	27	60
1982	38	3	62	33	16	3	24	105
180 to 219 acres 1987	17	3	30	12	14	-	17	43
1982	23	1	33	12	13	2	20	57
220 to 259 acres 1987	33	4	29	13	11	1	29	59
1982	30	4	41	14	16	2	20	73
260 to 499 acres 1987	97	19	105	88	98	31	116	263
1982	166	41	119	107	103	33	133	343
500 to 999 acres 1987	135	45	73	102	104	60	118	231
1982	153	57	73	144	105	64	140	252
1,000 to 1,999 acres 1987	69	77	23	105	45	88	74	99
1982	50	75	18	109	54	90	95	86
2,000 acres or more 1987	15	85	6	55	15	93	40	24
1982	16	83	4	42	12	80	32	18
TENURE OF OPERATOR								
Full owners farms, 1987	164	49	174	87	134	68	133	168
1982	169	73	182	112	121	83	144	248
acres, 1987	58 268	52 082	41 232	50 194	53 751	114 027	48 296	47 572
1982	65 109	57 205	39 991	57 149	48 696	126 208	69 178	63 225
Part owners farms, 1987	251	159	182	246	186	188	290	585
1982	294	167	182	260	204	160	312	660
acres, 1987	208 194	330 160	101 934	322 199	161 427	378 671	313 247	389 327
1982	207 366	335 348	103 440	305 218	158 458	371 149	344 842	398 966
Tenants farms, 1987	42	38	34	82	26	50	54	101
1982	61	36	47	99	25	41	57	149
acres, 1987	19 879	66 410	11 576	51 414	11 534	73 251	54 963	44 384
1982	21 870	49 186	16 998	60 540	16 194	44 447	31 402	51 209
OPERATOR CHARACTERISTICS								
Operators by place of residence:								
On farm operated 1987	338	142	328	293	262	153	392	651
1982	416	150	358	338	281	144	420	776
Not on farm operated 1987	93	81	40	93	52	110	61	151
1982	81	84	36	113	32	102	85	173
Not reported 1987	26	23	22	29	34	23	24	52
1982	25	42	17	40	37	38	28	108
Operators by principal occupation:								
Farming 1987	320	224	273	344	248	231	325	636
1982	414	247	278	404	252	238	399	750
Other 1987	137	22	117	71	100	55	152	218
1982	110	29	133	87	98	46	114	307
Operators by days of work off farm:								
None 1987	224	143	205	236	171	159	214	352
1982	263	161	211	255	165	137	237	388
Any 1987	211	77	169	154	138	100	231	440
1982	226	75	170	183	148	101	240	567
1 to 49 days 1987	40	23	24	48	21	30	43	83
1982	35	22	25	62	34	30	57	142
50 to 99 days 1987	20	10	6	6	9	9	17	49
1982	25	13	12	16	11	5	22	50
100 to 149 days 1987	10	13	10	16	8	9	12	44
1982	19	7	8	15	8	7	18	52

See footnotes at end of table.

Table 16. **Farms With Sales of $10,000 or More: 1987 and 1982**—Con.

[Data for 1987 include abnormal farms. For meaning of abbreviations and symbols, see introductory text]

Item	Marion	Marshall	Meade	Miami	Mitchell	Montgomery	Morris	Morton
1987 FARMS BY STANDARD INDUSTRIAL CLASSIFICATION								
Cash grains (011)	314	436	248	144	320	118	103	120
Field crops, except cash grains (013)	6	4	7	12	-	5	4	2
Cotton (0131)	-	-	-	-	-	-	-	-
Tobacco (0132)	-	-	-	-	-	-	-	-
Sugarcane and sugar beets; Irish potatoes: field crops, except cash grains, n.e.c. (0133, 0134, 0139)	6	4	7	12	-	5	4	2
Vegetables and melons (016)	-	2	-	-	-	2	-	-
Fruits and tree nuts (017)	-	-	-	-	-	-	-	-
Horticultural specialties (018)	2	-	-	10	2	4	1	-
General farms, primarily crop (019)	20	10	1	12	4	6	6	-
Livestock, except dairy, poultry, and animal specialties (021)	310	262	113	195	142	197	215	40
Beef cattle, except feedlots (0212)	183	129	102	161	80	159	158	35
Dairy farms (024)	64	33	2	20	7	15	28	-
Poultry and eggs (025)	6	2	-	-	-	-	-	-
Animal specialties (027)	-	1	-	4	1	2	1	-
General farms, primarily livestock and animal specialties (029)	7	19	1	6	-	1	6	-
FARMS BY SIZE								
1 to 9 acres _____ 1987	18	20	11	4	11	6	11	1
1982	21	22	7	2	13	7	7	3
10 to 49 acres _____ 1987	17	11	-	9	7	7	2	1
1982	11	7	1	12	5	9	7	2
50 to 69 acres _____ 1987	9	4	-	8	3	8	-	-
1982	2	4	-	4	2	6	-	-
70 to 99 acres _____ 1987	9	5	1	16	7	19	2	2
1982	18	6	3	16	12	19	7	-
100 to 139 acres _____ 1987	18	12	3	24	5	15	7	-
1982	16	21	2	20	9	20	7	4
140 to 179 acres _____ 1987	36	41	5	36	15	25	14	7
1982	46	57	12	39	30	23	15	2
180 to 219 acres _____ 1987	19	31	1	33	13	15	10	1
1982	31	39	-	24	8	25	11	-
220 to 259 acres _____ 1987	41	33	3	28	18	24	18	-
1982	46	46	5	26	19	25	22	1
260 to 499 acres _____ 1987	204	223	54	117	95	80	85	13
1982	275	260	80	125	105	83	94	12
500 to 999 acres _____ 1987	225	256	105	70	130	82	96	20
1982	255	279	106	102	132	96	112	33
1,000 to 1,999 acres _____ 1987	109	131	99	47	121	46	75	55
1982	90	114	106	47	116	54	89	65
2,000 acres or more _____ 1987	29	22	80	8	51	25	44	62
1982	25	8	67	9	41	19	31	56
TENURE OF OPERATOR								
Full owners _____ farms, 1987	136	255	82	150	130	133	105	26
1982	174	309	106	146	137	160	113	33
acres, 1987	50 779	102 122	83 813	37 536	70 857	53 139	66 799	19 024
1982	118 375	134 410	147 736	46 906	65 293	52 123	91 337	48 417
Part owners _____ farms, 1987	471	411	198	198	248	178	215	108
1982	521	398	201	231	277	211	229	105
acres, 1987	413 478	350 249	377 195	138 558	321 691	171 922	269 479	258 404
1982	358 924	287 636	343 873	153 308	305 017	183 334	251 080	213 208
Tenants _____ farms, 1987	124	125	92	54	98	39	44	28
1982	141	156	80	50	78	25	60	42
acres, 1987	63 561	66 235	94 199	22 916	64 480	22 315	27 784	51 151
1982	56 906	69 226	70 842	26 485	38 669	16 705	29 772	46 630
OPERATOR CHARACTERISTICS								
Operators by place of residence:								
On farm operated _____ 1987	584	594	204	311	304	271	293	98
1982	639	614	211	328	306	318	314	104
Not on farm operated _____ 1987	107	154	136	68	132	57	57	46
1982	106	159	128	68	127	51	55	46
Not reported _____ 1987	40	43	32	23	40	22	16	18
1982	91	90	52	31	59	27	31	30
Operators by principal occupation:								
Farming _____ 1987	576	661	309	258	376	227	294	141
1982	688	746	323	284	413	269	332	159
Other _____ 1987	155	130	63	144	96	123	70	21
1982	148	117	66	143	79	127	70	21
Operators by days of work off farm:								
None _____ 1987	364	430	203	194	255	157	189	99
1982	392	466	203	185	257	183	220	104
Any _____ 1987	307	307	133	184	185	170	140	44
1982	344	265	133	207	176	185	161	41
1 to 49 days _____ 1987	66	100	43	16	43	20	39	12
1982	98	110	48	27	56	31	51	10
50 to 99 days _____ 1987	39	39	19	15	17	12	16	5
1982	47	36	8	20	11	13	17	3
100 to 149 days _____ 1987	30	16	9	16	18	10	10	2
1982	24	16	6	12	13	11	14	4

See footnotes at end of table.

Table 16. **Farms With Sales of $10,000 or More: 1987 and 1982**—Con.

[Data for 1987 include abnormal farms. For meaning of abbreviations and symbols, see introductory text.]

Item	Nemaha	Neosho	Ness	Norton	Osage	Osborne	Ottawa	Pawnee
1987 FARMS BY STANDARD INDUSTRIAL CLASSIFICATION								
Cash grains (011)	267	187	209	216	204	232	169	273
Field crops, except cash grains (013)	2	2	-	1	7	-	6	24
Cotton (0131)	-	-	-	-	-	-	-	-
Tobacco (0132)	-	-	-	-	-	-	-	-
Sugarcane and sugar beets; Irish potatoes; field crops, except cash grains, n.e.c. (0133, 0134, 0139)	2	2	-	1	7	-	6	24
Vegetables and melons (016)	-	1	-	-	-	1	-	-
Fruits and tree nuts (017)	-	2	-	-	2	-	-	-
Horticultural specialties (018)	1	1	-	-	2	-	2	1
General farms, primarily crop (019)	9	9	5	4	5	9	5	12
Livestock, except dairy, poultry, and animal specialties (021)	437	149	211	141	201	205	162	92
Beef cattle, except feedlots (0212)	156	117	191	95	149	156	135	60
Dairy farms (024)	95	21	5	5	8	8	8	1
Poultry and eggs (025)	4	-	-	-	-	-	1	-
Animal specialties (027)	1	-	-	1	2	1	-	-
General farms, primarily livestock and animal specialties (029)	20	7	1	2	1	2	1	-
FARMS BY SIZE								
1 to 9 acres ... 1987	30	1	9	10	9	10	7	12
1982	33	6	14	16	8	10	6	6
10 to 49 acres ... 1987	19	5	-	10	6	2	1	5
1982	16	2	-	3	7	6	2	5
50 to 69 acres ... 1987	4	3	-	1	3	-	4	-
1982	9	1	-	2	6	2	4	5
70 to 99 acres ... 1987	19	10	-	2	8	1	4	6
1982	23	2	2	2	18	4	7	1
100 to 139 acres ... 1987	13	15	3	3	13	4	10	4
1982	25	6	3	3	12	4	6	4
140 to 179 acres ... 1987	77	29	1	9	34	9	8	17
1982	80	30	9	12	30	23	21	17
180 to 219 acres ... 1987	35	12	2	6	16	8	6	3
1982	32	17	7	7	19	10	13	7
220 to 259 acres ... 1987	58	23	9	7	34	13	13	6
1982	72	23	15	8	24	20	31	15
260 to 499 acres ... 1987	276	102	61	48	98	88	68	70
1982	290	113	76	65	121	81	101	106
500 to 999 acres ... 1987	241	109	102	98	129	123	107	120
1982	231	123	140	119	150	143	107	133
1,000 to 1,999 acres ... 1987	57	52	133	103	60	135	93	95
1982	49	54	144	125	66	121	110	115
2,000 acres or more ... 1987	7	18	111	73	22	65	37	65
1982	5	19	92	59	17	58	32	46
TENURE OF OPERATOR								
Full owners ... farms, 1987	345	150	76	95	134	129	76	88
1982	408	136	103	122	143	144	116	107
acres, 1987	120 895	76 175	60 347	67 633	54 219	96 690	39 995	47 462
1982	140 183	68 683	90 389	91 058	52 444	109 279	59 412	68 849
Part owners ... farms, 1987	356	202	281	234	258	252	217	225
1982	320	227	269	248	302	264	238	279
acres, 1987	225 526	169 220	500 572	387 467	233 391	366 805	266 640	330 578
1982	193 183	179 808	467 162	350 891	243 706	328 200	246 052	331 110
Tenants ... farms, 1987	135	27	74	41	40	77	61	90
1982	137	33	110	51	33	74	86	75
acres, 1987	51 241	12 312	70 853	31 962	13 696	56 653	54 287	83 126
1982	46 346	22 323	91 849	50 140	17 878	51 403	69 292	53 412
OPERATOR CHARACTERISTICS								
Operators by place of residence:								
On farm operated ... 1987	653	278	259	245	343	293	253	250
1982	666	303	308	293	386	298	264	301
Not on farm operated ... 1987	127	69	143	97	77	134	79	127
1982	108	55	150	85	69	132	113	110
Not reported ... 1987	56	32	29	28	12	31	22	26
1982	91	40	44	43	23	52	63	50
Operators by principal occupation:								
Farming ... 1987	699	285	346	307	290	385	290	338
1982	752	307	419	387	339	409	353	393
Other ... 1987	137	94	83	63	142	73	64	65
1982	113	91	83	54	139	73	87	68
Operators by days of work off farm:								
None ... 1987	480	173	244	194	192	270	186	243
1982	498	181	245	222	221	261	207	248
Any ... 1987	284	173	164	142	214	156	147	133
1982	261	169	200	131	230	166	166	152
1 to 49 days ... 1987	56	24	43	25	34	49	41	35
1982	95	40	69	46	53	60	58	46
50 to 99 days ... 1987	39	23	17	13	16	15	18	12
1982	21	15	18	24	10	18	26	13
100 to 149 days ... 1987	24	12	13	12	22	11	20	5
1982	20	9	21	11	15	11	21	15

See footnotes at end of table.

Table 16. Farms With Sales of $10,000 or More: 1987 and 1982—Con.

[Data for 1987 include abnormal farms. For meaning of abbreviations and symbols, see introductory text]

Item	Phillips	Pottawatomie	Pratt	Rawlins	Reno	Republic	Rice	Riley
1987 FARMS BY STANDARD INDUSTRIAL CLASSIFICATION								
Cash grains (011)	156	88	273	251	531	456	281	87
Field crops, except cash grains (013)	4	5	7	3	18	4	10	1
Cotton (0131)	-	-	-	-	-	-	-	-
Tobacco (0132)	-	-	-	-	-	-	-	-
Sugarcane and sugar beets; Irish potatoes; field crops, except cash grains, n.e.c. (0133, 0134, 0139)	4	5	7	3	18	4	10	1
Vegetables and melons (016)	-	1	-	-	5	-	1	3
Fruits and tree nuts (017)	-	-	-	-	1	2	-	-
Horticultural specialties (018)	-	3	1	-	6	-	1	2
General terms, primarily crop (019)	10	3	-	14	17	11	12	5
Livestock, except dairy, poultry, and animal specialties (021)	247	327	104	144	228	143	100	206
Beef cattle, except feedlots (0212)	165	210	81	89	153	66	66	104
Dairy farms (024)	4	23	2	6	80	9	10	15
Poultry and eggs (025)	-	1	1	1	8	-	-	-
Animal specialties (027)	-	1	1	-	4	-	-	2
General farms, primarily livestock and animal specialties (029)	5	4	2	4	8	2	2	2
FARMS BY SIZE								
1 to 9 acres ___ 1987	10	12	4	7	17	15	7	7
1982	9	15	10	10	23	14	11	10
10 to 49 acres ___ 1987	4	9	4	3	26	7	3	12
1982	2	12	1	2	28	3	1	12
50 to 69 acres ___ 1987	5	1	-	-	5	5	1	4
1982	-	3	-	1	6	1	3	2
70 to 99 acres ___ 1987	8	9	3	4	14	9	7	4
1982	6	22	2	1	33	13	5	13
100 to 139 acres ___ 1987	4	6	4	3	14	23	3	11
1982	6	14	4	3	32	15	8	21
140 to 179 acres ___ 1987	14	28	15	5	47	46	11	21
1982	8	19	20	11	84	45	26	23
180 to 219 acres ___ 1987	4	15	7	5	37	23	10	10
1982	8	13	9	2	62	32	10	6
220 to 259 acres ___ 1987	15	13	8	2	64	23	8	11
1982	20	29	11	8	76	47	25	14
260 to 499 acres ___ 1987	51	99	55	51	219	137	83	77
1982	89	110	71	62	287	201	85	76
500 to 999 acres ___ 1987	116	144	123	105	245	204	127	108
1982	144	169	142	150	252	196	151	112
1,000 to 1,999 acres ___ 1987	132	75	113	134	176	116	117	44
1982	140	82	130	180	174	92	122	36
2,000 acres or more ___ 1987	67	45	55	104	39	19	40	16
1982	54	37	37	82	34	20	35	16
TENURE OF OPERATOR								
Full owners ___ farms, 1987	110	166	92	107	211	168	61	114
1982	133	213	95	140	280	194	96	126
acres, 1987	70 269	91 652	64 313	97 758	79 543	62 951	25 140	48 585
1982	114 326	133 633	50 989	142 135	102 163	96 404	47 403	57 064
Part owners ___ farms, 1987	250	232	206	246	526	361	274	176
1982	279	254	251	278	630	376	298	177
acres, 1987	383 050	264 237	279 745	423 123	450 528	310 234	308 741	146 893
1982	346 989	250 984	303 908	421 943	471 672	277 429	298 840	142 820
Tenants ___ farms, 1987	58	58	93	70	169	96	82	35
1982	74	58	91	94	181	109	88	41
acres, 1987	58 948	42 030	96 194	94 152	113 907	46 993	70 965	25 160
1982	54 865	26 523	68 560	93 716	85 297	40 838	66 647	22 496
OPERATOR CHARACTERISTICS								
Operators by place of residence:								
On farm operated ___ 1987	329	350	256	269	698	420	316	260
1982	354	407	271	361	799	459	345	264
Not on farm operated ___ 1987	70	77	112	108	152	159	77	49
1982	88	74	119	103	194	146	78	49
Not reported ___ 1987	29	29	23	26	56	46	24	16
1982	44	44	47	46	98	74	59	31
Operators by principal occupation:								
Farming ___ 1987	367	338	324	371	704	526	334	254
1982	426	436	360	460	863	579	403	274
Other ___ 1987	61	118	67	52	202	101	83	71
1982	60	89	77	52	208	100	79	70
Operators by days of work off farm:								
None ___ 1987	254	263	211	243	431	311	208	179
1982	277	281	223	298	516	344	254	178
Any ___ 1987	142	164	157	154	414	281	180	121
1982	163	184	169	147	448	235	178	129
1 to 49 days ___ 1987	58	28	46	60	104	97	43	23
1982	65	60	40	56	126	83	45	43
50 to 99 days ___ 1987	11	11	13	22	45	34	23	6
1982	10	17	15	22	51	14	29	12
100 to 149 days ___ 1987	9	12	20	5	38	20	16	13
1982	15	3	22	12	41	21	17	10

See footnotes at end of table.

Table 16. **Farms With Sales of $10,000 or More: 1987 and 1982**—Con.

[Data for 1987 include abnormal farms. For meaning of abbreviations and symbols, see introductory text.]

Item	Rooks	Rush	Russell	Saline	Scott	Sedgwick	Seward	Shawnee
1987 FARMS BY STANDARD INDUSTRIAL CLASSIFICATION								
Cash grains (011)	196	256	168	216	180	474	139	152
Field crops, except cash grains (013)	2	4	3	5	16	20	7	7
Cotton (0131)	-	-	-	-	-	-	-	-
Tobacco (0132)	-	-	-	-	-	-	-	-
Sugarcane and sugar beets; Irish potatoes; field crops, except cash grains, n.e.c. (0133, 0134, 0139)	2	4	3	5	5	20	7	7
Vegetables and melons (016)	-	-	-	1	-	7	-	4
Fruits and tree nuts (017)	-	-	-	-	-	-	-	-
Horticultural specialties (018)	1	-	-	3	-	15	-	7
General farms, primarily crop (019)	11	6	11	13	1	18	1	7
Livestock, except dairy, poultry, and animal specialties (021)	115	94	143	145	116	151	61	153
Beef cattle, except feedlots (0212)	101	88	120	124	55	97	47	121
Dairy farms (024)	9	7	12	15	-	76	-	7
Poultry and eggs (025)	-	1	-	-	-	7	-	-
Animal specialties (027)	1	-	-	-	2	11	-	2
General farms, primarily livestock and animal specialties (029)	1	1	4	1	1	10	-	-
FARMS BY SIZE								
1 to 9 acres ... 1987	5	10	10	8	19	28	4	14
1982	10	7	9	8	19	40	10	12
10 to 49 acres ... 1987	2	1	-	-	2	30	2	9
1982	1	4	-	4	5	25	1	12
50 to 69 acres ... 1987	2	-	3	-	2	11	-	4
1982	1	-	1	6	2	10	1	4
70 to 99 acres ... 1987	-	3	-	7	3	14	-	10
1982	4	5	2	7	2	21	4	16
100 to 139 acres ... 1987	1	4	3	8	-	23	-	21
1982	2	3	5	17	-	42	2	10
140 to 179 acres ... 1987	4	10	9	13	10	52	4	29
1982	19	16	21	44	8	94	8	17
180 to 219 acres ... 1987	3	6	1	3	5	24	2	19
1982	8	9	7	23	1	36	-	14
220 to 259 acres ... 1987	5	8	6	12	4	46	3	20
1982	12	6	14	19	7	62	1	16
260 to 499 acres ... 1987	52	59	67	87	46	233	25	88
1982	58	117	83	119	44	259	34	98
500 to 999 acres ... 1987	77	116	91	136	61	212	50	83
1982	112	146	134	133	84	214	42	66
1,000 to 1,999 acres ... 1987	100	115	82	94	74	92	69	33
1982	106	112	94	75	83	110	61	39
2,000 acres or more ... 1987	85	37	69	29	87	24	49	9
1982	69	31	53	33	80	15	51	7
TENURE OF OPERATOR								
Full owners ... farms, 1987	55	86	75	76	88	207	49	111
1982	94	81	114	111	103	279	53	108
acres, 1987	52 656	54 952	53 152	44 414	59 541	74 274	63 353	24 134
1982	79 823	43 889	72 442	36 437	94 502	90 906	48 205	34 169
Part owners ... farms, 1987	214	222	194	254	148	434	97	184
1982	239	287	219	289	156	483	102	166
acres, 1987	386 099	275 869	286 631	269 916	299 649	310 241	161 184	127 810
1982	362 982	294 917	294 891	289 031	326 215	315 542	199 229	120 515
Tenants ... farms, 1987	67	59	72	69	80	148	82	44
1982	69	88	91	88	76	166	50	37
acres, 1987	74 020	52 334	76 785	50 059	93 591	73 117	67 198	23 359
1982	61 586	61 801	75 337	39 453	75 868	68 588	64 578	18 298
OPERATOR CHARACTERISTICS								
Operators by place of residence:								
On farm operated ... 1987	218	233	209	292	151	579	122	256
1982	229	275	238	328	162	680	113	240
Not on farm operated ... 1987	100	107	101	89	134	151	65	68
1982	117	132	132	118	122	146	67	42
Not reported ... 1987	20	29	31	18	31	59	21	15
1982	56	49	53	42	51	102	35	29
Operators by principal occupation:								
Farming ... 1987	269	297	285	311	264	547	182	231
1982	304	362	332	374	288	662	182	233
Other ... 1987	67	72	56	88	52	242	26	108
1982	98	94	91	114	47	266	33	78
Operators by days of work off farm:								
None ... 1987	173	165	183	205	190	362	112	171
1982	159	216	223	228	170	373	108	150
Any ... 1987	143	160	133	166	101	374	72	143
1982	180	181	161	222	105	442	59	134
1 to 49 days ... 1987	30	44	33	33	26	63	21	15
1982	37	48	41	50	41	86	22	26
50 to 99 days ... 1987	18	13	14	16	10	48	10	12
1982	15	13	9	22	5	42	9	8
100 to 149 days ... 1987	17	23	15	16	9	24	5	12
1982	23	16	8	25	6	34	5	11

See footnotes at end of table.

Table 16. **Farms With Sales of $10,000 or More: 1987 and 1982**—Con.

[Data for 1987 include abnormal farms. For meaning of abbreviations and symbols, see introductory text]

Item	Sheridan	Sherman	Smith	Stafford	Stanton	Stevens	Sumner	Thomas
1987 FARMS BY STANDARD INDUSTRIAL CLASSIFICATION								
Cash grains (011)	289	321	284	255	175	204	568	420
Field crops, except cash grains (013)	5	4	5	11	2	5	6	-
Cotton (0131)	-	-	-	-	-	-	-	-
Tobacco (0132)	-	-	-	-	-	-	-	-
Sugarcane and sugar beets; Irish potatoes; field crops, except cash grains, n.e.c. (0133, 0134, 0139)	5	4	5	11	2	5	6	-
Vegetables and melons (016)	-	-	-	1	-	-	1	-
Fruits and tree nuts (017)	-	-	-	-	-	-	1	-
Horticultural specialties (018)	-	-	-	1	-	-	1	-
General farms, primarily crop (019)	11	4	12	6	2	2	6	2
Livestock, except dairy, poultry, and animal specialties (021)	113	73	241	119	39	30	173	71
Beef cattle, except feedlots (0212)	75	39	152	90	26	20	108	42
Dairy farms (024)	4	2	10	-	-	-	14	-
Poultry and eggs (025)	-	-	-	-	-	-	-	-
Animal specialties (027)	-	3	-	-	-	2	-	-
General farms, primarily livestock and animal specialties (029)	-	2	3	1	-	-	2	-
FARMS BY SIZE								
1 to 9 acres ___ 1987	18	11	14	5	6	2	14	4
1982	14	6	10	-	5	-	16	7
10 to 49 acres ___ 1987	2	1	6	5	1	-	6	1
1982	3	5	16	2	-	1	8	3
50 to 69 acres ___ 1987	-	4	-	1	-	1	3	1
1982	4	4	2	2	-	1	4	-
70 to 99 acres ___ 1987	-	6	8	5	-	-	13	3
1982	2	3	9	2	-	1	19	2
100 to 139 acres ___ 1987	3	1	4	2	1	1	7	2
1982	5	1	8	6	-	-	31	1
140 to 179 acres ___ 1987	18	15	24	8	6	3	27	10
1982	22	21	26	32	7	2	77	40
180 to 219 acres ___ 1987	1	2	6	1	1	1	17	5
1982	7	8	15	11	-	-	30	2
220 to 259 acres ___ 1987	3	8	27	5	-	1	33	5
1982	4	10	23	10	-	2	41	5
260 to 499 acres ___ 1987	72	43	90	73	14	16	176	78
1982	101	72	124	112	12	32	241	97
500 to 999 acres ___ 1987	102	101	163	110	36	42	233	136
1982	142	108	192	134	31	67	323	144
1,000 to 1,999 acres ___ 1987	141	124	160	124	76	83	194	168
1982	134	133	156	126	65	101	198	138
2,000 acres or more ___ 1987	62	95	53	52	79	89	49	90
1982	57	90	41	41	83	70	29	80
TENURE OF OPERATOR								
Full owners ___ farms, 1987	128	119	145	74	37	36	144	150
1982	169	154	181	117	43	45	222	213
acres, 1987	95 685	113 117	82 174	52 715	37 941	36 349	64 792	163 332
1982	133 843	150 951	93 912	92 682	(D)	53 150	94 476	194 872
Part owners ___ farms, 1987	229	218	320	237	107	147	479	249
1982	245	216	334	250	107	166	595	237
acres, 1987	336 731	364 034	389 939	307 944	241 116	313 326	475 573	391 083
1982	304 028	408 009	368 864	287 660	(D)	314 896	507 028	367 960
Tenants ___ farms, 1987	65	72	90	83	76	58	149	94
1982	81	89	107	113	53	66	200	68
acres, 1987	55 430	96 575	63 901	71 489	131 201	93 366	106 375	92 456
1982	59 362	89 698	60 921	69 143	81 459	78 437	96 323	75 424
OPERATOR CHARACTERISTICS								
Operators by place of residence:								
On farm operated ___ 1987	255	249	392	257	123	147	583	273
1982	285	288	435	285	110	150	749	275
Not on farm operated ___ 1987	121	132	127	112	82	72	154	181
1982	150	127	138	132	61	89	190	191
Not reported ___ 1987	46	28	36	25	15	22	35	39
1982	60	44	49	63	32	38	78	63
Operators by principal occupation:								
Farming ___ 1987	354	338	470	337	207	201	571	396
1982	421	396	523	407	182	250	807	409
Other ___ 1987	68	71	85	57	13	40	201	97
1982	74	63	99	73	21	27	210	110
Operators by days of work off farm:								
None ___ 1987	216	234	328	216	143	150	355	261
1982	255	267	333	256	126	168	460	266
Any ___ 1987	154	144	189	135	56	72	371	202
1982	179	135	228	156	54	77	457	188
1 to 49 days ___ 1987	46	44	49	45	13	16	70	64
1982	69	41	75	43	18	27	90	52
50 to 99 days ___ 1987	25	18	20	12	8	10	26	15
1982	19	17	27	14	4	5	32	15
100 to 149 days ___ 1987	21	15	24	16	8	6	41	18
1982	17	5	10	21	3	4	72	13

See footnotes at end of table.

Table 16. **Farms With Sales of $10,000 or More: 1987 and 1982**—Con.

[Data for 1987 include abnormal farms. For meaning of abbreviations and symbols, see introductory text]

Item	Trego	Wabaunsee	Wallace	Washington	Wichita	Wilson	Woodson	Wyandotte
1987 FARMS BY STANDARD INDUSTRIAL CLASSIFICATION								
Cash grains (011)	215	91	165	291	209	190	98	13
Field crops, except cash grains (013)	3	9	-	-	8	2	7	1
Cotton (0131)	-	-	-	-	-	-	-	-
Tobacco (0132)	-	-	-	-	-	-	-	-
Sugarcane and sugar beets; Irish potatoes; field crops, except cash grains, n.e.c. (0133, 0134, 0139)	3	9	-	-	8	2	7	1
Vegetables and melons (016)	-	1	-	-	-	-	1	8
Fruits and tree nuts (017)	-	-	-	-	-	-	1	-
Horticultural specialties (018)	-	-	-	1	-	-	-	3
General terms, primarily crop (019)	10	2	4	3	1	3	7	1
Livestock, except dairy, poultry, and animal specialties (021)	137	235	68	368	84	137	107	10
Beef cattle, except feedlots (0212)	118	182	68	160	38	118	89	6
Dairy farms (024)	12	15	-	31	-	10	1	1
Poultry and eggs (025)	-	1	-	-	-	-	-	-
Animal specialties (027)	-	1	-	5	-	-	-	2
General terms, primarily livestock and animal specialties (029)	4	2	-	7	-	1	-	1
FARMS BY SIZE								
1 to 9 acres ... 1987	10	5	10	41	8	3	-	3
... 1982	7	12	2	20	10	2	3	-
10 to 49 acres ... 1987	1	7	2	11	2	1	2	7
... 1982	2	7	1	9	1	5	5	7
50 to 69 acres ... 1987	-	2	-	4	-	3	-	2
... 1982	-	4	-	6	1	3	-	2
70 to 99 acres ... 1987	1	5	-	8	1	11	6	6
... 1982	1	8	5	18	-	8	2	2
100 to 139 acres ... 1987	1	10	-	16	2	7	1	2
... 1982	1	18	-	4	-	9	2	3
140 to 179 acres ... 1987	6	17	4	28	9	17	7	1
... 1982	7	19	7	62	20	25	8	5
180 to 219 acres ... 1987	4	22	4	22	4	10	10	3
... 1982	1	12	1	26	5	14	4	2
220 to 259 acres ... 1987	5	16	-	34	-	19	10	1
... 1982	6	18	3	38	3	24	14	3
260 to 499 acres ... 1987	62	72	26	179	37	78	53	6
... 1982	55	81	41	224	43	85	54	10
500 to 999 acres ... 1987	121	104	52	208	66	110	56	5
... 1982	111	127	54	244	53	139	56	7
1,000 to 1,999 acres ... 1987	111	62	86	122	79	71	56	3
... 1982	132	73	67	105	77	81	48	4
2,000 acres or more ... 1987	50	35	73	33	74	13	22	2
... 1982	52	27	79	26	78	15	21	1
TENURE OF OPERATOR								
Full owners ... farms, 1987	89	129	70	227	66	123	66	20
... 1982	82	146	89	278	80	124	61	14
... acres, 1987	58 173	71 498	92 099	87 131	64 584	58 997	29 251	3 588
... 1982	58 991	78 676	151 403	126 498	87 809	52 927	47 771	1 964
Part owners ... farms, 1987	220	187	129	380	153	186	133	13
... 1982	219	203	120	394	151	237	142	21
... acres, 1987	337 902	278 351	330 432	340 682	278 159	182 160	186 336	9 822
... 1982	329 781	268 257	286 171	322 207	278 297	209 254	180 624	12 706
Tenants ... farms, 1987	72	41	56	99	63	34	24	8
... 1982	74	57	51	113	60	49	24	11
... acres, 1987	83 450	61 890	88 757	64 066	85 837	16 313	15 212	3 079
... 1982	69 698	48 158	53 034	52 095	49 215	21 391	18 469	3 488
OPERATOR CHARACTERISTICS								
Operators by place of residence:								
On farm operated ... 1987	266	271	154	519	162	259	169	27
... 1982	265	315	136	565	146	327	171	30
Not on farm operated ... 1987	96	56	95	137	95	60	35	9
... 1982	61	53	82	128	99	52	32	11
Not reported ... 1987	19	30	6	50	25	24	19	5
... 1982	29	38	42	92	44	31	24	5
Operators by principal occupation:								
Farming ... 1987	308	282	207	626	238	279	176	15
... 1982	305	318	229	672	241	329	184	33
Other ... 1987	73	75	50	80	43	64	47	26
... 1982	70	88	31	113	50	81	43	13
Operators by days of work off farm:								
None ... 1987	186	198	131	363	156	165	124	10
... 1982	192	205	137	446	149	213	117	21
Any ... 1987	178	134	117	242	103	154	82	30
... 1982	142	151	87	240	103	159	93	22
1 to 49 days ... 1987	44	20	34	80	30	42	21	3
... 1982	30	29	32	78	25	36	25	3
50 to 99 days ... 1987	28	13	7	27	14	15	4	1
... 1982	13	14	8	25	12	16	11	3
100 to 149 days ... 1987	10	13	7	25	12	8	7	2
... 1982	14	12	7	23	9	17	13	6

See footnotes at end of table.

Table 16. **Farms With Sales of $10,000 or More: 1987 and 1982**—Con.

[Data for 1987 include abnormal farms. For meaning of abbreviations and symbols, see Introductory text.]

Item	Kansas	Allen	Anderson	Atchison	Barber	Barton	Bourbon
OPERATOR CHARACTERISTICS— Con.							
Operators by days of work off farm—Con.							
Any—Con.							
150 to 199 days 1987	1 763	20	16	21	10	32	27
1982	1 650	18	16	11	9	32	22
200 days or more 1987	8 240	73	96	100	69	99	92
1982	8 332	70	73	94	81	130	62
Not reported 1987	3 087	31	39	35	37	47	25
1982	5 417	57	58	43	51	68	36
1987 operators by years on present farm:							
2 years or less	1 600	12	21	17	26	19	7
3 or 4 years	1 800	15	12	21	20	35	20
5 to 9 years	4 651	24	52	45	43	65	46
10 years or more	27 950	251	257	283	227	393	242
Average years on present farm	23.5	24.0	23.2	22.5	23.0	24.7	23.2
Not reported	6 727	54	72	65	65	105	62
1987 operators by age group:							
Under 25 years	945	6	13	19	7	15	7
25 to 34 years	6 161	45	61	65	56	98	39
35 to 44 years	7 754	66	73	87	74	86	75
45 to 54 years	7 827	58	94	88	50	106	69
55 to 64 years	10 758	103	109	107	111	176	90
65 years and over	9 263	78	94	65	81	136	97
Average age	51.6	52.7	51.5	49.0	51.8	52.0	53.7
TYPE OF ORGANIZATION							
Individual or family (sole proprietorship) .... farms, 1987	36 327	318	390	357	314	522	337
1982	40 949	357	416	383	351	604	360
acres, 1987	33 178 291	191 772	266 965	160 738	531 859	418 381	202 535
1982	33 951 129	199 858	271 914	163 312	523 612	412 822	216 649
Partnership .... farms, 1987	4 309	32	47	59	54	74	31
1982	5 010	40	43	59	51	82	44
acres, 1987	5 881 210	34 467	41 283	32 494	100 084	67 478	36 581
1982	5 962 690	(D)	46 285	33 211	69 376	80 165	34 144
Corporation:							
Family held .... farms, 1987	1 758	5	5	13	8	17	7
1982	1 664	7	3	8	11	14	8
acres, 1987	3 397 256	(D)	(D)	(D)	15 252	21 942	12 422
1982	3 182 393	(D)	(D)	11 378	25 815	(D)	19 207
Other than family held .... farms, 1987	122	1	-	-	-	2	1
1982	147	-	-	-	2	1	-
acres, 1987	152 533	(D)	-	-	(D)	(D)	(D)
1982	237 134	-	-	-	(D)	(D)	-
Other—cooperative, estate or trust, institutional, etc. .... farms, 1987	212	-	1	2	4	2	1
1982	225	-	1	-	2	3	-
acres, 1987	287 780	-	(D)	(D)	(D)	(D)	(D)
1982	326 961	-	(D)	-	(D)	2 538	-
1987 FARM PRODUCTION EXPENSES[1]							
Total farm production expenses .... farms	42 865	358	441	429	384	616	381
$1,000	5 378 664	16 595	23 266	19 436	40 007	102 912	18 171
Livestock and poultry purchased .... farms	18 117	146	179	156	256	235	163
$1,000	2 415 351	2 224	4 349	2 684	15 195	44 425	4 940
Feed for livestock and poultry .... farms	27 518	290	320	275	318	369	320
$1,000	877 309	2 188	1 893	2 037	4 856	29 033	2 527
Commercially mixed formula feeds .... farms	11 221	102	126	126	177	137	116
$1,000	161 449	567	851	974	667	3 135	648
Seeds, bulbs, plants, and trees .... farms	36 438	297	391	370	281	531	268
$1,000	91 270	696	1 028	1 065	580	900	501
Commercial fertilizer .... farms	35 204	320	379	381	290	512	286
$1,000	207 371	1 258	1 576	1 863	1 923	2 381	953
Agricultural chemicals .... farms	34 474	235	365	405	233	541	251
$1,000	118 865	844	1 221	1 314	720	1 565	475
Petroleum products .... farms	42 296	348	439	406	373	614	381
$1,000	227 993	1 157	1 593	1 570	2 128	2 891	1 094
Electricity .... farms	35 071	286	355	366	301	511	286
$1,000	50 132	329	296	360	325	779	223
Hired farm labor .... farms	20 551	156	189	201	221	264	128
$1,000	223 983	956	943	579	1 853	2 447	509
Contract labor .... farms	6 184	61	50	14	88	81	77
$1,000	22 375	118	421	60	243	326	154
Repair and maintenance .... farms	38 771	303	387	353	360	565	360
$1,000	235 054	1 584	1 768	1 794	2 140	4 142	1 203
Customwork, machine hire, and rental of machinery and equipment .... farms	23 220	185	171	215	184	267	133
$1,000	101 691	273	524	508	1 110	788	284
Interest .... farms	29 923	254	287	258	281	336	281
$1,000	295 316	1 920	2 840	2 530	3 408	2 863	2 619
Cash rent .... farms	17 942	144	192	137	210	238	179
$1,000	119 525	607	1 372	668	2 122	958	612
Property taxes .... farms	40 045	340	433	407	352	568	358
$1,000	96 361	684	855	723	1 086	1 367	684
All other farm production expenses .... farms	42 856	358	441	429	384	616	381
$1,000	296 067	1 757	2 586	1 672	2 319	8 047	1 394

See footnotes at end of table.

Table 16. **Farms With Sales of $10,000 or More: 1987 and 1982**—Con.

[Data for 1987 include abnormal farms. For meaning of abbreviations and symbols, see introductory text.]

Item	Brown	Butler	Chase	Chautauqua	Cherokee	Cheyenne	Clark
OPERATOR CHARACTERISTICS—Con.							
Operators by days of work off farm—Con.							
Any—Con.							
150 to 199 days .... 1987..	10	25	6	13	14	14	9
1982..	11	24	10	13	10	9	6
200 days or more .... 1987..	82	156	51	40	86	55	54
1982..	72	171	26	49	89	64	40
Not reported .... 1987..	34	30	13	8	22	32	11
1982..	68	50	23	27	42	53	29
1987 operators by years on present farm:							
2 years or less	24	11	11	10	10	18	11
3 or 4 years	25	23	11	10	12	15	18
5 to 9 years	54	80	28	25	43	31	38
10 years or more	372	461	135	126	249	251	130
Average years on present farm	23.7	23.2	22.4	21.5	23.0	24.8	20.8
Not reported	68	75	26	19	60	69	32
1987 operators by age group:							
Under 25 years	18	7	1	3	13	6	–
25 to 34 years	78	72	34	22	51	55	40
35 to 44 years	127	99	42	34	71	64	39
45 to 54 years	79	124	33	44	87	59	33
55 to 64 years	133	153	42	38	73	115	69
65 years and over	108	195	59	49	79	85	48
Average age	50.3	54.6	52.2	52.7	50.4	52.7	52.0
TYPE OF ORGANIZATION							
Individual or family (sole proprietorship) .... farms, 1987..	420	553	179	164	323	326	183
1982..	467	553	166	197	367	393	202
acres, 1987..	217 897	475 418	211 024	200 839	169 113	447 420	372 500
1982..	227 795	439 232	226 403	214 507	202 197	472 336	388 085
Partnership .... farms, 1987..	54	62	17	16	37	34	23
1982..	94	79	24	20	43	39	24
acres, 1987..	(D)	73 232	62 516	36 164	33 947	73 019	(D)
1982..	54 995	97 680	90 627	(D)	37 191	57 311	(D)
Corporation:							
Family held .... farms, 1987..	50	30	12	8	13	22	17
1982..	32	19	14	5	11	22	18
acres, 1987..	60 258	(D)	(D)	27 506	(D)	(D)	(D)
1982..	43 071	49 599	(D)	24 072	(D)	(D)	89 392
Other than family held .... farms, 1987..	3	2	1	1	–	1	4
1982..	1	2	1	1	–	–	2
acres, 1987..	3 293	(D)	(D)	(D)	–	–	21 270
1982..	(D)	(D)	(D)	(D)	–	(D)	(D)
Other—cooperative, estate or trust,							
institutional, etc. .... farms, 1987..	6	3	2	1	1	2	2
1982..	2	4	3	–	2	2	–
acres, 1987..	(D)	(D)	(D)	(D)	(D)	(D)	(D)
1982..	(D)	(D)	(D)	–	(D)	(D)	–
1987 FARM PRODUCTION EXPENSES[1]							
Total farm production expenses .... farms..	540	648	209	193	374	386	250
$1,000..	49 372	82 290	26 359	12 282	15 890	42 906	50 517
Livestock and poultry purchased .... farms..	228	342	108	112	122	155	193
$1,000..	12 652	39 683	14 092	2 193	1 574	17 881	29 631
Feed for livestock and poultry .... farms..	395	473	150	173	206	233	200
$1,000..	7 896	13 342	3 976	2 083	1 180	4 629	5 466
Commercially mixed formula feeds .... farms..	177	231	74	67	33	95	54
$1,000..	2 418	3 419	2 140	537	749	851	(D)
Seeds, bulbs, plants, and trees .... farms..	500	450	133	100	304	342	197
$1,000..	1 828	821	147	345	1 104	1 157	301
Commercial fertilizer .... farms..	476	496	133	94	332	306	176
$1,000..	3 263	2 669	330	330	2 048	1 993	766
Agricultural chemicals .... farms..	498	469	137	120	299	281	167
$1,000..	2 543	1 260	378	233	1 046	1 055	555
Petroleum products .... farms..	538	647	209	184	374	383	249
$1,000..	2 241	2 419	745	790	1 357	2 523	1 594
Electricity .... farms..	442	530	180	131	284	316	199
$1,000..	567	583	163	181	185	627	244
Hired farm labor .... farms..	309	306	80	84	108	173	115
$1,000..	4 585	3 386	1 089	1 433	1 166	1 826	1 933
Contract labor .... farms..	46	148	25	37	44	68	81
$1,000..	309	411	82	82	79	198	356
Repair and maintenance .... farms..	487	617	191	183	332	366	227
$1,000..	2 690	2 654	1 098	632	1 470	2 121	1 484
Customwork, machine hire, and rental of							
machinery and equipment .... farms..	354	290	85	74	156	271	126
$1,000..	963	520	301	229	422	1 391	727
Interest .... farms..	292	416	129	145	258	293	179
$1,000..	4 068	4 328	1 079	1 122	1 750	2 986	2 595
Cash rent .... farms..	184	306	75	76	135	120	170
$1,000..	1 044	2 336	755	472	608	810	1 769
Property taxes .... farms..	495	632	183	192	349	366	222
$1,000..	1 535	1 496	484	410	777	953	559
All other farm production expenses .... farms..	540	648	209	193	374	386	250
$1,000..	3 219	6 081	1 640	1 786	1 122	2 758	2 535

See footnotes at end of table.

Table 16. **Farms With Sales of $10,000 or More: 1987 and 1982**—Con.

[Data for 1987 include abnormal farms. For meaning of abbreviations and symbols, see introductory text]

Item	Clay	Cloud	Coffey	Comanche	Cowley	Crawford	Decatur
OPERATOR CHARACTERISTICS—Con.							
Operators by days of work off farm—Con.							
Any—Con.							
150 to 199 days ....1987..	18	11	19	4	30	16	14
1982..	19	16	22	10	36	27	24
200 days or more ....1987..	71	72	93	36	120	73	46
1982..	58	81	71	27	163	84	44
Not reported ....1987..	40	33	20	22	25	23	23
1982..	74	47	48	32	59	27	47
1987 operators by years on present farm:							
2 years or less	20	17	16	6	16	10	27
3 or 4 years	17	17	19	8	11	9	20
5 to 9 years	55	45	40	22	51	41	53
10 years or more	314	284	276	130	349	250	233
Average years on present farm	24.6	24.0	22.7	25.6	24.4	22.6	23.3
Not reported	82	73	53	36	72	66	56
1987 operators by age group:							
Under 25 years	17	12	10	-	4	13	8
25 to 34 years	81	86	54	24	63	56	67
35 to 44 years	87	81	90	31	83	60	64
45 to 54 years	74	71	71	37	82	81	66
55 to 64 years	121	97	100	43	142	84	86
65 years and over	108	90	79	69	125	82	96
Average age	50.8	50.1	50.8	55.7	53.5	50.8	51.4
TYPE OF ORGANIZATION							
Individual or family (sole proprietorship) ....farms, 1987..	424	368	370	163	436	347	314
1982..	477	422	374	169	578	391	345
acres, 1987..	291 130	307 428	273 058	316 354	408 144	207 349	376 858
1982..	299 272	306 102	257 580	290 414	490 263	229 308	388 870
Partnership ....farms, 1987..	53	49	49	24	50	19	38
1982..	45	76	31	32	67	43	54
acres, 1987..	(D)	(D)	16 500	95 816	87 301	13 930	47 388
1982..	35 552	59 573	35 469	108 655	105 988	(D)	(D)
Corporation:							
Family held ....farms, 1987..	11	16	10	6	11	6	41
1982..	8	9	10	6	16	5	33
acres, 1987..	(D)	(D)	16 357	(D)	42 707	(D)	(D)
1982..	7 990	13 569	(D)	(D)	42 640	(D)	(D)
Other than family held ....farms, 1987..	1	1	1	1	1	-	1
1982..	2	-	1	1	3	-	-
acres, 1987..	-	(D)	-	-	(D)	-	(D)
1982..	(D)	-	(D)	(D)	(D)	-	(D)
Other—cooperative, estate or trust, institutional, etc. ....farms, 1987..	-	-	-	1	1	2	-
1982..	1	3	-	1	2	-	-
acres, 1987..	(D)	840	-	(D)	(D)	(D)	-
1987 FARM PRODUCTION EXPENSES[1]							
Total farm production expenses ....farms..	487	440	402	205	503	377	369
$1,000..	26 812	22 163	24 444	21 578	48 643	15 084	61 237
Livestock and poultry purchased ....farms..	262	158	224	137	237	97	166
$1,000..	5 684	3 237	7 974	8 606	19 248	2 537	29 121
Feed for livestock and poultry ....farms..	383	250	291	179	388	238	263
$1,000..	5 310	1 996	3 405	2 453	8 266	1 721	10 912
Commercially mixed formula feeds ....farms..	115	109	125	61	143	95	76
$1,000..	1 926	266	1 346	486	2 196	447	817
Seeds, bulbs, plants, and trees ....farms..	457	390	365	140	392	331	372
$1,000..	765	619	927	289	468	683	932
Commercial fertilizer ....farms..	463	405	305	127	437	339	326
$1,000..	2 349	2 405	1 070	723	1 630	1 677	1 967
Agricultural chemicals ....farms..	431	384	337	129	340	275	310
$1,000..	1 222	1 029	1 013	366	677	759	1 147
Petroleum products ....farms..	486	433	402	204	488	368	376
$1,000..	2 046	2 034	1 507	1 130	1 893	1 221	2 303
Electricity ....farms..	429	366	325	174	370	291	369
$1,000..	477	365	283	161	361	236	(D)
Hired farm labor ....farms..	219	224	130	92	248	120	232
$1,000..	1 338	911	1 002	1 148	2 693	536	1 592
Contract labor ....farms..	38	59	39	43	97	37	62
$1,000..	122	(D)	42	42	324	64	(D)
Repair and maintenance ....farms..	407	384	352	191	439	346	353
$1,000..	2 096	2 027	1 482	978	2 579	1 280	2 182
Customwork, machine hire, and rental of machinery and equipment ....farms..	271	245	173	126	232	193	242
$1,000..	310	498	354	555	454	486	927
Interest ....farms..	350	352	309	154	371	227	269
$1,000..	2 513	2 858	2 013	1 743	3 608	1 484	3 519
Cash rent ....farms..	206	191	219	96	239	149	176
$1,000..	861	(D)	972	1 111	1 459	548	1 165
Property taxes ....farms..	458	417	396	183	490	370	356
$1,000..	1 109	1 009	546	562	1 296	830	954
All other farm production expenses ....farms..	487	440	402	205	503	377	389
$1,000..	2 410	1 929	1 837	1 673	3 346	1 222	3 506

See footnotes at end of table.

Table 16. **Farms With Sales of $10,000 or More: 1987 and 1982** – Con.

[Data for 1987 include abnormal farms. For meaning of abbreviations and symbols, see introductory text.]

Item	Dickinson	Doniphan	Douglas	Edwards	Elk	Ellis	Ellsworth
OPERATOR CHARACTERISTICS – Con.							
Operators by days of work off farm – Con.							
Any – Con.							
150 to 199 days .... 1987..	22	6	11	7	5	26	21
1982..	26	23	15	9	12	22	9
200 days or more .... 1987..	122	59	97	31	66	104	61
1982..	99	70	83	40	59	137	61
Not reported .... 1987..	34	30	28	34	22	38	24
1982..	97	42	35	45	24	56	48
1987 operators by years on present farm:							
2 years or less	17	24	8	13	6	10	2
3 or 4 years	29	12	13	12	8	16	11
5 to 9 years...............................	80	31	24	33	19	43	35
10 years or more	449	245	246	175	154	268	244
Average years on present farm	24.2	22.8	25.5	24.0	24.7	23.6	25.6
Not reported	65	57	42	50	39	103	63
1987 operators by age group:							
Under 25 years............................	12	12	7	11	2	2	5
25 to 34 years	111	68	38	42	18	56	46
35 to 44 years	139	72	50	45	26	80	61
45 to 54 years	96	67	60	42	41	102	61
55 to 64 years	168	92	86	68	60	113	87
65 years and over	134	58	92	75	79	87	95
Average age	50.6	49.0	54.0	52.2	57.4	51.8	53.8
TYPE OF ORGANIZATION							
Individual or family (sole proprietorship) .... farms, 1987..	575	295	275	245	196	386	324
1982..	684	332	297	297	219	453	354
acres, 1987..	367 034	135 197	122 360	308 287	222 677	405 183	315 740
1982..	398 663	135 771	130 517	305 042	251 260	408 854	299 215
Partnership .... farms, 1987..	53	44	43	28	24	42	17
1982..	83	78	44	30	24	43	26
acres, 1987..	50 930	(D)	37 547	43 656	51 640	45 750	38 093
1982..	63 859	32 302	25 831	44 124	(D)	42 047	36 096
Corporation:							
Family held .... farms, 1987..	14	29	12	9	5	5	10
1982..	18	33	15	8	6	8	7
acres, 1987..	(D)	44 339	11 070	(D)	(D)	33 729	26 181
1982..	(D)	(D)	(D)	(D)	(D)	(D)	(D)
Other than family held .... farms, 1987..	2	–	2	1	2	1	1
1982..	–	2	1	2	1	–	1
acres, 1987..	(D)	–	(D)	(D)	(D)	–	–
1982..	–	(D)	(D)	(D)	(D)	926	(D)
Other – cooperative, estate or trust,							
institutional, etc. .... farms, 1987..	6	1	1	–	1	6	4
1982..	3	2	1	–	–	3	2
acres, 1987..	(D)	(D)	(D)	–	(D)	(D)	17 922
1982..	(D)	(D)	(D)	–	–	(D)	(D)
1987 FARM PRODUCTION EXPENSES[1]							
Total farm production expenses .... farms..	654	369	332	302	226	446	358
$1,000..	52 687	24 264	20 452	48 563	13 210	39 183	17 330
Livestock and poultry purchased .... farms..	342	157	156	139	111	151	219
$1,000..	23 450	3 784	6 673	17 504	3 473	15 385	3 035
Feed for livestock and poultry .... farms..	457	187	225	190	208	294	251
$1,000..	6 245	1 822	2 027	5 476	2 590	7 426	1 245
Commercially mixed formula feeds .... farms..	175	77	101	93	89	128	127
$1,000..	1 374	552	690	581	1 103	1 550	566
Seeds, bulbs, plants, and trees .... farms..	548	355	260	266	137	376	325
$1,000..	673	1 475	867	560	179	378	343
Commercial fertilizer .... farms..	587	338	312	264	159	310	304
$1,000..	2 872	2 188	1 552	3 432	353	799	1 177
Agricultural chemicals .... farms..	587	351	267	238	122	365	330
$1,000..	1 198	2 187	924	1 706	174	877	731
Petroleum products .... farms..	646	360	332	302	226	437	358
$1,000..	2 529	1 678	1 085	2 692	683	1 778	1 442
Electricity .... farms..	514	304	249	262	181	356	336
$1,000..	475	(D)	332	552	114	434	226
Hired farm labor .... farms..	337	197	114	210	98	180	141
$1,000..	1 562	1 445	758	2 712	625	2 254	688
Contract labor .... farms..	64	53	12	77	56	83	57
$1,000..	138	(D)	56	329	148	101	50
Repair and maintenance .... farms..	595	330	307	278	200	406	319
$1,000..	2 840	2 214	1 250	2 183	729	2 220	2 029
Customwork, machine hire, and rental of							
machinery and equipment .... farms..	313	235	138	206	102	231	230
$1,000..	566	923	259	1 512	253	402	695
Interest.................................... farms..	496	236	254	243	165	242	256
$1,000..	4 075	2 656	1 913	3 808	1 073	2 151	1 592
Cash rent.................................. farms..	316	130	114	143	88	243	156
$1,000..	2 010	1 157	629	1 747	924	1 530	1 172
Property taxes .... farms..	613	338	313	319	292	213	356
$1,000..	1 070	813	728	779	699	921	709
All other farm production expenses................. farms..	654	369	331	302	226	446	358
$1,000..	3 183	1 450	1 399	2 573	1 193	2 527	2 194

See footnotes at end of table.

Table 16. Farms With Sales of $10,000 or More: 1987 and 1982—Con.

[Data for 1987 include abnormal farms. For meaning of abbreviations and symbols, see introductory text]

Item	Finney	Ford	Franklin	Geary	Gove	Graham	Grant
OPERATOR CHARACTERISTICS—Con.							
Operators by days of work off farm—Con.							
Any—Con.							
150 to 199 days .... 1987...	15	27	16	3	24	15	10
1982...	14	17	13	4	23	19	4
200 days or more .... 1987...	59	118	118	46	57	51	25
1982...	68	153	110	30	65	68	25
Not reported .... 1987...	32	53	29	14	33	18	24
1982...	61	78	37	19	59	54	26
1987 operators by years on present farm:							
2 years or less	19	32	16	3	28	5	17
3 or 4 years	18	36	7	8	19	24	15
5 to 9 years	55	55	34	24	50	33	27
10 years or more	268	347	306	116	252	200	135
Average years on present farm	21.9	22.2	24.0	23.6	22.9	22.9	19.2
Not reported	61	109	45	27	61	70	46
1987 operators by age group:							
Under 25 years	5	15	1	4	7	4	16
25 to 34 years	55	76	48	33	66	50	36
35 to 44 years	114	99	69	21	72	47	47
45 to 54 years	74	115	97	32	67	83	46
55 to 64 years	87	126	115	37	95	99	46
65 years and over	86	143	80	51	83	69	49
Average age	50.4	52.4	53.0	52.9	50.4	52.5	49.1
TYPE OF ORGANIZATION							
Individual or family (sole proprietorship) .... farms, 1987...	304	462	356	155	361	286	195
1982...	364	501	395	148	372	312	200
acres, 1987...	441 013	470 999	193 046	123 823	551 315	428 032	228 261
1982...	475 119	472 792	196 241	113 664	531 957	413 919	244 616
Partnership .... farms, 1987...	64	60	44	12	28	35	29
1982...	60	93	57	22	38	43	20
acres, 1987...	153 453	115 959	37 750	(D)	54 911	35 593	53 244
1982...	126 931	115 419	35 589	15 182	56 893	66 880	48 513
Corporation:							
Family held .... farms, 1987...	44	31	7	11	18	7	18
1982...	36	31	9	9	21	8	15
acres, 1987...	97 664	(D)	21 364	(D)	(D)	(D)	(D)
1982...	77 089	(D)	10 291	(D)	(D)	9 360	29 616
Other than family held .... farms, 1987...	5	5	4	1	-	-	1
1982...	8	2	4	1	-	-	2
acres, 1987...	(D)	(D)	-	-	-	-	(D)
1982...	(D)	(D)	(D)	(D)	-	-	(D)
Other—cooperative, estate or trust,							
institutional, etc. .... farms, 1987...	4	1	3	-	3	4	1
1982...	7	2	2	3	1	3	1
acres, 1987...	(D)	(D)	1 560	(D)	(D)	(D)	-
1982...	(D)	(D)	(D)	(D)	(D)	1 704	(D)
1987 FARM PRODUCTION EXPENSES[1]							
Total farm production expenses .... farms..	425	579	407	178	405	371	236
$1,000..	342 324	211 951	23 672	11 452	52 755	25 017	226 178
Livestock and poultry purchased .... farms..	114	231	151	79	167	115	72
$1,000..	213 484	131 074	4 056	2 718	23 654	5 301	159 444
Feed for livestock and poultry .... farms..	148	301	298	120	227	222	96
$1,000..	72 790	38 792	3 392	2 211	7 330	3 094	41 298
Commercially mixed formula feeds .... farms..	59	101	127	57	94	55	46
$1,000..	8 201	1 619	1 108	476	1 313	776	(D)
Seeds, bulbs, plants, and trees .... farms..	372	484	303	153	338	346	207
$1,000..	1 927	1 536	970	172	873	713	1 026
Commercial fertilizer .... farms..	341	464	300	159	304	308	195
$1,000..	4 313	3 627	1 509	840	1 606	1 289	1 937
Agricultural chemicals .... farms..	354	488	284	166	317	309	210
$1,000..	2 660	2 455	1 148	284	1 020	1 091	1 248
Petroleum products .... farms..	424	574	390	172	379	360	236
$1,000..	6 648	4 437	1 325	768	2 491	1 913	2 847
Electricity .... farms..	334	456	332	122	360	319	196
$1,000..	1 614	945	373	180	(D)	445	934
Hired farm labor .... farms..	298	257	174	71	207	216	163
$1,000..	13 115	4 952	1 846	832	2 171	1 240	5 010
Contract labor .... farms..	97	122	47	16	54	59	55
$1,000..	(D)	408	127	31	(D)	153	(D)
Repair and maintenance .... farms..	418	521	375	170	372	322	223
$1,000..	6 121	4 441	1 831	868	2 287	2 049	3 617
Customwork, machine hire, and rental of							
machinery and equipment .... farms..	285	327	225	65	219	211	144
$1,000..	3 616	2 467	612	235	1 577	860	1 497
Interest .... farms..	342	401	274	142	278	287	169
$1,000..	5 821	5 922	2 321	1 116	3 617	2 783	2 306
Cash rent .... farms..	133	176	187	69	142	253	70
$1,000..	(D)	1 872	1 062	344	(D)	1 110	(D)
Property taxes .... farms..	372	545	405	148	369	361	221
$1,000..	1 395	1 678	895	393	993	872	568
All other farm production expenses .... farms..	425	579	407	178	405	371	236
$1,000..	7 179	7 346	2 213	660	3 496	2 103	3 526

See footnotes at end of table.

Table 16. **Farms With Sales of $10,000 or More: 1987 and 1982**—Con.

[Data for 1987 include abnormal farms. For meaning of abbreviations and symbols, see introductory text]

Item	Gray	Greeley	Greenwood	Hamilton	Harper	Harvey	Haskell
OPERATOR CHARACTERISTICS—Con.							
Operators by days of work off farm—Con.							
Any—Con.							
150 to 199 days ....1987..	14	11	15	5	27	24	9
1982..	16	9	14	8	12	29	8
200 days or more ....1987..	72	35	93	28	89	109	30
1982..	68	21	95	34	89	156	35
Not reported ....1987..	32	15	32	15	36	24	29
1982..	38	26	32	23	66	47	59
1987 operators by years on present farm:							
2 years or less	28	16	6	12	24	11	13
3 or 4 years	21	13	13	10	15	17	11
5 to 9 years...	65	24	33	27	43	59	32
10 years or more	260	125	246	122	313	364	160
Average years on present farm	19.2	21.0	24.5	21.9	23.7	24.5	21.3
Not reported	74	38	57	43	77	55	53
1987 operators by age group:							
Under 25 years	34	–	4	5	5	7	9
25 to 34 years	87	31	26	35	61	67	53
35 to 44 years	112	43	52	46	70	97	59
45 to 54 years	71	37	59	51	95	89	41
55 to 64 years	87	59	97	41	130	133	77
65 years and over	57	46	117	36	111	113	30
Average age	46.0	52.6	56.5	49.4	53.0	52.0	46.2
TYPE OF ORGANIZATION							
Individual or family (sole proprietorship) ....farms, 1987..	341	153	316	161	387	445	195
1982..	374	160	344	183	470	540	231
acres, 1987..	348 166	268 707	397 227	366 193	338 832	228 995	235 753
1982..	348 824	279 074	440 964	421 185	385 115	238 156	261 276
Partnership ....farms, 1987..	51	25	26	32	55	46	46
1982..	54	33	29	21	51	55	41
acres, 1987..	(D)	101 213	66 388	(D)	74 377	34 603	74 354
1982..	(D)	102 323	67 335	58 260	52 959	39 182	(D)
Corporation:							
Family held ....farms, 1987..	51	33	10	17	26	12	22
1982..	41	12	4	15	17	11	18
acres, 1987..	90 072	(D)	(D)	(D)	43 114	17 981	(D)
Other than family held ....farms, 1982..	97 731	38 715	17 036	47 456	(D)	14 663	(D)
1987..	4	4	1	4	–	1	5
1982..	9	1	1	3	–	5	4
acres, 1987..	9 939	–	–	2 605	–	(D)	4 167
1982..	8 206	(D)	(D)	(D)	–	(D)	2 220
Other—cooperative, estate or trust,							
institutional, etc. ....farms, 1987..	1	5	2	–	4	2	1
1982..	1	2	2	1	5	1	6
acres, 1987..	(D)	(D)	(D)	–	2 440	(D)	(D)
1982..	(D)	(D)	(D)	(D)	(D)	(D)	2 536
1987 FARM PRODUCTION EXPENSES[1]							
Total farm production expenses ....farms..	450	218	349	216	471	506	251
$1,000..	217 759	75 141	26 398	49 864	46 167	39 424	221 026
Livestock and poultry purchased ....farms..	200	69	199	77	232	194	66
$1,000..	135 643	40 776	10 711	19 031	18 507	11 502	137 065
Feed for livestock and poultry ....farms..	247	92	296	92	321	277	89
$1,000..	35 504	13 104	4 320	(D)	4 931	6 779	43 742
Commercially mixed formula feeds ....farms..	80	45	141	24	145	144	37
$1,000..	4 201	1 829	1 441	391	373	2 734	9 694
Seeds, bulbs, plants, and trees ....farms..	395	190	217	169	340	475	206
$1,000..	2 142	918	268	755	757	988	1 554
Commercial fertilizer ....farms..	375	129	199	133	420	467	185
$1,000..	4 354	1 410	785	843	2 727	2 702	3 005
Agricultural chemicals ....farms..	362	157	194	141	262	481	208
$1,000..	2 813	925	367	525	798	1 230	2 217
Petroleum products ....farms..	449	215	347	208	470	502	250
$1,000..	6 087	2 192	1 144	1 675	2 716	2 178	4 248
Electricity ....farms..	361	146	272	166	362	455	204
$1,000..	1 353	498	245	512	297	567	914
Hired farm labor ....farms..	246	106	144	108	242	227	183
$1,000..	6 259	2 847	1 337	2 044	1 482	1 276	9 111
Contract labor ....farms..	114	27	72	36	39	56	69
$1,000..	(D)	330	252	(D)	305	145	(D)
Repair and maintenance ....farms..	413	181	318	193	405	473	244
$1,000..	4 460	2 063	1 462	1 750	2 719	2 437	4 497
Customwork, machine hire, and rental of							
machinery and equipment ....farms..	296	138	134	151	235	285	136
$1,000..	3 013	1 640	410	1 294	1 449	995	1 254
Interest ....farms..	339	163	211	172	343	391	197
$1,000..	5 987	2 935	2 254	1 602	4 367	3 569	4 041
Cash rent ....farms..	120	48	162	57	233	303	59
$1,000..	(D)	674	1 661	(D)	1 013	1 691	(D)
Property taxes ....farms..	415	191	324	182	415	452	243
$1,000..	1 499	538	684	555	1 097	919	831
All other farm production expenses ....farms..	449	216	349	216	471	506	251
$1,000..	6 974	4 189	2 259	1 937	3 001	2 445	7 356

See footnotes at end of table.

Table 16. **Farms With Sales of $10,000 or More: 1987 and 1982**—Con.

[Data for 1987 include abnormal farms. For meaning of abbreviations and symbols, see introductory text]

Item	Hodgeman	Jackson	Jefferson	Jewell	Johnson	Kearny	Kingman	Kiowa
OPERATOR CHARACTERISTICS—Con.								
Operators by days of work off farm—Con.								
Any—Con.								
150 to 199 days................ 1987..	6	24	18	20	12	11	27	5
1982..	12	30	16	22	5	7	32	10
200 days or more .... 1987..	54	154	120	75	80	34	106	40
1982..	66	126	120	81	74	22	110	42
Not reported .... 1987..	31	36	23	47	13	8	24	15
1982..	55	46	55	79	32	33	86	38
1987 operators by years on present farm:								
2 years or less	17	16	16	28	6	9	28	12
3 or 4 years	17	18	20	15	7	11	26	12
5 to 9 years........................	38	48	39	60	31	27	53	19
10 years or more	208	365	291	365	170	149	347	153
Average years on present farm	23.0	23.2	22.4	23.0	22.4	22.6	23.8	24.4
Not reported	54	71	56	75	47	32	83	38
1987 operators by age group:								
Under 25 years	20	13	15	16	7	2	5	2
25 to 34 years	61	64	40	91	25	23	91	33
35 to 44 years	62	100	63	97	43	50	95	42
45 to 54 years	49	96	95	89	59	58	99	39
55 to 64 years	78	142	123	141	63	59	122	59
65 years and over	64	103	86	109	64	36	125	59
Average age	49.4	51.8	52.7	50.9	53.1	51.1	51.5	52.5
TYPE OF ORGANIZATION								
Individual or family (sole proprietorship) .... farms, 1987..	276	464	384	467	210	169	480	191
1982..	319	484	397	565	238	177	571	250
acres, 1987..	358 137	227 636	174 329	382 122	91 756	308 861	364 514	266 672
1982..	356 577	268 524	179 496	394 542	89 851	316 993	400 767	299 899
Partnership .... farms, 1987..	39	46	30	61	31	30	51	31
1982..	34	50	39	60	47	35	56	34
acres, 1987..	(D)	30 496	(D)	(D)	15 440	(D)	75 683	73 059
1982..	63 482	32 582	22 311	65 207	21 310	117 584	57 854	97 850
Corporation:								
Family held .... farms, 1987..	17	6	7	14	14	26	4	11
1982..	18	3	8	13	15	18	6	4
acres, 1987..	49 160	(D)	(D)	22 473	(D)	(D)	(D)	(D)
1982..	37 303	1 440	(D)	(D)	17 164	65 414	6 940	10 110
Other than family held .... farms, 1987..	2	1	1	1	-	3	-	-
1982..	3	-	2	-	3	4	-	-
acres, 1987..	(D)	-	(D)	(D)	-	382	-	-
1982..	(D)	(D)	(D)	-	(D)	6 297	(D)	-
Other—cooperative, estate or trust, institutional, etc. .... farms, 1987..	-	2	-	-	5	-	2	1
1982..	5	2	2	2	-	1	3	3
acres, 1987..	-	(D)	-	-	778	-	(D)	(D)
1982..	(D)	(D)	(D)	(D)	-	(D)	242	5 176
1987 FARM PRODUCTION EXPENSES[1]								
Total farm production expenses .... farms..	337	519	425	544	256	226	539	239
$1,000..	83 167	21 434	19 127	31 370	15 216	102 863	29 582	20 368
Livestock and poultry purchased .... farms..	180	299	164	240	91	85	284	79
$1,000..	47 826	5 005	2 899	6 530	3 356	56 456	6 775	4 034
Feed for livestock and poultry .... farms..	233	443	300	383	159	105	402	122
$1,000..	12 540	4 031	2 456	4 637	1 606	18 214	2 559	908
Commercially mixed formula feeds .... farms..	58	166	134	179	86	31	194	24
$1,000..	1 169	1 045	935	1 323	511	2 063	888	136
Seeds, bulbs, plants, and trees .... farms..	324	380	327	482	211	198	405	233
$1,000..	842	799	845	831	651	1 255	749	897
Commercial fertilizer .... farms..	260	407	389	459	213	170	443	211
$1,000..	1 084	1 796	1 953	2 364	994	2 506	3 225	2 247
Agricultural chemicals .... farms..	293	416	343	448	200	177	383	172
$1,000..	1 090	1 003	1 091	1 246	818	1 499	917	870
Petroleum products .... farms..	331	507	425	538	256	225	539	238
$1,000..	2 827	1 278	1 186	2 173	910	3 707	2 432	1 675
Electricity .... farms..	257	426	370	491	227	181	443	146
$1,000..	521	300	291	602	293	668	444	194
Hired farm labor .... farms..	159	208	170	296	99	147	312	157
$1,000..	3 749	597	528	1 490	1 763	4 516	1 169	1 017
Contract labor .... farms..	49	70	50	67	53	80	77	62
$1,000..	163	115	95	154	225	532	131	166
Repair and maintenance .... farms..	298	464	374	523	(D)	215	498	224
$1,000..	3 644	1 444	1 439	2 368	1 138	3 036	2 629	1 527
Customwork, machine hire, and rental of machinery and equipment .... farms..	188	194	220	319	55	154	302	178
$1,000..	1 033	448	420	825	(D)	3 224	1 089	1 184
Interest............................... farms..	250	395	266	387	131	159	365	192
$1,000..	3 086	1 860	2 207	3 013	1 070	2 791	2 597	1 960
Cash rent.............................. farms..	159	206	182	259	123	92	233	111
$1,000..	961	570	749	1 626	538	1 057	1 475	1 543
Property taxes .... farms..	516	419	507	249	199	495	224	
$1,000..	1 094	728	774	1 232	615	573	1 020	473
All other farm production expenses .... farms..	337	519	425	544	256	226	539	239
$1,000..	2 906	1 561	1 906	2 239	1 165	2 826	2 352	1 692

See footnotes at end of table.

Table 16. **Farms With Sales of $10,000 or More: 1987 and 1982**—Con.

[Data for 1987 include abnormal farms. For meaning of abbreviations and symbols, see introductory text.]

Item	Labette	Lane	Leavenworth	Lincoln	Linn	Logan	Lyon	McPherson
OPERATOR CHARACTERISTICS—Con.								
Operators by days of work off farm—Con.								
Any—Con.								
150 to 199 days ... 1987..	19	7	16	18	13	15	24	70
1982..	25	11	19	14	10	12	29	77
200 days or more ... 1987..	122	24	113	67	87	37	135	194
1982..	122	22	106	76	85	47	114	246
Not reported ... 1987..	22	26	16	25	39	27	32	62
1982..	35	40	30	53	37	46	36	102
1987 operators by years on present farm:								
2 years or less	14	7	8	11	14	18	19	27
3 or 4 years	23	7	11	18	7	13	22	33
5 to 9 years	44	23	46	49	34	32	65	102
10 years or more	306	160	261	277	226	177	319	583
Average years on present farm	21.7	23.9	23.3	24.4	23.7	22.0	24.4	24.1
Not reported	68	49	64	60	67	48	62	109
1987 operators by age group:								
Under 25 years	11	5	8	2	-	6	7	22
25 to 34 years	57	24	52	66	23	42	70	110
35 to 44 years	85	53	61	96	65	67	88	165
45 to 54 years	76	48	84	53	65	39	91	151
55 to 64 years	132	63	113	127	94	74	112	218
65 years and over	96	55	82	71	101	58	109	188
Average age	52.0	52.1	52.7	51.0	56.0	50.6	51.8	51.6
TYPE OF ORGANIZATION								
Individual or family (sole proprietorship) ... farms, 1987..	405	195	332	359	331	238	413	761
1982..	460	230	350	425	330	254	443	945
acres, 1987..	238 584	312 363	114 371	326 801	208 728	465 465	310 564	412 040
1982..	247 967	346 171	121 107	342 896	199 241	463 075	330 186	441 932
Partnership ... farms, 1987..	42	33	48	37	12	26	49	80
1982..	56	24	52	49	17	22	50	62
acres, 1987..	36 143	92 757	28 722	62 451	10 043	52 858	68 214	57 010
1982..	41 539	60 932	29 132	52 683	(D)	(D)	60 885	51 333
Corporation:								
Family held ... farms, 1987..	6	17	8	12	3	15	12	11
1982..	5	18	9	8	3	7	15	22
acres, 1987..	(D)	(D)	(D)	26 841	(D)	(D)	(D)	(D)
1982..	(D)	(D)	10 190	(D)	(D)	24 746	(D)	15 647
Other than family held ... farms, 1987..	1	-	-	-	-	-	2	1
1982..	1	1	-	1	-	-	3	2
acres, 1987..	(D)	-	-	(D)	-	(D)	-	(D)
1982..	(D)	(D)	-	(D)	-	-	(D)	(D)
Other—cooperative, estate or trust, institutional, etc. ... farms, 1987..	3	1	2	7	2	3	3	1
1982..	2	3	-	8	-	1	2	6
acres, 1987..	(D)	(D)	(D)	7 714	(D)	(D)	(D)	(D)
1982..	(D)	3 955	-	(D)	-	-	(D)	(D)
1987 FARM PRODUCTION EXPENSES[1]								
Total farm production expenses ... farms..	454	250	396	415	352	283	481	858
$1,000..	38 692	79 423	18 190	30 596	15 608	18 343	48 034	57 812
Livestock and poultry purchased ... farms..	207	73	193	176	152	90	223	344
$1,000..	19 103	39 961	1 277	10 708	2 880	4 159	19 684	20 340
Feed for livestock and poultry ... farms..	359	138	311	251	316	145	382	439
$1,000..	5 390	19 200	2 482	3 150	2 238	1 207	7 901	8 775
Commercially mixed formula feeds ... farms..	115	53	103	115	134	50	101	174
$1,000..	1 360	(D)	1 105	563	693	334	1 514	3 591
Seeds, bulbs, plants, and trees ... farms..	345	214	348	383	251	243	384	758
$1,000..	752	513	1 253	560	543	457	788	1 173
Commercial fertilizer ... farms..	336	139	349	366	261	136	377	739
$1,000..	1 497	956	1 394	1 607	1 174	894	1 415	3 690
Agricultural chemicals ... farms..	270	198	329	371	252	175	365	730
$1,000..	718	996	1 012	942	747	566	925	1 473
Petroleum products ... farms..	445	249	396	414	351	282	481	852
$1,000..	1 391	2 246	1 362	1 947	1 065	1 592	1 722	2 336
Electricity ... farms..	333	216	335	314	303	227	391	695
$1,000..	241	336	354	331	273	326	238	918
Hired farm labor ... farms..	206	162	165	176	137	163	238	394
$1,000..	1 966	(D)	1 609	1 334	783	(D)	2 439	1 622
Contract labor ... farms..	34	43	33	66	57	34	78	59
$1,000..	54	77	77	72	104	(D)	213	223
Repair and maintenance ... farms..	438	225	359	361	333	247	430	751
$1,000..	1 766	2 032	1 651	1 850	1 117	1 731	2 329	3 440
Customwork, machine hire, and rental of machinery and equipment ... farms..	197	162	221	221	128	153	246	439
$1,000..	356	1 758	380	617	290	899	698	1 103
Interest ... farms..	310	191	315	302	251	202	343	616
$1,000..	1 764	2 714	1 818	2 717	1 666	2 676	3 265	4 488
Cash rent ... farms..	144	122	173	190	139	99	248	393
$1,000..	622	924	1 125	1 077	778	549	1 468	1 689
Property taxes ... farms..	423	246	381	402	337	241	463	806
$1,000..	891	878	620	996	482	733	865	1 504
All other farm production expenses ... farms..	454	250	395	415	352	263	461	858
$1,000..	1 762	3 134	1 776	2 667	1 447	1 435	3 968	3 936

See footnotes at end of table.

Table 16. Farms With Sales of $10,000 or More: 1987 and 1982—Con.

[Data for 1987 include abnormal farms. For meaning of abbreviations and symbols, see introductory text]

Item	Marion	Marshall	Meade	Miami	Mitchell	Montgomery	Morris	Morton
OPERATOR CHARACTERISTICS— Con.								
Operators by days of work off farm—Con.								
Any—Con.								
150 to 199 days .... 1987..	24	31	8	24	19	13	14	2
1982..	39	26	16	24	19	14	19	6
200 days or more .... 1987..	148	119	54	111	88	115	61	23
1982..	136	98	55	124	77	116	50	18
Not reported .... 1987..	60	54	36	24	36	23	35	19
1982..	100	112	53	35	59	28	31	35
1987 operators by years on present farm:								
2 years or less	11	20	16	15	17	13	14	2
3 or 4 years	21	30	17	13	37	12	13	7
5 to 9 years	92	83	47	50	49	40	37	19
10 years or more	492	542	209	265	291	245	252	101
Average years on present farm	24.4	22.6	22.8	22.9	24.1	22.8	25.4	25.3
Not reported	115	116	83	59	82	40	48	39
1987 operators by age group:								
Under 25 years	10	23	3	9	18	2	10	3
25 to 34 years	115	151	54	45	65	36	42	19
35 to 44 years	142	122	50	60	97	64	62	38
45 to 54 years	124	154	72	99	76	71	57	36
55 to 64 years	165	219	108	94	132	91	87	36
65 years and over	175	122	85	95	88	84	106	28
Average age	51.5	49.6	53.1	52.8	50.7	53.5	53.5	51.4
TYPE OF ORGANIZATION								
Individual or family (sole proprietorship) ...... farms, 1987..	657	702	295	347	407	319	310	132
1982..	741	783	328	364	415	350	345	150
acres, 1987..	447 170	448 384	405 157	159 683	367 892	200 379	278 456	240 480
1982..	430 118	433 499	417 615	175 865	331 241	197 582	304 634	244 607
Partnership .... farms, 1987..	61	84	55	44	37	18	46	20
1982..	80	88	44	47	51	38	54	26
acres, 1987..	56 834	46 839	76 077	29 471	42 273	18 061	77 024	57 674
1982..	78 552	43 695	(D)	35 997	53 838	39 239	83 395	(D)
Corporation:								
Family held .... farms, 1987..	13	24	19	8	27	10	7	8
1982..	13	10	13	12	22	7	1	4
acres, 1987..	23 926	(D)	(D)	9 362	44 711	(D)	(D)	24 200
1982..	(D)	(D)	(D)	52 906	(D)	(D)	(D)	(D)
Other than family held .... farms, 1987..	-	1	-	1	2	2	-	1
1982..	-	1	4	1	1	2	-	-
acres, 1987..	-	(D)	(D)	(D)	(D)	(D)	-	(D)
1982..	-	(D)	-	(D)	(D)	-	-	-
Other—cooperative, estate or trust,								
institutional, etc. .... farms, 1987..	-	-	3	2	3	1	1	1
1982..	2	3	-	3	2	1	2	(D)
acres, 1987..	-	-	(D)	(D)	(D)	(D)	(D)	(D)
1982..	(D)	1 630	-	2 520	(D)	(D)	(D)	-
1987 FARM PRODUCTION EXPENSES[1]								
Total farm production expenses .... farms..	728	793	372	403	478	354	364	141
$1,000..	43 389	41 881	44 117	15 474	47 129	17 457	34 630	17 527
Livestock and poultry purchased .... farms..	336	324	135	139	147	126	200	64
$1,000..	12 226	7 536	(D)	968	16 776	2 248	12 700	4 122
Feed for livestock and poultry .... farms..	487	486	182	293	237	269	289	82
$1,000..	6 242	5 188	5 378	1 404	7 064	2 959	6 687	2 454
Commercially mixed formula feeds .... farms..	208	213	50	130	92	120	165	29
$1,000..	2 511	1 146	918	589	2 446	1 441	1 104	126
Seeds, bulbs, plants, and trees .... farms..	669	758	314	297	444	249	316	119
$1,000..	749	1 450	1 227	1 197	845	536	481	883
Commercial fertilizer .... farms..	670	750	298	357	421	257	295	87
$1,000..	3 372	3 741	2 675	1 675	3 000	1 213	1 393	869
Agricultural chemicals .... farms..	609	739	310	303	420	220	297	102
$1,000..	1 341	2 023	1 558	1 289	1 648	679	644	712
Petroleum products .... farms..	708	783	369	396	475	347	363	139
$1,000..	2 402	2 984	3 480	1 256	2 620	1 284	1 739	1 376
Electricity .... farms..	650	633	299	345	405	281	316	117
$1,000..	625	689	493	271	487	367	367	202
Hired farm labor .... farms..	342	332	222	196	245	151	164	106
$1,000..	1 930	1 797	1 979	1 075	1 946	1 021	2 030	1 403
Contract labor .... farms..	103	77	68	62	51	74	41	41
$1,000..	160	174	179	160	22	165	109	(D)
Repair and maintenance .... farms..	671	703	365	390	419	328	340	129
$1,000..	2 825	3 320	2 428	1 388	2 420	1 596	1 980	1 533
Customwork, machine hire, and rental of								
machinery and equipment .... farms..	418	496	226	162	268	87	156	72
$1,000..	778	1 093	1 636	382	969	326	364	(D)
Interest .... farms..	546	615	227	238	367	235	236	96
$1,000..	3 613	4 835	2 189	1 735	3 841	1 871	2 221	1 176
Cash rent .... farms..	433	253	132	191	194	146	176	33
$1,000..	2 470	1 297	1 994	656	1 283	712	1 249	215
Property taxes .... farms..	672	747	341	392	419	345	344	131
$1,000..	1 291	1 597	699	626	1 293	732	753	257
All other farm production expenses .... farms..	728	793	372	403	478	354	364	141
$1,000..	3 367	4 078	2 896	1 172	2 775	1 818	1 943	1 370

See footnotes at end of table.

Table 16. **Farms With Sales of $10,000 or More: 1987 and 1982**—Con.

[Data for 1987 include abnormal farms. For meaning of abbreviations and symbols, see introductory text]

Item	Nemaha	Neosho	Ness	Norton	Osage	Osborne	Ottawa	Pawnee
OPERATOR CHARACTERISTICS—Con.								
Operators by days of work off farm—Con.								
Any—Con.								
150 to 199 days .... 1987..	23	17	23	13	26	17	11	14
1982..	18	14	14	5	23	17	22	9
200 days or more .... 1987..	142	97	68	79	116	54	57	67
1982..	107	91	80	45	129	80	59	69
Not reported .... 1987..	72	33	23	34	26	32	21	27
1982..	106	48	57	68	27	55	47	61
1987 operators by years on present farm:								
2 years or less	35	17	6	9	14	23	6	20
3 or 4 years	45	13	20	13	15	15	5	16
5 to 9 years	107	33	51	44	48	53	28	46
10 years or more	525	260	296	241	302	293	257	252
Average years on present farm	21.7	23.8	26.0	25.0	24.2	24.6	25.9	24.0
Not reported	124	56	58	63	53	74	58	70
1987 operators by age group:								
Under 25 years.......................................	28	8	10	5	8	17	1	5
25 to 34 years	162	46	52	59	54	64	39	53
35 to 44 years	147	64	71	63	72	78	56	75
45 to 54 years	157	74	75	72	93	74	79	56
55 to 64 years	218	97	129	86	117	116	86	101
65 years and over	124	90	94	85	88	109	93	112
Average age	48.8	52.8	52.7	51.8	52.0	51.8	54.1	53.1
TYPE OF ORGANIZATION								
Individual or family (sole proprietorship) .... farms, 1987..	715	339	369	324	381	404	304	339
1982..	741	346	436	377	426	424	379	365
acres, 1987..	324 488	212 072	545 906	405 838	233 025	448 889	288 076	349 018
1982..	316 949	207 904	530 404	417 518	251 898	420 652	305 676	363 447
Partnership .... farms, 1987..	102	27	53	19	48	38	25	44
1982..	91	40	56	17	50	43	40	57
acres, 1987..	(D)	(D)	71 369	(D)	63 958	49 996	(D)	74 897
1982..	44 345	46 186	93 423	18 826	(D)	42 814	35 854	69 783
Corporation:								
Family held .... farms, 1987..	19	6	8	26	3	7	22	16
1982..	24	10	6	20	2	8	17	14
acres, 1987..	(D)	16 856	(D)	(D)	4 925	(D)	42 959	34 216
1982..	(D)	(D)	(D)	(D)	(D)	(D)	33 217	17 462
Other than family held .... farms, 1987..	1	5	–	2	–	2	–	3
1982..	–	1	–	–	–	1	–	3
acres, 1987..	–	5 551	–	–	–	(D)	–	(D)
1982..	(D)	(D)	–	(D)	–	(D)	–	(D)
Other—cooperative, estate or trust,								
institutional, etc. .... farms, 1987..	–	2	1	1	–	7	3	1
1982..	8	1	2	5	–	6	4	2
acres, 1987..	–	(D)	(D)	(D)	–	2 997	(D)	(D)
1982..	(D)	(D)	(D)	9 120	–	5 286	2 009	(D)
1987 FARM PRODUCTION EXPENSES[1]								
Total farm production expenses .... farms..	832	378	428	370	438	459	353	405
$1,000..	45 082	18 070	20 022	27 445	22 756	29 369	31 139	71 848
Livestock and poultry purchased .... farms..	504	124	224	170	177	239	124	179
$1,000..	9 236	2 707	4 844	8 091	5 570	3 791	13 574	30 278
Feed for livestock and poultry .... farms..	651	301	300	297	283	326	216	212
$1,000..	9 531	2 637	1 366	3 379	2 213	2 403	3 809	13 591
Commercially mixed formula feeds .... farms..	350	126	103	98	97	170	100	75
$1,000..	3 313	507	251	781	504	902	625	573
Seeds, bulbs, plants, and trees .... farms..	735	316	365	310	387	427	301	388
$1,000..	1 205	716	461	582	680	717	401	1 131
Commercial fertilizer .... farms..	742	340	315	262	392	424	309	369
$1,000..	3 401	1 700	882	1 337	1 622	1 965	1 683	2 167
Agricultural chemicals .... farms..	751	288	317	264	400	406	282	361
$1,000..	1 716	671	751	804	1 505	1 291	717	1 310
Petroleum products .... farms..	825	378	419	366	438	459	345	394
$1,000..	2 799	1 464	1 814	1 790	1 364	2 235	1 700	2 598
Electricity .... farms..	730	327	330	345	366	398	316	336
$1,000..	800	308	234	471	253	341	266	690
Hired farm labor .... farms..	331	185	220	177	131	217	225	187
$1,000..	1 581	1 100	707	1 090	792	1 144	1 329	2 631
Contract labor .... farms..	82	24	59	49	47	27	60	65
$1,000..	213	115	48	146	605	51	105	179
Repair and maintenance .... farms..	748	343	372	304	407	437	317	374
$1,000..	3 289	1 396	1 606	1 801	1 555	1 950	1 828	3 211
Customwork, machine hire, and rental of								
machinery and equipment .... farms..	457	166	298	214	197	322	194	245
$1,000..	798	328	1 175	755	378	1 204	391	2 210
Interest .... farms..	527	244	311	277	326	338	275	316
$1,000..	3 983	1 592	2 205	2 599	2 307	2 968	2 111	4 068
Cash rent .... farms..	218	141	200	192	169	229	123	165
$1,000..	1 356	538	1 187	1 245	786	991	875	1 940
Property taxes .... farms..	782	355	388	339	430	423	329	384
$1,000..	1 365	677	990	937	879	1 074	694	1 372
All other farm production expenses .... farms..	832	378	428	370	437	459	353	405
$1,000..	3 805	1 922	1 752	2 119	2 047	3 234	1 655	4 476

See footnotes at end of table.

Table 16. Farms With Sales of $10,000 or More: 1987 and 1982—Con.

[Data for 1987 include abnormal farms. For meaning of abbreviations and symbols, see introductory text]

Item	Phillips	Pottawatomie	Pratt	Rawlins	Reno	Republic	Rice	Riley
OPERATOR CHARACTERISTICS—Con.								
Operators by days of work off farm—Con.								
Any—Con.								
150 to 199 days _____ 1987__	10	13	18	8	50	27	15	10
1982__	8	20	19	20	46	19	23	9
200 days or more _____ 1987__	54	100	60	59	177	103	83	69
1982__	65	84	73	37	184	98	64	55
Not reported _____ 1987__	32	29	23	26	61	35	29	25
1982__	46	60	45	67	127	100	50	37
1987 operators by years on present farm:								
2 years or less _____	9	17	9	15	21	24	19	6
3 or 4 years _____	15	21	19	10	41	27	20	16
5 to 9 years _____	35	55	39	46	100	70	40	25
10 years or more _____	282	288	266	291	569	406	277	216
Average years on present farm _____	25.4	23.7	24.7	24.2	23.9	23.8	23.7	24.1
Not reported _____	87	75	58	61	155	100	61	60
1987 operators by age group:								
Under 25 years _____	8	13	6	10	11	23	13	4
25 to 34 years _____	58	44	49	66	126	123	58	45
35 to 44 years _____	78	94	80	72	202	120	72	55
45 to 54 years _____	71	84	69	89	167	106	97	65
55 to 64 years _____	106	109	77	100	220	143	95	76
65 years and over _____	107	112	110	86	180	112	82	80
Average age _____	52.2	52.6	52.5	50.7	51.0	49.0	51.0	52.8
TYPE OF ORGANIZATION								
Individual or family (sole proprietorship) ____ farms, 1987__	370	383	324	345	774	556	356	272
1982__	417	435	369	414	926	590	405	289
acres, 1987__	409 357	283 911	349 941	476 621	514 300	360 773	340 210	163 106
1982__	389 490	299 665	351 832	483 651	544 150	344 563	334 003	167 827
Partnership _____ farms, 1987__	43	57	38	61	84	53	32	40
1982__	50	67	39	68	115	65	50	41
acres, 1987__	(D)	74 074	49 676	104 517	77 779	38 968	29 649	37 432
1982__	72 664	63 312	39 429	113 044	70 746	46 645	41 449	29 812
Corporation:								
Family held _____ farms, 1987__	15	15	25	16	44	15	24	10
1982__	18	17	24	21	42	22	23	12
acres, 1987__	(D)	(D)	39 467	(D)	48 227	(D)	(D)	(D)
1982__	(D)	(D)	(D)	(D)	42 412	(D)	(D)	(D)
Other than family held _____ farms, 1987__	–	1	1	3	3	1	–	2
1982__	–	2	1	2	5	1	3	1
acres, 1987__	–	(D)	(D)	(D)	(D)	(D)	(D)	(D)
1982__	–	(D)	(D)	(D)	(D)	(D)	(D)	(D)
Other—cooperative, estate or trust, institutional, etc. _____ farms, 1987__	–	–	2	1	1	2	4	1
1982__	1	4	4	7	1	2	1	1
acres, 1987__	–	–	(D)	(D)	(D)	(D)	3 470	(D)
1982__	(D)	(D)	2 520	11 510	(D)	(D)	(D)	(D)
1987 FARM PRODUCTION EXPENSES[1]								
Total farm production expenses _____ farms__	433	455	391	425	909	626	420	327
$1,000__	26 219	26 393	89 145	23 981	63 150	87 159	56 803	17 778
Livestock and poultry purchased _____ farms__	228	205	134	161	361	200	134	186
$1,000__	4 003	7 065	44 903	3 614	17 395	40 370	25 872	4 317
Feed for livestock and poultry _____ farms__	275	335	198	248	567	394	216	288
$1,000__	3 804	5 410	13 680	2 203	9 298	16 123	7 670	2 759
Commercially mixed formula feeds _____ farms__	100	162	85	77	263	165	70	95
$1,000__	738	1 606	2 349	634	5 815	1 219	1 219	1 015
Seeds, bulbs, plants, and trees _____ farms__	348	342	356	392	821	596	407	259
$1,000__	636	645	1 725	699	1 497	1 606	917	386
Commercial fertilizer _____ farms__	352	330	349	335	767	590	379	256
$1,000__	1 479	1 495	4 356	1 526	4 731	4 072	2 436	1 013
Agricultural chemicals _____ farms__	350	351	322	331	739	595	365	291
$1,000__	1 019	930	1 925	908	1 715	1 987	1 326	629
Petroleum products _____ farms__	422	454	383	408	906	618	413	321
$1,000__	1 972	1 534	3 232	2 215	3 995	3 150	2 337	977
Electricity _____ farms__	368	379	323	356	756	531	361	276
$1,000__	462	396	602	432	931	671	650	242
Hired farm labor _____ farms__	202	175	213	213	521	331	241	168
$1,000__	1 303	1 607	2 676	1 006	4 031	2 360	2 644	1 279
Contract labor _____ farms__	48	29	60	68	140	63	54	20
$1,000__	100	62	481	373	287	173	99	35
Repair and maintenance _____ farms__	383	396	367	382	859	546	382	310
$1,000__	1 794	2 047	3 364	2 207	4 574	3 097	3 160	1 821
Customwork, machine hire, and rental of machinery and equipment _____ farms__	275	173	234	240	467	411	294	167
$1,000__	761	275	1 709	1 493	1 209	1 449	1 422	276
Interest _____ farms__	252	282	286	294	627	433	301	202
$1,000__	3 012	2 378	3 764	2 100	5 077	4 600	3 199	1 306
Cash rent _____ farms__	199	152	177	153	418	319	213	106
$1,000__	1 625	1 227	1 319	877	1 875	2 339	899	524
Property taxes _____ farms__	396	411	340	415	834	590	365	326
$1,000__	999	771	1 060	1 241	1 543	1 659	927	612
All other farm production expenses _____ farms__	433	455	391	425	908	626	420	327
$1,000__	3 060	2 550	3 949	2 187	4 993	3 503	3 222	1 602

See footnotes at end of table.

Table 16. Farms With Sales of $10,000 or More: 1987 and 1982—Con.

[Data for 1987 include abnormal farms. For meaning of abbreviations and symbols, see introductory text.]

Item	Rooks	Rush	Russell	Saline	Scott	Sedgwick	Seward	Shawnee
OPERATOR CHARACTERISTICS— Con.								
Operators by days of work off farm—Con.								
Any—Con.								
150 to 199 days..........................1987..	14	19	19	23	12	35	6	13
1982..	13	23	23	27	13	50	5	9
200 days or more ....1987..	64	60	52	78	44	204	30	91
1982..	92	81	80	98	40	230	28	78
Not reported ....1987..	20	24	25	28	25	53	24	25
1982..	63	59	39	38	60	113	38	27
1987 operators by years on present farm:								
2 years or less	8	5	10	12	23	25	13	11
3 or 4 years	18	5	10	16	19	33	18	16
5 to 9 years...................................	34	46	28	48	34	90	29	36
10 years or more	225	239	241	281	179	510	101	232
Average years on present farm	25.4	26.6	25.1	24.5	20.9	23.1	17.5	23.0
Not reported	51	74	52	42	61	131	47	44
1987 operators by age group:								
Under 25 years................................	5	7	4	6	6	10	14	6
25 to 34 years	54	43	46	63	48	98	42	39
35 to 44 years	62	53	60	63	69	148	46	45
45 to 54 years	63	60	50	75	55	157	35	79
55 to 64 years	72	121	95	96	77	202	41	80
65 years and over	80	85	86	96	61	174	30	90
Average age	52.0	53.9	53.4	51.9	50.4	51.9	46.4	53.9
TYPE OF ORGANIZATION								
Individual or family (sole proprietorship) ....farms, 1987..	294	314	291	339	214	655	173	284
1982..	352	392	358	419	237	788	181	272
acres, 1987..	413 035	309 148	318 546	286 272	274 582	362 178	244 364	143 413
1982..	423 830	325 125	348 908	301 565	307 717	381 786	242 792	137 429
Partnership ....farms, 1987..	33	28	41	43	51	90	21	41
1982..	39	44	52	56	55	96	23	27
acres, 1987..	85 546	31 618	68 999	45 538	93 140	63 867	31 883	23 528
1982..	63 426	29 168	62 000	44 447	(D)	62 473	36 109	24 440
Corporation:								
Family held ....farms, 1987..	6	23	9	16	42	36	11	11
1982..	5	18	9	11	36	39	7	11
acres, 1987..	(D)	39 460	29 023	(D)	(D)	26 676	(D)	(D)
1982..	10 507	(D)	(D)	(D)	97 024	29 758	(D)	(D)
Other than family held ....farms, 1987..	-	-	-	-	5	6	1	1
1982..	1	2	-	1	4	2	2	-
acres, 1987..	-	-	-	-	772	(D)	(D)	(D)
1982..	(D)	(D)	-	(D)	1 047	(D)	(D)	-
Other—cooperative, estate or trust,								
Institutional, etc. ....farms, 1987..	3	4	-	1	4	2	2	2
1982..	5	-	3	1	3	1	2	1
acres, 1987..	(D)	2 929	-	(D)	(D)	(D)	(D)	(D)
1982..	(D)	-	(D)	(D)	(D)	(D)	(D)	(D)
1987 FARM PRODUCTION EXPENSES[1]								
Total farm production expenses ....farms..	336	367	337	399	313	787	240	339
$1,000..	16 991	13 813	13 903	23 627	249 184	43 846	123 491	13 717
Livestock and poultry purchased ....farms..	107	114	124	150	122	249	58	116
$1,000..	2 683	1 749	2 290	4 487	162 108	6 276	73 644	2 268
Feed for livestock and poultry ....farms..	212	220	203	250	161	388	78	176
$1,000..	1 279	706	937	2 911	51 537	5 678	22 097	1 043
Commercially mixed formula feeds ....farms..	74	60	100	110	68	230	94	79
$1,000..	343	137	330	713	13 084	2 534	(D)	433
Seeds, bulbs, plants, and trees ....farms..	271	288	302	356	255	681	212	257
$1,000..	475	312	400	596	767	1 416	(D)	1 033
Commercial fertilizer ....farms..	260	263	225	356	204	683	193	258
$1,000..	1 123	1 003	897	1 629	1 497	3 999	1 875	1 009
Agricultural chemicals ....farms..	264	305	270	355	225	660	190	269
$1,000..	904	888	703	782	977	1 837	1 113	978
Petroleum products ....farms..	338	366	316	396	311	785	232	339
$1,000..	1 505	1 492	1 279	1 650	3 426	3 529	2 677	962
Electricity ....farms..	235	270	249	343	212	664	177	251
$1,000..	257	164	170	402	1 166	1 037	1 484	202
Hired farm labor ....farms..	148	173	126	202	173	368	136	92
$1,000..	989	745	674	1 611	8 786	3 292	6 085	786
Contract labor ....farms..	28	41	80	33	53	190	42	44
$1,000..	50	96	187	99	619	458	(D)	108
Repair and maintenance ....farms..	294	356	241	371	284	735	185	278
$1,000..	1 510	1 594	988	1 961	2 824	3 563	2 663	1 313
Customwork, machine hire, and rental of machinery and equipment ....farms..	207	163	156	221	178	362	137	109
$1,000..	1 148	463	502	407	2 126	814	1 580	135
Interest ....farms..	205	216	215	252	224	512	192	161
$1,000..	1 902	1 747	1 409	2 074	4 317	4 369	2 034	1 391
Cash rent ....farms..	181	115	131	193	92	277	103	140
$1,000..	955	572	1 397	1 369	1 241	1 743	1 140	616
Property taxes ....farms..	300	346	295	370	287	734	190	323
$1,000..	653	821	623	646	826	1 789	695	618
All other farm production expenses ....farms..	336	367	337	399	313	787	240	339
$1,000..	1 558	1 463	1 446	2 999	6 966	4 047	5 369	1 217

See footnotes at end of table.

Table 16. **Farms With Sales of $10,000 or More: 1987 and 1982**—Con.

[Data for 1987 include abnormal farms. For meaning of abbreviations and symbols, see introductory text.]

Item	Sheridan	Sherman	Smith	Stafford	Stanton	Stevens	Sumner	Thomas
OPERATOR CHARACTERISTICS—Con.								
Operators by days of work off farm—Con.								
Any—Con.								
150 to 199 days .... 1987..	4	11	20	15	5	6	46	15
1982..	11	9	30	18	6	8	59	18
200 days or more .... 1987..	68	56	76	47	22	34	188	90
1982..	63	63	86	60	23	33	204	88
Not reported .... 1987..	42	31	38	43	21	19	46	30
1982..	61	57	61	68	23	32	100	67
1987 operators by years on present farm:								
2 years or less	23	25	12	14	21	7	11	39
3 or 4 years	20	17	25	16	13	11	42	28
5 to 9 years	58	49	57	52	33	20	76	57
10 years or more	242	243	375	251	118	163	540	292
Average years on present farm	22.3	22.2	24.0	24.2	19.4	23.9	23.4	22.3
Not reported	79	75	86	61	35	40	103	77
1987 operators by age group:								
Under 25 years	3	13	16	6	6	2	15	16
25 to 34 years	75	64	93	56	42	35	110	70
35 to 44 years	74	62	105	76	49	54	147	65
45 to 54 years	75	76	90	73	37	50	174	105
55 to 64 years	121	112	140	97	52	56	176	95
65 years and over	73	82	111	82	24	44	148	122
Average age	50.7	51.7	50.6	51.4	46.4	50.6	50.5	51.6
TYPE OF ORGANIZATION								
Individual or family (sole proprietorship) ..... farms, 1987..	364	333	488	322	182	174	674	401
1982..	431	359	533	387	155	219	909	431
acres, 1987..	412 669	460 831	418 697	321 582	278 410	295 916	529 793	468 886
1982..	415 720	445 802	394 666	327 526	300 281	328 765	604 450	462 311
Partnership .... farms, 1987..	26	26	35	36	30	46	77	34
1982..	38	58	54	62	34	41	84	39
acres, 1987..	34 466	59 878	(D)	65 634	80 525	113 199	92 441	62 543
1982..	42 659	(D)	53 211	74 543	(D)	79 903	66 733	55 594
Corporation:								
Family held .... farms, 1987..	25	37	31	29	26	13	17	46
1982..	21	37	33	27	12	14	18	40
acres, 1987..	(D)	(D)	71 657	(D)	(D)	30 377	18 027	(D)
1982..	(D)	(D)	(D)	(D)	60 548	28 437	(D)	(D)
Other than family held .... farms, 1987..	1	2	2	1	-	1	2	2
1982..	2	2	-	2	1	-	2	2
acres, 1987..	(D)	(D)	-	961	(D)	-	(D)	(D)
1982..	(D)	(D)	(D)	(D)	6 729	(D)	(D)	(D)
Other—cooperative, estate or trust, institutional, etc. .... farms, 1987..	6	9	1	2	2	4	2	10
1982..	3	3	-	3	-	2	6	7
acres, 1987..	2 621	3 903	(D)	(D)	(D)	(D)	(D)	(D)
1982..	(D)	(D)	-	6 729	-	(D)	5 361	26 924
1987 FARM PRODUCTION EXPENSES[1]								
Total farm production expenses .... farms..	420	411	554	393	226	242	771	494
$1,000..	47 291	55 580	36 994	61 316	77 534	86 711	44 657	63 353
Livestock and poultry purchased .... farms..	212	100	236	165	66	41	289	137
$1,000..	15 253	20 993	6 910	26 366	36 573	48 262	7 356	22 415
Feed for livestock and poultry .... farms..	294	155	378	227	72	82	447	183
$1,000..	7 344	5 604	4 123	10 249	12 367	(D)	4 382	6 521
Commercially mixed formula feeds ..... farms..	137	52	113	84	20	14	166	82
$1,000..	1 020	482	649	991	(D)	145	1 197	1 268
Seeds, bulbs, plants, and trees .... farms..	381	370	506	377	219	223	645	454
$1,000..	1 076	1 730	832	1 363	1 279	1 374	1 263	1 871
Commercial fertilizer .... farms..	336	321	485	359	194	221	679	366
$1,000..	2 067	2 702	2 495	3 904	2 538	3 043	4 479	2 852
Agricultural chemicals .... farms..	376	323	522	332	216	211	527	389
$1,000..	1 477	1 701	1 743	1 529	(D)	1 770	1 264	2 056
Petroleum products .... farms..	412	395	539	386	226	242	771	471
$1,000..	3 162	3 974	2 448	2 775	3 597	3 565	4 152	3 897
Electricity .... farms..	387	321	477	326	211	206	621	372
$1,000..	665	624	486	703	674	641	570	800
Hired farm labor .... farms..	223	181	266	230	137	155	411	255
$1,000..	1 870	2 374	2 067	2 075	5 145	3 349	1 926	3 471
Contract labor .... farms..	55	77	86	83	54	48	130	55
$1,000..	258	366	280	230	240	(D)	422	245
Repair and maintenance .... farms..	384	345	515	359	196	217	727	415
$1,000..	2 729	2 793	2 791	2 834	3 175	3 130	3 789	3 572
Customwork, machine hire, and rental of machinery and equipment .... farms..	289	315	419	213	149	117	442	350
$1,000..	1 761	3 040	1 031	956	1 565	879	1 839	3 627
Interest .... farms..	311	288	394	275	182	174	594	330
$1,000..	4 260	3 598	3 497	3 361	2 773	3 055	6 031	4 781
Cash rent .... farms..	153	105	280	175	61	73	363	129
$1,000..	969	1 224	1 476	1 231	(D)	1 055	1 903	1 414
Property taxes .... farms..	397	366	497	378	209	238	798	458
$1,000..	1 150	1 135	1 269	917	560	555	1 973	1 777
All other farm production expenses .... farms..	420	411	554	393	226	242	771	494
$1,000..	3 230	3 724	3 554	2 823	4 614	3 015	3 309	4 056

See footnotes at end of table.

Table 16. Farms With Sales of $10,000 or More: 1987 and 1982—Con.

[Data for 1987 include abnormal farms. For meaning of abbreviations and symbols, see introductory text.]

Item	Trego	Wabaunsee	Wallace	Washington	Wichita	Wilson	Woodson	Wyandotte
OPERATOR CHARACTERISTICS— Con.								
Operators by days of work off farm—Con.								
Any—Con.								
150 to 199 days .... 1987..	34	17	10	23	8	18	10	2
1982..	12	20	9	19	13	17	5	-
200 days or more .... 1987..	64	71	59	85	43	60	40	22
1982..	73	76	31	95	44	69	39	10
Not reported .... 1987..	17	25	9	71	21	24	17	1
1982..	41	50	36	99	39	38	17	3
1987 operators by years on present farm:								
2 years or less	15	12	16	37	19	7	7	3
3 or 4 years	18	8	11	27	21	7	9	6
5 to 9 years	54	36	33	65	32	24	18	4
10 years or more	242	236	162	456	163	252	149	19
Average years on present farm	22.1	25.2	20.4	23.7	20.2	25.7	23.6	14.4
Not reported	52	65	35	121	47	53	40	9
1987 operators by age group:								
Under 25 years	9	10	6	28	7	5	5	3
25 to 34 years	62	36	60	125	61	39	22	6
35 to 44 years	73	56	41	117	43	53	49	11
45 to 54 years	72	55	43	106	64	70	34	9
55 to 64 years	98	105	55	191	74	90	83	7
65 years and over	67	95	52	139	33	86	50	6
Average age	50.3	54.2	49.5	50.3	48.8	53.4	52.4	46.6
TYPE OF ORGANIZATION								
Individual or family (sole proprietorship) .... farms, 1987..	344	312	216	591	222	302	206	32
1982..	331	347	218	589	230	358	212	33
acres, 1987..	399 398	267 749	375 853	380 684	301 276	205 187	212 038	9 408
1982..	379 562	270 484	352 178	416 412	310 738	234 280	187 966	13 564
Partnership .... farms, 1987..	33	31	17	86	25	30	15	3
1982..	36	48	21	66	31	46	10	7
acres, 1987..	(D)	97 285	(D)	63 416	62 174	(D)	(D)	2 915
1982..	67 783	(D)	53 369	40 600	(D)	(D)	34 688	(D)
Corporation:								
Family held .... farms, 1987..	4	11	19	27	31	11	2	5
1982..	4	11	18	22	27	4	4	5
acres, 1987..	(D)	40 216	(D)	(D)	(D)	(D)	(D)	(D)
1982..	(D)	(D)	78 721	(D)	(D)	(D)	(D)	(D)
Other than family held .... farms, 1987..	-	2	1	1	1	-	-	1
1982..	-	-	-	2	3	-	-	1
acres, 1987..	-	(D)	(D)	(D)	(D)	-	-	(D)
1982..	-	-	-	1 521	-	-	(D)
Other—cooperative, estate or trust,								
institutional, etc. .... farms, 1987..	-	1	4	1	3	-	-	-
1982..	2	-	3	4	-	-	1	-
acres, 1987..	-	(D)	(D)	(D)	3 810	-	-	-
1982..	(D)	-	6 320	(D)	-	-	(D)	-
1987 FARM PRODUCTION EXPENSES[1]								
Total farm production expenses .... farms..	386	360	257	707	306	343	224	36
$1,000..	29 934	28 257	22 860	48 973	190 396	14 600	14 257	3 317
Livestock and poultry purchased .... farms..	164	199	81	351	109	146	88	1
$1,000..	11 182	9 366	4 916	10 619	(D)	1 872	5 067	(D)
Feed for livestock and poultry .... farms..	279	298	106	526	138	255	112	16
$1,000..	5 249	4 717	1 499	8 791	34 710	1 320	718	(D)
Commercially mixed formula feeds .... farms..	120	103	45	255	71	91	44	8
$1,000..	478	1 210	438	3 749	(D)	361	229	(D)
Seeds, bulbs, plants, and trees .... farms..	319	281	215	582	268	291	173	25
$1,000..	420	397	914	1 254	926	547	(D)	316
Commercial fertilizer .... farms..	289	303	179	577	184	293	177	18
$1,000..	940	1 000	1 494	3 433	1 421	1 663	771	197
Agricultural chemicals .... farms..	315	282	183	590	227	279	173	24
$1,000..	621	628	860	2 023	985	809	427	(D)
Petroleum products .... farms..	376	358	250	698	303	342	210	36
$1,000..	1 562	1 163	2 447	2 811	3 757	1 266	698	304
Electricity .... farms..	315	302	204	577	199	259	172	27
$1,000..	266	365	384	882	1 187	201	103	16
Hired farm labor .... farms..	153	166	121	282	127	91	103	28
$1,000..	796	1 653	1 147	2 403	4 738	410	540	757
Contract labor .... farms..	22	40	41	65	54	74	27	18
$1,000..	41	124	214	253	(D)	108	(D)	(D)
Repair and maintenance .... farms..	354	350	222	622	269	300	197	29
$1,000..	1 503	1 495	1 613	3 344	2 841	1 213	876	161
Customwork, machine hire, and rental of								
machinery and equipment .... farms..	247	170	183	363	191	183	107	15
$1,000..	765	350	1 411	892	1 975	275	498	(D)
Interest .... farms..	246	201	192	564	247	222	170	16
$1,000..	1 863	2 086	2 456	4 617	(D)	1 797	1 150	(D)
Cash rent .... farms..	185	151	109	310	76	177	131	4
$1,000..	1 001	1 400	1 000	1 996	(D)	1 194	959	74
Property taxes .... farms..	371	340	233	658	261	331	211	36
$1,000..	564	812	789	1 609	658	660	502	115
All other farm production expenses .... farms..	386	356	257	707	306	343	224	36
$1,000..	3 141	2 659	1 712	3 846	4 195	1 265	1 130	314

See footnotes at end of table.

Table 16. **Farms With Sales of $10,000 or More: 1987 and 1982**—Con.

[Data for 1987 include abnormal farms. For meaning of abbreviations and symbols, see introductory text]

Item	Kansas	Allen	Anderson	Atchison	Barber	Barton	Bourbon
MACHINERY AND EQUIPMENT[1]							
Estimated market value of all machinery and							
equipment .... farms, 1987..	42 831	358	441	429	384	618	381
1982..	48 043	404	463	450	417	704	412
$1,000, 1987..	3 028 837	20 771	24 520	23 136	25 697	50 556	13 668
1982..	3 432 446	25 404	26 336	29 483	29 130	51 324	19 586
Average per farm ....dollars, 1987..	70 716	58 018	55 601	53 929	66 918	82 071	35 873
1982..	71 445	62 882	56 880	65 518	69 857	72 904	47 538
Motortrucks, including pickups .... farms, 1987..	41 188	343	395	403	337	608	373
1982..	45 697	362	435	434	377	696	401
number, 1987..	123 782	873	1 028	1 192	1 101	1 875	777
1982..	127 663	894	1 061	1 079	1 119	2 157	740
Wheel tractors .... farms, 1987..	39 758	325	403	397	335	570	362
1982..	43 505	375	438	404	360	661	369
number, 1987..	113 793	913	1 082	1 357	883	1 791	808
1982..	117 817	1 018	1 325	1 344	897	2 104	793
Grain and bean combines[2] .... farms, 1987..	28 372	241	315	319	179	497	199
1982..	32 623	304	375	272	181	591	175
number, 1987..	35 670	281	364	365	232	697	231
1982..	40 246	322	389	296	245	815	191
LIVESTOCK AND POULTRY							
Cattle and calves inventory .... farms, 1987..	28 111	281	342	302	320	404	316
1982..	32 612	337	367	336	324	458	345
number, 1987..	5 266 525	25 184	31 419	26 208	87 388	52 606	39 076
1982..	5 481 532	29 664	38 093	29 433	90 481	80 437	38 875
Cows and heifers that had calved .... farms, 1987..	22 650	269	308	263	228	370	266
1982..	26 889	319	319	293	233	403	291
number, 1987..	1 314 791	12 753	14 282	10 691	28 130	14 361	14 932
1982..	1 485 313	15 127	16 853	10 835	27 545	14 312	14 004
Beef cows .... farms, 1987..	21 232	236	281	242	221	356	240
1982..	25 008	282	280	256	220	393	257
number, 1987..	1 219 830	10 365	12 643	9 384	27 319	13 428	13 563
1982..	1 364 535	12 455	14 849	9 356	26 734	13 813	11 791
Milk cows................................ farms, 1987..	2 514	43	43	40	13	26	43
1982..	3 685	63	64	59	17	39	65
number, 1987..	95 161	2 388	1 639	1 307	811	923	1 369
1982..	120 778	2 672	2 004	1 479	811	699	2 213
Heifers and heifer calves .... farms, 1987..	22 032	253	297	241	226	339	247
number, 1987..	1 564 381	6 981	9 203	7 709	22 827	32 747	9 766
Steers, steer calves, bulls, and bull calves ... farms, 1987..	24 681	261	301	241	273	381	274
number, 1987..	2 387 353	5 420	7 934	7 808	36 431	35 508	14 378
Cattle and calves sold .... farms, 1987..	29 267	290	353	305	331	414	333
1982..	33 511	341	369	339	331	449	357
number, 1987..	7 185 342	14 830	26 771	14 514	66 321	149 458	28 916
1982..	6 373 366	15 514	19 692	17 341	71 513	130 193	31 216
Calves .... farms, 1987..	11 574	165	171	139	119	218	168
number, 1987..	406 979	4 375	4 619	3 566	7 788	5 692	6 353
Cattle .... farms, 1987..	25 323	248	287	281	262	332	273
1982..	27 949	281	291	271	280	313	265
number, 1987..	6 776 363	10 455	22 152	10 926	60 533	143 576	22 563
number, 1987..	6 859 782	9 848	14 457	13 542	61 234	124 099	23 118
Fattened on grain and concentrates .... farms, 1987..	3 710	26	30	64	15	30	36
number, 1987..	4 547 436	1 028	2 566	3 759	(D)	(D)	5 170
Hogs and pigs inventory.................... farms, 1987..	5 480	47	44	106	27	51	47
1982..	7 327	53	59	146	18	62	71
number, 1987..	1 486 304	6 424	10 029	17 173	(D)	5 230	6 978
1982..	1 667 539	8 769	13 567	22 795	2 795	6 110	9 627
Used or to be used for breeding .... farms, 1987..	3 847	38	26	80	21	32	41
1982..	5 161	51	42	114	10	37	57
number, 1987..	184 633	890	870	2 062	(D)	956	1 041
1982..	199 217	1 286	1 026	2 619	(D)	820	1 196
Other .... farms, 1987..	5 187	45	40	101	26	49	44
1982..	6 889	61	57	141	17	54	67
number, 1987..	1 301 671	5 528	9 159	15 091	(D)	4 274	5 937
1982..	1 468 322	7 483	12 539	20 176	(D)	5 290	8 431
Hogs and pigs sold .... farms, 1987..	5 791	49	43	117	27	56	47
1982..	7 831	65	63	154	18	65	75
number, 1987..	2 713 592	11 585	16 589	27 629	5 345	14 596	10 904
1982..	2 967 268	16 244	22 358	34 105	4 879	14 567	16 146
Feeder pigs .... farms, 1987..	1 392	6	9	26	7	27	6
1982..	2 015	21	8	38	4	28	12
number, 1987..	489 501	1 090	2 004	2 969	(D)	6 395	2 474
1982..	517 609	2 596	359	4 659	(D)	6 301	2 855
Sheep and lambs inventory .... farms, 1987..	1 387	4	16	8	13	10	13
1982..	1 515	15	18	11	13	21	13
number, 1987..	217 992	(D)	707	2 160	5 100	1 280	477
1982..	245 670	910	965	(D)	(D)	(D)	1 574
Sheep and lambs sold .... farms, 1987..	1 436	4	13	7	12	6	11
1982..	1 536	17	18	11	11	22	13
number, 1987..	243 837	177	811	1 047	2 101	752	381
1982..	236 490	740	807	1 491	(D)	1 311	633
Hens and pullets of laying age inventory .... farms, 1987..	2 214	23	43	11	20	48	14
1982..	3 283	24	58	31	18	80	27
number, 1987..	1 745 164	(D)	(D)	(D)	(D)	(D)	(D)
1982..	1 708 080	(D)	(D)	(D)	(D)	(D)	(D)
Broilers and other meat-type chickens sold ... farms, 1987..	72	1	2	2	2	6	-
1982..	123	-	-	-	-	8	-
number, 1987..	166 899	(D)	(D)	(D)	(D)	(D)	-
1982..	88 298	-	-	(D)	(D)	3 339	-

See footnotes at end of table.

Table 16. **Farms With Sales of $10,000 or More: 1987 and 1982**—Con.

[Data for 1987 include abnormal farms. For meaning of abbreviations and symbols, see introductory text.]

Item	Brown	Butler	Chase	Chautauqua	Cherokee	Cheyenne	Clark
MACHINERY AND EQUIPMENT[1]							
Estimated market value of all machinery and							
equipment .... farms, 1987..	540	648	209	193	374	386	250
1982..	616	657	208	223	445	472	246
$1,000, 1987..	39 765	35 430	9 318	7 493	22 257	26 970	14 920
1982..	55 782	32 243	10 759	8 647	32 779	34 416	14 179
Average per farm ....dollars, 1987..	73 638	54 676	44 586	38 823	59 511	69 870	59 678
1982..	90 556	49 077	51 724	38 775	73 661	72 916	57 638
Motortrucks, including pickups .... farms, 1987..	505	640	207	183	373	369	240
1982..	572	642	208	223	441	446	236
number, 1987..	1 321	1 459	547	606	1 095	1 052	710
1982..	1 536	1 565	645	593	1 275	1 259	703
Wheel tractors .... farms, 1987..	529	608	200	176	358	348	223
1982..	583	595	187	166	392	395	199
number, 1987..	1 774	1 518	464	446	944	966	545
1982..	1 806	1 558	461	406	911	1 020	539
Grain and bean combines[2] .... farms, 1987..	416	345	117	98	269	218	83
1982..	454	402	115	123	325	261	114
number, 1987..	476	410	143	106	336	277	(D)
1982..	531	473	139	159	383	339	143
LIVESTOCK AND POULTRY							
Cattle and calves inventory .... farms, 1987..	347	469	156	171	244	219	170
1982..	436	499	177	209	290	258	172
number, 1987..	37 431	101 766	38 280	30 265	16 382	41 433	65 831
1982..	46 386	116 380	37 030	36 767	18 609	44 820	65 906
Cows and heifers that had calved .... farms, 1987..	290	349	118	149	214	183	86
1982..	365	370	145	194	263	222	97
number, 1987..	12 758	23 048	9 328	14 154	7 392	14 931	10 205
1982..	15 619	24 283	13 506	18 971	8 946	15 447	12 801
Beef cows .... farms, 1987..	262	325	114	146	211	183	85
1982..	324	330	140	188	255	216	95
number, 1987..	11 038	21 853	8 985	13 667	7 275	14 916	(D)
1982..	13 001	22 343	13 258	18 579	8 689	14 942	12 792
Milk cows... farms, 1987..	51	40	10	11	9	5	1
1982..	64	72	16	15	13	18	4
number, 1987..	1 720	1 195	343	487	117	15	(D)
1982..	2 618	1 940	248	392	257	505	9
Heifers and heifer calves .... farms, 1987..	265	361	122	156	195	161	106
number, 1987..	7 910	34 164	9 564	8 626	4 453	9 274	16 921
Steers, steer calves, bulls, and bull calves ___ farms, 1987..	293	411	140	159	219	189	146
number, 1987..	16 763	44 556	19 388	7 485	4 537	17 226	38 705
Cattle and calves sold .... farms, 1987..	362	517	180	170	245	226	188
1982..	444	517	186	221	287	271	191
number, 1987..	42 210	134 784	57 101	19 160	11 841	55 186	90 723
1982..	37 080	138 552	52 000	23 328	11 625	47 749	85 483
Calves .... farms, 1987..	134	198	53	79	153	93	29
number, 1987..	3 196	11 993	3 296	3 064	4 959	4 625	8 401
Cattle .... farms, 1987..	297	470	166	154	173	188	178
1982..	374	452	156	179	191	226	167
number, 1987..	39 014	122 791	53 803	16 096	6 882	50 561	82 322
1982..	33 046	127 628	47 139	18 282	6 451	42 339	76 652
Fattened on grain and concentrates .... farms, 1987..	89	115	19	15	16	26	21
number, 1987..	26 070	73 666	4 523	(D)	398	(D)	(D)
Hogs and pigs inventory.......................... farms, 1987..	123	106	31	33	34	30	5
1982..	154	116	31	34	50	44	7
number, 1987..	42 233	36 655	7 796	7 535	5 917	5 006	(D)
1982..	43 258	31 579	6 827	5 515	5 183	8 762	(D)
Used or to be used for breeding .... farms, 1987..	85	69	21	29	29	21	3
1982..	112	79	22	30	41	21	5
number, 1987..	5 326	3 819	633	1 102	618	593	27
1982..	5 162	3 058	464	825	734	724	(D)
Other .... farms, 1987..	117	104	29	32	33	30	5
1982..	144	109	30	30	48	44	5
number, 1987..	36 907	32 836	7 165	6 433	5 299	4 413	(D)
1982..	38 096	28 521	6 363	4 690	4 449	8 038	(D)
Hogs and pigs sold .... farms, 1987..	131	109	31	33	37	31	4
1982..	164	127	34	36	53	43	12
number, 1987..	77 204	60 079	15 721	11 137	9 609	8 338	(D)
1982..	75 261	56 398	14 560	12 148	8 636	15 719	(D)
Feeder pigs .... farms, 1987..	30	15	6	17	8	9	1
1982..	41	22	7	17	17	9	2
number, 1987..	14 959	4 205	(D)	4 468	965	(D)	(D)
1982..	17 138	4 741	(D)	5 327	2 337	1 049	(D)
Sheep and lambs inventory...................... farms, 1987..	17	21	11	9	3	10	5
1982..	14	21	5	7	3	6	2
number, 1987..	1 353	1 267	1 930	358	(D)	682	(D)
1982..	1 378	1 482	434	880	39	(D)	(D)
Sheep and lambs sold .... farms, 1987..	18	18	11	8	2	10	4
1982..	14	21	5	8	3	9	2
number, 1987..	1 255	1 271	1 648	154	(D)	532	(D)
1982..	919	1 074	187	414	55	(D)	(D)
Hens and pullets of laying age inventory .... farms, 1987..	22	44	7	12	13	17	6
1982..	32	58	12	15	15	31	10
number, 1987..	(D)	(D)	(D)	(D)	(D)	376	(D)
1982..	(D)	(D)	(D)	764	(D)	795	287
Broilers and other meat-type chickens sold ...... farms, 1987..	-	4	2	-	-	1	-
1982..	1	-	-	-	-	5	-
number, 1987..	-	-	(D)	-	-	(D)	-
1982..	(D)	(D)	(D)	-	-	269	-

See footnotes at end of table.

1987 CENSUS OF AGRICULTURE—COUNTY DATA

Table 16. **Farms With Sales of $10,000 or More: 1987 and 1982**—Con.

[Data for 1987 include abnormal farms. For meaning of abbreviations and symbols, see introductory text]

Item	Clay	Cloud	Coffey	Comanche	Cowley	Crawford	Decatur
MACHINERY AND EQUIPMENT[1]							
Estimated market value of all machinery and equipment ...... farms, 1987	487	434	402	205	503	377	389
1982	534	509	416	234	667	439	433
$1,000, 1987	35 477	31 194	19 265	12 505	27 113	21 992	35 984
1982	35 327	36 019	25 364	15 500	41 547	27 622	38 174
Average per farm ...... dollars, 1987	72 848	71 876	47 923	61 001	53 903	58 334	92 504
1982	66 155	74 694	60 971	66 239	62 290	62 920	88 161
Motortrucks, including pickups ...... farms, 1987	484	417	390	195	492	357	389
1982	482	484	394	219	643	434	420
number, 1987	1 371	1 274	1 068	566	1 460	987	1 350
1982	1 149	1 376	1 085	638	1 831	928	1 441
Wheel tractors ...... farms, 1987	455	406	346	204	473	367	346
1982	494	468	398	197	611	413	404
number, 1987	1 458	1 239	1 024	463	1 229	1 084	1 010
1982	1 589	1 621	1 070	435	1 439	892	1 211
Grain and bean combines[2] ...... farms, 1987	412	319	257	84	326	283	257
1982	411	360	308	107	468	331	266
number, 1987	493	469	294	96	428	357	345
1982	458	507	321	131	548	342	364
LIVESTOCK AND POULTRY							
Cattle and calves inventory ...... farms, 1987	365	274	259	171	355	293	271
1982	421	340	302	177	478	353	332
number, 1987	37 470	29 150	29 601	49 670	55 352	25 041	56 179
1982	44 065	35 616	35 578	37 942	65 918	34 089	67 347
Cows and heifers that had calved ...... farms, 1987	313	246	188	114	302	272	232
1982	345	303	231	128	409	321	270
number, 1987	14 022	12 963	7 610	14 699	16 454	11 861	16 406
1982	15 581	15 547	10 311	14 424	27 173	13 978	17 301
Beef cows ...... farms, 1987	296	240	183	111	296	260	230
1982	325	288	226	123	398	307	266
number, 1987	13 266	12 683	(D)	(D)	17 761	11 118	16 206
1982	14 541	14 717	9 885	14 211	26 305	13 004	16 489
Milk cows ...... farms, 1987	31	12	15	7	27	23	6
1982	38	31	28	10	35	26	18
number, 1987	756	280	(D)	(D)	693	743	202
1982	1 040	830	426	213	868	974	812
Heifers and heifer calves ...... farms, 1987	310	217	204	115	291	231	214
number, 1987	11 097	6 744	8 077	10 083	13 554	5 710	17 539
Steers, steer calves, bulls, and bull calves ... farms, 1987	329	250	234	156	311	267	243
number, 1987	12 351	9 443	13 914	24 888	23 344	7 470	22 232
Cattle and calves sold ...... farms, 1987	379	283	271	187	379	295	283
1982	433	349	314	184	494	350	336
number, 1987	24 088	19 620	26 785	46 221	69 148	18 552	84 945
1982	25 129	24 831	23 292	30 758	99 941	22 836	83 372
Calves ...... farms, 1987	93	107	51	49	173	157	103
number, 1987	3 590	3 165	1 209	3 176	5 912	3 992	4 609
Cattle ...... farms, 1987	344	249	253	171	315	236	246
1982	380	277	281	160	426	251	266
number, 1987	21 098	16 655	25 576	43 045	63 229	14 560	80 336
1982	20 973	18 820	21 759	24 972	90 583	17 044	77 019
Fattened on grain and concentrates ...... farms, 1987	58	21	57	16	46	20	60
number, 1987	7 195	4 110	8 573	4 807	21 000	546	(D)
Hogs and pigs inventory ...... farms, 1987	136	60	37	13	78	23	61
1982	141	79	87	18	89	76	67
number, 1987	41 535	16 509	5 644	1 896	23 305	2 592	12 397
1982	34 846	15 411	9 110	1 429	32 288	11 959	17 428
Used or to be used for breeding ...... farms, 1987	118	46	25	6	55	17	48
1982	105	57	47	9	70	63	46
number, 1987	5 077	2 188	821	341	3 067	505	(D)
1982	4 536	2 009	1 327	(D)	3 381	1 660	(D)
Other ...... farms, 1987	132	54	35	13	73	20	53
1982	139	75	83	16	78	72	64
number, 1987	36 458	14 321	4 623	1 555	20 238	2 087	(D)
1982	30 310	13 402	7 783	(D)	28 907	10 298	(D)
Hogs and pigs sold ...... farms, 1987	145	64	40	13	79	24	64
1982	144	65	74	21	100	74	71
number, 1987	75 017	32 709	11 370	3 257	47 187	5 018	29 672
1982	60 531	32 829	23 453	2 949	55 659	20 576	31 034
Feeder pigs ...... farms, 1987	37	21	10	2	23	6	20
1982	44	23	24	3	33	17	20
number, 1987	13 023	9 910	4 918	(D)	10 504	2 049	11 628
1982	13 167	7 910	10 288	(D)	4 850	7 116	(D)
Sheep and lambs inventory ...... farms, 1987	16	15	14	2	22	7	7
1982	20	12	7	6	26	12	8
number, 1987	1 383	2 022	1 062	(D)	5 068	710	(D)
1982	2 631	2 028	321	199	4 119	1 617	(D)
Sheep and lambs sold ...... farms, 1987	19	15	14	2	22	8	12
1982	23	13	6	8	24	12	8
number, 1987	1 306	921	603	(D)	3 403	520	(D)
1982	(D)	986	220	91	2 490	1 588	(D)
Hens and pullets of laying age inventory ...... farms, 1987	23	14	24	6	21	11	31
1982	36	24	25	17	36	18	38
number, 1987	(D)	(D)	708	(D)	(D)	325	1 326
1982	(D)	1 186	(D)	(D)	(D)	(D)	(D)
Broilers and other meat-type chickens sold ...... farms, 1987	2	2	-	-	-	-	1
1982	-	-	-	-	(D)	-	(D)
number, 1987	-	-	-	-	-	-	(D)
1982	(D)	(D)	-	-	(D)	-	(D)

See footnotes at end of table.

1987 CENSUS OF AGRICULTURE—COUNTY DATA

Table 16. Farms With Sales of $10,000 or More: 1987 and 1982—Con.

[Data for 1987 include abnormal farms. For meaning of abbreviations and symbols, see introductory text]

Item	Dickinson	Doniphan	Douglas	Edwards	Elk	Ellis	Ellsworth
MACHINERY AND EQUIPMENT[1]							
Estimated market value of all machinery and equipment ... farms, 1987..	654	358	332	302	226	439	358
1982..	766	444	353	337	250	506	390
$1,000, 1987..	42 030	23 480	17 842	28 940	7 729	28 133	20 886
1982..	50 241	30 909	22 501	29 014	7 354	35 485	21 743
Average per farm ... dollars, 1987..	64 267	65 585	53 742	95 828	34 199	64 083	57 781
1982..	63 758	69 516	63 742	86 095	29 417	70 128	55 751
Motortrucks, including pickups ... farms, 1987..	646	357	304	300	220	412	350
1982..	767	423	333	330	203	479	369
number, 1987..	1 677	953	676	1 279	583	1 185	1 025
1982..	1 857	1 080	776	1 047	504	1 313	932
Wheel tractors ... farms, 1987..	639	319	313	294	197	430	319
1982..	699	407	297	308	192	478	329
number, 1987..	1 863	991	922	920	637	1 078	967
1982..	2 041	1 120	846	823	485	1 243	866
Grain and bean combines[2] ... farms, 1987..	526	233	168	240	130	276	285
1982..	645	271	187	243	105	363	305
number, 1987..	645	252	192	349	151	405	439
1982..	852	302	200	316	126	510	425
LIVESTOCK AND POULTRY							
Cattle and calves inventory ... farms, 1987..	477	213	232	174	201	350	280
1982..	565	266	272	185	224	404	297
number, 1987..	70 234	18 600	22 031	50 745	33 794	51 313	35 354
1982..	75 104	21 398	26 512	53 673	38 080	55 982	32 628
Cows and heifers that had calved ... farms, 1987..	330	180	195	101	179	322	254
1982..	431	222	245	126	210	359	271
number, 1987..	14 908	7 477	7 864	4 708	15 057	20 729	16 753
1982..	16 565	8 168	10 201	6 691	18 800	23 514	14 664
Beef cows ... farms, 1987..	300	175	170	97	178	303	251
1982..	391	212	206	120	208	333	264
number, 1987..	(D)	(D)	5 787	4 524	(D)	(D)	(D)
1982..	14 612	7 539	7 440	(D)	18 672	22 236	14 216
Milk cows ... farms, 1987..	48	13	36	9	8	29	10
1982..	65	26	56	12	18	37	21
number, 1987..	(D)	(D)	2 077	184	(D)	(D)	(D)
1982..	1 953	629	2 761	(D)	126	1 276	448
Heifers and heifer calves ... farms, 1987..	347	168	185	123	167	259	236
number, 1987..	19 820	5 087	7 089	16 186	9 075	13 442	8 731
Steers, steer calves, bulls, and bull calves ... farms, 1987..	419	188	205	146	175	311	255
number, 1987..	35 706	6 036	7 078	29 851	9 662	17 142	9 870
Cattle and calves sold ... farms, 1987..	504	218	248	182	212	362	287
1982..	579	270	291	198	235	417	306
number, 1987..	75 571	14 539	19 237	61 653	27 369	62 360	22 106
1982..	65 683	14 714	21 238	69 612	21 970	43 268	17 259
Calves ... farms, 1987..	120	84	124	74	72	233	115
number, 1987..	3 198	2 185	2 749	2 369	3 124	6 167	4 156
Cattle ... farms, 1987..	470	192	212	149	202	271	248
1982..	523	221	246	156	208	316	263
number, 1987..	72 373	12 354	16 488	59 284	24 245	54 173	17 950
1982..	61 485	11 885	17 357	65 412	16 271	34 726	13 718
Fattened on grain and concentrates ... farms, 1987..	81	70	45	15	14	23	17
number, 1987..	19 220	8 027	6 850	25 706	(D)	(D)	967
Hogs and pigs inventory ... farms, 1987..	110	93	35	10	30	32	34
number, 1987..	18 682	17 862	7 808	(D)	9 437	3 898	6 727
1982..	23 736	22 408	18 419	(D)	14 077	4 088	8 562
Used or to be used for breeding ... farms, 1987..	80	59	25	8	19	20	20
1982..	104	88	41	7	41	18	31
number, 1987..	2 362	2 440	1 152	(D)	588	(D)	(D)
1982..	2 804	2 199	1 833	(D)	1 060	794	1 129
Other ... farms, 1987..	108	88	31	10	29	29	34
1982..	136	152	50	12	49	34	40
number, 1987..	16 320	15 422	6 656	(D)	8 849	(D)	(D)
1982..	20 934	20 209	16 586	(D)	13 017	3 294	7 433
Hogs and pigs sold ... farms, 1987..	117	97	37	13	30	29	32
1982..	157	166	56	15	57	33	43
number, 1987..	35 563	32 931	12 514	(D)	18 343	9 348	13 756
1982..	40 695	35 950	27 404	1 182	24 135	9 930	14 685
Feeder pigs ... farms, 1987..	25	18	10	8	9	9	13
1982..	41	27	19	2	17	13	17
number, 1987..	6 529	3 733	3 806	677	1 393	(D)	(D)
1982..	6 710	4 635	5 348	(D)	(D)	(D)	(D)
Sheep and lambs inventory ... farms, 1987..	33	13	17	5	6	11	8
1982..	27	21	14	8	5	11	4
number, 1987..	2 795	903	703	(D)	405	1 614	(D)
1982..	3 627	1 136	906	(D)	860	1 740	248
Sheep and lambs sold ... farms, 1987..	33	16	17	5	7	10	7
1982..	28	22	13	6	8	8	4
number, 1987..	2 060	653	466	(D)	381	1 088	(D)
1982..	2 777	838	1 077	(D)	872	839	193
Hens and pullets of laying age inventory ... farms, 1987..	31	22	13	8	14	60	41
1982..	49	30	28	18	17	68	42
number, 1987..	(D)	(D)	(D)	(D)	485	2 013	(D)
1982..	(D)	1 483	1 864	1 384	(D)	(D)	(D)
Broilers and other meat-type chickens sold ... farms, 1987..	1	-	4	2	1	-	1
1982..	2	-	-	2	-	-	-
number, 1987..	(D)	-	(D)	(D)	(D)	(D)	(D)
1982..	(D)	-	-	(D)	(D)	(D)	(D)

See footnotes at end of table.

Table 16. **Farms With Sales of $10,000 or More: 1987 and 1982**—Con.

[Data for 1987 include abnormal farms. For meaning of abbreviations and symbols, see introductory text]

Item	Finney	Ford	Franklin	Geary	Gove	Graham	Grant
MACHINERY AND EQUIPMENT[1]							
Estimated market value of all machinery and							
equipment .... farms, 1987..	425	579	407	178	405	371	236
1982..	475	629	467	183	431	364	238
$1,000, 1987..	55 163	82 791	22 227	10 540	29 705	25 126	35 683
1982..	59 651	48 345	24 541	10 540	38 601	26 863	33 802
Average per farm.............dollars, 1987..	129 795	142 989	54 611	59 212	73 346	67 725	151 200
1982..	125 581	76 860	52 550	57 598	89 562	73 799	142 024
Motortrucks, including pickups .... farms, 1987..	413	572	389	175	362	348	226
1982..	454	576	404	180	425	347	229
number, 1987..	1 818	1 918	1 020	538	1 232	1 206	856
1982..	1 924	1 691	873	443	1 307	1 045	1 025
Wheel tractors .... farms, 1987..	403	547	390	170	357	370	233
1982..	445	547	426	168	366	329	236
number, 1987..	1 325	1 293	1 223	556	694	993	646
1982..	1 319	1 284	1 117	483	1 024	910	668
Grain and bean combines[2] .... farms, 1987..	255	379	208	134	247	267	158
1982..	392	378	262	118	301	273	167
number, 1987..	308	486	277	145	291	342	206
1982..	510	449	305	126	429	340	(D)
LIVESTOCK AND POULTRY							
Cattle and calves inventory .... farms, 1987..	145	336	302	139	262	241	100
1982..	171	368	366	149	302	266	102
number, 1987..	193 176	135 922	29 343	20 559	79 562	35 542	148 696
1982..	147 360	144 483	36 728	18 059	86 196	41 391	76 155
Cows and heifers that had calved .... farms, 1987..	76	166	266	122	204	227	64
1982..	92	200	323	142	237	240	72
number, 1987..	6 088	14 058	12 747	8 751	16 460	16 694	3 694
1982..	5 286	9 689	14 598	8 270	20 460	18 084	6 007
Beef cows .... farms, 1987..	74	158	228	111	199	218	63
1982..	91	194	276	129	229	234	69
number, 1987..	(D)	13 453	9 433	7 965	15 830	(D)	(D)
1982..	5 275	8 867	11 263	7 383	(D)	(D)	(D)
Milk cows................ farms, 1987..	6	13	57	15	16	21	4
1982..	7	17	76	23	21	20	12
number, 1987..	(D)	605	3 314	786	630	(D)	(D)
1982..	11	822	3 315	887	(D)	(D)	(D)
Heifers and heifer calves .... farms, 1987..	106	207	256	113	207	203	79
number, 1987..	48 411	55 147	9 636	5 135	26 285	11 361	69 304
Steers, steer calves, bulls, and bull calves ..... farms, 1987..	127	284	252	132	235	203	84
number, 1987..	138 676	66 717	6 958	6 673	36 817	7 467	75 696
Cattle and calves sold .... farms, 1987..	151	366	316	139	270	248	98
1982..	178	384	374	147	314	268	103
number, 1987..	484 800	332 482	21 086	13 506	123 881	27 358	307 377
1982..	273 829	273 464	23 118	8 762	93 124	29 977	(D)
Calves .... farms, 1987..	37	75	140	61	97	126	25
number, 1987..	1 749	2 832	4 643	1 604	7 252	5 034	745
Cattle .... farms, 1987..	134	319	280	129	232	184	86
1982..	151	339	325	132	266	209	89
number, 1987..	482 851	329 650	16 443	11 902	116 629	22 324	306 631
1982..	268 719	268 773	19 838	7 203	87 309	24 621	(D)
Fattened on grain and concentrates .... farms, 1987..	41	48	53	17	47	13	14
number, 1987..	455 318	294 254	6 614	1 589	87 159	(D)	(D)
Hogs and pigs inventory................ farms, 1987..	23	23	56	36	33	15	25
1982..	19	40	97	52	42	30	23
number, 1987..	5 737	4 438	16 627	18 970	6 064	(D)	3 721
1982..	5 180	6 763	23 372	18 403	(D)	4 264	3 491
Used or to be used for breeding .... farms, 1987..	12	15	42	27	21	10	10
1982..	9	21	73	39	20	19	11
number, 1987..	626	512	2 146	4 515	765	(D)	428
1982..	475	726	2 958	2 200	(D)	(D)	507
Other .... farms, 1987..	20	18	53	34	30	12	25
1982..	18	38	87	49	42	26	23
number, 1987..	5 111	3 926	14 481	14 455	5 299	(D)	3 293
1982..	4 705	6 037	20 414	16 203	(D)	(D)	2 984
Hogs and pigs sold .... farms, 1987..	23	23	60	36	35	21	29
1982..	23	37	101	57	42	30	27
number, 1987..	10 622	9 690	32 529	35 438	10 720	(D)	5 703
1982..	8 147	11 621	43 961	36 391	15 171	9 555	7 001
Feeder pigs................ farms, 1987..	5	3	11	15	7	3	3
1982..	6	11	26	22	13	5	10
number, 1987..	785	100	13 182	3 798	2 972	(D)	(D)
1982..	1 046	921	18 071	5 965	2 559	(D)	(D)
Sheep and lambs inventory .... farms, 1987..	9	8	14	1	9	5	5
1982..	4	14	10	3	13	8	11
number, 1987..	445	150	551	(D)	4 137	(D)	(D)
1982..	505	(D)	1 240	266	(D)	264	(D)
Sheep and lambs sold .... farms, 1987..	10	7	15	1	9	5	4
1982..	8	12	11	3	15	7	11
number, 1987..	1 436	192	641	(D)	3 204	(D)	235
1982..	233	351	2 343	136	3 066	161	(D)
Hens and pullets of laying age inventory .... farms, 1987..	19	14	27	15	27	14	20
number, 1987..	7	28	46	11	39	24	29
1982..	(D)	(D)	1 656	1 426	(D)	(D)	(D)
Broilers and other meat-type chickens sold ..... farms, 1987..	-	1	2	1	4	-	6
1982..	-	3	3	(D)	1	-	(D)
number, 1987..	-	(D)	(D)	(D)	350	-	750
1982..	-	(D)	(D)	(D)	(D)	-	(D)

See footnotes at end of table.

Table 16. **Farms With Sales of $10,000 or More: 1987 and 1982**—Con.

[Data for 1987 include abnormal farms. For meaning of abbreviations and symbols, see introductory text]

Item		Gray	Greeley	Greenwood	Hamilton	Harper	Harvey	Haskell
MACHINERY AND EQUIPMENT¹								
Estimated market value of all machinery and equipment	farms, 1987..	450	215	349	216	471	506	251
	1982..	473	208	380	226	543	612	309
	$1,000, 1987..	49 971	24 210	12 234	24 185	33 936	41 811	42 604
	1982..	55 480	24 956	13 014	24 212	37 818	33 964	46 908
Average per farm	dollars, 1987..	111 046	112 606	35 055	111 966	72 051	82 236	169 736
	1982..	117 294	119 991	34 247	107 135	69 646	55 496	151 807
Motortrucks, including pickups	farms, 1987..	411	200	340	209	455	470	249
	1982..	462	184	350	200	524	591	303
	number, 1987..	1 603	684	852	921	1 491	1 311	1 130
	1982..	1 658	767	826	732	1 626	1 448	1 079
Wheel tractors	farms, 1987..	421	193	289	207	426	482	240
	1982..	425	180	326	197	467	569	279
	number, 1987..	1 086	559	660	547	1 205	1 379	710
	1982..	1 011	449	852	527	1 215	1 583	659
Grain and bean combines²	farms, 1987..	261	110	132	106	325	392	157
	1982..	327	108	172	161	326	439	170
	number, 1987..	315	141	153	174	469	463	168
	1982..	368	165	173	248	451	524	181
LIVESTOCK AND POULTRY								
Cattle and calves inventory	farms, 1987..	234	76	302	87	349	286	93
	1982..	220	74	330	107	398	342	104
	number, 1987..	147 660	51 960	60 120	57 710	69 004	31 309	134 100
	1982..	99 390	39 311	71 080	41 585	58 975	35 042	159 846
Cows and heifers that had calved	farms, 1987..	75	36	250	58	215	205	37
	1982..	90	48	269	73	285	264	42
	number, 1987..	5 621	6 676	24 895	4 803	11 625	6 760	2 422
	1982..	4 803	3 506	29 135	5 818	13 993	8 648	2 656
Beef cows	farms, 1987..	73	36	243	58	209	174	33
	1982..	89	46	280	73	275	221	39
	number, 1987..	(D)	6 668	23 948	(D)	(D)	5 433	(D)
	1982..	(D)	3 496	27 918	5 818	13 334	6 716	(D)
Milk cows	farms, 1987..	4	4	22	2	13	42	4
	1982..	10	5	36	-	23	57	3
	number, 1987..	(D)	8	947	(D)	(D)	1 327	(D)
	1982..	(D)	10	1 219	-	659	1 932	(D)
Heifers and heifer calves	farms, 1987..	125	50	225	62	243	219	59
	number, 1987..	34 113	16 622	16 689	17 038	17 711	8 105	42 662
Steers, steer calves, bulls, and bull calves	farms, 1987..	201	63	261	79	296	251	67
	number, 1987..	107 926	28 662	18 536	35 869	39 668	16 444	88 816
Cattle and calves sold	farms, 1987..	245	82	319	97	362	283	100
	1982..	223	80	346	109	417	337	112
	number, 1987..	313 936	90 805	55 020	110 286	68 904	36 608	328 871
	1982..	171 942	155 424	52 159	66 983	59 040	34 596	492 104
Calves	farms, 1987..	49	12	114	34	82	113	19
	number, 1987..	3 553	(D)	6 803	1 297	3 829	1 562	1 368
Cattle	farms, 1987..	225	76	283	80	325	252	91
		189	71	311	95	370	289	105
	number, 1987..	310 383	(D)	48 217	108 989	65 075	34 946	327 503
	1982..	168 429	154 685	45 601	65 665	55 391	32 353	(D)
Fattened on grain and concentrates	farms, 1987..	24	27	38	10	17	53	21
	number, 1987..	(D)	(D)	7 118	(D)	(D)	17 802	302 285
Hogs and pigs inventory	farms, 1987..	17	6	26	9	28	90	11
	1982..	29	15	46	13	35	103	12
	number, 1987..	(D)	951	5 714	(D)	4 111	29 854	4 882
	1982..	8 150	(D)	7 562	1 530	4 270	25 941	(D)
Used or to be used for breeding	farms, 1987..	8	3	14	3	16	48	7
	1982..	15	10	34	8	30	60	7
	number, 1987..	480	(D)	718	(D)	458	2 145	1 046
Other	farms, 1987..	533	(D)	795	(D)	877	2 681	(D)
	1982..	17	6	25	9	26	90	10
	number, 1987..	29	15	44	12	29	101	12
	1982..	(D)	(D)	4 996	(D)	3 653	27 709	3 836
	1982..	5 617	(D)	6 767	(D)	3 393	23 260	(D)
Hogs and pigs sold	farms, 1987..	20	6	26	10	25	96	12
	1982..	34	16	52	11	37	112	15
	number, 1987..	9 742	1 495	7 488	5 559	50 813	16 039
	1982..	10 823	(D)	14 265	2 548	9 286	54 214	14 863
Feeder pigs	farms, 1987..	1	-	3	2	4	17	4
	1982..	10	2	18	2	6	28	-
	number, 1987..	(D)	-	(D)	-	(D)	3 548	(D)
	1982..	(D)	(D)	(D)	(D)	4 205	12 939	-
Sheep and lambs inventory	farms, 1987..	10	4	13	2	21	38	8
	1982..	8	4	14	1	16	57	5
	number, 1987..	4 374	(D)	553	(D)	33 859	6 579	(D)
Sheep and lambs sold	farms, 1987..	(D)	(D)	509	(D)	2 098	11 833	595
	1982..	12	4	13	2	25	39	8
	number, 1987..	4	6	14	2	17	60	4
	1987..	2 200	(D)	326	(D)	(D)	5 589	(D)
	1982..	1 070	(D)	406	(D)	1 203	7 020	(D)
Hens and pullets of laying age inventory	farms, 1987..	19	4	8	5	12	32	10
	1982..	24	9	20	12	30	41	7
	number, 1987..	(D)	(D)	390	118	(D)	(D)	(D)
	1982..	(D)	269	684	(D)	500	(D)	205
Broilers and other meat-type chickens sold	farms, 1987..	3	-	1	-	1	-	1
	1982..	11	-	-	-	-	4	1
	number, 1987..	(D)	-	-	-	(D)	-	-
	1982..	(D)	-	(D)	-	-	(D)	(D)

See footnotes at end of table.

Table 16. **Farms With Sales of $10,000 or More: 1987 and 1982**—Con.

[Data for 1987 include abnormal farms. For meaning of abbreviations and symbols, see introductory text]

Item	Hodgeman	Jackson	Jefferson	Jewell	Johnson	Kearny	Kingman	Kiowa
MACHINERY AND EQUIPMENT[1]								
Estimated market value of all machinery and equipment .... farms, 1987..	337	519	425	544	256	226	539	239
1982..	377	540	449	630	303	235	636	285
$1,000, 1987..	24 296	19 695	22 168	32 527	19 520	35 511	33 487	22 107
1982..	29 010	24 918	22 491	45 715	19 266	33 455	41 728	22 172
Average per farm .... dollars, 1987..	72 094	37 948	52 161	59 792	76 251	157 126	62 129	92 497
1982..	76 949	46 140	50 091	72 564	63 583	142 362	65 610	77 795
Motortrucks, including pickups .... farms, 1987..	327	510	424	528	256	215	490	239
1982..	353	499	424	604	279	229	589	283
number, 1987..	1 424	1 157	1 024	1 400	657	1 084	1 526	716
1982..	1 233	1 140	949	1 656	708	1 105	1 600	848
Wheel tractors .... farms, 1987..	307	495	404	519	219	212	502	236
1982..	351	483	395	576	280	205	579	241
number, 1987..	931	1 143	1 201	1 552	736	801	1 414	566
1982..	794	1 185	1 119	1 604	763	715	1 473	623
Grain and bean combines[2] .... farms, 1987..	264	294	234	348	182	117	355	136
1982..	292	337	221	461	165	132	391	177
number, 1987..	373	371	272	422	186	161	491	154
1982..	409	399	236	570	169	185	512	(D)
LIVESTOCK AND POULTRY								
Cattle and calves inventory .... farms, 1987..	226	434	295	378	165	103	410	140
1982..	273	464	332	449	183	107	485	165
number, 1987..	82 425	35 020	25 405	42 079	15 569	77 420	48 765	30 255
1982..	74 677	45 461	31 362	53 969	17 212	79 539	46 664	34 699
Cows and heifers that had calved .... farms, 1987..	122	381	265	325	136	79	336	86
1982..	163	420	285	389	154	80	401	135
number, 1987..	8 110	15 867	11 753	18 333	6 114	7 983	20 110	7 845
1982..	9 263	20 748	12 674	20 323	6 371	5 172	18 276	11 213
Beef cows .... farms, 1987..	115	348	240	316	126	79	319	85
1982..	153	384	257	375	144	80	378	133
number, 1987..	(D)	14 504	10 069	17 540	5 341	(D)	(D)	7 838
1982..	8 474	18 422	10 607	19 288	5 615	(D)	17 630	(D)
Milk cows .... farms, 1987..	15	53	38	32	19	7	26	4
1982..	20	64	63	39	15	7	43	5
number, 1987..	(D)	1 363	1 684	793	773	(D)	(D)	8
1982..	789	2 324	2 067	1 035	756	(D)	1 646	(D)
Heifers and heifer calves .... farms, 1987..	173	341	234	321	131	77	308	97
number, 1987..	30 376	8 303	6 988	10 544	6 387	17 281	12 521	8 839
Steers, steer calves, bulls, and bull calves .... farms, 1987..	182	387	270	344	123	82	384	118
number, 1987..	43 939	10 650	6 664	13 202	3 068	52 156	16 134	13 570
Cattle and calves sold .... farms, 1987..	233	454	306	396	177	108	422	150
1982..	278	483	336	463	202	111	494	195
number, 1987..	122 217	26 480	17 534	29 534	15 322	136 817	35 385	23 738
1982..	112 786	26 481	19 314	33 470	16 004	185 330	32 889	22 850
Calves .... farms, 1987..	47	218	149	151	88	48	170	44
number, 1987..	2 324	6 674	5 359	3 950	2 832	3 295	6 009	3 906
Cattle .... farms, 1987..	211	402	266	353	135	86	353	134
1982..	241	400	279	387	169	98	400	164
number, 1987..	119 893	19 806	12 175	25 584	12 490	133 522	29 376	19 832
1982..	107 304	19 790	14 659	28 220	10 008	163 022	24 540	18 253
Fattened on grain and concentrates .... farms, 1987..	28	66	50	54	30	11	26	6
number, 1987..	89 787	4 109	2 371	6 944	3 309	118 106	1 217	(D)
Hogs and pigs inventory...................... farms, 1987..	16	100	58	142	35	8	83	10
1982..	21	149	110	189	36	19	87	16
number, 1987..	(D)	16 091	10 062	49 213	8 104	(D)	8 599	1 560
1982..	1 396	20 406	19 622	54 674	11 313	2 102	9 674	5 680
Used or to be used for breeding .... farms, 1987..	8	74	43	122	25	5	51	8
1982..	7	110	79	158	32	8	57	15
number, 1987..	(D)	2 006	1 379	6 569	1 337	164	1 003	(D)
1982..	115	2 627	2 316	7 837	1 506	236	956	512
Other .... farms, 1987..	13	89	53	134	33	7	70	10
1982..	21	140	99	174	34	19	83	18
number, 1987..	(D)	14 085	8 683	42 624	6 767	(D)	7 596	(D)
1982..	1 281	17 781	17 306	46 837	9 805	1 866	8 918	5 166
Hogs and pigs sold .... farms, 1987..	16	108	63	148	37	8	89	12
1982..	21	155	119	212	42	22	84	23
number, 1987..	(D)	31 807	16 237	84 320	16 580	1 845	17 012	2 941
1982..	3 726	36 641	32 135	84 135	19 026	5 386	14 292	10 530
Feeder pigs...................... farms, 1987..	1	21	16	32	11	2	17	3
1982..	2	51	34	55	13	3	19	7
number, 1987..	(D)	4 237	4 625	5 417	(D)	(D)	3 413	(D)
1982..	(D)	8 499	4 610	11 786	(D)	(D)	2 111	1 270
Sheep and lambs inventory .... farms, 1987..	7	13	10	26	5	6	23	2
1982..	5	13	16	32	8	5	19	2
number, 1987..	(D)	2 413	427	5 871	(D)	(D)	1 581	(D)
1982..	(D)	2 235	421	6 047	1 020	(D)	1 061	(D)
Sheep and lambs sold .... farms, 1987..	10	14	11	27	5	6	25	2
1982..	10	17	14	29	8	6	20	2
number, 1987..	(D)	1 866	361	6 693	60	(D)	3 121	(D)
1982..	548	2 193	347	5 156	319	(D)	988	(D)
Hens and pullets of laying age inventory .... farms, 1987..	21	25	22	32	12	13	32	2
1982..	21	41	34	51	17	23	58	10
number, 1987..	628	(D)	(D)	1 754	(D)	(D)	(D)	(D)
1982..	(D)	(D)	1 329	(D)	(D)	(D)	(D)	(D)
Broilers and other meat-type chickens sold ...... farms, 1987..	-	-	1	3	1	-	2	-
1982..	1	-	-	2	(D)	-	-	-
number, 1987..	(D)	(D)	(D)	(D)	(D)	(D)	(D)	-

See footnotes at end of table.

Table 16. **Farms With Sales of $10,000 or More: 1987 and 1982** — Con.

[Data for 1987 include abnormal farms. For meaning of abbreviations and symbols, see introductory text]

Item	Labette	Lane	Leavenworth	Lincoln	Linn	Logan	Lyon	McPherson
MACHINERY AND EQUIPMENT[1]								
Estimated market value of all machinery and								
equipment .... farms, 1987..	454	250	396	414	352	283	481	857
1982..	524	276	411	491	350	283	513	1 057
$1,000, 1987..	20 842	22 867	20 166	26 295	14 852	23 102	18 021	52 028
1982..	26 213	22 232	24 022	28 350	17 909	22 495	25 258	57 275
Average per farm.................. dollars, 1987..	45 909	91 468	50 923	63 515	42 193	81 631	37 465	60 710
1982..	50 026	80 549	58 449	57 739	51 167	79 488	49 233	54 167
Motortrucks, including pickups .... farms, 1987..	432	246	388	400	319	270	438	813
1982..	518	264	374	490	325	272	485	994
number, 1987..	1 156	921	1 017	1 147	776	897	1 120	2 344
1982..	1 257	924	957	1 293	784	974	1 218	2 322
Wheel tractors .... farms, 1987..	428	222	370	364	342	233	437	824
1982..	501	261	372	406	309	226	454	987
number, 1987..	1 068	625	1 031	1 111	828	646	1 269	2 269
1982..	1 221	678	1 086	1 177	838	591	1 358	2 357
Grain and bean combines[2] .... farms, 1987..	231	135	215	325	179	166	272	712
1982..	372	169	272	367	212	212	304	819
number, 1987..	322	176	234	409	190	252	310	899
1982..	415	224	290	477	241	272	323	976
LIVESTOCK AND POULTRY								
Cattle and calves inventory..................... farms, 1987..	364	116	307	311	272	153	342	482
1982..	412	154	327	360	295	168	396	601
number, 1987..	48 899	59 500	21 411	52 350	30 499	30 945	71 549	53 738
1982..	48 870	64 241	25 519	49 213	32 817	31 849	71 122	55 250
Cows and heifers that had calved .... farms, 1987..	320	74	290	287	240	134	258	359
1982..	371	100	307	328	· 267	141	310	476
number, 1987..	15 011	5 530	11 029	19 471	12 519	10 966	17 231	13 649
1982..	17 651	7 168	12 507	21 378	14 269	12 313	16 557	16 155
Beef cows .... farms, 1987..	307	71	248	263	230	132	246	307
1982..	350	89	251	316	254	139	295	403
number, 1987..	13 836	(D)	7 606	(D)	11 790	10 797	16 654	11 316
1982..	15 597	7 156	8 156	(D)	12 928	(D)	15 599	12 962
Milk cows................................. farms, 1987..	26	6	65	24	16	16	26	69
1982..	46	8	91	34	30	17	49	101
number, 1987..	1 175	(D)	3 423	(D)	729	169	577	2 533
1982..	2 054	12	4 351	(D)	1 361	(O)	958	3 193
Heifers and heifer calves..................... farms, 1987..	301	83	255	253	234	114	272	383
number, 1987..	15 733	16 508	5 812	14 585	8 210	7 585	24 446	17 995
Steers, steer calves, bulls, and bull calves .... farms, 1987..	328	106	257	282	253	131	293	404
number, 1987..	18 155	37 462	4 570	18 194	9 770	12 394	29 872	21 894
Cattle and calves sold .... farms, 1987..	372	130	311	320	283	166	365	496
1982..	435	184	337	371	301	181	419	612
number, 1987..	54 073	114 044	11 018	47 206	20 636	22 283	78 154	60 381
1982..	44 948	106 646	12 050	25 120	18 870	21 920	65 503	45 099
Calves .... farms, 1987..	201	38	190	113	134	79	114	192
number, 1987..	4 960	2 103	4 342	4 208	3 626	4 927	3 040	4 604
Cattle .... farms, 1987..	316	113	249	263	248	131	328	441
1982..	345	148	271	298	237	144	371	507
number, 1987..	49 093	111 941	6 676	42 998	16 710	17 356	75 114	55 777
1982..	37 670	104 654	7 706	19 515	12 146	17 113	60 769	38 443
Fattened on grain and concentrates .... farms, 1987..	23	21	41	28	44	15	85	53
number, 1987..	(D)	(D)	1 091	3 641	2 555	(D)	33 900	(D)
Hogs and pigs inventory..................... farms, 1987..	44	13	85	42	35	20	82	105
1982..	74	20	85	49	65	20	138	149
number, 1987..	13 842	(D)	16 677	6 340	15 350	1 883	10 630	21 725
1982..	19 980	2 666	13 369	7 928	18 680	2 874	16 750	24 712
Used or to be used for breeding .... farms, 1987..	31	7	61	24	24	14	62	66
1982..	54	12	72	35	47	10	92	91
number, 1987..	794	149	2 086	907	1 494	250	1 525	2 364
1982..	1 329	616	1 769	994	2 025	(D)	2 176	2 587
Other .... farms, 1987..	42	13	62	40	34	19	74	104
1982..	70	18	76	44	59	20	129	138
number, 1987..	13 148	(D)	14 589	5 433	13 856	1 633	9 105	19 361
1982..	18 651	2 050	11 600	6 934	16 655	(D)	14 674	22 125
Hogs and pigs sold .... farms, 1987..	47	14	90	41	42	20	84	115
1982..	75	19	94	59	70	19	146	159
number, 1987..	27 672	(D)	30 180	13 769	26 663	4 601	17 301	40 110
1982..	44 171	8 601	20 997	17 121	26 328	4 937	32 925	51 573
Feeder pigs .... farms, 1987..	19	3	16	13	5	4	17	31
1982..	21	4	22	15	23	4	33	31
number, 1987..	3 125	432	3 160	3 948	(D)	(D)	2 446	7 167
1982..	4 034	(D)	3 530	3 766	3 891	(D)	7 256	11 549
Sheep and lambs inventory .... farms, 1987..	13	2	8	21	6	2	10	43
1982..	19	8	12	29	6	11	8	48
number, 1987..	551	(D)	637	4 764	169	(D)	485	8 314
1982..	731	538	309	6 350	267	(D)	465	8 272
Sheep and lambs sold .... farms, 1987..	12	4	9	22	6	3	10	43
1982..	20	8	11	32	6	10	9	52
number, 1987..	358	162	356	643	130	(D)	427	5 546
1982..	565	477	271	3 978	268	625	431	15 007
Hens and pullets of laying age inventory .... farms, 1987..	14	13	19	23	15	22	29	46
1982..	26	19	27	38	19	26	37	89
number, 1987..	299	(D)	(D)	(D)	(D)	(D)	(D)	(D)
1982..	(D)	(D)	2 262	(D)	1 142	(D)	(D)	(D)
Broilers and other meat-type chickens sold ...... farms, 1987..	-	-	-	1	-	1	-	3
1982..	-	-	-	-	3	-	-	8
number, 1987..	-	-	-	(D)	-	(D)	-	(D)
1982..	-	-	-	-	(D)	-	-	(D)

See footnotes at end of table.

Table 16. **Farms With Sales of $10,000 or More: 1987 and 1982**—Con.

[Data for 1987 include abnormal farms. For meaning of abbreviations and symbols, see Introductory text]

Item	Marion	Marshall	Meade	Miami	Mitchell	Montgomery	Morris	Morton
MACHINERY AND EQUIPMENT[1]								
Estimated market value of all machinery and								
equipment .... farms, 1987..	728	793	372	403	478	354	364	141
1982..	838	863	388	427	492	396	402	180
$1,000, 1987..	44 099	43 601	31 214	19 773	37 506	20 045	19 301	18 624
1982..	45 004	57 319	35 119	27 042	43 718	27 471	24 634	18 231
Average per farm.......................... dollars, 1987..	60 576	54 983	83 909	49 064	78 464	56 624	53 024	132 084
1982..	53 833	66 418	90 513	63 330	88 857	69 370	61 278	101 283
Motortrucks, including pickups .... farms, 1987..	710	781	355	396	477	336	347	141
1982..	799	844	365	408	490	396	399	179
number, 1987..	1 931	1 865	1 169	899	1 443	896	964	696
1982..	2 004	1 705	1 285	962	1 537	1 042	983	729
Wheel tractors .... farms, 1987..	695	758	347	372	430	343	347	131
1982..	782	808	351	387	476	371	370	170
number, 1987..	2 102	2 172	833	960	1 082	855	1 084	444
1982..	2 430	2 173	964	936	1 221	868	1 075	427
Grain and bean combines[2] .... farms, 1987..	558	654	261	185	316	187	220	89
1982..	674	683	280	252	369	231	297	113
number, 1987..	741	702	356	208	509	230	289	145
1982..	811	722	322	290	587	306	342	150
LIVESTOCK AND POULTRY								
Cattle and calves inventory .... farms, 1987..	516	527	184	310	266	275	301	88
1982..	623	598	204	333	304	319	336	100
number, 1987..	62 557	46 862	49 536	23 966	46 431	23 118	53 142	14 884
1982..	73 314	46 143	45 758	31 346	46 563	28 955	59 106	16 847
Cows and heifers that had calved .... farms, 1987..	380	455	102	284	224	244	265	75
1982..	471	522	144	301	250	293	292	77
number, 1987..	19 217	17 405	8 729	12 091	12 221	11 702	17 532	5 157
1982..	22 656	18 071	11 339	13 362	12 658	13 923	19 118	5 385
Beef cows .... farms, 1987..	309	415	99	262	218	231	245	74
1982..	385	474	140	278	240	270	266	76
number, 1987..	15 391	14 762	(D)	10 504	(D)	10 779	15 892	(D)
1982..	17 880	15 215	11 030	11 319	(D)	12 770	17 517	(D)
Milk cows........................ farms, 1987..	91	69	5	35	14	17	45	5
1982..	128	84	9	46	23	34	55	1
number, 1987..	3 826	2 643	(D)	1 587	(D)	823	1 640	(D)
1982..	4 816	2 856	609	2 043	(D)	1 153	1 801	(D)
Heifers and heifer calves .... farms, 1987..	396	431	128	247	202	222	251	64
number, 1987..	16 104	15 433	12 935	5 488	11 916	6 117	12 713	2 482
Steers, steer calves, bulls, and bull calves .... farms, 1987..	437	469	160	280	243	256	278	80
number, 1987..	27 246	14 024	27 873	6 407	22 294	5 299	22 887	7 245
Cattle and calves sold .... farms, 1987..	538	538	199	326	277	294	310	93
1982..	644	614	212	343	309	329	347	104
number, 1987..	54 142	34 248	55 674	15 437	54 196	13 872	51 166	17 607
1982..	53 234	30 950	50 461	16 622	49 192	17 846	57 837	14 836
Calves .... farms, 1987..	192	202	57	137	81	159	102	33
number, 1987..	6 517	4 605	3 431	4 105	2 361	4 166	3 324	1 110
Cattle .... farms, 1987..	470	464	169	282	244	249	282	89
1982..	561	522	194	287	262	267	303	77
number, 1987..	47 625	29 443	52 243	11 331	51 835	9 686	47 842	16 497
1982..	47 699	25 730	47 229	12 611	45 368	11 577	49 998	12 437
Fattened on grain and concentrates .... farms, 1987..	87	52	13	37	28	26	47	7
1982..	7 226	10 672	26 218	780	(D)	975	23 741	(D)
Hogs and pigs inventory.................... farms, 1987..	140	244	11	44	78	47	88	3
1982..	178	254	27	69	93	63	106	3
number, 1987..	29 901	44 365	(D)	11 105	22 853	20 726	10 482	60
1982..	29 220	51 372	(D)	11 883	27 968	23 611	17 727	(D)
Used or to be used for breeding .... farms, 1987..	95	182	10	34	64	38	46	2
1982..	131	190	18	48	68	44	65	2
number, 1987..	4 310	5 799	400	1 293	2 603	2 315	2 458	(D)
1982..	3 752	5 707	(D)	1 344	2 641	2 170	2 418	(D)
Other .... farms, 1987..	135	231	11	42	73	44	85	3
1982..	168	239	26	68	88	57	97	3
number, 1987..	25 491	38 566	(D)	9 812	20 250	18 411	8 024	41
1982..	25 488	45 665	(D)	10 539	25 327	21 641	15 309	(D)
Hogs and pigs sold .... farms, 1987..	153	257	12	43	81	49	70	3
1982..	191	270	28	73	99	76	112	5
number, 1987..	56 431	84 609	(D)	16 112	41 970	43 097	20 971	(D)
1982..	51 543	98 171	(D)	18 760	47 132	50 258	29 983	851
Feeder pigs .... farms, 1987..	34	63	5	5	28	13	17	1
1982..	57	85	6	12	26	18	33	1
number, 1987..	15 531	18 084	361	1 585	10 521	2 329	5 832	(D)
1982..	10 003	19 430	921	1 636	15 036	4 566	(D)	(D)
Sheep and lambs inventory.................... farms, 1987..	43	18	5	14	26	9	8	3
1982..	31	18	7	17	31	7	16	1
number, 1987..	3 654	1 146	(D)	268	4 749	277	381	(D)
1982..	3 026	1 143	645	849	7 583	495	741	(D)
Sheep and lambs sold .... farms, 1987..	44	18	6	13	33	8	14	3
1982..	33	17	8	16	35	8	14	-
number, 1987..	2 511	870	(D)	276	3 548	359	320	(D)
1982..	2 635	906	699	584	5 822	311	507	(D)
Hens and pullets of laying age inventory .... farms, 1987..	50	39	12	18	23	11	27	6
1982..	66	44	20	31	21	30	27	18
number, 1987..	(D)	2 622	454	(D)	(D)	(D)	(D)	(D)
1982..	(D)	(D)	452	(D)	903	(D)	(D)	(D)
Broilers and other meat-type chickens sold....... farms, 1987..	1	1	1	4	-	1	-	-
1982..	3	1	(D)	-	(D)	1	-	-
number, 1987..	(D)	-	(D)	-	-	(D)	-	-
1982..	90	(D)	(D)	-	-	-	-	-

See footnotes at end of table.

Table 16. Farms With Sales of $10,000 or More: 1987 and 1982—Con.

[Data for 1987 include abnormal farms. For meaning of abbreviations and symbols, see introductory text]

Item	Nemaha	Neosho	Ness	Norton	Osage	Osborne	Ottawa	Pawnee
MACHINERY AND EQUIPMENT[1]								
Estimated market value of all machinery and equipment ... farms, 1987	832	378	428	370	438	459	353	405
1982	864	398	502	421	478	482	492	481
$1,000, 1987	48 660	18 778	26 757	22 277	23 295	33 650	19 174	36 746
1982	49 527	25 542	36 508	31 586	29 256	29 247	30 981	48 535
Average per farm ... dollars, 1987	58 485	49 679	62 517	60 209	53 184	73 311	54 317	90 730
1982	57 322	64 176	72 725	75 026	61 206	50 679	62 969	105 282
Motortrucks, including pickups ... farms, 1987	792	357	418	370	408	457	344	404
1982	780	386	444	402	473	462	481	441
number, 1987	1 622	942	1 314	1 180	1 064	1 393	1 054	1 474
1982	1 384	1 047	1 576	1 156	1 235	1 258	1 217	1 449
Wheel tractors ... farms, 1987	765	350	383	353	405	453	335	396
1982	810	367	482	371	417	420	452	436
number, 1987	2 272	889	1 058	962	1 181	1 181	823	1 385
1982	2 125	986	1 246	1 028	1 205	1 063	1 097	1 274
Grain and bean combines[2] ... farms, 1987	532	242	299	256	270	381	281	293
1982	573	312	311	331	340	345	366	332
number, 1987	576	270	405	332	300	468	429	432
1982	627	371	444	450	370	441	537	453
LIVESTOCK AND POULTRY								
Cattle and calves inventory ... farms, 1987	609	296	303	262	291	319	233	194
1982	698	322	368	319	367	360	286	236
number, 1987	57 217	29 339	41 362	37 082	29 954	46 347	39 371	58 436
1982	66 255	35 056	45 192	49 376	38 768	51 795	44 684	45 795
Cows and heifers that had calved ... farms, 1987	467	264	222	228	230	283	191	136
1982	567	303	275	291	285	319	233	182
number, 1987	19 356	12 137	15 206	15 798	9 809	19 237	13 481	9 846
1982	22 589	14 433	17 589	21 031	11 754	22 172	13 610	11 254
Beef cows ... farms, 1987	356	248	218	225	221	279	184	134
1982	446	262	270	273	276	310	224	177
number, 1987	13 383	10 771	14 923	(D)	9 356	18 876	12 983	(D)
1982	16 118	11 923	(D)	20 002	11 153	21 475	12 949	(D)
Milk cows ... farms, 1987	139	37	14	12	17	17	19	2
1982	172	50	16	31	25	32	20	9
number, 1987	5 973	1 366	283	(D)	453	561	498	(D)
1982	6 471	2 510	(D)	1 029	601	697	661	(D)
Heifers and heifer calves ... farms, 1987	465	256	266	211	231	266	186	161
number, 1987	18 290	8 827	11 998	10 273	9 630	13 145	12 434	15 061
Steers, steer calves, bulls, and bull calves ... farms, 1987	504	263	264	234	253	293	204	162
number, 1987	19 571	8 375	14 158	11 011	10 515	13 965	13 456	31 529
Cattle and calves sold ... farms, 1987	613	302	327	269	309	329	246	203
1982	716	331	388	324	375	370	302	234
number, 1987	38 270	18 878	30 323	31 369	25 317	35 183	44 826	130 217
1982	45 121	18 871	35 734	31 976	30 290	33 559	41 395	61 702
Calves ... farms, 1987	207	152	126	131	97	129	91	76
1982	4 743	4 267	5 210	4 574	2 333	5 363	4 114	3 533
Cattle ... farms, 1987	542	260	286	209	281	298	217	175
1982	573	264	303	271	325	323	262	189
number, 1987	33 527	14 611	25 113	26 795	22 984	29 820	40 814	126 684
1982	38 903	13 769	27 268	24 554	25 677	28 534	37 586	57 866
Fattened on grain and concentrates ... farms, 1987	126	25	18	22	45	35	26	21
number, 1987	12 632	1 677	(D)	13 603	5 612	9 852	(D)	(D)
Hogs and pigs inventory ... farms, 1987	291	40	15	55	58	49	19	31
1982	335	70	23	64	69	64	38	42
number, 1987	84 244	23 257	1 835	16 268	7 645	7 705	3 252	9 997
1982	75 823	26 971	(D)	11 710	13 001	8 197	7 705	11 604
Used or to be used for breeding ... farms, 1987	214	27	9	31	39	38	14	19
1982	295	40	13	36	71	38	23	27
number, 1987	9 762	2 719	(D)	(D)	1 249	1 498	431	1 217
1982	8 025	3 428	(D)	2 225	1 799	870	(D)	1 610
Other ... farms, 1987	278	37	15	52	52	46	18	30
1982	322	66	22	40	79	61	35	38
number, 1987	74 482	20 538	(D)	(D)	6 396	6 207	2 821	8 780
1982	67 798	23 543	1 012	9 485	11 202	7 327	(D)	9 994
Hogs and pigs sold ... farms, 1987	304	46	15	56	61	56	19	33
1982	343	76	23	63	93	70	41	43
number, 1987	150 512	33 180	(D)	34 880	15 736	13 409	8 439	17 480
1982	120 359	45 217	(D)	22 529	21 426	15 032	18 005	19 684
Feeder pigs ... farms, 1987	78	7	4	13	13	17	8	5
1982	69	22	7	6	25	20	11	10
number, 1987	28 663	(D)	(D)	17 930	3 664	3 892	434	(D)
1982	15 172	5 956	(D)	(D)	4 790	4 053	(D)	2 457
Sheep and lambs inventory ... farms, 1987	33	8	10	9	7	33	16	10
1982	24	7	12	17	6	29	12	13
number, 1987	1 805	508	(D)	1 247	98	3 265	2 231	2 013
Sheep and lambs sold ... farms, 1987	34	8	11	9	11	33	18	10
1982	24	6	11	16	5	27	12	14
number, 1987	1 800	411	828	973	58	2 657	1 449	1 493
1982	1 151	387	993	1 774	268	2 143	1 609	1 358
Hens and pullets of laying age inventory ... farms, 1987	34	20	24	28	18	31	25	9
1982	50	19	24	31	35	45	24	18
number, 1987	45 320	(D)	(D)	(D)	825	(D)	1 343	356
Broilers and other meat-type chickens sold ... farms, 1987	(D)	-	-	1 389	2 509	2	(D)	895
1982	2	-	1	-	-	2	-	-
number, 1987	(D)	-	-	-	-	(D)	-	-
1982	(D)	-	-	(D)	-	(D)	-	-

See footnotes at end of table.

Table 16. **Farms With Sales of $10,000 or More: 1987 and 1982**—Con.

[Data for 1987 include abnormal farms. For meaning of abbreviations and symbols, see introductory text]

Item	Phillips	Pottawatomie	Pratt	Rawlins	Reno	Republic	Rice	Riley
MACHINERY AND EQUIPMENT[1]								
Estimated market value of all machinery and								
equipment .... farms, 1987..	433	455	391	418	909	626	420	327
1982..	486	525	437	512	1 092	679	481	344
$1,000, 1987..	24 947	18 979	37 249	27 772	60 226	41 893	33 904	16 656
1982..	27 038	26 770	36 337	38 106	69 136	47 721	43 676	19 200
Average per farm .... dollars, 1987..	57 614	41 711	95 265	66 439	66 257	66 922	80 723	57 668
1982..	55 634	50 990	83 150	74 429	63 312	70 282	90 803	55 814
Motortrucks, Including pickups .... farms, 1987..	419	439	386	406	816	595	413	307
1982..	444	522	421	511	1 007	647	445	335
number, 1987..	1 257	1 124	1 401	1 259	2 639	1 542	1 310	841
1982..	1 123	1 219	1 259	1 429	2 683	1 718	1 390	837
Wheel tractors .... farms, 1987..	413	376	363	382	838	580	398	297
1982..	461	466	409	447	1 010	640	455	307
number, 1987..	1 574	1 208	948	1 284	2 552	1 780	1 258	1 118
1982..	1 306	1 361	1 051	1 303	2 692	1 877	1 306	1 098
Grain and bean combines[2] .... farms, 1987..	278	283	258	263	717	478	306	211
1982..	322	313	333	333	708	511	354	226
number, 1987..	353	302	355	366	909	567	394	272
1982..	414	350	404	444	944	610	489	278
LIVESTOCK AND POULTRY								
Cattle and calves inventory .... farms, 1987..	353	369	215	285	544	397	251	244
1982..	410	434	239	363	669	455	299	265
number, 1987..	49 844	53 075	59 711	44 056	64 300	56 346	48 090	29 105
1982..	63 125	65 160	56 794	46 333	71 235	57 565	54 211	33 029
Cows and heifers that had calved .... farms, 1987..	326	321	138	258	442	361	198	201
1982..	390	387	170	329	560	455	223	235
number, 1987..	24 911	20 509	5 371	19 164	19 518	13 323	9 048	11 880
1982..	28 472	22 702	7 062	22 879	22 670	15 912	9 810	11 129
Beef cows .... farms, 1987..	322	309	135	251	365	358	188	187
1982..	387	367	161	315	466	443	204	220
number, 1987..	(D)	19 189	5 102	(D)	15 335	12 486	8 175	10 779
1982..	28 069	20 724	6 610	21 290	16 672	15 179	8 636	9 765
Milk cows.................................... farms, 1982..	26	48	6	13	112	16	19	28
1982..	30	80	18	36	132	31	31	43
number, 1987..	(D)	1 320	259	(D)	4 183	837	671	1 101
1982..	998	1 978	452	1 589	4 196	733	1 174	1 364
Heifers and heifer calves .... farms, 1987..	286	306	149	225	421	322	192	208
number, 1987..	12 409	14 777	17 520	10 398	16 465	12 490	19 051	7 960
Steers, steer calves, bulls, and bull calves ..... farms, 1987..	313	345	184	260	450	362	225	222
number, 1987..	12 524	17 789	36 620	14 494	28 317	30 535	20 993	9 265
Cattle and calves sold .... farms, 1987..	359	379	224	287	554	416	263	257
1982..	413	436	238	376	666	510	313	272
number, 1987..	27 554	39 192	104 064	23 703	76 883	94 763	69 257	20 541
1982..	32 047	43 062	76 234	23 218	67 155	67 053	56 560	21 466
Calves .... farms, 1987..	146	157	38	162	292	160	101	83
number, 1987..	5 454	5 570	4 077	5 612	7 182	3 198	3 562	2 114
Cattle .... farms, 1987..	319	326	189	231	466	366	229	235
1982..	318	379	202	274	532	415	263	245
number, 1987..	22 100	33 622	99 967	18 091	69 701	91 565	65 695	18 427
1982..	24 315	35 907	72 633	14 429	58 965	62 150	52 631	19 001
Fattened on grain and concentrates .... farms, 1987..	30	51	29	40	52	42	22	64
number, 1987..	1 572	6 270	(D)	(D)	46 853	(D)	46 972	8 342
Hogs and pigs inventory......................... farms, 1987..	91	159	20	62	97	101	28	85
1982..	108	200	21	74	148	148	51	120
number, 1987..	40 945	35 529	17 857	11 409	20 825	19 360	(D)	29 392
1982..	34 851	42 625	19 101	10 365	21 789	32 247	20 392	22 621
Used or to be used for breeding .... farms, 1987..	58	126	16	53	69	59	24	68
1982..	91	172	14	52	94	103	32	89
number, 1987..	5 044	4 561	1 732	2 020	3 002	2 200	(D)	2 952
1982..	3 965	6 256	1 606	2 044	2 932	3 453	2 419	3 138
Other .... farms, 1987..	87	153	17	53	98	99	26	84
1982..	100	191	21	66	138	141	48	116
number, 1987..	35 901	30 966	16 125	9 389	17 823	17 160	(D)	26 440
1982..	30 886	36 369	17 495	8 321	18 857	28 794	17 973	19 683
Hogs and pigs sold .... farms, 1987..	100	168	22	62	106	111	34	97
1982..	114	211	26	73	156	162	55	130
number, 1987..	67 038	63 700	25 228	25 066	40 348	32 934	25 991	49 674
1982..	56 203	63 605	27 687	25 152	42 773	50 070	34 657	40 014
Feeder pigs .... farms, 1987..	10	25	2	3	32	23	9	21
1982..	24	38	4	33	45	36	21	33
number, 1987..	4 426	8 599	(D)	11 961	6 663	(D)	6 112	
1982..	(D)	10 962	(D)	8 381	(D)	7 294	6 394	
Sheep and lambs inventory .... farms, 1987..	13	5	12	5	88	26	10	14
1982..	13	5	10	12	113	21	6	9
number, 1987..	656	186	847	113	11 931	3 606	877	2 660
1982..	411	276	(D)	3 452	17 954	3 541	499	(D)
Sheep and lambs sold .... farms, 1987..	14	6	11	4	89	28	10	13
1982..	14	5	10	15	110	24	9	8
number, 1987..	584	295	615	(D)	7 559	2 850	610	2 356
1982..	267	567	(D)	1 939	10 481	2 526	534	1 794
Hens and pullets of laying age inventory .... farms, 1987..	27	32	15	34	66	30	13	24
1982..	47	44	22	60	123	31	19	35
number, 1987..	(D)	2 393	315	1 641	(D)	(D)	(D)	(D)
1982..	2 612	2 919	(D)	4 837	173 459	3 028	884	(D)
Broilers and other meat-type chickens sold .... farms, 1987..	1	-	1	2	6	-	-	-
1982..	3	1	-	-	5	-	-	(D)
number, 1987..	-	(D)	-	-	22 125	-	-	
1982..	(D)	(D)	(D)	(D)	(D)	-	-	

See footnotes at end of table.

Table 16. **Farms With Sales of $10,000 or More: 1987 and 1982**—Con.

[Data for 1987 include abnormal farms. For meaning of abbreviations and symbols, see introductory text]

Item	Rooks	Rush	Russell	Saline	Scott	Sedgwick	Seward	Shawnee
MACHINERY AND EQUIPMENT[1]								
Estimated market value of all machinery and								
equipment .... farms, 1987..	338	367	337	399	313	787	240	339
1982..	402	455	406	488	336	930	215	311
$1,000, 1987..	22 438	23 716	21 173	27 660	39 129	58 500	28 384	16 338
1982..	27 725	34 488	25 320	34 695	35 251	67 767	18 423	20 953
Average per term................... dollars, 1987..	66 384	64 622	62 827	69 323	125 014	74 333	118 265	48 188
1982..	68 967	75 797	62 363	71 095	105 228	72 868	85 687	67 374
Motortrucks, including pickups .... farms, 1987..	311	354	320	381	307	753	214	326
1982..	386	440	397	447	324	843	212	294
number, 1987..	1 056	1 090	895	1 178	1 219	2 195	813	866
1982..	1 178	1 475	1 001	1 185	1 250	2 224	625	840
Wheel tractors .... farms, 1987..	284	317	313	381	278	743	202	332
1982..	363	443	357	428	294	874	192	271
number, 1987..	690	867	744	1 135	837	2 225	586	863
1982..	970	1 225	862	1 125	791	2 207	424	791
Grain and bean combines[2] .... farms, 1987..	210	263	180	290	186	615	150	219
1982..	299	352	190	334	205	720	97	169
number, 1987..	249	402	238	419	218	779	179	242
1982..	336	490	288	447	246	877	125	183
LIVESTOCK AND POULTRY								
Cattle and calves inventory .... farms, 1987..	242	229	250	250	117	417	81	197
1982..	276	311	298	315	143	498	88	197
number, 1987..	34 407	20 790	32 534	34 030	189 601	37 165	85 541	15 346
1982..	38 179	32 214	34 584	42 803	142 545	42 440	78 516	16 666
Cows and heifers that had calved .... farms, 1987..	222	201	234	215	36	328	52	162
1982..	254	252	262	269	67	387	59	165
number, 1987..	16 526	9 522	16 183	14 464	5 029	15 608	3 104	5 874
1982..	17 431	11 675	15 192	14 470	4 727	16 475	5 202	6 621
Beef cows .... farms, 1987..	214	194	217	198	36	250	51	152
1982..	242	250	244	248	64	297	57	151
number, 1987..	15 738	(D)	(O)	13 067	(D)	8 650	(D)	5 516
1982..	16 200	11 461	14 206	12 880	4 689	9 667	5 196	5 946
Milk cows................................... farms, 1987..	20	11	25	25	1	84	3	15
1982..	31	11	28	40	6	112	4	21
number, 1987..	788	(D)	(D)	1 397	(D)	6 956	(D)	358
1982..	1 231	214	964	1 590	38	6 808	6	675
Heifers and heifer calves .... farms, 1987..	200	175	191	200	89	322	67	149
number, 1987..	8 271	4 756	8 614	8 815	76 517	11 509	29 276	3 647
Steers, steer calves, bulls, and bull calves .... farms, 1987..	222	207	222	228	85	341	74	178
number, 1987..	9 610	6 512	7 727	10 751	88 055	9 950	53 161	5 825
Cattle and calves sold .... farms, 1987..	254	241	256	264	131	434	87	219
1982..	288	324	315	322	156	498	91	211
number, 1987..	22 357	14 636	20 313	24 197	393 371	23 314	145 572	12 517
1982..	28 584	23 309	23 115	36 262	311 090	26 553	164 483	13 280
Calves .... farms, 1987..	126	114	140	103	25	206	24	85
1982..	5 002	2 784	4 802	3 975	851	6 080	2 123	1 956
Cattle .... 1987..	207	211	213	234	119	353	75	205
1982..	239	257	249	285	143	407	78	178
number, 1987..	17 355	11 854	15 511	20 222	392 520	17 234	143 449	10 561
1982..	23 888	17 026	16 915	33 856	308 431	21 841	160 042	10 895
Fattened on grain and concentrates .... farms, 1987..	17	8	21	13	46	84	13	31
number, 1987..	4 202	286	1 636	720	309 059	2 727	(D)	1 872
Hogs and pigs inventory....................... farms, 1987..	32	8	30	31	22	68	11	33
1982..	32	14	32	36	25	93	13	55
number, 1987..	2 814	(D)	4 060	21 040	29 964	14 500	(D)	4 297
1982..	5 783	1 500	3 305	24 919	25 368	16 666	10 368	8 608
Used or to be used for breeding .... farms, 1987..	19	2	23	20	14	43	8	20
1982..	22	7	19	22	20	49	11	42
number, 1987..	(O)	(D)	700	2 027	(D)	1 162	(D)	522
1982..	(O)	129	(D)	2 346	2 927	836	(D)	1 164
Other .... farms, 1987..	27	8	28	30	21	67	10	32
1982..	32	14	27	34	24	86	13	51
number, 1987..	(D)	(D)	3 360	19 013	(D)	13 338	(D)	3 775
1982..	(D)	1 371	(D)	22 573	22 441	15 830	(D)	7 442
Hogs and pigs sold .... farms, 1987..	33	9	29	34	21	74	11	34
1982..	38	17	34	43	24	103	16	60
number, 1987..	5 153	(D)	9 151	43 507	45 601	29 242	(D)	14 714
1982..	12 065	2 251	9 094	41 213	42 656	37 223	19 478	17 299
Feeder pigs................................... farms, 1987..	8	1	14	10	4	22	3	9
1982..	8	4	7	8	6	22	7	21
number, 1987..	(D)	(D)	(D)	(D)	4 059	(D)	3 666	
1982..	(O)	(D)	1 171	999	3 840	2 401	(D)	4 842
Sheep and lambs inventory .... farms, 1987..	10	6	7	11	2	42	-	-
1982..	8	13	7	11	5	51	-	1
number, 1987..	315	1 273	829	1 106	(D)	13 982	-	-
1982..	267	2 985	822	1 607	1 669	32 848	57	(D)
Sheep and lambs sold .... farms, 1987..	10	6	7	12	2	44	-	1
1982..	6	10	7	12	5	51	4	1
number, 1987..	250	1 045	404	1 895	(D)	14 150	-	-
1982..	(D)	2 208	610	1 120	792	43 155	(D)	(D)
Hens and pullets of laying age inventory .... farms, 1987..	18	17	22	17	4	27	4	12
1982..	28	37	30	41	14	53	15	14
number, 1987..	(D)	(D)	(D)	(D)	88	(D)	61	(D)
1982..	(D)	3	1 386	(D)	(D)	599	(D)	(D)
Broilers and other meat-type chickens sold ...... farms, 1987..	1	-	-	3	-	1	1	-
1982..	-	265	-	-	-	-	-	-
number, 1987..	(D)		-	-	-	1	1	-
1982..	-	-	-	(D)	-	(D)	(D)	-

See footnotes at end of table.

Table 16. Farms With Sales of $10,000 or More: 1987 and 1982—Con.

[Data for 1987 include abnormal farms. For meaning of abbreviations and symbols, see introductory text.]

Item	Sheridan	Sherman	Smith	Stafford	Stanton	Stevens	Sumner	Thomas
MACHINERY AND EQUIPMENT[1]								
Estimated market value of all machinery and equipment ... farms, 1987..	420	411	554	393	226	242	771	494
1982..	494	458	622	515	231	291	1 017	519
$1,000, 1987..	36 038	37 102	37 798	40 531	30 700	42 628	57 243	47 236
1982..	43 900	50 663	41 343	42 937	30 254	37 913	79 784	46 846
Average per farm ... dollars, 1987..	83 420	90 274	68 228	103 132	135 840	176 148	74 246	95 619
1982..	88 867	110 619	66 469	83 373	130 971	130 287	78 450	90 267
Motortrucks, Including pickups ... farms, 1987..	411	396	653	390	223	235	750	491
1982..	491	415	574	514	222	281	966	476
number, 1987..	1 373	1 251	1 740	1 332	918	1 151	2 402	1 623
1982..	1 574	1 412	1 622	1 567	867	1 051	2 938	1 536
Wheel tractors ... farms, 1987..	370	380	533	354	221	231	700	477
1982..	443	415	553	459	210	270	931	415
number, 1987..	1 095	1 018	1 747	1 082	637	745	1 969	1 247
1982..	1 174	1 237	1 560	1 364	626	699	2 460	1 067
Grain and bean,combines[2] ... farms, 1987..	280	198	418	307	123	173	564	324
1982..	365	264	460	400	141	201	811	265
number, 1987..	359	247	532	350	138	206	806	388
1982..	416	376	525	(D)	168	248	1 183	312
LIVESTOCK AND POULTRY								
Cattle and calves inventory ... farms, 1987..	260	145	396	218	80	95	419	187
1982..	318	184	479	248	71	104	573	212
number, 1987..	42 692	33 215	53 535	61 632	49 115	51 903	38 703	35 966
1982..	57 685	36 875	66 845	53 057	44 515	18 916	42 014	42 633
Cows and heifers that had calved ... farms, 1987..	214	110	346	152	38	75	300	153
1982..	284	143	429	192	45	89	438	166
number, 1987..	14 416	8 065	21 091	12 504	1 987	5 167	11 911	8 827
1982..	16 935	9 912	28 015	13 662	(D)	5 243	12 693	9 870
Beef cows ... farms, 1987..	209	107	331	152	38	75	283	153
1982..	277	139	410	190	45	67	422	165
number, 1987..	(D)	7 955	20 205	(D)	1 387	5 167	10 669	(D)
1982..	(D)	9 493	27 164	(D)	(D)	(D)	11 452	9 828
Milk cows ... farms, 1987..	14	11	38	3	-	-	26	10
1982..	42	15	42	8	2	5	33	9
number, 1987..	(D)	110	866	(D)	-	-	1 242	(D)
1982..	(D)	419	851	(D)	(D)	(D)	1 241	42
Heifers and heifer calves ... farms, 1987..	187	115	325	171	56	76	308	150
number, 1987..	11 852	7 470	12 689	19 361	28 021	14 261	10 276	8 690
Steers, steer calves, bulls, and bull calves ... farms, 1987..	229	120	359	190	53	84	362	153
number, 1987..	16 724	17 680	19 555	29 767	19 707	32 455	16 516	19 449
Cattle and calves sold ... farms, 1987..	266	147	414	224	84	103	435	197
1982..	331	187	495	256	78	108	590	221
number, 1987..	48 292	53 914	43 126	86 498	98 820	(D)	32 227	55 277
1982..	49 886	39 210	49 150	58 685	(D)	44 022	31 934	54 276
Calves ... farms, 1987..	90	67	140	55	21	30	161	79
number, 1987..	3 117	3 395	4 087	3 549	592	2 152	3 307	2 095
Cattle ... farms, 1987..	224	127	377	195	80	90	356	165
1982..	279	147	426	202	65	85	488	175
number, 1987..	45 175	50 519	39 039	82 947	98 228	(D)	28 920	53 182
1982..	45 111	34 722	43 534	55 816	75 666	42 217	28 992	50 941
Fattened on grain and concentrates ... farms, 1987..	46	27	45	34	15	5	57	43
number, 1987..	30 197	41 772	10 843	44 067	85 224	(D)	4 120	44 827
Hogs and pigs inventory ... farms, 1987..	52	18	93	24	6	6	69	17
1982..	82	39	138	21	12	6	100	31
number, 1987..	6 976	1 753	27 627	4 004	102	(D)	20 297	5 737
1982..	10 726	6 444	29 162	3 211	(D)	(D)	21 999	8 595
Used or to be used for breeding ... farms, 1987..	31	11	68	15	3	5	49	16
1982..	43	23	110	19	5	6	70	(D)
number, 1987..	897	594	3 661	(D)	23	448	2 482	(D)
1982..	1 438	732	3 996	(D)	(D)	6	2 224	902
Other ... farms, 1987..	52	17	90	22	4	6	64	15
1982..	78	37	125	20	12	8	90	26
number, 1987..	6 079	1 159	23 966	(D)	79	(D)	17 815	(D)
1982..	9 288	5 712	25 166	(D)	(D)	(D)	19 775	7 693
Hogs and pigs sold ... farms, 1987..	49	21	102	26	6	6	74	19
1982..	83	47	147	22	12	10	104	37
number, 1987..	11 860	12 168	63 104	8 137	230	5 132	47 353	12 374
1982..	19 906	18 268	55 830	5 337	(D)	4 929	36 786	17 258
Feeder pigs ... farms, 1987..	13	9	26	5	1	3	14	5
1982..	19	7	47	2	4	3	26	5
number, 1987..	(D)	(D)	9 357	(D)	(D)	(D)	3 151	(D)
1982..	2 342	(D)	13 557	(D)	(D)	(D)	7 002	1 290
Sheep and lambs inventory ... farms, 1987..	8	9	31	11	4	5	43	11
1982..	13	13	39	12	2	1	54	13
number, 1987..	(D)	(D)	2 286	1 054	64	(D)	8 853	1 495
1982..	(D)	(D)	5 397	1 532	(D)	(D)	8 533	3 881
Sheep and lambs sold ... farms, 1987..	9	12	33	9	4	2	40	12
1982..	13	15	39	10	2	1	50	14
number, 1987..	(D)	(D)	1 543	1 828	40	(D)	6 758	1 018
1982..	2 648	(D)	1 174	(D)	(D)	(D)	6 003	3 717
Hens and pullets of laying age inventory ... farms, 1987..	27	23	46	16	4	8	26	24
1982..	34	26	56	26	13	17	35	20
number, 1987..	(D)	548	(D)	(D)	(D)	(D)	(D)	472
1982..	(D)	(D)	(D)	772	(D)	(D)	(D)	699
Broilers and other meat-type chickens sold ... farms, 1987..	-	1	4	-	-	-	3	1
1982..	-	-	-	-	-	-	1	-
number, 1987..	-	(D)	(D)	-	-	-	(D)	(D)
1982..	-	(D)	-	-	-	-	(D)	-

See footnotes at end of table.

Table 16. **Farms With Sales of $10,000 or More: 1987 and 1982**—Con.

[Data for 1987 include abnormal farms. For meaning of abbreviations and symbols, see introductory text.]

Item	Trego	Wabaunsee	Wallace	Washington	Wichita	Wilson	Woodson	Wyandotte
MACHINERY AND EQUIPMENT[1]								
Estimated market value of all machinery and								
equipment .... farms, 1987..	386	360	257	707	306	343	224	36
1982..	375	406	250	785	298	410	227	50
$1,000, 1987..	27 056	15 693	21 199	45 071	29 505	19 117	10 816	3 002
1982..	27 977	22 162	24 055	52 636	29 704	23 115	13 358	3 396
Average per farm...................... dollars, 1987..	70 094	43 593	82 487	63 750	96 422	55 733	48 731	83 381
1982..	74 606	54 586	96 218	67 054	99 677	56 378	58 847	67 925
Motortrucks, including pickups .... farms, 1987..	356	345	244	677	292	336	212	36
1982..	352	393	240	715	259	398	221	49
number, 1987..	1 121	880	773	1 612	1 116	1 005	608	113
1982..	1 129	910	675	1 693	1 018	993	542	132
Wheel tractors .... farms, 1987..	350	316	240	631	256	319	222	32
1982..	346	339	206	733	231	383	220	44
number, 1987..	797	830	611	2 056	667	949	629	109
1982..	873	842	519	2 007	693	913	597	134
Grain and bean combines[2] .... farms, 1987..	307	203	138	459	160	241	131	5
1982..	287	253	109	576	146	326	142	12
number, 1987..	359	230	159	528	196	263	160	(D)
1982..	372	253	152	642	180	412	153	12
LIVESTOCK AND POULTRY								
Cattle and calves inventory .... farms, 1987..	293	271	127	538	120	250	173	17
1982..	292	322	141	598	143	314	193	20
number, 1987..	37 873	48 407	21 950	54 961	90 155	24 253	20 164	866
1982..	42 876	71 625	30 697	68 480	81 490	32 248	33 481	2 725
Cows and heifers that had calved .... farms, 1987..	263	223	105	442	80	220	151	15
1982..	263	277	104	502	99	298	174	18
number, 1987..	15 831	17 749	10 074	20 840	5 770	10 713	7 556	452
1982..	17 509	19 281	12 013	22 894	6 876	14 775	12 395	(D)
Beef cows .... farms, 1987..	243	210	101	413	80	213	150	14
1982..	243	260	101	452	95	277	167	15
number, 1987..	14 957	16 803	9 977	(D)	5 770	10 070	(D)	(D)
1982..	16 472	18 197	11 924	19 876	(D)	13 911	11 890	972
Milk cows .... farms, 1987..	30	32	11	45	–	13	5	3
1982..	42	43	18	88	6	28	19	4
number, 1987..	874	946	97	(D)	–	643	(D)	(D)
1982..	1 037	1 084	89	2 616	(D)	864	405	(D)
Heifers and heifer calves .... farms, 1987..	202	214	107	430	90	218	146	14
number, 1987..	10 029	12 488	5 706	15 189	26 664	6 752	6 215	240
Steers, steer calves, bulls, and bull calves .... farms, 1987..	250	242	112	478	102	235	159	14
number, 1987..	12 013	18 170	6 170	18 932	57 721	6 788	8 390	174
Cattle and calves sold .... farms, 1987..	298	285	141	548	121	256	181	18
1982..	298	341	143	603	144	315	196	19
number, 1987..	42 592	41 211	22 163	40 532	294 581	13 207	25 431	(D)
1982..	58 648	56 191	21 462	45 416	203 850	17 054	32 830	1 143
Calves .... farms, 1987..	165	93	74	181	42	101	63	11
number, 1987..	6 089	4 410	3 546	4 312	1 800	2 481	2 404	(D)
Cattle .... farms, 1987..	242	260	122	482	102	234	163	15
1982..	263	305	119	535	119	256	169	15
number, 1987..	36 503	36 801	18 617	36 220	292 781	10 726	23 027	1 137
1982..	50 989	52 175	16 958	40 408	201 580	11 989	29 784	949
Fattened on grain and concentrates .... farms, 1987..	6	34	14	92	24	18	24	7
number, 1987..	(D)	4 065	5 575	11 954	277 148	825	(D)	318
Hogs and pigs inventory........................ farms, 1987..	35	56	17	232	14	37	20	3
1982..	45	62	25	260	36	60	46	4
number, 1987..	(D)	19 246	2 363	92 855	(D)	12 199	2 500	(D)
1982..	5 300	16 651	1 900	77 959	4 868	17 388	5 292	(D)
Used or to be used for breeding .... farms, 1987..	19	39	7	155	8	26	14	3
1982..	20	51	17	191	19	45	37	3
number, 1987..	(D)	2 701	114	9 867	(D)	1 865	328	(D)
1982..	503	2 287	347	9 524	(D)	2 154	651	(D)
Other .... farms, 1987..	34	51	17	226	12	37	19	3
1982..	43	76	20	245	36	58	41	4
number, 1987..	(D)	16 545	2 239	82 788	(D)	10 534	2 172	(D)
1982..	4 797	14 364	1 553	68 435	(D)	15 234	4 641	(D)
Hogs and pigs sold .... farms, 1987..	34	60	23	239	14	37	24	4
1982..	47	92	25	277	40	64	52	3
number, 1987..	(D)	37 277	5 034	165 365	3 005	22 009	4 761	(D)
1982..	9 450	32 700	6 651	147 981	9 474	34 058	9 500	(D)
Feeder pigs................................... farms, 1987..	10	21	5	49	1	10	10	3
1982..	11	33	5	70	5	19	11	1
number, 1987..	1 124	9 375	(D)	29 992	(D)	(D)	(D)	(D)
1982..	975	9 765	(D)	25 955	(D)	11 140	1 363	(D)
Sheep and lambs inventory .... farms, 1987..	9	13	14	34	9	8	13	2
1982..	9	9	9	37	11	6	17	1
number, 1987..	569	3 614	2 967	2 786	578	765	1 155	(D)
1982..	1 547	2 220	6 485	4 777	5 185	845	1 326	(D)
Sheep and lambs sold .... farms, 1987..	9	13	14	33	8	9	12	2
1982..	7	9	14	35	10	11	16	–
number, 1987..	456	3 380	4 317	1 628	(D)	412	1 116	(D)
1982..	925	1 676	(D)	2 713	(D)	653	952	–
Hens and pullets of laying age inventory .... farms, 1987..	31	18	16	42	10	8	12	1
1982..	41	29	28	48	35	22	14	1
number, 1987..	(D)	(D)	(D)	(D)	(D)	(D)	189	100
1982..	(D)	(D)	611	(D)	918	(D)	321	(D)
Broilers and other meat-type chickens sold .... farms, 1987..	1	1	–	4	–	1	–	–
1982..	3	1	1	(D)	–	1	–	–
number, 1987..	(D)	(D)	–	(D)	–	(D)	–	–
1982..	75	(D)	(D)	210	–	(D)	(D)	–

See footnotes at end of table.

Table 16. **Farms With Sales of $10,000 or More: 1987 and 1982**—Con.

[Data for 1987 include abnormal farms. For meaning of abbreviations and symbols, see introductory text]

Item	Kansas	Allen	Anderson	Atchison	Barber	Barton	Bourbon
CROPS HARVESTED							
Corn for grain or seed ... farms, 1987	8 028	88	186	250	-	43	87
1982	7 635	93	218	222	6	33	79
acres, 1987	1 229 426	7 370	13 425	21 970	-	9 382	5 736
1982	1 151 181	4 816	15 054	15 981	(D)	6 679	5 180
bushels, 1987	143 105 352	590 938	1 098 743	1 867 547	-	1 188 648	470 886
1982	130 030 333	321 779	1 104 331	1 357 827	142 250	876 725	382 063
Sorghum for grain or seed ... farms, 1987	27 102	225	283	303	95	432	158
1982	23 836	207	241	301	71	441	172
acres, 1987	3 362 294	17 767	21 629	30 367	6 729	40 564	10 922
1982	3 104 201	16 752	16 897	26 441	(D)	48 599	13 425
bushels, 1987	221 096 837	1 325 862	1 653 391	2 426 647	339 468	2 817 736	642 475
1982	189 097 099	1 032 001	1 169 535	1 715 924	(D)	2 717 773	847 382
Wheat for grain ... farms, 1987	30 569	118	118	113	305	564	50
1982	39 957	299	305	319	368	647	231
acres, 1987	8 225 848	8 991	6 477	4 907	115 961	155 722	3 060
1982	11 218 194	35 648	25 539	21 164	159 384	207 851	25 011
bushels, 1987	280 906 698	259 948	191 314	130 447	3 214 687	5 086 901	78 242
1982	362 029 226	951 160	593 954	439 713	5 742 446	6 743 538	564 822
Oats for grain ... farms, 1987	4 491	63	75	91	12	47	44
1982	5 590	69	106	83	31	24	68
acres, 1987	117 316	1 813	2 033	2 388	(D)	813	1 190
1982	154 957	1 773	2 463	1 565	1 233	333	1 459
bushels, 1987	4 463 199	71 131	56 825	120 909	(D)	38 029	36 408
1982	7 299 415	98 995	102 168	67 060	44 462	14 711	68 658
Soybeans for beans ... farms, 1987	15 037	284	358	352	15	77	206
1982	13 825	320	391	361	8	37	272
acres, 1987	1 779 543	58 368	77 920	41 742	(D)	8 945	29 372
1982	1 601 824	49 681	63 544	39 652	1 358	(D)	39 512
bushels, 1987	53 527 794	1 711 364	2 552 843	1 420 412	(D)	266 240	745 166
1982	41 381 772	1 153 050	1 644 693	1 042 634	52 860	(D)	874 937
Hay—alfalfa, other tame, small grain, wild, grass silage, green chop, etc. (see text) ... farms, 1987	24 304	272	328	273	198	408	282
1982	27 363	310	357	324	200	467	299
acres, 1987	1 990 641	25 416	34 534	16 116	17 796	35 173	28 306
1982	1 979 606	23 643	36 621	16 961	16 757	35 988	23 769
tons, dry, 1987	4 689 290	42 159	54 494	31 839	50 593	102 620	48 236
1982	4 694 142	43 430	60 600	39 925	41 078	103 735	43 125

Item	Brown	Butler	Chase	Chautauqua	Cherokee	Cheyenne	Clark
CROPS HARVESTED							
Corn for grain or seed ... farms, 1987	318	40	37	9	66	95	-
1982	379	15	33	7	43	101	2
acres, 1987	47 695	3 138	(D)	610	5 037	18 568	-
1982	51 860	(D)	1 599	525	2 927	(D)	(D)
bushels, 1987	4 683 632	247 742	(D)	40 110	494 665	2 366 495	-
1982	5 139 204	(D)	79 816	26 880	224 063	(D)	(D)
Sorghum for grain or seed ... farms, 1987	309	391	99	52	203	121	101
1982	287	339	96	34	113	92	79
acres, 1987	27 635	65 268	7 264	4 892	19 613	10 880	9 161
1982	23 780	58 155	6 283	4 494	9 105	(D)	7 542
bushels, 1987	2 219 294	4 625 466	499 838	270 900	1 374 999	700 202	513 068
1982	1 823 175	2 852 857	363 979	187 609	584 670	(D)	287 640
Wheat for grain ... farms, 1987	334	387	110	56	118	342	181
1982	502	459	138	113	390	415	207
acres, 1987	28 001	60 943	11 194	7 070	16 357	103 801	67 546
1982	52 042	79 886	16 325	18 578	79 655	143 411	92 021
bushels, 1987	1 011 975	1 784 915	312 428	158 779	351 661	3 899 416	2 029 319
1982	1 466 877	2 608 999	444 773	618 674	2 170 507	5 189 654	2 641 582
Oats for grain ... farms, 1987	101	38	29	12	41	22	7
1982	146	81	53	35	57	12	2
acres, 1987	2 172	780	(D)	(D)	1 071	1 033	260
1982	2 893	2 423	932	972	1 509	1 153	(D)
bushels, 1987	97 208	24 833	(D)	(D)	31 163	54 676	7 718
1982	159 716	107 456	41 551	43 407	98 998	37 817	(D)
Soybeans for beans ... farms, 1987	464	233	101	39	306	35	3
1982	511	151	98	25	390	28	6
acres, 1987	76 115	22 657	9 159	8 052	93 234	4 029	(D)
1982	69 463	11 855	7 049	2 935	96 420	2 872	(D)
bushels, 1987	2 475 752	687 798	326 140	218 565	1 973 300	167 976	(D)
1982	2 028 845	198 000	156 970	61 048	1 706 953	91 162	(D)
Hay—alfalfa, other tame, small grain, wild, grass silage, green chop, etc. (see text) ... farms, 1987	305	410	142	122	231	143	99
1982	397	444	148	149	262	155	99
acres, 1987	15 043	44 790	11 481	10 606	13 363	10 877	11 032
1982	20 543	51 498	12 429	11 468	14 488	9 879	(D)
tons, dry, 1987	34 659	75 147	23 753	18 158	21 379	30 735	30 721
1982	49 311	86 420	26 406	19 761	18 659	32 620	(D)

See footnotes at end of table.

Table 16. Farms With Sales of $10,000 or More: 1987 and 1982—Con.

[Data for 1987 include abnormal farms. For meaning of abbreviations and symbols, see introductory text.]

Item	Clay	Cloud	Coffey	Comanche	Cowley	Crawford	Decatur
CROPS HARVESTED							
Corn for grain or seed .... farms, 1987..	70	58	126	7	10	91	109
1982..	91	65	129	1	2	91	69
acres, 1987..	7 349	(D)	7 732	609	(D)	7 502	16 925
1982..	(D)	(D)	7 004	(D)	(D)	6 466	(D)
bushels, 1987..	881 024	(D)	613 591	127 385	(D)	655 976	1 733 831
1982..	(D)	(D)	522 677	(D)	(D)	472 386	(D)
Sorghum for grain or seed........ farms, 1987..	396	339	290	76	263	259	290
1982..	330	254	226	63	260	249	227
acres, 1987..	40 372	35 907	23 861	(D)	26 618	24 294	36 139
1982..	30 111	23 575	19 328	(D)	24 476	23 482	28 462
bushels, 1987..	2 894 351	2 905 869	1 549 738	(D)	1 647 644	1 680 907	2 504 599
1982..	2 093 919	1 626 989	1 247 679	(D)	1 146 939	1 522 822	1 638 044
Wheat for grain .... farms, 1987..	424	384	161	159	353	51	343
1982..	490	450	317	184	551	303	388
acres, 1987..	75 279	104 907	11 204	69 838	85 529	3 559	89 823
1982..	104 891	141 988	36 327	94 669	138 957	31 408	115 577
bushels, 1987..	2 598 895	3 758 981	300 866	1 809 295	2 462 054	113 419	3 912 155
1982..	2 971 065	3 893 347	789 436	3 018 239	4 465 501	805 533	4 703 969
Oats for grain .... farms, 1987..	115	75	30	2	24	73	38
1982..	119	87	34	6	65	128	35
acres, 1987..	2 103	1 678	576	(D)	464	2 593	1 363
1982..	2 267	2 608	535	866	1 730	3 797	932
bushels, 1987..	100 394	76 371	17 673	(D)	10 622	98 637	54 566
1982..	96 638	124 936	23 123	23 341	82 227	226 381	53 635
Soybeans for beans .... farms, 1987..	304	207	345	8	99	307	12
1982..	257	153	340	4	48	369	4
acres, 1987..	22 416	11 778	67 748	(D)	5 227	52 562	954
1982..	15 497	8 718	57 597	1 469	(D)	63 131	259
bushels, 1987..	725 463	348 934	2 085 658	(D)	133 697	1 151 703	23 712
1982..	486 881	250 827	1 372 286	(D)	(D)	1 343 623	2 700
Hay—alfalfa, other tame, small grain, wild, grass silage, green chop, etc. (see text) ...... farms, 1987..	355	244	250	105	324	251	213
1982..	393	336	296	96	440	301	228
acres, 1987..	23 568	16 260	28 668	9 476	27 000	17 065	13 194
1982..	20 988	16 788	30 345	8 638	34 164	16 740	13 241
tons, dry, 1987..	48 187	36 428	38 392	27 114	54 486	29 999	42 173
1982..	47 902	48 191	43 540	20 254	71 079	28 927	41 873

Item	Dickinson	Doniphan	Douglas	Edwards	Elk	Ellis	Ellsworth
CROPS HARVESTED							
Corn for grain or seed .... farms, 1987..	40	307	148	100	7	2	5
1982..	92	347	152	51	7	9	3
acres, 1987..	1 849	55 033	15 283	38 522	(D)	(D)	(D)
1982..	3 233	55 771	14 247	16 525	149	1 445	(D)
bushels, 1987..	146 113	6 126 194	1 486 693	4 203 683	(D)	(D)	(D)
1982..	227 129	5 674 361	1 277 770	2 446 103	9 249	127 653	(D)
Sorghum for grain or seed........ farms, 1987..	515	71	172	171	81	256	244
1982..	422	84	153	183	62	165	198
acres, 1987..	45 458	4 195	17 342	20 007	4 986	20 702	17 579
1982..	35 288	5 553	12 912	34 213	5 345	16 371	15 054
bushels, 1987..	2 524 771	366 187	1 297 183	1 263 490	271 781	1 144 674	1 174 504
1982..	2 153 887	409 543	810 705	1 954 130	271 837	782 448	814 965
Wheat for grain .... farms, 1987..	594	113	61	246	78	394	313
1982..	720	286	233	298	128	438	363
acres, 1987..	124 910	7 894	2 581	83 959	5 717	67 079	79 933
1982..	182 759	27 143	21 193	111 482	18 036	107 108	107 060
bushels, 1987..	4 070 656	324 090	85 490	2 808 960	135 126	2 835 579	2 796 993
1982..	5 691 071	731 421	473 951	3 409 858	562 216	3 454 649	3 565 145
Oats for grain .... farms, 1987..	172	33	59	9	16	19	47
1982..	257	33	58	8	34	8	18
acres, 1987..	3 516	(D)	1 370	355	431	507	1 028
1982..	7 597	1 007	1 241	203	997	154	(D)
bushels, 1987..	119 050	(D)	43 591	10 060	11 277	17 375	34 022
1982..	304 396	55 500	60 637	(D)	38 646	6 788	(D)
Soybeans for beans .... farms, 1987..	298	324	241	90	75	–	28
1982..	241	361	219	84	56	3	13
acres, 1987..	14 100	51 480	39 118	21 083	8 658	–	1 530
1982..	10 506	51 965	28 921	24 177	4 815	695	(D)
bushels, 1987..	398 626	1 900 611	1 317 059	806 148	254 052	16 400	45 230
1982..	256 595	1 739 805	894 738	918 274	114 616	(D)	(D)
Hay—alfalfa, other tame, small grain, wild, grass silage, green chop, etc. (see text) ...... farms, 1987..	493	168	248	132	169	254	255
1982..	555	202	265	159	198	282	278
acres, 1987..	36 466	5 936	19 143	18 958	16 272	20 520	22 382
1982..	35 201	5 444	18 195	22 314	19 437	19 251	17 261
tons, dry, 1987..	85 366	15 569	38 054	76 301	24 045	47 751	46 833
1982..	91 505	14 588	38 142	87 329	31 480	46 660	37 120

See footnotes at end of table.

Table 16. **Farms With Sales of $10,000 or More: 1987 and 1982**—Con.

[Data for 1987 include abnormal farms. For meaning of abbreviations and symbols, see introductory text.]

Item	Finney	Ford	Franklin	Geary	Gove	Graham	Grant
CROPS HARVESTED							
Corn for grain or seed .... farms, 1987..	139	81	153	21	37	25	108
1982..	132	60	172	28	36	27	81
acres, 1987..	50 349	19 058	11 390	(D)	5 013	3 902	(D)
1982..	66 138	16 540	11 765	(D)	6 063	(D)	(D)
bushels, 1987..	6 716 727	2 317 716	898 124	(D)	547 514	375 964	(D)
1982..	8 874 784	1 997 590	938 350	(D)	722 974	(D)	(D)
Sorghum for grain or seed............ farms, 1987..	256	381	239	137	275	254	159
1982..	259	274	199	110	279	173	177
acres, 1987..	55 281	50 903	19 811	9 747	39 805	29 568	41 772
1982..	54 548	44 262	13 298	8 926	45 451	21 578	65 551
bushels, 1987..	3 938 051	3 854 986	1 443 327	660 173	2 476 478	1 802 752	2 331 269
1982..	4 104 308	2 870 163	839 349	667 734	2 690 915	1 102 447	· 4 051 461
Wheat for grain .... farms, 1987..	370	517	74	132	369	305	206
1982..	425	542	259	147	367	333	201
acres, 1987..	170 329	173 527	· 4 612	15 846	113 627	87 797	69 838
1982..	212 999	205 568	19 654	22 024	112 913	109 076	82 143
bushels, 1987..	7 024 551	6 207 927	126 874	572 486	4 373 033	3 404 004	2 576 267
1982..	7 890 243	6 583 201	389 972	726 102	3 311 504	3 550 041	3 592 549
Oats for grain .... farms, 1987..	6	23	90	53	14	19	3
1982..	5	9	143	42	17	16	3
acres, 1987..	(D)	(D)	1 647	1 106	(D)	765	(D)
1982..	375	649	3 171	851	(D)	(D)	45
bushels, 1987..	(D)	(D)	60 815	36 309	(D)	31 105	4 200
1982..	16 070	23 436	164 593	41 728	(D)	(D)	2 450
Soybeans for beans .... farms, 1987..	84	65	321	97	3	3	41
1982..	44	60	340	61	10	2	28
acres, 1987..	8 596	6 586	57 447	5 198	(D)	205	(D)
1982..	(D)	(D)	52 134	3 139	458	(D)	3 576
bushels, 1987..	261 431	233 727	1 781 482	157 908	15 294	(D)	(D)
1982..	(D)	(D)	1 130 054	90 663	14 089	(D)	116 642
Hay—alfalfa, other tame, small grain, wild, grass silage, green chop, etc. (see text) ...... farms, 1987..	155	234	315	132	147	148	59
1982..	181	184	352	134	170	175	65
acres, 1987..	29 793	19 241	26 545	12 192	14 637	11 601	7 046
1982..	39 522	14 600	26 543	10 915	13 691	11 563	(D)
tons, dry, 1987..	130 429	66 243	46 625	22 489	38 596	32 063	33 780
1982..	195 457	48 932	50 378	24 325	41 689	32 092	(D)

Item	Gray	Greeley	Greenwood	Hamilton	Harper	Harvey	Haskell
CROPS HARVESTED							
Corn for grain or seed .... farms, 1987..	195	37	24	22	1	78	152
1982..	202	18	22	9	2	58	158
acres, 1987..	(D)	(D)	1 102	4 574	(D)	10 908	55 783
1982..	(D)	(D)	1 144	(D)	(D)	(D)	80 411
bushels, 1987..	(D)	(D)	89 985	624 772	(D)	1 365 745	7 386 876
1982..	(D)	(D)	72 211	(D)	(D)	(D)	8 413 068
Sorghum for grain or seed............ farms, 1987..	249	104	139	114	76	399	146
1982..	230	46	124	81	41	415	164
acres, 1987..	48 796	16 260	11 796	18 223	3 576	52 715	32 471
1982..	51 724	16 733	11 017	14 752	3 291	61 731	43 901
bushels, 1987..	4 014 175	734 321	692 249	710 360	167 376	4 193 482	2 838 655
1982..	4 850 094	1 125 672	536 886	705 855	163 534	3 394 749	3 994 862
Wheat for grain .... farms, 1987..	386	190	132	174	443	445	237
1982..	424	191	218	195	520	555	260
acres, 1987..	129 181	139 831	9 156	122 861	201 868	95 964	97 033
1982..	182 014	155 309	20 388	173 982	263 404	121 505	126 893
bushels, 1987..	4 858 059	4 419 772	232 585	3 921 329	6 016 000	2 886 576	3 763 237
1982..	7 007 506	4 099 744	573 001	4 118 420	9 520 353	4 074 891	5 019 152
Oats for grain .... farms, 1987..	4	4	30	4	18	30	2
1982..	6		49		31	56	2
acres, 1987..	105	306	761	132	(D)	1 762	(D)
1982..	980	-	1 234	-	915	1 380	(D)
bushels, 1987..	2 450	6 187	21 462	2 493	(D)	21 562	(D)
1982..	70 975	-	45 382	-	33 685	75 046	(D)
Soybeans for beans .... farms, 1987..	65	9	154	2	3	195	52
1982..	84	1	134	2	3	183	71
acres, 1987..	5 388	499	18 274	(D)	(D)	12 594	(D)
1982..	10 084	(D)	10 896	(D)	(D)	14 519	6 937
bushels, 1987..	206 743	13 450	470 135	(D)	(D)	468 295	(D)
1982..	394 216	(D)	242 602	(D)	(D)	421 489	259 871
Hay—alfalfa, other tame, small grain, wild, grass silage, green chop, etc. (see text) ...... farms, 1987..	121	54	230	56	246	289	52
1982..	119	37	281	55	291	356	59
acres, 1987..	20 462	4 353	30 690	8 373	16 322	12 654	6 012
1982..	14 345	2 809	26 981	7 378	14 900	16 237	6 049
tons, dry, 1987..	103 303	10 689	46 715	26 707	39 268	32 895	23 801
1982..	61 494	6 610	44 285	24 567	34 289	34 267	22 335

See footnotes at end of table.

Table 16. **Farms With Sales of $10,000 or More: 1987 and 1982**—Con.

[Data for 1987 include abnormal farms. For meaning of abbreviations and symbols, see introductory text.]

CROPS HARVESTED

Item	Hodgeman	Jackson	Jefferson	Jewell	Johnson	Kearny	Kingman	Kiowa
Corn for grain or seed ... farms, 1987..	33	163	195	64	88	38	24	52
1982..	14	160	201	58	96	33	10	21
acres, 1987..	(D)	11 935	21 963	6 259	8 389	(D)	(D)	13 151
1982..	1 546	11 751	21 199	6 808	7 539	37 732	(D)	5 114
bushels, 1987..	(D)	822 623	1 975 749	735 945	733 038	(D)	(D)	1 742 065
1982..	161 916	799 354	1 736 769	681 424	696 356	5 118 081	(D)	670 085
Sorghum for grain or seed... farms, 1987..	255	268	189	444	75	135	204	156
1982..	163	243	170	407	75	115	178	159
acres, 1987..	30 716	21 202	15 453	56 772	4 185	25 178	11 226	21 030
1982..	21 302	16 524	11 498	47 270	4 632	21 726	12 335	26 366
bushels, 1987..	1 892 248	1 249 598	1 104 287	4 165 032	309 831	1 234 043	604 239	1 476 300
1982..	1 052 653	852 854	683 443	2 981 500	280 815	1 166 644	585 553	1 429 788
Wheat for grain ... farms, 1987..	308	120	72	467	39	193	467	208
1982..	352	323	264	557	162	208	594	257
acres, 1987..	101 843	8 263	3 675	104 595	2 352	118 652	161 520	71 298
1982..	122 857	30 926	22 929	155 751	17 841	136 892	214 101	88 740
bushels, 1987..	3 554 717	217 922	121 719	4 213 520	68 723	4 451 831	4 653 953	2 244 884
1982..	4 171 833	498 704	471 079	5 220 482	544 671	4 695 649	6 851 803	2 544 480
Oats for grain ... farms, 1987..	4	74	70	104	39	7	45	10
1982..	2	86	88	93	42	2	64	5
acres, 1987..	131	1 951	1 840	2 731	675	516	1 475	717
1982..	(D)	2 250	2 222	2 913	812	(D)	2 320	1 187
bushels, 1987..	3 670	84 269	60 515	125 586	21 769	12 519	50 115	18 010
1982..	(D)	96 412	93 176	118 740	36 506	(D)	105 978	29 100
Soybeans for beans ... farms, 1987..	30	276	251	152	160	14	42	60
1982..	12	285	276	74	179	9	16	49
acres, 1987..	(D)	23 402	33 854	8 761	31 290	1 596	(D)	6 698
1982..	704	23 223	33 159	3 592	33 852	865	(D)	9 320
bushels, 1987..	(D)	623 218	1 093 861	250 451	976 364	32 278	(D)	270 986
1982..	28 532	510 613	866 862	109 321	958 951	32 209	(D)	388 151
Hay—alfalfa, other tame, small grain, wild, grass silage, green chop, etc. (see text) ... farms, 1987..	156	394	287	359	143	92	338	96
1982..	145	433	321	427	192	76	390	111
acres, 1987..	10 401	32 950	22 309	21 451	12 221	19 904	24 557	10 907
1982..	7 723	38 600	23 369	24 151	13 335	14 243	22 045	11 601
tons, dry, 1987..	27 245	56 220	41 915	55 132	21 782	88 127	59 487	36 132
1982..	22 404	76 478	45 997	66 180	25 239	56 077	46 325	37 330

CROPS HARVESTED

Item	Labette	Lane	Leavenworth	Lincoln	Linn	Logan	Lyon	McPherson
Corn for grain or seed ... farms, 1987..	38	8	211	6	73	16	162	101
1982..	50	14	165	10	76	17	119	86
acres, 1987..	2 058	643	15 936	1 120	6 376	3 448	10 720	11 522
1982..	2 487	2 036	10 969	266	5 510	4 576	6 577	8 079
bushels, 1987..	166 714	66 966	1 432 452	36 540	477 467	368 547	790 820	1 495 266
1982..	152 338	165 724	942 304	27 769	438 621	527 785	424 790	954 342
Sorghum for grain or seed... farms, 1987..	255	161	173	308	193	159	336	567
1982..	179	95	198	237	171	111	320	505
acres, 1987..	23 299	25 949	12 395	23 716	15 825	20 514	33 116	42 825
1982..	13 145	(D)	14 880	14 926	16 748	23 525	28 486	43 723
bushels, 1987..	1 895 367	1 389 706	819 900	1 571 055	1 094 985	988 496	2 233 073	3 487 183
1982..	762 820	(D)	935 630	953 980	981 992	1 188 122	1 514 376	2 987 672
Wheat for grain ... farms, 1987..	130	226	49	374	47	258	211	774
1982..	415	257	240	462	214	256	380	970
acres, 1987..	10 916	108 369	2 675	92 729	2 203	106 639	16 610	166 659
1982..	75 884	126 083	17 649	125 159	20 144	123 534	37 132	229 860
bushels, 1987..	228 873	4 127 238	75 388	3 224 647	59 541	3 429 192	469 397	5 671 212
1982..	2 083 531	4 132 234	364 814	4 186 638	457 927	3 585 782	793 696	7 150 197
Oats for grain ... farms, 1987..	131	11	67	74	46	21	42	40
1982..	189	2	63	65	75	7	86	83
acres, 1987..	4 610	(D)	1 373	1 830	1 120	1 329	1 306	569
1982..	6 173	(D)	837	(D)	1 640	328	1 511	1 472
bushels, 1987..	150 369	(D)	46 048	71 266	42 110	46 655	43 218	24 202
1982..	333 701	(D)	33 205	(D)	72 140	12 975	63 456	57 254
Soybeans for beans ... farms, 1987..	310	4	258	42	223	2	347	305
1982..	349	11	268	42	253	3	336	274
acres, 1987..	60 248	174	28 576	(D)	38 756	(D)	40 281	15 597
1982..	54 831	924	25 809	1 988	43 489	425	32 627	17 308
bushels, 1987..	1 426 484	5 240	897 088	(D)	1 159 706	(D)	1 249 985	536 877
1982..	873 521	30 170	755 454	52 203	1 068 590	(D)	707 225	541 569
Hay—alfalfa, other tame, small grain, wild, grass silage, green chop, etc. (see text) ... farms, 1987..	304	64	287	285	253	104	313	492
1982..	352	65	305	336	259	94	382	584
acres, 1987..	21 991	4 420	20 408	25 086	21 641	7 323	37 616	23 547
1982..	19 062	3 560	19 760	24 113	21 840	6 052	38 929	23 788
tons, dry, 1987..	37 747	8 284	41 171	86 121	37 636	14 704	50 955	60 366
1982..	31 759	8 686	44 562	65 334	35 770	15 560	57 829	61 009

See footnotes at end of table.

Table 16. **Farms With Sales of $10,000 or More: 1987 and 1982**—Con.

[Data for 1987 include abnormal farms. For meaning of abbreviations and symbols, see introductory text]

Item	Marion	Marshall	Meade	Miami	Mitchell	Montgomery	Morris	Morton
CROPS HARVESTED								
Corn for grain or seed .... farms, 1987..	78	99	79	114	26	61	57	9
1982..	84	123	50	108	24	63	57	10
acres, 1987..	3 889	5 859	(D)	9 395	2 392	7 798	2 583	(D)
1982..	3 554	6 606	13 834	8 725	1 886	6 026	2 599	(D)
bushels, 1987..	314 484	508 889	(D)	821 274	255 985	704 271	203 113	(D)
1982..	227 500	550 388	1 907 057	749 546	211 373	473 523	211 975	(D)
Sorghum for grain or seed........ farms, 1987..	595	704	248	191	381	188	278	127
1982..	585	641	194	180	269	145	246	134
acres, 1987..	64 995	87 936	55 462	15 901	47 077	26 760	25 685	56 351
1982..	65 947	72 487	61 219	12 538	30 490	18 415	20 063	75 967
bushels, 1987..	4 359 942	6 146 455	4 603 505	1 125 922	3 515 790	1 840 261	1 413 142	2 501 339
1982..	3 357 929	4 963 898	5 121 129	778 266	1 972 364	1 089 896	1 000 488	2 700 996
Wheat for grain .... farms, 1987..	640	676	335	34	442	128	251	135
1982..	767	772	348	222	455	269	313	145
acres, 1987..	108 875	72 963	102 760	1 393	159 855	14 831	33 698	69 574
1982..	145 733	96 410	119 711	16 428	190 005	57 000	48 444	85 637
bushels, 1987..	3 459 739	2 514 145	3 357 409	36 497	6 106 140	342 989	951 710	1 980 195
1982..	4 062 338	2 903 629	3 740 701	429 127	5 981 744	1 641 558	1 004 974	2 002 641
Oats for grain .... farms, 1987..	124	132	2	84	75	47	70	4
1982..	241	192	2	90	47	82	111	-
acres, 1987..	2 628	2 232	(D)	1 209	1 491	1 316	1 637	268
1982..	5 804	4 494	(D)	1 850	1 491	2 436	2 511	-
bushels, 1987..	79 935	108 559	(D)	44 530	70 796	42 473	44 666	12 340
1982..	220 345	245 248	(D)	91 163	74 472	116 891	94 603	-
Soybeans for beans .... farms, 1987..	272	651	49	252	106	185	171	3
1982..	201	627	32	276	32	171	157	1
acres, 1987..	10 977	59 849	5 173	42 657	7 602	31 775	11 425	(D)
1982..	10 388	62 636	5 416	42 479	2 934	20 686	8 583	(D)
bushels, 1987..	267 289	1 594 110	201 350	1 372 126	190 763	849 593	304 774	(D)
1982..	213 670	1 733 412	183 530	1 054 769	101 227	386 764	204 788	(D)
Hay—alfalfa, other tame, small grain, wild, grass silage, green chop, etc. (see text) .... farms, 1987..	544	531	113	304	251	246	272	37
1982..	630	599	101	334	258	260	305	26
acres, 1987..	41 719	26 024	9 448	27 328	13 778	17 715	29 560	(D)
1982..	40 493	29 572	10 253	26 326	13 054	16 796	29 631	1 449
tons, dry, 1987..	85 176	56 095	25 405	51 000	35 047	29 531	57 125	(D)
1982..	90 941	71 667	26 886	93 151	34 016	99 856	59 079	4 602

Item	Nemaha	Neosho	Ness	Norton	Osage	Osborne	Ottawa	Pawnee
CROPS HARVESTED								
Corn for grain or seed .... farms, 1987..	212	72	2	67	86	21	11	52
1982..	287	55	4	36	89	21	17	27
acres, 1987..	10 002	4 822	(D)	9 058	4 479	1 097	2 232	13 077
1982..	13 508	3 217	633	8 825	4 451	(D)	(D)	7 163
bushels, 1987..	663 925	430 663	(D)	577 142	346 576	115 586	301 182	1 819 964
1982..	1 085 515	207 489	(D)	472 768	281 740	(D)	(D)	861 714
Sorghum for grain or seed........ farms, 1987..	687	256	304	220	317	367	188	302
1982..	653	183	179	198	308	269	140	282
acres, 1987..	85 417	27 576	31 089	23 329	37 177	34 375	11 667	45 135
1982..	78 964	15 414	17 695	23 681	30 988	22 530	7 854	49 454
bushels, 1987..	6 019 669	2 058 873	1 694 561	1 682 655	2 713 488	2 552 189	837 016	3 447 418
1982..	5 527 836	1 017 981	795 933	1 316 333	1 894 403	1 404 774	476 199	3 298 295
Wheat for grain .... farms, 1987..	577	114	402	320	131	425	319	354
1982..	655	329	474	380	342	443	397	422
acres, 1987..	33 517	12 676	127 403	95 174	7 201	111 466	104 860	120 383
1982..	50 509	53 450	174 676	118 492	32 477	125 225	148 249	154 565
bushels, 1987..	1 037 632	327 943	4 421 359	3 827 259	192 624	4 145 336	3 316 538	4 156 140
1982..	1 457 651	1 487 126	6 123 616	4 653 562	532 143	4 081 898	4 489 972	5 044 129
Oats for grain .... farms, 1987..	107	116	12	60	47	57	32	12
1982..	156	132	7	41	86	21	22	11
acres, 1987..	1 827	3 630	297	(D)	906	1 222	521	324
1982..	2 626	4 749	(D)	(D)	1 423	576	(D)	898
bushels, 1987..	79 864	151 916	5 780	(D)	31 233	58 536	22 981	10 876
1982..	127 683	267 804	(D)	(D)	60 991	31 722	(D)	33 820
Soybeans for beans .... farms, 1987..	520	288	11	9	338	71	104	95
1982..	428	309	3	4	364	39	48	88
acres, 1987..	30 135	47 047	969	344	47 292	3 196	5 047	11 605
1982..	25 935	41 086	262	182	41 854	(D)	2 388	11 772
bushels, 1987..	804 437	1 218 474	9 850	4 646	1 523 273	84 747	149 219	459 784
1982..	661 569	805 899	4 484	(D)	932 081	(D)	66 011	458 913
Hay—alfalfa, other tame, small grain, wild, grass silage, green chop, etc. (see text) .... farms, 1987..	552	284	239	197	279	293	238	200
1982..	604	278	228	248	312	282	280	229
acres, 1987..	29 660	20 744	17 411	12 036	31 035	19 827	17 264	26 829
1982..	29 138	17 454	13 212	14 913	31 103	18 428	16 872	29 014
tons, dry, 1987..	65 039	37 823	42 218	34 070	43 884	48 792	41 077	95 653
1982..	73 033	29 126	29 080	40 585	44 513	49 387	40 930	102 370

See footnotes at end of table.

Table 16. **Farms With Sales of $10,000 or More: 1987 and 1982**—Con.

[Data for 1987 include abnormal farms. For meaning of abbreviations and symbols, see introductory text.]

Item		Phillips	Pottawatomie	Pratt	Rawlins	Reno	Republic	Rice	Riley
CROPS HARVESTED									
Corn for grain or seed	farms, 1987	35	117	112	54	65	238	33	45
	1982	03	129	66	45	45	244	31	54
	acres, 1987	5 206	11 111	29 531	6 047	11 032	38 926	7 744	2 747
	1982	4 880	10 766	(D)	(D)	5 291	36 898	(D)	3 489
	bushels, 1987	599 536	1 152 276	2 996 866	639 516	1 241 468	5 057 412	1 005 194	254 312
	1982	632 700	976 747	(D)	(D)	556 907	3 838 000	(D)	304 191
Sorghum for grain or seed	farms, 1987	316	296	269	325	630	464	355	235
	1982	309	330	256	230	654	445	351	225
	acres, 1987	35 230	25 447	35 579	39 051	75 175	62 152	51 858	23 085
	1982	32 574	23 290	41 212	25 145	84 893	55 188	51 461	20 337
	bushels, 1987	2 604 500	1 595 337	2 277 656	2 316 992	5 033 336	5 117 306	4 062 215	1 610 473
	1982	1 720 587	1 481 040	2 417 211	1 427 450	4 833 102	3 980 415	3 215 395	1 433 201
Wheat for grain	farms, 1987	375	250	350	392	806	549	379	238
	1982	442	362	400	465	987	614	434	273
	acres, 1987	80 244	15 994	137 239	117 958	217 141	80 413	125 266	19 625
	1982	93 844	32 375	161 595	155 931	286 781	111 942	160 312	27 314
	bushels, 1987	3 323 304	495 853	4 111 539	4 631 173	6 366 728	3 259 055	4 323 684	676 242
	1982	3 493 544	834 044	4 897 680	5 094 068	9 175 241	3 451 272	5 306 181	833 727
Oats for grain	farms, 1987	73	81	10	54	46	99	18	56
	1982	73	90	22	23	107	171	11	68
	acres, 1987	1 818	1 294	(D)	2 074	1 098	1 987	856	971
	1982	1 602	1 453	(D)	205	4 324	3 900	938	1 267
	bushels, 1987	62 697	50 982	(D)	97 135	35 010	105 424	27 580	41 409
	1982	80 155	58 360	(D)	(D)	218 994	200 990	49 005	57 889
Soybeans for beans	farms, 1987	19	257	80	11	121	402	109	173
	1982	4	236	69	5	102	364	73	140
	acres, 1987	(D)	17 751	8 571	461	8 214	24 017	7 358	10 436
	1982	75	14 392	11 746	(D)	8 394	23 553	6 723	7 378
	bushels, 1987	(D)	562 312	334 145	8 451	290 455	838 977	250 044	326 736
	1982	2 502	380 988	492 624	(D)	265 460	766 399	245 793	229 626
Hay—alfalfa, other tame, small grain, wild, grass silage, green chop, etc. (see text)	farms, 1987	313	333	132	203	524	378	237	243
	1982	351	389	157	240	619	458	283	250
	acres, 1987	26 557	39 217	28 423	15 114	36 265	18 799	14 607	16 001
	1982	25 342	39 556	15 763	18 297	39 148	20 054	16 099	17 230
	tons, dry, 1987	72 476	66 328	126 986	47 181	99 168	50 130	43 524	31 615
	1982	66 435	78 026	53 334	49 473	103 221	57 623	48 411	39 178

Item		Rooks	Rush	Russell	Saline	Scott	Sedgwick	Seward	Shawnee
CROPS HARVESTED									
Corn for grain or seed	farms, 1987	11	15	4	21	52	75	51	134
	1982	9	22	2	33	48	65	21	125
	acres, 1987	1 303	966	(D)	1 250	(D)	12 968	11 367	19 863
	1982	(D)	1 446	(D)	1 550	(D)	6 341	(D)	19 475
	bushels, 1987	134 750	104 265	(D)	109 616	1 584 512	1 340 010	2 143 944
	1982	(D)	133 260	(D)	115 470	(D)	983 198	(D)	1 877 468
Sorghum for grain or seed	farms, 1987	246	269	225	250	187	531	152	168
	1982	185	224	185	161	172	450	144	126
	acres, 1987	29 208	28 064	20 966	15 295	35 139	58 611	48 762	18 005
	1982	19 864	21 875	16 551	10 029	34 521	55 935	60 190	13 650
	bushels, 1987	1 781 566	1 857 264	1 310 007	1 042 565	2 293 164	3 889 864	3 254 165	1 157 773
	1982	970 689	1 096 335	941 491	574 859	2 451 452	3 315 098	3 446 143	729 952
Wheat for grain	farms, 1987	317	351	294	347	270	677	180	102
	1982	371	416	383	450	290	812	180	202
	acres, 1987	95 005	104 751	83 943	116 673	112 226	170 983	66 565	6 897
	1982	121 409	130 007	117 820	156 366	139 416	228 095	78 722	23 593
	bushels, 1987	3 588 415	3 579 703	2 768 676	3 514 422	4 440 901	5 031 547	2 261 740	210 984
	1982	4 355 952	4 454 856	4 059 944	4 784 205	4 554 537	8 050 531	2 594 176	478 918
Oats for grain	farms, 1987	21	43	30	26	3	23	3	47
	1982	21	22	22	58	4	51		36
	acres, 1987	(D)	1 498	748	681	122	493	123	840
	1982	1 415	1 771	851	(D)	(D)	2 802	(D)	593
	bushels, 1987	44 273	28 414	24 407	6 500	14 025	3 777	24 584
	1982	65 875	73 782	29 161	(D)	(D)	105 136	(D)	20 119
Soybeans for beans	farms, 1987	9	33	17	157	14	221	16	205
	1982	9	22	2	100	24	150	21	186
	acres, 1987	880	3 135	659	7 204	1 046	20 627	824	27 480
	1982	246	(D)	4 210	4 352	13 481	3 153	15 199
	bushels, 1987	11 895	39 001	17 750	192 169	39 512	767 670	29 413	848 374
	1982	5 189	(D)	(D)	106 215	155 475	413 736	92 079	374 072
Hay—alfalfa, other tame, small grain, wild, grass silage, green chop, etc. (see text)	farms, 1987	182	177	208	254	79	414	50	166
	1982	205	195	254	300	69	503	50	189
	acres, 1987	15 362	10 758	18 830	21 102	6 795	29 877	9 445	16 743
	1982	14 402	9 452	16 587	17 623	5 077	29 873	6 638	16 547
	tons, dry, 1987	45 253	26 864	42 404	51 223	18 742	74 690	36 975	25 456
	1982	39 939	24 100	37 492	50 013	15 522	65 269	25 794	32 712

See footnotes at end of table.

Table 16. Farms With Sales of $10,000 or More: 1987 and 1982—Con.

[Data for 1987 include abnormal farms. For meaning of abbreviations and symbols, see introductory text]

Item	Sheridan	Sherman	Smith	Stafford	Stanton	Stevens	Sumner	Thomas
CROPS HARVESTED								
Corn for grain or seed — farms, 1987	128	183	48	105	96	65	17	180
1982	139	174	34	56	76	46	4	137
acres, 1987	(D)	35 505	(D)	(D)	30 940	25 418	997	48 898
1982	(D)	44 314	3 016	(D)	31 895	15 870	277	48 050
bushels, 1987	(D)	5 059 354	(D)	(D)	4 387 760	3 303 471	69 170	7 119 193
1982	(D)	4 895 715	249 683	(D)	4 269 541	2 056 099	20 110	5 952 726
Sorghum for grain or seed — farms, 1987	278	109	468	280	134	206	355	282
1982	230	95	449	322	126	248	229	169
acres, 1987	35 068	10 146	60 217	45 646	30 941	112 774	30 562	35 211
1982	26 043	9 189	54 132	60 347	38 862	178 384	17 278	27 176
bushels, 1987	2 514 391	616 057	5 179 603	2 945 458	1 919 428	5 544 068	1 440 002	2 290 431
1982	1 980 198	530 600	3 552 750	3 800 349	2 924 925	7 839 032	754 925	1 848 717
Wheat for grain — farms, 1987	367	364	505	351	206	206	722	454
1982	421	418	546	442	168	228	979	481
acres, 1987	91 623	148 347	104 484	118 347	110 208	88 052	335 829	173 361
1982	110 460	193 640	126 017	150 912	135 665	98 006	454 240	214 294
bushels, 1987	3 837 096	5 683 375	4 320 101	3 403 834	4 068 752	3 140 191	9 899 944	6 292 585
1982	4 344 339	6 976 400	4 706 047	5 043 474	4 435 052	3 474 152	15 292 060	7 698 006
Oats for grain — farms, 1987	24	19	107	15	-	2	5	34
1982	21	29	78	25	1	-	31	26
acres, 1987	(D)	(D)	2 828	(D)	-	(D)	396	(D)
1982	656	(D)	1 812	1 205	(D)	-	1 070	(D)
bushels, 1987	(D)	(D)	121 753	(D)	-	(D)	10 520	(D)
1982	46 386	(D)	109 277	63 488	(D)	-	45 624	(D)
Soybeans for beans — farms, 1987	53	44	165	85	19	16	159	70
1982	39	41	32	86	31	11	33	39
acres, 1987	(D)	(D)	10 476	8 681	2 360	890	13 603	5 742
1982	5 068	4 315	(D)	16 119	5 584	652	1 516	4 742
bushels, 1987	(D)	(D)	300 677	323 339	75 869	26 397	292 242	183 371
1982	189 277	130 979	(D)	536 800	214 535	20 265	36 219	172 243
Hay—alfalfa, other tame, small grain, wild, grass silage, green chop, etc. (see text) — farms, 1987	164	106	363	187	38	46	391	112
1982	187	124	411	243	33	46	478	91
acres, 1987	10 247	6 966	21 561	19 831	(D)	(D)	20 566	6 524
1982	10 411	6 922	23 239	22 757	3 567	6 540	22 772	4 640
tons, dry, 1987	30 996	23 103	61 342	52 031	(D)	(D)	45 807	17 271
1982	36 106	26 422	52 975	66 180	15 969	33 032	46 554	14 330

Item	Trego	Wabaunsee	Wallace	Washington	Wichita	Wilson	Woodson	Wyandotte
CROPS HARVESTED								
Corn for grain or seed — farms, 1987	10	68	95	117	92	36	25	13
1982	7	78	93	144	87	36	21	15
acres, 1987	520	6 664	(D)	8 080	(D)	(D)	1 498	1 974
1982	862	5 800	24 670	957	20 289	(D)	1 124	(D)
bushels, 1987	66 335	692 234	(D)	774 949	(D)	(D)	93 405	220 260
1982	87 010	466 488	2 763 152	924 087	2 515 016	185 843	65 545	(D)
Sorghum for grain or seed — farms, 1987	253	224	77	593	174	236	157	2
1982	172	236	82	626	166	232	140	11
acres, 1987	26 053	16 104	9 632	94 043	24 024	25 394	16 798	(D)
1982	18 935	20 072	18 670	80 499	(D)	20 434	12 737	(D)
bushels, 1987	1 467 366	1 198 769	459 087	6 954 602	1 683 165	1 741 255	1 207 097	(D)
1982	837 378	1 077 226	1 380 143	5 750 522	(D)	1 296 493	850 433	(D)
Wheat for grain — farms, 1987	352	167	226	561	258	169	102	6
1982	344	263	225	703	265	349	159	22
acres, 1987	87 537	10 174	90 009	71 426	116 319	16 011	7 543	424
1982	100 022	21 444	94 010	106 255	123 952	57 802	19 656	3 124
bushels, 1987	3 241 237	305 762	2 936 435	2 543 987	4 398 588	376 206	164 665	13 173
1982	3 145 814	509 362	3 329 188	3 277 781	4 386 742	1 609 149	527 164	95 094
Oats for grain — farms, 1987	27	61	11	138	11	26	35	3
1982	8	73	3	175	7	56	43	4
acres, 1987	(D)	1 049	(D)	2 609	757	787	674	(D)
1982	251	981	157	4 613	432	1 063	749	(D)
bushels, 1987	(D)	40 702	(D)	137 052	32 630	28 313	25 420	(D)
1982	11 769	37 792	10 460	216 960	(D)	57 205	31 801	(D)
Soybeans for beans — farms, 1987	2	177	13	428	23	251	166	20
1982	-	167	3	372	93	302	164	25
acres, 1987	(D)	13 345	845	29 924	1 295	50 532	28 634	4 822
1982	-	9 610	152	31 083	(D)	42 911	21 812	3 374
bushels, 1987	(D)	413 580	28 139	579 077	37 428	1 450 961	872 551	191 475
1982	(D)	223 339	(D)	943 830	(D)	934 132	516 267	111 323
Hay—alfalfa, other tame, small grain, wild, grass silage, green chop, etc. (see text) — farms, 1987	209	243	94	488	87	228	164	12
1982	193	317	84	590	85	276	173	16
acres, 1987	13 668	32 177	10 008	27 960	6 973	17 245	27 730	(D)
1982	11 178	36 078	8 488	33 191	(D)	19 855	28 802	1 839
tons, dry, 1987	31 845	57 270	21 737	61 910	20 717	29 208	34 784	(D)
1982	29 699	61 878	20 931	78 390	(D)	39 105	43 492	4 105

¹Data are based on a sample of farms.
²Data for 1982 include self-propelled only.

Table 17. Milk Goats—Inventory and Sales: 1987 and 1982

[For meaning of abbreviations and symbols, see introductory text]

Geographic area	Inventory		Sales					
			Milk goats		Goat milk			
	Farms	Number	Farms	Number	Farms	Gallons	Farms	Total sales ($1,000)
STATE TOTAL								
Kansas .... 1987..	438	2 297	106	552	79	36 773	144	104
1982..	733	3 312	193	1 147	41	(D)	(NA)	(D)

Table 18. Angora Goats—Inventory and Sales: 1987 and 1982

[For meaning of abbreviations and symbols, see introductory text]

Geographic area	Inventory		Sales					
			Angora goats		Mohair			
	Farms	Number	Farms	Number	Farms	Pounds	Farms	Total sales ($1,000)
STATE TOTAL								
Kansas .... 1987..	55	3 978	17	980	43	43 086	48	160
1982..	9	(D)	2	(D)	2	(D)	(NA)	(D)

Table 19. Mink and Their Pelts—Inventory and Sales: 1987 and 1982

[For meaning of abbreviations and symbols, see introductory text]

Geographic area	Inventory		Sales		
	Farms	Number	Farms	Number	Sales ($1,000)
STATE TOTAL					
Kansas .... 1987..	6	394	6	462	14
1982..	6	695	3	1 134	25

Table 20. **Colonies of Bees and Honey—Inventory and Sales: 1987 and 1982**

[For meaning of abbreviations and symbols, see introductory text]

Geographic area	Inventory		Sales					
			Colonies of bees		Honey			
	Farms	Number	Farms	Number	Farms	Pounds	Farms	Total sales ($1,000)
STATE TOTAL								
Kansas .... 1987..	544	24 943	25	3 992	199	1 433 699	210	1 627
1982..	683	22 851	22	271	147	1 134 878	(NA)	705
COUNTIES, 1987								
Allen	7	60	-	-	5	1 410	5	2
Anderson	7	(D)	-	-	4	(D)	4	(D)
Atchison	3	(D)	-	-	1	(D)	1	(D)
Barton	11	191	-	-	4	9 650	4	6
Bourbon	4	13	-	-	1	(D)	1	(D)
Butler	20	65	2	(D)	4	(D)	6	1
Chase	5	6	-	-	-	-	-	-
Chautauqua	6	11	-	-	-	-	-	-
Cherokee	4	33	1	(D)	2	(D)	2	(D)
Clay	4	(D)	-	-	2	(D)	2	(D)
Cloud	6	810	1	(D)	3	(D)	4	(D)
Coffey	6	(D)	-	-	2	(D)	2	(D)
Cowley	10	62	-	-	2	(D)	3	(D)
Crawford	7	(D)	-	-	3	(D)	3	(D)
Dickinson	4	25	1	(D)	1	(D)	1	(D)
Doniphan	4	(D)	-	-	2	(D)	2	(D)
Douglas	15	525	-	-	7	6 385	7	4
Elk	3	3	-	-	-	-	-	-
Ellsworth	3	(D)	1	(D)	2	(D)	2	(D)
Finney	3	5	-	-	-	-	-	-
Franklin	12	60	-	-	2	(D)	2	(D)
Greenwood	5	16	-	-	1	(D)	1	(D)
Harvey	12	(D)	1	(D)	6	(D)	6	(D)
Jackson	10	24	-	-	3	(D)	3	(D)
Jefferson	19	55	1	(D)	6	563	6	(D)
Jewell	3	(D)	-	-	2	(D)	2	(D)
Johnson	16	402	-	-	6	(D)	6	(D)
Labette	10	51	1	(D)	4	570	5	1
Leavenworth	12	177	1	(D)	5	4 163	5	3
Linn	6	49	-	-	3	(D)	3	(D)
Lyon	11	65	-	-	4	(D)	4	(D)
McPherson	12	146	1	(D)	5	4 982	5	4
Marion	7	66	-	-	1	(D)	1	(D)
Marshall	9	99	-	-	2	(D)	2	(D)
Meade	4	31	-	-	-	-	-	-
Miami	14	50	-	-	4	372	4	(D)
Mitchell	3	(D)	-	-	2	(D)	2	(D)
Montgomery	13	65	-	-	7	1 356	7	1
Morris	4	24	-	-	3	710	3	(D)
Nemaha	5	254	1	(D)	2	(D)	2	(D)
Neosho	11	74	-	-	6	1 503	6	1
Osage	12	(D)	1	(D)	4	(D)	4	(D)
Osborne	4	(D)	1	(D)	1	(D)	2	(D)
Ottawa	5	18	-	-	-	-	-	-
Pawnee	6	47	1	(D)	4	(D)	4	(D)
Pottawatomie	6	63	-	-	2	(D)	2	(D)
Pratt	3	(D)	-	-	2	(D)	2	(D)
Reno	17	117	-	-	5	(D)	5	(D)
Republic	4	44	1	(D)	-	-	1	(D)
Riley	13	(D)	2	(D)	6	(D)	7	(D)
Rooks	4	55	-	-	4	2 215	4	2
Saline	15	77	1	(D)	5	715	5	(D)
Sedgwick	16	580	-	-	5	(D)	5	2
Shawnee	13	503	2	(D)	7	29 235	7	26
Sumner....................	14	51	-	-	3	210	3	(D)
Trego	3	(D)	-	-	1	(D)	1	(D)
Wabaunsee	4	10	-	-	1	(D)	1	(D)
Washington	9	8 848	-	-	7	459 682	7	191
Wilson	9	168	2	(D)	6	(D)	7	2
Woodson	4	18	-	-	3	(D)	2	(D)
Wyandotte	7	233	-	-	3	5 956	3	5
All other counties	44	2 162	2	(D)	12	149 770	14	96

Table 21. **Fish Sales: 1987 and 1982**

[For meaning of abbreviations and symbols, see introductory text]

Geographic area	Farms	Pounds (1,000)	Farms	Number (1,000)	Farms	Sales ($1,000)
CATFISH						
State Total						
Kansas .... 1987..	35	879	7	67	40	817
1982..	28	536	9	52	36	680

Table 22. **Miscellaneous Poultry—Inventory and Sales: 1987 and 1982**

[For meaning of abbreviations and symbols, see introductory text]

Geographic area	Inventory			
	Farms	Number	Farms	Number
DUCKS				
State Total				
Kansas .... 1987..	700	9 826	80	5 982
1982..	602	9 742	106	4 985
GEESE				
State Total				
Kansas .... 1987..	533	3 936	65	1 772
1982..	549	4 867	79	2 829
PHEASANTS				
State Total				
Kansas .... 1987..	56	6 614	21	13 920
1982..	40	(D)	11	16 341
QUAIL				
State Total				
Kansas .... 1987..	39	15 088	23	31 162
1982..	19	8 241	8	12 840
OTHER POULTRY				
State Total				
Kansas .... 1987..	149	2 154	28	(D)
1982..	161	2 327	34	891
POULTRY HATCHED (SEE TEXT)				
State Total				
Kansas .... 1987..	157	1 602 998	272	4 398 897
1982..	175	1 863 826	350	3 749 602

Table 23. **Miscellaneous Livestock and Animal Specialties—Inventory and Sales: 1987 and 1982**

[For meaning of abbreviations and symbols, see introductory text]

Geographic area	Inventory		Sales		
	Farms	Number	Farms	Number	Sales ($1,000)
MULES, BURROS, AND DONKEYS					
State Total					
Kansas .... 1987..	533	1 308	62	175	58
1982..	193	453	26	130	51
Counties, 1987					
Allen	6	24	2	(D)	(D)
Anderson	4	10	3	7	1
Atchison	6	10	3	4	1
Barber	12	18	-	-	-
Barton	8	20	1	(D)	(D)
Bourbon	7	16	-	-	-
Brown	4	5	1	(D)	(D)
Butler	15	23	2	(D)	(D)
Chautauqua	13	52	2	(D)	(D)
Cherokee	6	14	1	(D)	(D)
Clark	10	11	-	-	-
Clay	4	9	-	-	-
Cloud	7	18	-	-	-
Comanche	4	7	-	-	-
Cowley	8	16	1	(D)	(D)
Crawford	9	19	1	(D)	(D)
Dickinson	7	16	-	-	-
Douglas	6	22	-	-	-
Elk	4	9	-	-	-
Ellsworth	4	5	-	-	-
Finney	3	4	1	(D)	(D)
Ford	9	13	2	(D)	(D)
Franklin	4	11	1	(D)	(D)
Geary	3	11	-	-	-
Gove	4	5	-	-	-
Gray	3	5	-	-	-
Greenwood	6	15	1	(D)	(D)
Harper	3	5	1	(D)	(D)
Harvey	8	20	-	-	-
Jackson	12	28	2	(D)	(D)
Jefferson	11	30	1	(D)	(D)
Jewell	7	10	-	-	-
Johnson	13	71	3	4	2
Kingman	4	8	2	(D)	(D)
Labette	6	13	-	-	-
Lane	3	4	-	-	-
Leavenworth	15	22	3	5	1
Linn	4	5	-	-	-
Logan	5	14	-	-	-
Lyon	9	16	-	-	-
McPherson	8	16	1	(D)	(D)
Marion	9	18	3	6	1
Marshall	6	12	-	-	-
Meade	5	7	-	-	-
Miami	7	9	-	-	-
Montgomery	4	7	2	(D)	(D)
Morris	4	16	-	-	-
Neosho	5	16	1	(D)	(D)
Ness	4	5	-	-	-
Norton	6	8	2	(D)	(D)
Osage	5	17	2	(D)	(D)
Osborne	3	8	-	-	-
Ottawa	4	7	-	-	-
Pawnee	3	8	-	-	-
Phillips	9	62	-	-	-
Pottawatomie	6	10	2	(D)	(D)
Pratt	4	14	-	-	-
Rawlins	4	7	-	-	-
Reno	17	119	7	65	(D)
Republic	3	5	-	-	-
Rice	6	21	-	-	-
Riley	6	18	-	-	-
Rooks	6	8	1	(D)	(D)
Saline	7	9	-	-	-
Scott	3	5	-	-	-
Sedgwick	18	32	1	(D)	(D)
Shawnee	11	17	1	(D)	(D)
Smith	3	6	-	-	-
Stafford	7	17	-	-	-
Sumner	9	35	-	-	-
Thomas	4	7	-	-	-
Trego	3	4	-	-	-
Wallace	3	3	-	-	-
Washington	5	8	-	-	-
Wilson	10	28	-	-	-
Woodson	6	19	-	-	-
Wyandotte	5	11	2	(D)	(D)
All other counties	30	49	4	8	3

[For meaning of abbreviations and symbols, see introductory text]

Geographic area	Inventory		Sales		
	Farms	Number	Farms	Number	Sales ($1,000)
GOATS, TOTAL					
State Total					
Kansas ....1987..	862	8 831	258	2 679	(NA)
1982..	891	4 841	237	1 640	(NA)
Counties, 1987					
Allen	11	27	3	15	(NA)
Anderson	7	(D)	3	(D)	(NA)
Atchison	9	117	-	-	(NA)
Barber	10	109	1	(D)	(NA)
Barton	18	51	3	(D)	(NA)
Bourbon	18	92	4	34	(NA)
Brown	13	(D)	4	16	(NA)
Butler..	16	291	7	40	(NA)
Chase	3	4	2	(D)	(NA)
Chautauqua	15	162	5	94	(NA)
Cherokee	14	47	1	(D)	(NA)
Cheyenne	5	(D)	2	(D)	(NA)
Clark	4	10	-	-	(NA)
Clay	4	17	1	(D)	(NA)
Cloud	11	86	6	41	(NA)
Coffey	4	10	2	(D)	(NA)
Cowley	21	825	7	29	(NA)
Crawford	7	26	1	(D)	(NA)
Decatur	2	(D)	3	5	(NA)
Dickinson	16	78	8	36	(NA)
Doniphan	9	24	3	9	(NA)
Douglas...	16	93	4	9	(NA)
Edwards	3	(D)	1	(D)	(NA)
Elk	8	155	5	26	(NA)
Ellis	3	(D)	1	(D)	(NA)
Ellsworth	7	(D)	-	-	(NA)
Finney	4	9	-	-	(NA)
Ford...	10	34	5	15	(NA)
Franklin...	12	76	-	-	(NA)
Geary	7	61	3	(D)	(NA)
Gove	7	47	5	43	(NA)
Grant	5	31	3	7	(NA)
Greenwood	10	36	1	(D)	(NA)
Harper	4	7	1	(D)	(NA)
Harvey...	8	63	3	36	(NA)
Hodgeman	4	(D)	-	-	(NA)
Jackson	22	276	10	83	(NA)
Jefferson	13	(D)	3	(D)	(NA)
Jewell	7	23	2	(D)	(NA)
Johnson	11	141	2	(D)	(NA)
Kearny..	9	23	3	12	(NA)
Kingman	12	113	3	44	(NA)
Labette	19	62	5	32	(NA)
Lane	3	(D)	1	(D)	(NA)
Leavenworth	15	71	4	32	(NA)
Lincoln	5	13	-	-	(NA)
Linn	11	59	3	17	(NA)
Logan	3	(D)	1	(D)	(NA)
Lyon	20	127	5	20	(NA)
McPherson...	10	(D)	3	(D)	(NA)
Marion	11	67	4	29	(NA)
Marshall	13	92	2	(D)	(NA)
Miami..	11	91	3	8	(NA)
Mitchell	9	108	1	(D)	(NA)
Montgomery..	19	124	4	52	(NA)
Morris	11	47	4	22	(NA)
Morton	3	(D)	-	-	(NA)
Nemaha	3	5	4	441	(NA)
Neosho	10	46	1	(D)	(NA)
Ness	5	12	2	(D)	(NA)
Norton	10	72	2	(D)	(NA)
Osage	8	29	3	66	(NA)
Osborne	13	51	2	(D)	(NA)
Ottawa	9	49	4	12	(NA)
Phillips..	10	27	4	6	(NA)
Pottawatomie	14	104	3	(D)	(NA)
Pratt	5	(D)	2	(D)	(NA)
Rawlins	4	(D)	1	(D)	(NA)
Reno	20	123	14	196	(NA)
Republic	6	(D)	-	-	(NA)
Riley	7	38	2	(D)	(NA)
Rooks	10	25	1	(D)	(NA)
Rush	3	12	-	-	(NA)
Russell	4	19	2	(D)	(NA)
Saline	8	36	2	(D)	(NA)
Sedgwick	16	204	6	64	(NA)
Seward	4	67	1	(D)	(NA)
Shawnee..	9	55	6	41	(NA)
Sherman..	9	500	3	(D)	(NA)
Smith..	10	47	4	9	(NA)

Table 23. Miscellaneous Livestock and Animal Specialties—Inventory and Sales: 1987 and 1982—Con.

[For meaning of abbreviations and symbols, see introductory text]

Geographic area	Inventory		Sales		
	Farms	Number	Farms	Number	Sales ($1,000)
GOATS, TOTAL—Con.					
Counties, 1987—Con.					
Stafford	3	(D)	3	21	(NA)
Stanton	4	14	1	(D)	(NA)
Stevens	6	22	-	-	(NA)
Sumner	15	90	5	13	(NA)
Thomas	4	(D)	-	-	(NA)
Trego	3	7	-	-	(NA)
Wallace	7	29	1	(D)	(NA)
Washington	16	95	5	27	(NA)
Wichita	9	151	-	-	(NA)
Wilson	12	101	4	25	(NA)
Woodson	6	13	2	(D)	(NA)
All other counties	16	464	5	24	(NA)
GOATS, EXCEPT ANGORA AND MILK					
State Total					
Kansas ... 1987	516	2 556	156	1 147	27
1982	219	(D)	58	(D)	(D)
RABBITS AND THEIR PELTS					
State Total					
Kansas ... 1987	268	8 214	104	20 430	74
1982	196	7 517	85	14 873	64
OTHER LIVESTOCK AND LIVESTOCK PRODUCTS					
State Total					
Kansas ... 1987	87	(X)	36	(X)	706
1982	(NA)	(X)	(NA)	(X)	(D)

Table 24. Grains—Corn, Sorghum, Wheat, and Other Small Grains: 1987 and 1982

[For meaning of abbreviations and symbols, see introductory text]

Geographic area	1987					1982				
	Harvested			Irrigated		Harvested			Irrigated	
	Farms	Acres	Quantity	Farms	Acres	Farms	Acres	Quantity	Farms	Acres
CORN FOR GRAIN OR SEED (BUSHELS)										
State Total										
Kansas	8 944	1 243 969	144 133 581	3 647	816 992	8 346	1 161 875	130 662 235	3 007	755 272
Counties										
Allen	103	7 562	600 173	1	(D)	100	4 855	324 550	1	(D)
Anderson	199	13 596	1 111 323	7	773	232	15 289	1 115 829	6	620
Atchison	285	22 627	1 910 556	4	192	248	16 396	1 385 378	-	-
Barton	43	9 362	1 186 648	37	8 731	33	6 679	876 725	29	5 582
Bourbon	105	5 937	482 711	5	379	101	5 501	395 711	6	(D)
Brown	349	48 227	4 726 726	-	-	412	52 287	5 180 537	-	-
Butler	43	3 180	250 012	2	(D)	16	1 195	81 609	2	(D)
Chase	38	2 323	163 141	-	-	40	1 703	82 895	-	-
Chautauqua	12	658	42 190	-	-	11	588	29 755	-	-
Cherokee	80	5 166	502 149	4	169	46	2 986	227 140	3	133
Cheyenne	98	18 604	2 367 733	88	17 474	102	17 710	1 937 921	95	16 845
Clay	75	7 405	866 470	36	5 236	92	8 660	844 479	45	5 524
Cloud	59	7 338	880 934	45	6 283	66	8 293	817 845	43	5 483
Coffey	136	7 862	620 771	1	(D)	143	7 227	536 151	4	(D)
Comanche	7	809	127 385	7	809	(NA)	(NA)	(NA)	(NA)	(NA)
Cowley	12	612	46 912	1	(D)	3	(O)	(O)	-	-
Crawford	108	7 737	675 502	9	1 004	110	6 726	486 704	7	671
Decatur	114	17 038	1 741 211	72	7 217	71	8 005	781 611	53	5 017
Dickinson	44	1 915	146 123	10	824	96	3 291	229 442	5	341
Doniphan	362	56 130	6 226 898	-	-	383	56 482	5 727 207	1	(D)
Douglas	175	15 643	1 513 650	5	580	186	14 746	1 309 935	3	(D)
Edwards	100	36 522	4 203 683	96	36 963	51	16 525	2 446 103	48	15 225
Elk	8	307	21 270	-	-	11	(D)	12 005	-	-
Ellis	4	207	9 840	-	-	9	1 445	127 653	4	(D)
Ellsworth	6	231	16 945	1	(D)	3	(O)	(O)	-	-
Finney	142	50 415	6 724 251	140	49 215	135	66 191	8 878 132	131	65 311
Ford	81	19 058	2 317 716	78	18 632	60	16 540	1 997 590	56	15 719
Franklin	182	11 765	920 810	4	(D)	205	12 143	960 559	6	(D)
Geary	22	952	84 624	6	321	29	1 159	96 162	9	(D)
Gove	37	5 013	547 514	36	4 721	36	6 063	722 974	32	5 571

Table 24. Grains—Corn, Sorghum, Wheat, and Other Small Grains: 1987 and 1982—Con.

[For meaning of abbreviations and symbols, see introductory text]

Geographic area	1987 Harvested Farms	1987 Harvested Acres	1987 Harvested Quantity	1987 Irrigated Farms	1987 Irrigated Acres	1982 Harvested Farms	1982 Harvested Acres	1982 Harvested Quantity	1982 Irrigated Farms	1982 Irrigated Acres

CORN FOR GRAIN OR SEED (BUSHELS)—Con.

Counties—Con.

Geographic area	Farms	Acres	Quantity	Farms	Acres	Farms	Acres	Quantity	Farms	Acres
Graham	25	3 302	375 964	19	2 875	29	4 491	456 266	25	4 201
Grant	110	28 238	4 104 121	105	27 776	83	29 204	4 007 668	82	29 129
Gray	196	51 161	6 327 646	194	50 995	203	62 515	8 720 968	193	59 515
Greeley	38	12 977	1 678 904	37	12 965	19	7 255	799 353	17	6 639
Greenwood	29	1 119	90 970	2	(D)	26	1 167	72 786	4	158
Hamilton	22	4 574	624 772	21	4 466	10	2 305	323 790	10	2 305
Harvey	82	11 053	1 370 794	66	9 806	59	6 619	840 834	50	6 254
Haskell	157	55 966	7 401 004	152	55 319	158	60 411	8 413 068	157	59 986
Hodgeman	35	2 826	343 924	33	2 779	14	1 546	161 916	12	1 386
Jackson	205	12 664	858 889	1	(D)	187	12 193	819 839	1	(D)
Jefferson	262	23 174	2 053 312	5	842	251	21 860	1 780 456	4	706
Jewell	67	6 361	742 577	47	5 113	63	6 917	689 861	39	4 693
Johnson	104	8 787	759 913	1	(C)	110	7 716	705 743	-	-
Kearny	39	24 651	3 148 328	38	24 631	33	37 732	5 118 081	30	37 549
Kingman	26	5 130	674 624	22	4 472	11	1 529	150 521	9	1 323
Kiowa	52	13 151	1 742 065	52	13 091	21	5 114	670 065	20	5 099
Labette	47	2 261	175 848	5	444	56	2 573	166 778	6	(D)
Lane	8	643	66 966	6	379	14	2 036	165 724	9	1 202
Leavenworth	292	17 320	1 525 704	-	-	232	11 835	1 000 720	-	-
Lincoln	9	1 131	37 506	-	-	10	266	27 769	6	142
Linn	92	6 544	485 739	-	-	89	5 723	448 443	-	-
Logan	16	3 448	368 647	16	3 436	17	4 578	527 785	13	(D)
Lyon	180	11 007	805 667	2	(D)	149	6 975	442 752	2	(D)
McPherson	106	11 579	1 498 266	92	10 935	86	8 079	954 942	72	7 539
Marion	65	3 765	319 364	14	1 189	90	3 618	231 036	12	743
Marshall	114	6 076	516 616	10	1 307	136	6 796	559 889	8	(D)
Meade	80	21 643	2 651 087	79	21 543	50	13 834	1 907 057	49	13 575
Miami	156	9 976	857 078	-	-	127	9 004	768 364	1	(D)
Mitchell	32	2 516	265 085	20	2 141	24	1 886	211 373	16	1 401
Montgomery	73	7 980	717 163	9	1 597	70	6 171	478 909	6	722
Morris	65	2 667	205 977	-	-	68	2 752	222 855	1	(D)
Morton	10	2 658	361 115	8	2 475	11	2 958	335 863	7	2 653
Nemaha	243	10 885	711 109	-	-	266	13 878	1 105 065	-	-
Neosho	88	5 010	443 841	1	(D)	62	3 321	211 436	-	-
Norton	70	9 097	881 532	39	4 655	36	3 825	472 768	33	3 132
Osage	98	4 676	360 132	-	-	107	4 662	292 600	1	(D)
Osborne	26	1 180	121 174	16	761	22	975	107 752	14	562
Ottawa	11	2 232	301 182	8	354	18	1 313	119 837	11	1 070
Pawnee	52	13 077	1 619 964	52	13 007	27	7 163	861 714	24	6 672
Phillips	38	5 261	604 232	28	3 729	36	4 942	635 845	24	3 051
Pottawatomie	133	11 352	1 167 310	36	6 305	140	10 913	984 007	34	4 367
Pratt	112	29 531	2 996 866	107	27 173	87	16 479	2 415 470	83	15 921
Rawlins	54	6 047	639 516	34	3 925	46	7 684	747 659	34	5 965
Reno	69	11 147	1 243 297	50	8 847	45	5 291	556 907	35	3 355
Republic	255	39 494	5 110 811	211	36 361	256	37 203	3 653 235	197	30 091
Rice	36	7 833	1 015 410	35	7 603	32	5 343	646 360	29	5 195
Riley	56	2 892	263 869	8	633	57	3 608	305 181	10	(D)
Rooks	11	1 303	134 760	8	971	10	1 678	106 081	6	288
Rush	15	966	104 265	12	849	18	1 446	133 260	10	704
Russell	8	102	6 047	-	-	8	(D)	(D)	1	(D)
Saline	27	1 324	115 318	7	305	38	1 575	116 340	10	276
Scott	53	8 948	1 137 275	52	8 801	49	11 902	1 444 365	46	11 800
Sedgwick	79	13 005	1 568 412	67	11 542	85	8 341	983 198	56	7 493
Seward	51	11 367	1 340 010	51	11 367	33	8 805	1 109 932	32	8 750
Shawnee	176	20 588	2 194 933	41	7 110	154	19 857	1 904 940	41	(D)
Sheridan	130	29 533	4 061 477	124	27 485	141	37 152	4 729 234	138	36 419
Sherman	188	35 617	5 066 990	182	34 781	177	44 346	4 896 661	171	43 584
Smith	50	3 039	353 379	37	2 270	39	3 096	251 513	24	1 705
Stafford	106	29 798	3 786 704	100	29 140	57	15 638	2 002 090	49	14 181
Stanton	96	30 940	4 387 760	95	30 360	76	31 695	4 269 541	74	31 542
Stevens	65	25 418	3 303 471	64	25 408	48	15 870	2 056 099	48	15 670
Sumner	17	997	69 170	3	432	4	277	20 110	1	(D)
Thomas	184	48 965	7 122 349	174	45 449	141	46 137	5 958 506	136	45 721
Trego	10	520	66 335	6	425	7	862	67 010	5	707
Wabaunsee	75	6 814	701 730	17	2 647	82	5 881	471 383	8	(D)
Wallace	96	22 478	3 210 151	95	22 148	83	24 670	2 763 152	74	23 976
Washington	129	8 272	785 743	45	3 716	152	10 151	932 294	31	3 540
Wichita	94	16 401	2 291 817	88	15 870	87	20 289	2 515 016	90	20 103
Wilson	38	2 231	176 995	4	272	45	2 338	189 458	3	(D)
Woodson	28	1 513	94 015	-	-	24	1 148	66 995	-	-
Wyandotte	21	2 104	229 180	-	-	16	1 504	134 923	-	-
All other counties	3	291	27 605	1	(D)	(NA)	(NA)	(NA)	(NA)	(NA)

SORGHUM FOR GRAIN OR SEED (BUSHELS)

State Total

	Farms	Acres	Quantity	Farms	Acres	Farms	Acres	Quantity	Farms	Acres
Kansas	32 492	3 399 564	228 045 100	3 137	464 119	26 908	3 187 148	192 400 229	3 474	643 658

[For meaning of abbreviations and symbols, see Introductory text]

Geographic area	1987					1982				
	Harvested			Irrigated		Harvested			Irrigated	
	Farms	Acres	Quantity	Farms	Acres	Farms	Acres	Quantity	Farms	Acres

SORGHUM FOR GRAIN OR SEED (BUSHELS)—Con.

Counties

Geographic area	Farms	Acres	Quantity	Farms	Acres	Farms	Acres	Quantity	Farms	Acres
Allen	294	19 291	1 392 031	-	(D)	254	17 669	1 075 727	1	(D)
Anderson	330	22 705	1 701 589	2	(D)	295	17 965	1 224 904	4	(D)
Atchison	381	32 153	2 556 518	1	(D)	355	27 756	1 783 258	-	-
Barber	104	6 932	348 987	8	746	72	5 359	239 986	6	500
Barton	501	41 882	2 893 658	71	7 967	484	49 778	2 747 676	86	12 924
Bourbon	213	12 311	707 820	-	-	225	14 386	694 551	-	-
Brown	354	28 762	2 296 531	-	-	310	24 208	1 850 117	-	-
Butler	496	68 302	4 789 767	3	260	401	60 154	2 919 375	4	(D)
Chase	122	7 794	521 325	-	-	114	6 658	375 443	-	-
Chautauqua	65	5 308	285 900	-	-	42	4 654	194 549	-	-
Cherokee	248	20 936	1 445 829	-	-	121	9 222	590 433	-	-
Cheyenne	131	11 063	707 778	34	3 889	94	11 420	730 686	37	5 713
Clark	108	9 362	521 390	17	1 556	86	7 888	292 140	12	1 548
Clay	464	41 625	2 964 750	13	579	357	30 662	2 127 030	16	(D)
Cloud	410	37 418	3 004 763	31	1 865	273	24 003	1 646 295	22	1 085
Coffey	342	24 807	1 592 593	3	80	268	20 346	1 297 139	-	-
Comanche	78	7 311	333 660	8	732	64	8 434	290 601	14	1 239
Cowley	365	29 662	1 796 900	9	826	283	25 101	1 165 822	5	800
Crawford	345	26 330	1 787 148	2	(D)	313	24 778	1 580 774	4	(D)
Decatur	326	37 248	2 567 910	15	763	233	26 712	1 648 332	25	1 445
Dickinson	619	47 319	2 702 408	16	825	465	35 952	2 180 955	9	(D)
Doniphan	80	4 352	378 074	-	-	102	5 999	435 442	-	-
Douglas	242	18 903	1 374 534	-	-	203	14 111	858 675	-	-
Edwards	194	20 630	1 290 566	53	5 309	193	34 666	1 966 382	91	14 624
Elk	104	5 465	290 331	-	-	77	5 650	288 866	1	(D)
Ellis	314	21 586	1 182 640	6	598	186	17 316	836 178	8	334
Ellsworth	291	18 469	1 227 419	4	188	212	15 416	832 497	2	(D)
Finney	268	55 632	3 950 820	140	28 229	265	54 674	4 108 566	174	36 103
Ford	428	52 001	3 911 021	115	17 879	289	44 701	2 878 152	121	23 192
Franklin	322	21 469	1 523 437	2	(D)	249	14 188	883 396	3	(D)
Geary	168	10 601	706 133	8	305	132	9 361	693 798	5	(D)
Gove	308	40 514	2 605 504	49	4 864	300	46 482	2 732 785	46	5 017
Graham	287	30 316	1 836 475	27	2 557	201	22 608	1 134 143	24	2 396
Grant	174	42 463	2 350 616	107	20 910	163	65 933	4 066 037	130	36 736
Gray	275	47 462	4 043 765	141	28 627	233	51 785	4 853 670	180	40 919
Greeley	124	16 705	745 922	19	3 214	53	16 951	1 137 342	22	10 512
Greenwood	174	12 603	723 755	1	(D)	151	11 826	563 702	-	-
Hamilton	127	18 681	724 726	17	1 264	86	14 927	710 637	36	5 091
Harper	78	10	(D)	-	-	44	3 329	164 334	2	(D)
Harvey	520	55 624	4 377 977	49	3 514	487	64 182	3 478 461	52	4 279
Haskell	151	32 584	2 843 263	97	23 034	168	44 207	4 001 362	135	35 148
Hodgeman	262	31 439	1 923 912	72	5 669	171	21 644	1 066 834	68	7 036
Jackson	365	23 760	1 362 502	1	(D)	304	17 746	899 661	2	(D)
Jefferson	279	17 596	1 219 455	4	277	225	12 529	733 212	-	-
Jewell	523	58 469	4 277 975	3	175	438	48 073	3 010 074	13	612
Johnson	103	4 799	346 105	-	-	95	5 086	308 046	-	-
Kearny	145	23 385	1 241 764	44	7 230	120	21 991	1 172 509	66	10 117
Kingman	231	11 834	622 839	27	2 317	189	12 527	591 613	30	3 424
Kiowa	190	21 760	1 501 690	41	5 778	168	26 727	1 438 103	30	10 728
Labette	342	25 624	1 819 205	5	372	210	13 652	784 421	3	300
Lane	176	26 210	1 400 041	27	4 030	98	15 993	896 852	40	6 455
Leavenworth	260	14 487	1 030 845	-	-	286	16 905	1 042 078	-	-
Lincoln	350	24 531	1 624 789	4	202	245	15 157	966 035	1	(D)
Linn	241	16 867	1 144 733	-	-	209	17 879	1 019 030	-	-
Logan	184	21 236	1 019 612	19	2 923	133	24 955	1 229 282	23	3 313
Lyon	459	35 421	2 360 796	-	-	408	30 521	1 594 448	1	(D)
McPherson	683	44 923	3 602 374	80	5 602	553	44 882	3 047 246	84	6 452
Marion	739	66 973	4 561 421	9	652	676	57 948	3 440 263	7	475
Marshall	824	91 784	6 350 013	2	(D)	720	74 616	5 086 555	2	(D)
Meade	269	58 143	4 632 870	141	38 130	204	61 501	5 126 686	140	49 606
Miami	262	17 421	1 208 594	1	(D)	259	14 174	850 254	3	112
Mitchell	429	48 067	3 569 899	8	305	283	30 793	1 990 375	8	797
Montgomery	255	28 613	1 921 024	1	(D)	189	19 516	1 130 559	2	(D)
Morris	347	27 744	1 494 922	1	(D)	284	21 146	1 029 188	-	-
Morton	148	59 159	2 546 003	57	13 656	145	16 801	710 914	47	15 296
Nemaha	822	90 326	6 298 279	2	(D)	730	82 005	5 651 871	-	-
Neosho	318	28 847	2 130 009	-	-	211	16 915	1 038 440	-	-
Ness	362	32 270	1 744 228	20	1 177	193	17 957	805 954	19	1 300
Norton	242	23 991	1 713 245	6	409	208	23 997	1 326 086	13	847
Osage	435	39 997	2 864 632	2	(D)	409	33 514	2 002 085	3	(D)
Osborne	417	35 310	2 602 595	58	1 190	291	23 290	1 431 002	24	1 400
Ottawa	211	12 192	869 169	11	615	147	8 065	481 779	3	(D)
Pawnee	337	48 296	3 497 382	117	16 439	290	49 953	3 313 821	135	22 090
Phillips	362	36 063	2 650 230	4	(D)	346	33 527	1 762 323	9	507
Pottawatomie	382	27 721	1 707 784	9	397	340	25 128	1 556 706	7	(D)
Pratt	292	36 214	2 301 925	72	8 625	280	41 923	2 434 254	73	10 838
Rawlins	354	40 057	2 357 618	26	3 223	245	25 618	1 452 558	40	4 344
Reno	785	80 060	5 271 212	78	7 851	754	87 852	4 932 141	84	8 034
Republic	538	64 091	5 252 038	25	1 148	500	56 484	4 021 235	29	1 601
Rice	418	53 304	4 174 853	31	2 779	393	52 500	3 267 617	22	3 094
Riley	312	25 050	1 717 217	3	63	263	21 155	1 476 890	3	(D)
Rooks	284	30 101	1 824 568	9	449	201	20 268	988 040	8	(D)
Rush	337	30 125	1 796 580	5	4 247	241	22 367	1 116 218	60	4 746
Russell	253	21 617	1 336 856	1	(D)	193	15 689	949 603	1	(D)
Saline	303	16 514	1 098 936	16	147	184	10 539	696 827	6	296
Scott	203	35 551	2 314 111	97	17 556	184	34 864	2 463 628	117	21 036
Sedgwick	709	63 831	4 162 363	48	4 030	516	57 698	3 380 245	61	7 934
Seward	185	49 622	3 281 751	100	25 160	157	61 383	4 271 463	83	30 557
Shawnee	260	20 453	1 279 717	6	147	189	14 800	774 951	3	(D)
Sheridan	304	35 704	2 549 482	71	8 434	241	26 324	1 988 008	92	11 220

Table 24. Grains—Corn, Sorghum, Wheat, and Other Small Grains: 1987 and 1982—Con.

[For meaning of abbreviations and symbols, see introductory text]

Geographic area	1987					1982				
	Harvested			Irrigated		Harvested			Irrigated	
	Farms	Acres	Quantity	Farms	Acres	Farms	Acres	Quantity	Farms	Acres
SORGHUM FOR GRAIN OR SEED (BUSHELS)—Con.										
Counties—Con.										
Sherman	115	10 329	620 775	42	4 033	95	9 189	530 600	51	4 826
Smith	507	61 188	6 249 221	49	2 962	473	54 710	3 584 964	26	1 571
Stafford	328	47 264	3 023 173	90	11 350	338	60 989	3 631 977	102	16 401
Stanton	146	31 419	1 937 190	95	20 217	131	39 102	2 933 275	103	27 637
Stevens	225	114 832	5 595 676	124	35 126	266	180 500	7 880 269	135	48 974
Sumner	412	31 913	1 506 504	5	460	246	17 557	763 645	8	(D)
Thomas	322	36 435	2 357 796	56	8 268	184	27 679	1 871 603	79	11 615
Trego	273	26 500	1 507 727	12	1 198	166	19 430	851 440	16	1 399
Wabaunsee	292	19 382	1 274 145	6	470	294	21 507	1 139 425	-	-
Wallace	81	9 731	463 198	28	3 100	85	18 732	1 382 213	50	14 278
Washington	689	96 823	7 110 326	26	3 021	690	82 730	5 853 379	10	(D)
Wichita	187	24 374	1 693 699	115	14 259	168	30 202	2 419 424	131	24 204
Wilson	269	26 603	1 798 323	2	(D)	253	20 866	1 312 404	1	(D)
Woodson	191	17 603	1 250 906	-	-	163	13 370	873 354	-	-
Wyandotte	6	(D)	(D)	-	-	13	511	39 956	-	-
WHEAT FOR GRAIN (BUSHELS)										
State Total										
Kansas	38 838	8 679 588	292 999 442	3 046	635 524	49 231	11 664 008	372 590 045	3 111	715 445
Counties										
Allen	141	9 519	273 355	1	(D)	403	38 549	1 011 938	1	(D)
Anderson	135	6 576	197 151	-	-	386	26 129	635 014	-	-
Atchison	133	5 160	137 915	-	-	397	22 948	467 804	-	-
Barber	375	121 445	3 341 963	5	416	411	161 844	5 813 295	4	275
Barton	750	167 887	5 428 175	37	3 859	781	216 460	6 965 195	52	9 990
Bourbon	65	3 442	65 687	-	-	315	27 231	608 342	-	-
Brown	367	26 577	1 030 105	-	-	566	54 048	1 504 957	-	-
Butler	486	63 948	1 885 760	1	(D)	651	87 703	2 789 142	2	(D)
Chase	136	11 898	330 110	-	-	178	17 804	477 274	-	-
Chautauqua	78	8 028	179 242	-	-	144	19 411	639 782	-	-
Cherokee	158	16 296	372 571	-	-	523	83 914	2 260 391	1	(D)
Cheyenne	409	109 225	4 063 922	42	5 127	459	145 981	5 255 519	51	8 519
Clark	213	70 665	2 097 680	7	1 857	237	94 556	2 683 999	14	2 544
Clay	519	79 221	2 715 122	7	520	598	111 394	3 104 666	6	700
Cloud	501	108 897	3 909 381	4	230	578	149 400	4 045 896	5	280
Coffey	182	11 740	313 311	-	-	404	38 862	832 133	-	-
Comanche	182	71 867	1 848 967	10	1 007	202	96 249	3 058 889	12	2 149
Cowley	549	95 945	2 695 979	3	220	730	147 415	4 682 442	3	350
Crawford	69	3 989	121 569	-	-	411	34 510	877 364	1	(D)
Decatur	396	93 716	3 999 819	8	1 110	428	117 804	4 790 172	9	775
Dickinson	816	135 344	4 377 284	-	-	927	194 101	5 980 097	-	-
Doniphan	118	7 949	326 510	-	-	329	26 108	756 627	-	-
Douglas	76	2 844	92 999	-	-	363	24 460	539 088	1	(D)
Edwards	296	87 995	2 921 112	61	11 093	338	114 098	3 467 145	71	13 147
Elk	99	6 405	148 994	-	-	181	19 781	606 202	-	-
Ellis	611	99 562	3 181 838	2	(D)	611	118 080	3 735 127	4	368
Ellsworth	405	85 816	2 976 878	2	(D)	439	111 611	3 674 534	3	335
Finney	431	174 488	7 146 392	229	61 592	463	214 825	7 947 679	233	62 464
Ford	644	181 190	6 427 347	111	22 320	667	214 227	6 779 134	111	25 597
Franklin	87	4 832	136 449	-	-	378	22 532	442 872	1	(D)
Geary	170	16 731	603 083	2	(D)	189	23 265	764 968	2	(D)
Gove	435	117 701	4 498 191	19	2 389	415	116 232	3 383 960	18	1 917
Graham	379	91 909	3 548 458	14	1 784	425	114 914	3 710 398	30	3 575
Grant	232	72 047	2 626 269	156	36 744	209	92 689	3 609 301	141	44 853
Gray	453	133 609	4 994 017	237	47 179	466	185 813	7 107 378	248	67 307
Greeley	252	145 703	4 553 923	31	6 651	252	161 289	4 204 899	22	7 557
Greenwood	160	9 895	249 303	1	(D)	293	23 006	629 403	1	(D)
Hamilton	207	125 546	3 977 998	32	6 878	219	176 830	4 155 467	33	9 343
Harper	579	212 192	6 247 571	1	(D)	596	267 854	9 640 603	3	380
Harvey	602	103 013	3 078 624	10	874	697	128 828	4 256 279	20	1 702
Haskell	269	99 081	3 800 254	185	60 292	267	127 700	5 032 452	194	66 589
Hodgeman	370	105 731	3 654 253	55	5 220	402	126 997	4 268 344	64	5 497
Jackson	155	9 222	240 021	1	(D)	459	34 356	555 193	3	650
Jefferson	83	3 836	126 760	-	-	367	25 522	516 446	-	-
Jewell	566	109 626	4 379 120	3	260	640	160 165	5 340 637	7	495
Johnson	50	2 575	74 530	-	-	231	13 687	577 681	-	-
Kearny	226	121 394	4 521 318	84	23 260	230	138 241	4 732 102	89	22 406
Kingman	661	176 798	4 985 931	15	3 945	713	221 474	7 020 389	12	1 502
Kiowa	252	74 613	2 338 400	49	7 715	286	90 420	2 586 715	55	9 534
Labette	171	11 815	252 913	-	-	595	62 529	2 225 675	1	(D)
Lane	280	111 527	4 240 788	26	3 904	291	128 244	4 186 591	37	5 695
Leavenworth	74	3 049	86 850	-	-	390	20 703	421 059	-	-
Lincoln	480	99 912	3 442 697	1	(D)	520	128 675	4 275 564	1	(D)
Linn	73	2 608	70 864	-	-	299	22 360	502 544	-	-
Logan	322	111 886	3 567 380	18	2 178	292	126 792	3 744 936	11	1 919
Lyon	274	17 825	498 181	-	-	553	41 908	884 017	-	(D)
McPherson	1 077	184 434	6 198 954	9	1 133	1 213	244 679	7 509 966	6	730
Marion	857	118 472	3 717 501	-	-	969	156 067	4 300 596	2	(D)
Marshall	766	75 311	2 580 342	1	(D)	901	101 052	3 019 208	1	(D)
Meade	391	106 765	3 452 545	152	31 487	410	125 027	3 861 636	130	29 088

Table 24. **Grains—Corn, Sorghum, Wheat, and Other Small Grains: 1987 and 1982**—Con.

[For meaning of abbreviations and symbols, see introductory text]

Geographic area	1987 Harvested Farms	Acres	Quantity	1987 Irrigated Farms	Acres	1982 Harvested Farms	Acres	Quantity	1982 Irrigated Farms	Acres
WHEAT FOR GRAIN (BUSHELS)—Con.										
Counties—Con.										
Miami	48	1 831	44 393	-	-	340	19 191	481 170	-	-
Mitchell	529	164 343	6 254 876	4	644	548	196 397	8 129 729	-	-
Montgomery	177	16 023	365 771	-	-	423	62 293	1 772 173	1	(D)
Morris	326	36 194	1 020 099	-	-	398	49 490	1 067 703	-	-
Morton	167	74 500	2 058 381	64	17 937	174	98 280	2 042 541	47	14 895
Nemaha	654	35 303	1 080 837	-	-	755	53 302	1 522 644	-	-
Neosho	136	13 064	335 523	1	(D)	475	58 446	1 575 703	-	-
Ness	519	135 612	4 654 378	14	745	567	180 184	6 279 479	17	1 800
Norton	376	98 468	3 942 666	2	(D)	421	121 570	4 720 905	6	1 037
Osage	160	7 688	205 292	1	(D)	528	37 407	711 880	1	(D)
Osborne	517	117 191	4 308 743	4	1 621	528	129 846	4 195 634	2	(D)
Ottawa	424	111 270	3 482 863	-	-	476	153 160	4 566 654	3	465
Pawnee	433	125 758	4 295 992	94	11 786	481	158 657	5 142 355	96	15 083
Phillips	473	84 316	3 467 434	-	-	532	97 804	3 610 923	3	(D)
Pottawatomie	301	16 968	524 558	1	(D)	465	35 466	898 003	1	(D)
Pratt	428	143 482	4 258 898	47	6 499	465	165 792	4 997 083	38	6 327
Rawlins	467	123 069	4 778 125	14	1 605	541	162 641	5 224 894	22	2 483
Reno	1 140	237 736	6 848 396	19	2 999	1 232	298 224	9 446 664	23	3 947
Republic	639	83 080	3 356 029	15	769	723	116 068	3 560 207	11	1 844
Rice	484	130 672	4 485 243	7	321	533	165 617	5 436 931	10	1 223
Riley	302	21 023	723 691	1	(D)	360	29 744	912 477	3	210
Rooks	408	100 707	3 769 144	1	(D)	455	126 965	4 593 142	6	1 217
Rush	461	113 315	3 815 969	30	1 461	494	135 769	4 619 455	24	1 300
Russell	414	92 100	2 995 383	2	(D)	466	123 359	4 217 092	2	(D)
Saline	541	126 775	3 770 758	5	198	606	166 557	5 039 990	1	(D)
Scott	315	115 140	4 521 676	88	16 013	336	141 976	4 626 370	111	18 063
Sedgwick	1 041	189 806	5 504 666	21	2 162	1 106	242 204	6 445 246	25	2 673
Seward	208	68 948	2 317 037	123	30 213	195	79 568	2 613 642	90	29 436
Shawnee	146	7 719	233 770	-	-	355	27 231	536 936	4	194
Sheridan	421	94 689	3 742 447	54	5 811	458	112 641	4 419 751	58	5 634
Sherman	445	155 862	5 887 056	120	17 196	478	198 634	7 112 290	122	21 348
Smith	579	107 735	4 438 271	1	(D)	513	128 944	4 794 127	6	519
Stafford	439	124 760	3 592 067	87	11 272	492	193 498	6 096 384	76	12 219
Stanton	233	113 050	4 136 357	157	51 671	205	137 229	4 469 170	127	49 338
Stevens	224	89 747	3 172 411	141	48 869	237	98 712	3 486 470	134	45 464
Sumner	1 040	356 942	10 409 785	7	418	1 188	476 013	15 510 050	3	(D)
Thomas	551	181 694	6 513 764	76	9 745	538	217 672	7 804 657	80	15 731
Trego	413	91 726	3 380 837	6	400	411	105 559	3 267 173	5	313
Wabaunsee	222	11 153	330 170	2	(D)	355	24 503	572 872	3	(D)
Wallace	287	93 419	3 009 097	89	12 340	255	96 483	3 392 212	67	16 220
Washington	652	74 196	2 636 117	1	(D)	784	109 298	3 356 641	4	207
Wichita	300	118 864	4 477 060	135	29 166	288	126 266	4 440 890	152	34 656
Wilson	210	16 950	394 873	-	-	439	61 262	1 662 195	2	(D)
Woodson	114	7 822	171 930	-	-	206	21 000	559 055	-	-
Wyandotte	9	482	14 156	-	-	36	3 473	103 314	-	-
BARLEY FOR GRAIN (BUSHELS)										
State Total										
Kansas	2 307	95 465	3 639 224	186	7 359	666	34 820	1 490 498	84	9 599
Counties										
Barber	4	(D)	(D)	-	-	11	443	17 114	-	-
Barton	19	528	14 200	-	-	8	307	20 095	-	-
Cheyenne	56	2 286	108 554	2	(D)	3	120	4 500	1	(D)
Clay	4	105	4 260	-	-	4	122	2 310	-	-
Cloud	7	245	8 366	-	-	3	70	2 800	-	-
Coffey	3	136	(D)	-	-	3	(D)	(D)	-	-
Comanche	4	123	4 320	-	-	6	(D)	(D)	2	(D)
Cowley	17	716	24 604	-	-	27	1 521	59 907	-	-
Decatur	53	1 242	44 587	1	(D)	3	125	5 500	-	-
Dickinson	41	871	34 173	-	-	30	914	34 970	-	-
Edwards	51	1 969	81 544	2	(D)	13	548	25 582	8	205
Ellis	16	165	6 702	-	-	(NA)	(NA)	(NA)	(NA)	(NA)
Ellsworth	16	442	21 143	-	-	9	45	2 700	-	-
Finney	52	2 536	95 395	12	681	1 028	42 310		5	900
Ford	95	2 476	93 682	4	205	12	1 077	36 716	2	(D)
Franklin	4	57	2 440	-	-	9	210	7 114	-	-
Geary	5	49	1 726	-	-	(NA)	(NA)	(NA)	(NA)	(NA)
Gove	96	4 539	194 869	2	(D)	12	591	24 798	-	-
Graham	35	1 380	38 749	-	-	5	893	42 260	2	(D)
Grant	29	1 088	40 696	21	546	3	108	3 277	3	106
Gray	7	154	3 611	-	-	5	117	2 142	-	-
Greeley	79	6 100	299 064	6	578	(NA)	(NA)	(NA)	(NA)	(NA)
Hamilton	25	1 592	63 210	8	(D)	7	1 026	26 364	5	75
Harper	11	344	10 840	-	-	10	437	19 480	-	-
Harvey	22	599	30 908	-	-	10	626	32 271	-	-
Haskell	8	577	13 124	4	142	(NA)	(NA)	(NA)	(NA)	(NA)
Hodgeman	67	2 303	81 587	3	(D)	5	283	17 166	1	(D)
Jackson	3	(D)	(D)	1	(D)	(NA)	(NA)	(NA)	(NA)	(NA)
Jefferson	4	26	621	-	-	(NA)	(NA)	(NA)	(NA)	(NA)
Jewell	18	947	50 989	-	-	9	263	12 247	-	-

Table 24. **Grains—Corn, Sorghum, Wheat, and Other Small Grains: 1987 and 1982**—Con.

[For meaning of abbreviations and symbols, see introductory text]

Geographic area	1987					1982				
	Harvested			Irrigated		Harvested			Irrigated	
	Farms	Acres	Quantity	Farms	Acres	Farms	Acres	Quantity	Farms	Acres

BARLEY FOR GRAIN (BUSHELS)—Con.

Counties—Con.

Kearny	57	4 146	176 547	10	397	(NA)	(NA)	(NA)	(NA)	(NA)
Kingman	12	675	31 138	-	-	23	1 055	47 940	5	362
Kiowa	8	223	7 710	1	(D)	9	277	14 772	3	180
Labette	3	(D)	(D)	-	-	7	141	5 005	-	-
Lane	92	4 742	176 954	5	310	14	834	30 651	5	320
Leavenworth	8	105	5 676	-	-	3	(D)	(D)	1	(D)
Lincoln	16	561	27 429	-	-	(NA)	(NA)	(NA)	(NA)	(NA)
Logan	48	1 975	58 549	-	-	5	194	11 379	-	-
Lyon	6	73	3 185	2	(D)	(NA)	(NA)	(NA)	(NA)	(NA)
McPherson	14	243	10 590	-	-	15	499	19 542	-	-
Marion	44	1 345	60 670	-	-	24	1 394	65 132	1	(D)
Meade	26	770	24 008	3	89	4	156	(D)	3	126
Mitchell	8	317	16 140	1	(D)	(NA)	(NA)	(NA)	(NA)	(NA)
Montgomery	3	64	(D)	-	-	9	429	14 886	-	-
Morris	4	55	1 685	-	-	6	260	5 525	-	-
Morton	12	1 083	26 951	2	(D)	(NA)	(NA)	(NA)	(NA)	(NA)
Nemaha	5	191	7 968	-	-	(NA)	(NA)	(NA)	(NA)	(NA)
Ness	99	4 077	107 211	-	-	10	407	13 900	-	-
Norton	66	1 959	76 595	-	-	4	395	18 925	1	(D)
Osborne	15	415	19 390	-	-	5	188	7 300	-	-
Ottawa	4	130	3 100	-	-	(NA)	(NA)	(NA)	(NA)	(NA)
Pawnee	19	655	23 681	1	(D)	5	548	20 975	1	(D)
Phillips	39	881	39 472	-	-	5	215	9 695	-	-
Pottawatomie	4	32	1 090	-	-	(NA)	(NA)	(NA)	(NA)	(NA)
Pratt	8	295	11 857	-	-	4	614	25 002	1	(D)
Rawlins	54	1 901	65 248	1	(D)	6	144	5 946	-	-
Reno	21	624	29 898	-	-	22	835	31 411	2	(D)
Rice	5	63	2 396	-	-	4	245	(D)	-	-
Riley	10	157	5 686	-	-	(NA)	(NA)	(NA)	(NA)	(NA)
Rooks	24	590	20 707	-	-	3	(D)	(D)	-	-
Rush	53	953	34 752	1	(D)	4	125	3 800	3	102
Russell	14	297	11 395	-	-	(NA)	(NA)	(NA)	(NA)	(NA)
Saline	13	521	24 287	-	-	4	200	(D)	-	-
Scott	87	4 517	206 928	9	354	(NA)	(NA)	(NA)	(NA)	(NA)
Sedgwick	17	290	8 598	-	-	25	1 076	43 762	-	-
Seward	14	711	24 575	4	123	(NA)	(NA)	(NA)	(NA)	(NA)
Sheridan	64	1 885	69 363	8	274	(NA)	(NA)	(NA)	(NA)	(NA)
Sherman	58	2 871	123 683	11	436	9	891	49 518	2	(D)
Smith	42	1 180	35 253	-	-	7	145	9 120	-	-
Stafford	16	560	19 417	1	(D)	9	467	19 990	-	-
Stanton	35	2 623	100 955	18	1 817	16	2 359	133 459	14	2 248
Stevens	25	1 380	48 456	8	237	(NA)	(NA)	(NA)	(NA)	(NA)
Sumner	28	1 312	50 193	-	-	39	2 431	112 195	-	-
Thomas	61	2 914	100 823	1	(D)	4	(D)	(D)	1	(D)
Trego	46	1 228	47 262	-	-	(NA)	(NA)	(NA)	(NA)	(NA)
Wallace	46	1 682	53 290	4	79	18	1 408	59 662	7	584
Wichita	83	4 600	188 694	12	276	(NA)	(NA)	(NA)	(NA)	(NA)
All other counties	31	840	29 691	2	(D)	(NA)	(NA)	(NA)	(NA)	(NA)

OATS FOR GRAIN (BUSHELS)

State Total

Kansas	5 313	126 091	4 775 729	48	2 276	6 644	186 982	7 799 056	108	7 176

Counties

Allen	77	1 965	75 541	-	-	92	2 042	111 540	-	-
Anderson	84	2 144	60 947	-	-	120	2 618	108 158	-	-
Atchison	107	2 589	127 246	-	-	100	1 829	76 244	-	-
Barber	14	779	29 834	-	-	38	1 360	47 062	-	-
Barton	52	880	39 723	-	-	27	361	15 391	2	(D)
Bourbon	63	1 434	45 437	-	-	91	1 737	77 622	-	-
Brown	114	2 277	101 456	-	-	183	3 089	167 930	-	-
Butler	49	951	27 956	-	-	103	2 729	113 895	1	(D)
Chase	31	527	20 226	-	-	54	1 112	47 674	-	-
Chautauqua	14	793	25 175	-	-	44	1 046	46 677	-	-
Cherokee	50	1 186	34 397	-	-	75	1 731	105 011	-	-
Cheyenne	25	1 107	58 106	5	257	12	1 153	37 817	3	191
Clark	7	260	7 718	-	-	(NA)	(NA)	(NA)	(NA)	(NA)
Clay	135	2 298	106 359	-	-	129	2 360	99 640	-	-
Cloud	82	1 769	80 251	-	-	91	2 646	126 326	-	-
Coffey	36	629	18 783	-	-	46	620	25 733	-	-
Cowley	33	667	15 647	-	-	74	1 865	88 729	-	-
Crawford	98	3 003	109 140	-	-	159	4 294	245 432	-	-
Decatur	42	1 448	57 297	-	-	35	932	53 635	-	-
Dickinson	201	4 012	126 951	-	-	294	6 273	319 736	2	(D)
Doniphan	34	425	22 486	-	-	36	1 036	56 697	-	-
Douglas	82	1 611	49 741	-	-	102	1 711	78 925	-	-
Edwards	9	355	10 060	1	(D)	6	203	(D)	3	(D)
Elk	24	507	13 300	-	-	40	1 068	41 226	-	-
Ellis	25	650	20 211	-	-	9	192	7 666	-	-
Ellsworth	51	1 046	34 586	-	-	19	562	27 570	-	-
Finney	-	372	13 838	1	(D)	5	375	16 070	3	335
Ford	24	975	24 292	1	(D)	9	649	23 438	4	267
Franklin	113	1 891	67 971	-	-	202	3 929	192 941	-	-
Geary	62	1 188	40 269	-	-	53	965	44 930	1	(D)

Table 24. Grains—Corn, Sorghum, Wheat, and Other Small Grains: 1987 and 1982—Con.

[For meaning of abbreviations and symbols, see introductory text]

Geographic area	1987					1982				
	Harvested			Irrigated		Harvested			Irrigated	
	Farms	Acres	Quantity	Farms	Acres	Farms	Acres	Quantity	Farms	Acres
OATS FOR GRAIN (BUSHELS)—Con.										
Counties—Con.										
Gove	16	1 005	32 069	1	(D)	18	1 371	35 528	4	330
Graham	22	776	31 190	-	-	17	1 124	49 744	4	500
Grant	3	(D)	4 200	2	(D)	3	45	2 450	2	(D)
Gray	4	105	2 450	2	(D)	9	980	70 975	8	910
Greeley	4	306	6 187	-	-	(NA)	(NA)	(NA)	(NA)	(NA)
Greenwood	96	891	24 087	-	-	60	1 496	54 182	-	-
Hamilton	4	132	2 492	4	132	(NA)	(NA)	(NA)	(NA)	(NA)
Harper	20	1 045	29 335	-	-	36	961	34 713	-	-
Harvey	33	854	25 612	-	-	66	1 446	76 885	2	(D)
Haskell	3	37	1 300	2	(D)	(NA)	(NA)	(NA)	(NA)	(NA)
Hodgeman	4	131	3 670	-	-	(NA)	(NA)	(NA)	(NA)	(NA)
Jackson	95	2 186	89 856	1	(D)	121	2 707	111 342	3	(D)
Jefferson	97	1 945	68 835	-	-	119	2 521	102 349	-	-
Jewell	116	2 973	132 983	-	-	97	3 099	124 515	-	-
Johnson	52	928	33 361	-	-	57	1 024	42 305	-	-
Kearny	7	516	12 519	-	-	(NA)	(NA)	(NA)	(NA)	(NA)
Kingman	53	1 540	51 915	-	-	68	2 387	107 413	1	(D)
Kiowa	10	717	19 010	1	(D)	5	1 187	29 100	-	-
Labette	179	5 485	172 356	-	-	247	7 155	376 383	-	-
Lane	13	645	21 405	1	(D)	3	(D)	(D)	2	(D)
Leavenworth	90	1 647	55 135	1	(D)	85	1 094	42 429	-	-
Lincoln	77	1 845	71 466	-	-	87	2 020	96 538	1	-
Linn	61	1 225	44 681	-	-	99	1 929	82 412	1	(D)
Logan	21	1 329	48 655	-	-	7	328	12 975	-	-
Lyon	47	1 332	43 923	-	-	105	1 655	68 062	2	-
McPherson	53	675	27 692	-	-	92	1 541	59 434	-	(D)
Marion	148	2 925	85 028	-	-	271	6 151	231 847	-	-
Marshall	145	2 320	112 692	-	-	215	4 852	256 400	-	-
Miami	89	1 520	53 858	-	-	125	2 188	103 223	-	-
Mitchell	79	1 503	71 498	2	(D)	54	1 572	78 372	-	-
Montgomery	64	1 552	48 806	-	-	110	2 823	132 680	1	(D)
Morris	83	1 759	48 007	-	-	131	2 789	101 638	-	-
Morton	4	268	12 940	2	(D)	(NA)	(NA)	(NA)	(NA)	(NA)
Nemaha	120	2 034	84 805	-	-	171	2 825	134 916	-	-
Neosho	147	4 216	168 894	-	-	162	5 260	291 000	-	-
Ness	12	297	5 780	-	-	9	258	16 810	-	-
Norton	62	2 996	103 836	1	(D)	42	1 798	88 502	-	-
Osage	63	1 040	34 658	-	-	114	1 713	69 534	-	-
Osborne	61	1 344	86 866	-	-	24	701	36 062	-	-
Ottawa	40	625	25 481	-	-	23	369	17 169	1	(D)
Pawnee	12	324	10 876	-	-	11	696	33 820	-	-
Phillips	77	1 834	63 457	-	-	78	1 671	82 750	-	-
Pottawatomie	95	1 421	56 179	-	-	109	1 643	63 992	-	-
Pratt	12	484	15 979	2	(D)	23	1 048	49 241	4	300
Rawlins	59	2 160	100 026	-	-	24	859	46 497	3	110
Reno	55	1 157	36 030	2	(D)	119	4 444	224 787	7	326
Republic	111	2 162	109 378	2	(D)	191	4 120	212 050	2	(D)
Rice	22	889	28 124	-	-	15	953	49 463	-	-
Riley	68	1 027	43 598	-	-	78	1 342	60 657	-	-
Rooks	22	736	23 120	-	-	21	1 415	65 875	1	(D)
Rush	50	1 569	46 850	2	(D)	29	1 919	83 902	5	118
Russell	39	827	30 517	-	-	26	909	31 256	-	-
Saline	33	703	25 625	-	-	59	1 244	52 017	-	-
Scott	3	122	6 500	1	(D)	5	220	11 302	4	197
Sedgwick	27	560	15 665	-	-	85	2 947	109 766	-	-
Seward	3	123	3 777	2	(D)	(NA)	(NA)	(NA)	(NA)	(NA)
Shawnee	73	1 086	30 440	-	-	64	894	29 082	-	-
Sheridan	26	1 038	33 054	3	(D)	24	1 103	67 288	3	(D)
Sherman	20	959	49 845	3	212	30	2 479	159 884	7	352
Smith	110	2 874	123 463	-	-	81	1 843	110 777	-	-
Stafford	16	792	21 679	2	(D)	26	1 222	64 388	2	(D)
Sumner	11	538	13 000	-	-	36	1 144	47 144	-	-
Thomas	36	2 369	113 468	1	(D)	27	2 131	105 113	10	784
Trego	28	875	24 243	-	-	8	251	11 769	1	(D)
Wabaunsee	66	1 122	42 686	-	-	85	1 067	42 862	-	-
Wallace	12	762	25 960	-	-	3	157	10 480	-	-
Washington	155	2 775	143 002	-	-	181	4 565	219 260	-	-
Wichita	11	757	32 630	2	(D)	7	432	(D)	1	(D)
Wilson	31	818	29 093	-	-	72	1 244	65 771	-	-
Woodson	38	740	27 145	-	-	51	883	37 292	-	-
Wyandotte	4	51	1 730	-	-	5	60	2 320	-	-
All other counties	6	(D)	6 100	-	-	(NA)	(NA)	(NA)	(NA)	(NA)
POPCORN (POUNDS, SHELLED)										
State Total										
Kansas	127	7 801	23 176 812	56	6 143	51	1 915	5 778 250	27	1 735

Table 24. Grains—Corn, Sorghum, Wheat, and Other Small Grains: 1987 and 1982—Con.

[For meaning of abbreviations and symbols, see introductory text]

Geographic area	1987					1982				
	Harvested			Irrigated		Harvested			Irrigated	
	Farms	Acres	Quantity	Farms	Acres	Farms	Acres	Quantity	Farms	Acres
POPCORN (POUNDS, SHELLED)—Con.										
Counties										
Anderson	3	(D)	(D)	-	-	(NA)	(NA)	(NA)	(NA)	(NA)
Clay	3	(D)	(D)	2	(D)	(NA)	(NA)	(NA)	(NA)	(NA)
Douglas	6	(D)	509 000	-	-	(NA)	(NA)	(NA)	(NA)	(NA)
Franklin	4	8	6 000	-	-	3	6	5 000	1	(D)
Grant	13	(D)	3 001 430	13	(D)	11	880	2 823 877	11	880
Haskell	4	(D)	2 032 400	4	(D)	(NA)	(NA)	(NA)	(NA)	(NA)
Jefferson	5	(D)	357 350	-	-	(NA)	(NA)	(NA)	(NA)	(NA)
Labette	6	156	552 536	3	152	(NA)	(NA)	(NA)	(NA)	(NA)
Leavenworth	4	103	164 820	-	-	(NA)	(NA)	(NA)	(NA)	(NA)
Lyon	3	(D)	(D)	1	(D)	(NA)	(NA)	(NA)	(NA)	(NA)
Nemaha	3	(D)	3 700	-	-	(NA)	(NA)	(NA)	(NA)	(NA)
Norton	3	183	349 716	1	(D)	(NA)	(NA)	(NA)	(NA)	(NA)
Phillips	8	105	202 300	-	-	(NA)	(NA)	(NA)	(NA)	(NA)
Shawnee	3	(D)	(D)	-	-	(NA)	(NA)	(NA)	(NA)	(NA)
Stanton	10	2 133	7 600 900	10	(D)	4	320	1 335 200	4	320
Stevens	6	823	3 127 880	8	823	(NA)	(NA)	(NA)	(NA)	(NA)
All other counties	45	1 414	3 624 710	16	969	(NA)	(NA)	(NA)	(NA)	(NA)
PROSO MILLET (BUSHELS)										
State Total										
Kansas	61	8 184	150 564	-	-	27	2 884	43 566	1	(D)
Counties										
Cheyenne	14	898	26 537	-	-	(NA)	(NA)	(NA)	(NA)	(NA)
Greeley	13	3 879	57 890	-	-	7	853	12 052	-	-
Hamilton	3	(D)	(D)	-	-	(NA)	(NA)	(NA)	(NA)	(NA)
Rawlins	3	190	6 640	-	-	(NA)	(NA)	(NA)	(NA)	(NA)
Sherman	7	(D)	16 095	-	-	11	744	12 233	1	(D)
Thomas	3	80	(D)	-	-	(NA)	(NA)	(NA)	(NA)	(NA)
Wallace	5	(D)	3 100	-	-	(NA)	(NA)	(NA)	(NA)	(NA)
Wichita	3	(D)	(D)	-	-	(NA)	(NA)	(NA)	(NA)	(NA)
All other counties	10	1 224	16 116	-	-	(NA)	(NA)	(NA)	(NA)	(NA)
RYE FOR GRAIN (BUSHELS)										
State Total										
Kansas	131	7 620	213 924	9	484	95	2 563	60 806	2	(D)
Counties										
Barton	3	(D)	(D)	-	-	4	(D)	2 752	1	(D)
Cheyenne	9	742	20 990	-	-	6	250	4 290	1	(D)
Gove	8	240	9 115	-	-	(NA)	(NA)	(NA)	(NA)	(NA)
Greeley	4	670	21 155	-	-	(NA)	(NA)	(NA)	(NA)	(NA)
Kearny	3	182	5 481	1	(D)	(NA)	(NA)	(NA)	(NA)	(NA)
Logan	4	554	14 350	2	(D)	(NA)	(NA)	(NA)	(NA)	(NA)
Morton	4	260	4 240	-	-	(NA)	(NA)	(NA)	(NA)	(NA)
Pawnee	3	74	(D)	-	-	(NA)	(NA)	(NA)	(NA)	(NA)
Phillips	3	145	4 675	1	(D)	(NA)	(NA)	(NA)	(NA)	(NA)
Rawlins	6	361	14 770	-	-	(NA)	(NA)	(NA)	(NA)	(NA)
Reno	3	(D)	(D)	-	-	6	67	2 124	-	-
Sheridan	9	172	3 155	-	-	(NA)	(NA)	(NA)	(NA)	(NA)
Sherman	3	207	4 369	1	(D)	(NA)	(NA)	(NA)	(NA)	(NA)
Stafford	20	1 081	19 815	-	-	8	375	6 800	-	-
Thomas	4	510	15 600	-	-	(NA)	(NA)	(NA)	(NA)	(NA)
Wichita	3	120	3 598	-	-	(NA)	(NA)	(NA)	(NA)	(NA)
All other counties	44	2 207	69 157	2	(D)	(NA)	(NA)	(NA)	(NA)	(NA)
SUNFLOWER SEED (POUNDS)										
State Total										
Kansas	1 196	113 449	134 339 654	140	13 088	380	42 328	48 509 547	147	15 463
Counties										
Cheyenne	106	11 437	15 649 351	8	938	(NA)	(NA)	(NA)	(NA)	(NA)
Clark	4	246	326 100	-	-	(NA)	(NA)	(NA)	(NA)	(NA)
Cloud	5	241	(D)	-	-	6	260	141 813	-	-
Decatur	105	(D)	15 972 688	3	70	(NA)	(NA)	(NA)	(NA)	(NA)
Edwards	3	346	464 260	1	(D)	3	(D)	(NA)	2	(D)
Ellis	5	431	411 785	-	-	(NA)	(NA)	(NA)	(NA)	(NA)
Ellsworth	5	224	235 600	-	-	(NA)	(NA)	(NA)	(NA)	(NA)
Finney	16	1 999	2 004 746	9	975	15	1 774	1 682 230	9	1 154
Ford	27	(D)	4 487 815	9	320	16	1 813	1 924 545	9	990
Gove	8	631	749 660	-	-	8	1 315	1 194 000	-	-

Table 24. Grains—Corn, Sorghum, Wheat, and Other Small Grains: 1987 and 1982—Con.

[For meaning of abbreviations and symbols, see introductory text]

| Geographic area | 1987 | | | | | 1982 | | | | |
| | Harvested | | | Irrigated | | Harvested | | | Irrigated | |
	Farms	Acres	Quantity	Farms	Acres	Farms	Acres	Quantity	Farms	Acres
SUNFLOWER SEED (POUNDS)—Con.										
Counties—Con.										
Graham	29	3 594	3 694 670	-	-	4	178	165 080	-	-
Grant	5	452	628 000	3	(D)	6	374	326 420	6	374
Gray	13	1 262	1 540 690	1	(D)	8	1 685	993 060	6	1 127
Greeley	12	670	862 850	3	247	7	1 015	619 060	-	-
Harvey	9	382	304 025	-	-	3	180	(D)	-	-
Hodgeman	5	(D)	270 325	-	-	(NA)	(NA)	(NA)	(NA)	(NA)
Jewell	19	703	567 810	-	-	6	422	330 750	-	-
Kearny	4	494	304 400	-	-	(NA)	(NA)	(NA)	(NA)	(NA)
Kiowa	6	(D)	311 515	1	(D)	5	383	360 660	4	320
Lincoln	4	(D)	242 080	-	-	(NA)	(NA)	(NA)	(NA)	(NA)
Logan	6	936	726 509	-	-	3	(D)	77 044	(NA)	(NA)
McPherson	3	46	14 450	-	-	(NA)	(NA)	(NA)	(NA)	(NA)
Marshall	3	(D)	73 800	-	-	(NA)	(NA)	(NA)	(NA)	(NA)
Meade	9	685	723 174	2	(D)	5	361	450 200	5	376
Mitchell	10	748	449 228	-	-	3	(D)	(D)	-	-
Morton	3	233	(D)	-	-	(NA)	(NA)	(NA)	(NA)	(NA)
Nemaha	3	155	108 500	-	-	(NA)	(NA)	(NA)	(NA)	(NA)
Ness	21	1 007	908 705	-	-	(NA)	(NA)	(NA)	(NA)	(NA)
Norton	46	3 567	4 956 713	-	-	(NA)	(NA)	(NA)	(NA)	(NA)
Osborne	18	1 427	1 800 265	1	(D)	(NA)	(NA)	(NA)	(NA)	(NA)
Ottawa	7	223	(D)	-	-	(NA)	(NA)	(NA)	(NA)	(NA)
Pawnee	23	1 715	1 893 597	2	(D)	(NA)	(NA)	(NA)	(NA)	(NA)
Phillips	30	3 134	3 989 613	-	-	(NA)	(NA)	(NA)	(NA)	(NA)
Rawlins	71	6 298	8 913 421	3	565	(NA)	(NA)	(NA)	(NA)	(NA)
Republic	29	(D)	1 365 462	-	-	8	441	395 500	-	-
Rice	4	202	214 770	-	-	(NA)	(NA)	(NA)	(NA)	(NA)
Rooks	36	2 778	2 466 019	-	-	(NA)	(NA)	(NA)	(NA)	(NA)
Rush	15	1 033	804 540	1	(D)	4	159	135 320	3	94
Russell	4	188	272 500	-	-	(NA)	(NA)	(NA)	(NA)	(NA)
Saline	5	(D)	95 950	-	-	(NA)	(NA)	(NA)	(NA)	(NA)
Scott	3	212	173 488	1	(D)	6	310	297 126	3	118
Seward	9	734	771 960	6	374	(NA)	(NA)	(NA)	(NA)	(NA)
Sheridan	61	(D)	7 096 133	5	439	5	699	568 683	4	420
Sherman	143	18 766	22 230 020	41	4 278	39	4 238	5 913 313	20	1 338
Smith	23	1 027	1 258 108	-	-	(NA)	(NA)	(NA)	(NA)	(NA)
Stanton	6	1 504	1 524 776	4	289	(NA)	(NA)	(NA)	(NA)	(NA)
Stevens	9	752	619 707	4	435	5	376	776 140	5	376
Sumner	7	417	257 605	-	-	(NA)	(NA)	(NA)	(NA)	(NA)
Thomas	79	10 071	10 691 684	10	838	9	887	885 900	6	550
Trego	13	1 353	978 880	-	-	(NA)	(NA)	(NA)	(NA)	(NA)
Wallace	24	3 076	3 123 390	5	615	26	7 769	9 254 970	12	1 813
Washington	13	1 014	773 957	-	-	18	1 210	1 059 110	1	(D)
Wichita	39	3 921	4 448 136	21	1 545	34	4 137	7 246 825	33	3 771
All other counties	26	998	888 586	2	(D)	(NA)	(NA)	(NA)	(NA)	(NA)
TRITICALE (BUSHELS)										
State Total										
Kansas	134	10 382	278 065	11	900	34	1 181	37 198	3	190
Counties										
Edwards	3	(D)	(D)	3	(D)	(NA)	(NA)	(NA)	(NA)	(NA)
Ellis	5	152	3 246	-	-	(NA)	(NA)	(NA)	(NA)	(NA)
Finney	5	(D)	26 162	-	-	(NA)	(NA)	(NA)	(NA)	(NA)
Gove	10	(D)	19 191	-	-	(NA)	(NA)	(NA)	(NA)	(NA)
Graham	4	(D)	5 310	-	-	(NA)	(NA)	(NA)	(NA)	(NA)
Greeley	16	(D)	53 509	-	-	(NA)	(NA)	(NA)	(NA)	(NA)
Lane	3	157	4 186	-	-	(NA)	(NA)	(NA)	(NA)	(NA)
Logan	3	(D)	(D)	-	-	(NA)	(NA)	(NA)	(NA)	(NA)
Ness	8	(D)	6 739	-	-	(NA)	(NA)	(NA)	(NA)	(NA)
Rooks	3	(D)	1 264	-	-	(NA)	(NA)	(NA)	(NA)	(NA)
Scott	13	(D)	55 215	2	(D)	(NA)	(NA)	(NA)	(NA)	(NA)
Trego	7	(D)	10 831	-	-	(NA)	(NA)	(NA)	(NA)	(NA)
Wichita	6	221	5 613	-	-	(NA)	(NA)	(NA)	(NA)	(NA)
All other counties	48	2 988	57 809	6	617	(NA)	(NA)	(NA)	(NA)	(NA)

Table 25. **Cotton, Tobacco, Soybeans, Dry Beans and Peas, Potatoes, Sugar Crops, and Peanuts: 1987 and 1982**

[For meaning of abbreviations and symbols, see introductory text]

Geographic area	1987 Harvested			1987 Irrigated		1982 Harvested			1982 Irrigated	
	Farms	Acres	Quantity	Farms	Acres	Farms	Acres	Quantity	Farms	Acres
COTTON (BALES)										
State Total										
Kansas	10	542	595	2	(D)	(NA)	(NA)	(NA)	(NA)	(NA)
TOBACCO (POUNDS)										
State Total										
Kansas	13	30	60 805	3	8	13	30	50 889	1	(D)
SOYBEANS FOR BEANS (BUSHELS)										
State Total										
Kansas	18 864	1 878 978	55 789 994	1 939	175 053	17 116	1 692 288	43 042 471	1 725	199 270
Counties										
Allen	398	61 809	1 787 211	1	(D)	423	52 354	1 205 004	1	(D)
Anderson	449	80 630	2 618 386	4	285	478	66 391	1 701 311	7	530
Atchison	435	43 701	1 474 034	3	308	439	41 718	1 091 792	–	–
Barber	16	1 416	45 929	11	1 098	8	1 358	52 860	7	1 270
Barton	77	6 945	266 240	52	5 239	38	5 875	260 007	32	5 277
Bourbon	317	32 777	817 832	1	(D)	392	42 966	932 787	5	250
Brown	539	78 311	2 532 198	–	–	567	71 005	2 065 005	–	–
Butler	279	23 825	714 386	1	(D)	181	12 798	211 960	–	–
Chase	121	9 639	339 233	–	–	111	7 422	163 247	2	(D)
Chautauqua	48	8 401	225 752	–	–	23	3 095	62 838	–	–
Cherokee	457	100 264	2 089 323	3	(D)	556	104 013	1 807 194	2	(D)
Cheyenne	33	4 029	167 976	30	3 785	26	2 872	91 162	21	2 480
Clark	3	(D)	(D)	2	(D)	3	228	(D)	2	(D)
Clay	349	23 155	743 352	34	3 196	276	15 639	494 782	35	2 437
Cloud	231	12 176	357 467	38	1 571	158	6 815	251 608	26	1 137
Coffey	434	70 461	2 150 726	3	275	446	61 131	1 440 911	4	145
Comanche	9	774	28 709	7	626	4	1 469	(D)	2	(D)
Cowley	123	5 627	141 824	4	216	50	2 350	48 639	1	(D)
Crawford	475	58 552	1 259 435	4	333	545	69 213	1 449 138	8	909
Decatur	12	954	23 712	8	204	4	259	2 700	5	(D)
Dickinson	336	14 637	413 709	14	420	259	10 798	262 516	6	310
Doniphan	376	52 547	1 931 717	–	–	423	53 287	1 772 646	1	(D)
Douglas	373	42 051	1 399 719	3	509	328	31 700	748 167	4	390
Edwards	90	21 063	806 148	83	16 363	84	24 177	918 274	78	19 336
Elk	98	9 348	269 817	–	–	82	5 482	123 578	–	–
Ellsworth	31	1 562	45 930	3	281	15	686	23 823	4	335
Finney	87	8 644	263 194	80	7 773	45	4 359	141 354	42	4 104
Ford	65	6 586	233 727	55	5 960	61	7 146	280 610	53	6 044
Franklin	498	62 225	1 871 238	6	643	521	57 240	1 226 234	5	347
Geary	113	5 462	163 290	9	504	67	3 280	93 238	7	307
Gove	3	(D)	15 294	2	(D)	10	458	14 089	7	410
Graham	3	205	(D)	1	(D)	(NA)	(NA)	(NA)	(NA)	(NA)
Grant	43	3 793	106 002	38	3 409	26	3 576	116 842	27	3 076
Gray	66	5 462	208 432	60	4 970	84	10 084	394 216	78	6 826
Greeley	9	499	13 450	7	479	(NA)	(NA)	(NA)	(NA)	(NA)
Greenwood	197	17 664	500 533	1	(D)	175	12 204	265 629	–	–
Harper	3	(D)	(D)	2	(D)	9	(D)	(D)	3	(D)
Harvey	217	12 996	479 136	68	6 055	198	14 858	425 503	78	7 586
Haskell	53	3 719	110 636	49	3 561	71	6 937	259 871	69	6 827
Hodgeman	31	1 918	59 874	23	1 516	12	704	28 632	11	682
Jackson	369	26 243	668 413	–	–	378	25 630	559 109	2	(D)
Jefferson	365	36 268	1 155 963	1	(D)	374	35 778	917 153	2	(D)
Jewell	164	8 942	254 175	23	1 262	77	3 665	110 101	15	1 064
Johnson	239	33 097	1 030 735	1	(D)	256	35 614	997 403	1	(D)
Kearny	14	1 595	32 276	12	1 396	9	665	32 209	7	585
Kingman	43	3 644	146 047	27	3 037	17	1 729	73 600	14	1 585
Kiowa	60	6 698	270 966	42	5 220	40	9 320	388 151	45	8 760
Labette	482	66 168	1 536 005	7	572	464	56 200	917 753	14	315
Lane	7	174	5 240	4	164	11	924	30 170	9	848
Leavenworth	381	31 563	974 966	2	(D)	392	29 060	833 186	1	(D)
Lincoln	4	1 895	48 261	2	(D)	42	1 588	52 203	3	120
Linn	297	40 829	1 206 979	–	–	358	46 600	1 135 792	–	–
Lyon	492	43 599	1 340 498	2	(D)	489	36 664	779 657	3	122
McPherson	352	16 498	554 623	90	5 259	295	18 290	548 366	101	7 915
Marion	321	11 732	301 506	5	166	218	10 745	218 155	6	249
Marshall	741	61 942	1 639 693	7	403	683	63 688	1 761 294	6	373
Meade	54	5 232	202 530	45	4 499	32	5 416	183 530	30	5 196
Miami	393	46 043	1 462 832	3	(D)	428	46 033	1 119 469	–	–
Mitchell	114	7 764	194 245	15	1 373	32	2 934	101 227	8	1 011
Montgomery	280	34 604	913 282	4	172	218	21 853	402 931	2	(D)
Morris	212	12 488	329 334	2	(D)	181	9 134	215 488	4	166
Morton	3	(D)	(D)	1	(D)	(NA)	(NA)	(NA)	(NA)	(NA)
Nemaha	613	31 953	839 157	1	(D)	479	27 259	587 201	–	–
Neosho	408	50 550	1 292 026	1	(D)	397	43 652	844 057	2	(D)
Ness	11	969	9 885	1	(D)	3	262	4 484	1	(D)
Norton	9	344	4 646	2	(D)	3	182	(D)	1	(D)
Osage	481	50 704	1 608 243	2	(D)	543	46 896	1 020 408	4	235
Osborne	74	3 224	84 719	20	852	40	2 122	63 435	10	408
Ottawa	117	5 250	155 104	10	588	40	2 534	68 566	7	571
Pawnee	98	11 666	461 282	77	10 000	91	11 878	458 598	77	11 042

Table 25. **Cotton, Tobacco, Soybeans, Dry Beans and Peas, Potatoes, Sugar Crops, and Peanuts: 1987 and 1982**—Con.

[For meaning of abbreviations and symbols, see introductory text]

Geographic area	1987					1982				
	Harvested			Irrigated		Harvested			Irrigated	
	Farms	Acres	Quantity	Farms	Acres	Farms	Acres	Quantity	Farms	Acres

SOYBEANS FOR BEANS (BUSHELS)—Con.

Counties—Con.

Phillips	20	904	26 818	2	(D)	4	75	2 502	2	(D)
Pottawatomie	311	18 726	584 291	23	1 719	282	15 180	396 678	10	1 043
Pratt	80	8 871	334 145	71	7 744	69	11 746	492 824	63	10 970
Rawlins	11	461	8 451	2	(D)	5	(D)	(D)	1	(D)
Reno	132	8 400	297 067	50	3 905	112	8 473	268 331	48	4 927
Republic	434	24 503	852 680	114	5 783	394	24 208	783 548	113	7 296
Rice	117	7 475	253 945	29	2 506	79	6 953	254 623	29	3 692
Riley	208	10 911	341 081	11	464	162	7 707	237 292	10	767
Rooks	9	860	11 895	3	(D)	6	246	5 189	3	(D)
Rush	36	3 179	40 534	12	316	23	690	24 077	18	463
Russell	17	659	17 750	1	(D)	3	70	1 038	–	–
Saline	183	7 565	199 976	15	715	111	4 396	108 781	2	(D)
Scott	14	1 046	39 512	13	1 006	24	4 352	155 475	21	3 097
Sedgwick	240	21 042	779 026	79	9 437	166	13 902	418 537	80	7 926
Seward	16	824	29 413	16	824	21	3 153	92 079	18	2 629
Shawnee	323	30 060	913 322	33	3 077	271	17 363	413 603	18	1 681
Sheridan	55	3 899	169 748	47	3 637	39	5 068	189 277	33	1 155
Sherman	46	5 071	211 544	43	4 656	41	4 315	130 979	33	3 686
Smith	175	10 597	307 315	20	1 200	34	1 225	35 803	12	446
Stafford	88	8 721	324 309	66	7 390	89	16 224	636 926	76	14 692
Stanton	19	2 360	75 869	18	2 310	31	5 584	214 535	30	5 534
Stevens	16	890	28 397	14	745	11	652	20 265	10	642
Sumner	196	14 494	305 850	9	1 263	39	1 620	38 298	3	(D)
Thomas	70	5 742	183 371	49	3 710	39	4 742	172 243	37	4 381
Wabaunsee	227	14 271	434 517	14	557	192	9 969	230 553	8	522
Wallace	13	845	28 139	12	759	3	152	(D)	2	(D)
Washington	475	30 869	902 105	22	879	400	31 776	962 189	12	1 346
Wichita	23	1 295	37 426	20	1 147	34	1 760	61 533	31	1 524
Wilson	329	52 601	1 505 453	7	697	356	44 558	963 660	4	279
Woodson	210	30 000	905 137	–	–	208	22 881	538 229	–	–
Wyandotte	35	5 417	204 728	–	–	37	3 611	117 513	–	–
All other counties	4	175	7 193	3	125	(NA)	(NA)	(NA)	(NA)	(NA)

DRY EDIBLE BEANS, EXCLUDING DRY LIMAS (CWT)

State Total

Kansas	192	30 460	441 318	167	26 182	223	25 287	262 041	186	23 111

Counties

Cheyenne	29	4 775	69 762	27	4 649	27	4 421	39 137	27	4 421
Reno	3	212	848	–	–	(NA)	(NA)	(NA)	(NA)	(NA)
Scott	4	632	7 180	4	632	(NA)	(NA)	(NA)	(NA)	(NA)
Sherman	81	12 694	195 301	77	12 142	96	10 479	114 907	90	10 075
Stanton	3	(D)	(D)	3	(D)	(NA)	(NA)	(NA)	(NA)	(NA)
Sumner	7	920	4 527	–	–	(NA)	(NA)	(NA)	(NA)	(NA)
Thomas	6	980	8 160	5	980	6	165	1 009	6	165
Wallace	26	3 760	55 637	24	3 615	20	2 201	24 004	17	1 897
Wichita	16	3 537	51 180	16	3 537	24	2 762	29 861	22	2 657
All other counties	18	(D)	(D)	11	(D)	(NA)	(NA)	(NA)	(NA)	(NA)

IRISH POTATOES (CWT)

State Total

Kansas	97	643	138 764	21	(D)	210	827	144 655	24	(D)

SWEETPOTATOES (BUSHELS)

State Total

Kansas	10	26	2 462	3	(D)	19	122	18 432	6	67

Table 26. Field Seeds, Grass Seeds, Hay, Forage, and Silage: 1987 and 1982

[For meaning of abbreviations and symbols, see introductory text]

Geographic area	1987 Harvested Farms	Harvested Acres	Harvested Quantity	Irrigated Farms	Irrigated Acres	1982 Harvested Farms	Harvested Acres	Harvested Quantity	Irrigated Farms	Irrigated Acres
FIELD SEED AND GRASS SEED CROPS										
State Total										
Kansas	1 188	56 460	(X)	12	2 222	1 049	36 382	(X)	12	1 227
Counties										
Allen	9	(D)	(X)	-	-	5	94	(X)	-	-
Anderson	9	613	(X)	-	-	10	151	(X)	-	-
Atchison	34	1 190	(X)	-	-	9	179	(X)	-	-
Barber	5	517	(X)	-	-	9	750	(X)	1	(D)
Barton	16	895	(X)	-	-	27	969	(X)	-	-
Bourbon	28	1 906	(X)	-	-	16	683	(X)	-	-
Brown	36	(D)	(X)	-	-	14	276	(X)	-	-
Butler	21	1 867	(X)	-	-	23	1 003	(X)	-	-
Chase	6	(D)	(X)	-	-	10	208	(X)	-	-
Cherokee	14	(D)	(X)	-	-	6	167	(X)	-	-
Clark	3	(D)	(X)	-	-	4	228	(X)	1	(D)
Clay	11	(D)	(X)	-	-	9	174	(X)	-	-
Cloud	18	(D)	(X)	-	-	16	646	(X)	-	-
Coffey	9	(D)	(X)	-	-	3	45	(X)	-	-
Comanche	3	329	(X)	-	-	10	627	(X)	1	(D)
Cowley	12	(D)	(X)	-	-	18	235	(X)	-	-
Crawford	31	(D)	(X)	-	-	30	2 287	(X)	-	-
Dickinson	19	(D)	(X)	-	-	49	879	(X)	-	-
Doniphan	9	(D)	(X)	-	-	(NA)	(NA)	(X)	(NA)	(NA)
Douglas	15	513	(X)	-	-	3	90	(X)	-	-
Edwards	3	(D)	(X)	1	(D)	3	133	(X)	1	(D)
Elk	3	205	(X)	-	-	4	125	(X)	-	-
Ellsworth	4	(D)	(X)	-	-	9	241	(X)	-	-
Ford	3	(D)	(X)	1	(D)	(NA)	(NA)	(X)	(NA)	(NA)
Franklin	21	745	(X)	-	-	5	71	(X)	-	-
Geary	16	113	(X)	1	(D)	6	76	(X)	-	-
Greenwood	6	(D)	(X)	-	-	(NA)	(NA)	(X)	(NA)	(NA)
Harper	7	(D)	(X)	-	-	14	410	(X)	1	(D)
Harvey	13	293	(X)	1	(D)	26	504	(X)	-	-
Jackson	76	(D)	(X)	-	-	16	778	(X)	-	-
Jefferson	28	784	(X)	-	-	10	310	(X)	-	-
Jewell	14	417	(X)	-	-	14	330	(X)	1	(D)
Johnson	11	(D)	(X)	-	-	4	100	(X)	-	-
Kingman	14	936	(X)	-	-	8	226	(X)	-	-
Labette	50	3 154	(X)	-	-	26	1 237	(X)	-	-
Leavenworth	17	509	(X)	-	-	11	133	(X)	-	-
Lincoln	8	453	(X)	-	-	9	211	(X)	-	-
Linn	23	(D)	(X)	-	-	15	453	(X)	-	-
Lyon	10	(D)	(X)	-	-	6	107	(X)	-	-
McPherson	24	(D)	(X)	-	-	80	1 833	(X)	-	-
Marion	38	(D)	(X)	-	-	52	1 484	(X)	-	-
Marshall	26	(D)	(X)	-	-	9	125	(X)	-	-
Miami	14	(D)	(X)	-	-	5	39	(X)	-	-
Mitchell	13	305	(X)	-	-	7	269	(X)	-	-
Montgomery	8	(D)	(X)	-	-	10	169	(X)	-	-
Morris	15	970	(X)	-	-	17	294	(X)	-	-
Nemaha	80	3 649	(X)	-	-	10	361	(X)	-	-
Neosho	38	(D)	(X)	-	-	14	1 189	(X)	-	-
Ness	3	(D)	(X)	1	(D)	3	41	(X)	-	-
Norton	3	22	(X)	-	-	10	359	(X)	-	-
Osage	18	(D)	(X)	-	-	(NA)	(NA)	(X)	(NA)	(NA)
Osborne	25	(D)	(X)	-	-	10	276	(X)	-	-
Ottawa	6	(D)	(X)	-	-	18	392	(X)	-	-
Pawnee	8	(D)	(X)	2	(D)	15	1 550	(X)	-	-
Phillips	13	849	(X)	-	-	37	1 062	(X)	-	-
Pottawatomie	12	(D)	(X)	-	-	(NA)	(NA)	(X)	(NA)	(NA)
Pratt	3	(D)	(X)	-	-	4	155	(X)	-	-
Reno	29	1 135	(X)	1	(D)	49	1 575	(X)	-	-
Republic	13	(D)	(X)	-	-	21	421	(X)	-	-
Rice	5	(D)	(X)	-	-	20	531	(X)	-	-
Riley	10	(D)	(X)	-	-	3	37	(X)	-	-
Rush	4	(D)	(X)	-	-	(NA)	(NA)	(X)	(NA)	(NA)
Russell	9	448	(X)	-	-	10	419	(X)	-	-
Saline	15	649	(X)	-	-	30	804	(X)	1	(D)
Sedgwick	6	322	(X)	-	-	28	943	(X)	-	-
Shawnee	10	(D)	(X)	-	-	(NA)	(NA)	(X)	(NA)	(NA)
Smith	18	498	(X)	-	-	29	1 126	(X)	-	-
Stafford	10	(D)	(X)	-	-	21	1 024	(X)	1	(D)
Sumner	4	(D)	(X)	-	-	4	81	(X)	-	-
Trego	4	(D)	(X)	-	-	(NA)	(NA)	(X)	(NA)	(NA)
Wabaunsee	22	2 063	(X)	-	-	12	415	(X)	-	-
Washington	10	(D)	(X)	-	-	15	179	(X)	-	-
Wilson	10	139	(X)	-	-	3	(D)	(X)	-	-
Woodson	11	(D)	(X)	-	-	(NA)	(NA)	(X)	(NA)	(NA)
All other counties	25	3 028	(X)	4	1 546	(NA)	(NA)	(X)	(NA)	(NA)

Table 26. **Field Seeds, Grass Seeds, Hay, Forage, and Silage: 1987 and 1982**—Con.

[For meaning of abbreviations and symbols, see introductory text]

| Geographic area | 1987 | | | | | 1982 | | | | |
| | Harvested | | | Irrigated | | Harvested | | | Irrigated | |
	Farms	Acres	Quantity	Farms	Acres	Farms	Acres	Quantity	Farms	Acres
ALFALFA SEED (POUNDS)										
State Total										
Kansas	357	11 060	963 184	6	(D)	774	24 065	2 376 363	10	918
Counties										
Barton	14	(D)	53 231	-	-	27	969	106 552	-	-
Butler	8	291	30 100	-	-	18	741	61 750	-	-
Clay	6	75	7 116	-	-	9	174	9 080	-	-
Cloud	11	235	22 993	-	-	16	646	66 932	-	-
Cowley	8	145	14 987	-	-	16	(D)	32 750	-	-
Dickinson	13	317	17 625	-	-	45	648	78 135	-	-
Geary	4	71	5 200	1	(D)	6	76	6 020	-	-
Harper	5	159	5 450	-	-	14	410	46 720	1	(D)
Harvey	6	105	16 680	1	(D)	26	(D)	39 206	-	-
Jewell	13	254	27 650	-	-	13	(D)	24 993	-	-
Kingman	8	266	10 069	-	-	8	226	17 320	-	-
Lincoln	6	167	30 500	-	-	9	211	29 600	-	-
McPherson	18	465	47 601	-	-	79	(D)	179 956	-	-
Marion	27	671	52 230	-	-	48	1 416	112 010	-	-
Marshall	5	76	(D)	-	-	6	84	4 295	-	-
Mitchell	11	253	21 445	-	-	7	289	14 536	-	-
Morris	10	(D)	24 360	-	-	17	294	31 950	-	-
Nemaha	5	(D)	1 820	-	-	(NA)	(NA)	(NA)	(NA)	(NA)
Ness	3	(D)	6 240	1	(D)	3	41	(D)	-	-
Osborne	21	496	49 625	-	-	10	276	26 052	-	-
Ottawa	5	137	12 796	-	-	17	(D)	37 870	-	-
Pawnee	8	(D)	54 933	2	(D)	15	1 550	153 866	-	-
Phillips	10	373	32 722	-	-	37	(D)	72 539	-	-
Pottawatomie	6	(D)	4 680	-	-	(NA)	(NA)	(NA)	(NA)	(NA)
Reno	26	731	53 306	-	-	46	(D)	165 974	-	-
Republic	3	55	(D)	-	-	20	346	26 917	-	-
Rice	4	140	6 692	-	-	20	531	54 143	-	-
Riley	8	119	8 170	-	-	3	37	1 800	-	-
Rush	3	80	5 500	-	-	(NA)	(NA)	(NA)	(NA)	(NA)
Russell	8	(D)	54 961	-	-	10	419	32 098	-	-
Saline	10	617	90 950	-	-	30	604	86 698	1	(D)
Sedgwick	5	(D)	39 060	-	-	27	(D)	108 260	-	-
Smith	17	(D)	44 444	-	-	29	(D)	90 076	-	-
Stafford	9	583	34 687	-	-	21	1 024	134 310	1	(D)
Sumner	4	(D)	(D)	-	-	4	81	8 140	-	-
Washington	3	46	2 590	-	-	14	(D)	7 934	-	-
All other counties	32	786	72 062	1	(D)	(NA)	(NA)	(NA)	(NA)	(NA)
BROMEGRASS SEED (POUNDS)										
State Total										
Kansas	435	17 872	3 413 485	3	440	70	2 273	444 684	1	(D)
Counties										
Atchison	22	923	184 810	-	-	(NA)	(NA)	(NA)	(NA)	(NA)
Bourbon	4	(D)	10 700	-	-	(NA)	(NA)	(NA)	(NA)	(NA)
Brown	27	672	167 212	-	-	(NA)	(D)	69 300	(NA)	(NA)
Butler	14	936	188 192	-	-	7	(D)	(NA)	-	-
Chase	5	83	8 100	-	-	(NA)	(NA)	(NA)	(NA)	(NA)
Clay	3	(D)	(D)	-	-	(NA)	(NA)	(NA)	(NA)	(NA)
Cloud	6	192	(D)	-	-	(NA)	(NA)	(NA)	(NA)	(NA)
Cowley	3	74	2 535	-	-	(NA)	(NA)	(NA)	(NA)	(NA)
Dickinson	6	147	26 630	-	-	3	(D)	(D)	-	-
Doniphan	5	159	18 940	-	-	(NA)	(NA)	(NA)	(NA)	(NA)
Douglas	6	345	61 120	-	-	3	90	12 000	-	-
Franklin	14	474	65 016	-	-	(NA)	(NA)	(NA)	(NA)	(NA)
Geary	3	42	10 822	-	-	(NA)	(NA)	(NA)	(NA)	(NA)
Greenwood	3	(D)	(D)	-	-	(NA)	(NA)	(NA)	(NA)	(NA)
Harvey	5	(D)	12 900	-	-	(NA)	(NA)	(NA)	(NA)	(NA)
Jackson	68	3 364	744 508	-	-	14	(D)	158 190	-	-
Jefferson	14	480	77 628	-	-	(NA)	(NA)	(NA)	(NA)	(NA)
Johnson	4	300	42 000	-	-	(NA)	(NA)	(NA)	(NA)	(NA)
Leavenworth	6	190	26 200	-	-	(NA)	(NA)	(NA)	(NA)	(NA)
Linn	7	266	25 200	-	-	(NA)	(NA)	(NA)	(NA)	(NA)
Lyon	5	237	74 900	-	-	(NA)	(NA)	(NA)	(NA)	(NA)
McPherson	7	(D)	30 360	-	-	(NA)	(NA)	(NA)	(NA)	(NA)
Marion	13	417	64 980	-	-	(NA)	(NA)	(NA)	(NA)	(NA)
Marshall	17	289	53 810	-	-	3	(D)	2 300	-	-
Miami	7	317	34 819	-	-	(NA)	(NA)	(NA)	(NA)	(NA)
Mitchell	4	52	7 000	-	-	(NA)	(NA)	(NA)	(NA)	(NA)
Nemaha	58	3 241	709 653	-	-	4	307	20 735	-	-
Osage	11	355	60 231	-	-	(NA)	(NA)	(NA)	(NA)	(NA)
Osborne	5	86	19 440	-	-	(NA)	(NA)	(NA)	(NA)	(NA)
Pottawatomie	9	643	67 320	-	-	(NA)	(NA)	(NA)	(NA)	(NA)
Republic	4	46	7 250	-	-	6	76	10 700	-	-
Russell	3	(D)	(D)	-	-	(NA)	(NA)	(NA)	(NA)	(NA)
Saline	7	132	17 660	-	-	(NA)	(NA)	(NA)	(NA)	(NA)
Shawnee	10	(D)	63 430	-	-	(NA)	(NA)	(NA)	(NA)	(NA)
Wabaunsee	20	933	178 981	-	-	10	(D)	68 756	-	-
Wilson	3	45	5 800	-	-	(NA)	(NA)	(NA)	(NA)	(NA)
All other counties	27	1 279	254 475	3	440	(NA)	(NA)	(NA)	(NA)	(NA)

[For meaning of abbreviations and symbols, see introductory text]

Geographic area	1987					1982				
	Harvested			Irrigated		Harvested			Irrigated	
	Farms	Acres	Quantity	Farms	Acres	Farms	Acres	Quantity	Farms	Acres
FESCUE SEED (POUNDS)										
State Total										
Kansas	139	10 026	1 614 514	-	-	54	3 772	445 913	-	-
Counties										
Allen	5	123	27 094	-	-	(NA)	(NA)	(NA)	(NA)	(NA)
Bourbon	23	1 703	301 910	-	-	6	425	87 400	-	-
Cherokee	6	(D)	(D)	-	-	3	85	14 080	-	-
Crawford	15	720	152 356	-	-	9	1 616	135 950	-	-
Labette	27	1 811	393 331	-	-	14	765	123 378	-	-
Linn	11	478	92 373	-	-	5	297	19 524	-	-
Miami	4	240	23 232	-	-	(NA)	(NA)	(NA)	(NA)	(NA)
Montgomery	5	1 047	(D)	-	-	4	76	16 500	-	-
Neosho	19	961	139 621	-	-	4	350	31 370	-	-
Wilson	3	(D)	(D)	-	-	(NA)	(NA)	(NA)	(NA)	(NA)
Woodson	9	596	141 099	-	-	(NA)	(NA)	(NA)	(NA)	(NA)
All other counties	12	450	35 126	-	-	(NA)	(NA)	(NA)	(NA)	(NA)
LESPEDEZA SEED (POUNDS)										
State Total										
Kansas	59	2 410	747 200	-	-	46	2 135	611 807	-	-
Counties										
Cherokee	5	253	91 549	-	-	(NA)	(NA)	(NA)	(NA)	(NA)
Crawford	14	387	111 341	-	-	21	641	169 097	-	-
Labette	23	1 062	320 510	-	-	9	341	80 890	-	-
Neosho	14	577	184 600	-	-	5	763	216 500	-	-
All other counties	3	131	39 200	-	-	(NA)	(NA)	(NA)	(NA)	(NA)
RED CLOVER SEED (POUNDS)										
State Total										
Kansas	209	4 273	475 350	-	-	112	1 942	150 443	-	-
Counties										
Allen	3	68	4 415	-	-	(NA)	(NA)	(NA)	(NA)	(NA)
Anderson	7	161	16 730	-	-	7	102	7 100	-	-
Atchison	15	267	39 760	-	-	9	179	9 565	-	-
Bourbon	4	81	7 400	-	-	7	(D)	20 100	-	-
Brown	14	204	20 784	-	-	14	276	21 620	-	-
Cherokee	5	62	8 150	-	-	(NA)	(NA)	(NA)	(NA)	(NA)
Coffey	4	80	7 328	-	-	(NA)	(NA)	(NA)	(NA)	(NA)
Doniphan	4	98	5 740	-	-	(NA)	(NA)	(NA)	(NA)	(NA)
Douglas	9	168	27 000	-	-	(NA)	(NA)	(NA)	(NA)	(NA)
Franklin	8	(D)	20 400	-	-	4	(D)	3 033	-	-
Jackson	12	181	22 355	-	-	(NA)	(NA)	(NA)	(NA)	(NA)
Jefferson	16	(D)	41 788	-	-	8	(D)	19 900	-	-
Johnson	8	147	13 505	-	-	4	100	6 780	-	-
Labette	12	209	23 800	-	-	5	(D)	6 500	-	-
Leavenworth	15	319	44 385	-	-	9	(D)	9 968	-	-
Linn	8	(D)	22 700	-	-	8	(D)	10 271	-	-
Marshall	7	(D)	8 300	-	-	(NA)	(NA)	(NA)	(NA)	(NA)
Miami	5	84	8 292	-	-	5	39	3 050	-	-
Nemaha	23	331	40 013	-	-	6	(D)	2 010	-	-
Neosho	10	218	22 880	-	-	6	76	8 014	-	-
Osage	7	289	20 070	-	-	(NA)	(NA)	(NA)	(NA)	(NA)
Wilson	3	56	4 650	-	-	(NA)	(NA)	(NA)	(NA)	(NA)
All other counties	7	429	(D)	-	-	(NA)	(NA)	(NA)	(NA)	(NA)
SWEETCLOVER SEED (POUNDS)										
State Total										
Kansas	4	132	10 700	-	-	11	82	8 300	-	-

[For meaning of abbreviations and symbols, see introductory text]

Geographic area	1987					1982				
	Harvested			Irrigated		Harvested			Irrigated	
	Farms	Acres	Quantity	Farms	Acres	Farms	Acres	Quantity	Farms	Acres

OTHER SEEDS (POUNDS)

State Total

Kansas	96	11 673	2 341 552	4	(D)	6	1 436	(D)	-	-

Counties

Barber	3	(D)	13 160	-	-	(NA)	(NA)	(NA)	(NA)	(NA)
Coffey	3	(D)	(D)	-	-	(NA)	(NA)	(NA)	(NA)	(NA)
Cowley	5	710	58 620	-	-	(NA)	(NA)	(NA)	(NA)	(NA)
Edwards	3	(D)	(D)	1	(D)	(NA)	(NA)	(NA)	(NA)	(NA)
Kingman	6	670	33 360	-	-	(NA)	(NA)	(NA)	(NA)	(NA)
Lyon	3	440	28 130	-	-	(NA)	(NA)	(NA)	(NA)	(NA)
Morris	4	407	26 000	-	-	(NA)	(NA)	(NA)	(NA)	(NA)
Republic	5	(D)	41 160	-	-	(NA)	(NA)	(NA)	(NA)	(NA)
Trego	4	(D)	(D)	-	-	(NA)	(NA)	(NA)	(NA)	(NA)
Washington	5	94	4 796	-	-	(NA)	(NA)	(NA)	(NA)	(NA)
All other counties	55	7 419	1 911 342	3	1 470	(NA)	(NA)	(NA)	(NA)	(NA)

HAY—ALFALFA, OTHER TAME, SMALL GRAIN, WILD, GRASS SILAGE, GREEN CHOP, ETC. (SEE TEXT) (TONS, DRY)

State Total

Kansas	33 964	2 254 082	5 080 847	1 492	206 961	37 341	2 233 631	5 092 039	1 841	187 173

Counties

Allen	435	30 385	48 927	-	-	460	27 363	48 867	1	(D)
Anderson	463	39 800	62 070	-	-	498	40 901	66 178	1	(D)
Atchison	395	19 182	36 644	-	-	457	19 595	44 666	-	-
Barber	222	18 355	51 611	10	454	216	17 185	41 872	10	473
Barton	492	37 437	106 817	26	1 777	560	37 622	107 071	39	4 596
Bourbon	522	36 721	61 439	1	(D)	543	32 187	56 390	-	-
Brown	364	16 003	36 477	-	-	475	21 667	51 561	-	-
Butler	676	54 005	86 301	2	(D)	774	63 362	100 627	3	138
Chase	180	12 737	26 011	-	-	190	13 589	27 834	1	(D)
Chautauqua	208	13 125	21 664	-	-	239	13 693	22 521	-	-
Cherokee	411	18 011	27 319	1	(D)	431	17 936	22 949	2	(D)
Cheyenne	156	11 353	31 386	46	3 299	168	10 220	33 757	57	4 194
Clark	110	11 161	31 065	12	1 197	100	8 864	22 374	7	337
Clay	424	25 074	50 497	1	(D)	451	22 167	50 066	6	(D)
Cloud	326	18 121	39 301	5	175	413	20 430	51 946	10	594
Coffey	330	31 082	41 420	-	-	380	33 163	47 073	-	-
Comanche	119	9 870	27 747	15	1 054	99	8 654	20 277	10	697
Cowley	500	31 618	61 034	2	(D)	607	38 093	76 682	-	-
Crawford	439	21 593	36 658	-	-	495	21 613	36 377	-	-
Decatur	228	13 517	42 846	16	529	247	13 633	42 845	27	1 271
Dickinson	650	39 564	90 833	9	279	692	37 623	96 418	2	(D)
Doniphan	210	6 512	16 496	-	-	250	6 137	15 976	2	(D)
Douglas	540	27 405	50 418	2	(D)	574	26 060	50 596	-	-
Edwards	146	19 249	76 879	50	12 517	165	22 480	87 712	63	13 501
Elk	250	19 341	27 687	1	(D)	295	23 589	36 835	1	(D)
Ellis	358	22 783	51 546	6	147	335	20 672	49 224	17	546
Ellsworth	312	23 590	48 605	-	-	315	18 327	38 455	4	146
Finney	169	30 042	130 943	117	25 700	193	39 690	155 955	156	24 668
Ford	273	19 770	67 161	54	8 778	212	15 268	50 665	62	7 379
Franklin	613	33 840	57 077	2	(D)	657	33 947	61 504	1	(D)
Geary	189	13 587	24 346	5	243	184	12 120	26 057	2	(D)
Gove	162	14 965	39 347	13	862	189	14 177	42 648	16	1 154
Graham	165	11 912	32 560	11	662	205	12 141	33 592	21	1 818
Grant	64	7 349	34 351	40	5 683	66	6 668	24 713	44	4 253
Gray	131	20 644	103 541	76	17 966	125	14 442	61 686	79	10 624
Greeley	65	4 570	11 021	4	(D)	41	2 943	6 734	9	1 003
Greenwood	331	35 069	51 958	1	(D)	415	32 077	51 455	-	-
Hamilton	69	8 479	26 944	28	5 148	62	7 617	24 849	32	4 943
Harper	294	17 327	41 069	2	(D)	317	15 378	35 103	10	514
Harvey	401	14 908	36 505	11	570	488	18 694	37 964	16	944
Haskell	58	6 126	23 904	48	5 565	59	6 049	22 335	44	4 637
Hodgeman	170	10 880	27 568	35	1 699	182	7 993	22 578	51	2 190
Jackson	708	43 691	71 748	3	364	782	50 122	94 726	1	(D)
Jefferson	638	32 019	56 692	3	56	656	32 429	59 660	1	(D)
Jewell	420	22 984	57 762	5	65	493	25 459	68 953	1	(D)
Johnson	336	17 728	30 095	2	(D)	398	18 774	33 366	3	86
Kearny	100	20 561	89 250	62	17 589	80	14 339	56 268	57	12 199
Kingman	426	26 571	62 799	17	937	458	23 089	48 194	27	1 067
Kiowa	102	11 051	36 268	25	5 190	120	11 937	37 778	23	5 025
Labette	545	28 555	47 709	-	-	587	24 601	39 857	4	51
Lane	75	4 653	6 716	12	372	70	3 616	8 774	15	389
Leavenworth	677	29 970	55 874	2	(D)	744	29 580	60 423	-	-
Lincoln	326	26 059	67 549	1	(D)	375	25 322	67 577	2	(D)
Linn	438	27 364	46 141	-	-	483	28 424	45 068	-	-
Logan	117	7 713	15 478	15	592	113	6 596	17 182	20	904
Lyon	492	44 903	59 188	1	(D)	562	44 655	64 654	1	(D)
McPherson	654	26 779	66 796	11	367	722	25 947	65 411	14	339
Marion	710	45 711	91 483	2	(D)	782	43 651	85 464	6	131
Marshall	617	29 463	58 624	3	(D)	728	32 231	77 057	2	(D)
Meade	125	9 648	25 891	36	2 976	112	10 475	27 169	57	4 856

Table 26. Field Seeds, Grass Seeds, Hay, Forage, and Silage: 1987 and 1982 — Con.

[For meaning of abbreviations and symbols, see introductory text]

Geographic area	1987					1982				
	Harvested			Irrigated		Harvested			Irrigated	
	Farms	Acres	Quantity	Farms	Acres	Farms	Acres	Quantity	Farms	Acres
HAY — ALFALFA, OTHER TAME, SMALL GRAIN, WILD, GRASS SILAGE, GREEN CHOP, ETC. (SEE TEXT) (TONS, DRY) — Con.										
Counties — Con.										
Miami	748	40 425	70 017	1	(D)	796	40 956	74 032	-	-
Mitchell	285	14 427	36 215	2	(D)	306	13 705	35 378	4	301
Montgomery	524	25 647	40 851	1	(D)	511	23 320	39 202	2	(D)
Morris	348	31 849	60 014	-	-	380	32 154	62 217	-	-
Morton	39	3 273	6 166	9	768	32	1 558	4 711	10	690
Nemaha	662	33 071	70 183	2	(D)	739	32 666	79 326	-	-
Neosho	462	26 155	45 326	1	(D)	440	21 837	35 817	-	-
Ness	272	16 306	43 749	13	385	254	13 853	30 019	21	732
Norton	220	12 510	34 952	11	358	272	15 306	41 469	14	376
Osage	489	37 888	52 307	-	-	559	38 207	54 892	2	(D)
Osborne	331	20 527	50 319	7	422	318	19 191	51 295	8	398
Ottawa	293	16 533	43 177	2	(D)	325	17 722	42 496	4	281
Pawnee	220	27 298	96 658	69	12 465	255	29 925	103 807	79	9 823
Phillips	368	27 505	74 247	10	251	407	26 768	71 308	9	193
Pottawatomie	459	43 089	71 446	5	342	540	45 063	85 774	-	-
Pratt	154	26 831	127 661	20	(D)	177	16 190	54 310	27	9 366
Rawlins	233	15 764	48 473	26	1 434	260	15 707	50 308	47	2 834
Reno	734	40 161	106 117	26	1 861	811	42 476	109 787	41	1 663
Republic	455	19 993	52 593	23	444	559	22 059	61 834	18	421
Rice	287	16 076	45 925	13	836	330	17 067	50 490	9	825
Riley	333	17 945	34 821	4	110	339	16 797	41 976	3	(D)
Rooks	208	16 051	46 623	4	(D)	232	14 951	41 007	11	451
Rush	213	12 066	26 721	23	517	220	9 826	24 760	40	1 234
Russell	265	20 371	44 657	2	(D)	301	17 725	39 468	2	(D)
Saline	362	22 883	54 221	6	162	393	19 167	53 219	10	263
Scott	86	6 975	19 126	32	2 364	76	5 181	15 775	43	2 485
Sedgwick	669	35 692	84 452	12	478	800	36 277	75 628	24	848
Seward	59	9 678	37 342	29	7 530	58	6 918	25 991	29	4 371
Shawnee	443	23 711	34 650	4	14	515	25 510	45 326	4	41
Sheridan	180	10 691	31 918	18	1 145	197	10 640	36 492	35	1 888
Sherman	113	9 169	23 389	54	3 007	136	8 548	26 808	71	4 302
Smith	401	22 323	63 066	9	737	449	24 089	65 095	12	892
Stafford	215	20 696	63 614	34	4 542	255	23 009	66 542	39	4 079
Stanton	40	3 794	11 464	22	2 477	33	3 567	15 969	25	3 149
Stevens	47	7 046	33 777	28	5 957	49	6 678	33 068	36	6 218
Sumner	489	22 666	49 487	2	(D)	585	24 890	50 358	5	152
Thomas	122	6 733	18 031	10	754	99	4 758	14 585	15	1 005
Trego	225	13 979	32 250	12	626	220	11 879	31 021	13	826
Wabaunsee	380	36 781	62 976	6	2 670	457	40 214	67 835	6	2 185
Wallace	105	10 267	22 017	23	1 914	91	8 676	21 278	30	2 937
Washington	581	29 903	64 738	8	255	683	34 928	82 357	8	431
Wichita	87	6 973	20 717	50	4 492	87	6 237	20 022	55	4 393
Wilson	353	20 675	34 169	7	260	397	23 016	43 556	3	74
Woodson	240	31 246	38 745	-	-	240	31 537	46 896	1	(D)
Wyandotte	66	2 063	3 215	-	-	89	3 180	5 929	-	-
ALFALFA HAY (TONS, DRY)										
State Total										
Kansas	15 484	741 856	2 529 635	1 174	180 952	20 032	875 567	2 820 549	1 530	162 974
Counties										
Allen	113	3 413	10 164	-	-	154	4 269	13 457	-	-
Anderson	121	3 926	11 151	-	-	187	5 616	17 219	1	(D)
Atchison	93	2 174	5 738	-	-	143	2 634	8 002	-	-
Barber	100	5 006	18 740	8	(D)	123	7 145	20 544	10	348
Barton	358	26 005	84 407	23	1 653	450	26 899	91 188	38	(D)
Bourbon	85	2 295	6 333	1	(D)	126	3 236	9 357	-	-
Brown	135	3 223	11 072	-	-	204	5 341	18 683	-	-
Butler	276	12 917	35 112	1	(D)	81	2 110	44 161	1	(D)
Chase	123	4 742	15 463	-	-	141	6 799	18 980	1	(D)
Chautauqua	49	2 228	5 933	-	-	80	2 629	7 790	-	-
Cherokee	16	295	692	-	-	18	353	700	-	-
Cheyenne	61	3 442	12 654	37	2 386	80	5 030	22 539	52	3 811
Clark	41	(D)	(D)	8	1 122	44	4 397	14 636	6	(D)
Clay	298	10 068	27 092	1	(D)	358	10 693	31 788	6	(D)
Cloud	239	9 497	26 417	4	(D)	345	12 941	39 534	10	594
Coffey	69	1 706	4 035	-	-	123	3 319	8 584	-	-
Comanche	60	3 990	13 819	12	862	55	4 116	12 821	8	(D)
Cowley	224	9 659	31 028	1	(D)	347	15 660	43 658	-	-
Crawford	25	913	2 233	-	-	81	2 110	5 370	-	-
Decatur	137	7 037	25 918	14	464	162	8 585	29 666	27	1 271
Dickinson	488	19 544	58 591	8	(D)	521	18 907	62 985	2	(D)
Doniphan	114	2 116	7 071	-	-	156	2 575	8 060	1	(D)
Douglas	100	2 992	6 862	1	(D)	150	3 529	9 752	-	-
Edwards	94	16 331	70 334	45	12 193	150	20 598	84 298	56	13 147
Elk	74	3 309	8 916	1	(D)	105	5 207	14 769	1	(D)
Ellis	130	4 725	12 461	6	(D)	170	6 473	19 685	14	412
Ellsworth	182	6 898	18 093	-	-	197	6 851	18 625	3	(D)
Finney	120	25 710	121 199	105	23 889	163	37 276	150 950	146	23 711
Ford	84	9 987	47 594	40	7 397	100	8 323	32 606	52	5 802
Franklin	135	2 773	7 092	1	(D)	166	3 820	9 908	1	(D)

[For meaning of abbreviations and symbols, see introductory text]

Geographic area	1987 Harvested			1987 Irrigated		1982 Harvested			1982 Irrigated	
	Farms	Acres	Quantity	Farms	Acres	Farms	Acres	Quantity	Farms	Acres
ALFALFA HAY (TONS, DRY) —Con.										
Counties—Con.										
Geary	144	4 657	13 358	5	(D)	143	4 879	16 803	2	(D)
Gove	55	2 616	8 194	9	407	86	6 147	19 312	9	562
Graham	76	3 223	10 722	8	714	139	4 954	15 810	15	735
Grant	41	5 668	31 395	36	5 424	49	5 577	22 729	37	3 702
Gray	48	16 673	96 911	42	16 406	54	10 988	53 537	49	9 110
Greeley	5	250	978	1	(D)	10	995	3 918	7	(D)
Greenwood	139	5 812	16 880	-	-	193	6 803	19 980	-	-
Hamilton	34	5 580	22 458	26	4 865	35	5 154	21 135	31	4 396
Harper	148	5 250	18 204	2	(D)	159	5 697	16 205	7	449
Harvey	239	7 030	21 231	10	(D)	325	9 258	23 204	10	621
Haskell	38	4 696	20 209	34	4 516	38	4 044	18 480	32	3 851
Hodgeman	50	2 583	8 934	21	1 332	61	2 387	9 916	36	1 477
Jackson	163	3 304	7 341	-	-	261	6 955	18 558	-	-
Jefferson	122	2 552	6 904	-	-	176	3 783	9 091	-	-
Jewell	317	11 872	35 672	4	(D)	407	14 007	46 362	1	(D)
Johnson	54	1 569	4 237	-	-	77	1 723	3 350	-	-
Kearny	61	17 034	83 747	59	16 816	52	12 089	52 372	49	11 659
Kingman	210	7 513	20 620	7	247	255	8 256	21 435	16	543
Kiowa	26	5 210	22 826	18	4 422	31	5 337	24 066	17	4 350
Labette	51	1 551	3 566	-	-	68	1 751	5 961	3	(D)
Lane	24	1 111	2 758	8	256	41	1 762	4 790	11	301
Leavenworth	136	2 733	7 819	1	(D)	218	5 047	13 598	-	-
Lincoln	237	11 692	35 776	1	(D)	293	13 700	46 088	2	(D)
Linn	64	1 916	4 959	-	-	68	2 203	4 722	-	-
Logan	20	(D)	2 776	8	231	26	1 267	4 085	14	500
Lyon	190	6 153	11 865	-	-	251	6 161	16 607	1	(D)
McPherson	471	16 726	45 856	8	293	570	16 277	48 521	12	206
Marion	491	21 127	53 672	2	(D)	566	19 543	46 709	3	36
Marshall	405	11 763	31 388	3	60	561	15 934	47 640	2	(D)
Meade	55	4 990	17 095	27	2 440	64	7 190	20 611	43	3 742
Miami	103	2 499	5 277	-	-	131	2 968	6 830	-	-
Mitchell	193	6 005	10 099	2	(?)	241	7 870	23 639	4	(D)
Montgomery	99	2 240	6 263	-	-	138	3 914	10 994	-	-
Morris	235	9 969	28 705	-	-	284	12 064	32 928	-	-
Morton	7	417	2 176	6	397	18	987	4 178	10	690
Nemaha	352	9 679	27 374	1	(D)	495	13 508	41 505	-	-
Neosho	61	1 732	5 000	-	-	66	1 584	3 616	-	-
Ness	87	1 912	5 336	11	284	120	4 021	11 686	18	653
Norton	121	4 095	14 137	10	(D)	170	7 691	20 930	13	270
Osage	87	2 309	4 594	-	-	145	2 995	7 166	2	(D)
Osborne	218	7 263	23 753	6	(D)	241	9 785	33 217	5	320
Ottawa	218	9 108	26 937	1	(D)	252	9 193	29 760	3	(D)
Pawnee	174	23 081	67 482	85	11 406	222	27 542	99 735	77	9 676
Phillips	315	16 942	49 092	8	219	366	17 435	49 454	7	(D)
Pottawatomie	300	10 477	31 307	5	342	385	14 442	43 085	-	-
Pratt	47	21 740	(D)	13	(D)	91	10 846	45 003	25	7 926
Rawlins	135	7 972	29 606	24	1 344	180	10 691	39 235	44	2 603
Reno	542	25 553	76 342	20	1 100	625	24 906	72 780	24	1 423
Republic	365	12 402	38 852	14	154	484	14 585	49 838	16	214
Rice	206	10 014	33 820	11	615	284	13 054	41 400	9	(D)
Riley	237	6 856	19 277	2	(D)	278	8 269	26 845	3	(D)
Rooks	113	6 587	23 832	2	(D)	165	8 429	26 044	7	(D)
Rush	86	4 181	14 072	18	416	114	4 239	14 058	33	1 036
Russell	136	5 585	16 235	-	-	177	6 610	19 045	2	(D)
Saline	272	12 028	34 836	4	126	317	11 773	38 336	8	(D)
Scott	36	2 924	10 052	26	2 001	41	2 984	9 926	33	2 145
Sedgwick	446	19 242	54 869	10	391	537	20 197	52 349	16	523
Seward	21	6 922	33 392	21	6 922	27	5 372	22 991	23	3 890
Shawnee	119	2 553	6 350	2	(D)	183	5 070	17 772	3	(D)
Sheridan	99	4 771	18 596	15	855	127	6 297	23 797	36	1 937
Sherman	60	3 943	14 572	45	2 371	73	4 673	18 057	58	3 323
Smith	299	10 751	35 819	7	267	373	13 933	44 642	12	762
Stafford	159	15 335	51 909	29	4 300	225	19 198	58 644	31	3 601
Stanton	14	1 562	7 700	12	1 519	24	2 996	15 272	22	2 964
Stevens	28	6 147	32 165	26	5 877	35	6 107	32 161	33	6 000
Sumner	222	7 768	23 163	2	-	295	11 437	30 049	4	(D)
Thomas	27	1 575	6 095	6	630	33	1 281	4 850	7	326
Trego	95	2 690	7 904	11	(D)	134	3 734	12 143	9	435
Wabaunsee	210	7 470	23 254	5	(D)	286	10 194	26 721	5	(D)
Wallace	39	2 518	9 925	21	1 694	50	3 292	12 041	27	2 376
Washington	391	11 673	33 404	7	(D)	548	20 008	55 061	6	(D)
Wichita	47	3 819	13 987	44	3 422	64	4 205	15 739	48	3 932
Wilson	134	3 788	11 477	3	(D)	154	6 666	21 342	3	74
Woodson	55	1 650	4 437	-	-	91	2 939	8 709	-	-
Wyandotte	11	196	446	-	-	27	415	1 028	-	-
SMALL GRAIN HAY (TONS, DRY)										
State Total										
Kansas	4 860	154 772	276 785	135	5 985	3 233	95 569	177 085	133	6 667

Table 26. **Field Seeds, Grass Seeds, Hay, Forage, and Silage: 1987 and 1982**—Con.

[For meaning of abbreviations and symbols. see introductory text]

Geographic area	1987					1982				
	Harvested			Irrigated		Harvested			Irrigated	
	Farms	Acres	Quantity	Farms	Acres	Farms	Acres	Quantity	Farms	Acres
SMALL GRAIN HAY (TONS, DRY)—Con.										
Counties										
Allen	39	979	1 666	-	-	24	269	652	-	-
Anderson	27	806	1 108	-	-	14	323	382	-	-
Atchison	22	409	388	-	-	11	155	263	-	-
Barber	84	4 619	8 320	-	-	49	2 655	5 246	2	(D)
Barton	85	1 872	3 720	-	-	56	1 357	2 494	-	-
Bourbon	45	1 368	1 843	-	-	25	744	1 593	-	-
Brown	13	(D)	(D)	-	-	16	282	394	-	-
Butler	43	856	1 276	-	-	55	1 462	2 302	-	-
Chase	16	(D)	(D)	-	-	15	197	233	-	-
Chautauqua	10	267	334	-	-	24	533	666	-	-
Cherokee	29	683	789	-	-	10	1 184	968	-	-
Cheyenne	57	2 618	6 692	3	(D)	20	555	1 021	-	-
Clark	24	2 314	3 227	-	-	24	659	1 316	-	-
Clay	36	728	1 049	-	-	43	824	1 733	-	-
Cloud	39	539	773	-	-	32	801	2 071	-	-
Coffey	13	231	238	-	-	10	(D)	(D)	-	-
Comanche	23	1 161	2 880	-	-	19	460	676	1	(D)
Cowley	50	1 145	1 801	1	(D)	40	1 164	2 335	-	-
Crawford	45	740	989	-	-	16	251	334	-	-
Decatur	48	1 164	2 515	-	-	25	(D)	(D)	-	-
Dickinson	52	1 154	1 802	-	-	53	1 940	4 559	-	-
Doniphan	10	175	179	-	-	7	74	110	-	-
Douglas	29	535	752	-	-	18	276	342	-	-
Edwards	36	1 211	(D)	2	(D)	13	410	407	4	(D)
Elk	27	640	878	-	-	30	520	846	-	-
Ellis	130	3 472	6 778	-	-	45	1 814	3 414	-	-
Ellsworth	94	2 070	4 493	-	-	43	1 048	2 153	-	-
Finney	96	2 213	4 549	8	819	17	772	1 590	6	(D)
Ford	111	3 633	5 636	6	(D)	39	1 515	(D)	6	115
Franklin	37	817	1 150	-	-	30	567	894	-	-
Geary	11	266	567	-	-	12	193	298	-	-
Gove	92	5 835	12 557	1	(D)	54	2 669	6 088	1	(D)
Graham	69	2 843	5 496	2	(D)	31	1 007	2 678	5	313
Grant	7	300	390	1	(D)	12	466	527	5	(D)
Gray	51	1 645	(D)	20	493	34	1 291	3 053	13	592
Greeley	33	2 239	3 809	-	-	13	(D)	(D)	1	(D)
Greenwood	29	745	931	-	-	23	654	1 053	-	-
Hamilton	21	1 806	2 315	2	(D)	10	687	740	2	(D)
Harper	93	3 296	5 504	-	-	58	(D)	(D)	-	-
Harvey	48	911	1 565	-	-	68	1 217	2 154	1	(D)
Haskell	17	601	1 167	14	(D)	18	526	(D)	9	211
Hodgeman	71	2 599	4 733	9	(D)	35	1 928	4 525	5	(D)
Jackson	17	462	546	-	-	24	344	512	1	(D)
Jefferson	34	719	954	-	-	28	716	1 215	-	-
Jewell	79	1 535	2 339	1	(D)	61	1 964	3 942	-	-
Johnson	16	(D)	979	-	-	4	63	59	-	-
Kearny	31	1 926	2 727	3	(D)	16	1 203	1 731	6	(D)
Kingman	129	4 285	8 613	1	(D)	100	3 317	6 234	3	160
Kiowa	34	1 542	3 060	4	(D)	23	966	1 583	2	(D)
Labette	61	1 309	1 842	-	-	50	955	1 384	-	-
Lane	33	1 929	2 618	4	(D)	9	249	778	1	(D)
Leavenworth	44	613	868	-	-	38	530	893	-	-
Lincoln	72	1 784	3 597	-	-	50	1 358	2 604	-	-
Linn	13	223	282	-	-	19	527	816	-	-
Logan	65	3 030	4 561	5	223	37	1 561	2 962	4	161
Lyon	26	815	1 321	1	(D)	22	425	492	-	-
McPherson	83	1 260	2 814	-	-	71	1 372	2 853	-	-
Marion	112	2 322	4 003	-	-	88	1 569	3 342	2	(D)
Marshall	30	411	673	-	-	29	569	1 401	-	-
Meade	52	2 310	3 586	3	107	21	815	1 685	4	(D)
Miami	29	486	886	-	-	22	364	437	-	-
Mitchell	44	958	2 135	-	-	38	1 084	2 569	-	-
Montgomery	32	666	678	-	-	48	870	1 531	-	-
Morris	38	817	1 427	-	-	32	840	1 476	-	-
Morton	15	926	(D)	2	(D)	9	373	376	-	-
Nemaha	47	1 037	1 546	-	-	31	643	1 457	-	-
Neosho	42	906	1 216	-	-	31	815	1 713	-	-
Ness	117	4 603	8 717	-	-	36	1 439	2 371	-	-
Norton	66	2 623	4 501	-	-	45	1 341	3 363	2	(D)
Osage	20	391	580	-	-	17	635	672	-	-
Osborne	55	1 992	4 456	-	-	37	(D)	4 126	-	-
Ottawa	40	656	1 448	-	-	34	1 135	2 280	-	-
Pawnee	32	(D)	(D)	-	-	18	(D)	(D)	1	(D)
Phillips	78	1 914	3 207	2	(D)	47	1 651	3 111	2	(D)
Pottawatomie	32	554	566	-	-	34	1 863	2 831	-	-
Pratt	51	2 940	6 561	1	(D)	41	2 206	3 049	1	(D)
Rawlins	64	2 027	3 674	-	-	21	761	1 298	1	(D)
Reno	112	2 871	5 473	3	(D)	98	2 750	4 705	4	95
Republic	31	816	1 867	1	(D)	39	680	1 170	-	-
Rice	60	1 139	2 593	1	(D)	30	646	1 554	-	-
Riley	27	475	909	1	(D)	28	502	939	-	-
Rooks	58	2 007	3 966	-	-	19	490	(D)	-	-
Rush	57	1 678	3 131	-	-	23	320	600	-	-
Russell	71	1 889	4 032	-	-	36	721	1 143	-	-
Saline	36	1 603	3 534	1	(D)	34	768	2 235	1	(D)
Scott	41	1 211	5 007	5	(D)	18	983	2 113	7	176
Sedgwick	67	1 595	3 193	1	(D)	64	1 463	2 060	2	(D)
Seward	21	1 058	1 550	4	(D)	11	(D)	(D)	4	(D)
Shawnee	23	(D)	412	-	-	12	211	243	-	-
Sheridan	58	2 360	4 653	2	(D)	21	665	1 706	-	-

[For meaning of abbreviations and symbols, see introductory text]

Geographic area	1987					1982				
	Harvested			Irrigated		Harvested			Irrigated	
	Farms	Acres	Quantity	Farms	Acres	Farms	Acres	Quantity	Farms	Acres
SMALL GRAIN HAY (TONS, DRY)—Con.										
Counties—Con.										
Sherman	49	2 968	6 051	6	352	32	988	1 630	6	178
Smith	60	1 484	2 713	1	(D)	37	854	1 383	1	(D)
Stafford	45	1 182	2 060	1	(D)	25	912	1 294	3	208
Stanton	18	(D)	(D)	8	(D)	6	308	347	1	(D)
Stevens	8	291	(D)	-	-	10	333	453	4	146
Sumner	70	1 982	3 303	-	-	67	1 720	3 096	-	-
Thomas	53	2 606	6 142	-	-	21	(D)	(D)	3	(D)
Trego	99	2 927	5 777	-	-	29	740	1 933	-	-
Wabaunsee	14	242	280	-	-	21	383	476	-	-
Wallace	54	2 722	4 473	2	(D)	18	762	1 067	3	(D)
Washington	44	913	2 875	-	-	45	839	1 465	-	-
Wichita	37	1 903	3 599	5	291	16	528	939	5	(D)
Wilson	26	662	688	-	-	34	795	1 157	-	-
Woodson	6	(D)	(D)	-	-	13	973	1 869	-	-
Wyandotte	4	101	164	-	-	(NA)	(NA)	(NA)	(NA)	(NA)
TAME HAY OTHER THAN ALFALFA, SMALL GRAIN, AND WILD HAY (SEE TEXT) (TONS, DRY)										
State Total										
Kansas	18 484	723 861	1 409 236	230	10 695	16 439	664 805	1 243 821	227	8 842
Counties										
Allen	250	8 737	14 938	-	-	251	8 530	15 098	1	(D)
Anderson	295	13 631	23 315	-	-	272	12 101	19 092	-	-
Atchison	345	15 144	28 060	-	-	396	15 283	33 089	-	-
Barber	115	7 358	21 311	2	(D)	96	5 896	13 782	1	(D)
Barton	213	6 026	13 325	2	(D)	201	4 424	8 764	1	(D)
Bourbon	367	16 230	32 714	1	(D)	344	15 381	28 066	-	-
Brown	298	10 784	22 077	-	-	378	13 966	26 421	-	-
Butler	276	11 310	18 456	-	-	327	13 798	19 992	-	-
Chase	76	3 910	6 532	-	-	69	3 305	4 792	-	-
Chautauqua	74	2 781	5 105	-	-	85	3 255	4 729	-	-
Cherokee	208	7 104	11 900	1	(D)	205	7 031	9 534	2	(D)
Cheyenne	84	4 786	11 709	12	(D)	80	3 789	7 737	5	(D)
Clark	62	4 016	10 248	4	75	50	2 887	5 678	2	(D)
Clay	264	7 428	12 655	-	-	207	4 703	7 605	-	-
Cloud	158	4 286	7 522	-	-	135	2 723	4 993	-	-
Coffey	140	5 634	7 807	-	-	166	7 114	9 781	-	-
Comanche	60	3 502	9 243	3	(D)	40	2 989	5 641	-	-
Cowley	199	7 987	11 820	-	-	194	6 852	9 461	-	-
Crawford	309	11 634	21 931	-	-	309	10 392	17 462	-	-
Decatur	111	3 868	11 564	3	(D)	101	3 594	10 402	-	-
Dickinson	346	9 087	15 664	-	-	342	8 350	15 040	-	-
Doniphan	142	3 984	8 385	-	-	127	2 998	6 215	-	-
Douglas	472	19 899	36 655	1	(D)	493	18 593	35 001	-	-
Edwards	47	1 054	2 492	-	-	39	1 085	1 800	7	176
Elk	89	3 134	4 298	1	(D)	108	4 307	6 888	1	(D)
Ellis	198	10 557	26 288	1	(D)	184	10 152	23 470	3	(D)
Ellsworth	188	6 201	13 323	-	-	151	4 465	8 587	1	(D)
Finney	34	1 384	(D)	13	(D)	27	1 375	3 121	11	477
Ford	139	3 750	8 782	9	250	98	2 113	4 242	6	(D)
Franklin	499	20 477	35 376	1	(D)	503	18 808	34 380	-	-
Geary	95	3 851	4 843	-	-	87	2 341	3 054	-	-
Gove	73	3 656	11 220	1	(D)	63	2 496	7 993	4	(D)
Graham	81	4 593	13 097	1	(D)	84	4 919	12 797	3	(D)
Grant	20	(D)	(D)	5	154	10	350	(D)	5	263
Gray	58	1 826	3 611	19	612	44	1 123	(D)	19	351
Greeley	26	1 270	2 749	2	(D)	21	1 049	1 645	1	(D)
Greenwood	138	9 156	12 452	1	(D)	164	7 671	10 445	-	-
Hamilton	12	1 173	(D)	1	(D)	18	1 114	1 105	2	(D)
Harper	149	7 158	16 566	-	-	189	8 391	14 515	3	65
Harvey	176	3 143	6 536	1	(D)	195	3 299	5 308	3	(D)
Haskell	19	609	2 149	15	507	15	1 157	1 203	9	258
Hodgeman	96	4 745	12 237	8	183	86	3 170	7 546	16	354
Jackson	601	31 320	53 556	3	364	635	32 610	62 456	-	-
Jefferson	535	23 587	41 373	2	(D)	545	22 971	40 287	1	(D)
Jewell	221	9 307	14 784	-	-	224	6 804	13 832	-	-
Johnson	295	14 860	23 662	2	(D)	352	16 295	29 930	2	(D)
Kearny	23	1 256	2 208	5	619	19	871	1 357	6	222
Kingman	234	10 310	26 081	5	(D)	239	9 093	15 577	4	(D)
Kiowa	60	3 808	9 299	4	255	72	4 843	10 672	6	375
Labette	342	14 657	26 619	-	-	334	11 205	17 528	1	(D)
Lane	29	1 374	2 975	1	(D)	23	(D)	(D)	2	(D)
Leavenworth	588	23 953	43 053	-	-	613	21 156	40 173	-	-
Lincoln	176	5 993	15 322	-	-	155	4 651	9 853	-	-
Linn	347	17 753	30 035	-	-	383	16 824	27 920	-	-
Logan	50	2 649	6 324	1	(D)	65	3 143	8 667	3	(D)
Lyon	148	5 632	9 571	-	-	232	8 429	10 925	-	-
McPherson	258	4 685	8 725	2	(D)	241	3 829	6 274	1	(D)
Marion	373	9 611	15 401	-	-	366	10 466	17 451	-	-
Marshall	310	7 651	12 692	-	-	311	7 025	13 898	-	-
Meade	39	1 516	3 727	6	96	33	979	1 643	7	127

Table 26. **Field Seeds, Grass Seeds, Hay, Forage, and Silage: 1987 and 1982**—Con.

[For meaning of abbreviations and symbols, see introductory text]

Geographic area	1987					1982				
	Harvested			Irrigated		Harvested			Irrigated	
	Farms	Acres	Quantity	Farms	Acres	Farms	Acres	Quantity	Farms	Acres

TAME HAY OTHER THAN ALFALFA, SMALL GRAIN, AND WILD HAY (SEE TEXT) (TONS, DRY)—Con.

Counties—Con.

Miami	659	34 015	59 059	1	(D)	669	33 063	59 541	-	-
Mitchell	146	4 326	10 057	-	-	130	3 112	7 134	1	(D)
Montgomery	256	8 503	16 093	1	(D)	240	6 955	12 339	2	(D)
Morris	169	5 647	9 041	-	-	154	5 906	9 456	-	-
Morton	18	1 379	2 082	2	(D)	6	(D)	(D)	-	-
Nemaha	444	16 481	31 407	1	(D)	414	12 734	27 306	-	-
Neosho	296	11 063	21 651	-	-	237	7 598	13 684	-	-
Ness	154	9 653	27 070	1	(D)	141	6 585	13 813	2	(D)
Norton	91	4 625	14 242	1	(D)	112	4 266	12 536	1	(D)
Osage	329	14 317	22 931	-	-	357	14 677	24 062	-	-
Osborne	195	6 581	14 436	-	-	150	4 243	8 864	2	(D)
Ottawa	130	3 384	7 064	-	-	113	2 651	4 356	1	(D)
Pawnee	60	1 673	4 316	3	(D)	41	1 208	2 742	2	(D)
Phillips	137	5 794	16 298	-	-	142	5 135	14 802	-	-
Potawatomie	168	7 269	11 147	-	-	168	5 415	13 584	-	-
Pratt	91	3 092	8 563	6	296	90	2 806	5 878	3	(D)
Rawlins	103	4 407	12 506	2	(D)	90	3 350	8 085	5	(D)
Reno	292	7 274	16 827	5	92	254	7 005	12 161	3	(D)
Republic	195	3 244	5 761	9	179	200	3 724	5 396	1	(D)
Rice	120	2 762	5 685	1	(D)	95	2 143	5 115	1	(D)
Riley	141	2 496	3 979	2	(D)	108	2 001	3 790	-	-
Rooks	102	6 206	14 697	2	(D)	109	4 439	11 464	2	(D)
Rush	110	4 020	8 328	5	(D)	118	3 739	7 177	6	76
Russell	151	8 155	18 755	1	(D)	143	5 497	12 495	-	-
Saline	146	3 971	8 896	1	(D)	129	2 979	5 955	-	-
Scott	16	(D)	(D)	-	-	17	(D)	(D)	4	(D)
Sedgwick	219	5 294	10 437	2	(D)	229	5 806	8 936	6	(D)
Seward	25	1 305	2 071	8	430	21	948	1 454	5	294
Shawnee	289	9 440	13 622	2	(D)	308	8 662	14 113	1	(D)
Sheridan	66	2 760	7 019	1	(D)	67	2 505	7 320	2	(D)
Sherman	30	1 318	2 181	2	(D)	38	1 489	3 592	5	214
Smith	182	4 974	15 146	1	(D)	180	5 361	12 342	2	(D)
Stafford	67	2 254	9 756	4	(D)	57	1 767	4 882	5	(D)
Stanton	15	1 014	1 721	6	378	7	263	350	3	(D)
Stevens	11	418	239	3	80	10	236	454	3	68
Sumner	212	6 532	12 373	-	-	229	5 443	9 056	-	-
Thomas	59	2 056	4 702	3	(D)	45	1 397	3 750	2	(D)
Trego	115	6 415	16 010	1	(D)	107	5 997	15 579	5	391
Wabaunsee	187	10 660	17 873	1	(D)	242	11 987	19 882	1	(D)
Wallace	41	2 750	4 936	4	(D)	32	1 867	4 093	3	100
Washington	299	7 626	13 655	-	-	294	6 234	12 901	-	-
Wichita	18	(D)	(D)	5	(D)	27	1 229	2 888	9	231
Wilson	168	5 654	9 535	4	60	174	5 175	6 111	-	-
Woodson	100	3 927	5 351	-	-	85	3 860	4 775	1	(D)
Wyandotte	47	1 571	2 358	-	-	61	2 510	4 635	-	-

WILD HAY (TONS, DRY)

State Total

Kansas	11 434	555 349	699 410	15	1 321	11 621	519 040	677 488	19	701

Counties

Allen	280	16 432	20 784	-	-	284	13 765	16 612	-	-
Anderson	303	21 114	25 736	-	-	311	20 396	26 650	-	-
Atchison	33	681	949	-	-	34	740	1 098	-	-
Barber	22	(D)	(D)	-	-	25	881	1 725	-	-
Barton	110	2 968	4 462	-	-	99	2 559	4 072	-	-
Bourbon	302	14 472	20 103	-	-	293	11 715	15 944	-	-
Brown	14	(D)	(D)	-	-	17	356	741	-	-
Butler	390	27 117	28 592	1	(D)	415	30 731	33 162	2	(D)
Chase	73	3 572	4 420	-	-	74	3 172	3 728	-	-
Chautauqua	154	7 667	9 872	-	-	158	7 052	8 560	-	-
Cherokee	253	9 778	13 852	-	-	274	9 202	11 600	-	-
Cheyenne	5	138	260	-	-	7	486	1 463	-	-
Clark	5	184	(D)	-	-	9	576	556	-	-
Clay	170	6 320	8 518	-	-	152	5 054	7 505	-	-
Cloud	104	3 210	3 457	-	-	106	3 310	4 420	-	-
Coffey	263	23 323	29 115	-	-	277	22 194	28 333	-	-
Comanche	12	(D)	(D)	-	-	11	399	465	-	-
Cowley	284	12 304	15 440	-	-	299	13 845	20 022	-	-
Crawford	232	8 173	11 592	-	-	262	8 720	12 602	-	-
Decatur	10	472	742	-	-	8	(D)	(D)	-	-
Dickinson	237	8 354	11 028	-	-	219	6 766	9 837	-	-
Doniphan	6	45	47	-	-	8	89	166	-	-
Douglas	136	3 591	5 340	1	(D)	112	2 377	3 418	-	-
Elk	193	12 091	13 447	-	-	202	13 125	14 061	-	-
Ellis	104	2 554	3 536	-	-	76	1 852	2 210	-	-
Ellsworth	165	7 958	11 197	-	-	152	5 219	7 720	-	-
Ford	8	155	134	1	(D)	12	558	(D)	1	(D)
Franklin	232	9 057	12 433	-	-	234	9 706	13 865	-	-
Geary	103	4 623	4 898	-	-	96	4 534	5 492	-	-
Gove	16	746	1 430	-	-	25	1 054	919	-	-

[For meaning of abbreviations and symbols, see introductory text]

Geographic area	1987					1982				
	Harvested			Irrigated		Harvested			Irrigated	
	Farms	Acres	Quantity	Farms	Acres	Farms	Acres	Quantity	Farms	Acres
WILD HAY (TONS, DRY)—Con.										
Counties—Con.										
Graham	17	(D)	978	–	–	27	781	1 512	–	–
Grant	4	200	(D)	1	(D)	4	(D)	613	1	(D)
Greenwood	217	19 038	21 160	1	(D)	265	16 690	19 377	–	–
Harper	16	(D)	376	–	–	34	979	(D)	–	–
Harvey	108	2 782	3 942	–	–	104	3 093	4 052	–	–
Haskell	4	(D)	(D)	1	(D)	(NA)	(NA)	(NA)	(NA)	(NA)
Hodgeman	3	(D)	(D)	–	–	4	(D)	(D)	–	–
Jackson	205	8 173	9 875	–	–	231	9 500	12 084	–	–
Jefferson	129	4 414	6 189	1	(D)	124	3 436	5 299	–	–
Jewell	89	2 383	3 441	–	–	81	1 909	2 523	–	–
Johnson	26	682	961	–	–	29	455	828	–	–
Kingman	94	2 944	3 770	–	–	90	2 413	2 912	1	(D)
Kiowa	5	151	150	–	–	14	556	661	–	–
Labette	312	10 778	15 372	–	–	324	10 218	14 226	–	–
Lane	4	(D)	(D)	–	–	8	186	(D)	–	–
Leavenworth	75	1 772	1 905	1	(D)	70	1 396	1 966	–	–
Lincoln	119	5 563	7 342	–	–	127	4 161	6 276	–	–
Linn	200	6 976	9 118	–	–	218	8 343	10 610	–	–
Logan	13	830	(D)	–	–	11	323	768	–	–
Lyon	373	32 521	36 147	–	–	359	28 656	35 596	–	–
McPherson	145	3 805	5 856	–	–	140	3 083	4 283	–	–
Marion	318	10 431	13 939	–	–	315	10 326	14 410	1	(D)
Marshall	271	8 106	11 103	–	–	276	7 791	11 996	–	–
Meade	5	(D)	(D)	–	–	6	330	810	2	(D)
Miami	144	3 006	4 115	–	–	167	3 821	6 001	–	–
Mitchell	41	1 240	1 916	–	–	33	862	1 344	–	–
Montgomery	324	13 991	17 523	–	–	283	11 140	13 818	1	(D)
Morris	225	14 435	18 323	–	–	221	11 953	15 931	–	–
Nemaha	116	4 092	5 667	–	–	120	4 348	6 118	–	–
Neosho	307	11 934	16 467	–	–	296	11 653	16 304	–	–
Ness	29	873	1 225	–	–	35	1 003	1 362	–	–
Norton	16	403	606	–	–	19	760	1 255	–	–
Osage	291	19 311	22 848	–	–	305	19 382	22 220	–	–
Osborne	84	3 606	5 065	–	–	61	2 409	3 641	–	–
Ottawa	86	4 320	6 000	–	–	97	4 157	4 571	–	–
Pawnee	3	(D)	(D)	–	–	4	(D)	(D)	–	–
Phillips	56	1 440	1 933	–	–	61	2 007	3 039	–	–
Pottawatomie	307	24 201	27 805	–	–	308	19 777	25 291	–	–
Pratt	10	199	(D)	–	–	(NA)	(NA)	(NA)	(NA)	(NA)
Rawlins	17	449	715	–	–	22	(D)	762	–	–
Reno	86	2 602	3 166	1	(D)	71	1 620	2 438	–	–
Republic	146	2 823	4 370	1	(D)	143	2 667	3 619	2	(D)
Rice	32	1 455	1 769	–	–	25	635	716	–	–
Riley	195	7 178	8 989	–	–	178	7 344	9 276	2	(D)
Rooks	49	1 512	2 417	–	–	36	(D)	(D)	–	–
Rush	51	1 973	2 724	–	–	48	1 060	1 507	–	–
Russell	109	4 204	4 616	–	–	114	4 348	5 933	–	–
Saline	105	4 285	5 477	–	–	100	2 508	4 254	–	–
Sedgwick	154	6 729	9 235	–	–	172	5 906	7 822	2	(D)
Seward	3	(D)	(D)	–	–	4	(D)	(D)	–	–
Shawnee	226	11 154	14 098	–	–	230	10 058	12 684	–	–
Sheridan	8	134	236	–	–	14	360	1 269	–	–
Sherman	7	(D)	437	–	–	10	561	768	–	–
Smith	70	3 903	6 308	1	(D)	80	3 162	4 516	–	–
Stafford	19	1 161	1 621	1	(D)	13	649	998	–	–
Sumner	133	4 346	6 183	–	–	157	4 992	6 147	–	–
Thomas	3	(D)	(D)	–	–	8	(D)	(D)	–	–
Trego	36	913	1 112	–	–	43	900	1 462	–	–
Wabaunsee	246	17 769	20 547	–	–	288	17 281	20 213	–	–
Wallace	21	1 987	2 397	–	–	22	2 057	3 279	–	–
Washington	272	8 197	11 755	1	(D)	273	6 477	9 549	2	(D)
Wilson	227	10 078	12 233	2	(D)	232	10 170	12 547	1	(D)
Woodson	187	25 261	28 688	–	–	186	23 532	30 505	1	(D)
Wyandotte	8	123	(D)	–	–	6	199	226	–	–
All other counties	11	595	1 243	–	–	(NA)	(NA)	(NA)	(NA)	(NA)
GRASS SILAGE, HAYLAGE, AND GREEN CHOP HAY (TONS, GREEN)										
State Total										
Kansas	1 577	78 244	491 391	105	8 008	1 507	78 650	519 336	117	7 989
Counties										
Allen	17	824	4 120	–	–	16	550	3 144	–	–
Anderson	8	261	2 262	–	–	21	1 965	8 506	–	–
Atchison	16	774	4 526	–	–	19	783	6 545	–	–
Barber	6	(D)	(D)	–	–	8	809	1 730	–	–
Barton	17	564	2 621	1	(D)	15	383	1 656	–	–
Bourbon	10	336	1 338	–	–	21	1 111	4 289	–	–
Brown	24	1 213	6 382	–	–	31	1 722	10 035	–	–
Butler	19	1 805	8 593	–	–	17	574	2 967	–	–
Chase	5	(D)	(D)	–	–	5	113	300	–	–
Chautauqua	8	162	1 259	–	–	5	224	2 330	–	–

[For meaning of abbreviations and symbols, see introductory text]

Geographic area	1987					1982				
	Harvested			Irrigated		Harvested			Irrigated	
	Farms	Acres	Quantity	Farms	Acres	Farms	Acres	Quantity	Farms	Acres

GRASS SILAGE, HAYLAGE, AND GREEN CHOP HAY (TONS, GREEN) — Con.

Counties — Con.

Cherokee	4	151	260	-	-	8	166	443	-	-
Cheyenne	6	369	3 216	4	245	6	360	2 993	3	(D)
Clark	5	(D)	655	-	-	3	303	566	-	-
Clay	17	530	3 558	-	-	18	693	4 314	-	-
Cloud	22	589	3 396	10	(D)	16	655	2 780	-	-
Coffey	5	188	676	-	-	5	(D)	(D)	-	-
Comanche	7	(D)	(D)	1	(D)	8	690	3 819	1	(D)
Cowley	12	513	2 836	-	-	16	572	3 621	-	-
Crawford	5	133	638	-	-	11	370	1 829	-	-
Decatur	13	976	6 325	1	(D)	12	757	2 813	-	-
Dickinson	43	1 825	11 245	1	(D)	47	1 860	11 997	-	-
Doniphan	6	192	2 442	-	-	12	401	4 270	1	(D)
Douglas	14	368	2 428	-	-	22	1 185	8 253	-	-
Edwards	10	(D)	4 817	3	(D)	6	(D)	(D)	1	(D)
Elk	8	167	445	-	-	6	430	1 412	-	-
Ellis	32	1 475	7 451	-	-	11	371	1 334	1	(D)
Ellsworth	19	453	4 498	-	-	11	744	4 114	1	(D)
Finney	7	(D)	7 060	4	(D)	(NA)	(NA)	(NA)	(NA)	(NA)
Ford	21	2 245	15 099	7	997	13	2 759	30 035	7	1 398
Franklin	20	718	3 065	-	-	31	1 155	7 377	-	-
Geary	7	190	2 040	1	(D)	6	173	1 229	-	-
Gove	15	2 132	17 838	2	(D)	19	1 811	25 008	5	350
Graham	9	(D)	6 861	-	-	12	480	2 383	3	(D)
Grant	4	(D)	780	3	(D)	(NA)	(NA)	(NA)	(NA)	(NA)
Gray	8	(D)	3 057	6	455	7	(D)	7 308	5	571
Greeley	8	611	10 452	1	(D)	(NA)	(NA)	(NA)	(NA)	(NA)
Greenwood	10	318	1 605	-	-	8	259	1 800	-	-
Hamilton	4	(D)	1 840	1	(D)	8	566	5 295	3	405
Harper	17	(D)	7 252	-	-	14	(D)	1 563	-	-
Harvey	35	1 042	9 696	-	-	37	1 827	9 735	6	297
Hodgeman	8	(D)	(D)	1	(D)	6	(D)	(D)	1	(D)
Jackson	12	432	1 268	-	-	10	513	3 346	-	-
Jefferson	13	747	3 621	-	-	24	1 523	11 301	-	-
Jewell	18	787	4 585	-	-	19	765	6 820	-	-
Johnson	3	(D)	590	-	-	6	238	1 496	1	(D)
Kingman	33	1 519	11 154	6	423	25	1 010	6 108	6	269
Kiowa	9	540	2 794	2	(D)	6	235	2 390	2	(D)
Labette	12	240	937	-	-	13	472	2 275	-	-
Leavenworth	21	898	6 692	-	-	29	1 461	11 370	-	-
Lincoln	16	1 030	7 537	-	-	24	1 252	8 270	-	-
Linn	8	494	3 444	-	-	11	527	2 404	-	-
Logan	8	(D)	(D)	3	(D)	6	302	2 099	1	(D)
Lyon	9	782	1 453	-	-	15	964	3 098	-	-
McPherson	45	1 283	10 627	1	(D)	34	1 386	10 439	3	(D)
Marion	43	2 220	13 398	-	-	36	1 747	10 653	-	-
Marshall	31	1 532	7 710	-	-	26	922	6 367	-	-
Meade	11	(D)	(D)	7	333	11	1 161	7 258	7	670
Miami	16	419	2 044	-	-	17	720	3 671	-	-
Mitchell	22	1 100	6 327	-	-	22	777	2 374	1	(D)
Montgomery	8	215	879	-	-	12	441	1 557	-	-
Morris	20	787	7 550	-	-	20	1 389	7 275	-	-
Morton	4	551	(D)	-	-	(NA)	(NA)	(NA)	(NA)	(NA)
Nemaha	66	1 582	12 473	1	(D)	46	1 433	8 831	-	-
Neosho	3	520	2 372	1	(D)	8	187	898	-	-
Ness	22	1 065	4 198	2	(D)	17	705	2 362	2	(D)
Norton	18	764	4 395	-	-	21	1 248	10 094	2	(D)
Osage	10	1 560	4 059	-	-	7	518	2 257	-	-
Osborne	28	1 086	7 773	-	-	16	(D)	4 345	2	(D)
Ottawa	21	1 067	6 080	1	(D)	17	586	4 592	-	-
Pawnee	13	1 259	7 122	5	(D)	8	215	546	2	(D)
Phillips	23	1 415	11 159	2	(D)	16	540	2 705	-	-
Pottawatomie	15	588	1 865	-	-	18	566	2 954	-	-
Pratt	11	860	5 255	1	(D)	8	(D)	(D)	-	-
Rawlins	16	909	5 830	-	-	13	(D)	2 784	-	126
Reno	52	1 851	12 936	5	157	56	6 193	53 050	2	(D)
Republic	21	706	5 229	3	(D)	11	403	2 439	2	(D)
Rice	17	706	6 172	-	-	11	589	5 119	-	-
Riley	28	940	4 998	-	-	10	677	3 376	-	-
Rooks	13	737	5 130	-	-	8	(D)	2 190	-	-
Rush	9	204	1 400	1	(D)	14	468	4 256	4	121
Russell	11	538	3 053	1	(D)	14	549	2 562	-	-
Saline	24	996	4 416	1	(D)	16	1 139	7 316	1	(D)
Scott	9	929	5 567	1	(D)	7	630	7 350	3	(D)
Sedgwick	52	2 832	20 158	1	(D)	63	2 905	13 383	2	(D)
Seward	5	(D)	(D)	2	(D)	4	135	1 701	1	(D)
Shawnee	5	(D)	478	-	-	9	509	1 542	-	-
Sheridan	14	666	4 245	1	(D)	14	813	7 201	2	(D)
Sherman	9	(D)	3 445	6	(D)	13	617	8 279	7	587
Smith	27	1 211	9 236	-	-	25	779	6 640	1	(D)
Stafford	14	764	6 810	-	-	9	493	2 170	2	(D)
Stevens	4	(D)	280	-	-	(NA)	(NA)	(NA)	(NA)	(NA)
Sumner	34	2 058	13 405	-	-	33	1 298	6 018	1	(D)
Thomas	8	(D)	(D)	1	(D)	10	910	12 230	3	(D)
Trego	12	1 034	4 340	-	-	10	508	1 513	-	-
Wabaunsee	13	640	3 066	1	(D)	8	369	1 630	-	-
Wallace	6	290	860	-	-	8	700	2 394	1	(D)
Washington	42	1 294	9 746	1	(D)	16	1 370	10 088	-	-
Wilson	42	293	705	-	-	16	270	1 198	-	-
Woodson	3	(D)	(D)	-	-	5	293	3 109	-	-
Wyandotte	3	72	(D)	-	-	3	(D)	(D)	-	-
All other counties	9	754	5 632	5	444	(NA)	(NA)	(NA)	(NA)	(NA)

Table 26. Field Seeds, Grass Seeds, Hay, Forage, and Silage: 1987 and 1982—Con.

[For meaning of abbreviations and symbols, see introductory text]

Geographic area	1987 Harvested Farms	1987 Harvested Acres	1987 Harvested Quantity	1987 Irrigated Farms	1987 Irrigated Acres	1982 Harvested Farms	1982 Harvested Acres	1982 Harvested Quantity	1982 Irrigated Farms	1982 Irrigated Acres
CORN FOR SILAGE OR GREEN CHOP (TONS, GREEN)										
State Total										
Kansas	2 009	109 230	1 669 413	659	53 214	3 020	154 307	2 280 790	903	71 132
Counties										
Allen	17	900	12 264	1	(D)	18	595	6 348	-	-
Anderson	32	1 484	18 280	-	-	39	1 159	12 464	-	-
Atchison	33	918	12 621	-	-	46	1 284	15 241	-	-
Barton	14	964	17 398	14	964	16	1 192	21 655	13	1 010
Bourbon	27	1 039	11 295	-	-	37	1 472	15 345	1	(D)
Brown	59	1 940	27 753	-	-	94	4 569	66 233	-	-
Butler	38	1 952	21 642	2	(D)	44	1 871	20 202	2	(D)
Chase	23	2 262	32 958	-	-	26	1 567	20 215	1	(D)
Chautauqua	5	123	1 410	-	-	5	200	3 170	-	-
Cherokee	9	97	1 563	1	(D)	9	106	1 110	-	-
Cheyenne	23	1 239	21 762	19	1 008	32	1 479	24 616	26	1 294
Clay	21	742	7 778	3	(D)	34	894	14 149	8	299
Cloud	10	267	3 678	6	103	20	880	10 934	7	310
Coffey	16	878	11 142	-	-	38	1 499	16 535	1	(D)
Cowley	8	379	4 880	-	-	9	(D)	5 351	2	(D)
Crawford	10	384	6 326	-	-	26	1 068	11 380	-	-
Decatur	13	474	6 434	8	270	22	1 046	15 701	16	496
Dickinson	85	3 208	35 499	9	340	173	6 186	70 841	4	245
Doniphan	25	806	15 706	-	-	47	1 564	24 464	1	(D)
Douglas	40	1 720	21 964	-	-	68	2 380	26 637	-	-
Edwards	13	708	12 130	10	522	9	690	10 306	7	543
Elk	3	31	248	-	-	(NA)	(NA)	(NA)	(NA)	(NA)
Ellsworth	9	189	2 785	2	(D)	8	(D)	3 370	2	(D)
Finney	20	2 065	45 427	19	2 055	23	3 120	51 209	23	3 110
Ford	17	1 900	27 268	16	1 770	16	1 571	27 110	12	956
Franklin	43	1 576	22 443	-	-	64	2 636	35 322	1	(D)
Geary	14	307	3 707	-	-	18	320	3 827	2	(D)
Gove	21	3 210	42 725	16	1 132	35	2 368	51 450	13	2 253
Graham	11	766	12 490	8	591	15	659	9 351	9	439
Grant	12	1 777	38 246	12	1 777	11	614	11 269	11	614
Gray	16	975	15 585	16	975	34	2 473	48 708	33	2 433
Greeley	6	706	14 418	6	706	5	2 407	41 576	4	2 107
Greenwood	16	815	8 755	2	(D)	31	1 775	23 384	3	75
Harvey	23	882	12 907	11	454	42	1 479	23 815	18	655
Haskell	25	2 326	45 243	24	2 300	35	3 815	78 826	34	3 813
Hodgeman	44	4 094	77 011	44	4 082	42	3 717	64 542	40	3 627
Jackson	24	773	10 139	1	(D)	30	1 192	11 488	-	-
Jefferson	29	844	10 436	-	-	55	1 791	23 346	-	-
Jewell	8	326	5 865	4	182	13	445	7 706	4	135
Johnson	14	1 029	10 582	-	-	12	622	9 730	-	-
Kearny	17	2 455	40 610	17	2 455	24	3 884	66 340	22	3 644
Kingman	12	496	6 146	7	295	11	362	4 792	5	202
Kiowa	3	146	2 685	3	146	4	310	6 315	4	310
Labette	16	561	6 854	2	(D)	25	1 169	11 905	1	(D)
Lane	17	3 690	66 540	16	3 530	15	2 179	37 288	11	1 317
Leavenworth	49	1 566	24 990	1	(D)	59	2 330	26 363	-	-
Lincoln	12	255	2 315	1	(D)	17	340	4 372	5	106
Linn	4	132	1 686	-	-	15	588	7 403	-	-
Logan	5	900	18 450	5	900	5	722	9 620	4	(D)
Lyon	55	3 783	49 028	-	-	90	5 633	58 513	-	-
McPherson	38	1 320	17 320	13	574	60	1 630	24 589	27	685
Marion	71	2 128	23 383	6	145	127	4 780	50 086	7	290
Marshall	20	514	5 364	-	-	35	1 064	13 838	1	(D)
Meade	12	909	14 726	12	909	14	1 135	19 500	14	1 138
Miami	26	1 063	12 678	-	-	36	1 487	18 247	-	-
Mitchell	8	207	3 384	6	195	8	360	5 848	6	215
Montgomery	7	351	3 731	-	-	8	299	3 235	-	-
Morris	31	896	13 074	1	(D)	43	1 140	12 977	1	(D)
Morton	4	881	(D)	3	(D)		(D)		2	(D)
Nemaha	104	3 625	41 155	1	(D)	172	4 867	61 863	-	-
Neosho	11	798	14 617	-	-	19	1 100	11 528	-	-
Norton	4	224	4 100	3	124	15	829	10 447	9	493
Osage	15	842	11 877	-	-	35	1 767	18 254	1	(D)
Osborne	6	68	730	5	40	17	512	9 699	10	261
Ottawa	4	136	1 530	3	110	17	896	11 029	4	250
Pawnee	8	411	8 496	8	411	15	839	16 196	13	767
Phillips	7	279	6 355	5	227	8	346	6 537	5	248
Pottawatomie	33	1 917	23 565	10	641	58	3 435	44 619	10	1 268
Pratt	7	810	12 610	7	810	13	877	16 955	12	852
Rawlins	16	496	6 665	8	192	23	1 243	18 735	19	981
Reno	36	614	10 796	13	480	38	1 314	17 400	18	596
Republic	13	260	3 977	8	159	46	2 357	39 832	30	1 834
Rice	12	1 069	21 416	11	939	22	1 798	30 854	21	1 789
Riley	47	1 349	19 932	2	(D)	49	1 321	16 219	1	(D)
Rooks	6	269	3 820	4	149	7	340	6 570	6	205
Rush	4	255	4 255	4	255	5	113	1 585	3	96
Saline	44	1 556	19 967	13	493	51	1 831	26 758	15	726
Scott	42	4 936	83 677	42	4 936	60	6 854	116 440	39	6 554
Sedgwick	28	1 823	25 336	10	583	46	1 822	23 171	20	838
Seward	7	1 020	17 700	5	350	7	458	8 596	7	458

[For meaning of abbreviations and symbols, see introductory text]

Geographic area	1987					1982				
	Harvested			Irrigated		Harvested			Irrigated	
	Farms	Acres	Quantity	Farms	Acres	Farms	Acres	Quantity	Farms	Acres
CORN FOR SILAGE OR GREEN CHOP (TONS, GREEN)—Con.										
Counties—Con.										
Shawnee	15	437	5 116	2	(D)	26	981	11 034	2	(D)
Sheridan	20	1 138	19 932	19	1 023	57	3 271	53 219	50	3 056
Sherman	33	1 741	34 885	30	1 663	70	4 264	74 702	65	4 027
Stafford	18	1 262	21 218	15	1 117	21	1 677	27 713	20	1 658
Stanton	13	1 854	37 442	13	1 854	10	1 253	27 820	9	1 133
Sumner	15	559	6 140	-	-	19	1 126	10 877	1	(D)
Thomas	27	2 719	47 201	25	2 665	31	2 687	44 100	29	2 654
Trego	4	67	837	1	(D)	11	699	11 532	6	512
Wabaunsee	33	1 098	14 641	2	(D)	44	1 462	18 623	2	(D)
Wallace	9	532	9 235	9	532	14	511	9 630	13	471
Washington	31	1 110	12 470	3	160	41	1 603	22 001	5	249
Wichita	25	2 281	47 466	24	2 246	25	3 967	85 712	25	3 967
Wilson	9	426	5 880	-	-	14	416	4 843	1	(D)
All other counties	20	1 379	(D)	8	661	(NA)	(NA)	(NA)	(NA)	(NA)

SORGHUM CUT FOR DRY FORAGE OR HAY (TONS, DRY)

State Total

| Kansas | 1 099 | 52 231 | 134 520 | 27 | 722 | 1 224 | 52 453 | 134 376 | 37 | 1 134 |

Counties

Barber	27	1 456	3 046	-	-	29	1 253	2 891	-	-
Barton	26	1 073	3 081	-	-	22	419	1 361	-	-
Bourbon	3	34	44	-	-	(NA)	(NA)	(NA)	(NA)	(NA)
Chase	3	70	84	-	-	(NA)	(NA)	(NA)	(NA)	(NA)
Cheyenne	23	958	1 796	1	(D)	19	1 218	2 793	-	-
Clark	10	463	1 043	2	(D)	16	1 147	2 288	-	(D)
Clay	7	177	623	-	-	3	(D)	(D)	2	-
Cloud	6	269	402	-	-	3	23	72	-	-
Comanche	17	1 999	4 361	1	(D)	12	1 103	1 650	-	-
Cowley	3	67	150	-	-	3	96	(D)	-	-
Crawford	3	100	189	-	-	(NA)	(NA)	(NA)	(NA)	(NA)
Decatur	41	1 712	5 296	-	-	41	1 316	4 621	-	-
Dickinson	3	57	(D)	-	-	(NA)	(NA)	(NA)	(NA)	(NA)
Edwards	8	168	306	1	(D)	12	(D)	461	2	(D)
Ellis	54	2 090	6 074	-	-	60	2 645	7 070	1	(D)
Ellsworth	18	504	1 263	-	-	33	1 335	3 772	-	-
Finney	7	240	528	3	90	4	184	474	1	(D)
Ford	17	616	1 253	-	-	26	(D)	1 844	4	61
Gove	28	1 238	3 480	3	47	25	1 466	3 899	1	(D)
Graham	46	4 655	8 665	-	-	48	3 388	8 413	-	-
Gray	5	190	347	1	(D)	3	60	170	-	-
Greeley	3	200	340	-	-	3	160	600	-	-
Harper	8	171	493	-	-	16	549	1 182	-	-
Harvey	4	17	62	-	-	(NA)	(NA)	(NA)	(NA)	(NA)
Hodgeman	16	539	905	4	70	14	(D)	1 849	3	94
Jewell	16	455	1 226	-	-	23	642	2 536	-	-
Kearny	5	225	265	-	-	6	(D)	846	3	140
Kingman	11	214	485	-	-	22	(D)	1 703	2	(D)
Kiowa	8	445	1 677	-	-	15	627	1 322	-	-
Lane	10	659	1 618	-	-	13	613	765	-	-
Lincoln	24	487	1 545	-	-	33	1 080	3 568	-	-
Logan	16	902	1 496	1	(D)	17	1 174	2 338	2	(D)
McPherson	14	216	454	-	-	5	67	135	-	-
Marshall	5	45	71	-	-	(NA)	(NA)	(NA)	(NA)	(NA)
Meade	7	176	505	-	-	8	486	490	-	-
Mitchell	14	209	728	-	-	15	(D)	1 055	-	-
Montgomery	3	26	47	-	-	3	50	83	-	-
Ness	47	2 669	8 090	2	(D)	51	2 973	6 045	1	(D)
Norton	32	1 684	5 129	-	-	30	1 245	3 675	-	-
Osborne	39	1 556	4 944	-	-	55	2 112	6 397	-	-
Ottawa	7	161	292	-	-	8	262	262	-	-
Pawnee	8	269	1 176	-	-	8	181	418	-	-
Phillips	63	3 654	13 503	-	-	70	3 544	8 325	-	-
Pratt	9	330	915	-	-	12	298	550	-	-
Rawlins	44	2 174	5 991	-	-	46	1 998	5 651	-	-
Reno	10	100	275	-	-	15	382	621	-	-
Rice	6	121	518	-	-	7	125	350	-	-
Rooks	46	4 582	10 360	-	-	42	2 876	7 664	-	-
Rush	26	943	2 047	3	100	27	941	2 231	2	(D)
Russell	26	1 136	3 238	-	-	40	1 912	6 760	-	-
Saline	8	343	424	-	-	5	105	226	-	-
Sedgwick	3	97	230	-	-	5	89	(D)	-	-
Seward	3	140	360	-	-	(NA)	(NA)	(NA)	(NA)	(NA)
Sheridan	27	1 513	3 476	1	(D)	29	958	2 779	2	(D)
Sherman	9	480	764	-	-	12	587	1 040	2	(D)
Smith	36	1 003	3 294	-	-	49	1 166	3 704	-	-
Stafford	5	98	212	1	(D)	5	(D)	686	1	(D)
Sumner	5	115	287	-	-	6	70	156	-	-
Thomas	17	792	2 219	-	-	24	888	2 474	1	(D)
Trego	50	3 640	9 961	-	-	51	2 694	7 233	-	-
Wallace	7	455	568	1	(D)	10	(D)	2 044	2	(D)
Washington	4	42	40	-	-	(NA)	(NA)	(NA)	(NA)	(NA)
Wichita	5	196	210	-	-	(NA)	(NA)	(NA)	(NA)	(NA)
All other counties	27	656	(D)	2	(D)	(NA)	(NA)	(NA)	(NA)	(NA)

[For meaning of abbreviations and symbols, see introductory text]

Geographic area	1987					1982				
	Harvested			Irrigated		Harvested			Irrigated	
	Farms	Acres	Quantity	Farms	Acres	Farms	Acres	Quantity	Farms	Acres
SORGHUM FOR SILAGE OR GREEN CHOP (TONS, GREEN)										
State Total										
Kansas	3 944	168 654	2 189 924	452	22 109	5 559	231 330	2 800 231	577	33 599
Counties										
Allen	6	132	1 456	–	–	19	334	3 422	–	–
Anderson	19	381	4 967	–	–	28	725	13 553	1	(D)
Atchison	17	464	6 045	–	–	31	765	9 222	–	–
Barber	17	984	12 275	2	(D)	33	2 162	19 964	4	166
Barton	42	1 353	13 086	4	99	86	1 934	16 547	3	75
Bourbon	20	477	5 976	1	(D)	36	1 208	12 963	1	(D)
Brown	37	692	9 771	–	–	45	1 410	19 489	–	–
Butler	52	2 468	36 723	–	–	62	3 261	36 613	–	–
Chase	11	308	4 029	–	–	24	1 136	14 311	–	–
Chautauqua	5	339	5 051	–	–	8	(D)	2 452	–	–
Cheyenne	23	1 272	16 644	11	454	27	1 395	15 879	7	277
Clark	14	896	12 551	3	192	13	1 256	16 168	5	(D)
Clay	64	2 004	27 045	–	–	92	2 598	31 846	2	(D)
Cloud	30	990	15 507	3	75	59	1 907	28 455	1	(D)
Coffey	21	952	13 219	–	–	22	(D)	9 246	–	–
Comanche	43	2 692	35 762	7	278	37	2 846	20 083	4	223
Cowley	16	843	10 840	–	–	26	1 538	23 074	–	–
Crawford	5	64	500	–	–	18	620	7 619	1	(D)
Decatur	41	2 102	29 932	5	180	55	2 346	25 629	13	494
Dickinson	176	6 391	86 251	3	87	186	5 302	73 482	1	(D)
Doniphan	4	57	910	–	–	8	103	1 840	–	–
Douglas	25	541	7 758	–	–	38	685	6 855	–	–
Edwards	26	1 569	25 112	12	955	26	1 531	15 783	5	(D)
Elk	4	236	1 780	–	–	5	307	1 459	–	–
Ellis	50	3 111	22 165	1	(D)	80	3 857	29 199	8	(D)
Ellsworth	30	659	8 952	2	(D)	55	1 466	12 324	1	(D)
Finney	13	992	11 622	7	444	19	1 623	26 855	10	700
Ford	38	2 245	33 802	11	481	56	2 617	35 143	19	1 081
Franklin	27	1 108	15 969	–	–	49	1 238	14 410	–	–
Geary	22	692	8 092	1	(D)	29	803	11 916	1	(D)
Gove	97	8 097	110 162	25	1 443	106	10 185	131 079	35	3 015
Graham	33	2 963	29 008	4	140	65	3 614	26 825	9	366
Grant	12	740	10 706	10	421	11	356	4 917	7	(D)
Gray	11	457	8 135	7	257	16	967	15 340	12	827
Greeley	14	1 771	29 392	7	967	18	1 610	20 804	10	596
Greenwood	19	1 174	18 213	–	–	27	1 281	14 523	–	–
Hamilton	13	1 285	16 885	5	310	12	1 658	19 605	7	(D)
Harper	34	1 925	18 745	1	(D)	48	2 719	23 778	–	–
Harvey	77	2 296	32 956	4	60	111	3 996	46 462	8	210
Haskell	12	557	8 943	12	527	12	1 139	19 965	8	1 139
Hodgeman	47	2 655	35 421	16	677	60	3 901	56 008	33	1 874
Jackson	26	640	5 693	–	–	34	(D)	9 765	–	–
Jefferson	13	407	4 658	–	–	18	535	6 026	–	–
Jewell	61	2 489	26 879	3	28	99	3 347	40 709	3	62
Johnson	3	(D)	1 340	–	–	4	84	1 005	–	–
Kingman	48	1 870	16 795	5	79	83	4 049	39 781	9	(D)
Kiowa	12	1 380	10 433	4	(D)	18	1 202	12 018	3	110
Labette	9	189	2 445	–	–	22	496	5 392	–	–
Lane	46	3 017	39 071	18	844	44	2 832	35 214	25	1 331
Leavenworth	17	284	4 584	1	(D)	47	1 074	12 768	–	–
Lincoln	73	2 615	36 344	2	(D)	100	4 088	59 567	1	(D)
Linn	7	163	2 321	–	–	16	(D)	4 274	–	–
Logan	20	1 252	17 997	6	340	33	1 884	19 584	11	(D)
Lyon	42	2 853	33 685	–	–	65	3 607	43 444	–	–
McPherson	125	3 946	64 030	12	153	178	4 326	57 327	14	236
Marion	148	4 625	65 908	1	(D)	200	6 485	74 904	–	–
Marshall	102	3 405	41 778	–	–	114	2 540	33 146	1	(D)
Meade	15	1 166	12 332	5	313	22	1 159	15 656	8	257
Miami	14	201	3 276	–	–	16	307	3 614	–	–
Mitchell	58	2 662	40 260	–	–	83	3 107	42 266	4	133
Montgomery	7	121	1 770	–	–	15	428	3 441	1	(D)
Morris	59	1 539	16 723	–	–	80	2 978	34 401	–	–
Nemaha	135	2 880	35 660	–	–	160	3 496	51 081	–	–
Neosho	7	183	2 120	–	–	15	(D)	2 799	–	–
Ness	33	2 065	24 459	2	(D)	50	2 683	20 824	4	(D)
Norton	46	2 539	31 249	3	61	66	3 422	38 626	9	287
Osage	21	644	8 087	–	–	28	1 261	15 797	–	–
Osborne	83	3 795	51 538	17	292	88	4 415	52 826	3	(D)
Ottawa	64	2 599	30 693	2	(D)	77	3 650	57 886	2	(D)
Pawnee	29	1 480	23 612	16	627	31	1 126	15 280	15	504
Phillips	55	2 733	42 638	1	(D)	94	4 168	44 165	4	91
Pottawatomie	44	1 529	19 184	2	(D)	89	2 718	34 756	1	(D)
Pratt	21	1 206	16 369	6	535	96	1 361	17 976	3	482
Rawlins	53	2 678	24 384	9	360	74	3 408	34 274	10	328
Reno	114	2 941	40 034	3	55	203	6 483	74 513	6	(D)
Republic	43	1 223	19 740	8	158	53	1 293	17 873	4	290
Rice	51	1 838	20 499	3	180	61	2 278	24 513	4	(D)
Riley	81	2 372	27 285	–	–	96	2 981	45 175	1	(D)
Rooks	52	3 320	39 629	1	(D)	57	3 606	34 942	1	(D)
Rush	22	596	8 446	5	124	49	1 867	18 104	12	(D)

1987 CENSUS OF AGRICULTURE—COUNTY DATA

Table 26. Field Seeds, Grass Seeds, Hay, Forage, and Silage: 1987 and 1982—Con.

[For meaning of abbreviations and symbols, see introductory text]

Geographic area	1987					1982				
	Harvested			Irrigated		Harvested			Irrigated	
	Farms	Acres	Quantity	Farms	Acres	Farms	Acres	Quantity	Farms	Acres
SORGHUM FOR SILAGE OR GREEN CHOP (TONS, GREEN)—Con.										
Counties—Con.										
Russell	43	2 011	19 852	-	-	82	3 887	44 198	-	-
Saline	72	2 259	25 836	4	99	93	3 251	40 024	5	134
Scott	51	4 440	67 777	35	2 766	56	5 501	78 390	39	4 111
Sedgwick	80	3 046	39 229	5	426	114	6 006	72 129	17	1 273
Seward	6	495	12 900	6	495	7	(D)	10 655	6	(D)
Shawnee	9	270	3 554	1	(D)	15	641	6 474	-	-
Sheridan	47	2 069	30 220	21	785	79	4 298	68 097	34	2 018
Sherman	11	404	6 925	5	235	30	1 657	19 582	18	(D)
Smith	109	4 552	74 815	18	337	140	5 942	88 704	11	547
Stafford	34	1 948	32 278	20	1 061	40	1 545	18 489	5	(D)
Stanton	6	511	6 910	2	(D)	(NA)	(NA)	(NA)	(NA)	(NA)
Sumner	58	2 128	24 283	-	-	95	3 585	33 760	1	(D)
Thomas	28	1 512	15 539	6	390	36	1 732	24 041	13	(D)
Trego	51	2 426	29 267	6	246	76	5 043	47 950	11	564
Wabaunsee	31	1 171	15 400	-	-	59	1 777	21 476	-	-
Wallace	10	462	5 306	4	122	12	1 501	12 391	5	337
Washington	141	4 437	50 560	1	(D)	192	5 090	72 177	1	(D)
Wichita	24	1 358	15 303	14	680	25	1 271	20 352	22	1 076
Wilson	8	315	4 190	-	-	16	381	4 420	1	(D)
All other counties	9	(D)	5 394	3	150	(NA)	(NA)	(NA)	(NA)	(NA)

Table 27. Vegetables, Sweet Corn, and Melons Harvested for Sale: 1987 and 1982

[For meaning of abbreviations and symbols, see introductory text]

Geographic area	1987				1982			
	Harvested		Irrigated		Harvested		Irrigated	
	Farms	Acres	Farms	Acres	Farms	Acres	Farms	Acres
LAND USED FOR VEGETABLES (SEE TEXT)								
State Total								
Kansas	418	4 834	167	1 803	362	4 273	123	1 201
Counties								
Allen	5	9	1	(D)	4	18	1	(D)
Anderson	4	4	-	-	(NA)	(NA)	(NA)	(NA)
Butler	7	22	3	18	3	(D)	3	(D)
Cloud	5	36	3	(D)	5	122	-	-
Cowley	13	104	1	(D)	10	56	2	(D)
Crawford	3	4	-	-	(NA)	(NA)	(NA)	(NA)
Dickinson	4	17	-	-	7	38	1	(D)
Doniphan	7	36	-	-	7	57	-	-
Douglas	13	147	2	(D)	12	71	2	(D)
Ellis	3	(D)	1	(D)	(NA)	(NA)	(NA)	(NA)
Ford	3	4	2	(D)	(NA)	(NA)	(NA)	(NA)
Franklin	5	7	3	3	6	12	-	(D)
Grant	5	15	4	7	(NA)	(NA)	(NA)	(NA)
Harvey	17	161	4	54	9	142	3	(D)
Jackson	3	(D)	-	-	(NA)	(NA)	(NA)	(NA)
Jefferson	12	127	4	(D)	10	17	1	(D)
Johnson	16	178	3	(D)	22	261	4	26
Kingman	5	12	3	6	4	(D)	3	(D)
Labette	4	7	2	(D)	10	25	1	(D)
Leavenworth	20	306	2	(D)	12	157	1	(D)
Linn	5	16	2	(D)	6	19	1	(D)
Lyon	3	7	-	-	(NA)	(NA)	(NA)	(NA)
McPherson	10	21	7	16	(NA)	(NA)	(NA)	(NA)
Marion	3	(D)	1	(D)	10	39	5	(D)
Miami	5	12	1	(D)	3	(D)	-	-
Mitchell	3	7	2	(D)	4	11	-	-
Montgomery	7	104	3	(D)	6	(D)	2	(D)
Neosho	13	86	2	(D)	5	24	1	(D)
Osage	8	12	2	(D)	3	4	2	(D)
Osborne	3	(D)	2	(D)	3	(D)	1	(D)
Pawnee	4	27	2	(D)	(NA)	(NA)	(NA)	(NA)
Phillips	4	22	2	(D)	3	(D)	2	(D)
Pottawatomie	7	40	2	(D)	11	44	4	11
Reno	26	193	11	87	26	123	10	24
Republic	5	(D)	4	(D)	3	8	1	-
Rice	3	(D)	2	(D)	4	8	-	-
Riley	15	314	8	245	8	332	2	(D)
Saline	9	48	5	22	4	8	3	(D)
Sedgwick	33	268	21	169	33	217	24	184
Shawnee	11	314	5	286	12	552	7	164

Table 27. **Vegetables, Sweet Corn, and Melons Harvested for Sale: 1987 and 1982**—Con.

[For meaning of abbreviations and symbols, see introductory text]

Geographic area	1987				1982			
	Harvested		Irrigated		Harvested		Irrigated	
	Farms	Acres	Farms	Acres	Farms	Acres	Farms	Acres
LAND USED FOR VEGETABLES (SEE TEXT) —Con.								
Counties—Con.								
Stafford	4	(D)	3	(D)	9	67	4	54
Sumner	8	46	4	33	8	48	6	38
Wabaunsee	3	44	2	(D)	4	21	1	(D)
Wilson	7	122	2	(D)	4	16	1	(D)
Woodson	4	16	1	(D)	(NA)	(NA)	(NA)	(NA)
Wyandotte	20	1 222	1	(D)	16	1 370	-	-
All other counties	45	311	30	206	(NA)	(NA)	(NA)	(NA)
VEGETABLES HARVESTED (SEE TEXT)								
State Total								
Kansas	418	5 424	166	1 851	362	4 808	123	1 201
Counties								
Allen	5	9	1	(D)	4	16	1	(D)
Anderson	4	4	-	-	(NA)	(NA)	(NA)	(NA)
Butler	7	24	3	20	3	10	3	(D)
Cloud	5	38	3	(D)	5	122	-	-
Cowley	13	112	1	(D)	10	56	2	(D)
Crawford	3	4	-	-	(NA)	(NA)	(NA)	(NA)
Dickinson	4	17	-	-	7	37	1	(D)
Doniphan	5	36	-	-	7	57	-	-
Douglas	13	170	2	(D)	12	70	2	(D)
Ellis	3	(D)	-	-	(NA)	(NA)	(NA)	(NA)
Ford	3	4	2	(D)	(NA)	(NA)	(NA)	(NA)
Franklin	5	10	3	3	6	12	-	-
Grant	5	15	4	7	(NA)	(NA)	(NA)	(NA)
Harvey	17	164	7	55	9	142	3	(D)
Jackson	3	(U)	-	-	(NA)	(NA)	(NA)	(NA)
Jefferson	12	126	4	(D)	6	16	1	4
Johnson	16	178	3	(D)	22	259	4	26
Kingman	5	12	-	-	4	(D)	3	(D)
Labette	4	7	1	(D)	10	25	1	(D)
Leavenworth	20	309	2	(D)	12	157	1	(D)
Linn	5	16	2	(D)	6	19	(NA)	(D)
Lyon	3	8	-	-	3	(NA)	(NA)	(NA)
McPherson	10	21	7	16	(NA)	(NA)	(NA)	(NA)
Marion	5	(D)	1	(D)	10	39	5	(D)
Miami	5	12	1	(D)	3	(D)	-	-
Mitchell	4	7	2	(D)	4	17	-	-
Montgomery	7	114	3	(D)	8	(D)	2	(D)
Neosho	13	86	2	(D)	5	24	1	(D)
Osage	5	12	2	(D)	3	9	2	(D)
Osborne	3	(D)	2	(D)	3	(D)	1	(D)
Pawnee	4	27	2	(D)	(NA)	(NA)	(NA)	(NA)
Phillips	7	22	2	(D)	3	5	2	(D)
Pottawatomie	7	40	2	(D)	11	42	4	11
Reno	26	194	11	67	26	123	10	24
Republic	5	(D)	4	(D)	3	6	-	-
Rice	3	(D)	2	(D)	4	6	1	(D)
Riley	15	337	6	267	8	332	2	(D)
Saline	9	49	5	22	4	5	3	(D)
Sedgwick	33	272	21	169	33	220	24	166
Shawnee	11	313	5	286	12	551	7	484
Stafford	4	(D)	3	(D)	9	68	4	55
Sumner	8	46	4	33	8	48	6	38
Wabaunsee	3	44	2	(D)	4	21	1	(D)
Wilson	7	123	2	(D)	4	(D)	1	(D)
Woodson	4	16	1	(D)	(NA)	(NA)	(NA)	(NA)
Wyandotte	20	1 732	1	(D)	16	1 898	-	-
All other counties	45	312	30	206	(NA)	(NA)	(NA)	(NA)
ASPARAGUS								
State Total								
Kansas	49	93	20	30	15	13	9	7
SNAP BEANS								
State Total								
Kansas	44	84	18	34	56	150	18	103
BEETS								
State Total								
Kansas	11	10	7	4	12	8	5	2

Table 27. **Vegetables, Sweet Corn, and Melons Harvested for Sale: 1987 and 1982**—Con.

[For meaning of abbreviations and symbols, see introductory text]

Geographic area	1987				1982			
	Harvested		Irrigated		Harvested		Irrigated	
	Farms	Acres	Farms	Acres	Farms	Acres	Farms	Acres
BROCCOLI								
State Total								
Kansas	22	35	12	27	8	8	7	7
HEAD CABBAGE								
State Total								
Kansas	30	77	15	36	17	38	12	24
CANTALOUPS								
State Total								
Kansas	146	415	65	235	137	429	56	194
Counties								
Cowley	3	(D)	-	-	6	15	1	(D)
Dickinson	3	(D)	-	-	5	6	1	(D)
Douglas	5	12	-	-	4	7	-	-
Ford	3	(D)	2	(D)	(NA)	(NA)	(NA)	(NA)
Grant	4	3	3	(D)	(NA)	(NA)	(NA)	(NA)
Harvey	6	17	-	-	4	(D)	1	(D)
Jefferson	5	8	2	(D)	(NA)	(NA)	(NA)	(NA)
Johnson	9	20	1	(D)	7	23	1	(D)
Leavenworth	9	32	2	(D)	4	(D)	-	-
Linn	4	2	-	-	(NA)	(NA)	(NA)	(NA)
Neosho	4	18	-	-	3	(D)	-	-
Phillips	3	(D)	2	(D)	(NA)	(NA)	(NA)	(NA)
Reno	8	26	5	21	12	21	4	(D)
Riley	9	53	4	44	4	33	2	(D)
Sedgwick	11	18	7	12	14	25	12	22
Shawnee	7	19	4	(D)	10	62	5	36
Sumner	4	(D)	2	(D)	5	13	4	12
Wyandotte	6	14	1	(D)	7	29	-	-
All other counties	43	139	30	119	(NA)	(NA)	(NA)	(NA)
CUCUMBERS AND PICKLES								
State Total								
Kansas	55	121	27	86	51	41	25	24
EGGPLANT								
State Total								
Kansas	17	14	9	7	16	8	13	7
HONEYDEW MELONS								
State Total								
Kansas	6	28	6	28	(NA)	(NA)	(NA)	(NA)
MUSTARD GREENS								
State Total								
Kansas	12	170	4	5	15	195	3	5
DRY ONIONS								
State Total								
Kansas	11	16	5	5	13	4	5	1
OKRA								
State Total								
Kansas	18	13	10	7	25	8	10	2
GREEN PEAS, EXCLUDING GREEN COWPEAS								
State Total								
Kansas	9	8	4	3	8	4	-	-

[For meaning of abbreviations and symbols, see introductory text]

Geographic area	1987 Harvested Farms	1987 Harvested Acres	1987 Irrigated Farms	1987 Irrigated Acres	1982 Harvested Farms	1982 Harvested Acres	1982 Irrigated Farms	1982 Irrigated Acres
HOT PEPPERS								
State Total								
Kansas	14	18	8	10	12	7	4	4
SWEET PEPPERS								
State Total								
Kansas	42	45	21	27	31	14	17	9
Counties								
Jefferson	4	(D)	3	(D)	(NA)	(NA)	(NA)	(NA)
Leavenworth	3	2	1	(D)	(NA)	(NA)	(NA)	(NA)
Sedgwick	3	3	1	(D)	4	2	4	2
Shawnee	4	4	2	(D)	(NA)	(NA)	(NA)	(NA)
Wyandotte	4	2	-	-	(NA)	(NA)	(NA)	(NA)
All other counties	24	(D)	14	21	(NA)	(NA)	(NA)	(NA)
PUMPKINS								
State Total								
Kansas	96	548	43	254	86	373	32	78
Counties								
Doniphan	3	(D)	-	-	4	18	-	-
Douglas	4	19	-	-	3	11	-	-
Harvey	5	55	3	(D)	3	23	-	-
Johnson	6	45	2	(D)	8	71	1	(D)
Leavenworth	9	(D)	-	-	3	(D)	-	-
Montgomery	4	5	2	(D)	(NA)	12	(NA)	(NA)
Reno	4	17	1	(D)	3	12	2	(D)
Riley	4	36	2	(D)	4	12	9	42
Sedgwick	13	84	9	71	13	54	(NA)	(NA)
Shawnee	4	19	1	(D)	(NA)	(NA)	(NA)	(NA)
Wabaunsee	3	(D)	2	(D)	(NA)	(NA)	(NA)	(NA)
Wyandotte	8	46	-	-	4	50	-	-
All other counties	32	93	21	79	(NA)	(NA)	(NA)	(NA)
SQUASH								
State Total								
Kansas	32	136	16	65	29	80	10	51
Counties								
Saline	3	3	2	(D)	(NA)	(NA)	(NA)	(NA)
Sedgwick	3	2	1	(D)	(NA)	(NA)	(NA)	(NA)
Shawnee	5	46	3	42	5	(D)	3	(D)
All other counties	21	85	10	22	(NA)	(NA)	(NA)	(NA)
SWEET CORN								
State Total								
Kansas	225	1 053	85	408	170	883	49	215
Counties								
Allen	3	(D)	-	-	3	6	-	-
Anderson	4	3	-	-	(NA)	(NA)	(NA)	(NA)
Butler	5	9	2	(D)	(NA)	(NA)	(NA)	(NA)
Cloud	3	11	1	(D)	4	72	(NA)	(NA)
Cowley	7	19	1	-	(NA)	(NA)	(NA)	(NA)
Crawford	3	(D)	-	-	(NA)	(NA)	(NA)	(NA)
Douglas	8	64	2	(D)	5	20	-	-
Franklin	4	2	2	(D)	4	7	-	-
Grant	3	5	3	5	(NA)	(NA)	(NA)	(NA)
Harvey	10	17	5	8	6	40	3	(D)
Jefferson	6	20	1	-	(NA)	(NA)	(NA)	(NA)
Johnson	11	67	1	(D)	6	62	1	(D)
Leavenworth	12	48	2	-	11	25	-	-
Linn	4	4	-	-	6	6	-	-
Lyon	3	7	-	-	(NA)	(NA)	(NA)	(NA)
McPherson	6	13	5	12	(NA)	(NA)	(NA)	(NA)
Miami	6	3	1	(D)	(NA)	(NA)	(NA)	(NA)
Montgomery	6	(D)	3	(D)	6	(D)	2	(D)
Neosho	3	(D)	2	(D)	(NA)	(NA)	(NA)	(NA)
Osage	3	(D)	2	(D)	(NA)	(NA)	(NA)	(NA)

1987 CENSUS OF AGRICULTURE—COUNTY DATA

[For meaning of abbreviations and symbols, see introductory text]

Geographic area	1987				1982			
	Harvested		Irrigated		Harvested		Irrigated	
	Farms	Acres	Farms	Acres	Farms	Acres	Farms	Acres
SWEET CORN—Con.								
Counties—Con.								
Reno	9	28	8	11	4	12	2	(D)
Republic	5	8	4	8	3	(D)	-	-
Riley	8	99	4	(D)	5	20	1	(D)
Saline	3	29	2	(D)	(NA)	(NA)	(NA)	(NA)
Sedgwick	15	35	10	25	14	42	7	24
Shawnee	7	38	4	(D)	7	80	4	55
Sumner	3	5	2	(D)	(NA)	(NA)	(NA)	(NA)
Wilson	7	82	2	(D)	3	(D)	1	(D)
Wyandotte	13	132	-	-	6	261	-	-
All other counties	48	229	19	66	(NA)	(NA)	(NA)	(NA)
TOMATOES								
State Total								
Kansas	174	186	80	90	143	135	60	60
Counties								
Cowley	6	(D)	-	-	3	1	2	-
Douglas	4	5	-	-	5	2	2	(D)
Franklin	4	2	2	(D)	3	2	-	-
Grant	3	(D)	2	(D)	(NA)	(NA)	(NA)	(NA)
Harvey	4	1	-	-	4	1	1	(D)
Jefferson	6	11	2	(D)	(NA)	(NA)	(NA)	(NA)
Johnson	7	4	1	(D)	6	10	-	-
Labette	4	2	1	(D)	5	4	1	(D)
Leavenworth	10	12	1	(D)	4	3	-	-
Linn	4	3	2	(D)	3	1	-	-
McPherson	3	(D)	2	(D)	(NA)	(NA)	(NA)	(NA)
Montgomery	6	7	3	(D)	5	(D)	2	(D)
Pawnee	3	(D)	2	(D)	(NA)	(NA)	(NA)	(NA)
Reno	6	1	3	(D)	6	5	(NA)	(NA)
Rice	3	(D)	2	(D)	(NA)	(NA)	(NA)	(NA)
Riley	10	11	3	7	4	3	1	(D)
Saline	4	6	3	(D)	(NA)	(NA)	(NA)	(NA)
Sedgwick	11	8	8	3	13	8	11	7
Shawnee	5	12	3	(D)	7	22	5	16
Sumner	6	4	4	(D)	5	3	3	2
Wyandotte	16	15	1	(D)	9	14	-	-
All other counties	51	54	29	34	(NA)	(NA)	(NA)	(NA)
TURNIPS								
State Total								
Kansas	23	130	7	(D)	22	197	8	(D)
MIXED VEGETABLES								
State Total								
Kansas	21	53	8	17	15	231	2	(D)
WATERMELONS								
State Total								
Kansas	179	841	64	346	161	636	49	205
Counties								
Cowley	7	35	-	-	8	27	1	(D)
Dickinson	3	9	-	-	6	29	1	(D)
Douglas	6	18	-	-	4	17	-	-
Grant	3	(D)	2	(D)	(NA)	(NA)	(NA)	(NA)
Harvey	6	53	1	(D)	5	27	1	(D)
Jefferson	5	5	3	(D)	(NA)	(NA)	(NA)	(NA)
Johnson	5	14	1	(D)	6	27	-	-
Kingman	3	4	1	(D)	3	9	3	9
Leavenworth	9	79	1	(D)	(NA)	(NA)	(NA)	(NA)
Montgomery	8	25	3	(D)	3	(D)	1	(D)
Neosho	9	46	-	-	3	16	-	-
Phillips	3	(D)	2	(D)	(NA)	(NA)	(NA)	(NA)
Pottawatomie	3	8	-	-	7	14	-	-
Reno	12	88	1	(D)	18	62	2	(D)
Rice	3	(D)	2	(D)	(NA)	(NA)	(NA)	(NA)
Riley	9	74	4	(D)	4	50	1	(D)
Sedgwick	19	51	11	20	18	46	10	27
Shawnee	7	24	4	(D)	6	45	5	40
Stafford	4	(D)	3	(D)	8	23	3	15
Sumner	4	17	3	(D)	6	18	3	14
Wabaunsee	3	10	2	(D)	4	18	1	(D)
Wyandotte	9	56	-	-	8	30	-	-
All other counties	40	97	21	69	(NA)	(NA)	(NA)	(NA)

Table 27. Vegetables, Sweet Corn, and Melons Harvested for Sale: 1987 and 1982—Con.

[For meaning of abbreviations and symbols, see introductory text]

Geographic area	1987				1982			
	Harvested		Irrigated		Harvested		Irrigated	
	Farms	Acres	Farms	Acres	Farms	Acres	Farms	Acres
OTHER VEGETABLES								
State Total								
Kansas	11	12	8	8	13	17	4	4

Table 28. Fruits and Nuts: 1987 and 1982

[For meaning of abbreviations and symbols, see introductory text]

Geographic area	Total			Trees or vines not of bearing age		Trees or vines of bearing age		Harvested	
	Farms	Acres	Trees or vines	Farms	Number	Farms	Number	Farms	Pounds
LAND IN ORCHARDS									
State Total									
Kansas 1987	503	5 999	(X)	(X)	(X)	(X)	(X)	(X)	(X)
1982	603	6 408	(X)	(X)	(X)	(X)	(X)	(X)	(X)
Counties, 1987									
Allen	6	15	(X)	(X)	(X)	(X)	(X)	(X)	(X)
Anderson	5	13	(X)	(X)	(X)	(X)	(X)	(X)	(X)
Bourbon	17	49	(X)	(X)	(X)	(X)	(X)	(X)	(X)
Butler	12	81	(X)	(X)	(X)	(X)	(X)	(X)	(X)
Chase	5	34	(X)	(X)	(X)	(X)	(X)	(X)	(X)
Chautauqua	6	(D)	(X)	(X)	(X)	(X)	(X)	(X)	(X)
Cherokee	18	1 176	(X)	(X)	(X)	(X)	(X)	(X)	(X)
Cloud	4	34	(X)	(X)	(X)	(X)	(X)	(X)	(X)
Coffey	3	16	(X)	(X)	(X)	(X)	(X)	(X)	(X)
Cowley	15	70	(X)	(X)	(X)	(X)	(X)	(X)	(X)
Crawford	4	27	(X)	(X)	(X)	(X)	(X)	(X)	(X)
Dickinson	4	9	(X)	(X)	(X)	(X)	(X)	(X)	(X)
Doniphan	10	377	(X)	(X)	(X)	(X)	(X)	(X)	(X)
Douglas	15	52	(X)	(X)	(X)	(X)	(X)	(X)	(X)
Elk	7	16	(X)	(X)	(X)	(X)	(X)	(X)	(X)
Ellsworth	3	10	(X)	(X)	(X)	(X)	(X)	(X)	(X)
Franklin	16	55	(X)	(X)	(X)	(X)	(X)	(X)	(X)
Greenwood	4	5	(X)	(X)	(X)	(X)	(X)	(X)	(X)
Harper	3	(D)	(X)	(X)	(X)	(X)	(X)	(X)	(X)
Harvey	12	78	(X)	(X)	(X)	(X)	(X)	(X)	(X)
Haskell	3	(D)	(X)	(X)	(X)	(X)	(X)	(X)	(X)
Jefferson	12	114	(X)	(X)	(X)	(X)	(X)	(X)	(X)
Johnson	11	30	(X)	(X)	(X)	(X)	(X)	(X)	(X)
Kingman	5	34	(X)	(X)	(X)	(X)	(X)	(X)	(X)
Labette	17	268	(X)	(X)	(X)	(X)	(X)	(X)	(X)
Leavenworth	15	81	(X)	(X)	(X)	(X)	(X)	(X)	(X)
Linn	24	384	(X)	(X)	(X)	(X)	(X)	(X)	(X)
Lyon	4	(D)	(X)	(X)	(X)	(X)	(X)	(X)	(X)
Marion	12	20	(X)	(X)	(X)	(X)	(X)	(X)	(X)
Marshall	10	21	(X)	(X)	(X)	(X)	(X)	(X)	(X)
Meade	3	(D)	(X)	(X)	(X)	(X)	(X)	(X)	(X)
Miami	9	72	(X)	(X)	(X)	(X)	(X)	(X)	(X)
Mitchell	4	12	(X)	(X)	(X)	(X)	(X)	(X)	(X)
Montgomery	15	179	(X)	(X)	(X)	(X)	(X)	(X)	(X)
Neosho	13	1 083	(X)	(X)	(X)	(X)	(X)	(X)	(X)
Osage	6	19	(X)	(X)	(X)	(X)	(X)	(X)	(X)
Pottawatomie	10	68	(X)	(X)	(X)	(X)	(X)	(X)	(X)
Reno	10	55	(X)	(X)	(X)	(X)	(X)	(X)	(X)
Republic	3	(D)	(X)	(X)	(X)	(X)	(X)	(X)	(X)
Riley	8	56	(X)	(X)	(X)	(X)	(X)	(X)	(X)
Sedgwick	35	402	(X)	(X)	(X)	(X)	(X)	(X)	(X)
Shawnee	4	8	(X)	(X)	(X)	(X)	(X)	(X)	(X)
Smith	3	3	(X)	(X)	(X)	(X)	(X)	(X)	(X)
Stafford	4	26	(X)	(X)	(X)	(X)	(X)	(X)	(X)
Sumner	17	209	(X)	(X)	(X)	(X)	(X)	(X)	(X)
Thomas	4	4	(X)	(X)	(X)	(X)	(X)	(X)	(X)
Trego	3	(D)	(X)	(X)	(X)	(X)	(X)	(X)	(X)
Wilson	9	35	(X)	(X)	(X)	(X)	(X)	(X)	(X)
Woodson	7	28	(X)	(X)	(X)	(X)	(X)	(X)	(X)
Wyandotte	14	123	(X)	(X)	(X)	(X)	(X)	(X)	(X)
All other counties	40	178	(X)	(X)	(X)	(X)	(X)	(X)	(X)

Table 28. Fruits and Nuts: 1987 and 1982—Con.

[For meaning of abbreviations and symbols, see introductory text.]

Geographic area	Total			Trees or vines not of bearing age		Trees or vines of bearing age		Harvested	
	Farms	Acres	Trees or vines	Farms	Number	Farms	Number	Farms	Pounds
APPLES									
State Total									
Kansas ....1987..	318	1 310	76 704	163	18 420	263	56 284	166	7 094 254
1982..	416	2 064	98 454	224	18 404	319	80 050	163	8 474 047
Counties, 1987									
Allen ------------------	6	9	315	2	(D)	6	(D)	3	(D)
Bourbon ----------------	9	8	428	6	56	6	370	4	1 590
Butler -----------------	7	19	898	2	(D)	5	(D)	5	109 800
Chase ------------------	3	(D)	(D)	1	(D)	2	(D)	2	(D)
Cherokee ---------------	4	(D)	635	2	(O)	3	(D)	2	(D)
Coffey -----------------	3	(D)	(D)	1	(O)	3	(D)	2	(O)
Cowley -----------------	10	21	1 303	6	322	7	981	7	118 330
Doniphan ---------------	9	361	17 091	3	(D)	9	(D)	9	3 309 890
Douglas ----------------	12	21	1 608	9	448	12	1 150	5	(D)
Elk --------------------	6	5	177	1	(D)	6	(D)	1	(D)
Ellsworth --------------	3	(D)	336	1	(D)	2	(D)	2	(D)
Franklin ---------------	14	32	1 251	8	(D)	9	(D)	6	3 029
Greenwood --------------	4	3	52	-	-	4	52	4	7 200
Harper -----------------	3	(D)	(D)	-	-	3	(D)	1	(D)
Harvey -----------------	8	39	3 949	3	(O)	7	(D)	6	132 416
Jefferson --------------	10	80	6 378	5	(D)	10	(D)	5	(D)
Johnson ----------------	9	19	1 484	4	(D)	6	(D)	2	(D)
Kingman ----------------	3	(D)	(D)	3	(D)	2	(D)	1	(D)
Labette ----------------	8	10	819	5	120	7	699	4	(D)
Leavenworth ------------	12	43	1 791	8	783	9	1 008	7	25 380
Linn -------------------	7	8	118	2	(D)	7	(D)	2	(D)
Marion -----------------	11	13	562	7	94	9	466	8	25 355
Marshall ---------------	8	4	102	4	56	4	44	2	(D)
Miami ------------------	6	7	353	2	(D)	5	(D)	4	(D)
Mitchell ---------------	4	9	(D)	3	(D)	1	(D)	-	-
Montgomery -------------	10	27	1 527	4	(D)	9	(D)	4	(D)
Neosho -----------------	4	(D)	(D)	4	(O)	4	(D)	3	(O)
Osage ------------------	6	(D)	(D)	3	(D)	5	(D)	3	3 540
Pottawatomie -----------	5	25	540	4	220	3	320	3	21 800
Reno -------------------	8	38	2 254	5	(D)	7	(D)	4	(D)
Republic ---------------	3	(D)	(D)	3	560	2	(D)	2	(D)
Riley ------------------	7	31	2 765	5	1 265	5	1 520	5	139 103
Sedgwick ---------------	13	26	1 317	4	(D)	11	(D)	3	(D)
Shawnee ----------------	3	4	210	3	(D)	1	(D)	-	-
Smith ------------------	3	3	185	3	(O)	2	(D)	2	(D)
Stafford ---------------	4	16	1 050	3	100	3	950	-	-
Sumner -----------------	8	50	1 360	6	(O)	7	(D)	6	(O)
Wilson -----------------	8	30	1 392	2	(D)	8	(D)	2	(D)
Woodson ----------------	3	7	260	1	(D)	3	(D)	3	(D)
Wyandotte --------------	9	28	1 609	5	563	8	1 046	3	(D)
All other counties -----	45	177	11 869	20	1 711	39	10 158	29	423 092
APRICOTS									
State Total									
Kansas ....1987..	47	10	406	33	278	23	126	4	(D)
1982..	77	21	1 170	60	375	46	795	3	3
CHERRIES, TOTAL (SEE TEXT)									
State Total									
Kansas ....1987..	83	38	2 137	52	713	60	1 424	32	21 610
1982..	126	58	2 768	84	925	92	1 863	38	10 883
GRAPES (SEE TEXT) (FRESH WEIGHT)									
State Total									
Kansas ....1987..	135	163	71 320	103	32 179	113	39 141	47	145 326
1982..	109	51	21 518	77	5 601	88	15 917	36	17 854
NECTARINES									
State Total									
Kansas ....1987..	15	3	189	8	140	7	49	3	(D)
1982..	22	10	410	15	158	12	252	-	-

Table 28. Fruits and Nuts: 1987 and 1982—Con.

[For meaning of abbreviations and symbols, see introductory text]

Geographic area	Total			Trees or vines not of bearing age		Trees or vines of bearing age		Harvested	
	Farms	Acres	Trees or vines	Farms	Number	Farms	Number	Farms	Pounds
PEACHES									
State Total									
Kansas 1987	242	752	51 249	133	10 440	184	40 809	75	450 893
1982	312	1 200	69 724	203	20 592	227	49 132	22	48 215
Counties, 1987									
Allen	3	(D)	(D)	1	(D)	2	(D)	2	-
Bourbon	7	3	110	5	59	7	51	2	(D)
Butler	4	6	(D)	2	(D)	2	(D)	-	(D)
Chase	3	(D)	(D)	1	(D)	2	(D)	-	-
Cherokee	4	9	(D)	2	(D)	3	(D)	1	(D)
Coffey	3	(D)	(D)	-	-	3	(D)	2	(D)
Cowley	5	7	340	5	150	3	190	2	(D)
Dickinson	4	6	406	2	(D)	4	(D)	3	(D)
Douglas	8	5	(D)	3	(D)	8	(D)	3	(D)
Elk	4	2	54	2	(D)	4	(D)	-	-
Franklin	9	7	366	6	86	6	280	3	(D)
Greenwood	4	1	14	-	-	4	14	2	(D)
Harper	3	(D)	(D)	-	-	3	(D)	-	-
Harvey	8	20	1 582	2	(D)	6	(D)	3	(D)
Haskell	3	(D)	(D)	3	(D)	3	(D)	1	(D)
Jefferson	6	(D)	(D)	3	19	4	(D)	1	(D)
Johnson	4	2	36	3	(D)	1	(D)	-	-
Kingman	4	(D)	(D)	4	(D)	2	(D)	1	(D)
Labette	6	7	(D)	2	(D)	6	(D)	3	(D)
Leavenworth	7	(D)	728	6	(D)	1	(D)	-	-
Linn	6	3	85	6	31	6	54	1	(D)
Marion	6	1	34	4	(D)	2	(D)	2	(D)
Marshall	7	2	42	4	32	3	10	-	-
Miami	4	2	37	4	(D)	4	(D)	2	(D)
Mitchell	4	1	37	2	37	-	-	-	-
Montgomery	5	2	59	3	(D)	4	(D)	1	(D)
Osage	4	(D)	42	3	(D)	3	(D)	1	(D)
Pottawatomie	3	1	(D)	2	(D)	1	(D)	-	-
Reno	5	10	661	4	142	4	519	-	-
Riley	5	(D)	643	2	(D)	3	(D)	3	(D)
Sedgwick	24	301	22 274	9	3 068	23	19 186	9	76 514
Stafford	4	(D)	708	3	148	3	560	2	(D)
Sumner	6	(D)	(D)	5	(D)	5	(D)	3	(D)
Woodson	4	(D)	(D)	2	(D)	4	26	4	(D)
Wyandotte	11	90	6 060	5	586	10	5 474	6	143 935
All other counties	45	57	2 686	23	338	35	2 348	12	34 355
PEARS									
State Total									
Kansas 1987	84	56	2 911	49	344	60	2 567	29	44 216
1982	116	55	3 198	74	691	79	2 507	13	4 927
PLUMS AND PRUNES (SEE TEXT) (FRESH WEIGHT)									
State Total									
Kansas 1987	40	12	831	28	529	22	302	7	176
1982	67	30	1 787	63	529	59	1 258	12	4 204
PECANS (IN SHELL)									
State Total									
Kansas 1987	131	3 570	89 889	83	27 169	109	62 720	84	599 562
1982	164	2 885	71 401	108	10 840	113	60 561	57	195 666
Counties, 1987									
Bourbon	5	23	420	3	(D)	3	(D)	3	500
Butler	5	48	2 267	5	(D)	1	(D)	1	(D)
Cherokee	15	1 156	30 747	11	10 645	15	20 102	13	323 205
Cowley	6	37	303	3	66	5	235	3	(D)
Douglas	3	(D)	(D)	1	(D)	2	(D)	2	(D)
Labette	8	240	5 972	6	619	8	5 353	6	48 250
Leavenworth	3	(D)	(D)	2	(D)	3	(D)	-	-
Linn	21	364	6 845	7	309	21	6 336	21	59 781
Miami	4	60	1 075	1	(D)	4	(D)	3	(D)
Montgomery	8	146	5 459	5	5 315	5	144	8	(D)
Neosho	11	(D)	(D)	8	4 147	11	(D)	8	(D)
Sedgwick	9	64	1 708	7	1 016	6	692	2	(D)
Sumner	7	79	2 329	5	957	7	1 372	7	16 150
All other counties	26	274	6 105	19	1 341	19	4 764	11	23 476

Table 28. **Fruits and Nuts: 1987 and 1982**—Con.

[For meaning of abbreviations and symbols. see introductory text]

Geographic area	Total			Trees or vines not of bearing age		Trees or vines of bearing age		Harvested	
	Farms	Acres	Trees or vines	Farms	Number	Farms	Number	Farms	Pounds
OTHER NUTS (IN SHELL)									
State Total									
Kansas .... 1987..	9	32	794	6	482	7	312	3	(D)
1962..	-	~	~	-	-	-	~	-	~
OTHER FRUITS AND NUTS (SEE TEXT)									
State Total									
Kansas .... 1987..	24	41	2 244	14	1 451	20	793	11	4 941
1962..	11	14	977	8	273	8	704	5	(D)

Table 29. **Berries Harvested for Sale: 1987 and 1982**

[For meaning of abbreviations and symbols, see introductory text]

Geographic area	1987					1982				
	Harvested			Irrigated		Harvested			Irrigated	
	Farms	Acres	Quantity	Farms	Acres	Farms	Acres	Quantity	Farms	Acres
BERRIES										
State Total										
Kansas	131	275	(X)	63	165	107	205	(X)	48	128
BLACKBERRIES (POUNDS)										
State Total										
Kansas	22	31	39 145	7	(D)	3	(D)	565	1	(D)
RASPBERRIES (POUNDS)										
State Total										
Kansas	17	21	11 211	9	16	5	(D)	(D)	1	(D)
STRAWBERRIES (POUNDS)										
State Total										
Kansas	115	219	449 780	59	142	106	199	542 644	46	(D)
Counties										
Butler	3	(D)	(D)	1	(D)	3	(D)	3 681	3	(D)
Cloud	3	(D)	(D)	1	(D)	(NA)	(NA)	(NA)	(NA)	(NA)
Doniphan	3	1	3 060	-	(D)	4	(D)	4 420	1	(D)
Douglas	3	(D)	(D)	1	(D)	4	1	1 300	2	(D)
Franklin	3	(D)	(D)	1	(D)	3	1	(D)	1	(D)
Harvey	3	(D)	(D)	2	(D)	3	1	(D)	1	(D)
Jefferson	4	4	(D)	1	(D)	(NA)	(NA)	(NA)	(NA)	(NA)
Johnson	4	(D)	(D)	2	(D)	(NA)	(NA)	(NA)	(NA)	(NA)
Kingman	3	4	10 970	2	(D)	(NA)	(NA)	(NA)	(NA)	(NA)
Labette	4	7	13 080	2	(D)	(NA)	(NA)	(NA)	(NA)	(NA)
Marshall	3	2	2 302	-	-	(NA)	(NA)	(NA)	(NA)	(NA)
Montgomery	4	18	29 950	2	(D)	3	14	16 350	3	14
Neosho	3	4	(D)	1	(D)	3	(D)	2 200	1	(D)
Reno	4	(D)	4 950	3	3	12	(D)	10 134	5	3
Republic	3	3	6 275	2	(D)	(NA)	(NA)	(NA)	(NA)	(NA)
Riley	5	15	12 092	3	(D)	4	(D)	(D)	2	(D)
Sedgwick	13	(D)	50 607	12	(D)	12	54	149 816	12	54
Shawnee	4	11	37 625	4	11	3	(D)	(D)	2	(D)
Wilson	3	8	16 900	2	(D)	(NA)	(NA)	(NA)	(NA)	(NA)
Woodson	3	(D)	(D)	1	(D)	(NA)	(NA)	(NA)	(NA)	(NA)
Wyandotte	4	5	8 030	-	-	6	(D)	14 440	-	-
All other counties	33	61	111 842	16	26	(NA)	(NA)	(NA)	(NA)	(NA)

1987 CENSUS OF AGRICULTURE—COUNTY DATA

Table 30. **Nursery and Greenhouse Crops, Mushrooms, and Sod Grown for Sale: 1987 and 1982**

[For meaning of abbreviations and symbols, see introductory text]

Geographic area	1987				1982			
	Farms	Sq. ft. under glass or other protection	Acres in the open	Sales ($1,000)	Farms	Sq. ft. under glass or other protection	Acres in the open	Sales ($1,000)
NURSERY AND GREENHOUSE CROPS (SEE TEXT)								
State Total								
Kansas	272	3 489 306	4 195	26 805	298	2 964 220	4 248	21 515
Counties								
Barton	5	(D)	(D)	(D)	6	(D)	(D)	(D)
Brown	3	16 500	-	(D)	(NA)	(NA)	(NA)	(NA)
Butler	9	(D)	(D)	120	9	(D)	(D)	132
Coffey	3	(D)	(D)	(D)	5	(D)	(D)	(D)
Cowley	8	68 200	26	306	3	(D)	(D)	(D)
Douglas	11	23 074	18	115	10	15 600	(D)	79
Ford	3	6 700	(D)	(D)	4	(D)	-	(D)
Franklin	4	(D)	(D)	(D)	7	(D)	(D)	(D)
Geary	3	(D)	(D)	(D)	5	(D)	(D)	(D)
Harvey	3	(D)	(D)	(D)	3	(D)	(D)	(D)
Jefferson	9	(D)	(D)	(D)	(NA)	(NA)	(NA)	(NA)
Johnson	22	179 904	(D)	3 159	40	293 177	1 514	2 646
Kingman	3	(D)	(D)	(D)	4	(D)	(D)	(NA)
Labette	4	(D)	(D)	47	(NA)	(NA)	(NA)	(NA)
Leavenworth	13	(D)	(D)	(D)	10	(D)	(D)	(D)
McPherson	7	(D)	(D)	59	3	(D)	(D)	(D)
Marion	4	(D)	(D)	(D)	(NA)	(NA)	(NA)	(NA)
Miami	16	(D)	(D)	2 056	18	2 600	534	626
Mitchell	5	(D)	(D)	67	3	(D)	(D)	(D)
Montgomery	5	95 000	9	395	7	(D)	(D)	500
Osage	5	13 620	-	41	(NA)	(NA)	(NA)	(NA)
Pottawatomie	3	(D)	(D)	(D)	7	(D)	(D)	596
Reno	9	446 550	7	2 516	11	(D)	(D)	1 537
Riley	7	115 263	8	(D)	5	(D)	(D)	678
Saline	5	(D)	(D)	135	5	(D)	(D)	259
Sedgwick	26	155 686	375	2 931	34	203 491	285	2 579
Shawnee	11	(D)	(D)	1 476	20	(D)	(D)	2 134
Stafford	9	(D)	(D)	(D)	(NA)	(NA)	(NA)	(NA)
Sumner	4	(D)	(D)	13	(NA)	(NA)	(NA)	(NA)
Wyandotte	8	(D)	(D)	(D)	8	(D)	(D)	(D)
All other counties	57	943 635	82	4 873	(NA)	(NA)	(NA)	(NA)
NURSERY, FLORICULTURE, VEGETABLE AND FLOWER SEED CROPS, SOD, ETC., GROWN IN THE OPEN, IRRIGATED (SEE TEXT)								
State Total								
Kansas	60	(X)	754	(X)	57	(X)	1 347	(X)
Counties								
Johnson	6	(X)	16	(X)	11	(X)	(D)	(X)
Miami	5	(X)	(D)	(X)	(NA)	(X)	(NA)	(X)
Sedgwick	12	(X)	541	(X)	13	(X)	61	(X)
Stafford	3	(X)	(D)	(X)	(NA)	(X)	(NA)	(X)
Wyandotte	4	(X)	(D)	(X)	(NA)	(X)	(NA)	(X)
All other counties	30	(X)	281	(X)	(NA)	(X)	(NA)	(X)
BEDDING PLANTS								
State Total								
Kansas	142	1 737 613	(D)	7 946	149	1 286 564	61	5 471
Counties								
Brown	3	(D)	-	(D)	(NA)	(NA)	(NA)	(NA)
Butler	5	11 140	-	31	4	(D)	-	(D)
Coffey	3	(D)	(D)	(D)	3	(D)	-	(D)
Cowley	3	32 000	-	105	(NA)	(NA)	(NA)	(NA)
Douglas	5	23 074	-	56	7	(D)	-	30
Ford	3	4 200	-	(D)	3	(D)	-	88
Franklin	3	25 500	-	36	4	23 000	-	188
Johnson	6	93 100	(D)	400	13	41 242	(D)	7
Kingman	3	(D)	-	6	4	(D)	-	(NA)
Leavenworth	8	101 640	-	(D)	(NA)	(NA)	(NA)	(NA)
McPherson	5	15 840	(D)	45	3	4 133	(D)	(NA)
Miami	4	(D)	-	3	3	(D)	(NA)	(NA)
Mitchell	4	16 440	-	40	(NA)	(NA)	(NA)	(D)
Montgomery	3	(D)	(D)	185	3	(D)	(D)	(NA)
Osage	5	13 620	-	41	(NA)	(NA)	(NA)	(NA)
Reno	4	(D)	-	1 000	7	98 450	(D)	352
Riley	5	(D)	(D)	(D)	(NA)	(NA)	(NA)	(NA)
Saline	3	15 300	-	45	(NA)	(NA)	(NA)	(NA)
Sedgwick	9	59 136	(D)	292	13	79 091	(D)	516
Shawnee	7	102 033	-	339	7	56 500	(D)	167
Sumner	3	(D)	-	(D)	(NA)	(NA)	(NA)	(NA)
All other counties	48	845 442	3	3 873	(NA)	(NA)	(NA)	(NA)

[For meaning of abbreviations and symbols, see introductory text]

Geographic area	1987				1982			
	Farms	Sq. ft. under glass or other protection	Acres in the open	Sales ($1,000)	Farms	Sq. ft. under glass or other protection	Acres in the open	Sales ($1,000)
CUT FLOWERS AND CUT FLORIST GREENS								
State Total								
Kansas	16	58 919	16	190	24	60 122	24	185
FOLIAGE AND POTTED FLOWERING PLANTS, TOTAL								
State Total								
Kansas	71	1 527 831	28	9 202	74	1 228 329	27	7 086
Counties								
Franklin	3	7 000	–	15	5	23 480	–	48
Johnson	5	49 000	(D)	254	6	(D)	(D)	87
Labette	3	(D)	(D)	(D)	(NA)	(NA)	(NA)	(NA)
Leavenworth	4	(D)	(D)	(D)	(NA)	(NA)	(NA)	(NA)
Reno	4	274 936	–	1 449	4	146 000	(D)	(D)
Sedgwick	8	92 600	–	537	5	109 800	–	750
Shawnee.............................	4	(D)	–	(D)	8	31 520	(D)	156
All other counties	40	591 868	8	3 381	(NA)	(NA)	(NA)	(NA)
FOLIAGE PLANTS								
State Total								
Kansas	31	324 521	(D)	2 580	(NA)	(NA)	(NA)	(NA)
POTTED FLOWERING PLANTS								
State Total								
Kansas	58	1 203 310	(D)	6 622	(NA)	(NA)	(NA)	(NA)
NURSERY CROPS								
State Total								
Kansas	88	67 704	1 410	3 864	91	245 003	1 826	5 314
Counties								
Butler...............................	4	–	(D)	(D)	6	–	(D)	104
Cowley	5	(D)	25	31	(NA)	(NA)	(NA)	(NA)
Douglas..............................	4	–	6	17	(NA)	(NA)	(NA)	(NA)
Johnson	10	(D)	204	263	17	(D)	98	740
Leavenworth	5	–	(D)	(D)	6	(D)	107	(D)
Pottawatomie	3	(D)	(D)	(D)	3	–	(D)	(D)
Riley	3	–	(D)	(D)	4	–	20	(D)
Sedgwick	14	(D)	(D)	(D)	17	(D)	114	613
Shawnee.............................	3	–	(D)	(D)	9	(D)	(D)	(D)
Wyandotte	4	–	(D)	(D)	3	–	48	289
All other counties	33	8 700	737	1 188	(NA)	(NA)	(NA)	(NA)
SOD HARVESTED								
State Total								
Kansas	26	(X)	2 721	5 344	45	(X)	2 310	3 198
Counties								
Johnson	4	(X)	(D)	(D)	12	(X)	1 363	1 613
Miami	11	(X)	1 180	2 028	15	(X)	527	816
Sedgwick	3	(X)	(D)	(D)	6	(X)	(D)	(D)
All other counties	8	(X)	53	98	(NA)	(NA)	(NA)	(NA)
VEGETABLE AND FLOWER SEEDS								
State Total								
Kansas	5	4 975	(D)	15	(NA)	(NA)	(NA)	(NA)
GREENHOUSE VEGETABLES								
State Total								
Kansas	10	68 014	(X)	138	21	143 032	(X)	218

Table 31. **Other Crops: 1987 and 1982**

[For meaning of abbreviations and symbols. see introductory text]

| Geographic area | 1987 | | | | | 1982 | | | | |
| | Harvested | | | Irrigated | | Harvested | | | Irrigated | |
	Farms	Acres	Quantity	Farms	Acres	Farms	Acres	Quantity	Farms	Acres
MUNGBEANS FOR BEANS (POUNDS)										
State Total										
Kansas	3	112	32 320	-	-	6	325	73 900	-	-
Counties										
Sumner	3	112	32 320	-	-	3	(D)	56 000	-	-
SORGHUM, HOGGED OR GRAZED										
State Total										
Kansas	49	1 975	(X)	1	(D)	53	2 904	(X)	7	307
Counties										
Barber	3	80	(X)	-	-	3	(D)	(X)	(NA)	(NA)
Decatur	3	54	(X)	-	-	(NA)	(NA)	(X)	(NA)	(NA)
Stafford	3	249	(X)	-	-	(NA)	(NA)	(X)	(NA)	(NA)
All other counties	40	1 592	(X)	1	(D)	(NA)	(NA)	(X)	(NA)	(NA)
OTHER										
State Total										
Kansas	12	105	(X)	3	(D)	11	276	(X)	1	(D)

Table 32. **Farms Operated by Black and Other Races by Value of Sales and Occupation: 1987 and 1982**

[For classification of social and ethnic groups, see text. For meaning of abbreviations and symbols, see introductory text]

| Geographic area | Land in farms | | Harvested cropland | | Market value of agricultural products sold ($1,000) | Farms by value of sales | | | | | |
| | | | | | | Occupation farming | | | Occupation other than farming | | |
	Farms	Acres	Farms	Acres		Less than $2,500	$2,500 to $9,999	$10,000 or more	Less than $2,500	$2,500 to $9,999	$10,000 or more
STATE TOTAL											
Kansas 1987	275	73 470	176	26 005	4 293	19	30	63	59	73	31
1982	269	94 052	192	36 025	6 482	23	18	76	65	62	22
COUNTIES, 1987											
Atchison	13	2 507	10	830	172	-	4	1	-	3	5
Brown	10	9 769	8	2 717	542	-	1	6	-	1	2
Butler	13	1 201	6	332	93	2	-	-	5	6	-
Chautauqua	7	1 454	4	144	191	-	3	2	2	-	-
Cherokee	8	999	6	545	297	-	-	3	1	4	-
Cowley	15	2 084	6	442	103	-	-	-	6	6	3
Crawford	6	179	4	57	60	-	-	-	2	2	2
Douglas	4	468	3	80	15	-	1	-	1	2	-
Finney	8	6 058	7	3 450	305	-	1	6	-	1	1
Franklin	4	340	1	(D)	17	2	-	-	-	1	1
Graham	12	3 817	9	957	86	4	1	4	1	1	1
Jackson	8	1 071	7	178	68	-	-	2	2	3	1
Jefferson	13	3 703	7	1 599	292	4	-	6	1	2	-
Jewell	4	2 264	4	1 250	189	-	-	3	-	1	-
Johnson	3	42	2	(D)	4	-	1	-	2	-	-
Labette	12	1 834	2	(D)	74	1	-	-	4	3	2
Leavenworth	12	1 328	10	576	104	-	2	1	-	5	3
Lyon	6	631	6	366	55	-	2	-	4	-	-
Marshall	4	801	4	779	161	-	1	2	-	1	-
Montgomery	5	258	1	(D)	35	1	1	-	1	1	1
Nemaha	3	339	3	335	75	-	-	2	-	1	-
Rice	3	180	1	(D)	8	-	-	-	2	1	-
Rooks	3	1 170	3	309	(D)	-	-	1	2	-	-
Russell	4	400	4	130	23	-	-	-	-	4	-
Saline	3	600	2	(D)	14	-	2	-	4	1	-
Sedgwick	8	878	3	496	149	-	1	1	-	3	2
Shawnee	9	1 590	9	711	51	2	3	1	2	1	-
Stevens	3	4 000	3	2 042	111	-	-	2	-	-	1
Sumner	6	675	4	(D)	41	-	1	-	2	2	1
Wyandotte	11	211	4	24	32	1	1	-	7	3	-
All other counties	55	21 619	34	7 163	(D)	2	4	16	10	15	8

Table 33. **Farms Operated by Black and Other Races by Tenure: 1987 and 1982**

[For classification of social and ethnic groups, see text. For meaning of abbreviations and symbols, see introductory text.]

Geographic area	Full owners			Part owners			Tenants		
	Number	Land in farms	Harvested cropland	Number	Land in farms	Harvested cropland	Number	Land in farms	Harvested cropland
STATE TOTAL									
Kansas .... 1987..	172	26 446	7 046	66	32 317	12 553	37	14 707	6 406
1982..	155	22 554	7 335	69	51 422	19 408	45	20 076	9 282
COUNTIES, 1987									
Atchison ------------------	11	(D)		2	(D)	(D)	-	-	-
Brown --------------------	3	4 610	(D)	4	4 614	1 277	3	545	-
Butler --------------------	11	(D)	(D)	2	(D)	(D)	-	-	(D)
Chautauqua --------------	5	(D)	(D)	2	(D)	(D)	-	-	-
Cherokee -----------------	3	(D)	(D)	3	640	(D)	2	(D)	(D)
Cowley --------------------	12	2 032	442	1	(D)	-	2	(D)	-
Crawford -----------------	4	(D)	(D)	2	(D)	(D)	-	-	-
Douglas ------------------	3	(D)	(D)	1	(D)	(D)	-	-	-
Finney --------------------	3	(D)	516	3	(D)	(D)	2	(D)	(D)
Franklin ------------------	3	(D)	-	1	(D)	(D)	-	-	-
Graham -------------------	5	650	(D)	4	2 057	466	3	1 110	(D)
Jackson -------------------	5	826	(D)	2	(D)	(D)	1	(D)	(D)
Jefferson -----------------	6	341	(D)	7	3 362	(D)	-	-	-
Labette -------------------	9	1 454	(D)	3	380	(D)	-	-	-
Leavenworth -------------	8	867	342	4	461	236	-	-	-
Lyon ---------------------	4	(D)	(D)	2	(D)	(D)	-	-	-
Marshall ------------------	3	(D)	(D)	1	(D)	-	-	-	-
Montgomery --------------	5	256	(D)	-	-	-	-	-	-
Rooks --------------------	-	-	-	3	1 170	309	-	-	-
Saline --------------------	3	600	(D)	-	-	-	-	-	-
Sedgwick -----------------	7	(D)	(D)	-	-	-	1	(D)	(D)
Shawnee -----------------	7	(D)	(D)	2	(D)	(D)	-	-	-
Sumner -------------------	6	(D)	-	-	-	-	1	(D)	(D)
Wyandotte ----------------	10	(D)	24	1	(D)	-	-	-	-
All other counties ---------	37	6 894	2 435	16	12 903	4 611	22	9 047	3 737

Table 34. **Operators by Selected Racial Groups: 1987 and 1982**

[For meaning of abbreviations and symbols, see introductory text.]

Geographic area	All farms		Farms with sales of $10,000 or more[1]	
	Farms	Land in farms	Farms	Land in farms
BLACK				
State Total				
Kansas .... 1987..	129	36 759	50	29 537
1982..	137	42 710	53	33 053
Counties, 1987				
Atchison	13	2 507	6	1 778
Butler..	6	(D)	-	-
Cherokee..	5	516	1	(D)
Cowley	4	480	-	-
Finney	3	(D)	2	(D)
Graham..	11	641	5	2 480
Jackson	3	641	3	641
Jefferson	6	1 693	3	(D)
Jewell	3	(D)	3	(D)
Leavenworth	10	(D)	4	449
Lyon	3	315	3	315
Rooks	3	1 170	1	(D)
Sedgwick..	4	606	1	(D)
Shawnee...	3	(D)	-	-
Stevens..	3	4 000	2	(D)
Sumner	3	475	1	(D)
Wyandotte	11	211	-	-
All other counties	35	15 003	15	12 747

See footnotes at end of table.

Table 34. **Operators by Selected Racial Groups: 1987 and 1982**—Con.

[For meaning of abbreviations and symbols, see introductory text]

Geographic area	All farms		Farms with sales of $10,000 or more[1]	
	Farms	Land in farms	Farms	Land in farms
AMERICAN INDIAN				
State Total				
Kansas 1987	121	26 897	34	19 616
1982	101	34 163	32	25 254
Counties, 1987				
Brown	9	(D)	8	(D)
Butler	6	743	-	-
Chautauqua	7	1 454	2	(D)
Cherokee	3	480	2	(D)
Cowley	11	1 604	3	1 236
Crawford	5	(D)	2	(D)
Jackson	4	(D)	-	-
Jefferson	5	(D)	2	(D)
Labette	12	1 834	2	(D)
Lyon	3	316	1	(D)
Montgomery	5	258	1	-
Saline	3	600	-	-
Shawnee	5	(D)	1	(D)
All other counties	43	7 768	10	5 331
ASIAN OR PACIFIC ISLANDER				
State Total				
Kansas 1987	9	5 616	4	(D)
1982	19	13 869	11	13 718
OTHER RACES (SEE TEXT)				
State Total				
Kansas 1987	16	4 198	8	(D)
1982	12	3 310	4	3 000

[1]Data for 1982 exclude abnormal farms.

Table 35. **Operators of Spanish Origin: 1987 and 1982**

[For classification of Spanish origin, see text. For meaning of abbreviations and symbols, see introductory text]

Geographic area	All farms		Farms with sales of $10,000 or more[1]	
	Farms	Land in farms	Farms	Land in farms
STATE TOTAL				
Kansas 1987	108	55 373	52	49 577
1982	113	50 850	56	46 478
COUNTIES, 1987				
Bourbon	3	540	3	540
Finney	4	3 098	4	3 098
Jefferson	5	397	1	(D)
Kearny	3	3 168	3	3 168
Leavenworth	5	1 617	2	(D)
Miami	3	217	1	(D)
Osage	4	230	-	-
Reno	3	220	-	-
Sedgwick	4	807	1	(D)
Shawnee	4	1 682	1	(D)
Sumner	5	(D)	-	-
Wallace	3	3 644	2	(D)
Wilson	3	793	1	(D)
All other counties	89	(D)	33	34 535

[1]Data for 1982 exclude abnormal farms.

Table 36. Farms With Grazing Permits: 1987

[For meaning of abbreviations and symbols, see introductory text]

Geographic area	Land in farms		Farms by land in farms						Source of permits			
	Farms	Acres	Less than 100 acres	100 to 259 acres	260 to 499 acres	500 to 999 acres	1,000 to 1,999 acres	2,000 acres or more	Forest service	Taylor grazing	Indian land	Other
Kansas	**641**	**576 372**	**135**	**99**	**101**	**119**	**110**	**77**	**72**	**44**	**35**	**541**
Allen	9	5 416	3	2	-	1	2	1	-	1	-	8
Anderson	9	4 332	-	5	1	2	1	-	1	1	1	9
Atchison	3	1 544	1	-	-	2	-	-	-	-	-	3
Barber	9	3 753	6	-	1	-	-	1	-	-	-	8
Barton	3	207	2	1	-	-	-	-	-	2	-	1
Bourbon	6	3 762	-	1	4	-	-	1	1	-	-	5
Butler	13	7 744	3	2	2	5	-	1	-	1	-	12
Chase	7	8 888	-	1	-	2	3	1	-	-	-	7
Chautauqua	4	4 629	-	-	1	2	-	1	-	-	-	4
Clark	3	9 560	-	-	-	-	1	2	-	-	-	3
Clay	12	8 305	-	2	2	5	3	-	-	-	-	12
Coffey	9	5 877	1	-	1	6	1	-	-	2	-	7
Cowley	6	4 106	3	-	1	-	1	1	1	-	-	4
Crawford	5	504	3	1	1	-	-	-	-	-	-	5
Decatur	5	13 160	-	1	-	-	2	2	-	-	-	5
Dickinson	13	12 445	-	-	6	3	4	1	-	-	-	13
Doniphan	3	1 372	-	2	-	-	1	-	-	-	-	3
Douglas	9	2 347	3	3	2	-	1	-	-	-	-	9
Elk	4	3 541	-	1	-	1	2	-	-	-	-	4
Ford	3	1 535	1	-	-	2	-	-	-	1	-	2
Franklin	4	878	1	1	2	-	-	-	-	-	-	4
Geary	11	7 426	-	2	3	3	3	-	-	-	-	11
Grant	6	2 495	-	-	5	1	-	-	1	-	1	4
Gray	3	4 826	1	-	-	-	1	1	-	-	-	3
Greenwood	10	6 321	-	6	2	-	-	1	-	-	-	10
Harper	10	15 043	1	2	-	1	3	3	-	-	-	10
Harvey	11	4 289	4	-	2	5	-	-	-	-	-	11
Hodgeman	3	7 030	-	-	-	-	2	1	-	-	-	3
Jackson	22	16 219	1	5	4	6	5	1	3	3	10	15
Jefferson	9	1 296	5	2	2	-	-	-	1	-	-	8
Jewell	8	5 295	3	2	1	1	-	1	-	3	-	5
Kingman	5	6 810	1	-	1	1	-	2	1	1	1	5
Kiowa	3	3 456	-	-	1	1	-	1	-	-	-	3
Labette	8	3 536	4	-	-	1	2	-	-	-	-	8
Lane	3	3 187	-	-	-	1	2	-	-	1	-	2
Leavenworth	9	1 208	6	2	-	1	-	-	1	1	3	6
Lincoln	3	1 035	-	-	2	1	-	-	2	-	3	2
Linn	6	3 635	2	-	2	1	-	1	-	-	-	6
Logan	6	3 373	3	-	1	-	2	-	1	1	1	6
Lyon	12	8 834	1	2	2	4	2	1	-	2	-	10
McPherson	10	2 622	4	1	4	1	-	-	-	-	1	9
Marion	18	11 361	3	1	4	7	2	1	-	1	-	18
Marshall	20	8 930	4	5	7	1	2	1	-	1	-	19
Meade	8	8 420	2	-	1	2	2	1	-	1	-	7
Mitchell	3	2 807	2	-	-	-	-	1	-	1	-	2
Montgomery	7	2 411	4	1	-	2	-	-	-	1	-	6
Morris	9	6 027	3	1	1	1	1	2	1	2	-	7
Morton	53	96 755	2	6	4	4	17	20	42	-	-	14
Nemaha	15	4 377	5	1	6	3	-	-	-	4	-	11
Neosho	5	1 456	3	1	-	-	1	-	-	-	-	5
Osage	10	9 377	5	1	1	1	1	1	-	1	1	9
Osborne	3	1 822	2	-	-	-	1	-	1	1	1	1
Ottawa	6	2 598	1	1	2	2	-	-	1	1	1	6
Pottawatomie	8	6 173	1	-	1	-	3	3	-	-	-	8
Reno	18	20 888	3	4	3	2	2	4	-	-	-	18
Republic	7	4 643	2	2	-	1	2	-	-	-	-	7
Rice	4	3 792	1	-	-	-	3	-	-	-	-	4
Riley	9	4 656	1	3	-	2	1	2	-	1	-	8
Saline	3	1 587	-	-	1	2	-	-	-	-	-	3
Sedgwick	15	13 193	6	4	1	3	-	1	1	2	2	14
Shawnee	11	2 567	5	3	1	1	1	-	-	1	-	9
Sherman	5	8 573	1	-	-	-	3	1	1	1	-	4
Stafford	6	11 746	-	-	-	-	3	3	3	-	-	6
Sumner	7	5 397	2	-	-	2	3	-	-	-	-	7
Wabaunsee	21	23 119	1	3	5	3	4	2	1	-	-	20
Washington	12	11 018	1	-	-	7	4	-	-	-	-	12
Wilson	14	7 335	3	6	2	-	2	1	3	1	3	12
All other counties	48	82 565	5	7	6	8	8	14	8	4	4	37

APPENDIX A.
General Explanation

DATA COLLECTION

Method of Enumeration

All agriculture censuses beginning with the 1969 census primarily have used mailout/mailback data collection. Direct enumeration methods, however, continue to be used for the agriculture census in Puerto Rico, Guam, the U.S. Virgin Islands, American Samoa, and the Commonwealth of the Northern Mariana Islands.

Mail List

The mail list for the 1987 census was comprised of individuals, businesses, and organizations that could be readily identified as being associated with agriculture. The list was assembled from the records of the 1982 census, administrative records of the Internal Revenue Service (IRS), and the statistical records of the U.S. Department of Agriculture (USDA). In addition, lists of large or specialized operations, such as nurseries and greenhouses, specialty crop farms, poultry farms, fish farms, livestock farms, and cattle feedlot operations, were obtained from State and Federal agencies, trade associations, and similar organizations. Lists of companies having one or more establishments (or locations) producing agricultural products were obtained from the 1982 census and updated using the information from the Standard Statistical Establishment List maintained by the Census Bureau. Exhaustive record linkage, unduplication, and mathematical modeling yielded a final mail list of 4.1 million names and addresses that had a substantial probability of being a farm operation.

Report Forms

In 1987, three different report forms were used—a two-page, a four-page, and a six-page form to minimize the reporting burden, particularly for small farms and places less likely to be farms. The six-page sample form and the four-page nonsample form are the same, except sections 23 through 28 have been added to the sample form to obtain supplemental information from a sample of farms.

The information collected in these sections will give the Bureau of the Census a good basis for making estimates of these data for other farms included in the census. The two-page form does not have as many questions or as much detail as the four-page and six-page forms. The four-page form has 11 regional versions and the six-page form has 13 regional versions. Both forms have different crops prelisted. Appendix D contains copies of both the two-page and six-page forms.

The six-page form was mailed to 1,104,000 addressees on the mail list, including all those expected to be large (based on expected sales or acreage) or unique (farms operated by multiestablishment companies or nonprofit organizations), all those in Alaska and Hawaii, and a sample of other addressees. The two-page form was mailed to 906,000 addressees. These were expected to be small farms or less likely to be farms. The four-page form was mailed to the remaining 2,079,000 addressees. Further discussion of the criteria used to determine which form was mailed to an addressee is provided in the Census Sample Design section of appendix C.

Initial Mailing

The report forms were mailed in mid-December 1987 to the approximately 4,089,000 individuals, businesses, and organizations on the mail list. The mail packages included a report form, a cover letter with a description of the purposes and uses of the census on the reverse side, an information sheet containing instructions for completing the form, and a postage-paid return envelope. Additional special instructions were included with report forms sent to grazing associations; feedlot operations; institutional organizations; indian reservations; firms with multiple farm or ranch operations; and producers of poultry under contract, bees and honey, fish, laboratory animals, and nursery and greenhouse crops.

To provide additional help to farmers in completing their reports, copies of an Agriculture Census Guide booklet were sent to vocational agriculture instructors, USDA county offices of the Agriculture Stabilization and Conservation Service, and the Cooperative Extension Service. The Guide contained descriptions and definitions of various items in more detail than the instructions included with each report form. Representatives of the above agencies graciously consented to assist farmers in completing their report forms.

Followup Procedures

A thank you/reminder card was mailed to those on the mail list in mid-January 1988. Five followup letters, three of which were accompanied by a report form, were sent to nonrespondents at 4-week intervals starting in mid-February and continuing until early June 1988.

Telephone calls were made to all large farms who had not responded. In addition, telephone calls were made to a sample of other nonrespondents in counties that had a response rate of less than 75 percent. A nonresponse adjustment procedure was used to represent the final nonrespondent farms in the census results. A description of this procedure is included in the Census Estimation section of appendix C.

DATA PROCESSING

Selected report forms were reviewed prior to keying the data. These included reports with attached correspondence and reports with remarks or no positive data on the front page.

The data from each report form were subjected to a detailed item-by-item computer edit. The edit performed comprehensive checks for consistency and reasonableness, corrected erroneous or inconsistent data, supplied missing data based on similar farms within the same county, and assigned farm classification codes necessary for tabulating the data. Substantial computer-generated changes to the data were clerically reviewed and verified.

In the computer edit, farms with sales, acreage, or commodities exceeding specified levels were tested for historical comparability. Key items, such as acreage and sales, were compared for substantial changes between 1982 and 1987. Sizeable historical differences were resolved or verified by telephone, if necessary. Respondents who reported sales or acreage above specified levels on non-sample forms were sent correspondence requesting the additional sample data. Prior to publication, tabulated totals were reviewed by statisticians to identify inconsistencies and potential coverage problems. Comparisons were made with previous census data, estimates published by the USDA, and other available data.

MAJOR DATA CHANGES

Prior to each agriculture census, the Census Bureau reviews the content of the census forms to eliminate questions no longer needed and to identify new items necessary to meet user needs and to better describe the agricultural situation in our Nation. Data requests are solicited from farmers, farm organizations, land grant colleges and universities, State and federal agencies, and members of the Census Advisory Committee on Agricultural Statistics. Each agency and organization is asked to identify and justify its specific data needs. The following data inquiries were added to the 1987 report form:

Income from farm-related sources
Acres under the Conservation Reserve Program
Payments received for participation in federal farm
  programs
Grazing permits by source

Additional data on production expenses were added in 1987:

Repair and maintenance expenses
Cash rent
Property taxes paid
All other production expenses

The following separate data inquiries were eliminated from the 1987 form:

Storage capacity for petroleum products
Number of hired farm and ranch workers
Value of agricultural products sold directly to individuals
  for human consumption
Source of irrigation water
Tons of commercially mixed feed
Expenditures for coal, wood, and coke
Selected machinery items: automobiles, corn heads for
  combines, and field forage harvesters
Chinchillas
Worms
Tropical and baitfish

FOLLOW-ON SURVEYS, SPECIAL CENSUSES, AND RELATED PUBLICATIONS

In addition to the 1987 Census of Agriculture for the 50 States, Puerto Rico, Guam, the U.S. Virgin Islands, American Samoa, and the Commonwealth of the Northern Mariana Islands, the census of agriculture program includes the 1988 Farm and Ranch Irrigation Survey, the 1988 Agricultural Economics and Land Ownership Survey, and the 1988 Census of Horticultural Specialties.

The 1988 Farm and Ranch Irrigation Survey provides data on water use by irrigated farms and ranches. Data include: the amount of water applied by crop, method of water distribution, source of water, and energy costs for pumping water. Data from this survey will be published as volume 3, part 1.

The 1988 Agricultural Economics and Land Ownership Survey provides detailed data on debts, expenses, taxes, credits, assets, land ownership, and farm and off-farm income for farm operators. Many of these items, as well as detailed data on landlord characteristics, are being collected from the landlords of the farms involved in the survey. Data from this survey will be published as volume 3, part 2.

The 1988 Census of Horticultural Specialties covers operations growing and selling $2,000 or more of horticultural products such as greenhouse products, outdoor-grown floricultural products, nursery products, mushrooms, and sod. These data will be published as volume 4.

Additional publications of the 1987 Census of Agriculture data include the Agricultural Atlas of the United States (previously called the Graphic Summary), Coverage Evaluation, Ranking of States and Counties, and Government Payments and Market Value of Agricultural Products Sold.

The Agricultural Atlas of the United States presents the Nation's agriculture graphically illustrated by dot and multicolor pattern maps. The maps provide displays on size and type of farm, land use, farm tenure, market value of products sold, crops harvested, livestock inventories, and other characteristics of farms. This report will be published as volume 2, part 1.

The Coverage Evaluation report provides estimates of the completeness of the 1987 Census of Agriculture for the United States, geographic regions, and selected States and groups of States. Estimates with their associated sample reliability are provided for farms not on the mail list, farms classified as nonfarms, duplicate farms, and nonfarms classified as farms. This report will be published as volume 2, part 2.

The Ranking of States and Counties report ranks the leading States and counties for selected items in the 1987 census and provides comparative data from the 1982 census. This report will be published as volume 2, part 3.

A new publication on Government Payments and Market Value of Agricultural Products Sold presents 1987 data for the United States and each State. The U.S. table has a format similar to volume 1, U.S. table 52 and presents summary data by size of farm. This report will be published as volume 2, part 5.

DEFINITIONS AND EXPLANATIONS

The following definitions and explanations provide a more detailed description of the terms used in this publication than are available in the tables or on the report form. For an exact wording of the questions on the 1987 census report forms and the information sheet which accompanied these forms, see appendix D. Most definitions of terms are the same as those used in earlier censuses. The more important exceptions are also noted here.

Farms or farms reporting—The term "farms" or "farms reporting" in the presentation of data denotes the number of farms reporting the item. For example, if there are 3,710 farms in a State and 842 of them had 28,594 cattle and calves, the data for those farms reporting cattle and calves would appear as:

Cattle and calves- - - - - - - -farms- -   842
number- -   28,594

Land in farms—The acreage designated in the tables as "land in farms" consists primarily of agricultural land used for crops, pasture, or grazing. It also includes woodland and wasteland not actually under cultivation or used for pasture or grazing, provided it was part of the farm operator's total operations. Large acreages of woodland or wasteland held for nonagricultural purposes were deleted from individual reports during the processing operations. Land in farms includes acres set aside under annual commodity acreage programs as well as acres in the Conservation Reserve Program for places meeting the farm definition.

Land in farms is an operating unit concept and includes land owned and operated as well as land rented from others. Land used rent free was to be reported as land rented from others. All grazing land, except land used under government permits on a per-head basis, was included as "land in farms" provided it was part of a farm or ranch. Land under the exclusive use of a grazing association was to be reported by the grazing association and included as land in farms. All land in Indian reservations used for growing crops or grazing livestock was to be included as land in farms. Land in reservations not reported by individual Indians or non-Indians was to be reported in the name of the cooperative group that used the land. In some instances, an entire Indian reservation was reported as one farm.

Land area—The approximate land area of counties and States represents the total land area as determined by records and calculations as of January 1, 1988. These data are updated periodically; however, the acreages shown for 1987 are essentially the same as for 1982. Any differences between the land area for 1987 and 1982 are due to annexations and other changes affecting county boundaries.

Land in two or more counties—With few exceptions, the land in each farm was tabulated as being in the operator's principal county. The principal county was defined as the one where the largest value of agricultural products was raised or produced. It was usually the county containing all or the largest proportion of the land in the farm or viewed by the respondent as his/her principal county. For a limited number of Midwest and Western States, this procedure has resulted in the allocation of more land in farms to a county than the total land area of the county. To minimize this distortion, separate reports were required for large farms identified from the 1982 census as having more than one farm unit. Other reports received showing land in more than one county were separated into two or more reports if the data would substantially affect the county totals.

Value of land and buildings—Respondents were asked to report their estimate of the current market value of land and buildings owned, rented or leased from others, and rented or leased to others. Market value refers to the value the land and buildings would sell for under current market conditions. If the value of land and buildings was not reported, it was estimated using the average value of land and buildings from a similar farm in the same geographic area.

Harvested cropland—This category includes land from which crops were harvested or hay was cut, and land in orchards, citrus groves, vineyards, nurseries, and greenhouses. Land from which two or more crops were harvested was counted only once, even though there was more than one use of the land.

Cropland used only for pasture or grazing—This category includes land used only for pasture or grazing that could have been used for crops without additional improvement. Included also was all cropland used for rotation pasture and land in government diversion programs that were pastured. However, cropland that was pastured before or after crops were harvested was to be included as harvested cropland rather than cropland for pasture or grazing.

Other cropland—This category includes cropland not harvested and not grazed which was used for cover crops, soil improvement crops, land on which all crops failed, cultivated summer fallow, idle cropland, and land planted in crops that were to be harvested after the census year.

Total woodland—This category includes natural or planted woodlots or timber tracts, cutover and deforested land with young growth which has or will have value for wood products, land planted for Christmas tree production, and woodland pastured. Land covered by sagebrush or mesquite was to be reported as other pastureland and rangeland or other land.

Woodland pastured—This category includes all woodland used for pasture or grazing during the census year. Woodland or forest land pastured under a per-head grazing permit was not counted as land in farms and therefore, was not included in woodland pastured.

Cropland in annual commodity acreage adjustment programs—This category includes land diverted or set aside under the provisions of the Federal Commodity Acreage Program. These data are for the acres of cropland taken out of production by growers of wheat, cotton, rice, corn, sorghum, barley, and oats, and devoted to conservation uses. Information was not obtained as to which crops would have been grown on the acres set aside.

Cropland in the Conservation Reserve Program (CRP)—This category includes acres of "highly erodible" cropland taken out of agricultural production and planted to protective cover crops or reforested. The CRP was established through the 1985 Food Security Act and provides for annual rental payments and shared costs of conservation practices through a 10-year contract with the USDA. Appendix B presents data on places with all their cropland enrolled in the Conservation Reserve Program and which were not counted as farms in the 1987 census.

Irrigated land—This category includes all land watered by any artificial or controlled means, such as sprinklers, furrows or ditches, and spreader dikes. Included are supplemental, partial, and preplant irrigation. Each acre was to be counted only once regardless of the number of times it was irrigated or harvested.

Operator—The term "operator" designates a person who operates a farm, either doing the work or making day-to-day decisions about such things as planting, harvesting, feeding, and marketing. The operator may be the owner, a member of the owner's household, a hired manager, a tenant, a renter, or a sharecropper. If a person rents land to others or has land worked on shares by others, he/she is considered the operator only of the land which is retained for his/her own operation. For partnerships, only one partner is counted as the operator. If it is not clear which partner is in charge, then the senior or oldest active partner is considered the operator. For census purposes, the number of operators is the same as the number of farms. In some cases, the operator was not the individual named on the address label of the report form, but another family member, a partner, or a hired manager who was actually in charge of the farm operation.

Operator characteristics—All operators were asked to report place of residence, principal occupation, days of off-farm work, year in which his/her operation of the farm began, age, race, sex, and Spanish origin. If race, age, sex, and principal occupation were not reported, they were imputed based on information reported by farms with similar acreage, tenure, and value of sales. No imputations were made for nonresponse to place of residence, Spanish origin, off-farm work, or year began operation. Operators of Spanish origin were tabulated by reported race.

Farm production expenses—In 1987, additional specific expense items and a category for all other farm production expenses were added to the selected farm production expenses collected in 1982. Consequently, we are publishing total farm production expenses in 1987. The expenses are limited to those incurred in the operation of the farm business. Expenses include the share of the expenditures provided by landlords, contractors, and partners in the operation of the farm business. Property taxes paid by landlords are excluded. Expenditures for nonfarm activities; farm-related activities such as providing customwork for others, the production and harvest of forest products, and recreational services; and household expenses are excluded. In 1987, as in other recent censuses, operators producing crops, livestock, or poultry under contract often were unable or unwilling to estimate the cost of production inputs furnished by the contractors. As a consequence, extensive estimation was required for contract producers.

Commercial fertilizer—The expense for commercial fertilizer is the amount spent on fertilizer during 1987 including the cost of custom application. The cost of custom application was excluded from the 1982 and 1978 data.

Agricultural chemicals—These expenses include the cost of all insecticides, herbicides, fungicides, and other pesticides, including the cost of custom application. Data exclude commercial fertilizer purchased. The cost of custom application was excluded from the 1982 and 1978 data. The cost of lime was excluded from the 1987 and 1982 data, but included in 1978.

Customwork, machine hire, and rental of machinery and equipment—These expenses include costs incurred for having customwork done on the place and for renting machines to perform agricultural operations. The cost of cotton ginning is excluded. The cost of labor involved in the customwork service is included in the customwork expense. The cost of custom application of fertilizer and chemicals was included in the 1982 and 1978 customwork data, but is included in expenditures for these items in 1987. The cost of hired labor for operating rented or hired machinery is included as a hired farm and ranch labor expense.

Interest—In 1987, separate data were collected for interest paid on debts secured by real estate and interest paid on debts not secured by real estate. In 1982, only total interest expenses were collected.

Market value of agricultural products sold—This category represents the gross market value before taxes and production expenses of all agricultural products sold or removed from the place in 1987 regardless of who received the payment. It includes sales by the operator as well as the value of any shares received by partners, landlords, contractors, or others associated with the operation. In addition, it includes receipts from placing commodities in the Commodity Credit Corporation (CCC) loan program in 1987. It does not include payments received for participation in federal farm programs nor does it include income from farm-related sources such as customwork and other agricultural services, or income from nonfarm sources.

The value of crops sold in 1987 does not necessarily represent the sales from crops harvested in 1987. Data may include sales from crops produced in earlier years and exclude some crops produced in 1987, but held in storage and not sold. For commodities, such as sugar beets and wool, sold through a co-op which made payments in several installments, respondents were requested to report the total value received in 1987.

The value of agricultural products sold was requested of all operators. If the operator failed to report this information, estimates were made based on the amount of crops harvested, livestock or poultry inventory or number sold. Extensive estimation was required for operators growing crops or livestock under contract.

Caution should be used when comparing sales in 1987 with sales reported in earlier censuses. Sales figures are expressed in current dollars and have not been adjusted for inflation or deflation.

Government payments—This category is limited to direct cash or generic commodity certificate (PIK) payments received by the farm operator in 1987. It includes deficiency and diversion payments; wool payments; payments from the Dairy Termination Program, the Conservation Reserve Program, other conservation programs, and all other federal farm programs under which payments were made directly to farm operators.

Other farm-related income—The 1987 report form included a new inquiry on income from farm-related sources. These data consist of gross income in 1987 before taxes and expenses from the sales of farm by-products and other sales and services closely related to the principal functions of the farm business. These data are for income producing activities that are primarily a by-product or supplemental to the farm operation. They exclude income from business activities that are separate from the farm business.

Customwork and other agricultural services—This income includes gross receipts received by farm operators for providing services for others such as planting, plowing, spraying, and harvesting. Income from customwork and other agricultural services is generally included in the agriculture census if it is closely related to the farming operation. However, it is excluded if it constitutes a separate business or is conducted from another location.

Rental of farmland—This income includes gross cash rent or share payments received from renting out farmland; payments received from the lease or sale of allotments for crops such as tobacco; and payments received for livestock pastured on a per-head, per-month, or per-pound basis. It excludes rental income from nonfarm property.

Sales of forest products—This income includes gross receipts from the sales of Christmas trees, standing timber, maple products, gum for naval stores, firewood, and other forest products from the farm business. It excludes income from nonfarm timber tracts and sawmill businesses.

Other farm-related income sources—This income includes gross receipts from hunting leases, fishing fees, camping, other recreational services, patronage dividends of cooperatives, sales of farm by-products, and other sales and services closely related to the farm business. It excludes income from nonfarm businesses.

Commodity Credit Corporations loans—This category includes loans for corn, wheat, soybeans, sorghum, barley, oats, cotton, peanuts, rye, rice, tobacco, and honey.

Agricultural chemicals used, including fertilizer and lime—For each type of agricultural chemical, the acres treated were to be reported only once even if the acres were fertilized or limed more than once. If multipurpose chemicals were used, the acres treated for each purpose were to be reported.

Fish and other aquacultural products—The raising of fish and other aquacultural products in captivity is included in the agriculture census. Production in salt water is considered not to be in captivity and is excluded from the census.

Bees and honey—Bee and honey production was enumerated and tabulated in the county in which the home farm was located even though hives are often moved from farm to farm over a wide geographic area.

Citrus enumeration—In the 1987 census, reports for selected citrus caretakers in Arizona, Florida, and Texas were obtained by direct enumeration. A citrus caretaker is an organization or person caring for or managing citrus groves for others. This special enumeration has been used in recent censuses because of the difficulty in identifying and enumerating absentee grove owners who often do not know the information that is needed to adequately complete the census report. Each citrus caretaker was enumerated as a farm operator and requested to complete one report form for all groves cared for and to furnish a list of grove owners' names, addresses, and acres of citrus. The names on the lists were matched to completed grove owners' report forms to eliminate duplication. The caretaker also was requested to inform the grove owner that he had already reported for the citrus under his care and that the grove owner was not to report the citrus again. In the 1987 census, 7 caretakers in Arizona reported 175 grove owners having 12,000 acres of citrus; the 65 caretakers in Florida reported 3,000 grove owners having 170,000 acres of citrus; and 20 caretakers in Texas reported 800 grove owners having 14,500 acres of citrus.

Crop year or season covered—Acres and quantity harvested are for the calendar year 1987 except for citrus fruits, avocados, olives; vegetables in Florida; sugarcane in Florida and Texas; and pineapples and coffee in Hawaii.

Citrus fruits—The data for Florida relate to the quantity harvested in the September 1986 through July 1987 harvest season, except limes that were harvested in the April 1987 through March 1988 harvest season. The data for Texas relate to the quantity harvested in the September 1986 through May 1987 harvest season. The data for States, other than Florida and Texas, relate to the quantity harvested in the 1986-87 harvest season.

Avocados—The data for California relate to the quantity harvested in the November 1986 through November 1987 harvest season and for Florida the April 1987 through March 1988 harvest season.

Olives—The data for California relate to the quantity harvested in the September 1986 through March 1987 harvest season.

Vegetables—The data for Florida relate to the crop harvested in the September 1986 through August 1987 harvest season.

Sugarcane for sugar—The data for Florida relate to the cuttings from November 1986 through April 1987, and for Texas the cuttings from October 1986 through April 1987.

Pineapples—The data for Hawaii relate to the quantity harvested in the year ending May 31, 1987.

Coffee—The data for Hawaii relate to the 1986-87 crop.

Acres and quantity harvested—Crops were reported in whole acres, except for the following crops which were reported in 10ths of acres: Irish potatoes, sweetpotatoes, tobacco, fruit and nut crops including land in orchards, berries, vegetables, and nursery and greenhouse crops; and in Hawaii, taro, ginger root, and lotus root. Totals for crops reported in 10ths of acres were rounded to whole acres at the aggregate level during the tabulation process.

If two or more crops were harvested from the same land during the year, the acres would be counted for each crop. Therefore, the total acres of all crops harvested generally exceeds the acres of cropland harvested. An exception to this procedure is hay crops. When more than one cutting of hay was taken from the same acres, the acres are counted only once but the quantity harvested includes all cuttings. However, hay cut for both dry hay and green chop or silage would be reported for each applicable crop. For interplanted crops or "skip-row" crops, acres were to be reported according to the portion of the field occupied by each crop.

If a crop was planted but not harvested, the acres were not to be reported as harvested. These acres were to be reported in the "land use" section under the appropriate cropland items—cropland used only for pasture or grazing, cropland used for cover crops, cropland on which all crops failed, or cropland idle.

Corn and sorghum hogged or grazed were to be reported as "cropland harvested" and not as "cropland used only for pasture or grazing." Crop residue left in fields and later hogged or grazed was not reported as cropland pasture.

Quantity harvested was not obtained for crops such as vegetables; nursery and greenhouse crops; corn cut for dry fodder, hogged or grazed; and sorghum, hogged or grazed.

Acres of land in bearing and nonbearing fruit orchards, citrus or other groves, vineyards, and nut trees were to be reported as harvested cropland regardless of whether the crop was harvested or failed. However, abandoned orchards were to be reported as cropland idle, not as harvested cropland and the individual abandoned orchard crop acres were not to be reported.

Land in orchards—This category includes land in bearing and nonbearing fruit trees, citrus or other groves, vineyards, and nut trees of all ages, including land on which all fruit crops failed. Respondents were instructed not to report abandoned plantings and plantings of less than 20 total fruit, citrus, or nut trees, or grapevines.

Crop units of measure—The regional report forms allowed the operator to report the quantity of field crops harvested in a unit of measure commonly used in the region. When the operator reported in a unit of measure different than the unit of measure published, the quantity harvested was converted to the published unit of measure.

Grapes could be reported in dry weight or fresh weight; plums and prunes in fresh weight, or prunes in dry weight; and in Hawaii, coffee in pounds parchment or pounds cherry, and macadamia nuts in pounds husked, unshelled or pounds shelled. For other fruit and nut crops and citrus, the operator was given a choice of units of measure of pounds, tons, or boxes. The quantity harvested for these crops is published in pounds.

Write-in crops—To reduce the length of the report form, only the major crops for the region were prelisted. For other crops, the respondent was requested to look at a list of crops in each section and write in the crop name and its code. For crops that had no individual code listed on the report form, the respondent was to write in the crop name and code the crop into the appropriate "all other" category for that section. Write-in crops coded as "all other" were reviewed and assigned a specific code when possible. Crops not assigned a specific code were left in the appropriate "all other" category.

In some cases, the reviewers were unable to determine the specific crop reported by the respondent because of incomplete or generalized crop names. To ensure proper coding, most of these respondents were telephoned. Reports for those not telephoned were changed on the basis of other reports for the area.

Misreported or miscoded crops—In a few instances, tabulated data may be inaccurate because respondents misunderstood or misinterpreted questions on the report form. Data may have been reported on the wrong line or in the wrong section, or the wrong crop code may have been placed beside the name of a write-in crop. Some of these errors as well as some keying errors may not have been identified during processing and therefore, were not corrected. Reports with significant acres of unusual crops for the area were examined to minimize the possibility that they were in error.

"See text" References

Items in the tables which carry the note "See text" are explained or defined in this section.

Data are based on a sample of farms—For 1987, 1982, and 1978, selected data were collected from only a sample of farms. These data are subject to sampling error. For 1987, the six-page sample form was mailed to all large and specialized farms (based on expected sales, acres, or standard industrial classification), all farms in Alaska and Hawaii, and approximately 17 percent of all other farms. Sample sections 23 through 28 of the 1987 census forms included inquiries on production expenses, commercial fertilizer and lime, chemicals, machinery and equipment, value of land and buildings, and income from farm-related sources. Estimates of the reliability of county totals for selected items are shown in table F of appendix C.

Operators of Spanish origin—No imputation was made for those not responding to the question on Spanish origin.

Farms operated by Black and other races—This category includes Blacks, American Indians, Asian and Pacific Islanders, and all other racial groups other than White.

All other races—This category is primarily limited to persons native to or of ancestry from Mexico, the Caribbean, and Central and South America.

Total sales—This item represents the gross market value of all agricultural products sold before taxes and expenses in the census year including livestock, poultry, and their products; and crops, including nursery crops and hay. Respondents were asked to include landlords' and contractors' shares. The value of commodities placed in CCC loans are included as sold. In 1987, all farms including abnormal farms were tabulated by size based on reported sales. In 1982 and 1978, abnormal farms were included in the total sales figure, but excluded from the detailed size breakdowns. Abnormal farms include institutional farms, experimental and research farms, and Indian reservations.

Farms with sales of less than $1,000—This category includes all farms with actual sales of less than $1,000, but having the production potential for sales of $1,000 or more. These farms normally could be expected to sell $1,000 or more of agricultural products.

Net cash return from agricultural sales for the farm unit—This category is derived by subtracting total operating expenditures from the gross market value of agricultural products sold. Depreciation and the change in inventory values are excluded from expenditures. Production expenditures may be understated on part owner and tenant farms because property taxes paid by landlords are excluded. Other landlord expenditures, such as insurance or rent paid, which are not readily known to renters may also be omitted or understated. Gross sales include sales by the operator as well as the share of sales received by partners, landlords, and contractors. Consequently, the net cash return is that of the farm unit rather than the net farm income of the operator.

Other livestock and livestock products—This category includes all livestock and livestock products not listed separately.

Value of livestock and poultry on farms—Data for the value of livestock and poultry on farms were obtained by multiplying the inventory of each major age and sex group by State average prices. The State average prices for cattle, hogs, sheep, Angora goats, hens and pullets of laying age, and turkeys were obtained primarily from data published by the National Agricultural Statistics Service, USDA. Prices applied to other livestock and poultry were census-derived averages based primarily on reported value of sales in the census.

Poultry hatched—This category includes all poultry hatched on the place during the year and placed or sold. Incubator egg capacity on December 31, 1987, is tabulated under the column heading "Inventory" and the number of poultry hatched and placed or sold is under the heading "Sales."

Hay—alfalfa, other tame, small grain, wild, grass silage, green chop, etc.—Data shown for hay represent all hay crops, including grass silage, haylage, and hay crops cut and fed green (green chop). In production data, dry tons represent dry tonnage for the various hay categories and dry weight equivalents for grass silage and hay cut and fed green. The conversion used was 3 tons of green weight to 1 ton of dry weight.

Tame hay other than alfalfa, small grain, and wild hay—Data shown represent dry tons of hay harvested from clover, lespedeza, timothy, Bermuda grass, Sudan grass, and other types of legume and tame grasses.

Grapes—Farm operators were given the option of reporting the quantity of grapes harvested in dry weight or fresh weight. For publication purposes, all quantities of grapes harvested have been converted to pounds of fresh weight. The conversion used was 4 pounds fresh weight to 1 pound dry weight.

Plums and prunes—Farm operators were given the option of reporting the quantity of plums and prunes harvested in dry weight or fresh weight. For publication purposes, all quantities of plums and prunes harvested have been converted to pounds of fresh weight. The conversion used was 3 pounds fresh weight to 1 pound dry weight.

Cherries—For 1987, cherries were reported as "sweet cherries," "tart cherries," or "cherries" depending on the regional form the respondent completed. On regional

forms for States where cherries are an important fruit crop, "sweet cherries" and "tart cherries" were listed separately. On the other regional forms, either "cherries" were listed or could be written in. For publication purposes, "cherries, total" could be shown along with the individual breakdown of "sweet cherries," "tart cherries," or "cherries, not specified." "Cherries, not specified" is used to account for cherries where the "sweet" and "tart" breakdown was not asked or where respondents wrote in "cherries" but did not specify or code the kind of cherry. All the individual cherry items may not be shown. Data for "sweet cherries," "tart cherries," and "cherries, not specified" are not available for 1982.

Other fruits and nuts—Data shown for other fruits and nuts relate to any fruits and nuts not having a specific code on the 1987 report form.

Land used for vegetables—Data are for the total land used for vegetable crops. The acres are reported only once, even though two or more harvests of a vegetable or more than one vegetable were harvested from the same acres.

Vegetables harvested for sale—The acres of vegetables harvested is the summation of the acres of individual vegetables harvested. All of the individual vegetable items may not be shown.

Nursery and greenhouse crops grown for sale—These data are a summation of the individual items reported. All of the individual items may not be shown.

Nursery, floriculture, vegetable and flower seed crops, sod, etc., grown in the open, Irrigated—Data refer to farms reporting irrigated nursery, floriculture, vegetable and flower seeds, sod, bedding plants, etc., grown in the open.

Other grains—These data are for the total market value of other grains sold including dry edible beans, dry lima beans, buckwheat, dry southern peas (cowpeas), emmer and spelt, flaxseed, mixed grains, lentils, mustard seed, dry edible peas, popcorn, proso millet, rice, rye for grain, safflower, sunflower seed, triticale, and wild rice.

Value of crop production—This item represents the estimated value of all crops harvested during the 1987 crop year. Data for the value of crops harvested were obtained by multiplying the average estimated value per unit by the reported acres or quantity harvested. Generally, harvested units of production (pounds, bushels, bales, etc.) were multiplied by State estimates of prices per unit. If only acres harvested were reported, State estimates for value of production per acre were used. The State average production price and production value per acre used in these calculations were obtained usually from publications of the National Agricultural Statistics Service, USDA. When

USDA estimates were not available, Bureau of the Census statisticians made estimates using available sources such as data from adjacent States, respondent report forms, county extension agents, and other persons knowledgeable about specific crops.

FARMS CLASSIFIED BY SPECIFIED CHARACTERISTICS

State tables 48 through 53 present detailed 1987 data for all farms classified by specified characteristics—tenure of operator, type of organization, age and principal occupation of operator, size of farm (acres), value of agricultural products sold, and standard industrial classification. Other tables include data classified by value of sales groups or other characteristics of the farm or the operator.

Farms by value of agricultural products sold or value of sales— In 1987, all farms were tabulated by size based on reported sales. In 1982 and earlier censuses, abnormal farms were not tabulated based on sales size. In the tables on market value of agricultural products sold, the sales of abnormal farms in 1982 and earlier censuses were included in the total sales figure, but excluded from the detailed size categories. Abnormal farms included institutional farms, experimental and research farms, and Indian reservations. The category "farms with sales of less than $1,000" included all farms with actual sales of less than $1,000 but having the production potential for sales of $1,000 or more. These farms normally could be expected to sell $1,000 or more of agricultural products.

The sales size categories used in this report are consistent with the standard business size categories issued by Office of Management and Budget (OMB) in 1982. In State table 52, data are presented for four sales size categories between $10,000 and $49,999. This provides users with bridge data under both the OMB and the 1978 census classifications. For the 1992 census, data will be presented only for the OMB sales size categories of $10,000 to $24,999 and $25,000 to $49,999.

Abnormal farms—This category includes institutional farms, experimental and research farms, and Indian reservations. Institutional farms include those operated by hospitals, penitentiaries, churches, schools, grazing associations, and government agencies. In 1987 and 1982, nongovernmental units such as church farms and Future Farmers of America camps were classified as abnormal farms only when 50 percent or more of their products produced and intended for human consumption were utilized by the organization.

Farms by tenure of operator—The classifications of tenure used in the 1987 census were:

Full owners, who operate only land they own.

Part owners, who operate land they own and also land they rent from others.

Tenants, who operate only land they rent from others or work on shares for others.

Farms by type of organization—All farms were classified by type of organization in the 1987 census. The classifications used were:

Individual or family (sole proprietorship), excluding partnership and corporation.

Partnership, including family partnership.

Corporation, including family corporation.

Other, cooperative, estate or trust, institutional, etc.

Corporations were subclassified by two additional characteristics into:

1. Family held
   Other than family held

2. More than 10 stockholders
   10 or less stockholders

Farms by age and principal occupation of operator—Data on age and principal occupation were requested from all operators in 1987. The principal occupation classifications used were:

Farming—The operator spent 50 percent or more of his/her worktime in 1987 in farming or ranching.

Other—The operator spent more than 50 percent of his/her worktime in 1987 in occupations other than farming or ranching.

Farms by size—All farms were classified into selected size groups according to the total land area in the farm. The land area of a farm is an operating unit concept and includes land owned and operated as well as land rented from others. Land rented to or assigned to a tenant was considered the tenant's farm and not the owner's.

Farms by standard industrial classification—In 1987, all agricultural production establishments (farms, ranches, nurseries, greenhouses, etc.) were classified by type of activity using the standard industrial classification (SIC) system. These classifications, found in the 1987 SIC Manual[1], are used to promote uniformity and comparability in the presentation of statistical data collected by various agencies.

---

[1]Standard Industrial Classification Manual: 1987. For sale by Superintendent of Documents, U.S. Government Printing Office, Washington, DC 20402. Stock No. 041-001-003-14-2.

An establishment primarily engaged in crop production (major group 01) or production of livestock and animal specialties (major group 02) is classified in the four-digit industry and three-digit industry group which accounts for 50 percent or more of the total value of sales of its agricultural products. If the total value of sales of agricultural products of an establishment is less than 50 percent from a single four-digit industry, but 50 percent or more from the products of two or more four-digit industries within the same three-digit industry group, the establishment is classified in the miscellaneous industry of that industry group. Otherwise, it is classified as a general crop farm in industry 0191 or a general livestock farm in industry 0291. Establishments that derive 50 percent or more of the value of sales from horticultural specialties of industry group 018 are classified in industry 0181 or 0182 according to their primary activity.

Characteristics of all farms by selected SIC groupings are shown in State tables 18 and 53. The SIC groupings shown in State table 53, together with the associated products (value of sales representing 50 percent or more of the value of agricultural products sold during the year) on which the classification is based, are as follows:

Cash grains (011)—Wheat, rice, corn, soybeans, barley, buckwheat, cowpeas, dry field and seed beans and peas, flaxseed, lentils, milo, mustard seed, oats, popcorn, rye, safflower, sorghum, sunflowers, and other small grains.

Cotton (0131)—Cotton and cottonseed.

Tobacco (0132)—Tobacco.

Sugarcane, sugar beets, Irish potatoes, hay, peanuts, and other field crops (0133, 0134, 0139)—Sugarcane, sugar beets, Irish potatoes, alfalfa, broomcorn, clover, grass seed, hay, hops, mint, peanuts, sweetpotatoes, timothy, and yams.

Vegetables and melons (016)—Vegetables and melons grown in the open.

Fruits and tree nuts (017)—Berries, grapes, tree nuts, citrus fruits, deciduous tree fruits, avocados, bananas, coffee, dates, figs, olives, pineapples, and tropical fruit.

Horticultural specialties (018)—Bedding plants, bulbs, florists' greens, flower and vegetable seeds, flowers, foliage, fruit stocks, nursery stock, ornamental plants, shrubberies, sod, mushrooms, and vegetables grown under cover.

General farms, primarily crops (019)—Crops, including horticultural specialties, but less than 50 percent of sales from any single three-digit industry group.

Livestock, except dairy, poultry, and animal specialties (021)—Cattle, calves, hogs, sheep, goats, goat's milk, mohair, and wool.

Beef cattle, except feedlots (0212)—Production or feeding of beef cattle, except feedlots.

Dairy farms (024)—Production of cows' milk and other dairy products and raising of dairy heifer replacements.

Poultry and eggs (025)—Chickens, chicken eggs, turkeys, ducks, geese, pheasants, pigeons, quail, and squab.

Animal specialties (027)—Fur-bearing animals, rabbits, horses, ponies, bees, fish in captivity except fish hatcheries, worms, and laboratory animals.

General farms, primarily livestock and animal specialties (029)— Livestock and animal specialties and their products, but less than 50 percent of sales from any single three-digit industry group.

The SIC manual was revised for 1987. Animal aquaculture (0273) was established as a new industry and horticultural specialties, not elsewhere classified (0189) was deleted.

APPENDIX B.
Places With All Cropland in the Conservation Reserve Program

The Food Security Act of 1985 established the Conservation Reserve Program (CRP). This program provides annual payments for highly erodible cropland enrolled in the program and meeting its conservation requirements. It also requires that the land be taken out of agricultural production for 10 years.

The 1987 Census of Agriculture includes Conservation Reserve acreage as land in farms on operations that meet the census farm definition. For census purposes, a farm is any place from which agricultural products of $1,000 or more were produced and sold or normally would have been sold during the census year. Operations which placed all of their cropland in the CRP and did not otherwise meet the farm definition based upon sales, livestock inventories, planted crops, or other criteria for potential sales were not included as farms in the census tabulations.

The following table provides CRP data for places not meeting the census farm definition ("whole farm" CRP places). It also contains separate but corresponding CRP data for farms included in the census tabulations. In addition to State data, detailed county data are presented for counties with three or more "whole farm" CRP places reported. For counties with less than three "whole farm" CRP places reported, their data are combined and reported in "all other counties."

The data for "whole farm" CRP places are not complete for all counties. The census mail list was developed from sources which indicated the farm had agricultural production activity. It was not designed to cover all "whole farm" CRP places. Therefore, the data for these places are limited to what was reported in the census and have not been adjusted to account for nonresponse, incomplete coverage, and reporting errors.

Land in Conservation Reserve Program: 1987

[For meaning of abbreviations and symbols, see introductory text]

Geographic area	Agricultural places excluded by farm definition with acres in the CRP			Farms with acres in the CRP		
	Number	Land in places (acres)	Land in CRP (acres)	Number	Land in farms (acres)	Land in CRP (acres)
Kansas	603	105 989	84 385	5 630	7 531 724	810 662
Allen	4	643	606	8	4 894	324
Atchison	6	890	620	24	15 581	854
Barton	11	1 041	773	69	96 212	8 987
Bourbon	14	2 035	1 781	70	40 668	5 970
Brown	4	560	392	44	46 497	4 733
Butler	3	154	85	27	22 734	1 655
Cheyenne	5	666	544	100	165 827	14 957
Clark	7	2 090	1 780	78	221 635	24 883
Clay	3	630	630	61	47 630	4 970
Cloud	9	673	525	41	36 653	2 292
Coffey	6	804	406	44	54 640	2 763
Comanche	3	480	357	89	217 998	23 525
Cowley	5	619	262	26	24 473	1 271
Crawford	5	437	209	71	55 176	6 663
Dickinson	4	799	745	60	51 108	3 129
Doniphan	10	968	587	26	14 139	2 200
Douglas	15	1 080	715	34	23 060	2 156
Edwards	7	1 602	1 479	57	86 648	12 542
Ellis	4	714	474	63	75 037	7 284
Ellsworth	5	478	393	98	111 450	7 054
Finney	4	4 528	4 413	58	131 973	20 946
Ford	7	1 063	1 010	62	116 588	10 670
Franklin	11	1 150	511	17	11 843	591
Graham	6	1 365	291	97	151 730	12 258
Grant	3	475	466	23	41 960	4 478
Gray	3	781	768	31	60 915	5 962
Greeley	3	985	965	30	87 038	15 491
Hamilton	21	7 832	7 335	106	281 105	67 832
Harper	5	1 285	1 179	42	56 254	5 285
Haskell	4	1 698	1 668	18	34 596	6 321
Hodgeman	3	534	534	63	108 690	7 880
Jackson	13	1 150	868	75	43 750	7 017
Jefferson	14	1 157	766	72	27 174	5 141
Jewell	3	55	55	54	52 267	3 419
Johnson	4	373	217	6	1 705	417
Kearny	9	2 992	2 453	58	165 491	18 125
Kingman	12	1 596	1 337	139	127 696	14 851
Kiowa	7	1 764	1 734	98	159 335	21 791
Lane	7	1 729	1 641	49	92 166	7 614
Lincoln	3	192	192	62	75 532	3 642
Linn	21	2 026	1 262	82	61 221	8 147
Lyon	15	1 566	892	89	87 941	6 929
McPherson	11	1 630	1 550	59	59 643	4 290
Marion	3	280	186	49	38 554	2 488
Marshall	6	453	240	53	37 576	4 359
Meade	7	1 349	1 261	53	101 187	12 129
Miami	22	4 092	1 736	78	40 300	3 682
Mitchell	3	274	260	37	46 438	2 711

Land in Conservation Reserve Program: 1987—Con.

[For meaning of abbreviations and symbols, see introductory text]

Geographic area	Agricultural places excluded by farm definition with acres in the CRP			Farms with acres in the CRP		
	Number	Land in places (acres)	Land in CRP (acres)	Number	Land in farms (acres)	Land in CRP (acres)
Morton	12	4 791	4 542	80	177 933	45 261
Nemaha	12	2 074	1 359	93	56 157	7 851
Neosho	6	262	161	73	48 158	5 458
Ness	4	620	568	77	132 469	9 967
Norton	5	635	606	97	171 570	10 924
Osage	20	1 153	573	108	59 556	7 459
Osborne	4	479	397	64	89 592	5 771
Ottawa	3	371	254	37	51 787	3 741
Phillips	6	392	334	71	97 332	5 909
Pottawatomie	9	657	387	66	67 295	3 656
Pratt	10	1 642	1 480	78	106 451	11 793
Rawlins	3	352	352	97	126 889	8 951
Reno	19	2 624	1 789	128	102 851	14 270
Riley	4	420	244	25	18 047	1 055
Rooks	12	1 231	1 177	106	178 998	12 998
Rush	7	729	354	56	69 332	3 781
Russell	7	2 151	1 233	106	152 896	12 743
Saline	3	223	168	73	67 926	5 611
Sedgwick	4	269	196	24	17 022	1 708
Seward	9	2 801	2 362	42	67 714	14 694
Shawnee	6	992	225	40	18 751	2 140
Stafford	7	1 350	1 320	43	53 687	6 359
Stanton	12	9 107	7 707	71	170 581	37 474
Stevens	5	2 650	2 409	74	137 566	21 410
Sumner	4	173	167	23	23 549	1 584
Thomas	3	192	191	26	62 859	5 991
Wabaunsee	6	478	224	43	22 430	2 274
Wichita	3	2 255	1 648	28	56 276	7 258
Wilson	4	191	181	36	27 289	3 041
Woodson	3	297	146	14	24 613	1 153
All other counties	31	3 466	2 668	979	1 371 390	107 899

APPENDIX C.
Statistical Methodology

MAIL LIST MODEL

A statistical discriminant model was developed to predict the probability that a mail list addressee operated a farm. The model was used to identify the 4.1 million records from the preliminary census mail list of 6.0 million records that would receive a census of agriculture report form. Records from the 1982 census mail list were used to build the model. Record characteristics such as the source of the mail list record (see appendix A for a description of record sources), number of source lists on which the record appeared, expected value of agricultural sales, and geographic location were used to separate mail list records into model groups. The proportion of 1982 census farm records in each group was calculated to provide an estimate of the probability that an addressee in the group operated a farm.

Using these same group definitions, the 1987 census mail list records were separated into groups, each with an associated estimate of farm probability from the model. The 4.1 million mail list records in groups with the largest estimate of farm probability were selected to receive the census report form. A large percentage of the 1.9 million records that were dropped from the 6.0 million preliminary census mail list were nonfarm records from the previous census. This procedure was used to obtain a more complete census enumeration without excessive respondent burden and data collection cost.

CENSUS SAMPLE DESIGN

Each of the 4.1 million name and address records on the census mail list was designated to receive one of three different types of census report forms. The three forms were the nonsample census form (a four-page form), the sample form (a six-page form), and the short form (a two-page form). Sections 1 through 22 of the sample form were identical to sections on the nonsample census form. However, the sample form contained additional sections on farm production expenditures, usage of fertilizers and insecticides, value of machinery and equipment, value of land and buildings, and farm-related income. The short form contained abbreviated versions of the sections on the nonsample census form. These three different forms were used to reduce the response burden of the census, while providing quality information on a large number of data items at the county level.

The sample form was mailed to all mail list records in Alaska and Hawaii and to a sample of records in other States identified when the mail list was constructed. Addresses were selected into the sample with certainty if they were expected to have large total values of agricultural products sold or large acreage, if they were firms with two or more farms, or if they had other special characteristics. When a nonsample large farm was identified during processing, a supplemental form that contained the additional data inquiries was mailed. All farms in counties with less than 100 farms in 1982 were included in the sample with certainty; counties containing 100 to 199 farms in 1982 were systematically sampled at a rate of 1 in 2; and counties containing 200 or more farms in 1982 were systematically sampled at a rate of 1 in 6. This differential sample scheme was used to provide reliable data for sections 23 through 28 of the report form for all counties.

To determine which mail list records would receive the short form, all mail list records not designated for the sample were sorted into model groups according to farm probability as specified by the mail list model. The 906,000 mail list records in the model groups with the lowest probability of being farms and with an expected total value of agricultural product sales less than $20,000 were designated to receive the short form. The remaining mail list records were selected to receive the nonsample census form.

CENSUS ESTIMATION

The 1987 Census of Agriculture used two types of statistical estimation procedures. These estimation procedures accounted both for nonresponse to the data collection and for the sample data collection. These procedures are used because some farm operators never respond to the census despite numerous attempts to contact them, and not all farm operators are requested to provide the sample data items.

Whole Farm Nonresponse Estimation

A statistical estimation procedure was used to account for the census farms among mail list nonrespondents that were not designated for telephone followup. A stratified systematic sample of eligible census nonrespondents were mailed a simplified report form. Five sample strata were defined based on form type, expected value of sales, and previous census status. The report form was designed to provide sufficient information to determine farm status. Additional mail and telephone contacts were made to survey nonrespondents to obtain sufficient response for survey estimates.

Estimates of the proportion of census nonrespondents that operated farms were made for each stratum in the State using survey results and applied to the total number of census nonrespondents in that stratum. A synthetic estimation procedure was used to estimate the number of census nonrespondents that operated farms for each county by stratum. This estimation procedure is based on the assumption that the distribution of farms in a stratum by county is the same for census nonrespondents as for census respondents.

Within each stratum in a county, a noninteger nonresponse weight was calculated and assigned to each eligible respondent farm record. The procedure used for calculating the nonresponse weight assumed the eligible census respondents and the nonrespondent farm operations in a county had similar characteristics within each stratum. The noninteger nonresponse weight was the ratio of the sum of the estimated number of nonrespondent farms (using nonresponse survey results) and the number of eligible census respondent farms to the number of eligible census respondent farms. Stratum controls were established to ensure that this weight was never greater than 2.0. The noninteger nonresponse weight was used in the estimation of the final weight for the sample items. It was randomly rounded to an integer weight of either 1 or 2 for each record for tabulating the complete count items.

The procedure assumed that we obtain complete response from large and unique farm operations because these cases received intensive telephone followup during census processing. In situations where addressees could not be contacted by telephone or refused to cooperate, secondary sources such as Agricultural Stabilization and Conservation Service offices or county extension agents were asked to provide information as to whether or not the addressee had agricultural activities. Data from previous census reports for the specific addressee, in conjunction with other information, were used to complete the census report form.

Table A quantifies the effect of the nonresponse estimation procedure on selected census data items. The percentage of the census value contributed by nonresponse estimation as provided in this table indicates the potential for bias in published figures resulting from this procedure. The estimates provided in these tables do not reflect the effect of nonresponse to individual data items on respondents' census report forms. The effect of this item nonresponse is discussed further under Census Nonsampling Error.

Table A. **Percent of State Totals Contributed by Whole Farm Nonresponse Estimation: 1987**

Item	Percent of total
Farms --------------------------------number--	12.4
Land in farms ----------------------------acres--	8.6
Value of land and buildings --------------$1,000--	8.2
Market value of agricultural products sold --$1,000--	3.6
Harvested cropland -----------------------acres--	8.7
Corn for grain or seed---------------------acres--	5.7
Wheat for grain---------------------------acres--	9.0
Livestock and poultry inventory:	
Cattle and calves --------------------number--	5.3
Hogs and pigs-----------------------number--	6.3
Hens and pullets of laying age --------number--	1.5

Sample Estimation

All respondent sample records received a sample weight. The sample data estimates the actual figures that would have resulted from a complete census of the items in sections 23 through 28 of the report form. The estimates were obtained from an iterative ratio estimation procedure that resulted in the assignment of a weight to each record containing sample items. For any given county, a sample item total was estimated by multiplying the data items for each farm in the county by the corresponding sample weight and summing overall sample records in the county.

Each sample farm was assigned one sample weight to be used to produce estimates for all sample items. For example, if the weight given to a sample farm had the value 5, all sample data items reported by that farm would be multiplied by 5. The weight assigned a certainty farm was 1. The estimation procedure used to assign weights was performed for each county.

Within a county, the ratio estimation procedure for farms was performed in three steps using three variables. The first variable contained eight 1987 total value of agricultural production (TVP) groups. Both the second and third variables, Standard Industrial Classification (SIC) code and farm acreage, contained two groups. The variable groups were as follows:

TVP	SIC	Acres
$1 to $999	01 All crops	0 to 69
$1,000 to $ 2,499	02 All livestock	70 or more
$2,500 to $ 4,999		
$5,000 to $ 9,999		
$10,000 to $24,999		
$25,000 to $49,999		
$50,000 to $99,999		
$100,000 or more		

The first step in the estimation procedure was to partition the sample records into 32 mutually exclusive initial post strata formed by combining the three variable groups. This produced a three dimensional array where the cells of the array corresponded to the initial post strata groups. Each sample farm record was assigned an initial weight equal to the ratio of the total farm count to the sample farm count, expanded for nonresponse estimation, for the cell containing the sample farm. This weight was approximately equal to the inverse of the probability of selecting a farm for the census sample.

The second step in the estimation procedure was to combine, if necessary, the cells of the array (prior to the repeated ratio estimation procedure) to increase the reliability of the ratio estimation procedure. Any cell within the array that either contained less than 10 sample farms or had a ratio of total farms to sample farms that was more than 2 times the mail sample rate was collapsed with another cell (in the same variable) according to a specified collapsing pattern. New total farm counts and sample farm counts were computed for each of the collapsed cells (final post strata) and were used in the ratio estimation procedure to calculate final sample weights.

In the third step in the ratio estimation procedure, complete counts for the three variables (TVP, SIC, acreage) were used to compute the marginals of the array defined by the final post strata. Factors were then applied to expanded sample totals in each cell of the array to obtain agreement with the row marginal (TVP) complete counts. The sample totals then had factors applied to obtain agreement with the column marginal (SIC) complete counts. Lastly, the sample totals had factors applied to obtain agreement with the depth marginal (acreage) complete counts. This procedure that requires the row totals, then the column totals, and then the depth totals to agree with the complete counts for the rows, columns, and depths, respectively, is continued iteratively until the process converges (the marginal totals agree with the complete count totals).

The ratio of the adjusted total farm count to the sample farm count obtained from the second iteration of the estimation procedure was the noninteger final post stratum sample weight assigned to the sample farm records in that post stratum. The noninteger sample weight, the product of the noninteger final post stratum sample weight and the nonresponse weight, was randomly rounded to an integer weight for tabulation. If, for example, the final weight for the

farms in a particular group was 7.2, then one-fifth of the sample farms in this group were randomly assigned a weight of 8 and the remaining four-fifths received a weight of 7.

CENSUS SAMPLING ERROR

Sampling error in the census data results from the nonresponse sample and the census sample data collection. Census items were classified as either complete count or sample data items. The complete count items were asked of all farm operators. The complete count data items included land in farms, harvested cropland, livestock inventory and sales, crop acreages, quantities harvested and crop sales, land use, irrigation, government loans and payments, conservation acreage, type of organization, and operator characteristics (sections 1 through 22 of the census report form). Variability in the complete count data items is considerably smaller than in the sample items as the variation is due only to the nonresponse sample estimation procedure. The sample items were asked of approximately 25 percent of the total census farm operators. The sample data items included farm production expenditures, fertilizer and chemical usage, farm machinery and equipment, value of land and buildings, and farm-related items (sections 23 through 28 of the census report form). Variability in the estimates of sample items is due both to the census sample selection and estimation procedure and the nonresponse sample estimation procedure.

The sample for the 1987 Census of Agriculture is one of a large number of possible samples of the same size that could have been selected using the same sample design. Estimates derived from the different samples would differ from each other. The difference between a sample estimate and the average of all possible sample estimates is called the sampling deviation. The standard error or sampling error of a survey estimate is a measure of the variation among the estimates from all possible samples, and thus is a measure of the precision with which an estimate from a particular sample approximates the average result of all possible samples. The percent relative standard error of estimate is defined as the standard error of the estimate divided by the value being estimated multiplied by 100. If all possible samples were selected, each of the samples were surveyed under essentially the same conditions, and an estimate and its standard error were calculated from each sample, then:

1. Approximately 67 percent of the intervals from one standard error below the estimate to one standard error above the estimate would include the average value of all possible samples.

2. Approximately 90 percent of the intervals from 1.65 standard errors below the estimate to 1.65 standard errors above the estimate would include the average value of all possible samples.

The computations involved to define the above confidence statements are illustrated in the following example. Assume that the estimate of number of farms for the State is 94,382 and the relative standard error of the estimate (percent) is .1 percent (0.001). Multiplying 94,382 by 0.001 yields 94, the standard error. Therefore, a 67-percent confidence interval is 94,288 to 94,476 (i.e., 94,382 plus or minus 94). If corresponding confidence intervals were constructed for all possible samples of the same size and design, approximately 2 out of 3 (67 percent) of these intervals would contain the figure obtained from a complete enumeration. Similarly, a 90 percent confidence interval is 94,227 to 94,538 (i.e., 94,382 plus or minus 1.65 x 94).

Tables B and C provide the reliability estimates of the estimated number of farms in a county reporting complete count and sample items, respectively. Both tables show the percent relative standard errors for selected estimated number of farms in a county reporting an item. These are derived from a regression equation. The parameters of the regression equation were estimated using the estimated number of farms in a county reporting the complete count or sample item as the independent variable and the standard error of that estimate as the dependent variable for all counties in the State.

Table B. Reliability Estimates for Number of Farms in a County Reporting a Complete Count Item: 1987

Farms	Relative standard error of estimate (percent)
Number of farms reporting:	
25	7.0
50	5.0
75	4.1
100	3.5
150	2.9
200	2.5
300	2.1
500	1.6
750	1.4
1,000	1.2
1,500	1.0
2,000	.9

Note: Complete count items are items in sections 1 to 22 of the report form.

To illustrate the use of these tables, assume that the estimate of the number of farms reporting hogs and pigs for a particular county, as given in county table 12, is 89. Since hogs and pigs is a complete count data item, refer to table B and select the estimated relative standard error of the estimate from the row whose value is equal to or just less than the estimated number of farms, 89. For this example, the relative standard error of the estimate comes from the row for 75 farms reporting. For sample data items, follow the same procedure using table C. In counties that had less than 100 farms in the 1982 Census of Agriculture, table C does not apply because the farms in these

counties were sampled with certainty (1 in 1), and thus, the reliability estimates for the number of farms in these counties are smaller than for counties that were sampled at lower rates (1 in 2 or 1 in 6).

Table C. Reliability Estimates for Number of Farms in a County Reporting a Sample Item: 1987

Farms	Relative standard error of estimate (percent)
Number of farms reporting:	
25	37.5
50	26.0
75	20.8
100	17.7
150	13.8
200	11.4
300	8.3
500	4.5
750	3.7
1,000	3.2
1,500	2.6
2,000	2.3

Note: Sample items are items in sections 23 to 28 of the report form.

Table D presents the relative standard error of selected State data items for all farms and for all farms with sales of $10,000 or more. The percent relative standard error of the estimate for complete count data measures the variation associated with the sample-based adjustment for whole farm nonresponse. The percent relative standard error of the estimate for sample items measures both the sampling error due to the nonresponse sample estimation procedure and the census sample selection and estimation procedure. The reliability of State estimates may vary substantially from State to State. Generally, State estimates for a given data item are less reliable than the corresponding U.S. estimate.

Table E presents the standard error (not relative standard error) for percent change in State totals from 1982 to 1987. The general purpose of the percent change estimate is to provide a relative measure of the difference in a characteristic between censuses. The relative change for a given characteristic is defined as the ratio of the difference of the 1987 and the 1982 estimate for that characteristic to the 1982 estimate. This ratio is multiplied by 100 to obtain the percent change. The percent standard error of a percent change estimate, then, is the standard error of the ratio multiplied by 100.

Table F presents the relative standard error for county totals for 10 major complete count items and 7 sample items. The relative standard error of the estimate (percent) for the same item differs among counties in a State. Reasons for this are differences among counties in (1) the total number of farms, (2) the number of large farms included with certainty, (3) the size classifications of the farms sampled, (4) the amount of nonresponse, (5) the general agricultural characteristics, and (6) the specific characteristic being measured.

CENSUS NONSAMPLING ERROR

The accuracy of the census counts are affected by the joint effects of the sampling errors described in the previous section and nonsampling errors. Extensive efforts were made to compile a complete and accurate mail list for the census, to design an understandable report form and instructions, and to minimize processing errors through the use of quality control, verification, and check measures on specific operations. Nonsampling errors arise from incompleteness of the census mail list, duplication in the mail list, incorrect data reporting, errors in editing of reported data, and errors in imputation for missing data. These specific nonsampling errors are further discussed in this section. Evaluation studies will be conducted to measure the extent of certain nonsampling errors such as coverage error, classification error, and item imputation.

Census Coverage

The main objective of the census of agriculture is to obtain a complete and accurate enumeration of U.S. farms with accurate data on all aspects of the agricultural operation. However, the cost and availability of resources for this enumeration place restrictions on operationally feasible data collection methodologies. The past five agriculture censuses have been conducted by mail enumeration with telephone contact for selected nonrespondents. The completeness of such an enumeration thus depends to a large extent on the coverage of farm operations by the census mail list.

Historically, the census of agriculture has included approximately 90 percent of the farms in the United States and over 96 percent of the agricultural production. Complete enumeration of agricultural operations satisfying the farm definition of $1,000 or more in agricultural sales is complicated by fluctuations in agricultural operations qualifying for enumeration, the variety of arrangements under which farms are operated, the multiplicity of names used by an operation, the number of operations in which an operator participates, the accuracy of data reporting, etc. A new mail list is compiled for each census because no current single list of agricultural operations is comprehensive.

An evaluation of census coverage has been conducted for each census of agriculture since 1945. The evaluation provides estimates of the completeness of census farm count and major census data items. In addition, the evaluation helps to identify problems in the census enumeration and provide information that can form the basis for improvements. The results of the 1987 Coverage Evaluation program will be published in volume 2, part 2.

The evaluation of coverage conducted in 1987 was designed to measure errors in the census mail list and in farm classification. Mail list error includes a measurement of farms not on the census mail list (undercount), and a measurement of farms enumerated more than once in the

census (overcount). Classification error includes a measurement of farms classified as nonfarms in the census (undercount) and of nonfarms classified as farms in the census (overcount). Classification error arises from reporting and processing errors. Mail list undercount dominates all coverage errors. Net coverage error is defined as the difference of undercounted and overcounted farms. Measurements of these errors, as well as a description of the complete coverage program, will be available in the Coverage Evaluation report.

Mail List Coverage

A major problem with the use of a mail list for the census of agriculture enumeration is the difficulties that are encountered in compiling a complete list. The percentage of farms on the census mail list varies considerably by State. Several reasons have contributed to farm operators' names not being included on the census mail list—the operation may have been started after the mail list was developed, the operation may be so small as not to appear in agricultural related source lists used in compiling the census list, or the operation may have been falsely classified as a nonfarm prior to mailout. A large proportion of the farms not included on the mail list were small in both acres and sales of agricultural products.

The 1987 Census of Agriculture Coverage Evaluation used the area segment sample of the 1987 June Enumerative Survey (JES) of the National Agricultural Statistical Service (NASS) to estimate farms not on the census mail list. The Census Bureau contracted with the NASS to augment the JES data collection and receive survey data under the confidentiality protection afforded by Title 13, U.S. Code, from all residents of area sample segments with agricultural activity. These survey records were matched to the census mail list. Records that did not match were mailed a census of agriculture report form to estimate mail list coverage. Estimates of farms not on the census mail list used the capture-recapture dual frame estimator that will be described in the Coverage Evaluation report.

Table G provides coverage evaluation estimates of the number of farms not on the mail list and selected characteristics of those farms with their percent relative standard error. The table also provides an estimate of characteristics of farms not on the mail list as a percentage of total farms in the State. The estimate of total farms in the State is based on census farm count and the estimated number of farms not on the census mail list. This estimate of total farms in the State was not adjusted for classification and list duplication errors. Estimates of these errors will be made at the regional rather than the State level and will be available in the Coverage Evaluation report. The table provides the standard error (not relative standard error) of this percent estimate.

Respondent and Enumerator Error

Incorrect or incomplete responses to the mailed census report form or to the questions posed by a telephone enumerator introduce error into the census data. Such incorrect information can lead, in some cases, to incorrect enumeration of farms. This type of reporting error is measured by the Classification Error Study discussed later in this section. To reduce all types of reporting error, questions were phrased as clearly as possible based on tests of the census report form, and detailed instructions for completing the report form were provided to each addressee. In addition, each respondent's answers were checked for completeness and consistency.

Item Nonresponse

Nonresponse to particular questions on the census report that we would logically or statistically expect to be present may create a type of nonsampling error in both complete count and sample data. When information reported for another farm with similar characteristics is used to edit or impute for item nonresponse, the data may be biased because the characteristics of the nonrespondents have not been observed and may differ from those reported by respondents. Any attempt to correct the data for nonresponse may not completely reflect this difference either at the element level (individual farm operation) or on the average.

Processing Error

The many steps of processing of each census report form are sources for the introduction of nonsampling error. The processing of the census report forms includes clerical screening for farm activity, computerized check-in of report forms and followup of nonrespondents, keying and transmittal of completed report forms, computerized editing of inconsistent and missing data, review and correction of individual records referred from the computer edit, review and correction of tabulated data, and electronic data processing. These operations undergo a number of quality control checks to ensure as accurate an application as possible, yet some errors are not detected and corrected.

Classification Error

An evaluation study of classification errors was conducted in the 1987 Census of Agriculture as part of the census coverage evaluation program. A sample of mail list respondents was selected, and these addresses reenumerated to determine whether they were a farm or nonfarm. A farm status determination was made based on the evaluation questionnaire and compared with the status based on the data reported on the census form. Differences in status were reconciled.

In past censuses, the proportion of farms undercounted due to classification errors was higher for farms with small values of sales. The classification error rate was higher for (1) livestock farms than crop farms, (2) farms with a small

number of acres than larger farms, or (3) tenant farms than full or part-owner farms. Results from the 1987 classification error study will be published in the Coverage Evaluation report.

EDITING DATA AND IMPUTATION FOR ITEM NONRESPONSE

For the 1987 Census of Agriculture, as in previous censuses, all reported data were keyed and then edited by computer. The edits were used to determine whether the reports met the minimum criteria to be counted as farms in the census. Computer edits also performed a series of complex, logical checks of consistency and completeness of item responses. They provided the basis for deciding to accept, impute (supply), delete, or alter the reported value for each data record item.

Whenever possible, edit imputations, deletions, and changes were based on component or related data on the respondent's report form. For some items, such as operator characteristics, data from the previous census were used when available. Values for other missing or unacceptable reported data items were calculated based on reported quantities and known price parameters.

When these and similar methods were not available and values had to be supplied, the imputation process used information reported for another farm operation in a geographically adjacent area with characteristics similar to those of the farm operation with incomplete data. For example, a farm operation that reported acres of corn harvested, but did not report quantity of corn harvested, was assigned the same bushels of corn per acre harvested as that of the last nearby farm with similar characteristics that reported acceptable yields during that particular execution of the computer edit. The imputation for missing items in each section of the report form was conducted separately; thus, assigned values for one operation could come from more than one respondent.

Prior to the imputation operation, a set of default values and relationships were assigned to the possible imputation variables. The relationships and values varied depending on the item being imputed. For example, different default values were assigned for several standard industrial classification and total value of sales categories when imputing hired farm labor expenses. These values and item relationships for the possible imputation variables were stored in the computer in a series of matrices. The computer records were sorted by reported State and county, where the county sequence was based on similar types of farms and agricultural practices.

Each execution of the computer edit consisted of records from only one State. For a given execution of the edit, the stored entries in the various matrices were retained in the computer only until a succeeding record having acceptable characteristics for some sections of the report form was processed by the computer. Then the acceptable responses of the succeeding operation replaced those previously stored. When a record processed through the edit had unreported or unacceptable data, the record was assigned the last acceptable ratio or response from an operation with a similar set of characteristics. Once each execution of the computer edit for a State was completed, the possible imputation variables were reset to the default values and relationships for subsequent executions.

After the initial computer edit, keyed reports not meeting the census farm definition were reviewed to ensure that the data were keyed correctly. Edit referrals were generated for about 30 percent of the reports included as farms, and they were also reviewed for keying accuracy and to ensure that the computer edit actions were correct. If the results of the computer edit were not acceptable, corrections were made and the record was reedited. More extensive discussions of the edit and item imputation methodology with measures of the extent of imputation in the census estimates will be provided in a separate research report.

Tables D through G follow.

[For meaning of abbreviations and symbols, see introductory text]

Item	All farms		Farms with sales of $10,000 or more	
	Total (number)	Relative standard error of estimate (percent)	Total (number)	Relative standard error of estimate (percent)
Farms .... number..	68 579	(Z)	42 728	.1
Land in farms .... acres..	46 628 519	.1	42 829 070	.1
Average size of farm .... acres..	680	.1	1 002	.1
Value of land and buildings[1] .... $1,000..	19 068 461	.5	16 828 379	.6
Average per farm .... dollars..	278 047	.6	392 590	.6
Average per acre .... dollars..	413	1.0	397	1.0
Estimated market value of all machinery and equipment[1] .... $1,000..	3 447 663	.7	3 028 837	.7
Average per farm .... dollars..	50 411	.8	70 716	.8
Farms by size:				
1 to 9 acres .... farms..	3 689	.6	1 104	1.2
acres..	9 327	.8	2 076	1.6
10 to 49 acres .... farms..	6 222	.4	578	1.6
acres..	172 040	.5	15 949	1.7
50 to 179 acres .... farms..	15 510	.3	3 802	.6
acres..	1 779 180	.3	494 007	.6
180 to 499 acres .... farms..	16 705	.3	11 720	.3
acres..	5 429 273	.3	3 998 702	.3
500 to 999 acres .... farms..	12 093	.3	11 352	.3
acres..	8 673 395	.3	8 186 240	.3
1,000 to 1,999 acres .... farms..	8 304	.3	9 152	.3
acres..	12 925 252	.3	12 727 104	.3
2,000 acres or more .... farms..	5 056	.2	5 020	.3
acres..	17 640 082	.2	17 404 992	.2
Total cropland .... farms..	61 615	.1	40 636	.1
acres..	31 385 090	.1	29 090 486	.1
Harvested cropland .... farms..	57 622	.1	39 674	.1
acres..	17 729 394	.1	16 758 210	.1
Acres harvested:				
1 to 9 acres .... farms..	2 149	.8	262	2.0
acres..	10 659	.9	1 034	2.7
10 to 49 acres .... farms..	10 223	.3	1 810	.8
acres..	276 879	.4	55 026	.9
50 to 99 acres .... farms..	8 853	.4	3 589	.6
acres..	634 388	.4	268 561	.6
100 to 199 acres .... farms..	10 361	.4	8 083	.4
acres..	1 472 924	.4	1 179 150	.4
200 to 499 acres .... farms..	14 761	.3	14 461	.3
acres..	4 750 260	.3	4 672 472	.3
500 to 999 acres .... farms..	9 160	.3	8 145	.3
acres..	5 613 200	.3	(D)	(D)
1,000 acres or more .... farms..	3 325	(Z)	3 324	(Z)
acres..	4 971 084	(Z)	(D)	(D)
Cropland used only for pasture or grazing .... farms..	22 575	.2	15 052	.2
acres..	3 485 445	.3	2 955 754	.3
Other cropland .... farms..	43 046	.1	32 826	.1
acres..	10 170 251	.2	9 379 524	.2
Irrigated land .... farms..	7 352	.3	6 788	.3
acres..	2 483 073	.2	2 447 138	.2
Acres irrigated:				
1 to 9 acres .... farms..	416	1.6	187	2.1
acres..	1 324	2.3	581	3.4
10 to 49 acres .... farms..	897	1.2	676	1.4
acres..	25 518	1.3	20 056	1.5
50 to 99 acres .... farms..	996	1.2	912	1.2
acres..	71 219	1.2	65 495	1.2
100 to 199 acres .... farms..	1 574	.9	1 546	.9
acres..	218 591	.9	(D)	(D)
200 to 499 acres .... farms..	1 953	.6	1 951	.6
acres..	623 475	.6	(D)	(D)
500 to 999 acres .... farms..	1 012	.6	1 012	.6
acres..	700 303	.6	700 303	.6
1,000 acres or more .... farms..	504	.2	504	.2
acres..	822 643	.1	822 643	.1
Market value of agricultural products sold .... $1,000..	6 476 669	(Z)	6 373 092	(Z)
Average per farm .... dollars..	94 441	.1	149 155	.1
Value of sales:				
Less than $2,500 .... farms..	9 502	.3	-	-
$1,000..	9 635	.3	-	-
$2,500 to $4,999 .... farms..	6 919	.4	-	-
$1,000..	25 267	.4	-	-
$5,000 to $9,999 .... farms..	9 430	.4	-	-
$1,000..	66 474	.4	-	-
$10,000 to $24,999 .... farms..	14 070	.3	14 070	.3
$1,000..	230 372	.3	230 372	.3
$25,000 to $49,999 .... farms..	10 262	.3	10 262	.3
$1,000..	367 349	.3	367 349	.3
$50,000 to $99,999 .... farms..	8 997	.4	8 997	.4
$1,000..	637 837	.4	637 837	.4
$100,000 or more .... farms..	9 379	.2	9 379	.2
$1,000..	5 137 533	(Z)	5 137 533	(Z)
Sales by commodity or commodity group:				
Crops, including nursery and greenhouse crops .... farms..	51 773	.1	37 640	.1
$1,000..	1 693 609	.1	1 641 827	.1
Grains .... $1,000..	1 550 403	.1	1 504 937	.1
Corn for grain .... $1,000..	255 791	.3	254 432	.3
Wheat .... $1,000..	694 147	.1	669 098	.1
Soybeans .... $1,000..	263 742	.3	253 858	.3
Sorghum for grain .... $1,000..	311 649	.2	302 968	.2
Barley .... $1,000..	3 953	.7	3 881	.7
Oats .... $1,000..	3 328	1.0	3 093	1.1
Other grains .... $1,000..	17 793	.7	17 606	.7

See footnotes at end of table.

Table D. Reliability Estimates of State Totals: 1987—Con.

[For meaning of abbreviations and symbols, see introductory text]

Item	All farms Total (number)	All farms Relative standard error of estimate (percent)	Farms with sales of $10,000 or more Total (number)	Farms with sales of $10,000 or more Relative standard error of estimate (percent)
Sales by commodity or commodity group—Con.				
Crops, including nursery and greenhouse crops—Con.				
Cotton and cottonseed .... $1,000..	166	8.4	166	8.4
Tobacco .... $1,000..	80	15.7	73	17.3
Hay, silage, and field seeds .... $1,000..	109 574	.4	104 350	.4
Vegetables, sweet corn, and melons .... $1,000..	4 151	2.1	3 664	2.3
Fruits, nuts, and berries .... $1,000..	1 693	5.7	1 442	6.6
Nursery and greenhouse crops.................................. $1,000..	26 805	-	26 474	-
Other crops .... $1,000..	716	1.1	701	1.1
Livestock, poultry, and their products .... farms..	45 882	.1	31 350	.1
	$1,000..	4 783 060	(Z)	4 731 265	(Z)
Poultry and poultry products .... $1,000..	25 284	1.2	24 998	1.2
Dairy products .... $1,000..	140 232	.5	139 998	.5
Cattle and calves .... $1,000..	4 305 335	(Z)	4 261 056	(Z)
Hogs and pigs .... $1,000..	284 375	.3	281 062	.3
Sheep, lambs, and wool .... $1,000..	16 561	.8	16 929	.8
Other livestock and livestock products (see text) .... $1,000..	9 273	1.5	7 212	1.9
Farms by standard industrial classification:				
Cash grains (011) .... farms..	31 789	.1	22 225	.2
	acres..	24 396 997	.2	22 691 525	.2
Field crops, except cash grains (013) .... farms..	2 010	.8	569	1.6
	acres..	641 893	1.0	458 114	1.2
Vegetables and melons (016) .... farms..	179	2.7	59	4.6
	acres..	12 759	3.4	8 951	4.2
Fruits and tree nuts (017) .... farms..	171	3.1	24	9.4
	acres..	8 923	7.6	3 572	17.6
Horticultural specialties (018) .... farms..	224	-	145	-
	acres..	19 302	-	17 581	-
General farms, primarily crop (019) .... farms..	1 463	1.0	718	1.3
	acres..	911 997	1.0	830 406	1.0
Livestock, except dairy, poultry, and animal specialties (021) .... farms..	29 037	.2	17 179	.2
	acres..	19 106 721	.2	17 691 353	.2
Dairy farms (024) .... farms..	1 391	.9	1 348	.9
	acres..	805 354	.9	802 421	.9
Poultry and eggs (025) .... farms..	197	2.2	83	2.6
	acres..	34 376	4.8	23 657	2.2
Animal specialties (027) .... farms..	1 452	1.0	104	3.7
	acres..	126 440	2.2	14 530	4.9
General farms, primarily livestock and animal specialties (029) .... farms..	666	1.5	274	2.1
	acres..	563 757	1.1	286 960	1.6
Farms by type of organization:				
Individual or family (sole proprietorship) .... farms..	60 202	.1	36 327	.1
	acres..	36 420 471	.1	33 110 291	.1
Partnership .... farms..	5 689	.5	4 309	.5
	acres..	6 151 580	.4	5 881 210	.4
Corporation .... farms..	2 100	.7	1 680	.8
	acres..	3 606 121	.4	3 549 789	.4
Other—cooperative, estate or trust, institutional, etc. .... farms..	388	1.8	212	2.5
	acres..	450 347	.9	267 780	1.4
Tenure of operator:				
Full owners .... farms..	29 956	.2	11 862	.3
	acres..	8 839 919	.3	6 717 681	.3
Part owners .... farms..	27 967	.2	23 793	.2
	acres..	30 896 557	.1	29 906 320	.1
Tenants .... farms..	10 656	.4	7 073	.4
	acres..	6 892 043	.4	6 204 869	.4
Operators by principal occupation:				
Farming .... farms..	42 607	.1	33 778	.1
	acres..	40 030 217	.1	38 259 435	.1
Other .... farms..	25 972	.2	8 950	.4
	acres..	6 599 302	.3	4 569 635	.4
Operators by sex:				
Male .... farms..	65 619	.1	41 577	.1
	acres..	45 488 481	.1	41 943 936	.1
Female .... farms..	2 960	.7	1 151	1.2
	acres..	1 140 038	1.0	885 134	1.2
Average age of operator .... years..	52.0	.1	51.6	.1
Cropland under federal acreage reduction programs:				
Annual commodity acreage adjustment programs .... farms..	34 656	.1	29 094	.1
	acres..	3 956 196	.1	3 812 266	.1
Conservation reserve program .... farms..	5 630	.4	4 403	.5
	acres..	810 862	.6	696 782	.7
Government payments:				
Amount received in cash .... $1,000..	247 737	.2	238 588	.2
Value of certificates received [1] .... $1,000..	325 910	.2	309 258	.2
Net cash return from agricultural sales [1]:				
Net cash return from agricultural sales for the farm unit (see text) .... farms..	68 580	.1	42 865	.2
Average per farm .... dollars..	922 225 13 447	.8 .9	956 266 22 309	.8 .9
Farms with net gains [2] .... number..	41 673 1 140 553	.2 .5	31 351 1 119 077	.2 .5
	$1,000..				
Farms with net losses.. number..	26 907 216 328	.2 1.2	11 514 162 909	.4 1.4
	$1,000..				
Total farm production expenses [1] .... farms..	68 580	.1	42 865	.2
	$1,000..	6 516 516	.2	5 378 664	.2
Livestock and poultry purchased .... farms..	23 380	1.1	18 117	1.2
	$1,000..	2 426 148	.2	2 415 351	.2
Feed for livestock and poultry .... farms..	38 347	.7	27 516	.7
	$1,000..	887 270	.2	877 309	.2
Seeds, bulbs, plants, and trees .... farms..	48 233	.6	36 438	.5
	$1,000..	95 302	.8	91 270	.8
Commercial fertilizer .... farms..	47 731	.6	35 204	.5
	$1,000..	216 166	.6	207 371	.6

See footnotes at end of table.

Table D. **Reliability Estimates of State Totals: 1987**—Con.

[For meaning of abbreviations and symbols, see introductory text]

Item	All farms		Farms with sales of $10,000 or more	
	Total (number)	Relative standard error of estimate (percent)	Total (number)	Relative standard error of estimate (percent)
Total farm production expenses—Con.				
Agricultural chemicals _____ farms__	46 318	.6	34 474	.6
$1,000__	125 003	.8	118 865	.8
Petroleum products _____ farms__	65 460	.2	42 296	.2
$1,000__	243 566	.5	227 993	.5
Electricity _____ farms__	48 797	.6	35 071	.6
$1,000__	54 103	.6	50 132	.6
Hired farm labor _____ farms__	24 715	1.1	20 551	1.1
$1,000__	226 075	.5	223 983	.5
Contract labor _____ farms__	7 862	2.2	6 184	2.4
$1,000__	23 691	2.0	22 375	2.0
Repair and maintenance _____ farms__	56 961	.4	36 771	.4
$1,000__	252 018	.6	235 054	.6
Customwork, machine hire, and rental of machinery and equipment _____ farms__	30 603	1.0	23 220	1.0
$1,000__	107 366	1.3	101 691	1.4
Interest _____ farms__	39 549	.8	29 923	.7
$1,000__	314 163	.8	295 316	.8
Cash rent _____ farms__	21 234	1.2	17 942	1.2
$1,000__	123 531	1.3	119 525	1.3
Property taxes _____ farms__	63 359	.3	40 045	.3
$1,000__	112 201	.7	96 361	.7
All other farm production expenses_____ farms__	64 491	.3	42 856	.2
$1,000__	309 914	.5	296 067	.5
Livestock and poultry:				
Cattle and calves inventory _____ farms__	40 785	.1	28 111	.1
number__	5 539 292	.1	5 266 525	.1
Beef cows _____ farms__	31 475	.2	21 232	.2
number__	1 354 649	.2	1 219 630	.2
Milk cows _____ farms__	3 093	.6	2 514	.7
number__	96 675	.6	95 161	.6
Cattle and calves sold _____ farms__	41 498	.1	29 267	.1
number__	7 310 338	(Z)	7 185 342	(Z)
Hogs and pigs inventory _____ farms__	6 768	.4	5 480	.4
number__	1 516 878	.3	1 466 304	.3
Hogs and pigs sold _____ farms__	7 090	.4	5 791	.4
number__	2 759 876	.3	2 713 592	.3
Sheep and lambs inventory _____ farms__	2 400	.7	1 387	.9
number__	249 903	.8	217 992	.9
Sheep and lambs sold _____ farms__	2 996	.7	1 406	.9
number__	267 152	.7	243 837	.7
Hens and pullets of laying age inventory ____ farms__	4 150	.6	2 214	.8
number__	1 797 313	.5	1 745 184	.5
Broilers and other meat-type chickens sold_____ farms__	132	3.0	72	3.8
number__	176 061	14.3	168 899	15.1
Horses and ponies inventory_____ farms__	12 879	.3	7 341	.4
number__	55 598	.5	29 705	.7
Selected crops harvested:				
Corn for grain or seed _____ farms__	8 944	.3	8 026	.3
acres__	1 243 969	.2	1 228 426	.2
bushels__	144 133 561	.3	143 105 352	.3
Corn for silage or green chop_____ farms__	2 009	.6	1 946	.6
acres__	109 230	.6	107 988	.6
tons, green__	1 669 413	.6	1 657 553	.6
Sorghum for grain or seed_____ farms__	32 492	.1	27 102	.1
acres__	3 399 564	.2	3 362 294	.2
bushels__	226 045 100	.2	221 098 837	.2
Wheat for grain _____ farms__	36 636	.1	30 559	.1
acres__	8 679 588	.1	8 225 848	.1
bushels__	292 999 442	.1	280 906 698	.1
Oats for grain _____ farms__	5 313	.5	4 491	.5
acres__	126 091	.6	117 316	.6
bushels__	4 775 729	.6	4 463 199	.7
Soybeans for beans _____ farms__	18 864	.2	15 037	.2
acres__	1 876 978	.3	1 779 543	.3
bushels__	55 769 994	.3	53 527 794	.3
Hay—alfalfa, other tame, small grain, wild, grass silage, green chop, etc. (see text) _____ farms__	33 964	.1	24 304	.2
acres__	2 254 082	.2	1 990 641	.2
tons, dry__	5 080 847	.2	4 669 290	.2

¹Data are based on a sample of farms.
²Farms with total production expenses equal to market value of agricultural products sold are included as farms with gains.

Table E. **Reliability Estimates of Percent Change in State Totals: 1982 to 1987**

[For meaning of abbreviations and symbols, see introductory text]

Item	All farms		Farms with sales of $10,000 or more	
	Percent change	Standard error of estimate (percent)	Percent change	Standard error of estimate (percent)
Farms .... number..	-6.5	.2	-10.8	.1
Land in farms .... acres..	-.9	.1	-1.9	.1
Value of land and buildings[1]:				
Average per farm .... dollars..	-27.8	.6	-25.9	6
Total cropland .... farms..	-7.3	.2	-11.7	.1
acres..	2.6	.1	1.2	.1
Harvested cropland .... farms..	-8.0	.2	-12.3	.1
acres..	-12.2	.1	-13.2	.1
Irrigated land .... farms..	1.3	.4	-.8	.3
acres..	-7.9	.2	-8.2	.2
Market value of agricultural products sold .... $1,000..	-6.5	.2	-10.8	.1
acres..	4.6	.1	4.7	(Z)
Crops, including nursery and greenhouse crops .... rm ..	-8.8	.1	-13.3	.1
$1,000..	-21.0	.1	-21.6	.1
Livestock, poultry, and their products .... farms..	-11.3	.2	-12.6	.1
$1,000..	18.2	(Z)	18.5	(Z)
Poultry and poultry products .... farms..	-35.0	.6	-37.2	.7
$1,000..	-1.8	1.1	-1.5	1.2
Selected farm production expenses[1]:				
Livestock and poultry purchased .... farms..	-13.1	1.4	-8.9	1.6
$1,000..	27.7	.5	28.0	.5
Feed for livestock and poultry .... farms..	-15.1	.9	-11.8	1.0
$1,000..	-3.6	.4	-3.2	.4
Seeds, bulbs, plants, and trees .... farms..	1.6	.6	-5.3	.7
$1,000..	14.1	1.4	13.5	1.4
Commercial fertilizer[2] .... farms..	-3.9	.8	-8.1	.7
$1,000..	-15.1	.8	-15.8	.8
Agricultural chemicals[2] .... farms..	36.0	1.5	22.0	1.3
$1,000..	31.6	1.7	28.3	1.6
Hired farm labor .... farms..	-2.2	1.5	-2.9	1.5
$1,000..	47.4	1.3	49.5	1.3
Interest[3] .... farms..	-2.5	1.1	-7.1	1.0
$1,000..	-32.7	.7	-34.2	.7
Livestock and poultry inventory:				
Cattle and calves .... farms..	-13.2	.1	-13.8	.1
number..	-4.5	.1	-3.6	.1
Hogs and pigs .... farms..	-26.8	.3	-25.2	.3
number..	-11.2	.3	-10.8	.3
Hens and pullets of laying age .... farms..	-30.7	.4	-32.6	.5
number..	.1	.5	2.2	.5
Selected crops harvested:				
Corn for grain or seed .... farms..	7.2	.3	5.1	.3
acres..	7.1	.3	6.7	.3
Sorghum for grain or seed .... farms..	20.8	.2	13.7	.2
acres..	6.7	.2	5.1	.2
Wheat for grain .... farms..	-21.5	.1	-23.5	.1
acres..	-25.6	.1	-26.7	.1
Soybeans for beans .... farms..	10.2	.3	8.8	.3
acres..	11.0	.4	11.1	.4
Hay—alfalfa, other tame, small grain, wild, grass silage, green chop, etc.				
(see text) .... farms..	-9.0	.2	-11.2	.2
acres..	.9	.2	.6	.2
Vegetables harvested for sale (see text) .... farms..	15.5	2.0	44.8	3.3
acres..	12.8	2.2	15.1	2.6
Land in orchards .... farms..	-16.6	1.4	-5.2	2.5
acres..	-6.4	3.7	13.2	6.1

[1]Data are based on a sample of farms.
[2]Data for 1987 include cost of custom applications.
[3]Data for 1982 do not include imputation for item nonresponse.

Geographic area	Farms Total (number)	Farms Relative standard error of estimate (percent)	Land in farms Total (acres)	Land in farms Relative standard error of estimate (percent)	Average value of land and buildings per farm Value (dollars)	Average value of land and buildings per farm Relative standard error of estimate (percent)	Estimated market value of all machinery and equipment Total ($1,000)	Estimated market value of all machinery and equipment Relative standard error of estimate (percent)	Harvested cropland Total (acres)	Harvested cropland Relative standard error of estimate (percent)	Irrigated land Total (acres)	Irrigated land Relative standard error of estimate (percent)
Allen	665	.4	276 555	1.2	177 737	4.2	24 742	6.0	125 078	1.4	(D)	(D)
Anderson	727	.4	352 141	1.0	172 156	5.4	26 522	8.7	161 985	1.1	1 152	12.0
Atchison	694	.4	233 619	1.1	176 069	4.4	26 695	8.8	122 717	1.3	478	11.9
Barber	535	.5	700 147	.9	371 298	4.5	29 420	6.8	149 449	1.2	2 954	4.0
Barton	937	.3	556 433	.8	260 449	4.8	57 811	5.6	262 060	.8	29 147	1.8
Bourbon	842	.4	318 958	1.2	145 606	5.3	18 815	6.4	90 939	1.6	763	6.0
Brown	728	.4	339 853	.9	308 734	6.8	43 538	5.4	197 847	1.0	(D)	(D)
Butler	1 300	.2	699 487	.7	261 728	5.4	44 368	4.8	210 975	.9	3 588	11.5
Chase	288	.5	328 905	1.0	320 139	3.7	10 263	9.2	45 580	2.0	--	--
Chautauqua	421	.5	320 956	1.2	187 026	3.8	9 837	7.1	35 741	2.8	31	38.7
Cherokee	841	.3	280 704	1.1	173 944	6.1	29 536	7.3	156 409	1.3	376	15.8
Cheyenne	493	.5	619 870	1.0	395 783	5.8	28 963	5.9	176 293	1.1	40 651	2.4
Clark	290	.4	587 574	.6	520 769	2.6	15 342	6.5	92 271	.9	6 030	3.4
Clay	672	.4	392 321	1.2	242 841	9.0	41 015	8.5	176 217	1.2	10 626	2.6
Cloud	658	.4	397 383	1.1	262 653	6.9	34 812	7.0	184 007	1.2	10 139	4.4
Coffey	606	.3	330 435	.8	195 295	8.6	21 329	5.6	142 668	1.0	486	3.4
Comanche	277	.7	481 136	1.0	417 993	2.1	13 108	3.6	93 062	1.3	4 424	4.3
Cowley	997	.3	619 647	.8	230 291	4.4	35 555	6.7	160 551	1.2	1 410	11.1
Crawford	909	.3	263 589	1.0	154 295	8.9	28 383	7.7	118 714	1.2	1 447	5.3
Decatur	486	.5	543 466	1.1	350 809	7.0	37 919	6.8	175 861	1.1	10 433	3.0
Dickinson	1 028	.3	513 946	.9	209 824	4.2	49 694	7.5	245 504	.9	2 792	4.0
Doniphan	530	.5	216 179	1.0	279 453	6.6	25 501	6.1	127 686	1.0	(D)	(D)
Douglas	852	.3	223 426	1.1	195 964	4.9	24 740	6.9	108 664	1.2	1 927	1.5
Edwards	381	.5	387 300	.6	455 709	4.8	31 087	5.9	186 513	.6	83 316	.6
Elk	409	.5	340 899	1.0	237 000	3.7	9 708	7.6	40 040	1.7	(D)	(D)
Ellis	795	.6	566 934	1.2	264 675	6.0	33 230	7.1	147 980	1.4	983	6.8
Ellsworth	499	.7	423 655	1.4	276 723	4.6	24 601	10.5	128 533	1.7	896	3.2
Finney	534	.5	722 746	.7	658 750	9.3	56 675	3.8	323 607	.7	184 177	1.1
Ford	812	.4	674 986	.8	341 901	5.7	85 178	2.6	284 042	.8	77 829	1.2
Franklin	979	.3	312 763	.9	181 876	5.2	28 721	4.9	135 087	.9	1 503	6.3
Geary	295	.8	170 339	1.4	237 777	4.3	13 652	16.4	48 216	1.5	1 616	12.2
Gove	534	.5	676 575	.9	350 782	5.0	31 683	5.1	194 726	.9	15 941	2.6
Graham	452	.6	503 589	1.2	412 626	3.6	26 086	8.1	148 177	1.3	8 519	3.3
Grant	303	.7	323 138	1.2	535 611	4.8	36 752	6.8	156 356	1.2	99 429	1.2
Gray	547	.4	532 264	.7	479 429	8.3	51 258	3.7	258 379	.6	154 369	.7
Greeley	294	.7	475 278	1.0	668 113	5.5	25 052	5.2	196 152	.9	25 410	2.2
Greenwood	587	.4	549 507	.8	314 348	6.2	14 895	6.3	73 937	1.7	819	6.5
Hamilton	279	.7	536 449	.8	568 527	7.6	25 488	8.0	150 504	1.0	18 805	2.9
Harper	648	.4	484 471	.7	314 046	5.4	36 385	5.2	233 900	.7	584	8.3
Harvey	874	.3	308 123	.8	253 936	4.0	45 966	6.3	197 917	.9	20 939	1.9
Haskell	315	.7	369 650	1.2	737 000	8.5	43 454	4.4	200 065	1.0	154 476	1.1
Hodgeman	423	.4	495 080	.9	385 870	6.2	25 901	6.4	139 900	1.0	22 795	2.1
Jackson	1 082	.3	335 142	1.2	127 956	5.5	26 018	7.4	114 691	1.4	2 776	2.0
Jefferson	1 017	.3	260 592	1.2	166 896	12.5	29 599	5.1	112 695	1.4	1 763	4.9
Jewell	736	.4	502 105	.9	245 574	6.9	36 979	5.7	208 645	1.0	7 087	3.6
Johnson	659	.4	151 763	1.4	322 914	9.2	26 019	8.6	69 445	1.6	250	11.8
Kearny	291	.6	549 371	.7	740 880	4.2	38 050	5.1	202 166	.8	83 178	1.1
Kingman	818	.4	517 652	.9	269 880	4.7	40 088	4.6	219 446	1.0	14 798	1.5
Kiowa	310	.5	392 245	.7	404 894	4.8	24 178	15.9	128 425	1.0	37 144	1.5
Labette	971	.3	350 010	1.0	153 151	4.3	27 312	5.5	139 963	1.2	1 905	4.0
Lane	322	.6	467 005	.9	592 398	8.4	25 201	8.3	154 979	1.0	14 902	2.1
Leavenworth	1 144	.3	211 370	1.0	170 089	8.0	28 553	7.3	96 700	1.2	310	12.4
Lincoln	578	.4	454 341	1.0	253 820	5.3	29 610	9.2	153 709	1.1	699	12.1
Linn	688	.4	273 211	1.3	157 301	5.1	21 368	8.6	93 665	1.5	(D)	(D)
Logan	362	.4	610 480	.7	382 249	4.0	24 164	11.1	153 682	1.0	10 982	3.1
Lyon	872	.3	489 926	.7	177 635	3.6	35 208	6.5	153 682	.8	(D)	(D)
McPherson	1 357	.2	533 432	.7	222 022	4.6	62 042	5.0	283 523	.7	24 006	2.0
Marion	1 119	.3	577 700	.7	214 544	4.7	50 013	5.5	252 314	.8	2 188	5.9
Marshall	1 061	.4	553 436	1.0	237 714	4.7	46 654	4.5	261 802	1.0	2 159	6.3
Meade	464	.5	582 454	.7	483 019	6.2	32 863	4.2	200 706	.7	100 309	1.2
Miami	1 151	.3	272 290	1.0	193 407	5.4	31 213	7.3	116 217	1.1	437	1.8
Mitchell	622	.4	478 829	.9	345 722	5.4	40 085	4.5	237 322	.9	4 867	7.9
Montgomery	974	.3	327 193	1.2	154 431	5.4	27 434	6.5	111 306	1.5	2 463	3.5
Morris	560	.4	396 556	1.1	241 545	5.8	23 234	6.8	112 525	1.4	228	6.6
Morton	226	.7	457 440	.8	563 862	5.6	20 164	13.3	139 396	1.1	35 799	1.1
Nemaha	1 127	.3	436 761	.8	167 203	6.4	54 084	7.1	203 290	.9	494	6.9
Neosho	751	.4	305 492	1.0	158 283	4.6	23 777	5.1	126 121	1.2	310	8.7
Ness	597	.4	673 189	.9	284 951	5.9	33 163	7.5	193 390	1.0	2 682	4.9
Norton	470	.5	507 626	.9	341 366	7.6	23 902	7.7	154 827	.9	5 893	2.8
Osage	885	.3	357 199	1.0	154 063	3.9	29 297	5.1	140 377	1.0	(D)	(D)
Osborne	607	.7	545 417	1.4	279 456	4.8	36 044	6.8	182 096	1.4	8 452	3.4
Ottawa	523	.5	385 542	1.2	266 295	5.6	21 725	5.6	149 979	1.3	1 741	6.7
Pawnee	509	.4	486 599	1.0	397 967	6.3	38 991	4.5	223 904	1.0	65 213	1.3
Phillips	591	.5	542 578	.8	274 172	5.1	27 290	6.9	162 736	.9	4 910	4.5
Pottawatomie	790	.4	443 660	1.2	204 275	4.2	22 246	4.7	116 376	1.1	9 573	1.4
Pratt	517	.3	466 245	1.0	418 988	7.1	30 499	4.7	242 460	.9	71 541	.9
Rawlins	541	.5	641 810	1.2	326 342	4.3	30 467	8.0	196 707	1.3	11 547	3.2
Reno	1 557	.3	717 764	.7	263 020	6.0	71 897	4.3	374 579	.7	27 576	2.0
Republic	633	.4	440 214	.9	262 151	5.2	47 432	5.2	230 517	.9	15 058	1.7
Rice	604	.4	429 065	.8	315 447	4.7	39 062	4.6	204 933	.9	36 416	1.4
Riley	546	.5	247 809	1.3	183 629	7.3	20 803	9.8	80 307	1.5	1 922	6.2
Rooks	473	.3	547 539	.8	328 368	7.0	24 725	7.2	157 823	.9	2 864	4.9
Rush	548	.4	422 828	1.2	306 872	6.5	27 725	7.2	160 253	1.2	7 975	5.5
Russell	534	.5	461 014	1.4	241 090	7.2	24 055	8.7	135 417	1.3	134	16.0
Saline	743	.4	423 150	.7	248 793	6.4	34 866	8.5	173 828	.8	3 152	4.3
Scott	391	.5	470 774	.8	489 652	4.8	40 961	7.3	180 540	1.0	59 739	1.5
Sedgwick	1 569	.3	523 580	.7	289 538	4.5	59 227	5.0	319 625	.7	24 739	1.9
Seward	285	.6	221 098	1.1	562 074	2.6	29 227	7.3	141 650	1.0	77 842	1.6
Shawnee	852	.3	221 098	1.1	189 910	5.0	22 227	5.0	101 139	1.4	11 382	4.4
Sheridan	518	.4	503 582	1.0	359 500	6.3	36 362	6.9	183 013	1.1	20 623	2.0
Sherman	424	.5	626 342	.7	403 073	3.0	38 810	5.4	251 334	.8	83 424	1.3
Smith	692	.3	555 678	.8	283 039	6.0	41 116	5.2	211 337	.9	7 812	3.9
Stafford	540	.5	461 213	1.0	427 813	5.9	43 600	5.5	230 807	1.0	112 728	.9
Stanton	260	.6	423 150	.7	591 809	5.2	31 445	7.2	184 791	.7	112 728	1.0
Stevens	300	.6	460 974	.7	682 130	4.9	43 599	7.0	236 568	.7	119 752	1.0
Sumner	1 271	.3	704 788	.7	297 971	3.5	71 514	6.3	415 440	.7	2 694	6.7
Thomas	644	.5	677 199	.9	410 301	3.9	49 941	4.3	296 047	.8	73 546	1.8

See footnotes at end of table.

Geographic area	Farms Total (number)	Farms Relative standard error of estimate (percent)	Land in farms Total (acres)	Land in farms Relative standard error of estimate (percent)	Average value of land and buildings per farm[1] Value (dollars)	Average value of land and buildings per farm[1] Relative standard error of estimate (percent)	Estimated market value of all machinery and equipment[1] Total ($1,000)	Estimated market value of all machinery and equipment[1] Relative standard error of estimate (percent)	Harvested cropland Total (acres)	Harvested cropland Relative standard error of estimate (percent)	Irrigated land Total (acres)	Irrigated land Relative standard error of estimate (percent)
Trego	482	.5	480 159	.9	249 226	5.7	28 303	11.2	139 768	1.1	3 076	3.8
Wabaunsee	633	.4	460 304	.9	286 829	6.1	18 599	5.5	90 028	1.3	6 749	2.4
Wallace	330	.8	529 749	1.0	558 106	2.3	22 563	8.4	146 695	1.4	45 733	2.1
Washington	939	.3	518 501	.7	216 607	5.1	50 343	4.2	239 242	.6	8 293	2.0
Wichita	355	.6	440 457	.9	488 511	5.9	30 803	6.6	182 673	1.0	73 436	1.5
Wilson	610	.4	299 462	1.1	178 589	4.7	23 623	6.9	114 733	1.4	1 555	6.5
Woodson	369	.4	263 967	1.1	228 190	4.7	12 715	5.3	85 309	1.4	(D)	(D)
Wyandotte	199	.9	23 936	3.3	159 588	3.8	5 065	16.5	12 112	4.1	14	8.4

Geographic area	Cattle and calves inventory Total (number)	Cattle and calves inventory Relative standard error of estimate (percent)	Hogs and pigs inventory Total (number)	Hogs and pigs inventory Relative standard error of estimate (percent)	Corn for grain or seed Total (acres)	Corn for grain or seed Relative standard error of estimate (percent)	Wheat for grain Total (acres)	Wheat for grain Relative standard error of estimate (percent)	Soybeans for beans Total (acres)	Soybeans for beans Relative standard error of estimate (percent)	Market value of agricultural products sold Total ($1,000)	Market value of agricultural products sold Relative standard error of estimate (percent)
Allen	30 062	1.2	6 612	4.9	7 562	3.1	9 519	3.1	61 809	2.0	23 025	.9
Anderson	35 758	1.1	10 240	3.1	13 596	1.6	6 576	2.4	80 630	1.3	34 226	.8
Atchison	29 344	1.4	17 675	3.0	22 627	1.8	5 160	4.7	43 701	1.6	26 252	1.1
Barber	89 515	.9	3 900	9.4	-	-	121 445	1.3	1 416	8.1	45 715	.6
Barton	85 041	.5	5 473	6.3	9 382	2.4	167 887	.9	6 945	2.8	125 117	.2
Bourbon	46 580	1.5	7 261	4.0	5 937	3.4	3 442	4.7	32 777	2.4	23 062	1.1
Brown	39 705	1.3	42 810	1.7	46 227	1.6	26 577	1.5	78 311	1.2	62 567	.5
Butler	107 777	.7	37 102	2.8	3 180	4.0	63 948	1.2	23 825	1.8	99 289	.3
Chase	39 591	1.5	7 829	8.7	2 323	4.2	11 898	2.7	9 639	4.7	34 012	.6
Chautauqua	34 230	1.4	7 682	7.0	658	12.3	8 028	3.5	8 401	5.1	15 707	1.1
Cherokee	22 329	1.5	6 217	5.4	5 166	4.8	16 296	4.2	100 264	1.5	22 029	1.5
Cheyenne	42 329	1.2	5 134	18.1	18 604	2.6	109 225	1.3	4 029	5.8	51 543	.5
Clark	66 325	.7	(D)	(D)	-	-	70 885	1.0	(D)	(D)	54 942	.3
Clay	39 466	1.5	42 511	2.2	7 405	2.2	79 221	1.4	23 155	1.9	39 675	.8
Cloud	31 448	1.6	16 703	2.8	7 338	4.8	109 897	1.4	12 176	2.6	30 872	.9
Coffey	31 584	1.2	5 827	3.6	7 862	2.4	11 740	1.7	70 461	1.2	32 459	.7
Comanche	50 945	.8	2 035	6.7	809	3.7	71 867	1.5	774	3.1	29 146	.7
Cowley	61 062	.8	24 267	2.0	612	17.7	95 945	1.3	5 827	3.3	55 906	.4
Crawford	31 162	1.2	2 859	10.0	7 737	3.5	3 989	3.3	58 552	1.6	21 741	.8
Decatur	57 326	1.0	12 545	4.3	17 036	1.4	93 716	1.4	954	3.3	72 560	.4
Dickinson	73 786	1.3	19 456	3.2	1 915	5.7	135 344	1.1	14 637	1.8	65 235	.6
Doniphan	20 301	1.4	18 452	2.8	56 130	1.1	7 949	2.0	52 547	1.2	34 650	.8
Douglas	27 845	1.3	8 120	3.0	15 643	2.1	2 844	3.1	42 051	1.6	28 024	.9
Edwards	51 127	.5	1 333	9.7	36 522	.9	87 995	.9	21 083	.7	57 867	.3
Elk	37 023	1.1	9 613	1.3	307	2.2	6 405	3.2	9 348	4.0	17 905	.8
Ellis	55 888	1.3	4 096	11.0	207	.2	99 562	1.5	-	-	46 993	.7
Ellsworth	36 668	2.1	6 985	5.1	231	17.1	85 816	1.8	1 582	8.8	21 446	1.4
Finney	193 533	.2	6 046	1.5	50 415	.9	174 488	.9	8 644	3.6	381 532	1.1
Ford	137 745	.4	4 936	3.8	19 058	1.8	181 190	.9	6 586	3.5	229 083	.2
Franklin	35 740	1.2	17 076	2.3	11 765	1.6	4 832	2.2	62 225	3.0	33 009	.8
Geary	22 321	1.3	19 063	2.1	952	4.0	16 731	2.1	5 462	3.0	16 506	.9
Gove	81 975	.8	6 628	8.5	5 013	5.4	117 701	1.1	(D)	(D)	93 924	.3
Graham	36 291	1.5	2 239	4.4	3 302	4.9	91 909	1.5	205	11.2	27 508	.8
Grant	149 230	.1	3 797	1.5	28 298	2.1	72 047	1.3	3 793	3.4	231 412	.1
Gray	148 250	.3	4 607	3.4	51 161	.9	133 609	.9	5 462	1.3	236 428	.1
Greeley	52 354	.8	1 030	4.9	12 877	2.9	145 703	.9	499	8.8	81 569	.3
Greenwood	63 675	1.0	5 848	17.9	1 119	5.5	9 865	3.2	17 664	3.8	35 362	.7
Hamilton	58 221	.5	1 007	4.0	4 574	6.0	125 546	1.1	(D)	(D)	80 154	.2
Harper	70 210	.7	4 205	5.1	(D)	(D)	212 192	.8	(D)	(D)	55 261	.5
Harvey	33 335	1.4	30 478	1.6	11 053	2.3	103 018	1.0	12 996	1.7	52 369	.5
Haskell	134 383	.2	4 882	9.0	55 966	1.1	99 081	1.4	3 719	4.5	248 969	.1
Hodgeman	83 072	.7	672	10.3	2 826	2.8	105 731	1.2	918	4.0	89 478	.3
Jackson	43 136	1.5	16 624	3.9	12 664	3.0	9 222	3.7	25 243	2.3	27 790	1.1
Jefferson	32 879	1.2	11 369	2.2	23 174	1.9	3 836	6.4	36 268	2.1	25 301	1.0
Jewell	44 080	1.4	49 577	1.6	6 361	3.7	109 626	1.2	8 942	2.9	44 073	.6
Johnson	19 542	1.9	8 292	4.9	8 767	2.7	2 675	3.7	33 097	2.6	22 878	.9
Kearny	77 869	.5	1 457	9.7	24 651	.4	121 394	1.0	1 596	1.5	119 990	.2
Kingman	51 395	1.4	9 076	4.6	5 130	2.3	176 798	1.1	3 844	2.6	35 979	.8
Kiowa	31 041	2.7	1 640	11.8	13 151	1.6	74 813	1.2	6 698	1.8	24 592	.8
Labette	58 329	1.0	14 152	2.7	2 261	3.9	11 615	4.5	56 166	1.6	48 962	.5
Lane	59 727	.8	1 922	14.7	643	4.4	111 527	1.2	174	24.3	88 214	.2
Leavenworth	30 300	1.2	17 890	3.1	17 320	2.0	3 049	3.7	31 563	2.4	26 702	.8
Lincoln	53 344	1.1	6 635	4.3	131	27.5	99 612	1.2	1 896	5.6	38 488	.6
Linn	35 037	1.5	15 530	2.4	6 544	5.5	2 608	4.8	40 929	2.0	21 703	1.0
Logan	31 593	.9	1 883	9.2	3 448	8.2	111 686	1.0	(D)	(D)	22 420	.8
Lyon	75 525	.7	11 099	3.6	11 007	1.6	17 825	1.4	43 599	1.4	39 138	.5
McPherson	56 948	.8	22 177	3.1	11 579	2.8	184 434	.8	16 498	1.5	77 962	.4
Marion	66 026	.9	30 622	2.8	3 765	3.5	118 472	.9	11 732	2.0	58 631	.6
Marshall	49 806	1.5	44 970	2.6	6 076	3.5	75 311	1.2	61 942	1.5	59 932	.4
Meade	50 379	.8	2 728	9.4	21 843	1.1	106 761	1.2	924	4.5	82 337	.3
Miami	33 569	1.3	11 243	2.9	9 978	1.6	1 631	5.4	46 043	1.7	24 920	1.0
Mitchell	47 246	.9	23 109	1.5	2 516	6.3	164 343	1.0	7 764	3.5	49 885	.4
Montgomery	32 459	1.4	20 989	2.1	7 860	3.3	16 023	2.5	36 804	2.0	22 988	1.1
Morris	55 338	1.0	10 777	4.1	2 667	4.0	36 194	1.5	12 488	3.1	39 229	.6
Morton	15 115	2.3	80	13.9	2 558	.3	74 500	1.5	(D)	(D)	27 667	.7
Nemaha	60 317	1.2	86 022	1.5	10 885	3.3	35 363	1.6	81 953	1.7	61 420	.7
Neosho	34 652	1.3	23 529	1.7	5 010	3.9	13 064	1.6	56 060	1.9	26 111	1.0
Ness	42 710	1.5	1 870	22.2	(D)	(D)	136 612	.9	2 456	5.2	55 820	.4
Norton	38 256	1.2	16 293	3.1	9 007	2.8	92 488	1.1	344	12.1	33 417	.7
Osage	34 842	1.4	8 067	3.3	4 676	3.4	7 668	2.3	50 704	1.4	30 765	.8
Osborne	47 252	1.9	7 984	4.2	1 180	7.2	117 191	1.6	3 224	5.6	37 539	.7
Ottawa	40 780	1.7	7 809	7.3	2 232	2.8	117 270	1.4	5 250	3.6	37 552	.5
Pawnee	57 425	1.0	10 136	6.4	13 077	1.8	125 758	1.2	11 666	2.2	91 433	.2
Phillips	51 554	1.1	41 030	1.1	5 261	4.2	84 316	1.0	9 920	4.5	40 563	.6
Pottawatomie	56 613	1.2	36 363	2.1	16 693	2.2	11 352	1.9	38 706	1.6	39 265	.7
Pratt	61 095	.6	18 001	2.8	29 531	1.5	143 482	1.2	8 871	1.8	97 669	.3

See footnotes at end of table.

Geographic area	Cattle and calves inventory Total (number)	Relative standard error of estimate (percent)	Hogs and pigs inventory Total (number)	Relative standard error of estimate (percent)	Corn for grain or seed Total (acres)	Relative standard error of estimate (percent)	Wheat for grain Total (acres)	Relative standard error of estimate (percent)	Soybeans for beans Total (acres)	Relative standard error of estimate (percent)	Market value of agricultural products sold Total ($1,000)	Relative standard error of estimate (percent)
Rawlins	44 947	1.9	11 548	7.3	6 047	3.8	123 069	1.4	461	8.2	31 808	1.1
Reno	68 838	.8	21 871	2.0	11 147	1.6	237 738	.9	8 400	2.7	82 925	.4
Republic	58 209	.9	19 475	3.7	39 494	1.6	83 080	1.1	24 503	1.6	97 295	.4
Rice	50 618	1.1	17 285	1.6	7 893	2.4	130 572	1.1	7 475	2.1	69 583	.4
Riley	31 205	1.7	29 764	2.1	2 892	5.2	21 023	2.1	10 911	2.4	25 444	1.0
Rooks	35 999	1.0	2 903	4.4	1 303	8.2	100 707	1.0	680	1.5	24 933	.8
Rush	23 531	2.2	581	10.4	966	16.5	113 315	1.4	3 179	2.6	20 057	1.2
Russell	34 604	2.7	4 125	10.7	102	19.3	92 100	1.4	659	12.6	20 315	1.3
Saline	36 119	1.9	21 121	1.4	1 324	4.5	126 775	1.2	7 565	3.5	30 700	.9
Scott	169 825	.1	29 994	3.0	8 948	3.6	115 140	1.0	1 048	11.7	280 233	.1
Sedgwick	41 135	1.1	15 370	3.1	13 005	2.8	189 806	.9	21 042	1.5	59 327	.5
Seward	86 120	.3	(D)		11 367	2.5	68 948	1.3	824	7.3	130 390	.1
Shawnee	19 849	1.8	4 620	5.1	20 568	2.8	7 719	2.8	30 060	2.1	21 869	1.1
Sheridan	43 899	.9	7 319	5.9	28 533	1.9	94 689	1.3	3 899	4.7	54 089	.5
Sherman	33 721	1.0	1 950	3.7	35 617	1.5	155 862	.9	5 071	3.4	67 429	.9
Smith	54 862	1.2	28 020	3.3	3 029	2.8	107 735	1.0	10 697	2.2	50 552	1.0
Stafford	62 373	.8	4 180	8.5	29 798	1.3	124 760	1.2	8 721	3.3	72 053	.5
Stanton	49 389	.3	185	15.5	30 940	.9	113 050	.8	2 360	3.7	86 972	.2
Stevens	52 216	.3	3 663	2.6	25 416	1.2	89 747	1.0	890	2.2	96 541	.2
Sumner	41 742	1.3	20 817	2.8	997	7.7	356 942	.7	14 494	2.5	53 409	.6
Thomas	36 649	1.4	5 696	1.3	48 965	1.5	181 694	1.0	5 742	5.0	74 749	.4
Trego	38 838	1.1	2 771	8.9	520	13.6	91 726	1.1	-	-	35 552	.5
Wabaunsee	51 872	1.1	19 702	2.1	6 814	2.5	11 153	2.5	14 271	3.7	34 210	.7
Wallace	22 920	1.8	2 528	11.7	22 478	2.2	93 419	1.5	845	11.6	28 601	.8
Washington	57 997	.7	92 927	.8	8 272	1.8	74 198	.8	30 669	1.0	62 837	.4
Wichita	90 559	.4	1 800	12.7	16 401	2.2	118 864	1.1	1 295	4.0	223 235	.1
Wilson	28 333	1.8	12 236	3.1	2 231	3.3	16 950	2.4	52 601	1.8	20 203	1.1
Woodson	22 297	1.4	2 585	5.5	1 515	2.8	7 822	2.3	30 000	1.8	21 103	.8
Wyandotte	1 887	5.6	1 052	7.4	2 104	3.6	482	9.8	5 417	5.8	5 015	2.9

Selected farm production expenses[1]

Geographic area	Livestock and poultry purchased Total ($1,000)	Relative standard error of estimate (percent)	Commercial fertilizer Total ($1,000)	Relative standard error of estimate (percent)	Hired farm labor Total ($1,000)	Relative standard error of estimate (percent)	Petroleum products Total ($1,000)	Relative standard error of estimate (percent)	Electricity for the farm business Total ($1,000)	Relative standard error of estimate (percent)
Allen	2 297	13.8	1 349	9.6	984	9.1	1 337	5.1	365	7.4
Anderson	4 534	14.5	1 650	8.5	947	15.4	1 774	5.2	364	7.7
Atchison	3 029	12.5	1 960	6.0	603	5.6	1 714	9.0	423	11.8
Barber	15 301	3.8	2 022	5.9	1 866	5.2	2 276	4.8	371	6.7
Barton	44 482	.4	2 477	4.2	2 486	2.6	2 095	3.6	820	3.9
Bourbon	5 035	6.3	1 070	7.8	537	7.1	1 340	6.7	287	8.1
Brown	12 706	2.6	3 353	4.6	4 637	5.8	2 320	3.5	610	5.4
Butler	40 379	2.3	2 913	4.7	3 525	7.0	2 685	3.8	677	4.1
Chase	14 097	3.9	356	10.6	1 091	1.9	797	8.3	175	7.9
Chautauqua	2 365	9.6	390	9.3	1 448	1.2	895	5.2	160	19.0
Cherokee	1 614	9.5	2 203	8.3	1 197	14.1	1 526	5.2	229	9.9
Cheyenne	17 917	2.7	2 012	6.5	1 835	2.7	2 629	3.6	642	5.0
Clark	29 671	4.3	773	7.4	1 933	2.7	1 630	8.6	503	12.8
Clay	5 969	5.6	2 436	4.9	1 338	3.0	2 159	6.4	503	4.1
Cloud	3 370	10.7	2 477	5.8	964	4.8	2 127	4.4	(D)	10.4
Coffey	8 061	11.7	1 118	8.9	1 022	12.4	1 623	10.4	311	10.4
Comanche	8 606	1.8	727	2.0	1 147	.2	1 158	3.5	193	3.8
Cowley	19 467	4.2	1 999	5.1	2 710	9.5	2 227	4.6	411	8.4
Crawford	2 756	3.6	1 770	10.3	561	4.9	1 411	6.9	281	8.8
Decatur	29 157	1.7	990	8.2	1 596	3.3	2 363	4.3	(D)	(D)
Dickinson	23 474	4.2	3 047	4.1	1 579	5.3	2 768	4.2	550	4.9
Doniphan	3 893	6.1	2 214	5.5	1 446	6.0	1 710	3.9	273	7.6
Douglas	6 970	11.4	1 750	5.4	790	2.3	1 267	5.6	377	11.8
Edwards	17 504	4.0	3 452	6.4	2 712	4.5	2 758	4.5	565	6.5
Elk	3 547	4.1	376	11.2	643	14.5	775	8.5	149	12.4
Ellis	15 491	1.2	851	7.4	2 265	5.4	2 102	5.4	550	7.5
Ellsworth	3 053	19.0	1 226	9.0	690	3.3	1 545	7.1	268	11.1
Finney	213 837	.2	695	3.6	13 120	1.0	6 740	2.1	1 630	1.5
Ford	131 226	.3	859	8.3	4 873	1.3	4 565	4.4	989	3.2
Franklin	4 332	19.1	1 810	7.3	1 922	11.0	1 643	5.1	464	6.6
Geary	2 743	13.9	648	10.8	838	20.6	803	11.2	207	14.5
Gove	23 984	2.6	1 874	9.8	2 181	8.5	2 567	7.0	(D)	(D)
Graham	6 301	5.7	1 396	13.1	1 250	8.9	1 974	4.8	452	6.6
Grant	159 445	(Z)	1 960	9.9	5 011	3.9	2 927	5.1	946	.8
Gray	135 695	.3	4 376	2.2	6 260	1.1	6 144	1.5	1 358	1.4
Greeley	40 783	.3	1 496	3.8	2 878	2.3	2 249	6.0	518	5.1
Greenwood	10 785	6.7	829	10.8	1 338	12.2	1 258	6.7	267	4.9
Hamilton	19 036	3.3	846	5.2	2 047	.6	1 712	9.0	562	4.3
Harper	16 668	3.0	2 794	5.4	1 466	3.2	2 862	4.4	640	5.1
Harvey	11 656	5.5	2 792	3.4	1 316	1.5	2 379	5.6	840	5.1
Haskell	137 078	.1	3 028	2.1	9 134	2.3	4 305	2.4	920	2.8
Hodgeman	47 975	1.6	1 095	5.4	3 750	1.0	2 921	3.6	504	5.1
Jackson	5 902	10.8	2 098	6.4	621	8.4	1 588	6.4	398	8.1
Jefferson	3 243	11.4	2 222	4.3	895	18.2	1 423	4.5	356	5.7
Jewell	6 554	7.4	2 458	5.8	1 521	3.0	2 343	4.5	516	5.6
Johnson	5 477	11.6	1 106	7.0	1 823	8.4	1 066	5.8	343	11.2
Kearny	55 507	.3	2 523	6.3	4 520	7.2	3 782	3.3	676	1.6
Kingman	7 009	9.6	2 456	5.4	1 180	5.5	2 676	6.0	502	5.8
Kiowa	4 083	12.9	3 276	6.8	1 020	5.5	1 724	6.0	206	3.3
Labette	19 254	3.8	1 694	7.2	1 983	5.7	1 661	5.2	301	7.1
Lane	39 368	.3	1 589	7.1	4 200	3.6	2 283	10.0	(D)	(D)
Leavenworth	1 636	13.2	1 599	7.1	1 629	4.0	1 715	5.0	473	5.7
Lincoln	10 948	2.9	1 704	8.1	1 368	9.3	2 072	4.1	353	5.8
Linn	2 995	6.6	1 309	7.7	865	7.0	1 263	6.5	312	7.8
Logan	4 159	5.3	895	13.7	(D)	(0)	1 659	7.1	342	9.8
Lyon	19 791	2.7	1 527	4.9	2 470	4.8	1 964	4.0	391	4.4

See footnotes at end of table.

[For meaning of abbreviations and symbols, see introductory text]

Geographic area	Selected farm production expenses[1]									
	Livestock and poultry purchased		Commercial fertilizer		Hired farm labor		Petroleum products		Electricity for the farm business	
	Total ($1,000)	Relative standard error of estimate (percent)	Total ($1,000)	Relative standard error of estimate (percent)	Total ($1,000)	Relative standard error of estimate (percent)	Total ($1,000)	Relative standard error of estimate (percent)	Total ($1,000)	Relative standard error of estimate (percent)
McPherson	20 430	2.2	3 900	4.3	1 827	6.2	3 498	3.6	993	3.7
Marion	12 416	3.5	3 559	4.6	1 947	9.5	2 597	4.7	693	5.0
Marshall	7 638	7.6	3 847	5.2	1 806	6.1	3 171	4.3	690	6.4
Meade	(D)	(D)	2 707	5.0	1 991	1.9	3 526	5.8	506	7.1
Miami	1 256	9.3	1 892	8.0	1 109	3.7	1 603	6.4	368	7.1
Mitchell	16 792	1.0	3 042	5.8	1 955	5.2	2 723	3.6	509	5.2
Montgomery	2 490	23.2	1 396	6.6	1 083	6.8	1 866	5.5	448	11.1
Morris	12 705	6.4	1 486	12.3	2 040	2.1	1 934	6.8	397	6.9
Morton	4 127	15.4	945	6.0	1 500	24.7	1 459	8.7	218	17.8
Nemaha	9 371	9.4	3 523	4.0	1 606	3.4	3 065	3.7	861	5.0
Neosho	2 856	7.8	1 861	6.7	1 126	7.4	1 716	4.7	396	4.6
Ness	4 846	12.1	929	5.9	713	5.3	2 034	4.8	269	7.7
Norton	8 114	2.3	1 363	5.4	1 096	4.7	1 855	4.9	465	6.2
Osage	5 796	6.1	1 721	5.2	823	4.9	1 583	4.7	325	9.8
Osborne	3 796	7.8	2 016	4.6	1 151	8.6	2 323	5.5	353	4.7
Ottawa	13 639	5.5	1 786	8.0	1 334	7.1	1 824	5.2	289	8.5
Pawnee	30 325	2.2	2 208	4.3	2 648	2.8	2 700	4.3	708	5.9
Phillips	4 033	9.6	1 519	7.9	1 313	2.6	2 044	5.8	481	6.4
Pottawatomie	7 190	5.1	1 612	5.3	1 623	7.7	1 723	5.9	456	6.2
Pratt	44 958	.9	4 447	4.2	2 891	1.6	3 349	2.6	620	3.3
Rawlins	3 548	7.9	1 628	6.7	1 007	9.4	2 330	7.0	447	6.4
Reno	17 666	2.1	4 932	5.8	4 077	6.1	4 373	2.7	1 010	7.9
Republic	40 424	.5	4 160	3.8	2 379	1.8	3 284	3.4	713	4.2
Rice	25 674	.8	2 505	4.4	2 694	5.9	2 451	3.7	681	2.8
Riley	4 343	10.3	1 106	6.1	1 301	3.9	1 052	4.4	249	5.4
Rooks	2 692	8.0	1 194	7.8	990	7.6	1 597	6.2	291	8.2
Rush	1 757	18.6	1 079	7.2	767	8.9	1 684	7.2	199	8.9
Russell	2 330	8.4	960	8.4	676	13.8	1 441	10.6	177	11.1
Saline	4 599	12.4	1 705	4.5	1 626	12.1	1 858	4.0	434	3.8
Scott	162 111	.4	1 515	3.7	8 789	.2	3 468	3.5	1 187	2.8
Sedgwick	6 495	4.4	4 291	3.9	3 391	2.8	3 973	2.7	1 198	5.1
Seward	73 731	.3	1 879	5.5	6 085	.6	2 713	6.8	1 507	7.0
Shawnee	2 487	8.5	1 180	7.8	810	11.4	1 197	4.4	290	8.8
Sheridan	15 292	2.2	2 081	4.5	1 887	9.4	3 214	3.5	680	3.0
Sherman	21 049	1.0	2 726	3.6	2 384	1.2	4 092	4.8	670	5.3
Smith	8 963	3.7	2 537	6.4	2 075	7.4	2 510	5.5	493	5.3
Stafford	26 390	2.6	4 002	3.8	2 084	3.2	2 928	3.4	726	6.1
Stanton	36 650	.4	2 553	4.7	5 152	2.6	3 627	5.1	875	5.9
Stevens	48 263	1.2	3 060	4.8	3 349	5.4	3 632	2.5	645	2.5
Sumner	7 786	6.9	4 759	4.0	1 956	3.2	4 601	3.5	647	6.1
Thomas	22 468	1.2	2 913	4.3	3 475	3.4	3 979	3.7	807	5.4
Trego	11 277	1.4	964	7.4	799	7.8	1 641	5.2	297	6.0
Wabaunsee	9 524	8.4	1 069	8.7	1 656	5.3	1 290	6.9	418	4.5
Wallace	4 936	2.6	1 507	8.7	1 147	6.9	2 510	6.9	395	4.6
Washington	10 678	3.9	3 541	4.0	2 407	4.9	2 948	4.7	919	4.6
Wichita	126 432	.2	1 426	4.8	4 739	.8	3 814	4.4	1 190	4.7
Wilson	1 883	18.7	1 832	7.6	419	5.5	1 422	5.5	241	9.6
Woodson	5 255	6.1	814	11.4	(D)	(D)	778	4.6	(D)	(D)
Wyandotte	(D)	(D)	225	6.8	765	13.3	373	8.7	(D)	(D)

[1]Data are based on a sample of farms.

Table G. **State Coverage Evaluation Estimates of Farms Not on the Mail List: 1987**

[Data are based on a sample of farms; see text. For meaning of abbreviations and symbols, see introductory text]

Item	Not on mail list		Percent not on mail list	
	Total number	Relative standard error of estimate (percent)	Total percent	Standard error of percent
Farms --- number..	1 882	4.7	2.7	.1
Land in farms --acres..	103 657	46.9	.2	.1
Farms by size:				
Less than 50 acres --- farms..	1 411	5.9	12.5	.7
50 acres or more -- farms..	471	8.2	.8	.1
Harvested cropland -- farms..	726	49.0	1.2	.6
acres..	41 882	60.3	.2	.2
Farms by value of sales:				
Less than $2,500 --- farms..	1 411	5.9	12.9	.8
$2,500 or more -- farms..	471	8.2	.8	.1
$2,500 to $9,999 --- farms..	(S)	(S)	(S)	(S)
$10,000 or more -- farms..	(S)	(S)	(S)	(S)
Market value of agricultural products sold ------------------------ $1,000..	6 556	53.2	.1	.
Farms by standard industrial classification:				
Crops (01) --- farms..	-	-	-	-
Livestock (02) --- farms..	1 882	4.7	5.4	.3
Farms by tenure of operator:				
Full owners --- farms..	1 882	4.7	5.9	.3
Part owners and tenants ------------------------------------- farms..	-	-	-	-
Operators by principal occupation:				
Farming -- farms..	509	1.6	1.2	(Z)
Other --- farms..	1 373	5.9	5.0	.3
Average age of operator --years..	38.3	(Z)	(X)	(X)

Note 1: Farms classified as nonfarms, nonfarms classified as farms, and farms appearing more than once in the census are not accounted for in these estimates, but will be provided in the 1987 Coverage Evaluation publication. See appendix C for further explanation.

Note 2: Detail may not add to total due to rounding.

APPENDIX D.
Report Form and Information Sheet

DUE BY FEBRUARY 1, 1988

FORM 87-A0202 (8-30-86)

U.S. DEPARTMENT OF COMMERCE
BUREAU OF THE CENSUS

UNITED STATES CENSUS OF AGRICULTURE

AG CENSUS USA

BUREAU OF THE CENSUS
1201 East Tenth Street
Jeffersonville, IN 47133

OMB No. 0607-0534 Approval Expires September 30, 1989

NOTICE — Response to this inquiry is required by law (title 13, U.S. Code). By the same law YOUR REPORT TO THE CENSUS BUREAU IS CONFIDENTIAL. It may be seen only by sworn Census employees and may be used only for statistical purposes. Your report CANNOT be used for purposes of taxation, investigation, or regulation. The law also provides that copies retained in your files are immune from legal process.

In correspondence pertaining to this report, please refer to your Census File Number (CFN)

87-A0202

Please complete this form and RETURN TO:

Note — If your records are not available, reasonable estimates may be used. If you cannot file by February 1, a time extension request may be sent to the above address. Include your 12-character Census File Number (CFN) as shown in your address label in all correspondence to us.

If you received more than one report form, enter extra Census File Number(s) here and return extra copies with your completed report.

A | | | | | — | | | |
A | | | | | — | | | |

CENSUS USE ONLY

035 | 036 | 037 | 038
039 | 040 | 041 | 042

Please correct errors in name, address, and ZIP Code. ENTER street and number if not shown.

SECTION 1 — **ACREAGE IN 1987** Report land owned, rented, or used by you, your spouse, or by the partnership, corporation, or organization for which you are reporting. Include ALL LAND, REGARDLESS OF LOCATION OR USE — cropland, pastureland, rangeland, woodland, idle land, house lots, etc.

If the acres you operated in 1987 changed during the year, refer to the INFORMATION SHEET, section 1.

	None	Number of acres
1. All land owned	☐	043
2. All land rented or leased FROM OTHERS, including land worked by you on shares, used rent free, in exchange for services, payment of taxes, etc. Include leased Federal, State, and railroad land. (DO NOT include land used on a per-head basis under a grazing permit.) Also complete item 5 below.	☐	044
3. All land rented or leased TO OTHERS, including land worked on shares by others and land subleased. Also complete item 6 below.	☐	045
4. **Acres in "THIS PLACE"** — ADD acres owned (item 1) and acres rented (item 2), then SUBTRACT acres rented TO OTHERS (item 3), and enter the result in this space.		046

For this census report these are the acres in "THIS PLACE." If the entry is zero please refer to the INFORMATION SHEET, section 1.

5. If you rented land FROM OTHERS (item 2), enter the following information for each landlord.

Name of landlord	Mailing address (include ZIP Code)	Number of acres

List additional landlords on a separate sheet of paper.

6. If you rented land TO OTHERS (item 3), enter the following information for each renter.

Name of renter	Mailing address (include ZIP Code)	Number of acres

List additional renters on a separate sheet of paper.

a. Of the land you rented or leased to others, how many acres did you own? .... None ☐ 053 ____ Acres

7. Did you have any grazing permits on a per-head basis?
054
1 ☐ Yes — Mark (X) all boxes which apply
2 ☐ No — Go to item 8

3 ☐ Forest Service
4 ☐ Taylor Grazing Sec. 3 (BLM)
5 ☐ Indian Land
6 ☐ Other — Specify

8. LOCATION OF AGRICULTURAL ACTIVITY FOR "THIS PLACE"

a. In what county was the largest value of your agricultural products raised or produced?

	County name	State	Number of acres
Principal county			056

b. If you also had agricultural operations in any other county(ies), enter the county name(s), etc.

	County name	State	Number of acres
Other counties			057
			058
			059

PENALTY FOR FAILURE TO REPORT

INSTRUCTIONS — Please report your crops in the appropriate section. Use section 7 to report ONLY those CROPS NOT listed in sections 2 through 6 and section 8. DO NOT INCLUDE crops grown on land rented to others.

SECTION 2 — Were any of the following CROPS harvested from "THIS PLACE" in 1987?

	None	Acres harvested	Quantity harvested	Acres irrigated
1. Corn (field) for grain or seed (Report quantity on a dry shelled-weight basis.)	☐	067	068 Bu.	069
2. Corn (field) for silage or green chop	☐	070	071 Tons, green	072
3. Soybeans for beans	☐	088	089 Bu.	090
4. Beans, dry edible	☐	554	555 Cwt.	556
5. Wheat for grain	☐	073	074 Bu.	075
6. Oats for grain	☐	076	077 Bu.	078
7. Barley for grain	☐	079	080 Bu.	081
8. Rye for grain	☐	688	687 Bu.	688
9. Sorghum for grain or seed (including milo)	☐	082	083 T --- OR --- Bu. Cwt.	084
10. Sorghum for silage or green chop (Do not include sorghum-sudan crosses.)	☐	085	086 Tons, green	087
11. Popcorn	☐	662	663 Lbs., shelled	664
12. Tobacco — all types	☐	094 /10	095 Lbs.	096 /10
13. Potatoes, Irish	☐	097 /10	098 Cwt.	099 /10

SECTION 3 — Was any DRY HAY, GRASS SILAGE, HAYLAGE, or GREEN CHOP cut or harvested from "THIS PLACE" in 1987?

Include sorghum-sudan crosses and hay cut from pastures.

53 ☐ 1 ☐ YES — Complete this section ☐ 2 ☐ NO — Go to section 4

If cuttings were made for both dry hay and grass silage, haylage, or green chop from the same acres, report the acreage in the appropriate items under DRY HAY and also under GRASS SILAGE, HAYLAGE, and GREEN CHOP.

		Acres harvested	Quantity harvested (Report either dry or green weight as indicated.)	Acres irrigated
1. **DRY HAY** (If two or more cuttings of dry hay were made from the same acres, report acres only once, but report total tons from all cuttings.)				
a. Alfalfa and alfalfa mixtures for hay or dehydrating		103	104 Tons, dry	105
b. Small grain hay — oats, wheat, barley, rye, etc.		106	107 Tons, dry	108
c. Other tame dry hay — clover, lespedeza, timothy, bromegrass, Sudangrass, millet, etc.		109	110 Tons, dry	111
d. Wild hay		112	113 Tons, dry	114
2. **GRASS SILAGE, HAYLAGE, AND GREEN CHOP** (If two or more cuttings were made from the same acres, report acres only once, but report total tons from all cuttings.)		115	116 Tons, green	117
3. **HAY SOLD** — Did you sell any hay or grass silage in 1987? (Report value of hay sold in section 8, item 4)	118		1 ☐ Yes	2 ☐ No

---

SECTION 4 — Were any VEGETABLES, SWEET CORN, MELONS, etc., harvested FOR SALE from "THIS PLACE" in 1987? (Do not include those grown for home use.)

54
1 ☐ YES — Complete this section
2 ☐ NO — Go to section 5

	Acres		Acres irrigated	
	Whole acres	Tenths	Whole acres	Tenths
1. Land from which vegetables were harvested in 1987	375 /10		376 /10	

2. From the list below, enter the crop name and code for each crop harvested in 1987. If more than one vegetable crop was harvested from the same acres, report acres for each crop. Report crops grown under protection in section 5.

Crop name	Code	Acres harvested		Acres irrigated	
Sweet corn	461	/10	482		/10
Tomatoes	463	/10	484		/10
		/10			/10
		/10			/10
		/10			/10
		/10			/10

If more space is needed, use a separate sheet of paper.

Crop name	Code	Crop name	Code	Crop name	Code
Asparagus	379	Eggplant	415	Peppers, hot	445
Beans, snap (bush and pole)	381	Honeydew melons	423	Pumpkins	449
Beets	383	Kale	425	Radishes	451
Broccoli	385	Lettuce and romaine	427	Spinach	457
Cabbage, head	391	Lima beans, green	429	Squash	459
Cantaloups and muskmelons	395	Mustard greens	431	Turnips	465
		Onions, dry	433	Turnip greens	467
Carrots	397	Onions, green	435	Watermelons	473
Cauliflower	399	Okra	437	Other vegetables —	
Celery	401	Parsley	439	Specify	475
Collards	407	Peas, green	441		
Cucumbers and pickles	411	Peppers, sweet	442		

SECTION 5 — Were any NURSERY and GREENHOUSE CROPS, MUSHROOMS, sod, bulbs, flowers, flower seeds, vegetable seeds and plants, vegetables under glass or other protection, GROWN FOR SALE on "THIS PLACE" in 1987?

55
1 ☐ YES — Complete this section
2 ☐ NO — Go to section 6

		Area Irrigated		
	None	Square feet	Acres	Tenths
1. Nursery and greenhouse crops irrigated in 1987 . . ☐		477	478	/10

2. From the list below, enter the crop name and code for each crop grown.

Crop name	Code	Square feet under glass or other protection in 1987	Acres in the open in 1987		Sales in 1987	
			Whole acres	Tenths	Dollars	Cents
				/10		00
				/10		00
				/10		00

If more space is needed, use a separate sheet of paper.

Crop name	Code	Crop name	Code
Bedding plants (include vegetable plants)	479	Potted flowering plants	710
Bulbs (Exclude bulb flowering plants)	482	Mushrooms	484
Cut flowers and cut florist greens	485	Sod harvested	487
Nursery crops — ornamentals, fruit and nut trees, and vines	488	Vegetable and flower seeds	500
		Greenhouse vegetables	503
Foliage plants	707	Other — Specify	506

SECTION 6 — Were any STRAWBERRIES or OTHER BERRIES harvested FOR SALE from "THIS PLACE" in 1987? (Do not include those grown for home use.)

56
1 ☐ YES — Complete this section
2 ☐ NO — Go to section 7

Crop name	Code	Acres harvested		Quantity harvested		Acres irrigated	
		Whole acres	Tenths			Whole acres	Tenths
Strawberries	536		/10	537 Lbs.		538	/10
Blackberries	509		/10	510 Lbs.		511	/10
Blueberries, tame	512		/10	513 Lbs.		514	/10
Raspberries	533		/10	534 Lbs.		535	/10
Other berries — Specify	539		/10	540 Lbs.		541	/10

If more space is needed, use a separate sheet of paper.

SECTION 7 — Were any OTHER CROPS harvested from "THIS PLACE" in 1987 — small grains, field seeds, sugar beets, sunflowers, mint, or other crops not previously reported? (Report fruit in section 8.)

57
1 ☐ YES — Complete this section
2 ☐ NO — Go to section 8

For those crops not listed enter the crop name and code from the list below. Report quantity harvested in unit specified with crop name.

Crop name	Code	Acres harvested	Quantity harvested	Acres irrigated
Sugar beets for sugar	719		720 Tons	721
Alfalfa seed	542		542 Lbs.	544
Red clover seed	671		672 Lbs.	673
Sorghum cut for dry forage or hay	698		699 Tons, dry	700
Sunflower seed	734		735 Lbs.	736
Proso millet	665		666 Bu.	667
Mint for oil	644		645 Lbs. of oil	646

If more space is needed, use a separate sheet of paper.

Crop name	Code	Crop name	Code
Bromegrass seed (pounds)	669	Redtop seed (pounds)	674
Buckwheat (bushels)	575	Sorghum hogged or grazed (report acres only)	701
Corn cut for dry fodder, hogged or grazed (report acres only)	581	Sweetclover seed (pounds)	737
Cotton (bales)	091	Timothy seed (pounds)	745
Emmer and spelt (bushels)	589	Triticale (bushels)	749
Fescue seed (pounds)	602	Vetch seed (pounds)	755
Grains, mixed (bushels)	614	Other crops (pounds) — Specify	752
Lespedeza seed (pounds)	638		

SECTION 8 — Was there a combined total of 20 or more FRUIT TREES, including GRAPEVINES and NUT TREES, on "THIS PLACE" in 1987?

58
1 ☐ YES — Complete this section
2 ☐ NO — Go to section 9

	Total acres		Acres irrigated	
	Whole acres	Tenths	Whole acres	Tenths
1. TOTAL ACRES in bearing and nonbearing fruit orchards, vineyards, and nut trees on this place. (Do not include abandoned acres.)	131 /10		132 /10	

2. For those crops not listed below, enter the name and code from the list at the right for other fruit and nut trees on this place in 1987. Report the requested information for each crop even if not harvested because of low prices, damage from hail, frost, etc.

Crop name	Code	NUMBER OF TREES OR VINES OF —		Acres in trees and vines of all ages		Quantity harvested	Unit of measure Mark one			
		Nonbearing age	Bearing age	Whole acres	Tenths		Lbs.	Tons	Boxes	Lbs. per box
Apples	123	124	125		/10	126	137 1☐ 2☐ 3☐			138
Peaches	225	226	227		/10	228	229 1☐ 2☐ 3☐			230
Grapes	177	178	179		/10	180	181 1☐ 2☐ 3☐			182
		1	2		/10	3	1☐ 2☐ 3☐			
		1	2		/10	3	1☐ 2☐ 3☐			
		1	2		/10	3	4 1☐ 2☐ 3☐			

Crop name	Code
Apricots	129
Cherries	047
Nectarines	201
Pears	231
Persimmons	237
Plums and prunes	243
Pecans	339
Other fruit and nuts — Specify	369

If more space is needed, use a separate sheet of paper.

FORM 87-A0202 (9-30-86)

Page 2

SECTION 9 — GROSS VALUE of CROPS SOLD from "THIS PLACE" in 1987, BEFORE taxes and expenses (Refer to the INFORMATION SHEET, section 9.)

Report your best estimate of the value for each of the following groups of crops sold from this place in 1987. Include the value of the landlord's and/or contractor's share, estimating if necessary. Include value of Government CCC loans.

	None	Dollars	Cents
1. Grains, soybeans and other beans sold in 1987		773	
a. Corn for grain	☐	9	00
b. Wheat	☐	774 9	00
c. Soybeans	☐	775 9	00
d. Sorghum for grain	☐	776 9	00
e. Barley	☐	777 9	00
f. Oats	☐	778 9	00
g. Other — rye, dry edible beans, sunflower seed, popcorn, proso millet, etc.	☐	779 9	00
2. Cotton and cottonseed	☐	780 9	00
3. Tobacco	☐	781 9	00
4. Hay, silage, field seeds, and grass seeds	☐	782 9	00
5. Vegetables, sweet corn, and melons — (Do not include Irish potatoes and sweetpotatoes, report them in item 7 below.)	☐	783 9	00
6. Fruits, nuts, and berries — apples, peaches, strawberries, etc.	☐	784 9	00
7. Other crops — potatoes, mint for oil, sugar beets, etc. (Do not include nursery and greenhouse crops.) —		785 9	
Specify	☐	9	00

SECTION 10 — How were the ACRES in this place USED in 1987?

1. Copy acres in "THIS PLACE" from section 1, item 4, page 1 _____ Acres

NOTE: For items 2 to 5 below, if land was used for more than one purpose in 1987 report it in the FIRST land use listed below that applies. For example, report cropland harvested and also pastured, only as "Cropland harvested."

2. CROPLAND	None	Number of acres
a. Cropland harvested — Include all land from which crops were harvested or hay was cut, and all land in orchards, citrus groves, vineyards, and nursery and greenhouse crops.	☐	787 9
b. Cropland used only for pasture or grazing — Include rotation pasture and grazing land that could have been used for crops without additional improvements.	☐	788 9
c. Cropland used for cover crops, legumes, and soil-improvement grasses, but NOT harvested and NOT pastured	☐	789 9
d. Cropland on which all crops failed — (Exception: Do not report here land in orchards and vineyards on which the crop failed. Such acreage is to be reported in item 2a.)	☐	790 9
e. Cropland in cultivated summer fallow	☐	791 9
f. Cropland idle	☐	793 9
3. Woodland — Include all {a. Woodland pastured woodlots and timber tracts and cutover and deforested land with young timber growth. {b. Woodland not pastured	☐ ☐	794 9 795 9
4. Other pastureland and rangeland — Include any pastureland other than cropland and woodland pasture.	☐	796 9
5. All other land — Land in house lots, ponds, roads, wasteland, etc. — Include any land not reported in items 2 through 4 above.	☐	797 9
6. TOTAL ACRES — Add the acres reported in items 2 through 5 (Should be the same as item 1 above.)		798 9

SECTION 11 — Was any LAND in this place IRRIGATED at any time in 1987?

Irrigated land is all land watered by any artificial or controlled means — sprinklers, furrows or ditches, spreader dikes, etc. Include supplemental, partial, and preplant irrigation.

511
1 ☐ YES — Complete this section
2 ☐ NO — Go to section 12

	None	Number of acres irrigated
1. How many acres of harvested land were irrigated? Include land from which hay was cut and land in bearing and nonbearing fruit and nut crops reported in section 10, item 2a.	☐	880
2. How many acres of pastureland, rangeland, and any other lands not included in item 1 above were irrigated?	☐	881

SECTION 12 — Were any ACRES in this place SET ASIDE, DIVERTED, OR IDLED under FEDERAL acreage reduction programs in 1987?

512
1 ☐ YES — Complete this section
2 ☐ NO — Go to section 13

	None	Number of acres
1. How many acres were set aside (or diverted) under ANNUAL commodity acreage adjustment programs?	☐	882
2. How many acres were under the CONSERVATION RESERVE PROGRAM (10 year, CRP)?	☐	883

FORM 87-A0202 (9-20-86)

SECTION 13 — Did you or anyone else have any CATTLE or CALVES on this place in 1987?

513
1 ☐ YES — Complete this section
2 ☐ NO — Go to section 14

• DECEMBER 31, 1987 INVENTORY	None	INVENTORY Number on this place Dec. 31, 1987
1. CATTLE AND CALVES of all ages (Total of a, b, c, and d below)	☐	803 Total
a. BEEF COWS — Include beef heifers that had calved.	☐	804 Beef cows
b. MILK COWS kept for production of milk or cream for sale or home use — Include dry milk cows and milk heifers that had calved.	☐	805 Milk cows
c. HEIFERS AND HEIFER CALVES — (Do not include heifers that had calved.)	☐	806 Heifers and heifer calves
d. STEERS, STEER CALVES, BULLS, AND BULL CALVES	☐	807 Steers and bulls of all ages

• CATTLE AND CALVES SOLD FROM THIS PLACE IN 1987 Include those fed on this place on a contract or custom basis. Also report as sold cattle moved from this place to a feedlot for further feeding.	None	Number sold in 1987	Gross value of sales Dollars	Cents
2. Calves weighing less than 500 pounds	☐	808	809 9	00
3. Cattle, including calves weighing 500 pounds or more	☐	810	811 9	00
a. Of the total cattle sold, how many were FATTENED on this place on GRAIN or CONCENTRATES for 30 days or more and SOLD for SLAUGHTER?	☐	812	813 9	00

• DAIRY PRODUCTS SOLD FROM THIS PLACE IN 1987	None	DAIRY PRODUCTS Gross value of sales Dollars	Cents
4. Gross value of sales of DAIRY PRODUCTS from this place in 1987 — Include milk, cream, butter, etc.	☐	6	00

SECTION 14 — Did you or anyone else have any HOGS or PIGS on this place in 1987?

514
1 ☐ YES — Complete this section
2 ☐ NO — Go to section 15

• DECEMBER 31, 1987 INVENTORY	None	INVENTORY Number on this place Dec. 31, 1987
1. HOGS and PIGS of all ages (Total of a and b below)	☐	815 Total
a. HOGS and PIGS used or to be used for BREEDING	☐	816 Breeding
b. OTHER HOGS and PIGS	☐	817 Other

• LITTERS FARROWED	None	Number of litters
2. LITTERS FARROWED on this place between —		
a. December 1, 1986 and May 31, 1987	☐	818
b. June 1, 1987 and November 30, 1987	☐	819

• HOGS AND PIGS SOLD	None	Number sold in 1987	Gross value of sales Dollars	Cents
3. HOGS and PIGS SOLD from this place in 1987	☐	820	821 9	00
4. Of the hogs and pigs sold, how many were sold as FEEDER PIGS for further feeding?	☐	822	823 9	00

SECTION 15 — Did you or anyone else have any SHEEP or LAMBS on this place in 1987?

515
1 ☐ YES — Complete this section
2 ☐ NO — Go to section 16

	None	INVENTORY Number on this place Dec. 31, 1987
1. SHEEP and LAMBS of all ages	☐	824
a. EWES 1 year old or older	☐	826

	None	Number shorn in 1987	Pounds of wool shorn in 1987
2. SHEEP and LAMBS SHORN	☐	827	

	None	Gross value of sales Dollars	Cents
3. What was the gross value of sales of SHEEP, LAMBS, and WOOL from this place in 1987?	☐	829 9	00

Page 3

SECTION 16 — Did you or anyone else have any HORSES, BEES, FISH, GOATS, OTHER LIVESTOCK, or ANIMAL SPECIALTIES on this place in 1987?

616 1 ☐ YES — Complete this section   2 ☐ NO — Go to section 17

	None	INVENTORY Number on this place Dec. 31, 1987	Total quantity sold in 1987	Gross value of sales	
				Dollars	Cents
1. Horses and ponies of all ages	☐	830	831 Number	832 $	00
2. Colonies of bees	☐	839	840 Number / 841 Pounds honey	842 $	00
3. Milk goats	☐	843	844 / 845 Gallons milk	846 $	00
4. Angora goats	☐	847	848 Number / 849 Pounds mohair	850 $	00
5. Other goats	☐	851	852 Number	853 $	00
6. Mules, burros, and donkeys	☐	833	834 Number	835 $	00
7. Mink and their pelts	☐	836	837 Number	838 $	00
8. Rabbits and their pelts	☐	854	855 Number	856 $	00
9. All other livestock and livestock products Specify _____	☐	857	858 Number	859 $	00

10. Fish and other aquaculture products (Enter name and code from list below.) Name _____ Code _____	Total quantity sold in 1987	Gross value of sales	
		Dollars	Cents
— OR —	860 Pounds / Number	2 $	00

Name	Code	Name	Code
Catfish	860	Other fish — Specify	866
Trout	863	Other aquaculture products — Specify	869

If more space is needed, use a separate sheet of paper.

SECTION 17 — Did you or anyone else have any POULTRY, such as CHICKENS, TURKEYS, DUCKS, etc., on this place in 1987? — Include poultry grown for others on a contract basis.

617 1 ☐ YES — Complete this section   2 ☐ NO — Go to section 18

		INVENTORY Number on this place Dec. 31, 1987	Total number sold in 1987
1. HENS and PULLETS of laying age	☐	892	893
2. PULLETS for laying flock replacement			
a. PULLETS 3 months old or older not yet of laying age	☐	894	895
b. PULLET CHICKS and PULLETS under 3 months old (Do not include commercial broilers.)	☐	896	
3. BROILERS, fryers, and other meat-type chickens including capons and roasters	☐	898	899
4. TURKEYS			
a. Turkeys for slaughter (Do not include breeders.)	☐	900	901
b. Turkey HENS kept for breeding	☐	902	903

5. OTHER POULTRY raised in captivity — ducks, geese, pigeons or squab, pheasants, quail, etc. (Enter poultry name and code from list below.)

Poultry name _____ Code _____

Poultry name _____ Code _____

Name	Code	Name	Code	Name	Code
Ducks	904	Pigeons or squab	908	Quail	912
Geese	905	Pheasants	910	All other poultry — Specify	914

6. POULTRY HATCHED on this place in 1987 and placed or sold — chickens, turkeys, ducks, etc. — Specify kind of poultry _____	None ☐	Number 916

7. Incubator egg capacity on December 31, 1987 . . ☐   917

8. What was the gross value of sales of poultry and poultry products (eggs, etc.) from this place in 1987?	None ☐	Gross value of sales	
		Dollars	Cents
		918 $	00

Form 87-A0202 (2-20-86)   Page 4

SECTION 18 — GOVERNMENT CCC LOANS
818

1. Amount received in 1987 from Government CCC loans for — Include regular and reserve loans, even if redeemed or forfeited.	None	Dollars	Cents
a. Corn	☐	866 $	00
b. Wheat	☐	867 $	00
c. Soybeans	☐	888 $	00
d. Sorghum, barley, and oats	☐	889 $	00
e. Cotton	☐	890 $	00
f. Tobacco, rye, and honey	☐	891 $	00

SECTION 19 — Payments received for participation in FEDERAL FARM PROGRAMS in 1987 (DO NOT INCLUDE CCC loans.) Refer to INFORMATION SHEET, section 19.

	None	Dollars	Cents
1. Amount received in cash	☐	884 $	00
2. Value of certificates received — payment-in-kind (PIK) or commodity certificates	☐	885 $	00

SECTION 20 — TYPE OF ORGANIZATION
820

Mark (X) the one item which best describes the type of organization for this place in 1987. Refer to the INFORMATION SHEET, section 20.

821
- FAMILY or INDIVIDUAL operation — (Do not include partnership and corporation.) . . . . 1 ☐
- PARTNERSHIP operation — Include family partnerships. . . . . 2 ☐   } Go to section 22
- INCORPORATED UNDER STATE LAW . . . . 3 ☐   Go to section 21
- OTHER, such as estate or trust, prison farm, grazing association, Indian reservation, etc. . . . . 4 ☐   Specify below then go to section 22

Specify _____

SECTION 21 — CORPORATE STRUCTURE (for incorporated operations only) Refer to the INFORMATION SHEET, section 21.

		821		822	
1. Is this a family-held corporation?		1 ☐ Yes	2 ☐ No		
2. Are there more than 10 stockholders?		3 ☐ Yes	4 ☐ No		

SECTION 22 — CHARACTERISTICS AND OCCUPATION OF OPERATOR (Senior partner or person in charge) Refer to the INFORMATION SHEET, section 22.

822
1. RESIDENCE — Does the operator (senior partner or person in charge) live on this place? . . . . 1 ☐ Yes   2 ☐ No

823
2. PRINCIPAL OCCUPATION — At which occupation did the operator spend the majority (50 percent or more) of his/her worktime in 1987? For partnerships consider all members of the partnership together. . . . . 1 ☐ Farming or ranching   2 ☐ Other

3. OFF-FARM WORK — How many days did the operator (senior partner or person in charge) work at least 4 hours per day off this place in 1987? — Include work at a nonfarm job, business, or on someone else's farm for pay. (Do not include exchange farmwork.) . . . .
- 1 ☐ None
- 2 ☐ 1—49 days
- 3 ☐ 50—99 days
- 4 ☐ 100—149 days
- 5 ☐ 150—199 days
- 6 ☐ 200 days or more

4. In what YEAR did the operator (or senior partner) begin to operate any part of this place? . . . . 080 _____ Year

5. AGE of operator (senior partner or person in charge) . . . 925 _____ Years old

924
6. RACE of operator (senior partner or person in charge) . .
- 1 ☐ White
- 2 ☐ Negro or Black
- 3 ☐ American Indian
- 4 ☐ Asian or Pacific Islander
- 5 ☐ Other — Specify

7. SEX of operator (senior partner or person in charge) . . . 926 1 ☐ Male   2 ☐ Female

8. SPANISH ORIGIN — Is the operator (senior partner or person in charge) of Spanish origin or descent (Mexican, Puerto Rican, Cuban, or other Spanish)? . . . . 927 1 ☐ Yes   2 ☐ No

Page 5

SECTION 23 — **PRODUCTION EXPENSES** paid by you and others for this place in 1987

823

Include your best estimates of expenses paid by you, your landlord, contractors, buyers, and others for production of crops, livestock, and other agricultural products in 1987. (DO NOT INCLUDE expenses connected with performing customwork for others; operation of nonfarm activities, businesses, or services; or household expenses not related to the farm business.)

	None	Dollars	Cents
1. **Livestock and poultry purchased** — cattle, calves, hogs, pigs, sheep, lambs, goats, horses, chicks, poults, started pullets, etc.	☐	871	00
2. **Feed purchased for livestock and poultry** — grain, hay, silage, mixed feeds, concentrates, etc.	☐	872	00
a. Commercially mixed formula feeds purchased — complete, supplement, concentrates, premixes.			

(Do not include ingredients purchased separately, such as soybean meal, cottonseed meal, and urea.)

	None	Dollars	Cents
	☐	873	00

	None	Dollars	Cents
3. **Seed cost** — for corn, other grains, soybeans, tobacco, cotton, etc. — Include plants and trees purchased.	☐	874	00
4. **Commercial fertilizer purchased** — all forms, including rock phosphate and gypsum. Include cost of custom applications.	☐	875	00
5. **Agricultural chemicals purchased** — Insecticides, herbicides, fungicides, other pesticides, etc. — Include cost of custom applications. (Do not include lime.)	☐	876	00
6. **Gasoline and other petroleum fuel and oil** purchased for the farm business —			
a. Gasoline and gasohol	☐	877	00
b. Diesel fuel	☐	878	00
c. Natural gas	☐	879	00
d. LP gas, fuel oil, kerosene, motor oil, grease, etc.	☐	880	00
7. **Electricity for the farm business** — (Do not include household expenses.)	☐	881	00
8. **Hired farm and ranch labor** — also include employer's cost for social security, workman's compensation, insurance premiums, pension plans, etc. (See INFORMATION SHEET)	☐	882	00
9. **Contract labor** — Include expenditures for labor, such as harvesting of fruit, vegetables, berries, etc., performed on a contract basis by a contractor, crew leader, a cooperative, etc.	☐	883	00
10. **Repair and maintenance expenses for the upkeep of buildings, motor vehicles, and farm equipment**	☐	884	00
11. **Customwork, machine hire and rental of machinery and equipment** — Include expenditures for use of equipment and for customwork such as grinding and mixing feed, plowing, combining, corn picking, drying, silo filling, spraying, dusting, fertilizing, etc. (Do not include cost of cotton ginning and application of fertilizer and chemicals.)	☐	885	00
12. **Interest paid on debts** — (See INFORMATION SHEET)			
a. Secured by real estate	☐	886	00
b. Not secured by real estate	☐	887	00
13. **Cash rent paid for land and buildings in 1987** — (Do not include grazing fees.)	☐	888	00
14. **Property taxes paid** — Include farm real estate, machinery, livestock, etc. for the farm business. (Do not include taxes paid by landlords.)	☐	889	00
15. **All other production expenses** — Include insurance, water, animal health costs, grazing fees, marketing charges, miscellaneous farm supplies, etc. (Do not include depreciation, household expenses, and expenses not associated with the farm business.)	☐	890	00

SECTION 24 — Was any COMMERCIAL FERTILIZER, including ROCK PHOSPHATE, or LIME used on this place during 1987?

824

1 ☐ YES — Complete this section   2 ☐ NO — Go to section 25

	None	Acres fertilized
1. Acres of cropland fertilized in 1987 — (Do not include cropland for pastures reported in section 10, item 2b.)	☐	932
2. Acres of pastureland and rangeland fertilized in 1987 reported in section 10, items 2b and 4	☐	933

	None	Tons of lime	Acres limed
3. LIME — tons of lime used and acres on which applied — (Do not include land plaster or gypsum or lime for sanitation.)	☐	934	935

FORM 87-A0202 (6-20-86)

SECTION 25 — Were any INSECTICIDES, HERBICIDES, FUNGICIDES, NEMATICIDES, OTHER PESTICIDES, or OTHER CHEMICALS used on this place in 1987?

825

1 ☐ YES — Complete this section   2 ☐ NO — Go to section 26

Include any materials provided by you, your landlords, or contractors. For each item listed, report acres only once. If multipurpose chemicals were used, report acreage treated for each purpose.

	None	Acres on which used
1. Sprays, dusts, granules, fumigants, etc., (fungicide, herbicide, insecticide, nematicide) to control —		
a. Insects on crops, including hay	☐	936
b. Nematodes in crops	☐	937
c. Diseases in crops and orchards (blights, smuts, rusts, etc.)	☐	938
d. Weeds, grass, or brush in crops and pasture — Include both pre-emergence and post emergence.	☐	939
2. Chemicals for defoliation or for growth control of crops or thinning of fruit	☐	940

SECTION 26 — MACHINERY AND EQUIPMENT on this place on December 31, 1987 — Include only equipment used for agricultural operations in 1986 or 1987.

826

• Value of ALL machinery and equipment on this place, December 31, 1987

		Estimated market value
		Dollars	Cents
1. What is the estimated market value of ALL machinery, equipment, and implements usually kept on this place and used for the farm or ranch business? — Include cars, trucks, tractors, combines, plows, disks, harrows, dryers, pumps, motors, irrigation equipment, dairy equipment including milkers and bulk tanks, livestock feeders, grinding and mixing equipment, etc.	943		00

• SELECTED machinery and equipment on this place, December 31, 1987. (Report only if used in 1986 or 1987.)	None	Total number on this place on December 31, 1987	Of the total, HOW MANY were manufactured in the last 5 years (1983-1987)?
2. Motortrucks — Include pickups	☐	944	945
3. Wheel tractors other than garden tractors and motor tillers —			
a. Less than 40 horsepower (PTO)	☐	946	947
b. 40 horsepower (PTO) or more	☐	948	949
4. Grain and bean combines, all types	☐	950	951
5. Cotton pickers and strippers	☐	956	957
6. Mower conditioners	☐	958	959
7. Pickup balers — Include rectangle and round balers	☐	960	961

SECTION 27 — ESTIMATED CURRENT MARKET VALUE OF LAND and BUILDINGS

827

Please give your best ESTIMATE of the CURRENT MARKET VALUE of land and buildings for all acres reported in section 1, items 1, 2, and 3, page 1.

	None	Estimated market value of land and buildings
		Dollars	Cents
1. All land owned	☐	996	00
2. All land rented or leased FROM OTHERS	☐	997	00
3. All land rented or leased TO OTHERS	☐	998	00

SECTION 28 — INCOME FROM FARM-RELATED SOURCES IN 1987 — Report amount received before taxes and expenses.

828

	None	Farm-related income
		Dollars	Cents
1. Customwork and other agricultural services provided for farmers and others — plowing, planting, spraying, harvesting, preparation of products for market, etc. (If customwork is a separate business, refer to INFORMATION SHEET, section 28)	☐	992	00
2. Gross cash rent or share payments received from renting out farmland or payments received from lease or sale of allotments — Include payments for livestock pastured on a per-head basis, per-month basis, per-pound basis, etc.	☐	993	00
3. Sales of forest products and Christmas trees — Include maple products, naval stores, firewood, etc.	☐	994	00
4. Recreational services, patronage dividends of cooperatives, and other income which is CLOSELY RELATED to the agricultural operation on this place – Specify	☐	995	00

SECTION 29 — PERSON COMPLETING THIS REPORT — Please print

Name _____ 999 Date _____

Telephone number | Area Code | Number

INFORMATION SHEET

U.S. DEPARTMENT OF COMMERCE
BUREAU OF THE CENSUS

1987 UNITED STATES CENSUS OF AGRICULTURE

Special Reporting Instructions

1. Who Should Report

WE NEED A REPLY FROM EVERYONE RECEIVING A REPORT FORM, INCLUDING individuals, landlords, tenants, partnerships, corporations, institutions, and THOSE NOT CONDUCTING AGRICULTURAL OPERATIONS. Each case included in the census has a unique Census File Number (CFN). In order to make the census results as complete and accurate as possible, we need to obtain information about every CFN.

2. If You Received More Than One Report Form for an Operation

Complete only ONE report form for an operation. Write "Duplicate" near the address label of each extra report form. Also, write the 11-digit census file number(s) of the DUPLICATE report(s) ON THE COMPLETED REPORT in the space provided to the left of the address label. Return the extra report(s) in the same envelope with your completed report form so that we can correct our records.

3. If You No Longer Farm

If you had agricultural operations **at any time during 1987,** please report all agricultural activity during the year. Report all land on your census form that you owned or rented. Also, report all 1987 crop and livestock production and 1987 sales.

Explain on the first page of the report form (or on a separate sheet of paper) that you quit farming or ranching and give the approximate date and the name and address of the present operator, if known.

4. If You Never Farmed or Have No Association With Agriculture

Please write a note on the report form near the address label explaining this and return the form so that we can correct our records. In our efforts to make the census as complete as possible, we obtained lists from various sources. We tried to eliminate duplicate and nonfarm addresses, however, it was not always possible to do so.

5. If You Have More Than One Agricultural Operation

Complete a report form for EACH SEPARATE and DISTINCT production unit, i.e., each individual farm, ranch, feedlot, greenhouse, etc., or combination of farms, etc., for which you maintain SEPARATE records of operating expenses and sales, livestock and other inventories, crop acreages, and production.

6. If You Have a Partnership Operation

Complete only ONE report for the entire partnership's agricultural operation and include all partners' shares on the one report. If members of the partnership also operate separate farms or ranches in addition to the partnership farming operation, separate report forms should be completed for each individual farm.

If two or more report forms were received for the same operation, mark each additional form as a "Duplicate." Return the duplicate report(s) in the same envelope with the completed partnership report, where possible, or write a note on the duplicate report, such as, *"(Name of partner)* has completed a report for the partnership *(provide name and CFN of partnership.)"*

7. Landlord's or Contractor's Share

If you rented or leased land from others or had a contract for the production of agricultural products, include both your share and the landlord's or contractor's share of the production, sales, and expenses so your census report form will be complete for "THIS PLACE."

If you do not know the landlord's or contractor's share, include your BEST ESTIMATE. If you do not have records available for all data items, use your best estimate.

How to Enter Your Response

Enter your replies in the proper spaces, on the correct lines, and in the units requested, i.e., dollars, bushels, tons, etc. Write any explanation outside the answer spaces or on a separate sheet of paper.

All dollar figures may be entered in whole dollars. CENTS ARE NOT REQUIRED.

Enter whole numbers except where tenths are requested, such as acres of potatoes harvested. If you have 1/2, 1/3, or 1/4 of an acre, convert to tenths. For example, convert 1/2 to 5/10, 1/3 to 3/10, 1/4 to 2/10.

The census report form will contain sections and questions which do not apply to you. When this occurs, mark the "None" or "No" box and go on to the next item or section.

Instructions For Specified Sections

▶ **Section 1 — ACREAGE IN 1987**

Your answers to this section will determine the land (Acres in "THIS PLACE") referred to in the rest of the report form.

When answering the acreage questions, include the land associated with your agricultural operations in 1987 whether in production or not. Include all land that you owned or rented during 1987 even if only for part of the year. Do not include any unrelated residential or commercial land.

IF YOU QUIT FARMING DURING 1987 — Complete the report form for the portion of the year that you did farm. Explain on the report form in the space to the left of the address label (or on another sheet of paper) when you stopped farming and include the name and address of the person now using the land.

Report all land in section 1 in whole acres.

Item 1 — All Land Owned — Report all land owned in 1987 whether held under title, purchase contract or mortgage, homestead law, or as heir or trustee of an undivided estate. Include all land owned by you and/or your spouse, or by the partnership, corporation, or organization for which you are reporting.

Item 2 — All Land Rented or Leased FROM OTHERS — Report all land rented by you or your operation even though the landlord may have supplied materials or supervision.

INCLUDE in item 2:

  a. Land for agricultural use that you rented from others for cash

  b. Land you worked on a share basis (crop or livestock)

  c. Land owned by someone else that you used rent-free

  d. Federal, State, Indian reservation, or railroad land rented or leased by the acre

DO NOT INCLUDE in item 2:

Land used on a per-head or animal unit license or permit basis, such as section 3 of the Taylor Grazing Act, National Forest, or Indian reservation permit land. If you had any of these permits, mark "yes" to item 7.

Item 3 — All Land Rented or Leased TO OTHERS — Include all land rented out for any purpose if it was part of the acreage reported in items 1 and 2. A report form will be obtained from each of your tenants to cover the operations on that land.

INCLUDE in item 3:

  a. Owned land rented to others for cash or a share of crops or livestock

  b. Land you rented from someone and then subleased to someone else

  c. Land worked for you by someone for a share of crops or livestock

  d. Land which you allowed others to use rent-free

Item 4 — Acres in "THIS PLACE" — This figure will show the total of all land you operated at any time in 1987.

If Item 4, Acres in "THIS PLACE" is "0" and:

  a. You raised any crops or had any livestock or poultry on "THIS PLACE" in 1987, complete the report.

  b. All your land was operated by a renter or sharecropper, complete item 29, and explain briefly, "all land rented out," etc. Mail form in return envelope.

  c. You did not have any agricultural activity on owned or rented land in 1987, complete section 29 and explain briefly, such as "retired," "sold farm," and date. Give name and address of current operator if known and return form.

▶ **Sections 2 through 8 — CROPS**

Sections 2 through 8 provide space for reporting crops harvested during the 1987 crop year from the land shown in section 1, Item 4 (Acres in "THIS PLACE") of your report. Please report your crops in the appropriate sections. Do NOT include any crops grown on land rented or leased TO OTHERS, or worked by others on shares during 1987.

Acres harvested — Enter the acres harvested in 1987. Round fractions to whole acres except where tenths are requested by "/10" in the reporting box, such as for potatoes.

Quantity harvested — If your unit of measure is different than the unit on the report form, please convert your figure for the quantity harvested to the unit requested. If the harvest was incomplete by December 31, 1987, please report the quantity harvested and estimated quantity to be harvested.

Acres Irrigated — For each crop irrigated, report number of acres irrigated. Irrigation is defined as land watered by artificial or controlled means — sprinklers, furrows or ditches, spreader dikes, purposeful flooding, etc. Include acres that received supplemental, partial, and/or preplant irrigation. Do not report water applied in transplanting tobacco plants, trees, or vegetables as irrigation. Leave "Acres irrigated" blank for crops that are not irrigated.

How to Report Crops Harvested

▶ **Sections 2 and 3** — Report only for the listed crops.

▶ **Sections 4 through 8** — To report: (1) find the crop name and the code number from the list in the section; (2) enter crop name and code in the first two columns of the first available answer line in the section; (3) enter the information that is requested in the remaining columns. If you harvested a crop not listed in sections 4 through 8, use the "Other" code in the appropriate section and specify the crop name.

Double Cropping — If two or more crops were harvested from the same land (double cropping) report the total acres and production of each harvested crop in the appropriate section(s) of the report form.

Example: In 1987 you harvested 1,230 bushels of wheat from 40 acres, then on the same 40 acres planted soybeans, from which you harvested 1,550 bushels.You irrigated the soybeans but not the wheat.

Section 2f 52	Were any of the following CROPS harvested from "THIS PLACE" in 1987?			
	None	Acres harvested	Quantity harvested	Acres irrigated
1. Cotton	☐	091	092 Bales	093
2. Soybeans for beans . . .	☐	088 *40*	089 *1,550* Bu.	090 *40*
3. Wheat for grain	☐	073 *40*	074 *1,230* Bu.	075
4. Oats for grain	☐	076	077 Bu.	078

Interplanted Crops — If two crops were grown at the same time in alternating strips in the same field, report the portion of the field used for each crop.

Example: A 60 acre field was planted in cotton and soybeans, with two rows of cotton followed by an area of the same width planted in soybeans. No irrigation was used. Thirty acres of soybeans and 30 acres of cotton would be reported in the appropriate section(s).

Skip Row Planting — If a crop is planted in an alternating pattern of planted and non-planted rows, such as two rows planted and two rows skipped (2 X 2), report the portion of the field occupied by the crop in the appropriate section for that crop, and report the skipped portion as "Cropland idle" in section 10, item 2f.

▶ **Section 4** — **VEGETABLES** — Report acres of vegetables harvested FOR SALE or commercial processing. Do not include vegetables grown for home use. Report the total acreage of each vegetable crop harvested.

Example: In 1987 you harvested 10 acres of lettuce from a field, then replanted the field in lettuce and harvested the 10 acres again. Both crops of lettuce were irrigated. Enter only 10 acres of land from which vegetables were harvested and 10 acres irrigated in item 1 of section 4, but write in 20 acres of lettuce harvested and 20 acres of lettuce irrigated in item 2 of section 4.

▶ **Section 8** — **FRUITS and NUTS** — In counting the combined total of 20 or more trees and vines, include those for home use as well as those maintained for sale of the production. Acres in trees or vines that have been abandoned should not be included; these acres should be included in section 10, item 2f "Cropland idle."

If crops other than fruit and nut trees and vines were interplanted with trees or vines, report the total acres for the orchard crop in section 8 and the total acres of the interplanted crop in the appropriate section.

▶ **Section 9** — **GROSS VALUE OF CROPS SOLD**

Report the value of all crops sold from "THIS PLACE" in 1987, regardless of the year they were harvested or who owned the land. Be sure to report gross values before deducting expenses and taxes. Include Government CCC loans received for "THIS PLACE" in 1987. Include payments received in 1987 from cooperatives or marketing organizations for crops produced on "THIS PLACE" regardless of the year in which the crops were harvested.

Also include as sales, your estimate of the value of any crop removed from "THIS PLACE" in trade for services, such as hay cut in exchange for fence repair, clearing, or other services. If the sale price or market value is not known, give your best estimate of the crop's market value when removed from "THIS PLACE."

DO NOT INCLUDE crops or crop products purchased from others and later sold.

▶ **Section 10** — **USE OF ACRES IN "THIS PLACE"**

This section is used to classify the acres in "THIS PLACE" reported in section 1, item 4. (Do not include any acres you rented to others reported in section 1, item 3). The sum of the acres entered in various categories should equal total acres in "THIS PLACE."

Land Used for More Than One Purpose — Do not report the same acreage for more than one of the listed purposes. If part or all of your land was used for more than one listed purpose in 1987, report that land only in the first category listed. For example, if you plowed under a cover crop, and planted and harvested a grain crop, report the land in item 2a, "Cropland harvested," but do NOT report as "Cropland used for cover crops, legumes, etc." (item 2c).

Double Cropping — When more than one crop was harvested from the same land in 1987, report that land only ONCE as "Cropland harvested," in item 2a.

Interplanted Crops — If you interplanted crops, such as cotton in an orchard, report the total land used for both crops only ONCE, as "Cropland harvested," in item 2a.

Skip Row Planted Crops — Report the acres that represent the total nonplanted or skipped rows as "Cropland idle," item 2f. The acres that represent the planted rows should be reported as "Cropland harvested," in item 2a.

▶ **Section 12** — **ACRES SET ASIDE, DIVERTED, OR IDLED UNDER FEDERAL ACREAGE REDUCTION PROGRAMS IN 1987**

Include in item 2 all acres in "THIS PLACE" retired from production and placed, by long-term contract, into the Conservation Reserve Program. Acres placed into the program during and prior to 1987 should be included.

▶ **Sections 13 through 17** — **LIVESTOCK, POULTRY, OTHER LIVESTOCK, OR ANIMAL SPECIALTIES**

Animals and Poultry to Include in the Report — Report all animals, poultry, and animal specialties on "this place" (section 1, item 4) on December 31, 1987. Include all owned by you and any kept by you for others. Include animals on unfenced lands, National Forest land, district land, cooperative grazing association land, or rangeland administered by the Bureau of Land Management on a per-head or lease basis. Animals in transit on December 31, 1987, or animals on a short-term pasture (such as wheat pasture or crop residue) on a per-head or lease basis should be reported by the person who had control of the animals.

Animals and Poultry to Exclude from the Report — Do not report animals or poultry kept on land rented to others or kept under a share arrangement on land rented to others. Do not include animals quartered in feedlots which are not a part of "this place." Animals kept on a place not operated by you are to be included on the report for that place.

Animals Bought and Sold — DO NOT REPORT ANY ANIMALS BOUGHT AND THEN RESOLD WITHIN 30 DAYS. Such purchases and sales are considered "dealer" transactions, and are not included in this census.

Number Sold — Report all animals and poultry sold or removed from "this place" in 1987, without regard to ownership or who shared in the receipts. Include animals sold for a landlord or given to a landlord or others in trade or in payment for goods or services. Do NOT report number sold for any livestock or poultry kept on another place.

Dairy Termination Program or "Whole-Herd Dairy Buy-Out Program" — The amount received in 1987 from the Government under the dairy termination program should be included in section 19, item 1. Dairy animals and products sold in 1987 should be reported in section 13.

Animals Moved to Another Place — For animals moved from "this place" to another place, such as for further feeding, report animals as "sold" and give your best estimate of their market value when they left "this place."

Fat Cattle Sold — Cattle fattened on grain or concentrates for 30 days or more and sold for slaughter are reported in section 13, item 3a.

DO NOT INCLUDE WITH FATTENED CATTLE SOLD:

  a. Cattle and calves sold for further feeding

  b. Veal calves, or any calves weighing less than 500 pounds

  c. Dairy cows fed only the usual dairy ration before being sold

Value of Sales — Report the total gross value of animals and poultry sold or removed from "this place" in 1987 without deducting production or marketing expenses (cost of feed, cost of livestock purchased, cost of hauling and selling, etc.). If the sale price or market value is not known, give your best estimate of their market value when they left "this place." Do NOT report the value of sales of any livestock and poultry owned by you but kept and sold from a place you did not operate.

Contract and Custom Feeding Operations — Livestock or poultry kept by you on "this place" on a contract or custom basis should be included on this report REGARDLESS OF OWNERSHIP. Report as "INVENTORY" numbers of animals or poultry on the place on December 31, 1987. Report as "SOLD" animals and poultry kept on a contract or custom basis and removed or sold from the place in 1987. If the sale price or market value is not known, give your best estimate of the market value of the animals or poultry when they left the place.

▶ **Section 16 — HORSES, BEES, FISH, GOATS, OTHER LIVESTOCK, OR ANIMAL SPECIALTIES**

Item 2 — If you owned BEES — Report all colonies or hives of bees and honey operations conducted by you, regardless of where the hives were kept most of the year. Report hives or colonies, pounds of honey sold, and value of sales.

Items 7 and 8 — Mink pelts and rabbit pelts should be included in number sold and value of sales, but not in inventory.

Item 9 — Other Livestock and Livestock Products — Include in all other livestock and livestock products manure, beeswax, and any other animal products sold from "this place" in 1987. Please indicate units used in reporting.

Item 10 — Fish and Other Aquaculture Products — Report number of pounds sold and gross value of sales for each. Enter name and code from list.

▶ **Section 17 — POULTRY**

The person who furnished the housing and labor should report the poultry operation on his/her report form regardless of who owns the birds. Report as sold poultry that were taken or moved from the place in 1987.

▶ **Section 18 — AMOUNT RECEIVED FROM GOVERNMENT CCC LOANS**

Item 1 — Report the amount received under the regular or reserve program for commodities placed under CCC loan during 1987. Include amount received even if commodity was redeemed or forfeited prior to December 31, 1987.

Do not include CCC loans received to build crop storage facilities or amount received for storage payments in the reserve program.

▶ **Section 19 — FEDERAL PAYMENTS RECEIVED**

Report all payments received from Federal Farm Programs in 1987 regardless of whether payment was made in cash or commodity certificates. Include cash payments in item 1. In item 2, include the value of any certificates held or the value received from sale or redemption of any certificates in 1987.

Federal payments include receipts from Federal programs such as deficiency payments, "Whole-herd dairy buy-out," support price payments, indemnity programs, disaster payments, paid land diversion, inventory reduction payments, payments received for approved soil and water conservation projects, etc.

▶ **Section 20 — TYPE OF ORGANIZATION**

Use the following definitions to determine the type of organization for your operation:

Family or Individual Operation — Defined as farm or business organization controlled and operated by an individual (sole proprietor). Include family operations that are not incorporated and not operated under a partnership agreement.

Partnership Operation — Defined as two or more persons who have agreed on the amount of their contribution (capital and effort) and the distribution of profits. Co-ownership of land by husband and wife or joint filing of income tax forms by husband and wife DOES NOT constitute a partnership, unless a specific agreement to share contributions, decisionmaking, profits, and liabilities exists. Production under contract or under a share rental agreement DOES NOT constitute a partnership.

Incorporated Under State Law — A corporation is defined as a legal entity or artificial person created under the laws of a State to carry on a business. This definition does not include cooperatives. Information on type of corporation should be reported in section 21.

Other — Such as cooperatives (defined as an incorporated or unincorporated enterprise or an association created and formed jointly by the members), estate or trust (defined as a fund of money or property administered for the benefit of another individual or organization), prison farm, grazing association, Indian reservation, institution run by a government or religious entity, etc.

▶ **Section 21 — CORPORATE STRUCTURE**

This section is to be answered by corporations only. Answer both items. A family-held corporation has more than 50 percent of its stock owned by persons related by blood or marriage.

▶ **Section 22 — CHARACTERISTICS AND OCCUPATION OF OPERATOR**

This section collects information about the operator of "this place" defined as the individual owner, the operator, the senior partner, or person in charge for the type of organization reported in section 20.

For Family or Individual Operation — Complete this section for the operator.

For Partnership Operations — Answer all items, except item 2, for the "Senior Partner." The "Senior Partner" is the individual who is mainly responsible for the agricultural operations on "this place," not necessarily the person senior in age. If each partner shares equally in the day-to-day management decisions, consider the oldest as the "Senior Partner." For item 2 (Principal Occupation) consider all members of the partnership together. Please include as "farming" worktime at all types of agricultural enterprises, including work at greenhouses, nurseries, mushroom production, ranching, feedlots, broiler feeding, etc.

For Corporations and Other Operations (Cooperatives, Estates, etc.) — Complete section 22 for the person in charge, such as a hired manager, business manager, or other person primarily responsible for the on-site, day-to-day operation of the farm or ranch business.

Item 4 — Year Began Operation — Report the first year the operator or senior partner began to operate any part of "this place" on a continuous basis. If the operator returned to a place previously operated, report the year operations were resumed.

▶ **Section 23 — PRODUCTION EXPENSES paid by you and others for "this place" in 1987**

Include farm production expenses paid by you, your landlord, contractors, or anyone else for crops, livestock, or poultry produced on "this place." Include expenses incurred in 1987 even if they were not paid for in 1987. Please estimate if exact figures are not known. Refer to the individual expenditure items below for further explanations.

Livestock and Poultry Purchased — Report the cost of cattle, calves, hogs, pigs, sheep, lambs, horses, goats, chicks, pullets, poults, etc., including breeding stock and dairy cows. Contract growers or custom feeders should not own or purchase the livestock or poultry themselves should estimate the value of the cattle, calves, pigs, baby chicks, pullets, etc. at the time they came onto the place.

Feed Purchased for Livestock and Poultry — Report the purchase cost of corn, sorghum, oats, barley, other grains, silage, hay, mixed feed, concentrates, etc., fed to livestock and poultry on "this place." Contract livestock and poultry growers should estimate the value of feed provided by the contracting company. Custom feedyards should include feed costs for all cattle fed even if the owners of the cattle were billed for the feed. Feed raised on "this place" should not be reported as purchased.

Cost of Hired Farm and Ranch Labor — Include gross salaries and wages, commissions, dismissal pay, vacation pay, and paid bonuses paid to hired workers, family members, hired managers, administrative and clerical employees, and salaried corporate officers. Also, include supplemental cost for benefits such as employer's social security contributions, unemployment compensation, workmen's compensation insurance, life and medical insurance, pension plans, etc.

Contract Labor — Includes the labor costs of workers furnished on a contract basis by a labor contractor, crew leader, or cooperative for harvesting vegetables or fruit, shearing sheep, or similar farm activities. Do not include costs for building or repair work done by a construction contractor. Include the cost of customwork or machine hire in item 11.

Repair and Maintenance Expenses for the Upkeep of Buildings, Motor Vehicles, and Farm Equipment — Include the cost of repairs and upkeep of farm machinery, vehicles, buildings, fences, and other equipment used in the farm business. Do not include repairs to vehicles not used in the farm business or for equipment used only for performing customwork for others. Do not include expenditures for the construction of new buildings or the cost of additions to existing buildings.

Interest Expense Paid on Debts — Report all interest expenses paid in 1987 for the farm business. Include interest on loans secured by land and buildings (real estate) in item 12a. Include all loans not secured by real estate such as for fertilizer, feed, and seed in item 12b. Include interest paid on CCC loans. Do not include interest associated with activities not related to production of crops or livestock on "this place" such as land or buildings rented to others, packing sheds, or feed mills that provide services to others. Do not include interest on owner/operator dwelling where amount is separated from interest on other land and buildings on "this place."

Cash Rent Paid for Land and Buildings in 1987 — Report rent paid in cash during 1987 for land and buildings in "this place." Do not include rent paid for operator dwelling or other nonfarm property. Do not include the value of shares of crops or livestock paid to landlords.

Property Taxes Paid — Include real estate property taxes you paid on the acres and buildings you operated and used in the farm business.

Do not include:

a. Property taxes on land or buildings rented to someone else

b. Taxes paid by landlords

c. Property taxes paid on other property not associated with the farm business

d. Income and excise taxes

All Other Production Expenses — Farm production costs not previously listed should be reported here. In addition to items listed on the report form, include bookkeeping charges, tax preparation fees, postage, advertising, commission for sale of cattle, and fees paid for farm-related advice or for farm consultants. Do not include depreciation or expenditures for the purchase of land and buildings or new or used machinery.

▶ **Section 24 — COMMERCIAL FERTILIZER AND LIME**

Report acres on which commercial fertilizer (items 1 and 2) or lime (item 3) was applied during 1987. If any acreage was fertilized or limed more than once, report acres ONLY ONCE in each item. Report expense for commercial fertilizer purchased, excluding lime, in section 23, item 4.

▶ **Section 26 — MACHINERY AND EQUIPMENT**

The estimated market value in item 1 refers to ALL machinery and equipment kept primarily on "this place" and used for the farm business. Report the value in its present condition, not the replacement or depreciated value. Specialized equipment, which is an integral part of a building, should be included as a part of the value of land and buildings.

▶ **Section 27 — ESTIMATED CURRENT MARKET VALUE OF LAND AND BUILDINGS**

The value for each of the three listed categories should be your estimate of the value of the land and buildings if they were sold in the current market. The real estate tax assessment value should not be used unless that value represents a full market value assessment and the land and buildings could reasonably be assumed to be sold at that price. Do not deduct real estate marketing charges from your estimate. Report the total value, not the value on a per acre basis.

▶ **Section 28 — INCOME FROM FARM—RELATED SOURCES IN 1987**

Item 1 through 4 refer only to those income producing activities for which you use part of the land, machinery, equipment, labor, or capital normally used on "this place," and which you do not consider as entirely separate from your farming activities. Report gross amounts received before taxes and expenses.

Item 1 — Customwork — Do not report income for customwork or agricultural services provided to others if operated as an entirely separate business from your agricultural operations.

Item 2 — Rental Income — Do not include rental income from nonfarm property.

Item 3 — Forest Products — Include only those forest products or Christmas trees cut from "this place," not items cut from other nonfarm timber acreage. Do not include income from saw mill business.

Item 4 — Other Farm-Related Income — Include income from hunting leases, fishing fees, and other recreational services, sales of farm by-products, and other business or income closely related to the agricultural operation on "this place." Include dividends for business done with farmer-owned cooperatives. Do not enter previously reported farm sales or income from investments not associated with the farm. Do not include retirement pensions or social security benefits received.

Form 87-A0400
(1-13-87)

U.S. DEPARTMENT OF COMMERCE
BUREAU OF THE CENSUS

OMB No. 0607-0524: Approval Expires September 30, 1989

NOTICE — Response to this inquiry is required by law (title 13, U.S. Code). By the same law YOUR REPORT TO THE CENSUS BUREAU IS CONFIDENTIAL. It may be seen only by sworn Census employees and may be used only for statistical purposes. Your report CANNOT be used for purposes of taxation, investigation, or regulation. The law also provides that copies retained in your files are immune from legal process.

In correspondence pertaining to this report, please refer to your Census File Number (CFN)

UNITED STATES
CENSUS
OF AGRICULTURE

AG CENSUS USA

87-A0400

Please complete this
form and RETURN TO:

BUREAU OF THE CENSUS
1201 East Tenth Street
Jeffersonville, IN 47133

Note — If your records are not available, reasonable estimates may be used. If you cannot file by February 1, a time extension request may be sent to the above address. Include your 12-character Census File Number (CFN) as shown in your address label in all correspondence to us.

If you received more than one report form, enter extra Census File Number(s) here and return extra copies with your completed report.

A
A

| CENSUS USE ONLY | 035 | 036 | 037 | 038 |
| | 039 | 040 | 041 | 042 |

Please correct errors in name, address, and ZIP code. ENTER street and number if not shown.

SECTION 1

1. At any time during 1987, did you plant, grow, or have any:
   - Hay or tobacco?
   - Corn, wheat, or other grains?
   - Other crops?
   - Fruit, nut, or citrus trees; grapevines?
   - Vegetables, melons, or berries?
   - Greenhouse or nursery crops?

   ☐ Yes ☐ No

2. At any time during 1987, did you raise, sell, or keep any:
   - Cattle, hogs, sheep, or goats?
   - Chickens or other poultry?
   - Bees?
   - Horses or ponies?
   - Fish in captivity?
   - Other animal specialties?

   ☐ Yes ☐ No

   If you answered YES to EITHER of these questions, go to SECTION 2.
   If you answered NO to BOTH of these questions, go to SECTION 10.

SECTION 2 ACREAGE IN 1987 Report land owned, rented, or used by you, your spouse, or by the partnership, corporation, or organization for which you are reporting. Include ALL LAND, REGARDLESS OF LOCATION OR USE — cropland, pastureland, rangeland, woodland, idle land, house lots, etc.

	None	Number of acres
1. All land owned	☐	043
2. All land rented or leased FROM OTHERS, including land worked by you on shares, used rent free, in exchange for services, payment of taxes, etc. Include leased Federal, State, and railroad land. (DO NOT include land used on a per-head basis under a grazing permit.)	☐	044
3. All land rented or leased TO OTHERS, including land worked on shares by others and land subleased. Also complete item 5 below.	☐	045
4. **Acres in "THIS PLACE"** — ADD acres owned (item 1) and acres rented (item 2), then SUBTRACT acres rented TO OTHERS (item 3), and enter the result in this space.		046

If the entry is zero please refer to the Information Sheet, section 2.

	None	Acres
5. Of the land you rented or leased to others, how many acres did you own?	☐	056

	County name	State
6. In what county was the largest value of your agricultural products raised or produced?		

SECTION 3 LAND USE and IRRIGATION

PART A — How were the ACRES in this place used in 1987?

	None	Number of acres
1. Cropland harvested — *Include all land from which crops were harvested or hay was cut, and all land in orchards, citrus groves, vineyards, and nursery and greenhouse crops.*	☐	787
2. Cropland on which all crops failed — *(Exception: Do not report here land in orchards and vineyards on which the crop failed.)*	☐	790
3. Cropland idle, cropland used for cover crops, or cropland in cultivated summer fallow	☐	793
4. Cropland used only for pasture, woodland pastured, and other pastureland and rangeland	☐	796
5. All other woodland, wasteland, houselots, etc. not reported in items 1 through 4 above	☐	797

PART B — IRRIGATION

	None	Number of acres irrigated
1. How many acres of harvested land were irrigated? *Include land from which hay was cut and land in bearing and nonbearing fruit and nut crops.*	☐	980
2. How many acres of pastureland, and any other lands not included in item 1 above were irrigated?	☐	981

PENALTY FOR FAILURE TO REPORT

SECTION 4

PART A — CROPS HARVESTED from "THIS PLACE" in 1987.
(Do not include crops grown on land rented to others.)

1. Hay crops —	None	Acres harvested	Quantity harvested		Gross value of crops sold
					Dollars Cents
a. Alfalfa and alfalfa mixtures	☐	103	104 Tons, dry	782	00
b. Small grain hay	☐	106	107 Tons, dry	782	00
c. Wild hay	☐	112	113 Tons, dry	783	00
d. Other hay — Specify kind	☐	109	110 Tons, dry	785	00
2. Corn for grain or seed	☐	067	068 Bu.	773	00
3. Soybeans for beans	☐	068	068 Bu.	775	00
4. Wheat for grain	☐	073	074 Bu.	774	00
5. Tobacco — all types	☐	094 /10	095 Lbs.	781	00
6. Potatoes, Irish — *(Do not include those grown for home use.)*	☐	097 /10	098 Cwt.	785	00

	None	Total acres	Dollars	Cents
7. All vegetables for sale *(Do not include those grown for home use.)*	☐	375	783	00
Specify kind(s)		/10		
		/10		

	None	Total acres	Quantity harvested		Dollars Cents
8. All fruit and nut orchards, vineyards, and berries	☐	121 /10		Lbs.	00
Specify kind(s)		/10		Lbs.	

9. **Other crops** — *For additional crops, enter the crop name and code from the list below.* Report quantity harvested in the unit specified with crop name.

Crop name	Code	Acres harvested	Quantity harvested	Gross value of crops sold Dollars Cents
		1		00
		2		00

If more space is needed, use a separate sheet of paper.

Crop name	Code	Crop name	Code
Barley for grain (bushels)	076	Oats for grain (bushels)	078
Corn for silage or green chop (tons, green)	070	Sorghum for grain-milo (bushels)	082
Cotton (bales)	091	Other crops (pounds) — *Specify*	762

PART B — NURSERY and GREENHOUSE CROPS GROWN FOR SALE on "THIS PLACE" in 1987

From the list below, enter the crop name and code for each crop grown.

Crop name	Code	Square feet under glass or other protection	Acres in the open in 1987 Whole acres Tenths	Sales in 1987 Dollars Cents
			/10	00

If more space is needed, use a separate sheet of paper.

Crop name	Code	Crop name	Code
Bedding plants (include vegetable plants)	479	Potted flowering plants	719
Cut flowers and cut florist greens	488	Foliage plants	707
Nursery crops — ornamentals, fruit and nut trees, and vines	488	Greenhouse vegetables	503
		Other — *Specify*	506

CONTINUE ON REVERSE SIDE →

PART A — CATTLE and CALVES

	None	INVENTORY Number on this place Dec. 31, 1987	
1. CATTLE and CALVES of all ages	☐	803	Total
a. BEEF COWS — Include beef heifers that had calved.	☐	804	Beef cows
b. MILK COWS kept for production of milk or cream for sale or home use — Include dry milk cows and milk heifers that had calved.	☐	805	Milk cows

	None	Gross value of sales	
		Dollars	Cents
2. Value of DAIRY PRODUCTS sold in 1987 — Include milk, cream, butter, etc.	☐	814	00

CATTLE and CALVES SOLD FROM THIS PLACE IN 1987
Include as sold cattle moved from this place to a feedlot for further feeding.

	None	Number sold in 1987	Gross value of sales	
			Dollars	Cents
3. Calves less than 500 pounds	☐	808	809	00
4. Cattle — Include calves 500 pounds or more	☐	810	811	00
a. Of ALL cattle sold, how many were FATTENED on this place on GRAIN or CONCENTRATES for 30 days or more and SOLD for SLAUGHTER?	☐	812	813	00

PART B — HOGS and PIGS

	None	INVENTORY Number on this place Dec. 31, 1987	
1. HOGS and PIGS of all ages	☐	815	Total
a. HOGS and PIGS used or to be used for breeding	☐	816	Breeding

	None	Number sold in 1987	Gross value of sales	
			Dollars	Cents
2. HOGS and PIGS SOLD from this place in 1987	☐	820	821	00
3. Of the hogs and pigs sold, how many were sold as FEEDER PIGS for further feeding?	☐	822	823	00

PART C — SHEEP and LAMBS

	None	INVENTORY Number on this place Dec. 31, 1987	NUMBER SOLD in 1987
1. SHEEP and LAMBS of all ages	☐	824	825
a. EWES 1 year old or older	☐	826	

	None	Number	Pounds wool
2. SHEEP and LAMBS SHORN in 1987	☐ 827	828	

	None	Gross value of sales	
		Dollars	Cents
3. What was the gross value of sales of SHEEP, LAMBS, and WOOL from this place in 1987?	☐	829	00

PART D — POULTRY

	None	INVENTORY Number on this place Dec. 31, 1987	Number sold in 1987
1. HENS and PULLETS	☐	892	893
a. HENS and PULLETS of laying age	☐		
b. PULLETS 3 months old or older not yet of laying age for layer replacement	☐	894	895
c. PULLETS under 3 months old for layer replacement	☐	896	
2. BROILERS, fryers, other meat-type chickens	☐	898	899
3. TURKEYS for slaughter (Do not include breeders.)	☐	900	901
4. OTHER POULTRY (Enter name/code from below.)			

Poultry name _____ Code _____

Name/code | Name/code | Name/code
Turkey hens kept for breeding ... 902 | Geese .... 908 | Quail 912
Ducks .... 904 | Pigeons or squabs .. 908 | All other poultry — Specify 914
| Pheasants .... 910 |

	None	Gross value of sales	
		Dollars	Cents
5. Value of POULTRY and POULTRY PRODUCTS (eggs, etc.) sold from this place in 1987?	☐	916	00

PART E — HORSES, OTHER LIVESTOCK, ANIMAL SPECIALTIES, and FISH

	None	INVENTORY Number on this place Dec. 31, 1987	Total quantity sold in 1987	Gross value of sales	
				Dollars	Cents
1. Horses and ponies of all ages	☐	830	831 Number	832	00
2. Colonies of bees	☐	839	840 Number	842	00
			841 Pounds honey		
3. Milk goats	☐	843	844 Number	846	00
			845 Gallons milk		
4. Angora goats	☐	847	848 Number	850	00
			849 Pounds mohair		
5. Other livestock, fish, animal products. (Enter name/code from below.)		1	2 Quantity	3	00

Name/code | Name/code | Name/code
Mules, burros, donkeys .. 833 | Rabbits and their pelts .. 884 | Other livestock, fish,
Mink and their pelts .... 836 | Other goats .... 881 | and their products ... 887

Amount received in 1987 from Government CCC loans. Include regular and reserve loans, even if redeemed or forfeited.

	None	Dollars	Cents
Specify crop(s) _____	☐		00

	None	Dollars	Cents
1. Amount received in cash	☐	884	00
2. Value of certificates received — payment-in-kind (PIK) or commodity certificates	☐	885	00

	None	Number of acres
1. How many acres were set aside (or diverted) under ANNUAL commodity acreage adjustment programs?	☐	552
2. How many acres were under the CONSERVATION RESERVE PROGRAM (10 year, CRP)?	☐	553

1. RESIDENCE — Does the operator live on this place? ... 923 ₁☐ Yes ₂☐ No

2. PRINCIPAL OCCUPATION — At which occupation did the operator spend the majority (50 percent or more) of his/her worktime in 1987? For partnerships consider all members of the partnership together. ... 928 ₁☐ Farming ₂☐ Other or ranching

3. OFF-FARM WORK — How many days did the operator work at least 4 hours per day off this place in 1987? — Include work at a nonfarm job, business, or on someone else's farm for pay. (Do not include exchange farmwork.) ... 929
₁☐ None
₂☐ 1 — 49 days
₃☐ 50 — 99 days
₄☐ 100 — 149 days
₅☐ 150 — 199 days
₆☐ 200 days or more

4. In what YEAR did the operator begin to operate any part of this place? ... 060 _____ Year

5. AGE of operator ... 925 _____ Years old

6. RACE of operator ... 924
₁☐ White
₂☐ Negro or Black
₃☐ American Indian
₄☐ Asian or Pacific Islander
₅☐ Other — Specify ₇

7. SEX of operator ... 928 ₁☐ Male ₂☐ Female

8. SPANISH ORIGIN — Is the operator of Spanish origin or descent (Mexican, Puerto Rican, Cuban, or other Spanish)? ... 927 ₁☐ Yes ₂☐ No

Name _____ 998 Date _____

Telephone number _____ Area code _____ Number _____

FORM 87-A0400 (3-13-87)

Page 2

INFORMATION SHEET
1987 UNITED STATES CENSUS OF AGRICULTURE

Special Reporting Instructions

1. Who Should Report

WE NEED A REPLY FROM EVERYONE RECEIVING A REPORT FORM, INCLUDING individuals, landlords, tenants, partnerships, corporations, institutions, and THOSE NOT CONDUCTING AGRICULTURAL OPERATIONS. Each case included in the Census has a unique Census File Number (CFN). In order to make the Census results as complete and accurate as possible, we need to obtain information about every CFN.

2. If You Received More Than One Report Form for an Operation

Complete only ONE report form for an operation. Write "Duplicate" near the address label of each extra report form. Also, write the 11-digit census file number(s) of the DUPLICATE report(s) ON THE COMPLETED REPORT in the space provided to the left of the address label. Return the extra report(s) in the same envelope with your completed report form so that we can correct our records.

3. If You No Longer Farm

If you had agricultural operations at any time during 1987, please report all agricultural activity during the year. Report all land on your Census form that you owned or rented. Also, report your 1987 crop and livestock production and 1987 sales.

Explain on the first page of the report form (or on a separate sheet of paper) that you quit farming or ranching and give the approximate date and the name and address of the present operator, if known.

4. If You Never Farmed or Have No Association With Agriculture

Please write a note on the report form near the address label explaining this and return the form so that we can correct our records. In our effort to make the Census as complete as possible, we obtained lists from various sources. We tried to eliminate duplicate and nonfarm addresses, however, it was not always possible to do so.

5. If You Have More Than One Agricultural Operation

Complete a report form for EACH SEPARATE and DISTINCT production unit, i.e., each individual farm, ranch, feedlot, greenhouse, etc., or combination of farms, etc., for which you maintain SEPARATE records of operating expenses and sales, livestock and other inventories, crop acreages, and production.

6. If You Have a Partnership Operation

Complete only ONE report for the entire partnership's agricultural operation and include all partners' shares on the one report. If members of the partnership also operate separate farms or ranches in addition to the partnership farming operation, separate report forms should be completed for each individual operation.

If two or more report forms were received for the same operation, mark each additional form as a "Duplicate." Return the duplicate report(s) in the same envelope with the completed partnership report, where possible, or write a note on the duplicate report, such as, "(Name of partner) has completed a report for the partnership (provide name and CFN of partnership)."

7. Landlord's or Contractor's Share

If you rented or leased land from others or had a contract for the production of agricultural products, include both your share and the landlord's or contractor's share of the production, sales, and expenses so your Census report form will be complete for "THIS PLACE."

If you do not know the landlord's or contractor's share, include your BEST ESTIMATE. If you do not have records available for all data items, use your best estimate.

8. How to Enter Your Response

Enter your replies in the proper spaces, on the correct lines, and in the units requested, i.e., dollars, bushels, tons, etc. Write any explanation outside the answer spaces or on a separate sheet of paper. All dollar figures may be entered in whole dollars. CENTS ARE NOT REQUIRED.

Enter whole numbers except where tenths are requested, such as acres of potatoes harvested. If you have 1/2, 1/3, or 1/4 of an acre, convert to tenths. For example, convert 1/2 to 5/10, 1/3 to 3/10, 1/4 to 2/10.

The census report form will contain sections and questions which do not apply to you. When this occurs, mark the "None" or "No" box and go on to the next item or section.

Instructions For Specified Sections

▶ Section 2 — ACREAGE IN 1987

Your answers to this section will determine the land (Acres in "THIS PLACE") referred to in the rest of the report form.

When answering the acreage questions, include the land associated with your agricultural operation in 1987 whether in production or not. Include all land that you owned or rented during 1987 even if only for part of the year. Do not include any unrelated residential or commercial land.

Report all land in section 2 in whole acres.

Item 1 — All Land Owned — Report all land owned in 1987 whether held under title, purchased contract or mortgage, homestead law, or as heir or trustee of an undivided estate. Include all land owned by you and/or your spouse, or by the partnership, corporation, or organization for which you are reporting.

Item 2 — All Land Rented or Leased FROM OTHERS — Report all land rented by you or your operation even though the landlord may have supplied materials or supervision.

INCLUDE in item 2:

a. Land for agricultural use that you rented from others for cash
b. Land you worked on a share basis (crop or livestock)
c. Land owned by someone else that you used rent-free
d. Federal, State, Indian reservation, or railroad land rented or leased by the acre

DO NOT INCLUDE in item 2:

Land used on a per-head or animal unit license or permit basis, such as section 3 of the Taylor Grazing Act, National Forest, or Indian reservation permit land.

Item 3 — All Land Rented or Leased TO OTHERS — Include all land rented out for any purpose if it was part of the acreage reported in items 1 and 2. A report form will be obtained from each of your tenants to cover the operations on that land.

INCLUDE in item 3:

a. Owned land rented to others for cash or a share of crops or livestock
b. Land you rented from someone and then subleased to someone else
c. Land worked for you by someone for a share of crops or livestock
d. Land which you allowed others to use rent-free

Item 4 — Acres in "THIS PLACE" — This figure will show the total of all land you operated at any time in 1987.

If item 4, Acres in "THIS PLACE" is "0" and:

a. You raised any crops or had any livestock or poultry on "THIS PLACE" in 1987, complete the report.
b. All your land was operated by a renter or sharecropper, skip to and complete section 10, and explain briefly, "All land rented out," etc. Mail form in return envelope.
c. You did not have any agricultural activity on owned or rented land in 1987, complete section 10 and explain briefly, such as "retired," "sold farm," and date. Give name and address of current operator if known and return form.

▶ Section 3 — LAND USE AND IRRIGATION

This section is used to classify the acres in "THIS PLACE" reported in section 2, item 4. Do not include any acres you rented to others reported in section 2, item 3. The sum of the acres entered in various categories should equal total acres in "THIS PLACE."

Land Used for More Than One Purpose — Do not report the same acreage for more than one of the listed purposes. If part or all of your land was used for more than one listed purpose in 1987, report that land only in the first category listed. For example, if you harvested a crop and later used the same land for pasture, report the land in part A, item 1, "Cropland harvested."

Double Cropping — When more than one crop was harvested from the same land in 1987, report that land only ONCE as "Cropland harvested," in part A, item 1 of this section.

Interplanted Crops — If you interplanted crops, such as cotton in an orchard, report the total land used for both crops only ONCE, as "Cropland harvested," in part A, item 1.

Skip Row Planted Crops — Report the acres that represent the total nonplanted or skipped rows as "Cropland idle," part A, item 3, the acres that represent the planted rows should be reported as "Cropland harvested," part A, item 1.

Irrigation is defined as land watered by artificial or controlled means — sprinklers, furrows or ditches, spreader dikes, prepared flooding, etc. Include acres that receive supplemental, partial, and/or preplant irrigation. Do not report water applied in transplanting tobacco plants, trees, or vegetables as irrigation.

▶ Section 4 — CROPS

This section provides space for reporting crops harvested during the 1987 crop year from the land shown in section 2, item 4 (Acres in "THIS PLACE") of your report. A few crops are already listed on the form. For these crops, just report acres harvested, quantity harvested, and value of sales. If you produced crops not listed, write the name of the crop and code from the list provided and report the acres harvested, quantity harvested, and the value of sales.

DO NOT INCLUDE:

a. Any crops grown on land rented or leased TO OTHERS, or worked by others on shares during 1987.

b. Crops or crop products purchased from others and later sold.

Acres Harvested — Enter the acres harvested in 1987. Round fractions to whole acres except where tenths are requested by "/10" in the reporting box, such as potatoes.

Quantity Harvested — If your unit of measure is different than the unit on the report form, please convert your figure for the quantity harvested to the unit requested. If the harvest was incomplete by December 31, 1987, please report the quantity harvested and the estimated quantity to be harvested.

Gross Value of Crops Sold — Report the value of all crops sold from "THIS PLACE" in 1987, regardless of the year they were harvested or who owned the land. Be sure to report gross value before deducting expenses and taxes. Include Government CCC loans received for "THIS PLACE" in 1987. Include payments received in 1987 from cooperatives or marketing organizations for crops produced on "THIS PLACE."

Item 7 — Vegetables — Report acres of vegetables harvested FOR SALE or commercial processing. Do not include vegetables grown for home use. Report the total acreage of each vegetable crop harvested.

Item 8 — Fruit Orchards, Citrus, Vineyards, and Nut Trees — Report only if total of 20 or more trees and vines. Include those for home use as well as those maintained for sale of their production. Acres in trees and vines that have been abandoned should not be included, these acres should be included in section 3, part A, item 3 "Cropland idle."

If crops other than fruit and nut trees and vines were interplanted with trees or vines, report the total acres for the orchard crop in item 8 and the total acres of the interplanted crop in the appropriate item.

Item 9 — Other Crops — To report: (1) find the crop name and the code number from the list under item 9; (2) enter crop name and code in the first two columns of the first available answer line under item 9; (3) enter the information that is requested in the remaining columns. If you harvested a crop not listed, use the "OTHER" code and specify the crop name. If you need additional space, use a separate sheet of paper to write the crop name(s), acres and quantity harvested, and gross value of crop(s) sold.

▶ **Section 5 — LIVESTOCK, POULTRY, OTHER LIVESTOCK, OR ANIMAL SPECIALTIES**

Parts A, B, C, and D — LIVESTOCK AND POULTRY

Animals and Poultry to Include in the Report — Report all animals, poultry, and animal specialties on "this place" (section 2, item 41) on December 31, 1987. Include all owned by you and any kept by you for others. Include animals on unfenced lands, National Forest land, district land, cooperative grazing association land, or rangeland administered by the Bureau of Land Management on a per-head or lease basis. Include animals in transit on December 31, 1987, or animals on a short-term pasture (such as wheat pasture or crop residue) on a per-head or lease basis should be reported by the person who had control of the animals.

Animals and Poultry to Exclude from the Report — Do not report animals or poultry kept on land rented to others or kept under a share arrangement on land rented to others. Do not include animals quartered in feedlots which are not a part of "this place," Animals kept on a place not operated by you are to be included on the report for that place.

Animals Bought and Sold — DO NOT REPORT ANY ANIMALS BOUGHT AND THEN RESOLD WITHIN 30 DAYS. Such purchases and sales are considered "dealer" transactions, and are not included in this census.

Number Sold — Report all animals and poultry sold or removed from "this place" in 1987, without regard to ownership or who shared in the receipts. Include animals sold for a landlord or given to a landlord or others in trade or in payment for goods or services. Do NOT report number sold for any livestock or poultry kept on another place.

Dairy Termination Program or "Whole-Herd Dairy Buy-Out Program" — The amount received in 1987 from the Government under the dairy termination program should be included in section 7, item 1. Dairy Cattle and Calves sold should be reported in section 5, part A.

Animals Moved to Another Place — For animals moved from "this place" to another place, such as for further feeding, report animals as "sold" and give your best estimate of their market value when they left "this place."

Fat Cattle Sold — Cattle fattened on grain or concentrates for 30 days or more and sold for slaughter are reported in section 5, part A, item 4a.

DO NOT INCLUDE WITH FATTENED CATTLE SOLD:

a. Cattle and calves sold for further feeding

b. Dairy cows fed only the usual dairy ration before being sold

c. Veal calves, or any calves weighing less than 500 pounds

Value of Sales — Report the total gross value of animals and poultry sold or removed from "this place" in 1987 without deducting production or marketing expenses (cost of feed, cost of livestock purchase, cost of hauling and selling, etc.). If the sale price or market value is not known, give your best estimate of their market value when they left "this place." Do NOT report the value of sales of any livestock and poultry owned by you but kept and sold from a place you did not operate.

Contract and Custom Feeding Operations — Livestock or poultry kept by you on "this place" on a contract or custom basis should be included on this report REGARDLESS OF OWNERSHIP. Report as "INVENTORY" numbers of animals or poultry on the place on December 31, 1987. Report as "SOLD" animals and poultry kept on a contract or custom basis and removed or sold from the place in 1987. If the sale price or market value is not known, give your best estimate of the market value of the animals or poultry when they left the place.

The person who furnished the housing and labor should report the poultry operation on his/her report form regardless of who owned the birds. Report as sold the number of poultry that were taken or moved from the place in 1987.

Part E — HORSES, OTHER LIVESTOCK, ANIMAL SPECIALTIES, AND FISH

If you owned BEES — Report all colonies or hives of bees and honey operations conducted by you, regardless of where the hives were kept most of the year. Report hives or colonies, pounds of honey sold, and value of sales.

Other Livestock and Livestock Products — Include in all other livestock and livestock products manure, beeswax, and any other animal products sold from "this place" in 1987. Mink pelts and rabbit pelts should be included in number sold and value of sales, but not in inventory.

Fish and Other Aquaculture Products — Report quantity sold and gross value of sales for each.

▶ **Section 6 — AMOUNT RECEIVED FROM GOVERNMENT CCC LOANS**

Item 1 — Report the amount received under the regular or reserve program for Commodities placed under CCC loan during 1987. Include amount received even if commodity was redeemed or forfeited prior to December 31, 1987.

Do not include CCC loans received to build crop storage facilities or amount received for storage payments in the reserve program.

▶ **Section 7 — FEDERAL PAYMENTS RECEIVED**

Report all payments received from Federal Farm Programs in 1987 regardless of whether payment was made in cash or commodity certificates. Include cash payments in item 1. In item 2, include the value of any certificates held or the value received from sale or redemption of any certificates in 1987.

Federal payments include receipts from Federal programs such as deficiency payments, "Whole-Herd Dairy Buy-Out," support price payments, indemnity programs, disaster payments, paid land diversion, inventory reduction payments, payments received for approved soil and water conservation projects, etc.

▶ **Section 8 — ACRES SET ASIDE, DIVERTED, OR IDLED UNDER FEDERAL ACREAGE REDUCTION PROGRAMS IN 1987**

Include in item 2 all acres in "this place" retired from production and placed, by long-term contract, into the Conservation Reserve Program. Acres placed into the program during and prior to 1987 should be included.

▶ **Section 9 — CHARACTERISTICS AND OCCUPATION OF OPERATOR**

This section collects information about the operator of "this place" defined as the individual owner, the operator, the senior partner, or person in charge.

For Family or Individual Operation — Complete this section for the operator.

For Partnership Operations — Answer all items, except item 2, for the "Senior Partner." The "Senior Partner" is the individual who is mainly responsible for the agricultural operations on "this place," not necessarily the person senior in age. If each partner shares equally in the day-to-day management decisions, consider the oldest as the "Senior Partner." For Item 2 (Principal Occupation) consider all members of the partnership together. Please include as "farming or ranching" worktime all types of agricultural enterprises, including work at greenhouses, nurseries, mushroom production, ranching, feedlots, broiler feeding, etc.

For Corporation and Other Operations (Cooperatives, Estates, etc.) — Complete section 9 for the person in charge, such as a hired manager, business manager, or other person primarily responsible for the on-site, day-to-day operation of the farm or ranch business.

Item 4 — Year Began Operation — Report the first year the operator or senior partner began to operate any part of "this place" on a continuous basis. If the operator returned to a place previously operated, report the year operations were resumed.

INDEX

(Index items not reported for the State will not appear in designated tables)

Item	State tables	County tables	Item	State tables	County tables
A			**B—Con.**		
Abnormal farms.........	19	–	Bluegrass seed, Kentucky.................	44	26
Acreage reduction program	7,10,48–53	5	Boysenberries...........	–	29
Age of operator	1,16,48–53	1,10,16	Breeding hogs and pigs	32,48–53	12,16
Agricultural products sold, market value..........	1,2,10,18,47,48–53	1,2,16	Broccoli...................	–	27
Agricultural services income	5,48–53	4	Broilers	1,20–22,48–53	1,14,16
Alfalfa hay..............	43,44,48–53	26	Bromegrass seed	–	26
Alfalfa seed	43,44	26	Brussels sprouts	–	27
Almonds.................	45,48–53	28	Buckwheat...............	–	24
American Indian operator	17	34	Bulbs.....................	46	30
Angora goats...........	41	18	Bulls, bull calves, steers, and steer calves......	20,25,48–53	11,16
Apples	45,48–53	28	Burros, donkeys, and mules	41	23
Apricots..................	42	28			
Aquacultural products ..	41	21	**C**		
Artichokes	–	27	Cabbage.................	–	27
Asian or Pacific Islander operator	17	34	Cantaloups	44	27
Asparagus...............	–	27	Carrots...................	–	27
Assets, value...........	1,10–12,18, 47,48–53	1,5,8,16	Cash, government farm programs payments ...	5	4
Austrian winter peas....	–	26	Cash rent, expenses....	3,10,48–53	3,16
Avocados................	45	28	Cash rent or share payments received, farm-related income ...	5,48–53	4
B			Catfish sales	–	21
			Cattle and calves	1,10,20,25,27,47, 48–53	1,11,16
Bahia grass seed	–	26	Cattle and calves sales, value....................	2,20,26,31,47, 48–53	2,11,16
Balers, pickup	13,48–53	8	Cauliflower...............	–	27
Bananas.................	45	28	Celery....................	–	27
Barley for grain.........	1,42–44,48–53	1,15,16,24	Certificates, government farm programs payments...............	5	4
Barley for grain sales, value....................	2,48–53	2,16	Chemicals, expenses...	1,3,10,15,47,48–53	3,16
Beans, dry edible	42–44,48–53	15,16,25	Chemicals used	15,48–53	9
Beans, dry lima	–	25	Cherries..................	45,48–53	28
Beans, green lima	–	27	Chickens 3 months old or older................	1,20,21,23,48–53	1,14
Beans, snap (bush and pole)....................	44,48–53	27	Chicory	–	27
Beans, soybeans.......	1,42–44,48–53	1,15,16,25	Chinese cabbage	–	27
Bedding plants	46	30	Chinese or ming peas ..	–	27
Beef cows..............	1,20,25,29,48–53	1,11,16	Christmas trees and forest products sales, farm-related income ...	5,48–53	4
Bees, colonies	41	20	Citrus fruit	45,48–53	28
Beets, sugar............	42–44,48–53	1,15,16,25	Clover seed	–	26
Beets, table	–	27	Coffee	45	28
Bentgrass seed	–	26	Collards..................	–	27
Bermuda grass seed....	–	26	Colonies of bees........	41	20
Berries..................	42,44,48–53	29	Combines, grain and bean, all types	13,48–53	16
Birdsfoot trefoil seed ...	–	26			
Blackberries.............	–	29			
Black operators and other races	16,17,48–53	32–34			
Blueberries	44	29			

INDEX—Con.

(Index items not reported for the State will not appear in designated tables)

Item	State tables	County tables	Item	State tables	County tables
C—Con.			**D**		
Commercially mixed formula feed purchased..	1,3,48–53	3,16	Daikon....................	–	27
Commodity Credit Corporation loans......	6,10,48–53	4	Dairy cows (milk cows).	1,10,20,25,30,47, 48–53	1,11,16
Conservation reserve programs..............	7,10,48–53	5	Dairy products sales, value....................	2,47,48–53	2,11,16
Contract labor expenses	3,10,48–53	3,16	Dates	–	28
Corn, field	1,42–44,48–53	1,15,16, 24,31	Dewberries	–	29
			Diesel fuel expenses ...	14,48–53	3
Corn for grain sales, value....................	2,48–53	2,16	Dill for oil	–	31
Corn, sweet	44,48–53	27	Disease control in crops and orchards....	15,48–53	9
Corn, sweet, for seed...	–	31	Donkeys, burros, and mules..................	41	23
Corporation, family held.....................	16,48–53	10,16	Ducks.....................	–	14,22
Corporation, nonfamily held....................	16,48–53	10,16	Ducks, geese, and other poultry	21	14,22
Corporation, type of organization...........	1,16,48–53	–	**E**		
Cotton	1,42,44,47,48–53	1,15,16,25	Eggplant..................	–	27
Cotton sales, value	2,47,48–53	2,16	Electricity expenses.....	10,47,48–53	3
Cottonpickers and strippers.................	13,48–53	8	Emmer and spelt........	–	24
Cowpeas for dry peas ..	–	25	Endive	–	27
Cowpeas, green.........	–	27	Equipment and machinery	1,10,12,18,47,48–53	1,8,16
Cows and heifers that had calved	20,25,48–53	11,16	Escarole	–	27
Cranberries..............	44	29	Ewes 1 year old or older....................	38	13
Cropland diverted, set aside....................	7,10,48–53	5	Expenses, farm production..............	1,3,10,47,48–53	1,3,16
Cropland for cover crops, legumes, and soil-improvement grasses..	7,48–53	5	**F**		
Cropland harvested.....	1,7,8,10,16,18,42, 47,48–53	1,3,5,6, 10,15,16	Family held corporations............	48–53	10,16
Cropland harvested, irrigated................	8–10	7	Family or individual, type of organization ...	1,16,48–53	10,16
Cropland idle...........	7,48–53	5	Farm-related income....	5,48–53	4
Cropland in cultivated summer fallow	7,48–53	5	Farms by age and principal occupation of operator	16,48–53	10,16
Cropland on which all crops failed.............	7,48–53	5	Farms by size of farm ..	8,47,48–53	6,16
Cropland pastured	7,48–53	5	Farms by standard industrial classification	18,48–53	16
Cropland total	1,7,10,47,48–53	1,5,16	Farms by tenure of operator	16,48–53	10,16
Crops, farms reporting, acres, production	42	15,16	Farms by type of organization...........	1,16,48–53	10,16
Cucumbers	44	27	Farms by value of agricultural products sold....................	1,2,10,18,47,48–53	1,2,16
Currants	–	29	Farms, number..........	1,7,8,10,16,18,47, 48–53	1,5,10,16
Customwork, machine hire, and rental of machinery and equipment, expenses........	3,10,48–53	3,16	Fattened cattle sales ...	26,29,31,48–53	11,16
Customwork and other agricultural services, farm-related income ...	5,48–53	16	Feed purchased........	1,3,47,48–53	3,16
			Feeder pigs sales.......	20,33,35–37,48–53	12

INDEX—Con.

(Index items not reported for the State will not appear in designated tables)

Item	State tables	County tables	Item	State tables	County tables
F—Con.			**G—Con.**		
Female operators	16,17,48–53	10	Grass silage, haylage, and green chop hay	43,44	26
Fertilizer applied	15,48–53	9	Grazing permits	–	36
Fertilizer expenses	3,10,15,47,48–53	3,16	Grease, LP gas, fuel oil, kerosene, motor oil, etc., expenses	14,48–53	3
Fescue seed	44	26	Greenhouse crops	42,46	30
Field seed crops	44,48–53	26	Greenhouse vegetables	46	30
Figs	–	28	Guar	–	31
Filberts	45	28	Guavas	45	28
Fish sales	41	21			
Flaxseed	42,44,48–53	24	**H**		
Florist greens and flowers, cut	46	30	Hatcheries	–	22
Flower and vegetable seeds	46	30	Hay crops	1,42–44,48–53	1,15,16,26
Flowering plants, potted	46	30	Hay, silage, and field seeds sales, value	2,47,48–53	2,16
Flowers and florist greens, cut	46	30	Haylage, grass silage, and green chop hay	43,44	26
Foliage plants	46	30	Hazelnuts	45	28
Forest products and Christmas trees sales, farm-related income	5,48–53	4	Heifers and heifer calves	20,25,48–53	11,16
Foxtail millet seed	–	26	Hens and pullets of laying age	20,21,48–53	14,16
Fruit crops	45	15,16,28	Herbs	–	31
Fruits, nuts, and berries sales, value	2,47,48–53	2,16	Hired farm labor expenses	3,10,47,48–53	3,16
Fuel oil, kerosene, motor oil, grease, LP gas, etc., expenses	14,48–53	3	Hogs and pigs	1,10,20,32,35,47, 48–53	1,12,16
Full owners	16,48–53	10,16	Hogs and pigs sales, value	2,20,33,36,47,48–53	2,12,16
			Hogs, litters farrowed	34,37,48–53	12
G			Honey sales	41	20
Garlic	–	27	Honey tangerines	–	28
Gas, natural, expenses	14,48–53	3	Honeydew melons	–	27
Gasoline and other petroleum fuel and oil expenses	14,48–53	3,16	Hops	44	31
Gasoline expenses	14,48–53	3	Horses and ponies	20,41,48–53	13
Geese	–	22			
Geese, ducks, and other poultry	41	14,22	**I**		
Ginger root	–	31	Income from farm-related sources	5,48–53	4
Goat milk sales	41	17	Income, see net cash return	4,48–53	4
Goats	41,48–53	23	Individual or family, type of organization	1,16,48–53	10,16
Goats, Angora	41	23	Insects, chemical control	15,48–53	9
Goats, milk	41	17	Interest, debt not secured by real estate	3,48–53	3
Goats, other	41	23	Interest, debt secured by real estate	3,48–53	3
Government farm programs payments	5,10,47,48–53	4	Interest expenses	1,3,10,47,48–53	3,16
Grain hay	43,44	26	Irish potatoes	1,42–44,48–53	1,15,16,25
Grain sales, value	2,47,48–53	2,16			
Grains	44,48–53	16			
Grapefruit	45	28			
Grapes	45,48–53	28			

(Index items not reported for the State will not appear in designated tables)

Item	State tables	County tables	Item	State tables	County tables
I—Con.			**M**		
Irrigated farms and acres	1,8–10	1,7	Macadamia nuts	45	28
			Machine hire, rental of machinery and equipment, and customwork expenses	3,10,48–53	3,16
J			Machinery and equipment	1,10,12,18,47,48–53	1,8,16
Jojoba	–	31	Male operators	16,17,48–53	10
K			Mangoes	–	28
Kale	–	27	Melons	–	27
Kentucky bluegrass seed	44	26	Milk cows (dairy cows)	1,10,20,25,30,47, 48–53	1,11,16
Kerosene, motor oil, grease, LP gas, fuel oil, etc., expenses	14,48–53	3	Milk goats	41	17
			Millet, proso	44	24
Kiwifruit	–	28	Millet seed, foxtail	–	26
Kumquats	–	28	Mink and their pelts	41	19
			Mint for oil	44	31
L			Mohair sales	41	18
Labor expenses	1,3,10,47,48–53	3,16	Motor oil, grease, LP gas, fuel oil, kerosene, etc., expenses	14,48–53	3
Land and buildings, value	1,10,11,47,48–53	5,16	Motortrucks, including pickups	13,48–53	8,16
Land in farms	1,7,8,10,16,18,47, 48–53	1,5,10,16	Mower conditioners	13,48–53	8
Land owned	10,48–53	–	Mules, burros, and donkeys	41	23
Land rented from others	48–53	–	Mungbeans for beans	–	31
Land rented to others	48–53	–	Mushrooms	46	30
Land set aside in federal farm programs	7,10,48–53	1	Mustard cabbage	–	27
Land use	7,8,10,47,48–53	5	Mustard greens	–	27
Lemons	45	28	Mustard seed	–	24
Lentils	44	25	**N**		
Lespedeza seed	–	26	Natural gas expenses	14,48–53	3
Lettuce and romaine	44	27	Nectarines	–	28
Lima beans, dry	–	25	Nematode control in crops	15,48–53	9
Lima beans, green	–	27	Net cash return from agricultural sales	4,48–53	4
Lime applied	15,48–53	9	Nonfamily held corporations	16,48–53	10,16
Limes	–	28	Number of farms	1,7,8,10,16,18,47, 48–53	1,5,10,16
Litters farrowed	34,37,48–53	12	Nursery and greenhouse crops	42,46	30
Livestock and livestock products sold	20	–	Nursery and greenhouse crops sales, value	2,42,46,47,48–53	2,16,30
Livestock and poultry	20	1,16	Nursery crops-shrubs, trees, etc.	46	30
Livestock and poultry purchased	1,3,10,47,48–53	3,16	**O**		
Livestock, poultry, and their products sales, value	1,2,10,18,20,47	1,2,16	Oat sales, value	2,48–53	2,16
Loans, Commodity Credit Corporation	6,10,48–53	4	Oats for grain	1,42–44,48–53	1,15,16,24
Loganberries	–	29	Occupation of operator	1,16,48–53	1,10,16
Lotus root	–	31			
LP gas, fuel oil, kerosene, motor oil, grease, etc., expenses	14,48–53	3			

INDEX—Con.

(Index items not reported for the State will not appear in designated tables)

Item	State tables	County tables	Item	State tables	County tables
O—Con.			**P—Con.**		
Off-farm work by			Pineapples..............	1,42,44–53	1,15,16,31
operator................	1,16,48–53	1,10,16	Pistachios	–	28
Okra	–	27	Plums....................	45	28
Olives...................	–	28	Pomegranates..........	–	28
Onions, dry and green..	44	27	Ponies and horses......	20,41,48–53	13
Operator characteristics–			Popcorn..................	44	24
residence, age, race,			Potatoes, Irish..........	1,42–44,48–53	1,15,16,25
occupation, off-farm			Potatoes, sweet........	42,44,48–53	25
work, sex, Spanish			Poultry and poultry		
origin, years on			products sales, value..	2,20,48–53	2,16
present farm	16,17,48–53	10,16	Poultry hatched	–	22
Oranges	45	28	Principal occupation		
Orchardgrass seed	–	26	of operator	1,16,48–53	1,10,16
Orchards................	1,42–44,48–53	1,15,16,28	Production expenses ...	1,3,10,47,48–53	1,3,16
Organization of farm....	1,16,48–53	10,16	Property taxes,		
Other farm production			expenses..............	3,10,48–53	3,16
expenses..............	5,48–53	3,16	Proso millet..............	44	24
Other field crops sales,			Prunes...................	45	28
value..................	2,48–53	2,16	Pullets	22	14
Other grains sales, value	2,48–53	2,16	Pumpkins	–	27
Other livestock and live-					
stock products sales,			**Q**		
value...................	2,47,48–53	2,16			
Other poultry	–	22	Quail.....................	–	22
Owned land	10,48–53	–			
			R		
P					
Papayas	45	28	Rabbits and their pelts .	41	23
Parsley..................	–	27	Race of operator........	16,48–53	34
Part owners	16,48–53	10,16	Radishes	–	27
Partnership, type of			Rangeland..............	7,48–53	5
organization............	1,16,48–53	10,16	Rapeseed	–	31
Passion fruit............	–	28	Raspberries	44	29
Pastureland and grazing			Redtop seed	–	26
land....................	7,48–53	5	Rent paid in cash,		
Pastureland and other			expenses..............	3,10,48–53	3,16
land irrigated..........	9	7	Rent received, farm-		
Payroll expenses........	1,3,10,47,48–53	3,16	related income........	5,48–53	4
Peaches	45,48–53	28	Repair and maintenance		
Peanuts for nuts	42–44,48–53	1,15,16,25	expenses..............	3,10,48–53	3,16
Pears	45	28	Residence of operator..	16,48–53	10,16
Peas, Austrian winter ...	–	26	Rhubarb	–	27
Peas, Chinese or ming .	–	27	Rice.....................	1,42–44,48–53	1,15,16,24
Peas, dry edible.........	44	25	Romaine and lettuce ...	44	27
Peas, green	44,48–53	27	Rye for grain	42,44	24
Pecans..................	45,48–53	28	Ryegrass seed	44	26
Peppers.................	–	27			
Persimmons.............	–	28	**S**		
Petroleum products					
expenses..............	3,10,14,48–53	3,16	Safflower	–	24
Pheasants..............	–	22	Sales of agricultural		
Pickup balers...........	13,48–53	8	products...............	1,2,10,18,47,48–53	1,2,16
Pigeons or squab	–	22	Salt hay.................	–	31
Pimientos...............	–	27			

INDEX—Con.

(Index items not reported for the State will not appear in designated tables)

Item	State tables	County tables	Item	State tables	County tables
S—Con.			**T—Con.**		
Seeds, bulbs, plants, and trees purchased	3,10,48–53	3	Tenure of operator......	16,48–53	10,16
Set aside programs, acreage.................	7,10,48–53	5	Timothy seed...........	–	26
Sex of operator	16,17,48–53	10	Tobacco	1,42–44,48–53	1,15,16,25
Shallots.................	–	27	Tobacco sales, value...	2,47,48–53	2,16
Sheep and lambs	10,20,38,39,48–53	1,13,16	Tomatoes................	44,48–53	27
Sheep and lambs shorn	38,48–53	13	Tractors, wheel.........	13,48–53	8,16
Sheep, lambs, and wool sales, value	2,20,38,47,48–53	2,13,16	Triticale	–	24
Size of farm, average...	1,48–53	1,16	Trout sales	–	21
Small grain hay	43,44	26	Trucks, including pickups	13,48–53	8,16
Snap beans, bush and pole....................	44,48–53	27	Turkeys	20,21,24,48–53	14
Sod	46	30	Turnip greens	–	27
Sorghum.................	1,42–44,48–53	1,15,16,24 26,31	Turnips..................	–	27
Sorghum for grain sales, value...................	2,48–53	2,16	Type of farm	18,48–53	16
Southern peas (cowpeas), dry	–	25	Type of organization....	1,16,48–53	1,10,16
Southern peas (cowpeas), green	–	27	**V**		
Soybeans................	1,42–44,48–53	1,15,16,25	Value of agricultural products sold	1,2,10,18,47,48–53	1,2,16
Soybeans sales, value..	2,48–53	2,16	Value of land and buildings...............	1,10,18,48–53	5,16
Spanish origin, operators of	16,17,48–53	35	Value of machinery and equipment........	1,10,12,18,47,48–53	1,8,16
Spelt and emmer	–	24	Vegetable and flower seeds..................	46	30
Spinach..................	–	27	Vegetables, greenhouse	46	30
Squash	–	27	Vegetables harvested for sale	1,42–44,48–53	1,15,16,27
Standard industrial classification of farms .	18,48–53	2,16	Vegetables, sweet corn, and melons sales, value	2,47,48–53	2,16
Steers, steer calves, bulls, and bull calves........	20,25,48–53	11,16	Vetch seed	–	26
Strawberries............	43,44	29	**W**		
Sudangrass seed	–	26	Walnuts, English	45,48–53	28
Sugar beets	42–44,48–53	1,15,16,25	Watercress	–	27
Sugarcane...............	1,42–44,48–53	1,15,16,25	Watermelons	44	27
Sunflower seed	1,42,44,48–53	1,15,16,24	Weeds, chemical control	15,48–53	9
Sweet corn	44,48–53	27	Wheat for grain	1,42–44,48–53	1,15,16,24
Sweet corn for seed....	–	31	Wheat sales, value	2,48–53	2,16
Sweet potatoes	42,44,48–53	25	Wheatgrass seed	–	26
T			Wheel tractors	13,48–53	8,16
			Wild hay	43,44	26
Tame dry hay	43,44	16,26	Wild rice	–	24
Tangelos................	–	28	Woodland................	1,7,48–53	5
Tangerines	–	28	Wool, pounds shorn	38,48–53	13
Taro.....................	–	31	Work off-farm by operator	1,16,48–53	1,10,16
Taxes, property, expenses...............	5,48–53	3	**Y**		
Tenant operated farms .	16,48–53	10,16	Years on present farm..	47,48–53	16

PUBLICATION PROGRAM

1987 CENSUS OF AGRICULTURE

Results of the 1987 Census of Agriculture are being published in a series of reports which provide data for each county (or equivalent), each State, the United States, Puerto Rico, Guam, the Virgin Islands of the United States, American Samoa, and the Northern Mariana Islands. The publications include statistics on the number of farms; land in farms; farm and operator characteristics; livestock, poultry, and their products; crop production and value; operating expenditures; irrigation; and other characteristics of farms.

Publication order forms may be obtained from Data User Services Division, Customer Services, Bureau of the Census, Washington, DC 20233, any U.S. Department of Commerce district office, or by calling (301) 763-1113.

ADVANCE REPORTS (AC87-A-01-000(A) TO 56-000(A)

Advance Reports are published separately for each county (or equivalent) in the United States with 10 farms or more, for each State, and the United States. The reports contain data for all agricultural operations with $1,000 or more in actual or potential sales of agricultural products in the census year. The Advance Reports contain final data for major data items together with comparable data from the 1982 census. Included in the reports are data on number of farms, land in farms, size of farms, land use practices, farm operator characteristics, sales expenditures, machinery and equipment, livestock, their products; tenure, age, and major crops harvested (which vary by State). No advance reports are available for Puerto Rico, Guam, or the U.S. Virgin Islands.

VOLUME 1. GEOGRAPHIC AREA SERIES (AC87-A-1 TO 56)

State and County Data (A-1 to 50) are published showing detailed data in national and State tables for the United States, and in county and State tables separately for each State. These reports include data on number and size of farms; crop production; livestock, poultry, and their products; tenure, age, and occupation of operators; types of organization; value of products sold; and standard industrial classification of farms.

Summary and State Data (A-51)
* Chapter 1. National level data
* Chapter 2. State level data

Outlying Areas (A-52 to 56) provide detailed data for the regions and municipios of Puerto Rico; the election districts of Guam; the U.S. Virgin Islands; American Samoa; and Northern Mariana Islands.

VOLUME 2. SUBJECT SERIES (AC87-S-1 TO 6)

Agricultural Atlas of the United States (AC87-S-1), formerly the *Graphic Summary*, presents a profile of the Nation's agriculture in a series of dot and multicolor pattern maps. The maps provide displays on size and type of farm, land use, farm tenure, market value of products sold, crops harvested, livestock inventories, and other characteristics of farms.

Coverage Evaluation (AC87-S-2) provides national and regional level estimates on the completeness of the census, in terms of both the number of farms missed and selected characteristics of those farms.

Ranking of States and Counties (AC87-S-3) presents the ranking of the top 20 States and the top 100 counties of importance of selected items from the 1987 census. Comparative data from the 1982 census are included in most tables. Tables also show cumulative totals for States and counties.

History (AC87-S-4) is a concise description of the major census operations together with facsimiles of selected data tables. It explains the history of the agriculture census, farm definition, data collection and processing, and dissemination of census data.

Government Payments and Market Value of Agricultural Products Sold (AC87-S-5) shows detailed data for farms cross-tabulated by combined market value of agricultural products sold and Government payments received, including detailed national data and selected data for each State.

ZIP Code Tabulations of Selected Items From the 1987 Census of Agriculture (AC87-S-6) provides tabulations by five-digit ZIP Code for selected items from the 1987 census. Data items include number of farms, land in farms, farms by size, market value of agricultural products sold by size of sale, livestock inventory, cropland harvested, and selected crops.

VOLUME 3. RELATED SURVEYS (AC87-RS-1 AND 2)

The Farm and Ranch Irrigation Survey (AC87-RS-1) provides statistical data collected from a sample of farm operations from the 1987 Census of Agriculture. The publication offers information on acres irrigated, land use, yields of specified crops, methods of water distribution, quantity of water used by its source, and other irrigation practices.

Agricultural Economics and Land Ownership Survey (AC87-RS-2) provides data on indebtedness, expenditures, income and assets for both farm operators and landlords. This report also includes measures of credit used for purchases and expenditures, debt by type of lender, assets, off-farm income, and other land ownership data.

VOLUME 4. CENSUS OF HORTICULTURAL SPECIALTIES (AC87-HOR-1)

This report includes detailed information on the horticultural establishments with production and sales of $2,000 or more. It provides data on number of establishments, value of sales of horticultural products, type of horticultural products, and kinds of horticultural businesses, for the United States, States, and counties.

ELECTRONIC MEDIA

Flexible Diskette—The Advance Reports of the 1987 Census of Agriculture are available on flexible diskettes. The files can be used with any compatible microcomputer employing the PC-DOS 2.0 or higher operating system. Diskettes can be obtained by calling (301) 763-4100.

Computer Tapes—Public-use computer tapes contain the same summary statistics that are found in the published reports. Two files are available for each State: data for counties and the aggregated State-level data. Order forms may be obtained from the Data User Services Division, Customer Services, Bureau of the Census, Washington, DC 20233 (or call (301) 763-4100).

Compact Disc-Read Only Memory (CD-ROM)— Data for the conterminous United States and Puerto Rico are available on CD-ROM. The CD-ROM can be obtained from the Data User Services Division, Customer Services, Bureau of the Census, Washington, DC 20233 (or call (301) 763-4100).

Online Access— National and State level data from the 1987 Census of Agriculture are available on CENDATA through two information vendors— CompuServe and DIALOG. In addition, the advance reports, highlights of the Subject Series, and Related Surveys reports, are available online from AGRIDATA. For information on these services call (301) 763-4100.